Consumer Behavior

100691

Consumer Behavior

Buying, Having, and Being

Eleventh Edition

Global Edition

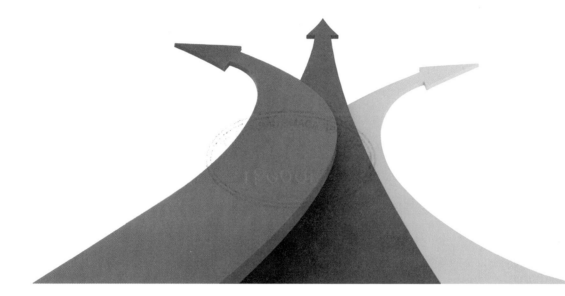

Michael R. Solomon

Saint Joseph's University

Boston   Columbus   Indianapolis   New York   San Francisco   Upper Saddle River

Amsterdam   Cape Town   Dubai   London   Madrid   Milan   Munich   Paris   Montréal   Toronto

Delhi   Mexico City   São Paulo   Sydney   Hong Kong   Seoul   Singapore   Taipei   Tokyo

Editor in Chief: Stephanie Wall
Acquisitions Editor: Mark Gaffney
Senior Acquisitions Editor, Global Editions:
Steven Jackson
Assistant Project Editor, Global Editions: Suchismita Ukil
Program Manager Team Lead: Ashley Santora
Program Manager: Jennifer M. Collins
Editorial Assistant: Daniel Petrino
Director of Marketing: Maggie Moylan
Executive Marketing Manager: Anne Fahlgren
Project Manager Team Lead: Judy Leale
Project Manager: Becca Groves
Head of Learning Asset Acquisition, Global Editions:
Laura Dent
Media Producer, Global Editions: M. Vikram Kumar

Senior Manufacturing Controller, Production, Global Editions: Trudy Kimber
Procurement Specialist: Nancy Maneri-Miller
Creative Director: Blair Brown
Sr. Art Director: Janet Slowik
Interior and Cover Designer: Karen Quigley
Cover Image: © indigolotos/Shutterstock
VP, Director of Digital Strategy & Assessment: Paul Gentile
Digital Editor: Brian Surette
Digital Development Manager: Robin Lazrus
Digital Project Manager: Alana Coles
MyLab Product Manager: Joan Waxman
Digital Production Project Manager: Lisa Rinaldi
Full-Service Project Management and Composition:
S4Carlisle Publishing Services

Credits and acknowledgments borrowed from other sources and reproduced, with permission, in this textbook appear on the appropriate page within text.

Pearson Education Limited
Edinburgh Gate
Harlow
Essex CM20 2JE
England

and Associated Companies throughout the world

Visit us on the World Wide Web at:
www.pearsonglobaleditions.com

© Pearson Education Limited 2015

ISBN 10: 1-292-01741-4
ISBN 13: 978-1-292-01741-9

British Library Cataloguing-in-Publication Data
A catalogue record for this book is available from the British Library

10 9 8 7 6 5 4 3 2 1
14

Typeset in 9.5/12 Utopia by S4Carlisle Publishing Services

Printed and bound by Courier Kendallville in The United States of America

BRIEF CONTENTS

Section 1 ● Foundations of Consumer Behavior   25

Chapter 1   Buying, Having, and Being: An Introduction to Consumer Behavior   26
Chapter 2   Decision Making and Consumer Behavior   58
Chapter 3   Cultural Influences on Consumer Decision Making   100
Chapter 4   Consumer and Social Well-Being   152

Section 2 ● Internal Influences on Consumer Behavior   193

Chapter 5   Perception   194
Chapter 6   Learning and Memory   228
Chapter 7   The Self   270
Chapter 8   Attitudes and Persuasion   322

Section 3 ● External Influences on Consumer Behavior   371

Chapter 9   Group and Situational Effects on Consumer Behavior   372
Chapter 10   Consumer Identity I: Sex Roles and Subcultures   426
Chapter 11   Consumer Identity II: Social Class and Lifestyles   476
Chapter 12   Networked Consumer Behavior: Word-of-Mouth, Social Media, and Fashion   522

CONTENTS

About the Author 11
New to this Edition! 13
Preface 15
Acknowledgments 21

Section 1 • Foundations of Consumer Behavior 25

Chapter 1 • Buying, Having, and Being: An Introduction to Consumer Behavior 26

Consumer Behavior: People in the Marketplace 27

What Is Consumer Behavior? 28
Consumer Behavior Is a Process 29

Consumers' Impact on Marketing Strategy 30
Consumers Are Different! How We Divide Them Up 30
Segmenting by Behavior: Welcome to Big Data 33

Marketing's Impact on Consumers 35
Popular Culture Is Marketing Is Popular Culture . . . 36
All the World's a Stage 37
What Does It Mean to Consume? 38
What Do We Need—Really? 41
How We Classify Consumer Needs 42
The Global "Always On" Consumer 45
The Digital Native: Living a Social [Media] Life 45

Consumer Behavior as a Field of Study 48
Where Do We Find Consumer Researchers? 48
Interdisciplinary Influences on the Study
    of Consumer Behavior 48
Two Perspectives on Consumer Research 51
Should Consumer Research Have an Academic
    or an Applied Focus? 52

Taking It from Here: The Plan of the Book 52

Chapter Summary 53
Key Terms 53
Review 54
Consumer Behavior Challenge 54
Case Study 55
Notes 56

Chapter 2 • Decision Making and Consumer Behavior 58

What's Your Problem? 59
Consumer Involvement 61
Types of Involvement 63

Cognitive Decision Making 69
Steps in the Cognitive Decision-Making
    Process 69

Habitual Decision Making 80
Priming and Nudging 81
Decision-Making Biases and Shortcuts 81
Heuristics: Mental Shortcuts 84

Affective Decision Making 85
Emotions and Consumption 86
Positive Affect 88
Negative Affect 88
How Social Media Tap into Our Emotions 89

Chapter Summary 90
Key Terms 91
Review 92
Consumer Behavior Challenge 92
Case Study 94
Notes 95

Chapter 3 • Cultural Influences on Consumer Decision Making 100

Cultural Systems 102

Cultural Values 102
Core Values 103
How Do Values Link to Consumer Behavior? 105

The Yin and Yang of Marketing and Culture 107
Cultural Movement 108
High and Low Culture 112
Cultural Formulae 113

Reality Engineering 115
Product Placement 117
Advergaming 118

Cultural Stories and Ceremonies 119
  Myths 120
  Rituals 124

Sacred and Profane Consumption 131
  Sacralization 131
  Domains of Sacred Consumption 133
  From Sacred to Profane, and Back Again 134

Global Consumer Culture 135
  It's a BRAND New World 136
  Adopt a Standardized Strategy 138
  Adopt a Localized Strategy 138
  Cross-Cultural Differences Relevant to Marketers 140
  Does Global Marketing Work? 140

Chapter Summary 141
Key Terms 142
Review 143
Consumer Behavior Challenge 143
Case Study 145
Notes 146

Chapter 4 ● Consumer and Social Well-Being 152

Business Ethics and Consumer Rights 153
  *Needs and Wants: Do Marketers Manipulate
    Consumers?* 154

Consumers' Rights and Product Satisfaction 158
  Market Regulation 160
  Consumerism 162
  *Social Marketing and Corporate Social Responsibility
    (CSR)* 164

Major Policy Issues Relevant to Consumer Behavior 165
  Data Privacy and Identity Theft 165
  Market Access 167
  Sustainability and Environmental Stewardship 169

The Dark Side of Consumer Behavior 177
  Consumer Terrorism 178
  Addictive Consumption 179
  Consumed Consumers 181
  Illegal Acquisition and Product Use 182

Chapter Summary 184
Key Terms 184
Review 184
Consumer Behavior Challenge 185
Case Study 186
Notes 187
Nielsen Nugget 191

Section 2 ● Internal Influences on Consumer Behavior 193

Chapter 5 ● Perception 194

Sensation 195
  Vision 197
  Dollars and Scents 200
  Sound 202
  Touch 203
  Taste 204

The Stages of Perception 206
  Stage 1: Exposure 206
  Stage 2: Attention 209
  Stage 3: Interpretation 215

Chapter Summary 222
Key Terms 223
Review 223
Consumer Behavior Challenge 223
Case Study 224
Notes 225

Chapter 6 ● Learning and Memory 228

Learning 229
  Behavioral Learning Theories 230
  *Marketing Applications of Classical Conditioning
    Principles* 233
  *Marketing Applications of Instrumental Conditioning
    Principles* 238
  Gamification 238
  Cognitive Learning Theory 240
  How Do We Learn to Be Consumers? 243
  Cognitive Development 245

Memory 247
  How Our Brains Encode Information 248
  Memory Systems 250
  How Our Memories Store Information 250
  *How We Retrieve Memories When We Decide
    What to Buy* 253
  What Makes Us Forget? 255
  *How We Measure Consumers' Recall of Marketing
    Messages* 258
  *Bittersweet Memories: The Marketing Power of
    Nostalgia* 259

Chapter Summary 262
Key Terms 263
Review 263

Consumer Behavior Challenge 263
Case Study 264
Notes 265

Chapter 7 • The Self 270

The Self 271
Does the Self Exist? 271
Self-Concept 272
Fantasy: Bridging the Gap Between the Selves 274
Symbolic Interactionism 275
The Extended Self 276
The Digital Self 279

Personality 280
*Consumer Behavior on the Couch: Freudian
    Theory 282*
Neo-Freudian Theories 285
Trait Theory 286

Brand Personality 294
Socializing with Brands 296
Are We What We Buy? 297

Body Image 301
Ideals of Beauty 301
Working on the Body 308
Body Image Distortions 311

Chapter Summary 314
Key Terms 315
Review 315
Consumer Behavior Challenge 315
Case Study 316
Notes 317

Chapter 8 • Attitudes and Persuasion 322

The Power of Attitudes 323
The ABC Model of Attitudes 324
Hierarchies of Effects 325

How Do We Form Attitudes? 327
All Attitudes Are Not Created Equal 327
The Consistency Principle 328
Motivational Conflicts 329
Self-Perception Theory 330
Social Judgment Theory 331
Balance Theory 331
Attitude Models 333
Do Attitudes Predict Behavior? 336
Trying to Consume 339

How Do Marketers Change Attitudes? 340
*Decisions, Decisions: Tactical Communications
    Options 340*
The Elements of Communication 341
An Updated View: Interactive Communications 341
New Message Formats 342
The Source 343
The Message 349
Types of Message Appeals 353
*The Source versus the Message: Do We Sell the
    Steak or the Sizzle? 358*

Chapter Summary 359
Key Terms 360
Review 361
Consumer Behavior Challenge 361
Case Study 363
Notes 364
Nielsen Nugget 369

Section 3 • External Influences on Consumer Behavior 371

Chapter 9 • Group and Situational Effects on Consumer Behavior 372

Situational Effects on Consumer Behavior 374
Our Social and Physical Surroundings 376
Temporal Factors 376
Waiting Time 378

The Shopping Experience 379
When the Going Gets Tough, the Tough Go Shopping 379
E-Commerce: Clicks Versus Bricks 380
Retailing as Theater 383
Store Image 384
In-Store Decision-Making 385
The Salesperson: A Lead Role in the Play 388

The Social Power of Groups 389
Reference Groups Aren't Just Any Groups 390
Conformity 396

Collective Decision-Making 397
B2B Decision-Making 397
Family Decision-Making 402
Animals Are People Too! Nonhuman Family Members 406
The Family Life Cycle 407
The Intimate Corporation: Family Decision-Making 408
*Sex Roles and Family Decision-Making
    Responsibilities 410*

Chapter Summary 413
Key Terms 415

Review 415
Consumer Behavior Challenge 416
Case Study 419
Notes 420

Chapter 10 ● Consumer Identity I: Sex Roles and Subcultures 426

Consumer Identity 427

Gender Identity 428
Sex Role Socialization 429
Gender Identity Versus Sexual Identity 431
Sex-Typed Products 432

Ethnic and Racial Subcultures 438
Ethnic and Racial Stereotypes 439
Ethnicity and Acculturation 440
The "Big Three" American Ethnic Subcultures 442

Religious Subcultures 446
Organized Religion and Consumption 447
Born-Again Consumers 447
Islamic Marketing 448

Age Subcultures 449
Children as Decision-Makers: Consumers-in-Training 450
The Youth Market 451
Gen Y 453
Gen X 457
The Mature Market 457

Place-Based Subcultures 463

Chapter Summary 465
Key Terms 466
Review 467
Consumer Behavior Challenge 467
Case Study 470
Notes 471

Chapter 11 ● Consumer Identity II: Social Class and Lifestyles 476

Income and Consumer Identity 477
Income Patterns 477
To Spend or Not to Spend, That Is the Question 478
The Great Recession and Its Aftermath 479
Materialism and Economic Conditions 481

Social Class and Consumer Identity 481
Pick a Pecking Order 481
Components of Social Class 484
Social Class in the United States 491
Social Class Around the World 491
How Do We Measure Social Class? 495

Status Symbols and Social Capital 497
"What Do You Use That Fork For?" Taste Cultures, Codes, and Cultural Capital 499
Social Capital 500
Status Symbols 502

Lifestyles and Consumer Identity 506
Product Complementarity and Co-Branding Strategies 509
Psychographics 510

Chapter Summary 515
Key Terms 516
Review 516
Consumer Behavior Challenge 517
Case Study 518
Notes 519

Chapter 12 ● Networked Consumer Behavior: Word-of-Mouth, Social Media, and Fashion 522

Word-of-Mouth Communication 523
Buzz Building 526
Negative WOM: The Power of Rumors 527

Opinion Leadership 529
How Influential Is an Opinion Leader? 530
Types of Opinion Leaders 531
How Do We Find Opinion Leaders? 532

The Social Media Revolution 535
Social Media and Community 536
The Structure of Social Networks 539
The Power of Online Communities 540
Online Opinion Leaders 543

The Diffusion of Innovations 547
How Do We Decide to Adopt an Innovation? 547
Behavioral Demands of Innovations 548
What Determines If an Innovation Will Diffuse? 549
The Fashion System 550

Chapter Summary 556
Key Terms 557
Review 557
Consumer Behavior Challenge 558
Case Study 559
Notes 560
Nielsen Nugget 563

Glossary 565
Index 579

Michael R. Solomon, Ph.D., is Professor of Marketing and Director of the Center for Consumer Research in the Haub School of Business at Saint Joseph's University in Philadelphia. Before joining the Saint Joseph's faculty in the fall of 2006, he was the Human Sciences Professor of Consumer Behavior at Auburn University. Before moving to Auburn in 1995, he was chair of the Department of Marketing in the School of Business at Rutgers University, New Brunswick, New Jersey. Professor Solomon began his academic career in the Graduate School of Business Administration at New York University, where he also served as Associate Director of NYU's Institute of Retail Management. He earned his B.A. degrees in psychology and sociology *magna cum laude* at Brandeis University and a Ph.D. in social psychology at the University of North Carolina at Chapel Hill. In 1996 he was awarded the Fulbright/FLAD Chair in Market Globalization by the U.S. Fulbright Commission and the Government of Portugal, and he served as Distinguished Lecturer in Marketing at the Technical University of Lisbon. He held an appointment as Professor of Consumer Behaviour at The University of Manchester (U.K.) from 2007–2013.

Professor Solomon's primary research interests include consumer behavior and lifestyle issues; branding strategy; the symbolic aspects of products; the psychology of fashion, decoration, and image; services marketing; marketing in virtual worlds; and the development of visually oriented online research methodologies. He has published numerous articles on these and related topics in academic journals, and he has delivered invited lectures on these subjects in Europe, Australia, Asia, and Latin America. His research has been funded by the American Academy of Advertising, the American Marketing Association, the U.S. Department of Agriculture, the International Council of Shopping Centers, and the U.S. Department of Commerce. He currently sits on the editorial or advisory boards of *The Journal of Consumer Behaviour, Journal of Marketing Theory and Practice, Critical Studies in Fashion and Beauty,* and *Journal for Advancement of Marketing Education,* and he served an elected six-year term on the Board of Governors of the Academy of Marketing Science. Professor Solomon has been recognized as one of the 15 most widely cited scholars in the academic behavioral sciences/fashion literature, and as one of the 10 most productive scholars in the field of advertising and marketing communications.

Professor Solomon is a frequent contributor to mass media. His feature articles have appeared in such magazines as *Psychology Today, Gentleman's Quarterly,* and *Savvy.* He has been quoted in numerous national magazines and newspapers, including *Allure, Elle, Glamour, Mademoiselle, Mirabella, Newsweek,* the *New York Times, Self, USA Today,* and the *Wall Street Journal.* He frequently appears on television and speaks on radio to comment on consumer behavior issues, including appearances on *The Today Show, Good Morning America, Inside Edition, Newsweek on the Air,* the *Entrepreneur Sales and Marketing Show,* CNBC, Channel One, the *Wall Street Journal* Radio Network, the WOR Radio Network, and National Public Radio. He acts as consultant to numerous companies on consumer behavior and marketing strategy issues and often speaks to business groups throughout the United States and overseas. In addition to this text, Professor Solomon is coauthor of the widely used textbook *Marketing: Real People, Real Choices.* He has three children, Amanda, Zachary, and Alexandra; a son-in-law, Orly; and two granddaughters, Rose and Evey. He lives in Philadelphia with his wife Gail and their "other child," a pug named Kelbie Rae.

The eleventh edition of *Consumer Behavior* has been extensively revised and updated to reflect the major trends and changes in marketing that impact the study of consumer behavior. The most significant changes to the edition are highlighted below:

- A totally reorganized Table of Contents that now presents a comprehensive overview of the field in 12 chapters. The new structure organizes material into three sections of four chapters each, so that instructors can easily cover one chapter per week in a typical semester. The first section presents a framework of consumer decision-making that incorporates both micro and macro influences on how people choose products and services. The second section dives deeper into micro influences such as perception and learning, and the third section examines macro variables such as group dynamics and lifestyles.
- Six new end-of-chapter cases and six updated end-of-chapter cases.
- A strong focus on social media platforms and how they change consumer behavior.
- A new chapter on Consumer and Social Well-Being that highlights pressing ethical issues relevant to consumer behavior such as privacy, sustainability, and addiction.
- Significant coverage of major emerging topics including Big Data, the Digital Self, gamification, and contextual influences on decision-making such as priming and nudging.
- New content added to every chapter, including the following topics:

  - Ch. 1
    - Big Data
    - Social shopping
    - Productivity orientation
  - Ch. 2
    - Emotional oracle effect
    - Counteractive construal
    - Priming and nudging
    - Self-regulation
  - Ch. 3
    - Wedding rituals and social media
  - Ch. 4
    - Curation
    - Cyberbullying
    - Cyberterrorism
    - Identity theft
    - Locational privacy
    - Market access
    - Media literacy
    - Phantom vibration syndrome
    - Provenance
    - Recommerce
    - Red market
    - Regulatory agencies
    - Real-time bidding
    - Social media addiction

Ch. 5   • Context effects

        • Eyeball economy

Ch. 6   • Gamification

Ch. 7   • Big Five personality dimensions

        • Digital self

        • Lifestream

        • Mark and Pearson brand archetypes

        • Myers-Briggs Type Indicator

        • Social footprint

Ch. 9   • Showrooming

Ch. 10 • Minimal group paradigm

        • Social identity theory

Ch. 11 • Bottom of the pyramid

        • Limited social mobility

        • One Percenter

Ch. 12 • FOMO (fear of missing out)

        • Pure play retailer

        • Reverse innovation

I love to people-watch, don't you? People shopping, people flirting, people consuming. Consumer behavior is the study of people and the products that help to shape their identities. Because I'm a consumer myself, I have a selfish interest in learning more about how this process works—and so do you.

In many courses, students are merely passive observers; they learn about topics that affect them indirectly, if at all. Not everyone is a plasma physicist, a medieval French scholar, or a marketing professional. But we are all consumers. Many of the topics in this book have both professional and personal relevance to the reader, regardless of whether he or she is a student, professor, or businessperson. Nearly everyone can relate to the trials and tribulations of last-minute shopping; primping for a big night out; agonizing over an expensive purchase; fantasizing about a week in the Caribbean; celebrating a holiday or commemorating a landmark event, such as graduating or getting a driver's license; or (dreaming about) winning the lottery.

In this edition, I have tried to introduce you to the latest and best thinking by some very bright scientists who develop models and studies of consumer behavior. But that's not enough. Consumer behavior is an applied science, so we must never lose sight of the role of "horse sense" when we apply our findings to life in the real world. That's why you'll find a lot of practical examples to back up these fancy theories.

What Makes This Book Different: Buying, Having, and Being

As this book's subtitle suggests, my vision of consumer behavior goes well beyond studying the act of *buying—having* and *being* are just as important, if not more so. Consumer behavior is more than buying things; it also embraces the study of how having (or not having) things affects our lives and how our possessions influence the way we feel about ourselves and about each other—our state of being. I developed the *wheel of consumer behavior* that appears at the beginning of text sections to underscore the complex—and often inseparable—interrelationships between the individual consumer and his or her social realities.

In addition to understanding why people buy things, we also try to appreciate how products, services, and consumption activities contribute to the broader social world we experience. Whether we shop, cook, clean, play basketball, hang out at the beach, or even look at ourselves in the mirror, the marketing system touches our lives. As if these experiences aren't complex enough, the task of understanding the consumer increases when we take a multicultural perspective.

CONSUMER BEHAVIOR

3. External Influences on Consumer Behavior

2. Internal Influences on Consumer Behavior

1. Foundations of Consumer Behavior

for a hospitalization, to mark movements from one life stage to another (e.g., weddings, birthdays), and as greetings (e.g., when one meets a visitor). They give company gifts to commemorate the anniversary of a corporation's founding, the opening of a new building, or the announcement of new products. In keeping with the Japanese emphasis on saving face, the recipient doesn't open the present in front of the giver so that he won't have to hide any disappointment with what he gets.[106]

Holiday Rituals

On holidays, we step back from our everyday lives and perform ritualistic behaviors unique to those occasions.[107] Each cultural celebration typically relates to the adventures of one or more special characters, such as St. Patrick in Ireland or Yue Lao in China. These special events require tons of ritual artifacts and scripts. The Thanksgiving holiday script includes serving (in gluttonous portions) foods such as turkey and cranberry sauce that many of us consume only on that day, complaining about how much we've eaten (yet rising to the occasion to find room for dessert), and (for many) a postmeal trip to the couch for the obligatory football game.

Most holidays commemorate a cultural myth, often with a historical (e.g., Miles Standish on Thanksgiving) or imaginary (e.g., Cupid on Valentine's Day) character as the story's hero. These holidays persist because their basic elements appeal to our deep-seated needs.[108]

- **Christmas**—Myths and rituals fill the Christmas holiday, from Santa's adventures at the North Pole to others' adventures under the mistletoe. The meaning of Christmas evolved quite dramatically during the past few hundred years. In colonial times, Christmas celebrations resembled carnivals and public rowdiness was the norm. Most notable was the tradition of "wassailing," in which roving packs of rowdy young men laid siege to the rich and demanded food and drink. By the end of the 1800s, the mobs were so unruly that city fathers in Protestant America invented a tradition whereby families conducted Christmas gatherings around a tree, a practice they "borrowed" from early pagan rites. In an 1822 poem Clement Clarke Moore, the wealthy son of a New York Episcopal bishop, invented the modern-day myth of Santa Claus. The Christmas ritual slowly changed to a focus on children and gift-giving.[109] One of the most important holiday rituals, of course, stars Santa, a mythical figure for whose arrival children eagerly await (even if their house doesn't have a fireplace). Indeed, an Australian study

This McDonald's ad from Hong Kong celebrates a holiday. The literal translation is "April Fool's Day: the best day to take the piss out of your friends."
Source: Courtesy of DDB Hong Kong.

We'll explore these ideas with intriguing and current examples as we show how the consumer behavior discipline relates to your daily life. Throughout the eleventh edition, you'll find up-to-the-minute discussions of topics such as red markets, Phantom Vibration Syndrome, sexting, bromances, helicopter moms, cosplay, the sheconomy, and headbanging rituals. If you can't identify all of these terms, I can suggest a textbook that you should read immediately!

Going Global

The American experience is important, but it's far from the whole story. This book also considers the many other consumers around the world whose diverse experiences with buying, having, and being we must understand. That's why you'll find numerous examples of marketing and consumer practices relating to consumers and companies outside the United States throughout the book. If we didn't know it before the tragic events of September 11, 2001, we certainly know it now: Americans also are global citizens, and it's vital that we all appreciate others' perspectives.

Digital Consumer Behavior: A Virtual Community

As more of us go online every day, there's no doubt the world is changing—and consumer behavior evolves faster than you can say "the Web." The eleventh edition continues to highlight and celebrate the brave new world of digital consumer behavior. Today, consumers and producers come together electronically in ways we have never known before. Rapid transmission of information alters the speed at which new trends develop and the direction in which they travel, especially because the virtual world lets consumers participate in the creation and dissemination of new products.

One of the most exciting aspects of the new digital world is that consumers can interact directly with other people who live around the block or around the world. As a result, we need to radically redefine the meaning of community. It's no longer enough to acknowledge that consumers like to talk to each other about products. Now we share opinions and get the buzz about new movies, CDs, cars, clothes—you name it—in electronic communities that may include a housewife in Alabama, a disabled senior citizen in Alaska, or a teen loaded with body piercings in Amsterdam. And many of us meet up in computer-mediated environments (CMEs) such as Facebook, Twitter, and Foursquare. I'm totally fascinated by what goes on in virtual worlds, and you'll see a lot of material in this edition that relates to these emerging consumer playgrounds.

We have just begun to explore the ramifications for consumer behavior when a Web surfer can project her own picture onto a Web site to get a virtual makeover or a corporate purchasing agent can solicit bids for a new piece of equipment from vendors around the world in minutes. These new ways of interacting in the marketplace create bountiful opportunities for businesspeople and consumers alike. You will find illustrations of the changing digital world sprinkled liberally throughout this edition. In addition, each chapter features boxes that I call *Net Profit,* which point to specific examples of the Internet's potential to improve the way we conduct business.

But is the digital world always a rosy place? Unfortunately, just as in the "real world," the answer is no. The potential to exploit consumers, whether by invading their privacy, preying on the curiosity of children, or simply providing false product information, is always there. That's why you'll also find boxes called *The Tangled Web* that point out some of the abuses of this fascinating new medium. Still, I can't imagine a world without the Web, and I hope you'll enjoy the ways it's changing our field. When it comes to the new virtual world of consumer behavior, you're either on the train or under it.

Consumer Research Is a Big Tent: The Importance of a Balanced Perspective

Like most of you who will read this book, the field of consumer behavior is young, dynamic, and in flux. It is constantly cross-fertilized by perspectives from many different disciplines: The field is a big tent that invites many diverse views to enter. I try to express the field's staggering diversity in these pages. Consumer researchers represent virtually every social science discipline, plus a few from the physical sciences and the arts for good measure. From this blending of disciplines comes a dynamic and complex research perspective, including viewpoints regarding appropriate research methods, and even deeply held beliefs about what are and what are not appropriate issues for consumer researchers to study in the first place.

The book also emphasizes how strategically vital it is to understand consumers. Many (if not most) of the fundamental concepts in marketing emanate from a manager's ability to know people. After all, if we don't understand why people behave as they do, how can we identify their needs? If we can't identify their needs, how can we satisfy their needs? If we can't satisfy people's needs, we don't have a marketing concept, so we might as well fold up our big tent and go home!

To illustrate the potential of consumer research to inform marketing strategy, the text contains numerous examples of specific applications of consumer behavior concepts by marketing practitioners, as well as examples of windows of opportunity where we could use these concepts (perhaps by alert strategists after they take this course!). The *Marketing Opportunity* boxes you'll find in each chapter highlight the fascinating ways in which marketing practitioners translate the wisdom they glean from consumer research into actual business activities.

The Good, the Bad, and the Ugly

A strategic focus is great, but this book doesn't assume that everything marketers do is in the best interests of consumers or of their environment. Likewise, as consumers we do many things that are not so positive, either. We suffer from addictions, status envy, ethnocentrism, racism, sexism, and many other -isms. Regrettably, there are times when marketing activities—deliberately or not—encourage or exploit these human flaws. This book deals with the totality of consumer behavior, warts and all. We'll highlight marketing mistakes or ethically suspect activities in boxes that I call *Marketing Pitfall*.

On a more cheerful note, marketers create wonderful (or at least unusual) things, such as holidays, comic books, Krispy Kreme donuts, nu-jazz music, Webkinz, and the many stylistic options that beckon to us in the domains of clothing, home design, the arts, and cuisine. I also take pains to acknowledge the sizable impact of marketing on popular culture. Indeed, the final section of this book captures very recent work in the field that

The Tangled Web

A Japanese food and soy sauce brand launched a Facebook app that allows people to "Asianate" themselves. To give yourself an "Urban Asian look," you upload your photo and software merges your features with those of a Japanese sumo wrestler. The app was created in the Netherlands, as "Your portal to Asia's city life today."[164]

Marketing Opportunity

Successful companies understand that needs are a moving target. No organization—no matter how renowned for its marketing prowess—can afford to rest on its laurels. *Everyone* needs to keep innovating to stay ahead of changing customers and the marketplace. BMW is a great example. No one (not even rivals like Audi or Mercedes-Benz) would argue that the German automaker knows how to make a good car (though they may not agree with the company's claim to be "the ultimate driving machine"). Still, BMW's engineers and designers know they have to understand how drivers' needs will change in the future—even those loyal owners who love the cars they own today. The company is highly sensitive to such key trends as:

- A desire for environmentally friendly products
- Increasingly congested roadways and the movement by some cities such as London to impose fees on vehicles in central areas
- New business models that encourage consumers to rent products only while they need them rather than buying them outright

BMW's response: The company committed more than $1 billion to develop electric models like its new i3 commuter car and i8 sports car. These futuristic-looking vehicles are largely made from lightweight carbon fiber to maximize the distance they can go between battery charges, and 25 percent of the interior plastic [is from] renewable raw material[s]. [BMW] started a car-sharing [service] it calls DriveNow: D[rivers can] chip in their licenses [and use cars] wherever they are wh[en they need] it. That's forward think[ing].

Marketing Pitfall

When Hurricane Sandy devastated cities on the East Coast in 2012, some marketers rose to the occasion while others stumbled in the wind. Gap, for example, tweeted, "We'll be doing lots of Gap.com shopping today. How about you?" American Apparel offered an incentive to shoppers: "In case you're bored during the storm, just Enter SANDYSALE at Checkout." Many of the storm victims were not amused. One tweeted, "Hey @americanapparel people have died and others are in need. Shut up about your #Sandy sale."

In contrast, Allstate ran radio commercials to let policyholders know how to file claims quickly. JetBlue Airways waived change and cancellation fees for people who had to rebook. How's this for a relationship builder: Duracell batteries sent a truck to New York City that offered free batteries and access to charging lockers for mobile devices and computers to desperate people who had been without power (or even worse, access to social media).[18]

scrutinizes, criticizes, and sometimes celebrates consumers in their everyday worlds. I hope you will enjoy reading about such wonderful things as much as I enjoyed writing about them. Welcome to the fascinating world of consumer behavior!

CB AS I SEE IT
Professor Gavan Fitzsimmons, *Duke University*

For many years consumer researchers have thought of the consumer largely as a conscious, thinking machine. Consumers consider what is important to them, evaluate choice options on those alternatives on those dimensions, and make a decision. Recently, however, a growing group of consumer researchers has started to revisit an old idea that had been largely considered debunked: namely, that much of what goes on in the life of a consumer occurs outside of his or her conscious awareness.

The idea that consumers are influenced outside of their conscious awareness is frightening to many consumers, and has thus received considerable resistance. And yet, the data become more and more clear that consumers influenced by stimuli they don't realize they have been exposed to, processes occur in the consumers' minds they are unaware of, and consumers even engage in behavior that they are not conscious of (e.g., consider many habitual behaviors). These nonconscious processes are often adaptive and helpful for the consumer, but can also at times be detrimental.

One interesting recent example from our own lab involved subliminally exposing consumers to brand logos—in several studies, either an Apple or an IBM logo. Incidental brand exposures occur every day (recent estimates range between 3,000 and 10,000 times in a single day for the typical American consumer) and thus we were curious if they could influence consumer behavior in meaningful ways. Apple or IBM logos were flashed on a screen for very brief intervals—from 10 to 50 milliseconds—to mimic this real-world incidental brand exposure. Participants had no conscious experience of seeing a brand, and believed they were only seeing a box on the left or right of the screen. Our results showed that nonconscious exposure to the Apple logo led consumers to be significantly more creative than consumers similarly exposed to an IBM logo. This incidental brand exposure activated a goal in consumers that they actively pursued until they could satisfy it. Similar studies have shown dramatic increases in choices of one brand versus another as a result of incidental brand exposure.

The future of research on unconscious consumer behavior is likely to continue to document domains in which the consumer is influenced outside of his or her awareness. Contexts in which consumers find themselves taxed, exhausted, or overwhelmed are all ripe for unconscious influence, which sadly have become the default rather than the exception for most consumers. Some of the most interesting questions remaining deal with exactly how nonconscious processes work, and when they may be adaptive versus harmful. If helpful, how can consumers, firms, and public policymakers embrace and encourage them? For example, many consumers might like to be more creative, or faster, for example, and thus might strategically surround themselves with Apple or Speedo logos. Over time, exposure to these logos will become incidental and they may find themselves increasingly creative or faster. If such exposures are harmful, what can these groups do to minimize their effects? Preliminary evidence suggests that warnings preceding exposure can, at least in part, dampen these nonconscious effects.

Consumer Behavior in the Trenches

I'm a huge believer in the value of up-to-date information. Our field changes so rapidly that often yesterday's news is no news at all. True, there are "timeless" studies that demonstrate basic consumer behavior constructs as well today as they did 20 years ago or more (I may even have authored some of them!). Still, I feel a real obligation to present students and their professors with a current view of research, popular culture, and marketing activities whenever I can. For this reason, each time I start to contemplate my next edition, I write to colleagues to ask for copies of papers they have in press that they believe will be important in the future. Their cooperation with my request allows me to include a lot of fresh research examples; in some cases, these articles will not yet have been published when this book comes out.

I've also taken this initiative to the next level with a feature I call *CB As I See It*. In every chapter you'll find a "flesh-and-blood" consumer behavior professor who shares his or her perspective as a leading researcher in a particular area of specialization about an appropriate topic. I've let these esteemed colleagues largely speak for themselves, so now students can benefit from other voices who chime in on relevant research issues.

SECTION 1 NIELSEN NUGGET

In a unique partnership with The Nielsen Company, you have access to data-driven exercises that allow you to analyze actual data gathered by one of the world's leading consumer research organizations.

For nearly a century, Nielsen has enabled organizations in various industries to make strategic decisions based on information it gathers through evolving research methodologies. Nielsen helps media companies better understand viewers, listeners, and the industry as a whole by providing insights for audience measurement, advertising effectiveness, and overall marketing performance and cross-platform strategies. Nielsen's broad range of consumer packaged goods (CPG) analytics and consulting services are specifically designed for, and with, top CPG manufacturers and retailers, to ensure that they have the most accurate view of the consumer and the marketplace. Spanning 80 countries across five continents, Nielsen maintains its leadership position by providing customized solutions based on local marketing research.

Scenario: Awesome Beans is a manufacturer with offerings across many categories. Although they have experienced flat sales in coffee over the past few years, the category has recently begun to show slight growth. Awesome Beans would like to capitalize on this trend, to make sure they are receiving at least their fair share of the category growth. The company recently conducted an attitudinal segmentation study. Survey research resulted in differentiating coffee consumers into four categories based on their common needs and buying motivation.

2. Determine which of the household types identified would be the most appropriate demographically to target with promotions.
3. Which of the demographic dimensions should be considered as potential segment-defining variables?

Attitudinal Group	% Buyers	% Value	Index	$ Value (000s)
Coffee Bingers	29	25	86	$ 74,323
Café Callers	33	27	83	$ 80,295
Flavour Followers	13	12	96	$ 36,433
Premium People	24	35	145	$102,471

Attitudinal groups were segmented based on their responses to survey questions. The data in the previous table show:
- The size of each group, in terms of share of coffee buyers (% Buyers)
- The percent of coffee dollar sales (% value)
- Dollar Index (% Value/% Buyers × 100). A score of 100 is average.
- $ Value—Total coffee $ spent by consumer segment

Buyer Index vs. All Shoppers	Coffee Bingers	Café Callers	Flavour Followers	Premium People
AWESOME BEANS	103	100	104	96
COMPETITOR 1	98	97	110	100
COMPETITOR 2	95	101	95	105
COMPETITOR 3	88	113	103	100

Nielsen Nuggets

The folks at Nielsen, a leading global provider of consumer and market research, have partnered with us to provide you with actual data the company obtained from recent consumer surveys. Each exercise contains Nielsen data and some suggestions about how to use it to come up with answers to specific marketing questions. Your challenge is to make sense of what the numbers tell us about how people actually consume.

Critical Thinking in Consumer Behavior: Case Study

Learning by doing is an integral part of the classroom experience. You'll find a *case study* at the end of each chapter, along with discussion questions to help you apply the case to the chapter's contents. Also included in the eleventh edition are the following items that will enhance the student learning experience:

> ### Case Study
>
> **NETFLIX**
>
> Netflix, a company initially known for distributing movies through the mail, recently joined major television studios in having it's original programs nominated for the 65th annual Primetime Emmy Awards. It was an unprecedented accomplishment for an Internet-based company. Netflix earned 14 nominations for their original content series and stood alongside studio giants HBO, CBS, ABC, and NBC. Although 14 is a small number of nominations when compared to HBO's 108 nominations, Netflix certainly caught the industry's attention as a successful producer of television content.
>
> How did this company, an outsider to the system, become such a major force in the entertainment industry? It's because consumer viewing behavior is changing and Netflix is driving the evolution. Consider the steps of the cognitive decision-
>
> reveals traditional and online viewing are both increasing and the average American watches five hours of video per day. Furthermore, people want to watch what people are talking about. Netflix's Emmy nominations for *House of Cards, Arrested Development*, and *Hemlock Grove* created interest among viewers and increased their desire to watch those shows.
>
> Viewing needs are changing in some other significant ways. In addition to quality programming and increased choice, viewers want to be able to watch multiple episodes of a show in one sitting. Referred to as "binge viewing," consumers would rather not wait a week for the next episode of a show. They want to sit down and watch multiple episodes, a full season, or multiple seasons. Netflix noticed this change in viewing style and made the decision to release all their shows as entire seasons rather than weekly episodes.
>
> Consider other stages of the cognitive decision-making pro-

- **Chapter Objectives** at the beginning of each chapter
  provide an overview of key issues to be covered in the chapter. Each *chapter summary* is then organized around the objectives to help you integrate the material you have read.
- **Review** at the end of each chapter helps you to study key issues.
- **The Consumer Behavior Challenge** at the end of each chapter is divided into two sections:
  - **Discuss** poses thoughtful issues that encourage you to consider pragmatic and ethical implications of the material you have read.
  - **Apply** allows you to "get your hands dirty" as you conduct mini-experiments and collect data in the real world to better grasp the application of consumer behavior principles.

Instructor Supplements

Instructor's Manual—This Instructor's Manual includes lecture outlines, answers to all end-of-chapter questions, additional activities, and assignments for your students. This manual is available for download by visiting ***www.pearsonglobaleditions.com/Solomon***.

Test Item File—The Test Item File contains more than 1,000 questions, including multiple-choice, true/false, and essay. Each question is followed by the correct answer, the learning objective it ties to, an AACSB category, a course learning outcome, and the difficulty rating. It has been thoroughly reviewed by an assessment expert. The Test Item File is available for download by visiting ***www.pearsonglobaleditions.com/Solomon***.

TestGen—Pearson Education's test-generating software is available from ***www.pearsonglobaleditions.com/Solomon***. The software is PC/MAC compatible and preloaded with all of the Test Item File questions. You can manually or randomly view test questions and drag and drop to create a test. You can also add or modify test-bank questions as needed.

Instructor PowerPoints—This presentation includes basic outlines and key points from each chapter. It includes figures from the text but no forms of rich media, which makes the file size manageable and easier to share online or via email. This set was also designed for the professor who prefers to customize PowerPoints and who wants to be spared from having to strip out animation, embedded files, and other media-rich features.

Video Library—Videos illustrating the most important subject topics are available at:
  MyLab–available for instructors and students; provides round the clock instant access to videos and corresponding assessment and simulations for Pearson textbooks. Contact your local Pearson representative to request access.

Student Supplements

CourseSmart[*]—CourseSmart textbooks were developed for students looking to save on required or recommended textbooks. Students simply select their eText by title or author and purchase immediate access to the content for the duration of the course, using any major credit card. With a CourseSmart eText, students can search for specific keywords or page numbers, take notes online, print out reading assignments that incorporate lecture notes, and bookmark important passages for later review. For more information or to purchase a CourseSmart eTextbook, visit *www.coursesmart.co.uk*.

MyMarketingLab—MyMarketingLab (www.mymktlab.com) is an easy-to-use online tool that personalizes course content and provides robust assessment and reporting to measure individual and class performance. All of the resources that students need for course success are in one place—flexible and easily adapted for your students' course experience.

[*]This product may not be available in all markets. For more details, please visit www.coursesmart.co.uk or contact your local Pearson representative.

Justin Goss, a doctoral student at The University of Texas at San Antonio, did yeoman service as he helped me to review recently published academic articles. I'm also grateful for the many helpful comments on how to improve the eleventh edition that my peer reviewers provided. Special thanks go to the following individuals:

Anthony Patino, University of Baltimore
Cynthia Webster, Mississippi State University
Dawn Valentine, Georgia Southwestern State University
Ed Langlois, Palm Beach Atlantic University
Jeffrey Harper, Texas Tech University
Joshua Coplen, Santa Monica College
Linda Crosby, Davenport University
Mark Blake, York College of PA
Mary Jean Koontz, Golden Gate University
Rebecca Legleiter, Tulsa Community College
Sari Silvanto-Ryan, University of Redlands
Summer Elsinger, Upper Iowa University

These colleagues generously contributed their thoughts to my *CB As I See It* boxes:

Alladi Venkatesh, University of California, Irvine
Americus Reed, University of Pennsylvania
Aradhna Krishna, University of Michigan
Cele Otnes, University of Illinois at Urbana-Champaign
Donna Hoffman, The George Washington University
Edward McQuarrie, Santa Clara University
Gavan Fitzsimmons, Duke University
George Loewenstein, Carnegie Mellon University
George Moschis, Georgia State University
Gordon Bruner, Southern Illinois University
Jennifer Aaker, Stanford University
John Schouten, Aalto University
Julie Ozanne, Virginia Tech
Kathy LaTour, University of Nevada–Las Vegas
Lauren Block, Baruch College of The City University of New York
Laurie Meamber, George Mason University
Lisa Bolton, The Pennsylvania State University
Michael LaTour, University of Nevada–Las Vegas
Praveen Aggarwal, University of Minnesota–Duluth
Sonya Grier, American University
Susan Dobscha, Bentley University
William Baker, University of Akron

I thank Tracy Tuten of East Carolina University for the creation of the PowerPoint Presentation, Instructor's Manual, and Test Item File, and Deb Utter of Boston University for revising and creating the new chapter cases.

I would also like to thank the good people at Pearson who, as always, have done great work on this edition. A special thanks to Mark Gaffney, Stephanie Wall, and Anne Fahlgren for their support; Becca Groves did a great job keeping me on course, and Melissa Pellerano was her usual conscientious self.

Without the tolerance of my friends and colleagues, I would never have been able to sustain the illusion that I was still an active researcher while I worked on this edition. I am grateful to my department chair, Dave Allan, and to Dean Joe DiAngelo for supporting their high-maintenance faculty member. Also, I am grateful to my students, who have been a prime source of inspiration, examples, and feedback. The satisfaction I garnered from teaching them about consumer behavior motivated me to write a book I felt they would like to read.

Last but not least, I would like to thank my family and friends for sticking by me during this revision. They know who they are; their names pop up in chapter vignettes throughout the book. My apologies for "distorting" their characters in the name of poetic license! My gratitude and love go out to my parents, Jackie and Henry, and my in-laws, Marilyn and Phil. Ditto to my super children, Amanda, Zachary, and Alexandra—and my high-tech son-in-law Orly—who always made the sun shine on gray days (not to mention my favorite pug, Kelbie Rae). My fabulous granddaughters Rose and Evey added a special thrill. Finally, thanks above all to the love of my life: Gail, my wonderful wife, best friend, and the hottest grandmother on earth: I still do it all for you.

M.R.S.
Philadelphia, Pennsylvania
November 2013

Pearson would like to thank and acknowledge the following people for their work on the Global Edition:

Contributors

Adele Berndt, Jönköping International Business School, Sweden
Ali Hallak, Head of Digital Marketing, Samsung Gulf Electronics, UAE
Diane and Jon Sutherland, Writers, UK
Hamed Shamma, American University in Cairo, Egypt
Jimmy Wong, Monash University, Australia
Xavier Pierron, Coventry University, UK

Reviewers

Alan Au, The Open University of Hong Kong, China
Frederick Hong-kit Yim, Hong Kong Baptist University, China
Osman GÖK, Yasar University, Turkey

Consumer Behavior

Section 1 • Foundations of Consumer Behavior

This introductory section provides an overview of the field of consumer behavior (CB). In Chapter 1, we look at how consumers influence the field of marketing and at how marketers influence us. We describe the discipline of consumer behavior and some of the different approaches to understanding what makes consumers tick. In Chapter 2 we'll take a closer look at how each of us decides what to buy (or what not to buy), and then in Chapter 3 we'll zoom out and examine how the culture in which we live influences those decisions. Chapter 4 will focus on what these choices mean for each of us and for the world in which we live.

CHAPTERS AHEAD

Chapter 1 • **Buying, Having, and Being: An Introduction to Consumer Behavior**

Chapter 2 • **Decision Making and Consumer Behavior**

Chapter 3 • **Cultural Influences on Consumer Decision Making**

Chapter 4 • **Consumer and Social Well-Being**

Chapter 1 • Buying, Having, and Being: An Introduction to Consumer Behavior

Chapter Objectives

When you finish reading this chapter you will understand why:

1. Consumer behavior is a process.

2. Marketers have to understand the wants and needs of different consumer segments.

3. Our choices as consumers relate in powerful ways to the rest of our lives.

4. Our motivations to consume are complex and varied.

5. Technology and culture create a new "always on" consumer.

6. Many different types of specialists study consumer behavior.

7. There are differing perspectives regarding how and what we should understand about consumer behavior.

MyMarketingLab™

⭐ Improve Your Grade!

Over 10 million students improved their results using the Pearson MyLabs.
Visit **mymktlab.com** for simulations, tutorials, and end-of-chapter problems.

Source: Supri Suharjoto/Shutterstock.com.

Gail has some time to kill before her Accounting class, so she pulls out her trusty iPhone to see what's going on in her social networks. Between studying for her Accounting and Marketing exams, she hasn't checked out anything interesting in days—even her Facebook friends around campus have been quiet. Enough of the serious stuff, she decides. It's time for some *really* educational surfing.

So, where to go first? Gail figures she'll start at one of the popular women's portals and see what happens. She goes to iVillage.com, where she quickly scans a feature on the top 10 virtual makeovers. At Oxygen.com she watches a streaming video preview about a new reality show and some scenes from the latest episode of *Bad Girls Club*. She flicks over to HerCampus ("a collegiette's guide to life[SM]") to quickly check out the male students they're featuring in today's Eye Candy section. Just then Gail gets a text from Jewelmint.com to notify her that the site has a new jewelry option for her that's based on the profile she filled out when she registered—and it's recommended by actress Kate Bosworth. Wow, a gorgeous pendant for only $29.99! With her PayPal account, it doesn't take Gail long to throw the pendant in the cart and order it—and to share a photo of her haul on Facebook. As Gail glances at the clock, she realizes she'd better come back to the real world or she'll miss her exam. OK, enough time for one quick post before she runs to catch the campus shuttle: Gail logs on to RateMyProfessors.com and writes a quick but glowing paragraph about how great her Consumer Behavior professor has been this semester . . . not to mention that awesome textbook they've been using.[1]

OBJECTIVE 1
Consumer behavior is a process.

Consumer Behavior: People in the Marketplace

This book is about people like Gail—and *you*. It concerns the products and services we buy and use, and the ways these fit into our lives. The introductory chapter describes some important aspects of the field of consumer behavior and some reasons why it's essential to understand how people interact with the marketing system. For now, though, let's return to one "typical" consumer: Gail, the business major. The preceding vignette allows us to highlight some aspects of consumer behavior that we will cover in the rest of the book.

Gail is a consumer; so let's compare her to other consumers. For some purposes, marketers find it useful to categorize her in terms of her age, gender, income, or occupation. These are descriptive characteristics of a population, or **demographics**. In other cases, marketers would rather know something about Gail's interests in clothing or music, or the way she spends her leisure time. Knowledge of consumer characteristics plays an extremely important role in many marketing applications, such as when a manufacturer defines the market for a product or an advertising agency decides upon the appropriate techniques to employ when it targets a certain group of consumers.

Gail's sorority sisters strongly influence her purchase decisions. The conversations we have with others transmit a lot of product information, as well as recommendations to use or avoid particular brands; this content often is more influential than what we see on television commercials, magazines, or billboards. The growth of the Web has created thousands of online **consumption communities**, where members share opinions and recommendations about anything from Barbie dolls to baseball fantasy league team lineups to iPhone apps. Gail forms bonds with fellow group members because they use the same products. There is also pressure on each group member to buy things that will meet with the group's approval. A consumer may pay a steep price in the form of group rejection or embarrassment when she doesn't conform to others' conceptions of what is good or bad, "in" or "out."

As members of a large society, such as the United States, people share certain cultural values, or strongly held beliefs about the way the world should function. Members of subcultures, or smaller groups within the culture, also share values; these groups include Hispanics, teens, Midwesterners, and even Lady Gaga's "Little Monsters."

Everyday—like all of us—Gail comes into contact with information about many competing *brands*. Some don't capture her attention at all, whereas others are just a turnoff because they don't relate to "looks," people, or ideas with which she identifies. The use of **market segmentation strategies** means an organization targets its product, service, or idea only to specific groups of consumers rather than to everybody—even if it means that other consumers who don't belong to this target market aren't attracted to it. That's why they make chocolate and vanilla ice cream (and even candied bacon flavor!).

Brands often have clearly defined images, or "personalities," that advertising, packaging, branding, and other marketing elements help to shape. Even the choice of a favorite Web site is very much a *lifestyle* statement: It says a lot about a person's interests, as well as something about the type of person she would like to be. People often purchase a product because they like its image or because they feel its "personality" somehow corresponds to their own. Moreover, a consumer may believe that if she buys and uses the product or service, its desirable qualities will "magically" rub off onto her. When a product or service succeeds in satisfying our specific needs or desires, we may reward it with many years of *brand loyalty*, a bond between product and consumer that is very difficult for competitors to break.

The appearance, taste, texture, or smell of the item influences our evaluations of products. A good Web site helps people to feel, taste, and smell with their eyes. We may be swayed by the shape and color of a package on the store shelf, as well as by more subtle factors, such as the symbolism in a brand name, in an advertisement, or even in the choice of a cover model for a magazine. These judgments are affected by—and often reflect—how a society feels people should define themselves at that point in time. Many product meanings lurk below the surface of the packaging and advertising; we'll discuss some of the methods marketers and social scientists use to discover or apply these meanings.

Like Gail, we shape our opinions and desires based upon a mix of voices from around the world, which is becoming a much smaller place as a result of rapid advancements in communications and transportation systems. In today's global culture, consumers often prize products and services that "transport" them to different places and allow them to experience the diversity of other cultures—even if only to watch others brush their teeth on YouTube.

What Is Consumer Behavior?

The field of **consumer behavior** covers a lot of ground: *It is the study of the processes involved when individuals or groups select, purchase, use, or dispose of products, services, ideas, or experiences to satisfy needs and desires.* Consumers take many forms, ranging from an 8-year-old child who begs her mother for a Webkinz stuffed animal to an executive in a large corporation who helps to decide on a multimillion-dollar computer system. The items we consume include anything from canned peas to a massage, democracy,

Juicy jeans, Reggaeton music, or a celebrity like Adele. The needs and desires we satisfy range from hunger and thirst to love, status, and even spiritual fulfillment. Also, as we'll see throughout this book, people get passionate about a broad range of products. Whether it's vintage Air Jordans, that perfect yoga mat, or the latest computer tablet, there's no shortage of brand fans who will do whatever it takes to find and buy what they crave.

Consumer Behavior Is a Process

In its early stages of development, researchers referred to the field as *buyer behavior;* this reflected the emphasis at that time (back in the 1960s and 1970s) on the interaction between consumers and producers at the time of purchase. Most marketers now recognize that consumer behavior is in fact an ongoing *process*, not merely what happens at the moment a consumer hands over money or a credit card and in turn receives some good or service.

The **exchange**, a transaction in which two or more organizations or people give and receive something of value, is an integral part of marketing.[2] Although *exchange theory* remains an important part of consumer behavior, the expanded view emphasizes the *entire* consumption process, which includes the issues that influence the consumer before, during, and after a purchase. Figure 1.1 illustrates some of the issues that we address during each stage of the consumption process.

A **consumer** is a person who identifies a need or desire, makes a purchase, and then disposes of the product during the three stages of the consumption process. In many cases, however, different people play a role in this sequence of events. The purchaser and user of a product might not be the same person, as when a parent picks out clothes for a teenager (and makes selections that can result in "fashion suicide" in the view of the teen). In other cases, another person may act as an *influencer* by recommending certain products without actually buying or using them. A friend's grimace when you try on that new pair of pants may be more influential than anything your mother might say.

Finally, consumers may take the form of organizations or groups. One or several persons may select products that many will use, as when a purchasing agent orders a company's office supplies. In other organizational situations, a large group of people may make purchase decisions: for example, company accountants, designers, engineers, sales personnel, and others—all of whom will have a say in the various stages of the consumption

Figure 1.1 STAGES IN THE CONSUMPTION PROCESS

Marketing Opportunity

Successful companies understand that needs are a moving target. No organization—no matter how renowned for its marketing prowess—can afford to rest on its laurels. *Everyone* needs to keep innovating to stay ahead of changing customers and the marketplace. BMW is a great example. No one (not even rivals like Audi or Mercedes-Benz) would argue that the German automaker knows how to make a good car (though they may not agree with the company's claim to be "the ultimate driving machine"). Still, BMW's engineers and designers know they have to understand how drivers' needs will change in the future—even those loyal owners who love the cars they own today. The company is highly sensitive to such key trends as:

- A desire for environmentally friendly products
- Increasingly congested roadways and the movement by some cities such as London to impose fees on vehicles in central areas
- New business models that encourage consumers to rent products only while they need them rather than buying them outright

BMW's response: The company committed more than $1 billion to develop electric models like its new i3 commuter car and i8 sports car. These futuristic-looking vehicles are largely made from lightweight carbon fiber to maximize the distance they can go between battery charges, and 25 percent of the interior plastic comes from recycled or renewable raw materials. In addition, BMW started a car-sharing service (now in Munich) it calls DriveNow: Drivers use a computer chip in their licenses to hire a car and leave it wherever they are when they no longer need it. That's forward thinking.[3]

process. As we'll see in Chapter 9, one important type of organization is the family, where different family members weigh in about products and services that all will use.

Consumers' Impact on Marketing Strategy

Why should managers, advertisers, and other marketing professionals bother to learn about consumer behavior? Very simply, *it's good business*. The basic marketing concept that you (hopefully) remember from your basic Marketing class states that organizations exist to satisfy needs. Marketers can satisfy these needs only to the extent that they understand the people or organizations that will use the products and services they sell. Voila! That's why we study consumer behavior.

OBJECTIVE 2
Marketers have to understand the wants and needs of different consumer segments.

Consumers Are Different! How We Divide Them Up

Our society is evolving from a *mass culture* in which many consumers share the same preferences to a diverse one in which we each have almost an infinite number of choices—just think about how many shades of lipstick or necktie patterns compete for your attention. This change makes it more important than ever to identify distinct market segments and to develop specialized messages and products for those groups.

As we'll see later, building loyalty to a brand is a very smart marketing strategy, so sometimes companies define market segments when they identify their most faithful customers or **heavy users**. As a rule of thumb, marketers use the **80/20 rule**: 20 percent of users account for 80 percent of sales. This guideline often holds up well, and in some cases even this lopsided split isn't big enough: A study of 54 million shoppers reported that only 2.5 percent of consumers account for 80 percent of sales for the average packaged-goods brand. The 1 percent of pet owners who buy 80 percent of Iams pet food spend $93 a year on the brand, and the 1.2 percent of beer drinkers who account for 80 percent of Budweiser sales spend $170 on Bud each year. Of the 1,364 brands the researchers studied, only 25 had a consumer base of more than 10 percent that accounted for 80 percent of volume.[4] So, just think of the 80/20 rule as a general rule of thumb.

Aside from heavy usage of a product, we use many other dimensions to divide up a larger market. As we've already seen, *demographics* are statistics that measure observable aspects of a population, such as birth rate, age distribution, and income. The U.S. Census Bureau is a major source of demographic data on U.S. families, but many private firms gather additional data on specific population groups as well. The changes and

BMW anticipated changes in consumer behavior as it develops electric car models like the i8 that satisfy dual desires for style and environmental responsibility.
Source: BMW of North America, LLC.

trends that demographic studies reveal are of great interest to marketers because they can use the data to locate and predict the size of markets for many products, ranging from home mortgages to brooms and can openers. Imagine trying to sell baby food to a single male, or an around the world cruise to a couple making $15,000 a year!

In this book we explore many of the important demographic variables that make one consumer the same as or different from others. We also consider other important characteristics that are a bit subtler, such as differences in consumers' personalities and tastes that we can't objectively measure, yet may hugely impact our product choices. For now, let's summarize a few of the most important demographic dimensions, each of which we'll describe in more detail in later chapters.

Age

Consumers of different *age groups* obviously have very different needs and wants. Although people who belong to the same age group differ in many other ways, they do tend to share a set of values and common cultural experiences that they carry throughout life.[5]

In some cases, marketers initially develop a product to attract one age group and then try to broaden its appeal later on. That's what the high-octane energy drink Red Bull does. The company aggressively introduced it in bars, nightclubs, and gyms to the product's core audience of young people. Over time, it became popular in other contexts, and the company began to sponsor the PGA European Tour to broaden its reach to older golfers (who probably aren't up partying all night). It also hands out free cans to commuters, cab drivers, and car rental agencies to promote the drink as a way to stay alert on the road.[6]

Gender

We start to make gender distinctions at a very early age—even diapers come in pink versions for girls and blue for boys. Many products, from fragrances to footwear, target either men or women. An all-female marketing team at Procter & Gamble (P&G), who jokingly call themselves "chicks in charge," introduced Crest Rejuvenating Effects, the first mass-market toothpaste positioned just for women. P&G communicates that this product is feminine when the company packages it in a teal tube nestled inside a glimmering "pearlescent" box. The toothpaste is sparkly, teal-toned, and tastes like vanilla and cinnamon.[7]

Family Structure

A person's family/marital status is yet another important demographic variable, because this has a huge effect on consumers' spending priorities. Not surprisingly, young bachelors and newlyweds are the most likely to exercise; go to bars, concerts, and movies; and consume alcohol (enjoy it while you can!). Families with young children are big purchasers of health foods and fruit juices, whereas single-parent households and those with older children buy more junk food. Older couples and bachelors are most likely to use home maintenance services.[8]

Social Class and Income

People who belong to the same *social class* are approximately equal in terms of income and social standing in the community. They work in roughly similar occupations, and they tend to have similar tastes in music, clothing, leisure activities, and art. They also tend to socialize with one another, and they share many ideas and values regarding the way they should live.[9] The distribution of wealth is of great interest to marketers because it determines which groups have the greatest buying power and market potential.

Race and Ethnicity

African Americans, Hispanic Americans, and Asian Americans are the three fastest-growing ethnic groups in the United States. As our society becomes increasingly multi-cultural, new opportunities develop to deliver specialized products to racial and ethnic

Net Profit

Consider how one of the world's largest food chains adapts to changing times: McDonald's now devotes a third of its U.S. marketing budget to television, compared with two-thirds a few years ago. The company uses that left-over money to sponsor closed-circuit sports programming it pipes into Hispanic bars and for ads in *Upscale*, a custom-published magazine distributed to barber shops that cater to African American consumers. McDonald's advertises on Foot Locker's in-store video network to reach young men, and it zeroes in on mothers through ads in women's magazines such as *O: The Oprah Magazine* and Web sites such as iVillage.com. McDonald's even sponsored one of the first global **alternate reality games (ARGs)**, called *The Lost Ring*. An ARG integrates multiple media channels, ranging from TV, email, SMS, and snail mail, to engage a community of players who collaborate to solve a complex puzzle. *The Lost Ring* was the story of six amnesiac Olympians who competed in an ancient, lost Olympic sport: labyrinth running. Gamers from all over the world found clues hidden both online, in places like YouTube and Flickr and story microsites, as well as in offline locations. McDonald's strategically placed 27 game artifacts in the United States, Germany, Australia, China, France, Spain, Switzerland, Japan, Canada, Argentina, England, Singapore, Korea, South Africa, Sweden, Italy, the Netherlands, and Mexico; the final story lines were not revealed until the final artifact was discovered. By the end of the campaign, the game's Web site had received 4.8 million visits, and almost 3 million people in 110 countries participated.[10] Unlike most McDonald's advertising, which makes it clear that you need to buy a burger, there was no mention of the company's sponsorship in the campaign (this is known as a "dark-play ARG"). Still, the chain benefited from a substantial boost in favorability ratings when people learned who was behind the global game.[11]

According to a survey done by the marketing company Porter Novelli,[12] a heavy user in the fast food industry is a person who spends around $40 a day in fast food restaurants. Thus, this person may visit them more than once in a day. Firms compete with each other to obtain the loyalty of these users by producing specialized products to attract them.[13] The following are relevant examples of such products. Mo'men, an Egyptian fast food chain, created the Max Meal that includes a large sandwich of the client's choosing (chicken, beef, or fish) served with fries, a soft drink, a salad, and a cookie. Sultan Ayub, famous for its shawarmas in Egypt, introduced the largest shawarma sandwich along with a 50 percent discount on any additional sandwich. And finally Quick, a Belgian chain of hamburger fast food restaurants, introduced "The Giant" sandwich, which now constitutes about 50 percent of Quick's burger orders.[14]

When Hurricane Sandy devastated cities on the East Coast in 2012, some marketers rose to the occasion while others stumbled in the wind. Gap, for example, tweeted, "We'll be doing lots of Gap.com shopping today. How about you?" American Apparel offered an incentive to shoppers: "In case you're bored during the storm, just Enter SANDYSALE at Checkout." Many of the storm victims were not amused. One tweeted, "Hey @americanapparel people have died and others are in need. Shut up about your #Sandy sale."

In contrast, Allstate ran radio commercials to let policyholders know how to file claims quickly. JetBlue Airways waived change and cancellation fees for people who had to rebook. How's this for a relationship builder: Duracell batteries sent a truck to New York City that offered free batteries and access to charging lockers for mobile devices and computers to desperate people who had been without power (or even worse, access to social media).[18]

Consumers from the same social class tend to gravitate toward similar artistic or recreational outlets.
Source: CD: Karpat Polat; AD: Cuneyt Ozalp.

groups and to introduce other groups to these offerings. McDonald's, for example, regards ethnic consumers as trendsetters. The restaurant chain often assesses their reactions to new menu items or advertisements before it rolls them out to the Caucasian market. For example, the fruit combinations in McDonald's smoothies are based upon preferences they discovered in ethnic communities.[15]

Geography

Many national marketers tailor their offerings to appeal to consumers who live in different parts of the country. Some southerners are fond of a "good ol' boy" image that leaves others scratching their heads. Although many northerners regard the name "Bubba" as a negative term, businesses in Dixie proudly flaunt the name. Bubba Co. is a Charleston-based firm that licenses products such as Bubba-Q-Sauce. In Florida, restaurants, sports bars, nightclubs, and a limousine firm all proudly bear the name Bubba.[16]

Lifestyles

Consumers also have very different *lifestyles,* even if they share other demographic characteristics such as gender or age. The way we feel about ourselves, the things we value, the things we like to do in our spare time—all of these factors help to determine which products will push our buttons, or even those that make us feel better. Procter & Gamble developed its heartburn medicine Prilosec OTC with an ideal customer in mind based on a lifestyle analysis. Her name is Joanne, and she's a mother over the age of 35 who's more likely to get heartburn from a cup of coffee than from an overdose of pizza and beer. A P&G executive observed, "We know Joanne. We know what she feels. We know what she eats. We know what else she likes to buy in the store."[17]

Marketers carefully define customer segments and listen to people in their markets as never before. Many of them now realize that a key to success is building relationships between brands and customers that will last a lifetime. Marketers who subscribe to this philosophy of **relationship marketing** interact with customers on a regular basis and give them solid reasons to maintain a bond with the company over time. A focus on relationships is even more vital during the nasty economic conditions we've recently experienced—when times are tough, people tend to rely on their good friends for support!

The Redneck Bank takes a unique approach to social class segmentation (yes, this is a real bank).

Source: Courtesy of www.redneckbank.com.

Segmenting by Behavior: Welcome to Big Data

Database marketing tracks specific consumers' buying habits very closely and crafts products and messages tailored precisely to people's wants and needs based on this information. Walmart stores massive amounts of information on the 100 million people who visit its stores each week, and the company uses these data to fine-tune its offerings. For example, when the company analyzed how shoppers' buying patterns react when forecasters predict a major hurricane, it discovered that people do a lot more than simply stock up on flashlights. Sales of strawberry Pop-Tarts increase by about 700 percent, and the top-selling product of all is . . . beer. Based on these insights, Walmart loads its trucks with toaster pastries and six-packs to stock local stores when a big storm approaches.[19]

At this very moment (and every moment thereafter until we croak), we all generate massive amounts of information that holds tremendous value for marketers. You may not see it, but we are practically buried by data that comes from many sources—sensors that collect climate information, the comments you and your friends make to your favorite social media sites, the credit card transactions we authorize, and even the GPS signals in our smartphones that let organizations know where most of us are pretty much anytime day or night. This incredible amount of information has created a new field that causes tremendous excitement among marketing analysts (and other math geeks). The

CAPTURE THE DREAM.

WWW.AZIMUTYACHTS.COM

AZIMUT YACHTS

This Italian ad for a yacht company appeals to people who have money or who dream they will someday have enough to buy a yacht.

Source: Courtesy of Azimut Yachts.

collection and analysis of extremely large datasets is called **Big Data**, and you'll be hearing a lot more about it in the next few years. Hint: If you have aptitude and/or interest in quantitative topics, this will be a very desirable career path for you.

In a single day, consumers create 2.5 quintillion bytes of data (or 2.5 exabytes). New data pops up so quickly that this number doubles about every 40 months—and 90 percent of the data in the world today was created in the last 2 years alone. In addition to the huge *volume* of information marketers now have to play with, its *velocity* (speed) also enables companies to make decisions in real time that used to take months or years. For example, one group of researchers used the GPS phone signals that were coming from Macy's parking lots on Black Friday to estimate whether the department store was going to meet or exceed its sales projections for the biggest shopping day of the year—before the stores even reported their sales. This kind of intelligence allows financial analysts and marketing managers to move very quickly as they buy and sell stocks or make merchandising decisions.

It's safe to say this data explosion will profoundly change the way we think about consumer behavior. Companies, nonprofits, political parties, and even governments now have the ability to sift through massive quantities of information that enables them to make very precise predictions about what products we will buy, what charities we will donate to, what candidates we will vote for—and what levers they need to push to make this even more likely to happen. Walmart alone collects more than 2.5 petabytes of data every hour from its customer transactions (the equivalent of about 20 million filing cabinets' worth of text). Here are a few varied examples that illustrate how Big Data influences what we know and do:[20]

- When they monitor blips in Google queries for words like *flu* and *fever*, epidemiologists at the Centers for Disease Control can identify specific areas of the United States that have been hit by flu outbreaks even before the local authorities notice a rise in hospital admissions.
- Analysts for city police departments use massive amounts of crime data to identify "hot zones," where an abnormal amount of crimes occur. This intelligence enables them to assign and reassign law enforcement agents exactly where they need them.

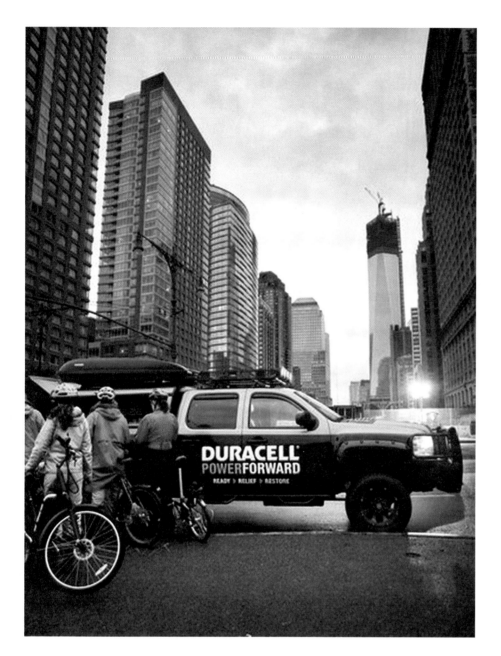

Duracell met a legitimate consumer need—and generated a lot of goodwill—when the company provided power to people who were cut off of the grid by Hurricane Sandy.

Source: The Procter & Gamble Company.

● Although the Republicans outspent the Democrats during the 2012 presidential campaign, many attribute President Obama's reelection to his campaign's masterful use of Big Data. The Democratic campaign systematically used huge datasets to help it decide exactly which voters needed an extra "nudge" to go to the polls and pull the lever for Obama.

OBJECTIVE 3
Our choices as consumers relate in powerful ways to the rest of our lives.

Marketing's Impact on Consumers

Does marketing imitate life, or vice versa? After the movie *Wedding Crashers* became a big hit, hotels, wedding planners, and newlyweds reported an outbreak of uninvited guests who tried to gain access to parties across the United States.[21] For better or for worse, we all live in a world that the actions of marketers significantly influence.

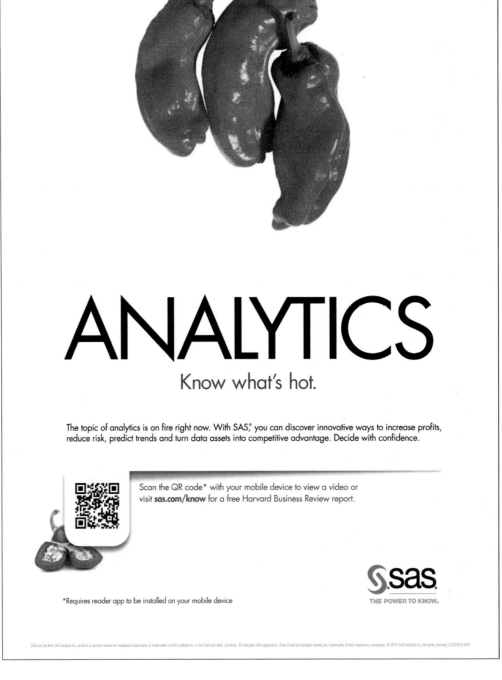

Popular Culture Is Marketing Is Popular Culture . . .

Marketing stimuli surround us as advertisements, stores, and products compete for our attention and our dollars. Marketers filter much of what we learn about the world, whether through the affluence they depict in glamorous magazines, the roles actors play in commercials, or maybe the energy drink that rock star just "happens" to hold during a photo shoot. Ads show us how we should act with regard to recycling, alcohol consumption, the types of houses and cars we might wish to own—and even how to evaluate others based on the products they buy or don't buy. In many ways we are also at the mercy of marketers, because we rely on them to sell us products that are safe and that perform as promised, to tell us the truth about what they sell, and to price and distribute these products fairly.

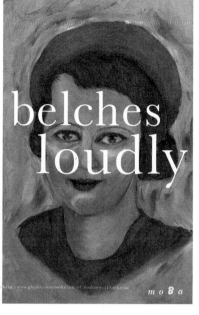

Some art speaks to you.
Some just belches loudly in your face.

mo8a   museum of bad art

We are surrounded by elements of popular culture—the good, the bad, and the ugly. This ad for the Museum of Bad Art reminds us of that.
Source: With permission of Museum of Bad Art.

Popular culture—the music, movies, sports, books, celebrities, and other forms of entertainment that the mass market produces and consumes—is both a product of and an inspiration for marketers. It also affects our lives in more far-reaching ways, ranging from how we acknowledge cultural events such as marriage, death, or holidays to how we view social issues such as global warming, gambling, and addictions. Whether it's the Super Bowl, Christmas shopping, national health care, newspaper recycling, medical marijuana, body piercing, cigarette smoking, tweeting, or online video games, marketers play a significant role in our view of the world and how we live in it.

This cultural impact is hard to overlook, although many people do not seem to realize how much marketers influence their preferences for movie and musical heroes; the latest fashions in clothing, food, and decorating choices; and even the physical features that they find attractive or ugly in men and women. For example, consider the product icons that companies use to create an identity for their products. Many imaginary creatures and personalities, from the Pillsbury Doughboy to the Jolly Green Giant, at one time or another have been central figures in popular culture. In fact, it is likely that more consumers could recognize such characters than could identify past presidents, business leaders, or artists. Although these figures never really existed, many of us feel as if we "know" them, and they certainly are effective *spokescharacters* for the products they represent.

All the World's a Stage

The sociological perspective of **role theory** takes the view that much of consumer behavior resembles actions in a play.[23] As in a play, each consumer has the lines, props, and costumes necessary to put on a good performance. Because people act out many different roles, they sometimes alter their consumption decisions depending on the particular "play" they are in at the time. The criteria they use to evaluate products and services in one of their roles may be quite different from those they use in other roles. That's why it's important for marketers to provide each of us "actors" with the props we need to play all of our varied roles; these might include "up-and-coming executive," "geek," or "big man on campus."

As we have seen, one trademark of marketing strategies today is that many organizations try very hard to build relationships with customers. The nature of these relationships can vary, but these bonds help us to understand some of the possible meanings

Marketing Opportunity

The interplay between marketing/media and "real life" is obvious when you consider the history of the cultural observance American college students know as "Spring Break." Back in 1958 an English professor at Michigan State University heard some students talking about their Easter trip to Fort Lauderdale, Florida. He decided to go along to observe (they probably loved that), and upon his return he wrote a novel he called *Where the Boys Are.* That turned into a hit movie and the title song by Connie Francis rocked the charts. The year after the movie debuted in 1960, the number of students who visited Florida on their spring vacation ballooned from 20,000 to 50,000. MTV hosted a concert at Daytona Beach in 1986 that attracted major advertisers—thus began the commercialization of a rite that now attracts hundreds of thousands of devotees every year.[22]

Marketers contribute to Spring Break frenzy.
Source: Kzenon/Shutterstock.

products have for us. Furthermore, researchers find that, like friendships and love affairs with other people, our relationships with brands evolve over time. Some resemble deep friendships, whereas others are more like exciting but short-lived flings.[24]

Here are some of the types of relationships a person might have with a product:

- **Self-concept attachment**—The product helps to establish the user's identity.
- **Nostalgic attachment**—The product serves as a link with a past self.
- **Interdependence**—The product is a part of the user's daily routine.
- **Love**—The product elicits emotional bonds of warmth, passion, or other strong emotion.[25]

OBJECTIVE 4
Our motivations to consume are complex and varied.

What Does It Mean to Consume?

What's the poop on Peeps? Every year, people buy about 1.5 billion of these mostly tasteless marshmallow chicks; about two-thirds of them sell around Easter. They have no nutritional value, but they do have a shelf life of 2 years. Maybe that's why not all Peeps get eaten. Devotees use them in decorations, dioramas, online slide shows, and sculptures. Some fans feel challenged to test their physical properties: On more than 200 Peeps Web sites, you can see fetishists skewering, microwaving, hammering, decapitating, and otherwise abusing the spongy confections.[26]

This fascination with a creepy little candy chick illustrates one of the fundamental premises of the modern field of consumer behavior: *People often buy products not for what they do but for what they mean.* This principle does not imply that a product's basic function is unimportant, but rather that the roles products play in our lives extend well beyond the tasks they perform. The deeper meanings of a product may help it to stand out from other similar goods and services. All things being equal, we choose the brand that has an image (or even a personality!) consistent with our underlying needs.

For example, although most people probably couldn't run faster or jump higher if they wear Nikes instead of Reeboks, many die-hard loyalists swear by their favorite brand. People choose between these archrivals (or other competitors) largely due to their *brand images*—meanings that have been carefully crafted with the help of legions of rock stars, athletes, slickly produced commercials, and many millions of dollars. So, when you buy a Nike "swoosh," you are doing more than choosing shoes to wear to the

Many products help to define our identities. Are you what you drive?
Source: Courtesy of Automobile Magazine, Source Interlink.

Nothing says more about how you see yourself than the car you choose to drive. And no publication understands this better than Automobile Magazine. It isn't about cars. It's for drivers. And dreamers. Automobile Magazine is where aspiration comes looking for inspiration. Make sure our readers get to see how your brand fits.

WHAT KIND OF CAR ARE YOU?

mall: you also make a lifestyle statement about the type of person you are or wish you were. For a relatively simple item made of leather and laces, that's quite a feat!

Our allegiances to sneakers, musicians, and even soft drinks help us define our place in modern society, and these choices also help each of us to form bonds with others who share similar preferences. This comment by a participant in a focus group captures the curious bonding that can be caused by consumption choices: "I was at a Super Bowl party, and I picked up an obscure drink. Somebody else across the room went 'yo!' because he had the same thing. People feel a connection when you're drinking the same thing."[27]

Motivation refers to the processes that lead people to behave as they do. It occurs when a need is aroused that the consumer wishes to satisfy. The need creates a state of tension that drives the consumer to attempt to reduce or eliminate it. This need may be *utilitarian* (i.e., a desire to achieve some functional or practical benefit, as when a person loads up on green vegetables for nutritional reasons) or it may be *hedonic* (i.e., an experiential need, involving emotional responses or fantasies). The desired end state is

This ad for electronics products by Samsung focuses on pure desire—consuming as experience.
Source: Courtesy of Samsung Electronics America, Inc. Reprinted by permission.

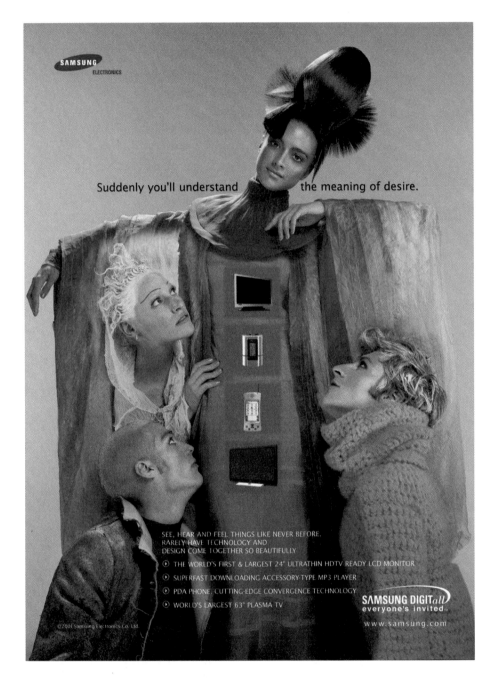

the consumer's **goal**. Marketers try to create products and services to provide the desired benefits and help the consumer to reduce this tension.

Whether the need is utilitarian or hedonic, the magnitude of the tension it creates determines the urgency the consumer feels to reduce it. We call this degree of arousal a **drive**. **Drive theory** focuses on biological needs that produce unpleasant states of arousal (e.g., your stomach grumbles during a morning class). The arousal this tension causes motivates us to reduce it. Some researchers believe that this need to reduce arousal is a basic mechanism that governs much of our behavior.

If a behavior reduces the drive, we naturally tend to repeat it. Your motivation to leave class early to grab a snack would be greater if you hadn't eaten in 24 hours than if you had eaten only 2 hours earlier. If you did sneak out and got indigestion afterward, say, from wolfing down a package of Twinkies, you would be less likely to repeat this behavior the next time you want a snack. One's degree of motivation, then, depends on the distance between one's present state and the goal.

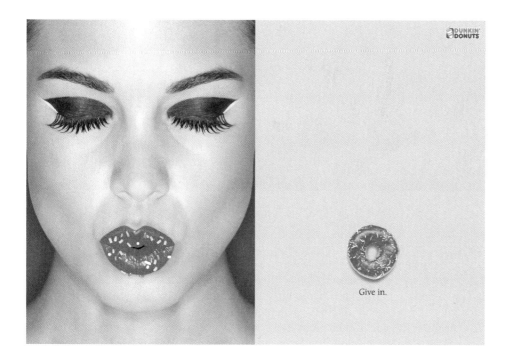

Drive theory runs into difficulties when it tries to explain some facets of human behavior that run counter to its predictions. People often do things that increase a drive state rather than decrease it. For example, we may *delay gratification.* If you know you are going out for a lavish dinner, you might decide to forego a snack earlier in the day even though you are hungry at that time.

Most current explanations of motivation focus on cognitive factors rather than biological ones to understand what motivates behavior. **Expectancy theory** suggests that expectations of achieving desirable outcomes—positive incentives—rather than being pushed from within motivate our behavior. We choose one product over another because we expect this choice to have more positive consequences for us. Thus, we use the term *drive* here loosely to refer to both physical and cognitive processes.

Motives have direction as well as strength. They are goal-oriented in that they drive us to satisfy a specific need. We can reach most goals by a number of routes, and the objective of a company is to convince consumers that the alternative it offers provides the best chance to attain the goal. For example, a consumer who decides that she needs a pair of jeans to help her reach her goal of being admired by others can choose among Levi's, Wranglers, True Religion, Diesel, Seven for All Mankind, and many other alternatives, each of which promises to deliver certain benefits.

What Do We Need—*Really*?

What is the difference between needing something and wanting it? The answer to this deceptively simple question actually explains a lot of consumer behavior! A **want** is a specific manifestation of a need that personal and cultural factors determine. For example, hunger is a basic need that all of us must satisfy; a lack of food creates a tension state that a person is motivated to reduce. But, the way he or she chooses to do that can take a lot of forms: One person's "dream meal" might include a cheeseburger, fries, and double-fudge Oreo cookies, while another might go for sushi. We describe motivation in terms of its *strength,* or the pull it exerts on the consumer; and its *direction,* or the particular way the consumer attempts to reduce it.

When we focus on a *utilitarian need,* we emphasize the objective, tangible attributes of products, such as miles per gallon in a car; the amount of fat, calories, and protein in a cheeseburger; or the durability of a pair of blue jeans. *Hedonic needs* are subjective and experiential; here we might look to a product to meet our needs for excitement,

One utilitarian need is very simple—we need to replenish products when we run out of them.
Source: Shalmor Avnon Amichay/Y&R.

self-confidence, or fantasy—perhaps to escape the mundane or routine aspects of life.[28] Many items satisfy our hedonic needs (there's even a popular resort called Hedonism). Luxury brands in particular thrive when they offer the promise of pleasure to the user—how badly do you "need" that Armani suit or Tiffany brooch?[29]

Of course, we can also be motivated to purchase a product because it provides *both* types of benefits. For example, a woman (perhaps a politically incorrect one) might buy a mink coat because of the luxurious image it portrays and because it also happens to keep her warm through the long, cold winter. Indeed, recent research on novel consumption experiences indicates that even when we choose to do unusual things (like eating bacon ice cream or staying in a freezing ice hotel), we may do so because we have what the authors term a **productivity orientation**. This refers to a continual striving to use time constructively: Trying new things is a way to check them off our "bucket list" of experiences we want to achieve before we move on to others.

How We Classify Consumer Needs

Some analysts set out to define a universal inventory of needs they could trace systematically to explain virtually all behavior. One such inventory that the psychologist Henry Murray developed delineates a set of 20 *psychogenic needs* that (sometimes in combination) result in specific behaviors. These needs include such dimensions as *autonomy* (being independent), *defendance* (defending the self against criticism), and even *play* (engaging in pleasurable activities).[30]

Other motivational approaches focus on specific needs and their ramifications for behavior. For example, individuals with a high *need for achievement* strongly value personal accomplishment.[31] They place a premium on products and services that signify success because these consumption items provide feedback about the realization of their goals. These consumers are good prospects for products that provide evidence of their achievement. One study of working women found that those who were high in achievement motivation were more likely to choose clothing they considered businesslike and less likely to be interested in apparel that accentuated their femininity.[32] Some other important needs that are relevant to consumer behavior include:

- **Need for affiliation**—(to be in the company of other people).[33] The need for affiliation is relevant to products and services for people in groups, such as those participating in team sports, frequenting bars, and hanging out at shopping malls.
- **Need for power**—(to control one's environment).[34] Many products and services allow us to feel that we have mastery over our surroundings (to quote the famous line from the TV show *Seinfeld*, we are "masters of our domain")! These products range from "hopped-up" muscle cars and loud boom boxes (large portable radios that impose one's musical tastes on others) to luxury resorts that promise to respond to every whim of their pampered guests.

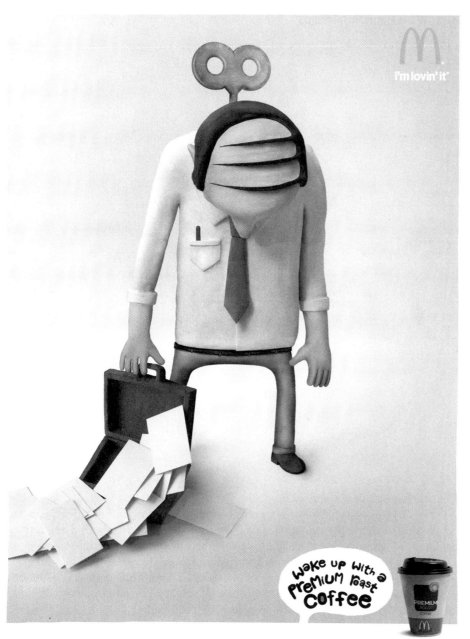

McDonald's promises its coffee will satisfy a physiological need—to wake up.

Source: Courtesy of McDonald's.

- **Need for uniqueness**—(to assert one's individual identity).[35] Products satisfy the need for uniqueness when they pledge to bring out our distinctive qualities. For example, Cachet perfume claims to be "as individual as you are."

Psychologist Abraham Maslow originally developed his influential **Hierarchy of Needs** to understand personal growth and how people attain spiritual "peak experiences." Marketers later adapted his work to understand consumer motivations.[36] Maslow's *hierarchical* structure implies that the order of development is fixed—that is, we must attain a certain level before we activate a need for the next, higher one. Marketers embraced this perspective because it (indirectly) specifies certain types of product benefits people might look for, depending on their stage of mental or spiritual development or on their economic situation.[37]

Figure 1.2 presents this model. At each level, the person seeks different kinds of product benefits. Ideally, an individual progresses up the hierarchy until his or her dominant motivation is a focus on "ultimate" goals, such as justice and beauty. Unfortunately, this state is difficult to achieve (at least on a regular basis); most of us have to be satisfied

Figure 1.2 MASLOW'S HIERARCHY OF NEEDS

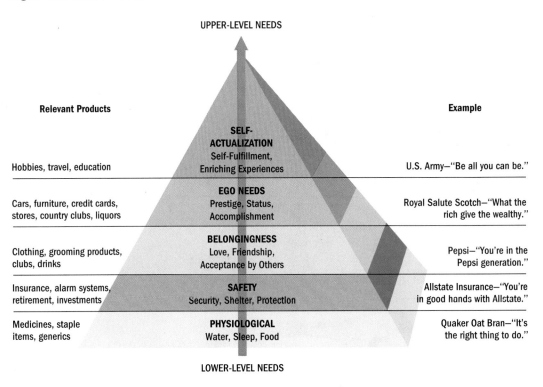

with occasional glimpses, or *peak experiences*. One study of men aged 49 to 60 found that these respondents engaged in three types of activities to attain self-fulfillment: (1) *sport and physical activity,* (2) *community and charity,* and (3) *building and renovating.* Regardless of whether these activities were related to their professional work, these so-called *magnetic points* gradually took the place of those that were not as fulfilling.[38]

Marketers' application of this hierarchy has been somewhat simplistic, especially as the same product or activity can gratify different needs. For example, one study found that gardening could satisfy needs at every level of the hierarchy:[39]

- **Physiological**—"I like to work in the soil."
- **Safety**—"I feel safe in the garden."
- **Social**—"I can share my produce with others."
- **Esteem**—"I can create something of beauty."
- **Self-actualization**—"My garden gives me a sense of peace."

Another problem with taking Maslow's Hierarchy of Needs too literally is that it is culture-bound; its assumptions may apply only to Western culture. People in other cultures (or, for that matter, even some in Western cultures) may question the order of the levels it specifies. A religious person who has taken a vow of celibacy would not necessarily agree that physiological needs must be satisfied before self-fulfillment can occur.

Similarly, many Asian cultures value the welfare of the group (belongingness needs) more highly than needs of the individual (esteem needs). The point is that this hierarchy, although marketers widely apply it, is helpful primarily because it reminds us that consumers may have different need priorities in different consumption situations and at different stages in their lives—not because it *exactly* specifies a consumer's progression up the ladder of needs.

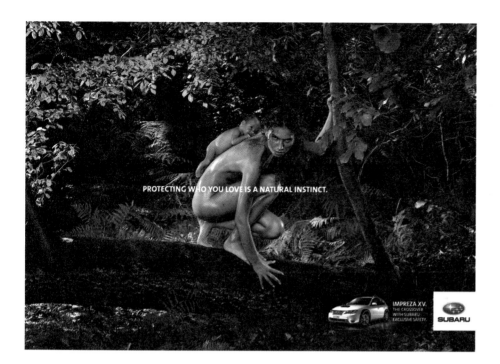

This Italian ad reinforces the need for safety in Maslow's Hierarchy of Needs.
Source: Courtesy of Subaru Italy.

The Global "Always On" Consumer

OBJECTIVE 5
Technology and culture create a new "always on" consumer.

Today many of us take for granted things that our grandparents only dreamed about. We instantly access people, places, and products with the click of a link. Many consumers travel to remote countries in a day rather than the weeks or months our ancestors needed—if they ever left their places of birth at all.

The majority of us now live in urban centers that bustle with people from many countries and that offer exotic foods from around the world. The United Nations defines a **megacity** as a metropolitan area with a total population of more than 10 million people. By 2011, there were already 20 such areas in the world. Researchers estimate that by 2030 three out of five people will live in cities—and more than 2 billion people will live in slums. Already, China boasts four shopping centers that are larger than the massive Mall of America in Minnesota, and very soon it will be home to seven of the world's largest malls.[40] This concentration in urban centers, combined with population growth in developing countries and increasing demands for modernization by billions of people in booming economies such as China, India, and Brazil, is both a blessing and a curse. Quality of life for many everyday citizens is better than even the elite who lived several centuries ago (even kings only bathed once a month). On the other hand, millions live in squalor, children around the world go to bed hungry, and we all feel the effects unbridled growth contributes to pollution of our air, soil, and water. As we'll see later in the book, all of these issues relate directly to our understanding of consumer behavior—and to the impact companies and customers have on our future and the world that we will leave to our children.

The Digital Native: Living a Social [Media] Life

There's little doubt that the digital revolution is one of the most significant influences on consumer behavior, and the impact of the Web will continue to expand as more and more people around the world log in. Many of us are avid Web surfers, and it's hard to imagine a time when texting, tweeting, Facebooking, or pinning favorite items on Pinterest weren't an accepted part of daily life—not to mention those of us who compulsively check in on FourSquare at their local Starbucks 10 times a day!

Wir melden unsere Lieblinge bei Facebook an.

Sind wir reif für eine neue Zeitung?

sind-wir-reif.de

KURZ. ANDERS. GEDRUCKT.

WELT KOMPAKT

The explosion of online communications changes the media landscape as traditional media platforms try to adapt. This German newspaper ad says "We sign our pets on Facebook. Are we ready for a new newspaper? *Welt Kompakt.* Concise. Different. Printed."

Source: Courtesy of WELT KOMPAKT.

Electronic marketing makes our lives a lot easier. You can shop 24/7 without leaving home, you can read today's newspaper without getting drenched picking up a hard copy in a rainstorm, and you don't have to wait for the 6:00 p.m. news to find out what the weather will be like tomorrow—whether at home or around the globe. With the increasing use of handheld devices and wireless communications, you can get that same information—from stock quotes to the weather—even when you're away from your computer.

Also, it's not all about businesses selling to consumers (**B2C e-commerce**). The cyberspace explosion has created a revolution in consumer-to-consumer activity (**C2C e-commerce**): Welcome to the world of *virtual brand communities.* Just as e-consumers are not limited to local retail outlets in their shopping, they are not limited to their local communities when they look for friends or fellow fans of wine, hip-hop, or skateboarding.

Picture a small group of local collectors who meet once a month at a local diner to discuss their shared interests over coffee. Now multiply that group by thousands, and include people from all over the world who are united by a shared passion for sports memorabilia, Barbie dolls, Harley-Davidson motorcycles, refrigerator magnets, or massive multiplayer online games (MMOGs) such as *World of Warcraft.* The Web also provides an easy way for consumers around the world to exchange information about their experiences with products, services, music, restaurants, and movies. The Hollywood Stock Exchange (hsx.com) offers a simulated entertainment stock market where traders predict the 4-week box office take for each film.[41] Amazon.com encourages shoppers to write reviews of books, and (just as Gail did) you can even rate your professors at RateMyProfessors.com (don't tell your prof about this one; it'll be our secret).[42] The popularity of chat rooms where consumers can go to discuss various topics with like-minded "Netizens" around the world grows every day, as do immersive **virtual worlds** such as Second Life, Habbo Hotel, and Kaneva. News reports tell us of the sometimes wonderful and sometimes horrific romances that have begun on the Internet as people check out potential mates on sites such as Match.com or OKCupid. In one month, the dating site Plenty of Fish alone had 122 million visits.[43]

If you're a typical student, you probably can't recall a time when the Internet was just a static, one-way platform that transmitted text and a few sketchy images. And, believe it or not, in the last century even *that* crude technique didn't exist. You may have read about this in a history class: People actually *hand-wrote* letters to each other and waited for printed magazines to arrive in their mailboxes to learn about current events! The term **digital native** originated in a 2001 article to explain a new type of student who was starting to turn up on campus. These consumers grew up "wired" in a highly networked, always-on world where digital technology had always existed.[44]

Fast-forward a decade: Today the Internet is the backbone of our society. Widespread access to devices like personal computers, digital video and audio recorders, webcams, and smartphones ensures that consumers of practically any age who live in virtually any part of the world can create and share content. But information doesn't just flow from big companies or governments down to the people; today each of us can communicate with huge numbers of people by a click on a keypad, so information flows *across* people as well.

That's what we mean by a **horizontal revolution**. This horizontal revolution is characterized in part by the prevalence of social media. **Social media** are the online means of communication, conveyance, collaboration, and cultivation among interconnected and interdependent networks of people, communities, and organizations enhanced by technological capabilities and mobility.

The Internet and its related technologies that gave birth to Web 2.0 make what we know today as social media possible and prevalent. Every day the influence of social media expands as more people join online communities. Facebook, a social utility that offers **synchronous interactions** (those that occur in real time, like when you text back-and-forth with a friend) and **asynchronous interactions** (those that don't require all participants to respond immediately, like when you text a friend and get an answer the next day), photo-sharing, games, applications, groups, e-retailing, and more, has more than one billion active users.[46]

People aren't just joining social communities. They are contributing too! Users upload 72 hours of video to YouTube every minute. In just 30 days on YouTube, more video is broadcast than in the past 60 years on the CBS, NBC, and ABC broadcasting networks combined.[47] Consider these mind-boggling social media stats:[48]

- If you were paid $1 for every time an article was posted on Wikipedia, you would earn $156.23 per hour.
- It took radio 38 years to reach 50 million listeners. TV took 13 years to reach 50 million users. The Internet took 4 years to reach 50 million people. In less than 9 months, Facebook added 100 million users.
- About 70 percent of Facebook users are outside the United States.
- Social networks have overtaken porn as the number-one online activity.
- One out of eight couples that married last year met on a social media site.
- 80 percent of companies use LinkedIn as their primary recruiting tool.
- 25 percent of search results for the world's top 10 brands are to user-generated content.
- People share more than 1.5 billion pieces of content on Facebook—*every day*.
- 80 percent of Twitter usage is from mobile devices, and 17 percent of users have tweeted while on the toilet.

This is all exciting stuff, especially because social media platforms enable a **culture of participation**; a belief in democracy; the ability to freely interact with other people, companies, and organizations; open access to venues that allow users to share content

Net Profit

Do you remember all those crazy Mentos/Diet Coke videos? At least 800 of them flooded YouTube after people discovered that when you drop the quarter-size candies into bottles of Diet Coke, you get a geyser that shoots 20 feet into the air. Needless to say, Mentos got a gusher of free publicity out of the deal, too.[45] Probably the biggest marketing phenomenon of this decade is **user-generated content**, whereby everyday people voice their opinions about products, brands, and companies on blogs, podcasts, and social networking sites such as Facebook and Twitter, and even film their own commercials that thousands view on sites such as YouTube. This important trend helps to define the era of **Web 2.0**: the rebirth of the Internet as a social, interactive medium from its original roots as a form of one-way transmission from producers to consumers.

from simple comments to reviews, ratings, photos, stories, and more; and the power to build on the content of others from your own unique point of view. Of course, just like democracy in the real world, we have to take the bitter with the sweet. There are plenty of unsavory things going on in cyberspace, and the hours people spend on Facebook, on online gambling sites, or in virtual worlds like Second Life have led to divorce, bankruptcy, or jail in the real world.

OBJECTIVE 6

Many different types of specialists study consumer behavior.

Consumer Behavior as a Field of Study

By now it should be clear that the field of consumer behavior encompasses many things, from the simple purchase of a carton of milk to the selection of a complex networked computer system; from the decision to donate money to a charity to devious plans to rip off a company.

There's an awful lot to understand, and many ways to go about it. Although people have certainly been consumers for a long time, it is only recently that consumption *per se* has been the object of formal study. In fact, although many business schools now require that marketing majors take a consumer behavior course, most colleges did not even offer such a course until the 1970s.

Where Do We Find Consumer Researchers?

Where do we find consumer researchers? Just about anywhere we find consumers. Consumer researchers work for manufacturers, retailers, marketing research firms, governments and nonprofit organizations, and of course colleges and universities. You'll find them in laboratories, running sophisticated experiments that involve advanced neural imaging machinery, or in malls interviewing shoppers. They may conduct focus groups or run large-scale polling operations. For example, when the advertising agency began to work on a new campaign for retailer JC Penney, it sent staffers to hang out with more than 50 women for several days. They wanted to really understand the respondents' lives, so they helped them to clean their houses, carpool, cook dinner, and shop. As one of the account executives observed, "If you want to understand how a lion hunts, you don't go to the zoo—you go to the jungle."[49]

Researchers work on many types of topics, from everyday household products and high-tech installations to professional services, museum exhibits, and public policy issues such as the effect of advertising on children. Indeed, no consumer issue is too sacred for researchers: Some intrepid investigators bravely explore "delicate" categories like incontinence products and birth control devices. The marketing director for Trojan condoms noted that, "Unlike laundry, where you can actually sit and watch people do their laundry, we can't sit and watch them use our product." For this reason, Trojan relies on clinical psychologists, psychiatrists, and cultural anthropologists to understand how men relate to condoms.[50]

Interdisciplinary Influences on the Study of Consumer Behavior

Many different perspectives shape the young field of consumer behavior. Indeed, it is hard to think of a field that is more interdisciplinary. You can find people with training in a very wide range of disciplines—from psychophysiology to literature—doing consumer research. Universities, manufacturers, museums, advertising agencies, and governments employ consumer researchers. Several professional groups, such as the Association for Consumer Research and the Society for Consumer Psychology, have been formed since the mid-1970s.

To gain an idea of the diversity of interests of people who do consumer research, consider the list of professional associations that sponsor the field's major journal, the

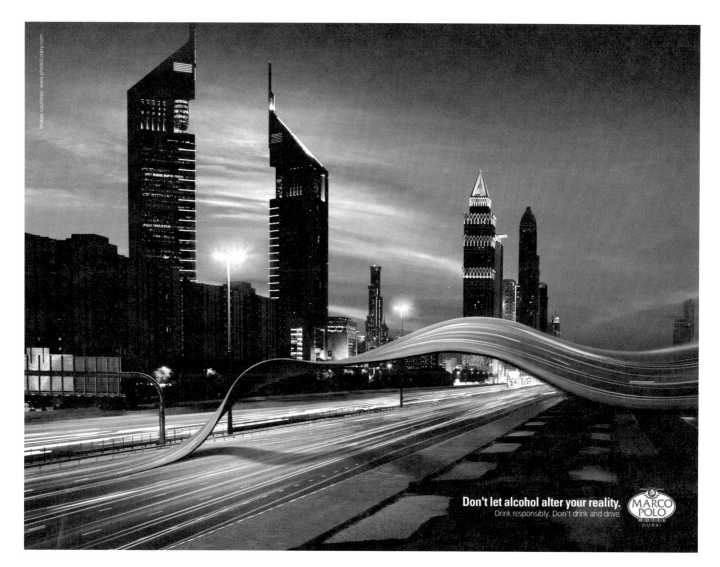

Don't let alcohol alter your reality.
Drink responsibly. Don't drink and drive.
MARCO POLO HOTEL DUBAI

The expanded view of consumer behavior embraces much more than the study of what and why we buy; it also focuses on how marketers influence consumers and how consumers use the products and services marketers sell. In this case, a hotel in Dubai promotes responsible behavior.
Source: Courtesy of Marco Polo Hotel/Dubai; Brandcom Agency.

Journal of Consumer Research: the American Association of Family and Consumer Sciences, the American Statistical Association, the Association for Consumer Research, the Society for Consumer Psychology, the International Communication Association, the American Sociological Association, the Institute of Management Sciences, the American Anthropological Association, the American Marketing Association, the Society for Personality and Social Psychology, the American Association for Public Opinion Research, and the American Economic Association. That's a pretty mixed bag.

Clearly there are a lot of researchers from diverse backgrounds who are into the study of consumer behavior. So, which is the "correct" discipline to look into these issues? You might remember a children's story about the blind men and the elephant. The gist of the story is that each man touched a different part of the animal and, as a result, the descriptions each gave of the elephant were quite different. This analogy applies to consumer research as well. Depending on the training and interests of the researchers studying it, they will approach the same consumer phenomenon in different ways and at different levels. Table 1.1 illustrates how we can approach a "simple" topic such as magazine usage from a range of perspectives.

Figure 1.3 provides a glimpse of some of the disciplines that work in the field and the level at which each tackles research issues. We can roughly characterize them in terms of their focus on micro versus macro consumer behavior topics. The fields closer to the top of the pyramid concentrate on the individual consumer (micro issues), and those toward

TABLE 1.1	Interdisciplinary Research Issues in Consumer Behavior

Disciplinary Focus	Magazine Usage Sample Research Issues
Experimental Psychology: product role in perception, learning, and memory processes	How specific aspects of magazines, such as their design or layout, are recognized and interpreted; which parts of a magazine people are most likely to read.
Clinical Psychology: product role in psychological adjustment	How magazines affect readers' body images (e.g., do thin models make the average woman feel overweight?)
Microeconomics/Human Ecology: product role in allocation of individual or family resources	Factors influencing the amount of money a household spends on magazines.
Social Psychology: product role in the behavior of individuals as members of social groups	Ways that ads in a magazine affect readers' attitudes toward the products depicted; how peer pressure influences a person's readership decisions
Sociology: product role in social institutions and group relationships	Pattern by which magazine preferences spread through a social group (e.g., a sorority)
Macroeconomics: product role in consumers' relations with the marketplace	Effects of the price of fashion magazines and expense of items advertised during periods of high unemployment
Semiotics/Literary Criticism: product role in the verbal and visual communication of meaning	Ways in which underlying messages communicated by models and ads in a magazine are interpreted
Demography: product role in the measurable characteristics of a population	Effects of age, income, and marital status of a magazine's readers
History: product role in societal changes over time	Ways in which our culture's depictions of "femininity" in magazines have changed over time
Cultural Antropology: product role in a society's beliefs and practices	Ways in which fashions and models in a magazine affect readers' definitions of masculine versus feminine behavior (e.g., the role of working women, sexual taboos)

Figure 1.3 THE PYRAMID OF CONSUMER BEHAVIOR

**MICRO CONSUMER BEHAVIOR
(INDIVIDUAL FOCUS)**

Experimental Psychology
Clinical Psychology
Developmental Psychology
Human Ecology
Microeconomics
Social Psychology
Sociology
Macroeconomics
Semiotics/Literary Criticism
Demography
History
Cultural Anthropology

**MACRO CONSUMER BEHAVIOR
(SOCIAL FOCUS)**

the base are more interested in the collective activities that occur among larger groups of people, such as consumption patterns shared by members of a culture or subculture (macro issues). As we make our way through this book, we'll focus on the issues at the top (micro) and then make our way to the bottom of the pyramid by the end of the course. Hang in there!

OBJECTIVE 7
There are differing perspectives regarding how and what we should understand about consumer behavior.

Two Perspectives on Consumer Research

One general way in which we classify consumer research is in terms of the fundamental assumptions the researchers make about what they study and how to study it. We call a set of beliefs that guide our understanding of the world a **paradigm**. As in other fields of study, a paradigm dominates the discipline of consumer behavior. However, some believe the discipline is in the middle of a *paradigm shift*, which occurs when a competing paradigm challenges the dominant set of assumptions.

The basic set of assumptions underlying the dominant paradigm at this point in time is **positivism** (sometimes called *modernism*). This perspective has significantly influenced Western art and science since the late 16th century. It emphasizes that human reason is supreme and that there is a single, objective truth that science can discover. Positivism encourages us to stress the function of objects, to celebrate technology, and to regard the world as a rational, ordered place with a clearly defined past, present, and future.

The newer paradigm of **interpretivism** (or *postmodernism*) questions these assumptions.[51] Proponents of this perspective argue that our society emphasizes science and technology too much, and they feel that this ordered, rational view of behavior denies or ignores the complex social and cultural world in which we really live. Others feel that positivism puts too much emphasis on material well-being and that its logical outlook is directed by an ideology that stresses the homogenous views of a culture dominated by (dead) white males. And, as we'll see in the next chapter, some adherents to this view also believe researchers should not just study consumer issues, but act on them as well.

Interpretivists instead stress the importance of symbolic, subjective experience, and the idea that meaning is in the mind of the person—that is, we each construct our own meanings based on our unique and shared cultural experiences, so there are no right or wrong answers. In this view, the world in which we live is a **pastiche**, or mixture of images and ideas.[52] This perspective rejects the value we assign to products because they help us to create order; instead, it focuses on regarding consumption as offering a set of diverse experiences. Table 1.2 summarizes the major differences between these two perspectives on consumer research.

To understand how an interpretive framework helps us to understand marketing communications, let's refer to an analysis of one of the best-known and longest-running (1959–1978) advertising campaigns of all time: the work the advertising agency Doyle Dane Bernbach (DDB) did for the Volkswagen Beetle. This campaign, widely noted for its self-mocking wit, found many ways to turn the Beetle's homeliness, small size, and lack of power into positive attributes at a time when most car ads were emphasizing just the opposite.

An interpretative analysis of these messages used concepts from literature, psychology, and anthropology to ground the appeal of this approach within a broader cultural context. Analysts linked the image DDB created for the humble car to other examples of what scholars of comedy call the "Little Man" pattern. This is a type of comedic character who is related to a clown or a trickster, a social outcast who is able to poke holes in the stuffiness and rigidity of bureaucracy and conformity. Other examples of the "Little Man" character include Hawkeye in the classic TV sitcom *M*A*S*H*, the comedian Woody Allen, and Charlie Chaplin. When one looks at the cultural meaning of marketing messages this way, it is perhaps no coincidence that IBM chose the Charlie Chaplin character some years later to help it "soften" its stuffy, intimidating image as it tried to convince consumers that its new personal computer products were user-friendly.

| TABLE 1.2 | Positivist versus Interpretivist Approaches to Consumer Behavior |

Assumptions	Positivist Approach	Interpretivist Approach
Nature of reality	Objective, tangible Single	Socially constructed Multiple
Goal	Prediction	Understanding
Knowledge generated	Time-free, context independent	Time-bound Context dependent
View of causality	Existence of real causes	Multiple, simultaneous shaping events
Research relationship	Separation between researcher and subject	Interactive, cooperative with researcher being part of phenomenon under study

Source: Adapted from Laurel A. Hudson and Julie L. Ozanne, "Alternative Ways of Seeking Knowledge in Consumer Research," *Journal of Consumer Research* 14 (March 1988): 508–21. Reprinted with the permission of the University of Chicago Press. Copyright © 1988 JCR, Inc.

Should Consumer Research Have an Academic or an Applied Focus?

Many researchers regard the field of consumer behavior as an applied social science. They argue that the value of the knowledge we generate should be judged in terms of its ability to improve the effectiveness of marketing practice. However, others argue that consumer behavior should not have a strategic focus at all; the field should not be a "handmaiden to business." It should instead focus on the understanding of consumption for its own sake rather than marketers applying this knowledge to making a profit.[53] Most consumer researchers do not hold this rather extreme view, but it has encouraged many to expand the scope of their work beyond the field's traditional focus on the purchase of consumer goods such as food, appliances, and cars to embrace social problems such as homelessness or preserving the environment. Certainly, it has led to some fiery debates among people working in the field!

Taking It from Here: The Plan of the Book

This book covers many facets of consumer behavior, and in the chapters to come we will highlight many of the research perspectives that we only briefly described in this one. The plan of the book is simple: It goes from micro to macro. Think of it as a sort of photograph album of consumer behavior: Each chapter provides a "snapshot" of consumers, but the lens used to take each picture gets successively wider. First we'll anchor the study of consumer behavior in the remaining three chapters of Section 1 as we explore how consumers make decisions, how our world around us influences those decisions, and some of the consequences of those decisions for ourselves and our environment. In Section 2 we'll dive deeper into the facets of individual decision—making as we look at the internal factors such as how we learn about products and services and then use this information to decide how we feel about them. In Section 3 we expand the lens to consider external influences on these decisions such as the groups to which we belong and the opinions of others we access via both traditional and new media.

CHAPTER SUMMARY

Now that you have finished reading this chapter, you should understand why:

1. Consumer behavior is a process.

Consumer behavior is the study of the processes involved when individuals or groups select, purchase, use, or dispose of products, services, ideas, or experiences to satisfy needs and desires. A consumer may purchase, use, and dispose of a product, but different people may perform these functions. In addition, we can think of consumers as role players who need different products to help them play their various parts.

2. Marketers have to understand the wants and needs of different consumer segments.

Market segmentation is an important aspect of consumer behavior. Consumers can be segmented according to many dimensions, including product usage, demographics (the objective aspects of a population, such as age and sex), and psychographics (psychological and lifestyle characteristics). Emerging developments, such as the new emphasis on relationship marketing and the practice of database marketing, mean that marketers are much more attuned to the wants and needs of different consumer groups.

3. Our choices as consumers relate in powerful ways to the rest of our lives.

Marketing activities exert an enormous impact on individuals. Consumer behavior is relevant to our understanding of both public policy issues (e.g., ethical marketing practices) and the dynamics of popular culture.

4. Our motivations to consume are complex and varied.

Marketers try to satisfy consumer needs, but the reasons people purchase any product can vary widely. The identification of consumer motives is an important step to ensure that a product will satisfy appropriate needs.

Traditional approaches to consumer behavior focus on the abilities of products to satisfy rational needs (utilitarian motives), but hedonic motives (e.g., the need for exploration or for fun) also play a key role in many purchase decisions. As Maslow's Hierarchy of Needs demonstrates, the same product can satisfy different needs for different people and in different situations.

5. Technology and culture create a new "always on" consumer.

The Web and social media transform the way consumers interact with companies and with each other. Online commerce allows us to locate obscure products from around the world, and consumption communities provide forums for people to share opinions and product recommendations.

6. Many different types of specialists study consumer behavior.

The field of consumer behavior is interdisciplinary; it is composed of researchers from many different fields who share an interest in how people interact with the marketplace. We can categorize these disciplines by the degree to which their focus is micro (the individual consumer) or macro (the consumer as a member of groups or of the larger society).

7. There are differing perspectives regarding how and what we should understand about consumer behavior.

Researchers who study consumer behavior do so both for academic purposes and to inform marketing organizations about practical decisions. We can roughly divide research orientations into two approaches: The positivist perspective emphasizes the objectivity of science and the consumer as a rational decision maker. The interpretivist perspective, in contrast, stresses the subjective meaning of the consumer's individual experience and the idea that any behavior is subject to multiple interpretations rather than to one single explanation.

KEY TERMS

alternate reality games (ARGs), 31
asynchronous interactions, 47
B2C e-commerce, 46
Big Data, 34
C2C e-commerce, 46
consumer, 29
consumer behavior, 28
consumption communities, 28
culture of participation, 47
database marketing, 33
demographics, 27
digital native, 47
drive, 40

drive theory, 40
80/20 rule, 30
exchange, 29
expectancy theory, 41
goal, 40
heavy users, 30
Hierarchy of Needs, 43
horizontal revolution, 47
interpretivism, 51
market segmentation strategies, 28
megacity, 45
motivation, 39
paradigm, 51

pastiche, 51
popular culture, 37
positivism, 51
productivity orientation, 42
relationship marketing, 32
role theory, 37
social media, 47
synchronous interactions, 47
user-generated content, 47
virtual worlds, 47
want, 41
Web 2.0, 47

REVIEW

1-1 Provide a definition of consumer behavior.

1-2 What are demographics? Give three examples of demographic characteristics.

1-3 What is market segmentation? Give three examples of market segments.

1-4 What is role theory, and how does it help us to understand consumer behavior?

⭐ 1-5 What do we mean by an exchange?

⭐ 1-6 Why is it important for businesses to learn about their heavy users?

1-7 How practical and useful is database marketing for most businesses?

1-8 Identify the three stages of the consumption process.

1-9 Have traditional patterns of consumption been radically changed by globalization?

1-10 How could interdisciplinary research in consumer behavior explain the profile of a national newspaper or television news channel?

1-11 Name two different disciplines that study consumer behavior. How would their approaches to the same issue differ?

CONSUMER BEHAVIOR CHALLENGE

■ DISCUSS

1-12 There are different ways of consuming products and services, based on an individual's tastes and preferences, but also dependent upon variables such as country, region, language, culture, market and so on. This affects the way a particular product or service is marketed and sold. Are there specific ways in which consumers in your country or region consume or demand products and services?

1-13 Each country or region will have a core of products and services that are consumed. Collectively, the consumption of these infers some kind of group bond. Identify examples of these specific products and services and comment on how they help to maintain group bonds.

1-14 Why should managers, advertisers, and marketers want to learn about the behavior of their consumers? Is it their role to modify and drive that behavior?

⭐ 1-15 What aspects of consumer behavior would interest a financial planner? A university administrator? A graphic arts designer? A social worker in a government agency? A nursing instructor?

1-16 Individuals can have different relationships with brands and products. It is suggested that an individual can have a self-concept attachment, a nostalgic attachment, interdependence, or love. Choose eight to 10 brands or products that you use and comment on whether you feel any of these attachments toward them. What do your findings tell you about the power of each brand?

1-17 Some researchers have sought to create a universal inventory to explain broader behavior that encompasses consumer behavior. Henry Murray developed 20 different psychogenic needs. It seems that theories such as this have significance in developed economies where the basic needs of most individuals have been met and there is scope to focus on psychogenic needs. But do these psychogenic needs run deeper than simple consumer consumption trends? Can we explain any level of consumer behavior in terms of psychogenic needs? Are they relevant when the basic needs are for shelter, food, and safety? To what extent is the theory valuable in understanding people in your own country or region? As noted in Brenda Geren's look at China, the country has needs and value systems not fully realized. Is this the case in your country or region?[54]

1-18 Businesses using social media as a means by which they can seem relevant and present in the lives of their consumers have seen some tremendous successes. Some, however, have exposed themselves to threats they could not have imagined and have suffered huge losses in consumer perception.[55] Yet, it seems that businesses cannot afford to ignore social media; they need to have a visible and vibrant presence. The major problems are that the businesses become the subject of discussion. In these discussions, businesses have little control, and deleting comments is seen as exercising unreasonable censorship. Do you agree or disagree with this assertion?

1-19 According to Internet World Stats, the world's population is just over 7 billion. Of that total, over 2.4 billion have access to the Internet.[56] The penetration of the Internet across the world is patchy. Africa, with over 1 billion people, shows that less than 170 million have Internet access. Compared to the rest of the globe, this is the lowest penetration as a percentage of the population at just 15.6 percent. North America leads the way with a penetration of 78.6 percent. Globally, the figure is 34.3 percent. But how is Internet access changing the way in which we interact with one another and with businesses wanting to sell us products and services?

According to Kenneth Dixon, writing in the *Stanford News* back in 2005, a change in the way we run our lives was already under way and recognizable.[57] Dixon's research, focusing on U.S. citizens, suggested that those with access to the Internet spent 70 minutes less per day interacting with their family members. They also skimped on sleep and watched less television. This was at a time when the Internet penetration of the U.S. population was just 31 percent.

It would seem that Internet addiction is a global phenomenon, according to a study that analyzed Internet use in Europe in 2013.[58] The research suggested that across Europe the addiction rate was around 12.7 percent. The study also identified a new potential term to explain this addiction: Dysfunctional Internet Behavior (DIB). What is the rate of Internet penetration in your country or region? Has it changed the way in which people interact? Has it changed their consumption behavior? If so, what are the consequences of these changes?

▦ APPLY

1-21   National marketers will often adapt the ways in which they market and promote products and services on a geographical basis. Is this the case in your country? Discuss with a company example.

1-22   The specific way we choose to satisfy a need depends on our unique history, learning experiences, and cultural environment. For example, two classmates may feel their stomachs rumble during a lunchtime lecture. If neither person has eaten since the night before, the strength of their respective needs (hunger) would be about the same. However, the ways each person goes about satisfying this need might be quite different. Conduct this exercise with classmates: "As you probably know, a prisoner who is sentenced to die traditionally gets to choose his or her 'last meal.' If you had to do this (let's hope not), describe your 'last meal' in detail." Compare the responses you get, especially among people from different ethnic or cultural backgrounds. What similarities and differences emerge?

1-23   Our online behaviors also can satisfy needs at different levels of Maslow's Hierarchy of Needs, especially when we participate in social networks like Facebook. Web-based companies can build loyalty if they keep these needs in mind when they design their offerings:

1-20   The basic lesson of Maslow's Hierarchy of Needs is that we must first satisfy basic needs before we progress up the ladder (a starving man is not interested in status symbols, friendship, or self-fulfillment). This implies that consumers value different product attributes depending on what is currently available to them. In today's economic environment, the hierarchy helps to explain why many consumers take a closer look at the price and reliability of a product rather than whether it will impress their friends. How do you believe the recession has changed the way consumers evaluate products? Do you agree that the priorities many now place on "value-priced" brands is "The New Normal" or will our attitudes change when the economy improves?

- We satisfy physiological needs when we use the Web to research topics such as nutrition or medical questions.
- The Web enables users to pool information and satisfy safety needs when they call attention to bad practices, flawed products, or even dangerous predators.
- Profile pages on Facebook let users define themselves as individuals.
- Online communities, blogs, and social networks provide recognition and achievement to those who cultivate a reputation for being especially helpful or expert in some subject.
- Users can seek help from others and connect with people who have similar tastes and interests.
- Access to invitation-only communities provides status.
- Spiritually based online communities can provide guidance to troubled people.[59]

Interview people you know about their motivations to participate in social media. Ask them to provide a list of the platforms they access most, then for each probe about their reasons to visit these. What needs do these sites appear to satisfy? How might these insights help you to devise ideas for new social media products?

Case Study

LINKING BRITISH POPULAR CULTURE AND BRAND-BUILDING STRATEGIES

As the accelerating forces of globalization and technology cross national borders, awareness of, interest in, and participation in popular culture(s) have steadily grown worldwide. Furthermore, the growth of the Web has revolutionized the spreading of new cultural influences globally by creating thousands of online communities where people of all ages share information one-on-one or with large, worldwide groups using blogs, podcasts, and social networking sites such as Facebook, Twitter, and You-Tube. As a result, popular culture has become an attractive tool for marketers and brand managers.

British popular culture in particular holds an important place globally, and much of it appeals to many age groups, regardless of their social class, educational background, or religious affiliation. Early notable movements, such as The Beatles, the British rock band of the 1960s, and, later, Britpop, an era that saw the rise of the British guitar bands in the 1990s, helped establish the British popular music industry as an international center of musical creativity. In recent years, British popular culture has become a source of popular literature, fashion, television entertainment, and film. For instance, in both its book and film formats, J. K. Rowling's Harry Potter series has attracted a huge following in various parts of the world; the James Bond series of books and movies also remain very popular. The British have also been responsible for some of the most popular television entertainment formats that the global mass market consumes, including game shows such as *The Weakest Link* and *Who Wants to Be a Millionaire* and talent shows like *Britain's Got Talent* and *The X Factor*. Adaptations of these shows have appeared on the airwaves of many countries, including the United States, China, and India. The quirky British sense of humor has traveled well, too, with television situation comedy series such as *The Office* and comedy films like *Four Weddings and a Funeral.* The influence of popular culture on brand management is hard to overlook, in particular in the digital age where consumers can create buzz, pass on viral messages, and bring brands alive in the popular culture using Web-based consumer-generated content. It is increasingly clear that brands that combine traditional brand management with an updated popular culture appeal are among the most successful and relevant. British companies such as Aston Martin, manufacturer of luxury sports cars, the Barclays Bank PLC, and fashion house Burberry have benefited from an understanding of how British popular culture is perceived in their target markets and from exploring the international branding potential of popular culture. By way of example, in 2010, the fashion company Burberry used Emma Watson, the actress who played the young Harry Potter heroine Hermione Granger, and George Craig, the lead musician of the indie band One Night Only, to represent the modernity of its heritage brand. The popular culture attributes, images, and symbols associated with these characters helped breathe life into the iconic Burberry brand and transform it into readily identifiable British products, giving the company a competitive advantage in the international marketplace.

DISCUSSION QUESTIONS

CS 1–1 Many cultural critics have dismissed popular culture as merely a symptom or side effect of mass consumerism. Discuss.

CS 1–2 To what extent do you agree with the statement that the Internet has become a major carrier of what's popular among the masses, and why?

CS 1–3 Describe a popular culture that you are familiar with, noting its key components, and discuss how it has influenced the branding strategy of a national and/or global brand of your choice. In your view, can more synergy be achieved in marketing terms by linking the two more closely?

Sources: Stephen Brook, "Britain Leads the Way in Selling Global TV Formats," *The Guardian* (April 5, 2010); Roblyn Simeon, "A Conceptual Model Linking Brand Building Strategies and Japanese Popular Culture," *Marketing Intelligence and Planning* 24, no. 5 (2006): 463–76.

MyMarketingLab

Go to **mymktlab.com** for the following Assisted-graded writing questions:

1-24 This chapter states "people often buy products not for what they do but for what they mean." Explain the meaning of this statement and provide an example.

1-25 What are the major differences between the positivist and interpretivist paradigms in consumer research?

1-26 MyMktlab only—comprehensive writing assignment for this chapter.

NOTES

1. http://www.jewelmint.com, accessed July 18, 2013; http://www.oxygen .com, accessed July 18, 2013; http://www.ivillage.com, accessed July 18, 2013; http://www.hercampus.com, accessed July 18, 2013; http://www .RateMyProfessors.com, accessed July 18, 2013.
2. Michael R. Solomon and Elnora W. Stuart, *Marketing: Real People, Real Choices*, 2nd ed. (Upper Saddle River, NJ: Prentice Hall, 2000): 5-6.
3. Joann Muller, "BMW's Car of the Future: Glued, Screwed & Rented," *Forbes* (November 3, 2011), http://www.forbes.com/sites/joannmuller/2011/11/03/ bmws-vision-for-the-future-of-automobiles/, accessed December 21, 2012.
4. Jack Neff, "Study: Package-Goods Brands' Consumer Bases Very Small, Yet Diverse," *Advertising Age* (December 8, 2008), http://www.adage.com, accessed December 8, 2008.
5. Natalie Perkins, "Zeroing in on Consumer Values," *Advertising Age* (March 22, 1993): 23.
6. Hannah Karp, "Red Bull Aims at an Older Crowd," *Wall Street Journal* (June 7, 2004): B3.
7. Jack Neff, "Crest Spinoff Targets Women," *Advertising Age* (June 3, 2002): 1.
8. Charles M. Schaninger and William D. Danko, "A Conceptual and Empirical Comparison of Alternative Household Life Cycle Models," *Journal of Consumer Research* 19 (March 1993): 580–94; Robert E. Wilkes, "Household Life-Cycle Stages, Transitions, and Product Expenditures," *Journal of Consumer Research* 22 (June 1995): 27–42.
9. Richard P. Coleman, "The Continuing Significance of Social Class to Marketing," *Journal of Consumer Research* 10 (December 1983): 265–80.

10. Anthony Bianco, "The Vanishing Mass Market," *BusinessWeek* (July 12, 2004): 61–67.

11. Tracy Tuten and Michael R. Solomon, *Social Media Marketing* (Upper Saddle River, NJ: Pearson, 2013); some material provided by Julie Channing, head planner at AKQA for The Lost Ring campaign.

12. Porter Novelli company Web site, http://www.porternovelli.com.

13. Jennifer Ordonez, "A taste for convenience: Fast food companies seek more "heavy users"," *Sarasota Herald-Tribune* (January 13, 2000), http://tinyurl.com/mzv4pau.

14. Quick company Web site, http://groupe.quick.fr/en.

15. Burt Helm, "Ethnic Marketing: McDonald's Is Lovin' It," *Bloomberg-Businessweek* (July 8, 2010), http://www.businessweek.com/magazine/content/10_29/b4187022876832.htm, accessed December 21, 2012.

16. Motoko Rich, "Region's Marketers Hop on the Bubba Bandwagon," *Wall Street Journal Interactive Edition* (May 19, 1999).

17. Sarah Ellison, "Prilosec OTC Blitz by P&G Represents New Drug Foray," *Wall Street Journal* (September 12, 2003), http://www.wsj.com, accessed September 12, 2003.

18. Stuart Elliott, "Capitalizing on Disaster, Sometimes With Results That Match," *New York Times* (October 31, 2012), http://www.nytimes.com/2012/11/01/business/media/marketers-ride-the-coattails-of-a-storm-not-all-successfully.html, accessed December 21, 2012.

19. Constance L. Hayes, "What Wal-Mart Knows About Customers' Habits," *New York Times* (November 14, 2004), http://www.nytimes.com, accessed November 14, 2004.

20. Andrew McAfee and Erik Brynjolfsson, *Big Data: The Management Revolution, Harvard Business Review* (October 2012), http://hbr.org/2012/10/big-data-the-management-revolution/ar/1, accessed December 21, 2012; "Bringing Big Data to the Enterprise," IBM, http://www-01.ibm.com/software/data/bigdata/, accessed December 21, 2012; Geoff Nunberg, "Forget YOLO: Why 'Big Data' Should Be the Word of the Year," *NPR* (December 20, 2012), http://www.npr.org/2012/12/20/167702665/geoff-nunbergs-word-of-the-year-big-data, accessed December 21, 2012.

21. Mylene Mangalindan, "Hollywood's 'Wedding Crashers' Inspires the Invitationless," *Wall Street Journal* (December 28, 2005): B1.

22. Pagan Kennedy, "Who Made That? (Spring Break)," *The New York Times Magazine* (March 24, 2013).

23. Erving Goffman, *The Presentation of Self in Everyday Life* (Garden City, NY: Doubleday, 1959); George H. Mead, *Mind, Self, and Society* (Chicago: University of Chicago Press, 1934); Michael R. Solomon, "The Role of Products as Social Stimuli: A Symbolic Interactionism Perspective," *Journal of Consumer Research* 10 (December 1983): 319–29.

24. Jennifer Aaker, Susan Fournier, and S. Adam Brasel, "When Good Brands Do Bad," *Journal of Consumer Research* 31 (2004): 1–16.

25. Susan Fournier, "Consumers and Their Brands. Developing Relationship Theory in Consumer Research," *Journal of Consumer Research* 24 (March 1998): 343–73.

26. http://www.marshmallowpeeps.com/products/valentines-day, accessed December 22, 2012; Thomas Vinciguerra, "Soft, Chewy and Taking Over the World," *New York Times* (July 5, 2006): Sec. 4, p. 2.

27. Quoted in "Bringing Meaning to Brands," *American Demographics* (June 1997): 34.

28. Russell W. Belk, Guliz Ger, and Søren Askegaard, "The Fire of Desire: A Multisited Inquiry into Consumer Passion," *Journal of Consumer Research* 30 (2003): 326–51; cf. also Yu Chen, "Possession and Access: Consumer Desires and Value Perceptions Regarding Contemporary Art Collection and Exhibit Visits," *Journal of Consumer Research* 35 (April 2009): 925–40.

29. Henrik Hagtvedt and Vanessa M. Patrick, "The Broad Embrace of Luxury: Hedonic Potential as a Driver of Brand Extendibility," *Journal of Consumer Psychology* 19, no. 4 (2009): 608–18.

30. See Paul T. Costa and Robert R. McCrae, "From Catalog to Classification: Murray's Needs and the Five-Factor Model," *Journal of Personality & Social Psychology* 55 (1988): 258–65; Calvin S. Hall and Gardner Lindzey, *Theories of Personality*, 2nd ed. (New York: Wiley, 1970); James U. McNeal and Stephen W. McDaniel, "An Analysis of Need-Appeals in Television Advertising," *Journal of the Academy of Marketing Science* 12 (Spring 1984): 176–90.

31. See David C. McClelland, *Studies in Motivation* (New York: Appleton-Century-Crofts, 1955).

32. Mary Kay Ericksen and M. Joseph Sirgy, "Achievement Motivation and Clothing Preferences of White-Collar Working Women," in Michael R. Solomon, ed., *The Psychology of Fashion* (Lexington, MA: Lexington Books, 1985): 357–69.

33. See Stanley Schachter, *The Psychology of Affiliation* (Stanford, CA: Stanford University Press, 1959).

34. Eugene M. Fodor and Terry Smith, "The Power Motive as an Influence on Group Decision Making," *Journal of Personality & Social Psychology* 42 (1982): 178–85.

35. C. R. Snyder and Howard L. Fromkin, *Uniqueness: The Human Pursuit of Difference* (New York: Plenum, 1980).

36. Abraham H. Maslow, *Motivation and Personality*, 2nd ed. (New York: Harper & Row, 1970).

37. An integrative view of consumer goal structures and goal-determination processes proposes six discrete levels of goals wherein higher-level (versus lower-level) goals are more abstract, more inclusive, and less mutable. In descending order of abstraction, these goal levels are life themes and values, life projects, current concerns, consumption intentions, benefits sought, and feature preferences. See Cynthia Huffman, S. Ratneshwar, and David Glen Mick, "Consumer Goal Structures and Goal-Determination Processes: An Integrative Framework," in S. Ratneshwar, David Glen Mick, and Cynthia Huffman, eds., *The Why of Consumption* (London: Routledge, 2000): 9–35.

38. Paul Henry, "Magnetic Points for Lifestyle Shaping: The Contribution of Self-Fulfillment, Aspirations and Capabilities," *Qualitative Market Research* 9, no. 2 (2006): 170.

39. Study conducted in the Horticulture Department at Kansas State University, cited in "Survey Tells Why Gardening's Good," *Vancouver Sun* (April 12, 1997): B12; see also Paul Hewer and Douglas Brownlie, "Constructing 'Hortiporn': On the Aesthetics of Stylized Exteriors," *Advances in Consumer Research* 33, no. 1 (2006).

40. "Megacities," http://webs.schule.at/website/megacities/megacities_index_en.htm, accessed December 22, 2012; David Barbosa, "China, New Land of Shoppers, Builds Malls on Gigantic Scale," *New York Times* (May 25, 2005), http://www.nytimes.com, accessed May 25, 2005.

41. http://www.hsx.com, accessed December 22, 2012.

42. http://www.RateMyProfessors.com/, accessed December 23, 2012.

43. http://www.pof.com/inbox.aspx, accessed December 16, 2012; Irina Slutsky, "Get Hooked up with the Big Business of Online Dating," *Advertising Age* (February 14, 2011), http://adage.com/article/ad-age-graphics/online-dating-a-a-1-3-billion-market/148845/, accessed May 7, 2011.

44. Marc Prensky, "Digital Natives, Digital Immigrants," *On the Horizon* 9, no. 5 (October 2001): 1–6.

45. Keith Schneider, "Recipe for Success: Take Mentos, Diet Coke. Mix," *New York Times* (February 20, 2007), http://www.nytimes.com/2007/02/20/business/smallbusiness/20eep.html, accessed December 22, 2012; Steve Spangler, "Mentos Diet Coke Geyser," SteveSpanglerScience.com, http://www.stevespanglerscience.com/experiment/original-mentos-diet-coke-geyser, accessed May 7, 2011; Suzanne Vranica and Chad Terhune, "Mixing Diet Coke and Mentos Makes a Gusher of Publicity," *Wall Street Journal* (June 12, 2006): B1.

46. http://newsroom.fb.com/Key-Facts, accessed December 22, 2012.

47. http://www.youtube.com/t/press_statistics, accessed December 22, 2012.

48. Parts of this section are adapted from Tracy Tuten and Michael R. Solomon, *Social Media Marketing* (Upper Saddle River, NJ: Pearson Education, 2012).

49. Suzanne Vranica, "Ad Houses Will Need to Be More Nimble, Clients Are Demanding More and Better Use of Consumer Data, Web," *Wall Street Journal* (January 2, 2008): B3.

50. Jack Neff, "Mucus to Maxi Pads: Marketing's Dirtiest Jobs, Frank Talk about Diapers and Condoms Lifts Taboos and Helps Make a Difference in Consumers' Lives, Say Those in the Trenches," *Advertising Age* (February 17, 2009), http://www.adage.com, accessed February 17, 2009.

51. For an overview, see Eric J. Arnould and Craig J. Thompson, "Consumer Culture Theory (CCT): Twenty Years of Research," *Journal of Consumer Research* 31 (March 2005): 868–82.

52. Alladi Venkatesh, "Postmodernism, Poststructuralism and Marketing," paper presented at the American Marketing Association Winter Theory Conference, San Antonio, February 1992; see also Stella Proctor, Ioanna Papasolomou-Doukakis, and Tony Proctor, "What Are Television Advertisements Really Trying to Tell Us? A Postmodern Perspective," *Journal of Consumer Behavior* 1 (February 2002): 246–55; A. Fuat Firat and Alladi Venkatesh, "The Making of Postmodern Consumption," in Russell W. Belk and Nikhilesh Dholakia, eds., *Consumption and Marketing: Macro Dimensions* (Boston: PWS-Kent, 1993).

53. Morris B. Holbrook, "The Consumer Researcher Visits Radio City: Dancing in the Dark," in Elizabeth C. Hirschman and Morris B. Holbrook, eds., *Advances in Consumer Research* 12 (Provo, UT: Association for Consumer Research, 1985): 28–31.

54. Brenda Geren, "Motivation: Chinese theoretical perspectives," *Journal of Behavioral Studies in Business,* New York Institute of Technology Bahrain, http://www.aabri.com/manuscripts/10692.pdf, accessed December 16, 2013.

55. Maxwell Chi, "Reducing the Risks of Social Media to Your Organization: Security Policy and Social Media Use," SANS Institute Reading Room (2011), http://www.sans.org/reading-room/whitepapers/policyissues/reducing-risks-social-media-organization-33749.

56. http://www.internetworldstats.com/stats.htm, accessed December 16, 2013.

57. Kenneth M. Dixon, "Researchers link use of Internet, social isolation," *Stanford News* (February 23, 2005), http://news.stanford.edu/news/2005/february23/internet-022305.html, accessed December 16, 2013.

58. Nerea Rial, "Spanish teenagers lead European Internet addiction," *New Europe* (January 18, 2013), http://www.neurope.eu/article/spanish-teenagers-lead-european-internet-addiction, accessed December 16, 2013.

59. Adapted in part from Jack Loechner, "Emotional Business Bonding on Social Networks," *Research Brief*, Center for Media Research (December 27, 2007), http://blogs.mediapost.com/research_brief/?p=1603, accessed December 27, 2007.

Chapter 2 • Decision Making and Consumer Behavior

Chapter Objectives

When you finish reading this chapter you will understand why:

1. The three categories of consumer decision making are cognitive, habitual, and affective.

2. A cognitive purchase decision is the outcome of a series of stages that results in the selection of one product over competing options.

3. We often rely upon "rules-of-thumb" or cues in the environment to make routine decisions.

4. We make some decisions on the basis of an emotional reaction rather than as the outcome of a rational thought process.

Richard has had it! There's only so much longer he can go on watching TV on his tiny, antiquated set. It was bad enough trying to squint at *The Walking Dead.* The final straw was when he couldn't tell the Titans from the Jaguars during an NFL football game. When he went next door to watch the second half on Mark's home theater setup, he finally realized what he was missing. Budget or not, it was time to act: A man has to have his priorities.

Where to start looking? The Web, naturally. Richard checks out a few comparison-shopping Web sites, including pricegrabber.com and bizrate.com. After he narrows down his options, he ventures out to check on a few sets in person. He figures he'll probably get a decent selection (and an affordable price) at one of those huge "big box" stores. Arriving at Zany Zack's Appliance Emporium, Richard heads straight for the Video Zone in the back—he barely notices the rows of toasters, microwave ovens, and stereos on his way. Within minutes, a smiling salesperson in a cheap suit accosts him. Even though he could use some help, Richard tells the salesperson he's only browsing. He figures these guys don't know what they're talking about, and they're simply out to make a sale no matter what.

Richard examines some of the features on the 60-inch color sets. He knew his friend Evey had a set by Prime Wave that she really liked, and his sister Rose warned him to stay away from the Kamashita. Although Richard finds a Prime Wave model loaded to the max with features such as a sleep timer, on-screen programming menu, cable-compatible tuner, and picture-in-picture, he chooses the less expensive Precision 2000X because it has one feature that really catches his fancy: stereo broadcast reception.

Later that day, Richard is a happy man as he sits in his easy chair and watches Sheldon match wits with Leonard, Howard, and the others on *The Big Bang Theory.* If he's going to be a couch potato, he's going in style.

OBJECTIVE 1
The three categories of consumer decision making are cognitive, habitual, and affective.

What's Your Problem?

Every consumer decision we make is a response to a problem. Of course, the type and scope of these problems varies enormously; our needs range from simple physiological priorities like quenching thirst to abstract intellectual or aesthetic quandaries like choosing a college major—or perhaps what to wear to that upcoming Rihanna concert.

Because some purchase decisions are more important than others, the amount of effort we put into each differs. Sometimes the decision-making process is almost automatic; we seem to make snap judgments based on very little information. At other times the decision process resembles a full-time job. A person may literally spend days or weeks agonizing over an important purchase such as a new home, a car, or even an iPhone versus an Android phone. We make some decisions very thoughtfully and rationally as we carefully weigh the pros and cons of different choices—while in other cases we let our emotions guide us to one choice over another as we react to a problem with great enthusiasm or even disgust.

Given the range of problems we all confront in our lives, clearly it is difficult to apply a "one size fits all" explanation to the complexities of consumer behavior. Researchers now realize that decision makers actually possess a *repertoire* of strategies. In a thought process we call **constructive processing**, we evaluate the effort we'll need to make a particular choice and then tailor the amount of cognitive "effort" we expend to get the job done.[1] When the task requires a well-thought-out, rational approach, we'll invest the brainpower to do it. Otherwise, we look for shortcuts such as "just do what I usually do," or perhaps we make "gut" decisions based on our emotional reactions. In some cases we may actually create a **mental budget** that helps us to estimate what we will consume over time so that we can regulate what we do in the present—if the dieter knows he will be chowing down at a big BBQ tomorrow, he may decide to skip that tempting candy bar today. Case closed.[2]

So, let's think about consumer decision making in terms of three "buckets" as Figure 2.1 shows. We're going to consider each of these types of decision making in turn, but keep in mind that they don't necessarily work independently of one another. Think for example about Ken, who has decided to embark on a weight-loss program. A person's efforts to change or maintain his actions over time, whether these involve dieting, living on a budget, or training to run a marathon, involve planning that is a form of **self-regulation**. He may engage in cognitive decision making as he carefully selects a diet and perhaps compiles a list of foods that are "banned" from his kitchen. In addition, he may have to recognize that he has a behavioral pattern of snacking on junk food in the mid-afternoon whether he's really hungry or not. Ken may have to "argue" with himself as he weighs the long-term benefits of a successful diet against short-term temptations like that inviting candy bar sitting on his desk. In some cases this involves some creative tinkering with the facts—for example, consumers engage in **counteractive construal** when they exaggerate the negative aspects of behaviors that will interfere with the ultimate goal.[3] Ken may inflate the number of calories the snack contains as one way to resist its lure. As every dieter knows, we don't always win this argument.

Finally, emotional issues such as feelings of inferiority or low self-esteem may be the primary motivator. In some situations people consume products (especially food) as a reaction to prior life experiences such as loss of a loved one or perhaps abuse as a child. A British man whom the U.K. news media once dubbed "the world's fattest man" when he weighed in at 980 pounds is a case in point. He explained that as an adult his insatiable desire to constantly eat stemmed from an abusive father and sexual abuse by a relative: "I still had all these things going around in my head from my childhood. Food replaced the love I didn't get from my parents." (The good news: after a gastric bypass operation this man has lost almost two-thirds of his body weight).[4] Obviously this is an extreme case, and it certainly doesn't mean that everyone who struggles with his or her weight is

Figure 2.1 THE THREE "BUCKETS" OF CONSUMER DECISION MAKING a victim of abuse! Nonetheless, emotion often plays a role—a dieter may feel elated when he weighs in at three pounds less than last week; however, if he fails to make progress he may become discouraged and actually sabotage himself with a Krispy Kreme binge.[5]

Consumer Involvement

We'll explore each of these decision-making "buckets" in more detail, but first we need to take a step back and ask *why* different consumers may approach the same choice situation from very different perspectives. For example, imagine this conversation between two shoppers at a car dealership:

Consumer #1: I want the one I read about in the latest issue of *Car and Driver* magazine: It has a six-cylinder turbo engine, a double-clutch transmission, a 90 strokebore, and 10:1 compression ratio.

Consumer #2: I want a red one.

Involvement is "a person's perceived relevance of the object based on their inherent needs, values, and interests."[6] We use the word *object* in the generic sense to refer to a product (or a brand), an advertisement, or a purchase situation. Consumers can find involvement in all these objects. Figure 2.2 shows that different factors may create involvement. These factors can be something about the person, something about the object, or something about the situation.

Our motivation to attain a goal increases our desire to acquire the products or services that we believe will satisfy it. However, as we see in the case of Consumer #2, not everyone is motivated to the same extent. Involvement reflects our level of motivation to process information about a product or service we believe will help us to solve a problem

Figure 2.2 CONCEPTUALIZING INVOLVEMENT

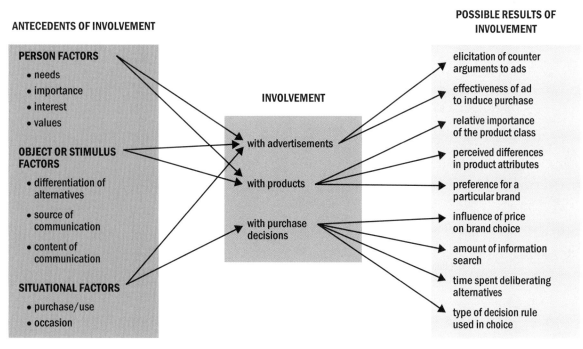

INVOLVEMENT = f (Person, Situation, Object)

The level of involvement may be influenced by one or more of these three factors. Interactions among persons, situation, and object factors are likely to occur.

or reach a goal.[7] Think of a person's degree of involvement as a continuum that ranges from absolute lack of interest in a marketing stimulus at one end to obsession at the other. **Inertia** describes consumption at the low end of involvement, where we make decisions out of habit because we lack the motivation to consider alternatives. Table 2.1 shows one of the most widely used scales to assess level of involvement.

Depending on whether the need we want to satisfy is utilitarian or hedonic (see Chapter 1), as our involvement increases we think more about the product ("I've spent the last three days researching mortgage interest rates") or we experience a strong emotional response ("I get goose bumps when I imagine what my daughter will look like in that bridal gown").[8] Figure 2.3 summarizes the relationship between involvement and our three types of decision making. Not surprisingly, we tend to find higher levels of involvement in product categories that demand a big investment of money (like houses) or self-esteem (like clothing) and lower levels for mundane categories like household cleaners or hardware.[9] Still, bear in mind that virtually anything can qualify as highly involving to some people—just ask a "tool guy" to talk about his passion for hammers or plumbing supplies.

TABLE 2.1	A Scale to Measure Involvement

To Me [Object to Be Judged] Is

1. important	_:_:_:_:_:_:_	unimportant*
2. boring	_:_:_:_:_:_:_	interesting
3. relevant	_:_:_:_:_:_:_	irrelevant*
4. exciting	_:_:_:_:_:_:_	unexciting*
5. means nothing	_:_:_:_:_:_:_	means a lot to me
6. appealing	_:_:_:_:_:_:_	unappealing*
7. fascinating	_:_:_:_:_:_:_	mundane*
8. worthless	_:_:_:_:_:_:_	valuable
9. involving	_:_:_:_:_:_:_	uninvolving*
10. not needed	_:_:_:_:_:_:_	needed

Figure 2.3 INVOLVEMENT AND DECISION MAKING

This Brazillian ad for hair-loss product appeals to men who take their impending baldness seriously.

Source: Art Director: Pedro Vargens, Creative Directors: Bruno Richter and Victor Vicente.

Types of Involvement

A freelance software programmer who calls himself Winter is on a mission to visit every Starbucks in the world. To date he's been to more than 11,000 outlets in numerous countries. When he learned that a Starbucks store in British Columbia was scheduled to close the next day, he spent $1,400 to fly there immediately just to order a cup of coffee in the nick of time. He chronicles his odyssey on his Web site, starbuckseverywhere.net.[13]

OK, maybe Winter needs to get a life. Still, his passion demonstrates that involvement takes many forms. It can be cognitive, as when a "gearhead" is motivated to learn all she can about the latest specs of a new tablet, or emotional, as when the thought of a new Armani suit gives a clotheshorse the chills.[14] What's more, the very act of *buying* the Armani may be highly involving for people who are passionately devoted to shopping.

To further complicate matters, advertisements such as those Nike or Adidas produce may themselves be involving for some reason (e.g., because they make us laugh or cry, or inspire us to exercise harder). So, it seems that involvement is a fuzzy concept, because it overlaps with other things and means different things to different people. Indeed, the consensus is that there are actually several broad types of involvement we can relate to the product, the message, or the perceiver.[15]

Product Involvement

Product involvement is a consumer's level of interest in a particular product. The more closely marketers can tie a brand to an individual, the higher the involvement they will create.

As a rule, product decisions are likely to be highly involving if the consumer believes there is **perceived risk**. This means the person believes there may be negative consequences if he or she chooses the wrong option. Risk is greater when a product is expensive or complicated. In some cases perceived risk also is a factor when others can see what we choose, and we may be embarrassed if we make the wrong choice.[16] This means that a product does not necessarily have to cost a fortune or be hard to use to be risky—for example, a college senior who is going to a job interview may obsess about sweating too much and give a lot of thought to the brand of deodorant he or she uses that morning.

Minolta features a no-risk guarantee as a way to reduce the perceived risk in buying an office copier.

Source: Courtesy of Minolta Corporation.

MAYBE THE BEST WAY TO HANDLE RISK IS TO AVOID IT ALTOGETHER.

That's why Minolta created the No-Risk Guarantee. It takes you out of harm's way by letting you decide whether you're happy with the copier's performance.

Even better, it covers our EP 9760 Pro Series Copier, which was recently voted first overall in productivity in the high-volume class.*

Here's how it works: If you're not completely satisfied with our copier within the first three years of normal operation, we will replace it with an identical or comparably equipped model, free of charge. In other

words, it works or it walks. An award-winning copier combined with an iron-clad guarantee? The only risk involved is passing this opportunity up.

For more information, call 1-800-9-MINOLTA.

NO-RISK COPIERS
ONLY FROM THE MIND OF MINOLTA

MINOLTA

Mass customization describes the personalization of products and services for individual customers at a mass-production price.[17] This product involvement strategy applies to a wide range of products and services, from newspaper Web sites that allow readers to choose which sections of the paper they want to see, to Dell computers that you can configure, to Levi's blue jeans that have a right leg one inch shorter than a left leg to fit an asymmetrical body (this is more common than you think).[18] Mars Snackfood USA introduced M&M's Faces to encourage consumers to bond with its chocolates: At mymms.com, you can upload a photo and order a batch of M&Ms with a face and personal message printed on the candy shell.

Figure 2.4 lists five kinds of risk—including objective (e.g., physical danger) and subjective (e.g., social embarrassment) factors—as well as the products each type tends to affect. Perceived risk is less of a problem for consumers who have greater "risk capital," because they have less to lose from a poor choice. For example, a highly self-confident person might worry less than a vulnerable, insecure person who chooses a brand that peers think isn't cool.

When a consumer is highly involved with a specific product, this is The Holy Grail for marketers because it means he or she exhibits **brand loyalty**: Repeat purchasing behavior that reflects a conscious decision to continue buying the same brand.[19] Note that this definition states that the consumer not only buys the brand on a regular basis, but that he or she also has a strong positive attitude toward it rather than simply buying it out of habit. In fact, we often find that a brand-loyal consumer has more than simply a positive attitude; frequently she is passionate about the product. "True-blue" users react more vehemently when a company alters, redesigns, or (God forbid) eliminates a

Figure 2.4 FIVE TYPES OF PERCEIVED RISK

	BUYERS MOST SENSITIVE TO RISK	PURCHASES MOST SUBJECT TO RISK
MONETARY RISK	Risk capital consists of money and property. Those with relatively little income and wealth are most vulnerable.	High-ticket items that require substantial expenditures are most subject to this form of risk.
FUNCTIONAL RISK	Risk capital consists of alternative means of performing the function or meeting the need. Practical consumers are most sensitive.	Products or services whose purchase and use requires the buyer's exclusive commitment are most sensitive.
PHYSICAL RISK	Risk capital consists of physical vigor, health, and vitality. Those who are elderly, frail, or in ill health are most vulnerable.	Mechanical or electrical goods (such as vehicles or flammables), drugs and medical treatment, and food and beverages are most sensitive.
SOCIAL RISK	Risk capital consists of self-esteem and self-confidence. Those who are insecure and uncertain are most sensitive.	Socially visible or symbolic goods, such as clothes, jewelry, cars, homes, or sports equipment are most subject to social risk.
PSYCHO-LOGICAL RISK	Risk capital consists of affiliations and status. Those lacking self-respect or attractiveness to peers are most sensitive.	Expensive personal luxuries that may engender guilt, durables, and services whose use demands self-discipline or sacrifice are most sensitive.

favorite brand. One simple test to find out if you're brand loyal: If the store is temporarily out of your favorite brand, will you buy a different product or hold off until you can get your first choice?

Message Involvement

Media vehicles possess different qualities that influence our motivation to pay attention to what they tell us, known as **message involvement**. Print is a *high-involvement medium* (whether it appears on a "dead tree" or in an e-book). The reader actively processes the information and (if desired) he or she is able to pause and reflect on it before turning the page.[23] In contrast, television is a *low-involvement medium* because it requires a passive viewer who exerts relatively little control (remote-control "zipping" notwithstanding) over content.

TV's passive nature explains why advertisers try to place their ads in shows such as *American Idol* that engage viewers—they want to increase the likelihood their audience will pay attention when their messages come on the screen. Research evidence indicates that a viewer who is more involved with a television show will respond more positively to commercials he sees during that show, and that these spots will have a greater chance to influence his purchase intentions.[24] In fact, some messages (including really well-made advertisements) are so involving that they trigger a stage of **narrative transportation**, where people become immersed in the storyline. One recent study showed that people who are feeling lucky engage in this process when they look at an advertisement for a lottery; once immersed, it is hard to distract them from the message.[25] Not a great thing for compulsive gamblers, but a powerful effect nonetheless.

Marketing Pitfall

Although everyone wants to cultivate a set of brand-loyal customers, there is a wrinkle that sometimes confounds even the most effective marketers. We often engage in *brand switching*, even if our current brand satisfies our needs. When researchers for British brewer Bass Export studied the American beer market, they discovered that many drinkers have a repertoire of two to six favorite brands rather than one clear favorite.[20]

Sometimes, it seems we simply like to try new things—we crave variety as a form of stimulation or to reduce boredom. **Variety seeking**, the desire to choose new alternatives over more familiar ones, even influences us to switch from our favorite products to ones we like less! This can occur even before we become *satiated*, or tired, of our favorite. Research supports the idea that we are willing to trade enjoyment for variety because the unpredictability *itself* is rewarding.[21]

We're especially likely to look for variety when we are in a good mood, or when there isn't a lot of other stuff going on.[22] So, even though we have favorites, we still like to sample other possibilities. However, when the decision situation is ambiguous, or when there is little information about competing brands, we tend to opt for the safe choice.

This British ad appeals to social risk.
Source: © Abbot Mead Vickers BBD, London. Ad created and produced by Simon Langley, Richard Morgan, and John Offenbach.

Marketing Opportunity

Competitions are one way to get customers involved with the organization and its products. In a bag of licorice allsorts, there are a variety of types of licorice sweets. Beacon, a popular South African confectioner, decided to sell bags of just one of them, but didn't have a name for it. As this is an important decision, Beacon decided to involve customers through social media, specifically Facebook, to come up with a name for the product. Consumers voted to call them "Liq-O-Dots."[26]

Although consumers' involvement levels with a product message vary, marketers do not have to simply sit back and hope for the best. If they are aware of some basic factors that increase or decrease attention, they can take steps to increase the likelihood that product information will get through. A marketer can boost a person's motivation to process relevant information via one or more of the following techniques:[27]

- **Use novel stimuli, such as unusual cinematography, sudden silences, or unexpected movements, in commercials.** When a British firm called Egg Banking introduced a credit card to the French market, its ad agency created unusual commercials to make people question their assumptions. One ad stated, "Cats always land on their paws," and then two researchers in white lab coats dropped a kitten off a rooftop—never to see it again (animal rights activists were not amused).[28]
- **Use prominent stimuli, such as loud music and fast action, to capture attention.** In print formats, larger ads increase attention. Also, viewers look longer at colored pictures than at black-and-white ones.
- **Include celebrity endorsers.** As we'll see in Chapter 8, people process more information when it comes from someone they admire (or maybe even Kim Kardashian).
- **Provide value that customers appreciate.** Charmin bathroom tissue set up public toilets in Times Square that hordes of grateful visitors used. Thousands more people (evidently with time on their hands) visited the brand's Web site to view the display.[29]

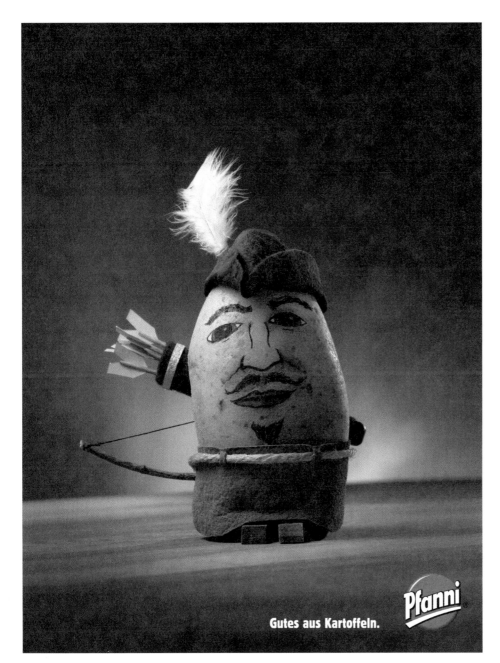

Gutes aus Kartoffeln.

Pfanni

This German ad hopes to ramp up involvement with potatoes, a low-involvement product. The ad for ready-to-serve potato dishes declares, "Good stuff from potatoes."
Source: Courtesy of Unilever/Germany.

- **Invent new media platforms to grab attention.** Procter & Gamble printed trivia questions and answers on its Pringles snack chips with ink made of blue or red food coloring, and a company called Speaking Roses International patented a technology to laser-print words, images, or logos on flower petals.[30] An Australian firm creates hand stamps that nightclubs use to identify paying customers; the stamps include logos or ad messages so partiers' hands become an advertising platform.[31]

- **Create spectacles where the message is itself a form of entertainment**. In the early days of radio and television, ads literally were performances—show hosts integrated marketing messages into the episodes. Today live advertising is making a come-back as marketers try harder and harder to captivate jaded consumers:[32] Axe body products sponsored a posh Hamptons (New York) nightclub for the whole season; it became The Axe Lounge, sporting branding on the DJ booth and menu and Axe products in the restrooms.

Situational Involvement

Situational involvement takes place with a store, Web site, or a location where people consume a product or service. One way to increase this kind of involvement is to personalize the messages shoppers receive at the time of purchase. For example, a few marketers tailor the recommendations they give shoppers in a store based on what they picked up from a shelf. At some Dunkin' Donuts locations, a person who orders a morning coffee sees an ad at the cash register that pushes hash browns or breakfast sandwiches.

New facial-recognition technology in billboards classifies passersby on the street based on their approximate age and their likely gender (some hairstyles and facial piercings will make this challenge interesting). The technology analyzes features like the size and shape of the nose, eyes, cheekbones, and jaw line and compares these to databases to make a guess as to which category the person should belong in. After the technology categorizes the consumer, he or she sees a message tailored to that category.[33]
Source: Photo by Alex Grimm/Getty Images.

Product involvement often depends on the situation we're in. The Charmin toilet tissue brand sponsors a Web site, appropriately named SitOrSquat.com. The site helps travelers find the cleanest public restrooms wherever they happen to be on Earth. The brand manager explains, "Our goal is to connect Charmin with innovative conversations and solutions as a brand that understands the importance of bringing the best bathroom experience to consumers, even when they're away from home." According to Charmin, SitOrSquat lists over 52,000 toilets in 10 countries.
Source: Courtesy of P&G/Charmin.

OBJECTIVE 2
A cognitive purchase
decision is the outcome
of a series of stages that
results in the selection
of one product over
competing options.

Cognitive Decision Making

Now, it's time to consider the three different decision-making perspectives we described earlier, starting with the classic cognitive decision-making approach. Traditionally, consumer researchers approached decision making from an **information-processing perspective**. According to this view, people calmly and carefully integrate as much information as possible with what they already know about a product, painstakingly weigh the pluses and minuses of each alternative, and arrive at a satisfactory decision. This kind of careful, deliberate thinking is especially relevant to activities like financial planning that call for a lot of attention to detail and many choices that impact a consumer's quality of life (unfortunately, most of us seem to be better at planning for the short-term than thinking ahead to the future).[34]

When marketing managers believe that their customers in fact do undergo this kind of planning, they should carefully study steps in decision making to understand just how consumers weigh information, form beliefs about options, and choose criteria they use to select one option over others. With these insights in hand, they can develop products and promotional strategies that supply the specific information people look for in the most effective formats.[35]

However, even the traditional view of decision making recognizes that we tend to be "cognitive misers" who do what we can to simplify our choices if possible. The **economics of information** perspective assumes that we collect just as much data as we need to make an informed decision. We form expectations of the value of additional information and continue to search to the extent that the rewards of doing so (what economists call the *utility*) exceed the costs. This utilitarian assumption also implies that we collect the most valuable units of information first. We absorb additional pieces only to the extent that we think they will add to what we already know.[36] In other words, we'll put ourselves out to collect as much information as we can, so long as the process isn't too onerous or time-consuming.[37]

Steps in the Cognitive Decision-Making Process

Let's think about Richard's process of buying a new TV that we described at the beginning of the chapter. He didn't suddenly wake up and crave a new TV. Richard went through several steps between the time he felt the need for a new boob tube and when he actually brought one home. We describe these steps as (1) problem recognition, (2) information search, (3) evaluation of alternatives, and (4) product choice. Of course, after we make a decision, its outcome affects the final step in the process, in which learning occurs based on how well the choice worked out (more on that in Chapter 6). This learning process, of course, influences the likelihood that we'll make the same choice the next time the need for a similar decision occurs. And so on and so on. . . . Figure 2.5 provides an overview of this decision-making process. Let's briefly look at each step.

Step #1: Problem Recognition

Ford's plan to promote its Fusion hybrid model focused on people who aren't thinking about buying a new car—at least not right now. Its TV commercials target what the auto industry terms the "upper funnel," or potential buyers down the road. Ford's research found that a large number of U.S. drivers still are unaware of the Fusion. The company is confident that it can close sales if and when customers decide to buy a new car. But, its weak spot is to get people into the frame of mind where they want to do that. To create desire where none exists yet, visitors to a special Web site entered to win a trip and a new Fusion. Ford publicized the sweepstakes on Twitter and Facebook; during the first two weeks of the promotion, almost 70,000 people requested more information about the car.[38]

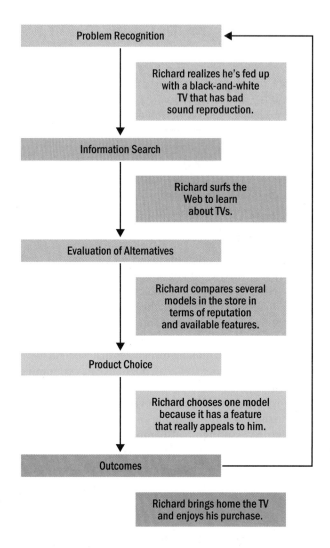

Figure 2.5 STAGES IN CONSUMER DECISION MAKING

Problem recognition occurs at what Ford terms "the upper funnel," when we experience a significant difference between our current state of affairs and some state we desire. As we noted at the beginning of the chapter, this problem requires a solution. A person who unexpectedly runs out of gas on the highway has a problem, as does the person who becomes dissatisfied with the image of his car, even though there is nothing mechanically wrong with it. Although the quality of Richard's TV had not changed, he altered his *standard of comparison,* and as a result he had a new problem to solve: how to improve his TV experience.

Figure 2.6 shows that a problem arises in one of two ways. The person who runs out of gas experiences a decline in the quality of his *actual state* (*need recognition*). In contrast, the person who craves a newer, flashier car moves his *ideal state* upward (*opportunity recognition*). Either way, there is a gulf between the actual state and the ideal state.[39] Richard perceived a problem due to opportunity recognition: He moved his ideal state upward in terms of the quality of TV reception he craved.

Step #2: Information Search

Once a consumer recognizes a problem, he or she needs the 411 to solve it. **Information search** is the process by which we survey the environment for appropriate data to make a reasonable decision. You might recognize a need and then search the marketplace for specific information (a process we call *prepurchase search*). However, many of us,

Figure 2.6 PROBLEM RECOGNITION: SHIFTS IN ACTUAL OR IDEAL STATES

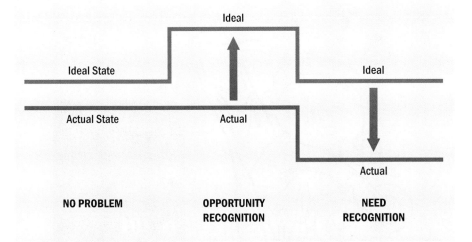

An Italian sushi company reminds us that problem recognition can occur in unexpected places.
Source: Touché Advertising Agency, Bologna, Italy; Sosushi brand.

especially veteran shoppers, enjoy browsing just for the fun of it or because we like to stay up-to-date on what's happening in the marketplace. Those shopaholics engage in *ongoing search.*[40]

Whether we're hard-core shoppers or not, each of us has some degree of knowledge already in memory about many products. When a purchase decision confronts us, we may engage in *internal search* as we scan our own memory banks to assemble information about different product alternatives (more on this in Chapter 6). Usually, though, even those of us who are the most market-savvy need to supplement this knowledge with external search, so we also obtain information from advertisements, friends, or just plain people watching. A Finnish study demonstrated that what our neighbors buy affects our own decision making. The researchers discovered that when one of a person's 10 nearest neighbors bought a car, the odds that the person would buy a car of the same make during the next week and a half jumped 86 percent.[41]

Product labels assist us with problem solving, but some are more useful than others. Here are some examples of the not-so-helpful variety:[44]

- Instructions for folding up a portable baby carriage: "Step 1: Remove baby."
- On a Conair Pro Style 1600 hair dryer: "WARNING: Do not use in shower. Never use while sleeping."
- At a rest stop on a Wisconsin highway: "Do not eat urinal cakes."
- On a bag of Fritos: "You could be a winner! No purchase necessary. Details inside."
- On some Swanson frozen dinners: "Serving suggestion: Defrost."
- On Tesco's Tiramisu dessert (printed on bottom of box): "Do not turn upside down."
- On Marks & Spencer bread pudding: "Product will be hot after heating."
- On packaging for a Rowenta iron: "Do not iron clothes on body."
- On Nytol sleeping aid: "Warning: May cause drowsiness."

Some product labels are more useful than others.

Source: Hachette Book Group, Inc.

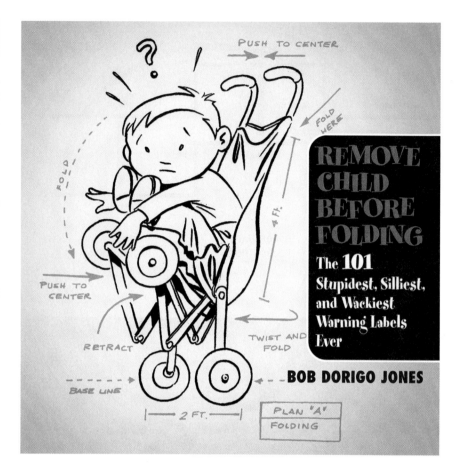

How Much Do We Search? As a general rule, we search more when the purchase is important, when we have more of a need to learn more about the purchase, or when it's easy to obtain the relevant information.[42] Consumers differ in the amount of search they tend to undertake, regardless of the product category in question. All things equal, younger, better-educated people who enjoy the shopping/fact-finding process tend to conduct more information searches. Women are more inclined to search than are men, as are those who place greater value on style and the image they present.[43]

Does knowing something about the product make it more or less likely that we will engage in search? The answer to this question isn't as obvious as it first appears: Product experts and novices use very different strategies when they make decisions. "Newbies" who know little about a product should be the most motivated to find out more about it. However, experts are more familiar with the product category, so they should be better able to understand the meaning of any new product information they might acquire.

So, who searches more? The answer is neither: Search tends to be greatest among those consumers who are *moderately knowledgeable* about the product. Typically we find an inverted-U relationship between knowledge and external search effort, as Figure 2.7 shows. People with very limited expertise may not feel they are competent to search extensively. In fact, they may not even know where to start. Richard, who did not spend a lot of time researching his purchase, is typical. He visited one store, and he looked only at brands with which he was already familiar. In addition, he focused on only a small number of product features.[45]

Because experts have a better sense of what information is relevant to the decision, they engage in *selective search*, which means their efforts are more focused and efficient. In contrast, novices are more likely to rely on the opinions of others and on "nonfunctional" attributes, such as brand name and price, to distinguish among alternatives. Finally, novice consumers may process information in a "top-down" rather than a "bottom-up" manner—they focus less on details than on the big picture. For instance,

Figure 2.7 THE RELATIONSHIP BETWEEN AMOUNT OF INFORMATION SEARCH AND PRODUCT KNOWLEDGE

(Graph: vertical axis labeled AMOUNT OF SEARCH, horizontal axis labeled PRODUCT KNOWLEDGE, showing an inverted-U curve.)

they may be more impressed by the sheer amount of technical information an ad presents than by the actual significance of the claims it makes.[46]

Cybermediaries. As anyone who's ever Googled a phrase like "home theaters" knows, the Web delivers enormous amounts of product and retailer information in seconds. In fact, the biggest problem Web surfers face these days is to narrow down their choices, not to beef them up. In cyberspace, simplification is key.

With the tremendous number of Web sites available and the huge number of people surfing the Web each day, how can people organize information and decide where to click? A **cybermediary** often is the answer. This term describes a Web site or app that helps to filter and organize online market information so that customers can identify and evaluate alternatives more efficiently.[47] Many consumers regularly link to comparison-shopping sites, such as Bizrate.com or Pricegrabber.com, for example, that list many online retailers that sell a given item along with the price each charges.[48] *Directories* and *portals,* such as Yahoo! or The Knot, are general services that tie together a large variety of different sites. *Forums, fan clubs*, and *user groups* offer product-related discussions to help customers sift through options. **Intelligent agents** are sophisticated software programs that use *collaborative filtering* technologies to learn from past user behavior in order to recommend new purchases.[49] When you let Amazon.com suggest a new book, the site uses an intelligent agent to propose novels based on what you and others like you have bought in the past.

Today social media platforms play a major role in the search process. Although about 60 percent of consumers now start their online process by typing queries into a search engine such as Google or Bing, 40 percent now continue their quest for more information in other places such as blogs, YouTube, Twitter, and Facebook. The goal here is not to collect more technical or performance information, but to get other people's opinions about options in the product category—and to eliminate some brands from consideration when others ding them. What's more, after they buy a brand, about three-fourths of shoppers who use social media in the process choose to follow it on the company's Facebook page so they can continue to engage with it in the future.[50]

Step #3: Evaluate Alternatives

Much of the effort we put into a purchase decision occurs at the stage where we have to put the pedal to the metal and actually choose a product from several alternatives. This may not be easy; modern consumer society abounds with choices. In some cases, there

Net Profit

Customer product reviews are a key driver of satisfaction and loyalty. In one large survey, about half of the respondents who bought an item from a major Web site remembered seeing other buyers' reviews.[51] Another advantage these reviews provide is that consumers learn about other, less popular options they may like as well—and at the same time products such as movies, books, and CDs that aren't "blockbusters" are more likely to sell. At the online DVD rental company Netflix, for example, fellow subscribers recommend about two-thirds of the films that people order. In fact, between 70 and 80 percent of Netflix rentals come from the company's back catalog of 38,000 films rather than recent releases.[52]

This aspect of online customer review is one important factor that's fueling a new way of thinking, which one writer calls the **long tail**.[53] The basic idea is that we no longer need to rely solely on big hits (such as blockbuster movies or best-selling books) to find profits. Companies can also make money if they sell small amounts of items that only a few people want—*if* they sell enough different items. For example, Amazon.com maintains an inventory of 3.7 million books, compared to the 100,000 or so you'll find in a Barnes & Noble retail store. Most of these will sell only a few thousand copies (if that), but the 3.6 million books that Barnes & Noble *doesn't* carry make up a quarter of Amazon's revenues! Other examples of the long tail include successful microbreweries and TV networks that make money on reruns of old shows on channels such as the Game Show Network.

Is there a "buy button" in your brain? Some corporations, including Google, CBS, Disney, and Frito-Lay, have teamed up with neuroscientists to find out.[57] **Neuromarketing** uses *functional magnetic resonance imaging* (or *fMRI*), a brain-scanning device that tracks blood flow as we perform mental tasks. In recent years, researchers have discovered that regions in the brain, such as the amygdala, the hippocampus, and the hypothalamus, are dynamic switchboards that blend memory, emotions, and biochemical triggers. These interconnected neurons shape the ways in which fear, panic, exhilaration, and social pressure influence our choices.

Scientists know that specific regions of the brain light up in these scans to show increased blood flow when a person recognizes a face, hears a song, makes a decision, or senses deception. Now they hope to harness this technology to measure consumers' reactions to movie trailers, automobiles, the appeal of a pretty face, and even their loyalty to specific brands. DaimlerChrysler took brain scans of men as they looked at photos of cars and confirmed that sports cars activated their reward centers. The company's scientists found that the most popular vehicles—the Porsche- and Ferrari-style sports cars—triggered activity in a section of the brain they call the *fusiform face area*, which governs facial recognition. A psychiatrist who ran the study commented, "They were reminded of faces when they looked at the cars. The lights of the cars look a little like eyes."

A study that took brain scans of people as they drank competing soft-drink brands illustrates how loyalty to a brand affects our reactions, even at a very basic, physiological level. When the researchers monitored brain scans of 67 people who took a blind taste test of Coca-Cola and Pepsi, each soft drink lit up the brain's reward system, and the participants were evenly split as to which drink they preferred—even though three out of four participants *said* they preferred Coke. When told they were drinking Coke, the regions of the brain that control memory lit up, and this activation drowned out the area that simply reacts to taste cues. In this case, Coke's strong brand identity trumped the sensations coming from respondents' taste receptors.

may be literally hundreds of different brands (as in cigarettes) or different variations of the same brand (as in shades of lipstick).

Ask a friend to name all the brands of perfume she can think of. The odds are she will reel off three to five names rather quickly, then stop and think awhile before she comes up with a few more. She's probably very familiar with the first set of brands, and in fact she probably wears one or more of these. Her list may also contain one or two brands that she doesn't like; to the contrary, they come to mind because she thinks they smell nasty or are unsophisticated. Note also that there are many, many more brands on the market that she did not name at all.

If your friend goes to the store to buy perfume, it is likely that she will consider buying some or most of the brands she listed initially. She might also entertain a few more possibilities if these come to her attention while she's at the fragrance counter (for example, if an employee "ambushes" her with a scent sample as she walks down the aisle).

We call the alternatives a consumer knows about the **evoked set** and the ones he or she seriously considers the **consideration set**.[54] Recall that Richard did not know much about the technical aspects of television sets, and he had only a few major brands in memory. Of these, two were acceptable possibilities and one was not.

Consumers often consider a surprisingly small number of alternatives, especially with all the choices available to us. A cross-national study found that people generally include just a few products in their consideration set, although this amount varies by product category and across countries. For example, on average American beer consumers considered only three brands, whereas Canadian consumers typically considered seven brands. In contrast, whereas auto buyers in Norway studied two alternatives, American consumers on average looked at more than eight models before they decided.[55] We seem to be a lot pickier about our wheels than our brews.

For obvious reasons, a marketer who finds that his brand is not in his target market's evoked set has cause to worry. You often don't get a second chance to make a good first impression; a consumer isn't likely to place a product in his evoked set after he has already considered it and rejected it. Indeed, we're more likely to add a new brand to the evoked set than one that we previously considered but passed over, even after a marketer has provided additional positive information about it.[56] For marketers, a consumer's reluctance to give a rejected product a second chance underscores the importance of ensuring that it performs well from the time the company introduces it.

How Do We Put Products into Categories? Remember that when consumers process product information, they don't do it in a vacuum. They evaluate its attributes in terms of what they already know about the item or other similar products. A person who thinks about a particular 35 mm camera will most likely compare it to *other* 35 mm cameras rather than to a disposable camera. Because the *category* in which a consumer places a product determines the other products she will compare it to, the way we classify a brand in our minds plays a big role in how we evaluate it.[58]

The products in a consumer's evoked set are likely to share some similar features. This process can either help or hurt a product, depending on what people compare it to. For example, in one survey, about 25 percent of consumers said they would be less likely to buy a product made of hemp if they know it's derived from the same plant from which marijuana comes (but without any of the latter's effects). When we come across a new product, we tend to place it into an existing category rather than create a new category.[59] Of course, that's one of the big hurdles a new form of technology has to clear: Before people will buy a microwave oven, MP3 player, or GPS, they need to make sense out of the category to which it belongs.

It is important to understand how we cognitively represent this information in a **knowledge structure**. This term refers to a set of beliefs and the way we organize these beliefs in our minds.[60] Their makeup matters to marketers because they want to ensure that customers correctly group their products. For example, General Foods brought out

Figure 2.8 LEVELS OF ABSTRACTION IN DESSERT CATEGORIES

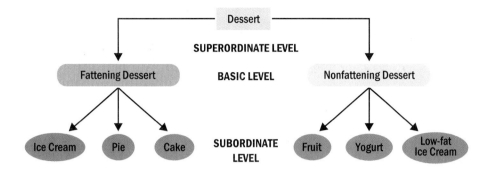

Many researchers remain skeptical about how helpful this technology will be for consumer research. However, if indeed researchers can reliably track consumers' brand preferences by seeing how their brains react, there may be many interesting potential opportunities for new research techniques that rely on what we (or at least our brains) do rather than what we say.

• • • • • • • • • • • • • • • •

a new line of Jell-O flavors, such as Cranberry Orange, that it called Jell-O Gelatin Flavors for Salads. Unfortunately, the company discovered that people used the product only for salad, because the name encouraged them to put the product in their "salad" structure rather than in their "dessert" structure. General Foods dropped the product line.[61]

Typically we represent a product in a cognitive structure at one of three levels. To understand this idea, consider how someone might respond to these questions about an ice cream cone: What other products share similar characteristics, and which would you consider as alternatives to eating a cone? These questions may be more complex than they first appear. At one level, a cone is similar to an apple because you could eat both as a dessert. At another level, a cone is similar to a piece of pie because you could eat either for dessert and both are fattening. At still another level, a cone is similar to an ice cream sundae—you could eat either for dessert, both are made of ice cream, and both are fattening. Figure 2.8 depicts these three levels.

It's easy to see that the foods a person associates with the category "fattening dessert" influence his or her decision about what to eat after dinner. The middle level, or *basic level category*, is typically the most useful for classifying products. At this level, the items we group together tend to have a lot in common with each other, but still permit us to consider a broad enough range of alternatives. The broader *superordinate category* is more abstract, whereas the more specific *subordinate category* often includes individual brands.[62] Of course, not all items fit equally well into a category. Apple pie is a better example of the subordinate category "pie" than is rhubarb pie, even though both are types of pies. This is because it's more *prototypical*, and most people would think of apple as a pie flavor before they thought of rhubarb. In contrast, true pie experts probably know a lot about both typical and atypical category examples.[63]

Strategic Implications of Product Categorization. The way we categorize products has a lot of strategic implications. That's because this process affects which products consumers will compare to our product and also the criteria they'll use to decide if they like us or the other guys.

Position a Product. The success of a *positioning strategy* hinges on the marketer's ability to convince the consumer to consider its product within a given category. For example, the orange juice industry tried to reposition orange juice as a drink people can enjoy all day long ("It's not just for breakfast anymore"). However, soft-drink companies attempt the opposite when they portray sodas as suitable for breakfast consumption. They are trying to make their way into consumers' "breakfast drink" category, along with orange juice, grapefruit juice, and coffee. Of course, this strategy can backfire, as Pepsi-Cola discovered when it introduced Pepsi A.M. and positioned it as a coffee substitute. The company did such a good job of categorizing the drink as a morning beverage that customers wouldn't drink it at any other time, and the product failed.[64]

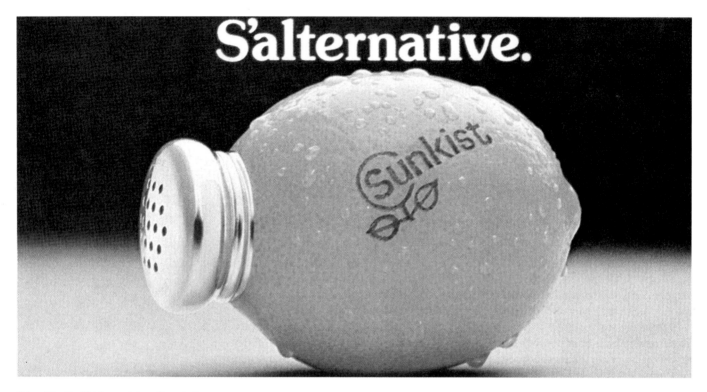

This ad for Sunkist lemon juice attempts to establish a new category for the product by repositioning it as a salt substitute.
Source: Courtesy of Sunkist Growers.

Identify Competitors. At the abstract, superordinate level, many different product forms compete for membership. The category "entertainment" might comprise both bowling and the ballet, but not many people would substitute one of these activities for the other. Products and services that on the surface are quite different, however, actually compete with each other at a broad level for consumers' discretionary dollars. Although bowling or ballet may not be a likely tradeoff for many people, a symphony might try to lure away season ticket holders to the ballet by positioning itself as an equivalent member of the superordinate category "cultural event."[65]

We're often faced with choices between noncomparable categories, where we can't directly relate the attributes in one to those in another (the old problem of comparing apples and oranges). When we can create an overlapping category that encompasses both items (e.g., entertainment, value, usefulness) and then rate each alternative in terms of that superordinate category comparison, the process is easier.[66]

Create an Exemplar Product. As we saw with the case of apple pie versus rhubarb pie, if a product is a really good example of a category, then it is more familiar to consumers and they more easily recognize and recall it.[67] The characteristics of **category exemplars** tend to exert a disproportionate influence on how people think of the category in general.[68] In a sense, brands we strongly associate with a category get to "call the shots": They define the criteria we use to evaluate all category members.

Being a bit less than prototypical is not necessarily a bad thing, however. Products that are moderately unusual within their product category may stimulate more information processing and positive evaluations because they are neither so familiar that we will take them for granted nor so different that we won't consider them at all.[69] A brand that is strongly discrepant (such as Zima, a clear malt beverage) may occupy a unique niche position, whereas those that are somewhat different (e.g., local microbrews) remain in a distinct position within the general category.[70]

Locate Products in a Store. Product categorization also can affect consumers' expectations regarding the places where they can locate a desired product. If products do not clearly fit into categories (e.g., is a rug furniture?), this may diminish our ability to find them or figure out what they're supposed to be once we do. For instance, a frozen dog food that pet owners had to thaw and cook before they served it to Fido failed in the market, partly because people could not adapt to the idea of buying dog food in the "frozen foods for people" section of their grocery stores.

Evaluative Criteria. When Richard looked at different television sets, he focused on one or two product features and completely ignored several others. He narrowed down his choices as he only considered two specific brand names, and from the Prime Wave and Precision models, he chose one that featured stereo capability.

Evaluative criteria are the dimensions we use to judge the merits of competing options. When he compared alternative products, Richard could have chosen from among many criteria that ranged from very functional attributes ("Does this TV come with remote control?") to experiential ones ("Does this TV's sound reproduction make me imagine I'm in a concert hall?").

Another important point is that criteria on which products *differ* from one another carry more weight in the decision process than do those where the alternatives are *similar*. If all brands a person considers rate equally well on one attribute (e.g., if all TVs come with remote control), Richard needs to find other reasons to choose one over another. **Determinant attributes** are the features we actually use to differentiate among our choices.

Marketers often educate consumers about which criteria they should use as determinant attributes. For example, consumer research from Church & Dwight indicated that many consumers view the use of natural ingredients as a determinant attribute. As a result, the company promoted its toothpaste made from baking soda, which the company already manufactured for Church & Dwight's Arm & Hammer brand.[71]

Sometimes a company actually invents a determinant attribute: Pepsi-Cola accomplished this when it stamped freshness dates on soda cans. It spent about $25 million on an advertising and promotional campaign to convince consumers that there's nothing quite as horrible as a stale can of soda—even though people in the industry estimate that drinkers consume 98 percent of all cans well before this could be a problem. Six months after it introduced the campaign, lo and behold, an independent survey found that 61 percent of respondents felt that freshness dating is an important attribute for a soft drink![72] To effectively recommend a new decision criterion, a marketer should convey three pieces of information:[73]

1   It should point out that there are significant differences among brands on the attribute.
2   It should supply the consumer with a decision-making rule, such as *if* . . . (deciding among competing brands), *then* . . . (use the attribute as a criterion).

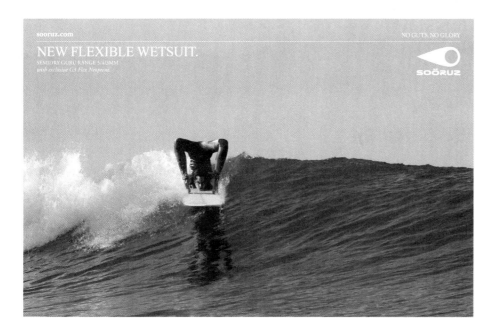

This French ad provides a vivid way to suggest an evaluative criterion.
Source: SOORUZ/PUBLICIS Conseil Paris/ Photographers: Cesar Ancelle-Hancelle/Jacques Demarcillac—Producer: Charles Denis.

3 It should convey a rule that is consistent with how the person made the decision on prior occasions. Otherwise, she is likely to ignore the recommendation because it requires too much mental work.

Under conditions of high cognitive involvement, people tend to think carefully about the pros and cons of different options, almost like a computer that would follow a somewhat complicated formula to make a decision. When we make habitual or emotional decisions we probably use a .**noncompensatory rule**[74] This means that if an option doesn't suit us on one dimension, we just reject it out of hand and move on to something else rather than think about how it might meet our needs in other ways: "I've never heard of that brand," or maybe "That color is gross."

To explain this idea, Table 2.2 summarizes the attributes of the TV sets that Richard considered. Now, let's see how some of these rules result in different brand choices—starting with noncompensatory rules.

Consumers often simplify choices when they use heuristics such as automatically choosing a favorite color or brand.

Source: Courtesy of iParty Retail Store Corp.

| TABLE 2.2 | Hypothetical Alternatives for a TV Set |

Attribute	Importance Ranking	Brand Ratings		
		Prime Wave	Precision	Kamashita
Size of screen	1	Excellent	Excellent	Excellent
Stereo broadcast capability	2	Poor	Excellent	Good
Brand reputation	3	Excellent	Excellent	Poor
Onscreen programming	4	Excellent	Poor	Poor
Cable-ready capability	5	Good	Good	Good
Sleep timer	6	Excellent	Poor	Good

The Lexicographic Rule. When a person uses the *lexicographic rule*, he selects the brand that is the best on the most important attribute. If he feels that two or more brands are equally good on that attribute, he then compares them on the second most important attribute. This selection process goes on until the tie is broken. In Richard's case, because both the Prime Wave and Precision models were tied on his most important attribute (a 60-inch screen), he chose the Precision because of its rating on his second most important attribute: its stereo capability.

The Elimination-by-Aspects Rule. Using the *elimination-by-aspects rule*, the buyer also evaluates brands on the most important attribute. In this case, though, he imposes specific cutoffs. For example, if Richard had been more interested in having a sleep timer on his TV (i.e., if it had a higher importance ranking), he might have stipulated that his choice "must have a sleep timer." Because the Prime Wave model had one and the Precision did not, he would have chosen the Prime Wave.

The Conjunctive Rule. Whereas the two former rules involve processing by attribute, the *conjunctive rule* entails processing by brand. As with the elimination-by-aspects procedure, the decision maker establishes cutoffs for each attribute. He chooses a brand if it meets all the cutoffs, but rejects a brand that fails to meet any one cutoff. If none of the brands meet all the cutoffs, he may delay the choice, change the decision rule, or modify the cutoffs he chooses to apply.

If Richard stipulated that all attributes had to be rated "good" or better, he would not have been able to choose any of the available options. He might then have modified his decision rule, conceding that it was not possible to attain these high standards in his price range. In this case, perhaps Richard could decide that he could live without on-screen programming, so he would reconsider the Precision model.

If we're willing to allow good and bad product qualities to cancel each other out, we arrive at a very different choice. For example, if Richard were not concerned about having stereo reception, he might have chosen the Prime Wave model. But because this brand doesn't feature this highly ranked attribute, it doesn't stand a chance when he uses a noncompensatory rule.

Step #4: Product Choice

Once we assemble and evaluate the relevant options in a category, eventually we have to choose one.[75] Recall that the decision rules that guide our choices range from very simple

Satisfaction or dissatisfaction is more than a reaction to how well a product or service performs. According to the **expectancy disconfirmation model**, we form beliefs about product performance based on our prior experience with the product or communications about the product that imply a certain level of quality.[81] When something performs the way we thought it would, we may not think much about it. If it fails to live up to expectations, this may create negative feelings. However, if performance happens to exceed our expectations, we're happy campers.

This perspective underscores how important it is to manage expectations. We often trace a customer's dissatisfaction to his or her erroneous expectations of the company's ability to deliver a product or service. NO company is perfect. It's just not realistic to think that everything will always turn out perfectly (although some firms don't even come close!). For a while the hotel chain Holiday Inn adopted the slogan "No surprises" to assure guests of flawless service. Inevitably, there were surprises (no operator to answer the phone, an unmade bed) and the company had to drop its promise of perfection.

and quick strategies to complicated processes that require a lot of attention and cognitive processing.[76] Our job isn't getting any easier as companies overwhelm us with more and more features. We deal with 50-button remote controls, digital cameras with hundreds of mysterious features and book-length manuals, and cars with dashboard systems worthy of the space shuttle. Experts call this spiral of complexity **feature creep**. As evidence that the proliferation of gizmos is counterproductive, Philips Electronics found that at least half of the products buyers return have nothing wrong with them—consumers simply couldn't figure out how to use them! What's worse, on average the buyer spent only 20 minutes trying to figure out how to use the product and then gave up.

Why don't companies avoid this problem? One reason is that we often assume the more features the better. It's only when we get the product home that we realize the virtue of simplicity. In one study, consumers chose among three models of a digital device that varied in terms of how complex each was. More than 60 percent chose the one with the most features. Then, when the participants got the chance to choose from up to 25 features to customize their product, the average person chose 20 of these add-ons. But when they actually used the devices, it turns out that the large number of options only frustrated them; they ended up being much happier with the simpler product. As the saying goes, "Be careful what you wish for. . . ."[77]

Step #5: Postpurchase Evaluation

As the old saying goes, "the proof of the pudding is in the eating." In other words, the true test of our decision-making process is whether we are happy with the choice we made after we undergo all these decision-making stages. **Postpurchase evaluation** closes the loop; it occurs when we experience the product or service we selected and decide whether it meets (or maybe even exceeds) our expectations.

Our overall reactions to a product after we've bought it—what researchers call **consumer satisfaction/dissatisfaction (CS/D)**—obviously play a big role in our future behavior. It's a lot easier to sell something once than to sell it again if it bombed the first time. We evaluate the things we buy as we use them and integrate them into our daily consumption activities.[78] What exactly do consumers look for in products? That's easy: They want quality and value.[79] However, these terms have slippery meanings that are hard for us to pin down. We infer quality when we rely on cues as diverse as brand name, price, product warranties, and even our estimate of how much money a company invests in its advertising.[80]

OBJECTIVE 3
We often rely upon "rules-of-thumb" or cues in the environment to make routine decisions.

Habitual Decision Making

The decision-making steps we've reviewed are well and good, but common sense tells us we don't undergo this elaborate sequence every time we buy something.[82] If we did, we'd spend our entire lives making these decisions. This would leave us very little time to enjoy the things we eventually decide to buy. Some of our buying behaviors simply don't seem "rational" because they don't serve a logical purpose (you don't use that navel ring to hold a beach towel).

We purchase some items with virtually no advance planning at all—have you ever impulsively thrown a fattening candy bar into your cart while you wait at the grocery checkout? (Hint: That's why candy bars and celeb magazines are placed there.)

Still other actions actually contradict what those rational models predict. For example, **purchase momentum** occurs when our initial impulse purchases actually increase the likelihood that we will buy even more (instead of less as we satisfy our needs); it's like we get "revved up" and plunge into a spending spree (we've all been there!).[83]

Habitual decision making describes the choices we make with little or no conscious effort. Many purchase decisions are so routine we may not realize we've made them until we look in our shopping carts![84] In fact, the amount of external search we do for most products is surprisingly small.[85] Although decisions we make on the basis of little conscious thought may seem dangerous or at best stupid, this process actually is quite efficient in many cases. The journalist Malcolm Gladwell hit the bestseller list with his book *Blink,* which demonstrated how snap judgments that occur in the blink of an eye can be surprisingly accurate.[86]

Priming and Nudging

Today there is a lot of interest among both researchers and policy makers in the power of the unconscious to influence our daily decisions.[87] In particular, many focus on the role of **priming**: Cues in the environment that make us more likely to react in a certain way even though we're unaware of these influences. Consider this example: A study of the influence of computer company logos found that, when consumers were primed with either an Apple or an IBM logo briefly flashed on a screen, their behaviors changed even though they weren't even aware they had seen the logo. Creativity, nonconformity, and innovation are traits many consumers associate with the Apple brand, while they link tradition, intelligence, and responsibility with IBM.[88] Sure enough, those who saw the Apple logo subsequently provided more creative and innovative responses than those who saw the IBM logo.

Researchers continue to identify factors that bias our decisions—and many of these are factors that operate beneath the level of conscious awareness. In one study, respondents' attitudes toward an undesirable product—curried grasshoppers!—improved when they were asked to approach it. This physical movement typically links to liking; even our own body movements or other physiological reactions can influence what goes on in our minds.[89] To help understand this process, try to force yourself to smile or frown and then carefully gauge your feelings—you may find that the old prescription to "put on a happy face" to cheer yourself up may actually have some validity.[90]

This perspective implies that subtle changes in a consumer's environment can change behavior; some refer to such a change as a **nudge** that results in a dramatic effect. For example, one "nudge" that changes how people act is to switch from asking consumers to "opt in" to a program to asking them to "opt out" of a program if they don't want to participate. In Europe, countries that ask drivers to indicate if they want to be an organ donor convince less than 20 percent of drivers to do so. In contrast, those that require drivers to opt out if they *don't* want to be donors get more than 95 percent participation.

This **default bias**—where we are more likely to comply with a requirement than to make the effort not to comply—is potentially a powerful way to encourage a variety of behaviors. For example, people are more likely to save for retirement if their employers automatically deduct a set amount from their paychecks than if they have to set up this process themselves. It is also how many software companies and social media platforms encourage users to adopt their products and privacy policies (e.g., when you must opt out of Facebook's right to share your data with others).[91]

Decision-Making Biases and Shortcuts

The default bias we previously described illustrates that we often take the easy way out when we make decisions. Unlike the cognitive decision strategies we've already described we use when we want to arrive at the best result—a **maximizing solution**—in fact we often are quite content to exert less mental effort and simply receive an adequate outcome—a **satisficing solution**. This "good enough" perspective on decision making is called **bounded rationality**. In recent years, the recognition that many decisions are not based on a maximization strategy has contributed to the huge resurgence of the field of **behavioral economics**, a blend of psychology and economics that studies how consumers make economic decisions.[92] Like the default bias, which contrasts an opt-in with an opt-out situation, many of the principles in behavioral economics deal with the way a choice is put into context–the process of **framing**.[93]

CB AS I SEE IT

Professor Gavan Fitzsimmons, *Duke University*

For many years consumer researchers have thought of the consumer largely as a conscious, thinking machine. Consumers consider what is important to them, evaluate choice options on those alternatives on those dimensions, and make a decision. Recently, however, a growing group of consumer researchers has started to revisit an old idea that had been largely considered debunked: namely, that much of what goes on in the life of a consumer occurs outside of his or her conscious awareness.

The idea that consumers are influenced outside of their conscious awareness is frightening to many consumers, and has thus received considerable resistance. And yet, the data become more and more clear that consumers are influenced by stimuli they don't realize they have been exposed to, processes occur in the consumers' minds they are unaware of, and consumers even engage in behavior that they are not conscious of (e.g., consider many habitual behaviors). These nonconscious processes are often adaptive and helpful for the consumer, but can also at times be detrimental.

One interesting recent example from our own lab involved subliminally exposing consumers to brand logos— in several studies, either an Apple or an IBM logo. Incidental brand exposures occur every day (recent estimates range between 3,000 and 10,000 times in a single day for the typical American consumer) and thus we were curious if they could influence consumer behavior in meaningful ways. Apple or IBM logos were flashed on a screen for very brief intervals—from 10 to 50 milliseconds—to mimic this real-world incidental brand exposure. Participants had no conscious experience of seeing a brand, and believed they were only seeing a box on the left or right of the screen. Our results showed that nonconscious exposure to the Apple logo led consumers to be significantly more creative than consumers similarly exposed to an IBM logo. This incidental brand exposure activated a goal in consumers that they actively pursued until they could satisfy it. Similar studies have shown dramatic increases in choices of one brand versus another as a result of incidental brand exposure.

The future of research on unconscious consumer behavior is likely to continue to document domains in which the consumer is influenced outside of his or her awareness. Contexts in which consumers find themselves taxed, exhausted, or overwhelmed are all ripe for unconscious influence, which sadly have become the default rather than the exception for most consumers. Some of the most interesting questions remaining deal with exactly how nonconscious processes work, and when they may be adaptive versus harmful. If helpful, how can consumers, firms, and public policymakers embrace and encourage them? For example, many consumers might like to be more creative, or faster, for example, and thus might strategically surround themselves with Apple or Speedo logos. Over time, exposure to these logos will become incidental and they may find themselves increasingly creative or faster. If such exposures are harmful, what can these groups do to minimize their effects? Preliminary evidence suggests that warnings preceding exposure can, at least in part, dampen these nonconscious effects.

To see how framing works, consider the following scenario: You've scored a free ticket to a sold-out football game. At the last minute, though, a sudden snowstorm makes it somewhat dangerous to get to the stadium. Would you still go? Now, assume the same game and snowstorm—except this time you paid a small fortune for the ticket. Would you head out in the storm in this case?

Analyses of people's responses to this situation and to other similar puzzles illustrate principles of **mental accounting**. This means that the way we pose a problem and whether it's phrased in terms of gains or losses influences our decisions.[94] In this case, researchers find that people are more likely to risk their personal safety in the storm if they *paid* for the football ticket than if it's a freebie. Only the most die-hard fan would fail to recognize that this is an irrational choice, because the risk is the same regardless of whether you got a great deal on the ticket. Researchers call this decision-making bias the *sunk-cost fallacy:* If we've paid for something, we're more reluctant to waste it.

Loss aversion is another bias. This means that we emphasize our losses more than our gains. For example, for most people losing money is more *unpleasant* than gaining money is *pleasant*. **Prospect theory** describes how people make choices; it defines utility in terms of gains and losses. We evaluate the riskiness of a decision differently if it's put to us in terms of what we stand to gain rather than what we stand to lose.[95] To illustrate this bias, consider the following choices. For each, would you take the safe bet or choose to gamble?

- **Option 1**—You're given $30 and a chance to flip a coin: Heads you win $9, tails you lose $9.
- **Option 2**—You get $30 outright or you accept a coin flip that will win you either $39 or $21.

In one study, 70 percent of those who got option 1 chose to gamble, compared to only 43 percent of those who got option 2—yet the odds are the same for both options! The difference is that we prefer to "play with the house money"; we're more willing to take risks when we think we're using someone else's resources. So, contrary to a rational decision-making perspective, we value money differently depending on its source. This explains, for example, why the same person who chooses to blow an unexpected bonus on a $2,000 pair of Manolo Blahnik heels would never consider taking that same amount out of her savings account to buy shoes.

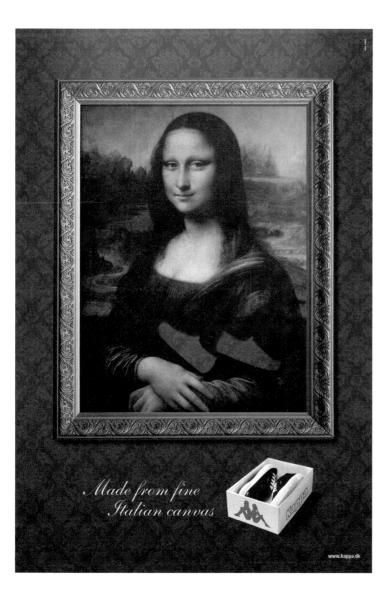

A Dutch shoe ad reminds us that a product's address matters.

Source: Courtesy of Grey/Copenhagen.

Heuristics: Mental Shortcuts

We've seen that many habitual decisions we make are subject to mental accounting biases. In addition, we often fall back on other shortcuts to simplify our choices. For example, Richard made certain assumptions instead of conducting an extensive information search. In particular, he assumed that the selection at Zany Zack's was more than sufficient, so he did not bother to shop at any other stores.[96]

We refer to these shortcuts as **heuristics**. These "mental rules-of-thumb" range from the very general ("higher-priced products are higher-quality products" or "buy the same brand I bought last time") to the very specific ("buy Domino, the brand of sugar my mother always bought").[97] Sometimes these shortcuts may not be in our best interests. A car shopper who personally knows one or two people who have had problems with a particular vehicle, for example, might assume that he would have similar trouble with it rather than taking the time to find out that it actually has an excellent repair record.[98] Table 2.3 lists a set of market beliefs that many of us share. Let's summarize a few of the most prevalent heuristics we commonly use:

- **Covariation.** A person who sells a used car probably makes sure the car's exterior is clean and shiny: Potential buyers often judge the vehicle's mechanical condition by its appearance, even though this means they may drive away in a clean, shiny clunker.[99] When we only have incomplete product information, we often base our judgments on our beliefs about **covariation**—our associations among events that may or may not actually influence one another.[100]
- **Country of origin.** A product's "address" matters. We Americans like to buy Italian shoes, Japanese cars, and microwave ovens built in South Korea. Consumers strongly associate certain items with specific countries, and products from those countries often attempt to benefit from these linkages. **Ethnocentrism** refers to the tendency to prefer products (or people) of one's own culture to those of other countries. Ethnocentric consumers are likely to feel it is wrong to buy products made elsewhere, particularly because this may have a negative effect on the domestic economy.[101]
- **Familiar brand names.** In a study the Boston Consulting Group conducted of the market leaders in 30 product categories, 27 of the brands that were number one in 1930 (such as Ivory Soap and Campbell's Soup) still were at the top more than 50 years later.[102]
- **Higher prices.** Many people assume that a higher-priced alternative is better quality than a lower-priced option.[103] This assumption is often correct; you do tend to get what you pay for. However, let the buyer beware: The price–quality relationship is not always justified.[104]

Zumba exercise routines focus on providing an emotional experience.

Source: Photo by Danny Martindale/WireImage/Getty Images.

TABLE 2.3	Market Beliefs
Brand	All brands are basically the same. Generic products are just name brands sold under a different label at a lower price. The best brands are the ones that are purchased the most. When in doubt, a national brand is always a safe bet.
Store	Specialty stores are great places to familiarize yourself with the best brands; but once you figure out what you want, it's cheaper to buy it at a discount outlet. A store's character is reflected in its window displays. Salespeople in specialty stores are more knowledgeable than other sales personnel. Larger stores offer better prices than small stores. Locally owned stores give the best service. A store that offers a good value on one of its products probably offers good values on all of its items. Credit and return policies are most lenient at large department stores. Stores that have just opened usually charge attractive prices.
Prices/Discounts/Sales	Sales are typically run to get rid of slow-moving merchandise. Stores that are constantly having sales don't really save you money. Within a given store, higher prices generally indicate higher quality.
Advertising and Sales Promotion	"Hard-sell" advertising is associated with low-quality products. Items tied to "giveaways" are not a good value (even with the freebie). Coupons represent real savings for customers because they are not offered by the store. When you buy heavily advertised products, you are paying for the label, not for higher quality.
Product/Packaging	Largest-sized containers are almost always cheaper per unit than smaller sizes. New products are more expensive when they're first introduced; prices tend to settle down as time goes by. When you are not sure what you need in a product, it's a good idea to invest in the extra features, because you'll probably wish you had them later. In general, synthetic goods are lower in quality than goods made of naturals materials. It's advisable to stay away from products when they are new to the market; it usually takes the manufacturer a little time to work the bugs out.

Source: Adapted from Calvin P. Duncan, "Consumer Market Beliefs: A Review of the Literature and an Agenda for Future Research," in Marvin E. Goldberg. Gerald Gorn, and Richard W. Pollay eds., *Advances in Consumer Research* 17 (Provo, UT: Association for Consumer Research, 1990):729–35.

OBJECTIVE 4

We make some decisions on the basis of an emotional reaction rather than as the outcome of a rational thought process.

Affective Decision Making

Zumba began in the 1990s as a Colombian dance fitness program, but today it's an international sensation. Every week about 14 million people in more than 150 countries take classes that combine elements of dance moves adapted from various sources such as hip-hop, salsa, merengue, mambo, belly dancing, and Bollywood, with some squats and lunges thrown in for good measure. The Zumba company started as an infomercial producer, but the regimen was popularized when the CEO's brother, an out-of-work advertising executive, had a revelation and convinced him to change focus. The brother recalls that he saw a movie billboard with some exuberant dancers: "Immediately, I called my brother and said, 'You're selling the wrong thing. You're selling fitness when you should be selling this emotion.' I wanted to turn Zumba into a brand where people felt that kind of free and electrifying joy." The two invented the tagline, "Ditch the workout; join the party!" The rest is history.[105]

Marketers like this Danish restaurant often rely on consumers' expectations based on country-of-origin cues.

Source: Courtesy of Reef 'N Beef/Saatchi.

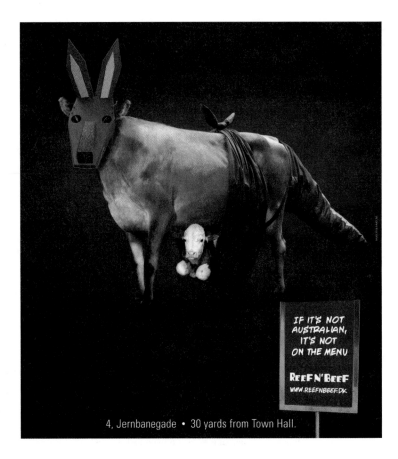

IF IT'S NOT AUSTRALIAN, IT'S NOT ON THE MENU

REEF N' BEEF
WWW.REEFNBEEF.DK

4, Jernbanegade • 30 yards from Town Hall.

Marketing Opportunity

A recent study shows that this emotional element is especially potent for decisions that involve outcomes the person will experience shortly as opposed to those that involve a longer time frame.[109] Another study attests to the interplay between our emotions and how we access information in our minds that allows us to make smarter decisions. These researchers reported evidence for what they call an **emotional oracle effect**: People who trusted their feelings were able to predict future events better than those who did not; this occurred for a range of situations including the presidential election, the winner of *American Idol*, movie box office success, and the stock market. The likely reason is that those with more confidence were better able to access information they had learned that could help them make an informed forecast.[110]

Emotions and Consumption

We may not all be in good enough shape to endure a Zumba workout, but many of our decisions are driven by our emotional responses to products. Social scientists refer to these raw reactions as **affect**. That explains why so many marketing activities and messages focus on altering our moods or linking their products to an affective response—although different types of emotional arousal may be more effective in some contexts than others.[106] These connections make sense to anyone who has ever teared up during a sappy TV commercial or written an angry letter after getting shabby treatment at a hotel. Here are a few recent examples:

- LUSH Cosmetics introduced "Emotional Brilliance," the company's first cosmetics line, and markets the products by mood. The shopper picks a mood, like "Confident," and this guides her to the day's color choice.[107]
- The American Red Cross launched a "storytellers" campaign that features unscripted stories created and filmed by people actually helped by the charity. Ads provide moving personal accounts of people who have been touched by the Red Cross.[108]
- A television commercial by the paint company Valspar never shows an interior, or people painting a wall. It opens with a couple walking on white sand toward a white wall, which resembles a drive-in movie screen, as a voiceover begins, "To some, a wall is just a wall—a divider between here and there." The couple interacts with the wall to bring up a series of spectacular landscapes. As one of the advertising agency executives explained, "What you see in almost every paint commercial is couples

[sic] in blue jeans and flannel shirts holding rollers and going up and down on the wall and whistling while they work, and Valspar didn't need to go there. We don't show people painting walls, or interiors, or any of the kind of mundane aspects of the chore. It's more about the mind-space of the consumer—we're talking to their imagination and emotions."[111]

CB AS I SEE IT

Professor Laurie Meamber, *George Mason University*

Have you ever attended a live performance and been bombarded by sensorial content: the sights and sounds of the performers, their costumes, and the staging that surrounds them? Have you ever visited a place, such as a theme park or a historical site, and been amazed at the way it has been designed to engage your senses? Have you ever bought a car and enjoyed its looks and feel both inside and out? These are all instances of aesthetic consumption. Aesthetics is a term that derives from the Greek word aesthesis and means perceiving the world with the senses. Aesthetic experiences are sensorial in nature and include everyday consumption of places, products, and events, including art and performance. Consumers are ensconced in aesthetic experiences as they go about their daily lives and often make choices based on aesthetic factors. Aesthetic value has become important in the late 20th and early 21st centuries. Some writers assert that the aesthetic age

was reborn during this period with the increasing attention to design of everyday objects and experiences by companies such as Apple, Disney, and even General Motors, which marketed the iconic Hummer brand vehicles from the late 1990s until the retirement of the brand in 2010. Objects and experiences contain aesthetic value when they offer unique aesthetic identities that appeal to the consumer's senses. Aesthetic value does not replace other values, such as performance value, symbolic value, and monetary value or other consumption-specific or product-specific values. Instead, aesthetic value supplements these other forms of value. My own research with several collaborators examines various instances of aesthetic consumption in the realm of the arts, experiences, and consumer products. In the realm of the arts, we are witnessing an explosion of immersive and interactive artistic experiences, whether it is an installation that engages consumers' senses through a multimedia experience or a live performance that uses computer-generated projections to alter scale, time, location, commingling with live performers, connecting with remote performers, and audiences, such as those developed by Cyburbia Productions.

Involving consumers in sensorial experiences is nothing new in the arts, but sophisticated immersive offerings have increased as new

media technology has become readily accessible. Themed environments, likewise, are creating a particular experience of the world for their visitors using a range of aesthetic experiences to delight consumer sensibilities. For example, at many historic homes open to the public, interactive exhibits—such as those that allow visitors to animate the milling process at a gristmill or films shown in theaters replete with seats that shake to replicate the jolt from cannon fire—allow consumers to get a sense of what life was like for those living this history. Also, consumer products are ripe with sensorial content. As mentioned previously, Hummer-brand vehicles, which were based on the look of the Humvee military vehicle, are noted for their unique design, inside and out. Consumers in our study conducted on the Hummer brand indicated that these vehicles had a rugged interior and the looks of a body builder. Even mundane consumer products contain sensorial qualities that offer aesthetic value. For example, consumers we interviewed discussed how objects such as coffeemakers inspired emotional reactions because of their beautiful appearance. This research suggests that consumers do not always separate art products from craft products when making consumption choices, and experience similar emotional reactions to both original pieces and mass-produced products.

Positive Affect

Our feelings also can serve as a source of information when we weigh the pros and cons of a decision. Put simply, the fact that the prospect of owning a specific brand will make a person feel good is a determinant attribute—even if the brand is similar on a functional level to other competing brands. That helps to explain why many of us will willingly pay a premium for a product that on the surface seems to do the same thing as a less expensive alternative—whether in the case of the hottest new Apple iPhone, a Ralph Lauren shirt, or even a pricey university. A passionate commitment to one brand has famously been termed a **lovemark** by the head of the Saatchi & Saatchi advertising agency.

Negative Affect

Many researchers believe that the primitive emotion of disgust evolved to protect us from contamination; we learned over the years to avoid putrid meat and other foul substances linked to pathogens. As a result, even the slight odor of something nasty elicits a universal reaction—the wrinkling of the nose, curling of the upper lips, and protrusion of the tongue. Wrinkling the nose has been shown to prevent pathogens from entering through the nasal cavity, and sticking out the tongue aids in the expulsion of tainted food and is a common precursor to vomiting.

Marketing Opportunity

As part of its global "Open Happiness" campaign, Coca-Cola set up a vending machine at the National University of Singapore that trades free coke beverages for hugs. The machine, which is outfitted in Coca-Cola's signature colors and fonts, reads "hug me" in large letters on the front. "Reactions were amazing . . . at one point we had four to five people hugging the machine at the same time as well as each other! In fact, there was a long line of people looking to give hugs—it was really fantastic and heartwarming," observed Leonardo O'Grady, ASEAN IMC director of Coca-Cola. The machine is one of a number of "Happiness Machines" Coca-Cola has deployed around the world since 2009. A machine set up at a U.S. university handed out (literally) multiple cokes as well as flowers and air balloons in early 2010, racking up 4.5 million views on YouTube.[112]

· · · · · · · · · · · · · · · ·

Coke's vending machine trades free beverages for hugs.
Source: Coca-Cola Singapore/Solent News/ Rex Features/AP Images.

Talk about a rude awakening—and the need to make a quick decision! This unforgiving clock brings new meaning to the phrase, "you snooze, you lose." If you don't get up to turn off the alarm when it sounds, it's going to cost you.
Source: wireframe.ru.

OK, now that you're sufficiently grossed out, what (you may ask in disgust) does this have to do with marketing and persuasion? Well, disgust also exerts a powerful effect on our judgments. People who experience this emotion become harsher in their judgments of moral offenses and offenders. In one experiment, people who sat in a foul-smelling room or at a desk cluttered with dirty food containers judged acts like lying on a résumé or keeping a wallet found on the street as more immoral than individuals who were asked to make the same judgments in a clean environment. In another study, survey respondents who were randomly asked to complete the items while they stood in front of a hand sanitizer gave more conservative responses than those who stood in another part of the hallway.[113]

Advertisers used to avoid using negative imagery so they wouldn't turn people off, but many now realize that it actually can be productive to elicit extreme feelings such as disgust in order to get their message across.

- The New York City Department of Health ran a spot that included images of a soft drink turning into gobs of fat as a man drinks it (the Department claims that sugar-rich beverage consumption dropped 12 percent after the campaign).
- A Febreze TV spot shows blindfolded volunteers sitting in an ultra-filthy room—but fooled into thinking that they smell something pleasant, thanks to the household odor killer.
- A spot for Lamisil, which fights toenail fungus, stars "Digger," a creepy, yellow rat-like creature that digs under human toenails and causes athlete's foot.[114]

How Social Media Tap into Our Emotions

A lot of our social media activity involves expressing affect, both positive and negative. We may share particularly good or bad feelings on Facebook or Twitter, or even resort to corny emoticons like :) in texts or emails, to convey how we feel. To push sales of its Jell-O brand, Kraft unveiled a "Mood Monitor" on Twitter, in which it will randomly send

Net Profit

As uses of big data proliferate (see Chapter 1), we can expect to see more services that monitor consumers' moods on a large scale. Already, one startup company called Ginger.io uses smartphone data to monitor patients' moods. The app collects information about the user's text message habits, call frequencies, and call locations. If a patient stops calling his friends or perhaps he doesn't go to work for a few days, this pattern might trigger his doctor to check in on him. The doctor also can send out simple surveys to patients (e.g., "How did you sleep last night on a scale of 1 to 10?") to track their status.[115]

coupons to users it finds who type in a :(emoticon. Kraft will monitor the Twittersphere and the company will launch coupons whenever the national average of smiley faces dips below 51 percent.[116] LOL!

In fact, it's so common for people to express their moods and also their emotional reactions to products that these posts can be a treasure trove for marketers who want to learn more about how their offerings make people feel. A technique called **sentiment analysis** refers to a process (sometimes also called *opinion mining*) that scours the social media universe to collect and analyze the words people use when they describe a specific product or company. When people feel a particular way, they are likely to choose certain words that tend to relate to the emotion. From these words, the researcher creates a **word-phrase dictionary** (sometimes called a *library*) to code the data. The program scans the text to identify whether the words in the dictionary appear.

Consider this example based on Canon's PowerShot A540. A review on *Epinions*, a product review site, included this statement: "The Canon PowerShot A540 had good aperture and excellent resolution." A sentiment analysis would extract the entities of interest from the sentence, identifying the product as the Canon PowerShot A540 and the relevant dimensions as aperture and resolution. The sentiment would then be extracted for each dimension: the sentiment for aperture is *good* while that for resolution is *excellent*. Text-mining software would collect these reactions and combine them with others to paint a picture of how people are talking about the product. There are several sentiment analysis programs that do similar things; a new one called ToneCheck even reports on the emotions it detects in people's emails.[117]

MyMarketingLab

Go to **mymktlab.com** to complete the problems marked with this icon ⭐.

CHAPTER SUMMARY

Now that you have finished reading this chapter, you should understand why:

1. The three categories of consumer decision making are cognitive, habitual, and affective.

Consumer decision making is a central part of consumer behavior, but the way we evaluate and choose products (and the amount of thought we put into these choices) varies widely, depending on such dimensions as the degree of novelty or risk related to the decision. We almost constantly need to make decisions about products. Some of these decisions are very important and entail great effort, whereas we make others on a virtually automatic basis. Perspectives on decision making range from a focus on habits that people develop over time to novel situations involving a great deal of risk in which consumers must carefully collect and analyze information before making a choice. Many of our decisions are highly automated; we make them largely by habit. The way we evaluate and choose a product depends on our degree of involvement with the product, the marketing message, and/or the purchase situation. Product involvement can range from very low, where purchase decisions are made via inertia, to very high, where consumers form very strong bonds with what they buy.

2. A cognitive purchase decision is the outcome of a series of stages that results in the selection of one product over competing options.

A typical decision involves several steps. The first is problem recognition, when we realize we must take some action. This recognition may occur because a current possession malfunctions or perhaps because we have a desire for something new. Once the consumer recognizes a problem and sees it as sufficiently important to warrant some action, he or she begins the process of information search. This search may range from performing a simple memory scan to determine what he or she has done before to resolve the same problem to extensive fieldwork during which he or she consults a variety of sources to amass as much information as possible. The World Wide Web has changed the way many of us search for information.

Today, our problem is more likely to weed out excess detail than to search for more information. Comparative search sites and intelligent agents help to filter and guide the search process. We may rely on cybermediaries, such as Web portals, to sort through massive amounts of information as a way to simplify the decision-making process. In the evaluation of alternatives stage, the options a person considers constitute his or her evoked set. Members of the evoked set usually share some characteristics; we categorize them similarly. The way the person mentally groups products influences which alternatives she will consider, and usually we associate some brands more strongly with these categories (i.e., they are more prototypical). When the consumer eventually must make a product choice from among alternatives, he uses one of several decision rules. Noncompensatory rules eliminate alternatives that are deficient on any of the criteria we've chosen. **Compensatory rules**, which we are more likely to apply in high-involvement situations, allow us to consider each alternative's good and bad points more carefully to arrive at the overall best choice. Once the consumer makes a choice, he or she engages in postpurchase evaluation to determine whether it was a good one; this assessment in turn influences the process the next time the problem occurs.

3. We often rely upon "rules-of-thumb" or cues in the environment to make routine decisions.

In many cases, people engage in surprisingly little search. Instead, they rely on various mental shortcuts, such as brand names or price, or they may simply imitate others' choices. We may use heuristics, or mental rules-of-thumb, to simplify decision making. In particular, we develop many market beliefs over time. One of the most common beliefs is that we can determine quality by looking at the price. Other heuristics rely on well-known brand names or a product's country of origin as signals of product quality. When we consistently purchase a brand over time, this pattern may be the result of true brand loyalty or simply inertia because it's the easiest thing to do. Principles of mental accounting demonstrate that the way a problem is framed and whether it is put in terms of gains or losses influences what we decide. In addition, other cues in the environment—including very subtle ones of which we may not even be aware—may prime us to choose one option over another.

4. We make some decisions on the basis of an emotional reaction rather than as the outcome of a rational thought process.

Affective decision making occurs when our emotional reactions determine how we react to a product. Marketers often try to elicit a positive emotional response via advertising or other communication channels so that consumers form a bond (or love mark) with their offering. A lot of the content on social media reflects affective responses that people post, so these platforms are a rich source of information for marketers to gauge how consumers feel about their brands.

KEY TERMS

affect, 86
behavioral economics, 81
bounded rationality, 81
brand loyalty, 64
category exemplars, 76
compensatory rules, 91
consideration set, 74
constructive processing, 60
consumer satisfaction/dissatisfaction (CS/D), 80
counteractive construal, 60
country of origin, 84
covariation, 84
cult products, 82
cybermediary, 73
default bias, 81
determinant attributes, 77
economics of information, 69
emotional oracle effect, 86
ethnocentrism, 84

evaluative criteria, 77
evoked set, 74
expectancy disconfirmation model, 80
feature creep, 80
framing, 81
habitual decision-making, 80
heuristics, 84
inertia, 62
information search, 70
information-processing perspective, 69
intelligent agents, 73
involvement, 61
knowledge structure, 74
long tail, 73
lovemark, 88
mass customization, 64
maximizing solution, 81
mental accounting, 82
mental budget, 60
message involvement, 65

narrative transportation, 65
neuromarketing, 74
noncompensatory rule, 78
nudge, 81
perceived risk, 63
postpurchase evaluation, 80
priming, 81
problem recognition, 70
product involvement, 63
prospect theory, 83
purchase momentum, 80
satisficing solution, 81
self-regulation, 60
sentiment analysis, 90
situational involvement, 68
spectacles, 67
variety seeking, 65
word-phrase dictionary, 90

REVIEW

2-1 Why do we say that "mindless" decision making can actually be more efficient than devoting a lot of thought to what we buy?

2-2 List the steps in the model of cognitive decision making.

2-3 What is purchase momentum, and how does it relate (or not relate) to the model of rational decision making?

2-4 Give an example of the type of purchase that each of the three types of decision making—cognitive, habitual and affective—would most likely explain.

2-5 Name two ways in which a consumer problem arises.

2-6 Give an example of the sunk-cost fallacy.

2-7 What is prospect theory? Does it support the argument that we are rational decision makers?

⭐ **2-8** Describe the relationship between a consumer's level of expertise and how much she is likely to search for information about a product.

2-9 List three types of perceived risk, and give an example of each.

2-10 "Marketers need to be extra sure their product works as promised when they first introduce it." How does this statement relate to what we know about consumers' evoked sets?

2-11 Describe the difference between a superordinate category, a basic level category, and a subordinate category.

2-12 What is an example of an exemplar product?

2-13 List three product attributes that consumers use as product quality signals and provide an example of each.

2-14 How does a brand name work as a heuristic?

2-15 Describe the difference between inertia and brand loyalty.

2-16 What is the difference between a noncompensatory and a compensatory decision rule? Give one example of each.

2-17 What is consumer involvement? How does this concept relate to consumer decision making?

2-18 What are some strategies marketers can use to increase consumers' involvement with their products?

CONSUMER BEHAVIOR CHALLENGE

■ DISCUSS

2-19 If people are not always rational decision makers, is it worth the effort to study how they make purchasing decisions?

⭐ **2-20** Why is it difficult to place a product in a consumer's evoked set after the person has already rejected that product? What strategies might a marketer use to accomplish this goal?

2-21 Technology has the potential to make our lives easier as it reduces the amount of clutter we need to work through to access the information on the Internet that really interests us. However, perhaps intelligent agents that make recommendations based only on what we and others like us have chosen in the past limit us, in that they reduce the chance that we will stumble on something (e.g., a book on a topic we've never heard of or a music group that's different from the style we usually listen to) through serendipity. Will the proliferation of "shopping bots" make our lives too predictable by only giving us more of the same? If so, is this a problem?

2-22 Anonymous product endorsement postings and reviews can be seen across the Internet, on social networking sites, blogs, and even product review Web sites. It is becoming increasingly clear that many of these are generated by the business providing the products and services. Is this an ethical means of marketing products and services? Is this a practice that is common in your country or region?

2-23 The chapter notes that people respond to very subtle cues in the environment even when they are totally unaware of these effects. Can or should marketers exploit these influences?

2-24 The chapter mentions new facial recognition technology that marketers will soon use to classify shoppers in terms of their appearance so they can serve up ads that appeal to people in certain demographic categories. This makes advertising more useful because it reduces the amount of irrelevant information we will see. However, is there a downside to this technique? Do you see any potential for negative applications that use (for example) racial profiling to decide what information consumers should receive? Do the potential benefits outweigh these negative applications?

2-25 Commercial Alert, a consumer group, is highly critical of neuromarketing. The group's executive director wrote, "What would happen in this country if corporate marketers and political consultants could literally peer inside our brains and chart the neural activity that leads to our selections in the supermarket and voting booth? What if they then could trigger this neural activity by various means, so as to modify our behavior to serve their own ends?"[118] What do you think? Is neuromarketing dangerous?

■ APPLY

2-26 Choose a niche product or service culturally specific to your country. Suggest ways in which it could be marketed abroad, and identify potential consumers.

2-27 Use an online review Web site such as Trip Advisor and search for hotels, restaurants, and attractions in your own town or city. How useful are the reviews, and do they match up with your own opinions?

2-28 Individually, choose a very familiar product or service that is popular in your own country or region. Keeping the brand name of the product or service to yourself, describe its attributes to the group or another individual. You cannot use any of the taglines or slogans used to identify the brand. Is the brand recognizable?

2-29 Choose a product or service associated with your country and region and suggest how it fits into product categorization.

2-30 Just how strongly are you attracted to recognizable brands? Is your purchasing determined by brand names, and do you seek out those brands regardless of other products or services that fulfill the same purpose? To what extent do you automatically pick those brands without actually thinking about it? Do you think the marketing has worked and the brand is uppermost in your mind at the point of purchase?

2-31 Apply the concept of consumer involvement to a typical product or service. Outline how marketers can manipulate the antecedents of involvement through marketing activities to produce definable outcomes in terms of sales and positive image. Is this approach too process-oriented to work in some cases?

2-32 Although some purchases are impulse buys, many need careful thought, as there are various options open to the consumer. If time, to some extent, was not a factor, how would you eliminate options and settle on the ideal purchase?

2-33 Particular countries are associated with specific products and services. These perceptions differ from region to region, largely influenced by traditional trading arrangements between countries in a region. To illustrate this point, choose five countries other than your own from your region and identify at least two specific products for which those countries have a reputation. What are your perceptions of those products in terms of quality and reliability? How likely are you to buy them from those countries? Some of the choices may be based on stereotypical images of the products manufactured, but are they true reflections of what the country has to offer?

2-34 What decision rule do you use when making a purchasing choice between two competing brands? What is the usual process that leads you to choose one brand over another? What are the influences behind this decision?

2-35 The default bias, according to the chapter, infers that we are more likely to comply with a requirement than make the effort not to comply. How true is this?

2-36 In a global economic environment the tendency is toward purchasing in non-traditional ways. Increasingly, consumers will purchase products and services online without actually seeing or feeling the product before the purchase. There may be "cooling-off periods" offered in case the consumers change their minds or feel that the product or service is not suitable. Is this sufficient compensation for not being able to touch before buying?

2-37 The chapter notes that marketers continue to push the envelope in order to create spectacles that will increase consumer involvement with their messages.

- A British show broadcast a group of skydivers who performed a dangerous jump to create a human formation in the air that spelled out the letters *H*, *O*, *N*, *D*, and *A*.
- Honda built a musical road in Lancaster, PA; grooves in the cement create a series of pitches that play the William Tell Overture when a car drives over them.
- A New York campaign for Jameson Irish Whiskey projects an ad onto a wall—an operator scans the street for pedestrians who fit the brand's profile and inserts live text messages directed at them into the display.
- To promote the 25th anniversary of the Michael Jackson album *Thriller*, which featured zombies dancing in a music video of the title song, Sony BMG staged a performance on the London Underground. A group of "passengers" suddenly burst into a zombie-like dance before they disappeared into

the crowd—and this videotaped scene was posted online. The video inspired similar performances in other countries, and within a week more than a million people had downloaded these films. In a similar stunt for T-Mobile, several hundred commuters at the Liverpool rail station broke into a dance; more than 15 million people watched the performance on YouTube in the following weeks. These (not so) spontaneous *flashmobs* have become increasingly common.

Can you top these? Imagine that a client hires you to launch a new energy drink. Propose a *spectacle* you could engineer that would attract potential customers to learn more about your product.

2-38   Can you replicate Richard's decision-making process as he chose a TV brand for other consumers and/or other products? Create a grid for a different product category that lists available brands and the features each offers. (Hint: Product Web sites for computers, cars, and other complex products often generate these grids when they allow you to choose the "compare products" option.) Present this grid to several respondents and ask each to talk aloud as they evaluate their options. Based on their description, can you identify which decision rule they seem to use?

2-39   Extraneous characteristics of the choice situation can influence our selections, even though they wouldn't *if* we were totally rational decision makers. Create two versions of this scenario (alternate the text you see in parentheses as directed) and ask a seprate group of people to respond to each:

> You are lying on the beach on a hot day. All you have to drink is ice water. For the past hour you have been thinking about how much you would enjoy a nice cold bottle of your favorite brand of beer. A companion gets up to go make a phone call and offers to bring back a beer from the only nearby place where beer is sold (either a fancy resort hotel or a small, run-down grocery store, depending on the version you're given). He says that the beer might be expensive and so asks how much you are willing to pay for it. What price do you tell him?

When researchers gave both versions of this question to respondents, they found that the median price participants who read the fancy-resort version gave was $2.65, but those who got the grocery-store version were only willing to pay $1.50. In both versions, the consumption act is the same, the beer is the same, and they don't consume any "atmosphere" because they drink the beer on the beach.[119] How do these results compare to yours?

Case Study

NETFLIX

Netflix, a company initially known for distributing movies through the mail, recently joined major television studios in having it's original programs nominated for the 65th annual Primetime Emmy Awards. It was an unprecedented accomplishment for an Internet-based company. Netflix earned 14 nominations for their original content series and stood alongside studio giants HBO, CBS, ABC, and NBC. Although 14 is a small number of nominations when compared to HBO's 108 nominations, Netflix certainly caught the industry's attention as a successful producer of television content.

How did this company, an outsider to the system, become such a major force in the entertainment industry? It's because consumer viewing behavior is changing and Netflix is driving the evolution. Consider the steps of the cognitive decision-making process and you can see why more viewers are subscribing to the service and why existing viewers are logging more of their television viewing hours on Netflix.

The first step, problem recognition, is clear to most players in the entertainment industry. Consumers want quality entertainment. And they want a lot of it! Recent data from Nielsen reveals traditional and online viewing are both increasing and the average American watches five hours of video per day. Furthermore, people want to watch what people are talking about. Netflix's Emmy nominations for *House of Cards, Arrested Development,* and *Hemlock Grove* created interest among viewers and increased their desire to watch those shows.

Viewing needs are changing in some other significant ways. In addition to quality programming and increased choice, viewers want to be able to watch multiple episodes of a show in one sitting. Referred to as "binge viewing," consumers would rather not wait a week for the next episode of a show. They want to sit down and watch multiple episodes, a full season, or multiple seasons. Netflix noticed this change in viewing style and made the decision to release all their shows as entire seasons rather than weekly episodes.

Consider other stages of the cognitive decision-making process and how Netflix differentiates themselves from traditional television. When you want to watch traditional television, you most likely pull up a grid listing television shows and the time they air. With Netflix, you can search shows by genre and evaluate them by using the ratings of other viewers. You can also let Netflix's sophisticated recommender system suggest shows to you based on the data of billions of consumer ratings. According to college freshman Lydia Utter, "I prefer Netflix over traditional television because it helps me decide what to watch."

What is the future of television viewing and how will traditional television adapt? Will they be able to convince consumers of a benefit in waiting one week for the next episode? What's next for Netflix and how will they handle other streaming video competitors including Hulu and Amazon?

DISCUSSION QUESTIONS

CS 2–1 How do you split your time between traditional television and streaming video? Has it changed? If so, how?

CS 2–2 How might consumers use heuristics when choosing television shows to watch on Netflix?

Sources: "The Cross Platform Report: A Look Across Screens," June 6, 2013, www.nielsen.com, http://www.nielsen.com/us/en/reports/2013/the-cross-platform-report--a-look-across-screens.html, accessed August 7, 2013; Braeme McMillan, "Netflix Scores Big in Emmy Nominations, But Wall Street Not Impressed," www.wired.com (July 24, 2013), http://www.wired.com/underwire/2013/07/netflix-emmy-nominations/, accessed August 7, 2013; Xavier Amatriain and Justin Basilico, "Netflix Recommendations: Beyond the 5 Stars," http://techblog.netflix.com/2012/06/netflix-recommendations-beyond-5-stars.html, accessed August 7, 2013.

MyMarketingLab

Go to **mymktlab.com** for the following Assisted-graded writing questions:

2-40 Describe how a man's level of involvement with his car would affect how different marketing stimuli influence him. How might you design a strategy for a line of car batteries for a segment of low-involvement consumers, and how would this strategy differ from your attempts to reach a segment of men who are very involved in working on their cars?

2-41 In the past few years, several products made in China (including toothpaste and toys) have been recalled because they are dangerous or even fatal to use. In one survey, about 30 percent of American respondents indicated that they have stopped purchasing some Chinese goods as a result of the recalls.[120] Essentially these consumers use country of origin as a heuristic to avoid Chinese products. If the Chinese government hired you as a consultant to help it repair some of the damage to the reputation of products made there, what actions would you recommend?

2-42 Mymktlab Only—comprehensive writing assignment for this chapter.

NOTES

1. James R. Bettman, "The Decision Maker Who Came in from the Cold" (presidential address), in Leigh McAllister and Michael Rothschild, eds., *Advances in Consumer Research* 20 (Provo, UT: Association for Consumer Research, 1993): 7–11; John W. Payne, James R. Bettman, and Eric J. Johnson, "Behavioral Decision Research: A Constructive Processing Perspective," *Annual Review of Psychology* 4 (1992): 87–131.

2. Parthasarathy Krishnamurthy and Sonja Prokopec, "Resisting That Triple-Chocolate Cake: Mental Budgets and Self-Control," *Journal of Consumer Research* 37 (June 2010): 68–79.

3. Ying Zhang, Szu-chi Huang, and Susan M. Broniarczyk, "Counteractive Construal in Consumer Goal Pursuit," *Journal of Consumer Research* 37 (June 2010): 129–42.

4. Quoted in Sarah Lyall, "One-Third the Man He Used to Be, and Proud of It," *New York Times* (February 6, 2013), http://www.nytimes.com/2013/02/06/world/europe/paul-mason-is-one-third-the-man-he-used-to-be.html?_r=0, accessed February 6, 2013.

5. Claudia Townsend and Wendy Liu, "Is Planning Good for You? The Differential Impact of Planning on Self-Regulation," Journal of Consumer Research 38 (December 2012): 688–703.

6. Judith Lynne Zaichkowsky, "Measuring the Involvement Construct in Marketing," *Journal of Consumer Research* 12 (December 1985): 341–52.

7. Andrew Mitchell, "Involvement: A Potentially Important Mediator of Consumer Behavior," in William L. Wilkie, ed., *Advances in Consumer Research* 6 (Provo, UT: Association for Consumer Research, 1979): 191–96.

8. Richard L. Celsi and Jerry C. Olson, "The Role of Involvement in Attention and Comprehension Processes," *Journal of Consumer Research* 15 (September 1988): 210–24.

9. Barbara J. Phillips and Edward F. McQuarrie, (2010). "Narrative and Persuasion in Fashion Advertising," *Journal of Consumer Research* 37 (October 2010): 368–92; Goldsmith, Ronald E., Leisha R. Flynn, and Ronald A. Clark, "Materialistic, Brand Engaged, and Status Consuming

Consumers and Clothing Behaviors," *Journal of Fashion Marketing and Management* 16, no. 1 (forthcoming): 102–20.

10. Jeremy W. Peters, "Gave Up Sleep and Maybe a First-Born, but at Least I Have an iPhone," *New York Times Online* (June 30, 2007), http://www.nytimes.com/2007/06/30/technology/30phone.html?scp=1&sq=Gave%20up%20Sleep%20and%20Maybe%20a%20First-Born,%20but%20at%20Least%20I%20Have%20an%20iPhone&st=Search, accessed August 24, 2011.

11. Robert W. Pimentel and Kristy E. Reynolds, "A Model for Consumer Devotion: Affective Commitment with Proactive Sustaining Behaviors," *Academy of Marketing Science Review*, no. 5 (2004), www.amsreview.org/articles/pimentel05-2004.pdf, accessed date.

12. Tanya Irwin, "'Breakout Brands' Connect With Customers," *Marketing Daily* (November 4, 2012), http://www.mediapost.com/publications/article/186468/breakout-brands-connect-with-customers.html?edition=53137#ixzz2HcbTBfx7, accessed January 10, 2013.

13. www.starbuckseverywhere.net, accessed February 6, 2013; Julie Jargon, "A Fan Hits a Roadblock on Drive to See Every Starbucks," *Wall Street Journal* (May 23, 2009), http://online.wsj.com/article/SB124301100481847767.html, accessed May 25, 2009.

14. Judith Lynne Zaichkowsky, "The Emotional Side of Product Involvement," in Paul Anderson and Melanie Wallendorf, eds., *Advances in Consumer Research* 14 (Provo, UT: Association for Consumer Research): 32–35.

15. For a discussion of interrelationships between situational and enduring involvement, see Marsha L. Richins, Peter H. Bloch, and Edward F. McQuarrie, "How Enduring and Situational Involvement Combine to Create Involvement Responses," *Journal of Consumer Psychology* 1, no. 2 (1992): 143–53. For more information on the involvement construct, see "Special Issue on Involvement," *Psychology & Marketing* 10, no. 4 (July–August 1993).

16. Alba and Hutchinson, "Dimensions of Consumer Expertise"; Bettman and Park, "Effects of Prior Knowledge and Experience and Phase of the Choice Process on Consumer Decision Processes"; Merrie Brucks, "The Effects of Product Class Knowledge on Information Search Behavior," *Journal of Consumer Research* 12 (June 1985): 1–16; Joel E. Urbany, Peter R. Dickson, and William L. Wilkie, "Buyer Uncertainty and Information Search," *Journal of Consumer Research* 16 (September 1989): 208–15.

17. Joseph B. Pine, II, and James H. Gilmore, *Markets of One: Creating Customer-Unique Value through Mass Customization* (Boston: Harvard Business School Press, 2000), www.managingchange.com/masscust/overview.htm, accessed May 30, 2005.

18. Neeraj Arora, Xavier Dréze, Anindya Ghose, James D. Hess, Reghuram Iyengar, Bing Jing, Yogesh Joshi, V. Kumar, Nicholas Lurie, Scott Neslin, S. Sajeesh, Meng Su, Niladri Syam, Jacquelyn Thomas, and Z. John Zhang, "Putting One-to-One Marketing to Work: Personalization, Customization, and Choice," *Marketing Letters* (2008): 305–21; Mike Beirne, "Mars Gives M&M's a Face," *Brandweek* (May 22, 2008), www.Brandweek.Com/Bw/News/Recent_Display.Jsp?Vnu_Content_Id=1003807134, accessed May 22, 2008.

19. Jacob Jacoby and Robert Chestnut, *Brand Loyalty: Measurement and Management* (New York: Wiley, 1978).

20. David F. Midgley, "Patterns of Interpersonal Information Seeking for the Purchase of a Symbolic Product," *Journal of Marketing Research* 20 (February 1983): 74–83.

21. Cyndee Miller, "Scotland to U.S.: 'This Tennent's for You,'" *Marketing News* (August 29, 1994): 26.

22. Rebecca K. Ratner, Barbara E. Kahn, and Daniel Kahneman, "Choosing Less-Preferred Experiences for the Sake of Variety," *Journal of Consumer Research* 26 (June 1999): 1–15.

23. Herbert E. Krugman, "The Impact of Television Advertising: Learning Without Involvement," *Public Opinion Quarterly* 29 (Fall 1965): 349–56.

24. Kevin J. Clancy, "CPMs Must Bow to 'Involvement' Measurement," *Advertising Age* (January 20, 1992): 26.

25. Brent McFerran, Darren W. Dahl, Gerald J. Gorn, and Heather Honea, "Motivational Determinants of Transportation into Marketing Narratives," *Journal of Consumer Psychology* 20, no. 3 (2010): 306–16.

26. Beacon Allsorts Facebook page, https://www.facebook.com/Beaconallsorts/posts/636796316338040.

27. David W. Stewart and David H. Furse, "Analysis of the Impact of Executional Factors in Advertising Performance," *Journal of Advertising Research* 24 (1984): 23–26; Deborah J. MacInnis, Christine Moorman, and Bernard J. Jaworski, "Enhancing and Measuring Consumers' Motivation, Opportunity, and Ability to Process Brand Information from Ads," *Journal of Marketing* 55 (October 1991): 332–53.

28. Elaine Sciolino, "Disproving Notions, Raising a Fury," *New York Times* (January 21, 2003), www.nytimes.com, accessed January 21, 2003.

29. Louise Story, "Times Sq. Ads Spread via Tourists' Cameras," *New York Times* (December 11, 2006), www.nytimes.com, accessed December 11, 2006.

30. "Read My Chips? Pringles Has Plans to Print Jokes, Trivia on Its Potatoes," *Wall Street Journal* (May 20, 2004): C13; David Serchuk, "A Rose with Another Name," *Forbes* (December 27, 2004): 52.

31. "Ads That Stay with You," *Newsweek* (November 19, 2007), www.newsweek.com/Id/68904, accessed November 19, 2007.

32. Stephanie Clifford, "Axe Body Products Puts Its Brand on the Hamptons Club Scene," *New York Times* (May 22, 2009): B6; Alana Semuels, "Honda Finds a Groovy New Way to Pitch Products: The Musical Road," *Los Angeles Times* (October 13, 2008), www.latimes.com/Business/La-Fi-Roads13-2008oct13,0,4147014.Story, accessed October 13, 2008; Eric Pfanner, "A Live Promotion, At 14,000 Feet," *New York Times* (June 6, 2008), www.nytimes.com, accessed June 6, 2008; Les Luchter, "Jameson Whiskey Texts Targets on N.Y. Streets," *Marketing Daily* (August 8, 2008), www.mediapost.com, accessed August 8, 2008; Doreen Carvajal, "Dancers in the Crowd Bring Back 'Thriller,'" *New York Times* (March 10, 2008), www.nytimes.com, accessed March 10, 2008; Eric Pfanner, "When Consumers Help, Ads Are Free," *New York Times* (June 21, 2009), www.nytimes.com, accessed June 22, 2009.

33. "Billboards with Face Recognition Collect Demographic Data in Japan" (July 19, 2010), http://adverlab.blogspot.com/2010/07/billboards-with-face-recognition.html, accessed May 12, 2011; Emily Steel, "The Ad Changes with the Shopper in Front of It," *Wall Street Journal* (August 21, 2008): B7.

34. John G. Lynch, Richard G. Netemeyer, Stephen A. Spiller, and Alessandra Zammit, "A Generalizable Scale of Propensity to Plan: The Long and the Short of Planning for Time and for Money," *Journal of Consumer Research* 37 (June 2010): 108–128; Bosmans, Anick, Rik Pieters, and Hans Baumgartner, "The Get Ready Mind-Set: How Gearing Up for Later Impacts Effort Allocation Now," *Journal of Consumer Research* 37 (June 2010): 98–107.

35. John C. Mowen, "Beyond Consumer Decision-Making," *Journal of Consumer Marketing* 5, no. 1 (1988): 15–25.

36. Itamar Simonson, Joel Huber, and John Payne, "The Relationship between Prior Brand Knowledge and Information Acquisition Order," *Journal of Consumer Research* 14 (March 1988): 566–78.

37. John R. Hauser, Glenn L. Urban, and Bruce D. Weinberg, "How Consumers Allocate Their Time when Searching for Information," *Journal of Marketing Research* 30 (November 1993): 452–66; George J. Stigler, "The Economics of Information," *Journal of Political Economy* 69 (June 1961): 213–25. For a set of studies focusing on online search costs, see John G. Lynch, Jr., and Dan Ariely, "Wine Online: Search Costs and Competition on Price, Quality, and Distribution," *Marketing Science* 19, no. 1 (2000): 83–103.

38. Jean Halliday, "With Fusion Campaign, Ford Targets 'Upper Funnel' Car Buyers: $60M to $80M Ad Blitz Aimed at Consumers Not Yet Ready to Buy New Vehicle," *Advertising Age* (March 2, 2009), www.advertisingage.com, accessed March 2, 2009.

39. Gordon C. Bruner, II, and Richard J. Pomazal, "Problem Recognition: The Crucial First Stage of the Consumer Decision Process," *Journal of Consumer Marketing* 5, no. 1 (1988): 53–63.

40. Peter H. Bloch, Daniel L. Sherrell, and Nancy M. Ridgway, "Consumer Search: An Extended Framework," *Journal of Consumer Research* 13 (June 1986): 119–26.

41. David Leonhardt, "The Neighbors as Marketing Powerhouses," *New York Times* (June 13, 2005), www.nytimes.com, accessed June 13, 2005.

42. Thaler, "Mental Accounting and Consumer Choice," p. 206.

43. Girish N. Punj and Richard Staelin, "A Model of Consumer Search Behavior for New Automobiles," *Journal of Consumer Research* 9 (March 1983): 366–80. For recent work on online search that decomposes search strategies in terms of type of good, cf. Peng Huang, Nicholas H. Lurie, and Sabyasachi Mitra, "Searching for Experience on the Web: An Empirical Examination of Consumer Behavior for Search and Experience Goods," *Journal of Marketing* 73 (March 2009): 55–69.

44. Examples provided by Dr. William Cohen, personal communication, October 1999.

45. Cobb and Hoyer, "Direct Observation of Search Behavior"; Moore and Lehmann, "Individual Differences in Search Behavior for a Nondurable"; Punj and Staelin, "A Model of Consumer Search Behavior for New Automobiles"; Brian T. Ratchford, M. S. Lee, and D. Toluca, "The Impact of the Internet on Information Search for Automobiles," *Journal of Marketing Research* 40, no. 2 (2003): 193–209.

46. James R. Bettman and C. Whan Park, "Effects of Prior Knowledge and Experience and Phase of the Choice Process on Consumer Decision Processes: A Protocol Analysis," *Journal of Consumer Research* 7 (December 1980): 234–48.

47. www.neurosciencemarketing.com/blog, accessed June 7, 2009; Hotz, "Searching for the Why of Buy"; Blakeslee, "If You Have a 'Buy Button' in

Your Brain, What Pushes It?"; Thompson, "There's a Sucker Born in Every Medial Prefrontal Cortex."

48. Michael Porter, *Competitive Advantage* (New York: Free Press, 1985).

49. Jeffrey M. O'Brien, "You're Soooooooo Predictable," *Fortune* (November 27, 2006): 230.

50. Greg Sterling, "Search + Social Media Increases CTR by 94 Percent: Report," *Search Engine Land* (February 28, 2011), http://searchengineland.com/search-social-media-increases-ctr-by-94-percent-report-66231?utm_source=feedburner&utm_medium=feed&utm_campaign=Feed%3A+searchengineland+%28Search+Engine+Land%3A+Main+Feed%29, accessed April 30, 2011.

51. Material in this section was adapted from Michael R. Solomon and Elnora W. Stuart, *Welcome to Marketing.com: The Brave New World of E-Commerce* (Upper Saddle River, NJ: Prentice Hall, 2001).

52. "Customer Product Reviews Drive Online Satisfaction and Conversion," *Marketing Daily* (January 24, 2007), www.mediapost.com, accessed January 24, 2007.

53. Chris Anderson, *The Long Tail: Why the Future of Business Is Selling Less of More* (New York: Hyperion, 2006).

54. Mary Frances Luce, James R. Bettman, and John W. Payne, "Choice Processing in Emotionally Difficult Decisions," *Journal of Experimental Psychology: Learning, Memory, & Cognition* 23 (March 1997): 384–405; example provided by Professor James Bettman, personal communication (December 17, 1997).

55. Some research suggests that structural elements of the information available, such as the number and distribution of attribute levels, will influence how items in a consideration set are processed; cf. Nicholas H. Lurie, "Decision-Making in Information-Rich Environments: The Role of Information Structure," *Journal of Consumer Research* 30 (March 2004): 473–86.

56. John R. Hauser and Birger Wernerfelt, "An Evaluation Cost Model of Consideration Sets," *Journal of Consumer Research* 16 (March 1990): 393–408.

57. Natasha Singer, "Making Ads That Whisper to the Brain," *New York Times* (November 13, 2010), http://www.nytimes.com/2010/11/14/business/14stream.html?_r=1&ref=technology, accessed April 17, 2011; Martin Reimann, Andreas Aholt, Carolin Neuhaus, Thorsten Teichert, and Bernd Weber, "On the Use of Functional Magnetic Resonance Imaging in Consumer Research: Review, Procedures and Own Empirical Results" (unpublished manuscript, 2009); Robert Lee Hotz, "Searching for the Why of Buy," *Los Angeles Times Online* (February 27, 2005), www.latimes.com/news/science/la-sci-brain27feb27,0,3899978.story?coll=la-home-headlines; Sandra Blakeslee, "If You Have a 'Buy Button' in Your Brain, What Pushes It?" *New York Times* (October 19, 2004), www.nytimes.com, accessed October 19, 2004; Clive Thompson, "There's a Sucker Born in Every Medial Prefrontal Cortex," *New York Times* (October 26, 2003), www.nytimes.com, accessed September 29, 2007.

58. Cait Poynor and Stacy Wood, "Smart Subcategories: How Assortment Formats Influence Consumer Learning and Satisfaction," *Journal of Consumer Research* 37 (June 2010): 159–175; Kenneth C. Manning and David E. Sprott, "Price Endings, Left-Digit Effects, and Choice," *Journal of Consumer Research* 36, no. 2 (2009): 328–35; Sandra J. Milberg, Francisca Sinn, and Ronald C. Goodstein, "Consumer Reactions to Brand Extensions in a Competitive Context: Does Fit Still Matter?" *Journal of Consumer Research* 37, no. 3 (2010): 543–53; David Sleeth-Keppler and S. Christian Wheeler, "A Multidimensional Association Approach to Sequential Consumer Judgments," *Journal of Consumer Psychology* 21, no. 1 (2011): 14–23; Aner Sela, Jonah Berger, and Wendy Liu, "Variety, Vice, and Virtue: How Assortment Size Influences Option Choice," *Journal of Consumer Research* 35, no. 6 (2009): 941–51.

59. Stuart Elliott, "A Brand Tries to Invite Thought," *New York Times* (September 7, 2007), www.nytimes.com, accessed September 7, 2007.

60. Cyndee Miller, "Hemp Is Latest Buzzword," *Marketing News* (March 17, 1997): 1.

61. Alba and Hutchison, "Dimensions of Consumer Expertise"; Joel B. Cohen and Kunal Basu, "Alternative Models of Categorization: Toward a Contingent Processing Framework," *Journal of Consumer Research* 13 (March 1987): 455–72.

62. Robert M. McMath, "The Perils of Typecasting," *American Demographics* (February 1997): 60.

63. Eleanor Rosch, "Principles of Categorization," in E. Rosch and B. B. Lloyd, eds., *Recognition and Categorization* (Hillsdale, NJ: Erlbaum, 1978); cf. also Joseph Lajos, Zsolt Katona, Amitava Chattopadhyay, and Miklos Savary, "Category Activation Model: A Spreading Activation Network Model of Subcategory Positioning when Categorization Uncertainty Is High," *Journal of Consumer Research* 36, no. 1 (June 2009): 122–36.

64. Michael R. Solomon, "Mapping Product Constellations: A Social Categorization Approach to Symbolic Consumption," *Psychology & Marketing* 5, no. 3 (1988): 233–58.

65. McMath, "The Perils of Typecasting."

66. Elizabeth C. Hirschman and Michael R. Solomon, "Competition and Cooperation among Culture Production Systems," in Ronald F. Bush and Shelby D. Hunt, eds., *Marketing Theory: Philosophy of Science Perspectives* (Chicago: American Marketing Association, 1982): 269–72.

67. Michael D. Johnson, "The Differential Processing of Product Category and Noncomparable Choice Alternatives," *Journal of Consumer Research* 16 (December 1989): 300–39.

68. Mita Sujan, "Consumer Knowledge: Effects on Evaluation Strategies Mediating Consumer Judgments," *Journal of Consumer Research* 12 (June 1985): 31–46.

69. Rosch, "Principles of Categorization."

70. Joan Meyers-Levy and Alice M. Tybout, "Schema Congruity as a Basis for Product Evaluation," *Journal of Consumer Research* 16 (June 1989): 39–55.

71. Ronald Alsop, "How Boss's Deeds Buff a Firm's Reputation," *Wall Street Journal* (January 31, 2007): B1.

72. Jack Trout, "Marketing in Tough Times," *Boardroom Reports* 2 (October 1992): 8.

73. Stuart Elliott, "Pepsi-Cola to Stamp Dates for Freshness on Soda Cans," *New York Times* (March 31, 1994): D1; Emily DeNitto, "Pepsi's Gamble Hits Freshness Dating Jackpot," *Advertising Age* (September 19, 1994): 50.

74. C. Whan Park, "The Effect of Individual and Situation-Related Factors on Consumer Selection of Judgmental Models," *Journal of Marketing Research* 13 (May 1976): 144–51.

75. Mita Sujan and James R. Bettman, "The Effects of Brand Positioning Strategies on Consumers' Brand and Category Perceptions: Some Insights from Schema Research," *Journal of Marketing Research* 26 (November 1989): 454–67.

76. See William P. Putsis, Jr., and Narasimhan Srinivasan, "Buying or Just Browsing? The Duration of Purchase Deliberation," *Journal of Marketing Research* 31 (August 1994): 393–402.

77. Robert E. Smith, "Integrating Information from Advertising and Trial: Processes and Effects on Consumer Response to Product Information," *Journal of Marketing Research* 30 (May 1993): 204–19.

78. Rama Jayanti and Anita Jackson, "Service Satisfaction: Investigation of Three Models," in Rebecca H. Holman and Michael R. Solomon, eds., *Advances in Consumer Research* 18 (Provo, UT: Association for Consumer Research, 1991): 603–10; David K. Tse, Franco M. Nicosia, and Peter C. Wilton, "Consumer Satisfaction as a Process," *Psychology & Marketing* 7 (Fall 1990): 177–93. For a recent treatment of satisfaction issues from a more interpretive perspective, see Susan Fournier and David Mick, "Rediscovering Satisfaction," *Journal of Marketing* 63 (October 1999): 5–23.

79. Robert Jacobson and David A. Aaker, "The Strategic Role of Product Quality," *Journal of Marketing* 51 (October 1987): 31–44. For a review of issues regarding the measurement of service quality, see J. Joseph Cronin, Jr., and Steven A. Taylor, "Measuring Service Quality: A Reexamination and Extension," *Journal of Marketing* 56 (July 1992): 55–68.

80. Amna Kirmani and Peter Wright, "Money Talks: Perceived Advertising Expense and Expected Product Quality," *Journal of Consumer Research* 16 (December 1989): 344–53; Donald R. Lichtenstein and Scot Burton, "The Relationship Between Perceived and Objective Price-Quality," *Journal of Marketing Research* 26 (November 1989): 429–43; Akshay R. Rao and Kent B. Monroe, "The Effect of Price, Brand Name, and Store Name on Buyers' Perceptions of Product Quality: An Integrative Review," *Journal of Marketing Research* 26 (August 1989): 351–57; Shelby Hunt, "Post-Transactional Communication and Dissonance Reduction," *Journal of Marketing* 34 (January 1970): 46–51; Daniel E. Innis and H. Rao Unnava, "The Usefulness of Product Warranties for Reputable and New Brands," in Rebecca H. Holman and Michael R. Solomon, eds., *Advances in Consumer Research* 18 (Provo, UT: Association for Consumer Research, 1991): 317–22; Terence A. Shimp and William O. Bearden, "Warranty and Other Extrinsic Cue Effects on Consumers' Risk Perceptions," *Journal of Consumer Research* 9 (June 1982): 38–46.

81. Gilbert A. Churchill, Jr., and Carol F. Surprenant, "An Investigation into the Determinants of Customer Satisfaction," *Journal of Marketing Research* 19 (November 1983): 491–504; John E. Swan and I. Frederick Trawick, "Disconfirmation of Expectations and Satisfaction with a Retail Service," *Journal of Retailing* 57 (Fall 1981): 49–67; Peter C. Wilton and David K. Tse, "Models of Consumer Satisfaction Formation: An Extension," *Journal of Marketing Research* 25 (May 1988): 204–12. For a discussion of what may occur when customers evaluate a new service for which comparison standards do not yet exist, see Ann L. McGill and Dawn Iacobucci, "The Role of Post-Experience Comparison Standards in the Evaluation of Unfamiliar Services," in John F. Sherry, Jr., and Brian Sternthal, eds., *Advances in Consumer Research* 19 (Provo, UT: Association for Consumer Research,

1992): 570–78; William Boulding, Ajay Kalra, Richard Staelin, and Valarie A. Zeithaml, "A Dynamic Process Model of Service Quality: From Expectations to Behavioral Intentions," *Journal of Marketing Research* 30 (February 1993): 7–27.

82. Richard W. Olshavsky and Donald H. Granbois, "Consumer Decision-Making—Fact or Fiction," *Journal of Consumer Research* 6 (September 1989): 93–100.

83. Ravi Dhar, Joel Huber, and Uzma Khan, "The Shopping Momentum Effect," paper presented at the Association for Consumer Research, Atlanta, GA, October 2002.

84. Malcolm Gladwell, *Blink: The Power of Thinking without Thinking* (New York: Little Brown & Company, 2005): 48–71.

85. Geoffrey C. Kiel and Roger A. Layton, "Dimensions of Consumer Information Seeking Behavior," *Journal of Marketing Research* 28 (May 1981): 233–39; see also Narasimhan Srinivasan and Brian T. Ratchford, "An Empirical Test of a Model of External Search for Automobiles," *Journal of Consumer Research* 18 (September 1991): 233–42; Alex Mindlin, "Buyers Search Online, but Not by Brand," *New York Times* (March 13, 2006), www.nytimes.com, accessed March 13, 2006; Cathy J. Cobb and Wayne D. Hoyer, "Direct Observation of Search Behavior," *Psychology & Marketing* 2 (Fall 1985): 161–79; Sharon E. Beatty and Scott M. Smith, "External Search Effort: An Investigation across Several Product Categories," *Journal of Consumer Research* 14 (June 1987): 83–95; William L. Moore and Donald R. Lehmann, "Individual Differences in Search Behavior for a Nondurable," *Journal of Consumer Research* 7 (December 1980): 296–307.

86. Gladwell, 2005, op. cit.

87. J. A. Bargh and T. L. Chartrand, "The Unbearable Automaticity of Being," *American Psychologist* 54, no. 7 (1999): 462–79; J. A. Bargh and M. J. Ferguson, "Beyond Behaviourism: On the Automaticity of Higher Mental Processes," *Psychological Bulletin* 126, no. 6 (2000): 925–45.

88. Tanya L. Chartrand, Joel Huber, Baba Shiv, and Robin J Tanner, "Nonconscious Goals and Consumer Choice," *Journal of Consumer Research* 35, no. 2 (August 2008): 189–201.

89. Aparna A. Labroo and Jesper H. Nielsen, "Half the Thrill Is in the Chase: Twisted Inferences from Embodied Cognitions and Brand Evaluations," *Journal of Consumer Research* 37 (June 2010): 143–58.

90. Leslie Z. McArthur, Michael R. Solomon, and Rebecca H. Jaffe, "Weight Differences in Emotional Responsiveness to Proprioceptive and Pictorial Stimuli," *Journal of Personality and Social Psychology* 39, no. 2 (1980): 308–19.

91. Richard H. Thaler and Cass R. Sunstein, *Nudge: Improving Decisions About Health, Wealth, and Happiness* (New York: Penguin Books, 2009); Rob Girling, *Design's Next Frontier: Nudging Consumers Into Making Better Life Choices, Co. Design* (February 29, 2012), http://www.fastcodesign .com/1669055/designs-next-frontier-nudging-consumers-into-making-better-life-choices?partner=homepage_newsletter, accessed February 16, 2013.

92. Steven J. Levitt and Stephen G. Dubner, *Freakonomics: A Rogue Economist Explores the Hidden Side of Everything* (New York, NY: Harper Perennial, 2009); Dan Ariely, *Predictably Irrational: The Hidden Forces That Shape Our Decisions* (New York, NY: HarperCollins, 2008).

93. Beth Snyder Bulik, "Behavioral Economics Helping Marketers Better Understand Consumers Practice Gives Advertisers Insight into Shoppers' Brand Selection," *Ad Age CMO Strategy* (July 26, 2010), http://adage. com/article/cmo-strategy/behavioral-economics-helping-marketers-understand-consumers/145091/, accessed April 17, 2011; cf. also Robin L. Soster, Ashwani Monga, and William O. Bearden, "Tracking Costs of Time and Money: How Accounting Periods Affect Mental Accounting," *Journal of Consumer Research* 37, no. 4 (2010): 712–21.

94. J. Jeffrey Inman, "The Role of Sensory-Specific Satiety in Consumer Variety Seeking among Flavors" (unpublished manuscript, A. C. Nielsen Center for Marketing Research, University of Wisconsin–Madison, July 1999).

95. Chip Heath and Jack Soll, "Mental Budgeting and Consumer Decisions," *Journal of Consumer Research* 23 (1996): 40–52; Richard Thaler and Eric J. Johnson, "Gambling with the House Money or Trying to Break Even: The Effects of Prior Outcomes on Risky Choice," *Management Science* 36 (June 1990): 643–60; Richard Thaler, "Mental Accounting and Consumer Choice," *Marketing Science* 4 (Summer 1985): 199–214.

96. Laurie J. Flynn, "Like This? You'll Hate That (Not All Web Recommendations Are Welcome)," *New York Times* (January 23, 2006), www .nytimes.com, accessed January 23, 2006. For fairly recent work that uses consumers' self-reported need for cognition as a moderator of heuristic usage, cf. Aimee Drolet, Mary Frances Luce, and Itamar Simonson, "When Does Choice Reveal Preference? Moderators of Heuristic vs. Goal Based Choice," *Journal of Consumer Research* (June 2009): 137–47.

97. Robert A. Baron, *Psychology: The Essential Science* (Boston: Allyn & Bacon, 1989); Valerie S. Folkes, "The Availability Heuristic and Perceived Risk," *Journal of Consumer Research* 15 (June 1989): 13–23; Kahneman and Tversky, "Prospect Theory: An Analysis of Decision under Risk."

98. Wayne D. Hoyer, "An Examination of Consumer Decision-Making for a Common Repeat Purchase Product," *Journal of Consumer Research* 11 (December 1984): 822–29; Calvin P. Duncan, "Consumer Market Beliefs: A Review of the Literature and an Agenda for Future Research," in Marvin E. Goldberg, Gerald Gorn, and Richard W. Pollay, eds., *Advances in Consumer Research* 17 (Provo, UT: Association for Consumer Research, 1990): 729–35; Frank Alpert, "Consumer Market Beliefs and Their Managerial Implications: An Empirical Examination," *Journal of Consumer Marketing* 10, no. 2 (1993): 56–70.

99. Michael R. Solomon, Sarah Drenan, and Chester A. Insko, "Popular Induction: When Is Consensus Information Informative?" *Journal of Personality* 49, no. 2 (1981): 212–24.

100. Beales et al., "Consumer Search and Public Policy," *Journal of Consumer Research* 8, no. 1 (June 1981): 11–22.

101. Items excerpted from Terence A. Shimp and Subhash Sharma, "Consumer Ethnocentrism: Construction and Validation of the CETSCALE," *Journal of Marketing Research* 24 (August 1987): 282.

102. Adam Bryant, "Message in a Beer Bottle," *Newsweek* (May 29, 2000): 43.

103. Duncan, "Consumer Market Beliefs."

104. Chr. Hjorth-Andersen, "Price as a Risk Indicator," *Journal of Consumer Policy* 10 (1987): 267–81; David M. Gardner, "Is There a Generalized Price-Quality Relationship?" *Journal of Marketing Research* 8 (May 1971): 241–43; Kent B. Monroe, "Buyers' Subjective Perceptions of Price," *Journal of Marketing Research* 10 (1973): 70–80.

105. Quoted in Alexandra Bruell, "How Zumba Built a Brand with a Cult Following in Just a Few Years," *Ad Age/CMO Strategy* (August 20, 2012), http:// adage.com/article/cmo-interviews/zumba-built-a-cult-a-years/236737/, accessed January 11, 2013.

106. Fabrizio Di Muro and Kyle B. Murray, "An Arousal Regulation Explanation of Mood Effects on Consumer Choice," *Journal of Consumer Research* 39, no. 3 (October 2012): 574–84, http://www.jstor.org/stable/10.1086/ 664040; Cassie Mogilner, Jennifer Aaker, and Sepandar D. Kamvar, "How Happiness Affects Choice," *Journal of Consumer Research* 39, no. 2 (August 2012): 429–43, http://www.jstor.org/stable/10.1086/663774; For a study that looks at cross-cultural differences in expression of emotion, cf. Ana Valenzuela, Barbara Mellers, and Judi Strebel, "Pleasurable Surprises: A Cross-Cultural Study of Consumer Responses to Unexpected Incentives," *Journal of Consumer Research* 36, no. 5 (2010): 792–805; cf. also Samuel K. Bonsu, Aron Darmody, and Marie-Agnes Parmentier, "Arrested Emotions in Reality Television," *Consumption Markets & Culture* 13, no. 1 (2010): 91–107. Parts of this section were adapted from Michael R. Solomon, Rebekah Russell-Bennett, and Josephine Previte, *Consumer Behaviour: Buying, Having, Being*, 3rd ed. (Frenchs Forest, NSW: Pearson Australia, 2012).

107. Sarah Mahoney, "LUSH Launches Mood-Boosting Color Line," *Marketing Daily* (June 15, 2012), http://www.mediapost.com/publications/ article/176899/lush-launches-mood-boosting-color-line.html?edition= 48051#ixzz2HhTpLLNg, accessed January 11, 2013.

108. Tanya Irwin, "American Red Cross Tells Emotional Stories," *Marketing Daily* (December 13, 2012), http://www.mediapost.com/publications/ article/189241/american-red-cross-tells-emotional-stories.html?edition =54496#ixzz2HhNKzoOg, accessed January 11, 2013.

109. Hannah H. Chang and Michel Tuan Pham, "Affect as a Decision-Making System of the Present," *Journal of Consumer Research* 2013, vol. 40, issue 1, pages 42–63.

110. Michel Tuan Pham, Leonard Lee, and Andrew T. Stephen, "Feeling the Future: The Emotional Oracle Effect," *Journal of Consumer Research* 39, no. 3 (October 2012): 461–77.

111. Steffan Postaer quoted in Andrew Adam Newman, "Using Appeals to Emotions to Sell Paint," *New York Times* (June 7, 2010), http://www .nytimes.com/2010/06/08/business/media/08adco.html?_r=1&adxn nl=1&emc=eta1&adxnnlx=1304103633-mStFlnofYaYKKni2WfWtLA, accessed April 29, 2011.

112. Lauren Indvik, "Hug a Vending Machine, Get a Free Coke," April 9, 2012, http://mashable.com/2012/04/09/coca-cola-hug-machine/?WT.mc_ id=en_business&utm_campaign=Business&utm_medium=email&utm_ source=newsletter, accessed January 11, 2013.

113. Peter Lieberman and David Pizarro, "All Politics Is Olfactory," *New York Times* (October 23, 2010), http://www.nytimes.com/2010/ 10/24/opinion/24pizarro.html?_r=1&ref=todayspaper, accessed April 29, 2011.

114. Andrea C. Morales, Eugenia C. Wu, and Gavan J. Fitzsimons, "How Disgust Enhances the Effectiveness of Fear Appeals," *Journal of Marketing*

Research 49, no. 3 (2012): 383–93; Bruce Horowitz, "Gross Ads Disgust Consumers into Action," *USA Today* (February 27, 2012), http://usatoday30.usatoday.com/money/advertising/story/2012-02-27/gross-ads-fear-vs-disgust/53275918/1, accessed January 11, 2013.

115. Ariel Schwartz, "This App Uses Cell Phone Data To Track How You're Feeling," *Fast Company*, http://www.fastcoexist.com/1680969/this-app-uses-cell-phone-data-to-track-how-youre-feeling, accessed January 11, 2013.

116. E. J. Schultz, "Turning the Frown Upside Down: Kraft's Jell-O Plans Twitter Mood Monitor," *Advertising Age* (May 8, 2011), http://adage.com/article/news/kraft-s-jell-o-plans-twitter-mood-monitor/227439/, accessed May 10, 2011.

117. Tracy Tuten and Michael R. Solomon, *Social Media Marketing* (Upper Saddle River, NJ: Pearson Education, 2012); Jennifer Van Grove,

"How a Sentiment Analysis Startup Profits by Checking Emotion in E-mail," *Mashable* (January 20, 2011), http://mashable.com/2011/01/20/lymbix/?utm_source=feedburner&utm_medium=email&utm_campaign=Feed%3A+Mashable+%28Mashable%29, accessed April 29, 2011.

118. Blakeslee, "If You Have a 'Buy Button' in Your Brain, What Pushes it?"

119. Daniel Kahneman and Amos Tversky, "Prospect Theory: An Analysis of Decision under Risk," *Econometrica* 47 (March 1979): 263–91; Timothy B. Heath, Subimal Chatterjee, and Karen Russo France, "Mental Accounting and Changes in Price: The Frame Dependence of Reference Dependence," *Journal of Consumer Research* 22, no. 1 (June 1995): 90–97.

120. "Americans Are Open to Chinese Goods, Poll Finds," *New York Times* (October 22, 2007), www.nytimes.com/2007/10/22/business/22bizpoll.html?ex=1350705600&en=1615df5334b6437f&ei=5088&partner=rssnyt&emc=rss, accessed October 22, 2007.

Chapter 3 • Cultural Influences on Consumer Decision Making

Chapter Objectives

When you finish reading this chapter you will understand why:

1. A culture is a society's personality.

2. Our deeply held cultural values dictate the types of products and services we seek out or avoid.

3. We distinguish between high culture and low culture.

4. Many modern marketers are *reality engineers*.

5. Myths are stories that express a culture's values, and in modern times marketing messages convey these values to members of the culture.

6. Many of our consumption activities—including holiday observances, grooming, and gift-giving—are rituals.

7. We describe products as either sacred or profane, and it's not unusual for some products to move back and forth between the two categories.

8. Products that succeed in one culture may fail in another if marketers fail to understand the differences among consumers in each place.

9. Western (and particularly American) culture has a huge impact around the world, although people in other countries don't necessarily ascribe the same meanings to products as we do.

Stephanie is at her wits' end. It's bad enough that she has a deadline looming on that new Christmas promotion for her gift shop. Now, there's trouble on the home front as well: Her son Mark had to go and flunk his driver's license road exam, and he's just about suicidal because he feels he can't be a "real man" if he doesn't have a license. To top things off, now she'll have to postpone her much-anticipated vacation to Disney World with stepdaughter Melissa because she just can't find the time to get away.

When Stephanie meets up with her buddy Anne at their local Starbucks for their daily "retreat," her mood starts to brighten. Somehow the calm of the café rubs off as she savors her *grande cappuccino*. Anne consoles her with the ultimate remedy to beat the blues: Go home, take a nice long bath, and then consume a quart of Starbucks Espresso Swirl ice cream. Yes, that's the ticket. It's amazing how the little things in life can make such a big difference. As she strolls out the door, Stephanie makes a mental note to get Anne a really nice Christmas gift this year. She's earned it.

OBJECTIVE 1
A culture is a society's personality.

While on tour in New Zealand, the Spice Girls (remember them?) created a stir among New Zealand's indigenous Maoris when they performed a war dance that only men can do. A tribal official indignantly stated, "It is not acceptable in our culture, and especially by girlie pop stars from another culture."[1] Americans had a somewhat similar reaction when Posh Spice came to the United States with her husband David Beckham to teach us Yanks about the joys of soccer!

Sensitivity to cultural issues, whether among rock stars or brand managers, can only occur when we understand these underlying dimensions—and that's this chapter's goal. **Culture** is a society's personality. It includes both abstract ideas, such as values and ethics, and material objects and services, such as the automobiles, clothing, food, art, and sports a society produces. Put another way, it's the accumulation of shared meanings, rituals, norms, and traditions among the members of an organization or society.

We simply can't understand consumption unless we consider its cultural context: Culture is the "lens" through which people view products. Ironically, the effects of culture on consumer behavior are so powerful and far-reaching that it's sometimes difficult to grasp their importance. Like a fish immersed in water, we don't always appreciate this power until we encounter a different culture. Suddenly, many of the assumptions we take for granted about the clothes we wear, the food we eat, or the way we address others no longer seem to apply. The effect when we encounter such differences can be so great that the term *culture shock* is not an exaggeration.

Our culture determines the overall priorities we attach to different activities and products, and it also helps us decide whether specific products will make it. A product that provides benefits to members of a culture at any point in time has a much better chance to achieve marketplace acceptance. For example, American culture began to emphasize the concept of a fit, trim body as an ideal of appearance in the mid-1970s. The premium consumers put on thinness, which stemmed from underlying values such as mobility, wealth, and a focus on the self, greatly contributed to Miller's success when the brewer launched its Lite beer. However, when Gablinger's introduced a similar low-cal beer in the 1960s, the product failed. This beverage was "ahead of its time" because

American beer drinkers at that time (who were almost all men) weren't worried about cutting down on calories.

The relationship between consumer behavior and culture is a two-way street. On the one hand, consumers are more likely to embrace products and services that resonate with a culture's priorities at any given time. On the other hand, it's worthwhile for us to understand which products do get accepted because this knowledge provides a window into the dominant cultural ideals of that period. Consider, for example, some American products that successfully reflected dominant values during their time:

● The TV dinner reflected changes in family structure and the onset of a new informality in American home life.
● Cosmetics made from natural materials without animal testing reflected consumers' apprehensions about pollution, waste, and animal rights.
● Condoms marketed in pastel carrying cases for female buyers signaled changes in attitudes toward sexual responsibility and openness.

Cultural Systems

Culture is not static. It evolves continually as it synthesizes old ideas with new ones. A *cultural system* consists of these functional areas:[2]

● **Ecology**—The way a system adapts to its habitat. The technology a culture uses to obtain and distribute resources shapes its ecology. The Japanese, for example, greatly value products that make efficient use of space, because of the cramped conditions in their urban centers.[3]
● **Social structure**—The way people maintain an orderly social life. This includes the domestic and political groups that dominate the culture (e.g., the nuclear family versus the extended family; representative government versus dictatorship).
● **Ideology**—The mental characteristics of a people and the way they relate to their environment and social groups. They share a common *worldview* that includes ideas about principles of order and fairness. They also share an *ethos*, or a set of moral and aesthetic principles. A theme park in Bombay called Water Kingdom that caters to India's emerging middle class illustrates how distinctive a culture's worldview can be. Many consumers there are unfamiliar with mixed-sex swimming in public, so the park rents swimsuits to women who have never worn them before. No thongs here, though: The suits cover the women from wrists to ankles.[4]

Cultural Values

A religious official in Saudi Arabia decreed that children there should not be allowed to watch Mickey Mouse, because the cartoon character is a "soldier of Satan."[5] This observation may surprise most of us, but then again we don't live in this deeply conservative Islamic culture. A **value** is a belief that some condition is preferable to its opposite. For example, it's safe to assume that most people prefer freedom to slavery. Others avidly pursue products and services that will make them look younger rather than older. A person's set of values plays a very important role in consumption activities. Consumers purchase many products and services because they believe these products will help to attain a value-related goal.

Two people can believe in and exhibit the same behaviors (e.g., vegetarianism), but their underlying *belief systems* may be quite different (e.g., animal activism versus health concerns). The extent to which people share a belief system is a function of individual, social, and cultural forces. Advocates of a belief system often seek out others with similar beliefs so that social networks overlap; as a result, believers tend to be exposed to information that supports their beliefs (e.g., tree-huggers rarely hang out with loggers).[6]

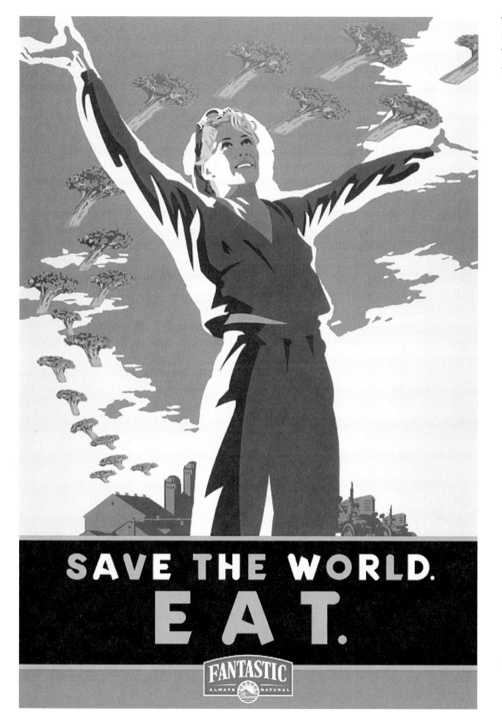

This ad for a line of veggie foods borrows the look of World War II propaganda art to imply that eating our broccoli is an heroic act.
Source: Courtesy of Fantastic Foods.

OBJECTIVE 2
Our deeply held cultural values dictate the types of products and services we seek out or avoid.

Core Values

The actress Kim Kardashian wasn't pleased when her picture ran on the cover of *Cosmopolitan Turkey*, especially when it was released on the same date that some countries commemorate the alleged Armenian genocide in the last days of the Ottoman Empire. Because *Cosmopolitan* publishes in 64 different countries, it is difficult to be sure readers everywhere experience the content the same way. In addition to political differences, marketers have to be sensitive to cultural values: In some countries, because of local norms about modesty,

Marketing Opportunity

Everyone wants to be clean, but some societies are more fastidious than others and won't accept products and services that they think cut corners. Italian women on average spend 21 hours a week on household chores other than cooking—compared with only 4 hours for Americans, according to Procter & Gamble's research. The Italian women wash kitchen and bathroom floors at least four times a week, Americans only once. Italian women typically iron nearly all their wash, even socks and sheets, and they buy more cleaning supplies than women elsewhere do.

Because of these traits, they should be ideal customers for cleaning products, right? That's what Unilever thought when it launched its all-purpose Cif spray cleaner there, but it flopped. Similarly, P&G's best-selling Swiffer wet mop bombed big time. Both companies underestimated this market's desire for products that are tough cleaners, not timesavers. Only about 30 percent of Italian households have dishwashers, because many women don't trust machines to get dishes as clean as they can get them by hand, manufacturers say. Many of those who do use machines tend to thoroughly rinse the dishes before they load them into the dishwasher The explanation for this value: After World War II, Italy remained a poor country until well into the 1960s, so labor-saving devices, such as washing machines, which had become popular in wealthy countries, arrived late. Italian women joined the workforce later than many other European women and in smaller numbers. Young Italian women increasingly work outside the home, but they still spend nearly as much time as their mothers did on housework.

When Unilever did research to determine why Italians didn't take to Cif, they found that these women weren't convinced that a mere spray would do the job on tough kitchen grease or that one product would adequately clean different surfaces (it turns out that 72 percent of Italians own more than eight different cleaning products). The company reformulated the product and reintroduced it with different varieties instead of as an all-in-one. It also made the bottles 50 percent bigger, because Italians clean so frequently, and changed its advertising to emphasize the products' cleaning strength rather

some female readers have to hide the magazine from their husbands! Different cultures emphasize varying belief systems that define what it means to be female, feminine, or appealing—and what people consider appropriate to see in print on these matters. Publishers of the Chinese version aren't even permitted to mention sex at all, so they replace articles about uplifting cleavage with uplifting stories about youthful dedication. Ironically, there isn't much down-and-dirty material in the Swedish edition either—but for the opposite reason: The culture is so open about this topic that it doesn't grab readers' attention the way it would in the United States.[7]

In many cases, of course, values are universal. Who does not desire health, wisdom, or world peace? What sets cultures apart is the *relative importance*, or ranking, of these universal values. This set of rankings constitutes a culture's **value system**.[8] For example, one study found that North Americans have more favorable attitudes toward advertising messages that focus on self-reliance, self-improvement, and the achievement of personal goals as opposed to themes stressing family integrity, collective goals, and the feeling of harmony with others. Korean consumers exhibited the reverse pattern.[9]

We characterize every culture in terms of its members' endorsement of a value system. Not every individual will endorse these values equally; in some cases, values may even seem to contradict one another (e.g., Americans appear to value both conformity and individuality, and try to find some accommodation between the two). Nonetheless, it is usually possible to identify a general set of **core values** that uniquely define a culture. Core values such as freedom, youthfulness, achievement, materialism, and activity characterize American culture.

In contrast, most Japanese are happy to trade off a bit of independence for security and a feeling of safety—especially when it comes to their children. It's common for communities to post guards along school routes and for parents to place global positioning system (GPS) devices and safety buzzers in their kids' backpacks. Numerous indoor parks in Japan are highly secure environments designed to ease parents' minds. At a typical one called the Fantasy Kids Resort, there are uniformed monitors, security cameras, and antibacterial sand. Visitors spray their stroller wheels with antiseptic soap, and guards require identification from visitors before they admit them.[10] Despite living under enormous stress and deprivation after the 2011 earthquake and tsunami, thousands of Japanese who were marooned in public shelters still found ways to maintain order and hygiene to the greatest extent possible.[11]

How do we determine what a culture values? We term the process of learning the beliefs and behaviors endorsed by one's own culture **enculturation**. In contrast, we call the process of learning the value system and behaviors of another culture (often a priority for those who wish to understand consumers and markets in foreign countries) **acculturation**. *Socialization agents*, including parents, friends, and teachers, impart these beliefs to us. In one study, for example, the researchers explored the domain of hunting. They described the process by which family members and friends mentor young men as they learn how to hunt. These socialization agents used stories and traditions to guide the men as they moved through the stages of pre-hunter, neophyte, and apprentice, until they finally become competent hunters.[12]

The media are another important socialization agent; we learn a lot about a culture's priorities when we look at the values that advertising communicates. For example, sales strategies differ significantly between the United States and China. U.S. commercials are more likely to present facts about products and suggestions from credible authorities, whereas Chinese advertisers tend to focus more on emotional appeals without bothering too much about substantiating their claims. U.S. ads tend to be youth-oriented, whereas Chinese ads are more likely to stress the wisdom of older people.[13]

As we've seen, *values* are very general ideas about good and bad goals. From these flow *norms*, or rules that dictate what is right or wrong, acceptable or unacceptable. We explicitly decide on *enacted norms*, such as the rule that a green traffic light means "go" and a red one means "stop." Many norms, however, are much more subtle.

We discover these **crescive norms** as we interact with others. The following are all types of crescive norms:[14]

- A **custom** is a norm that controls basic behaviors, such as division of labor in a household or how we practice particular ceremonies.
- A **more** ("mor-ay") is a custom with a strong moral overtone. It often involves a *taboo*, or forbidden behavior, such as incest or cannibalism. Violation of a more often meets with strong sanctions. In Islamic countries such as Saudi Arabia, people consider it sacrilege to display underwear on store mannequins or to feature a woman's body in advertising, so retailers have to tread lightly; one lingerie store designed special headless and legless mannequins with only the slightest hint of curves to display its products.[16]
- **Conventions** are norms that regulate how we conduct our everyday lives. These rules often deal with the subtleties of consumer behavior, including the "correct" way to furnish one's house, wear one's clothes, or host a dinner party. The Chinese government tried to change citizens' conventions when the country geared up for the Olympics in Beijing: Local habits were at odds with what planners knew foreign visitors expected to encounter. For one, it's common to spit on the sidewalk; the sinus-clearing, phlegmy pre-spit hawking sound is so common that one foreigner dubbed it "the national anthem of China." In addition to the extensive cleanup the government conducted (it even restricted city traffic to reduce smog levels), it imposed a hefty fine for public spitting to get people accustomed to holding in their saliva before hordes of fans descended on the city.[17]

All three types of crescive norms may jointly define a culturally appropriate behavior. For example, a more may tell us what kind of food it's okay to eat. These norms vary across cultures, so a meal of dog is taboo in the United States, Hindus shun steak, and Muslims avoid pork products. A custom dictates the appropriate hour at which we should serve the meal. Conventions tell us how to eat the meal, including such details as the utensils we use, table etiquette, and even the appropriate apparel to wear at dinnertime. We often take these conventions for granted. We just assume that they are the "right" things to do (again, until we travel to a foreign country!). Much of what we know about these norms we learn *vicariously* as we observe the behaviors of actors in television commercials, sitcoms, print ads, and other media. That reminds us why the marketing system is such an important element of culture.

How Do Values Link to Consumer Behavior?

Despite their importance, values haven't helped us to understand consumer behavior as much as we might expect. One reason is that broad-based concepts such as freedom, security, or inner harmony are more likely to affect general purchasing patterns than to differentiate between brands within a product category. This is why some researchers distinguish among broad-based *cultural values* such as security or happiness, *consumption-specific values* such as convenient shopping or prompt service, and *product-specific values* such as ease of use or durability, which affect the relative importance people in different cultures place on possessions.[18]

A study of product-specific values looked in depth at Australians who engage in extreme sports such as surfing, snowboarding, and skateboarding. The researchers identified four dominant values that drove brand choice: freedom, belongingness, excellence, and connection. For example, one female surfer they studied embraced the value of belongingness. She expressed this value when she wore popular brands of surfing apparel even when these major brands had lost their local roots by going mainstream. In contrast, another surfer in the study valued connection: he expressed this as he selected only locally made brands and supported local surfing events.[19]

than convenience. P&G also reintroduced its Swiffer, this time adding beeswax and a Swiffer duster that is now a bestseller. It sold 5 million boxes in the first 8 months, twice the company's forecasts.[15]

Some aspects of brand image, such as sophistication, tend to be common across cultures, but others are more likely to be relevant in specific places. The Japanese tend to value peacefulness, whereas Spaniards emphasize passion, and the value of ruggedness appeals to Americans.[20] Because values drive much of consumer behavior (at least in a very general sense), we might say that virtually *all* consumer research ultimately relates to identifying and measuring values. Let's briefly describe some specific attempts by researchers to measure cultural values and apply this knowledge to marketing strategy.

The Rokeach Value Survey

The psychologist Milton Rokeach identified a set of **terminal values**, or desired end states, that apply to many different cultures. The *Rokeach Value Survey* also includes a set of **instrumental values**; actions we need to take to achieve these terminal values.[21] Table 3.1 lists these two sets of values.

Some evidence indicates that differences in these global values do translate into product-specific preferences and differences in media usage. Nonetheless, marketing researchers have not widely used the Rokeach Value Survey.[22] One reason is that our society is evolving into smaller and smaller sets of *consumption microcultures* within a larger culture, each with its own set of core values (more on this in Chapter 10). For example, in the United States, a sizable number of people are strong believers in natural health practices and alternative medicine. This focus on wellness instead of mainstream

| TABLE 3.1 | Terminal and Instrumental Values |

Instrumental Values	Terminal Values
Ambitious	A comfortable life
Broad-minded	An exciting life
Capable	A sense of accomplishment
Cheerful	A world of peace
Clean	A world of beauty
Courageous	Equality
Forgiving	Family security
Helpful	Freedom
Honest	Happiness
Imaginative	Inner harmony
Independent	Mature love
Intellectual	National security
Logical	Pleasure
Loving	Salvation
Obedient	Self-respect
Polite	Social recognition
Responsible	True friendship
Self-controlled	Wisdom

Source: Richard W. Pollay, "Measuring the Cultural Values Manifest in Advertising," *Current Issues and Research in Advertising* (1983): 71–92. Reprinted by permission, CtC Press. All rights reserved.

medical approaches to sickness influences many of their behaviors, from food choices to the use of alternative medical practitioners, as well as their opinions on political and social issues.[23]

The List of Values (LOV)

The **list of values (LOV) scale** isolates values with more direct marketing applications. This instrument identifies nine consumer segments based on the values members endorse and relates each value to differences in consumption behaviors. These segments include consumers who place priorities on such values as a sense of belonging, excitement, warm relationships with others, and security. For example, people who endorse the sense-of-belonging value are older, are more likely to read *Reader's Digest* and *TV Guide*, drink and entertain more, and prefer group activities more than people who do not endorse this value as highly. In contrast, those who endorse the value of excitement are younger and prefer *Rolling Stone* magazine.[24]

The Means–End Chain Model

The **means–end chain model** assumes that people link very specific product attributes (indirectly) to terminal values: We choose among alternative means to attain some end state that we value (such as freedom or safety). Thus, we value products to the extent that they provide the means to some end we desire. A technique researchers call **laddering** uncovers consumers' associations between specific attributes and these general consequences. Using this approach, they help consumers climb up the "ladder" of abstraction that connects functional product attributes with desired end states.[25] Based on consumer feedback, they then create *hierarchical value maps* that show how specific product attributes get linked to end states.

The laddering technique illustrates stark differences among product/values links across cultures.[26]

Syndicated Surveys

A number of companies track changes in values through large-scale surveys. They sell the results of these studies to marketers, who receive regular updates on changes and trends. This approach originated in the mid-1960s, when Playtex was concerned about sagging girdle sales (pun intended). The company commissioned the market research firm of Yankelovich, Skelly & White to see why sales had dropped. Their research linked the decline to a shift in values regarding appearance and naturalness. Playtex went on to design lighter, less restrictive garments, while Yankelovich went on to track the impact of these types of changes in a range of industries. Gradually, the firm developed the idea of one big study to track U.S. attitudes. In 1970, it introduced the Yankelovich *Monitor*™, which is based on 2-hour interviews with 4,000 respondents.[27]

Today, many other syndicated surveys also track changes in values. Advertising agencies perform some of these so that they can stay on top of important cultural trends and help shape the messages they craft for clients. These services include VALS2™ (more on this in Chapter 11), GlobalScan (operated by the advertising agency Backer Spielvogel Bates), New Wave (the Ogilvy & Mather advertising agency), and the Lifestyles Study conducted by the DDB World Communications Group.

OBJECTIVE 3
We distinguish between high culture and low culture.

The Yin and Yang of Marketing and Culture

Even though inner-city teens represent only 8 percent of all people in that age group and have incomes significantly lower than their white suburban counterparts, their influence on young people's musical and fashion tastes is much greater than these numbers suggest. "Urban" fashion now is a mainstay in the heartland, as major retail chains pick up on the craze and try to lure legions of young middle-class shoppers. Macy's and JC Penney carry Sean John and FUBU ("for us by us"); labels like Versace, Tommy Hilfiger, Enyce, Ecko, Nautica, and Affliction are standard issue for junior high kids. Web sites such as hiphopcapital.com sell other emblems of hip-hop such as "pimp cups," gold plated "grillz," and Bellagio spoke rims.[28] Why does this subculture influence the mass market so strongly?

Outsider heroes—whether John Dillinger, James Dean, or Dr. Dre—who achieve money and fame without being hemmed in by societal constraints have always fascinated Americans. That helps to explain the devotion of many white suburban teens to the urban music scene. As one executive of a firm that researches urban youth noted, "People resonate with the strong anti-oppression messages of rap, and the alienation of blacks."[29] It's common for mainstream culture to modify symbols from "cutting-edge" subcultures for a larger audience to consume. As this occurs, these cultural products undergo a process of **cooptation**, in which outsiders transform their original meanings.[30] The spread of hip-hop fashions and music is only one example of what happens when the marketing system takes a set of subcultural meanings, reinterprets them, and reproduces them for mass consumption.

Of course, the countercultures that originate these movements don't just sit still for this. They develop strategies to reclaim and repoliticize their symbols and practices. For example, large food manufacturers and retailers today recognize shifting consumer tastes as they co-opt vegan or organic food cultures and repackage food products for mainstream grocery shoppers. Walmart sells organic food, and the huge conglomerate ConAgra purchased Ben & Jerry's ice cream. In response, adherents of a "locavore" lifestyle that emphasizes locally produced meat and vegetables may find alternative channels of distribution, such as farmers' markets, to sell their "authentic" versions to true believers.[31]

In this section we'll look at how our culture creates these meanings—which often reside in everyday products—and how these meanings move through a society. As Figure 3.1 shows, the advertising and fashion industries play a key role in this process; they link functional products with symbolic qualities such as sexiness, sophistication, or just plain "cool." These goods, in turn, impart their meanings to us as we use these products to create and express our identities.[32]

Cultural Movement

Aztec tats. Tory Burch flats. Cage-free eggs. Rihanna. High-tech furniture. Gangnam style. Postmodern architecture. *Angry Birds*. Foursquare checkins. Tablets. Hybrid cars. Costa Rican ecotours. We inhabit a world that brims with different styles and possibilities. The food we eat, the cars we drive, the clothes we wear, the places we live and work, the music we listen to—the ebb and flow of popular culture and fashion influences all of them.

Figure 3.1 THE MOVEMENT OF MEANING

New fashion sites like Garmz, Fabricly, Threadless, and ModCloth illustrate the growing influence that customers and fans play as cultural gatekeepers. As we also will see in Chapter 10, they use a crowdsourcing model that empowers buyers to determine what styles they should actually manufacture and sell. Indeed, the fashion site ModaOperanda labels itself a **pretailer**. It works with an exclusive base of fashionistas to encourage designers to manufacture dress designs that otherwise appeared only on catwalks.[33]

Source: Courtesy of Garmz GMBH.

At times we may feel overwhelmed by the sheer number of choices available to us in the marketplace. A person who wants to choose something as routine as a necktie or a color of lipstick may look at hundreds of alternatives! Despite this seeming abundance, however, the options available to us at any point in time actually represent only a small fraction of the *total* set of possibilities. Figure 3.2 shows that when we select certain

Figure 3.2 THE CULTURE PRODUCTION PROCESS

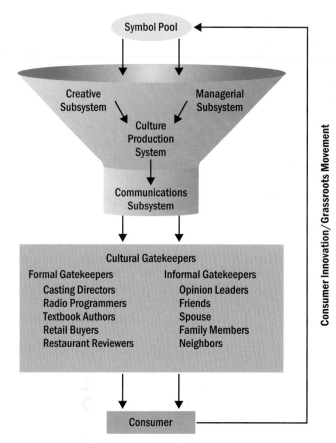

alternatives over others—whether automobiles, dresses, computers, recording artists, political candidates, religions, or even scientific methodologies—our choice actually is only the culmination of a complex filtration process that resembles a funnel. Many possibilities initially compete for adoption; most of them drop out of the mix as they make their way down the path from conception to consumption. We call this winnowing-out process **cultural selection**.

We don't form our tastes and product preferences in a vacuum. The many images mass media present to us drive our choices, as well as our observations of those around us, and even our desires to live in the fantasy worlds marketers create in the ads we see all around us. These options constantly evolve and change. A clothing style or type of cuisine that is "hot" one year may be "out" the next.

The widespread adoption of hip-hop style illustrates some of the characteristics of fashion and popular culture:

● Styles reflect more fundamental societal trends (e.g., politics and social conditions).
● A style begins as a risky or unique statement by a relatively small group of people and then spreads as others become aware of it.
● Styles usually originate as an interplay between the deliberate inventions of designers and businesspeople and spontaneous actions by ordinary consumers who modify these creations to suit their own needs. Designers, manufacturers, and merchandisers who anticipate what consumers want will succeed in the marketplace. In the process, they help to fuel the fire when they encourage distribution of the item—especially if they persuade opinion leaders to use it first.
● Cultural products travel widely, often across countries and even continents.
● Influential people in the media and increasingly everyday "influencers" who are active in social media play a significant role in deciding which items will succeed.

- Most styles eventually wear out as people continually search for new ways to express themselves and marketers scramble to keep up with these desires.
- The cultural selection process never stops, so when styles become obsolete others wait to replace them in popular culture.

No single designer, company, or advertising agency creates popular culture. Many parties contribute to every hit song, hot car, or new clothing style. A **culture production system (CPS)** is the set of individuals and organizations that create and market a cultural product.[34] The structure of a CPS determines the types of products it creates. Factors such as the number and diversity of competing systems and the amount of innovation versus conformity each influence the selection of products from which we choose at any point in time. For example, an analysis of the country/western music industry showed that the hit records it produces are similar to one another when a few large companies dominate the industry, but when a greater number of labels compete we see more diversity in musical styles.[35] Table 3.2 illustrates some of the many cultural specialists that jointly create a hit CD like singer Beyoncé's platinum album *4*.

A culture production system has three major subsystems:

1 A *creative subsystem* to generate new symbols and products
2 A *managerial subsystem* to select, make tangible, produce, and manage the distribution of new symbols and products
3 A *communications subsystem* to give meaning to the new product and provide it with a symbolic set of attributes

An example of the three components of a culture production system for a music release is (1) a singer (e.g., singer Beyoncé, a creative subsystem); (2) a company (e.g., Columbia Records distributes Beyoncé's CDs, a managerial subsystem); and

| TABLE 3.2 | Cultural Specialists in the Music Industry |

Specialist	Functions
Songwriter(s)	Compose music and lyrics; must reconcile artistic preferences with estimates of what will succeed in the marketplace
Performer(s)	Interpret music and lyrics; may be formed spontaneously, or may be packaged by an agent to appeal to a predetermined market (e.g., The Monkees, Menudo, and New Kids on the Block)
Teachers and coaches	Develop and refine performers' talents
Agents	Represent performers to record companies
A&R (artist & repertoire) executives	Acquire artists for the record label
Publicists, image consultants, designers, stylists	Create an image for the group that is transmitted to the buying public
Recording technicians, producers	Create a recording to be sold
Marketing executives	Make strategic decisions regarding performer's appearances, ticket pricing, promotional strategies, and so on
Video directors	Interpret the song visually to create a music video that will help to promote the record
Music reviewers	Evaluate the merits of a recording for listeners
Disc jockeys, radio program directors	Decide which records will be given airplay and/or placed in the radio stations' regular rotations
Record store owners	Decide which of the many records produced will be stocked and/or promoted heavily in the retail environment

(3) the advertising agencies and corporations such as PepsiCo that work with the singer's company Parkwood Entertainment to promote her music and arrange for her appearances in venues including the Super Bowl and even on a limited edition set of Pepsi soda cans.[36]

Many judges or "tastemakers" have a say in the products we consider. These **cultural gatekeepers** filter the overflow of information as it travels down the "funnel." Gatekeepers include movie, restaurant, and car reviewers; interior designers; disc jockeys; retail buyers; magazine editors; and increasingly a fan base that obsessively follows and shares the latest gossip, styles, TV and film plots, and other pieces of popular culture. Collectively, social scientists call this set of agents the *throughput sector*.[37]

High and Low Culture

Question: What do Beethoven and Kanye West have in common? Although we associate both the famous composer and the rap singer with music, many would argue that the similarity stops there. Culture production systems create many kinds of products, but we make some basic distinctions.

An **art product** is an object we admire strictly for its beauty or because it inspires an emotional reaction in us (perhaps bliss, or perhaps disgust). In contrast, we admire a **craft product** because of the beauty with which it performs some function (e.g., a ceramic ashtray or hand-carved fishing lures).[38] A craft tends to follow a formula that permits rapid production.[39]

To appreciate this distinction, consider the phenomenal success of the late artist Thomas Kinkade. This painter sold 10 million digital reproductions of his work. Even after his death in 2012, his studio manufactures pictures at a factory in California, where workers reproduce a digital photograph of each original thousands of times onto thin plastic film they glue to canvasses. Then "high-lighters" sit along an assembly line where they dab oil paint onto set spots. The company also licenses images that appear on coffee mugs, La-Z-Boy recliners, and even a romance novel cover.[40]

As Kinkade's "formula for success" demonstrates, the distinction between high and low culture is not as clear as it used to be. In addition to the possible class bias that drives such a distinction (i.e., we assume that the rich have culture but the poor do not), today high and low culture blend together in interesting ways. In addition to the appliances, tires, and cereals it sells by the case, the warehouse club Costco stocks fine art, including limited-edition lithographs by Pablo Picasso, Marc Chagall, and Joan Miró.[41]

A multinational team of consumer researchers extended the study of high and low art to the realm of *street art*, where artists create paintings, murals, and other pieces in public places. They identified numerous sites where the art became an instrument

Characters from popular culture often serve as a form of "shorthand" for companies the world over to communicate with their customers. This ad is from Nigeria but the figures in it are familiar to people in many countries.

Source: Noah's Ark Communications Ltd.

that was used for "transactions" between the artists and the people who lived in the area. Although not all reactions were positive, it was common to observe that people's experiences of public spaces were enhanced because the street art created a feeling of empowerment and ownership in formerly barren places.[42]

Marketers often invoke high-art imagery to promote products. They may feature works of art on shopping bags or sponsor artistic events to build public goodwill.[43] When observers from Toyota watched customers in luxury car showrooms, the company found that these consumers view a car as an art object. The company then used this theme in an ad for the Lexus with the caption, "Until now, the only fine arts we supported were sculpture, painting, and music."[44]

Cultural Formulae

Mass culture, in contrast, churns out products specifically for a mass market. These products aim to please the average taste of an undifferentiated audience. Rather than being unique, they are predictable because they follow a well-defined pattern. Many popular art forms, such as detective stories or science fiction, follow a **cultural formula**, where familiar roles and props occur consistently.[45] For example, we expect to see characters in a classic western use horses to get around, while in a science fiction movie they use spaceships; hard-boiled detectives drive a beat-up car and characters in a family sitcom ride in a station wagon. Similarly, a six-gun or rifle is the weapon in a classic western, ray guns appear in science fiction movies, a hard-boiled detective uses a pistol or his fists, and the actors in a family sitcom fight one another with verbal insults. Romance novels

As this British ad illustrates, high art merges with popular art in interesting ways.

Source: Courtesy of Eddis Trailers c/o The Explorer Group.

At home in the world's great landscapes. Eddis

are an extreme case of a cultural formula. Computer programs even allow users to "write" their own romances by systematically varying certain set elements of the story.

As members of the creative subsystem rely on these formulae, they tend to *recycle* images as they reach back through time for inspiration. Thus, young people watch retro shows like *Gilligan's Island* as well as remakes such as *The Real Gilligan's Island*; designers modify styles from Victorian England or colonial Africa; hip-hop deejays sample sound bits from old songs and combine them in new ways; and Gap runs ads that feature celebrities in khaki pants, including Humphrey Bogart, Gene Kelly, and Pablo Picasso. With easy access to CD burners, digital cameras, and imaging software, virtually anyone can "remix" the past.[46]

This British ad borrows the cultural formula of a horror movie poster.
Source: MCBD and Elvis.

OBJECTIVE 4
Many modern marketers
are reality engineers.

Reality Engineering

People love the GEICO caveman. He appears in commercials dressed in "yuppie" clothing as he struggles against GEICO's insensitivity when its ads claim, "It's so easy even a caveman can do it." How much do viewers love him? ABC developed a (short-lived) sitcom about a group of caveman roommates who battle prejudice in modern-day America. GEICO receives hundreds of letters and emails about the characters, and fans at college sporting events hold up signs that say, "Beating [team name] is so easy, even a caveman can do it." The cavemen continue to appear in commercials and were featured in a music video by the band 3 Doors Down.[47]

Reality engineering occurs when marketers appropriate elements of popular culture and use them as promotional vehicles.[49] It's hard to know what's real anymore; specialists even create "used jeans" when they apply chemical washes, sandpaper, and other techniques to make a new pair of jeans look like they're ready for retirement. The industry even has a term for this practice that sums up the contradiction: *new vintage!*[50]

Reality engineers have many tools at their disposal; they plant products in movies, pump scents into offices and stores, attach video monitors in the backs of taxicabs, buy ad space on police patrol cars, or film faked "documentaries" such as *The Blair Witch Project.*[51] This process is accelerating: Historical analyses of Broadway plays, best-selling novels, and the lyrics of hit songs, for example, clearly show large increases in the use of real brand names over time.[52]

Here are some examples of reality engineering:

- Mattel announced that it was putting a "for sale" sign on the Barbie Malibu Dreamhouse, where the doll character supposedly has lived in comfort since the introduction of Malibu Barbie in 1971. The company plans to announce the location of Barbie's new home, which will be brought to life in a play set.

    The campaign mixes actual and imaginary elements. A section of the real estate Web site Trulia will carry the for-sale listing for what is being called "the dreamiest of dreamhouses." Josh Altman, a cast member on a real estate reality series on the Bravo cable channel, will list the house.[53]

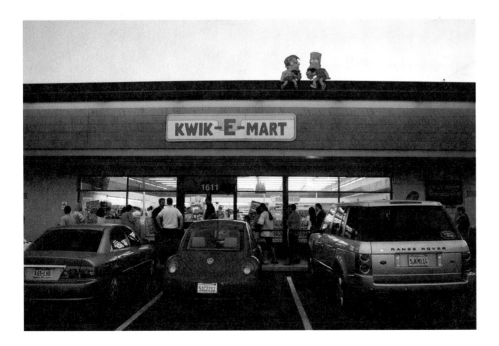

The mythical Simpsons family debuted in real life as 7-Eleven transformed many of its stores into Kwik-E-Marts to promote the cartoon series' movie. During the promotion customers snapped up Krusty O's cereal, Buzz Cola, and ice Squishees, all products from the show.[48]
Photo by David McNew/Getty Images.

Singer Hatsune Miku always sells out her concerts as hordes of screaming fans crowd the aisles. One hitch: Miku doesn't exist. She is an avatar who is supposedly 16 years old and five feet two inches tall. Her songs are digitally remastered from the voice of a Japanese actress. She is so popular that three metal plates with her image etched on them were placed on board the Japanese spacecraft Akatsuki and sent into space.[54]

Source: © Crypton Future Media, Inc. www.crypton.net.

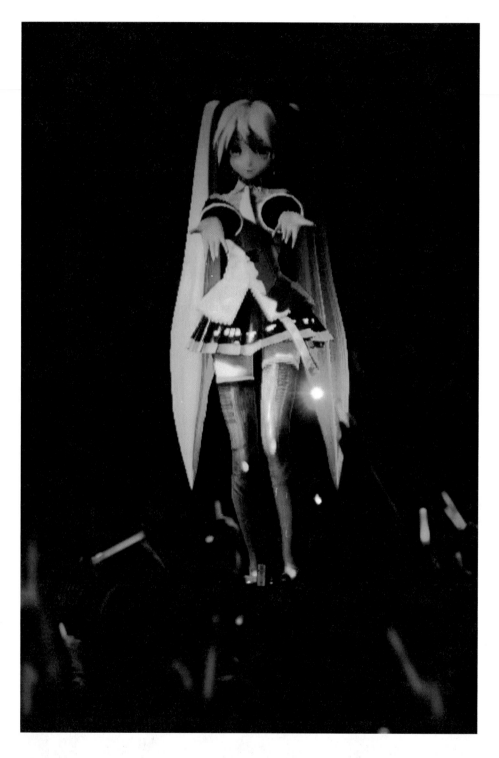

- The Quill.com division of the office supply retail chain Staples carries a line of products from the Dunder Mifflin Paper Company of Scranton, Pa. As any fan knows, that is the fictional setting of the TV show *The Office*, which recently went off the air after nine seasons.[55]
- The 2012 Coachella music festival made headlines with a "virtual performance" (via hologram) of the deceased performer Tupac Shakur. YouTube reported over 15 million views of the spectacle within 48 hours, and Tupac's greatest hits album made the Billboard 200 for the first time in 12 years. Plans are underway to debut holograms of other dead stars including Elvis Presley and Michael Jackson.[56]

● A New York couple funded their $80,000 wedding by selling corporate plugs; they inserted coupons in their programs and tossed 25 bouquets from 1-800-FLOWERS.

Product Placement

The Pennsylvania city of Altoona temporarily renamed itself "POM Wonderful Presents: The Greatest Movie Ever Sold" to promote a popular movie that parodies product-placement advertising; the movie's producers sold the title to the maker of POM Wonderful pomegranate juice for $1 million.[57] Lady Gaga prominently shows off a Virgin Mobile phone, Miracle Whip dressing, and several other brands in her hit video "Telephone."[58]

That's quite a change: Back in the day, TV networks demanded that producers "geek" (alter) brand names before they appeared in a show, as when *Melrose Place* changed a Nokia cell phone to a "Nokio."[60] Today, real products pop up everywhere. Well-established brands lend an aura of realism to the action, while upstarts benefit tremendously from the exposure. In the movie version of *Sex and the City,* Carrie's assistant admits that she "borrows" her pricey handbags from a rental Web site called Bag Borrow or Steal. The company's head of marketing commented about the mention, "It's like the *Good House-keeping* Seal of Approval. It gives us instant credibility and recognition."[61]

Bag Borrow or Steal got a free plug (oops, they got another one here!). In many cases, however, these "plugs" are no accident. **Product placement** is the insertion of real products in fictional movies, TV shows, books, and plays. Many types of products play starring (or at least supporting) roles in our culture; the most visible brands range from Coca-Cola

The Food Hotel in Germany is completely done in a food theme, from can-shaped furniture to barstools made of beer crates. Each guest room is sponsored by a food brand. A room by the chocolate manufacturer Ferrero re-creates the scene of a TV commercial for its Raffaello coconut candies set on a desert island, with palm trees, shells, summer hats, photos of sandy beaches, and books about beach holidays. Another room by potato-chip brand Chio features a rotating mirrored disco ball and flashing bathroom lights with an integrated sound system.[59]

Source: Courtesy of epa european pressphoto agency b.v.

and Nike apparel to the Chicago Bears football team and the Pussycat Dolls band.[62] The TV shows that feature the most placements include *The Biggest Loser* (it showed about 4,000 brands in just a three-month period), *American Idol* (how subtle is that Coca-Cola glass each judge holds?), *The Apprentice, America's Next Top Model,* and *One Tree Hill.*

Product placement is by no means a casual process: Marketers pay about $25 billion per year to plug their brands in TV and movies. Several firms specialize in arranging these appearances; if they're lucky, they manage to do it on the cheap when they get a client's product noticed by prop masters who work on the shows. For example, in a cafeteria scene during an episode of *Grey's Anatomy,* it was no coincidence that the character Izzie Stevens happened to drink a bottle of Izze Sparkling Pomegranate fruit beverage. The placement company that represents PepsiCo paid nothing to insert the prop in that case, but it probably didn't get off so easily when the new brand also showed up in HBO's *Entourage* and CBS's *The Big Bang Theory* and *The New Adventures of Old Christine.*[63]

Today, most major releases brim with real products, even though a majority of consumers believe the line between advertising and programming is becoming too fuzzy and distracting (though as we might expect, concerns about this blurring of boundaries are more pronounced among older people than younger).[64] A study reported that consumers respond well to placements when the show's plot makes the product's benefit clear. Similarly, audiences had a favorable impression when a retailer provided furniture, clothes, appliances, and other staples for the struggling families who get help on ABC's *Extreme Makeover: Home Edition.*[65]

Some researchers claim that product placement aids consumer decision making because the familiarity of these props creates a sense of cultural belonging while they generate feelings of emotional security. Another study found that placements consistent with a show's plot do enhance brand attitudes, but incongruent placements that aren't consistent with the plot affect brand attitudes *negatively* because they seem out of place.[66]

Advergaming

If you roar down the streets in the *Need for Speed Underground 2* video racing game, you'll pass a Best Buy store as well as billboards that hawk Old Spice and Burger King.[67] *America's Army*, produced by the U.S. government as a recruitment tool, is one of the most successful advergames. Twenty-eight percent of those who visit the *America's Army* Web page click through to the recruitment page.

About three-quarters of American consumers now play video games, yet to many marketers the idea of integrating their brands with the stories that games tell is still a well-kept secret. Others, including Axe, Mini Cooper, and Burger King, have figured this out: They create game narratives that immerse players in the action. Orbitz offers playable banner-games that result in the highest click-through rate of any kind of advertising the online travel site does. However, these linkages sometimes draw criticism if they seem to encourage violent behavior. Recently, as the game maker Electronic Arts took steps to launch its *Medal of Honor Warfighter* game, the company put up a Web site that included links to the catalogs of the manufacturers of the real kinds of guns, knives, and combat-style gear the game includes, such as a powerful sniper's rifle and accessories for assault weapons. After gamers protested, EA disabled the links.[68]

Even so, it's likely that the future is bright for **advergaming**, where online games merge with interactive advertisements that let companies target specific types of consumers. These placements can be short exposures such as a billboard that appears around a racetrack, or they can take the form of branded entertainment and integrate the brand directly into the action. The mushrooming popularity of user-generated videos on YouTube and other sites creates a growing market to link ads to these sources as well. This strategy is growing so rapidly that there's even a new (trademarked) term for it. **Plinking**™ is the act of embedding a product or service link in a video.

Why is this new medium so hot?[69]

● Compared to a 30-second TV spot, advertisers can get viewers' attention for a much longer time. Players spend an average of 5 to 7 minutes on an advergaming site.

Renault may have discovered the secret to making electric vehicles more palatable for the masses: Stick them in video games. The automaker's Twizy Z.E. concept vehicle isn't going on sale in Europe until next year, but Sims players can soon download the car as part of the upcoming Electric Vehicle Pack, a free add-on that also includes solar panels and windmills—all of which cut down on weekly virtual household bills.

Source: Renault Communications.

- Physiological measures confirm that players are highly focused and stimulated when they play a game.
- Marketers can tailor the nature of the game and the products in it to the profiles of different users. They can direct strategy games to upscale, educated users, while they gear action games to younger users.
- The format gives advertisers great flexibility, because game makers now ship PC video games with blank spaces in them to insert virtual ads. This allows advertisers to change messages on the fly and pay only for the number of game players that actually see them. Sony Corporation now allows clients to directly insert online ads into PlayStation 3 videogames; the in-game ads change over time through a user's Internet connection.
- There's great potential to track usage and conduct marketing research. For example, an inaudible audio signal coded into Activision's *Tony Hawk's Underground 2* skating game on PCs alerts a Nielsen monitoring system each time the test game players view Jeep product placements within the game.

Cultural Stories and Ceremonies

Every culture develops *stories* and *ceremonies* that help its members to make sense of the world. When we hear about some strange practice that goes on in another place, it may be hard to figure out just what these people think they're doing. Yet, our own cultural practices seem quite normal—even though a visitor may find them equally bizarre! Just take a European to a NASCAR event and you'll understand that culture is relative.

To appreciate how "primitive" belief systems influence our supposedly "modern" rational society, consider the avid interest many of us have in magic. Marketers of health foods, anti-aging cosmetics, exercise programs, and gambling casinos often imply that their offerings have "magical" properties that prevent sickness, old age, poverty, or just plain bad luck. People by the millions play their "lucky numbers" in the lottery, carry rabbits' feet and other amulets to ward off "the evil eye," and own "lucky" clothing.[70] In one study, Asian consumers who were primed with lucky numbers influenced their estimates of how likely they were to win a lottery and the amount of money they were willing to invest in different financial options.[71]

Interest in the occult tends to spike when members of a society feel overwhelmed or powerless; magical remedies simplify our lives when they give us "easy" answers. Many consumers even regard the computer with awe as a sort of "electronic magician" with the ability to solve our problems (or, in other cases, to cause data to magically disappear!).[72] Software developers even supply "wizards" that guide the uninitiated through their programs! Or, we may even think a person's soul inhabits an object: Kids (and maybe some

Advertisements like these for Canadian plays build on familiar stories.

Source: Courtesy of Saatchi Toronto.

adults as well) believe that when they put on their Air Nikes they magically absorb some of the athletic ability of Michael Jordan or Dwyane Wade. Sound preposterous? The movie *Like Mike* had this exact storyline. In this section, we'll discuss myths and rituals, two aspects of culture common to all societies from the ancients to the modern world.

OBJECTIVE 5

Myths are stories that express a culture's values, and in modern times marketing messages convey these values to members of the culture.

Myths

People in Thailand are preoccupied with supernatural forces. One common sight is a "spirit house," a miniature dwelling intended for protective ghosts. Some include electric wiring and indoor lighting; you will even find them in 7-Eleven convenience stores throughout the country. Thais spend about $63 million per year on visits to fortune tellers. Stores sell amulets for good luck next to breath mints, and horoscope books next to junk food. There are YouTube channels devoted to fortune telling and computer programs like "Feng Shui Master," which supposedly helps to predict the future of gold prices.[73]

A **myth** is a story with symbolic elements that represents a culture's ideals. The story often focuses on some kind of conflict between two opposing forces, and its outcome serves as a moral guide for listeners. In this way, a myth reduces anxiety because it provides consumers with guidelines about their world. Most members of a culture learn these stories, but usually we don't really think about their origins.

The familiar *Little Red Riding Hood* myth started as a peasant's tale in 16th-century France, where a girl meets a werewolf on her way to Granny's house (there

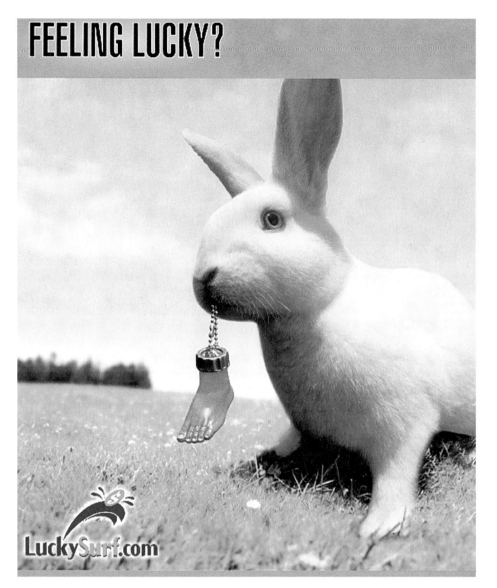

is historical evidence for a plague of wolf attacks during this time, including several incidents where men were put on trial because they allegedly turned themselves into the deadly animals). The werewolf has already killed Granny, stored her flesh in the pantry, and poured her blood in a bottle. Contrary to the version we know, however, when the girl arrives at the house she snacks on Granny, strips naked, and climbs into bed with the wolf! To make the story even more scandalous, some versions refer to the wolf as a "gaffer" (a contraction of "grandfather"), implying incest as well. This story first appeared in print in 1697; it was a warning to the loose ladies of Louis XIV's court (the author puts her in red in this version because this color symbolizes harlots). Eventually, the Brothers Grimm wrote their own version in 1812, but they substituted violence for sex in order to scare kids into behaving. And to reinforce the sex-role standards of that time, in the Grimm version a man rescues the girl from the wolf.[74] So, this myth sends vivid messages about such cultural no-no's as cannibalism, incest, and promiscuity.

In some cases marketers adapt these stories and (perhaps unconsciously) pattern their messages along a mythic structure. Consider, for example, the way that McDonald's takes on "mythical" qualities.[75] The "golden arches" are virtually synonymous with American culture. They offer sanctuary to Americans around the world, who know exactly what to expect once they enter. Basic struggles involving good versus evil play out in the fantasy world McDonald's advertising creates; for example, when Ronald McDonald confounds the Hamburglar. McDonald's even has a "seminary" (Hamburger University) where inductees go to learn the ways of The Golden Arches.

This ad for Norwegian trade unions borrows from the Little Red Riding Hood myth. It says, "There are many advantages in being many."
Source: Lofavor Norway - Supertanker (SMFB Norway) Photo: Petrus Olsson, Adamsky.

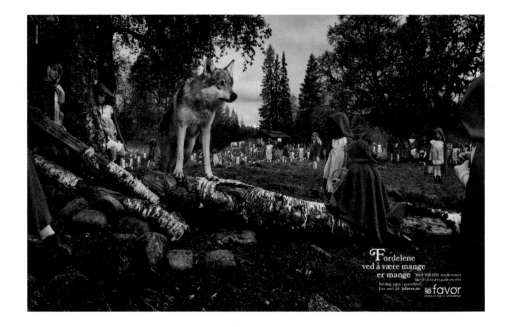

Corporations often have myths and legends in their history, and some teach them to newcomers. Nike designates senior executives as "corporate storytellers" who explain the company's heritage to the hourly workers at Nike stores. They recount tales about the coach of the Oregon track team who poured rubber into his family waffle iron to make better shoes for his team—the origin of the Nike waffle sole. The stories emphasize the dedication of runners and coaches to reinforce the importance of teamwork. Rookies even visit the track where the coach worked to help them appreciate the importance of the Nike legends. And rumor has it that senior Nike executives (including the CEO) have a "swoosh" tattoo on their backsides.[76]

Myths serve four interrelated functions in a culture:[77]

1 **Metaphysical**—They help to explain the origins of existence.
2 **Cosmological**—They emphasize that all components of the universe are part of a single picture.
3 **Sociological**—They maintain social order because they authorize a social code for members of a culture to follow.
4 **Psychological**—They provide models for personal conduct.

When we analyze myths, we examine their underlying structures, a technique the French anthropologist Claude Lévi-Strauss (no relation to the blue jeans company) pioneered. Lévi-Strauss noted that many stories involve **binary opposition**, which represents two opposing ends of some dimension (e.g., good versus evil, nature versus technology).[78] Often a *mediating figure* resolves the conflict between mythical opposing forces; this links the opposites as it shares characteristics of each. For example, many myths are about animals that have human abilities (e.g., a talking snake) to bridge the gap between humanity and nature, just as marketers often give cars (technology) animal names (nature) such as Cougar, Cobra, or Mustang.

We associate myths with the ancient Greeks and Romans, but in reality comic books, movies, holidays, and yes, even commercials embody our own cultural myths. Furthermore, researchers report that some people create their own *consumer fairy tales:* They tell stories that include magical agents, donors, and helpers to overcome villains and obstacles as they seek out goods and services in their quest for happy endings.[79]

Smart marketers are more than happy to help us live out these fairy tales. Consider the popularity of the elaborate weddings Disney stages for couples who want to reenact their own version of a popular myth: At Disney World, the princess bride wears a tiara and rides to the park's lakeside wedding pavilion in a horse-drawn coach, complete with

This Italian jeans ad evokes imagery from a modern myth that involves an animal character.
Source: Courtesy Meltin' Pot Jeans/Armando Testa, Milan.

two footmen in gray wigs and gold lamé pants. At the exchange of vows, trumpets blare as Major Domo (he helped the Duke in his quest for Cinderella) walks up the aisle with two wedding bands he gently places in a glass slipper on a velvet pillow. Disney stages about 2,000 of these extravaganzas each year. The company continues to expand the appeal of this myth as it moves into the bridal gown business. It sells a line of billowing princess gowns complete with crystal tiaras. Fairy-tale brides can walk down the aisle costumed as Cinderella, Snow White, Belle, Sleeping Beauty, Jasmine, or Ariel.[80]

Many "blockbuster" movies and hit TV shows draw directly on mythic themes. Although dramatic special effects and attractive stars certainly don't hurt, a number of these movies also owe their huge appeal to their presentation of characters and plot structures that follow mythic patterns. Here are three examples of mythic blockbusters:[81]

- *Gone with the Wind*—Myths often take place in times of upheaval such as wars. In this story, the North (which represents technology and democracy) battles the South (which represents nature and aristocracy). The movie depicts a romantic era (the antebellum South) when love and honor were virtues. Following the war, newer values of materialism and industrialization (i.e., modern consumer culture) replace these priorities. The movie paints a picture of a lost era where man and nature existed in harmony.
- *E.T.: The Extra-Terrestrial*—*E.T.* represents a familiar myth involving messianic visitation. The gentle creature from another world visits Earth and performs miracles (e.g., he revives a dying flower). His "disciples" are neighborhood children; they help him combat the forces of modern technology and an unbelieving secular society. The myth teaches that the humans God chooses are pure and unselfish.
- *Star Trek*—The multiple television series and movies, prequels, and sequels that document the adventures of the starship *Enterprise* also link to myths, such as the story of the New England Puritans who explore and conquer a new continent ("the final frontier"). Encounters with the Klingons mirror skirmishes with Native Americans. In addition, at least 13 out of the original 79 episodes employed the theme of a quest for paradise.[82]

Advertisements sometimes represent mythic themes. Commercials for Pepperidge Farm ask consumers to "remember" the good old days (lost paradise) when products were wholesome and natural. Avis famously used the theme of the underdog prevailing over the stronger foe (i.e., David and Goliath).[83] A commercial that encouraged Hispanic consumers to buy more milk featured a female phantom who wails as she walks through a home. She is *La Llorona* (the crying one), a character in a Hispanic myth who murders her children, commits suicide, and roams for all eternity as she seeks her lost family. In this version, however, the moaning phantom makes her way to the refrigerator, only to find an empty milk carton.[84]

OBJECTIVE 6

Many of our consumption activities—including holiday observances, grooming, and gift-giving—are rituals.

Rituals

A **ritual** is a set of multiple, symbolic behaviors that occurs in a fixed sequence and is repeated periodically.[85] Bizarre tribal ceremonies, perhaps involving animal or human sacrifice, may come to mind when you think of rituals, but in reality many contemporary consumer activities are ritualistic.

Many colleges boast unique rituals in which students engage in some scripted group activity, but in recent years some institutions have abolished these because of safety concerns or because they encourage underage drinking. Casualties include spring couch burning at the University of Vermont and Princeton's Nude Winter Olympics. The death of 12 people from collapsing logs ended the tradition of Texas A&M's bonfire on the eve of the annual football game against the University of Texas (the bonfire ritual has since been revived off campus). Some campus rituals that survive include the following:

- **MIT**—Each spring students haul a steer into a dorm courtyard, put it on a spit, and light a fire under it with a flaming roll of toilet paper they lower from the roof.
- **Wesleyan College (Connecticut)**—Students honor the pot-smoking Doonesbury character Zonker Harris each spring with a day of live music, face painting, and plenty of open marijuana use.
- **Simon Fraser University (British Columbia)**—Costumed engineering students throw one another in the reflection pond during February's Polar Plunge.

Marketing Opportunity

Tailgating at college and pro ballgames is one of the most visible group rituals around today. According to legend, this practice started in the 19th century when fans had no choice but to cook meals in their carriages after they journeyed to the site of a football game. Now, tailgating is also big business. A survey Coca-Cola sponsored reported that 41 percent of tailgaters spend more than $500 a season on food and supplies, whereas a Ragu survey found that more than half of the fans prefer the party to the actual game! Now, everyone from food conglomerates to camping suppliers tries to get a piece of these boisterous pregame rituals:[86] The NFL sells $100 million a year of tailgating merchandise, including keg-shaped grills. The Buffalo Bills provide showers and changing rooms in the parking lot, and the Denver Broncos pick a "most valuable tailgater" at each home game. The Houston Texans sponsor "Tailgating 101" classes at a local sporting goods store. For the truly hard-core, California customizer Galpin Motors sells a tailgaters' pickup truck complete with a huge grill, taps for two beer kegs, a blender, and a flip-down TV screen for "only" $70,000.

Source: Photo by Mike Stobe/NHLI via Getty Images.

Consider a ritual that many beer drinkers in the United Kingdom and Ireland hold near and dear to their hearts: the spectacle of a pub bartender "pulling" the perfect pint of Guinness. According to tradition, the slow pour takes exactly 119.5 seconds as the bartender holds the glass at a 45-degree angle, fills it three-quarters full, lets it settle, and tops it off with its signature creamy head. Guinness wanted to make the pull faster so the bar could serve more drinks on a busy night, so it introduced FastPour, an ultrasound technology that dispenses the dark brew in only 25 seconds. You probably guessed the outcome: The brewer had to scrap the system when drinkers resisted the innovation. Note: Diageo (which owns Guinness) hasn't given up, and it continues to experiment with more efficient techniques in markets where this ritual isn't so inbred. A system it calls Guinness Surger shows up in Tokyo bars, many of which are too small to accommodate kegs: The bartender pours a pint from a bottle, places the glass on a special plate, and zaps it with ultrasound waves that generate the characteristic head.[87]
Source: Photo by Oli Scarff/Getty Images.

- **University of California at Santa Barbara**—Students run naked across campus on the first rainy day of the year. Princeton and the University of Michigan have banned nude sprints, but at Yale seniors still run naked through two campus libraries at the end of each semester and toss candy at underclass students as they cram for finals.

A study the BBDO Worldwide advertising agency conducted illustrates the close relationship between brands and rituals.[88] It labels items that we use to perform our rituals **fortress brands** because once they become embedded in our ceremonies—whether we use them to brush our teeth, drink a beer, or shave—we're unlikely to replace them. The study ran in 26 countries, and the researchers found that, overall, people worldwide practice roughly the same consumer rituals. The agency claims that 89 percent of people always use the same brands in their sequenced rituals; three out of four are disappointed or irritated when something disrupts their ritual or their brand of choice isn't available. For example, the report identifies one common ritual category it calls *preparing for battle*. For most of us this means getting ready for work. Relevant rituals include brushing the teeth, taking a shower or bath, having something to eat or drink, talking to a family member or partner, checking email, shaving, putting on makeup, watching TV or listening to the radio, and reading a newspaper.

Rituals occur at several levels. Some reinforce broad cultural or religious values. Public rituals such as the Super Bowl, presidential inaugurations, and graduation ceremonies are communal activities that affirm our membership in the larger group and reassure us that we are reading from the same script as everyone else.[89] In one study, researchers documented the collective ritual of *head banging* at heavy metal music concerts. They showed how participants, who tend to come from lower economic classes and feel disempowered in other settings, participate collectively in a performance that is a cathartic experience where they are rejuvenated and validated (perhaps this presents an opportunity for companies that sell headache remedies?).[90]

Other rituals occur in small groups or even in isolation. Market researchers discovered that for many people the act of late-night ice cream eating has ritualistic elements that often involve a favorite spoon and bowl![91] Rituals are not set in stone, though; they change with the times. For example, when we throw rice at a wedding we express our desire for the couple to be fertile.[92]

Many businesses benefit because they supply **ritual artifacts** to consumers. These are items we need to perform rituals, such as wedding rice, birthday candles, diplomas, specialized foods and beverages (e.g., wedding cakes, ceremonial wine, or even hot dogs at the ball park), trophies and plaques, band uniforms, greeting cards, and retirement watches.[93] In addition, we often follow a *ritual script* to identify the artifacts we need, the sequence in which we should use them, and who uses them. Examples include graduation programs, fraternity manuals, and etiquette books.

Grooming Rituals

Whether you brush your hair 100 strokes a day or give yourself a pep talk in the mirror before a big date, virtually all of us practice private **grooming rituals**. These ceremonies help us to transition from our private self to our public self, or back again. Grooming rituals help to inspire confidence before we face the world, and they "cleanse" us of impurities. When consumers talk about their grooming rituals, some of the dominant themes that emerge from these stories reflect the almost mystical qualities we attribute to grooming products and behaviors. Many people emphasize a before-and-after phenomenon, whereby the person feels magically transformed after she uses certain products (similar to the Cinderella myth).[95]

Some companies that make personal care products understand the power of these rituals and supply the artifacts we need to make them happen. Nair, the depilatory maker, expanded its customer base when it targeted younger girls with its Nair Pretty product—a market the industry calls "first-time hair removers." Researchers conducted focus groups with mothers and their daughters, where they learned that "[w]hen a girl removes hair for the first time, it's a life-changing moment." Some of the respondents actually held hair removal slumber parties, where the moms bought products for the teens to remove their hair. So, instead of a focus on boys or romance, ads for Nair Pretty suggest that the depilatory is a stubble-free path to empowerment. "I am a citizen of the world," reads the ad copy. "I am a dreamer. I am fresh. I am so not going to have stubs sticking out of my legs."[96]

Grooming rituals express two kinds of binary opposition: *private/public* and *work/leisure*. Many beauty rituals reflect a transformation from a natural state to the social world (as when a woman "puts on her face") or vice versa. To her, a bath may be a cleansing time, a way to wash away the "sins" of the profane world.[97] In these daily rituals, women reaffirm the value their culture places on personal beauty and the quest for eternal youth. This cleansing ritual is clear in ads for Oil of Olay Beauty Cleanser that proclaim, "And so your day begins. The Ritual of Oil of Olay."

Gift-Giving Rituals

In a **gift-giving ritual**, we procure the perfect object, meticulously remove the price tag, carefully wrap the object (where we symbolically change the item from a commodity to a unique good), and deliver it to the recipient.[98] Gifts can be store-bought objects, homemade items, or services. Some recent research even argues that music file-sharing systems such as Megaupload (which the government shut down), KaZaa, or Morpheus are really all about gifting. This work finds, for example, clear evidence of the gift-giving norm of *reciprocity*; people who download files but who don't leave their own files available to others are "leeches."[99]

Researchers view gift-giving as a form of *economic exchange* in which the giver transfers an item of value to a recipient, who in turn must reciprocate. However, gift-giving also involves *symbolic exchange*. In fact, researchers who analyzed the personal memoirs of World War II concentration camp inmates found that even in such a brutal environment, where people had to focus primarily on survival, a need to express humanity through

You don't want it. He can't have it back.

The courtship process often involves gift-giving from men to women, but what happens when the relationship ends? The founders of the Web site ExBoyfriendJewelry.com provide a market for jilted women who want to make some money and perhaps vent about their ex-partners. The site proclaims "You don't want it. He can't have it back." Users sell, auction, trade, or simply give away the refuse of their former romances—but they also have to share the story behind every gift.

Source: Courtesy of exboyfriendjewelry.com.

generosity prevailed. The authors found that gift-giving, which symbolized recognition of others' plight as well as one's own, was an act of defiance against the dehumanizing existence the camps forced on their prisoners.[100]

Some research indicates that gift-giving evolves as a form of social expression. It is more exchange oriented (instrumental) in the early stages of a relationship (where we keep track of exactly what we give and receive to be sure we're not getting ripped off), but it becomes more altruistic as the relationship develops.[101]

Every culture dictates certain occasions and ceremonies to give gifts, whether for personal or professional reasons. The birthday gift ritual alone is a significant contributor to our economy. Each American on average buys six birthday gifts a year—about 1 billion gifts in total.[102] Business gifts are an important way to define and maintain professional relationships. Expenditures on business gifts exceed $1.5 billion per year, and givers take great care to ensure that they purchase the appropriate gifts (sometimes with the aid of professional gift consultants). Most executives believe that corporate gift-giving provides both tangible and intangible results, including improved employee morale and higher sales.[103]

The gift-giving ritual proceeds in three distinct stages:[104]

1 During *gestation,* the giver procures an item to mark some event. This event may be either *structural* (i.e., prescribed by the culture, as when people buy Christmas presents) or *emergent* (i.e., the decision is more personal and idiosyncratic).

2 The second stage is *presentation,* or the process of gift exchange. The recipient responds to the gift (either appropriately or not), and the donor evaluates this response.

3 In the *reformulation* stage, the giver and receiver redefine the bond between them (either looser or tighter) to reflect their new relationship after the exchange. Negativity can arise if the recipient feels the gift is inappropriate or of inferior quality. For example, the hapless husband who gives his wife a vacuum cleaner as an anniversary present is just asking to sleep on the couch, and the new suitor who gives his girlfriend intimate apparel probably won't score many points. The donor may feel that the response to the gift was inadequate or insincere or a violation of the **reciprocity norm**, which obliges people to return the gesture of a gift with one of equal value.[105]

Japanese gift-giving rituals show how tremendously important these acts are in that culture, where the wrapping is as important (if not more so) than the gift itself. The Japanese view gifts as an important aspect of one's duty to others in one's social group. Giving is a moral imperative (*giri*). Highly ritualized acts occur when a person gives both household/personal gifts and company/professional gifts. Each individual has a well-defined set of relatives and friends with which he shares reciprocal gift-giving obligations (*kosai*). People give personal gifts on social occasions, such as at funerals, for a hospitalization, to mark movements from one life stage to another (e.g., weddings, birthdays), and as greetings (e.g., when one meets a visitor). They give company gifts to commemorate the anniversary of a corporation's founding, the opening of a new building, or the announcement of new products. In keeping with the Japanese emphasis on saving face, the recipient doesn't open the present in front of the giver so that he won't have to hide any disappointment with what he gets.[106]

Holiday Rituals

On holidays, we step back from our everyday lives and perform ritualistic behaviors unique to those occasions.[107] Each cultural celebration typically relates to the adventures of one or more special characters, such as St. Patrick in Ireland or Yue Lao in China. These special events require tons of ritual artifacts and scripts. The Thanksgiving holiday script includes serving (in gluttonous portions) foods such as turkey and cranberry sauce that many of us consume only on that day, complaining about how much we've eaten (yet rising to the occasion to find room for dessert), and (for many) a postmeal trip to the couch for the obligatory football game.

Most holidays commemorate a cultural myth, often with a historical (e.g., Miles Standish on Thanksgiving) or imaginary (e.g., Cupid on Valentine's Day) character as the story's hero. These holidays persist because their basic elements appeal to our deep-seated needs.[108]

● **Christmas**—Myths and rituals fill the Christmas holiday, from Santa's adventures at the North Pole to others' adventures under the mistletoe. The meaning of Christmas evolved quite dramatically during the past few hundred years. In colonial times, Christmas celebrations resembled carnivals and public rowdiness was the norm. Most notable was the tradition of "wassailing," in which roving packs of rowdy young men laid siege to the rich and demanded food and drink. By the end of the 1800s, the mobs were so unruly that city fathers in Protestant America invented a tradition whereby families conducted Christmas gatherings around a tree, a practice they "borrowed" from early pagan rites. In an 1822 poem Clement Clarke Moore, the wealthy son of a New York Episcopal bishop, invented the modern-day myth of Santa Claus. The Christmas ritual slowly changed to a focus on children and gift-giving.[109] One of the most important holiday rituals, of course, stars Santa, a mythical figure for whose arrival children eagerly await (even if their house doesn't have a fireplace). Indeed, an Australian study

This McDonald's ad from Hong Kong celebrates a holiday. The literal translation is "April Fool's Day: The best day to take the piss out of your friends."
Source: Courtesy of DDB Hong Kong.

that analyzed the letters children write to Santa found they specify their brand preferences quite carefully and often employ sophisticated request strategies to be sure they get what they want from the Big Guy.[110] In opposition to Christ, Santa is a champion of materialism. Perhaps it is no coincidence, then, that he appears in stores and shopping malls—secular temples of consumption. Whatever his origins, the Santa Claus myth socializes children as it teaches them to expect a reward when they are good and that people get what they deserve (which may be a lump of coal).

● **Halloween**—Halloween began as a pagan religious ceremony, but it's clearly a secular event today. However, in contrast to Christmas, the rituals of Halloween (e.g., trick-or-treating and costume parties) primarily involve nonfamily members. Halloween is an unusual holiday because its rituals are the opposite of many other cultural occasions. In contrast to Christmas, it celebrates evil instead of good and death rather than birth. It encourages revelers to extort treats with veiled threats of "tricks" rather than rewards for the good. Because of these oppositions, Halloween is an **antifestival**—an event that distorts the symbols we associate with other holidays. For example, the Halloween witch is an inverted mother figure. The holiday also parodies the meaning of Easter because it stresses the resurrection of ghosts, and it mocks Thanksgiving as it transforms the wholesome symbolism of the pumpkin pie into the evil jack-o-lantern.[111] Furthermore, Halloween provides a ritualized, and therefore socially sanctioned, context that allows people to try on new roles: Children can go outside after dark, stay up late, and eat all the candy they like for a night. The otherwise geeky guy who always sits in the back of class dresses as Jason from *Friday the 13th* and turns out to be the life of the party.

● **Valentine's Day**—On Valentine's Day, we relax our standards about sex and love and we express feelings we may hide during the rest of the year (in Japan, it's the women who send gifts to the men). A study that investigated Valentine's Day rituals explored how marketing communications help to shape the holiday. The authors identify five familiar classes of rituals:

1 Exchanging gifts and cards
2 Showing affection
3 Going out
4 Preparing and consuming food and drink
5 Special attention to grooming and clothing

Many of their informants (primarily men) understood the holiday as an obligatory occasion for them to buy their partners expensive, "romantic" gifts. One guy posted this warning: "If you want her happy always remember: the gift has to shine or smell [good] or she should be able to wear it! Otherwise, you're doomed." Some informants expressed negative associations with the holiday, including painful emotions because of broken relationships (or a lack of relationships altogether) and aversion to the "forced" consumption and artificial displays of affection the day requires.[112] But, as much as some of us may grumble about it, this holiday ritual is too powerful to ignore (unless you like sleeping on the couch).

Rites of Passage

What does a dance for recently divorced people have in common with a fraternity Hell Week? Both are modern **rites of passage**: rituals we perform to mark a change in social status. Every society, both primitive and modern, sets aside times for these changes. Some may occur as a natural part of our life cycles (e.g., puberty or death), whereas others are more individual (e.g., getting divorced and reentering the dating market).

Much like the metamorphosis of a caterpillar into a butterfly, a rite of passage consists of three phases. Let's see how this works for a young person who changes his social status to become a college student:[113]

1 In the first stage, *separation*, he detaches from his original group or status as a high school kid and leaves home for campus.

CB AS I SEE IT

Professor Lauren Block, *Baruch College, City University of New York*

Do you have any rituals you perform for good luck? I know a college student who will only walk up the left staircase of her university building on exam days. This student won't take the elevator or use the staircase on the right side of the building for fear that she will jinx her good performance on tests. I know another student who turns off the football game with three minutes left in the fourth quarter if his team is winning. It's not that he doesn't want to watch his team win, it's that he doesn't want to jinx them in the final moments and have a loss be his fault. Make sense? Of course not. But does it feel familiar? Probably.

Research has recently begun to document just how common and ordinary such superstitious or magical thinking is among people. Superstitions are beliefs that run counter to rational thought or are inconsistent with known laws of nature. While many superstitions are culturally shared and socially transmitted from generation to generation, others consist of relatively more idiosyncratic beliefs or rituals, like the examples described previously. My colleague Tom Kramer and I study how peoples' superstitious beliefs influence their behavior as consumers. For example, common superstitions among Taiwanese include beliefs about lucky colors (e.g., red) and lucky numbers (e.g., 8). In research Tom and I conducted in Taiwan, we found that Taiwanese consumers are more likely to purchase a product that is red than the same exact product in another color, and purchasers have higher expectations for the red product than for, say, a green product. In other words, consumers expect the red product to work better than the green one and would be more upset if the product failed or broke. Our research also demonstrated that Taiwanese consumers are willing to pay a higher price for a package with a "lucky" number of items inside (8 tennis balls) than the same package with a greater but neutral number of items (10 tennis balls). Taiwanese consumers were willing to spend over 50 percent more for 25 percent fewer tennis balls because of their positive superstitious beliefs regarding the number 8 (versus 10). Similarly, we found that Taiwanese consumers are willing to pay more to avoid unlucky numbers. They would rather pay TW$555 (5 is a neutral number) than TW$444 (4 is an unlucky number), foregoing a discount for the same product.

Would you be willing to spend more money to avoid unlucky numbers?

American consumers don't have the same beliefs as Taiwanese, but they do think 13 is an unlucky number. Many American buildings don't have a 13th floor, and U.S. businesses lose a large amount of money every Friday the 13th because people avoid important transactions on that day. Tom Kramer and I studied whether superstitious beliefs about Friday the 13th influence the choices American students make. Students were asked to choose between two bets: In the first bet students knew they could win a small sum of money and in the second bet students had to gamble to win either a large amount or nothing. For example, students were asked to choose between receiving $18 for sure versus a 20 percent chance of winning $240 and an 80 percent chance of winning nothing. It turns out that most American students prefer the riskier option in the hopes of winning the large amount of money. But when we asked this question on Friday the 13th, their choice switched to the not risky smaller amount.

Using this knowledge of how superstitious beliefs influence behavior can help managers make better business decisions. How much more profit could Taco Bell have earned if it had altered its seven-layer Crunchwrap Supreme into an eight-layer one for Chinese consumers? Similarly, the $4/$4/$4 promotion by Domino's Pizza was probably not well received by Chinese consumers.

2 *Liminality* is the middle stage, where he is in limbo between statuses. Think of those bewildered new first-year students who try to find their way around campus during orientation.

3 In the *aggregation* stage, he returns to society with his new status. Our hero returns home for Thanksgiving break as a cocky college "veteran."

Many types of people undergo rites of passage, including fraternity pledges, recruits at boot camp, or novitiates at a convent. We observe a similar transitional state when people prepare for occupational roles. For example, athletes and fashion models typically undergo a "seasoning" process. They leave their normal surroundings (athletes go to training camps, young models move to Paris or New York), they get indoctrinated into a new subculture, and then they return to the real world in their new roles (if they successfully pass the trials of their initiation and don't "get cut").

Death also involves rites of passage. Funeral ceremonies help the living organize their relationships with the deceased. Action is tightly scripted, down to the costumes (e.g., the ritual black attire, black ribbons for mourners, the body laid out in its best clothes) and specific behaviors (e.g., sending condolence cards or holding a wake). Passing motorists award special status to the *cortege* (the funeral motorcade) when they obey the strong social norm that prohibits cutting in as the line of cars proceeds to the cemetery.[114]

Funeral practices vary across cultures, but they're always rich in symbolism. For example, a study of funeral rituals in Ghana found that the community there determines a person's social value *after* he dies; this status depends on the type of funeral his family gives him. One of the main purposes of death rituals is to negotiate the social identities of deceased persons. This occurs as mourners treat the corpse with a level of respect that indicates what they think of him. The Asante people who were the subjects of the study don't view death as something to fear; it's just part of a broader, ongoing process of identity negotiation.[115] People in parts of Madagascar go a step further: They regularly remove the bodies of their ancestors from their tombs so that family members can caress the skeletal outlines that protrude through their burial shrouds. This ritual is called *a famadihana* many believe this is a time to convey the latest family news to the deceased and ask them for blessings and guidance.[116]

OBJECTIVE 7
We describe products as either sacred or profane, and it's not unusual for some products to move back and forth between the two categories.

Sacred and Profane Consumption

As we saw when we discussed the structure of myths, many types of consumer activities involve the demarcation, or binary opposition, of categories, such as good versus bad, male versus female—or even regular cola versus diet. One of the most important distinctions we find is between the sacred and the profane. **Sacred consumption** occurs when we "set apart" objects and events from normal activities and treat them with

respect or awe. Note that in this context the term *sacred* does not necessarily carry a religious meaning, although we do tend to think of religious artifacts and ceremonies as "sacred." **Profane consumption**, in contrast, describes objects and events that are ordinary or everyday; they don't share the "specialness" of sacred ones. Again, note that in this context we don't equate the word *profane* with obscenity, although the two meanings do share some similarities.

Again, often we're unaware of the distinction between these two domains—until they conflict with one another. Then, the sparks fly—sort of like the collision between matter and antimatter on *Star Trek*. A conflict in Thailand illustrates this process. It seems that several Bangkok nightclubs, inspired by the film *Coyote Ugly* about women who dance seductively on a New York bar, began to feature their own "Coyote Girls" dancers. The trend caught on and soon the dancers showed up at auto shows, in shopping malls, and at outdoor festivals. That's when the trouble started: Thailand's queen learned of one performance the girls put on near a Buddhist temple on a holy day that marks the end of a 3-month period where Buddhists refrain from impure thoughts and deeds (sort of like the Christian season of Lent). When the queen saw TV news reports about a motorcycle shop that hired Coyote Girls to promote its wares, she was outraged by the intrusion of profane activity into a sacred domain. Coyote Girls are now banned from dancing in public places.[117]

Sacralization

Sacralization occurs when ordinary objects, events, and even people take on sacred meaning. Many consumers regard events such as the Super Bowl and people such as Elvis Presley as sacred. Indeed, virtually anything can become sacred. Skeptical? Consider the

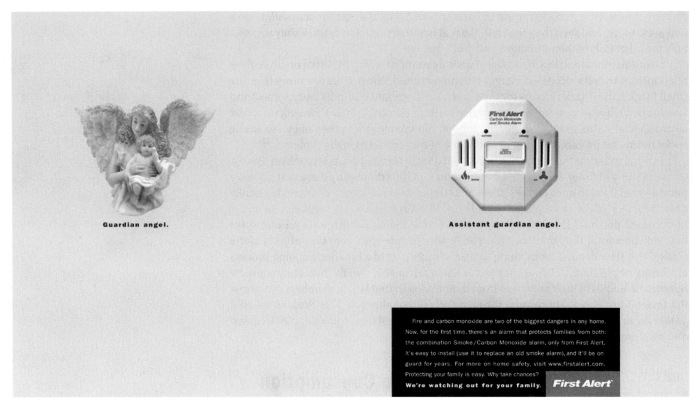

Guardian angel.

Assistant guardian angel.

Fire and carbon monoxide are two of the biggest dangers in any home. Now, for the first time, there's an alarm that protects families from both: the combination Smoke/Carbon Monoxide alarm, only from First Alert. It's easy to install (use it to replace an old smoke alarm), and it'll be on guard for years. For more on home safety, visit www.firstalert.com. Protecting your family is easy. Why take chances?

We're watching out for your family.   **First Alert**

This ad for an alarm system uses sacred imagery to sell a profane product.

Source: Courtesy of First Alert Corp.

Web site that sells *unlaundered* athletic wear that members of the Dallas Cowboys football team have worn. Former quarterback Troy Aikman's shoes sold for $1,999, and an unwashed practice jersey that retains the sweat of an unknown player goes for $99. Used socks fly out the door at $19.99 a pair. Says the owner, "Fans who have never been able to touch the Cowboys before now have an opportunity."[118]

Objectification occurs when we attribute sacred qualities to mundane items (such as smelly socks). One way that this process occurs is via **contamination**, whereby objects we associate with sacred events or people become sacred in their own right. This explains many fans' desire for items that belonged to (or were even touched by) famous people. Even the Smithsonian Institution in Washington, DC, maintains a display that features such "sacred items" as the ruby slippers from *The Wizard of Oz*, a phaser from *Star Trek*, and Archie Bunker's chair from the television show *All in the Family*—all reverently protected behind sturdy display glass.[119]

In addition to museum exhibits that display rare objects, we often set apart mundane, inexpensive things in *collections;* when we do so we transform them from profane items to sacred ones. An item is sacralized as soon as it enters a collection, and it takes on special significance to the collector that outsiders may find hard to comprehend. For example, you may know someone who collects matchbooks that mark visits to out-of-town restaurants: Just try to use one of these books if you actually need to light a match.

Collecting refers to the systematic acquisition of a particular object or set of objects. We distinguish this from **hoarding**, which reflects a reluctance to discard used objects.[120] Hoarding is a problem in some cities where residents' refusal to properly dispose of old newspapers, food, or even deceased pets results in fires, eviction, and even the removal of children from the home. A dozen cities run hoarding task forces to combat this problem.[121]

Collecting typically involves both rational and emotional components. On the one hand, avid collectors carefully organize and exhibit their treasures.[122] On the other hand, they are ferociously attached to their collections. A teddy bear collector summed up this fixation: "If my house ever burns down, I won't cry over my furniture, I'll cry over the bears."[123]

Some consumer researchers feel that collectors acquire their "prizes" to gratify their materialism in a socially acceptable manner. When he systematically amasses a collection, the collector "worships" material objects but he doesn't have to feel guilty or petty. Another perspective argues that collecting is actually an aesthetic experience; for many collectors, the pleasure comes from creating the collection. Whatever the motivation, hard-core collectors often devote a great deal of time and energy to maintaining and expanding their collections, so for many this activity becomes a central component of their extended selves (see Chapter 7).[124]

Domains of Sacred Consumption

Sacred consumption events permeate many aspects of our lives. We find ways to "set apart" all sorts of places, people, and events. In this section, we'll look at ways that "ordinary" consumption is sometimes *not* so ordinary after all.

Sacred Places

A society "sets apart" sacred places because they have religious or mystical significance (e.g., Bethlehem, Mecca, Stonehenge) or because they commemorate some aspect of a country's heritage (e.g., the Kremlin, the Emperor's Palace in Tokyo, the Statue of Liberty, or, more recently, Ground Zero in Manhattan). *Contamination* makes these places sacred: Something sacred happened on that spot, so the place itself takes on sacred qualities. Hard-core fans buy Yankees Sod, the first officially licensed grass. Although it costs a few thousand dollars to fill out a good-sized lawn, proud fans can boast of turf that grows from the same seeds the groundskeepers use at the stadium, and the sod comes with a certificate of authenticity from Major League Baseball and a counterfeit-proof hologram that declares it the official grass of the New York Yankees.[125]

Still other places start out as profane, but we endow them with sacred qualities. Grauman's Chinese Theater in Hollywood, where movie stars leave their footprints in concrete for posterity, is one such place. Theme parks are a form of mass-produced fantasy that take on aspects of sacredness. In particular, Disney World and Disneyland (and their outposts in Europe, Japan, and China) are destinations for "pilgrimages" by consumers around the globe. Disney World displays many characteristics of more traditional sacred places. Some even believe it has healing powers, which helps to explain why a trip to the park is the most common "last wish" for terminally ill children.[126]

As the saying goes, "Home is where the heart is."[127] In many cultures, the home is a particularly sacred place. It's a barrier between the harsh, external world and consumers' "inner space." Americans spend more than $50 billion a year on interior decorators and home furnishings, and our home is a central part of our identity. People all over the world go to great lengths to create a feeling of "homeyness." They personalize their dwellings with door wreaths, mantel arrangements, and a "memory wall" for family photos.[128] Even public places such as Starbucks cafés strive for a homelike atmosphere to shelter customers from the harshness of the outside world.

Sacred People

At her Web site livingoprah.com, superfan Robyn Okrant blogs about her devotion to Oprah Winfrey—and the year she spent living her life completely guided by Oprah's advice about what to eat, wear, and read. In her mission statement she speculates, "I wonder, will I find bliss if I commit wholeheartedly to her lifestyle suggestions?"[129]

We idolize sacred people as we set them apart from the masses, and sometimes people come to believe that these individuals have "superhuman" abilities. Souvenirs, memorabilia, and even mundane items these celebrities have touched acquire special meanings (the celebrities "contaminate" the items). Newspapers pay paparazzi hundreds of thousands of dollars for candid shots of stars or royalty. Indeed, many businesses thrive on our desire for products we associate with the famous. There is a flourishing market for celebrity autographs, and objects that celebrities owned, such as Princess Diana's gowns or John Lennon's guitars, sell on eBay for astronomical prices.

Sacred Events

Sometimes public events resemble sacred, religious ceremonies. Think about fans who hold their hands over their hearts and solemnly recite the "Pledge of Allegiance" before a ballgame, or how others reverently light matches (or hold up illuminated cell phones) during a rock concert.[130]

The world of sports is sacred to many of us (recent doping and gambling scandals aside). We find the roots of modern sports events in ancient religious rites, such as fertility festivals (e.g., the original Olympics).[131] And it's not uncommon for teams to join in prayer prior to a game. The sports pages are like the scriptures (and we all know ardent fans who read them "religiously"), the stadium is a house of worship, and the fans are members of the congregation. Devotees engage in group activities, such as tailgate parties and the "Wave," where sections of the stadium take turns standing up. The athletes and coaches that fans come to see are godlike; devotees believe they have almost superhuman powers. One study documented more than 600 children whose parents named them after the legendary University of Alabama coach Paul "Bear" Bryant![132]

Athletes are central figures in a common cultural myth known as the *hero tale*. In these stories, the player must prove himself under strenuous circumstances, and he achieves victory only through sheer force of will. On a more mundane level, devotees consume certain ritual artifacts during these ceremonies (such as hot dogs at the ballpark). Sales of snack foods and beverages spike around the time of the Super Bowl; people spend $10 million more on tortilla chips than during a normal 2-week period and more than $15 million extra on beer in the weeks surrounding the big game.[133]

Tourism is another category of sacred experience. People occupy sacred time and space when they travel on vacation (though you may not think so if you get stuck sleeping on an airport floor because of a plane delay). The tourist searches for "authentic" experiences that differ from his normal world (think of Club Med's motto, "The antidote to civilization").[134] This traveling experience involves binary oppositions between work and leisure and being "at home" versus "away." Often, we relax everyday (profane) norms regarding appropriate behavior as tourists, and participate in illicit or adventurous experiences we would never engage in at home ("What happens in Vegas, stays in Vegas").

The desire of travelers to capture these sacred experiences in objects forms the bedrock of the souvenir industry, which really sells sacred memories. Whether it's a personalized matchbook from a wedding or New York City salt-and-pepper shakers, a souvenir represents a tangible piece of the consumer's sacred experience.[135] In addition to personal mementos, such as ticket stubs you save from a favorite concert, these are some other sacred souvenir icons:[136]

- Local products (e.g., wine from California)
- Pictorial images (e.g., postcards)
- "Piece of the rock" (e.g., seashells, pine cones)
- Symbolic shorthand in the form of literal representations of the site (e.g., a miniature Statue of Liberty)
- Markers (e.g., Hard Rock Cafe T-shirts)

From Sacred to Profane, and Back Again

Just to make life interesting, some consumer activities move back and forth between the sacred and profane spheres over time.[137] A study of tea preparation in Turkey illustrates this movement. Although we are more likely to think of thick Turkish coffee, in reality Turks consume more tea *per capita* than any other country. In Turkish culture people drink tea continuously, like (or instead of) water. Tea is an integral part of daily life; many households and offices boil water for tea in the traditional *çaydanlik* (double teapot) first thing in the morning, and keep it steaming all day so that the beverage is ready at any time. The tea drinking process links to many symbolic meanings—including the traditional glasses, clear to appreciate the tea's color, and hourglass-shaped like a woman's body—and rituals, such as blending one's own tea, knowing how finely to grind the tea leaves, and how long to steep the tea for optimal flavor. When Lipton introduced the modern tea bag in 1984, Turkey was intent on modernization and soon consumers snapped up electric *çaydanliks* and mugs instead of small, shapely tea glasses. Tea became a symbol of the quick and convenient, and the drinking act became more of a fashion statement. Now, many Turkish consumers opt to return to the sacred, traditional rituals as a way to preserve authenticity in the face of rapid societal changes.[138]

The transition of Turkish tea to a mass-market product illustrates the process of **desacralization**. This occurs when we remove a sacred item or symbol from its special place or duplicate it in mass quantities so that it loses its "specialness" and becomes profane. Souvenir reproductions of sacred monuments such as the Washington Monument or the Eiffel Tower, artworks such as the *Mona Lisa* or Michelangelo's *David*, or reproductions of sacred symbols such as the American flag on T-shirts eliminate their special aspects. They become inauthentic commodities with relatively little value.

Religion itself has to some extent become desacralized. Religious symbols like stylized crosses or New Age crystals often pop up on fashion jewelry.[139] Critics often charge that Christmas has turned into a secular, materialistic occasion devoid of its original sacred significance. A similar process occurs in relatively Westernized parts of the Islamic Middle East, where the holy month of Ramadan (that people traditionally observe by fasting and praying) is starting to look like Christmas: People buy lights in the shape of an Islamic crescent moon, send Ramadan cards to one another, and attend lavish fast-breaking feasts at hotels.[140]

Global Consumer Culture

OBJECTIVE 8
Products that succeed in one culture may fail in another if marketers fail to understand the differences among consumers in each place.

As if understanding the dynamics of one's own culture weren't hard enough, these issues get even more complicated when we consider what drives consumers in other cultures. The consequences of ignoring cultural sensitivities can be costly. Think about problems a prominent multinational company such as McDonald's encounters as it expands globally—even as today the iconic American chain's worldwide operations are far bigger than its U.S. domestic business:

● During the 1994 soccer World Cup, the fast-food giant reprinted the Saudi Arabian flag, which includes sacred words from the Koran, on disposable packaging it used in promotions. Muslims around the world protested this borrowing of sacred imagery, and the company had to scramble to correct its mistake.

● In 2002, McDonald's agreed to donate $10 million to Hindu and other groups as partial settlement of litigation involving its mislabeling of French fries and hash browns as vegetarian (it cooked them in oil tainted with meat residue).

● Also in 2002, the company abruptly cancelled its plans to introduce its new McAfrika sandwich in its Norwegian restaurants. The CEO of McDonald's in Norway acknowledged on national television that introducing this menu item at a time of growing famine in Africa was "coincidental and unfortunate."

● In India, the company doesn't sell any of its famous beef hamburgers. Instead, it offers customized entrées such as a Pizza McPuff, McAloo Tikki (a spiced-potato burger), Paneer Salsa McWrap, and even a Crispy Chinese burger, to capitalize on the great popularity of Chinese food in India. It makes its mayonnaise without eggs, and all stores maintain separate kitchen sections for vegetarian and nonvegetarian dishes. Workers from the nonvegetarian section must shower before they cross over to the other area.

● In 2005, McDonald's introduced the spicy Prosperity Burger in nine countries, from South Korea to Indonesia, in recognition of the Lunar New Year.

● Today the chain's Big Tasty burger is an 840-calorie behemoth that consists of a 5.5-ounce beef patty slathered in smoky barbecue sauce and topped with three slices of cheese. The menu entrée was first introduced in Sweden, and it's now available in other parts of Europe as well as in Latin America and Australia.[141]

- Although the Japanese are well-known for their healthy diets, McDonald's numerous customers there are clamoring for high-calorie sandwiches—even as the company's American consumers welcome new diet-friendly entrées like the Fruit 'n Walnut salad. As part of its new Big America 2 campaign, McD's in Japan offer the 713-calorie Idaho burger (topped with melted cheese, a deep-fried hash brown, strips of bacon, onions, and pepper-and-mustard sauce) and several other U.S.-themed items.[142] It seems there's more than one way to translate "Big America."
- A McDonald's ad in France created some *sangfroid* because it features the French hero, Asterix, and his merry band of warriors eating in the restaurant. The character has been the topic of numerous movies and an Asterix theme park is very popular. The spot deliberately does not show the characters cramming burgers or fries, but some French bloggers are not amused.[143]
- McDonald's recently introduced a new entrée to the German market: The McCurrywurst is a mix of pork bratwurst chunks in a spicy tomato sauce accompanied by shaker packs of either mild or sharp curry powder. This follows on the mini Nürnburger brat sandwich the chain introduced a few years ago. Germans love their bratwurst, so now they can eat it Golden Arches style.[144]

More than 60 countries have a gross national product of less than $10 billion. There are at least 135 transnational companies that post more revenue than that figure. Many multinational firms are household names, widely recognized (though not necessarily liked) by literally billions of people. The dominance of these marketing powerhouses creates a **global consumer culture** that unites people around the world by their common devotion to brand-name consumer goods, movie stars, celebrities, and leisure activities.[145] Even during a global recession, sales of luxury goods remain quite healthy. Consumers spend about $272 billion on upscale products each year—Asian sales increased by almost 20 percent from 2011 to 2012.[146]

Tempting images of luxury cars, glam rock stars on MTV, and modern appliances that make life easier surround us wherever we turn. People the world over begin to share the ideal of a material lifestyle and value well-known brands that symbolize prosperity. Shopping evolves from a wearying, task-oriented struggle to locate even basic necessities to a leisure activity. Possessing these coveted items becomes a mechanism to display one's status—often at great personal sacrifice. Consumers around the world increasingly share the same aspirations, media, and even brands.

OBJECTIVE 9

Western (and particularly American) culture has a huge impact around the world, although people in other countries don't necessarily ascribe the same meanings to products as we do.

It's a BRAND New World

Coca-Cola is the drink of choice among young people in Asian countries, and McDonald's is their favorite restaurant.[147] The National Basketball Association sells $500 million of licensed merchandise every year *outside* of the United States.[148] Patrons of the Starlite Urban Drive-In in London sit in rows of cars as they watch American "classics" like *Grease* and *Dirty Dancing* while they chow down on burgers, meatloaf, and sweet potato pie, followed by ice cream sundaes or chocolate brownies and cream.[149]

Walk the streets of Lisbon or Buenos Aires, and the sight of Nike hats, Gap T-shirts, and Levi's jeans will accost you at every turn. The allure of American consumer culture spreads throughout the world—but with a lot of pushback in many places. Critics in other countries deplore the creeping Americanization of their cultures because of what they view as excessive materialism. One French critic summarized this resistance to the diffusion of American culture: He described the Euro Disney theme park as "a horror made of cardboard, plastic, and appalling colors—a construction of hardened chewing gum and idiotic folklore taken straight out of a comic book written for obese Americans."[150]

A survey in Beijing found that nearly half of all children under 12 think McDonald's is a domestic Chinese brand![151] The West (and especially the United States) is a net exporter of popular culture. Many consumers equate Western lifestyles in general and the English language in particular with modernization and sophistication, and numerous American brands slowly but surely insinuate themselves into local cultures. Indeed, some global brands are so widespread that many are only vaguely aware of their countries of origin. In surveys, consumers routinely guess that Heineken is German (it's really Dutch) and that Nokia is Japanese (it's Finnish).[152]

One study, conducted in 2009, looked at how Chinese consumers think about Western brands. The researchers found that their interpretations depended on their unique perspective about the history of relations between China and the West. The researchers in fact identified four different *narratives* (themes) in their sample: West as liberator, as oppressor, as subjugated, and as partner. Depending on which view they endorsed, respondents viewed Western brands as instruments of democratization, domination, a symbol of Asian ascendancy as Chinese domestic brands start to gain traction, or as instruments of economic progress that will help China to grow its economy in partnership with the United States and Western Europe.[153]

As the global consumption ethic spreads, rituals and product preferences in different cultures become homogenized. For example, some urbanites in Muslim Turkey now celebrate Christmas even though gift-giving is not customary in many parts of the country—even on birthdays. In China, Christmas fever grips China's newly rising urban middle class as an excuse to shop, eat, and party. People there snap up Christmas trees, ornaments, and Christian religious objects (even though the street vendors who peddle images of Jesus and Mary can't always identify who they are). Chinese consumers embrace Christmas because to them the holiday is international and modern, not because it's a traditional Christian celebration. The government encourages this practice because it stimulates consumer spending. To make the holiday even merrier, China exports about $1 billion worth of Christmas products every year, and its factories churn out $7.5 billion of the toys people worldwide put under their trees.[154]

Does this homogenization mean that in time consumers who live in Nairobi, New Guinea, or the Netherlands will all be indistinguishable from those in New York or Nashville? Probably not, because the meaning of consumer goods mutates to blend with local customs and values. For example, in Turkey some urban women use their ovens to dry clothes and their dishwashers to wash muddy spinach. A person in Papua New Guinea may combine a traditional clothing style such as a *bilum* with Western items such as Mickey Mouse shirts or baseball caps.[155] These processes make it unlikely that global homogenization will overwhelm local cultures, but it is likely that there will be multiple consumer cultures, each of which blends global icons such as Nike's pervasive "swoosh" with indigenous products and meanings. In Vietnam, for example, local fast-food chains dominate the market as they duplicate a McDonald's approach but add a local flavor. The country's hugely successful Kinh Do red and yellow outlets sell specialties like dried squid buns. In the Philippines, the Jollibee Foods Corp. burger chain also copies the McDonald's look—and it outsells McDonald's there.[156]

Creolization occurs when foreign influences integrate with local meanings. In India, handicapped beggars sell bottles of Coke from tricycles, and Indipop, a popular music hybrid, mixes traditional styles with rock, rap, and reggae.[157] Young Hispanic Americans bounce between hip-hop and *Rock en Español*, blend Mexican rice with spaghetti sauce, and spread peanut butter and jelly on tortillas.[158] In Argentina, Coca-Cola launched Nativa, a soft drink flavored with the country's traditional *yerba mate* herbal tea, as part of a strategy to broaden its portfolio with products it makes from indigenous ingredients.[159]

The creolization process sometimes results in bizarre permutations of products and services when locals modify them to be compatible with their customs. Consider these creolized adaptations, for example:[160]

- In Peru, Indian boys carry rocks painted to look like transistor radios.
- In highland Papua New Guinea, tribespeople put Chivas Regal wrappers on their drums and wear Pentel pens instead of nosebones.

- Bana tribespeople in the remote highlands of Kako, Ethiopia, pay to watch *Pluto the Circus Dog* on a View-Master.
- When an African Swazi princess marries a Zulu king, she wears a traditional costume of red touraco wing feathers around her forehead and a cape of windowbird feathers and oxtails. But guests record the ceremony on a Kodak movie camera while the band plays "The Sound of Music."
- The Japanese use Western words as a shorthand for anything new and exciting, even if they do not understand what the words mean. They give cars names such as Fairlady, Gloria, and Bongo Wagon. Consumers buy *deodoranto* (deodorant) and *appuru pai* (apple pie). Ads urge shoppers to *stoppu rukku* (stop and look), and products claim to be *yuniku* (unique).[161] Coca-Cola cans say, "I feel Coke & sound special," and a company called Cream Soda sells products with the slogan, "Too old to die, too young to happy."[162] Other Japanese products with English names include Mouth Pet (breath freshener), Pocari Sweat ("refreshment water"), Armpit (electric razor), Brown Gross Foam (hair-coloring mousse), Virgin Pink Special (skin cream), Cow Brand (beauty soap), and Mymorning Water (canned water).[163]

Rather than ignore the global characteristics of their brands, firms have to manage them strategically. That's critical, because future growth for most companies will come from foreign markets. In 2002, developed countries in North America, Europe, and East Asia accounted for 15 percent of the world's population of 6.3 billion. By 2030, according to the World Bank, the planet's population will rise to 9 billion—and 90 percent of these people will live in developing countries.

As corporations compete in many markets around the world, the debate intensifies: Should an organization develop separate marketing plans for each culture, or should it craft a single plan to implement everywhere? Let's briefly consider each viewpoint.

Adopt a Standardized Strategy

As Procter & Gamble strategizes about the best way to speak to consumers around the world, the company finds large segments in many countries that share the same outlooks, style preferences, and aspirations. These include teenagers, working women who try to juggle careers and families, and baby boomers. As the head of P&G's Global Health and Feminine Care division explained, "We're seeing global tribes forming around the world that are more and more interconnected through technology. If you focus on the similarities instead of the differences [in these tribes], key business opportunities emerge." For example, brand managers find that teenage girls everywhere have the same concerns and questions about puberty, so the company makes the same content available in 40 countries.[165]

Proponents of a standardized marketing strategy argue that many cultures, especially those of industrialized countries, are now so homogenized that the same approach will work throughout the world. If it develops one approach for multiple markets, a company can benefit from economies of scale, because it does not have to incur the substantial time and expense to develop a separate strategy for each culture.[166] This viewpoint represents an **etic perspective**, which focuses on commonalities across cultures. An etic approach to a culture is objective and analytical; it reflects impressions of a culture as outsiders view it.

Adopt a Localized Strategy

Unlike Disney World in Orlando, visitors to the Walt Disney Studios theme park at Disneyland Paris don't hear the voices of American movie stars narrating their guided tours. Instead, European actors such as Jeremy Irons, Isabella Rossellini, and Nastassja Kinski provide commentary in their native tongues.

Disney learned the hard way about the importance of being sensitive to local cultures after it opened its Euro Disney Park in 1992. The company got slammed because its new location didn't cater to local customs (such as serving wine with meals). Visitors to Euro Disney from many countries took offense, even at what seem to be small slights. For example, initially the park only sold a French sausage, which drew complaints from Germans, Italians, and others who believed their own local versions to be superior. Euro Disney's CEO explained, "When we first launched there was the belief that it was enough to be Disney. Now we realize that our guests need to be welcomed on the basis of their own culture and travel habits."[167]

Disney applied the lessons it learned in cultural sensitivity to its newer Hong Kong Disneyland. Executives shifted the angle of the front gate by 12 degrees after they consulted a *feng shui* specialist, who said the change would ensure prosperity for the park. Disney also put a bend in the walkway from the train station to the gate to make sure the flow of positive energy, or *chi*, did not slip past the entrance and out to the China Sea. Cash registers are close to corners or along walls to increase prosperity. The company burned incense as it finished each building, and it picked a lucky day (September 12) for the opening. One of the park's main ballrooms measures 888 square meters, because eight is a lucky number in Chinese culture. And because the Chinese consider the number four bad luck, you won't find any fourth-floor buttons in hotel elevators. Disney also recognizes that Chinese family dynamics are different, so it revamped its advertising: Print ads showed a grandmother, mother, and daughter who wore tiaras at the park. In China, bonding between parents and children is difficult because of the culture's hierarchical nature, so an executive explained, "We want to say it's OK to let your hair down." Camping out with stopwatches, the company's designers discovered that Chinese people take an average of 10 minutes longer to eat than Americans, so they added 700 extra seats to dining areas. Now, Disney is building another theme park and resort in Shanghai—but it's making more big changes to please Chinese visitors. The Chinese government insisted that the new venue not resemble Disneyland, which is a symbol of American culture. This one will be the only Disney park without classic American features like a Main Street.[168]

Disney's experience supports the view of marketers who endorse an **emic perspective** that stresses variations across cultures. They feel that each culture is unique, with its own value system, conventions, and regulations. This perspective argues that each country has a *national character*; a distinctive set of behavior and personality characteristics.[169] A marketer must therefore tailor its strategy to the sensibilities of each specific culture. An emic approach to a culture is subjective and experiential: It attempts to explain a culture as insiders experience it.

Sometimes this strategy means that a manufacturer has to modify what it makes or a retailer has to change the way it displays the product so that it's acceptable to local tastes. When Walmart started to open stores abroad in the early 1990s, it offered a little piece of America to foreign consumers—and that was the problem. It promoted golf clubs in soccer-mad Brazil and pushed ice skates in Mexico. It trained its German clerks to smile at customers—who thought they were flirting. Now Walmart tries to adapt to local preferences. Its Chinese stores sell live turtles and snakes and lure shoppers who come on foot or bicycle with free shuttle buses and home delivery for refrigerators and other large items.[170]

In some cases, consumers in one place simply do not like some products that are popular elsewhere, or their different lifestyles require companies to rethink their designs. IKEA finally realized that Americans use a lot of ice in their drinks and so didn't buy the smaller European glasses the stores stocked. The Swedish furniture chain also figured out that compared to Europeans, Americans sleep in bigger beds, need bigger bookshelves, and like to curl up on sofas rather than sit on them.[171] Snapple failed in Japan because the drink's cloudy appearance and the floating pulp in the bottles were a turnoff. Similarly, Frito-Lay stopped selling Ruffles potato chips (too salty) and Cheetos (the Japanese didn't appreciate orange fingers after they ate a handful).[172] The company still makes Cheetos in China, but the local version doesn't contain any cheese, which is not a staple of the Chinese diet. Instead, local flavors come in varieties such as Savory American Cream and Japanese Steak.[173]

Marketing Pitfall

The language barrier is one of the main obstacles that marketers face when they want to enter a new market outside of their region. The way the English language is used in China is a case in point. For instance, in a restaurant the waiter may ask a guest to eat slowly while meaning to say "enjoy your meal." In hotels, bellmen might say "don't see me out" to the residents while leaving their rooms when they actually mean "no need to walk me out." In a shopping mall in China, a placard placed near the escalator contained the message: "slip and fall down carefully," which meant to convey the following: "be careful not to slip and fall." Another sign on a bin indicated "un-recycled" instead of "nonrecyclables."[174]

An example of a company that faced a language barrier is Lada, the car manufacturer that introduced Lada Nova in Latin America. There, the word "nova" means "no go," which has a negative implication for a car.

One technique marketers use to avoid this problem is back-translation, in which a different interpreter retranslates a translated ad back into its original language to catch errors. Braniff Airlines would definitely have benefited from this. The company aimed to advertise the leather seats it had installed in First Class with the slogan "Fly in leather." Translated for Spanish-speaking markets as "*Vuela en cuero*," it literally meant "Fly naked!"[175]

Cross-Cultural Differences Relevant to Marketers

So, which perspective is correct, the emic or the etic? As you might guess, the best bet probably is a combination of both.[176] Some researchers argue that the relevant dimension to consider is **consumer style**: a pattern of behaviors, attitudes, and opinions that influences all of a person's consumption activities—including attitudes toward advertising, preferred channels of information and purchase, brand loyalty, and price consciousness. These researchers identified four major clusters of consumer styles when they looked at data from the United States, the United Kingdom, France, and Germany:[177]

- Price-sensitive consumers
- Variety seekers
- Brand-loyal consumers
- Information seekers

Given the sizable variations in tastes within the United States alone, it is hardly surprising that people around the world develop their own unique preferences. Panasonic touted the fact that its rice cooker kept food from getting too crisp—until the company learned that consumers in the Middle East *like* to eat their rice this way. Unlike Americans, Europeans favor dark chocolate over milk chocolate, which they think of as a children's food. Sara Lee sells its pound cake with chocolate chips in the United States, raisins in Australia, and coconuts in Hong Kong. Crocodile handbags are popular in Asia and Europe but not in the United States.[178]

One of the most widely used measures of cross-cultural values is an instrument a Dutch researcher developed called **Hofstede Dimensions of National Culture**.[179] This measure scores a country in terms of its standing on six dimensions so that users can compare and contrast values:[180]

- **Power distance**—The extent to which the less powerful members of organizations and institutions (like the family) accept and expect that power is distributed unequally.
- **Individualism**—The degree to which individuals are integrated into groups.
- **Masculinity**—The distribution of roles between the genders.
- **Uncertainty avoidance**—A society's tolerance for uncertainty and ambiguity.
- **Long-term orientation**—Values associated with Long-Term Orientation are thrift and perseverance; values associated with Short-Term Orientation are respect for tradition, fulfilling social obligations, and protecting one's "face."
- **Indulgence versus restraint**—The extent to which a society allows relatively free gratification of basic and natural human drives related to enjoying life and having fun. A culture high on restraint suppresses gratification of needs and regulates it by means of strict social norms.

Does Global Marketing Work?

So, what's the verdict? Does global marketing work or not? Perhaps the more appropriate question is, "*When* does it work?" Although the argument for a homogenous world culture is appealing in principle, in practice it hasn't worked out too well. One reason is that consumers in different countries have varying conventions and customs, so they simply do not use products the same way. Kellogg, for example, discovered that in Brazil people don't typically eat a big breakfast—they're more likely to eat cereal as a dry snack.

In fact, significant cultural differences even show up within the same country. We certainly feel that we've traveled to a different place as we move around the United States. Advertisers in Canada know that when they target consumers in French-speaking Quebec, their messages must be much different from those addressed to residents of English-speaking regions. Ads in Montreal tend to be a lot racier than those in Toronto, reflecting differences in attitudes toward sexuality between consumers with French versus British roots.[181]

Some large corporations, such as Coca-Cola, have successfully crafted a single, international image. Still, even the soft-drink giant must make minor modifications to the way it presents itself in each culture. Although Coke commercials are largely standardized, the company permits local agencies to edit them so they highlight close-ups of local faces.[182] To maximize the chances of success for these multicultural efforts, marketers must locate consumers in different countries who nonetheless share a common *worldview*. This is more likely to be the case among people whose frame of reference is relatively more international or cosmopolitan, or who receive much of their information about the world from sources that incorporate a worldwide perspective.

Who is likely to fall into this category? Two consumer segments are particularly good candidates: (1) affluent people who are "global citizens" and who come into contact with ideas from around the world through their travels, business contacts, and media experiences; and (2) young people whose tastes in music and fashion are strongly influenced by MTV and other media that broadcast many of the same images to multiple countries. For example, viewers of MTV Europe in Rome or Zurich can check out the same "buzz clips" as their counterparts in London or Luxembourg.[183]

A large-scale study of consumers in 41 countries identified the characteristics that people associate with global brands, and it also measured the relative importance of those dimensions when consumers buy products.[184] The researchers grouped consumers who evaluate global brands in the same way. They identified four major segments:

- **Global citizens**—The largest segment (55 percent of consumers) uses the global success of a company as a signal of quality and innovation. At the same time, they are concerned about whether companies behave responsibly on issues such as consumer health, the environment, and worker rights.
- **Global dreamers**—The second-largest segment, at 23 percent, consists of consumers who see global brands as quality products and readily buy into the myths they author. They aren't nearly as concerned with social responsibility as are the global citizens.
- **Antiglobals**—Thirteen percent of consumers are skeptical that transnational companies deliver higher-quality goods. They dislike brands that preach American values, and they don't trust global companies to behave responsibly. They try to avoid doing business with transnational firms.
- **Global agnostics**—The remaining 9 percent of consumers don't base purchase decisions on a brand's global attributes. Instead, they evaluate a global product by the same criteria they use to judge local brands and don't regard its global nature as meriting special consideration.

MyMarketingLab

Go to **mymktlab.com** to complete the problems marked with this icon ⭐.

CHAPTER SUMMARY

Now that you have finished reading this chapter, you should understand why:

1. A culture is a society's personality.

A society's culture includes its values, ethics, and the material objects its members produce. It is the accumulation of shared meanings and traditions among members of a society. We describe a culture in terms of ecology (the way

people adapt to their habitat), its social structure, and its ideology (including moral and aesthetic principles).

2. Our deeply held cultural values dictate the types of products and services we seek out or avoid.

Underlying values often drive consumer motivations. Products thus take on meaning because a person thinks they will help him or her to achieve some goal that is linked to a value, such as individuality or freedom. A set of core values characterizes each culture, to which most of its members adhere.

3. We distinguish between high culture and low culture.

Social scientists distinguish between high (or elite) forms and low (or popular) forms of culture. Products of popular culture tend to follow a cultural formula and contain predictable components. However, these distinctions blur in modern society as marketers increasingly incorporate imagery from "high art" to sell everyday products.

4. Many modern marketers are reality engineers.

Reality engineering occurs when marketers appropriate elements of popular culture to use in their promotional strategies. These elements include sensory and spatial aspects of everyday existence, whether in the form of products that appear in movies, scents pumped into offices and stores, billboards, theme parks, or video monitors attached to shopping carts.

5. Myths are stories that express a culture's values, and in modern times marketing messages convey these values to members of the culture.

Myths are stories with symbolic elements that express the shared ideals of a culture. Many myths involve a binary opposition, defining values in terms of what they are and what they are not (e.g., nature versus technology). Advertising, movies, and other media transmit modern myths.

6. Many of our consumption activities—including holiday observances, grooming, and gift-giving—are rituals.

A ritual is a set of multiple, symbolic behaviors that occur in a fixed sequence and that we repeat periodically. Ritual is related to many consumption activities that occur in popular culture. These include holiday observances, gift-giving, and grooming.

A rite of passage is a special kind of ritual that marks the transition from one role to another. These passages typically entail the need to acquire ritual artifacts to facilitate the transition. Modern rites of passage include graduations, fraternity initiations, weddings, debutante balls, and funerals.

7. We describe products as either sacred or profane, and it's not unusual for some products to move back and forth between the two categories.

We divide consumer activities into *sacred* and *profane* domains. Sacred phenomena are "set apart" from everyday activities or products. *Sacralization* occurs when we set apart everyday people, events, or objects from the ordinary. *Objectification* occurs when we ascribe sacred qualities to products or items that sacred people once owned. *Desacralization* occurs when formerly sacred objects or activities become part of the everyday, as when companies reproduce "one-of-a-kind" works of art in large quantities.

8. Products that succeed in one culture may fail in another if marketers fail to understand the differences among consumers in each place.

Because a consumer's culture exerts such a big influence on his or her lifestyle choices, marketers must learn as much as possible about differences in cultural norms and preferences when they do business in more than one country. One important issue is the extent to which we need to tailor our marketing strategies to each culture. Followers of an etic perspective believe that people in many cultures appreciate the same universal messages. Believers in an emic perspective argue that individual cultures are too unique to permit such standardization; marketers must instead adapt their approaches to local values and practices. Attempts at global marketing have met with mixed success. In many cases this approach is more likely to work if the messages appeal to basic values or if the target markets consist of consumers who are internationally rather than locally oriented.

9. Western (and particularly American) culture has a huge impact around the world, although people in other countries don't necessarily ascribe the same meanings to products as we do.

The United States is a net exporter of popular culture. Consumers around the world eagerly adopt American products, especially entertainment vehicles and items they link to an American lifestyle (e.g., Marlboro cigarettes, Levi's jeans). Despite the continuing "Americanization" of world culture, some people resist globalization because they fear it will dilute their own local cultures. In other cases, they practice creolization as they integrate these products with existing cultural practices.

KEY TERMS

acculturation, 104
advergaming, 118
antifestival, 129
art product, 112
binary opposition, 122

collecting, 132
consumer style, 140
contamination, 132
conventions, 105
cooptation, 108

core values, 104
craft product, 112
creolization, 137
crescive norms, 105
cultural formula, 113

cultural gatekeepers, 112
cultural selection, 110
culture, 101
culture production system (CPS), 111
custom, 105
desacralization, 135
ecology, 102
emic perspective, 139
enculturation, 104
etic perspective, 138
fortress brands, 125
gift-giving ritual, 126
global consumer culture, 136
grooming rituals, 126

hoarding, 132
Hofstede Dimensions of National
    Culture, 140
ideology, 102
instrumental values, 106
laddering, 107
list of values (LOV) scale, 107
means–end chain model, 107
more, 105
myth, 120
objectification, 132
Plinking™, 118
pretailer, 109

product placement, 117
profane consumption, 131
reality engineering, 115
reciprocity norm, 127
rites of passage, 129
ritual, 124
ritual artifacts, 126
sacralization, 131
sacred consumption, 131
social structure, 102
terminal values, 106
value, 102
value system, 104

REVIEW

3-1 What is culture? List three dimensions that social scientists use to describe a culture and give an example of each.

3-2 A myth is a special kind of story. What makes it special? What is an example of a modern myth?

3-3 Give an example of a marketer that uses the principle of binary opposition.

3-4 What is a ritual? Describe three kinds of rituals and provide an example of each.

3-5 List the three stages of a ritual.

3-6 What is the difference between sacred and profane consumption? Provide one example of each.

⭐ **3-7** How is a collection sacred? What is the difference between collecting and hoarding?

3-8 What is collective selection? Give an example.

3-9 Describe a culture production system and list its three components. What is an example of a CPS with these three components?

3-10 Define a cultural gatekeeper, and give three examples.

3-11 Describe the difference between arts and crafts.

3-12 What is a cultural formula? Give an example.

3-13 Define product placement and list three examples of it. How is this practice the same or different from branded entertainment?

3-14 What is advergaming? Give an example.

3-15 What are the influencing factors of CPS?

3-16 Who are innovators? Early adopters? Laggards?

3-17 What are the differences among *fashion, a fashion,* and *in fashion*?

⭐ **3-18** Summarize some of the major approaches we can use to understand fashion from the perspectives of psychologists, economists, and sociologists.

3-19 What is an example of a meme?

3-20 What is the trickle-down effect? List some reasons why this theory is no longer as valid as it used to be.

3-21 What is the difference between a fad, a fashion, and a classic fashion life cycle?

CONSUMER BEHAVIOR CHALLENGE

■ DISCUSS

3-22 What is culture shock? Has this phenomenon occurred in your country as a result of increasing globalization? Discuss its impact on your society and the reactions to it.

3-23 Why is culture not static, even in the most traditional countries? What drives cultural changes over time?

3-24 Every culture dictates certain occasions and ceremonies to give gifts, whether for personal or professional reasons. Identify examples in your own country.

3-25 Is it possible for a commercial building or attraction to attain a status that borders on the sacred? Give an example from your country or region.

3-26 Illustrate the concepts of separation, liminality, and aggregation in relation to your own specific culture. Are the concepts readily applicable?

3-27 Some products can be classified as being either sacred or profane. It is not unusual for some products to move back and forth between the two categories. Why?

3-28 Particularly in subcultures there is a tradition of having to go through some kind of entry rite at one point of time. Identify an example from your own country to illustrate this process.

3-29 How is sports portrayed in advertising in your country?

3-30 Religious festivals and ceremonies are not immune to marketing. Many have become another opportunity for businesses to make sales. To what extent is this true? Give reasons for your answer.

3-31 Often when a couple marry, the choice of gift is defined either by a wedding list, from which the guest will have to choose, or determined by cultural pressure to provide a certain level of financial gift. How does this work in your own country?

3-32 In Pamplona, Spain, there is an annual nine-day festival, unique in its nature and its potential dangers.[185] Yet it attracts tens of thousands of people. The Running of the Bulls has taken place since 1910. This is not bull-fighting, a popular spectator sport in Spain and much of Latin America. This event puts the spectator in much more jeopardy. The event involves penning up bulls and then letting them run freely through the packed streets of Pamplona. Literally, the whole crowd is in danger. Since the event began over 100 years ago, a conservative estimate of 15 deaths has been attributed to the event. Every year anywhere between 200 and 300 people are hurt in the stampede. Some are gored by the bulls, but more are injured as the crowds seek to run from the bulls. Are there similar examples of dangerous events involving crowds in your country? Should these types of events be banned?

3-33 Over the course of the next week, look out for overt signs of product placement on TV shows. Some will be more obvious than others, particularly in commercial productions and films. Identify examples of actors asking for a specific brand of product rather than a generic one. How do you feel about these subliminal advertising messages? Compare your observations with others in your group. Is the occurrence of product placement more obvious in domestically produced TV shows compared to imported productions? In international productions, such as films, are the products placed popular in your own country? Is this technique of any real value to the brand?[186]

3-34 Is advertising an art or a craft? Which should it be?

★ **3-35** Movie companies often conduct market research when they produce big-budget films. If necessary, they will reshoot part of a movie when viewers say they don't like it. Some people oppose this practice: They claim that movies, like books, songs, plays, and other artistic endeavors, should not conform to what the market wants, lest they sacrifice their integrity. What do you think?

3-36 Comment on the growing practice of reality engineering. Do marketers "own" our culture? Should they?

3-37 One of the most controversial intersections between marketing and society occurs when companies provide "educational materials" to schools.[187] Many firms, including Nike, Hershey, Crayola, Nintendo, and Foot Locker, provide free book covers swathed in ads. Standard art supplies, blocks, trucks, and dolls get supplemented with Milton Bradley and Care Bears worksheets, Purell hand-cleaning activities, and Pizza Hut reading programs. Clearasil provides sample packets of its acne medication along with brochures to educate high school students about proper skin care; the handouts also direct students to the Clearasil Web site where they can register for music downloads and iPods. Other companies contract with schools to run focus groups with their students during the school day in order to get reactions to new product ideas. Some schools encourage kids to practice their math as they count Tootsie Rolls, and the kids use reading software that bears the logos of Kmart, Coke, Pepsi, and Cap'n Crunch cereal. Many educators argue that these materials are a godsend for resource-poor schools that otherwise could not provide computers and other goodies to their students. However, a California law bans the use of textbooks with brand names and company logos. This legislation was prompted by complaints from parents about a middle-school math book that uses names such as Barbie, Oreos, Nike, and Sony PlayStation in word problems. What's your position on these practices? Should corporations be allowed to promote their products in schools in exchange for donations of educational materials, computers, and so on?

3-38 One way to clearly see the impact of shifting cultural values on consumption is to look at the increasing emphasis on the importance of health and wellness. In recent years, top-performing new food/beverage products featured items with natural or organic ingredients, such as Chobani yogurt and Nature's Pride bread.[188] Where is this trend going—is it just temporary or does it reflect a more permanent change in how Americans look at what they eat and drink?

■ APPLY

3-39 When you go out on a first date, identify the crescive norms that you follow. Write a report (preferably when the date is over) describing specific behaviors each person performed that made it clear you were on a first date. What products and services do those norms affect?

3-40 Interview people you know about any "magic" items they own (e.g., how many of your friends have a lucky charm or hang a St. Christopher medal or some other object from their rearview mirrors?). Get them to describe their feelings about these objects and tell how

they acquired their magical properties. How would they feel if they lost these special items?

3-41 Identify modern-day myths that corporations create. How do they communicate these stories to consumers?

3-42 Interview people you know who collect some kind of object. How do they organize and describe their collections? Do you see any evidence of sacred versus profane distinctions?

3-43 Ask friends to describe an incident in which they received a gift they thought was inappropriate. Why did they feel this way, and how did this event influence the relationship between them and the gift giver?

3-44 How might the rise of peer-to-peer music sharing influence the structure of the music CPS? One guess is that this method erodes the dominance of the big labels because listeners are more likely to access music from lesser-known groups. Survey your friends to determine whether this in fact is happening. Do they listen to a wider variety of artists, or simply download more from the big-time groups?

3-45 Read several romance or action novels to see if you can identify a cultural formula at work. Do you see parallels among the roles different characters play (e.g., the hero, the evildoer, the temptress, etc.)?

3-46 Watch 12 hours of TV and keep a log of all product placements you see. What are the dominant products that shows insert?

3-47 Collect a sample of ads that appeal to consumers' values. What value is being communicated in each ad, and how is this done? Is this an effective approach to designing a marketing communication?

3-48 American television inspires knockoffs around the world. But to be fair, many U.S. viewers don't realize that American reality show hits such as *Big Brother* and *American Idol* started out as European concepts that U.S. producers imported. In fact, the U.K. version of *Big Brother* briefly went off the air after a fight broke out and housemates threatened to kill each other. The German version attracted accusations of "shameless voyeurism" after a female contestant had her nipple pierced on live TV—without anesthetic.[189] In contrast, a Malaysian show that borrows the *American Idol* format is called *Imam Muda* (Young Leader). Contestants debate religious topics and recite passages from the Koran. The winner doesn't get a recording contract. Instead, he receives a job as an imam, or religious leader; a scholarship to study in Saudi Arabia; and an all-expenses-paid pilgrimage to Mecca, Islam's holiest city.[190] See if you can identify foreign versions of familiar reality shows. You should be able to find them online. How have the creators of these programs adapted them to appeal to local customs?

Case Study

CHEERIOS

Cheerios has topped the list of breakfast brands since it was introduced as the first ready-to-eat cereal in 1941. Originally called CheeriOats, the product's positioning was boosted in 1992 when the Food and Drug Administration claimed that Cheerios and other oat products could lower the risk of heart disease. With that news, Cheerios became heart healthy!

Millions of Americans include Cheerios in their daily rituals, whether it's breakfast or a snack bag for a toddler. Cheerios' success relies, in part, on an advertising message that focuses on one prominent American value: family. Although the brand stuck with their formula, they sparked a national dialog about modern racism when they used a biracial family to advertise the heart healthy benefits of the cereal in a television commercial.

The ad that sparked the conversation, "Just Checking," opens with a happy girl eating breakfast with her Mom, who is white, and learning about the heart healthy benefits of Cheerios. In a later scene you see the girl's dad, who is black, wake up to find that his daughter had placed Cheerios over his heart to make him healthier. The ad was aired nationally on television and posted on the Cheerios' YouTube channel. A small, but vocal group used the comments section of YouTube to harshly air their dissatisfaction with the casting in the commercial. Cheerios quickly disabled the comments section of the online commercial, but not before a portion of the four

million viewers read the racist comments and became engaged in the discussion.

The commercial was the topic of countless blogs, television shows, radio broadcasts, and news outlets. With research supporting the growing number of interracial families, most critics applauded General Mills for the ad. General Mills executives said they were genuinely surprised to see the negative reactions as they felt they were just reflecting the changing face of the American family.

Fueled by the negative responses to the commercial, online producers Benny and Rafi Fine, known as The Fine Brothers, produced their own video related to the Cheerios commercial. In their video, kids are asked to react to the ad and speculate on why it is controversial. The kids have no idea why the biracial couple is controversial; all they see is a happy and loving family. This response is certainly an encouraging reflection on the values of our youngest generation. The Fine Brothers video received over 10 million views, more than twice the views of the original ad.

Overall, most advertising critics would agree the video has helped the Cheerios brand. Online data company Kontera is reporting that Cheerios beat the average content views of their competitors by 137 percent with this commercial. Others say this might be more attention than Cheerios would like to see directed to their brand. Time will tell whether Cheerios continues their attempts to bring more realism to its advertising.

DISCUSSION QUESTIONS

CS 3-1 Should Cheerios have been more sensitive to cultural issues?

CS 3-2 Do you think this ad will increase sales of Cheerios?

Sources: "Mixed-Race Ad for Cheerios Does the Brand Some Good Despite YouTube Uproar," June 10, 2013, www.kontera.com, accessed August 7, 2013; Timm Nudd, "Cheerios Finds Its Sweet Spot Once Again First New Ad Since Interracial Family," July 18, 2013, http://www.adweek.com/news/advertising-branding/ad-day-cheerios-finds-its-sweet-spot-once-again-151264, accessed August 7, 2013; Kevin Hunt, "New Cheerios Commercial Celebrates Family," http://www.blog.generalmills.com/2013/05/new-cheerios-commercial-celebrates-family/, accessed August 7, 2013; www.cheerios.com, http://www.cheerios.com/our-story, accessed August 7, 2013.

MyMarketingLab

Go to **mymktlab.com** for the following Assisted Graded writing questions:

3-49 Describe the differences among continuous innovations, dynamically continuous innovations, and discontinuous innovations, and provide an example of each. Which type are consumers least likely to adopt as an innovation?

3-50 Some market analysts see a shift in values among young people. They claim that this generation has not had a lot of stability in their lives. They are fed up with superficial relationships and yearn for a return to tradition. What's your take on this? Are young people indeed returning to the values of their parents (or even their grandparents)? How have these changes influenced your perspective on marriage and family?

3-51 MymktlabOnly—comprehensive writing assignments for this chapter.

NOTES

1. "Spice Girls Dance into Culture Clash," *Montgomery Advertiser* (April 29, 1997): 2A.
2. Clifford Geertz, *The Interpretation of Cultures* (New York: Basic Books, 1973); Marvin Harris, *Culture, People and Nature* (New York: Crowell, 1971); John F. Sherry, Jr., "The Cultural Perspective in Consumer Research," in Richard J. Lutz, ed., *Advances in Consumer Research* 13 (Provo, UT: Association for Consumer Research, 1985): 573–75.
3. William Lazer, Shoji Murata, and Hiroshi Kosaka, "Japanese Marketing: Towards a Better Understanding," *Journal of Marketing* 49 (Spring 1985): 69–81.
4. Celia W. Dugger, "Modestly, India Goes for a Public Swim," *New York Times* (March 5, 2000), www.nytimes.com, accessed March 5, 2000; cf. also Marius K. Luedicke, Craig J. Thompson, and Markus Giesler, "Consumer Identity Work as Moral Protagonism: How Myth and Ideology Animate a Brand-Mediated Moral Conflict," *Journal of Consumer Research* 36, no. 6 (2010): 1016–32.
5. Robert F. Worth, "Arab TV Tests Societies' Limits with Depictions of Sex and Equality," *New York Times* (September 26, 2008), www.nytimes.com/2008/09/27/World/Middleeast/27beirut.Html?_R=1&Scp=1&Sq=N..., accessed September 26, 2008.
6. Ajay K. Sirsi, James C. Ward, and Peter H. Reingen, "Microcultural Analysis of Variation in Sharing of Causal Reasoning about Behavior," *Journal of Consumer Research* 22 (March 1996): 345–72.
7. Vercihan Zifliog˘lu, "TV Celebrity Kardashian Lashes Out at Turkish Cosmo Cover," *Hürriyet Daily News* (April 12, 2011), http://www.hurriyetdailynews.com/n.php?n=american-tv-personality-angry-for-her-ghotos-on-turkish-magazine-2011-04-12, accessed May 10, 2011; David Carr, "Romance in *Cosmo*'s World Is Translated in Many Ways," *New York Times* (May 26, 2002), www.nytimes.com, accessed May 26, 2002.
8. Milton Rokeach, *The Nature of Human Values* (New York: Free Press, 1973).
9. Sang-Pil Han and Sharon Shavitt, "Persuasion and Culture: Advertising Appeals in Individualistic and Collectivistic Societies," *Journal of Experimental Social Psychology* 30 (1994): 326–50.
10. Chisaki Watanabe, "Japanese Parents Embrace Ultra-Secure Children's Park," *Philadelphia Inquirer* (September 4, 2006): A2.
11. Jay Alabaster and Ryan Nakashima, "Japanese Comforted or Cramped in Evacuee Shelters," MSNBC.com (April 19, 2011), http://www.msnbc.msn.com/id/42672467/ns/world_news-asia-pacific/t/japanese-comforted-or-cramped-evacuee-shelters/, accessed May 10, 2011.
12. Jon Littlefield and Julie L. Ozanne, "Socialization into Consumer Culture: Hunters Learning to Be Men," *Consumption Markets & Culture* 14, no. 4 (2011): 333–60.
13. Carolyn A. Lin, "Cultural Values Reflected in Chinese and American Television Advertising," *Journal of Advertising* 30 (Winter 2001): 83–94.
14. George J. McCall and J. L. Simmons, *Social Psychology: A Sociological Approach* (New York: Free Press, 1982).
15. Deborah Ball, "Women in Italy Like to Clean but Shun the Quick and Easy: Convenience Doesn't Sell When Bathrooms Average Four Scrubbings a Week," *Wall Street Journal* (April 25, 2006): A1.
16. Arundhati Parmar, "Out from Under," *Marketing News* (July 21, 2003): 9–10.
17. Jim Yardley, "No Spitting on the Road to Olympic Glory, Beijing Says," *New York Times* (April 17, 2007), www.nytimes.com, accessed April 17, 2007.
18. Donald E. Vinson, Jerome E. Scott, and Lawrence R. Lamont, "The Role of Personal Values in Marketing and Consumer Behavior," *Journal of Marketing* 41 (April 1977): 44–50; John Watson, Steven Lysonski, Tamara Gillan, and Leslie Raymore, "Cultural Values and Important Possessions: A Cross-Cultural Analysis," *Journal of Business Research* 55 (2002): 923–31.
19. Pascale Quester, Michael Beverland, and Francis Farrelly, "Brand-Personal Values Fit and Brand Meanings: Exploring the Role Individual Values Play in Ongoing Brand Loyalty in Extreme Sports Subcultures," *Advances in Consumer Research* 33, no. 1 (2006): 21–28.
20. Jennifer Aaker, Veronica Benet-Martinez, and Jordi Garolera, "Consumption Symbols as Carriers of Culture: A Study of Japanese and Spanish Brand Personality Constructs," *Journal of Personality & Social Psychology* 81, no. 3 (2001): 492–508.

21. Milton Rokeach, *Understanding Human Values* (New York: Free Press, 1979); see also J. Michael Munson and Edward McQuarrie, "Shortening the Rokeach Value Survey for Use in Consumer Research," in Michael J. Houston, ed., *Advances in Consumer Research* 15 (Provo, UT: Association for Consumer Research, 1988): 381–86.

22. B. W. Becker and P. E. Conner, "Personal Values of the Heavy User of Mass Media," *Journal of Advertising Research* 21 (1981): 37–43; Vinson, Scott, and Lamont, "The Role of Personal Values in Marketing and Consumer Behavior."

23. Craig J. Thompson and Maura Troester, "Consumer Value Systems in the Age of Postmodern Fragmentation: The Case of the Natural Health Microculture," *Journal of Consumer Research* 28 (March 2002): 550–71.

24. Sharon E. Beatty, Lynn R. Kahle, Pamela Homer, and Shekhar Misra, "Alternative Measurement Approaches to Consumer Values: The List of Values and the Rokeach Value Survey," *Psychology & Marketing* 2 (1985): 181–200; Lynn R. Kahle and Patricia Kennedy, "Using the List of Values (LOV) to Understand Consumers," *Journal of Consumer Marketing* 2 (Fall 1988): 49–56; Lynn Kahle, Basil Poulos, and Ajay Sukhdial, "Changes in Social Values in the United States During the Past Decade," *Journal of Advertising Research* 28 (February–March 1988): 35–41; see also Wagner A. Kamakura and Jose Alfonso Mazzon, "Value Segmentation: A Model for the Measurement of Values and Value Systems," *Journal of Consumer Research* 18 (September 1991): 28; Jagdish N. Sheth, Bruce I. Newman, and Barbara L. Gross, *Consumption Values and Market Choices: Theory and Applications* (Cincinnati, OH: South-Western, 1991).

25. Thomas J. Reynolds and Jonathan Gutman, "Laddering Theory, Method, Analysis, and Interpretation," *Journal of Advertising Research* (February–March 1988): 11–34; Beth Walker, Richard Celsi, and Jerry Olson, "Exploring the Structural Characteristics of Consumers' Knowledge," in Melanie Wallendorf and Paul Anderson, eds., *Advances in Consumer Research* 14 (Provo, UT: Association for Consumer Research, 1986): 17–21; Tania Modesto Veludo-de-Oliveira, Ana Akemi Ikeda, and Marcos Cortez Campomar, "Laddering in the Practice of Marketing Research: Barriers and Solutions," *Qualitative Market Research: An International Journal* 9, no. 3 (2006): 297–306. For a recent critique of this technique, cf. Elin Brandi Sørenson and Søren Askegaard, "Laddering: How (Not) to Do Things with Words," *Qualitative Market Research: An International Journal* 10, no. 1 (2007): 63–77.

26. This example was adapted from Michael R. Solomon, Gary Bamossy, and Søren Askegaard, *Consumer Behaviour: A European Perspective*, 2nd ed. (London: Pearson Education Limited, 2002).

27. "25 Years of Attitude," *Marketing Tools* (November–December 1995): 38–39.

28. www.hiphopcapital.com, accessed February 16, 2013.

29. Marc Spiegler, "Marketing Street Culture: Bringing Hip-Hop Style to the Mainstream," *American Demographics* (November 1996): 29–34.

30. Elizabeth M. Blair, "Commercialization of the Rap Music Youth Subculture," *Journal of Popular Culture* 27 (Winter 1993): 21–34; Basil G. Englis, Michael R. Solomon, and Anna Olofsson, "Consumption Imagery in Music Television: A Bi-Cultural Perspective," *Journal of Advertising* 22 (December 1993): 21–34.

31. Craig Thompson and Gokcen Coskuner-Balli, "Countervailing Market Responses to Corporate Co-optation and the Ideological Recruitment of Consumption Communities," *Journal of Consumer Research* 34 (August 2007): 135–52.

32. Grant McCracken, "Culture and Consumption: A Theoretical Account of the Structure and Movement of the Cultural Meaning of Consumer Goods," *Journal of Consumer Research* 13 (June 1986): 71–84.

33. Alisa Gould-Simon, "How Fashion Retailers Are Redefining E-Commerce with Social Media," Mashable.com (March 7, 2011), http://mashable.com/2011/03/07/fashion-retailers-social-e-commerce/, accessed April 28, 2011.

34. Richard A. Peterson, "The Production of Culture: A Prolegomenon," in Richard A. Peterson, ed., *The Production of Culture, Sage Contemporary Social Science Issues* 33 (Beverly Hills, CA: Sage, 1976); Elizabeth C. Hirschman, "Resource Exchange in the Production and Distribution of a Motion Picture," *Empirical Studies of the Arts* 8, no. 1 (1990): 31–51; Michael R. Solomon, "Building Up and Breaking Down: The Impact of Cultural Sorting on Symbolic Consumption," in J. Sheth and E. C. Hirschman, eds., *Research in Consumer Behavior* (Greenwich, CT: JAI Press, 1988): 325–51. For a study that looked at ways consumers interact with marketers to create cultural meanings, cf. Lisa Peñaloza, "Consuming the American West: Animating Cultural Meaning and Memory at a Stock Show and Rodeo," *Journal of Consumer Research* 28 (December 2001): 369–98. Cf. also Markus Giesler, "Conflict and Compromise: Drama in Marketplace Evolution," *Journal of Consumer Research* 34 (April 2007): 739–53.

35. Richard A. Peterson and D. G. Berger, "Entrepreneurship in Organizations: Evidence from the Popular Music Industry," *Administrative Science Quarterly* 16 (1971): 97–107.

36. *Ben Sisario, "In Beyoncé Deal, Pepsi Focuses on Collaboration," New York Times* (December 9, 2012), http://www.nytimes.com/2012/12/10/business/media/in-beyonce-deal-pepsi-focuses-on-collaboration.html?smid=tw-nytimesmusic&seid=auto&_r=1&, accessed February 16, 2013.

37. Paul M. Hirsch, "Processing Fads and Fashions: An Organizational Set Analysis of Cultural Industry Systems," *American Journal of Sociology* 77, no. 4 (1972): 639–59; Russell Lynes, *The Tastemakers* (New York: Harper & Brothers, 1954); Michael R. Solomon, "The Missing Link: Surrogate Consumers in the Marketing Chain," *Journal of Marketing* 50 (October 1986): 208–19.

38. Howard S. Becker, "Arts and Crafts," *American Journal of Sociology* 83 (January 1987): 862–89.

39. Herbert J. Gans, "Popular Culture in America: Social Problem in a Mass Society or Social Asset in a Pluralist Society?" in Howard S. Becker, ed., *Social Problems: A Modern Approach* (New York: Wiley, 1966).

40. http://www.thomaskinkadeonline.com/?gclid=CO65vf7XvbUCFVGf4Ao dSGYArg, accessed February 16, 2013; Karen Breslau, "Paint by Numbers," *Newsweek* (May 13, 2002): 48.

41. Martin Forstenzer, "In Search of Fine Art Amid the Paper Towels," *New York Times on the Web* (February 22, 2004), www.nytimes.com.

42. Luca M. Visconti, John F. Sherry Jr., Stefania Borghini, and Laurel Anderson, "Street Art, Sweet Art? Reclaiming the 'Public' in Public Place," *Journal of Consumer Research* 37, no. 3 (2010): 511–29.

43. Annetta Miller, "Shopping Bags Imitate Art: Seen the Sacks? Now Visit the Museum Exhibit," *Newsweek* (January 23, 1989): 44.

44. Kim Foltz, "New Species for Study: Consumers in Action," *New York Times* (December 18, 1989): A1.

45. Arthur A. Berger, *Signs in Contemporary Culture: An Introduction to Semiotics* (New York: Longman, 1984).

46. Michiko Kakutani, "Art Is Easier the 2d Time Around," *New York Times* (October 30, 1994): E4.

47. www.geico.com/about/commercials/music/cavemen, accessed June 25, 2009.

48. Brooks Barnes and Suzanne Vranica, "Why Advertising's Cavemen Are Going Totally Hollyrock," *Wall Street Journal* (March 5, 2007): B1; Nina M. Lentini, "Doh! Looks Like 7-Eleven Stores May Get Homered," *Marketing Daily* (March 30, 2007), www.mediapost.com, accessed March 30, 2007.

49. Michael R. Solomon and Basil G. Englis, "Reality Engineering: Blurring the Boundaries Between Marketing and Popular Culture," *Journal of Current Issues & Research in Advertising* 16, no. 2 (Fall 1994): 1–17.

50. Austin Bunn, "Not Fade Away," *New York Times* (December 2, 2002), www.nytimes.com, accessed December 2, 2002.

51. Marc Santora, "Circle the Block, Cabby, My Show's On," *New York Times* (January 16, 2003), www.nytimes.com, accessed January 16, 2003; Wayne Parry, "Police May Sell Ad Space," *Montgomery Advertiser* (November 20, 2002): A4.

52. This process is described more fully in Michael R. Solomon, *Conquering Consumerspace: Marketing Strategies for a Branded World* (New York: AMACOM, 2003); cf. also T. Bettina Cornwell and Bruce Keillor, "Contemporary Literature and the Embedded Consumer Culture: The Case of Updike's Rabbit," in Roger J. Kruez and Mary Sue MacNealy, eds., *Empirical Approaches to Literature and Aesthetics: Advances in Discourse Processes* 52 (Norwood, NJ: Ablex, 1996), 559–72; Monroe Friedman, "The Changing Language of a Consumer Society: Brand Name Usage in Popular American Novels in the Postwar Era," *Journal of Consumer Research* 11 (March 1985): 927–37; Monroe Friedman, "Commercial Influences in the Lyrics of Popular American Music of the Postwar Era," *Journal of Consumer Affairs* 20 (Winter 1986): 193.

53. Stuart Elliott, "Leaving Behind Malibu in Search of a New Dream Home," *New York Times* (February 6, 2013), http://www.nytimes.com/2013/02/07/business/media/barbie-to-sell-her-malibu-dreamhouse.html?_r=0, accessed February 17, 2013.

54. Niall Firth, "Japanese 3D Singing Hologram Hatsune Miku Becomes Nation's Strangest Pop Star," *Mail Online* (November 12, 2010), http://www.dailymail.co.uk/sciencetech/article-1329040/Japanese-3D-singinghologram-Hatsune-Miku-nations-biggest-pop-star.html, accessed April 28, 2011.

55. Stuart Elliott, "Expanding Line of Dunder Mifflin Products Shows Success in Reverse Product Placement," *New York Times* (November 23, 2012), http://mediadecoder.blogs.nytimes.com/2012/11/23/expanding-line-of-dunder-mifflin-products-shows-success-in-reverse-product-placement/, accessed February 17, 2013.

56. Mark J. Miller, "Hologram Virtual Performances Put Dead Celebs on the Comeback Trail," *Brandchannel* (June 19, 2012), http://www.brandchannel.com/home/post/2012/06/19/Hologram-Virtual-Performances-061912.aspx, accessed February 17, 2013.

57. Erica Orden, "This Book Brought to You by . . .," *Wall Street Journal* (April 26, 2011), http://professional.wsj.com/article/SB100014240527 48704132220457628537 2092660548.html?mg=reno-WallStreetJournal, accessed April 28, 2011.

58. Joseph Plambeck, "Product Placement Grows in Music Videos," *New York Times* (July 5, 2010), http://www.nytimes.com/2010/07/06/business/media/06adco.html, accessed November 3, 2013.

59. Jennifer Sokolowsky, "Germany's Food Hotel: A La Carte Blanche for Brands," *BrandChannel* (November 25, 2010), http://www.brandchannel.com/home/post/2010/11/25/Germany-Food-Hotel.aspx, accessed April 28, 2011.

60. Fara Warner, "Why It's Getting Harder to Tell the Shows from the Ads," *Wall Street Journal* (June 15, 1995): B1.

61. Quoted in Simona Covel, "Bag Borrow or Steal Lands the Role of a Lifetime, Online Retailer Hopes to Profit from Mention in 'Sex and the City,'" *Wall Street Journal* (May 28, 2008), http://online.wsj.com/article/SB121184149016921095.html?mod=rss_media_and_marketing, accessed May 28, 2008; www.bagborroworsteal.com, accessed June 25, 2009.

62. "Top 10 Product Placements in First Half of '07," *Marketing Daily* (September 26, 2007), www.mediapost.com, accessed September 26, 2007.

63. Brian Steinberg, "Getting Izze to Izzie on 'Grey's Anatomy': How PepsiCo Placed Beverage Brand in ABC Show without Paying a Thing," *Advertising Age* (April 1, 2009), www.adage.com, accessed April 1, 2009.

64. Claire Atkinson, "Ad Intrusion Up, Say Consumers," *Advertising Age* (January 6, 2003): 1.

65. Motoko Rich, "Product Placement Deals Make Leap from Film to Books," *New York Times* (June 12, 2006), www.nytimes.com, accessed June 12, 2006.

66. Cristel Antonia Russell, "Investigating the Effectiveness of Product Placements in Television Shows: The Role of Modality and Plot Connection Congruence on Brand Memory and Attitude," *Journal of Consumer Research* 29 (December 2002): 306–18; Denise E. DeLorme and Leonard N. Reid, "Moviegoers' Experiences and Interpretations of Brands in Films Revisited," *Journal of Advertising* 28, no. 2 (1999): 71–90; Barbara B. Stern and Cristel A. Russell, "Consumer Responses to Product Placement in Television Sitcoms: Genre, Sex and Consumption," *Consumption, Markets & Culture* 7 (December 2004): 371–94.

67. Louise Story, "More Marketers Are Grabbing the Attention of Players During Online Games," *New York Times* (January 24, 2007), www.nytimes.com, accessed January 24, 2007; Shankar Gupta, "King of the Advergames," www.mediapost.com, accessed December 22, 2006; "Plinking," *Fast Company* (April 2007): 31; Sarah Sennott, "Gaming the Ad," *Newsweek* (January 31, 2005): E2; "Advertisements Insinuated into Video Games," *New York Times* (October 18, 2004), www.nytimes.com, accessed October 18, 2004; Jack Loechner, "Advergaming," *Research Brief* (October 24, 2007), http://www.mediapost.com/publications/?fa=Articles.showArticle&art_aid=69570&passFuseAction=PublicationsSearch.showSearchReslts&art_searched=&page_number=0, accessed September 13, 2011; Tim Zuckert, "Become One with the Game, Games Offer Brands a Unique Way to Be the Entertainment—Not Just Sponsor It," *Advertising Age* (June 16, 2008), www.adage.com, accessed June 16, 2008.

68. Barry Meier and Andrew Martin, "Real and Virtual Firearms Nurture a Marketing Link," *New York Times* (December 24, 2012), http://www.nytimes.com/2012/12/25/business/real-and-virtual-firearms-nurture-marketing-link.html, accessed February 17, 2013.

69. Nick Wingfield, "Sony's PS3 to Get In-Game Ads," *Wall Street Journal* (June 4, 2008): B7; Jeffrey Bardzell, Shaowen Bardzell, and Tyler Pace, *Player Engagement and In-Game Advertising* (November 23, 2008), http://class.classmatandread.net/pp/oto.pdf, accessed September 13, 2011.

70. Cf. Karen V. Fernandez and John L. Lastovicka, "Making Magic: Fetishes in Contemporary Consumption," *Journal of Consumer Research* (August 2011), 38, no. 2: 278–99.

71. Jiang Yuwei, Angela Cho, and Rashmi Adaval, "The Unique Consequences of Feeling Lucky: Implications for Consumer Behavior," *Journal of Consumer Psychology* 19, no. 2 (2009): 171–84.

72. Molly O'Neill, "As Life Gets More Complex, Magic Casts a Wider Spell," *New York Times* (June 13, 1994): A1.

73. Thomas Fuller, "Thais Look to the Supernatural," *New York Times* (December 28, 2010), http://www.nytimes.com/2010/12/29/world/asia/29iht-ghost29.html?_r=1&scp=5&sq=Thailand&st=cse, accessed April 28, 2011.

74. Susannah Meadows, "Who's Afraid of the Big Bad Werewolf?," *Newsweek* (August 26, 2002): 57.

75. Conrad Phillip Kottak, "Anthropological Analysis of Mass Enculturation," in Conrad P. Kottak, ed., *Researching American Culture* (Ann Arbor: University of Michigan Press, 1982), 40–74; cf. also Teresa Davis and Olga Kravets, "Bridges to Displaced Meaning: The Reinforcing Roles of Myth

76. and Marketing in Russian Vodka Labels," *Advances in Consumer Research* 32, no. 1 (2005): 480.

76. Eric Ransdell, "The Nike Story? Just Tell It!" *Fast Company* (January–February 2000): 44.

77. Joseph Campbell, *Myths, Dreams, and Religion* (New York: E. P. Dutton, 1970).

78. Claude Lévi-Strauss, *Structural Anthropology* (Harmondsworth, England: Peregrine, 1977).

79. Tina Lowrey and Cele C. Otnes, "Consumer Fairy Tales and the Perfect Christmas," in Cele C. Otnes and Tina M. Lowrey, eds., *Contemporary Consumption Rituals: A Research Anthology* (Mahwah, NJ: Lawrence Erlbaum, 2003).

80. Merissa Marr, "Fairy-Tale Wedding? Disney Can Supply the Gown," *Wall Street Journal* (February 22, 2007): B1; Laura M. Holson, "For $38,000, Get the Cake, and Mickey, Too," *New York Times Web* (May 24, 2003), www.nytimes.com, accessed May 24, 2003.

81. Elizabeth C. Hirschman, "Movies as Myths: An Interpretation of Motion Picture Mythology," in Jean Umiker-Sebeok, ed., *Marketing and Semiotics: New Directions in the Study of Signs for Sale* (Berlin: Mouton de Gruyter, 1987), 335–74.

82. See William Blake Tyrrell, "Star Trek as Myth and Television as Mythmaker," in Jack Nachbar, Deborah Weiser, and John L. Wright, eds., *The Popular Culture Reader* (Bowling Green, OH: Bowling Green University Press, 1978): 79–88.

83. Bernie Whalen, "Semiotics: An Art or Powerful Marketing Research Tool?" *Marketing News* (May 13, 1983): 8.

84. Eduardo Porter, "New 'Got Milk?' TV Commercials Try to Entice Hispanic Teenagers," *Wall Street Journal* (December 28, 2001), www.wsj.com, accessed December 28, 2001.

85. See Dennis W. Rook, "The Ritual Dimension of Consumer Behavior," *Journal of Consumer Research* 12 (December 1985): 251–64; Mary A. Stansfield Tetreault and Robert E. Kleine, III, "Ritual, Ritualized Behavior, and Habit: Refinements and Extensions of the Consumption Ritual Construct," in Marvin Goldberg, Gerald Gorn, and Richard W. Pollay, eds., *Advances in Consumer Research* 17 (Provo, UT: Association for Consumer Research, 1990): 31–38.

86. Nancy Keates and Charles Passy, "Tailgating, Inc.," *Wall Street Journal* (August 29, 2003), www.wsj.com, accessed August 29, 2003; www.tailgating.com, accessed June 23, 2009.

87. Deborah Ball, "British Drinkers of Guinness Say They'd Rather Take It Slow," *Wall Street Journal* (May 22, 2003), www.wsj.com, accessed May 22, 2003.

88. Karl Greenberg, "BBDO: Successful Brands Become Hard Habit for Consumers to Break," *Marketing Daily* (May 14, 2007), www.mediapost.com, accessed May 14, 2007.

89. Virginia Postrel, "From Weddings to Football, the Value of Communal Activities," *New York Times* (April 25, 2002), www.nytsimes.com, accessed April 25, 2002.

90. Paul Henry and Marylouise Caldwell, "Headbanging as Resistance or Refuge: A Cathartic Account," *Consumption, Markets, and Culture*, 10 (June 2007): 159–74.

91. Kim Foltz, "New Species for Study: Consumers in Action," *New York Times* (December 18, 1989): A1.

92. For a study that looked at updated wedding rituals in Turkey, see Tuba Ustuner, Güliz Ger, and Douglas B. Holt, "Consuming Ritual: Reframing the Turkish Henna-Night Ceremony," in Stephen J. Hoch and Robert J. Meyers, eds., *Advances in Consumer Research* 27 (Provo, UT: Association for Consumer Research, 2000): 209–14.

93. For a study that looked specifically at rituals pertaining to birthday parties, see Cele Otnes and Mary Ann McGrath, "Ritual Socialization and the Children's Birthday Party: The Early Emergence of Gender Differences," *Journal of Ritual Studies* 8 (Winter 1994): 73–93.

94. www.OurWeddingDay.com, accessed June 23, 2011; "Poll: Weddings Get More Social," *Marketing Daily* (January 14, 2011), http://www.mediapost.com/publications/?fa=Articles.showArticle&art_aid=143017&nid=122685, accessed April 29, 2011; Karl Greenberg, "JC Penney Inks Deal with Wedding Site," *Marketing Daily* (March 27, 2009), www.mediapost.com, accessed March 27, 2009; Laura M. Holson, "For Funerals Too Far, Mourners Gather on the Web," *New York Times* (January 24, 2011), http://www.nytimes.com/2011/01/25/fashion/25death.html?_r=2&hp=&adxnnl=1&adxnnlx=1295960444-LJmi3sSA0KtI0cBEmmh+tw, accessed April 28, 2011.

95. Dennis W. Rook and Sidney J. Levy, "Psychosocial Themes in Consumer Grooming Rituals," in Richard P. Bagozzi and Alice M. Tybout, eds., *Advances in Consumer Research* 10 (Provo, UT: Association for Consumer Research, 1983): 329–33.

96. Quoted in Andrew Adam Newman, "Depilatory Market Moves Far Beyond the Short-Shorts Wearers," *New York Times* (September 14, 2007), www.nytimes.com, accessed September 14, 2007.

97. Diane Barthel, *Putting on Appearances: Gender and Advertising* (Philadelphia: Temple University Press, 1988).

98. Russell W. Belk, Melanie Wallendorf, and John F. Sherry, Jr., "The Sacred and the Profane in Consumer Behavior: Theodicy on the Odyssey," *Journal of Consumer Research* 16 (June 1989): 1–38; Jean-Sebastien Marcoux, "Escaping the Gift Economy," *Journal of Consumer Research* 36, no. 4 (December 2009): 671–85.

99. Markus Giesler and Mali Pohlmann, "The Anthropology of File Sharing: Consuming Napster as a Gift," in Punam Anand Keller and Dennis W. Rook, eds., *Advances in Consumer Research* 30 (Provo, UT: Association for Consumer Research 2003); Markus Giesler, "Consumer Gift Systems," *Journal of Consumer Research* 33, no. 2 (2006): 283.

100. Jill G. Klein and Tina M. Lowrey, "Giving and Receiving Humanity: Gifts among Prisoners in Nazi Concentration Camps," *Advances in Consumer Research* 33, no. 1 (2006): 659.

101. Tina M. Lowrey, Cele C. Otnes, and Julie A. Ruth, "Social Influences on Dyadic Giving over Time: A Taxonomy from the Giver's Perspective," *Journal of Consumer Research* 30 (March 2004): 547–58; Russell W. Belk and Gregory S. Coon, "Gift Giving as Agapic Love: An Alternative to the Exchange Paradigm Based on Dating Experiences," *Journal of Consumer Research* 20 (December 1993): 393–417. See also Cele Otnes, Tina M. Lowrey, and Young Chan Kim, "Gift Selection for Easy and Difficult Recipients: A Social Roles Interpretation," *Journal of Consumer Research* 20 (September 1993): 229–44; Burcak Ertimur and Ozlem Sandikci, "Giving Gold Jewelry and Coins as Gifts: The Interplay of Utilitarianism and Symbolism," *Advances in Consumer Research* 32, no. 1 (2005).

102. Monica Gonzales, "Before Mourning," *American Demographics* (April 1988): 19.

103. Alf Nucifora, "'Tis the Season to Gift One's Best Clients," *Triangle Business Journal* (December 3, 1999): 14.

104. John F. Sherry, Jr., "Gift Giving in Anthropological Perspective," *Journal of Consumer Research* 10 (September 1983): 157–68.

105. Daniel Goleman, "What's Under the Tree? Clues to a Relationship," *New York Times* (December 19, 1989): C1; John F. Sherry, Jr., Mary Ann-McGrath, and Sidney J. Levy, "The Dark Side of the Gift," *Journal of Business Research* (1993): 225–44.

106. Colin Camerer, "Gifts as Economics Signals and Social Symbols," *American Journal of Sociology* 94 (Supplement 1988): 5, 180–214; Robert T. Green and Dana L. Alden, "Functional Equivalence in Cross-Cultural Consumer Behavior: Gift Giving in Japan and the United States," *Psychology & Marketing* 5 (Summer 1988): 155–68; Hiroshi Tanaka and Miki Iwamura, "Gift Selection Strategy of Japanese Seasonal Gift Purchasers: An Explorative Study," paper presented at the Association for Consumer Research, Boston, October 1994; cf. also Tonya Williams Bradford, "Intergenerationally Gifted Asset Dispositions," *Journal of Consumer Research* 36 (June 2009): 93–111.

107. See, for example, Russell W. Belk, "Halloween: An Evolving American Consumption Ritual," in Richard Pollay, Jerry Gorn, and Marvin Goldberg, eds., *Advances in Consumer Research* 17 (Provo, UT: Association for Consumer Research, 1990): 508–17; Melanie Wallendorf and Eric J. Arnould, "We Gather Together: The Consumption Rituals of Thanksgiving Day," *Journal of Consumer Research* 18 (June 1991): 13–31.

108. Bruno Bettelheim, *The Uses of Enchantment: The Meaning and Importance of Fairy Tales* (New York: Alfred A. Knopf, 1976).

109. Kenneth L. Woodward, "Christmas Wasn't Born Here, Just Invented," *Newsweek* (December 16, 1996): 71.

110. Aron O'Cass and Peter Clarke, "Dear Santa, Do You Have My Brand? A Study of the Brand Requests, Awareness and Request Styles at Christmas Time," *Journal of Consumer Behavior* 2 (September 2002): 37–53.

111. Theodore Caplow, Howard M. Bahr, Bruce A. Chadwick, Reuben Hill, and Margaret M. Williams, *Middletown Families: Fifty Years of Change and Continuity* (Minneapolis: University of Minnesota Press, 1982).

112. Angeline Close and George M. Zinkhan, "A Holiday Loved and Loathed: A Consumer Perspective of Valentine's Day," *Advances in Consumer Research* 33, no. 1 (2006): 356–65.

113. Arnold Van Gennep, *The Rites of Passage*, trans. Maika B. Vizedom and Shannon L. Caffee (London: Routledge & Kegan Paul, 1960; orig. published 1908); Michael R. Solomon and Punam Anand, "Ritual Costumes and Status Transition: The Female Business Suit as Totemic Emblem," in Elizabeth C. Hirschman and Morris Holbrook, eds., *Advances in Consumer Research* 12 (Washington, DC: Association for Consumer Research, 1995): 315–18.

114. Walter W. Whitaker, III, "The Contemporary American Funeral Ritual," in Ray B. Browne, ed., *Rites and Ceremonies in Popular Culture* (Bowling Green, OH: Bowling Green University Popular Press, 1980): 316–25. For an examination of funeral rituals, see Larry D. Compeau and Carolyn Nicholson, "Funerals: Emotional Rituals or Ritualistic Emotions,"

paper presented at the Association of Consumer Research, Boston, October 1994.

115. Samuel K. Bonsu and Russell W. Belk, "Do Not Go Cheaply into That Good Night: Death-Ritual Consumption in Asante, Ghana," *Journal of Consumer Research* 30 (June 2003): 41–55; cf also Stephanie O'Donohoe and Darach Turley, "Till Death Do Us Part? Consumption and the Negotiation of Relationships Following a Bereavement," *Advances in Consumer Research* 32, no. 1 (2005): 625–26.

116. Barry Bearak, "Dead Join the Living in a Family Celebration," *New York Times* (September 5, 2010), http://nytimes.com/2010/09/06/world/africa/06madagascar.html?scp=2&sq=madagascar&st=cse, accessed April 28, 2011.

117. "Queen Prompts Thailand to Restrict 'Coyote Ugly' Dance Troupes," *New York Times* (December 28, 2006), www.nytimes.com, accessed December 28, 2006.

118. J. C. Conklin, "Web Site Caters to Cowboy Fans by Selling Sweaty, Used Socks," *Wall Street Journal* (April 21, 2000), www.wsj.com, accessed April 21, 2000.

119. George E. Newman, Gil Diesendruck, and Paul Bloom, "Celebrity Contagion and the Value of Objects," *Journal of Consumer Research* 38, no. 2 (August 2011): 215–228.

120. Dan L. Sherrell, Alvin C. Burns, and Melodie R. Phillips, "Fixed Consumption Behavior: The Case of Enduring Acquisition in a Product Category," in Robert L. King, ed., *Developments in Marketing Science* 14 (1991): 36–40.

121. Anne Underwood, "Hoarders Pack It In," *Newsweek* (July 26, 2004): 12.

122. Russell W. Belk, "Acquiring, Possessing, and Collecting: Fundamental Processes in Consumer Behavior," in Ronald F. Bush and Shelby D. Hunt, eds., *Marketing Theory: Philosophy of Science Perspectives* (Chicago: American Marketing Association, 1982): 85–90.

123. Ruth Ann Smith, *Collecting as Consumption: A Grounded Theory of Collecting Behavior* (unpublished manuscript, Virginia Polytechnic Institute and State University, 1994): 14.

124. For a discussion of these perspectives, see Smith, *Collecting as Consumption*.

125. John Branch, "Yankees Grass Is Now a Brand," *New York Times* (March 21, 2009), www.nytimes.com/2009/03/22/sports/baseball/22grass.html?scp=1&sq=Yankees%20Grass%20Is%20Now%20a%20Brand&st=cse, accessed March 21, 2009.

126. Kottak, "Anthropological Analysis of Mass Enculturation."

127. Joan Kron, *Home-Psych: The Social Psychology of Home and Decoration* (New York: Clarkson N. Potter, 1983); Gerry Pratt, "The House as an Expression of Social Worlds," in James S. Duncan, ed., *Housing and Identity: Cross-Cultural Perspectives* (London: Croom Helm, 1981): 135–79; Michael R. Solomon, "The Role of the Surrogate Consumer in Service Delivery," *Service Industries Journal* 7 (July 1987): 292–307.

128. Grant McCracken, "'Homeyness': A Cultural Account of One Constellation of Goods and Meanings," in Elizabeth C. Hirschman, ed., *Interpretive Consumer Research* (Provo, UT: Association for Consumer Research, 1989): 168–84.

129. http://livingoprah.com/, accessed June 22, 2011; quoted in Jessica Grose, "Life in the Time of Oprah," *New York Times* (August 15, 2008), www.nytimes.com/2008/08/17/fashion/17oprah.html?scp=1&sq=Jessica%20Grose,%20%93Life%20in%20the%20Time%20of%20Oprah&st=cse, accessed August 17, 2008.

130. Emile Durkheim, *The Elementary Forms of the Religious Life* (New York: Free Press, 1915).

131. Susan Birrell, "Sports as Ritual: Interpretations from Durkheim to Goffman," *Social Forces* 60, no. 2 (1981): 354–76; Daniel Q. Voigt, "American Sporting Rituals," in Browne, ed., *Rites and Ceremonies in Popular Culture*.

132. Ronald W. Pimentel and Kristy E. Reynolds, "A Model for Consumer Devotion: Affective Commitment with Proactive Sustaining Behaviors," *Academy of Marketing Science Review* 5 (2004): 1.

133. Mark A. Stein, "Block That Snack," *New York Times* (February 4, 2007): 2.

134. Dean MacCannell, *The Tourist: A New Theory of the Leisure Class* (New York: Shocken Books, 1976).

135. Belk et al., "The Sacred and the Profane in Consumer Behavior."

136. Beverly Gordon, "The Souvenir: Messenger of the Extraordinary," *Journal of Popular Culture* 20, no. 3 (1986): 135–46.

137. Belk et al., "The Sacred and the Profane in Consumer Behavior"; Amber M. Epp and Linda L. Price, "The Storied Life of Singularized Objects: Forces of Agency and Network Transformation," *Journal of Consumer Research* 36, no. 5 (2010): 820–37.

138. Güliz Ger and Olga Kravets, "Rediscovering Sacred Times in the Mundane: Tea Drinking in Turkey," *Consuming Routines: Rhythms, Ruptures, and the Temporalities of Consumption*, International Workshop, European University Institute, Florence, Italy, May 3–5, 2007; cf. also Güliz Ger,

"Religion and Consumption: The Profane Sacred," *Advances in Consumer Research* 32, no. 1 (2005): 79–81.

139. Deborah Hofmann, "In Jewelry, Choices Sacred and Profane, Ancient and New," *New York Times* (May 7, 1989), www.nytimes.com, accessed October 11, 2007.

140. Lee Gomes, "Ramadan, a Month of Prayer, Takes on a Whole New Look," *Wall Street Journal* (December 4, 2002), www.wsj.com, accessed December 4, 2002.

141. Peter Gumbel, "Big Mac's Local Flavor," CNNmoney.com (May 2, 2008), http://money.cnn.com/2008/04/29/news/companies/big_macs_local.fortune/index.htm, accessed May 2, 2008; Geoffrey A. Fowler, "For Prosperity Burger, McDonald's Tailors Ads to Asian Tastes," *Wall Street Journal* (January 24, 2005), www.wsj.com, accessed January 24, 2005; Saritha Rai, "Tastes of India in U.S. Wrappers," *New York Times* (April 29, 2003), www.nytimes.com, accessed April 29, 2003; Gerard O'Dwyer, "McD's Cancels McAfrika Rollout," *Advertising Age* (September 9, 2002): 14; "McDonald's to Give $10 Million to Settle Vegetarian Lawsuit," *Wall Street Journal* (June 4, 2002), www.wsj.com, accessed June 4, 2002; "Packaging Draws Protest," *Marketing News* (July 4, 1994): 1.

142. Mariko Sanchanta and Yoree Koh, "Beefing Up McDonald's," *Wall Street Journal* (January 12, 2011), http://online.wsj.com/article/SB10001424052748703791904576075450692538030.html, accessed April 10, 2011.

143. Charles Onians, "By Toutatis! Asterix McDonald's Ad Irks French" (August 19, 2010), http://www.google.com/hostednews/afp/article/ALeqM5hmwaTJFdWfl0_J3N6qe2YA6Vximw, accessed April 28, 2011.

144. "McCurrywurst Time in Germany," *Burger Business* (February 18, 2013), http://www.burgerbusiness.com/?p=13289, accessed February 20, 2013.

145. For a discussion of this trend, see Russell W. Belk, "Hyperreality and Globalization: Culture in the Age of Ronald McDonald," *Journal of International Consumer Marketing* 8 (1995): 23–38.

146. "Bain Projects Global Luxury Goods Market Will Grow Overall by 10% in 2012, Though Major Structural Shifts in Market Emerge," Bain & Company (October 15, 2012), http://www.bain.com/about/press/press-releases/bain-projects-global-luxury-goods-market-will-grow-ten-percent-in-2012.aspx, accessed March 30, 2013.

147. Normandy Madden, "New GenerAsians Survey Gets Personal with Asia-Pacific Kids," *Advertising Age International* (July 13, 1998): 2.

148. Adam Thompson and Shai Oster, "NBA in China Gets Milk to Sell Hoops," *Wall Street Journal* (January 22, 2007): B1; "They All Want to Be Like Mike," *Fortune* (July 21, 1997): 51–53.

149. Emma Hall, "Volvo Parks Brits at the Drive-in Movie: 'Starlite' Promo Allows Locals to Soak up American Car Culture," *Ad Age Global* (July 7, 2010), http://adage.com/article/global-news/marketing-volvo-parks-brits-drive-movie/144824/, accessed April 28, 2011.

150. Alan Riding, "Only the French Elite Scorn Mickey's Debut," *New York Times* (April 13, 1992): A1.

151. Elisabeth Rosenthal, "Buicks, Starbucks and Fried Chicken, Still China?" *New York Times* (February 25, 2002), www.nytimes.com, accessed February 25, 2002.

152. Special Report, "Brands in an Age of Anti-Americanism," *BusinessWeek* (August 4, 2003): 69–76.

153. Lily Dong and Kelly Tian, "The Use of Western Brands in Asserting Chinese National Identity," *Journal of Consumer Research* 36 (October 2009).

154. David Murphy, "Christmas's Commercial Side Makes Yuletide a Hit in China," *Wall Street Journal* (December 24, 2002), www.wsj.com, accessed December 24, 2002.

155. This example courtesy of Professor Russell Belk, University of Utah, personal communication, July 25, 1997.

156. James Hookway, "In Vietnam, Fast Food Acts Global, Tastes Local," *Wall Street Journal* (March 12, 2008), http://online.wsj.com/article/Sb120528509133029135.html?mod=mm_hs_marketing_strat, accessed March 12, 2008.

157. Miriam Jordan, "India Decides to Put Its Own Spin on Popular Rock, Rap and Reggae," *Wall Street Journal* (January 5, 2000), www.wsj.com, accessed January 5, 2000; Rasul Bailay, "Coca-Cola Recruits Paraplegics for 'Cola War' in India," *Wall Street Journal* (June 10, 1997).

158. Rick Wartzman, "When You Translate 'Got Milk' for Latinos, What Do You Get?" *Wall Street Journal* (June 3, 1999).

159. Charles Newbery, "Coke Goes Native with New Soft Drink," *Advertising Age* (December 1, 2003): 34.

160. Eric J. Arnould and Richard R. Wilk, "Why Do the Natives Wear Adidas: Anthropological Approaches to Consumer Research," *Advances in Consumer Research* 12 (Provo, UT: Association for Consumer Research, 1985): 748–52.

161. John F. Sherry, Jr., and Eduardo G. Camargo, "May Your Life Be Marvelous: English Language Labelling and the Semiotics of Japanese Promotion," *Journal of Consumer Research* 14 (1987): 174–88.

162. Bill Bryson, "A Taste for Scrambled English," *New York Times* (July 22, 1990): 10; Rose A. Horowitz, "California Beach Culture Rides Wave of Popularity in Japan," *Journal of Commerce* (August 3, 1989): 17; Elaine Lafferty, "American Casual Seizes Japan: Teen-agers Go for N.F.L. Hats, Batman and the California Look," *Time* (November 13, 1989): 106.

163. Lucy Howard and Gregory Cerio, "Goofy Goods," *Newsweek* (August 15, 1994): 8.

164. Abe Sauer, "'Asianate Yourself' with Amoy. Actually, Please Don't," *Brandchannel* (March 9, 2011), http://www.brandchannel.com/home/post/2011/03/09/Asianate-Yourself-With-Amoy.aspx, accessed April 30, 2011; http://www.amoy.nl/web/#/home, accessed May 11, 2011.

165. www.beinggirl.com/en_US/home.jsp, accessed June 25, 2009; Carol Hymowitz, "Marketers Focus More on Global 'Tribes' than on Nationalities," *Wall Street Journal* (December 10, 2007): B1.

166. Theodore Levitt, *The Marketing Imagination* (New York: Free Press, 1983).

167. Geoffrey A. Fowler, "Main Street, H.K.: Disney Localizes Mickey to Boost Its Hong Kong Theme Park," *Wall Street Journal* (January 23, 2008): B1; Merissa Marr, "Small World: Disney Rewrites Script to Win Fans in India; China, Latin America Are Also in Turnaround," *Wall Street Journal* (June 11, 2007): A1; Laura M. Holson, "The Feng Shui Kingdom," *New York Times* (April 25, 2005), www.nytimes.com, accessed April 25, 2005; Keith Bradsher, "Disneyland for Chinese Offers a Soup and Lands in a Stew," *New York Times* (June 17, 2005): A1; Paulo Prada and Bruce Orwall, "Disney's New French Theme Park Serves Wine—and Better Sausage," *Wall Street Journal* (March 12, 2002), www.wsj.com, accessed March 12, 2002.

168. David Barboza and Brooks Barnes, "Disney Plans Lavish Park in Shanghai," *New York Times* (April 7, 2011), http://www.nytimes.com/2011/04/08/business/media/08disney.html?pagewanted=1&_r=1&ref=business, accessed April 10, 2011.

169. Terry Clark, "International Marketing and National Character: A Review and Proposal for an Integrative Theory," *Journal of Marketing* 54 (October 1990): 66–79.

170. Geraldo Samor, Cecilie Rohwedder, and Ann Zimmerman, "Innocents Abroad? Walmart's Global Sales Rise as It Learns from Mistakes; No More Ice Skates in Mexico," *Wall Street Journal* (May 16, 2006): B1.

171. Marc Gobé, *Emotional Branding: The New Paradigm for Connecting Brands to People* (New York: Allworth Press, 2001).

172. Norihiko Shirouzu, "Snapple in Japan: How a Splash Dried Up," *Wall Street Journal* (April 15, 1996): B1.

173. Glenn Collins, "Chinese to Get a Taste of Cheese-Less Cheetos," *New York Times* (September 2, 1994): D4.

174. http://carlgene.com/blog/2012/02/45-mandarin-sentences-with-chinese-characteristics/; http://www.oddee.com/item_97732.aspx; http://www.buzzfeed.com/nataliemorin/chinese-signs-that-got-seriously-lost-in-tranlsation.

175. Adam Wooten, "International Business: In global airline marketing, idioms must be handled carefully," *Deseret News* (January 1, 2011), http://www.deseretnews.com/article/705363635/In-global-airline-marketing-idioms-must-be-handled-carefully.html?pg=all.

176. For a case study that explores how the Guinness brand does this, cf. John Amis and Michael L. Silk, "Transnational Organization and Symbolic Production: Creating and Managing a Global Brand," *Consumption Markets & Culture* 13, no. 2 (2010): 159–79.

177. Martin McCarty, Martin I. Horn, Mary Kate Szenasy, and Jocelyn Feintuch, "An Exploratory Study of Consumer Style: Country Differences and International Segments," *Journal of Consumer Behaviour* 6, no. 1 (2007): 48.

178. Julie Skur Hill and Joseph M. Winski, "Goodbye Global Ads: Global Village Is Fantasy Land for Marketers," *Advertising Age* (November 16, 1987): 22.

179. Geert Hofstede, *Culture's Consequences: Comparing Values, Behaviors, Institutions, and Organizations across Nations* (Thousand Oaks, CA: Sage, 2001). For a recent critique of this instrument, cf. Aron M. Levin, Irwin P. Levin, and Michael P. Cook, "Measuring and Accounting for Cross-Country Response Biases in Marketing Food and Drink Products," *International Journal of Consumer Marketing*, in press.

180. Adapted from "What Are Hofstede's Five Cultural Dimensions?" www.geert-hofstede.com, accessed February 17, 2013.

181. Clyde H. Farnsworth, "Yoked in Twin Solitudes: Canada's Two Cultures," *New York Times* (September 18, 1994): E4.

182. Hill and Winski, "Goodbye Global Ads."

183. MTV Europe, personal communication, 1994; see also Teresa J. Domzal and Jerome B. Kernan, "Mirror, Mirror: Some Postmodern Reflections

on Global Advertising," *Journal of Advertising* 22 (December 1993): 1–20; Douglas P. Holt, "Consumers' Cultural Differences as Local Systems of Tastes: A Critique of the Personality-Values Approach and an Alternative Framework," *Asia Pacific Advances in Consumer Research* 1 (1994): 1–7.

184. Douglas B. Holt, John A. Quelch, and Earl L. Taylor, "How Global Brands Compete," *Harvard Business Review* (September 2004): 68–75.

185. "Three people gored during Pamplona bull run," *The Independent U.K.* (July 13, 2013), http://www.independent.co.uk/news/world/europe/three-people-gored-during-pamplona-bull-run-8705591.html.

186. http://www.channel4.com/info/press/news/research-shows-product-placement-can-shift-brand-perception.

187. Jack Neff, "Clearasil Marches into Middle-School Classes, *Advertising Age* (November 2006): 8; Bill Pennington, "Reading, Writing and Corporate Sponsorships," *New York Times on the Web* (October 18, 2004); Caroline E. Mayer, "Nurturing Brand Loyalty: With Preschool Supplies, Firms Woo Future Customers and Current Parents," *Washington Post* (October 12, 2003): F1.

188. Karlene Lukovitz, "New-Product Hits Tap In-Home, Health Trends," *Marketing Daily* (April 1, 2011), http://www.mediapost.com/publications/?fa=Articles.showArticle&art_aid=147857&nid=125349, accessed April 10, 2011.

189. Suzanne Kapner, "U.S. TV Shows Losing Potency around World," *New York Times* (January 2, 2003), www.nytimes.com, accessed January 2, 2003; "Big Brother Nipple Sparks Outrage," *BBCNews* (September 10, 2004), www.bbcnews.com, accessed September 10, 2004.

190. Liz Gooch, "A Reality Show Where Islam Is the Biggest Star," *New York Times* (July 28, 2010), http://www.nytimes.com/2010/07/29/world/asia/29imam.html?scp=1&sq=islamic%20reality%20show&st=cse, accessed April 10, 2011.

Chapter 4 • Consumer and Social Well-Being

Chapter Objectives

When you finish reading this chapter you will understand why:

1. Ethical business is good business.

2. Marketers have an obligation to provide safe and functional products as part of their business activities.

3. Consumer behavior impacts directly on major public policy issues that confront our society.

4. Consumer behavior can be harmful to individuals and to society.

Source: Art Allianz/Shutterstock.

Tracy wheels her cart down the grocery aisles, absent-mindedly throwing in the usual fill-ins she always buys on her weekly trip. She reaches for a box of Tide laundry detergent and is about to toss it into the cart when she stops herself in midair: She just remembered her resolution to think a little more about the environmental impact of the cleaning products and other groceries she's bringing into the house. When her son Jon came home from school and asked her how she was helping to preserve the world for the next generation, she was embarrassed that she couldn't answer him. From the mouths of babes! Time for this 33-year-old to learn a lesson.

Might as well start with detergents—Tracy thinks about that news report she saw last week about the excessive use of chemicals and other additives that are bad for the water supply, not to mention the huge amount of fresh water American consumers waste just to wash their clothes.

Tracy has always bought Tide; it's the same product her mother used for years. Now as she takes a closer look in the detergent section she notices a lot of other brands, including some "tree-hugger" ones she's never seen before like Dropps, Ecos, Method, and Seventh Generation. When she looks at each box, Tracy notices that some carry different "ecolabels" including one issued by the U.S. Environmental Protection Agency called DfE (Design for the Environment). Hmmm. . . . Tide doesn't have that on its box. On the other hand, the Tide package does recommend just using cold water instead of hot for the laundry, and Procter & Gamble now sells a concentrated version that doesn't require as much soap to do the wash. Tracy also notices that the "green" brands seem to cost a bit more. Today every penny counts—how much of her precious grocery budget is worth sacrificing for a slightly less sudsy wash? All of these choices are really confusing. Maybe she should stick with what she knows and let others worry about the environment. Then again, what will she tell Jon the next time he asks about how "green" she is?

Business Ethics and Consumer Rights

OBJECTIVE 1
Ethical business is good business.

Mainstream U.S. shoppers like Tracy increasingly choose "green" products that are better for the environment. On the other hand, there has been a lot of hype about "the green revolution"; since the recession, consumers are a lot more cost-conscious. To add to the confusion, even well-intended shoppers have trouble figuring out which brands really are better. It's practically a full-time job to sort out all the competing claims. One solution is for independent rating agencies to develop labeling systems that the shopper can use to decide among options—but even these systems can be overwhelming. There are more than 430 eco-label systems worldwide, and about a quarter of those are in North America. The U.S. Government is trying to encourage businesses and consumers to select green cleaning products; the EPA even signed a promotion agreement with NASCAR to raise awareness of the DfE label. In addition to DfE certification and other rating systems the cleaning industry sponsors, a few manufacturers and retailers even offer their own labels, such as SC Johnson's Greenlist and Eco-Scale by the Whole Foods grocery chain. Other major brands, like Procter & Gamble's Tide, sell highly concentrated versions that are formulated to work with cold water. It's tough to make apples-to-apples comparisons, and these competing systems threaten to "throw the baby out with the bath water" if consumers like Tracy throw up their hands and just stick to what they know. Is it possible for marketers to "do good" and still "do well"; can they provide profits and still do what's right for customers and the environment?

The answer is simple: Ethical business is good business. A Conference Board survey of U.S. consumers found that the most important criterion they use to form opinions about corporations is social responsibility in such areas as labor practices, business ethics, and environmental issues.[1] Consumers think better of the products a firm sells when the organization behaves ethically.[2]

Business ethics are rules of conduct that guide actions in the marketplace; these are the standards against which most people in a culture judge what is right and what is wrong, good or bad. These universal values include honesty, trustworthiness, fairness, respect, justice, integrity, concern for others, accountability, and loyalty.

Of course, notions of right and wrong differ among people, organizations, and cultures. Some businesses believe it is OK for salespeople to pull out all the stops to persuade customers to buy, even if this means they mislead them; other firms feel that anything less than total honesty with customers is terribly wrong. Because each culture has its own set of values, beliefs, and customs, companies around the world define ethical business behaviors quite differently. For example, one study found that because of differences in values (as we discussed in Chapter 3), Mexican firms are less likely to have formal codes of ethics and they are more likely to bribe public officials than are U.S. or Canadian companies. However, because of different attitudes about work and interpersonal relationships, these companies also are more likely to treat lower-level employees better than do their northern neighbors.[3]

These cultural differences certainly influence whether business practices such as bribery are acceptable. Since 1977 the Foreign Corrupt Practices Act makes it illegal for American executives to bribe foreigners to gain business. The Organization for Economic Cooperation and Development (OECD), to which most industrialized countries belong, also outlaws bribery. Still, these practices are common in many countries. In Japan, it's called *kuroi kiri* (black mist); in Germany, it's *schmiergeld* (grease money), whereas Mexicans refer to *la mordida* (the bite), the French say *pot-de-vin* (jug of wine), and Italians speak of the *bustarella* (little envelope). They're all talking about *baksheesh*, the Middle Eastern term for a "tip" to grease the wheels of a transaction. Giving "gifts" in exchange for getting business from suppliers or customers is acceptable and even expected in many countries.

Regardless of whether they do it intentionally, some marketers do violate their bonds of trust with consumers. In some cases, these actions are actually illegal, as when a manufacturer deliberately mislabels the contents of a package. Or a retailer may adopt a "bait-and-switch" selling strategy that lures consumers into the store when it offers inexpensive products with the sole intent to get them to switch to higher-priced goods.

In other cases, marketing practices have detrimental effects on society even though they are not explicitly illegal. Some companies erect billboards for alcohol and tobacco products in low-income neighborhoods; others sponsor commercials that objectify women as they pander to male viewers.

Needs and Wants: Do Marketers Manipulate Consumers?

One of the most common and stinging criticisms of marketing is that companies convince consumers they "need" many material things, and that they will be unhappy and inferior people if they do not have these "necessities." The issue is a complex one and is certainly worth considering: Do marketers give people what they want, or do they tell people what they *should* want?

Who controls the market, companies or consumers? This question is even more complicated as new ways of buying, having, and being are invented every day. It seems that the "good old days" of *marketerspace*—a time when companies called the shots and decided what they wanted their customers to know and do—are dead and gone. Many people now feel empowered to choose how, when, or if they will interact with corporations as they construct their own **consumerspace**. In this new environment, individuals dictate to companies the types of products they want and how, when, and where (or even if) they want to learn about those products. In turn, companies need to develop and leverage brand equity in bold new ways to attract the loyalty of these consumer "nomads." People still "need" companies—but in new ways and on their own terms. As we'll see throughout this book, profound changes in consumer behavior are influencing how people search for product information and evaluate alternative brands. In the brave new world of consumerspace, we have much greater potential to shape our own marketing destinies.[4]

Do Marketers Create Artificial Needs?

The marketing system has come under fire from both ends of the political spectrum. On the one hand, some members of the Religious Right believe that marketers contribute to the moral breakdown of society when they present images of hedonistic pleasure and encourage the pursuit of secular humanism at the expense of spirituality and the environment. A coalition of religious groups called the National Religious Partnership for the Environment claims that gas-guzzling cars and other factors that cause climate change are contrary to Christian moral teachings about protecting people and the Earth.[5]

On the other hand, some leftists argue that the same deceitful promises of material pleasure function to buy off people who would otherwise be revolutionaries working to change the system.[6] According to this argument, the marketing system creates demand—demand that only its products can satisfy.

A Response. As we saw in Chapter 1, *a need is a basic biological motive; a want represents one way that society has taught to satisfy the need.* For example, thirst is a biologically based need. Marketers teach us to want Coca-Cola to satisfy that thirst rather than, say, goat's milk. Thus, the need is already there; marketers simply recommend ways to satisfy it. A basic objective of marketing is to create awareness that needs exist, not to create needs.

Are Advertising and Marketing Necessary?

More than 50 years ago, the social critic Vance Packard wrote, "Large-scale efforts are being made, often with impressive success, to channel our unthinking habits, our purchasing decisions, and our thought processes by the use of insights gleaned from psychiatry and the social sciences."[7] The economist John Kenneth Galbraith charged that radio and television are important tools to accomplish this manipulation of the masses. Because consumers don't need to be literate to use these media, repetitive and compelling communications can reach almost everyone. This criticism may even be more relevant to online communications, where a simple click delivers a world of information to us.

Some people charge that marketers arbitrarily link products to desirable social attributes, so they foster a materialistic society where what we own defines our value as a person. One influential critic even argued that the problem is that we are not materialistic *enough*: We do not sufficiently value goods for the utilitarian functions they deliver but instead focus on the irrational value of goods for what they symbolize. According to this view, for example, "Beer would be enough for us, without the additional promise that in drinking it we show ourselves to be manly, young at heart, or neighborly. A washing machine would be a useful machine to wash clothes, rather than an indication that we are forward-looking or an object of envy to our neighbors."[8]

This ad was created by the American Association of Advertising Agencies to counter charges that ads create artificial needs.

Source: Used with permission of American Association of Advertising Agencies.

A Response. *Products meet existing needs, and advertising only helps to communicate their availability.*[9] The *economics of information* perspective we discussed in Chapter 2 regards advertising as an important source of consumer information.[10] This view emphasizes the economic cost of the time we spend to search for products. Accordingly, advertising is a service for which consumers are willing to pay because the information it provides reduces their search time.

Do Marketers Promise Miracles?

Advertising leads us to believe that products have magical properties (see Chapter 3); the things we buy will transform our lives. We will be beautiful, successful, perhaps even live forever. In this respect, advertising functions as mythology does in primitive societies: It provides simple, anxiety-reducing answers to complex problems.

A Response. *Advertisers simply do not know enough about people to manipulate them.* Consider that the failure rate for new products ranges from 40 to 80 percent. Although people think that advertisers have an endless source of magical tricks and scientific techniques to manipulate them, in reality the industry is successful when it tries to sell good products and unsuccessful when it sells poor ones.[11]

Materialism: Are You What You Own?

During World War II, members of "cargo cults" in the South Pacific literally worshiped cargo they salvaged from crashed aircraft or that washed ashore from ships. They believed that their ancestors piloted the ships and planes that passed near their islands, so they tried to attract them to their villages. They went so far as to construct fake planes from straw to lure the real ones overhead![12]

We may not worship products to that extent, but many of us certainly work hard to attain our vision of the good life, which abounds in material comforts. Most young people can't imagine a life without cell phones, MP3 players, and other creature comforts. In fact, we can think of marketing as a system that provides certain standards of living to consumers. To some extent, then, the standards of living we expect and desire influence our lifestyles, either by personal experience or as a result of the affluent characters we see on TV in "reality shows" like *Keeping Up With the Kardashians,* in movies, and in the pages of *Vogue* or *GQ.*[13] Exhibit A: The popular bumper sticker that reads "He Who Dies with the Most Toys Wins."

Our possessions play a central role in our lives, and our desire to accumulate them shapes our value systems. **Materialism** refers to the importance people attach to worldly possessions.[14] We sometimes take the bounty of products and services for granted, until we remember how recent this abundance is. For example, in 1950, two of five American homes did not have a telephone, and in 1940 only half of all households had indoor plumbing.

Materialistic values tend to emphasize the well-being of the individual versus the group, which may conflict with family or religious values. That conflict may help to explain why people with highly material values tend to be less happy.[15] Furthermore, materialism is highest among early adolescents (12 to 13 years old) in comparison to children or late adolescents—perhaps it's no coincidence that this is the age group that also has the lowest level of self-esteem.[16]

Materialists are more likely to value possessions for their status and appearance-related meanings, whereas those who do not emphasize this value tend to prize products that connect them to other people or that provide them with pleasure when they use them.[17] As a result, high materialists prefer expensive products that they publicly consume. A study comparing specific items that low versus high materialists value found that people who were non-materialists cherished items with personal significance, such as a mother's wedding gown, picture albums, a rocking chair from childhood, or a garden. In contrast, high materialists preferred prestige goods such as jewelry, china, or a vacation home.[18]

Materialistic people appear to link more of their self-identity to products. One study found that when people who score high on this value fear the prospect of dying, they form even stronger connections to brands.[19] Another study reported that consumers who are "love-smitten" with their possessions tend to use these relationships to compensate for loneliness and a lack of affiliation with social networks.[20] Yet another found that materialists tend to value a product before they buy it because they believe it will make them happy, but their satisfaction with it diminishes after the purchase when they realize this didn't happen.[21]

Nonetheless, consumers' appetites for material goods continue to grow—especially in developing markets where luxury goods reign supreme. One major industry analyst estimates steady growth in sales of luxury products in Europe and the United States, but with huge growth in China as well as solid gains in new markets such as Azerbaijan, Brazil, Indonesia, Kazakhstan, Malaysia, Mexico, South Africa, Turkey, and Vietnam. Asian consumers now account for more than 50 percent of global luxury sales.[26]

Even so, consumers' thinking about the importance of accumulating products, as well as which products are important, clearly is changing. In the United States, the big political debates about the so-called "1 percenters" at the top of the pyramid whose

Marketing Pitfall

In the early 1980s, the Romanian Communist government broadcast the American TV show *Dallas* to point out the decadence of Western capitalism. This strategy backfired: The devious (but rich!) J. R. Ewing became a revered icon in parts of Eastern Europe and the Middle East. A popular tourist attraction outside of Bucharest includes a big white log gate that announces (in English) the name, "Southfork Ranch."[22] Western "decadence" appears to be infectious.[23]

After the downfall of communism, Eastern Europeans emerged from a long winter of deprivation into a springtime of abundance. The picture is not all rosy, however. It's not easy for many people who live in **transitional economies** to attain consumer goods. This term describes countries such as China, Portugal, and Romania that struggle as they adapt from a controlled, centralized economy to a free-market system. In these situations, rapid changes occur in social, political, and economic dimensions as the populace suddenly is exposed to global communications and external market pressures.[24]

Some of the consequences of the transition to capitalism include a loss of confidence and pride in the local culture, as well as alienation, frustration, and increased stress as citizens sacrifice their leisure time to work ever harder to buy consumer goods. The yearning for the trappings of Western material culture is perhaps most evident in parts of Eastern Europe, where citizens who threw off the shackles of communism now have direct access to coveted consumer goods from the United States and Western Europe—if they can afford them. One analyst observed, "As former subjects of the Soviet empire dream it, the American dream has very little to do with liberty and justice for all and a great deal to do with soap operas and the Sears Catalogue."[25]

incomes rise while the rest of the country struggles to fuel the fire. In addition, our definition of luxury is changing, especially among affluent younger people.

One advertising executive argues that today an upscale grocery store like Whole Foods in its own way sells luxury products, but with a different twist. In his words, "Instead of cold, intimidating retail vaults awash in tastefully, restrained colors, Whole Foods provides a hip, eclectic sort of vibe that feels like a Berkeley revival with no credit limit. Funky music blares, dreadlocked associates staff checkout aisles, and shoppers are a mix of artsy-looking moms, retirees in pricey but well-cushioned running shoes, and a constant stream of suits taking a quick break from corporate America while awaiting a $15 turkey sub and some curried sweet potato couscous."

Thus, materialists value (or perhaps even obsess about) the inherent qualities of what they buy, whether their purchases are diamonds or organic yogurt. One important dimension today is **provenance**: Shoppers are willing to pay more for an item when they know exactly where it comes from, and they are assured that "real people" have thoughtfully selected the things from which they choose. This process of **curation**, which used to refer to an expert who carefully chooses pieces to include in a museum exhibit, now applies to a range of consumer products such as food, clothing, and travel. Whole Foods personalizes its inventory as it features the names of store employees on chalkboards throughout the store and often specifies the farms that grew the products.[27] Table 4.1 summarizes some of the similarities and differences between "old" and "new" materialism:

OBJECTIVE 2
Marketers have an obligation to provide safe and functional products as part of their business activities.

Consumers' Rights and Product Satisfaction

Fifty-four million dollars for a pair of missing pants? A judge in Washington, D.C., made headlines when he filed a $54 million lawsuit against his neighborhood dry cleaner because it lost a pair of his pinstriped suit pants. He claimed that a local

TABLE 4.1	Old Versus New Materialism	
	Neiman Marcus	**WHOLE FOODS** MARKET
Same	● Offers rare items not available anywhere else ● Plays at the top price range in its category ● Located in affluent zip codes ● Occasional shopper is there for a taste of the good life	
Different	● Core shoppers are affluent, and like to flaunt it ● Exclusive and intimidating ● High-style design ● Prefers designer labels ● Anonymous service ● Price-conscious consumers look for sales ● Indifferent ● Bespoke ● Geometric ● Spare	● Core shoppers are affluent, but prefer to hide it ● Egalitarian and welcoming ● High-touch design ● Prefers unknown producers ● Personally identified service ● Price-conscious consumers look for private label ● Humane ● Intentionally mismatched ● Kinetic ● Piled high

Source: Michael Pavone, "How Whole Foods Became the Luxury Brand of Millennials," *Fastcoexist.com* (February 23, 2012), http://www.fastcoexist.com/1679351/how-whole-foods-became-the-luxury-brand-of-millennials, accessed March 1, 2013.

consumer protection law entitled him to thousands of dollars for each day over nearly four years in which signs at the shop promised "same day service" and "satisfaction guaranteed." The suit dragged on for several months, but at the end of the day the plaintiff went home with empty pockets.[28] And some people claim we have too many lawsuits in this country!

If you're not happy with a product or service, what can you do about it? You have three possible courses of action (though sometimes you can take more than one):[29]

1 **Voice response**—You can appeal directly to the retailer for redress (e.g., a refund).
2 **Private response**—You can express your dissatisfaction to friends and boycott the product or the store where you bought it.
3 **Third-party response**—Like the pantless judge, you can take legal action against the merchant, register a complaint with the Better Business Bureau, or write a letter to the newspaper.

In one study, business majors wrote complaint letters to companies. When the firm sent a free sample in response, this action significantly improved how the students felt about it. This didn't happen, however, when they *only* received a letter of apology—but no swag. Even worse, students who got no response reported an even more negative image than before. This shows that *any* kind of response is better than none.[31]

A number of factors influence which route we choose. People are more likely to take action if they're dissatisfied with expensive products such as household durables, cars, and clothing than for problems with inexpensive products.[32] Ironically, consumers who are satisfied with a store in general are more likely to complain if they experience something bad; they take the time to complain because they feel connected to the store. And, if a company resolves the problem, a customer feels even better about it than if she hadn't complained in the first place![33] The moral: Although nobody likes criticism, organizations should encourage people to complain for these reasons:

1 They get the chance to correct the situation.
2 They will avoid an escalating problem that results when consumers take to social media to let others know they've been treated badly. People are more likely to spread the word about unresolved negative experiences to their friends than they are to boast about positive occurrences.

The Tangled Web

From ihatestarbucks .com to boycottwalmart .meetup.com, irritated customers have launched hundreds of **gripe sites** to air their grievances against companies. The practice is so widespread that some firms proactively buy unflattering domain names to keep other people from buying them. Xerox, for example, registered xeroxstinks.com, xeroxcorporationsucks.com, and ihatexerox.net. One study identified about 20,000 domain names that end in "sucks.com." About one-third of these sites are registered to none other than the companies they slam; owners include Walmart Stores, Coca-Cola, Toys "R" Us, Target, and Whole Foods Market.[30]

* * * * * * * * * * * * * *

Source: © Michael Matthews/Alamy.

Marketing Opportunity

Many analysts who study consumer satisfaction, or those who design new products or services to increase it, recognize that it is crucial to understand how people actually interact with their environment to identify potential problems. To do so, they typically conduct **focus groups**, in which a small set of consumers comes into a facility to try a new item while company personnel observe them from behind a mirror. However, some researchers advocate a more up-close-and-personal approach that allows them to watch people in the actual environment where they consume the product. This perspective originated in the Japanese approach to **total quality management (TQM)**—a complex set of management and engineering procedures that aims to reduce errors and increase quality.

To help companies achieve more insight, researchers go to the **gemba**, which to the Japanese means "the one true source of information." According to this philosophy, it's essential to send marketers and designers to the precise place where consumers use the product or service rather than to ask laboratory subjects to use it in a simulated environment.

Figure 4.1 illustrates this idea in practice. Host Foods, which operates food concessions in major airports, sent a team to the gemba—in this case, an airport cafeteria—to identify problem areas. Employees watched as customers entered the facility, and then followed them as they inspected the menu, procured silverware, paid, and found a table. The findings were crucial to Host's redesign of the facility. For example, the team identified a common problem that many people traveling solo experience: the need to put down one's luggage to enter the food line and the feeling of panic you get because you're not able to keep an eye on your valuables when you get your meal. This simple insight allowed Host to modify the design of its facilities to improve a patron's line-of-sight between the food area and the tables.[37]

● ● ● ● ● ● ● ● ● ● ● ● ● ● ●

3 They collect valuable insights about customers' experiences that will (hopefully) help them to improve for future customers.

4 If the consumer does not believe that the store will respond to her complaint, she will be more likely to simply switch than fight as she just takes her business elsewhere.

Companies that score high in customer satisfaction often benefit from a big competitive advantage—especially when so many firms skimp on the attention they pay to customers. A 5-year study of customer satisfaction in the Canadian banking industry provides typical results: Banks that provided better service commanded a larger "share of wallet" than did others (i.e., their customers entrusted them with a larger proportion of their money).[34]

Even so, over half of the chief marketing officers (CMOs) who participated in a large survey reported that their companies *do not reward their employees* if customer satisfaction improves. More than one-third said they have no way to track word of mouth among customers, and less than three in ten said their firms are good at resolving customers' complaints.[35] What is wrong with this picture?

When a product doesn't work as we expect or turns out to be unsafe (like the recent spate of hazardous products from China, ranging from toothpaste to dog food), it's the understatement of the year to say we're not satisfied. In these situations, marketers must immediately take steps to reassure us, or they risk losing a customer for life. If the company confronts the problem truthfully, we are often willing to forgive and forget. But if the firm seems to be dragging its heels or covering up, our resentment grows. This is what happened during the BP oil spill or when a disabled Carnival cruise ship sat at sea in 2013 while 4,200 passengers and crew suffered through five days with no plumbing or electricity, and little food, in the glare of an unrelenting media spotlight.[36]

Market Regulation

The subprime mortgage meltdown that led to the collapse of major investment banking and insurance companies such as Bear Stearns, Lehman Brothers, and AIG, as well as triggered The Great Recession of 2008 (and beyond), illustrates why many people look

Figure 4.1 GOING TO THE GEMBA

Source: © Quality Function Deployment Institute. Used with permission.

to governments and industry watchdogs to provide oversight and regulation rather than relying strictly on businesses to police themselves. Concern for the welfare of consumers has been an issue since at least the beginning of the 20th century, and activists continue to voice concerns about a range of issues such as child labor, exploitative advertising, and genetically engineered food.[38] Recent deaths due to salmonella-infected peanut butter and contaminated toothpaste add fuel to the fire.

Partly as a result of consumers' efforts, the U.S. government established many federal agencies to oversee consumer-related activities. These include the Department of Agriculture, the Federal Trade Commission, the Food and Drug Administration, the Securities and Exchange Commission, and the Environmental Protection Agency. After Upton Sinclair's 1906 book *The Jungle* exposed the awful conditions in the Chicago meatpacking industry, Congress was prompted to pass important pieces of legislation— the Pure Food and Drug Act in 1906 and the Federal Meat Inspection Act a year later— to protect consumers. A summary of some important consumer legislation enacted since that time appears in Table 4.2. You can find other information about consumer-related issues at consumerreports.org and cpsc.gov (the Consumer Product Safety Commission).

TABLE 4.2   Sample of Federal Legislation Intended to Enhance Consumers' Welfare

Year	Act	Purpose
1953	Flammable Fabrics Act	Prohibits the transportation of flammable fabrics across state lines.
1958	National Traffic and Safety Act	Creates safety standards for cars and tires.
1958	Automobile Information Disclosure Act	Requires automobile manufacturers to post suggested retail prices on new cars.
1966	Fair Packaging and Labeling Act	Regulates packaging and labeling of consumer products. (Manufacturers must provide information about package contents and origin.)
1966	Child Protection Act	Prohibits sale of dangerous toys and other items.
1967	Federal Cigarette Labeling and Advertising Act	Requires cigarette packages to carry a warning label from the Surgeon General.
1968	Truth-in-Lending Act	Requires lenders to divulge the true costs of a credit transaction.
1969	National Environmental Policy Act	Established a national environmental policy and created the Council on Environmental Quality to monitor the effects of products on the environment.
1972	Consumer Products Safety Act	Established the Consumer Product Safety Commission to identify unsafe products, establish safety standards, recall defective products, and ban dangerous products.
1975	Consumer Goods Pricing Act	Bans the use of price maintenance agreements among manufacturers and resellers.
1975	Magnuson-Moss Warranty-Improvement Act	Creates disclosure standards for consumer product warranties and allows the Federal Trade Commission to set policy regarding unfair or deceptive practices.
1990	The Nutrition Labeling and Education Act	Reaffirms the legal basis for the Food and Drug Administration's new rules on food labeling and establishes a timetable for the implementation of those rules. Regulations covering health claims became effective May 8, 1993. Those pertaining to nutrition labeling and nutrient content claims went into effect May 8, 1994.
1998	Internet Tax Freedom Act	Established a moratorium on special taxation of the Internet, including taxation of access fees paid to America Online and other Internet Service Providers.
2010	Dodd-Frank Wall Street Reform and Consumer Protection Act	Prompted by the recession that began in 2008, intends to promote the financial stability of the United States by improving accountability and transparency in the financial system, to end "too big to fail," to protect the American taxpayer by ending bailouts, and to protect consumers from abusive financial services practices.

Marketing Pitfall

Advertisers, retailers, and manufacturers typically try to police themselves to ensure that their messages and products are not harmful or inaccurate. In addition to good intentions, they have a very practical reason to do so: They don't want governments to do it for them. Indeed, sometimes these efforts even seem to go a bit over the top. Consider, for example, a ruling by the National Advertising Division (NAD) of the Council of Better Business Bureaus, which is one of these industry watchdogs. Acting on a complaint by rival Kimberly-Clark, Procter & Gamble must add little flecks of cartoon toilet paper to the backsides of its Charmin cartoon bears in future ads for its toilet paper. Although P&G supported its claim that Charmin leaves "fewer pieces behind" than the Cottonelle brand (and showed the results of its test on the brand's Web site), the NAD decided that the test "did not accurately reflect the results consumers normally see and experience."[40]

The Food and Drug Administration (FDA) polices advertising claims as well as the contents of edible products and pharmaceuticals, and its efforts have been more aggressive under the Obama administration. For example, as part of an FDA crackdown on consumer drug advertising, Bayer HealthCare Pharmaceuticals launched a $20 million **corrective advertising** campaign for Yaz, the most popular birth control pill in the United States. This term means that the company must inform consumers that previous messages were wrong or misleading. The TV commercials, which ran during primetime shows like *Grey's Anatomy* and on cable networks, warn that nobody should take Yaz hoping that it will also cure pimples or premenstrual syndrome. Bayer was required to run these ads to correct previous messages after regulators decided the previous ads overstated the drug's ability to improve women's moods and clear up acne.[39]

However, many regulatory issues are a lot more important than flecks of toilet paper, and they require active monitoring by policymakers. For example, a hot button topic right now involves efforts to curb child obesity by encouraging advertisers to limit the messages they send to kids about foods that are high in sodium, saturated fat, and added sugars. The Obama administration issued a set of voluntary guidelines, and it's likely that most companies will comply with these suggestions, which will affect commercials on about 1,700 television programs. The guidelines stipulate that food products targeted to children ages 2 to 17 would have to provide a "meaningful contribution" to a healthy diet and would have to meet limits for harmful ingredients (e.g., no trans fats allowed).[41] Table 4.3 lists major U.S. regulatory agencies and what they do.

Consumerism

"Absolut Impotence." So reads a parody of a vodka ad created by Adbusters, a nonprofit organization that advocates for "the new social activist movement of the information age." The editor of the group's magazine argues that America is no longer a country, but rather a multitrillion-dollar brand subverted by corporate agendas. He claims that "America™" is no different from McDonald's, Marlboro, or General Motors.[42]

Adbusters sponsors numerous initiatives, including Buy Nothing Day and TV Turnoff Week, that try to discourage rampant commercialism. These efforts, along with biting ads and commercials that lampoon advertising messages, are examples of

TABLE 4.3 US Regulatory Agencies and Responsibilties	
Regulatory Agency	**Responsibilities**
Consumer Product Safety Commission (CPSC)	Protects the public from potentially hazardous products. Through regulation and testing programs, the CPSC helps firms make sure their products won't harm customers.
Environmental Protection Agency (EPA)	Develops and enforces regulations aimed at protecting the environment. Such regulations have a major impact on the materials and processes that manufacturers use in their products and thus on the ability of companies to develop products.
Federal Communications Commission (FCC)	Regulates telephone, radio, and television. FCC regulations directly affect the marketing activities of companies in the communications industries, and they have an indirect effect on all firms that use broadcast media for marketing communications.
Federal Trade Commission (FTC)	Enforces laws against deceptive advertising and product labeling regulations. Marketers must constantly keep abreast of changes in FTC regulations to avoid costly fines.
Food and Drug Administration (FDA)	Enforces laws and regulations on foods, drugs, cosmetics, and veterinary products. Marketers of pharmaceuticals, over-the-counter medicines, and a variety of other products must get FDA approval before they can introduce products to the market.
Interstate Commerce Commission (ICC)	Regulates interstate bus, truck, rail, and water operations. The ability of a firm to efficiently move products to its customers depends on ICC policies and regulation.

V1: THE CLASSIC BLACKSPOT SNEAKER

culture jamming; a strategy to disrupt efforts by the corporate world to dominate our cultural landscape. The movement believes that "culture jamming" will change the way information flows; the way institutions wield power; the way TV stations are run; and the way the food, fashion, automobile, sports, music, and culture industries set their agendas.[43] The *Culture Jammers Manifesto* proclaims opposition to the "mind-polluters": "On the rubble of the old culture, we will build a new one with non-commercial heart and soul."[44]

Although some in corporate America may dismiss these extreme sentiments as the ravings of a lunatic fringe, their proponents deserve to be taken seriously. The recent scandals involving such corporate icons as BP, AIG, Enron, Martha Stewart, Arthur Andersen, and Bear Stearns fueled a growing bonfire of mistrust and skepticism among the consuming public.

President John F. Kennedy ushered in the modern era of consumerism with his "Declaration of Consumer Rights" in 1962. These include the right to safety, the right to be informed, the right to redress, and the right to choice. The 1960s and 1970s were a time of consumer activism as consumers began to organize to demand better-quality products (and to boycott companies that did not provide them).

The publication of books such as Rachel Carson's *Silent Spring* in 1962, which attacked the irresponsible use of pesticides, and Ralph Nader's *Unsafe at Any Speed* in 1965, which exposed safety defects in General Motors' Corvair automobile, prompted these movements. Many consumers have a vigorous interest in consumer-related issues, ranging from environmental concerns such as global warming and climate change, toxic waste, and so on, to excessive violence and sex on television or in the lyrics of popular rock and rap songs. Recent controversies surrounding "shock jocks" such as Don Imus or Glenn Beck, who use the public airwaves to hurl insults about racial or religious groups, illustrate that people take these issues very seriously.

Indeed, some consumer researchers are themselves organizing, not only to study but also to rectify what they see as pressing social problems in the marketplace. This perspective is called *participatory action research (PAR)* or **transformative consumer research (TCR)**. It promotes research projects that include the goal of helping people or bringing about social change. Scientists who subscribe to this perspective view consumers as collaborators who work with them to realize this change rather than as a "phenomenon" upon which to conduct research. Adherents of TCR work with at-risk populations, such as children, the disadvantaged, and the disabled, or on such topics as materialism, consumption of dangerous products, and compulsive consumption.[46]

To protest against what the organization claims are Nike's unfair labor practices, Adbusters sells its own Blackspot sneakers. They are made from hemp in a Portuguese factory where workers receive pay higher than the country's minimum wage and where many employees belong to a union.[45]

Source: Image courtesy of adbusters.org.

CB AS I SEE IT

Professor Julie Ozanne, *Virginia Tech*

If you want to work to make the world a better place, then it is essential to understand consumers' behavior. Consumption lies at the heart of the most important problems facing the global community. In economically developed countries, we are drowning in a sea of things that are depleting our limited global resources at an alarming rate. We are overconsuming food and raising a generation of overweight and unhealthy children. We are engaging in risky consumption behaviors such as smoking, drinking, and gambling. Yet most of the people in the world face limited consumption opportunities and struggle to meet even basic nutritional needs.

Transformative Consumer Research is a new movement of consumer researchers who want to improve consumer well-being. Transformative consumer researchers engage in rigorous research to understand the nature of these pressing social problems. But then they seek to move outside the university to forge alliances with external stakeholders who can build programs of social change to improve the quality of life. Consumer researchers stand in a unique position because they understand and respect the interests of both consumers and businesses. Thus, they have the potential to act as honest brokers working with consumer interest groups, makers of public policy, and business leaders to foster positive social transformation.

This is an exciting time in which to create new models of business and new forms of consumption that are more sustainable and can strengthen our communities. Nobel Peace Prize winner Muhammad Yunis envisioned offering microcredit loans to poor consumers who wanted to start their own businesses, which is a new model of consumer financing that has literally pulled millions of people out of poverty. New models of consumption are also being created. Paris encourages bike-sharing by distributing bikes throughout the city, and does not charge for the first half-hour of rental, so that short trips are free. Similarly, car-sharing, in which a fleet of cars is collectively owned and used, has spread to 600 cities worldwide.

My own research examines how the sharing of possessions can build and strengthen communities. For instance, toy-lending libraries operate similarly to book libraries by making toys available to children for a nominal fee. Networks of families form communities of sharing that become an important neighborhood resource for advice and support. Children get to enjoy a wide range of toys while learning important lessons, such as the pleasures of sharing and a respect for collective goods.

Social Marketing and Corporate Social Responsibility (CSR)

As the emerging TCR perspective shows, the field of consumer behavior can help to improve our lives as consumers.[47] **Social marketing** strategies use the techniques that marketers normally employ to sell beer or detergent to encourage positive behaviors such as increased literacy and to discourage negative activities such as drunk driving.[48] Many researchers help to evaluate or create public policies to ensure that products are labeled accurately, to certify that people can comprehend important information in advertising messages, or to prevent children from being exploited by program-length toy commercials that masquerade as television shows. For example, American Airlines and the American Association of People with Disabilities (AAPD) are joining forces to create television commercials that portray people with disabilities in a positive light.[49]

Many firms today try to integrate **corporate social responsibility (CSR)** into their business models. CSR describes processes that encourage the organization to make a positive impact on the various stakeholders in its community including consumers, employees, and the environment. For example, the shoe company TOMS is well-known for its promise to give a needy child a pair of shoes for every pair it sells.

CSR is more than a good idea; it's also good business. Consumer research convincingly shows that, all things equal, people are likely to choose a brand that gives back to the community. **Cause marketing** is a popular strategy that aligns a company or brand with a cause to generate business and societal benefits. Indeed, one survey reported that three out of five consumers bought a product or service in the previous year because of its association with a cause. An executive observed, "As a whole, Americans do have a heightened sensitivity to how they can help make a difference, and if anything, (the recession) exacerbated the point that we live in a fragile society right now."[50]

Another recent survey reported that the top brands consumers purchase due to their affiliation with a cause are:[51]

1 Yoplait
2 Anything affiliated with breast cancer
3 **and 4** (tied) Susan G. Komen for the Cure & Newman's Own
5 General Mills
6 Yogurt in general
7 **and 8** (tied) P&G and RED
9 Boxtops for Education
10 **11 and 12** (tied) Kellogg's, Campbell's, & Girl Scouts
13 Dawn
14 Avon

OBJECTIVE 3

Consumer behavior impacts directly on major public policy issues that confront our society.

Major Policy Issues Relevant to Consumer Behavior

It's hard to divorce consumer behavior from most of what goes on around us. The field intersects with many of the big issues we read about and debate every day. These range from human rights and humane working conditions to the safety of what we eat, the future of our environment, and our relationships with governments, corporations, and other organizations. In this section, we'll introduce three major issues—without pretending to cover *all* of the important ones.

Data Privacy and Identity Theft

One of the biggest ethical issues many marketers face today relates to how much they can—or should—know about their customers. Virtually anyone who surfs the Web or who carries a cell phone (especially a smartphone with GPS capability) shares reams of personal information with all sorts of companies (whether they know it or not).

Clearly, we all benefit from technologies that allow companies to precisely tailor their messages to our needs based upon the product information we look for. Indeed, industry researchers report that a lot of people actually don't mind the ads if they are personally relevant.[52] But some consumer advocates argue that we pay a very high cost for this convenience. As the director of one consumer group phrased it in a complaint to the Federal Trade Commission, "Online consumers are being bought and sold like chattel."[53]

Are we for sale? In some sense, yes. If you surf the Web (and who doesn't today?), it's likely that someone is carefully tracking your clicks—the search items you Google, the sites you visit, perhaps even the comments you post on Facebook. Your digital actions have actual financial value, because of the industry called **real-time bidding**; an electronic trading system that sells ad space on the Web pages people click on at the very moment they visit them.

In the early days of the Internet, advertisers simply bought space on Web sites that generally matched the demographics of their target audience. Then they showed the same ad to everyone who came to the site—an inefficient approach people in the industry call "spray and pray." Today that picture has changed as companies develop complex algorithms that predict where consumers with specific profiles (e.g., "Asian-Americans who make over $100,000 a year, live in Los Angeles, and are in the market for a luxury car") will visit and serve up precisely tailored messages to these customers. By the way, these are not "live auctions" like you might see on eBay—they are conducted automatically on powerful computers that receive several million bids every second. Each auction typically takes less than 30 milliseconds. And, since not all customers are as likely to buy or to spend as much as are others, these algorithms attach different values to them so higher value customers command higher auction prices. As the CEO of one of these trading companies explained, "The first impression seen by a high-value person on the opening page of a major newspaper first thing in the morning has a different value than a user from China who is 12 and has been on the Web all day long playing games." The real-time bidding business is growing rapidly: Analysts estimate that by 2017, the American market alone will reach $8.3 billion.[54]

Identity theft occurs when someone steals your personal information and uses it without your permission. They may charge items on a credit card or perhaps access medical services via your health benefits. Identity theft is the most common consumer complaint according to the Federal Trade Commission. It accounts for almost 20 percent of all problems reported.[55] Experts estimate that approximately 15 million Americans fall victim to identity theft each year, with financial losses exceeding $50 billion. And, as any victim knows, the financial aspects are not the only pain points since cancelling credit cards or otherwise correcting the situation can result in huge hassles.

Identity thieves get more sophisticated every day. They used to be content with stealing wallets and "dumpster diving" to obtain account numbers. Today, we increasingly experience high-tech **phishing** scams where people receive fraudulent emails that ask them to supply account information, as well as **botnets** (a set of

This Brazilian ad seeks to raise awareness of predators on the internet who masquerade as kids.
Source: Advertising Agency: Intertotal Comunicação, Brazil
Executive Creative Director: Guga Almeida
Creative Director: Helder França
Art Director: Eder Pessoa
Copywriter: Carlos Augusto
Director: Jackson Carvalho.

computers that are penetrated by malicious software known as *malware* that allows an external agent to control their actions) that hijack millions of computers without any trace. Recently we've witnessed numerous hacks of corporate and government databases including Apple, Best Buy, *The New York Times*, Sony Pictures, and even NASA.

Locational privacy is a related issue. Every one of us who walks around with a phone transmits his or her approximate location, and those of us with GPS-enabled phones leave nothing to chance. In addition, many cars now have GPS devices that can share their location with a centralized service. We can purchase GPS trackers to keep tabs on our kids, aged relatives, or wayward pets. Some insurance companies offer steep discounts to drivers who use GPS tracking technology. The companies provide a small tracker in the car that reports driving habits and in some cases even whether the driver is cruising through unsafe neighborhoods. Other services allow anxious parents to track a teenager's driving and provide a "report card" on use of the family car.[56] A school district in Brazil goes a step farther: It requires 20,000 grade school students to wear uniforms embedded with GPS chips similar to those used in pet trackers. The chips automatically send parents a text message as soon as their children enter the school grounds, or if their children are more than 20 minutes late.[57]

For all intents and purposes in today's wired world, consumers can run, but we can't hide: If someone wants to know where we are or where we've been, the data are there for the asking. As with Web tracking, there is value here: We can easily identify by looking at hundreds or even thousands of reviews the best sushi place within a block of our current location, or perhaps get a heads up on that policeman with the radar gun who is hiding behind that billboard up the highway. However, this is a mixed blessing if this information gets into the wrong hands. Consumers need to make tough tradeoffs between convenience and constant surveillance.

Market Access

Many of us take for granted that we are free to shop anywhere we want or that we can easily learn about our purchase options—everything we need is just a click of a mouse away, right? In reality, however, large numbers of people can't make this claim. For one reason or another their **market access** (i.e., their ability to find and purchase goods and services) is limited due to physical, mental, economic, or social barriers.

Disabilities

Disabled people are the largest minority market in the United States. One in five American adults lives with a disability that interferes with daily life.[58] The Census Bureau reports that there are 54 million adults with disabilities who spend almost $200 billion annually, yet companies pay remarkably little attention to the unique needs of this vast group. Fully 11 million American adults have a condition that makes it difficult for them to leave home to shop, so they rely almost exclusively on catalogs and the Internet to purchase products. Many people have limited mobility and are unable to gain easy access to stores, entertainment venues, educational institutions, and other locations. Bodily limitations or disfigurements may result in real or imagined stigmatization, so self-concept and interpersonal relationships may be problematic.[59] People who rely upon wheelchairs for mobility often encounter barriers when they try to enter stores, move around the aisles, or enter dressing rooms that are too narrow to accommodate a chair. Others have mental illnesses, such as excessive anxiety in public places. These issues touch many of us; for example, 15 percent of Vietnam and 1991 Gulf War Veterans have been diagnosed with *PTSD (post-traumatic stress disorder)*, and 20 percent of veterans who served in Afghanistan and Iraq received care at a VA facility for the disorder since their return home. Large numbers of children also encounter difficulties with market access, whether offline or online.

This British social marketing campaign tries to change how people look at individuals with physical deformities.
Source: Courtesy of Changing Faces U.K. DDB, London; Photograph by Robert Wilson.

Net Profit

Virtual reality exposure therapy uses a program called "Virtual Iraq" to help soldiers with PTSD (post-traumatic stress disorder) who experience behavioral problems when they return home by recreating battle conditions so that therapists can help to manage the anxiety these memories provoke. Patients wear a head-mounted display, while the therapist controls the simulation—helicopters overhead, gunfire, or even a call to prayer.[62]

The good news is that technology holds the potential to improve market access. Here are a few exciting new developments:

● The touch screen is a breakthrough for people who have problems with motor skills. They no longer need to manipulate a mouse, keyboard, or pen to use programs. A device like the iPad makes *touch-to-speak technology* affordable and easy to use. For example, a person who is unable to speak can communicate his or her preferences for meals, activities, and so on just by touching the screen. Other apps amplify sounds for the hard-of-hearing, or even encourage children with motor skills disabilities to engage in physical therapy.[60] The LookTel Money Reader app makes it possible for blind people to pay for products in cash; it can "read money" and tell the person the value of the bills he or she holds.[61]

● Dating Web sites for singles with health problems allow people with an array of disabilities, including paralysis and multiple sclerosis, to find partners. Dating 4 Disabled caters to people with physical diseases, while NoLongerLonely focuses on those with mental illness. Sites like these and others allow users to be blunt and honest about their own issues and what they seek in a partner. One site was created by a man whose brother suffered from Crohn's disease. He observed, "He was a good-looking boy, but when do you tell a girl that you have a colostomy bag? The first date? The third? There's no good time."[63]

Food Deserts

The Department of Agriculture defines a **food desert** as a Census tract where 33 percent of the population or 500 people, whichever is less, live more than a mile from a grocery store in an urban area or more than 10 miles away in a rural area. Healthy food options in these communities are hard to find or are unaffordable. Researchers estimate that in the United States about 23.5 million people live in food deserts.

Limited access to healthy choices can lead to poor diets and higher levels of obesity and other diet-related diseases. More broadly, this *food insecurity* increases the number of low- and moderate-income families who struggle to purchase the diet they need to sustain a healthy and active life.[64]

Literacy

Media literacy refers to a consumer's ability to access, analyze, evaluate, and communicate information in a variety of forms, including print and non-print messages.[65]

Media literacy empowers people to be both critical thinkers and creative producers of an increasingly wide range of messages using image, language, and sound. This movement reminds us that we are bombarded with thousands of messages every day that espouse a particular point of view or try to persuade us to buy this or that. It's our job to critically evaluate this information and not everyone has the skills to do that. This task is even more difficult in the age of Google, where many of us assume that whatever comes up in a Google search or on Wikipedia is completely true and accurate (Hint: not by a long shot). As the tried-but-true phrase says, "*Caveat Emptor*"—let the buyer beware!

Unfortunately, some of us have an even bigger problem than evaluating the source of a message: We can't read it in the first place. The U.S. Education Department estimates that about 1 in 7 American adults are **functionally illiterate**.[66] This term describes a person whose reading skills are not adequate to carry out everyday tasks, such as reading the newspaper or the instructions on a pill bottle. Almost half of Americans read below a sixth grade level. This limitation impedes market access for a couple of reasons: First, the illiterate or "low literate" consumer is at a disadvantage because he or she encounters difficulty in learning about the best purchase options. Second, this person may experience feelings of shame and embarrassment and avoid market situations where he or she will be forced to reveal the inability to read a label or other written material.[67] Some of these people (whom researchers term *social isolates*) cope with the stigma of illiteracy by avoiding situations in which they will have to reveal this problem. They may choose not to eat at a restaurant with an unfamiliar menu, for example. Low-literate consumers rely heavily on visual cues, including brand logos and store layouts, to navigate in retail settings, but they often make mistakes when they select similarly packaged products (for example, brand line extensions). They also encounter problems with *innumeracy* (understanding numbers); many low-literate people have difficulty knowing, for example, whether they have enough money to purchase the items in their cart and unethical merchants may cheat them out of the correct amount of change. Not surprisingly, these challenges create an emotional burden for low-literate consumers, who experience stress, anxiety, fear, shame, and other negative emotions before, during, and after they shop.[68]

Sustainability and Environmental Stewardship

Kraft's experience illustrates the value of a *sustainable business model*. Sustainability is not just about "do-gooder" efforts that reduce a company's carbon footprint or the amount of plastic that goes into landfills. Indeed, about six out of every 10 companies that convert to a sustainable business model report that they have profited financially as well.[69] A **triple bottom-line orientation** refers to business strategies that strive to maximize return in three ways:

1 **The financial bottom line:** Provide profits to stakeholders.
2 **The social bottom line:** Return benefits to the communities where the organization operates.

This ad from The Slovak Republic underscores the growing priority consumers place upon organic foods.
Source: Courtesy of JANDL.

3 **The environmental bottom line:** Minimize damage to the environment or even improve natural conditions.

The U.S. Environmental Protection Agency (EPA) defines the concept this way: "**Sustainability** is based on a simple principle: Everything that we need for our survival and well-being depends, either directly or indirectly, on our natural environment. Sustainability creates and maintains the conditions under which humans and nature can exist in productive harmony, that permit fulfilling the social, economic and other requirements of present and future generations."[70] Some people refer to this way of thinking as *cradle to cradle*; the target to aim for is a product made from natural materials that is fully reusable or recyclable so that the company actually uses zero resources to make it.

That is a tough goal, but many organizations work hard to get as close to it as they can—and consumers increasingly take notice. Many of us are much more mindful of these issues when we shop and when we make decisions about the foods we eat, the clothes we wear, the buildings in which we live and work, and the cars we drive. The consumer's focus on personal health is merging with a growing interest in global health. Some analysts call this new value **conscientious consumerism**.[71]

Green Marketing and Greenwashing

Because sustainability and related issues such as climate change, pollution, and toxic products are so pervasive, it is important to distinguish this term from another widely used buzzword: **Green marketing** describes a strategy that involves the development and promotion of environmentally friendly products—and stressing this attribute when the manufacturer communicates with customers. Although some specialized companies like Seventh Generation have successfully built a following around their green products, this strategy has not fared well in recent years. Nonetheless, there still is demand for environmentally friendly products: American consumers spend more than $40 billion a year on them. This estimate includes $29.2 billion for organic food; more than $10 billion for hybrid, electric, and clean-diesel vehicles; more than $2 billion on energy-efficient light bulbs; and $640 million on green cleaning products.[72] However, sales are flat or lower than in prior years.

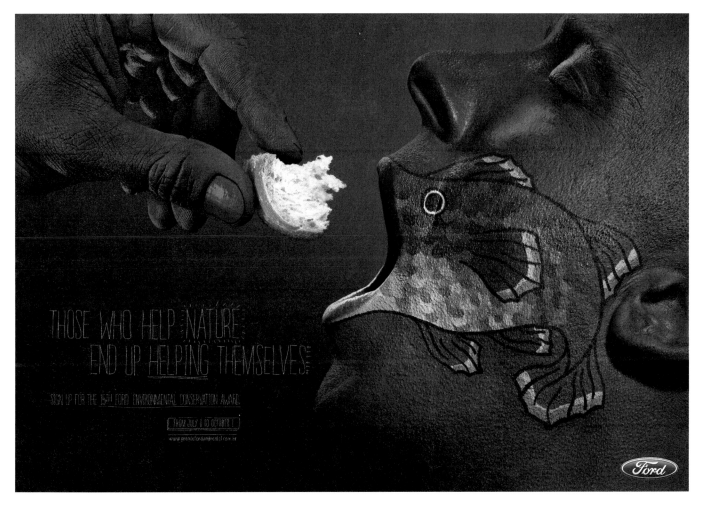

A Ford ad in Brazil promotes conservation.
Source: Courtesy of J. Walter Thompson Publicidade LTDA–Sao Paulo-Brazil.

Why would this be? We know that consumers increasingly pay more attention to environmental issues, and many even say they will pay more for products that manufacturers produce under ethical conditions (e.g., in humane workplaces and without harmful chemicals). In one typical study, the researchers gave subjects a description of a coffee company that either used or did not use Fair Trade principles to buy its beans. They found that participants were willing to pay an additional $1.40 for a pound of the coffee if it was ethically sourced and were very negative about the company if it did not adhere to these principles. The study obtained similar results for shirts that were made with organic cotton.[73]

Still—as we'll see in more detail in Chapter 8—it is common to witness a disconnect between consumers' attitudes and their actual behavior. As the old saying goes, "the road to hell is paved with good intentions." Despite consumers' best intentions to "buy green," we can point to two major reasons for the gap between saying and doing:

1 Green products are more expensive because the ingredients tend to cost more than their more conventional counterparts, and transportation costs are higher too because they are sold in smaller volumes than the big brands. Although many consumers profess a desire to buy environmentally friendly products, especially in tough economic times they have a tendency not to back these preferences with their cash. When The Great Recession hit in 2008, it took a lot of the steam out of the green movement. For example in 2009, S.C. Johnson introduced a line of green products called Nature's Source and the company spent more than $25 million to advertise them. By 2010 the company slashed the line's advertising budget to zero.[74] Figure 4.2 illustrates the declining demand for green products.

Figure 4.2 THE DECLINE OF GREEN

Source: GFK Green Gauge Survey.

Green marketing today focuses less on selling and more on conserving. Unilever launched a campaign on Facebook and YouTube tied to its Axe brand to encourage reduced usage of hot water. The "Showerpooling" campaign asks fans to take a pledge to share a shower with a like-minded acquaintance or attractive stranger.[75]

2 Unfortunately, the second reason for the lackluster showing of green products is largely self-inflicted. **Greenwashing** occurs when companies make false or exaggerated claims about how environmentally friendly their products are. Think about the old story of the "boy who cried wolf": Consumers simply don't believe most of the green claims companies make about their brands. Almost one-fourth of American consumers say they have "no way of knowing" if a product is green or actually does what it claims. Their skepticism is probably justified: According to one report, more than 95 percent of consumer companies that market as "green" make misleading or

inaccurate claims. Another survey found that the number of products that claim to be green has increased by 73 percent since 2009—but of the products investigated, almost one-third had fake labels, and 70 made green claims without offering any proof to back them up.[77] One survey reported that 71 percent of respondents say they will stop buying a product if they feel they've been misled about its environmental impact, and 37 percent are so angry about greenwashing that they believe this justifies a complete boycott of everything the company makes.[78]

As we saw in Chapter 1, it is typical to find that a relatively small number of consumers account for a large amount of the action with regard to a certain consumption activity or purchase. This certainly is true when we look at people who walk the walk, in addition to talking the talk, about modifying their behaviors to help the environment. Marketers point to a segment of consumers they call **LOHAS** —an acronym for "lifestyles of health and sustainability." This label refers to people who worry about the environment, want products to be produced in a sustainable way, and spend money to advance what they see as their personal development and potential. These so-called "Lohasians" (others refer to this segment as *cultural creatives*) represent a great market for products such as organic foods, energy-efficient appliances, and hybrid cars, as well as alternative medicine, yoga tapes, and ecotourism. One organization that tracks this group estimates that they make up between 13–19 percent of the adults in the United States; it values the market for socially conscious products at $290 billion.[79] Table 4.4 shows that the LOHAS market divides into six different sectors.

Product Disposal

Green issues don't end at the cash register. There is also the matter of what we do with our things when we're done with them. **Product disposal** is also an important element of consumer behavior.

Because we do form strong attachments to some products, it can be painful to get rid of them. Our possessions anchor our identities; our past lives on in our things.[80] Some Japanese people ritually "retire" worn-out sewing needles, chopsticks, and even computer chips when they burn them in a ceremony to thank them for years of good service.[81]

TABLE 4.4	LOHAS Market Sectors

Personal Health	Green Building
$117 billion	**$100 billion**
Natural, organic products	Home certification
Nutritional products	Energy Star appliances
Integrative health care	Sustainable flooring
Dietary supplements	Renewable energy systems
Mind body spirit products	Wood alternatives
Eco Tourism	**Natural Lifestyles**
$42 billion	**$10 billion**
Eco-tourism travel	Indoor & outdoor furnishings
Eco-adventure travel	Organic cleaning supplies
	Compact fluorescent lights
	Social change philanthropy
	Apparel
Alternative Transportation	**Alternative Energy**
$20 billion	**$1 billion**
Hybrid vehicles	Renewable energy credits
Biodiesel fuel	Green pricing
Car sharing programs	

Source: www.lohas.com/about.htm, accessed March 2, 2013.

Marketing Opportunity

Our demand for sustainable products that don't harm the environment when we're done with them creates new markets and new opportunities for entrepreneurs who find a better alternative. For example, TerraCycle sells an "exotic" product: A key ingredient on its label is "liquefied worm poop." A 25-year-old college dropout founded the company. (Company literature confesses that he was trying to grow "certain plants" in a worm bin inside his college apartment in order to "harvest the buds" when he stumbled on the idea. Inspiration comes from many sources!) TerraCycle makes fertilizer products that it packages in used plastic bottles, many of which the company itself collects through a nationwide recycling program it organized. TerraCycle claims that waste packaged in waste makes it the "ultimate eco-friendly" product. The fertilizer comes from containers filled with shredded newspaper, food scraps—and worms that eat this waste and digest it. The resulting "poop" happens to make great plant food.[82]

Still, we all have to get rid of our "stuff" at some point, either because it has served its purpose or perhaps because it no longer fits with our view of ourselves (as when newlyweds "upgrade" to a real place). Concern about the environment, coupled with a need for convenience, makes ease of product disposal a key attribute in categories from razors to diapers.

In many cases we acquire a new product even though the old one still functions—that's one of the hallmarks of our materialistic society. Some reasons to replace an item include a desire for new features, a change in the individual's environment (e.g., a refrigerator is the wrong color for a freshly painted kitchen), or a change in the person's role or self-image.[83]

The issue of product disposition is vital because of its enormous public policy implications. We live in a throwaway society, which creates problems for the environment and also results in a great deal of unfortunate waste. One study reported that we never use as much as 12 percent of the grocery products we buy; consumers buy nearly two-thirds of these **abandoned products** for a specific purpose such as a particular recipe and then they change their plans. Because we don't use these items immediately, they slowly get pushed to the back of the cupboard and forgotten.[84] Some of those "science projects" that grow in the back of your refrigerator might qualify. In another survey, 15 percent of adults admitted they are *pack rats,* and another 64 percent said they are selective savers. In contrast, 20 percent say they throw out as much garbage as they can. The consumers most likely to save things are older people and those who live alone.[85]

TerraCycle is the epitome of a sustainable product.
Source: TerraCycle®, Inc.

Training consumers to recycle has become a priority in many countries. In Japan, residents sort their garbage into as many as 44 different categories; for example, if they discard one sock, it goes into a bin for burnables, but if they throw out a pair it goes into used cloth, though only if the socks "are not torn, and the left and right sock match."[86]
Source: Bev Schellenberg, Photographer.

A study examined the relevant goals consumers have when they recycle. It used a means–end chain analysis of the type we described in Chapter 3 to identify how consumers link specific instrumental goals to more abstract terminal values. Researchers identified the most important lower-order goals to be "avoid filling up landfills," "reduce waste," "reuse materials," and "save the environment." They linked these to the terminal values of "promote health/avoid sickness," "achieve life-sustaining ends," and "provide for future generations."

Another study reported that the perceived effort involved in recycling was the best predictor of whether people would go to the trouble. This pragmatic dimension outweighed general attitudes toward recycling and the environment in predicting one's intention to recycle.[87] When researchers apply these techniques to study recycling and other product disposal behaviors, it will be easier for social marketers to design advertising copy and other messages that tap into the underlying values that will motivate people to increase environmentally responsible behavior.[88] Of course, one way to ease the pain is to reward consumers for recycling. Gap tried this when it teamed up with Cotton Incorporated to collect old denim, which will be turned into insulation and donated to communities to help them build new houses. The sweetener in the deal: Those who donated got a 30 percent discount on new jeans purchases, and a 40 percent discount went to those who bought the pants on Gap's Facebook page.[89]

During **lateral cycling**, one consumer exchanges something she owns for something the other person owns. Reusing other people's things is especially important in our throwaway society because, as one researcher put it, "there is no longer an 'away' to throw things to."[90] Although traditional marketers don't pay much attention to used-product sellers, factors such as concern about the environment, demands for quality, and cost and fashion consciousness make these "secondary" markets more important.[91] In fact, economic estimates of this **underground economy** range from 3 to 30 percent of

Product disposal is a major issue for used electronic items.
Source: With permission from RecycleYour Electronics.ca and Ontario Electronic Stewardship.

Source: Courtesy of www.sharesomesugar.com.

Net Profit

Social media platforms offer new ways to recycle. Numerous **sharing sites** like *Snap-Goods, NeighborGoods.com,* and *ShareSomeSugar* base their business models around allowing people to share, exchange, and rent goods in a local setting. In fact, some research indicates that people who participate in these sites also benefit because they feel they are part of a community. One study found that when people post messages on Twitter (also part of a community), this releases oxytocin, a neurotransmitter that evokes feelings of contentment and is thought to help induce a sense of positive social bonding. The researcher observed that this interaction "reduces stress hormones, even through the Web. You're feeling a real physiological relationship to that person, even if they are online."[94]

the gross national product of the United States and up to 70 percent of the gross domestic product of other countries. In the United States alone, there are more than 3,500 flea markets—including at least a dozen huge operations such as the 60-acre Orange County Marketplace in California—that operate nationwide to produce upward of $10 billion in gross sales.[92] The new trend of **recommerce** (a play on the term *e-commerce*) shows that many consumers want to squeeze more value out of their possessions by selling or trading them. Others are more conscious of the resale value of an item before they decide to buy it.[93]

The Dark Side of Consumer Behavior

OBJECTIVE 4
Consumer behavior can be harmful to individuals and to society.

In January 2012, a large crowd gathered overnight outside the first official Apple Store in Beijing, China, eager to be the first to own the latest smartphone—the Apple iPhone 4s. As more poured in from different parts of the country, queue lines started to get blurred and tempers rose as many had waited overnight bracing the cold Beijing winter. Eventually, fights broke out and riot police had to be called to the scene. For the sake of the consumers' safety as well as the Apple employees, the management announced that the store would remain closed until further notice. Chaos erupted immediately. The fans and the riot police came to blows; many of them threw eggs at the storefront. While several were led away by security, the remaining stood outside the store chanting "open the door." Although such negative publicity may not sound all too unfamiliar, it does raise the issue: is product fanaticism healthy?

Recent research has shown that products are purchased not only for their functionality but also for their ability to showcase the consumer's self-identity.[95] Because of their desire to showcase their self-image, consumers sometimes create a self-brand

CB AS I SEE IT

Professor John Schouten, *University of Portland*

There is no such thing as purely personal significance. To the extent that we create individual meaning at all, we do so from a shared language of objects, words, feelings, and experiences whose meanings have already been constructed by social groups. Similarly, there is no such thing as an individual consumer decision. We make our choices from assortments that society has provided, based on values and expectations that we have learned, questioned, embraced, or rejected as members of social groups.

Some groups or communities we choose. Others choose us. Ultimately, the character of our membership in any group is a matter of constant negotiation. Communities of any kind often coincide with or create markets. In response to shared needs and desires, humans come together, harness creativity and labor, and produce new goods and services. In the best cases, the creative power of community can accomplish tremendous good through cultural change. The LOHAS (Lifestyles of Health and Sustainability) community is one such social group, made up of both consumers and businesses. See lohas.com for more about the community's goals and impact.

Our biggest challenge today, in my view, is the collision between escalating human consumption and the rapidly declining capacity of the earth's natural systems to support it. I believe the best real hope for a tolerable human future lies in the ability of communities to redefine acceptable modes of consumer behavior and to participate actively and creatively in making them not only possible but also preferable to those practices that currently undermine the foundation of our existence.

For me, the most exciting aspects of communities are their dynamism and their power to effect change at levels ranging from individual purchases to global movements for social and environmental justice. Recently my studies have turned to such "communities of purpose." For example, for more than three years now Diane Martin and I have been engaged with groups of people determined to make Walmart more environmentally sustainable. Self-selecting community members include Walmart executives and associates, key members of its supply chain, environmental activists, academics, and others. Uniting these diverse participants are shared goals of carbon neutrality, zero waste, and products that support the sustainable use of the earth's finite resources. So far these groups have achieved impressive results, helping Walmart to divert millions of tons of waste from landfills, radically reduce its use of fossil fuels, develop more sustainable products, and (true to Walmart's mission) continue to profit, even in times of economic recession, with low prices to its customers. Explore walmartstores.com/sustainability and its link to Sustainable Value Networks for more about the results of these ongoing efforts.

connection in their minds. The stronger these psychological connections, the more likely it is that these consumers will defend their brands against negative publicity, and the more often they will engage in extreme behaviors similar to the Apple fans just described. While we would like to consider ourselves as rational individuals capable of making practical decisions, our consumption decisions sometimes do more harm without us knowing it.

Consumer Terrorism

The terrorist attacks of 9/11 were a wake-up call to the free-enterprise system. They revealed the vulnerability of nonmilitary targets and reminded us that disruptions of our financial, electronic, and supply networks can potentially be more damaging to our way of life than the fallout from a conventional battlefield. Assessments by the Rand Corporation and other analysts point to the susceptibility of the nation's food supply as a potential target of **bioterrorism**.[96] More recently, many concerned policymakers, executives, and military commanders have added the prospect of **cyberterrorism** to the list of pressing concerns, especially in the light of high-profile attacks on the computer systems of large financial institutions such as American Express.[97]

Even before the anthrax scares of 2001, toxic substances placed in products threatened to hold the marketplace hostage. This tactic first drew public attention in the United States in 1982, when seven people died after taking Tylenol pills that had been laced with cyanide. A decade later, Pepsi weathered its own crisis when more than 50 reports of syringes found in Diet Pepsi cans surfaced in 23 states. In that case, Pepsi pulled off a public relations *coup de grace* by convincing the public that the syringes could not have been introduced during the manufacturing process. The company even showed an in-store surveillance video that caught a customer slipping a syringe into a Diet Pepsi can while the cashier's head was turned.[98] Pepsi's aggressive actions underscore the importance of responding to such a crisis head-on and quickly.

More recently, a publicity campaign for a late-night cartoon show backfired when it aroused fears of a terrorist attack and temporarily shut down the city of Boston. The "guerrilla marketing" effort consisted of 1-foot-tall blinking electronic signs with hanging wires and batteries that marketers used to promote the Cartoon Network TV show *Aqua Teen Hunger Force* (a surreal series about a talking milkshake, a box of fries, and a meatball). The signs were placed on bridges and in other high-profile spots in several U.S. cities. Most depicted a boxy, cartoon character giving passersby the finger. The bomb squads and other police personnel required to investigate the mysterious boxes cost the city of Boston more than $500,000—and a lot of frayed nerves.[99]

Addictive Consumption

Though we usually equate substance abuse with addiction to alcohol, drugs, or nicotine, it seems we can become dependent on almost anything—there is even a Chapstick Addicts support group with 250 active members![100] **Consumer addiction** is a physiological or psychological dependency on products or services. Many companies profit from selling addictive products or from selling solutions for kicking a bad habit.

This ad from Singapore discourages young people from using ketamine, an animal tranquilizer.
Source: Used with permission of Saatchi & Saatchi of Singapore.

The Tangled Web

Internet addiction has been a big headache for several years already in South Korea, where 90 percent of homes connect to cheap, high-speed broadband. Many young Koreans' social lives revolve around the "PC *bang*," dim Internet parlors that sit on practically every street corner. A government study estimates that up to 30 percent of South Koreans under 18 are at risk of Internet addiction. Many already exhibit signs of actual addiction, including an inability to stop themselves from using computers, rising levels of tolerance that drive them to seek ever-longer sessions online, and withdrawal symptoms such as anger and craving when they can't log on. Some users have literally dropped dead from exhaustion after playing online games for days on end.[103]

. . . .

Addiction to Technology

Even technology can be addicting, as anyone with a BlackBerry can attest: Some people call this little device by the nickname of "CrackBerry" because it's so hard to stop checking it constantly. Psychologists compare **social media addiction** to chemical dependency, to the point of inducing symptoms of withdrawal when users are deprived of their fix. As one noted, "Everyone is a potential addict—they're just waiting for their drug of choice to come along, whether heroin, running, junk food or social media."[101] Indeed, a survey reported one in three smartphone owners would rather give up sex than their phones![102]

Other problems arise when people become overly involved in playing online games or posting on social network sites:

- In the U.K., a 33-year-old widowed mother let her two dogs starve to death and neglected her three kids after becoming hooked on the online game *Small World*. A judge banned her from going on the Internet. The woman slept only two hours a night as she played the virtual reality game (in which dwarves and giants battle to conquer the world) almost nonstop for six months. Her children—aged 9, 10, and 13—had no hot food and "drank" cold baked beans from tins. When the family's two dogs died from neglect, she left their bodies rotting in the dining room for two months.[104]
- An American woman pled guilty to a charge of second-degree murder in the death of her three-month-old son. The 22-year-old mother lost her temper when her child began crying while she was playing *FarmVille* on Facebook; she shook the baby until it died.
- **Cyberbullying** refers to the ". . . willful and repeated harm inflicted through the use of computer, cell phones, and other electronic devices."[105] One study reported that one in five middle-school students in the United States were subject to cyberbullying. As one seventh-grade girl observed, "It's easier to fight online, because you feel more brave and in control. On Facebook, you can be as mean as you want."[106]

This Brazilian ad is part of a campaign to combat cigarette addiction. It looks like we're actually ahead of schedule!
Source: Courtesy of ADESF Association for Smoker Awareness; Neoqama/BBH.

- **Phantom Vibration Syndrome** describes the tendency to habitually reach for your cell phone because you feel it vibrating, even if it is off or you are not even wearing it at the time. One researcher reports that 70 percent of people who report heavy usage of mobile devices say they experience this phenomenon. The name derives from *phantom limb syndrome,* a condition in which someone who has lost a limb experiences sensory hallucinations that it is still attached to the body and functioning.[107]

Compulsive Consumption

Some consumers take the expression "born to shop" quite literally. They shop because they are compelled to do so rather than because shopping is a pleasurable or functional task. **Compulsive consumption** refers to repetitive and often excessive shopping performed as an antidote to tension, anxiety, depression, or boredom.[108] "Shopaholics" turn to shopping much the way addicted people turn to drugs or alcohol.[109] One man diagnosed with *compulsive shopping disorder* (*CSD*) bought more than 2,000 wrenches and never used any of them. Therapists report that women clinically diagnosed with CSD outnumber men by four to one. They speculate that women are attracted to items such as clothes and cosmetics to enhance their interpersonal relationships, whereas men tend to focus on gadgetry, tools, and guns to achieve a sense of power.

One out of 20 U.S. adults is unable to control the buying of goods that he or she does not really want or need. Some researchers say compulsive shopping may be related to low self-esteem. It affects an estimated 2 to 16 percent of the adult U.S. population.[110] In some cases, the consumer has little or no control over his or her consumption, much like a drug addict. Whether it is alcohol, cigarettes, chocolate, diet colas, or even Chapstick, the products control the consumer. Even the act of shopping itself is an addicting experience for some people. Three common elements characterize many negative or destructive consumer behaviors:[111]

1 The behavior is not done by choice.
2 The gratification derived from the behavior is short-lived.
3 The person experiences strong feelings of regret or guilt afterward.

Gambling is an example of a consumption addiction that touches every segment of consumer society. Whether it takes the form of casino gambling, playing the "slots," betting on sports events with friends or through a bookie, or even buying lottery tickets, excessive gambling can be quite destructive. Taken to extremes, gambling can result in lowered self-esteem, debt, divorce, and neglected children. According to one psychologist, gamblers exhibit a classic addictive cycle: They experience a "high" while in action and depression when they stop gambling, which leads them back to the thrill of the action. Unlike drug addicts, however, money is the substance that hard-core gamblers abuse. We can probably expect the problem to grow as the movement to legalize online gambling in some U.S. states picks up steam (it already is legal in Nevada, Delaware, and New Jersey).[112] There already is a built-in market for this new format: Analysts estimate more than 170 million people play simulated casino games on social networks, more than triple the number of real money online gamblers.[113]

Consumed Consumers

Consumed consumers are people who are used or exploited, willingly or not, for commercial gain in the marketplace. Here are some examples:

- **Prostitutes**—Expenditures on prostitution in the United States alone are estimated at $20 billion annually. These revenues are equivalent to those in the domestic shoe industry.[114]
- **Organ, blood, and hair donors**—There is a lively global **red market** for body parts. By one estimate, you could make about $46 million if you donated every reusable part of your body (do not try this at home).[115] In the United States, millions of people sell

their blood. A lively market also exists for organs (e.g., kidneys), and some women sell their hair to be made into wigs. Bidding for a human kidney on eBay went to more than $5.7 million before the company ended the auction (it's illegal to sell human organs online . . . at least so far). The seller wrote, "You can choose either kidney. . . . Of course only one for sale, as I need the other one to live. Serious bids only."[116] Here is the retail price for some typical red market transactions in the United States (often much cheaper elsewhere):[117]

- A pint of blood: $337
- Hair (for extensions): $308
- Cornea: $24,400
- Heart: $997,700

- **Babies for sale**—Several thousand surrogate mothers have been paid to be medically impregnated and carry babies to term for infertile couples. A fertile woman between the ages of 18 and 25 can "donate" one egg every 3 months and rake in $7,000 each time. Over 8 years, that's 32 eggs for a total of $224,000.[118] In one case in Germany, police arrested a couple when they tried to auction their 8-month-old son on eBay. The parents claimed that the offer, which read "Baby—collection only. Offer my nearly new baby for sale because it cries too much. Male, 70 cm long" was just a joke.[119]

Illegal Acquisition and Product Use

In addition to being self-destructive or socially damaging, many consumer behaviors are illegal as well. Analysts estimate the cost of crimes that consumers commit against business at more than $40 billion per year. A survey conducted by the McCann-Erickson advertising agency revealed the following tidbits:[120]

- Ninety-one percent of people say they lie regularly. One in three fibs about his or her weight, one in four about income, and 21 percent lie about their age. Nine percent even lie about their natural hair color.
- Four out of ten Americans have tried to pad an insurance bill to cover the deductible.
- Nineteen percent say they've snuck into a theater to avoid paying admission.
- More than three out of five people say they've taken credit for making something from scratch when they have done no such thing. According to Pillsbury's CEO, this "behavior is so prevalent that we've named a category after it—speed scratch."

Consumer Theft and Fraud

Who among us has never received an email offering us fabulous riches if we help to recover a lost fortune from a Nigerian bank account? Of course, the only money changing hands will be yours if you fall for the pitch from a so-called *advance-fee fraud artist*. These con men have successfully scammed many victims out of hundreds of millions of dollars. However, a small but intrepid group of "counterscammers" sometimes give these crooks a taste of their own medicine by pretending to fall for a scam and humiliating the perpetrator. One common strategy is to trick the con artist into posing for pictures holding a self-mocking sign and then posting these photos on Internet sites. Both online and offline, fraud is rampant.

Stealing from stores is the most common scam. Someone commits a retail theft every 5 seconds. **Shrinkage** is the industry term for inventory and cash losses from shoplifting and employee theft (it does not refer to the condition George experienced in a famous episode of the *Seinfeld* TV show). This is a massive problem for businesses that gets passed on to consumers in the form of higher prices (about 40 percent of the losses can be attributed to employees rather than shoppers). Shopping malls spend $6 million annually on security, and a family of four spends about $300 extra per year because of markups to cover shrinkage.[121]

Indeed, shoplifting is America's fastest-growing crime. A comprehensive retail study found that shoplifting is a year-round problem that costs U.S. retailers $9 billion annually. The most frequently stolen products are tobacco products, athletic shoes, logo and brand-name apparel, designer jeans, and undergarments. The average theft amount per incident is $58.43, up from $20.36 in a 1995 survey.[122] The problem is equally worrisome in Europe; retailers there catch well over 1 million shoplifters every year. The United Kingdom has the highest rate of shrinkage (as a percent of annual sales), followed by Norway, Greece, and France. Switzerland and Austria have the lowest rates.[123]

The large majority of shoplifting is not done by professional thieves or by people who genuinely need the stolen items.[124] About 2 million Americans are charged with shoplifting each year, but analysts estimate that for every arrest, 18 unreported incidents occur.[125] About three-quarters of those shoplifters authorities catch are middle- or high-income people who shoplift for the thrill of it or as a substitute for affection. Shoplifting is also common among adolescents. Research evidence indicates that teen shoplifting is influenced by factors such as having friends who also shoplift. It is also more likely to occur if the adolescent does not believe that this behavior is morally wrong.[126]

And what about shoppers who commit fraud when they abuse stores' exchange and return policies? Some big companies, such as Guess, Staples, and Sports Authority, use new software that lets them track a shopper's track record of bringing items back. They are trying to crack down on **serial wardrobers** "who buy an outfit, wear it once, and return it"; customers who change price tags on items, then return one item for the higher amount; and shoppers who use fake or old receipts when they return a product. The retail industry loses approximately $16 billion a year to these and other forms of fraudulent behavior. Retail analysts estimate that about 9 percent of all returns are fraudulent.[127]

Counterfeiting, where companies or individuals sell fake versions of real products to customers (who may or may not be aware of the switch), accounts for over $600 billion in global losses annually. Many of us think of counterfeiters as guys who sell *faux* designer handbags or watches on the street, but in fact the problem is much more widespread—and often deadly. About 200,000 people in China die per year because they ingest fake pharmaceuticals.[128]

Anticonsumption

Some types of destructive consumer behavior are **anticonsumption**; events in which people deliberately deface or mutilate products and services. Some of these actions are relatively harmless, as when a person goes online at dogdoo.com to send a bag of dog manure to a lucky recipient. This site even lets customers calibrate the size of the "gift" by choosing among three "Poo Poo Packages": Econo-Poop (20-pound dog), Poo Poo Special (50-pound dog), and the ultimate in payback, the Poo Poo Grande (110-pound dog).[129] The moral: Smell your packages before opening.

Anticonsumption ranges from relatively mild acts like spray-painting graffiti on buildings and subways to serious incidences of product tampering or even the release of computer viruses that can bring large corporations to their knees. It can also take the form of political protest in which activists alter or destroy billboards and other advertisements that promote what they feel to be unhealthy or unethical acts. For example, some members of the clergy in areas heavily populated by minorities have organized rallies to protest the proliferation of cigarette and alcohol advertising in their neighborhoods; these protests sometimes include the defacement of billboards promoting alcohol or cigarettes.

CHAPTER SUMMARY

Now that you have finished reading this chapter, you should understand why:

1. Ethical business is good business.

Business ethics are rules of conduct that guide actions in the marketplace; these are the standards against which most people in a culture judge what is right and what is wrong, good or bad. Marketers must confront many ethical issues, especially ones that relate to how much they make consumers "want" things they don't need or are not good for them. A related issue is materialism, which refers to the importance people attach to worldly possessions, and the role of business in encouraging this outlook.

2. Marketers have an obligation to provide safe and functional products as part of their business activities.

It is both ethically and financially smart to maximize customer satisfaction. In some cases, external bodies such as the government or industry associations regulate businesses to ensure that their products and advertising are safe, clear, and accurate. Consumer behavior researchers may play a role in this process and those who do transformative consumer research (TCR) may even work to bring about social change. Companies also play a significant role in addressing social conditions through their corporate social responsibility (CSR) practices and social marketing campaigns that promote positive behaviors.

3. Consumer behavior impacts directly on major public policy issues that confront our society.

Our relationships with companies and other organizations are complex and many issues that impact quality-of-life relate directly to marketing practices. These include the tradeoff between our privacy and the ability of companies to tailor their offerings to our individual needs. Other issues revolve around market access as many people are unable to navigate the marketplace due to disabilities, illiteracy, or other conditions. In addition, our fragile environment requires a commitment to sustainable business practices that attempt to maximize the triple bottom-line that emphasizes financial, social, and environmental benefits.

4. Consumer behavior can be harmful to individuals and to society.

Although textbooks often paint a picture of the consumer as a rational, informed decision-maker, in reality many consumer activities are harmful to individuals or to society. The "dark side" of consumer behavior includes terrorism, addiction, the use of people as products (consumed consumers), and theft or vandalism (anticonsumption).

KEY TERMS

abandoned products, 174
anticonsumption, 183
bioterrorism, 178
botnets, 166
business ethics, 154
cause marketing, 164
compulsive consumption, 181
conscientious consumerism, 170
consumed consumers, 181
consumer addiction, 179
consumerspace, 155
corporate social responsibility (CSR), 164
corrective advertising, 162
counterfeiting, 183
culture jamming, 163
curation, 158
cyberbullying, 180

cyberterrorism, 178
focus groups, 160
food desert, 169
functionally illiterate, 169
gemba, 160
green marketing, 170
greenwashing, 172
gripe sites, 159
identity theft, 166
lateral cycling, 176
locational privacy, 167
LOHAS, 173
market access, 167
materialism, 157
media literacy, 169
Phantom Vibration Syndrome, 181
phishing, 166

product disposal, 173
provenance, 158
real-time bidding, 165
recommerce, 177
red market, 181
serial wardrobers, 183
sharing sites, 177
shrinkage, 182
social marketing, 164
social media addiction, 180
sustainability, 170
total quality management (TQM), 160
transitional economies, 157
transformative consumer
    research (TCR), 163
triple bottom-line orientation, 169
underground economy, 176

REVIEW

⭐ **4-1** The economics of information perspective argues that advertising is important. Why?

4-2 Why should companies encourage consumers to complain? How can this benefit the business?

4-3 What is green-washing, and is it ethical? Are consumers likely to be convinced?

CONSUMER BEHAVIOR CHALLENGE

■ DISCUSS

✪ **4-4** "College students' concerns about the environment and vegetarianism are simply a passing fad; a way to look 'cool.'" Do you agree?

✪ **4-5** Marketers continue to push the envelope as they challenge society's norms regarding what topics are appropriate to discuss in public. Products that people only used to whisper about now pop up in ads and billboards; these include feminine hygiene products, condoms, lubricants, grooming aids, and pregnancy tests. A commercial for a digital home-pregnancy test kit even broke a taboo when it showed urination on TV. As a stream of liquid flows onto the device, a voiceover says, "Introducing the most sophisticated piece of technology...you will ever pee on." Ads for feminine hygiene products used to barely hint at their function (typically they depicted a smiling woman who wore white to subtly signal how well the item worked). Today, Procter & Gamble's Always line of menstrual pads advertises with the cheerful theme, "Have a happy period."[130] Where do we cross the line in what we show in advertising?

4-6 Across Europe, lawyers estimate that around 10 million consumers are entitled to U.S. $5 billion in compensation from airline companies. The reason for the compensation claim is for when their flights have either been delayed or cancelled, unless this was due to extraordinary circumstances out of the control of the airline. The claims can date back as long as six years. In order to be eligible for a claim, the consumer had to have flown out of a European Union (EU) airport on an EU-registered airline. Despite the clear rulings on the compensation rights of consumers, thousands of claimants have found that their claims have been rejected by the airlines. The EU even clarified the ruling in 2012 and streamlined the claim process. Does your justice system adequately meet the needs of both consumers and companies in terms of how it awards damages?[131]

4-7 The U.K.-based price comparison Web site uSwitch estimates that 5.9 million people in the U.K. have homes fitted with a prepayment energy meter. According to the newspaper *The Guardian*, these energy customers are paying upwards of U.S. $500 per year more than customers who do not have these meters and are able to choose cheaper tariffs. In the U.K., average energy bills are nearly U.S. $3,000 per year. It is estimated that at least 5 million energy customers are indebted to their suppliers. When this is the case, prepayment meters are often installed, and this changeover is rising at a rate of 6 percent per year.[132] Is it fair to classify consumers in this way so that some get access to more attractive options than others?

4-8 In Chile, McDonald's, Burger King, and other fast food outlets have fallen afoul of a new law passed in the summer of 2012. The companies are being sued for including toys in their children's meals.[133] What do you think of this lawsuit? Follow up the story.

4-9 In the summer of 2013, Manchester United announced that it had agreed to an eight-year sponsorship contract with AON worth U.S. $245 million to have its name on the club's training ground at Carrington. The deal will see the facility renamed the AON Training Complex. This was a part of a complicated deal in which Manchester United would appear in the Far East for matches, wearing AON-sponsored shirts. The deal was worth double the amount that AON had paid in 2009 for its four-year shirt sponsorship. However, the name Old Trafford, the club's home, was not for sale at any price. Naming rights, claimed the executive vice-chairman of the club, were not up for negotiation.[134] Have sports clubs in your country or region sold their stadium names to sponsors? What is the reaction of fans to this move?

4-10 The Creative Bloq Web site (www.creativebloq.com/) featured a collection of the most controversial ad campaigns of 2013. All of them attracted a lot of criticism. The 10 chosen advertisements appeared across the world and were designed by a number of different agencies. What is your take on them? Are they offensive or controversial? Why did the brands approve them?

4-11 One of the fastest growing new technologies in marketing is facial recognition. In 2013, the market was estimated to be worth around U.S. $1.92 billion. This is confidently expected to grow to U.S. $6.5 billion by 2018. This represents a staggering growth of some 27.7 percent over the next five years. The biggest adopters of facial recognition are likely to be governments and utilities; however, marketers are increasingly recognizing the value of facial recognition as a marketing tool. The most obvious applications for facial recognition are the growth of the surveillance market and massive global spending on biometrics. However, there are huge opportunities for consumer electronics, hand-held devices, and innovative cloud-based services.

Advertisers have also begun to use facial recognition. Advertisements can be paused if the viewer looks away from the advertisement. Advertisers will soon have the ability to segment and target messages to specific individuals when their faces are recognized by the software. This can be an incredibly personalized marketing tool. With the chance to target customers based on their facial recognition, the race is on to create workable technologies.

Tarun Wadhwa, of Singularity University, claims that it will not be long before consumers look at a billboard and find that the image is looking back at them. Already, Immersive Labs has created a software package for digital billboards that measures the age, gender, and attention level of people passing the billboard. This is designed to scientifically quantify the effectiveness of the outdoor campaign. Is the trade-off in terms of our privacy worth it, or are companies simply going to be collecting too much data, without consent?[135]

■ APPLY

4-12 According to a 2012 report by Enisa, the European Information Security Agency, 93 percent of consumers were concerned as to whether businesses protected the information they hold about them. According to the report, 47 percent of service providers actively use personal data as a commercial asset. Around the same percentage share that data with third parties. If they were given the choice, consumers would be inclined to choose a business that required more personal data over one that did not in exchange for lower prices. The consumers also thought that giving more information would provide them with a more personalized service.[136]

    The Special Euro Barometer study in 2011 stated that 90 percent of customers revealed their names and addresses online to businesses. At the same time, the Enisa study suggested that 60 percent of consumers would choose a more data-friendly business, but if they gained better deals, this figure rose to 83 percent.

    Conduct a poll among 10 car owners of various ages, where you describe these programs, and ask respondents if they would like to participate in order to receive a discount on their purchases. What are the pros and cons? Share your findings with the class.

4-13 Many college students "share" music by downloading clips from the Internet. Interview at least five people who have downloaded at least one song or movie without paying for it. Do they feel they are stealing? What explanations do they offer for this behavior? Try to identify any common themes as a result of these interviews. If you were devising an ad campaign to discourage free downloading, how might you use what you have learned to craft a convincing message?

4-14 Corporate social responsibility (CSR) is gradually becoming a key element of business strategy across the world. In some developing economies CSR is considerably less well-developed than others. This is understandable since businesses in these countries have been more focused on becoming globally competitive in their struggle to survive. In Malaysia, a major study in the *Labuan e-Journal of Muamalat and Society* in 2011 specifically looked at whether Malaysian companies were in a position to consider CSR.[137] The study concluded that in the fields of welfare, environment, education, and human rights, some Malaysian companies were already being addressed. Malaysian businesses were aware of CSR, but despite some progress they were still way behind some of their competitors. What is the situation in your own country or region? Is CSR a main part of corporate strategy?

Case Study

UNICEF WAGES GUERRILLA WARFARE

Source: U.S. Fund for UNICEF.

New Yorkers rush through Manhattan's Union Square on their way to work. As they move quickly through the crowds, they pass a water vending machine on the sidewalk, something very appealing on a hot day in the city. But there's a catch: This brightly colored vending machine dispenses water in flavors such as malaria, cholera, typhoid, dengue, hepatitis, dysentery, salmonella, and yellow fever! The machine is part of UNICEF's Dirty Water campaign. The organization wants Americans to realize that about 2 billion people worldwide lack access to clean water, and more than 4,000 children die daily due to waterborne disease. UNICEF also informs people, via a sign on the machine, that if they insert $1, they provide a child with clean water for 40 days.

    UNICEF is a global humanitarian relief organization that provides children with health care and immunizations, clean water, nutrition, education, and emergency relief in more than 150 countries. This nonprofit has adopted so-called **guerrilla marketing** tactics: nontraditional methods to break through the clutter of competing messages in public areas (just as guerrillas use the element of surprise to overwhelm traditional armies with superior firepower). Being heard is an extra challenge for organizations like UNICEF; they have a more serious message to deliver and it's tough to compete against the thousands of ads for glamorous clothes or cool cars with which we're confronted every day.

Another major initiative for UNICEF is reducing the dangers of landmines throughout the world. These hidden explosives (usually left over from former wars) kill or injure 15,000 people a year, many of them children. UNICEF's street campaign for landmine awareness used another guerrilla tactic; this time it involved placing stickers on the streets of Zurich. The stickers, which matched the color of the sidewalk, were not easily noticed by pedestrians. A passerby would step on the sticker and it would stick to the bottom of his or her shoe. When the pedestrian turned a foot to see the sticker, he or she viewed a message from UNICEF that said, "In many other countries you would now be mutilated! Help the victims of landmines!"

Guerrilla marketing gets the attention of the jaded pedestrian, but it also has the potential to spread a message to many others as well with the help of social media. Wouldn't you tweet, post a video to YouTube, or upload a picture to your Facebook page if you saw something really cool and different, like malaria-flavored water or a landmine sticker on your way to class? Many of us learned as superstitious kids not to step on a crack in the sidewalk; maybe today other things we step on will result in good luck for worthy organizations like UNICEF.

DISCUSSION QUESTIONS

CS 4-1 Do you think UNICEF's campaigns will be effective? Why or why not?

CS 4-2 Guerrilla marketing tactics deliberately intend to "ambush" consumers in public places. Is this an effective marketing technique, or is it a violation of our right to go about our business undisturbed? Do these tactics intrude on our lives? In other words, is there a point where they cross a line?

CS 4-3 What are other ways UNICEF could spread the word about its causes such as the dangers of dirty water?

Sources: Leon Kaye, "UNICEF's Dirty Water Vending Machines Raises Manhattan," www.triplepundit.com (July 19th, 2010), accessed June 24, 2011. "Unicef Landmine," www.yayeveryday.com, accessed June 24, 2011. www.unicef.com, accessed June 24, 2011.

MyMarketingLab

Go to **mymktlab.com** for the following Assisted-graded writing questions:

4-15 Because of higher competition and market saturation, marketers in industrialized countries try to develop Third World markets. Asian consumers alone spend $90 billion a year on cigarettes, and U.S. tobacco manufacturers push relentlessly into these markets. We find cigarette advertising, which often depicts glamorous Western models and settings, just about everywhere—on billboards, buses, storefronts, and clothing—and tobacco companies sponsor many major sports and cultural events. Some companies even hand out cigarettes and gifts in amusement areas, often to preteens. Should governments allow these practices, even if the products may be harmful to their citizens or divert money that poor people should spend on essentials? If you were a trade or health official in a Third World country, what guidelines, if any, might you suggest to regulate the import of luxury goods from advanced economies?

4-16 What is the primary difference between transformative consumer research and other kinds of consumer research?

4-17 **Mymktlab Only**—comprehensive writing assignment for this chapter.

NOTES

1. Reported in *American Demographics* (December 1999): 18.
2. Valerie S. Folkes and Michael A. Kamins, "Effects of Information about Firms' Ethical and Unethical Actions on Consumers' Attitudes," *Journal of Consumer Psychology* 8 (1999): 243–59.
3. Jacqueline N. Hood and Jeanne M. Logsdon, "Business Ethics in the NAFTA Countries: A Cross-Cultural Comparison," *Journal of Business Research* 55 (2002): 883–90.
4. Michael R. Solomon, *Conquering Consumerspace: Marketing Strategies for a Branded World* (New York: AMACOM, 2003).
5. Jeffrey Ball, "Religious Leaders to Discuss SUVs with GM, Ford Officials," *Wall Street Journal Interactive Edition* (November 19, 2002); Danny Hakim, "The S.U.V. Is a Beast, and It's Hairy, Too," *New York Times* (February 2, 2005), www.nytimes.com, accessed February 2, 2005; www.nrpe.org/issues, accessed May 11, 2009.
6. William Leiss, Stephen Kline, and Sut Jhally, *Social Communication in Advertising: Persons, Products, and Images of Well-Being* (Toronto: Methuen, 1986); Jerry Mander, *Four Arguments for the Elimination of Television* (New York: William Morrow, 1977).
7. Packard (1957), quoted in Leiss et al., *Social Communication*, 11.
8. Raymond Williams, *Problems in Materialism and Culture: Selected Essays* (London: Verso, 1980).
9. Leiss et al., *Social Communication*.

10. George Stigler, "The Economics of Information," *Journal of Political Economy* (1961): 69.

11. Leiss et al., *Social Communication*, 11.

12. Russell W. Belk, "Possessions and the Extended Self," *Journal of Consumer Research* 15 (September 1988): 139–68; Melanie Wallendorf and Eric J. Arnould, "'My Favorite Things': A Cross-Cultural Inquiry into Object Attachment, Possessiveness, and Social Linkage," *Journal of Consumer Research* 14 (March 1988): 531–47.

13. L. J. Shrum, Jaehoon Lee, James E. Burroughs, and Aric Rindfleisch, "Online Process Model of Second-Order Cultivation Effects: How Television Cultivates Materialism and Its Consequences of Life Satisfaction," *Human Communication Research* 37 (January 2011): 34–57; L. J. Shrum, James E. Burroughs, and Aric Rindfleisch, "Television's Cultivation of Material Values," *Journal of Consumer Research* 32, no. 3 (2005): 473–79.

14. Susan Schultz Kleine and Stacy Menzel Baker, "An Integrative Review of Material Possession Attachment," *Academy of Marketing Science Review*, no. 1 (2004).

15. James E. Burroughs and Aric Rindfleisch, "Materialism and Well-Being: A Conflicting Values Perspective," *Journal of Consumer Research* 29 (December 2002): 348–70.

16. Lan Nguyen Chaplin and Deborah Roedder John, "Growing Up in a Material World: Age Differences in Materialism in Children and Adolescents," *Journal of Consumer Research* 34 (December 2007): 480–93.

17. Marsha L. Richins, "Special Possessions and the Expression of Material Values," *Journal of Consumer Research* 21 (December 1994): 522–33.

18. Ibid.

19. Aric Rindfleisch, James E. Burroughs, and Nancy Wong, "The Safety of Objects: Materialism, Existential Insecurity, and Brand Connection," *Journal of Consumer Research* 36 (June 2009): 1–16.

20. John L. Lastovicka and Nancy J. Sirianni, "Truly, Madly, Deeply: Consumers in the Throes of Material Possession Love," *Journal of Consumer Research* (in press).

21. Marsha L. Richins, "When Wanting Is Better than Having: Materialism, Transformation Expectations, and Product-Evoked Emotions in the Purchase Process," *Journal of Consumer Research* 40, no. 1 (June 2013): 1–18.

22. Professor Russell Belk, University of Utah, personal communication, July 25, 1997.

23. Material in this section adapted from Güliz Ger and Russell W. Belk, "I'd Like to Buy the World a Coke: Consumptionscapes of the 'Less Affluent World,'" *Journal of Consumer Policy* 19, no. 3 (1996): 271–304; Russell W. Belk, "Romanian Consumer Desires and Feelings of Deservingness," in Lavinia Stan, ed., *Romania in Transition* (Hanover, NH: Dartmouth Press, 1997): 191–208; see also Güliz Ger, "Human Development and Humane Consumption: Well-Being Beyond the Good Life," *Journal of Public Policy & Marketing* 16 (1997): 110–25.

24. Professor Güliz Ger, Bilkent University, Turkey, personal communication, July 25, 1997.

25. Erazim Kohák, "Ashes, Ashes . . . Central Europe after Forty Years," *Daedalus* 121 (Spring 1992): 197–215; Belk, "Romanian Consumer Desires and Feelings of Deservingness."

26. "Luxury Goods Market Predicted to Grow Six to Seven Percent in 2012, Defying Global Turmoil and Spreading to New Markets, According to Spring Update of Bain & Company's Luxury Goods Worldwide Market Study," Bain & Company, May 15, 2012, http://www.bain.com/about/press/press-releases/luxury-goods-market-predicted-to-grow-six-to-seven-percent-in-2012.aspx, accessed March 1, 2013.

27. Quoted in Michael Pavone, "How Whole Foods Became the Luxury Brand of Millennials," Fastcoexist.com, February 23, 2012, http://www.fastcoexist.com/1679351/how-whole-foods-became-the-luxury-brand-of-millennials, accessed March 1, 2013.

28. Ariel Sabar, "In Case of Missing Trousers, Aggrieved Party Loses Again," *New York Times* (June 26, 2007), www.nytimes.com, accessed June 26, 2007.

29. Mary C. Gilly and Betsy D. Gelb, "Post-Purchase Consumer Processes and the Complaining Consumer," *Journal of Consumer Research* 9 (December 1982): 323–28; Diane Halstead and Cornelia Droge, "Consumer Attitudes Toward Complaining and the Prediction of Multiple Complaint Responses," in Rebecca H. Holman and Michael R. Solomon, eds., *Advances in Consumer Research* 18 (Provo, UT: Association for Consumer Research, 1991): 210–16; Jagdip Singh, "Consumer Complaint Intentions and Behavior: Definitional and Taxonomical Issues," *Journal of Marketing* 52 (January 1988): 93–107.

30. Emily Steel, "How to Handle 'IHateYourCompany.com': Some Firms Buy Up Negative Domain Names to Avert 'Gripe Sites,'" *Wall Street Journal* (September 5, 2008), http://online.wsj.com/news/articles/SB12205776068830214763.djreprints.com/2574430594663.html, accessed September 5, 2008.

31. Gary L. Clark, Peter F. Kaminski, and David R. Rink, "Consumer Complaints: Advice on How Companies Should Respond Based on an Empirical Study," *Journal of Services Marketing* 6 (Winter 1992): 41–50.

32. Alan Andreasen and Arthur Best, "Consumers Complain—Does Business Respond?" *Harvard Business Review* 55 (July–August 1977): 93–101.

33. Tibbett L. Speer, "They Complain Because They Care," *American Demographics* (May 1996): 13–14; cf. also Yany Grégoire, Thomas M. Tripp, and Renaud Legoux, "When Customer Love Turns into Lasting Hate: The Effects of Relationship Strength and Time on Customer Revenge and Avoidance," *Journal of Marketing* 73 (November 2009): 18–32; Ingrid Martin, "Expert-Novice Differences in Complaint Scripts," in Rebecca H. Holman and Michael R. Solomon, eds., *Advances in Consumer Research* 18 (Provo, UT: Association for Consumer Research, 1991): 225–31; Marsha L. Richins, "A Multivariate Analysis of Responses to Dissatisfaction," *Journal of the Academy of Marketing Science* 15 (Fall 1987): 24–31; John A. Schibrowsky and Richard S. Lapidus, "Gaining a Competitive Advantage by Analyzing Aggregate Complaints," *Journal of Consumer Marketing* 11 (1994): 15–26; Clay M. Voorhees, Michael K. Brady, and David M. Horowitz, "A Voice from the Silent Masses: An Exploratory and Comparative Analysis of Noncomplainers," *Journal of the Academy of Marketing Science* 34 (Fall 2006): 514–27.

34. Bruce Cooil, Timothy L. Keiningham, Lerzan Aksoy, and Michael Hsu, "A Longitudinal Analysis of Customer Satisfaction and Share of Wallet: Investigating the Moderating Effect of Customer Characteristics," *Journal of Marketing* 71 (January 2007): 67–83. For a study that looks at consumer variables moderating this relationship, cf. Kathleen Seiders, Glenn B. Voss, Dhruv Grewal, and Andrea L. Godfrey, "Do Satisfied Customers Buy More? Examining Moderating Influences in a Retailing Context," *Journal of Marketing* 69 (October 2005): 26–43.

35. "Voice of the Consumer Not Leveraged," Center for Media Research (February 3, 2009), www.mediapost.com, accessed February 3, 2009.

36. Robbie Brown, Kim Severson, and Barry Meier, "Cruise Line's Woes Are Far From Over as Ship Makes Port," *New York Times* (February 14, 2013), http://www.nytimes.com/2013/02/15/us/carnival-cruise-line-ship-triumph-towed-into-port.html?pagewanted=all&_r=0, accessed February 20, 2013.

37. Material adapted from a presentation by Glenn H. Mazur, QFD Institute, 2002.

38. Robert V. Kozinets and Jay M. Handelman, "Adversaries of Consumption: Consumer Movements, Activism, and Ideology," *Journal of Consumer Research* 31 (December 2004): 691–704; cf. also Paul C. Henry, "How Mainstream Consumers Think about Consumer Rights and Responsibilities," *Journal of Consumer Research* 37, no. 4 (2010), 670–687.

39. Natasha Singer, "A Birth Control Pill That Promised Too Much," *New York Times* (February 10, 2009), www.nytimes.com, accessed February 10, 2009.

40. Jack Neff, "NAD to Charmin: No Bare Bear Bottoms: P&G Must Show Some Pieces of TP on Bruin's Bums," *Advertising Age* (August 12, 2010), http://adage.com/article/adages/advertising-p-g-show-pieces-charmin-bears/145379/, accessed April 29, 2011.

41. Janet Adamy, "Tough New Rules Proposed on Food Advertising for Kids," *Wall Street Journal* (April 29, 2011), http://professional.wsj.com/article/NA_EP_PUB:SB10001424052748704330404576291091782255946.html?lpe5WSJ_PRO&mg5com-wsj, accessed April 29, 2011.

42. "Adbusters," Adbusters Media Foundation, www.adbusters.org, accessed June 29, 2009.

43. Ibid.

44. www.nikesweatshop.net, accessed June 29, 2002.

45. Nat Ives, "Anti-Ad Group Tries Advertising," *New York Times* (September 21, 2004), www.nytimes.com, accessed September 21, 2004.

46. Julie L. Ozanne and Bige Saatcioglu, "Participatory Action Research," *Journal of Consumer Research* 35 (October 2008): 423–39.

47. For consumer research and discussions related to public policy issues, see Paul N. Bloom and Stephen A. Greyser, "The Maturing of Consumerism," *Harvard Business Review* (November–December 1981): 130–39; George S. Day, "Assessing the Effect of Information Disclosure Requirements," *Journal of Marketing* (April 1976): 42–52; Dennis E. Garrett, "The Effectiveness of Marketing Policy Boycotts: Environmental Opposition to Marketing," *Journal of Marketing* 51 (January 1987): 44–53; Michael Houston and Michael Rothschild, "Policy-Related Experiments on Information Provision: A Normative Model and Explication," *Journal of Marketing Research* 17 (November 1980): 432–49; Jacob Jacoby, Wayne D. Hoyer, and David A. Sheluga, *Misperception of Televised Communications* (New York: American Association of Advertising Agencies, 1980); Gene R. Laczniak and Patrick E. Murphy, *Marketing Ethics: Guidelines for Managers* (Lexington, MA: Lexington Books, 1985): 117–23; Lynn Phillips and Bobby Calder, "Evaluating Consumer Protection Laws: Promising Methods," *Journal of Consumer Affairs* 14 (Summer 1980): 9–36; Donald P. Robin and Eric Reidenbach, "Social Responsibility, Ethics, and Marketing Strategy: Closing the Gap Between Concept and Application," *Journal of Marketing* 51 (January 1987): 44–58; Howard Schutz and Marianne Casey, "Consumer Perceptions of Advertising as Misleading," *Journal of Consumer Affairs* 15 (Winter 1981): 340–57; Darlene Brannigan Smith and Paul N. Bloom, "Is Consumerism Dead or Alive? Some New Evidence," in Thomas C. Kinnear, ed., *Advances in Consumer Research* 11 (1984): 369–73.

48. Cf. Philip Kotler and Alan R. Andreasen, *Strategic Marketing for Nonprofit Organizations*, 4th ed. (Upper Saddle River, NJ: Prentice Hall, 1991); Jeff B. Murray and Julie L. Ozanne, "The Critical Imagination: Emancipatory

Interests in Consumer Research," *Journal of Consumer Research* 18 (September 1991): 192–244; William D. Wells, "Discovery-Oriented Consumer Research," *Journal of Consumer Research* 19 (March 1993): 489–504.

49. Karl Greenberg, "American Airlines, AAPD to Create Positive Ads Featuring Disabled People," *Marketing Daily* (March 30, 2009), www.mediapost .com, accessed March 30, 2009.

50. Quoted in Chuck Raasch, "'Conscientious Consumption' Survives Recession," *USA Today* (November 29, 2012), http://www.usatoday.com/story/ news/nation/2012/11/28/giving-back-post-great-recession/1634703/, accessed January 2, 2013; http://www.causemarketingforum.com/site/ c.bkLUKcOTLkK4E/b.6443937/k.41E3/Background_and_Basics.htm, accessed February 16, 2013.

51. "Cause Marketing Does Affect Brand Purchase," Posted by Sheila Shayon on August 26, 2011, Brand Channel, http://www.brandchannel.com/ home/post/2011/08/26/Cause-Marketing-Does-Affect-Brand-Purchase .aspx, accessed November 3, 2013.

52. Karl Greenberg, "Fewer People Find Social Ads Annoying," *Marketing Daily* (December 10, 2012), http://www.mediapost.com/publications/ article/188850/fewer-people-find-social-ads-annoying.html?edition= 54351#axzz2Ekc0H7Ua, accessed January 4, 2013.

53. Quoted in Natasha Singer, "YOU FOR SALE: Your Online Attention, Bought in an Instant," *New York Times* (November 17, 2012), http://www .nytimes.com/2012/11/18/technology/your-online-attention-bought-in-an-instant-by-advertisers.html?pagewanted=1, accessed January 4, 2013.

54. Ibid.

55. "Identity Theft Action Plan, Pennsylvania Commission on Crime and Delinquency," http://www.portal.state.pa.us/portal/server.pt/community/what_ is_id_theft_/12993/identity_theft_statistics/587724, accessed February 16, 2013; "Identity Theft," Federal Trade Commission, http://www.consumer .ftc.gov/features/feature-0014-identity-theft, accessed February 16, 2013; "Identity Theft Victim Statistics," http://www.identitytheft.info/victims .aspx, accessed February 16, 2013; "Hacker 'Botnet' Hijacked Online Searches," Phys.org (February 7, 2013), http://phys.org/news/2013-02-hacker-botnet-hijacked-online.html, accessed February 16, 2013; Nicole Perlroth, "Hackers in China Attacked the *Times* for Last 4 Months," *New York Times* (January 30, 2013), http://www.nytimes .com/2013/01/31/technology/chinese-hackers-infiltrate-new-york-times-computers.html?pagewanted=all, accessed February 16, 2013.

56. "Save Money on Car Insurance Through GPS Tracking, LiveView GPS" (February 9, 2012), http://www.liveviewgps.com/blog/save-money-on-car-insurance-through-gps-tracking/, accessed February 16, 2013; http:// www.motosafety.com/, accessed February 16, 2013.

57. Mariella Moon, "Uniforms with Microchip Notify Parents If Their Children Skip School," Mashable (March 26, 2012), http:// mashable.com/2012/03/26/uniforms-with-microchip/?utm_ medium=email&utm_source=newsletter, accessed January 4, 2013.

58. Susannah Fox, "Americans Living with Disability and Their Technology Profile," PewInternet (January 21, 2011), http://pewinternet.org/ Reports/2011/Disability.aspx, accessed January 2, 2013; Terry L. Childers and Carol Kaufman-Scarborough, "Expanding Opportunities for Online Shoppers with Disabilities," *Journal of Business Research* 62 (2009), 572–78.

59. Michael R. Solomon, Kel Smith, Nadine Vogel, and Natalie T. Wood, "Virtual Freedom for People with Disabilities," Society for Disability Studies, Philadelphia (June 2010).

60. Zoe Fox, "4 Ways iPads Are Changing the Lives of People with Disabilities," Mashable (July 25, 2011), http://mashable.com/2011/07/25/ipads-disabilities/?utm_source=feedburner&utm_medium=email&utm_camp aign=Feed%3A+Mashable+%28Mashable%29, accessed January 2, 2013.

61. Nick Bilton," An iPhone App Helps the Blind Identify Currency," *New York Times* (March 9, 2011), http://bits.blogs.nytimes.com/2011/03/09/ an-iphone-app-helps-the-blind-identify-currency/?scp=1&sq=app%20 help%20to%20blind&st=cse, accessed January 2, 2013.

62. David Zax, "'Virtual Iraq' Helps Soldiers Overcome PTSD," Fast Company (February 17, 2011), http://www.fastcompany.com/1728656/Virtual-Iraq-Helps-Soldiers-Overcome-PTSD, accessed January 2, 2013.

63. Quoted in Karen Barrow, "Difference Is the Norm on These Dating Sites," *New York Times* (December 27, 2010), http://www.nytimes .com/2010/12/28/health/28dating.html?emc=eta1, accessed January 2, 2013.; http://www.dating4disabled.com/, accessed February 16, 2013; http://www.nolongerlonely.com/, accessed February 16, 2013.

64. "Healthy Food Financing Initiative," Office of Community Services, U.S. Department of Health and Human Services (January 18, 2011), http:// www.acf.hhs.gov/programs/ocs/resource/healthy-food-financing-initiative-0, accessed January 4, 2013.

65. National Association for Media Literacy Education, http://namle.net/ publications/media-literacy-definitions/, accessed March 1, 2013.

66. Robert Roy Britt, "14 Percent of U.S. Adults Can't Read," *Live Science* (January 10, 2009), http://www.livescience.com/3211-14-percent-adults-read.html, accessed March 1, 2013.

67. Natalie Ross Adkins and Julie L. Ozanne, "The Low Literate Consumer," *Journal of Consumer Research* 32, no. 1 (June 2005): 93–105.

68. Natalie Ross Adkins and Julie L. Ozanne, "The Low Literate Consumer," *Journal of Consumer Research* 32, no. 1 (2005): 93; Madhubalan Viswanathan, José Antonio Rosa, and James Edwin Harris, "Decision-Making and Coping of Functionally Illiterate Consumers and Some Implications for Marketing Management," *Journal of Marketing* 69, no. 1 (2005): 15.

69. "5 Lessons From the Companies Making Sustainability More Profitable Than Ever," Fast Company Co.Exist (February 5, 2013), http://www .fastcoexist.com/1681339/5-lessons-from-the-companies-making-sustainability-more-profitable-than-ever, accessed March 1, 2013.

70. Quoted in "What Is Sustainability?" United States Environmental Protection Agency," http://www.epa.gov/sustainability/basicinfo.htm, accessed March 1, 2013.

71. Emily Burg, "Whole Foods Is Consumers' Favorite Green Brand," *Marketing Daily*, www.mediapost.com, accessed May 10, 2007.

72. Jack Neff, "As More Marketers Go Green, Fewer Consumers Willing to Pay For It," *Advertising Age* (September 24, 2012), http://adage.com/article/news/ marketers-green-fewer-consumers-pay/237377/, accessed January 4, 2013.

73. Remi Trudel and June Cotte, "Does It Pay to Be Good?," *MIT Sloan Management Review* 61 (Winter 2009): 61–68.

74. Stephanie Clifford and Andrew Martin, "As Consumers Cut Spending, 'Green' Products Lose Allure," *New York Times* (April 21, 2011), http:// www.nytimes.com/2011/04/22/business/energy-environment/22green .html?hp&_r=0, accessed March 1, 2013.

75. Bruce Horovitz, "Axe Showerpool Promo Raises Eyebrows," *USA Today* (September 17, 2012), http://usatoday30.usatoday.com/ money/business/story/2012/09/17/axe-showerpool-promo-raises-eyebrows/57797640/1, accessed March 1, 2013.

76. "Amazon Starts a Shopping Site for the Environmental Crowd," *New York Times* (September 26, 2012), http://bits.blogs.nytimes.com/2012/ 09/26/amazon-starts-a-shopping-site-for-the-environmental-crowd/?ref=technology, accessed January 4, 2013.

77. Wendy Koch, "'Green' Product Claims Are Often Misleading," *USA Today* (October 26, 2010), http://content.usatoday.com/communities/greenhouse/ post/2010/10/green-product-claims/1?csp=34money&utm_ source=feedburner&utm_medium=feed&utm_campaign=Feed%3A+ UsatodaycomMoney-TopStories+%28Money+-+Top+Stories%29, accessed April 10, 2011.

78. Mark Dolliver, "Thumbs Down on Corporate Green Efforts," *Adweek* (August 31, 2010), http://www.adweek.com/aw/content_display/news/ client/e3i84260d4301c885f91b2cd8a712f323cf, accessed April 10, 2011; Sarah Mahoney, "Americans Hate Faux Green Marketers," *Marketing Daily* (March 25, 2011), http://www.mediapost.com/publications/?fa=Articles .showArticle&art_aid=147415&nid=125122, accessed April 10, 2011.

79. www.lohas.com/about.htm, accessed March 2, 2013.

80. Russell W. Belk, "The Role of Possessions in Constructing and Maintaining a Sense of Past," in Marvin E. Goldberg, Gerald Gorn, and Richard W. Pollay, eds., *Advances in Consumer Research* 17 (Provo, UT: Association for Consumer Research, 1989): 669–76.

81. David E. Sanger, "For a Job Well Done, Japanese Enshrine the Chip," *New York Times* (December 11, 1990): A4.

82. Rob Walker, "The Worm Turns," *New York Times Magazine* (May 20, 2007), accessed May 20, 2007; www.terracycle.net, accessed June 4, 2011.

83. Jacob Jacoby, Carol K. Berning, and Thomas F. Dietvorst, "What About Disposition?" *Journal of Marketing* 41 (April 1977): 22–28.

84. Brian Wansink, S. Adam Brasel, and Steven Amjad, "The Mystery of the Cabinet Castaway: Why We Buy Products We Never Use," *Journal of Family & Consumer Sciences* 92, no. 1 (2000): 104–7.

85. Jennifer Lach, "Welcome to the Hoard Fest," *American Demographics* (April 2000): 8–9.

86. Norimitsu Onishi, "How Do Japanese Dump Trash? Let Us Count the Myriad Ways," *New York Times* (May 12, 2005), www.nytimes.com, accessed May 12, 2005.

87. Debra J. Dahab, James W. Gentry, and Wanru Su, "New Ways to Reach Non-Recyclers: An Extension of the Model of Reasoned Action to Recycling Behaviors," in Frank R. Kardes and Mita Sujan, eds., *Advances in Consumer Research* 22 (Provo, UT: Association for Consumer Research): 251–56.

88. Richard P. Bagozzi and Pratibha A. Dabholkar, "Consumer Recycling Goals and Their Effect on Decisions to Recycle," *Psychology & Marketing* 11, no. 4 (1994): 313–40; see also L. J. Shrum, Tina M. Lowrey, and John A. McCarty, "Recycling as a Marketing Problem: A Framework for Strategy Development," *Psychology & Marketing* 11 (July–August 1994): 393–416; Dahab, Gentry, and Su, "New Ways to Reach Non-Recyclers."

89. "Gap Asks Consumers to Recycle Their Jeans," *RetailingToday.com* (October 5, 2010), http://www.retailingtoday.com/article/gap-asks-consumers-recycle-their-jeans, accessed April 18, 2011.

90. John F. Sherry, Jr., "A Sociocultural Analysis of a Midwestern American Flea Market," *Journal of Consumer Research* 17 (June 1990): 13–30.

91. Allan J. Magrath, "If Used Product Sellers Ever Get Organized, Watch Out," *Marketing News* (June 25, 1990): 9; Kevin McCrohan and James D. Smith, "Consumer Participation in the Informal Economy," *Journal of the Academy of Marketing Science* 15 (Winter 1990): 62.

92. John F. Sherry, Jr., "Dealers and Dealing in a Periodic Market: Informal Retailing in Ethnographic Perspective," *Journal of Retailing* 66 (Summer 1990): 174.

93. "Recommerce," Trendwatching.com, October 2011, http://www.trendwatching.com/trends/recommerce/, accessed March 1, 2013.

94. Quoted in Jenna Wortham, "Neighborly Borrowing, Over the Online Fence," *New York Times* (August 28, 2010), http://www.nytimes.com/2010/08/29/business/29ping.html?_r51&scp51&sq5collaborative%20consumption&st5cse, accessed April 18, 2011; www.snapgoods.com, accessed June 4, 2011; www.neighborgoods.com, accessed June 4, 2011; www.sharesomesugar.com, accessed June 4, 2011.

95. J. E. Escalas and J. R. Bettman, "You Are What They Eat: The Influence of Reference Groups on Consumers' Connections to Brands," *Journal of Consumer Research* 13 (2003): 339–48.

96. Kenneth E. Nusbaum, James C. Wright, and Michael R. Solomon, "Attitudes of Food Animal Veterinarians to Continuing Education in Agriterrorism," paper presented at the 53rd Annual Meeting of the Animal Disease Research Workers in Southern States, University of Florida (February 2001).

97. Sean Gallagher, "Security Pros Predict "Major" Cyber Terror Attack This Year," *Ars Technica* (January 4, 2013), http://arstechnica.com/security/2013/01/security-pros-predict-major-cyberterror-attack-this-year/, accessed April 3, 2013.

98. Betty Mohr, "The Pepsi Challenge: Managing a Crisis," *Prepared Foods* (March 1994): 13.

99. "Boston Officials Livid Over Ad Stunt," *New York Times* (February 1, 2007), www.nytimes.com, accessed February 1, 2007.

100. http://www.experienceproject.com/groups/Am-Addicted-To-Chapstick/34083, accessed May 29, 2011.

101. Erik Sass, "Woman Kills Baby for Interrupting FarmVille," *Social Media & Marketing Daily* (October 28, 2010), http://www.mediapost.com/publications/?fa=Articles.showArticle&art_aid=138502&nid=120184, accessed April 30, 2011.

102. Bob Al-Greene, "Late-Night Gadget Use Damages Your Sleep Cycle," *Mashable* (November 19, 2012), http://mashable.com/2012/11/19/gadgets-sleep/, accessed January 4, 2013.

103. Martin Fackler, "In Korea, A Boot Camp Cure for Web Obsession," *New York Times* (November 18, 2007), www.nytimes.com/2007/11/18/Technology/18rehab.html, accessed November 19, 2007.

104. Chris Pollard, "A Cruel World," *The Sun (U.K.)* (September 13, 2010), http://www.diigo.com/cached?url=http%3A%2F%2Fwww.thesun.co.uk%2Fsol%2Fhomepage%2Fnews%2F3135278%2FMum-addicted-to-Small-World-neglected-kids-and-let-dogs-starve-to-death.html, accessed February 23, 2011.

105. Quoted in http://cyberbullying.us/, accessed March 2, 2013.

106. Quoted in Jan Hoffman, "Online Bullies Pull Schools Into the Fray," *New York Times* (June 27, 2010), http://www.nytimes.com/2010/06/28/style/28bully.html?pagewanted=1&_r=0&emc=eta1, accessed January 4, 2013.

107. Matt Petronzio, "Do You Suffer From These 4 Tech Afflictions?" Mashable (June 1, 2012), http://mashable.com/2012/06/01/tech-addiction/?WT.mc_id=en_top_stories&utm_campaign=Top%2BStories&utm_medium=email&utm_source=newsletter, accessed January 4, 2013.

108. Derek N. Hassay and Malcolm C. Smith, "Compulsive Buying: An Examination of the Consumption Motive," *Psychology & Marketing* 13 (December 1996): 741–52.

109. Nancy M. Ridgway, Monika Kukar-Kinney, and Kent B. Monroe, "An Expanded Conceptualization and a New Measure of Compulsive Buying," *Journal of Consumer Research* 35, no. 4 (2008): 622–39; Thomas C. O'Guinn and Ronald J. Faber, "Compulsive Buying: A Phenomenological Explanation," *Journal of Consumer Research* 16 (September 1989): 154.

110. Curtis L. Taylor, "Guys Who Buy, Buy, Buy," *Newsday* (October 6, 2006): Jim Thornton, "Buy Now, Pay Later," *Men's Health* (December, 2004): 109–12.

111. Georgia Witkin, "The Shopping Fix," *Health* (May 1988): 73; see also Arch G. Woodside and Randolph J. Trappey III, "Compulsive Consumption of a Consumer Service: An Exploratory Study of Chronic Horse Race Track Gambling Behavior," working paper #90-MKTG-04, A. B. Freeman School of Business, Tulane University (1990); Rajan Nataraajan and Brent G. Goff, "Manifestations of Compulsiveness in the Consumer-Marketplace Domain," *Psychology & Marketing* 9 (January 1992): 31–44; Joann Ellison Rodgers, "Addiction: A Whole New View," *Psychology Today* (September–October 1994): 32.

112. Deena Beasley and Nichola Groom, "States Race to Legalize Online Gambling," *The Huffington Post* (February 28, 2013), http://www.huffingtonpost.com/2013/03/01/online-gaming-legalized-in-new-jersey_n_2784866.html, accessed March 1, 2013.

113. Spencer E. Ante and Alexandra Berzon, "Gambling Industry Bets Virtual Money Turns Real," *Wall Street Journal* (December 20, 2012), http://professional.wsj.com/article/SB100014241278873247313045781 91741064162164.html, accessed January 4, 2013.

114. Helen Reynolds, *The Economics of Prostitution* (Springfield, IL: Thomas, 1986).

115. Patrick Di Justo, "How to Sell Your Body for $46 Million," *Wired* (August 2003): 47.

116. Amy Harmon, "Illegal Kidney Auction Pops Up on eBay's Site," *New York Times* (September 3, 1999), www.nytimes.com, accessed September 3, 1999.

117. Scott Carney, "Inside the Business of Selling Human Body Parts," *Wired* (January 31, 2011), http://www.wired.com/magazine/2011/01/ff_redmarkets/2, accessed March 1, 2013.

118. Di Justo, "How to Sell Your Body for $46 Million."

119. Reuters, "German Parents Offer Baby on eBay," *New York Times* (May 25, 2008), www.nytimes.com/2008/05/25/world/europe/25ebayby.html?_r=1&scp=1&sq=baby . . . , accessed May 25, 2008.

120. "Advertisers Face Up to the New Morality: Making the Pitch," *Bloomberg* (July 8, 1997).

121. "Shoplifting: Bess Myerson's Arrest Highlights a Multibillion-Dollar Problem That Many Stores Won't Talk About," *Life* (August 1988): 32.

122. "New Survey Shows Shoplifting Is a Year-Round Problem," *Business Wire* (April 12, 1998).

123. "Customer Not King, But Thief," *Marketing News* (December 9, 2002): 4.

124. Catherine A. Cole, "Deterrence and Consumer Fraud," *Journal of Retailing* 65 (Spring 1989): 107–20; Stephen J. Grove, Scott J. Vitell, and David Strutton, "Non-Normative Consumer Behavior and the Techniques of Neutralization," in Terry Childers et al., eds., *Marketing Theory and Practice,* 1989 AMA Winter Educators' Conference (Chicago: American Marketing Association, 1989): 131–35.

125. Mark Curnutte, "The Scope of the Shoplifting Problems," *Gannett News Service* (November 29, 1997).

126. Anthony D. Cox, Dena Cox, Ronald D. Anderson, and George P. Moschis, "Social Influences on Adolescent Shoplifting—Theory, Evidence, and Implications for the Retail Industry," *Journal of Retailing* 69 (Summer 1993): 234–46.

127. Stephanie Kang, "New Return Policy: Retailers Say 'No' to Serial Exchangers," *Wall Street Journal* (November 29, 2004): B1.

128. Leo Burnett, "Behind New System to Blunt Counterfeiting in China '1-Tag' Lets Consumers Authenticate Products and Avoid Potentially Hazardous Ripoffs," *AdAge Global* (January 31, 2011), http://adage.com/article/global-news/leo-burnett-creates-system-stop-counterfeiting-china/148571/, accessed January 2, 2013.

129. www.dogdoo.com, accessed March 1, 2013.

130. Nina M. Lentini, "Products No Longer So Personal," *Marketing Daily* (February 9, 2007), www.mediapost.com, accessed February 9, 2007; Karin Bittar, "'Pee Ship' Enterprise for Clearblue Pregnancy Test," *Marketing Daily* (December 20, 2006), www.mediapost.com, accessed December 20, 2006.

131. "Airline Operators Still Fighting Legal Compensation Claims," *BBC News U.K.* (October 9, 2013), http://www.bbc.co.uk/programmes/b006mg74/features/flight-compensation-thomas-cook-monarch, accessed December 17, 2013.

132. http://www.uswitch.com/gas-electricity/news/2013/04/22/are-prepay-meters-costing-consumers-more/, accessed December 17, 2013.

133. Dan Levine and Lisa Baertlein, "Judge Tosses Happy Meal Lawsuit Against McDonald's," *Reuters* San Francisco (April 4, 2012), http://www.reuters.com/article/2012/04/04/us-mcdonalds-lawsuit-idUSBRE8331DX20120404.

134. Simon Stone, "Naming Rights to Old Trafford will not be Sold Insist Manchester United After New Sponsorship Deal is Agreed," *The Independent U.K.* (April 8, 2013), http://www.independent.co.uk/sport/football/premier-league/naming-rights-to-old-trafford-will-not-be-sold-insist-manchester-united-after-new-sponsorship-deal-is-agreed-8564063.html.

135. Ann-Christine Diaz, "Facial Recognition Technology Makes Marketers a Fun Big Brother," *Advertising Age*, http://adage.com/article/news/brands-facial-recognition-campaigns/244233/, accessed December 17, 2013.

136. European Union Agency for Network and Information Security Web site, http://www.enisa.europa.eu/.

137. Bryan Ching-Wing Lo and Kim-Len Yap, "Are Malaysian Companies Ready for Corporate Social Responsibility?" *Labuan e-Journal of Muamalat and Society* 5 (2011): 11–15, http://wwwkal.ums.edu.my/ljms/2011/LJMS_vol5_2011_2.pdf, accessed December 17, 2013.

SECTION 1 NIELSEN NUGGET

In a unique partnership with The Nielsen Company, you have access to data-driven exercises that allow you to analyze actual data gathered by one of the world's leading consumer research organizations.

For nearly a century, Nielsen has enabled organizations in various industries to make strategic decisions based on information it gathers through evolving research methodologies. Nielsen helps media companies better understand viewers, listeners, and the industry as a whole by providing insights for audience measurement, advertising effectiveness, and overall marketing performance and cross-platform strategies. Nielsen's broad range of consumer packaged goods (CPG) analytics and consulting services are specifically designed for, and with, top CPG manufacturers and retailers, to ensure that they have the most accurate view of the consumer and the marketplace. Spanning 80 countries across five continents, Nielsen maintains its leadership position by providing customized solutions based on local marketing research.

Scenario: Awesome Beans is a manufacturer with offerings across many categories. Although they have experienced flat sales in coffee over the past few years, the category has recently begun to show slight growth. Awesome Beans would like to capitalize on this trend, to make sure they are receiving at least their fair share of the category growth. The company recently conducted an attitudinal segmentation study. Survey research resulted in differentiating coffee consumers into four categories based on their common needs and buying motivation.

Challenge: Awesome Beans wants to identify which of the four segments offers the greatest opportunity for sales growth. In addition, the company hopes to better understand this attitudinal segment demographically, so it can determine how best to reach these coffee buyers in terms of placement and message.

After reviewing the data provided:

1 Determine which segment Awesome Beans should choose to target more aggressively.

2 Determine which of the household types identified would be the most appropriate demographically to target with promotions.

3 Which of the demographic dimensions should be considered as potential segment-defining variables?

Attitudinal Group	% Buyers	% Value	Index	$ Value (000s)
Coffee Bingers	29	25	86	$ 74,323
Café Callers	33	27	83	$ 80,295
Flavour Followers	13	12	96	$ 36,433
Premium People	24	35	145	$102,471

Attitudinal groups were segmented based on their responses to survey questions. The data in the previous table show:

- The size of each group, in terms of share of coffee buyers (% Buyers)
- The percent of coffee dollar sales (% value)
- Dollar Index (% Value/% Buyers $\times$ 100). A score of 100 is average.
- $ Value—Total coffee $ spent by consumer segment

Buyer Index vs. All Shoppers	Coffee Bingers	Café Callers	Flavour Followers	Premium People
AWESOME BEANS	103	100	104	96
COMPETITOR 1	98	97	110	100
COMPETITOR 2	95	101	95	105
COMPETITOR 3	88	113	103	100

Buyer Index = % Buyers within each group/% Buyers of Total Respondents *100

Demographic	Coffee Bingers	Café Callers	Flavour Followers	Premium People
Young Families	20	12	16	24
Older Families	15	25	13	10
Older Singles and Couples	33	35	45	25

YOU SLEPT THROUGH HALF OF CHEMISTRY INSTEAD OF ALL OF IT 👍

REWARD YOURSELF **WITH** *SIRLOIN!*

SIRLOIN STEAK 'N' CHEDDAR CIABATTA

Section 2 • Internal Influences on Consumer Behavior

In this section, we focus on the internal dynamics of consumers. Although "no man is an island," each of us is to some degree "self-contained" in terms of receiving information about the outside world. We are constantly confronted by advertising messages, products, and other people—not to mention our own thoughts about ourselves—that affect our moods. Each chapter in this section looks at some aspect that may be "invisible" to others, but that we find very important.

Chapter 5 describes the process of perception; the way we absorb and interpret information about products and other people from the outside world. Chapter 6 focuses on how we store this information and how it adds to our existing knowledge about the world. Chapter 7 explores how our views about ourselves—particularly our sexuality and our physical appearance—affect what we do, want, and buy. Chapter 8 goes on to consider how we combine what we feel, think, and do to form attitudes toward the things we buy.

CHAPTERS AHEAD

Chapter 5 • **Perception**

Chapter 6 • **Learning and Memory**

Chapter 7 • **The Self**

Chapter 8 • **Attitudes and Persuasion**

Chapter 5 • Perception

Chapter Objectives

When you finish reading this chapter you will understand why:

1. The design of a product is now a key driver of its success or failure.

2. Products and commercial messages often appeal to our senses, but because of the profusion of these messages most of them won't influence us.

3. Perception is a three-stage process that translates raw stimuli into meaning.

4. Subliminal advertising is a controversial—but largely ineffective—way to talk to consumers.

5. We interpret the stimuli to which we do pay attention according to learned patterns and expectations.

6. The field of semiotics helps us to understand how marketers use symbols to create meaning.

MyMarketingLab™
⭐ Improve Your Grade!

Over 10 million students improved their results using the Pearson MyLabs.
Visit **mymktlab.com** for simulations, tutorials, and end-of-chapter problems.

Source: LensKiss/Shutterstock.

The European vacation has been wonderful, and this stop in Lisbon is no exception. Still, after two weeks of eating his way through some of the Continent's finest pastry shops and restaurants, Gary's getting a bit of a craving for his family's favorite snack—a good old American box of Oreos and an ice-cold carton of milk. Unbeknownst to his wife, Janeen, he had stashed away some cookies "just in case"—this was the time to break them out.

Now all he needs is the milk. On an impulse, Gary decides to surprise Janeen with a mid-afternoon treat. He sneaks out of the hotel room while she's napping and finds the nearest *grosa.* When he heads to the small refrigerated section, though, he's puzzled—no milk here. Undaunted, Gary asks the clerk, *"Leite, por favor?"* The clerk quickly smiles and points to a rack in the middle of the store piled with little white square boxes. No, that can't be right—Gary resolves to work on his Portuguese. He repeats the question, and again he gets the same answer.

Finally, he investigates and, sure enough, he sees that the boxes have labels saying they contain something called ultra heat treated (UHT) milk. Nasty! Who in the world would drink milk out of a little box that's been sitting on a warm shelf for who knows how long? Gary dejectedly returns to the hotel, his snack-time fantasies crumbling like so many stale cookies.

Sensation

Although news to Gary, many people in the world do drink milk out of a box every day. UHT, pasteurized milk that has been heated until the bacteria that cause it to spoil are destroyed, can last for 5 to 6 months without refrigeration if unopened. The milk tastes slightly sweeter than fresh milk but otherwise it's basically the same.

Shelf-stable milk is particularly popular in Europe, where there is less refrigerator space in homes and stores tend to carry less inventory than in the United States. Seven out of ten Europeans drink it routinely. Manufacturers keep trying to crack the U.S. market as well, though analysts doubt their prospects. To begin with, milk consumption in the United States is declining steadily as teenagers choose soft drinks instead, even though the Milk Industry Foundation pumped $44 million into an advertising campaign to promote milk drinking ("Got Milk?").

Beyond that, it's hard to convince Americans to drink milk out of a box. In focus groups, U.S. consumers say they have trouble believing the milk is not spoiled or unsafe. In addition, they consider the square, quart-sized boxes more suitable for dry food. Nonetheless, many schools and fast-food chains do buy UHT milk because of its long shelf life.[1] Still, although Americans may not think twice about drinking a McDonald's

McFlurry made with shelf-stable milk, it's going to be a long, uphill battle to change their minds about the proper partner for a bagful of Oreos.

Whether we experience the taste of Oreos, the sight of a Viva La Juicy perfume ad, or the sound of the music group the Black Eyed Peas, we live in a world overflowing with sensations. Wherever we turn, a symphony of colors, sounds, and odors bombards us. Some of the "notes" in this symphony occur naturally, such as the loud barking of a dog, the shades of the evening sky, or the heady smell of a rose bush. Others come from people: The person who plops down next to you in class might wear swirling tattoos, bright pink pants, and enough nasty perfume to make your eyes water.

Marketers certainly contribute to this commotion. Consumers are never far from pop-up ads, product packages, radio and television commercials, and billboards—all clamoring for our attention. Sometimes we go out of our way to experience "unusual" sensations: feeling thrills from bungee jumping; playing virtual reality games; or going to theme parks such as Universal Studios, which offers "Fear Factor Live" attractions in which vacationers swallow gross things or perform stomach-churning stunts.[2]

However, only a select few try to cram down as many peanut butter and banana sandwiches, Moon Pies, or cheesesteaks as (in)humanly possible in events sponsored by MLE/FOCE (Major League Eating/Federation of Competitive Eating). Others happily blast teeth-rattling Lupe Fiasco cuts from their booming car speakers. Each of us copes with this bombardment of sensations by paying attention to some stimuli and tuning out others. The messages to which we *do* pay attention often wind up affecting us differently from what the sponsors intended; we each put our personal "spin" on things as we assign meanings consistent with our own unique experiences, biases, and desires. This chapter focuses on the process of absorbing sensations and then using these to interpret the surrounding world.

Sensation refers to the immediate response of our sensory receptors (eyes, ears, nose, mouth, fingers, skin) to basic stimuli such as light, color, sound, odor, and texture. **Perception** is the process by which people select, organize, and interpret these sensations. The study of perception, then, focuses on what we *add* to these raw sensations in order to give them meaning.

Our brains receive external stimuli, or *sensory inputs,* on a number of channels. We may see a billboard, hear a jingle, feel the softness of a cashmere sweater, taste a new flavor of ice cream, or smell a leather jacket. These inputs are the raw data that begin the perceptual process. Sensory data from the external environment (e.g., hearing a tune on the radio) can generate internal sensory experiences; a song might trigger a young man's memory of his first dance and bring to mind the smell of his date's perfume or the feel of her hair on his cheek.

Marketers' messages are more effective when they appeal to several senses. For example, in a recent study one group read ad copy for potato chips that only mentioned the taste, whereas another group's ad copy emphasized the product's smell and texture, in addition to its taste. The participants in the second group came away thinking the chips would taste better than did those whose ad message only touched on taste.[3]

Each product's unique sensory qualities help it to stand out from the competition, especially if the brand creates a unique association with the sensation. The Owens-Corning Fiberglass Corporation was the first company to trademark a color when it used bright pink for its insulation material; it adopted the Pink Panther as its spokescharacter.[4] Harley-Davidson actually tried to trademark the distinctive sound a "hog" makes when it revs up. These responses are an important part of **hedonic consumption**: multisensory, fantasy, and emotional aspects of consumers' interactions with products.[5] Remember that in earlier chapters we talked about how physical cues "prime" us to react even when we're not aware of this impact. The sensations we experience are **context effects** that subtly influence how we think about products we encounter. Here are some recent examples from consumer research:

● Respondents evaluated products more harshly when they stood on a tile floor rather than a carpeted floor.[6]

● Fans of romance movies rate them higher when they watch them in a cold room (the researchers explain this is because they compensate for the low physical temperature with psychological warmth the movie provides).[7]

● When a product is scented, consumers are more likely to remember other attributes about it after they encounter it.[8]

OBJECTIVE 1

The design of a product is now a key driver of its success or failure.

When guests at Omni luxury hotels visit the hotel chain's Web site to reserve a room, they hear the sound of soft chimes playing. The signature scent of lemongrass and green tea hits them as they enter the lobby. In their rooms, they will find eucalyptus bath salts and Sensation Bars, minibars stocked with items such as mojito-flavored jellybeans, and miniature Zen gardens.

Welcome to the new era of **sensory marketing**, where companies think carefully about the impact of sensations on our product experiences. From hotels to carmakers to brewers, companies recognize that our senses help us decide which products appeal to us—and which ones stand out from a host of similar offerings in the marketplace. In this section, we'll take a closer look at how some smart marketers use our sensory systems to create a competitive advantage.

Vision

Sure, Apple's products usually work pretty well—but that's not why many people buy them. Sleek styling and simple, compact features telegraph an aura of modernity, sophistication, and just plain "cool." Marketers rely heavily on visual elements in advertising, store design, and packaging. They communicate meanings on the *visual channel* through a product's color, size, and styling.

Colors may even influence our emotions more directly. Evidence suggests that some colors (particularly red) create feelings of arousal and stimulate appetite, and others (such as blue) create more relaxing feelings. American Express launched its Blue card after its research found that people describe the color as "providing a sense of limitlessness and peace."[9] Advertisements of products presented against a backdrop of blue are better liked than the same ads shown against a red background, and cross-cultural research indicates a consistent preference for blue whether people live in Canada or Hong Kong.[10]

Marketing Opportunity

The sensory experiences we receive from products and services play an increasingly key role when we choose among competing options. As manufacturing costs go down and the amount of "stuff" that people accumulate goes up, consumers want to buy things that will provide hedonic value in addition to simply doing what they're designed to do. A *Dilbert* comic strip poked fun at this trend when it featured a product designer who declared: "Quality is yesterday's news. Today we focus on the emotional impact of the product." Fun aside, the new focus on emotional experience is consistent with psychological research finding that people prefer additional *experiences* to additional *possessions* as their incomes rise.[11]

In this environment, form *is* function. Two young entrepreneurs named Adam Lowry and Eric Ryan discovered that basic truth when they quit their day jobs to develop a line of house-cleaning products they called Method. Cleaning products—what a yawn, right?

Think again: For years, companies such as Procter & Gamble have plodded along, peddling boring boxes of soap powder to generations of housewives who suffered in silence, scrubbing and buffing, yearning for the daily respite of martini time. Lowry and Ryan gambled that they could offer an alternative: cleaners in exotic scents such as cucumber, lavender, and ylang-ylang that come in aesthetically pleasing bottles. The bet paid off. Within two years, the partners were cleaning up, taking in more than $2 million in revenue. Shortly thereafter, they hit it big when Target contracted to sell Method products in its stores.[12]

There's a method to Target's madness. Design is no longer the province of upper-crust sophisticates who never got close enough to a cleaning product to be revolted by it. The store chain helped to make designers such as Karim Rashid, Michael Graves, Philippe Starck, Todd Oldham, and Isaac Mizrahi household names. In fact, recent research evidence suggests that our brains are wired to appreciate good design: Respondents who were hooked up to a brain apparatus called an fMRI (functional magnetic resonance imaging) scanner showed faster reaction times when they saw aesthetically pleasing packages even compared to well-known brands like Coca-Cola.[13] Mass-market consumers thirst for great design, and they reward those companies that give it to them with their enthusiastic patronage and loyalty. From razor blades such as the Gillette Sensor to the Apple iPad2 and even to the lowly trash can, design *is* substance. Form *is* function.

• • • • • • • • • • • • • • • • • •

Source: Courtesy of Method Products.

People who complete tasks when the words or images appear on red backgrounds perform better when they have to remember details; however, they excel at tasks requiring an imaginative response when the words or images are displayed on blue backgrounds. Olympic athletes who wear red uniforms are more likely to defeat competitors in blue uniforms, and men rate women who wear red as more attractive than those who wear blue. In one study, interior designers created bars decorated primarily in red, yellow, or blue and invited people to choose one to hang out in. More people chose the yellow and red rooms, and these guests were more social and active—and ate more. In contrast, partygoers in the blue room stayed longer.[14] Maybe the moral is: Get your prof to give you multiple-choice exams on red paper, essays on blue paper, and then celebrate afterward in a red room!

Some reactions to color come from learned associations (which we'll tackle in the next chapter). In Western countries, black is the color of mourning, whereas in some Eastern countries, notably Japan, white plays this role. In addition, we associate the color black with power. Teams in both the National Football League and the National Hockey League who wear black uniforms are among the most aggressive; they consistently rank near the top of their leagues in penalties during the season.[15]

Other reactions are a result of biological and cultural differences. Women are drawn toward brighter tones and they are more sensitive to subtle shadings and patterns. Some scientists attribute this to biology; females see color better than males do, and men are 16 times more likely to be color-blind. Age also influences our responsiveness to color. As we get older, our eyes mature and our vision takes on a yellow cast. Colors look duller to older people, so they prefer white and other bright tones. This helps to explain why mature consumers are much more likely to choose a white car; Lexus, which sells heavily in this market, makes 60 percent of its vehicles in white. The trend toward brighter and more complex colors also reflects the increasingly multicultural makeup of the United States. For example, Hispanics tend to prefer brighter colors as a reflection of the intense lighting conditions in Latin America; strong colors keep their character in strong sunlight.[16] That's why Procter & Gamble uses brighter colors in makeup it sells in Latin countries.[17]

Scientists and philosophers have talked about the meanings of colors since the time of Socrates in the 5th century B.C., but it took Sir Isaac Newton in the early 17th century to shine light through a prism and reveal the color spectrum. Even then, Newton's observations weren't totally scientific; he identified seven major colors to be consistent with the number of planets known at that time, as well as the seven notes of the diatonic scale.

BLACK CAKE
White is for virgins.

Jan 30 – Feb 10
SAN FRANCISCO BALLET
Helgi Tomasson, Artistic Director

Stephen Legate and Lucia Lacarra photographed by Stan Musilek.

In Western culture the color black is often associated with sophistication while white connotes innocence.
Source: Used with permission of the San Francisco Ballet.

We now know that perceptions of a color depend on both its physical wavelength and how the mind responds to that stimulus. Yellow is in the middle of wavelengths the human eye can detect, so it is the brightest and attracts attention. The *Yellow Pages* originally were colored yellow to heighten the attention level of bored telephone operators.[18] However, our culture and even our language affect the colors we see. For example, the Welsh language has no words that correspond to green, blue, gray, or brown in English, but it uses other colors that English speakers don't (including one that covers part of green, part of gray, and the whole of our blue). The Hungarian language has two words for what we call red; Navajo has a single word for blue and green, but two words for black.[19]

Because colors elicit such strong emotional reactions, the choice of a *color palette* is a key issue in package design. Companies used to arrive at these choices casually. For example, Campbell's Soup made its familiar can in red and white because a company executive liked the football uniforms at Cornell University! Today, however, color choices are a serious business. These decisions help to "color" our expectations of what's inside the package. When it launched a white cheese as a "sister product" to an existing blue "Castello" cheese, a Danish company introduced it in a red package under the name of Castello Bianco. They chose this color to provide maximum visibility on store shelves. Although taste tests were very positive, sales were disappointing. A subsequent analysis of consumer interpretations showed that the red packaging and the name gave the consumers wrong associations with the product type and its degree of sweetness. Danish consumers had trouble associating the color red with the white cheese. Also, the name *Bianco* connoted a sweetness that was incompatible with the actual taste of the product. The company relaunched it in a white package and named it "White Castello." Almost immediately, sales more than doubled.[20]

Some color combinations come to be so strongly associated with a corporation that they become known as the company's **trade dress**, and courts may even grant exclusive use of specific color combinations: Eastman Kodak's trade dress protects its usage of its distinctive yellow, black, and red boxes. As a rule, however, judges grant trade dress protection only when consumers might be confused about what they buy because of similar coloration of a competitor's packages.[21]

Of course, fashion trends strongly influence our color preferences, so it's no surprise that we tend to encounter a "hot" color on clothing and in home designs in one season that something else replaces the next season (as when the *fashionistas* proclaim, "Brown is the new black!"). These styles do not happen by accident; most people don't know (but now *you* do) that a handful of firms produce *color forecasts* that manufacturers and retailers buy so they can be sure they stock up on the next hot hue. For example, Pantone, Inc. (one of these color arbiters) listed these colors as among its favorites for 2013:[22]

- Linden Green: "brings a lightness and brightness to the deeper shades of fall."
- Mykonos Blue: "a bold, meditative blue, for a classic and relaxed fall look."
- Samba: "red for an expressive and dramatic look."

Dollars and Scents

Odors stir emotions or create a calming feeling. They invoke memories or relieve stress. Perhaps that explains why a French perfume company launched a Sex Pistols scent to commemorate the punk rocker band that created a cult following in the 1970s.[23] One study found that consumers who viewed ads for either flowers or chocolate and who also were exposed to flowery or chocolaty odors spent more time processing the product information and were more likely to try different alternatives within each product category.[24] Another reported that subjects showed higher recall of a test brand's attributes if it was embedded with a scent—and this effect persisted as long as two weeks after the experiment.[25]

Many consumers control the odors in their environments, and this growing interest has spawned a lot of new products since Glade marketed the first air freshener to suburban families in 1956. Today, younger people are at the forefront of scented air as they take advantage of plug-ins, fragrance fans, diffusers, and potpourri. Almost anything is fair game to be scented today; even the country of Lithuania created a perfume (cleverly called "Lithuania") that it will use in embassies, hotels, and other public buildings to convey the country's image. In addition to a blend of sandalwood, cedar, and musk, the designer noted that the fragrance carries the smell of wood fires that is intended to remind users of pagan rituals.[26] Then again, for a while Burger King sold Flame, a body spray with "the scent of seduction" and a "hint of flame broiled meat."[27]

Some of our responses to scents result from early associations that call up good or bad feelings, and that explains why businesses explore connections among smell, memory, and mood.[28] Researchers for Folgers found that for many people the smell of coffee summons up childhood memories of their mothers cooking breakfast, so the aroma reminds them of home. The company turned this insight into a commercial in which a young man in an army uniform arrives home early one morning. He goes to the kitchen, opens a Folgers' package, and the aroma wafts upstairs. His mother opens her eyes, smiles, and exclaims, "He's home!"[29]

Speaking of coffee, Starbucks reverted to its old policy that requires *baristas* to grind a batch of coffee beans each time they brew a new pot instead of just once each morning. The idea is to reclaim lost customers by intensifying the smell of the beans when they enter the store. As the chain grew and adopted more efficient techniques that automated the process, the chain's founder reversed course. He declared that a switch to pre-ground coffee had taken the "romance and theatre" out of a trip to Starbucks: "We achieved fresh-roasted bagged coffee, but at what cost? The loss of aroma—perhaps the most powerful nonverbal signal we had in our stores."[30]

We process fragrance cues in the *limbic system,* the most primitive part of the brain and the place where we experience immediate emotions. One study even found that the scent of fresh cinnamon buns induced sexual arousal in a sample of male students![31]

CB AS I SEE IT

Professor Aradhna Krishna, *University of Michigan*

What is *sensory marketing*, what makes it important, and why is it so fascinating? I define it as "marketing that engages the consumers' senses and affects their behavior." The sensory characteristics of products such as the touch, smell, taste, sound, and look of products have a large impact on consumer behavior. These sensory inputs affect how we feel, how we think, what we remember, what we like, and even how we choose and use products. Specifically, by emphasizing the sensory characteristics of products and services, or even creating new sensations entirely, we can greatly enhance consumers' attitudes, perceptions, and satisfaction.

This concept of sensory marketing has received great attention from many top companies. Advertising within the food industry alone provides some illustrative examples, as companies try to incorporate more senses than just taste into their product experiences, A new brand of chewing gum that

produces a seemingly one-dimensional sensory experience (taste) is named "5" for all five senses, and the tagline reiterates this approach ("stimulate your senses"). Other examples include ads for Magnum 5 Senses Ice Cream and Denny's breakfast ("taste it with all five senses"). Other products that provide a single sensory experience also try to stimulate the other senses. Axe Dark Temptation deodorant spray is advertised with an irresistible chocolate man that appeals to all the girls ("Become as irresistible as chocolate"). Even electronic products want to stimulate our senses, with names like BlackBerry, Chocolate, and Touch.

With this increasing attention to sensory marketing, products and businesses need to act quickly to establish a **sensory signature**. Managers need to ask themselves, "Is there something about my brand that leaves a sensory impression in people's mind?" What sensory characteristic of the product sticks with consumers, helping them to remember the product in a positively unique way? Do they emphasize a sensory experience with the product, or have they constructed a new one entirely? Do they own a sensory experience and thus establish a sensory signature? A terrific example of a company with a definitive sensory signature, and consequently one of the most commonly cited by consultants

in this area, is Singapore Airlines, The airline focuses on creating a distinct visual signature, but perhaps more interesting and memorable is its signature aroma, Floridian Waters. This fragrance was developed specifically for use by Singapore Airlines, and is infused into their hot towels, dispersed throughout the planes, and even worn by flight attendants. The smell is not only invigorating; it also remains in passengers' minds, leading to positive responses upon future exposure to the aroma.

Sensory signatures are just one aspect of sensory marketing. Managers need to look at their offerings and ask themselves whether they can emphasize any sensory aspect of the product to make the product more appealing or create a new sensation completely. An example of the latter is Dippin' Dots: The company's Web site claims that "*After overcoming the sight of their ice cream beads 'pouring' into a cup there's the took of amazement that ice cream can be 'tingly and almost crunchy' [their words!], When the smooth, creamy ice cream begins to melt in their mouth . . . a fan is born!*" Another example is the new fish spas that are opening all over the world, where tiny fish bite the dead skin off customers' feet and offer a different type of pedicure. There's more than one path to a distinctive sensory experience!

In another study, women sniffed T-shirts that men had worn for two days (wonder how much they paid them to do that?) and reported which they preferred. The women were most attracted to the odor of men who were genetically similar to them, though not *too* similar. The researchers claimed the findings were evidence that we are "wired" to select compatible mates, but not those so similar as to cause inbreeding problems.[32]

As scientists continue to discover the powerful effects of smell on behavior, marketers come up with ingenious ways to exploit these connections. Ad companies spend about $80 million per year on scent marketing; the Scent Marketing Institute estimates that number will reach more than $500 million by 2016.[33] This form of *sensory marketing* takes interesting turns as manufacturers find new ways to put scents into products, including men's suits, lingerie, detergents, and aircraft cabins.

OBJECTIVE 2

Products and commercial messages often appeal to our senses, but because of the profusion of these messages most of them won't influence us.

Sound

Coca-Cola chose the song "Wavin' Flag" by an obscure Somalian musician named K'naan to be the centerpiece of its $300 million global advertising campaign linked to the 2010 World Cup. The company rerecorded the song in more than 20 regional flavors that included duets with local musicians (the U.S. version featured David Guetta and Will.I.Am). The tune became embedded with the world games as people around the world found themselves singing it. As a music industry executive explained, "Coke has used a technique we call **audio watermarking**. This is a popular and well-known trick that has been around for centuries and used by composers and producers to weave a

The classic, contoured Coca-Cola bottle also attests to the power of touch. The bottle was designed approximately 90 years ago to satisfy the request of a U.S. bottler for a soft-drink container that people could identify even in the dark.
Source: © Rufus Stone/Alamy.

sound/motif into a piece of music . . . [W]atermarking acts like an 'earworm,' which gets inside our brains and becomes so compulsive that we go around humming it as we walk down the street and not understanding why. We effectively become living, walking, singing commercials for Coke."[34]

Music and other sounds affect people's feelings and behaviors. Some marketers who come up with brand names pay attention to **sound symbolism**; the process by which the way a word sounds influences our assumptions about what it describes and attributes, such as size. For example, consumers are more likely to recognize brand names that begin with a hard consonant like a K (Kellogg's) or P (Pepsi). We also tend to associate certain vowel and consonant sounds (or *phonemes*) with perceptions of large and small size. Mental rehearsal of prices containing numbers with small phonemes results in overestimation of price discounts, whereas mental rehearsal of prices containing numbers with large phonemes results in underestimation.[35]

Touch

Hint to retailers: Follow Apple's lead and encourage customers to handle your products in the store! One recent study demonstrated the potential power of touch: The researchers found that participants who simply touched an item (an inexpensive coffee mug) for 30 seconds or less created a greater level of attachment to the product; this connection in turn boosted what they were willing to pay for it.[36] Britain's Asda grocery chain removed the wrapping from several brands of toilet tissue in its stores so that shoppers could feel and compare textures. The result, the retailer says, was soaring sales for its own in-store brand, resulting in a 50 percent increase in shelf space for the line.[37]

Sensations that reach the skin, whether from a luxurious massage or the bite of a winter wind, stimulate or relax us. Researchers even have shown that touch can influence sales interactions. In one study, diners whom wait staff touched gave bigger tips, and the same researchers reported that food demonstrators in a supermarket who lightly touched customers had better luck in getting shoppers to try a new snack product and to redeem coupons for the brand.[38] On the other hand, an accidental touch from a stranger (especially a male) leads to more negative evaluations of products a shopper encounters in a store.[39]

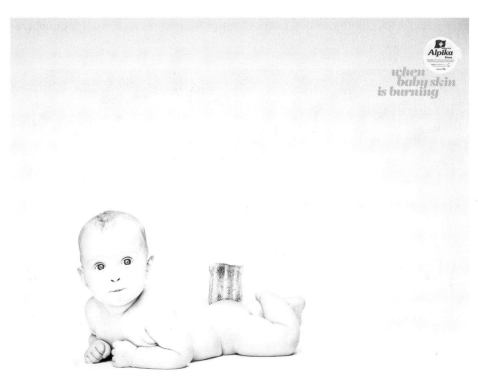

A Polish diaper rash cream.
Source: Courtesy of McCann Erickson Polska.

Some anthropologists view our experience of touch much like a primal language, one we learn well before writing and speech. Indeed, researchers are starting to identify the important role the **haptic** (touch) sense plays in consumer behavior. Haptic senses appear to moderate the relationship between product experience and judgment confidence. This confirms the commonsense notion that we're more sure about what we perceive when we can touch it (a major problem for those who sell products online). Individuals who score high on a "Need for Touch" (NFT) scale respond strongly to the haptic dimension. These people respond positively to such statements as:

● When walking through stores, I can't help touching all kinds of products.
● Touching products can be fun.
● I feel more comfortable purchasing a product after physically examining it.[40]

The Japanese take this idea a step farther with their practice of **Kinsei engineering**, a philosophy that translates customers' feelings into design elements. The designers of the Mazda Miata focused on young drivers who saw the car as an extension of their body, a sensation they call "horse and rider as one." After extensive research they discovered that making the stick shift exactly 9.5 centimeters long conveys the optimal feeling of sportiness and control.[41] Similar thinking went into the driver's seat of the Chrysler 300C, which is designed to make you feel a bit taller. In auto-industry speak, the car has a higher *H-point,* which refers to the location of the seated driver's hip. The change was prompted by the popularity of SUVs, pickups, and minivans that make drivers feel they are riding high on the highway. Ford calls its version "Command Seating" to reinforce the feeling of power it wants drivers to feel as they look down on all those little vehicles buzzing around below them.[42]

Taste

Our taste receptors obviously contribute to our experience of many products. So-called "flavor houses" develop new concoctions to please the changing palates of consumers. Scientists are right behind them as they build new devices to test these flavors. Alpha M.O.S. sells a sophisticated electronic tongue for tasting, and the company is working on what its executives call an electronic mouth, complete with artificial saliva, to chew food and to dissect its flavor. Coca-Cola and PepsiCo use the tongue to test the quality of

Marketing Opportunity

We have a tendency to want to touch objects, although typing or using a mouse are skills we have to learn. The proliferation of touchscreens on computers, ATM machines, digital cameras, GPS devices, and e-readers is an outgrowth of the **natural user interface** philosophy of computer design. This approach incorporates habitual human movements that we don't have to learn. Sony decided to offer touchscreens on its e-readers after its engineers repeatedly observed people in focus groups automatically swipe the screen of its older, nontouch models. Touchscreens also appear on exercise machines, in hospitals, at airport check-in terminals, and on Virgin America airplanes.[43]

• • • • • • • • • • •

Source: grafvision/shutterstock.com.

corn syrups, and Bristol-Myers Squibb and Roche use the device to devise medicines that don't taste bitter.[44]

Cultural factors also determine the tastes we find desirable. A food item's image and the values we attach to it (such as how vegans regard beef menu items, which is not kindly) influence how we experience the actual taste.[45] For example, consumers' greater appreciation of different ethnic dishes contributes to increased desires for spicy foods, so the quest for the ultimate pepper sauce continues. More than 50 stores in the United States supply fiery concoctions with names such as Sting and Linger, Hell in a Jar, and Religious Experience (comes in Original, Hot, and Wrath).[46]

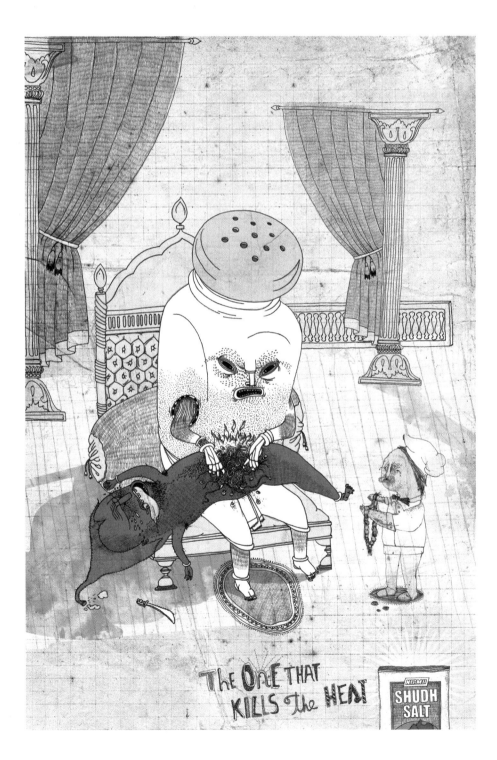

In India salt combats the sensory assault of spicy food.
Source: Courtesy of Taproot India. Contributors: Santosh Padhi, Agnello Dias, Pranan Bhide, and Chintan Ruparel.

OBJECTIVE 3

Perception is a three-stage process that translates raw stimuli into meaning.

The Stages of Perception

Like computers, we undergo stages of *information processing* in which we input and store stimuli. Unlike computers, though, we do *not* passively process whatever information happens to be present. In the first place, we notice only a very small number of the stimuli in our environment, simply because there are so many different ones out there vying for our attention. Of those we do notice, we attend to an even smaller number—and we might not process the stimuli that do enter consciousness objectively. Each individual interprets the meaning of a stimulus in a manner consistent with his or her own unique biases, needs, and experiences. As Figure 5.1 shows, these three stages of *exposure, attention*, and *interpretation* make up the process of perception.

Stage 1: Exposure

Exposure occurs when a stimulus comes within the range of someone's sensory receptors. Consumers concentrate on some stimuli, are unaware of others, and even go out of their way to ignore some messages. We notice stimuli that come within range for even a very short time—*if* we so choose. However, getting a message noticed in such a short time (or even in a longer one) is no mean feat. Before we consider what else people may choose not to perceive, let's consider what they are *capable* of perceiving. By this we mean that stimuli may be above or below a person's **sensory threshold**, or the point at which it is strong enough to make a conscious impact in his or her awareness.

If you have ever blown a dog whistle and watched your pooch respond to a sound you cannot hear, you won't be surprised to learn that there are some stimuli that people simply can't perceive. Some of us pick up sensory information that others, whose sensory channels have diminished due to disability or age, cannot. The science of **psychophysics** focuses on how people integrate the physical environment into their personal, subjective worlds.

It sounds like a great name for a rock band, but the **absolute threshold** refers to the minimum amount of stimulation a person can detect on a given sensory channel. The sound a dog whistle emits is at too high a frequency for human ears to pick up, so this stimulus is beyond our auditory absolute threshold. The absolute threshold is an important consideration when we design marketing stimuli. A highway billboard might have the most entertaining copy ever written, but this genius is wasted if the print is too small for passing motorists to see it. In contrast, the **differential threshold** refers to the ability of a sensory system to detect changes in or differences between two stimuli. The minimum difference we can detect between two stimuli is the **j.n.d. (just noticeable difference)**.

The dual issues of *if* and *when* consumers will notice a difference between two stimuli is relevant to many marketing situations. Sometimes a marketer may want to

Figure 5.1 AN OVERVIEW OF THE PERCEPTUAL PROCESS

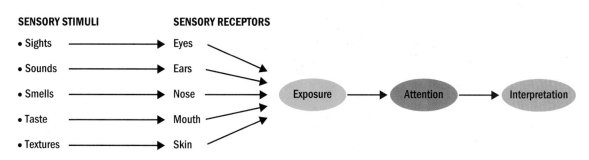

ensure that consumers notice a change, as when a retailer offers merchandise at a discount. In other situations, the marketer may want to downplay the fact that it has made a change, such as when a store raises a price or a manufacturer reduces the size of a package. As recession lingers and the cost of raw materials skyrockets due to shortages caused by natural disasters like the Tokyo earthquake and manmade ones like the conflict in the Middle East, some companies try to camouflage price increases as they shrink the size of packages instead of charging more. Sometimes marketers use code words to announce a change: they may label the smaller packages as greener because there is less plastic or cardboard in a smaller box, more "portable" when they squeeze products into little carry bags, or "healthier" because smaller amounts translate into fewer calories. For example, Kraft brought out "Fresh Stacks" packages for its Nabisco Premium saltines and Honey Maid graham crackers. Each holds about 15 percent fewer crackers than the standard boxes for the same price. But, Kraft notes that since the new packages include more sleeves of crackers, they are more portable—and the company notes that as an added benefit the smaller boxes supply crackers that will be fresher when you get around to eating them. A packaging expert noted that typically, when the economy recovers, companies respond with a new "jumbo" size product that is usually even more expensive per ounce. Then the process begins again: "It's a continuous cycle, where at some point the smallest package offered becomes so small that perhaps they're phased out and replaced by the medium-size package, which has been shrunk down."[47] Figure 5.2 shows the evolution of the Pepsi label over time.

Figure 5.2 THE PEPSI LOGO OVER TIME

A consumer's ability to detect a difference between two stimuli is relative. A whispered conversation that might be unintelligible on a noisy street can suddenly become public and embarrassingly loud in a quiet library. It is the *relative difference* between the decibel level of the conversation and its surroundings, rather than the absolute loudness of the conversation itself, that determines whether the stimulus will register.

In the 19th century, a psychophysicist named Ernst Weber found that the amount of change required for the perceiver to notice a change systematically relates to the intensity of the original stimulus. The stronger the initial stimulus, the greater a change must be for us to notice it. This relationship is **Weber's Law**.

Consider how Weber's Law works for a product when it goes on sale. If a retailer believes that a markdown should be at least 20 percent for the reduction to make an impact on shoppers, she should cut the price on a pair of socks that retails for $10 to $8 (a $2 discount) for shoppers to realize a difference. However, a sports coat that sells for $100 would not benefit from a $2 discount; the retailer would have to mark it down $20 to achieve the same impact.

Weber's Law, ironically, is a challenge to green marketers who try to reduce the sizes of packages when they produce concentrated (and more earth-friendly) versions of their products. Makers of laundry detergent brands have to convince their customers to pay the same price for about half the detergent. Also, because of pressure from powerful retailers such as Walmart that want to fit more bottles on their shelves, the size of detergent bottles is shrinking significantly. Procter & Gamble, Unilever, and Henkel all maintain that their new concentrated versions will allow people to wash the same number of loads with half the detergent. One perceptual trick they're using to try to convince consumers of this is the redesign of the bottle cap: Both P&G and Church & Dwight use a cap with a broader base and shorter sides to persuade consumers that they need a smaller amount.[48]

OBJECTIVE 4

Subliminal advertising is a controversial—but largely ineffective—way to talk to consumers.

Subliminal Perception

Most marketers want to create messages *above* consumers' thresholds so people will notice them. Ironically, a good number of consumers instead believe that marketers design many advertising messages so they will be perceived unconsciously, or *below* the threshold of recognition. Another word for threshold is *limen,* and we term stimuli that fall below the limen *subliminal.* **Subliminal perception** refers to a stimulus below the level of the consumer's awareness.

This topic has captivated the public for more than 50 years, despite the fact that there is virtually no proof that this process has *any* effect on consumer behavior. A survey of American consumers found that almost two-thirds believe in the existence of subliminal advertising, and more than one-half are convinced that this technique can get them to buy things they do not really want.[49] ABC rejected a Kentucky Fried Chicken (KFC) commercial that invited viewers to slowly replay the ad to find a secret message, citing the network's long-standing policy against subliminal advertising. KFC argued that the ad wasn't subliminal at all because the company told viewers about the message and how to find it. The network wasn't convinced.[50]

Like this KFC ad, most examples of subliminal advertising that people "discover" are not subliminal at all—on the contrary, the images are quite apparent. Remember, if you can see it or hear it, it's not subliminal; the stimulus is above the level of conscious awareness. Nonetheless, the continuing controversy about subliminal persuasion has been important in shaping the public's beliefs about advertisers' and marketers' abilities to manipulate consumers against their will.

Subliminal Messaging Techniques

Marketers supposedly send subliminal messages on both visual and aural channels. **Embeds** are tiny figures they insert into magazine advertising via high-speed photography or airbrushing. These hidden images, usually of a sexual nature, supposedly exert strong but unconscious influences on innocent readers. Some limited evidence hints at the possibility that embeds can alter the moods of men when they're exposed to sexually suggestive subliminal images, but the effect (if any) is very subtle—and may even work in the opposite direction if this creates negative feelings among viewers.[51] To date, the only real impact of this interest in hidden messages is to sell more copies of "exposés" written by a few authors and to make some consumers (and students taking a consumer behavior class) look a bit more closely at print ads, perhaps seeing whatever their imaginations lead them to see.

Does Subliminal Perception Work?

Some research by clinical psychologists suggests that subliminal messages can influence people under very specific conditions, though it is doubtful that these techniques would be of much use in most marketing contexts. For this kind of message to have a prayer of working, an advertiser has to tailor it specifically to an individual rather than the mass messages suitable for the general public.[52] The stimulus should also be as close to the liminal threshold as possible. Here are other discouraging factors:

- There are wide individual differences in threshold levels. For a message to avoid conscious detection by consumers who have low thresholds, it would have to be so weak that it would not reach those who have high thresholds.
- Advertisers lack control over consumers' distance and position from a screen. In a movie theater, for example, only a small portion of the audience would be in exactly the right seats to be exposed to a subliminal message.
- The viewer must pay absolute attention to the stimulus. People who watch a television program or a movie typically shift their attention periodically, and they might not even notice when the stimulus appears.
- Even if the advertiser induces the desired effect, it works only at a very general level. For example, a message might increase a person's thirst—but not necessarily for a specific drink. Because the stimulus just affects a basic drive, a marketer could find that after all the bother and expense of creating a subliminal message, demand for competitors' products increases as well!

Clearly, there are better ways to get our attention—let's see how.

Stage 2: Attention

As you sit in a lecture, you might find your mind wandering (yes, even you!). One minute you are concentrating on the professor's words, and the next you catch yourself daydreaming about the upcoming weekend. Suddenly, you tune back in as you hear your name being spoken. Fortunately, it's a false alarm—the professor has called on another "victim" who has the same first name. But she's got your attention now.

    Attention refers to the extent to which processing activity is devoted to a particular stimulus. As you know from sitting through both interesting and "less interesting" lectures, this allocation can vary depending on both the characteristics of the stimulus (i.e., the lecture itself) and the recipient (i.e., your mental state at the time).

This Canadian beer ad pokes fun at subliminal advertising.
Source: © 2005. Molson USA, LLC.

Although we live in an "information society," we can have too much of a good thing. Consumers often live in a state of **sensory overload**; we are exposed to far more information than we can process. In our society, much of this bombardment comes from commercial sources, and the competition for our attention is steadily increasing. The average adult is exposed to about 3,500 pieces of advertising information every single day—up from about 560 per day 30 years ago.

That means the fight for your attention—or what some marketers refer to as an **eyeball economy**—gets tougher every day. Technology that helps us to avoid these messages makes the job even harder.

Multitasking

Getting the attention of young people in particular is a challenge—as your professor probably knows! More than half of teens report that they engage in **multitasking**,

YOU MAY NOT BE AWARE OF IT, BUT RIGHT NOW YOUR SUBCONSCIOUS IS JONESING FOR A COLD, CRISP MOLSON. WHY? BECAUSE WE SLIPPED THROUGH THE BACK DOOR OF YOUR BRAIN AND PLANTED A FEW VISUAL CUES DEEP IN YOUR MIND. ANY OF THE IMAGES BELOW SEEM STRANGELY FAMILIAR? 🍁

MAGNIFIED AT 100X HOWEVER, WE BEGIN TO SEE SOMETHING.

AN IMAGE OF JOHN MOLSON PRINTED ON THE PAPER FIBER OF THE BEER LABEL. THOUGH MINUTE, YOUR BRAIN PICKED UP ON THIS SUBLIMINAL CUE TO A 219-YEAR HERITAGE OF BREWING GREAT-TASTING BEER.

AH, THERE IT IS: AN IMAGE OF PEOPLE SOCIALIZING WITH AN ICE-COLD MOLSON.

A MICROSCOPIC REMINDER THAT MOLSON HAS BEEN BRINGING FRIENDS TOGETHER SINCE 1786. SHOULD YOU SUDDENLY AWAKEN IN A CROWDED BAR ORDERING A ROUND OF MOLSON FOR EVERYONE, WE DID THAT. AND YOU'RE WELCOME.

where they process information from more than one medium at a time as they alternate among their cell phones, TVs, and laptops.[53] One study observed 400 people for a day and found that 96 percent of them were multitasking about a third of the time they used media.[54]

What impact does all this multitasking have on consumers' ability to absorb, retain, and understand information? One possible consequence: These bursts of stimulation provoke the body to secrete dopamine, which is addicting. When we go without these squirts, we feel bored. Some scientists warn that our cravings for more stimulation distract us from more prolonged thought processes and reduce our ability to concentrate (don't text and drive!). Researchers find that heavy multitaskers have more trouble focusing, and they experience more stress. One study found that people who are interrupted by email report significantly more stress than those who were allowed to focus on a task.

Before you panic, there is some good news: Evidence suggests that the brains of Internet users become more efficient at finding information, while some videogame players develop better eyesight. One team of researchers found that players of fast-paced video games could track the movement of a third more objects on a screen than nonplayers. They say the games can improve reaction and the ability to pick out details amid clutter. For better or worse, technology seems to be rewiring our brains to try to pay attention to more stimuli. Today we consume three times as much information each day as people did in 1960. We constantly shift attention: Computer users at work change windows or check email or other programs nearly 37 times an hour. Computer users visit an average of 40 Web sites a day.[55]

How Do Marketers Get Our Attention?

Marketers constantly search for ways to break through the clutter and grab people's attention. Some tactics are straightforward, as when manufacturers try to get their brands shelved at eye level in a store and toward the center of a display because they know that is where shoppers are most likely to look.[57] Here are some other ideas:

- Networks try to engage viewers during commercial breaks when they wedge original content into the blocks of advertising time so that viewers will anticipate seeing something fun if they sit through a few ads. Fox Broadcasting televised a series of clips about an animated character named Oleg, a New York cab driver, who popped up in 8-second vignettes during commercial breaks in series such as *24*. In a Greek accent, Oleg urged viewers to visit Fox's Web site. In one clip, Oleg sang about himself to the Barry Manilow tune "Copacabana." In others, he drove celebrities such as Tom Cruise and Rosie O'Donnell. Although Oleg generated more than 100,000 Web site hits on some nights, some viewers complained that he was an ethnic stereotype and others couldn't understand what he was saying—so Oleg is history. But it was a good idea in principle.[58]

- In the online world, advertisers keep innovating to get visitors to watch their messages. One of the most popular today is **rich media**, the use of animated .gif files or video clips to grab viewers' attention. LowerMyBills.com is notorious for its endless loops of silhouetted dancers and surprised office workers, whereas other ads spring into action when you move the cursor over them. Other rich media are online versions of familiar TV commercials that sit frozen on the Web site until you click them. *Teaser ads,* much like those you see on TV that give you a taste of the story but make you return later for the rest, also turn up on Web sites.[59]

- Of course, a sure-fire way to grab our attention is to do something outrageous, or at least unusual, in a public place. We talked about these *spectacles* in Chapter 2. To promote a new class at the New York Health and Racquet Club, six men and women stood outside the city's Grand Central Terminal flashing their underwear at strangers. The garments featured the club's logo and "Booty Call," the name of the class.

Because the brain's capacity to process information is limited, consumers are very selective about what they pay attention to. The process of **perceptual selection** means that people attend to only a small portion of the stimuli to which they are exposed. Consumers practice a form of "psychic economy" as they pick and choose among stimuli to avoid being overwhelmed. How do we choose? Both personal and stimulus factors help to decide.

Personal Selection Factors

How do marketers "know" when you're hungry and choose those times to bombard you with food ads? The answer is they don't—at least not yet. **Perceptual vigilance** means we are more likely to be aware of stimuli that relate to our current needs.

The flip side of perceptual vigilance is **perceptual defense**. This means that we tend to see what we want to see—and we don't see what we don't want to see. If a stimulus threatens us in some way, we may not process it, or we may distort its meaning so that it's more acceptable. For example, a heavy smoker may block out images of cancer-scarred lungs because these vivid reminders hit a bit too close to home.

Still another factor is **adaptation**, the degree to which consumers continue to notice a stimulus over time. The process of adaptation occurs when we no longer pay attention to a stimulus because it is so familiar. A consumer can "habituate" and require increasingly stronger "doses" of a stimulus to notice it. A commuter who is en route to work might read a billboard message when the board is first installed, but after a few days it simply becomes part of the passing scenery. Several factors can lead to adaptation:

- **Intensity**—Less-intense stimuli (e.g., soft sounds or dim colors) habituate because they have less sensory impact.
- **Discrimination**—Simple stimuli habituate because they do not require attention to detail.
- **Exposure**—Frequently encountered stimuli habituate as the rate of exposure increases.
- **Relevance**—Stimuli that are irrelevant or unimportant habituate because they fail to attract attention.

Stimulus Selection Factors

In addition to the receiver's mindset, characteristics of the stimulus itself play an important role to determine what we notice and what we ignore. Marketers need to understand these factors so they can create messages and packages that will have a better chance to cut through the clutter. For example, when researchers using infrared eye-tracking equipment measured what ads consumers look at, they found that visually complex ads are more likely to capture attention.[60]

In general, we are more likely to notice stimuli that differ from others around them (remember Weber's Law). A message creates **contrast** in several ways:

- **Size**—The size of the stimulus itself in contrast to the competition helps to determine if it will command attention. Readership of a magazine ad increases in proportion to the size of the ad.[61]
- **Color**—As we've seen, color is a powerful way to draw attention to a product or to give it a distinct identity. Black & Decker developed a line of tools it called DeWalt to target the residential construction industry. The company colored the new line yellow instead of black; this made the equipment stand out against other "dull" tools.[62]
- **Position**—Not surprisingly, we stand a better chance of noticing stimuli that are in places we're more likely to look. That's why the competition is so heated among suppliers to have their products displayed in stores at eye level. In magazines, ads that are placed toward the front of the issue, preferably on the right-hand side, also win out in the race for readers' attention. (Hint: The next time you read a magazine, notice which pages you're more likely to spend time looking at.)[63] A study that tracked consumers' eye movements as they scanned telephone directories also illustrates the importance of message position. Consumers scanned listings in alphabetical order, and they noticed 93 percent of quarter-page display ads but only 26 percent of plain listings. Their eyes were drawn to color ads first, and these were viewed longer than black-and-white ones. In addition, subjects spent 54 percent more time viewing ads for businesses they ended up choosing, which illustrates the influence of attention on subsequent product choice.[64]
- **Novelty**—Stimuli that appear in unexpected ways or places tend to grab our attention. One solution is to put ads in unconventional places, where there will be less competition for attention. These places include the backs of shopping carts, walls of tunnels, floors of sports stadiums, and yes, even public restrooms.[66] An outdoor

Figure 5.3 THE GOLDEN TRIANGLE

Eye-tracking studies reveal that people typically spend most of their time on a website looking at the "golden triangle" outlined by yellow, orange and red.

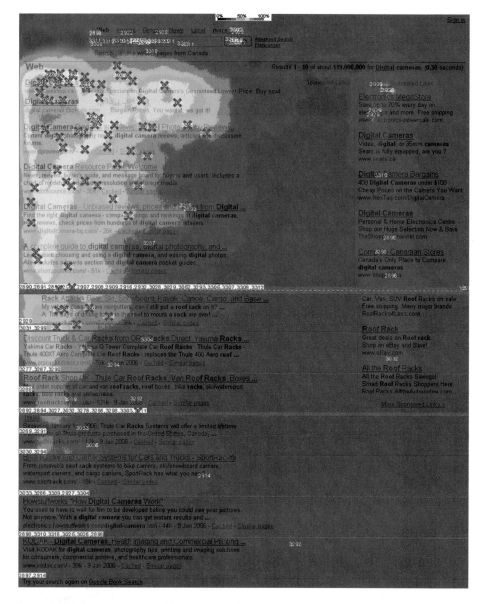

Source: Enquiro Search Solutions, Inc. (Now Mediative Performance LP).

advertising agency in London constructs huge ads in deserts and farm fields adjacent to airports so that passengers who look out the window can't help but pay attention. It prints the digital ads on pieces of PVC mesh that sit on frames a few inches above the ground.[67]

Indeed, one study indicates that novelty in the form of interruptions actually *intensifies* our experiences; distraction increases our enjoyment of pleasant stimuli as it amplifies our dislike of unpleasant stimuli. According to this research, people actually enjoy TV shows *more* when commercials interrupt them. A group of undergraduates watched an episode of an old sitcom (*Taxi*) with which they were unfamiliar. Half viewed the original broadcast, which included ads for a jeweler, a lawyer, and other businesses; the other half saw the show with all commercials deleted. Students who saw the original actually gave it higher evaluations. The researchers found a similar pattern when they interrupted people who were getting a massage. In contrast, subjects reported that the irritating sound of a vacuum cleaner was even worse when they got a break from listening to it and then had to hear it resume! The researchers interpret these results as the outcome of adaptation: We experience events more intensely at first but then get used to them. When we experience an interruption and then start over, we revert to the original intensity level.[68]

OBJECTIVE 5
We interpret the stimuli to which we do pay attention according to learned patterns and expectations.

Stage 3: Interpretation

Interpretation refers to the meanings we assign to sensory stimuli. Just as people differ in terms of the stimuli that they perceive, the meanings we assign to these stimuli vary as well. Two people can see or hear the same event, but their interpretation of it can be as different as night and day, depending on what they had expected the stimulus to be. In one study, kids ages 3 to 5 who ate McDonald's French fries served in a McDonald's bag overwhelmingly thought they tasted better than those who ate the same fries out of a plain white bag. Even carrots tasted better when they came out of a McDonald's bag—more than half the kids preferred them to the same carrots served in a plain package! Ronald would be proud.[69]

The meaning we assign to a stimulus depends on the **schema**, or set of beliefs, to which we assign it. As we saw in Chapter 2, *priming* certain properties of a stimulus evokes a schema. This in turn leads us to compare the stimulus to other similar ones we encountered in the past.

Identifying and evoking the correct schema is crucial to many marketing decisions, because this determines what criteria consumers will use to evaluate the product, package, or message. Extra Strength Maalox Whip Antacid flopped even though a spray can is a pretty effective way to deliver the product. To consumers, aerosol whips mean dessert toppings, not medication.[70] However, a college cafeteria gave menu items descriptive labels (e.g., Red Beans with Rice versus Traditional Cajun Red Beans with Rice, Chocolate Pudding versus Satin Chocolate Pudding) so that diners had more information about each option and were able to better categorize it. As a result, sales increased by more than 25 percent.[71]

A popular British retailer called French Connection relies on the priming process to evoke a response to its advertising by using an acronym that closely resembles another word.

Source: Used with permission TWBA London on behalf of French Connection.

Even the location of a product's image on a package influences the way our brains make sense of it. For example, due to what we have learned about the law of gravity (heavy objects sink and light objects float), we assume that products that are lower down in a frame weigh more than products that appear higher in a frame. In addition, objects on the right of a frame appear heavier than products that appear on the left of a frame. This interpretation results from our intuition about levers: We know that the farther away an object is from a lever's fulcrum, the more difficult it is to raise the item. Because we read from left to right, the left naturally becomes the visual fulcrum and thus we perceive objects on the right as heavier. Manufacturers should bear these *package schematics* in mind, as they may influence our feelings about the contents in a package for better or worse. Think, for example, about a diet food marketer who wants shoppers to regard her menu items as lighter.[72]

As we'll see later in Chapter 7, products often assume a "brand personality" because we tend to assign them common human traits such as sophistication or sexiness. In other words, we *anthropomorphize* objects when we think of them in human terms, and this thought process may encourage us to evaluate products using schemas we apply to classify other people. A recent study illustrates how this works: Subjects saw an advertisement with a picture of a car that had been modified to make it appear as though it was either "smiling" or "frowning." In some cases, the text of the ad was written in the first person, to activate a human schema, while others saw the same ad written in the third person. When the human schema was active, those who saw the "smiling" car rated it more favorably than when they saw a "frowning" car.[73]

Stimulus Organization

One factor that determines how we will interpret a stimulus is the relationship we assume it has with other events, sensations, or images in memory. When RJR Nabisco introduced a version of Teddy Grahams (a children's product) for adults, it used understated packaging colors to reinforce the idea that the new product was for grown-ups. But sales were disappointing. Nabisco changed the box to bright yellow to convey the idea that this was a fun snack, and buyers' more positive association between a bright primary color and taste prompted adults to start buying the cookies.[74]

The stimuli we perceive are often ambiguous. It's up to us to determine the meaning based on our past experiences, expectations, and needs. A classic experiment demonstrated the process of "seeing what you want to see": Princeton and Dartmouth students separately viewed a movie of a particularly rough football game between the two rival

We recognize patterns of stimuli, such as familiar words. In this Austrian ad consumers will tend to see the word "kitchen" even though the letters are scrambled.
Source: Client: XXXLutz; Head of Marketing: Mag. Thomas Saliger; Agency: Demner, Merlicek & Bergmann; Account Supervisor: Andrea Kliment; Account Manager: Albin Lenzer; Creative Directors: Rosa Haider, Tolga Buyukdoganay; Art Directors: Tolga Buyukdoganay, Rene Pichler; Copywriter: Alistair Thompson.

schools. Although everyone was exposed to the same stimulus, the degree to which students saw infractions and the blame they assigned for those they did see depended on which college they attended.[75]

As this experiment demonstrates, we tend to project our own desires or assumptions onto products and advertisements. This interpretation process can backfire for marketers. Planters LifeSavers Company found this out when it introduced Planters Fresh Roast, a vacuum-packed peanuts package. The idea was to capitalize on consumers' growing love affair with fresh-roast coffee by emphasizing the freshness of the nuts in the same way. A great idea—until irate supermarket managers began calling to ask who was going to pay to clean the peanut gook out of their stores' coffee-grinding machines.[76]

The Eye of the Beholder: Interpretational Biases

Our brains tend to relate incoming sensations to others already in memory, based on some fundamental organizational principles. These principles derive from *Gestalt psychology*, a school of thought based upon the notion that people interpret meaning from the *totality* of a set of stimuli rather than from any individual stimulus. The German word **Gestalt** roughly means *whole, pattern,* or *configuration,* and we summarize this term as "the whole is greater than the sum of its parts." A piecemeal perspective that analyzes each component of the stimulus separately can't capture the total effect. The

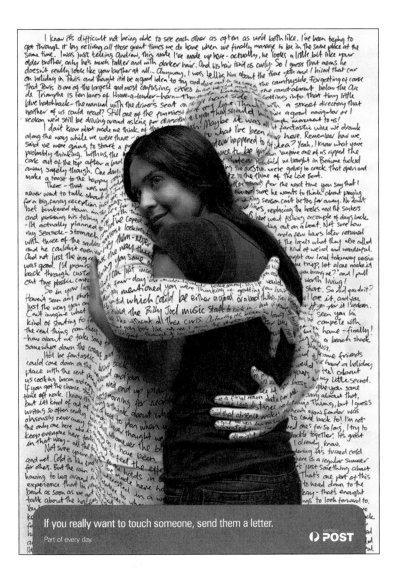

The Australian postal service uses a unique application of the figure-ground principle.
Source: © M&C Saatchi, 2007.

Gestalt perspective provides several principles that relate to the way our brains organize stimuli:

- The **closure principle** states that people tend to perceive an incomplete picture as complete. That is, we tend to fill in the blanks based on our prior experience. This principle explains why most of us have no trouble reading a neon sign even if several of its letters are burned out. The principle of closure is also at work when we hear only part of a jingle or theme. Marketing strategies that use the closure principle encourage audience participation, which increases the chance that people will attend to the message.
- The **principle of similarity** tells us that consumers tend to group together objects that share similar physical characteristics. Green Giant relied on this principle when the company redesigned the packaging for its line of frozen vegetables. It created a "sea of green" look to unify all of its different offerings.

This Indian paper ad relies on the principle of similarity to create an image of a man.
Source: Courtesy of Taproot India. Contributors: Santosh Padhi, Agnello Dias, Ananth Nanavre, Amol Jadhav, and Amol Kamble.

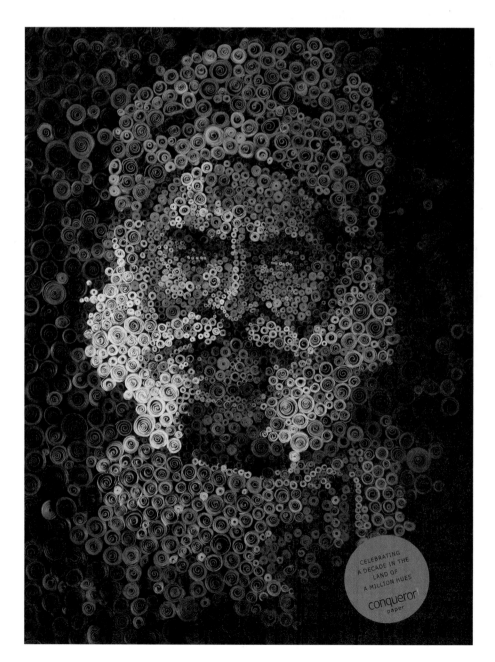

● The **figure-ground principle** states that one part of a stimulus will dominate (the *figure*), and other parts recede into the background (the *ground*). This concept is easy to understand if one thinks literally of a photograph with a clear and sharply focused object (the figure) in the center. The figure is dominant, and the eye goes straight to it. The parts of the configuration a person will perceive as figure or ground can vary depending on the individual consumer, as well as other factors. Similarly, marketing messages that use the figure-ground principle can make a stimulus the focal point of the message or merely the context that surrounds the focus.

OBJECTIVE 6

The field of semiotics helps us to understand how marketers use symbols to create meaning.

Semiotics: The Meaning of Meaning

As we've seen, when we try to "make sense" of a marketing stimulus we interpret it in light of our prior associations. An experiment demonstrated how our assumptions influence our experiences; in this case, the study altered beer drinkers' taste preferences simply by telling them different stories about a specific brew's ingredients. The researcher offered bar patrons free beer if they would participate in a taste test (guess what: very few refused the offer). Participants tasted two beers each, one a regular draft of Budweiser or Samuel Adams and the other the same beer with a few drops of balsamic vinegar added. Although most beer *aficionados* would guess that vinegar makes the drink taste bad, in fact 60 percent of the respondents who did not know which beer contained the vinegar actually preferred the doctored version to the regular one! But when tasters knew in advance which beer had vinegar in it before they took a swig, only one-third preferred that version.[77]

Much of the meaning we take away influences what we make of the symbolism we perceive. After all, on the surface many marketing images have virtually no literal connection to actual products. What does a cowboy have to do with a bit of tobacco rolled into a paper tube? How can a celebrity such as the basketball player LeBron James or the singer Rihanna enhance the image of a soft drink or a fast-food restaurant?

To help them understand how consumers interpret the meanings of symbols, some marketers turn to **semiotics**, a discipline that studies the correspondence between signs and symbols and their roles in how we assign meanings.[78] Semiotics is a key link to consumer behavior because consumers use products to express their social identities. Products carry learned meanings, and we rely on marketers to help us figure out what those meanings are. As one set of researchers put it, "Advertising serves as a kind of culture/consumption dictionary; its entries are products, and their definitions are cultural meanings."[79]

From a semiotic perspective, every marketing message has three basic components: an *object,* a *sign* (or symbol), and an *interpretant.* The **object** is the product that is the focus of the message (e.g., Marlboro cigarettes). The **sign** is the sensory image that represents the intended meanings of the object (e.g., the Marlboro cowboy). The **interpretant** is the meaning we derive from the sign (e.g., rugged, individualistic, American). Figure 5.4 diagrams this relationship.

According to semiotician Charles Sanders Peirce, signs relate to objects in one of three ways: They can resemble objects, connect to them, or tie to them conventionally. An **icon** is a sign that resembles the product in some way (e.g., the Ford Mustang has a galloping horse on the hood). An **index** is a sign that connects to a product because they share some property (e.g., the pine tree on some of Procter & Gamble's Spic and Span cleanser products conveys the shared property of fresh scent). A **symbol** is a sign that relates to a product by either conventional or agreed-on associations (e.g., the lion in Dreyfus Fund ads provides the conventional association with fearlessness and strength that it carries [or hopes to carry] over to the company's approach to investments).[80]

A lot of time, thought, and money go into creating brand names and logos that clearly communicate a product's image (even when a name like Exxon is generated by a computer!). Starbucks removed the words *Starbucks Coffee* as it introduced a new logo

Marketing Opportunity

In Chapter 3 we addressed the popular strategy of *product placement*, where TV shows and movies incorporate real products on sets and in plotlines. **Reverse product placement** is a great example of hyperreality; in these cases, fictional products that appear in shows become popular in the real world. The e-commerce site LastExitToNowhere.com sells T-shirts that bear the logos of companies featured in works of fiction. These include such made-up companies as Tyrell (the manufacturer of genetic replicants in the movie classic *Blade Runner*), Polymer Records (a music label in the cult movie *This Is Spinal Tap*), and the Weyland-Yutani Corporation (it made the spaceship freighter Nostromo in the *Alien* movies). Another online store—80sTees.com—proclaimed Duff beer, from *The Simpsons* TV show, the number-one fake brand. Coming in second was Dunder Mifflin, the paper company on *The Office* series.[81] Other fake-to-real products include:

● Bertie Bott's Every Flavor Beans, which originated in the *Harry Potter* book series before the product moved to actual retail shelves.

● The movie *Forrest Gump* inspired the Bubba Gump Shrimp Company restaurant chain.

● Nestlé sells Wonka candy (from the *Willy Wonka* movie).[82]

Figure 5.4 SEMIOTIC RELATIONSHIPS

Augmented reality (AR) refers to media that superimpose one or more digital layers of data, images, or video over a physical object. If you've ever watched a 3D movie with those clunky glasses, you've experienced one form of augmented reality. Or, if you've seen that yellow line in an NFL game that shows the first down marker, you've also encountered AR in a simple form.

More likely, though, in the next few years you'll live in AR through your smartphone or tablet. New apps like Google Goggles (for Android phones) and Layar (for Android and Apple devices) impose a layer of words and pictures on whatever you see in your phone's viewer. Google Glasses allow consumers to interact with digital content as an extension of things that you do every day, such as walking down the street.

Augmented reality apps open new worlds of information (and marketing communications). Do you want to know the bio of the singer you see on a CD cover? Who painted that cool mural in your local bar? How much did that house you were looking at sell for last month? Just point your smartphone at each and the information will be superimposed on your screen.[87] AR is about to be big business: Analysts project that revenue from augmented reality apps will hit $5.2 billion by 2017.[88]

that features only the famous siren character. The CEO explained this change means the company is thinking "beyond coffee."[83]

The choice of a logo is even more difficult when the brand has to travel across cultures. For example, as Chinese business becomes more global, companies refashion ancient Chinese pictograms into new corporate logos that resonate with both the East and the West. Chinese pictograms really are icons because the ancient symbols were once graphic depictions of the words they signify. China Telecom's logo features two interlocking letter *C*s that together form the Chinese character for China but also represent the concept of "customer" and "competition." In addition, though, the symbol also resembles the horns of an ox, a hard-working animal. When the software company Oracle redesigned its logo for the Chinese market, it added three Chinese characters that signify the literal translation of the word *oracle:* "writing on a tortoise shell." The expression dates back to ancient China when mystics scrawled prophecies on bones. The California firm was enthusiastic about the translation because it conveyed Oracle's core competency—data storage.[84]

Hyperreality

Designer Tommy Hilfiger now has his own (fictional) family called the Hilfigers; a clan of preppy-looking people who turn up at store openings and in advertisements (you can guess whose clothes they wear).[85] One of the hallmarks of modern advertising is that it creates a condition of **hyperreality**. This refers to the process of making real what is initially simulation or "hype." Advertisers create new relationships between objects and interpretants when they invent connections between products and benefits, such as when an ad equates Marlboro cigarettes with the American frontier spirit. In a hyperreal environment, over time it's no longer possible to discern the true relationship between the symbol and reality. The "artificial" associations between product symbols and the real world take on lives of their own. For example, a furniture designer launched a dining room set inspired by the TV series *Dexter*—the main character is a police blood splatter analyst who moonlights as a serial killer. The all-white table and chairs are festooned with big splotches of red.[86]

Last Exit to Nowhere sells T-shirts that bear the logos of companies featured in works of fiction.

Source: Images from LastExittoNowhere.com.

Perceptual Positioning

So, we know that we often interpret a product stimulus in light of what we've learned about a product category and the characteristics of existing brands. Our perception of a brand comprises both its functional attributes (e.g., its features, its price, and so on) and its symbolic attributes (its image and what we think it says about us when we use it). We'll look more closely at issues such as brand image in later chapters, but for now it's important to keep in mind that (as we stated in Chapter 1) our evaluation of a product typically is the result of what it means rather than what it does. This meaning—as consumers perceive it—constitutes the product's market position, and it may have more to do with our expectations of product performance as communicated by its color, packaging, or styling than with the product itself.

When a marketer understands how consumers think about a set of competing brands, it can use these insights to develop a **positioning strategy**, which is a fundamental component of a company's marketing efforts as it uses elements of the marketing mix (i.e., product design, price, distribution, and marketing communications) to influence the consumer's interpretation of its meaning in the marketplace relative to its competitors.

For example, although consumers' preferences for the taste of one product over another are important, this functional attribute is only one component of product evaluation.

Marketers can use many dimensions to carve out a brand's position in the marketplace. These include:[89]

- **Lifestyle.** Grey Poupon mustard is a "higher-class" condiment.
- **Price leadership.** L'Oréal sells its Noisôme brand face cream in upscale beauty shops, whereas its Plenitude brand is available for one-sixth the price in discount stores—even though both are based on the same chemical formula.[90]
- **Attributes.** Bounty paper towels are "the quicker picker-upper."
- **Product class.** The Spyder Eclipse is a sporty convertible.
- **Competitors.** Northwestern Insurance is "the quiet company."
- **Occasions.** Wrigley's gum is an alternative at times when smoking is not permitted.
- **Users.** Levi's Dockers target men in their 20s to 40s.
- **Quality.** At Ford, "Quality is job 1."

MyMarketingLab

Go to **mymktlab.com** to complete the problems marked with this icon ⭐.

CHAPTER SUMMARY

Now that you have finished reading this chapter, you should understand why:

1. The design of a product is now a key driver of its success or failure.

In recent years, the sensory experiences we receive from products and services have become a high priority when we choose among competing options. Consumers increasingly want to buy things that will give them hedonic value in addition to functional value. They often believe that most brands perform similarly, so they weigh a product's aesthetic qualities heavily when they select a brand.

2. Products and commercial messages often appeal to our senses, but because of the profusion of these messages most of them won't influence us.

Marketing stimuli have important sensory qualities. We rely on colors, odors, sounds, tastes, and even the "feel" of products when we evaluate them. Not all sensations successfully make their way through the perceptual process. Many stimuli compete for our attention, and we don't notice or accurately interpret the majority of them.

3. Perception is a three-stage process that translates raw stimuli into meaning.

Perception is the process by which physical sensations, such as sights, sounds, and smells, are selected, organized, and interpreted. The eventual interpretation of a stimulus allows it to be assigned meaning. A perceptual map is a widely used marketing tool that evaluates the relative standing of competing brands along relevant dimensions.

4. Subliminal advertising is a controversial—but largely ineffective—way to talk to consumers.

So-called subliminal persuasion and related techniques that expose people to visual and aural messages below the sensory threshold are controversial. Although evidence that subliminal persuasion is effective is virtually nonexistent, many consumers continue to believe that advertisers use this technique. Some of the factors that determine which stimuli (above the threshold level) do get perceived include the amount of exposure to the stimulus, how much attention it generates, and how it is interpreted. In an increasingly crowded stimulus environment, advertising clutter occurs when too many marketing-related messages compete for attention.

5. We interpret the stimuli to which we do pay attention according to learned patterns and expectations.

We don't attend to a stimulus in isolation. We classify and organize it according to principles of perceptual organization. A *Gestalt*, or overall pattern, guides these principles. Specific grouping principles include closure, similarity, and figure-ground relationships. The final step in the process of perception is interpretation. Symbols help us make sense of the world by providing us with an interpretation of a stimulus that others often share. The degree to which the symbolism is consistent with our previous experience affects the meaning we assign to related objects.

6. The field of semiotics helps us to understand how marketers use symbols to create meaning.

Marketers try to communicate with consumers by creating relationships between their products or services and desired attributes. A semiotic analysis involves the correspondence between stimuli and the meaning of signs. The intended meaning may be literal (e.g., an icon such as a street sign with a picture of children playing). Or it may be indexical if it relies on shared characteristics (e.g., the red in a stop sign means danger). Meaning also can be conveyed by a symbol in which an image is given meaning by convention or by agreement of members of a society (e.g., stop signs are octagonal, whereas yield signs are triangular). Marketer-created associations often take on lives of their own as consumers begin to believe that hype is, in fact, real. We call this condition hyperreality.

KEY TERMS

absolute threshold, 206
adaptation, 213
attention, 209
audio watermarking, 202
augmented reality (AR), 220
closure principle, 218
context effects, 196
contrast, 213
differential threshold, 206
embeds, 209
exposure, 206
eyeball economy, 210
figure-ground principle, 219
gestalt, 217
golden triangle, 213
haptic, 204
hedonic consumption, 196

hyperreality, 220
icon, 219
index, 219
interpretant, 219
interpretation, 215
j.n.d. (just noticeable difference), 206
Kinsei engineering, 204
multitasking, 210
natural user interface, 204
object, 219
perception, 196
perceptual defense, 213
perceptual selection, 212
perceptual vigilance, 212
positioning strategy, 221
principle of similarity, 218

psychophysics, 206
reverse product placement, 219
rich media, 212
schema, 215
semiotics, 219
sensation, 196
sensory marketing, 197
sensory overload, 210
sensory signature, 201
sensory threshold, 206
sign, 219
sound symbolism, 203
subliminal perception, 208
symbol, 219
trade dress, 200
Weber's Law, 208

REVIEW

5-1 Define hedonic consumption and provide an example.

5-2 Products and commercial messages often aim to appeal to our senses. How does this work?

✪ 5-3 How does the sense of touch influence consumers' reactions to products?

5-4 Identify and describe the three stages of perception.

5-5 What is the difference between an absolute threshold and a differential threshold?

5-6 Does subliminal perception work? Why or why not?

5-7 Consumers practice a form of "psychic economy." What does this mean?

5-8 Describe two factors that can lead to stimulus adaptation.

5-9 "The whole is greater than the sum of its parts." Explain this statement.

5-10 How do you identify a product's object, sign (or symbol), and interpretant?

5-11 With so many marketing messages and advertisements, how do marketers gain our attention? How do they break through the clutter?

✪ 5-12 What is a positioning strategy? What are some ways marketers can position their products?

CONSUMER BEHAVIOR CHALLENGE

■ DISCUSS

✪ 5-13 Many studies have shown that our sensory detection abilities decline as we grow older. Discuss the implications of the absolute threshold for marketers who want to appeal to the elderly.

5-14 Subliminal advertising is not illegal in the U.S., but it is in the U.K. and Australia. Should it be made illegal globally, considering there is no proof it actually works?

5-15 In July 2012, the Web site Food Oddity served up an infographic illustrating the stark differences in diet and the typical portion size in the U.S. and Asian countries. With around 30 percent of U.S. citizens being obese, the problem is portion size. U.S. portion sizes are enormous compared to those in Asia, Europe, and most of the rest of the world. In the U.S., the average fast food meal size is four times bigger than it was 60 years ago, and people have the highest per capita calorie consumption. Even tourists are not immune, with the average visitor to the country putting on weight during the trip.

Japan has the lowest obesity rate in the world. It has been estimated that an average adult in Japan consumes at least 200 calories less than his or her counterpart in the U.S. This is despite the fact that there is plenty of fast food available in Japan.[91]

Do you think that big portion size is a typically U.S. phenomenon? What are the preferences in your own country, and is it a sound marketing strategy to offer large portion sizes?

5-16 In a 2010 article in the journal *Problems and Perspectives in Management*, the toy giant Mattel was highlighted as having had severe problems with its products that were manufactured in China. In 2007, Mattel was forced to recall 80 product lines that had dangerous levels of lead in the paint used to decorate them. At the time, Mattel produced some 65 percent of its output via manufacturers in China.[92] The reasoning behind this is clear. It is far cheaper to produce toys and many other products in China than it is to center production in the U.S. or Europe. Wage rates are lower, as are many other costs. Some would also argue that legislation is not so stringent, which also helps keep costs down. Around 75 percent of all toys sold globally are manufactured in China. In the Guangdong province there are nearly 10,000 manufacturing plants with an estimated 1.5 million workers. Should toymakers take advantage of the cheaper rates in China? Is this ethical?

5-17 Analysts believe that augmented reality (AR) apps will be worth U.S. $5.2 billion (approximately) by 2017. This might be the case, but AR will not be available to everyone. Is your country's infrastructure ready for this next leap in technology?

5-18 Identify a locally produced brand that has retained its normal packaging size despite having lesser contents. Did the manufacturer make this change clear?

▣ APPLY

5-19 Interview three to five male and three to five female friends about their perceptions of mobile phones and their functionality. Construct a perceptual map for each model. Based on your map of mobile phones, do you see any areas that are not adequately served by current offerings? What (if any) gender differences did you notice regarding both the relevant dimensions raters use and how they place specific models along these dimensions?

5-20 Choose one of your favorite products that you have been buying versions of for some years. How has it changed over the years? Is it better, bigger, smaller, easier to use, better tasting?

5-21 Colors and designs of products are created so that they appeal to particular target groups. Colors are used to attract male or female consumers. The design of logos and packaging are also created so that they are attractive and appealing. What is your view of the ideal color, design, and packaging that would attract male consumers compared to female ones?

5-22 Finding new locations for advertisements is a constant quest. Consider your own country or region. Where are advertisements appearing today where there were no advertisements in the past?

Case Study

THE BRAVE NEW WORLD OF SUBWAY ADVERTISING

What do American Express, Target Stores, Coca-Cola, the Discovery Channel, Cadillac, Minute Maid, the Cartoon Network, Royal Caribbean, and Calvin Klein have in common? They all break through the clutter of traditional ad spaces to grab the attention of potential customers. And in the process, they dazzle them right out of the boredom of riding the subway.

Subway advertising has been around nearly as long as the subway itself. But advertising media pioneers Submedia and Sidetrack Technologies give the old venue a new twist. By employing an innovative technology similar to that of a childhood flip book, they illuminate dark subway tunnels and turn them into valuable showcases for major advertisers.

At the core of this new method is a series of lit panels that contain static images. The panels occupy 500 to 1,000 feet of space that normally holds only graffiti, grime, and the occasional rat. When you view one from a standstill, it appears as a simple still image. But when a subway train passes by, the series comes to life for riders as a 15- to 30-second full-motion commercial.

Having just another place to air a commercial might not seem so appealing to advertisers. But in a media environment where consumers increasingly skip or fast-forward through ads, the placement of these messages in subway tunnels presents exceptional possibilities. Advertisers clamor for opportunities to break through the typical clutter. Since these ads are really unique, they're likely to grab the attention of even the most jaded commuter. "We think this will catch people so totally by surprise that when they see them, they can't help but watch them," said Dan Hanrahan, Royal Caribbean's senior vice president of marketing and sales.

But the uniqueness of this medium is only part of the formula that makes these ad agencies believe they're on to something. The rest is based on the nature of the subway audience: captive and bored. "Everybody overwhelmingly says it takes away from the boredom of the ride," said Joshua Spodek, founder of New York City-based Submedia. "It's not like it's taking away from a beautiful view, like a billboard as you're driving around a beautiful area in Vermont. A subway tunnel is a semi-industrial environment."

Whether it's because the ads give a bored audience something to do or because this new wave of out-of-home advertisements is truly cutting-edge, industry officials claim that the public reaction has been overwhelmingly positive. Submedia reports that 87 percent of riders look forward to seeing the next Submedia advertisement and 60 percent said the ad made their ride more enjoyable.

Comments like these make it easy to believe the claims of underground advertising agencies. One estimate asserts that more than 92 percent of consumers remember the advertised product, whereas only 13 percent have that same level of recall for televisions ads. This means big ad revenues, and not just for the agencies. Mass transit organizations potentially can realize a big source of secondary income when they lease out this unused real estate.

Currently brightening the tunnels of numerous mass transit systems in North and South America, Asia, and Europe, these advertisements represent something every advertiser dreams of: an ad that people go out of their way to look at. In a world that is increasingly skeptical about too much advertising, this new platform is an express ride to success.

DISCUSSION QUESTIONS

CS 5-1 Based on the principles of attention the chapter presents, explain why riders receive these new ads so positively.

CS 5-2 Using the same principles, what should the ads' creators consider to avoid the potential burnout of this medium?

Sources: www.submediaworld.com/submediaworld/Tunnel_Advertising, accessed July 23, 2013; Katy Bachman, "Underground Film," *Mediaweek* 18, no. 15 (April 14, 2008): 24; Louis M. Brill, "Subway In-Tunnel Advertising Gives Outdoor a New Direction," www.sub-media.com/press, accessed May 23, 2009.

MyMarketingLab

Go to **mymktlab.com** for the following Assisted-graded writing questions:

5-23 Define a "schema" and provide an example of how this concept is relevant to marketing.

5-24 Assume that you are a consultant for a marketer who wants to design a package for a new premium chocolate bar targeted to an affluent market. What recommendations would you provide in terms of such package elements as color, symbolism, and graphic design? Give the reasons for your suggestions.

5-25 **Mymktlab Only**—comprehensive writing assignment for this chapter.

NOTES

1. http://www.milkunleashed.com/shelf-safe-milk/aseptic-packaging-uht-milk.html, accessed July 22, 2013; http://wiki.answers.com/Q/What_is_the_difference_between_fresh_milk_and_uht_treated_milk_and_any_advantages_and_disadvantages, accessed March 28, 2011; Craig Baumrucker, "Why Does Organic Milk Last So Much Longer Than Regular Milk?," *Scientific American* (June 6, 2008), www.scientificamerican.com/article.cfm?id=experts-organic-milk-lasts-longer, accessed June 30, 2009.

2. http://www.universalorlando.com/Theme_Parks/Universal_Studios_-Orlando/Attractions/fear_factor_live.aspx, accessed March 28, 2011; Nat Ives, "Putting Some Terror in Family Outings," *New York Times* (January 17, 2005), www.nytimes.com, accessed January 17, 2005.

3. Ryan S. Elder and Aradhna Krishna, "The Effects of Advertising Copy on Sensory Thoughts and Perceived Taste," *Journal of Consumer Research* 36, no. 5 (2010), 748–56.

4. Glenn Collins, "Owens-Corning's Blurred Identity," *New York Times* (August 19, 1994): D4.

5. Elizabeth C. Hirschman and Morris B. Holbrook, "Hedonic Consumption: Emerging Concepts, Methods, and Propositions," *Journal of Marketing* 46 (Summer 1982): 92–101.

6. Joan Myers-Levy, Rui (Juliet) Zhu, and Lan Jiang, "Context Effects From Bodily Sensations: Examining Bodily Sensations Induced by Flooring and the Moderating Role of Product Viewing Distance," *Journal of Consumer Research* 37 (June 2010): 1–14.

7. Jiewen Hong and Yacheng Sun, "Warm It Up with Love: The Effect of Physical Coldness on Liking of Romance Movies," *Journal of Consumer Research* 39, no. 2 (August 2012): 293–306.

8. Aradhna Krishna, May O. Lwin, and Maureen Morrin, "Product Scent and Memory," *Journal of Consumer Research* 37 (2010, June): 57–67.

9. Adam Bryant, "Plastic Surgery at AmEx," *Newsweek* (October 4, 1999): 55.

10. Amitava Chattopadhyay, Gerald J. Gorn, and Peter R. Darke, *Roses Are Red and Violets Are Blue—Everywhere? Cultural Universals and Differences in Color Preference among Consumers and Marketing Managers* (unpublished manuscript, University of British Columbia, Fall 1999); Joseph Bellizzi and Robert E. Hite, "Environmental Color, Consumer Feelings, and Purchase Likelihood," *Psychology & Marketing* 9 (1992): 347–63; Ayn E. Crowley, "The Two-Dimensional Impact of Color on Shopping," *Marketing Letters* 4 (January 1993); Gerald J. Gorn, Amitava Chattopadhyay, and Tracey Yi, *Effects of Color as an Executional Cue in an Ad: It's in the Shade* (unpublished manuscript, University of British Columbia, 1994).

11. Virginia Postrel, "The New Trend in Spending," *New York Times* (September 9, 2004), www.nytimes.com, accessed September 9, 2004.

12. Emily Cadei, "Cleaning Up: S. F. Duo Putting a Shine on Its Product Line," *San Francisco Business Times Online Edition* 17, no. 16 (December 6, 2002).

13. Martin Reimann, Judith Zaichkowsky, Carolin Neuhaus, Thomas Bender, and Bernd Weber, "Aesthetic Package Design: A Behavioral, Neural, and Psychological Investigation," *Journal of Consumer Psychology* 20 (2010): 431–41.

14. Pam Belluck, "Reinvent Wheel? Blue Room. Defusing a Bomb? Red Room," *New York Times* (February 5, 2009), www.nytimes.com, accessed February 5, 2009.

15. Mark G. Frank and Thomas Gilovich, "The Dark Side of Self and Social Perception: Black Uniforms and Aggression in Professional Sports," *Journal of Personality & Social Psychology* 54 (1988): 74–85.

16. Pamela Paul, "Color by Numbers," *American Demographics* (February 2002): 31–36.

17. Paulette Thomas, "Cosmetics Makers Offer World's Women an All-American Look with Local Twists," *Wall Street Journal* (May 8, 1995): B1.

18. Marc Gobé, *Emotional Branding: The New Paradigm for Connecting Brands to People* (New York: Allworth Press, 2001).

19. Dirk Olin, "Color Cognition," *New York Times* (November 30, 2003), www.nytimes.com, accessed November 30, 2003.

20. "Ny Emballage og Ny Navn Fordoblede Salget," *Markedsforing* 12 (1992): 24. Adapted from Michael R. Solomon, Gary Bamossy, and Soren Askegaard, *Consumer Behavior: A European Perspective*, 2nd ed. (London: Pearson Education, 2001).

21. Meg Rosen and Frank Alpert, "Protecting Your Business Image: The Supreme Court Rules on Trade Dress," *Journal of Consumer Marketing* 11 (1994): 50–55.

22. Excerpted from http://www.pantone.com/pages/fcr.aspx?pg=21058&ca=4, accessed March 2, 2013.

23. Ana Teriz, "Smells Like Celeb Spirit," *BrandChannel* (October 29, 2010), http://www.brandchannel.com/home/post/2010/10/29/Smells-like-Celeb-Spirit.aspx, accessed March 27, 2011.

24. Deborah J. Mitchell, Barbara E. Kahn, and Susan C. Knasko, "There's Something in the Air: Effects of Congruent or Incongruent Ambient Odor on Consumer Decision-Making," *Journal of Consumer Research* 22 (September 1995): 229–38; for a review of olfactory cues in store environments, see also Eric R. Spangenberg, Ayn E. Crowley, and Pamela W. Henderson, "Improving the Store Environment: Do Olfactory Cues Affect Evaluations and Behaviors?" *Journal of Marketing* 60 (April 1996): 67–80.

25. Krishna Aradhna, May O. Lwin, and Maureen Morrin, "Product Scent and Memory," *Journal of Consumer Research* 37, no. 1 (2010), 57–67.

26. "Lithuania Launches National Perfume," *Newstalk ZB/ONE News* (January 5, 2011), http://tvnz.co.nz/world-news/lithuania-launches-national-perfume-3992387, accessed March 27, 2011.

27. Emily Bryson York, "Make Your Man a Flamer, Mmmmmmm. Fresh Meat," *Advertising Age* (December 15, 2008), http://adage.com/adages/post?article_id=133264, accessed December 15, 2008.

28. Pam Scholder Ellen and Paula Fitzgerald Bone, "Does It Matter if It Smells? Olfactory Stimuli as Advertising Executional Cues," *Journal of Advertising* 27 (Winter 1998): 29–40.

29. Jack Hitt, "Does the Smell of Coffee Brewing Remind You of Your Mother?" *New York Times Magazine* (May 7, 2000): 73–77.

30. Quoted in Julie Jargon, "At Starbucks, It's Back to the Grind," *Wall Street Journal* (June 17, 2009), online at wsj.com/article/SB124517480498919731.html, accessed June 17, 2009.

31. Maxine Wilkie, "Scent of a Market," *American Demographics* (August 1995): 40–49.

32. Nicholas Wade, "Scent of a Man Is Linked to a Woman's Selection," *New York Times* (January 22, 2002), www.nytimes.com, accessed January 22, 2002.

33. Kara Newman, "How to Sell with Smell," *Business 2.0* (April 2007): 36.

34. Quoted in Sheila Shayon, "World Cup Winner: Coca-Cola for Sonic Branding," *BrandChannel* (July 12, 2010), http://www.brandchannel.com/home/post/2010/07/12/Coca-Cola-World-Cup-Wavin-Flag.aspx, accessed March 28, 2011.

35. Bruce G. Vanden Bergh, Janay Collins, Myrna Schultz, and Keith Adler, "Sound Advice on Brand Names," *Journalism Quarterly* 61, no. 4 (1984): 835–40; Eric Yorkston and Geeta Menon, "A Sound Idea: Phonetic Effects of Brand Names on Consumer Judgments," *Journal of Consumer Research* 31 (June 2004): 43–51; Keith S. Coulter and Robin A. Coulter, "Small Sounds, Big Deals: Phonetic Symbolism Effects in Pricing," *Journal of Consumer Research* 37, no. 2 (2010): 315–28.

36. "You Can Look—But Don't Touch," *Science Daily* (January 20, 2009), www.sciencedaily.com, accessed January 30, 2009; Joann Peck and Suzanne B. Shu, "The Effect of Mere Touch on Perceived Ownership," *Journal of Consumer Research* 36, no. 3 (2009): 434–47.

37. Sarah Ellison and Erin White, "'Sensory' Marketers Say the Way to Reach Shoppers Is the Nose," *Advertising Age* (November 24, 2000): 1–3.

38. Jacob Hornik, "Tactile Stimulation and Consumer Response," *Journal of Consumer Research* 19 (December 1992): 449–58.

39. Brett A. S. Martin, "A Stranger's Touch: Effects of Accidental Interpersonal Touch on Consumer Evaluations and Shopping Time," *Journal of Consumer Research* 39, no. 1 (June 2012): 174–184.

40. J. Peck and T. L. Childers, "Individual Differences in Haptic Information Processing: The 'Need for Touch' Scale," *Journal of Consumer Research* 30, no. 3 (2003): 430–42.

41. Material adapted from a presentation by Glenn H. Mazur, QFD Institute, 2002.

42. Joseph B. White, "Taller in the Saddle: Higher Driver's Seats in Sedans Are Effort to Appeal to Fans of SUVs and Minivans," *Wall Street Journal* (August 23, 2004), www.wsj.com, accessed August 23, 2004.

43. Claire Cain Miller, "To Win Over Users, Gadgets Have to Be Touchable," *New York Times* (September 1, 2010), http://www.nytimes.com/2010/09/01/technology/01touch.html?_r=1&emc=tnt&tntemail0=y, accessed March 27, 2011.

44. John Tagliabue, "Sniffing and Tasting with Metal and Wire," *New York Times* (February 17, 2002), www.nytimes.com, accessed February 17, 2002.

45. Michael W. Allen, Richa Gupta, and Arnaud Monnier, "The Interactive Effect of Cultural Symbols and Human Values on Taste Evaluation," *Journal of Consumer Research* 35 (August 2008): 294–308.

46. Becky Gaylord, "Bland Food Isn't So Bad—It Hurts Just to Think about This Stuff," *Wall Street Journal* (April 21, 1995): B1.

47. Stephanie Clifford and Catherine Rampell, quoted in "Food Inflation Kept Hidden in Tinier Bags," *New York Times* (March 28, 2011), http://www.nytimes.com/2011/03/29/business/29shrink.html?pagewanted=all, accessed March 29, 2011.

48. Ellen Byron, "Selling Detergent Bottles' Big Shrink Suds Makers' Challenge: Convince Consumers Less Isn't Really Less," *Wall Street Journal* (May 21, 2007), www.wsj.com, accessed May 21, 2007.

49. Michael Lev, "No Hidden Meaning Here: Survey Sees Subliminal Ads," *New York Times* (May 3, 1991): D7.

50. "ABC Rejects KFC Commercial, Citing Subliminal Advertising," *Wall Street Journal* (March 2, 2006), www.wsj.com, accessed March 2, 2006.

51. Andrew B. Aylesworth, Ronald C. Goodstein, and Ajay Kalra, "Effect of Archetypal Embeds on Feelings: An Indirect Route to Affecting Attitudes?" *Journal of Advertising* 28, no. 3 (Fall 1999): 73–81.

52. Joel Saegert, "Why Marketing Should Quit Giving Subliminal Advertising the Benefit of the Doubt," *Psychology & Marketing* 4 (Summer 1987): 107–20; see also Dennis L. Rosen and Surendra N. Singh, "An Investigation of Subliminal Embed Effect on Multiple Measures of Advertising Effectiveness," *Psychology & Marketing* 9 (March–April 1992): 157–73; for a more recent review, see Kathryn T. Theus, "Subliminal Advertising and the Psychology of Processing Unconscious Stimuli: A Review of Research," *Psychology & Marketing* (May–June 1994): 271–90.

53. Joseph Burris, "Plugged-in Generation Multi-Tasking Big Time," *Baltimore Sun* (February 17, 2010), http://articles.baltimoresun.com/2010-02-17/features/bal-md.pa.kids17feb17_1_cell-phones-multi-tasking-parental-controls, accessed May 5, 2011.

54. Sharon Waxman, "At an Industry Media Lab, Close Views of Multitasking," *New York Times* (May 15, 2006), http://www.nytimes.com/2006/05/15/technology/15research.html, accessed August 22, 2011

55. Matt Richtel, "Attached to Technology and Paying a Price," *New York Times* (June 6, 2010), http://www.nytimes.com/2010/06/07/technology/07brain.html?pagewanted=1, accessed April 17, 2011.

56. Brian Steinberg, "How to Keep Ad Skippers from Fast-Forwarding Your Ad," *Advertising Age* (March 31, 2009), www.adage.com, accessed March 31, 2009.

57. A. Selin Atalay, H. Onur Bodur, and Dina Rasolofoarison, "Shining in the Center: Central Gaze Cascade Effect on Product Choice," *Journal of Consumer Research* 39, no. 4 (December 2012): 848–866.

58. Stuart Elliott, "Trying to Keep the Viewers When the Ads Come On," *New York Times* (May 14, 2007), www.nytimes.com, accessed May 14, 2007.

59. Lee Gomes, "As Web Ads Grow, Sites Get Trickier about Targeting You," *Wall Street Journal* (May 9, 2007): B1.

60. Rik Pieters, Michel Wedel, and Rajeev Batra, "The Stopping Power of Advertising: Measures and Effects of Visual Complexity," *Journal of Marketing* 74 (September 2010): 48–60.

61. Roger Barton, *Advertising Media* (New York: McGraw-Hill, 1964).

62. Suzanne Oliver, "New Personality," *Forbes* (August 15, 1994): 114.

63. Adam Finn, "Print Ad Recognition Readership Scores: An Information Processing Perspective," *Journal of Marketing Research* 25 (May 1988): 168–77.

64. Gerald L. Lohse, "Consumer Eye Movement Patterns on Yellow Pages Advertising," *Journal of Advertising* 26 (Spring 1997): 61–73.

65. Chris Sherman, "A New F-Word for Google Search Results," *Search Engine Watch* (March 8, 2005), http://searchenginewatch.com/3488076, accessed June 29, 2010.

66. Michael R. Solomon and Basil G. Englis, "Reality Engineering: Blurring the Boundaries Between Marketing and Popular Culture," *Journal of Current Issues & Research in Advertising* 16, no. 2 (Fall 1994): 1–18; Michael McCarthy, "Ads Are Here, There, Everywhere: Agencies Seek Creative Ways to Expand Product Placement," *USA Today* (June 19, 2001): 1B.

67. Linda Stern, "Bigger Than at Times Square," *Newsweek* (March 24, 2008), www.newsweek.com.

68. Benedict Carey, "Liked the Show? Maybe It Was the Commercials," *New York Times* (March 2, 2009), http://topics.nytimes.com/topics/reference/timestopics/people/c/benedict_carey/index.html, accessed March 3, 2009.

69. Nicholas Bakalar, "If It Says McDonald's, Then It Must Be Good," *New York Times* (August 14, 2007), www.nytimes.com, accessed August 14, 2007.

70. Robert M. McMath, "Image Counts," *American Demographics* (May 1998): 64.

71. Brian Wansink, James Painter, and Koert van Ittersum, "Descriptive Menu Labels' Effect on Sales," *Cornell Hotel & Restaurant Administration Quarterly* (December 2001): 68–72.

72. Xiaoyan Deng and Barbara E. Kahn, "Is Your Product on the Right Side? The 'Location Effect' on Perceived Product Heaviness and Package Evaluation," *Journal of Marketing Research* 46, no. 6 (December 2009): 725–738.

73. Pankaj Aggarwal and Ann L. McGill, "Is That Car Smiling at Me? Schema Congruity as a Basis for Evaluating Anthropomorphized Products," *Journal of Consumer Behavior* 34 (December 2007): 468–79.

74. Anthony Ramirez, "Lessons in the Cracker Market: Nabisco Saved New Graham Snack," *New York Times* (July 5, 1990): D1.

75. Albert H. Hastorf and Hadley Cantril, "They Saw a Game: A Case Study," *Journal of Abnormal & Social Psychology* 49 (1954): 129–34; see also Roberto Friedmann and Mary R. Zimmer, "The Role of Psychological Meaning in Advertising," *Journal of Advertising* (1988): 31–40.

76. Robert M. McMath, "Chock Full of (Pea)nuts," *American Demographics* (April 1997): 60.

77. Benedict Carey, "Knowing the Ingredients Can Change the Taste," *New York Times* (December 12, 2006), www.nytimes.com, accessed December 12, 2006.

78. See David Mick, "Consumer Research and Semiotics: Exploring the Morphology of Signs, Symbols, and Significance," *Journal of Consumer Research* 13 (September 1986): 196–213.

79. Teresa J. Domzal and Jerome B. Kernan, "Reading Advertising: The What and How of Product Meaning," *Journal of Consumer Marketing* 9 (Summer 1992): 48–64.

80. Arthur Asa Berger, *Signs in Contemporary Culture: An Introduction to Semiotics* (New York: Longman, 1984); David Mick, "Consumer Research and Semiotics," 196–213; Charles Sanders Peirce, in Charles Hartshorne, Paul Weiss, and Arthur W. Burks, eds., *Collected Papers* (Cambridge, MA: Harvard University Press, 1931–1958); cf. also V. Larsen, D. Luna, and L. A. Peracchio, "Points of View and Pieces of Time: A Taxonomy of Image Attributes," *Journal of Consumer Research* 31, no. 1 (2004): 102–11.

81. Rob Walker, "False Endorsement," *New York Times Magazine* (November 18, 2007), www.nytimes.com/2007/11/18/magazine/18wwln-consumed-t.html?_r=1&, accessed November 24, 2007; David Edery, "Reverse Product Placement in Virtual Worlds," *Harvard Business Review* (December 2006), http://hbr.org/2006/12/reverse-product-placement-in-virtual-worlds/ar/1, accessed August 22, 2011.

82. Walker, "False Endorsement."

83. Steven Heller, "A Makeover for the Starbucks Mermaid," *New York Times* (January 8, 2011), http://www.nytimes.com/2011/01/09/weekinreview/09heller.html?_r=1&scp=2&sq=starbucks&st=cse, accessed March 27, 2011.

84. Gabriel Kahn, "Chinese Characters Are Gaining New Meaning as Corporate Logos," *Wall Street Journal Interactive Edition* (July 18, 2002).

85. Natalie Zmuda, "Why Tommy Hilfiger Boosted Ad Budget by 60%, Aired First Branded TV Spot Since 2005," *Ad Age CMO Strategy*, http://adage.com/article/cmo-strategy/marketing-tommy-hilfiger-boosted-ad-budget-60/147258/, accessed April 28, 2011.

86. Dexter Dining Room and Kitchen, *Metropolitan Home* (March 2009), www.metropolitanhome.com, accessed January 27, 2009.

87. Bob Teheschi, "Seeing the World Around You Through Your Phone," *New York Times* (July 28, 2010), http://www.nytimes.com/2010/07/29/technology/personaltech/29smart.html?emc=tnt&tntemail0=y, accessed March 28, 2011.

88. Lauren Johnson, "Augmented Reality Apps Predicted to Generate $300M in 2013: study," *Mobile Marketer* (November 7, 2012), http://www.mobilemarketer.com/cms/news/research/14159.html, accessed January 21, 2013.

89. Adapted from Michael R. Solomon and Elnora W. Stuart, *Marketing: Real People, Real Choices*, 2nd ed. (Upper Saddle River, NJ: Prentice Hall, 2000).

90. William Echikson, "Aiming at High and Low Markets," *Fortune* (March 22, 1993): 89.

91. Jenny H. Ledikwe, Julia A. Ello-Martin, and Barbara J. Rolls, "Portion Sizes and the Obesity Epidemic," *The Journal of Nutrition* 135, no. 4 (April 1, 2005): 905–09, http://jn.nutrition.org/content/135/4/905.long.

92. Sarah D. Stanwick and Peter A. Stanwick, "The Ethics of Outsourcing at Mattel," *Problems and Perspectives in Management* 8, no. 4 (2010): 179–83, http://businessperspectives.org/journals_free/ppm/2010/PPM_EN_2010_04_cont_Stanwick.pdf, accessed on December 17, 2013.

Chapter 6 · Learning and Memory

Chapter Objectives

When you finish reading this chapter you will understand why:

1. It is important to understand how consumers learn about products and services.

2. Conditioning results in learning.

3. Learned associations with brands generalize to other products, which is important to marketers.

4. There is a difference between classical and instrumental conditioning, and both processes help consumers learn about products.

5. We learn about products by observing others' behavior.

6. Our brains process information about brands to retain them in memory.

7. The other products we associate with an individual product influence how we will remember it.

8. Products help us to retrieve memories from our past.

9. Marketers measure our memories about products and ads.

Source: Photos.com/Thinkstock.

Ah, Sunday morning! The sun is shining, the birds are singing, and Joe is feeling groovy! He puts on his vintage Levi's 501 jeans (circa 1968) and his Woodstock T-shirt (the "real" Woodstock, not that fake abomination they put on in 2009, thank you) and saunters down to the kitchen. Joe smiles in anticipation of his morning plans. He's just returned from his college reunion and now it's time to "process" all the people he's seen and the stories he heard about their old antics. Joe cranks up the Lava Lamp, throws a Jefferson Airplane record on the turntable (ah, the sublime joys of vinyl), and sits back on his Barcalounger as he clutches a huge bowl filled to the brim with his all-time favorite cereal, Cap'n Crunch. Let the memories begin!

OBJECTIVE 1

It is important to understand how consumers learn about products and services.

Learning

Joe journeys through time with the aid of many products that make him feel good because they remind him of earlier parts of his life. Products have capitalized on this nostalgia, too. PepsiCo launched its "Throwback" campaign; now it sells Pepsi Throwback, Mountain Dew Throwback, and Doritos Taco-Flavored chips in authentic packages from the past. Hostess brought back its 1970s characters Twinkie the Kid, Captain CupCake, King Ding Dong, and Happy Ho Ho to adorn its snack cake packages. Disney is trying to revive its Tron franchise. As a PepsiCo marketing executive explained, "Retro is very cool with 20-somethings, because it ties in with their desire for simpler, cleaner, more authentic lives. Many of them are engaged in identity self-creation through their Facebook pages, Instagrams, Twitter and other social media, and they see nostalgia as a way to differentiate themselves."[1]

Learning is a relatively permanent change in behavior caused by experience. The learner need not have the experience directly, however; we can also learn when we observe events that affect others.[2] We learn even when we don't try: We recognize many brand names and hum many product jingles, for example, even for products we don't personally use. We call this casual, unintentional acquisition of knowledge **incidental learning**.

Learning is an ongoing process. Our knowledge about the world constantly updates as we are exposed to new stimuli and as we receive ongoing feedback that allows us to modify our behavior when we find ourselves in similar situations at a later time. The concept of learning covers a lot of ground, ranging from a consumer's simple association between a stimulus such as a product logo (e.g., Coca-Cola) and a response (e.g., "refreshing soft drink") to a complex series of cognitive activities (e.g., writing an essay on learning for a consumer behavior exam).

Psychologists who study learning advance several theories to explain the learning process. These theories range from those that focus on simple stimulus–response connections (*behavioral theories*) to perspectives that regard consumers as solvers of complex problems who learn abstract rules and concepts when they observe what others say and do (*cognitive theories*). It's important for marketers to understand these theories as well, because basic learning principles are at the heart of many consumer purchase decisions.

The Chinese middle class is booming, but young consumers still have a lot to learn about the ins and outs of shopping. They look for basic appliances and TV sets to fill their first apartments, save more than 30 percent of their income, and rarely use credit cards. Many Chinese shoppers expect to haggle over prices—a barrier that U.S. companies must overcome as they set up shop there, since this is a foreign concept for U.S. companies. As one shopper observed, "We need to learn about all these features because our parents didn't have most of this stuff."

That's why Best Buy decided to build up the local Five Star Brand when the chain expanded to China. In these stores, the employees coddle shoppers and help to guide them through the process as they consider big-ticket items their families never owned. A clerk will offer the shopper cherry tomatoes, a cup of hot water to sip, or some time in a massage chair. Later, the clerk will try to persuade the customer to buy the chair. Five Star offers "solution experts," who help customers sort through the conflicting claims of manufacturers' representatives who work in the stores, where goods are organized by manufacturer rather than by product. These guides aim to build a web of loyal shoppers as they rely on the Chinese custom of turning to a network of trusted acquaintances for input on big decisions.[3]

• • • • • • • • • • • • • • • •

Source: dotshock/Shutterstock.

OBJECTIVE 2
Conditioning results in learning.

Behavioral Learning Theories

Behavioral learning theories assume that learning takes place as the result of responses to external events. Psychologists who subscribe to this viewpoint do not focus on internal thought processes. Instead, they approach the mind as a "black box" and emphasize the observable aspects of behavior. The observable aspects consist of things that go into the box (the stimuli or events perceived from the outside world) and things that come out of the box (the responses, or reactions to these stimuli).

Two major approaches to learning represent this view: *classical conditioning* and *instrumental conditioning*. According to the behavioral learning perspective, the feedback we receive as we go through life shapes our experiences. Similarly, we respond to brand names, scents, jingles, and other marketing stimuli because of the learned connections we form over time. People also learn that actions they take result in rewards and punishments; this feedback influences the way they will respond in similar situations in the future. Consumers who receive compliments on a product choice will be more likely to buy that brand again, while those who get food poisoning at a new restaurant are not likely to patronize that restaurant in the future.

Classical conditioning occurs when a stimulus that elicits a response is paired with another stimulus that initially does not elicit a response on its own. Over time, this second stimulus causes a similar response because we associate it with the first stimulus. Ivan Pavlov, a Russian physiologist who conducted research on digestion in animals, first demonstrated this phenomenon in dogs. Pavlov induced classically conditioned learning when he paired a neutral stimulus (a bell) with a stimulus known to cause a salivation response in dogs (he squirted dried meat powder into their mouths). The powder was an **unconditioned stimulus (UCS)** because it was naturally capable of causing the response. Over time, the bell became a **conditioned stimulus (CS)**—it did not initially cause salivation, but the dogs learned to associate the bell with the meat powder and began to salivate at the sound of the bell only. The drooling of these canine consumers because of a sound, now linked to feeding time, was a **conditioned response (CR)**.

This basic form of classical conditioning that Pavlov demonstrated primarily applies to responses controlled by the *autonomic* (e.g., salivation) and *nervous* (e.g., eye blink) *systems*. That is, it focuses on visual and olfactory cues that induce hunger, thirst, sexual

Some advertising messages appeal to our motivation to avoid negative outcomes like bad breath. This Indian ad for a mint certainly does.
Source: McCann Erickson India.

arousal, and other basic drives. When marketers consistently pair these cues with conditioned stimuli, such as brand names, consumers may learn to feel hungry, thirsty, or aroused when they encounter these brand cues at a later point.

Classical conditioning can have similar effects for more complex reactions, too. Even a credit card becomes a conditioned cue that triggers greater spending, especially because as a stimulus it's present only in situations where we spend money. People learn they can make larger purchases with credit cards, and they also leave larger tips than when they pay by cash.[4] Small wonder that American Express reminds us, "Don't leave home without it."

Repetition

Conditioning effects are more likely to occur after the conditioned (CS) and unconditioned (UCS) stimuli have been paired a number of times.[5] Repeated exposures—**repetition**—increase the strength of stimulus–response associations and prevent the decay of these associations in memory. Some research indicates that the intervals between exposures may influence the effectiveness of this strategy as well as the type of medium the marketer uses; the most effective repetition strategy is a combination of spaced exposures that alternate in terms of media that are more and less involving, such as television advertising complemented by print media.[6]

Many classic advertising campaigns consist of product slogans that companies repeat so often they are etched in consumers' minds. Conditioning will not occur or will take longer if the CS is only occasionally paired with the UCS. One result of this lack of association is **extinction**, which occurs when the effects of prior conditioning diminish and finally disappear. This can occur, for example, when a product is overexposed in the marketplace so that its original allure is lost. The Izod Lacoste polo shirt, with its distinctive crocodile crest, is a good example of this effect. When the once-exclusive crocodile started to appear on baby clothes and many other items, it lost its cachet. Other contenders, such as the Ralph Lauren polo player, successfully challenged it as a symbol of casual elegance. Now that Izod is being more careful about where its logo appears, the brand is starting to regain its "cool" in some circles.

Stimulus Generalization

Stimulus generalization refers to the tendency of stimuli similar to a CS to evoke similar, conditioned responses. For example, Pavlov noticed in subsequent studies that his dogs would sometimes salivate when they heard noises that only resembled a bell, such as keys jangling.

People also react to other, similar stimuli in much the same way they responded to the original stimulus; we call this generalization a **halo effect**. A drugstore's bottle of private-brand mouthwash that is deliberately packaged to resemble Listerine mouthwash may evoke a similar response among consumers, who assume that this "me-too" product shares other characteristics of the original. Indeed, consumers in one study on shampoo brands tended to rate those with similar packages as similar in quality and performance as well.[8] This "piggybacking" strategy can cut both ways: When the quality of the me-too product turns out to be lower than that of the original brand, consumers may exhibit even more positive feelings toward the original. However, if they perceive the quality of the two competitors to be about equal, consumers may conclude that the price premium they pay for the original is not worth it.[9]

Stimulus Discrimination

Stimulus discrimination occurs when a UCS does not follow a stimulus similar to a CS. When this happens, reactions weaken and will soon disappear. Part of the learning process involves making a response to some stimuli but not to other, similar stimuli. Manufacturers of well-established brands commonly urge consumers not to buy "cheap imitations" because the results will not be what they expect.

CB AS I SEE IT

Prof. William E. Baker, *University of Akron*

Brand awareness and familiarity are important. Brands with high awareness are more likely to be in the consumers' consideration set. Brands that are familiar are more likely to be trusted. However, the first and most critical step in brand development may be **brand-name imprinting**.

A brand must own a niche in memory; a space that anchors it to a *specific* category (e.g., Porsche to sports car) or usage occasion (nighttime pain relief). Some researchers refer to this space as a "brand node." Weak imprinting occurs when the brand node is not clearly linked to a product category or usage occasion, *or* when it is linked to too broad a category (e.g., automobile) or usage situation (whenever you have pain).

Research has shown that if a new brand's name is imprinted by flashing it several times to consumers before they receive a presentation of the new brand's benefits, the information is better learned and linked to the brand than if the brand name is not imprinted prior to the presentation. Other research shows that if a brand node is ignited (i.e., cued) to memory by presenting the brand name/logo at the beginning of a video advertisement, the information that follows will be better linked to the brand than when the brand name is not revealed until the end of the advertisement.

OBJECTIVE 3
Learned associations with brands generalize to other products, which is important to marketers.

Marketing Applications of Classical Conditioning Principles

Behavioral learning principles apply to many consumer phenomena, such as when a marketer creates a distinctive brand image or links a product to an underlying need. The transfer of meaning from an unconditioned stimulus to a conditioned stimulus explains why "made-up" brand names, such as Marlboro, Coca-Cola, or Adidas, exert such powerful effects on consumers. The association between the Marlboro man and the cigarette is so strong that in some cases the company no longer even bothers to include the brand name in its ads that feature the cowboy riding off into the sunset. Indeed, recent research shows that these linkages cement early on; scans of children show how the pleasure and appetite centers of their brains light up when they view advertising images of fast-food companies such as the McDonald's logo.[10]

When researchers pair *nonsense syllables* (meaningless sets of letters) with such evaluative words as *beauty* or *success*, the meaning transfers to the fake words. This change in the symbolic significance of initially meaningless words shows that fairly simple associations can condition even complex meanings, and the learning that results can last a long time.[11] These associations are crucial to many marketing strategies that rely on the creation and perpetuation of **brand equity**, in which a brand has strong positive associations in a consumer's memory and commands a lot of loyalty as a result.[12]

Marketing Applications of Repetition

One advertising researcher argued that any more than three exposures to a marketing communication are wasted. The first exposure creates awareness of the product, the second demonstrates its relevance to the consumer, and the third reminds him or her of the product's benefits.[13] However, even this bare-bones approach implies that we need repetition to ensure that the consumer is actually exposed to (and processes) the message at least three times. As we've seen, this exposure is by no means guaranteed, because people tend to tune out or distort many marketing communications. Marketers that attempt to condition an association must ensure that the consumers they target will be exposed to the stimulus a sufficient number of times to make it "stick."

However, it is possible to have too much of a good thing. Consumers can become so used to hearing or seeing a marketing stimulus that they no longer pay attention to it. Varying the way in which the marketer presents the basic message can alleviate this problem of **advertising wear-out**. Toyota ran a commercial featuring a reworked version of The Fixx's song "Saved by Zero" to promote its no-interest payment options so many times that close to 10,000 fed-up viewers organized a Facebook group to petition the company for mercy. As one worn-out group member posted, "There have been worse commercials, and there have been commercials that were played this often; but never before has a commercial this bad been aired so much."[15]

How often should an advertiser repeat the ads it places on Web sites? Recent research indicates that the answer depends on whether the ad relates to the Web site's content, and whether or not competing ads are also present on the site. The study found support for the general idea that repetitive ad messages resulted in higher recall and interest in learning more about the advertised product (in this case, a laptop). However, repeating the same ad was primarily effective when competitors also showed ads on the site. Otherwise, it was better to vary the ad messages for the laptop (presumably because people tuned out the ad if it appeared repeatedly). These ads were also more effective when they appeared on a site where the content related to the advertised product.[16]

Marketing Applications of Conditioned Product Associations

Advertisements often pair a product with a positive stimulus to create a desirable association. Various aspects of a marketing message, such as music, humor, or imagery, can affect conditioning. In one study, for example, subjects who viewed a slide of pens paired

Marketing Pitfall

At least on the surface, it's easier to accept some brand extensions than others. Consider the line of wines that now sell under the Ed Hardy brand—better known for tattoo-themed streetwear. As one reviewer wrote, "Wine is a cultivated taste of a delicately cultivated product, a source of savored satisfaction and nuance, a living liquid that rewards reflection and restraint. The *haute-trash* Ed Hardy brand—as near as I can parse it—represents getting wasted in Las Vegas and leaving your $50 trucker hat in the cab on the way to the airport."[14] Cheers!

with either pleasant or unpleasant music were more likely later to select the pen that appeared with the pleasant music.[17]

Because of the danger of extinction, a classical conditioning strategy may not be as effective for products that consumers frequently encounter, because there is no guarantee that the CS will accompany them. A bottle of Pepsi paired with the refreshing sound of a carbonated beverage poured over ice may seem like a good application of conditioning. Unfortunately, people would also see the product in many other contexts in which this sound was absent, so this reduces the effectiveness of that conditioning strategy.

Marketing Applications of Stimulus Generalization

The process of stimulus generalization often is central to branding and packaging decisions that try to capitalize on consumers' positive associations with an existing brand or company name. We can clearly appreciate the value of this kind of linkage when we look at universities with winning sports teams: Loyal fans snap up merchandise, from clothing to bathroom accessories, emblazoned with the school's name. This business did not even exist 20 years ago when schools were reluctant to commercialize their images. Texas A&M was one of the first schools that even bothered to file for trademark protection, and that was only after someone put the Aggie logo on a line of handguns. Today it's a different story. Many college administrators crave the revenue they receive from sweatshirts, drink coasters, and even toilet seats emblazoned with school logos. Strategies that marketers base on stimulus generalization include:

- **Family branding**—Many products capitalize on the reputation of a company name. Companies such as Campbell's, Heinz, and General Electric rely on their positive corporate images to sell different product lines.
- **Product line extension**—Marketers add related products to an established brand. Dole, which we associate with fruit, introduced refrigerated juices and juice bars, whereas Sun Maid went from raisins to raisin bread. The gun manufacturer Smith & Wesson launched its own line of furniture and other home items. Starbucks Corp. and Jim Beam Brands teamed up to make Starbucks Coffee Liqueur. Meanwhile, Procter & Gamble cleans up with its Mr. Clean brand of liquid cleanser; it aggressively puts the name on new products such as Mr. Clean Magic Eraser, for removing crayon marks from walls and scuff marks from chair rails; and Mr. Clean Autodry, for leaving a freshly washed car spot-free without hand drying.[19]
- **Licensing**—Companies often "rent" well-known names, hoping that the learned associations they have forged will "rub off" onto other kinds of products. Jamba Juice launched a clothing line.[21] Zippo Manufacturing Co., long known for its "windproof" cigarette lighters, markets a men's fragrance—and no, it doesn't smell like lighter fluid.[22]
- **Look-alike packaging**—Distinctive packaging designs create strong associations with a particular brand. Companies that make generic or private-label brands and want to communicate a quality image often exploit this linkage when they put their products in packages similar to those of popular brands.[24] How does this strategy affect consumers' perceptions of the original brand? One study found that a negative experience with an imitator brand actually *increased* consumers' evaluations of the original brand, whereas a positive experience with the imitator had the opposite effect of decreasing evaluations of the original brand.[25] Another study found that consumers tend to react positively to "copycat brands" as long as the imitator doesn't make grandiose claims that it can't fulfill.[26]

Of course, this strategy can make a lot of work for lawyers if the copycat brand gets *too* close to the original. Marketers of distinctive brands work hard to protect their designs and logos, and each year companies file numerous lawsuits in so-called *Lanham Act* cases that hinge on the issue of **consumer confusion**: How likely is it that one company's logo, product design, or package is so similar to another that the typical shopper would mistake one for the other? For example, Levi Strauss has sued almost 100 other apparel manufacturers that it claims have borrowed its trademark pocket design of a

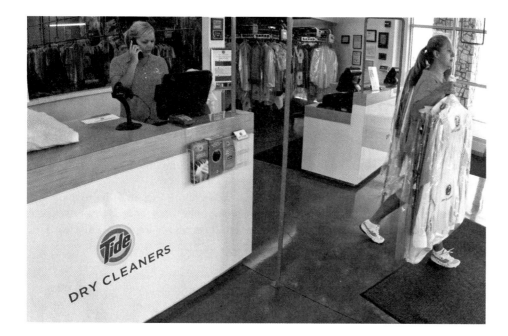

Procter & Gamble opened a new line of Tide Dry Cleaners, named after its bestselling laundry detergent. P&G will rely on the more than 800,000 Facebook fans of Tide (what else do these people "like" on Facebook?) and other loyal detergent users to trust their clothes to the franchise stores. P&G plans to infuse the stores and its dry cleaning fluids with the familiar Tide scent just to underscore the connection.
Source: Courtesy of Boomburg via Getty Images.

pentagon surrounding a drawing of a seagull in flight or its distinctive tab that it sews into its garments' vertical seams.[27]

Companies with a well-established brand image try to encourage stimulus discrimination when they promote the unique attributes of their brand—hence the constant reminders for American Express Travelers Cheques: "Ask for them by name." However, a brand name that a firm uses so widely that it is no longer distinctive becomes part of the public domain and competitors are free to borrow it: think of well-worn names such as aspirin, cellophane, yo-yo, escalator, and even google (which started as a noun and is now also a verb). This high degree of acceptance can be a tough barrier to jump when you're a competitor: Microsoft hopes that over time we will choose to "bing" rather than "google" when we want information.

OBJECTIVE 4

There is a difference between classical and instrumental conditioning, and both processes help consumers learn about products.

Instrumental Conditioning

Instrumental conditioning (or *operant conditioning*) occurs when we learn to perform behaviors that produce positive outcomes and avoid those that yield negative outcomes. We most closely associate this learning process with the psychologist B. F. Skinner, who demonstrated the effects of instrumental conditioning by teaching pigeons and other animals to dance, play Ping-Pong, and perform other activities when he systematically rewarded them for desired behaviors.[28]

Whereas responses in classical conditioning are involuntary and fairly simple, we make those in instrumental conditioning deliberately to obtain a goal, and these may be more complex. We may learn the desired behavior over a period of time as a **shaping** process rewards our intermediate actions. For example, the owner of a new store may award prizes to shoppers who simply drop in; she hopes that over time they will continue to drop in and eventually even buy something.

Also, whereas classical conditioning involves the close pairing of two stimuli, instrumental learning occurs when a learner receives a reward *after* she performs the desired behavior. In these cases, learning takes place over time, while the learner attempts and abandons other behaviors that don't get reinforced. A good way to remember the difference is to keep in mind that in instrumental learning the person makes a response because it is *instrumental* to gain a reward or avoid a punishment. Over time, consumers come to associate with people who reward them and to choose products that make them feel good or satisfy some need.

Instrumental conditioning occurs in one of three ways:

1 When the environment provides **positive reinforcement** in the form of a reward, this strengthens the response and we learn the appropriate behavior. For example, a woman who gets compliments after wearing Obsession perfume learns that using this product has the desired effect, and she will be more likely to keep buying the product.

2 **Negative reinforcement** also strengthens responses so that we learn the appropriate behavior. A perfume company might run an ad showing a woman sitting home alone on a Saturday night because she did not wear its fragrance. The message this conveys is that she could have avoided this negative outcome if only she had used the perfume.

3 In contrast to situations where we learn to do certain things in order to avoid unpleasantness, **punishment** occurs when unpleasant events follow a response (such as when our friends ridicule us if we wear a nasty-smelling fragrance). We learn the hard way not to repeat these behaviors.

Positive reinforcement occurs after consumers try a new product and like it.
Source: Provided courtesy of Frito-Lay North America, Inc.

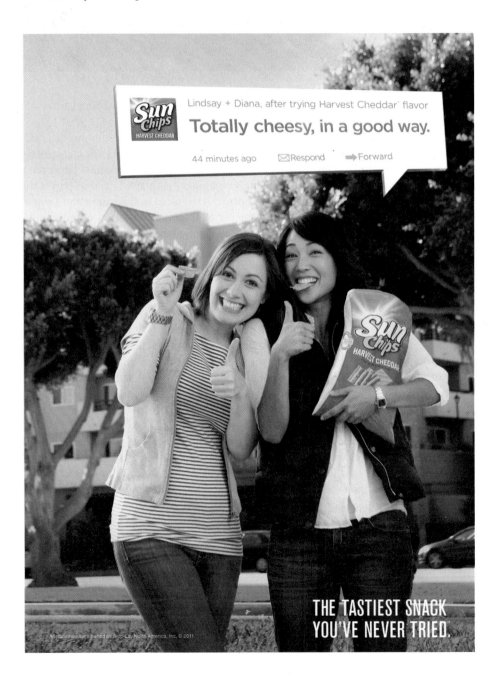

operant

these mechanisms, keep in mind that
ner behavior can be either positive or
negative, and that marketers can either apply or remove these outcomes (or anticipated outcomes). That is, under conditions of both positive reinforcement and punishment, the person receives a reaction when he or she does something. In contrast, negative reinforcement occurs when the person avoids a negative outcome—the removal of something negative is pleasurable and hence is rewarding.

Finally, when a person no longer receives a positive outcome, *extinction* is likely to occur, and the learned stimulus–response connection will not be maintained (as when a woman no longer receives compliments on her perfume). Thus, positive and negative reinforcement strengthen the future linkage between a response and an outcome because of the pleasant experience. This tie is weakened under conditions of both punishment and extinction because of the unpleasant experience. Figure 6.1 will help you to "reinforce" the relationships among these four conditions.

It's important for marketers to determine the most effective reinforcement schedule to use. This decision relates to the amount of effort and resources they must devote when they reward consumers who respond as they hope to their requests. Several schedules are possible:

- **Fixed-interval reinforcement**—After a specified time period has passed, the first response you make brings the reward. Under such conditions, people tend to respond slowly right after they get reinforced, but their responses get faster as the time for the next reinforcement approaches. For example, consumers may crowd into a store for the last day of its seasonal sale and not reappear until the next one.
- **Variable-interval reinforcement**—The time that must pass before you get reinforced varies based on some average. Because you don't know exactly when to expect

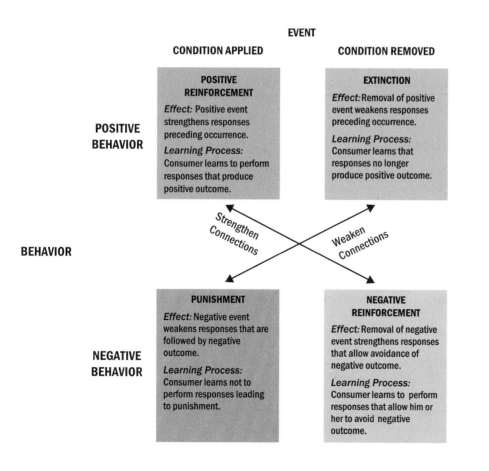

Figure 6.1 TYPES OF REINFORCEMENT

the reinforcement, you have to respond at a consistent rate. This is the logic behind retailers' use of so-called *secret shoppers:* people who periodically test for service quality when they pose as customers at unannounced times. Because store employees never know exactly when to expect a visit, they must maintain high quality constantly "just in case."

● **Fixed-ratio reinforcement**—Reinforcement occurs only after a fixed number of responses. This schedule motivates you to continue performing the same behavior over and over. For example, you might keep buying groceries at the same store in order to earn a prize when you collect 50 register receipts.

● **Variable-ratio reinforcement**—You get reinforced after a certain number of responses, but you don't know how many responses are required. People in such situations tend to respond at very high and steady rates, and this type of behavior is very difficult to extinguish. This reinforcement schedule is responsible for consumers' attractions to slot machines. They learn that if they keep throwing money into the machine, they will eventually win something (if they don't go broke first).

Marketing Applications of Instrumental Conditioning Principles

Principles of instrumental conditioning are at work when a marketer rewards or punishes a consumer for a purchase decision. Businesspeople shape behavior when they gradually reinforce the appropriate actions consumers take. A car dealer might encourage a reluctant buyer to simply sit in a floor model, then suggest a test drive, and then try to close the deal.

Marketers have many ways to reinforce consumers' behaviors, ranging from a simple "thank you" after a purchase to substantial rebates and follow-up phone calls. For example, a life insurance company obtained a much higher rate of policy renewal among a group of new customers who received a thank-you letter after each payment, compared to a control group that did not receive any reinforcement.[29]

Frequency marketing is a popular technique that rewards regular purchasers with prizes that get better as they spend more. The airline industry pioneered this instrumental learning strategy when it introduced "frequent flyer" programs in the early 1980s to reward loyal customers. The practice has spread to many other businesses as well, ranging from video stores to fast-food places.

Gamification

Many of us grew up playing games, and some of us never stopped. In some sense, all of life is a game, insofar as there are winners and losers and challenges we must solve to reach various objectives. Many organizations are going to the next level; they're borrowing from basic principles of gaming to motivate consumers and employees across a broad spectrum of activity.

The fast-growing strategy of **gamification** turns routine actions into experiences as it adds gaming elements to tasks that might otherwise be boring or routine. Millennials have grown up playing games; these activities structure their learning styles and influence the platforms to which they will gravitate.[30] Important elements of gaming include:

● A dynamic digital environment (whether in-store, on a laptop, or on a tablet or phone) that resembles a sophisticated videogame platform
● Multiple short- and long-term goals
● Rapid and frequent feedback
● A reward for most or all efforts in the form of a badge or a virtual product
● Friendly competition in a low-risk environment
● A manageable degree of uncertainty

Aherk! is a goal-oriented self-blackmailing service in three easy steps:

STEP 2:
Put your ass on the line.

Upload a compromising picture that will be posted to Facebook in case you fail to achieve your goal.

Net Profit

Aherk! helps people to reach their objectives by engaging in a bit of self-blackmail: You post a goal and a deadline on the site. You also post an embarrassing photo of yourself (they call it "the bomb"). When the deadline hits, your Facebook friends vote on whether you achieved your goal. If the vote is negative, boom!—up goes your photo for all to see. Other apps that dole out a dose of negative reinforcement include the GymPact, where missed workouts (tracked via smartphone) cost the user real money, and Write or Die, a cure for writer's block that unwrites the words on your laptop if you sit too long without adding more. Finally there's the Virtual Fridge Lock—it attaches to your refrigerator and posts to your Facebook timeline every time you open the door.[31]

Source: Aherk! (http://aherk.com).

Fitocracy is one of a new generation of apps that integrates gamification principles to encourage weight loss and physical fitness as it awards badges and provides a steady stream of feedback to the user. Another is Keas; it encourages workers to stay healthy by grouping themselves into teams of six and collecting points for achieving mental and physical fitness goals. Among the challenges Keas assigns: laughing randomly for 30 seconds. In South Africa, consumers play Vitality that allows them to accumulate points for healthy behaviors they can redeem for groceries and airline tickets.[32]

Source: Courtesy of Fitocracy, Inc.

Many domains of human activity (and business) share the common need to motivate and reward people to achieve ascending levels of mastery. These include:

- **Store and brand loyalty.** Foursquare gives people virtual badges when they check in at a local cafe or restaurant. Some of them check in as often as they can to compete for the honor of being named "mayor" of the location.
- **Social marketing.** More than 75 utilities have begun using a service from a company called Opower that awards badges to customers when they reduce their energy consumption. Customers can compare their progress with their neighbors' and broadcast their achievements on Facebook.
- **Employee performance.** Some restaurants use a service called Objective Logistics to rank the performances of waiters on a leader board, rewarding the good ones with plum shifts and more lucrative tables.[33]

Cognitive Learning Theory

Unlike behavioral theories of learning, **cognitive learning theory** approaches stress the importance of internal mental processes. This perspective views people as problem-solvers who actively use information from the world around them to master their environments. Supporters of this view also stress the role of creativity and insight during the learning process.

An Ocean Spray commercial for diet cranberry juice illustrates how marketers can harness their knowledge of cognitive theories to tweak marketing messages. The spot

This French ad for Pictionary requires the viewer to invest a fair amount of effort to understand it.
Source: Courtesy of Ogilvy & Mather, Paris.

features two men, in the role of cranberry growers, who stand knee-deep in a bog. A group of women who are exercising joins them. Originally, the ad depicted the women having a party, but a cognitive scientist who worked on the campaign nixed that idea; she argued that the exercise class would send the diet message more quickly, whereas the party scene would confuse viewers who would spend too much time trying to figure out why the group was celebrating. This extra cognitive activity would distract from the ad's message. And, contrary to standard practice in advertising that the actors name the product as early as possible, she decided that the main characters should wait a few seconds before they mention the new diet product. She reasoned that viewers would need a second or so more time to process the images because of the additional action in the ad (the exercising). In a test of which ads got remembered best, this new version scored in the top 10 percent.[34]

Is Learning Conscious or Not?

A lot of controversy surrounds the issue of whether or when people are aware of their learning processes.[35] Whereas behavioral learning theorists emphasize the routine, automatic nature of conditioning, proponents of cognitive learning argue that even these simple effects are based on cognitive factors: They create expectations that a response will follow a stimulus (the formation of expectations requires mental activity). According to this school of thought, conditioning occurs because subjects develop conscious hypotheses and then act on them.

There is some evidence to support the existence of *nonconscious procedural knowledge*. People apparently do process at least some information in an automatic, passive way, a condition that researchers call "mindlessness" (we've all experienced that!).[36] When we meet someone new or encounter a new product, for example, we have a tendency to respond to the stimulus in terms of existing categories we have learned, rather than taking the trouble to formulate new ones. In these cases a *trigger feature*—some stimulus that cues us toward a particular pattern—activates a reaction. For example, men in one study rated a car in an ad as superior on a variety of characteristics if a seductive woman (the trigger feature) was present, despite the fact that the men did not believe the woman's presence actually had an influence on their evaluations.[37] We discussed these triggers in the context of *priming* in earlier chapters.

Nonetheless, many modern theorists regard some instances of automatic conditioning as cognitive processes, especially when people form expectations about the linkages between stimuli and responses. Indeed, studies using *masking effects*, which make it difficult for subjects to learn CS/UCS associations, show substantial reductions in conditioning.[38] An adolescent girl may observe that women on television and in real life seem to be rewarded with compliments and attention when they smell nice and wear alluring clothing. She figures out that the probability of these rewards occurring is greater when she wears perfume, so she deliberately wears a popular scent to obtain the reward of social acceptance. For now, the jury is out regarding the true impact of nonconscious processing and priming as this question currently is one of the hottest debates in the field of psychology.[39]

OBJECTIVE 5

We learn about products by observing others' behavior.

Observational Learning

Observational learning occurs when we watch the actions of others and note the reinforcements they receive for their behaviors. In these situations, learning occurs as a result of *vicarious* rather than direct experience. This type of learning is a complex process; people store these observations in memory as they accumulate knowledge and then they use this information at a later point to guide their own behavior. **Modeling** (not the runway kind) is the process of imitating the behavior of others. For example, a woman who shops for a new kind of perfume may remember the reactions her friend received when she wore a certain brand several months earlier, and she will mimic her friend's behavior in the hope that she will get the same feedback.

The modeling process is a powerful form of learning, and people's tendencies to imitate others' behaviors can have negative effects. Of particular concern is the potential of television shows and movies to teach violence to children. Children may be exposed to new methods of aggression by models (e.g., cartoon heroes) in the shows they watch. At some later point, when the child becomes angry, he may imitate these behaviors. A classic study demonstrates the effect of modeling on children's actions. Kids who watched an adult stomp on, knock down, and otherwise torture a large inflated "Bobo doll" repeated these behaviors when later left alone in a room with the doll; children who did not witness these acts did not.[40] Unfortunately, the relevance of this study to violent TV shows seems quite clear.

Figure 6.2 shows that for observational learning in the form of modeling to occur, the marketer must meet four conditions:[41]

1 The consumer's attention must be directed to the appropriate model, whom, for reasons of attractiveness, competence, status, or similarity, he must want to emulate.
2 The consumer must remember what the model says or does.
3 The consumer must convert this information into actions.
4 The consumer must be motivated to perform these actions.

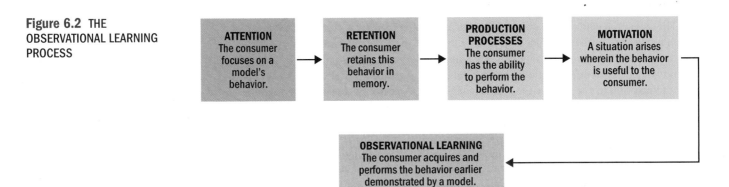

Figure 6.2 THE OBSERVATIONAL LEARNING PROCESS

ATTENTION The consumer focuses on a model's behavior. → **RETENTION** The consumer retains this behavior in memory. → **PRODUCTION PROCESSES** The consumer has the ability to perform the behavior. → **MOTIVATION** A situation arises wherein the behavior is useful to the consumer.

OBSERVATIONAL LEARNING The consumer acquires and performs the behavior earlier demonstrated by a model.

Marketing Applications of Cognitive Learning Principles

Our ability to learn vicariously when we observe the outcomes of what others do makes the lives of marketers much easier. They don't necessarily have to directly reward or punish consumers when they make a purchase (think how expensive or even ethically questionable that might be!). Instead, they can show what happens to desirable models who use or do not use their products; they know that consumers often will imitate these actions at a later time. For example, a perfume commercial might depict a throng of admirers who compliment a glamorous woman when she wears a certain fragrance. Needless to say, this learning process is more practical than providing the same attention to each woman who actually buys the perfume (unless your brand's market share is really, really small!).

Consumers' evaluations of the people they model go beyond simple stimulus–response connections. For example, a celebrity's image elicits more than a simple reflexive response of good or bad.[42] It is a complex combination of many attributes. In general, the degree to which a person emulates someone else depends on that model's level of *social attractiveness*. Attractiveness comes from several components, including physical appearance, expertise, or similarity to the evaluator (more on this in Chapter 8).

How Do We Learn to Be Consumers?

As kids, we don't spring from the womb with consumer skills in place. **Consumer socialization** is the process "by which young people acquire skills, knowledge, and attitudes relevant to their functioning in the marketplace."[43] From where does this knowledge come? Friends and teachers certainly participate in this process. For instance, children talk to one another about consumer products, and this tendency increases as the kids age.[44] Especially for young children, though, the family and the media are two primary socialization sources.

Parents' Influence

Parents influence consumer socialization both directly and indirectly. They deliberately try to instill their own values about consumption in their children ("You're going to learn the value of a dollar!"). Parents also determine the degree to which their children come into contact with other information sources, such as television, salespeople, and peers.[45] Cultural expectations regarding children's involvement in purchase decisions influence when and how parents socialize their kids as consumers. For example, parents in traditional cultures such as Greece and India rely on later development timetables for consumer-related skills and understanding of advertising practices than do American and Australian parents.[46]

Grown-ups also serve as significant models for observational learning. Children learn about consumption as they watch their parents' behaviors and imitate them. Marketers encourage this process when they package adult products in child versions. This "passing down" of product preferences helps to create brand loyalty; researchers find evidence of intergenerational influence when they study the product choices of mothers and their daughters.[47]

The process of consumer socialization begins with infants; within the first two years, children request products they want. By about age 5, most kids make purchases with the help of parents and grandparents, and by age 8 most buy things on their own.[48] Figure 6.3 summarizes the sequence of stages as kids turn into consumers.

Parents exhibit different styles when they socialize their children:[49]

- *Authoritarian parents* are hostile, restrictive, and emotionally uninvolved. They do not have warm relationships with their children, they censor the types of media their children see, and they tend to have negative views about advertising.
- *Neglecting parents* also are detached from their children, and the parents don't exercise much control over what their children do.
- *Indulgent parents* communicate more with their children about consumption-related matters and are less restrictive. They believe that children should be allowed to learn about the marketplace without much interference.

Figure 6.3 FIVE STAGES OF CONSUMER DEVELOPMENT BY EARLIEST AGE AT ONSET AND MEDIAN AGE AT ONSET

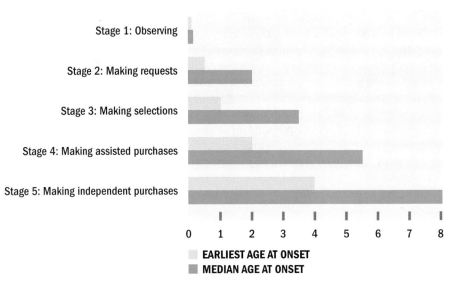

A CONSUMER IS BORN

Children start accompanying parents to the marketplace as early as one month old and begin to make independent purchases as early as four years old.

Television and the Web: Electric Babysitters

Advertising starts to influence us at a very early age. As we've seen, many marketers push their products on kids to encourage them to build a lifelong habit. One controversial exception occurred in France. An ad McDonald's placed in the magazine *Femme Actuelle* actually encouraged parents to limit kids' visits to its outlets when it proclaimed, "There is no reason to eat excessive amounts of junk food, nor go more than once a week to McDonald's." A spokesperson for McDonald's in the United States said the company did not agree with the views the ad expressed.[50] That's unfortunate: One study funded by the National Institutes of Health projected that a ban on fast-food advertising to children would cut the national obesity rate by as much as 18 percent.[51]

In two studies, British researchers compared the effects of television advertising on the eating habits of 152 kids between the ages of 5 and 11. In both studies, the kids watched 10 ads followed by a cartoon. In one session, the kids saw ads for toys before they watched a video. In another session, the researchers replaced the toy ads with food ads that commonly run during children's programs. After both viewings, held two weeks apart, the kids were allowed to snack as much as they wanted from a table of low-fat and high-fat snacks, including grapes, cheese-flavored rice cakes, chocolate buttons, and potato chips. The 5- to 7-year-old kids who saw the food ads ate 14 to 17 percent more calories than those who saw the toy ads. The results were even more dramatic among 9- to 11-year-olds. Those in the food ad condition ate from 84 to 134 percent more calories than did those in the toy ad condition.[52]

Today most kids divide their time among the TV set, the computer, and their cell phones. In the United States, about 80 percent of children age 5 and under use the Internet at least once a week. What's more, like their older brothers and sisters, little kids are avid multitaskers: A Nielsen study reported that 36 percent of kids ages 2 to 11 watch online content and TV at the same time.[53]

Now, to hasten kids' introduction to social media, a team of Finnish designers invented a block-sorting toy that also works like Twitter. It allows preverbal kids to grab colorful blocks with icons for sleeping, eating, or brushing their teeth; the kids then fit them into slots to indicate what they're up to. The device then transmits the "status update" to light up the corresponding block-shape on the same toy in another household.[54]

Cognitive Development

A child's ability to make mature, "adult" consumer decisions obviously increases with age (not that grown-ups always make mature decisions). Marketers segment kids in terms of their **stage of cognitive development**, or their ability to comprehend concepts of increasing complexity. Some evidence indicates that very young children learn consumption-related information surprisingly well.[55]

The Swiss psychologist Jean Piaget was the foremost proponent of the idea that children pass through distinct stages of cognitive development. He believed that a certain cognitive structure characterizes each stage as the child learns to process information.[56] In one classic demonstration of cognitive development, Piaget poured the contents of a short, squat glass of lemonade into a taller, thinner glass that actually held the same amount of liquid. Five-year-olds, who still believed that the shape of the glass determined its contents, thought this glass held more liquid than the first glass. They are in what Piaget termed a *preoperational stage of development*. In contrast, 6-year-olds tended to be unsure, but 7-year-olds knew the amount of lemonade had not changed.

Many developmental specialists no longer believe that children necessarily pass through these fixed stages at the same time. An alternative view proposes that they differ in information-processing capability, or ability to store and retrieve information from memory. Researchers who advocate this approach identify three developmental stages:[57]

1 **Limited**—Children who are younger than age 6 do not employ storage and retrieval strategies.
2 **Cued**—Children between the ages of 6 and 12 employ these strategies but only when prompted to do so.
3 **Strategic**—Children 12 and older spontaneously employ storage and retrieval strategies.

This sequence of development underscores the notion that children do not think in the same way adults do, and we can't expect them to use information the same way either. It also reminds us that they do not necessarily form the same conclusions as adults when they encounter product information. Kids are not as likely to realize that something they see on TV is not "real," and as a result they are more vulnerable to persuasive messages. Younger kids aren't able to distinguish media depictions from reality, so the more a child watches MTV's *Teen Mom 2* or Nickelodeon's *SpongeBob SquarePants*, the more he will accept the images it depicts as real.[58] Kids also see idealized images of what it is like to be an adult. Because children over the age of 6 do about a quarter of their television viewing during prime time, adult programs and commercials have a big effect on them. For example, young girls who see adult lipstick commercials associate lipstick with beauty.[59]

Research underscores the idea that children's understanding of brand names evolves as they age. Kids learn to relate to brand names at an early age; they recognize brand names in stores, develop preferences for some brands over others, and request branded items by name. However, brand names function as simple perceptual cues for these children that let them identify a familiar object with particular features. *Conceptual brand meanings*, which specify the nonobservable abstract features of the product, enter into the picture in middle childhood (about age 8); children incorporate them into their thinking and judgments a few years later. By the time a child reaches 12 years of age, she thinks about brands on a conceptual or symbolic level and she's likely to incorporate these meanings into brand-related judgments.[60]

Several business ventures illustrate that using sound principles of consumer psychology can also make good financial sense. The trend started a long time ago with public television's *Sesame Street*, but today the for-profit networks are in the game as well. The first successful foray into the preschool market was *Blue's Clues* in 1996, which turned into a huge hit as viewers abandoned the smarmy *Barney & Friends*.

Now, when millions of preschoolers tune in to Nickelodeon's hit show *Dora the Explorer*, they don't realize that they view content based on **multiple-intelligence theory**. This influential perspective argues for other types of intelligence, such as athletic prowess or musical ability, beyond the traditional math and verbal skills psychologists use to measure IQ. Thus, when Dora consults her map, she promotes "spatial" skills. And when she asks her young viewers to help her count planks to build a bridge, Dora builds "interpersonal intelligence."[61]

Message Comprehension

Because children differ in their abilities to process product-related information, advertisers' direct appeals to them raise many serious ethical issues.[62] Children's advocacy groups argue that kids younger than age 7 do not understand the persuasive intent of commercials, and (as we've seen) younger children cannot readily distinguish between a commercial and programming. Kids' cognitive defenses are not yet sufficiently developed to filter out commercial appeals, so in a sense, altering their brand preferences may be likened to "shooting fish in a barrel," as one critic put it.[63] Figure 6.4 shows one attempt to assess whether kids can tell that a commercial is trying to persuade them.

Beginning in the 1970s, the Federal Trade Commission (FTC) took action to protect children. The agency limited commercials during "children's" programming (most often Saturday morning television) and required "separators" to help children discern when a program ended and a commercial began (e.g., "We'll be right back after these commercial messages"). The FTC reversed itself in the early 1980s during the deregulatory, pro-business climate of the Reagan administration. The 1990 Children's Television Act restored some of these restrictions. Still, critics argue that rather than sheltering children

Figure 6.4 EXAMPLES OF SKETCHES RESEARCHERS USE TO MEASURE CHILDREN'S PERCEPTIONS OF COMMERCIAL INTENT from marketplace influences, the dominant way that marketers view them is as what one calls "kid customers."[65]

On the bright side, however, it seems that food companies are finally taking action to combat the growing problem of childhood obesity that they helped to create. Numerous corporations, including Sara Lee, Burger King, Campbell Soup Company, Coca-Cola, Pepsi, Dannon, General Mills, Hershey, Kellogg, Kraft Foods, Mars, McDonald's, and Nestlé, have joined the Council of Better Business Bureau's Children's Food and Beverage Initiative. They have pledged to market to kids 11 and under only products that meet government or American Heart Association standards for "healthy" foods. In addition, this agreement restricts the use of third-party licensed characters in ads targeted to child audiences, and sharply limits the usage of product images in places like elementary schools and video games.[66] In addition, the FTC recently strengthened privacy safeguards that cover mobile apps and Web sites targeted to children; now companies must obtain parental consent before they collect data from kids that could be used to identify, contact, or locate them.[67]

OBJECTIVE 6
Our brains process information about brands to retain them in memory.

Memory

Memory is a process of acquiring information and storing it over time so that it will be available when we need it. Contemporary approaches to the study of memory employ an *information-processing approach*. They assume that the mind is in some ways like a computer: Data are input, processed, and output for later use in revised form. In the **encoding** stage, information enters in a way the system will recognize. In the **storage** stage, we integrate this knowledge with what is already in memory and "warehouse" it until it is needed. During **retrieval**, we access the desired information.[68] Figure 6.5 summarizes the memory process.

Many of our experiences are locked inside our heads, and they may surface years later if the right cues prompt them. Marketers rely on consumers to retain information they collect about products and services so they will apply it to future purchase decisions. During the consumer decision-making process we discussed in Chapter 2, we combine this *internal memory* with *external memory*. This includes all the product details on packages and other marketing stimuli that permit us to identify and evaluate brand alternatives in the marketplace.[69]

Figure 6.5 TYPES OF MEMORY

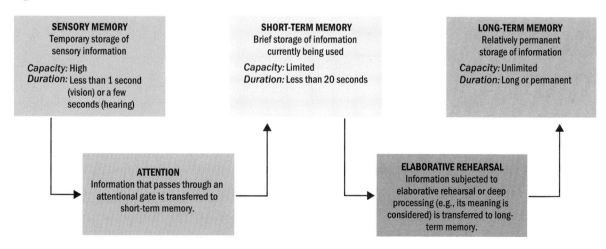

SENSORY MEMORY
Temporary storage of sensory information

Capacity: High
Duration: Less than 1 second (vision) or a few seconds (hearing)

SHORT-TERM MEMORY
Brief storage of information currently being used

Capacity: Limited
Duration: Less than 20 seconds

LONG-TERM MEMORY
Relatively permanent storage of information

Capacity: Unlimited
Duration: Long or permanent

ATTENTION
Information that passes through an attentional gate is transferred to short-term memory.

ELABORATIVE REHEARSAL
Information subjected to elaborative rehearsal or deep processing (e.g., its meaning is considered) is transferred to long-term memory.

An Australian ad for hair products evokes memories of an earlier time—that some of us might prefer to forget.

Source: Courtesy of Fudge Australia.

The grocery-shopping list is a good example of a powerful external memory aid. When consumers use shopping lists, they buy approximately 80 percent of the items on the list. The likelihood that a shopper will purchase a particular list item is higher if the person who wrote the list also participates in the shopping trip. This means that if marketers can induce a consumer to plan to purchase an item before she goes shopping, there is a high probability that she will buy it. One way to encourage this kind of advance planning is to provide peel-off stickers on packages so that, when the consumer notices the supply is low, she can simply peel off the label and place it directly on a shopping list.[70] Or, a retailer can support a phone app that generates a shopping list for the user (already more than 40 of these are available for the iPhone alone).[71]

How Our Brains Encode Information

The way we *encode*, or mentally program, information helps to determine how our brains will store this information. In general, it's more likely that we'll retain incoming data when we associate it with other things already in memory. For example, we tend to remember brand names that we link to physical characteristics of a product category (e.g., Coffee-Mate creamer or Sani-Flush toilet bowl cleaner) or that we can easily visualize (e.g., Tide detergent or Ford Mustang cars) compared to more abstract brand names.[72]

Types of Meaning

Sometimes we process a stimulus simply in terms of its *sensory meaning*, such as the literal color or shape of a package. We may experience a feeling of familiarity when, for example, we see an ad for a new snack food we have recently tasted. In many cases, though,

CB AS I SEE IT

Profs. Kathryn and Michael LaTour, The University of Nevada at Las Vegas

In our view, consumer research is about "digging deeper" for insight into the mind of the market in a way that elicits useful knowledge for the marketing manager. Our research embraces this proposition by expanding knowledge about the complexities of consumer memory and framing that understanding in a way that enhances how practitioners approach their consumers.

A particular focus of our research is on consumer experience, particularly memory for experience. Experience is *noeic*, coming from Greek *nous* meaning intellect or understanding; knowledge as experienced directly with a feeling of certitude. Consumers genuinely believe that their experiences drive their decision-making, and external

information like advertising has little impact. Our research has found otherwise. In early research, Kathy LaTour (formerly Braun) introduced the *theory of memory reconstruction* to marketing, and looked at how postexperience advertising could alter what consumers remembered about their direct tasting experience. In one experiment she had participants taste a sample of orange juice that had been doctored with vinegar, salt, and excess water. She found that when participants received advertising after that taste experience suggesting that the juice was fresh and flavorful, they "remembered" having tasted a better juice—in fact, identifying a better quality juice as the one they had tasted earlier in the hour. In other research with Elizabeth Loftus (one of the most prominent cognitive psychologists studying human memory), we found that autobiographical advertising for Disneyland that included a false reference (to Bugs Bunny) led a significant portion of participants to "recall" that they had themselves met and shook Bugs Bunny's hand when they visited a Disney park as a child (an impossible event, as Bugs is a Warner Bros. character and so is not allowed to set foot on a Disney property).

Memory is paradoxical: Sometimes people remember great details about events, other times (as evidenced in our research mentioned earlier) people can be quite suggestible. Though the memory of Bugs Bunny was false in our experiments, the participants believed that they had had that experience, and in fact listed

the overall Disney vacation as one of their most significant childhood events. In our qualitative research, we have looked at how certain childhood experiences can extend their influence into adulthood, ranging from preference to car design to fast-food choice to cola choice to gambling style.

Our most recent research has looked at how marketers can teach consumers to better learn from their experiences. In that research we looked at wine aficionados, whom we define as drinking a lot of wine but having little conceptual knowledge about it. We found aficionados to be overconfident in their ability to judge a wine, acting more similarly to novices than expert sommeliers in blind taste tests. However, we found that providing these aficionados with a vocabulary (wine aroma wheel) led them to better retention of their taste experience, making them overall more accurate and less likely to be swayed by misleading marketing communication. Currently Kathy LaTour is training for her *sommelier* certification as a means both to understand the processes involved in obtaining expertise in wine and to learn important issues from a practitioner perspective that might guide future research projects (and Mike is enjoying the wine learning as well!). One of our goals is to develop research projects that can guide managers in their experience design in order to provide consumers experiences that are more memorable. The larger framework we work under is to develop innovative research projects and have fun in the process.[73]

we encode meanings at a more abstract level. *Semantic meaning* refers to symbolic associations, such as the idea that rich people drink champagne or that fashionable women have navel piercings. Let's take a closer look at how we encode these deeper meanings.

Episodic memories relate to events that are personally relevant.[74] As a result, a person's motivation to retain these memories will likely be strong. Couples often have "their song," which reminds them of their first date or wedding. We call some especially vivid associations *flashbulb memories* (for example, where were you when you first heard that

Osama bin Laden was dead?). In addition, recall of the past may affect future behavior. A college fund-raising campaign can raise more money when it evokes pleasant college memories than when it reminds alumni of unpleasant ones.

A **narrative**, or a description of a product that is written as a story, is often an effective way to convey product information. Our memories store a lot of the social information we acquire in story form; it's a good idea to construct ads in the form of a narrative so they res-onate with the audience. Narratives persuade people to construct mental representations of the information they see or hear. Pictures aid in this construction and allow us to develop more detailed mental representations.[75] Research supports the idea that we are more likely to positively evaluate and purchase brands when they connect with us like this.[76]

Memory Systems

Researchers describe three distinct memory systems: *sensory memory*, *short-term mem-ory (STM)*, and *long-term memory (LTM)*. Each plays a role in processing brand-related information (see Figure 6.5).

Sensory Memory

Sensory memory stores the information we receive from our senses. This storage is very temporary; it lasts a couple of seconds at most. For example, a man who walks past a donut shop gets a quick, enticing whiff of something baking inside. Although this sensa-tion lasts only a few seconds, it is sufficient to allow him to consider whether he should investigate further. If he retains this information for further processing, it transfers to short-term memory.

Short-Term Memory

Short-term memory (STM) also stores information for a limited period of time, and it has limited capacity. Similar to a computer, this system is *working memory*; it holds the information we are currently processing. Our memories can store verbal input *acousti-cally* (in terms of how it sounds) or *semantically* (in terms of what it means).

We store this information as we combine small pieces into larger ones in a process we call **chunking**. A *chunk* is a configuration that is familiar to the person and that he or she can think about as a unit. For example, a brand name like Seven For All Mankind is a chunk that summarizes a great deal of detailed information about the product.

Initially, researchers believed that our STM was capable of processing between five and nine chunks of information at a time; they described this basic property as "the mag-ical number $7 +/- 2$." This is the reason our phone numbers today (at least in the United States) have seven digits.[77] It now appears that three to four chunks is the optimal size for efficient retrieval (we remember seven-digit phone numbers because we chunk the indi-vidual digits, so we may remember a three-digit exchange as one piece of information).[78] Phone calls aside, chunking is important to marketers because it helps determine how consumers keep prices in short-term memory when they comparison-shop.[79]

Long-Term Memory

Long-term memory (LTM) is the system that allows us to retain information for a long period of time. A cognitive process of **elaborative rehearsal** allows information to move from short-term memory into long-term memory. This involves thinking about the meaning of a stimulus and relating it to other information already in memory. Marketers sometimes assist in the process when they devise catchy slogans or jingles that consum-ers repeat on their own.

How Our Memories Store Information

The relationship between short-term memory and long-term memory is a source of some controversy. The traditional *multiple-store* perspective assumes that STM and LTM are separate systems. More recent research has moved away from the distinction between the two types of memory; it emphasizes the interdependence of the systems. According to **activation models of memory**, depending on the nature of the processing task different levels of processing occur that activate some aspects of memory rather than others.[81] The more effort it takes to process information (so-called *deep processing*), the more likely it is that information will transfer into LTM.

OBJECTIVE 7

The other products we associate with an individual product influence how we will remember it.

Associative Networks

According to activation models of memory, an incoming piece of information gets stored in an **associative network** that contains many bits of related information. We each have organized systems of concepts that relate to brands, manufacturers, and stores stored in our memories; the contents, of course, depend on our own unique experiences.

Think of these storage units, or *knowledge structures*, as complex spider webs filled with pieces of data. Incoming information gets put into nodes that connect to one another (if you haven't guessed, this is also why we call cyberspace the World Wide Web). When we view separate pieces of information as similar for some reason, we chunk them together under some more abstract category. Then, we interpret new, incoming information to be consistent with the structure we have created (recall the discussion in Chapter 5 about how prior expectations influence current experiences).[82] This helps explain why we are better able to remember brands or stores that we believe "go together"; for example, when Titleist rather than Chanel sponsors a golf tournament. Recent research indicates that people can recall brands that are not as obviously linked (for example, when an unlikely product sponsors an event), but in these cases marketers have to work harder to justify why the two things go together.[83]

In the associative network, links form between nodes. For example, a consumer might have a network for "perfumes." Each node represents a concept related to the category. This node can be an attribute, a specific brand, a celebrity the consumer identifies with a specific perfume brand, or even a related product. A network for perfumes might include concepts such as the brand names Viva La Juicy by Juicy Couture, Calvin Klein Eternity, and Elizabeth Arden Red Door, as well as attributes such as sexy and elegant.

When we ask the consumer to list perfumes, this consumer recalls only those brands that show up in the appropriate category. We referred to this group in Chapter 2 as an *evoked set*. The task of a new entrant that wants to position itself as a category member (e.g., a new luxury perfume) is to provide cues that facilitate its placement in the appropriate category.

Figure 6.6 shows a sample network for perfumes.

Spreading Activation

A marketing message may activate our memory of a brand directly (for example, when it shows us a picture of the package), or it may do so indirectly when it links to something else that's related to the brand in our knowledge structure. If it activates a node, it will also activate other linked nodes, much as tapping a spider's web in one spot sends movement reverberating across the web. Meaning thus spreads across the network, and we recall concepts, such as competing brands and relevant attributes, that we use to form attitudes toward the brand.

This process of **spreading activation** allows us to shift back and forth among levels of meaning. The way we store a piece of information in memory depends on the type of meaning we initially assign to it. This meaning type, in turn, will determine how and when something activates the meaning. Thus, we could store the memory trace for an Axe men's fragrance ad in one or more of the following ways:

- **Brand-specific**—Memory is stored in terms of claims the brand makes ("it's macho").
- **Ad-specific**—Memory is stored in terms of the medium or content of the ad itself (a macho-looking guy uses the product).
- **Brand identification**—Memory is stored in terms of the brand name (e.g., "Axe").

Figure 6.6 AN ASSOCIATIVE NETWORK
FOR PERFUMES

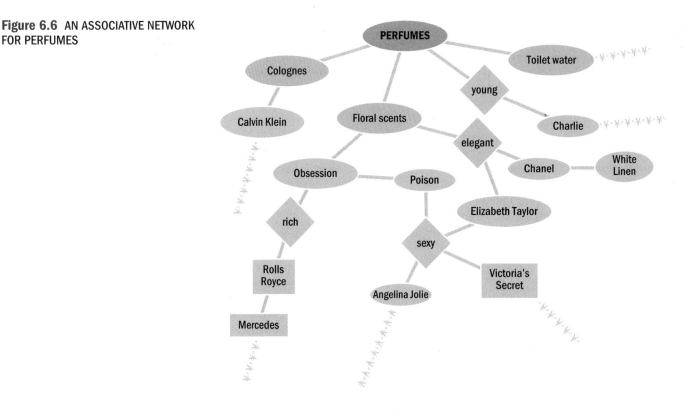

- **Product category**—Memory is stored in terms of how the product works or where it should be used (a bottle of Axe sits in a guy's medicine cabinet).
- **Evaluative reactions**—Memory is stored as positive or negative emotions ("that looks cool").[84]

Levels of Knowledge

Within a knowledge structure, we code elements at different levels of abstraction and complexity. *Meaning* concepts (such as "macho") get stored as individual nodes. We may combine these concepts into a larger unit we call a *proposition* (or a *belief*). A proposition links two nodes together to form a more complex meaning, which can serve as a single chunk of information. For example, "Axe is cologne for macho men" is a proposition (though not necessarily a correct one!).

In turn, we integrate propositions to produce an even more complex unit called a **schema**. A schema is a cognitive framework we develop through experience. We encode information more readily when that information is consistent with an existing schema.[85] The ability to move up and down among levels of abstraction greatly increases processing flexibility and efficiency. For this reason, young children who do not yet have well-developed schemas are not able to make as efficient use of purchase information as are older children.[86]

One type of schema especially relevant to consumer behavior is a **script**, a sequence of events an individual expects to occur. As consumers we learn *service scripts* that guide our behavior in commercial settings. We expect a certain sequence of events, and we may become uncomfortable if the service departs from our script. A service script for a visit to the dentist might include such events as (1) drive to the dentist, (2) read old magazines in the waiting room, (3) hear name called and sit in dentist's chair, (4) dentist injects something into gums, (5) dentist turns on high-pitched drill, and so on. This desire to follow a script helps to explain why such service innovations as automatic bank machines, self-service gas stations, or "scan-your-own" grocery checkouts have met with resistance by some consumers who have trouble adapting to new sequences of events.[87]

How We Retrieve Memories When We Decide What to Buy

In one major study, only 23 percent of the respondents could recall a new product introduced in the past year.[90] That's not an encouraging finding for marketers.

Retrieval is the process whereby we recover information from long-term memory. As evidenced by the popularity of the board game *Trivial Pursuit* or the TV show *Are You Smarter Than a Fifth Grader?,* we have a vast quantity of information stored in our heads—a lot of which is not very useful unless you play the game! Although most of the information that enters long-term memory does not go away, it may be difficult or impossible to retrieve unless the appropriate cues are present. What factors influence the likelihood that we will remember the marketing messages that organizations work so hard to create?

Situational factors also influence retrieval; these relate to the environment in which we encounter the message. Not surprisingly, recall is enhanced when we pay more attention to the message in the first place. Some evidence indicates that we can more easily retrieve information about a *pioneering brand* (the first brand to enter a market) from memory than we can for *follower brands,* because the first product's introduction is likely to be distinctive and, for the time being, no competitors divert our attention.[91] In addition, we are more likely to recall descriptive brand names than those that do not provide adequate cues as to what the product is.[92]

Not surprisingly, the way a marketer presents her message influences the likelihood that we'll be able to recall it later. The **spacing effect** describes the tendency for us to recall printed material more effectively when the advertiser repeats the target item periodically, rather than presenting it repeatedly in a short time period.[93] The viewing environment of a marketing message also affects recall. For example, commercials we see during baseball games yield the lowest recall scores among sports programs, because the activity is stop-and-go rather than continuous. Unlike football or basketball, the pacing of baseball gives many opportunities for attention to wander even during play. General Electric discovered that its commercials fared better in television shows with continuous activity, such as stories or dramas, compared to variety shows or talk shows that are punctuated by a series of acts.[94] A large-scale analysis of TV commercials found that viewers recall commercials shown first in a series of ads better than those they see last.[95]

Finally, it goes without saying that the nature of the ad itself plays a big role in determining whether it's memorable. One study on print advertising reported that we are far more likely to remember spectacular magazine ads, including multipage spreads, three-dimensional pop-ups, scented ads, and ads with audio components. For example, a Pepsi Jazz two-page spread, which incorporated a three-dimensional pop-up of the opened bottle, a small audio chip that played jazz music from the bottle's opening, and a scratch-and-sniff tab that let readers smell its black cherry vanilla flavor, scored an amazing 100 percent in reader recall.[96] Unfortunately, that kind of multimedia treatment is very expensive; not every ad can mimic a Broadway production!

CB AS I SEE IT
Professor Jennifer Aaker, *Stanford University*

Imagine you are at Disneyland about to board the Space Mountain ride. As you climb into your rocket, you feel joy and apprehension—a mixed feeling that persists even after the ride is over. You grip the safety bar, at once thrilled and frightened. You leave the Space Mountain ride dizzy with mixed emotions. How will you recall your experience a week later? Will you remember the mixed emotions you experienced on the ride? Or will the memory of those mixed emotions fade?

Questions regarding the memory of mixed emotions are important. Many of life's most important events are defined by mixtures of emotions where people find themselves feeling both positive and negative emotions—e.g., graduating from college ("I'm making progress, but leaving my friends and family"), moving ("I'm starting a

new life, but losing my old one"), or achieving major life goals ("I'm thrilled to have reached the destination, but I'm sad the journey is over").

To address these questions, we conducted a set of longitudinal experiments which show that the intensity of mixed emotions is underestimated at the time of recall—an effect that appears to increase over time and does not occur to the same degree with uniformly happy or sad emotions. Together, these results indicate that, as time passes, mixed emotions are increasingly difficult to recall, that memory for them fades, and that felt conflict underlies this recall bias.

The results of this work speak to several domains of research. For example, the results imply that individuals who are comfortable with inconsistency should recall mixed emotions more accurately. Similarly, if there is an increased desire to resolve the emotion of felt conflict, the effects documented here should be muted for individuals who are not disturbed by the ambiguity associated with mixed emotions. Also, the effects should dissipate if the mixed emotions we experience consist of a dominant emotion (e.g., strong feelings of

anger), thereby reducing the conflict we feel.

The results also speak to ongoing research in marketing, which suggests that emotional experiences can fundamentally affect purchase intent as well as foster brand loyalty. For example, the amount of warmth that emanates from a brand or the fun derived from a brand (e.g., iPhone) can fundamentally influence our relationship with it. However, in reality, most consumer–brand relationships are defined, at some point or another, by a transgression that gives rise to negative feelings among consumers, such as when something you buy breaks. Our research suggests that the degree to which a negative event is categorized as part of a mixed experience (as opposed a single negative event) affects the probability that the consumer will remember that experience and be influenced by it. If the transgression is mentally clumped together with positive interactions with the brand, the memory of the mixed emotional experience may indeed fade— which would not be the case if the transgression stood alone as an isolated negative event.

What Makes Us Forget?

Marketers obviously hope that consumers will not forget about their products. However, in a poll of more than 13,000 adults, more than half were unable to remember any specific ad they had seen, heard, or read in the past 30 days. How many can you remember right now? Clearly, forgetting by consumers is a big headache for marketers (not to mention a problem for students when they study for exams!).

Early memory theorists assumed that memories simply fade with the passage of time. In a process of **decay**, the structural changes that learning produces in the brain simply go away. Forgetting also occurs as a result of **interference**; as we learn additional information, it displaces the earlier information. Consumers may forget stimulus–response associations if they subsequently learn new responses to the same or similar stimuli; we call this process *retroactive interference*. Or, prior learning can interfere with new learning, a process we term *proactive interference*. Because we store pieces of information in memory as nodes that link to one another, we are more likely to retrieve a meaning concept that is connected by a larger number of links. But as we learn new responses, a stimulus loses its effectiveness in retrieving the old response.[97]

These interference effects help to explain problems in remembering brand information. Consumers tend to organize attribute information by brand.[98] Additional attribute information regarding a brand or similar brands may limit the person's ability to recall old brand information. Recall may also be inhibited if the brand name is composed of frequently used words. These words cue competing associations; as a result, we retain less brand information.[99] In one study, brand evaluations deteriorated more rapidly when ads for the brand appeared with messages for 12 other brands in the same category than when researchers showed the ad along with ads for 12 dissimilar products.[100] Thus, when we increase the uniqueness of one brand, it impairs the recall of other brands.[101] However, when we call a competitor by name, this can result in poorer recall for our own brand.[102]

State-Dependent Retrieval

Is it true that you'll do better on an exam if you study for it in the classroom in which you'll take the test? Perhaps. The process of **state-dependent retrieval** illustrates that we are better able to access information if our internal state is the same at the time of recall as when we learned the information. So, we are more likely to recall an ad if our mood or level of arousal at the time of exposure is similar to that in the purchase environment. When marketers re-create the cues that were present when they first presented the information, they can enhance recall. For example, on its box Life cereal uses a picture of "Mikey" from its commercial, which facilitates recall of brand claims and favorable brand evaluations.[103]

Familiarity and Recall

As a general rule, when we are already familiar with an item we're more likely to recall messages about it. Indeed, this is one of the basic goals of marketers who try to create and maintain awareness of their products. The more experience a consumer has with a product, the better use he or she makes of product information.[104] However, there is a possible fly in the ointment: As we noted earlier in this chapter, some evidence indicates that extreme familiarity can result in inferior learning and recall. When consumers are highly familiar with a brand or an advertisement, they may not pay much attention to a message for it, because they do not believe that any additional effort will increase their knowledge.[105] We call this process *automaticity*.[106] For example, when researchers expose consumers to a radio ad that repeats the audio track from a television ad they've already seen, they do very little critical, evaluative processing; they just mentally replay the video portion of the ad.[107]

We also tend to observe a **highlighting effect**, which occurs when the order in which consumers learn about brands determines the strength of association between these brands and their attributes. Consumers more strongly associate common attributes with early-learned brands and unique attributes with late-learned brands. More generally, we are more likely to recognize words, objects, and faces we learn early in life than similar items we learn later. This applies to brands as well; managers who introduce new entries into a market with well-established brand names need to work harder to create learning and memory linkages by exposing consumers to information about them more frequently.[108]

Salience and Recall

The **salience** of a brand refers to its prominence or level of activation in memory. Stimuli that stand out in contrast to their environments are more likely to command attention, which, in turn, increases the likelihood that we will recall them. The **von Restorff Effect** is well known to memory researchers; it shows that almost any technique that increases the novelty of a stimulus also improves recall. This explains why unusual advertising or distinctive packaging tends to facilitate brand recall.[109]

The tactic of introducing a surprise element in an ad can boost recall, even if the new information is not relevant to the remaining material.[110] In addition, *mystery ads*, in which the ad doesn't identify the brand until the end, are more effective if we want to build associations in memory between the product category and that brand—especially in the case of relatively unknown brands.[111]

Furthermore, the *intensity* and type of emotions we experience at the time also affect the way we recall the event later. We recall **mixed emotions** (e.g., those with positive and negative components) differently than **unipolar emotions** (e.g., those that are either wholly positive or wholly negative). The latter become even more polarized over time, so that we recall good things as even better than they really were and bad things as even worse (maybe the "good old days" weren't really so good after all!).[112]

The Viewing Context

Regardless of how awesome a commercial is, the show in which it appears influences its impact. Nielsen (the company that measures who watches which media) reports that viewers who enjoy a program are more likely to respond positively to a commercial and to say they want to buy the advertised product. The research firm Nielsen studied the responses of 10,000 people across 50 shows and 200 brands. Viewers are almost one-third more likely to remember brands whose products were placed in shows they enjoy. The impact of this factor varies across show format; it's weaker in sitcoms but much stronger in "lifestyle programs" such as *Extreme Makeover Home Edition*.[113]

It also helps when the marketer's message is consistent with the theme or events in the program—and it's even better when the advertised product actually makes a reference to the show. The Discovery Channel documented this effect during a broadcast of its program *Mythbusters*, which uses science to test the validity of urban legends. The network ran a brief ad for Guinness beer in which a character asked another whether it was a "myth that Guinness only has 125 calories." Viewers who saw this ad remembered the name of the Guinness brand 41 percent more often than they did when they saw a traditional ad for the beer. Other similar **hybrid ads** that include a program tie-in deliver similar results.[114]

Pictorial Versus Verbal Cues: Is a Picture Worth a Thousand Words?

There is some evidence for the superiority of visual memory over verbal memory, but this advantage is unclear because it is more difficult to measure recall of pictures.[115] However, the available data indicate that we are more likely to recognize information we see in picture form at a later time.[116] Certainly, visual aspects of an ad are more likely to grab a consumer's attention. In fact, eye-movement studies indicate that about 90 percent of viewers look at the dominant picture in an ad before they bother to view the copy.[117]

Although pictorial ads may enhance recall, they do not necessarily improve comprehension. One study found that television news items presented with illustrations (still

Visual aspects of an ad grab a consumer's attention, especially when they are novel. That is certainly the case for this "pile of trash" that is actually an outdoor ad on a Dutch street for the MINI Cooper.
Source: Courtesy of UbachsWisbrun/JWT.

pictures) as a backdrop result in improved recall for details of the news story, even though understanding of the story's content does not improve.[118] Another study confirmed that consumers typically recall ads with visual figures more often and they like them better.[119]

OBJECTIVE 8
Products help us to retrieve memories from our past.

Products as Memory Markers

The Disney theme parks' 2012 marketing campaign was called "Let the Memories Begin." It focused on vacation memories; TV commercials, online ads, and brochures featured photos and videos shot by park guests. Disney projected images of visitors on building facades each night.[120] The company understands just how powerful memories can be.

The pictures we take of ourselves using products and services (like when we pose with Mickey at Disney World) can themselves serve as powerful retrieval cues. Indeed, the three types of possessions consumers most value are furniture, visual art, and photos. These objects are likely to jog memories of the past.[121] Researchers find that valued possessions can evoke thoughts about prior events on several dimensions, including sensory experiences, friends and loved ones, and breaking away from parents or former partners.[122] That helps to explain the popularity of photo-sharing sites like Flickr and Instagram—Flickr alone hosts more than 5 billion pictures and offers "Share This" tools for use on Facebook and Twitter.[123]

Even food can facilitate recall: One study looked at how favorite recipes stimulate memories of the past. When the researchers asked informants to list three of their favorite recipes and to talk about these choices, they found that people tended to link them with memories of past events, such as childhood memories, family holidays, milestone

Marketing Opportunity

Proust.com is a memory-sharing service that targets nostalgic seniors. The social network is designed to help family members and close friends tell their life stories. The site guides users through the process of generating memories by providing prompts such as "When was your first kiss?"[125]

- - - - - - - - - - - - - -

events (such as dishes they only make on special holidays, like corned beef and cabbage on St. Patrick's Day), heirlooms (recipes handed down across generations), and the passing of time (e.g., only eating blueberry cobbler in the summer).[124] Indeed, one of the most famous literary references is from the classic (3,000-page!) novel *Remembrance of Things Past* by Marcel Proust. The narrator dips a pastry (a "madeleine") into his tea, and this action unleashes a flood of memories that drive the rest of the book.

Products are particularly important as markers when our sense of the past is threatened, as, for example, when an event such as divorce, relocation, or graduation challenges a consumer's current identity.[126] Our cherished possessions often have *mnemonic* qualities that serve as a form of external memory when they prompt us to retrieve episodic memories. For example, family photography allows consumers to create their own retrieval cues; the 11 billion amateur photos we take annually form a kind of external memory bank for our culture. A stimulus is, at times, able to evoke a weakened response even years after we first perceived it. We call this effect **spontaneous recovery**, and this reestablished connection may explain consumers' powerful emotional reactions to songs or pictures they have not been exposed to in quite a long time.

OBJECTIVE 9

Marketers measure our memories about products and ads.

How We Measure Consumers' Recall of Marketing Messages

Because marketers pay so much money to place their messages in front of consumers, they hope that people will actually remember these ads later on. It seems that they have good reason to be concerned. In one study, fewer than 40 percent of television viewers made positive links between commercial messages and the corresponding products, only 65 percent noticed the brand name in a commercial, and only 38 percent recognized a connection to an important point.[127]

Even more sadly, only 7 percent of television viewers can recall the product or company featured in the most recent television commercial they watched. This figure represents less than half the recall rate recorded in 1965. We can explain this drop-off in terms of such factors as the increase of 30- and 15-second commercials and the practice of airing television commercials in clusters rather than in single-sponsor programs.[128]

The news is a bit brighter for online marketing messages, especially when they repeat commercials that first appeared on television. Research by Google shows that recall

Facebook's Timeline feature helps consumers to recall the brands they have liked over time.[129]

Source: Justin Sullivan/Getty Images.

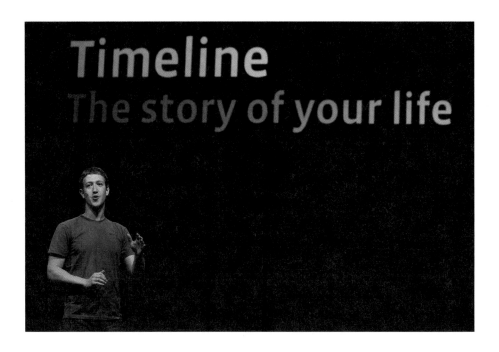

improves when spots reappear before YouTube videos.[130] Apple reports similar results for "iAds," mobile ads that pop up on iPhones and iPods.[131]

Recognition versus Recall

One indicator of good advertising is, of course, the impression it makes on us. But how can we define and measure this impact? Two basic measures of impact are **recognition** and **recall**. In the typical *recognition test*, researchers show ads to subjects one at a time and ask if they have seen them before. In contrast, *free recall tests* ask consumers to independently think of what they have seen without being prompted for this information first; obviously, this task requires greater effort on their part.

Under some conditions, these two memory measures tend to yield the same results, especially when the researchers try to keep the viewers' interest in the ads constant (though that may be an overly artificial way to study true memory for ads).[132] Generally, though, recognition scores tend to be more reliable and do not decay over time the way recall scores do.[133] Recognition scores are almost always better than recall scores because recognition is a simpler process and the consumer has more retrieval cues available.

Both types of retrieval play important roles in purchase decisions, however. Recall tends to be more important in situations in which consumers do not have product data at their disposal, so they must rely on memory to generate this information.[134] However, recognition is more likely to be an important factor in a store, where retailers confront consumers with thousands of product options (i.e., external memory is abundantly available) and the task simply may be to recognize a familiar package. Unfortunately, package recognition and familiarity can have negative consequences; for example, consumers may ignore warning labels because they take those messages for granted and don't really notice them.[135]

Problems with Memory Measures

Although measuring an ad's memorability is important, analysts have questioned whether existing measures accurately assess these dimensions, for several reasons. First, the results we obtain from a measuring instrument are not necessarily based on what we measure, but rather on something else about the instrument or the respondent. This form of contamination is a **response bias**. For example, people tend to give "yes" responses to questions, regardless of what the item asks. In addition, experimental subjects often are eager to be "good subjects": They try to figure out what the experimenter is looking for and give the response they think they are supposed to give. This tendency is so strong that in some studies the rate at which subjects claim they recognize *bogus ads* (ads they have not seen before) is almost as high as their recognition rate for those they really have seen![136]

Memory Lapses

People are also prone to forget information or retain inaccurate memories (yes, even younger people). Typical problems include *omitting* (leaving facts out), *averaging* (the tendency to "normalize" memories by not reporting extreme cases), and *telescoping* (inaccurate recall of time).[137] These distortions are not just a problem in court cases that rely on eyewitness testimony; they also call into question the accuracy of product usage databases that rely on consumers to recall their purchase and consumption of food and household items. For example, one study asked people to describe what portion of various foods—small, medium, or large—they ate in a typical meal. However, the researchers used different definitions of "medium." Regardless of the definition they gave, about the same number of people claimed they typically ate "medium" portions.[138]

Bittersweet Memories: The Marketing Power of Nostalgia

Marketers often resurrect popular characters and stories from days gone by; they hope that consumers' fond memories will motivate them to revisit the past. We had a 1950s revival in the 1970s, and consumers in the 1980s got a heavy dose of memories from

Fossil's product designs evoke memories of earlier, classic styles.

Source: Used with permission of Fossil Inc. Photography by Thom Jackson and Jon Kirk.

the 1960s. Today, it seems that popular characters only need to be gone for a few years before someone tries to bring them back. Many companies have responded as they dig deep into their vaults to bring back old favorites. New commercials position Chevrolet as a classic American brand. Planters Peanuts recruited the actor Robert Downey, Jr., as the new voice of Mr. Peanut. "Retired" brand names, including Meister Brau beer, the brokerage firm Shearson, Handi-Wrap plastic wrap, and Wonder Bread were sold at auction to companies that want to bring them back to life.[139] The biggest retro success story in recent years: the Old Spice Guy campaign that went viral and revived a men's deodorant brand that is more than 70 years old.

Nostalgia describes the bittersweet emotion that arises when we view the past with both sadness and longing.[140] References to "the good old days" are increasingly common, as advertisers call up memories of youth—and hope that these feelings will translate to what they're selling today. A **retro brand** is an updated version of a brand from a prior historical period. These products trigger nostalgia, and researchers find that they often inspire consumers to think back to an era when (at least in our memories) life was more stable, simple, or even utopian. Very simply, they let us "look backward through rose-colored glasses."[141]

Our prior experiences also help to determine what we like today. Consumer researchers created a nostalgia *index* that measures the critical ages during which our preferences are likely to form and endure over time. It turns out that a good predictor of whether a person will like a specific song is how old she was when that song was popular. On average, we are most likely to favor songs that were popular when we were 23.5 years old (so pay attention to the hot songs if you haven't turned 23 yet). Our preferences for fashion models peak at age 33, and we tend to like movie stars who were popular when we were 26 or 27 years old.[142]

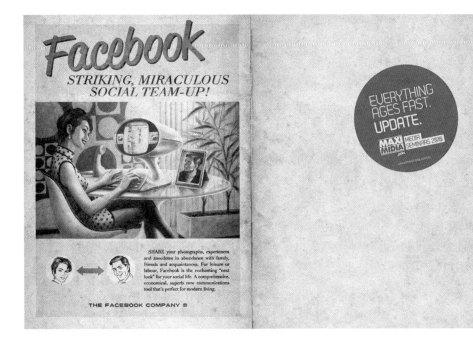

A Brazilian company uses nostalgic imagery to promote a high-tech product—seminars on social media.
Source: Courtesy of MaxiMidia.

This ad from Chile uses a retro appeal.
Source: Courtesy of Volkswagen.

MyMarketingLab
Go to **mymktlab.com** to complete the problems marked with this icon ⭐.

CHAPTER SUMMARY

Now that you have finished reading this chapter, you should understand why:

1. It is important to understand how consumers learn about products and services.

Learning is a change in behavior caused by experience. Learning can occur through simple associations between a stimulus and a response or via a complex series of cognitive activities.

2. Conditioning results in learning.

Behavioral learning theories assume that learning occurs as a result of responses to external events. Classical conditioning occurs when a stimulus that naturally elicits a response (an unconditioned stimulus) is paired with another stimulus that does not initially elicit this response. Over time, the second stimulus (the conditioned stimulus) elicits the response even in the absence of the first.

3. Learned associations with brands generalize to other products, which is important to marketers.

This response can also extend to other, similar stimuli in a process we call stimulus generalization. This process is the basis for such marketing strategies as licensing and family branding, where a consumer's positive associations with a product transfer to other contexts.

4. There is a difference between classical and instrumental conditioning, and both processes help consumers learn about products.

Operant, or instrumental, conditioning occurs as the person learns to perform behaviors that produce positive outcomes and avoid those that result in negative outcomes. Whereas classical conditioning involves the pairing of two stimuli, instrumental learning occurs when a response to a stimulus leads to reinforcement. Reinforcement is positive if a reward follows a response. It is negative if the person avoids a negative outcome by not performing a response. Punishment occurs when an unpleasant event follows a response. Extinction of the behavior will occur if reinforcement no longer occurs.

5. We learn about products by observing others' behavior.

Cognitive learning occurs as the result of mental processes. For example, observational learning occurs when the consumer performs a behavior as a result of seeing someone else performing it and being rewarded for it.

6. Our brains process information about brands to retain them in memory.

Memory is the storage of learned information. The way we encode information when we perceive it determines how we will store it in memory. The memory systems we call sensory memory, short-term memory, and long-term memory each play a role in retaining and processing information from the outside world.

7. The other products we associate with an individual product influence how we will remember it.

We don't store information in isolation; we incorporate it into a knowledge structure where our brains associate it with other related data. The location of product information in associative networks, and the level of abstraction at which it is coded, help to determine when and how we will activate this information at a later time. Some factors that influence the likelihood of retrieval include the level of familiarity with an item, its salience (or prominence) in memory, and whether the information was presented in pictorial or written form.

8. Products help us to retrieve memories from our past.

Products also play a role as memory markers; consumers use them to retrieve memories about past experiences (autobiographical memories), and we often value them because they are able to do this. This function also encourages the use of nostalgia in marketing strategies.

9. Marketers measure our memories about products and ads.

We can use either recognition or recall techniques to measure memory for product information. Consumers are more likely to recognize an advertisement if it is presented to them than they are to recall one without being given any cues. However, neither recognition nor recall automatically or reliably translates into product preferences or purchases.

KEY TERMS

activation models of memory, 251
advertising wear-out, 233
associative network, 251
behavioral learning theories, 230
brand equity, 233
brand-name imprinting, 232
chunking, 250
classical conditioning, 230
cognitive learning theory, 240
conditioned response (CR), 230
conditioned stimulus (CS), 230
consumer confusion, 234
consumer socialization, 243
decay, 255
elaborative rehearsal, 250
encoding, 247
episodic memories, 249
extinction, 232
family branding, 234
fixed-interval reinforcement, 237
fixed-ratio reinforcement, 238
frequency marketing, 238
gamification, 238

halo effect, 232
highlighting effect, 255
hybrid ads, 256
incidental learning, 229
instrumental conditioning, 235
interference, 255
learning, 229
licensing, 234
long-term memory (LTM), 250
memory, 247
mixed emotions, 256
modeling, 242
multiple-intelligence theory, 246
narrative, 250
negative reinforcement, 236
nostalgia, 260
observational learning, 242
positive reinforcement, 236
product line extension, 234
punishment, 236
recall, 259
recognition, 259
repetition, 231

response bias, 259
retrieval, 247
retro brand, 260
salience, 256
schema, 252
script, 252
sensory memory, 250
shaping, 235
short-term memory (STM), 250
spacing effect, 253
spontaneous recovery, 258
spreading activation, 251
stage of cognitive development, 245
state-dependent retrieval, 255
stimulus discrimination, 232
stimulus generalization, 232
storage, 247
unconditioned stimulus (UCS), 230
unipolar emotions, 256
variable-interval reinforcement, 237
variable-ratio reinforcement, 238
von Restorff Effect, 256

REVIEW

6-1 What is the difference between an unconditioned stimulus and a conditioned stimulus?

6-2 People react to other, similar stimuli in much the same way as they responded to an original stimulus. What is this phenomenon, and how does it work?

6-3 What are the dangers of advertising wear-out, and how might a marketer avoid it?

6-4 Advertisers like to use celebrities and well-known faces to help promote their products and services. Is this a good idea?

6-5 What is the difference between classical conditioning and instrumental conditioning?

6-6 What is the major difference between behavioral and cognitive theories of learning?

6-7 Name the three stages of information processing.

⭐ **6-8** What is external memory and why is it important to marketers?

6-9 Give an example of an episodic memory.

6-10 Why do phone numbers have seven digits?

6-11 List the three types of memory, and explain how they work together.

6-12 How is associative memory like a spider web?

6-13 How does the likelihood that a person wants to use an ATM machine relate to a schema?

6-14 Why does a pioneering brand have a memory advantage over follower brands?

⭐ **6-15** If a consumer is familiar with a product, advertising for it can work by either enhancing or diminishing recall. Why?

6-16 Why are retro brands so popular? What is the key ingredient that makes them successful?

6-17 What is a schema? Give an example.

6-18 How would you explain the terms *salience* and *recall*?

CONSUMER BEHAVIOR CHALLENGE

▣ DISCUSS

6-19 According to Gianfranco Zaccai of Continuum, focus groups kill innovation. He claims that in the 40 years he has been involved in the marketing industry, working with some of the most brilliant minds, he has never seen an innovation developed as a result of a focus group. He maintains that this is because of what focus groups can and cannot do. Do you agree?

6-20 Using commercial music for advertising is nothing new, but advertisers need to be very careful with their choices, as sometimes things can go wrong unexpectedly. In 2013, General Motors was forced to pull an advertisement for one of its Chevrolet models in China amid accusations of racism. The company had chosen the 2012 song "Booty Swing" by Parov Stelar, which sampled heavily from "Oriental Swing" by Lil Hardin Armstrong and Her Swing Orchestra. In the lyrics, there were lines that suggested that the Chinese were "ching-chong, chop-suey" and that the Japanese could not pronounce the letter "r."[143]

Although many musicians embrace the opportunity to earn royalties from the use of their music in advertising, some are adamant that their music should never be used. Once such example is Adam Yauch aka MCA, an original member of the Beastie Boys who died in 2012. His will left his entire estate to his widow with the caveat that in no event could his music or any of his creations be used in advertising. It was clear he did not approve.[144]

Some musicians are only too happy to accept an additional revenue stream from the use of their music in advertisements. Not only do they receive royalties for its use, but it might also stimulate sales. What is your view on use of popular music in advertisements?

▪ APPLY

6-21 Just how well do you recall jingles and tunes used by brands in commercials? As a group, compile a list and see how many of these you can remember. Is there something specific that triggers recall? Are they original jingles or tunes or are they "borrowed"?

6-22 In 2012, 14 of Singapore's biggest food and beverage businesses committed themselves to a radical rethinking of the way in which they advertise to children. The pledge, called the "Responsible Advertising to Children Pledge" was part of a commitment made by the companies to assist Singaporeans to attain a healthy and active lifestyle. The signatories were all renowned brands – Coca-Cola, Ferrero, General Mills, Kellogg's, Kerry, Mars, McCain, McDonald's, Mondelēz, Nestlé, Pepsico, FrieslandCampina, Suntory, and Unilever. They all agreed to advertise their products incorporating nutrient details that were based on independently verifiable scientific tests. Further, they undertook to apply these guidelines to any advertising aimed at under-12-year-olds or not advertise at all.[145]

The commitments were in place at the beginning of 2013 and were fully supported by the advertising industry. Speaking on behalf of the World Federation of Advertisers, Will Gilroy, Director of Communications, pointed out that self-regulation was the way forward. Third-party monitoring would ensure compliance, with the outcome of children being exposed to fewer advertisements of foods that could harm their health.

Clearly, brands and advertisers would prefer the self-regulation route, but this is not always possible in highly competitive markets. The proof, however, will be in the consumption of food products in Singapore. Whether this initiative will have a marked effect on health remains to be seen. Is self-regulation likely to work? Should it be swept aside in exchange for legislation and government control?

6-23 Choose a well-established product sold in your country. Identify its key attributes. How could the brand be leveraged? Can you suggest any brand extensions that could be developed? What about licensing? Just how far could you go with the development?

6-24 As a group, identify at least 10 long-established local brands that are specific to your country or region. What is it about them that has ensured their longevity? Identify the features and attributes of each brand, from the packaging and design to the product itself.

Case Study

DO AVATARS DREAM ABOUT VIRTUAL SHEEP?

When he ventures online, he's a muscular, bronzed, 23-year-old surfer. But, after a few hours chilling in the virtual world of *The Sims*, it's time for this shy, 110-pound student to get back to work. Sound weird? It's not. He is one of the well over one billion people worldwide who inhabit a virtual world in digital form. Welcome to the world of avatars! Marketers are just beginning to understand how the time people spend in virtual worlds influences the way they learn about brands.

In *The Sims* and other sites, users create an avatar to represent themselves online. Some people create avatars that look a lot like them in the real world, but many residents choose avatars that represent the person they would like to be, fantasy creatures, or even individuals of the opposite gender. With these alternate personalities they go out and explore virtual worlds. So what does this mean to marketers? A lot more than some pixels on a computer screen. Avatars interact with real brands in these virtual worlds. They can purchase products such as jeans for their avatars, and they can attend events such as concerts or lectures.

But it's not just virtual worlds that want to understand how to make money from the legions of avatars out there. Web site designers and developers also realize the importance of avatars that interact with visitors on corporate Web sites. Several companies such as Sitepal offer software applications that design avatars to greet and guide visitors. Some of these avatars take the form of famous people, including rock stars, actors, and historical figures. Research suggests that these avatars might increase users' satisfaction with the Web sites and affect purchases.

Organizations and educators are just beginning to realize the impact of avatars and virtual worlds. Many companies now host their business meetings online; they encourage employees to develop their own avatars when they attend the meetings. Several university presidents hold online forums with students and create avatars to discuss current issues of concern with their students. The world of avatars and virtual worlds will continue to challenge marketers in the years to come.

DISCUSSION QUESTIONS

CS 6-1 How might classical conditioning operate for a consumer who visits a new tutoring Web site and is greeted by the Web site's avatar who resembles Albert Einstein?

CS 6-2 How might a consumer who purchases a new outfit for his avatar on a virtual world be influenced by instrumental conditioning?

CS 6-3 Do consumers build associative networks from their avatar's experience? Do you think this network is part of the consumer's overall associative network for that brand, or is it a separate network?

Sources: Audrey Waters, "Number of Virtual World Users Breaks 1 Billion, Roughly Half Under Age 15," readwrite.com (October 1, 2010), http://readwrite.com/2010/10/01/number_of_virtual_world_users_breaks_the_1_billion#awesm=~omeiEn2UL1brEV, accessed November 4, 2013; www.sitepal.com, accessed November 4, 2013; Natalie T. Wood and Michael R. Solomon, (2011), "Adonis or Atrocious: Spokesavatars and Source Effects in Immersive Digital Environments," in eds. Matthew S. Eastin, Terry Daugherty, and Neal M. Burns, *Handbook of Research on Digital Media and Advertising: User Generated Content Consumption*, IGI Global, 521–534.

MyMarketingLab

Go to **mymktlab.com** for the following Assisted-graded writing questions:

6-25 How do different types of reinforcement enhance learning? How does the strategy of frequency marketing relate to conditioning?

6-26 How does learning new information make it more likely that we'll forget things we've already learned?

6-27 **Mymktlab Only**—comprehensive writing assignment for this chapter.

NOTES

1. Jenna Goudreau, "These Old Brands Are Poised for a 2011 Comeback: Nostalgia Will Help Sell to Consumers Who Aren't Happy with the Present," *Forbes* (December 31, 2010), http://today.msnbc.msn.com/id/40856091/ns/today-entertainment, accessed July 22, 2013.
2. Robert A. Baron, *Psychology: The Essential Science* (Boston: Allyn & Bacon, 1989).
3. Laurie Burkitt, "Chasing China's Shoppers," *Wall Street Journal* (June 14, 2012), http://professional.wsj.com/article/SB10001424052702303444204577460693377819420.html?mg=reno64-wsj, accessed January 7, 2013.
4. Richard A. Feinberg, "Credit Cards as Spending Facilitating Stimuli: A Conditioning Interpretation," *Journal of Consumer Research* 13 (December 1986): 348–56; Jenna Goudreau, "These Old Brands Are Poised for a 2011 Comeback: Nostalgia Will Help Sell to Consumers Who Aren't Happy with the Present," *Forbes* (December 31, 2010), http://today.msnbc.msn.com/id/40856091/ns/today-entertainment, accessed July 22, 2013.
5. R. A. Rescorla, "Pavlovian Conditioning: It's Not What You Think It Is," *American Psychologist* 43 (1988): 151–60; Elnora W. Stuart, Terence A. Shimp, and Randall W. Engle, "Classical Conditioning of Consumer Attitudes: Four Experiments in an Advertising Context," *Journal of Consumer Research* 14 (December 1987): 334–39.
6. C. Janiszewski, H. Noel, and A. G. Sawyer, "A Meta-analysis of the Spacing Effect in Verbal Learning: Implications for Research on Advertising Repetition and Consumer Memory," *Journal of Consumer Research* 30, no. 1 (2003): 138–49.
7. Yaveroglu Donthu and Naveen Donthu, "Advertising Repetition and Placement Issues in On-Line Environments," *Journal of Advertising* 37 (Summer 2008): 31–43.
8. James Ward, Barbara Loken, Ivan Ross, and Tedi Hasapopoulous, "The Influence of Physical Similarity of Affect and Attribute Perceptions from National Brands to Private Label Brands," in Terence A. Shimp et al., eds., *American Marketing Educators' Conference* (Chicago: American Marketing Association, 1986): 51–56.
9. Judith Lynne Zaichkowsky and Richard Neil Simpson, "The Effect of Experience with a Brand Imitator on the Original Brand," *Marketing Letters* 7, no. 1 (1996): 31–39.
10. Roger Dobson, "Logos 'Brand' Youthful Minds: Children's Brains Are Found to Light Up at the Sight of Fast-Food Logos," *The Independent* (September 23, 2012), http://www.independent.co.uk/news/science/logos-brand-youthful-minds-8165962.html, accessed January 21, 2013.
11. Randi Priluck Grossman and Brian D. Till, "The Persistence of Classically Conditioned Brand Attitudes," *Journal of Advertising* 21, no. 1 (1998): 23–31; Chris T. Allen and Thomas J. Madden, "A Closer Look at Classical Conditioning," *Journal of Consumer Research* 12 (December 1985): 301–15; Chester A. Insko and William F. Oakes, "Awareness and the Conditioning of Attitudes," *Journal of Personality & Social Psychology* 4 (November 1966): 487–96; Carolyn K. Staats and Arthur W. Staats, "Meaning Established by Classical Conditioning," *Journal of Experimental Psychology* 54 (July 1957): 74–80.
12. Kevin Lane Keller, "Conceptualizing, Measuring, and Managing Customer-Based Brand Equity," *Journal of Marketing* 57 (January 1993): 1–22.

13. Herbert Krugman, "Low Recall and High Recognition of Advertising," *Journal of Advertising Research* (February–March 1986): 79–80.

14. http://www.edhardywines.com/, accessed April 6, 2011; quoted in Dan Neil, "Ed Hardy Wines? Christian Audigier's Branding Machine Grinds On," *Los Angeles Times* (April 28, 2009), www.latimes.com/business, accessed April 28, 2009.

15. Brian Steinberg, "Ad Nauseam: Repetition of TV Spots Risks Driving Consumers Away, Fragmenting Media, Smaller Budgets Make for More of the Same Ads," *Crain's Detroit Business* (December 1, 2008), www.Crainsdetroit.Com/Article/20081201/Email01/812010278/1092, accessed December 1, 2008.

16. Yaveroglu Donthu and Naveen Donthu, "Advertising Repetition and Placement Issues in On-Line Environments," *Journal of Advertising* 37 (Summer 2008): 31–43.

17. Gerald J. Gorn, "The Effects of Music in Advertising on Choice Behavior: A Classical Conditioning Approach," *Journal of Marketing* 46 (Winter 1982): 94–101.

18. Stuart Elliot, "Gap Inc. Puts 'GAP' Back in Logo," *New York Times (October 12, 2010),* http://mediadecoder.blogs.nytimes.com/2010/10/12/gap-inc-puts-gap-back-in-logo/?scp_1&sq_gap%20logo&st_cse, accessed March 27, 2011.

19. Andrew Martin, "Smelling an Opportunity," *New York Times* (December 8, 2010), http://www.nytimes.com/2010/12/09/business/09tide.html?_r=1&ref=business, accessed May 7, 2011; Anand Natarajan, "Branding: Interiors by Smith & Wesson," *BusinessWeek* (November 10, 2003): 16; James B. Arndorfer, "Starbucks Wakes Up to Liquor Possibilities," *Advertising Age* (November 22, 2004): 4; Claudia Deutsch, "Will Real Men Buy Mr. Clean?," *New York Times* (September 24, 2003), www.nytimes.com, accessed September 24, 2003.

20. Kirk Johnson, "A University Steak to Go With That Sweatshirt?" *New York Times* (March 2, 2013), http://www.nytimes.com/2013/03/03/us/how-about-a-university-steak-with-your-sweatshirt.html?ref=todayspaper, accessed March 4, 2013.

21. Dan Macsai, "Jamba Juice Launches Clothing Line," *Fast Company* (July 1, 2010), http://www.fastcompany.com/magazine/147/unwanted-wear-your-smoothie.html?partner=homepage_newsletter, accessed April 6, 2011.

22. http://www.zippofragrances.com/VediMacro.phtml?goTo=1&IDMacro=1321&sLang=EN, accessed March 4, 2013; James R. Hagerty, "Zippo Preps for a Post-Smoker World," *Wall Street Journal* (March 8, 2011), http://online.wsj.com/article/SB10001424052748704076804576180411173921454.html?mod=dist_smartbrief&mod=WALLSTREETJOURNAL_hp_MIDDLENexttoWhatsNewsThird, accessed April 6, 2011.

23. Mark J. Miller, "Bob Marley Brand Expands from Music to Coffee to Swimwear," Brandchannel (February 21, 2012), http://www.brandchannel.com/home/post/2012/02/21/Bob-Marley-Brand-Extensions-022112.aspx, accessed January 7, 2013.

24. "Look-Alikes Mimic Familiar Packages," *New York Times* (August 9, 1986): D1.

25. Zaichkowsky and Simpson, "The Effect of Experience with a Brand Imitator on the Original Brand," 31–39.

26. Luk Warlop and Joseph W. Alba, "Sincere Flattery: Trade-Dress Imitation and Consumer Choice," *Journal of Consumer Psychology* 14, nos. 1 & 2 (2004): 21–27.

27. Michael Barbaro and Julie Creswell, "Levi's Turns to Suing Its Rivals," *New York Times* (January 29, 2007), www.nytimes.com/2007/01/29/business/29jeans.html, accessed June 30, 2009.

28. For a comprehensive approach to consumer behavior-based operant conditioning principles, see Gordon R. Foxall, "Behavior Analysis and Consumer Psychology," *Journal of Economic Psychology* 15 (March 1994): 5–91.

29. J. Blaise Bergiel and Christine Trosclair, "Instrumental Learning: Its Application to Customer Satisfaction," *Journal of Consumer Marketing* 2 (Fall 1985): 23–28.

30. Several books have recently been published on this topic; for example, *Implementing Game Mechanics in Web and Mobile Apps* (G. Zichermann and C. Cunningham), *Reality Is Broken: Why Games Make Us Better and How They Can Change the World* (J. McGonigal), and *Total Engagement: Using Games and Virtual Worlds to Change the Way People Work and Businesses Compete* (B. Reeves and L. Read).

31. Lini S. Kadaba, "Aherk! Uses Power of Shame to Motivate Users to Pledge a Goal. If They Fail, the Website Posts an Embarrassing Photo on Facebook. It's a Negative Reinforcement Trend—or 'almost blackmail,'" *Philadelphia Inquirer* (September 27, 2012), http://articles.philly.com/2012-09-27/news/34103610_1_facebook-timeline-website-posts-social-media, accessed January 8, 2013.

32. Sandra Mardin, "Points-Based Wellbeing," *Canvas* (September 11, 2011), http://www.canvas8.com/content/2011/11/09/discovery-vitality.html, accessed January 7, 2013.

33. Nick Wingfield, "All the World's a Game, and Business Is a Player," New York Times (December 23, 2012), http://www.nytimes.com/2012/12/24/technology/all-the-worlds-a-game-and-business-is-a-player.html?emc=eta1, accessed January 7, 2013.

34. Suzanne Vranica, "Agencies Don Lab Coats to Reach Consumers, Firms Deploy Scientists Within Creative Groups to Make Messages Stick," *Wall Street Journal* (June 4, 2007): B8.

35. Cf., for example, E. M. Eisenstein and J. W. Hutchinson, "Action-Based Learning: Goals and Attention in the Acquisition of Market Knowledge," *Journal of Marketing Research* 43, no. 2 (2006): 244–58.

36. Ellen J. Langer, *The Psychology of Control* (Beverly Hills, CA: Sage, 1983).

37. Robert B. Cialdini, *Influence: Science and Practice*, 2nd ed. (New York: William Morrow, 1984); Y. Rottenstreich, S. Sood, and L. Brenner, "Feeling and Thinking in Memory-Based versus Stimulus-Based Choices," *Journal of Consumer Research* 33, no. 4 (2007): 461–69.

38. Chris T. Allen and Thomas J. Madden, "A Closer Look at Classical Conditioning," *Journal of Consumer Research* 12 (December 1985): 301–15; see also Terence A. Shimp, Elnora W. Stuart, and Randall W. Engle, "A Program of Classical Conditioning Experiments Testing Variations in the Conditioned Stimulus and Context," *Journal of Consumer Research* 18 (June 1991): 1–12.

39. Sally L. Satel, "Primed for Controversy," *New York Times* (February 23, 2013), http://www.nytimes.com/2013/02/24/opinion/sunday/psychology-research-control.html, accessed March 4, 2013.

40. Terence A. Shimp, "Neo-Pavlovian Conditioning and Its Implications for Consumer Theory and Research," in Thomas S. Robertson and Harold H. Kassarjian, eds., *Handbook of Consumer Behavior* (Upper Saddle River, NJ: Prentice Hall, 1991).

41. Albert Bandura, *Social Foundations of Thought and Action: A Social Cognitive View* (Upper Saddle River, NJ: Prentice Hall, 1986).

42. Ibid.

43. Scott Ward, "Consumer Socialization," in Harold H. Kassarjian and Thomas S. Robertson, eds., *Perspectives in Consumer Behavior* (Glenview, IL: Scott, Foresman, 1980), 380; cf. also Patricia Robinson and Steven Maxwell Kates, "Children and Their Brand Relationships," *Advances in Consumer Research* 32, no. 1 (2005); Terry O'Sullivan, "Advertising and Children: What Do the Kids Think?," *Qualitative Market Research* 8, no. 4 (2005): 371.

44. Thomas Lipscomb, "Indicators of Materialism in Children's Free Speech: Age and Gender Comparisons," *Journal of Consumer Marketing* (Fall 1988): 41–46.

45. George P. Moschis, "The Role of Family Communication in Consumer Socialization of Children and Adolescents," *Journal of Consumer Research* 11 (March 1985): 898–913.

46. Gregory M. Rose, Vassilis Dalakas, and Fredric Kropp, "A Five-Nation Study of Developmental Timetables, Reciprocal Communication and Consumer Socialization," *Journal of Business Research* 55 (2002): 943–49.

47. Elizabeth S. Moore, William L. Wilkie, and Richard J. Lutz, "Passing the Torch: Intergenerational Influences as a Source of Brand Equity," *Journal of Marketing* 66 (April 2002): 17–37.

48. James U. McNeal and Chyon-Hwa Yeh, "Born to Shop," *American Demographics* (June 1993): 34–39.

49. Kari Greenberg, "Study: Kids Influence Family's Use of Media," *Marketing Daily* (June 10, 2010), http://www.mediapost.com/publications/?fa=Articles.showArticle&art_aid=129877, accessed April 19, 2011; Les Carlson, Sanford Grossbart, and J. Kathleen Stuenkel, "The Role of Parental Socialization Types on Differential Family Communication Patterns Regarding Consumption," *Journal of Consumer Psychology* 1, no. 1 (1992): 31–52; cf. also Sonya A. Grier, Janell Mensinger, Shirley H. Huang, Shiriki K. Kumanyika, and Nicolas Stettler, "Fast-Food Marketing and Children's Fast-Food Consumption: Exploring Parents' Influences in an Ethnically Diverse Sample," *Journal of Public Policy & Marketing* 26 (Fall 2007): 221–235.

50. Marian Burros, "McDonald's France Puts Its Mouth Where Its Money Is," *New York Times* (October 30, 2002), www.nytimes.com, accessed October 30, 2002.

51. Emily Bryson York, "NIH: Banning Fast Food Ads Will Make Kids Less Fat," *Advertising Age* (November 19, 2008), http://adage.com/results.php?endeca=1&return=endeca&search_offset=0&search_order_by=score&search_advanced=1&searchprop=AdAgeAll&search_phrase=banning+fast+food+ads+will+make+kids+less+fat&searchmode=match all&sortby=date&range=adage&variable=90&date_range=specific&date_begin=11%2F19%2F08&date_end=&x=42&y=20, accessed November 24, 2008.

52. Andrew Martin, "Kellogg to Curb Marketing of Foods to Children," *New York Times* (June 14, 2007), www.nytimes.com, accessed June 14, 2007; Tara Parker-Pope, "Watching Food Ads on TV May Program Kids to Overeat," *Wall Street Journal* (July 10, 2007): D1.

53. Erik Sass, "Four Out of Five Kids Ages Five and Under Are on the Web," *Marketing Daily* (March 17, 2011), http://www.mediapost.com/

publications/?fa=Articles.showArticle&art_aid=146941&nid=124844, accessed April 19, 2011.

54. http://passiripatti.com/2010/11/social-media-for-toddlers/, accessed June 14, 2011; "Sign of the Times: Toy Blocks That Teach Toddlers Social Networking," *Fast Company* (November 30, 2010), http://www.fastcodesign.com/1662781/toy-blocks-become-twitter-for-toddlers?partner=homepage_newsletter, accessed April 19, 2011.

55. Laura A. Peracchio, "How Do Young Children Learn to Be Consumers? A Script-Processing Approach," *Journal of Consumer Research* 18 (March 1992): 425–40; Laura A. Peracchio, "Young Children's Processing of a Tele-vised Narrative: Is a Picture Really Worth a Thousand Words?," *Journal of Consumer Research* 20 (September 1993): 281–93; see also M. Carole Macklin, "The Effects of an Advertising Retrieval Cue on Young Children's Memory and Brand Evaluations," *Psychology & Marketing* 11 (May–June 1994): 291–311.

56. Jean Piaget, "The Child and Modern Physics," *Scientific American* 196, no. 3 (1957): 46–51; see also Kenneth D. Bahn, "How and When Do Brand Perceptions and Preferences First Form? A Cognitive Developmental Investigation," *Journal of Consumer Research* 13 (December 1986): 382–93.

57. Deborah L. Roedder, "Age Differences in Children's Responses to Television Advertising: An Information-Processing Approach," *Journal of Consumer Research* 8 (September 1981): 144–53; see also Deborah Roedder John and Ramnath Lakshmi-Ratan, "Age Differences in Children's Choice Behavior: The Impact of Available Alternatives," *Journal of Marketing Research* 29 (May 1992): 216–26; Jennifer Gregan-Paxton and Deborah Roedder John, "Are Young Children Adaptive Decision Makers? A Study of Age Differences in Information Search Behavior," *Journal of Consumer Research* 21, no. 4 (1995): 567–80.

58. For a study on the effects of commercial programming on creative play, cf. Patricia M. Greenfield, Emily Yut, Mabel Chung, Deborah Land, Holly Kreider, Maurice Pantoja, and Kris Horsley, "The Program-Length Commercial: A Study of the Effects of Television/Toy Tie-Ins on Imaginative Play," *Psychology & Marketing* 7 (Winter 1990): 237–56.

59. Gerald J. Gorn and Renee Florsheim, "The Effects of Commercials for Adult Products on Children," *Journal of Consumer Research* 11 (March 1985): 962–67. For a study that assessed the impact of violent commercials on children, see V. Kanti Prasad and Lois J. Smith, "Television Commercials in Violent Programming: An Experimental Evaluation of Their Effects on Children," *Journal of the Academy of Marketing Science* 22, no. 4 (1994): 340–51.

60. Gwen Bachmannn Achenreiner and Deborah Roedder John, "The Meaning of Brand Names to Children: A Developmental Investigation," *Journal of Consumer Psychology* 13, no. 3 (2003): 205–19.

61. Paula Lyon Andruss, "'Dora' Translates Well," *Marketing News* (October 13, 2003): 8.

62. Gary Armstrong and Merrie Brucks, "Dealing with Children's Advertising: Public Policy Issues and Alternatives," *Journal of Public Policy & Marketing* 7 (1988): 98–113.

63. Bonnie Reece, "Children and Shopping: Some Public Policy Questions," *Journal of Public Policy & Marketing* (1986): 185–94.

64. Stuart Elliott, "If Philip Morris Becomes Altria, Its Corporate Image May Lose Some of the Odor of Stale Smoke," *New York Times* (November 19, 2001). http://www.nytimes.com/2001/11/19/business/media-business-advertising-if-philip-morris-becomes-altria-its-corporate-image.html, accessed August 24, 2011.

65. Daniel Cook, University of Illinois, personal communication, December 2002; Daniel Cook, "Contradictions and Conundrums of the Child Consumer: The Emergent Centrality of an Enigma in the 1990s," paper presented at the Association for Consumer Research, October 2002.

66. http://www.bbb.org/us/children-food-beverage-advertising-initiative/, accessed June 14, 2011; John Eggerton, "Sara Lee Agrees to Limit Food Marketing to Kids," *Broadcasting & Cable* (September 23, 2010), http://www.broadcastingcable.com/article/457541-Sara_Lee_Agrees_to_Limit_Food_Marketing_to_Kids.php, accessed April 19, 2011.

67. Natasha Singer, "New Online Privacy Rules for Children," *New York Times* (December 19, 2012), http://www.nytimes.com/2012/12/20/technology/ftc-broadens-rules-for-online-privacy-of-children.html, accessed January 4, 2013.

68. R. C. Atkinson and I. M. Shiffrin, "Human Memory: A Proposed System and Its Control Processes," in K. W. Spence and J. T. Spence, eds., *The Psychology of Learning and Motivation: Advances in Research and Theory*, vol. 2 (New York: Academic Press, 1968): 89–195.

69. James R. Bettman, "Memory Factors in Consumer Choice: A Review," *Journal of Marketing* (Spring 1979): 37–53. For a study that explores the relative impact of internal versus external memory on brand choice, see Joseph W. Alba, Howard Marmorstein, and Amitava Chattopadhyay, "Transitions in Preference over Time: The Effects of

Memory on Message Persuasiveness," *Journal of Marketing Research* 29 (1992): 406–16.

70. Lauren G. Block and Vicki G. Morwitz, "Shopping Lists as an External Memory Aid for Grocery Shopping: Influences on List Writing and List Fulfillment," *Journal of Consumer Psychology* 8, no. 4 (1999): 343–75.

71. Rob Griffiths, "Shop Shop Shopping List Review," macworld.com, http://www.macworld.com/appguide/app.html?id=71541&expand=false, accessed May 7, 2011.

72. Kim Robertson, "Recall and Recognition Effects of Brand Name Imagery," *Psychology & Marketing* 4 (Spring 1987): 3–15.

73. Kathryn A. Braun, "Post-Experience Advertising Effects on Consumer Memory," *Journal of Consumer Research* 25 (March 1999), 319–34; Kathryn A. Braun-LaTour, Michael S. LaTour, Jacqueline Pickrell, and Elizabeth F. Loftus, "How (and When) Advertising Can Influence Memory for Consumer Experience," *Journal of Advertising* 33, no. 4 (2004): 7–26; Kathryn A. Braun-LaTour, Michael S. LaTour, and George M. Zinkhan, "Using Childhood Memories to Gain Insight into Brand Meaning," *Journal of Marketing* 71 (April 2007): 45–60.

74. Endel Tulving, "Remembering and Knowing the Past," *American Scientist* 77 (July–August 1989): 361.

75. Rashmi Adaval and Robert S. Wyer, Jr., "The Role of Narratives in Consumer Information Processing," *Journal of Consumer Psychology* 7, no. 3 (1998): 207–46; cf. also R. F. Baumeister and L. S. Newman, "How Stories Make Sense of Personal Experiences: Motives that Shape Autobiographical Narratives," *Personality & Social Psychology Bulletin* 20, no. 6 (1994): 676–90; J. Bruner, *Actual Minds, Possible Worlds* (Cambridge, MA: Harvard University Press, 1986).

76. Jennifer Edson Escalas, "Narrative Processing: Building Consumer Connections to Brands," *Journal of Consumer Psychology* 14, nos. 1 & 2 (2004): 168–80.

77. George A. Miller, "The Magical Number Seven, Plus or Minus Two: Some Limits on Our Capacity for Processing Information," *Psychological Review* 63 (1956): 81–97.

78. James N. MacGregor, "Short-Term Memory Capacity: Limitation or Optimization?" *Psychological Review* 94 (1987): 107–8.

79. M. Vanhuele, G. Laurent, and X. Dréze, "Consumers' Immediate Memory for Prices," *Journal of Consumer Research* 33, no. 2 (2006): 163–72.

80. Beth Snyder Bulik, "What's in a (Good) Product Name? Sales Cellphone Study Finds 'Cognitive' Monikers Work; Numerics Flop," February 2, 2009, www.namedevelopment.com/Articles/Good-Cellphone-Names.html, accessed February 27, 2009.

81. See Catherine A. Cole and Michael J. Houston, "Encoding and Media Effects on Consumer Learning Deficiencies in the Elderly," *Journal of Marketing Research* 24 (February 1987): 55–64; A. M. Collins and E. F. Loftus, "A Spreading Activation Theory of Semantic Processing," *Psychological Review* 82 (1975): 407–28; Fergus I. M. Craik and Robert S. Lockhart, "Levels of Processing: A Framework for Memory Research," *Journal of Verbal Learning & Verbal Behavior* 11 (1972): 671–84.

82. Walter A. Henry, "The Effect of Information-Processing Ability on Processing Accuracy," *Journal of Consumer Research* 7 (June 1980): 42–48.

83. T. B. Cornwell, M. S. Humphreys, A. M. Maguire, C. S. Weeks, and C. L. Tellegen, "Sponsorship-Linked Marketing: The Role of Articulation in Memory," *Journal of Consumer Research* 33, no. 3 (2006): 312–21.

84. Kevin Lane Keller, "Memory Factors in Advertising: The Effect of Advertising Retrieval Cues on Brand Evaluations," *Journal of Consumer Research* 14 (December 1987): 316–33. For a discussion of processing operations that occur during brand choice, see Gabriel Biehal and Dipankar Chakravarti, "Consumers' Use of Memory and External Information in Choice: Macro and Micro Perspectives," *Journal of Consumer Research* 12 (March 1986): 382–405.

85. Susan T. Fiske and Shelley E. Taylor, *Social Cognition* (Reading, MA: Addison-Wesley, 1984).

86. Deborah Roedder John and John C. Whitney Jr., "The Development of Consumer Knowledge in Children: A Cognitive Structure Approach," *Journal of Consumer Research* 12 (March 1986): 406–17.

87. Michael R. Solomon, Carol Surprenant, John A. Czepiel, and Evelyn G. Gutman, "A Role Theory Perspective on Dyadic Interactions: The Service Encounter," *Journal of Marketing* 49 (Winter 1985): 99–111.

88. S. Danziger, S. Moran, and V. Rafaely, "The Influence of Ease of Retrieval on Judgment as a Function of Attention to Subjective Experience," *Journal of Consumer Psychology* 16, no. 2 (2006): 191–95.

89. Roger W. Morrell, Denise C. Park, and Leonard W. Poon, "Quality of Instructions on Prescription Drug Labels: Effects on Memory and Comprehension in Young and Old Adults," *The Gerontologist* 29 (1989): 345–54.

90. Aaron Baar, "New Product Messages Aren't Making Intended Impressions," *Marketing Daily* (March 6, 2008), http://publications.mediapost.com/Index.Cfm?Fuseaction=Articles.Showarticle&Art_Aid=779, accessed March 6, 2008.

91. Frank R. Kardes, Gurumurthy Kalyanaram, Murali Chandrashekaran, and Ronald J. Dornoff, "Brand Retrieval, Consideration Set Composition, Consumer Choice, and the Pioneering Advantage" (unpublished manuscript, The University of Cincinnati, Ohio, 1992).

92. Judith Lynne Zaichkowsky and Padma Vipat, "Inferences from Brand Names," paper presented at the European meeting of the Association for Consumer Research, Amsterdam (June 1992).

93. H. Noel, "The Spacing Effect: Enhancing Memory for Repeated Marketing Stimuli," *Journal of Consumer Psychology* 16, no. 3 (2006): 306–20; for an alternative explanation, see S. L. Appleton-Knapp, R. A. Bjork, and T. D. Wickens, "Examining the Spacing Effect in Advertising: Encoding Variability, Retrieval Processes, and Their Interaction," *Journal of Consumer Research* 32, no. 2 (2005): 266–76.

94. Herbert E. Krugman, "Low Recall and High Recognition of Advertising," *Journal of Advertising Research* (February–March 1986): 79–86.

95. Rik G. M. Pieters and Tammo H. A. Bijmolt, "Consumer Memory for Television Advertising: A Field Study of Duration, Serial Position, and Competition Effects," *Journal of Consumer Research* 23 (March 1997): 362–72.

96. Erik Sass, "Study Finds Spectacular Print Ads Get Spectacular Recall," *Marketing Daily* (February 23, 2007), www.mediapost.com, accessed February 23, 2007.

97. Raymond R. Burke and Thomas K. Srull, "Competitive Interference and Consumer Memory for Advertising," *Journal of Consumer Research* 15 (June 1988): 55–68.

98. Eric J. Johnson and J. Edward Russo, "Product Familiarity and Learning New Information," *Journal of Consumer Research* 11 (June 1984): 542–50.

99. Joan Meyers-Levy, "The Influence of Brand Name's Association Set Size and Word Frequency on Brand Memory," *Journal of Consumer Research* 16 (September 1989): 197–208.

100. Michael H. Baumgardner, Michael R. Leippe, David L. Ronis, and Anthony G. Greenwald, "In Search of Reliable Persuasion Effects: II. Associative Interference and Persistence of Persuasion in a Message-Dense Environment," *Journal of Personality & Social Psychology* 45 (September 1983): 524–37.

101. Joseph W. Alba and Amitava Chattopadhyay, "Salience Effects in Brand Recall," *Journal of Marketing Research* 23 (November 1986): 363–70.

102. Margaret Henderson Blair, Allan R. Kuse, David H. Furse, and David W. Stewart, "Advertising in a New and Competitive Environment: Persuading Consumers to Buy," *Business Horizons* 30 (November–December 1987): 20.

103. Kevin Lane Keller, "Memory Factors in Advertising: The Effect of Advertising Retrieval Cues on Brand Evaluations," *Journal of Consumer Research* 14 (December 1987): 316–33.

104. Eric J. Johnson and J. Edward Russo, "Product Familiarity and Learning New Information," *Journal of Consumer Research* 11 (June 1984): 542–50.

105. Eric J. Johnson and J. Edward Russo, "Product Familiarity and Learning New Information"; John G. Lynch and Thomas K. Srull, "Memory and Attentional Factors in Consumer Choice: Concepts and Research Methods," *Journal of Consumer Research* 9 (June 1982): 18–37.

106. Joseph W. Alba and J. Wesley Hutchinson, "Dimensions of Consumer Expertise," *Journal of Consumer Research* 13 (March 1988): 411–54; Julie A. Edell and Kevin Lane Keller, "The Information Processing of Coordinated Media Campaigns," *Journal of Marketing Research* 26 (May 1989): 149–64; cf. also Jeff Galak, Joseph P. Redden, and Justin Kruger, "Variety Amnesia: Recalling Past Variety Can Accelerate Recovery from Satiation," *Journal of Consumer Research* 36, no. 4 (2009): 575–84.

107. Marcus Cunha, Jr., and Juliano Laran, "Asymmetries in the Sequential Learning of Brand Associations: Implications for the Early Entrant Advantage," *Journal of Consumer Research* 35, no. 5 (2009): 788–99; Julie A. Edell and Kevin Lane Keller, "The Information Processing of Coordinated Media Campaigns," *Journal of Marketing Research* 26 (May 1989): 149–64; cf. also Galak, Redden, and Kruger, "Variety Amnesia: Recalling Past Variety Can Accelerate Recovery from Satiation."

108. Cunha, Jr., and Laran, "Asymmetries in the Sequential Learning of Brand Associations: Implications for the Early Entrant Advantage"; Andrew W. Ellis, Selina J. Holmes, and Richard L. Wright, "Age of Acquisition and the Recognition of Brand Names: On the Importance of Being Early," *Journal of Consumer Psychology* 20, no. 1 (2010): 43–52.

109. John G. Lynch and Thomas K. Srull, "Memory and Attentional Factors in Consumer Choice: Concepts and Research Methods," *Journal of Consumer Research* 9 (June 1982): 18–37; Joseph W. Alba and Amitava Chattopadhyay, "Salience Effects in Brand Recall," *Journal of Marketing Research* 23 (November 1986): 363–70; Elizabeth C. Hirschman and Michael R. Solomon, "Utilitarian, Aesthetic, and Familiarity Responses to Verbal versus Visual Advertisements," in Thomas C. Kinnear, ed., *Advances in Consumer Research* 11 (Provo, UT: Association for Consumer Research, 1984): 426–31.

110. Susan E. Heckler and Terry L. Childers, "The Role of Expectancy and Relevancy in Memory for Verbal and Visual Information: What Is Incongruency?" *Journal of Consumer Research* 18 (March 1992): 475–92.

111. Russell H. Fazio, Paul M. Herr, and Martha C. Powell, "On the Development and Strength of Category-Brand Associations in Memory: The Case of Mystery Ads," *Journal of Consumer Psychology* 1, no. 1 (1992): 1–13.

112. Jennifer Aaker, Aimee Drolet, and Dale Griffin, "Recalling Mixed Emotions," *Journal of Consumer Research* 35 (August 2008): 268–78.

113. Alex Mindlin, "Commercials Bask in a Show's Glow," *New York Times Online* (December 17, 2007), www.nytimes.com, accessed December 17, 2008.

114. Suzanne Vranica, "New Ads Take on Tivo, Tie-Ins to TV Shows Aim to Prevent Fast-Forwarding," *Wall Street Journal* (October 5, 2007): B4.

115. Hirschman and Solomon, "Utilitarian, Aesthetic, and Familiarity Responses to Verbal versus Visual Advertisements."

116. Terry Childers and Michael Houston, "Conditions for a Picture-Superiority Effect on Consumer Memory," *Journal of Consumer Research* 11 (September 1984): 643–54; Terry Childers, Susan Heckler, and Michael Houston, "Memory for the Visual and Verbal Components of Print Advertisements," *Psychology & Marketing* 3 (Fall 1986): 147–50.

117. Werner Krober-Riel, "Effects of Emotional Pictorial Elements in Ads Analyzed by Means of Eye Movement Monitoring," in Thomas C. Kinnear, ed., *Advances in Consumer Research* 11 (Provo, UT: Association for Consumer Research, 1984): 591–96.

118. Hans-Bernd Brosius, "Influence of Presentation Features and News Context on Learning from Television News," *Journal of Broadcasting & Electronic Media* 33 (Winter 1989): 1–14.

119. Edward F. McQuarrie and David Glen Mick, "Visual and Verbal Rhetorical Figures under Directed Processing versus Incidental Exposure to Advertising," *Journal of Consumer Research* 29 (March 2003): 579–87; cf. also Ann E. Schlosser, "Learning Through Virtual Product Experience: The Role of Imagery on True Versus False Memories," *Journal of Consumer Research* 33, no. 3 (2006): 377–83.

120. Hugo Martin, "Disney's 2011 Marketing Campaign Centers on Family Memories," *Los Angeles Times* (September 23, 2010), http://latimesblogs.latimes.com/money_co/201009/disney-to-market-on-memories.html, accessed April 4, 2011.

121. Russell W. Belk, "Possessions and the Extended Self," *Journal of Consumer Research* 15 (September 1988): 139–68.

122. Morris B. Holbrook and Robert M. Schindler, "Nostalgic Bonding: Exploring the Role of Nostalgia in the Consumption Experience," *Journal of Consumer Behavior* 3, no. 2 (December 2003): 107–27.

123. Alexia Tsotsis, "Flickr Dips Its Toes into Social with Twitter and Facebook 'Share This' Features," *TechCrunch* (March 30, 2011), http://techcrunch.com/2011/03/30/flickr-dips-its-toes-into-social-with-twitter-and-facebook-share-this-features/, accessed April 6, 2011.

124. Stacy Menzel Baker, Holli C. Karrer, and Ann Veeck, "My Favorite Recipes: Recreating Emotions and Memories Through Cooking," *Advances in Consumer Research* 32, no. 1 (2005): 304–5.

125. Proust.com, accessed March 4, 2013; Austin Carr, "Barry Diller, IAC Launch Proust, A Social Network for Nostalgic Seniors," *Fast Company* (July 19, 2011), http://www.fastcompany.com/1767926/barry-diller-iac-launch-proust-social-network-nostalgic-seniors, accessed January 7, 2013.

126. Russell W. Belk, "The Role of Possessions in Constructing and Maintaining a Sense of Past," in Marvin E. Goldberg, Gerald Gorn, and Richard W. Pollay, eds., *Advances in Consumer Research* 16 (Provo, UT: Association for Consumer Research, 1989): 669–78.

127. "Only 38% of T.V. Audience Links Brands with Ads," *Marketing News* (January 6, 1984): 10.

128. "Terminal Television," *American Demographics* (January 1987): 15.

129. Meet the Coolest Facebook Brand Timelines From Coke to ESPN to Ford *Brands: With Facebook Timeline, You Shall Know Our Illustrious History By: Michael Learmonth, Ad Age/Digital*, http://adage.com/article/digital/meet-coolest-facebook-brand-timelines-coke-espn-ford/233015/?utm_source=digital_email&utm_medium=newsletter&utm_campaign=adage, accessed January 7, 2013.

130. Susan Kuchinskas, "Home > Media > Video Brands Increase Recall with TV/Digital Mix, Google Says," *ClizkZ* (December 6, 2011), http://www.clickz.com/clickz/news/2130484/brands-increase-recall-tv-digital-mix-google, accessed January 7, 2013.

131. Kunur Patel, "Apple, Campbell's Say iAds Twice as Effective as TV A Nielsen Study Shows iPhone Users Are Paying Attention, While TV Viewers Not So Much," *Ad Age/Digital* (February 3, 2011), http://adage.com/article/digital/apple-campbell-s-iads-effective-tv/148630/, accessed January 7, 2013.

132. Richard P. Bagozzi and Alvin J. Silk, "Recall, Recognition, and the Measurement of Memory for Print Advertisements," *Marketing Science* 2 (1983): 95–134.

133. Adam Finn, "Print Ad Recognition Readership Scores: An Information Processing Perspective," *Journal of Marketing Research* 25 (May 1988): 168–77.

134. James R. Bettman, "Memory Factors in Consumer Choice: A Review," *Journal of Marketing* (Spring 1979): 37–53.

135. Mark A. Deturck and Gerald M. Goldhaber, "Effectiveness of Product Warning Labels: Effects of Consumers' Information Processing Objectives," *Journal of Consumer Affairs* 23, no. 1 (1989): 111–25.

136. Surendra N. Singh and Gilbert A. Churchill, Jr., "Response-Bias-Free Recognition Tests to Measure Advertising Effects," *Journal of Advertising Research* (June–July 1987): 23–36.

137. William A. Cook, "Telescoping and Memory's Other Tricks," *Journal of Advertising Research* 27 (February–March 1987): 5–8.

138. "On a Diet? Don't Trust Your Memory," *Psychology Today* (October 1989): 12.

139. Martinne Geller, "Exclusive: Flowers Foods to win Hostess' Wonder Bread," *Chicago Tribune* (February 27, 2013), http://articles.chicagotribune.com/2013-02-27/business/sns-rt-us-hostess-flowers-bre91q0tf-20130227_1_bread-brands-beefsteak-brand-hostess-brands, accessed March 4, 2013; Stuart Elliot, "From Retired Brands, Dollars and Memories," *New York Times* (December 8, 2010), http://www.nytimes.com/2010/12/09/business/media/09adco.html?_r=1&adxnnl=1&ref=media&adxnnlx=1301951891-EMjJs87oEc62npAZxAn7Gw, accessed April 4, 2011; Goudreau, "These Old Brands Are Poised for a 2011 Comeback."

140. Susan L. Holak and William J. Havlena, "Feelings, Fantasies, and Memories: An Examination of the Emotional Components of Nostalgia," *Journal of Business Research* 42 (1998): 217–26.

141. Stephen Brown, Robert V. Kozinets, and John F. Sherry, "Teaching Old Brands New Tricks: Retro Branding and the Revival of Brand Meaning," *Journal of Marketing* 67 (July 2003): 19–33.

142. Robert M. Schindler and Morris B. Holbrook, "Nostalgia for Early Experience as a Determinant of Consumer Preferences," *Psychology & Marketing* 20, no. 4 (April 2003): 275–302; Morris B. Holbrook and Robert M. Schindler, "Some Exploratory Findings on the Development of Musical Tastes," *Journal of Consumer Research* 16 (June 1989): 119–24; Morris B. Holbrook and Robert M. Schindler, "Market Segmentation Based on Age and Attitude Toward the Past: Concepts, Methods, and Findings Concerning Nostalgic Influences on Consumer Tastes," *Journal of Business Research* 37 (September 1996)1: 27–40.

143. Clark Bowling, "General Motors apologises after Chevrolet ad includes Chinese, Japanese racist stereotypes," *NY Daily News* (May 1, 2013), http://www.nydailynews.com/autos/ching-chong-chop-suey-gm-pulls-racist-ad-article-1.1332381, accessed on December 17, 2013.

144. "Beastie Boys star Adam Yauch's will bans music in ads," *BBC News U.K.* (August 10, 2012), http://www.bbc.co.uk/news/entertainment-arts-19206509, accessed on December 17, 2013.

145. "The Singapore Food & Beverage Industry—'Responsible Advertising to Children' Initiative," Food Industry Asia, http://foodindustry.asia/industry-pledge-in-singapore.

Chapter 7 • **The Self**

Chapter Objectives

When you finish reading this chapter you will understand why:

1. The self-concept strongly influences consumer behavior.

2. Products often define a person's self-concept.

3. A consumer's personality influences the way he responds to marketing stimuli, but efforts to use this information in marketing contexts meet with mixed results.

4. Brands have personalities.

5. The way we think about our bodies (and the way our culture tells us we should think) is a key component of self-esteem.

6. Every culture dictates certain types of body decoration or mutilation.

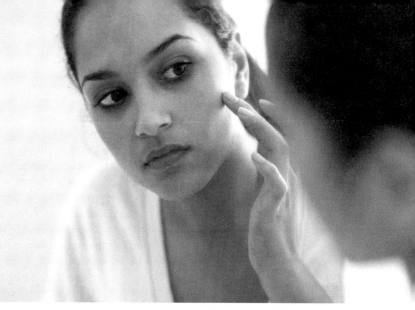

Lisa is trying to concentrate on the report her client expects by 5:00. She has worked hard to maintain this important account for the firm, but today she is distracted thinking about her date with Eric last night. Although things seemed to go OK, she couldn't shake the feeling that Eric regards her more as a friend than as a potential romantic partner. As she leafs through *Glamour* and *Cosmopolitan* during her lunch hour, Lisa is struck by all the articles about ways to become more attractive by dieting, exercising, and wearing sexy clothes. She begins to feel depressed as she looks at the svelte models in the many advertisements for perfumes, apparel, and makeup. Each woman is more glamorous and beautiful than the last. Surely they've had "adjustments"—women simply don't look that way in real life. Then again, it's unlikely that Eric could ever be mistaken for Brad Pitt on the street. Still, in her down mood, Lisa actually thinks that maybe she should look into cosmetic surgery. Even though she's never considered herself unattractive, maybe if she got a new nose or removed that mole on her cheek she'd feel better about herself. Who knows, she might look so good she'll get up the nerve to submit a photo to that Web site that everyone's talking about. But on second thought, is Eric even worth it?

OBJECTIVE 1

The self-concept strongly influences consumer behavior.

The Self

Are you what you buy? Lisa isn't the only person who feels that her physical appearance and possessions affect her "value" as a person. We choose many products, from cars to cologne, because we want to highlight or hide some aspect of the self. In this chapter, we'll focus on how consumers' feelings about themselves shape their consumption practices, particularly as they strive to fulfill their society's expectations about how a male or female should look and act.

Does the Self Exist?

Most of us can't boast of coming close to Lady Gaga's 10 million followers on Twitter, but many of us do have hundreds of followers, in addition to legions of Facebook friends.[1] The explosion of these and other social networking services enables everyone to focus on himself or herself and share mundane or scintillating details about his or her life with anyone who's interested (*why* they are interested is another story!).

Today it seems natural to think of ourselves as potential celebs waiting for our 15 minutes of fame (as the pop icon Andy Warhol once predicted). However, the idea that each single human life is unique rather than a part of a group only developed in late medieval times (between the 11th and 15th centuries). Furthermore, the emphasis on the unique nature of the self is much greater in Western societies.[2] Many Eastern cultures stress the importance of a *collective self,* where a person derives his or her identity in large measure from a social group. Both Eastern and Western cultures believe that the self divides into an inner, private self and an outer, public self. Where cultures differ is in terms of which part they see as the "real you"; the West tends to subscribe to an independent understanding of the self, which emphasizes the inherent separateness of each individual.

Non-Western cultures, in contrast, tend to focus on an interdependent self where we define our identities largely by our relationships with others.[3] For example, a Confucian perspective stresses the importance of "face": others' perceptions of the self and maintaining one's desired status in their eyes. One dimension of face is *mien-tzu*, the reputation one achieves through success and ostentation. Some Asian cultures developed explicit rules about the specific garments and even colors that certain social classes and occupations were allowed to display. These traditions live on today in Japanese style manuals that set out very detailed instructions for dressing and how to address people of differing status.[4]

That orientation is a bit at odds with such Western conventions as "casual Friday," which encourages employees to express their unique selves through dress (at least short of muscle shirts and flip-flops). To further illustrate these cross-cultural differences, a Roper Starch Worldwide survey compared consumers in 30 countries to see which were the most and least vain. Women who live in Venezuela were the chart toppers: 65 percent said they thought about their appearance all the time.[5] Other high-scoring countries included Russia and Mexico. The lowest scorers lived in the Philippines and in Saudi Arabia, where only 28 percent of consumers surveyed agreed with this statement.

Self-Concept

The **self-concept** summarizes the beliefs a person holds about his own attributes and how he evaluates the self on these qualities. Although your overall self-concept may be positive, there certainly are parts of it you evaluate more positively than others. For example, Lisa feels better about her professional identity than she does about her feminine identity.

The self-concept is a very complex structure. We describe attributes of self-concept along such dimensions as *content* (e.g., facial attractiveness versus mental aptitude), *positivity* (i.e., self-esteem), *intensity and stability* over time, and *accuracy* (i.e., the degree to which one's self-assessment corresponds to reality).[6] As we'll see later in this chapter, consumers' self-assessments can be quite distorted, especially with regard to their physical appearance. In addition, our own estimates of how much we change over time vary as well: A recent study that included both young and old people asked over 19,000 respondents about their preferences in the past (foods, vacations, hobbies, and bands) and also to predict how their tastes will change in the future. Regardless of age, people acknowledged that their prior choices had changed quite a bit over time, but they still tended to predict that they would not change as they got older.[7]

Self-Esteem

Self-esteem refers to the positivity of a person's self-concept. People with low self-esteem expect that they will not perform very well, and they will try to avoid embarrassment, failure, or rejection. When it developed a new line of snack cakes, for example, Sara Lee found that consumers low in self-esteem preferred portion-controlled snack items because they felt they lacked self-control.[8] In contrast, a more recent study found that individuals who are made to feel powerful spend more money on themselves ("because I'm worth it!"), whereas those who experience a feeling of powerlessness spend more on others than on themselves.[9]

Alberto-Culver uses a self-esteem appeal to promote a product that reflects our changing society: Soft & Beautiful Just for Me Texture Softener, an alternative to hair pressing or relaxing. It's targeted to white mothers who don't know how to care for the hair of their multiracial children who have "hair texture" issues. The self-esteem portion of the campaign, dubbed "Love Yourself. Love Your Hair," includes a Web site, texturesoftener.com, that offers "conversation starters" to help parents find ways to talk to their daughters about self-image.[10]

How do marketers influence self-esteem? Exposure to ads such as the ones Lisa checked out can trigger a process of **social comparison**, in which the person tries to evaluate her appearance by comparing it to the people depicted in these artificial images.[11] This is a basic human tendency, and many marketers tap into our need for benchmarks when they supply idealized images of happy, attractive people who just happen to use their products. An ad campaign for Clearasil is a good example. In one typical ad, two teenage boys enter a kitchen where a 40-ish mother is mixing something in a bowl. When her son leaves the room, his friend hits on Mom. The ad's tagline: "Clearasil may cause confidence."

In a study that illustrates the social comparison process, female college students who were exposed to beautiful women in advertisements afterward expressed lowered satisfaction with their own appearance, as compared to other participants who did not view ads with attractive models.[12] Another study reported that young women alter their perceptions of their own body shapes and sizes after they watch as little as 30 minutes of TV programming.[13] Researchers report similar findings for men.[14] This process even operates when we decide how much to eat: A study found that people who were served food by a server who was either fat or thin choose different portion sizes.[15]

Real and Ideal Selves

When a consumer compares some aspect of himself to an ideal, this judgment influences his self-esteem. He might ask, "Am I as good-looking as I would like to be?" or "Do I make as much money as I should?" The **ideal self** is a person's conception of how he would like to be, whereas the **actual self** refers to our more realistic appraisal of the qualities we do and don't have. We choose some products because we think they are consistent with our actual self, while we buy others to help us reach an ideal standard. We also often engage in a process of **impression management** in which we work hard to "manage" what others think of us; we strategically choose clothing and other products that will show us off to others in a good light.[16]

Impression management applies to all sorts of behaviors, from professional contexts and dating to markers of religious observance. For example, an increasing number of Islamic men in Egypt have a *zebibah* (Arabic for "raisin")—a dark circle of callused skin or a bump—between the hairline and the eyebrows. It marks the spot where the worshipper repeatedly presses his forehead into the ground during his daily prayers (observant Muslims pray five times a day). Some add prayers so that the bump will become even more pronounced; the owner of the mark thus broadcasts his degree of piousness on his head. As an Egyptian newspaper editor explains, "there is a kind of statement in it. Sometimes as a personal statement to announce that he is a conservative Muslim and

• • • • • • • • • • • • • • • • •

A German shampoo helps users to fantasize.
Source: Courtesy of JWT/Frankfurt.

sometimes as a way of outbidding others by showing them that he is more religious or to say that they should be like him."[17]

Fantasy: Bridging the Gap Between the Selves

Most people experience a discrepancy between their real and ideal selves, but for some consumers this gap is especially large. These people are especially good targets for marketing communications that employ *fantasy appeals*.[19] A **fantasy** or daydream is a self-induced shift in consciousness, which is sometimes a way to compensate for a lack of external stimulation or to escape from problems in the real world.[20] Many products and services succeed because they appeal to our fantasies. An ad may transport us to an unfamiliar, exciting situation; things we purchase may permit us to "try on" interesting or provocative roles. And, with today's technology, such as the *virtual makeovers* that several Web sites offer, consumers can experiment with different looks before they actually take the plunge in the real world.[21]

Multiple Selves

In a way, each of us really is a number of different people—for example, your mother probably would not recognize the "you" that emerges at a party at 2:00 a.m.! We have as many selves as we do different social roles. Depending on the situation, we act differently, use different products and services, and even vary in terms of how much we *like* the aspect of ourselves we put on display. A person may require a different set of products to play each of her roles: She may choose a sedate, understated perfume when she plays

A message about multiple selves from Chile.
Source: Courtesy of Redoff.

her professional self, but splash on something more provocative on Saturday night as she transitions to her *femme fatale* self.

The *dramaturgical perspective* on consumer behavior views people as actors who play different roles. We each play many roles, and each has its own script, props, and costumes.[22] The self has different components, or *role identities,* and only some of these are active at any given time. Some identities (e.g., husband, boss, student) are more central to the self than others, but other identities (e.g., dancer, gearhead, or advocate for the homeless) may dominate in specific situations.[23] Indeed, some roles may conflict with one another. For example, one study of Iranian young people who live in the U.K. described what the authors termed the **torn self**, where respondents struggle with retaining an authentic culture while still enjoying Western freedom (and dealing with assumptions of others who believe they might be terrorists).[24]

Strategically, this means a marketer may want to ensure that the appropriate role identity is active before she pitches products that customers need to play a particular role. One obvious way to do this is to place advertising messages in contexts in which people are likely to be well aware of that role identity; for example, when fortified drink and energy bar product companies hand out free product samples to runners at a marathon.

Symbolic Interactionism

If each person potentially has many social selves, how does each develop? How do we decide which self to "activate" at any point in time? The sociological tradition of **symbolic interactionism** stresses that relationships with other people play a large part to form the self.[26] According to this perspective, we exist in a symbolic environment. We assign meaning to any situation or object when we interpret the symbols in this environment. As members of society, individuals learn to agree on shared meanings. Thus, we "know" that a red light means stop, the "golden arches" mean fast food, and "blondes have more fun." That knowledge is important in order to understand consumer behavior because it implies that our possessions play a key role as we evaluate ourselves and decide "who we are."[27]

Each of us, then, interprets our identity, and this assessment continually evolves as we encounter new situations and people. In symbolic interactionist terms, we *negotiate* these meanings over time. Essentially, each of us poses the question: "Who am I in this situation?" Those around us greatly influence how we answer this query, and we ask, "Who do *other people* think I am?" We tend to pattern our behavior on the perceived

Marketing Opportunity

Several major retailers are testing a "virtual mirror" that simulates what makeup and hair dye would look like on shoppers. With the EZFace system, a person stands in front of the screen and an internal camera takes a picture. Then the person scans the barcodes of various cosmetics—such as mascara, foundation, eye shadow, blush, and lip gloss—and each automatically appears on the appropriate part of the face. The customer can print out the image, send it by email, or post it on Facebook.

Marketing Pitfall

The automaker Renault avoided a big problem when a French judge ruled that the company could go forward with its plan to release a new electric car named Zoe—even though the two plaintiffs in the case already had the name Zoe Renault. The lawyer who brought the unsuccessful suit argued that the girls would endure a lifetime of grief, as would the other 35,000 people in France who are also named Zoe He claimed, "Can you imagine what little Zoes would have to endure on the playground, and even worse, when they get a little bit older and someone comes up to them in a bar and says, 'Can I see your air bags?' or 'Can I shine your bumper?'"[25]

expectations of others, as a form of *self-fulfilling prophecy*. When we act the way we assume others expect us to act, we often confirm these perceptions.

The Looking-Glass Self

Some clothing stores are testing an interactive mirror that doubles as a high-resolution digital screen. When you choose a garment, the mirror superimposes it on your reflection so that you can see how it would look on your body. A camera relays live images of you modeling your virtual outfit to an Internet site where your friends can log in to instant message (IM) you to tell you what they think; their comments pop up on the side of the mirror for you to read. They can also select virtual items for you to try on that the "magic" mirror will reflect.[28]

Sociologists call the process of imagining others' reactions "taking the role of the other," or the **looking-glass self**.[29] According to this view, our desire to define ourselves operates as a sort of psychological sonar: We take readings of our own identity when we "bounce" signals off others and try to project their impression of us. Like the distorted mirrors in a funhouse, our appraisal of who we are varies depending on whose perspective we consider and how accurately we predict their evaluations of us. A confident career woman may sit morosely at a nightclub, imagining that others see her as a dowdy, unattractive woman with little sex appeal (regardless of whether these perceptions are true). A *self-fulfilling prophecy* like the one we described comes into play here because these "signals" influence the woman's actual behavior. If she doesn't believe she's attractive, she may choose frumpy, unflattering clothing that actually does make her less attractive. The next morning at work, however, her self-confidence at the office may cause her to assume that others hold her "executive self" in even higher regard than they actually do (we all know people like that)!

Self-Consciousness

If you have ever walked into a class in the middle of a lecture and been convinced that all eyes were on you as you awkwardly searched for a seat, you can understand the feeling of *self-consciousness*. In contrast, sometimes we behave with shockingly little self-consciousness. For example, we may do things in a stadium, at a riot, or at a fraternity party that we would never do if we were highly conscious of our behavior (and add insult to injury when we post these escapades to our Facebook page!).[30]

Some people seem to be more sensitive in general to the image they communicate to others. However, we all know people who act as if they're oblivious to the impression they are making. A heightened concern about the nature of one's public "image" also results in more concern about the social appropriateness of products and consumption activities.

Consumers who score high on a scale of *public self-consciousness* express more interest in clothing and use more cosmetics than others who score lower.[31] In one study, highly self-conscious subjects expressed greater willingness to buy personal products, such as a douche or a gas-prevention remedy, that are somewhat embarrassing to buy but may avoid awkward public incidents later.[32]

Similarly, high *self-monitors* are more attuned to how they present themselves in their social environments, and their estimates of how others will perceive their product choices influence what they choose to buy.[33] A scale to measure self-monitoring asks consumers how much they agree with statements such as "I guess I put on a show to impress or entertain others" or "I would probably make a good actor." Perhaps not surprisingly, publicly visible types such as college football players and fashion models tend to score higher on these dimensions.[34]

OBJECTIVE 2
Products often define a person's self-concept.

The Extended Self

As we noted earlier, many of the props and settings consumers use to define their social roles become parts of their selves. Those external objects that we consider a part of us constitute the **extended self**. In some cultures, people literally incorporate objects into the self: they lick new possessions, take the names of conquered enemies (or in some cases eat them), or bury the dead with their possessions.[35]

We don't usually go that far, but some people do cherish possessions as if they were a part of them. In fact, some of us willingly (and perhaps eagerly) label ourselves as *fanatics* about a cherished product.[37] Consider shoes, for example: You don't have to be Carrie of *Sex and the City* fame to acknowledge that many people feel a strong bond to their footwear. One study found that people commonly view their shoes as magical emblems of self, Cinderella-like vehicles for self-transformation. Based on data collected from consumers, the researcher concluded that (like their sister Carrie) women tend to be more attuned to the symbolic implications of shoes than men. A common theme that emerged was that a pair of shoes obtained when younger—whether a first pair of leather shoes, a first pair of high heels, or a first pair of cowboy boots—had a big impact even later in life. These experiences were similar to those that occur in such well-known fairy tales and stories as Dorothy's red shoes in *The Wizard of Oz* (1939), Karen's magical red shoes in Hans Christian Anderson's *The Red Shoes* (1845), and Cinderella's glass slippers.[38]

In addition to shoes, of course, many material objects—ranging from personal possessions and pets to national monuments or landmarks—help to form a consumer's identity. Just about everyone can name a valued possession that has a lot of the self "wrapped up" in it, whether it is a beloved photograph, a trophy, an old shirt, a car, or a cat. Indeed, usually we can construct a pretty accurate "biography" of someone when we simply catalog the items he displays in his bedroom or office. A study illustrates that the product/self doesn't even have to be that strong to influence a consumer's self-concept. In one experiment, researchers approached women in a shopping mall and gave them one of two shopping bags to walk around with for an hour. Women who received a bag from Victoria's Secret later reported to the researchers that they felt more sensual and glamorous. In another experiment, M.B.A. students were asked to take notes for six weeks using a pen embossed with the MIT logo; they reported feeling smarter at the end of the term.[39]

We describe four levels of the extended self, ranging from very personal objects to places and things that allow people to feel as though they are rooted in their larger social environments:[40]

1 **Individual level**—Consumers include many of their personal possessions in self-definition. These products can include jewelry, cars, clothing, and so on. The saying "You are what you wear" reflects the belief that one's things are a part of one's identity.

Net Profit

Many consumers try to bolster their self-esteem as they accumulate evidence of their achievements. In a results-oriented and competitive society, we continue to find ways to trumpet our successes. We display these **badges** by way of car bumper stickers ("My son is an honor student") or even grownup equivalents of the merit badges that the Boy Scouts award. Adults can buy their own Nerd Merit Badges recognizing geeky achievements, including "Open Source" (contribution to an open-source project), "Family Tech Support," or "I Have an Actual Human Skeleton in My Office." When they go online to **geospatial platforms** that use their smartphones to identify their physical locations, consumers earn pins on Gowalla to certify that they've eaten in certain restaurants, or badges on FourSquare that testify to personal qualities such as "Photogenic," "Gossip Girl," or even "Crunked" (for hitting more than four bars in a single night).[36]

A spouse often becomes part of a person's extended self—for better or worse.
Source: Courtesy of Clemenger BBDO.

2 **Family level**—This part of the extended self includes a consumer's residence and the furnishings in it. We can think of the house as a symbolic body for the family, and the place where we live often is a central aspect of who we are.

3 **Community level**—It is common for consumers to describe themselves in terms of the neighborhood or town from which they come. For farm families or other residents with close ties to a community, this sense of belonging is particularly important.

4 **Group level**—We regard our attachments to certain social groups as a part of the self; we'll consider some of these consumer *subcultures* in later chapters. A consumer also may feel that landmarks, monuments, or sports teams are a part of the extended self.

This Italian ad demonstrates that our favorite products are part of the extended self.
Source: Used with permission of Francesco Biasia and D'Adda, Lorenzini, Vigorelli BBDO.

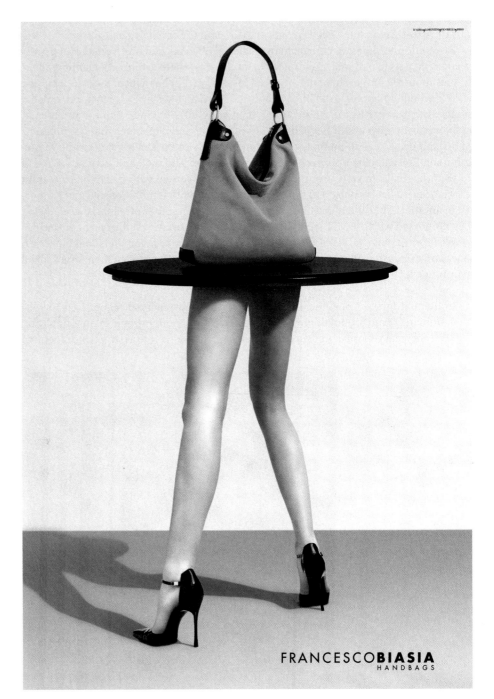

The Digital Self

With new platforms like Microsoft's Kinect that eliminate the need for hand controllers, our online and offline selves will continue to fuse. Already, scientists have been able to transmit the minds of volunteers from their physical bodies to their avatars. In one study, volunteers wore skullcaps that contained electrodes to monitor brain activity while they also wore a set of goggles that showed them as a different body in a virtual world. Researchers found that the subjects started to react as if their avatars were their real bodies.[41]

Earlier in the chapter we discussed the strategic process of *impression management*, where each of us selectively edits the personal cues he or she makes available to others.[42] In our wired world, this process is on steroids. Today we have access to "post-production" tools to engineer our identities. These free or inexpensive applications allow virtually any layman to dramatically modify his or her online persona at will. The ability to master the art of **digital identity management** changes the game as it adds a brand new layer to the extended self.[43] As a result, we also have to consider the existence of a **digital self** that expresses our online identities. Social media theorists use terms like *social footprints* and *lifestreams* to describe this new form of digital identity. A **social footprint** is the mark a consumer leaves after she occupies a specific digital space (e.g., today's Facebook posts), while her **lifestream** is the ongoing record of her digital life across platforms (e.g., registrations in virtual worlds, tweets, blog posts, etc.).

In the influential cyberpunk novel *Snow Crash,* author Neal Stephenson envisioned a virtual world he called the *Metaverse* as a successor to the Internet. In the Metaverse, everyday people take on glamorous identities in a 3-D immersive digital world. The book's main character delivers pizza in real life (RL), but in the Metaverse, he's a warrior prince and champion sword fighter.[44] The hugely popular *Matrix* movie trilogy paints a similar (though more sinister) picture of a world that blurs the lines between physical and digital reality, as did *Avatar* when the hero transformed from a disabled soldier to a 10-foot-tall blue warrior. In a less dramatic context, the clothing chain H&M now uses only virtual models on its Web site. The men and women look extremely realistic, but they are all computer-generated.[45]

Net Profit

One factor that propels consumers' creations of digital selves is the tremendous growth of real-time, interactive virtual worlds that allow us to assume **virtual identities** in cyberspace. More than 11 million people worldwide belong to the virtual world of *Second Life*, more than 8 million play the online game *World of Warcraft*, and the majority of Korean adults belong to *CyWorld*. Add to that the millions more who play *The Sims Online* or who visit other **computer-mediated environments (CMEs)** such as *Webkinz, Habbo, The Sims*, and more than 200 other virtual worlds, and you're looking at a lot of serious role-playing.[46]

On these sites people assume visual identities, or **avatars**, that range from realistic versions of their actual appearance to tricked-out versions with exaggerated physical characteristics or winged dragons or superheroes. Researchers are just starting to investigate how these online selves will influence consumer behavior and how the identities we choose in CMEs relate to our RL identities. Already we know that when people take on avatar forms, they tend to interact with other avatars much as their physical selves interact with other RL people. For example, just as in the RL, males in *Second Life* leave more space between

The popular online role-playing game *The Sims* allows a player to assume a virtual identity.

Source: The Sims 3 image used with permission of Electronic Arts Inc.

TABLE 7.1	The Impact of the Digital Self on Consumer Behavior	
Domain	**Consequences**	**Examples**
Decision making	Proactive information flows to personalize a consumer's access to market information, interactions, and transactions.	● Push technologies (e.g., automated email alerts about prescription medicine schedules).[50] ● Health monitors (e.g., motion sensors in smart homes that detect when an elderly person has fallen; Toto's "Intelligence Toilet" system measures sugar levels in urine, blood pressure, body fat, and weight).[51] ● Smartphone apps customize recipes based on an individual's budget, nutritional objectives, and medical conditions (e.g., Weight Watchers).[52]
Information search	Market fragmentation and personalized search exposes the user to artificially similar standards for social comparison.	● Customized searches only provide results that mesh with the user's predetermined preferences. One writer refers to this constricting process as "the filter bubble."[53]
Shopping	a. Crowdsourcing of purchase options so that product selections (both online and in-store) are made in consultation with a "shadow cabinet" of trusted advisors. b. Vicarious evaluation of product attributes in online shopping environments.	● Thousands of young women post "haul videos" on YouTube that meticulously document clothing they have bought in a recent shopping trip.[54] ● Social shopping sites provide online group feedback on items prior to purchase (e.g., *Fashism, The Fancy, GoTryitOn*).[55] ● Haptic gloves simulate tactile properties of merchandise in digital spaces.[56] ● Augmented reality mirrors allow shoppers to superimpose products on their digital reflections.[57] ● Online personal assistants learn the user's unique preferences over time (e.g., Apple's Siri).
Product usage	Customized products adapt to the individual.	● Pharmacogenetic drugs and DNA sequencing tailor a patient's medication and dosage based on his/her unique genetic blueprint.[58] ● Interactive car windows allow passengers to use them as a whiteboard and augmented reality platform.[59] ● Digitized living room walls encourage the resident to change artwork via touchscreen.[60] ● Smart homes automatically adjust thermostats and lighting.[61]

Source: Adapted from Jagdish N. Sheth and Michael R. Solomon, "Extending the Extended Self in a Digital World," *Journal of Marketing Theory and Practice,* Volume 2, 2014, in press.

them when they talk to other males versus females, and they are less likely to maintain eye contact than females are. When avatars get very close to one another, they tend to look away from each other—the norms of the RL steadily creep into the virtual world.[47] On the other hand, when people take on virtual identities they may behave quite differently, perhaps to compensate for restrictions they live with in their daily lives. One study that tracked the actions of more than 400 people who spent time in an online world reported that 71 percent of male avatars kept between 75 to 100 percent of their bodies covered, while 5 percent of females did.[48]

As our digital selves evolve, these changes mean we have to consider how these new identities impact on consumer decision-making. Table 7.1 summarizes some of these changes.[49]

OBJECTIVE 3
A consumer's personality influences the way he responds to marketing stimuli, but efforts to use this information in marketing contexts meet with mixed results.

Personality

At a party, it's likely that some people will thrust themselves into the spotlight, while other guests lurk on the sidelines—and others avoid these gatherings altogether. Just what makes people act so differently from one another, even when they are in the same social situation? One answer is the concept of **personality**, which refers to a person's unique psychological makeup and how it consistently influences the way a person responds to her environment.

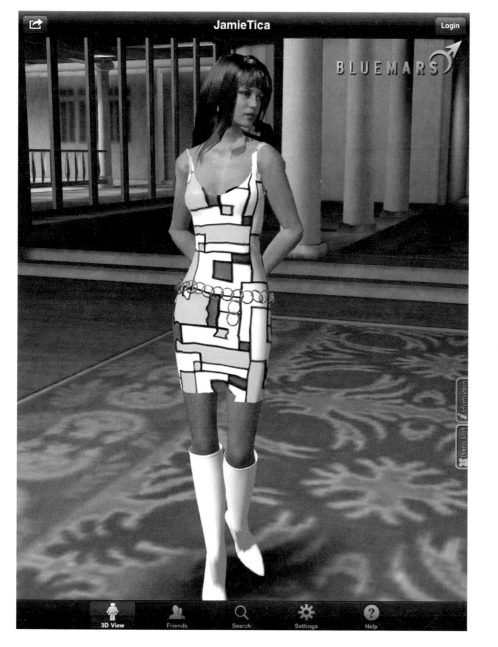

The Hot or Not Web site was an early web sensation when it debuted in 2000, letting you rate how attractive women or men were with a simple voting system. Now Avatar Reality, the maker of the Blue Mars virtual world, lets iPhone users vote on how hot, or not, your avatar is.
Source: Courtesy of Avatar Reality, Inc.

Do all people *have* unique, consistent personalities? Certainly we can wonder about some we meet! Actually, even though the answer seems like a no-brainer, some psychologists argue that the concept of personality may not be valid. Many studies find that people do not seem to exhibit stable personalities. Because people don't necessarily behave the same way in all situations, they argue that this is merely a convenient way to categorize people.

Intuitively, this argument is a bit hard to accept, because we tend to see others in a limited range of situations, and so they *do* appear to act consistently. However, we each know that we ourselves are not all *that* consistent; we may be wild and crazy at times and serious and responsible at others. Although certainly not all psychologists have abandoned the idea of personality, many now recognize that a person's underlying characteristics are but one part of the puzzle, and situational factors often play a very large role in determining behavior.[62] Although we may undergo dramatic changes as we grow up, in adulthood measures of personality stay relatively stable. Studies of thousands of people's scores on the widely used measurement instrument the *Minnesota Multiphasic Personality Inventory (MMPI)* confirm that our personalities tend to stabilize by the age of 30. For example, most of us become less interested in thrill seeking as we focus more on self-discipline. Enjoy it while you can![65]

Consumer Behavior on the Couch: Freudian Theory

The famous psychologist Sigmund Freud proposed that much of one's adult personality stems from a fundamental conflict between a person's desire to gratify her physical needs and the necessity to function as a responsible member of society. This struggle plays out in the mind among three systems. (Note: These systems do *not* refer to physical parts of the brain.) Let's quickly review each.

Freudian Systems

The **id** is about immediate gratification—it is the "party animal" of the mind. It operates according to the **pleasure principle**; that is, our basic desire to maximize pleasure and avoid pain guides our behavior. The id is selfish and illogical. It directs a person's psychic energy toward pleasurable acts without any regard for consequences.

The **superego** is the counterweight to the id. This system is essentially the person's conscience. It internalizes society's rules (especially as parents teach them to us) and tries to prevent the id from seeking selfish gratification. Finally, the **ego** is the system that mediates between the id and the superego. It's basically a referee in the fight between temptation and virtue. The ego tries to balance these opposing forces according to the **reality principle**, which means it finds ways to gratify the id that the outside world will find acceptable. (Hint: This is where Freudian theory applies to marketing.) These conflicts occur on an unconscious level, so the person is not necessarily aware of the underlying reasons for his or her behavior.

How is Freud's work relevant to consumer behavior? In particular, it highlights the potential importance of unconscious motives that guide our purchases. The implication is that consumers cannot necessarily tell us their true motivation when they choose products, even if we can devise a sensitive way to ask them directly. The Freudian perspective also raises the possibility that the ego relies on the symbolism in products to compromise between the demands of the id and the prohibitions of the superego. The person channels her unacceptable desire into acceptable outlets when she uses products that signify these underlying desires. This is the connection between product symbolism and motivation: The product stands for, or represents, a consumer's true goal, which is socially unacceptable or unattainable. By acquiring the product, the person vicariously experiences the forbidden fruit.

"Sometimes a Cigar Is Just a Cigar"

Most Freudian applications in marketing relate to a product's supposed sexual symbolism. For example, some analysts speculate that owning a sports car is a substitute for sexual gratification (especially for men going through a "midlife crisis"). Indeed, some people do seem inordinately attached to their cars, and they may spend many hours lovingly washing and polishing them. An Infiniti ad reinforces the belief that cars symbolically satisfy consumers' sexual needs in addition to their functional ones when it describes one model as "what happens when you cross sheet metal and desire." Other approaches focus on male-oriented symbolism—so-called *phallic symbols*—that appeals to women. Although Freud joked that "sometimes a cigar is just a cigar," many popular applications of Freud's ideas revolve around the use of objects that resemble sex organs (e.g., cigars, trees, or swords for male sex organs; tunnels for female sex organs). This focus stems from Freud's analysis of dreams, which he believed communicate repressed desires in the form of symbolically rich stories.

THE ID | THE SUPEREGO

Crave the party life | Better get to work

Long for a good movie | Better call the office

Thirst for Mozart on CD | Better call the client

Covet caviar canapés | Better write the brief

Yearn for filet mignon | Better make the brief better

Clamor for a liqueur | Better fax the brief

Hunger for Godiva Chocolate | Better E-mail the brief

Desire deep sleep | Better relax, briefly

In conflict? Gratify both sides. Coast to coast.

Work or play. From LAX to New York's JFK. Three-class service. Loaded with options. Nine times a day. From the employee-owners of United. We don't just work here. Come fly our friendly skies.

UNITED AIRLINES

This ad focuses on the conflict between the desire for hedonic gratification (represented by the id) versus the need to engage in rational, task-oriented activities (represented by the superego).

Source: Used with permission of United Airlines.

Motivational Research

In the 1950s, **motivational research** borrowed Freudian ideas to understand the deeper meanings of products and advertisements. This approach adapted psychoanalytical (Freudian) interpretations with a heavy emphasis on unconscious motives. It basically assumed that we channel socially unacceptable needs into acceptable outlets—including product substitutes.

This perspective relies on *depth interviews* with individual consumers. Instead of asking many consumers a few general questions about product usage and combining these responses with those of many other consumers in a representative statistical sample, a motivational researcher talks to only a few people, but probes deeply into each respondent's purchase motivations. A depth interview might take several hours, and it's based on the assumption that the respondent cannot immediately articulate his *latent* or underlying motives. A carefully trained interviewer can derive these only after extensive questioning and interpretation.

| TABLE 7.2 | A Motivational Researcher Identifies Consumption Motives |

Motive	Associated Products
Power-masculinity-virility	Power: Sugary products and large breakfasts (to charge oneself up), bowling, electric trains, hot rods, power tools Masculinity-virility: Coffee, red meat, heavy shoes, toy guns, buying fur coats for women, shaving with a razor
Security	Ice cream (to feel like a loved child again), full drawer of neatly ironed shirts, real plaster walls (to feel sheltered), home baking, hospital care
Eroticism	Sweets (to lick), gloves (to be removed by woman as a form of undressing), a man lighting a woman's cigarette (to create a tension-filled moment culminating in pressure, then relaxation)
Moral purity-cleanliness	White bread, cotton fabrics (to connote chastity), harsh household cleaning chemicals (to make housewives feel moral after using), bathing (to be equated with Pontius Pilate, who washed blood from his hands), oatmeal (sacrifice, virtue)
Social acceptance	Companionship: Ice cream (to share fun), coffee, Love and affection: Toys (to express love for children), sugar and honey (to express terms of affection) Acceptance: Soap, beauty products
Individuality	Gourmet foods, foreign cars, cigarette holders, vodka, perfume, fountain pens
Status	Scotch: ulcers, heart attacks, indigestion (to show one has a high-stress, important job!), carpets (to show one does not live on bare earth like peasants)
Femininity	Cakes and cookies, dolls, silk, tea, household curios
Reward	Cigarettes, candy, alcohol, ice cream, cookies
Mastery over environment	Kitchen appliances, boats, sporting goods, cigarette lighters
Disalienation (a desire to feel connectedness to things)	Home decorating, skiing, morning radio broadcasts (to feel "in touch" with the world)
Magic-mystery	Soups (having healing powers), paints (change the mood of a room), carbonated drinks (magical effervescent property), vodka (romantic history), unwrapping of gifts

Source: Adapted from Jeffrey F. Durgee, "Interpreting Dichter's Interpretations: An Analysis of Consumption Symbolism," in The Handbook of Consumer Motivation, Marketing and Semiotics: Selected Papers from the Copenhagen Symposium, eds. Hanne Hartvig-Larsen, David Glen Mick, and Christian Alstead (Copenhagen, 1991).

Ernest Dichter, a psychoanalyst who trained with Freud's disciples in Vienna in the early part of the 20th century, pioneered this work. Dichter conducted in-depth interview studies on more than 230 different products, and actual marketing campaigns incorporated many of his findings.[66] For example, Esso (now Exxon in the United States) for many years reminded consumers to "Put a Tiger in Your Tank" after Dichter found that people responded well to this powerful animal symbolism containing vaguely sexual undertones. Table 7.2 provides a summary of major consumption motivations he identified.

Some critics reacted to the motivational studies that ad agencies conducted in much the same way they did to subliminal perception studies (see Chapter 5). They charged that this approach gave advertisers the power to manipulate consumers.[67] However, many consumer researchers felt the research lacked sufficient rigor and validity because the interpretations are so subjective.[68] Because the analyst bases his conclusions on his own judgment after he interviews a small number of people, critics were dubious about whether the findings would generalize to a larger market. In addition, because the original motivational researchers were heavily influenced by orthodox Freudian theory, their interpretations usually involved sexual themes. This emphasis tends to overlook other plausible causes for behavior. Still, motivational research had great appeal to at least some marketers for several reasons:

- Motivational research is less expensive to conduct than large-scale, quantitative survey data collection because interviewing and data-processing costs are relatively minimal.
- The knowledge a company derives from motivational research may help it develop marketing communications that appeal to deep-seated needs and thus provide a more powerful hook to reel in consumers. Even if they are not necessarily valid for all consumers in a target market, these insights can still be valuable to an advertiser who wants to create copy that will resonate with customers.
- Some of the findings seem intuitively plausible after the fact. For example, motivational studies concluded that we associate coffee with companionship, that we avoid prunes because they remind us of old age, and that men fondly equate the first car they owned as an adolescent with the onset of their sexual freedom.

Other interpretations were hard for some researchers to swallow, such as the observation that women equate the act of baking a cake with birth, or that men are reluctant to give blood because they feel it drains their vital fluids. However, we do sometimes say a pregnant woman has "a bun in the oven," and Pillsbury claims that "nothing says lovin' like something from the oven." When the Red Cross hired motivational researcher Dichter to boost blood donation rates, he reported that men (but not women) tended to drastically overestimate the amount of blood they gave. As a result, the Red Cross counteracted men's fear of losing their virility when the organization symbolically equated the act of giving blood with fertilizing a female egg: "Give the gift of life." Despite its drawbacks, some ad agencies today still use some forms of motivational research. The approach is most useful, however, when we use it as an exploratory technique to provide insights that inform more rigorous research approaches.

Neo-Freudian Theories

Freud's work had a huge influence on subsequent theories of personality. Although he opened the door to the realization that explanations for behavior may lurk beneath the surface, many of his colleagues and students felt that an individual's personality is more influenced by how he handles relationships with others than by how he resolves sexual conflicts. We call these theorists *neo-Freudian* (meaning following from or being influenced by Freud).

Karen Horney

One of the most prominent neo-Freudians was Karen Horney. This pioneering psychotherapist described people as moving toward others (*compliant*), away from others (*detached*), or against others (*aggressive*).[69] Indeed, one early study found that compliant people are more likely to gravitate toward name-brand products, detached types are more likely to be tea drinkers, and males the researchers classified as aggressive preferred brands with a strong masculine orientation (e.g., Old Spice deodorant).[70] Other well-known neo-Freudians include Alfred Adler, who proposed that a prime motivation is to overcome feelings of inferiority relative to others; and Harry Stack Sullivan, who focused on how personality evolves to reduce anxiety in social relationships.[71]

Carl Jung

Carl Jung was also one of Freud's disciples. However, Jung didn't accept Freud's emphasis on sexual aspects of personality. He went on to develop his own method of psychotherapy that he called *analytical psychology*. Jung believed that the cumulative experiences of past generations shape who we are today. He proposed that we each share a *collective unconscious,* a storehouse of memories we inherit from our ancestors. For example, Jung would argue that many people are afraid of the dark because their distant ancestors had good reason to fear it. These shared memories create **archetypes**, or universally recognized ideas and behavior patterns. Archetypes involve themes, such as birth, death, or the devil, that appear frequently in myths, stories, and dreams.

Jung's ideas may seem a bit far-fetched, but advertising messages do in fact often include archetypes. For example, some of the archetypes Jung and his followers identified include the "old wise man" and the "earth mother."[72] These images appear frequently in marketing messages that feature characters such as wizards, revered teachers, or even Mother Nature. Our culture's current infatuation with stories such as *Harry Potter* and *The Lord of the Rings* speaks to the power of these images—to say nothing of the "wizard" who helps you repair your laptop.

Young & Rubicam (Y&R), a major advertising agency, uses the archetype approach in its BrandAsset® Archetypes model, as depicted in Figure 7.1. The model proposes healthy relationships among Archetypes as well as unhealthy ones. A healthy personality is one in which the *Archetypes* overwhelm their corresponding *Shadows*; a sick personality results when one or more Shadows prevail. When a brand's Shadows dominate, this cues the agency to take action to guide the brand to a healthier personality, much as one would try to counsel a psychologically ill person.[73]

A second, similar approach that applies archetype theory to brand personality employs a typology of 12 brand archetypes. This perspective draws upon theories of human motivation to create two sets of contrasts: belonging/people versus independence/self-actualization, and risk/mastery versus stability/control:[74] Table 7.3 summarizes some of these archetype/brand relationships.

Trait Theory

Popular online matchmaking services such as match.com and eharmony.com offer to create your "personality profile" and then hook you up with other members whose profiles are similar. This approach to personality focuses on the quantitative measurement of **personality traits**, which we define as the identifiable characteristics that define a person.

What are some crucial personality traits? One is that we tend to describe people in terms of whether they are socially outgoing (the trait of *extroversion*).[76] Some research evidence suggests that ad messages that match how a person thinks about himself are more persuasive.[77]

Another trait relevant to consumer behavior is *frugality*. Frugal people deny short-term purchasing whims; they choose instead to resourcefully use what they already own. For example, this personality type tends to favor cost-saving measures such as timing showers and bringing leftovers from home to have for lunch at work.[78] Obviously, during tough economic times many people reveal their "inner frugalista" as they search for ways to save money. Indeed, as the Great Recession invaded, Google searches for the term *frugality* increased by roughly 2,500 percent. Whereas many of us splurged on expensive cars or Jimmy Choo shoes (or both) in the past, many analysts predict that more of us will be frugal down the road, even if/when the economy improves. They expect to see us buy smaller houses and (gasp!) live within our means as we forsake heavy credit card debt. How accurate is this prediction? Maybe the answer depends on how many of us truly have frugal personality traits versus those who are merely "taking a break" until the economy improves.

According to the research firm Mindset Media, personality traits are better predictors of the type of media consumers choose than are demographic variables such as age, gender, and income. The company also claims that the TV shows you watch offer marketers insights into your personality and the types of brands you're likely to prefer, based upon your dominant personality traits and the (perceived) matchup with

Figure 7.1 BRANDASSET VALUATOR® ARCHETYPES

Characteristics

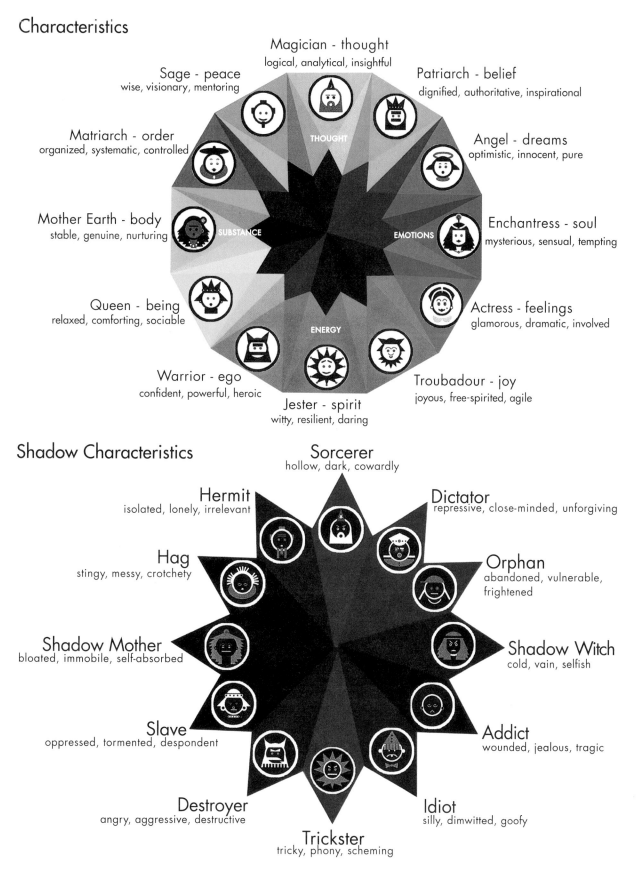

Magician - thought
logical, analytical, insightful

Sage - peace
wise, visionary, mentoring

Patriarch - belief
dignified, authoritative, inspirational

Matriarch - order
organized, systematic, controlled

Angel - dreams
optimistic, innocent, pure

Mother Earth - body
stable, genuine, nurturing

Enchantress - soul
mysterious, sensual, tempting

Queen - being
relaxed, comforting, sociable

Actress - feelings
glamorous, dramatic, involved

Warrior - ego
confident, powerful, heroic

Troubadour - joy
joyous, free-spirited, agile

Jester - spirit
witty, resilient, daring

THOUGHT

SUBSTANCE

EMOTIONS

ENERGY

Shadow Characteristics

Sorcerer
hollow, dark, cowardly

Hermit
isolated, lonely, irrelevant

Dictator
repressive, close-minded, unforgiving

Hag
stingy, messy, crotchety

Orphan
abandoned, vulnerable, frightened

Shadow Mother
bloated, immobile, self-absorbed

Shadow Witch
cold, vain, selfish

Slave
oppressed, tormented, despondent

Addict
wounded, jealous, tragic

Destroyer
angry, aggressive, destructive

Idiot
silly, dimwitted, goofy

Trickster
tricky, phony, scheming

Source: BrandAsset® Consulting: A Young & Rubican Brands Company.

TABLE 7.3   Mark and Pearson Brand Archetypes

Archetype	Description	Example Brands	As Consumers
Yearning for Paradise			
"Innocent" **Core desire:** Experience paradise **Goal:** To be happy **Fear:** Doing wrong **Strategy:** Do things right	The promise of the Innocent is that life does not need to be hard. The Innocent is extraordinarily attractive in this hectic, stressful age because it promises that you can get out of the fast lane and truly enjoy your life.	Innocent brands include movie stars: Reese Witherspoon, Meg Ryan, Tom Hanks, the movies *Baby Boom, Forrest Gump,* and *Local Hero.* Other innocent brands are the PBS network, Keds, Disney, Ronald McDonald, and Baskin-Robbins. Such brands promise that life can be simple, uncomplicated, and good.	Innocent consumers generally like to find brands they can trust and stick to, believing that "if it ain't broke, don't fix it." Innocent archetypes also like brands and products that make life simple; for example, products such as user-friendly computers.
"Explorer" **Core desire:** Freedom **Goal:** To experience a better, more authentic and fulfilling life **Fear:** Becoming trapped **Strategy:** Journey, seek out, and explore	The Explorer, by nature, goes out seeking a better world. The journey Explorers are experiencing is simultaneously inner and outer, because they are motivated by a deep desire to find what in the outer world fits with their inner needs. Their motto is: "Don't fence me in."	Great Exploring brand literature includes: *The Adventures of Huckleberry Finn, The Great Gatsby,* and *The Invisible Man.* Explorer brand television shows include *Survivor* and *Star Trek.* Branded products that serve the Explorers' needs include: Jeep Wrangler and The North Face.	Explorers are independent minded and curious. This archetype likes to try new things, so to gain their loyalty it is important to provide continual novelty and improvements in products. For example, many software companies such as Microsoft and IBM have this down pat.
"Sage" **Core desire:** The discovery of truth **Goal:** Use intelligence and analysis to understand the world **Fear:** Being duped, misled, or ignored **Strategy:** Seek out information and knowledge and become self-reflective	Sage archetypes have their own way of finding paradise. Their faith is in the capacity of humankind to learn and grow in ways that allow us to create a better world. In the process, they want to be free to think for themselves and to hold their own opinions. They are also known as expert scholars. Their motto is: "The truth will set you free."	Sage brands include: Harvard University, high-end consulting firms such as McKinsey and Arthur Andersen, and Google. Famous Sage personalities include: Al Gore, Albert Einstein, Oprah Winfrey, and Morgan Freeman.	Sage archetypes like to have all the relevant information they need to make informed decisions about brands. These types of consumers also enjoy learning, so products that require a learning curve (for example, computers) appeal to them. The Sage consumer, as with the Innocent and the Explorer, emphasize self over others and autonomy over belonging.
Leaving a Thumbprint on the World			
"Hero" **Core desire:** To prove worth through courageous action **Goal:** Exert mastery in a way that improves the world **Fear:** Weakness, vulnerability, and wimping out **Strategy:** Become strong and competent	Everything seems lost . . . but then the Hero rides over the hill and saves the day. The Hero triumphs over evil, adversity, and challenges; in doing so, the Hero inspires others. Heroes are ambitious and seek out challenges. The Hero generally wants to make the world a better place. Their motto is: "Where there is a will, there's a way."	Hero brands include: the Marines, the Olympics, the NASA space program, Nike, Red Cross, and Under Armour. Hero movies include: *Star Wars* and *Saving Private Ryan.* Famous Heroes include: Martin Luther King, Nelson Mandela, John F. Kennedy, and Superman.	Hero consumers expect companies, and indeed brands, to articulate their values, mission, and vision in a clear way. Increasingly, Hero consumers expect those corporate visions to reflect some sense of social responsibility. Heroes evaluate brands and companies not just on the quality of the product or service but also on the strengths and ethics of the firm's convictions.

TABLE 7.3 (continued)

Archetype	Description	Example Brands	As Consumers
"Outlaw" **Core desire:** Revenge or revolution **Goal:** To destroy what is not working **Fear:** Being powerless **Strategy:** Disrupt, destroy, or shock	The Outlaw has the enticement of forbidden fruit. People who give up on getting what they want in a healthy and socially acceptable way may turn to illegal or unethical strategies in order to prevail. The Outlaw's motto is: "Rules are meant to be broken."	Outlaw brands include: MTV, ABC, NBC, CBS, Jack Daniels, Southern Comfort, *Rolling Stone*, Harley-Davidson, and Mick Jagger. Famous Outlaw movies include: *The Godfather, Bonnie and Clyde,* and *Scarface.*	The Outlaw in each of us wants to get away with things. Therefore, slash-and-burn sales are great marketing strategies that are likely to appeal to Outlaws. Outlaws are attracted to edgy product images that are dark, shadowy, and feature intense colours.
"Magician" **Core desire:** Knowledge of fundamental laws and how the world works **Goal:** Make dreams come true **Fear:** Unanticipated negative consequences **Strategy:** Develop vision and live it	Most basic to the Magician is the desire to search out the fundamental laws of how things work and to apply these principles to getting things done. The most typical applications of magical lore are to heal the mind, heart, and body; to find the fountain of youth and the secret of longevity. Or to invent products to make things happen. The Magician's motto is: "It can happen."	Magician brands include all those that foster "magical moments": Sony, Google, Moët and Chandon, Verve Clicquot, MasterCard, and Disney. Television shows characterized by the Magician include: *City of Angels, Touched by an Angel,* and *Seventh Heaven.*	As customers, Magicians believe that who you are is as important as the quality of your products or services. You are always, therefore, selling yourself, your values, and your own consciousness when marketing to Magicians. Magicians are motivated by personal transformation; therefore, firms offering transformative experiences will appeal most to Magicians.

No Man Is an Island

Archetype	Description	Example Brands	As Consumers
"Regular Guy/Gal" **Core desire:** Connection with others **Goal:** To belong and fit in **Fear:** Standing out, seeming to put out airs, and being exiled or rejected as a result **Strategy:** Develop ordinary solid virtues and to blend in	This archetype demonstrates the virtues of simply being an ordinary person, just like others. The Regular Guy/Gal archetype is an active individual, usually dressing in working-class or otherwise ordinary attire and speaking in colloquial ways. The Regular Guy/Gal is the fundamental archetype for democracy. Their motto is: "All men and women are created equal."	Regular Guy/Gal brands include: VISA, Target, Sizzler, and Toyota. Films celebrating the Regular Guy/Gal ethos include: *The Full Monty, Local Hero,* and *Raising Ned Devine.*	Logos can be linked to status. To the Explorer, the logo may be a statement of identity. To the Regular Guy/Gal, the logo or brand is a means of affiliating a way of demonstrating one's connection with others who use that product and identify with its brand meaning. The Regular Guy/Gal archetype image is middle-class. These consumers prefer connections with people in order for brand loyalty to be increased.
"Lover" **Core desire:** Attain intimacy and experience sensual pleasure **Goal:** Being in a relationship with people **Fear:** Being alone, a wall-flower unwanted and unloved **Strategy:** Become more and more attractive physically, emotionally, and in every other way	The Lover archetype governs all sorts of love, from parental love, to friendship, to spiritual love, but most important is romantic love. The Lover is always active in intense and personal friendships. Lovers think of themselves as being wonderfully appreciative of others. They also typically dislike competition. This can often lead to jealousy and mean-spirited behavior. The Lover's motto is: "I only have eyes for you."	Lover brands include: Coco Chanel, Christian Dior, The Body Shop, Revlon, Godiva, Victoria's Secret, Hallmark, and Häagen Dazs. Lover archetypes in movies include: *Titanic, Pretty Woman,* and *Casablanca.* Famous Lover people include: Sofia Vergara, Sophia Loren, Elizabeth Taylor, and George Clooney.	The Lover wants a deeper kind of connection—one that is intimate, genuine, and personal (sometimes also sensual). Lovers often identify products with certain relationships. Lovers develop deep relationships with products and companies, especially those that help them feel special and loved. These types of consumers also like being singled out for attention; for example: "mailing to special customers only."

(continued)

TABLE 7.3 (continued)

Archetype	Description	Example Brands	As Consumers
"Jester" **Core desire:** To live in the moment with full enjoyment **Goal:** To have a great time and lighten up the world **Fear:** Boredom and being boring **Strategy:** Play, make jokes, and be funny	The Jester archetype includes: the clown, the trickster, and anyone at all who loves to play or act up. While it is possible to have fun on our own, the Jester calls us out to come and play with one another. Jester figures enjoy life and interaction for their own sake. They also love being the life of the party! The Jester's motto is: "If I can't dance, I don't want to be a part of your revolution."	Jester brands include: M&Ms, Snickers, Skittles, Pringles, Coke, Pepsi, and Bud Light. Famous Jester people include: Robin Williams, Johnny Carson, Chris Rock, and Will Smith.	The Jester in every one of us loves humor. Jesters like funny commercials because they entertain them and make them feel good, creating a halo effect around the product. Jester ads and packaging highlight bright colors and lots of action—the more outrageous, the better. Overall, the Jester loves the fun of marketing. They are not frightened by knowing we are in a new time.
Providing Structure to the World			
"Caregiver" **Core desire:** Protect people from harm **Goal:** To help others **Fear:** Selfishness and ingratitude **Strategy:** Do things for others	The Caregiver is an altruist, moved by compassion, generosity, and a desire to help others. The Caregiver fears instability and difficulty not so much for themselves but for others. Their worst fear could be something happening to their mothers. Generally speaking, the Caregiver's motto is: "Love your neighbor as yourself."	Caregiver brands include: Campbell's Soup, Avon, Hallmark, and Weight Watchers. Famous Caregivers include: Princess Diana, Mother Teresa, Florence Nightingale, and Angelina Jolie. Famous Caregiver television shows and movies include: *Sesame Street*, *Mrs. Doubtfire*, and *The First Wives Club*.	One of the least effective ways to market to Caregivers is to tell them straight out that you care. Caregivers are often cynical about these statements. Caregivers instead react better to emotive statements. The Caregiver is also related to the Innocent.
"Creator" **Core desire:** Create something of enduring value **Goal:** Give form to a vision **Fear:** Having a mediocre vision or execution **Strategy:** Develop artistic skill and control	"If it can be imagined, it can be created" is the motto of the Creator. The Creator archetype is often seen in the artist, the writer, the innovator, and the entrepreneur. The Creator's passion is self-expression in material form. They are often compelled to create or innovate—anything else and they feel stifled. They can also express creativity in their clothing, their homes, and their offices.	Creative brands are nonconformist. These brands include: Crayola, Martha Stewart, and M.A.C cosmetics. Famous Creators include Sir Richard Branson (CEO of Virgin) and Steve Jobs.	Creators love brands that help them create and release the Creator within. Any kind of artistic product will satisfy the creator. It is important for businesses communicating with Creators to see advertising and marketing communication as an art form.
"Ruler" **Core desire:** Control **Goal:** Create a prosperous, successful family, company, or community **Fear:** Chaos and being over-thrown **Strategy:** Exert leadership	When you imagine the Ruler archetype, think of the King and Queen, CEOs, or the president of a country. The Ruler lives and breathes the motto: "Power isn't everything. It's the only thing." The Ruler knows the best thing to do to avoid chaos is to take control.	Ruler brands include: Microsoft, Citibank, Cadillac, and Brooks Brothers. Famous Rulers include: Mark Zuckerberg (Facebook), Queen Elizabeth II, and Bill Gates.	Rulers like control. But, they do not like being told what to do. Ideally, the brand strategy, brand promise, brand essence, character, and personality should be well thought out and articulated in writing before it is communicated with Rulers (as in with all the archetypes).

Source: Adapted from: Michael R. Solomon, Rebekah Russell-Bennett, and Josephine Previte, *Consumer Behaviour: Buying, Having, Being,* 3rd ed., Frenchs Forest, NSW: Pearson Australia, 2012.

After elfa
The same space — with the same contents — is transformed into a well-functioning and beautiful closet!

Your design is customized to suit your unique storage needs.

Real wood accents add warmth to your space.

All of the vertical space is used to create additional storage.

Shoes are organized, easy to access and take up little space.

You have visibility to what you've stored, which saves time.

The Container Store®   containerstore.com | 800.733.3532

Products like these from a German company appeal to people who like to be well-organized.
Source: Photo provided courtesy of The Container Store.

a brand's image. To find out which personalities are attracted to which TV shows, it recently analyzed self-reported data from about 25,000 TV viewers across more than 70 TV shows. These are some of the media/trait/brand linkages the company generated in its analysis:[79]

- Viewers of *Mad Men* are emotionally sensitive and intellectually curious types who often tend to be dreamers rather than realists. Good brand matches are Apple and the Audi A6.
- Viewers of *Family Guy* are rebels who don't like authority, rules, or structure they deem unfair, and usually won't hesitate to make their feelings known with anger or sarcasm. Good brand matches are DiGiorno and the Ford F150.
- Viewers of *Glee* are open people who believe that imagination and intellectual pursuits contribute to a good life, and go out in search of unique and varied experiences. They are in touch with their own feelings and may even feel happiness or sadness more intensely than others. Good brand matches are Evian and the Volkswagen Jetta.
- Viewers of *Dancing with the Stars* are traditionalists who prefer stability and the tried-and-true. They respect authority and generally have their feet firmly grounded. Good brand matches are Kraft and the Chrysler Town and Country.

● Viewers of *The Office* consider themselves superior to others and like to brag about their accomplishments. They also like to be in charge. Good brand matches are Starbucks and the BMW Series 3.

The Big Five

The most widely recognized approach to measuring personality traits is the so-called **Big Five** (also known as the Neo-Personality Inventory). This is a set of five dimensions that form the basis of personality: openness to experience, conscientiousness, extroversion, agreeableness, and neuroticism. Table 7.4 describes these dimensions.

The **Myers-Briggs Type Indicator**, which is based on Carl Jung's work, is another widely used personality test. When you apply for a job it is quite possible your potential employer will ask you to take this test. The Myers-Briggs classifies people into 16 categories based upon whether they fall into one group or another on these dimensions:[80]

1 Focus of attention
   Introversion: Internal focus
   Extraversion: External focus
2 Information processing
   Sensing: Take in information in a sequential, step-by-step manner
   Intuition: Take in information in a snapshot or big-picture manner
3 Decision-making
   Thinking: Make decisions by stepping back from a situation and taking an objective view
   Feeling: Make decisions by stepping into a situation and taking a subjective view
4 Dealing with the outer world
   Judging: A systematic approach to meeting deadlines and achieving objectives
   Perceiving: A spontaneous approach to meeting deadlines and achieving objectives with a sudden rush of activity

TABLE 7.4   Description of Big Five Personality Dimensions

	Description	Example of Measurement Items (agree/disagree)
Openness to experience	The degree to which a person is open to new ways of doing things	Love to think up new ways of doing things
Conscientiousness	The level of organization and structure a person needs	Am always prepared
Extroversion	How well a person tolerates stimulation from people	Talk to a lot of different people at parties
Agreeableness	The degree to which we defer to other people	Take time out for others
Neuroticism (emotional instability)	How well a person copes with stress	Get upset easily

Source: Michael R. Solomon, Rebekah Russell-Bennett, and Josephine Previte, *Consumer Behaviour: Buying, Having, Being*, 3rd ed., Frenchs Forest, NSW: Pearson Australia, 2012.

The publishers of the Myers-Briggs test also relate these dimensions to social media usage. For example, they report that people who use platforms such as Facebook, Twitter, and LinkedIn are more likely to be Extraverts, use Intuition, and arrive at decisions by Thinking.[81]

Problems with Trait Theory in Consumer Research

Because consumer researchers categorize large numbers of consumers according to whether they exhibit various traits, we can apply this approach to segment markets. If a car manufacturer, for example, determines that drivers who fit a given trait profile prefer a car with certain features, it can use this information to great advantage. The notion that consumers buy products that are extensions of their personalities makes intuitive sense. As we'll see shortly, many marketing managers endorse this idea as they try to create *brand personalities* to appeal to different types of consumers.

Unfortunately, the use of standard personality trait measurements to predict product choices has met with mixed success at best. In general, marketing researchers simply have not been able to predict consumers' behaviors on the basis of measured personality traits. These are some logical explanations for these less-than-stellar results:[82]

- Many of the scales are not sufficiently valid or reliable; they do not adequately measure what they are supposed to measure, and their results may not be stable over time.
- Psychologists typically develop personality tests for specific populations (e.g., people who are mentally ill); marketers then "borrow" them to apply to a more general population where they have questionable relevance.
- Often marketers don't administer the tests under the appropriate conditions; people who are not properly trained may give them in a classroom or at a kitchen table.
- The researchers often make changes in the instruments to adapt them to their own situations and needs; in the process, they may add or delete items and rename variables. These *ad hoc* changes dilute the validity of the measures and also reduce researchers' ability to compare results across consumer samples.
- Many trait scales measure gross, overall tendencies (e.g., emotional stability or introversion); marketers then use these results to make predictions about purchases of specific brands.
- In many cases, marketers ask consumers to respond to a large number of scales with no advance thought about how they will relate these measures to consumer behavior. The researchers then use a "shotgun approach," as they follow up on anything that happens to look interesting. As any statistician will tell you, this approach capitalizes on chance and can produce distorted results that may not be reproducible (or surface at all) in other studies.

Although marketing researchers largely abandoned the use of personality measures after many studies failed to yield meaningful results, some researchers have not given up on the early promise of this line of work. More recent efforts (mainly in Europe) try to learn from past mistakes. Researchers use more specific measures of personality traits that they have reason to believe are relevant to economic behavior. They try to increase the validity of these measures, primarily by including multiple measures of behavior rather than just a single personality scale. In addition, these researchers tone down their expectations of what personality traits can tell them about consumers. They now recognize that traits are only part of the solution; they have to incorporate personality data with information about people's social and economic conditions for it to be useful.[83] As a result, some more recent research has had better success at relating personality traits to such consumer behaviors as alcohol consumption among young men or shoppers' willingness to try new, healthier food products.[84] Table 7.5 provides some examples of consumer research studies that tie personality traits to product purchase and use.

| TABLE 7.5 | Lifestyle Dimensions |

Personality Trait	Influence on Consumer Behavior
Superstition	Sports fan behavior such as "lucky socks," the direction of one's cap on the head, purchase of good luck charms, refusal to purchase particular items because of bad luck (i.e., opals, peacock feathers, apricots)
Pro-environment	Individual recycling efforts, decreased car usage, increased use of public transport
Romanticism	Movie genre choice, more likely to take risks, prefer warm countries to visit, prefer luxury travel
Willingness to spend money	Spendthrifts save less money and carry more debt than tightwads, so they are higher users of credit cards; more likely to buy hedonic items than tightwads
Enjoyment of shopping	People who enjoy shopping are more likely to spend time searching for products, resulting in increased product knowledge
Need for cognition (enjoyment of thinking)	People who enjoy thinking respond better to words than pictures and are more motivated to spend time processing the words and reading the "fine print."
Need for affect (enjoyment of processing feelings)	People who enjoy feelings respond better to pictures than words; more likely to engage in compulsive behavior; pictures may encourage impulse buying
Impulsiveness	More likely to experience pleasure than guilt when overeating
Need for uniqueness	People who want to "stand out from the crowd" tend to be opinion leaders; they are more likely to be sources of information about brands and products for other people
Susceptibility to interpersonal influence (how influenced a person is by another)	A person who is easily influenced by others is more likely to prefer wines that offer social benefits such as prestige
Self-consciousness	People who are concerned with the way they appear to others are less likely to complain directly to a business or in front of others
Extroversion	Extroverts experience more positive emotions when consuming
Neuroticism	Neurotic people are less likely to repurchase or complain (they just leave), regardless of their level of satisfaction

Source: Michael R. Solomon, Rebekah Russell-Bennett, and Josephine Previte, *Consumer Behaviour: Buying, Having, Being*, 3rd ed., Frenchs Forest, NSW: Pearson Australia, 2012.[85]

OBJECTIVE 4
Brands have personalities.

Brand Personality

Are Apple users better than the rest of us? Many of us know an "Apple-holic" who likes to turn up his or her nose at the uneducated masses that have to get by with their primitive PCs or Android phones. In fact, a survey of 20,000 people claims that iPad users are unkind and have little empathy; it labels them a "selfish elite." It also described them as "six times more likely to be wealthy, well-educated, power-hungry, over-achieving, sophisticated, unkind and non-altruistic 30- to 50-year-olds. They are self-centered workaholics with an overwhelming interest in business and finance who cherish 'power and achievement' and will not cross the street to help others."[86] Ouch! That's a pretty harsh way to describe people who happen to gravitate toward a successful brand. Do products as well as their owners actually have personalities? Let's step back to explore this intriguing question.

In 1886, a momentous event occurred in marketing history: The Quaker Oats man first appeared on boxes of hot cereal. Quakers had a reputation in 19th-century America for being shrewd but fair, and peddlers sometimes dressed as members of this religious group to cash in on their credibility. When the cereal company

Personality Traits		Low	High
Sincerity	Down-to-earth Honest Wholesome Cheerful		
Excitement	Daring Spirited Imaginative Up-to-date		
Competence	Reliable Intelligent Successful		
Sophistication	Upper class Charming		
Ruggedness	Outdoorsy Tough		

A study found that consumers infer strong differences in a wine's "personality" based on the bottle's label design.

Source: Reprinted with permission from *Journal of Marketing*, published by the American Marketing Association, Ulrich R. Orth & Keven Malkewitz, May 2008, Vol. 72, p. 73.

decided to "borrow" this imagery for its packages, it hoped customers might make the same association.[87]

Today, thousands of brands also borrow personality traits of individuals or groups to convey an image they want customers to form of them. A **brand personality** is the set

Even colleges have brand personalities—though, as with other products, these images aren't always an accurate (or desirable) reflection of the place. ESPN had to pull the plug on an advertising campaign for its collegiate basketball coverage after managers learned that Anomaly, the advertising agency ESPN had retained for the campaign, intended to recruit actors who would play the stereotypical students at numerous schools. The idea was to have the students stationed at a call center; they would phone consumers to convince them to watch their school play on TV. Here are just a few of the "brand personalities" a leaked memo described:

- Tennessee: "a slutty girl who would hang out at the cowgirl hall of fame."
- Duke: "a smart, with it, young white male. He's handsome. He's from money. He is, in short, the kind of guy everyone can't stand. He is the kind of guy everyone wants to be."
- Oklahoma: "is awesome and he thinks everything is awesome. He's very enthusiastic about all things call center and all things life and he wants to share this contagious enthusiasm with everyone he meets. Wide-eyed, as naive as they come."
- Purdue: "child prodigy. 14-year-old. Or open to an 18-year-old who looks 14. Aeronautical engineering. Wiz kid. Think McLovin from *Superbad*."
- Kansas: "straight off the farm. However, he takes great pains to point out that Kansas is very cosmopolitan, as witnessed by their record, their burgeoning tech industry, and their hybrid corns (bonus: modified by fish genes!)."
- Villanova: "the poor man's Duke—he's not quite as handsome, he's not quite as rich, he's not quite as dapper. After 2 or 3 beers though, who cares? . . . he's friendly enough."
- Pittsburgh: "a tomboy. She obviously grew up in the neighborhood and isn't going to take any guff from anyone and she'll wallop you in the eye with a crowbar if you suggest different. So don't. Think Tina Fey type."
- Georgetown: "a 4.36 GPA who's lived in 9 world-class cities, but all the time in her sister's shadow (her GPA is 4.37). She's sort of the female Duke, except most people like her. Think Reese Witherspoon."[90]

of traits people attribute to a product as if it were a person.[88] An advertising agency wrote the following memo to help it figure out how to portray one of its clients. Based on this description of the "client," can you guess who he is? "He is creative . . . unpredictable . . . an imp. . . . He not only walks and talks, but has the ability to sing, blush, wink, and work with little devices like pointers. . . . He can also play musical instruments. . . . His walking motion is characterized as a 'swagger.' . . . He is made of dough and has mass."[89] Of course, we all know today that packaging and other physical cues create a "personality" for a product (in this case, the Pillsbury Doughboy).

Anthropomorphism refers to the tendency to attribute human characteristics to objects or animals. We may think about a cartoon character or mythical creation as if it were a person and even assume that it has human feelings. Again, consider familiar spokescharacters such as the Cheetah from Pringles, the Keebler Elves, or the Michelin Man—or the frustration some people feel when they come to believe their computer is smarter than they are or even that it's "conspiring" to make them crazy! In research for its client Sprint Business Services, Grey Advertising found that when customers imagined long-distance carriers as animals, they envisioned AT&T as a lion, MCI as a snake, and Sprint as a puma. Grey used these results to position Sprint as a company that could "help you do more business" rather than taking the more aggressive approach of its competitors.[91]

In a sense, a brand personality is a statement about the brand's market position. Understanding this is crucial to marketing strategy, especially if consumers don't see the brand the way its makers intend them to and they must attempt to *reposition* the product (i.e., give it a personality makeover). That's the problem Volvo now faces: Its cars are renowned for safety, but drivers don't exactly see them as exciting or sexy. A safe and solid brand personality makes it hard to sell a racy convertible like the C70 model, so a British ad tried to change that perception with the tagline, "Lust, envy, jealousy. The dangers of a Volvo." Just as with people, however, you can only go so far to convince others that your personality has changed. Volvo has been trying to jazz up its image for years, but for the most part consumers aren't buying it. In an earlier attempt in the United Kingdom, the company paired action images like a Volvo pulling a helicopter off a cliff with the headline "Safe Sex"—but market research showed that people didn't believe the new image. As one brand consultant observed, "You get the sort of feeling you get when you see your grandparents trying to dance the latest dance. Slightly amused and embarrassed."[92] Still, Volvo keeps trying to morph into a sexy brand. It calls its new S60 model the Naughty S60, and to launch the car in Europe the company hosted underground parties in London, Paris, Milan, Berlin, and Madrid. What the partygoers didn't know was that at each event Volvo created—and filmed—a series of experiments, "carefully designed to measure guests' naughtiness, conformity, daring, confidence, curiosity and desire." More than 3,000 partygoers were secretly filmed (check out the videos on Volvo's Subject360 YouTube channel) to see which city's residents were most likely to break the rules. Spoiler alert: Paris is officially the "Naughty Capital of Europe."[93]

Socializing with Brands

Many of the most recognizable figures in popular culture are spokescharacters for long-standing brands, such as the Jolly Green Giant, the Keebler Elves, Mr. Peanut, or Charlie the Tuna.[94] These personalities periodically get a makeover to keep their meanings current. For example, Bayer recast Speedy Alka-Seltzer: In the 1950s and later, he was an all-around good guy who was ready to help with any sort of indigestion. Today, he appears as a "wing man" for men in their 20s and 30s who tend to "overindulge" on food and drink. (Do you know anyone who fits this description?) The creative director on the campaign explained that the goal is to introduce Speedy as "the good-times enabler who shows up whenever guys are being guys."[95]

Forging a successful brand personality often is key to building brand loyalty, but it's not as easy to accomplish as it might appear. One reason is that many consumers (particularly younger ones) have a very sensitive "BS detector" that alerts them when a brand doesn't live up to its claims or is somehow inauthentic. When this happens, the strategy may backfire as consumers rebel. They may create Web sites to attack the brand or post parodies that make fun of it on YouTube. One set of researchers terms this phenomenon a **Doppelgänger brand image** (one that looks like the original but is in fact a critique of it). For example, many consumers were immensely loyal to the Snapple brand until Quaker purchased it. These loyalists felt that Quaker had stripped the brand of its offbeat, grassroots sensibility; one shock jock renamed it "Crapple" on his radio show.[96]

So, how do people think about brands? We use some personality dimensions to compare and contrast the perceived characteristics of brands in various product categories, including these:[97]

- Old-fashioned, wholesome, traditional
- Surprising, lively, "with it"
- Serious, intelligent, efficient
- Glamorous, romantic, sexy
- Rugged, outdoorsy, tough, athletic

Indeed, consumers appear to have little trouble assigning personality qualities to all sorts of inanimate products, from personal care products to more mundane, functional ones—even kitchen appliances. Whirlpool's research showed that people saw its products as more feminine than they saw competing brands. When respondents were asked to imagine the appliance as a person, many of them pictured a modern, family-oriented woman living in the suburbs—attractive but not flashy. In contrast, they envisioned the company's Kitchen Aid brand as a modern professional woman who was glamorous, wealthy, and enjoyed classical music and the theater.[98]

A product that creates and communicates a distinctive brand personality stands out from its competition and inspires years of loyalty. However, personality analysis helps marketers identify a brand's weaknesses that have little to do with its functional qualities: Adidas asked kids in focus groups to imagine that the brand came to life and was at a party, and to tell what they would expect the brand to be doing there. The kids responded that Adidas would be hanging around the keg with its pals, talking about girls. Unfortunately, they also said Nike would *be with* the girls![99] The results reminded Adidas' brand managers that they had some work to do. We compare this process to **animism**, the common cultural practice whereby people attribute to inanimate objects qualities that make them somehow alive.[100]

Are We What We Buy?

Self-image congruence models suggest that we choose products when their attributes match some aspect of the self.[101] These models assume a process of *cognitive matching* between product attributes and the consumer's self-image.[102] Over time we tend to form relationships with products that resemble the bonds we create with other people: These include love, unrequited love (we yearn for it but can't have it), respect, and perhaps even fear or hate ("why is my computer out to get me?").[103] Researchers even report that after a "breakup" with a brand, people tend to develop strong negative feelings and will go to great lengths to discredit it, including bad-mouthing and even vandalism.[104]

Research tends to support the idea of congruence between product usage and self-image. One of the earliest studies to examine this process found that car owners' ratings of themselves tended to match their perceptions of their cars: Pontiac drivers saw themselves as more active and flashy than did Volkswagen drivers.[105] Indeed, a German study found that observers were able to match photos of male and female drivers to pictures of the cars they drove almost 70 percent of the time.[106] Researchers also report congruity between consumers and their most preferred brands of beer, soap, toothpaste, and

Some consumers might say that what we wear defines who we are. Modcloth.com is one web site that offers unique fashions for women who use style to express themselves. *Source:* Courtesy of Modcloth.com.

Marketing Opportunity

Identity marketing is a promotional strategy whereby consumers alter some aspects of their selves to advertise for a branded product. Air New Zealand created "cranial billboards" in exchange for a round-trip ticket to New Zealand—30 Los Angeles participants shaved their heads and walked around with an ad for the airline on their skulls.[111]

cigarettes relative to their least preferred brands, as well as between consumers' self-images and their favorite stores.[107] Some specific attributes useful to describe matches between consumers and products include rugged/delicate, excitable/calm, rational/emotional, and formal/informal.[108]

Although these findings make some intuitive sense, we cannot blithely assume that consumers will always buy products whose characteristics match their own. It is not clear that consumers really see aspects of themselves in down-to-earth, functional products that don't have very complex or humanlike images. It is one thing to consider a brand personality for an expressive, image-oriented product, such as perfume, and quite another to impute human characteristics to a toaster.

Another problem is the old "chicken-and-egg" question: Do people buy products because they see these as similar to themselves, or do people assume that these products must be similar to themselves because they bought them? The similarity between a person's self-image and the images of products he purchases does tend to increase over the time he owns the product, so we can't rule out this explanation.

Remember that the reflected self helps shape self-concept, which implies that people see themselves as they imagine others see them. Because what others see includes a person's clothing, jewelry, furniture, car, and so on, it stands to reason that these products also help to create the perceived self. A consumer's possessions place her into a social role, which helps to answer the question, "Who am I now?"

People use an individual's consumption behaviors to identify that person's social identity. In addition to checking out a person's clothes and grooming habits, we make inferences about personality based on her choice of leisure activities (e.g., squash versus bowling), food preferences (e.g., tofu and beans versus steak and potatoes), cars, and home decorating choices. When researchers show people pictures of someone's living room, for example, study participants make surprisingly accurate guesses about the occupant's personality.[109] In the same way that a consumer's use of products influences others' perceptions, the same products can help to determine his own self-concept and social identity.[110]

We are *attached* to an object to the extent we rely on it to maintain our self-concept.[112] Objects act as a security blanket when they reinforce our identities, especially in unfamiliar situations. For example, students who decorate their dorm rooms with personal items are less likely to drop out of college. This coping process may protect the self from being diluted in a strange environment.[113] When a pair of researchers asked children of various ages to create "who am I?" collages, for which they chose pictures that represented their selves, older kids between middle childhood and early adolescence inserted more photos of branded merchandise. Also, as they aged, their feelings about these objects evolved from concrete relationships (e.g., "I own it") to more sophisticated, abstract relationships (e.g., "It is like me").[114]

Our use of consumption information to define the self is especially important when we have yet to completely form a social identity, such as when we have to play a new role in life. Think, for example, of the insecurity many of us felt when we first started college or reentered the dating market after leaving a long-term relationship. **Symbolic self-completion theory** suggests that people who have an incomplete self-definition tend to complete this identity when they acquire and display symbols they associate with that role.[115]

Adolescent boys, for example, may use "macho" products such as cars and cigarettes to bolster their developing masculinity; these items act as a "social crutch" during a period of uncertainty about their new identity as adult males. As we mature into a role, we actually rely less on the products people associate with it: For example, when kids start to skateboard, they often invest in pro skateboard "decks" with graphics and branding that cost between $40 and $70 even without the "trucks" (wheels and axles). But—to

To promote its Double Down chicken filet sandwich, KFC recruited female college students to serve as human billboards. The brand ambassadors wore sweatpants bearing a branded message for the bun-less sandwich on their backsides.[116]

Source: Photo Courtesy KFC Corporation.

the chagrin of the skateboard industry—as they get more serious about boarding, many think it's just fine to buy *blank decks*, the plain wood boards that cost only $15 to $30.[117]

The contribution of possessions to self-identity is perhaps most apparent when we lose these treasured objects. One of the first acts of institutions that want to repress individuality and encourage group identity, such as prisons or the military, is to confiscate personal possessions.[118] Victims of burglaries and natural disasters commonly report feelings of alienation, depression, or of being "violated." One consumer's comment after she was robbed is typical: "It's the next worse thing to being bereaved; it's like being raped."[119] Burglary victims exhibit a diminished sense of community, lowered feelings of privacy, and less pride in their houses' appearance than do their neighbors.[120]

A study of postdisaster conditions, where consumers may have lost literally everything but the clothes on their backs following a fire, hurricane, flood, or earthquake, highlights the dramatic impact of product loss. Some people are reluctant to undergo the process of re-creating their identities by acquiring new possessions. Interviews with disaster victims reveal that some hesitate to invest the self in new possessions and so become more detached about what they buy. This comment from a woman in her 50s is representative of this attitude: "I had so much love tied up in my things. I can't go through that kind of loss again. What I'm buying now won't be as important to me."[121]

CB AS I SEE IT

Professor Lisa Bolton, *Penn State University*
Professor Americus Reed II, *The University of Pennsylvania*

The concept of "branding" is fundamental to marketing. It communicates benefits and establishes differentiation between product offerings in a category. However, sometimes the category label itself can have unforeseen consequences for consumers. Take the situation of consumers who seek to pursue a "healthy lifestyle"— especially those who are at high risk for consumer health complications (such as cholesterol and obesity).

We have been investigating how the labeling of health remedies affect healthy lifestyles. Imagine how consumers react to the same health remedy, labeled as either a "drug" or a "supplement." Do you think it will affect their plans to exercise and what they eat? If so, how?

When they consider a health remedy labeled as a "DRUG," consumers tend to discount the health risks associated with the remedy (such as health risks of high-fat foods). As a result, consumers are more likely to engage in risky behavior (such as high-fat eating). Ironically, this "boomerang" effect of drug marketing is more pronounced for consumers who are at greater risk (such as consumers with high cholesterol or obesity problems). In other words, the drug remedy hurts most the consumers it is designed to help!

At-risk consumers perceive the drug as a "get out of jail free card" that takes the risk out of risky behavior—in other words, bring on the cheesecake![122] Indeed, the boomerang effect has also been observed on actual behavior—for example, in one study consumers ate more M&M candy after a single exposure to a drug remedy advertisement.[123]

In contrast, the label "SUPPLEMENT" does not boomerang.[124] Consumers seem to realize that the label "means" that the remedy must be taken in conjunction with some kind of change in lifestyle (healthier eating, more exercise). Although supplements do not appear to undermine a healthy lifestyle, the researchers acknowledge other issues with supplement marketing (the category is somewhat notorious!) that merit future research.

Aside from the negative consequences for consumer health and welfare, the boomerang effect has important implications for marketers. Will a more responsible approach help to "undo" the boomerang effect on healthy behavior?

OBJECTIVE 5
The way we think about our bodies (and the way our culture tells us we should think) is a key component of self-esteem.

Body Image

For many women, trying on jeans is a painful exercise. Levi Strauss launched an online fitting service called the Curve ID System to make the process a little more comfortable. The digital offering is available in 20 languages and 50 countries; it is based on 60,000 women's figures worldwide and its goal is to provide a more customized experience to ease the frustration many women feel as they search for the perfect pair of jeans.[125] This allows you to consider some Spanx shapewear for some "tummy-taming," "butt boosting," or "thigh trimming" before you wear your new pants in public.[126]

A person's physical appearance is a large part of his self-concept. **Body image** refers to a consumer's subjective evaluation of his physical self. Our evaluations don't necessarily correspond to what those around us see. A man may think of himself as being more muscular than he really is, or a woman may feel she appears fatter than is actually the case.

Some marketers exploit consumers' tendencies to distort their body images when they prey on our insecurities about appearance. They try to create a gap between the real and the ideal physical selves and consequently motivate a person to purchase products and services he thinks will narrow that gap. Even social media apparently impacts how we feel about our bodies. A recent study of Facebook users reported that one-half of them felt more self-conscious about their body images after they looked at photos of themselves and others on the site.[127]

Ideals of Beauty

Our satisfaction with the physical image we present to others depends on how closely we think the image corresponds to the ideal our culture values. An **ideal of beauty** is a particular model, or *exemplar,* of appearance. Ideals of beauty for both men and women may include physical features (e.g., big breasts or small, bulging muscles) as well as clothing styles, cosmetics, hairstyles, skin tone (pale versus tan), and body type (petite, athletic, voluptuous, etc.).

Our desires to match up to these ideals—for better or worse—drive a lot of our purchase decisions. What's more, the pressure to exhibit these traits starts earlier and earlier: The retailer Abercrombie & Fitch first came under fire a few years ago for selling thongs to preteens. More recently, critics blasted the chain because it offers padded bikini tops to the same age group.[128] Judgments of the attractiveness of both men and women exert profound influences on their lives, and not just when it comes to who gets to hang out with "the beautiful people." One study reported that on average an American worker who was among the bottom one-seventh in looks, as assessed by randomly chosen observers, earned 10 to 15 percent less per year than a similar worker whose looks were assessed in the top one-third—a lifetime difference, in a typical case, of about $230,000.[129] Another cross-country examination found that beautiful people generally are happier.[130] Who says you can't judge a book by its cover?

Is Beauty Universal?

Virtually every culture displays this beauty bias, even though the standards by which people judge what is hot and what is not may differ. Communist China once banned beauty contests as "spiritual pollution," but then again China recently hosted the "Miss World" pageant. The Chinese consider appearance so important that they view plastic surgery as a commercial investment, and it's common for people to take out loans to fund procedures.[131]

A growing number of studies report evidence that preferences for some physical features rather than others are "wired in" genetically, and that these preferences tend to be the same among people around the world. When researchers show babies as young as

This Japanese anti-smoking ad appeals to women's concerns about appearance to drive home a message.

Source: Courtesy of McCann Worldgroup Holdings Japan.

5 hours old pictures of faces that adults rate as beautiful and not so beautiful, they spend more time looking at the attractive faces.

To what cues do people respond? Specifically, they appear to favor features we associate with good health and youth—attributes we link to reproductive ability and strength. These characteristics include large eyes, high cheekbones, and a narrow jaw. Believe it or not, another cue that people across ethnic and racial groups use to signal sexual desirability is whether the person's facial features are balanced (i.e., if the two sides of the face are in proportion to one another). This is a signal of health. Sure enough, people with symmetrical features on average start having sex 3 to 4 years earlier than those with unbalanced features.[132]

Men also use a woman's body shape as a sexual cue; an evolutionary explanation is that feminine curves provide evidence of reproductive potential. During puberty, a typical female gains almost 35 pounds of "reproductive fat" around the hips and thighs that supply the approximately 80,000 extra calories she will need to support a pregnancy. Most fertile women have waist–hip ratios of 0.6 to 0.8, an hourglass shape that also happens to be the one men rank highest. Even though preferences for overall weight change over time, waist–hip ratios tend to stay in this range. Even the superthin model Twiggy (who pioneered the "waif look" decades before Kate Moss) had a ratio of 0.73.[133]

How do women infer that a potential male mate has desirable characteristics of strength and health? They tend to favor men with heavy lower faces (an indication of a high concentration of androgens that impart strength), those who are slightly above average in height, and those with prominent brows. In one study, women viewed a series of male headshots that had been digitally altered to exaggerate or minimize masculine traits. They saw men with square jaws and well-defined brow ridges as good short-term partners, whereas they preferred those with feminine traits, such as rounder faces and fuller lips, for long-term mates. Overwhelmingly, participants said those with more masculine features were likely to be risky and competitive and also more apt to fight, challenge bosses, cheat on spouses, and put less effort into parenting. They assumed that men with more feminine faces would be good parents and husbands, hard workers, and emotionally supportive mates.[134]

Bear in mind that these preferences may not be at a conscious level; research offers evidence that hormonal changes trigger them. In one study, researchers tested female university students who came to their lab when they were ovulating and when they were not. They photographed each woman twice—once in her fertile phase and once in her least-fertile phase. Then the researchers asked a separate panel of men and women to look at these pairs of photos (with the faces blacked out) and choose the one in which they think the person tries to look more attractive. These judges were more likely to select the photo of each woman when she was ovulating. In these pictures, the women tended to wear flashier clothing and jewelry; the researchers compared this behavior to animals that commonly signal when they are fertile via scents or changes in skin color. In another study, researchers showed women in Japan and Scotland a series of computer-generated photos of male faces that were systematically altered in terms of such dimensions as the size of the jaw and the prominence of the eyebrow ridge.[135] Again, women in the study preferred the heavier masculine features when they were ovulating, but these choices shifted during other parts of their monthly cycles. Most recently, researchers reported that women who are at peak fertility choose sexy rather than conservative clothing, apparently as a way to lure males away from other women.[136]

Jaw size aside, the way we "package" our bodies still varies enormously, and that's where marketers come in: Advertising and other forms of mass media play a significant role in determining which forms of beauty we consider desirable at any point in time. An ideal of beauty functions as a sort of cultural yardstick. Consumers compare themselves to some standard (often one the fashion media advocate at that time), and they are dissatisfied with their appearance to the extent that they don't match up to it. This may lower their own self-esteem or, in some cases, possibly diminish the effectiveness of an ad because of negative feelings a highly attractive model arouses.[137]

Our language provides phrases to sum up these cultural ideals. We may talk about a "bimbo," a "girl-next-door," or an "ice queen," or we may refer to specific women who have come to embody an ideal, such as J-Lo, Gwyneth Paltrow, the late Princess Diana, and before her the late Princess Grace.[138] Similar descriptions for men include "jock," "pretty boy," and "bookworm," or a "Brad Pitt type," a "Wesley Snipes type," and so on.

The Western Ideal of Beauty

Beauty is about more than aesthetics. We use cues such as skin color and eye shape to make inferences about a person's status, sophistication, and social desirability. People in less powerful cultures tend to adopt the standards of beauty prevalent in dominant cultures. For example, an ad on Malaysian television showed an attractive college student who can't get a second glance from a boy at the next desk. "She's pretty," he says to himself, "but. . . . " Then she applies Pond's Skin Lightening Moisturizer by Unilever PLC, and she reappears looking several shades paler. Now the boy wonders, "Why didn't

I notice her before?" In many Asian cultures, people historically equate light skin with wealth and status, and they associate dark skin with the laboring class that toils in the fields. This stereotype persists today: In a survey, 74 percent of men in Malaysia, 68 percent in Hong Kong, and 55 percent in Taiwan said they are more attracted to women with fair complexions. About a third of the female respondents in each country said they use skin-whitening products. Olay has a product it calls White Radiance, and L'Oréal sells a White Perfect line.[139]

As media images of glamorous American (Caucasian) celebrities proliferate around the globe, women who buy into the Western ideal of beauty—big round eyes, tiny waists, large breasts, blond hair, and blue eyes—literally go under the knife to achieve these attributes:

- A model, who was the local spokeswoman for Lux soap and Omega watches, became the first blue-eyed Miss Thailand. She's one of a generation of racially mixed Thais who now dominate the local fashion and entertainment industries as the public abandons the round face, arched eyebrows, and small mouth of the classical Thai look in favor of a Western ideal. Many buy blue contact lenses to enhance their looks. In a poll to name the sexiest men and the sexiest women in Thailand, seven out of the nine top scorers were of mixed blood.[140] The Thai language reflects the stigma of darker skin. One common insult is *tua dam,* or "black body," and another is *dam tap pet,* or "black like a duck's liver."[141]

- Year after year, winners of the Most Beautiful Girl in Nigeria performed very poorly in the Miss World competition. Local organizers had about given up on the idea that an African woman could win a contest that Western beauties dominated. Then a Nigerian woman went on to win the Miss World title. She was the first African winner in the contest's 51-year history. However, pride mixed with puzzlement: The new Miss World didn't possess the voluptuous figure African culture prized. In West and Central Africa, people revere big women; many beauty contestants weigh more than 200 pounds. In Niger, women even eat livestock feed or special vitamins to bulk up. The Calabari in southeastern Nigeria send prospective brides to fattening farms, where they are fed huge amounts of food and massaged into rounder shapes. After weeks of this regimen, the bigger brides proudly parade in the village square.[142] As one African explained, "Plumpness means prosperity. Thin represents everything you don't want: poverty, AIDS, and other diseases, misery and hunger." In contrast, the contest winner is 6 feet tall and skinny. Older Nigerians did not find the winner especially attractive at all, and some bitingly described her as a white girl in black skin. But younger people feel different. For them, thin is in. In Lagos, fashionable thin girls are called *lepa* and there is even a popular song with this title. A movie called *Lepa Shandi* celebrates the more svelte look—the title means a girl as slim as a 20-naira bill.[143]

- Japanese retailers are scrambling to stock larger dress sizes to keep up with a new look the fashion industry calls *bonkyu-bon.* This means "big-small-big" and it stands for a change in that culture's body ideal: Japanese women are getting curvier. Today, the average Japanese woman's hips, at 35 inches, are about an inch wider than those of women a generation older. Women in their 20s wear bras at least two sizes larger than those of their mothers, whereas waist sizes have gotten smaller. The government reports that the average 20-year-old is also nearly 3 inches taller than she was in 1950. These changes are the result of a diet that is becoming more Westernized; the traditional meal of fish, vegetables, and tofu is now more likely to have been replaced by a meal of red meat, dairy, and decadent desserts such as Krispy Kreme doughnuts and Cold Stone Creamery ice cream. Juicy Couture, known for its figure-hugging terrycloth tracksuits, opened one of its biggest stores in Tokyo, and other department stores feature larger sizes from other American designers. Wacoal Corp., Japan's largest lingerie company, was once known for its super-padded brassieres. Now the company has a new bestseller: the "Love Bra," a cleavage-boosting creation with less padding, aimed at curvier women in their 20s.[144]

While Americans spend billions of dollars per year to fix less-than-perfect teeth, a new craze among Japanese women is to pay to have straight teeth made crooked. People in the U.S. refer negatively to this look as "snaggleteeth," or "fangs," but many Japanese men find what they call *yaeba* (double tooth) attractive. Blogs celebrate the *yaeba* look and woman pay dentists to attach pieces of plastic to their real teeth to achieve it.[145]
Source: © Philip Bigg/Alamy.

Ideals of Beauty Evolve Over Time

Although beauty may "only be skin deep," throughout history women have worked very hard to attain it. They starved themselves; painfully bound their feet; inserted plates into their lips; spent countless hours under hair dryers, in front of mirrors, and beneath tanning lights; and opted for breast reduction or enlargement operations.

We characterize periods of history by a specific "look," or ideal of beauty. Often these relate to broader cultural happenings, such as today's emphasis on fitness and toned bodies. A look at U.S. history reveals a succession of dominant ideals. For example, in sharp contrast to today's emphasis on health and vigor, in the early 1800s it was fashionable to appear delicate to the point of looking ill. The poet John Keats described the ideal woman of that time as "a milk white lamb that bleats for man's protection." Other past looks include the voluptuous, lusty woman that Lillian Russell made popular; the athletic Gibson Girl of the 1890s; and the small, boyish flapper of the 1920s exemplified by the silent movie actress Clara Bow.[146] Marilyn Monroe died in 1962, but she represents a cultural ideal of beauty that persists to this day. The TV series *Smash* revolves around the making of a Broadway musical based on her controversial life, and M.A.C. recently

Marketing Opportunity

The size and shape of the "average" U.S. consumer today is dramatically different from what it was 60 years ago. The U.S. government estimates that two-thirds of American adults are overweight or obese. Nevertheless, apparel companies still develop clothing lines based on a 1941 military study that set sizing standards based on a small sample of mostly white, young (and presumably physically fit) female soldiers.

Those standards are finally starting to change, because the typical woman's body is no longer as "petite" as it used to be. The most commonly purchased dress today is a size 14; it was a size 8 in 1985! Slowly but surely, standards change as many women reject the unrealistic body ideal of the waif and subscribe to the battle cry: "Big is beautiful!" The popularity of "full-figured" women, such as Oprah, Queen Latifah, and Rosie O'Donnell, and plus-size spokesmodels, such as Emme, also has helped to improve the self-esteem of larger women. In reality, plus-size clothes have been available for more than 90 years, ever since a Lithuanian immigrant, Lena Bryant (her name was later misspelled as "Lane" on a business form), transformed a maternity-wear business into a line for stout women in the 1920s. Today, mass-market stores like Forever 21 and Target and expensive designers like Elie Tahari have turned their attention to the larger woman, and with good reason: In a recent 12-month period, the plus-size market increased 1.4 percent while the market for overall women's apparel declined 0.8 percent.

In addition, standards based on this outdated snapshot of U.S. women need to recognize the diversity of today's ethnic population: According to current criteria, 78 percent of African American women and 72 percent of Hispanic women are overweight, compared with 58 percent of white women. Non-Caucasian body shapes differ as well: for example, Hispanic Americans and Asian Americans tend to be shorter than their Caucasian counterparts.

The clothing industry can't take the market potential of this segment lightly. Women spend about $47 billion on plus-size garments each year, which accounts for 20 percent of the total apparel market. Still, the plus-size market can be a tough sell. Larger women have some shopping issues their smaller counterparts don't worry about.

introduced a line of cosmetics named after her. Macy's recently got into the act with the launch of a Marilyn clothing line.[147]

In much of the 19th century, the desirable waistline for U.S. women was 18 inches, a circumference that required the use of corsets pulled so tight that they routinely caused headaches, fainting spells, and possibly even the uterine and spinal disorders common among women of the time. Although modern women are not quite as "straight-laced," many still endure such indignities as high heels, body waxing, eyelifts, and liposuction. In addition to the millions women spend on cosmetics, clothing, health clubs, and fashion magazines, these practices remind us that—rightly or wrongly—the desire to conform to current standards of beauty is alive and well.

Our culture communicates these standards—subtly and not so subtly—virtually everywhere we turn: on magazine covers, in department store windows, on TV shows. Feminists argue that fashion dolls, such as the ubiquitous Barbie, reinforce an unnatural ideal of thinness. When we extrapolate the dimensions of these dolls to average female body sizes, indeed they are unnaturally long and thin.[148] If the traditional Barbie doll were a real woman, her dimensions would be 38–18–34! Mattel conducted "plastic surgery" on Barbie to give her a less pronounced bust and slimmer hips, but she is still not exactly dumpy.[149] The company now sells an even more realistic Barbie featuring wider hips and a smaller bust.[150]

As we've seen, the ideal body type of Western women changes over time—check out portraits of models from several hundred years ago by Botticelli and others to appreciate by just how much. These changes periodically cause us to redefine *sexual dimorphic markers*—those aspects of the body that distinguish between the sexes. The first part of the 1990s saw the emergence of the controversial "waif" look in which successful models (most notably Kate Moss) were likely to have bodies that resembled those of young boys. Using heights and weights from winners of the Miss America pageant, nutrition experts concluded that many beauty queens were in the undernourished range. In the 1920s, contestants had a body mass index in the range now considered normal (20 to 25). Since then, an increasing number of winners have had indexes under 18.5, which is the World Health Organization's standard for undernutrition.[151]

Similarly, a study of almost 50 years of *Playboy* centerfolds shows that the women have become less shapely since Marilyn Monroe graced the first edition with a voluptuous hourglass figure of 37–23–36. However, a magazine spokesman comments, "As time has gone on and women have become more athletic, more in the business world and more inclined to put themselves through fitness regimes, their bodies have changed, and we reflect that as well. . . ."[152] Fair enough. Indeed, a recent reexamination of centerfold data shows that the trend toward increasing thinness seems to have stabilized and may actually have begun to reverse. Still, although the women shown in the magazine became somewhat heavier over the 21-year period the researchers reviewed, the Playmates remain markedly below weights medical experts consider normal for their age group.[153] Ironically, when researchers ask women to predict how men will rate women of different body shapes, women choose thinner figures than do men. In other words, they think men prefer skinny fashion model types, when in fact the shapes men choose come closer to the "real" women.[154]

Is the Ideal Getting Real?

The teen-oriented magazine *Seventeen* recently pledged to always feature "real girls" in its pages. This change was in response to an online petition that gathered nearly 85,000 signatures in just four days. The 14-year-old reader who posted the petition stated, "For the sake of all the struggling girls all over America, who read *Seventeen* and think these fake images are what they should be, I'm stepping up. I know how hurtful these photo-shopped images can be."[155]

For several years Dove's Campaign for Real Beauty has drawn attention to unrealistic beauty ideals as it features women with imperfect bodies in advertising. One ad read, "Let's face it, firming the thighs of a size 8 supermodel wouldn't have been much of a challenge." Unilever initiated the campaign after its research showed that many women

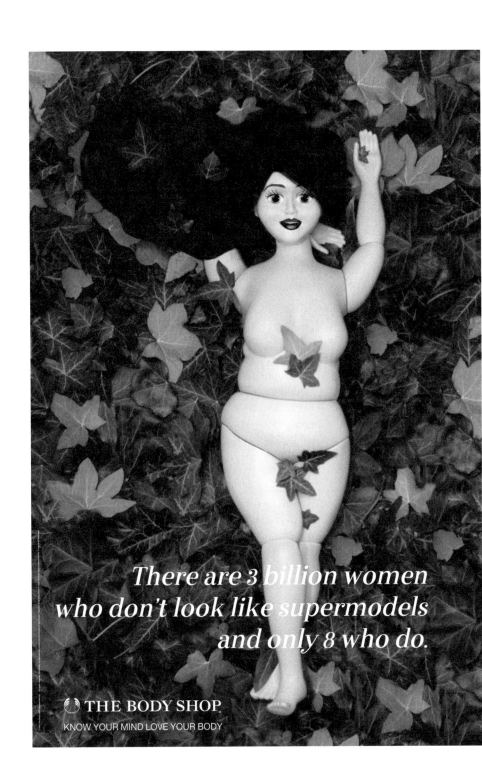

There are 3 billion women who don't look like supermodels and only 8 who do.

THE BODY SHOP
KNOW YOUR MIND LOVE YOUR BODY

The Body Shop taps into the growing sentiment against unrealistic ideals of beauty.
Source: Reproduced with the kind permission of The Body Shop International, plc.

didn't believe its products worked because the women who used them in its ads didn't look realistic.[156] When the company asked 3,200 women around the world to describe their looks, most summed themselves up as "average" or "natural." Only 2 percent called themselves "beautiful."

However, Unilever's experience with Chinese women reminds us again that appearance norms are strongly rooted in culture. Dove's Campaign for Real Beauty flopped in China; after the fact Unilever's research showed that many Chinese women *do* believe they can attain the kind of airbrushed beauty they see in advertising. As a result, the company scrapped the campaign there and instead launched a Chinese version of *Ugly Betty*—a successful American sitcom, which was in turn adapted from a Colombian

Some don't like to try on clothes in the same fitting rooms as smaller women. Plus-size stocks take up valuable storage space, and not everyone is big in the same way, meaning stores cannot count on, say, a size 16 dress fitting most 180-pound women—one might have a larger torso, another bigger thighs, and another wider hips. One hindrance to plus-size shoppers—which retailers are just starting to address—is that shopping can be an emotionally complex experience. When a plus-sized customer goes to a mall, she realizes most clothes there won't fit her, and "that's a bummer," says Liz Muñoz, chief merchant at Torrid, a plus-size brand with trendy clothes aimed at 18- to 35-year-olds.[157]

telenovela. The show, *Ugly Wudi*, focuses on fictional ad agency employee Lin Wudi, who strives to unveil her own beauty, aided by the numerous Dove products that appear in the show. As you might expect, it helps that the actress who played Wudi has perfect skin and actually is quite attractive once you strip away the oversized glasses and the fake braces.[158]

Male Ideals of Beauty

We also distinguish among ideals of beauty for men in terms of facial features, musculature, and facial hair—who could confuse Justin Bieber with Johnny Depp? In fact, one national survey that asked both men and women to comment on male aspects of appearance found that the dominant standard of beauty for men is a strongly masculine, muscled body—though women tend to prefer men with less muscle mass than men themselves strive to attain.[160]

Advertisers appear to have the males' ideal in mind; a study of men who appear in advertisements found that most sport the strong and muscular physique of the male stereotype.[161] More than 40 percent of boys in middle school and high school say they exercise regularly in order to increase muscle mass. Perhaps more troubling, 38 percent say they use protein supplements, and nearly 6 percent admit they have experimented with steroids.[162]

Working on the Body

The Japanese company Wacoal launched a men's girdle to flatten big stomachs. Levi Strauss introduced Levi's Ultimate Lift 544, a figure-enhancing jean for women. The new style creates a cup shape in each seat panel to mold the wearer's derriere.[163] No doubt, there's a lot of shaping going on out there.

Because many consumers experience a gap between their real and ideal physical selves, they often go to great lengths to change aspects of their appearance. From girdles to bras, cosmetics to plastic surgery, tanning salons to diet drinks, a multitude of products and services promise to alter aspects of the physical self. It is difficult to overstate the importance of the physical self-concept (and consumers' desires to improve their appearances) to many marketing activities.

Fattism

As the expression "You can never be too thin or too rich" reminds us, it's no secret that our society has an obsession with weight. The media continually bombard us

Advertising often reflects a dominant standard of beauty for men.
Source: Courtesy of Simplot Australia.

with images of thin, happy people. In one survey, more than twice as many female respondents said they were concerned about their weight than about cancer, heart disease, or diabetes. Only 40 percent said they were satisfied with their physical appearance.[164]

Fattism is deeply ingrained in our culture: As early as nursery school age, children prefer drawings of peers in wheelchairs, on crutches, or with facial disfigurements to those of fat children. One survey of girls aged 12 to 19 reported that 55 percent said they see ads "all the time" that make them want to go on a diet.[165] One recent advertising controversy testifies to our thinness mania: It was bad enough when Pepsi unveiled its new "skinny" diet soda can. When the company paired the launch with Fashion Week—the huge promotion for an industry that celebrates skinny models (some of whom have died from anorexia)—the National Eating Disorders Association protested and Pepsi had to apologize. The organization also persuaded Apple to shut down its first iPod ad campaign because it was built around the message, "You can never be too thin or too powerful."[166]

Although Americans' obsession with weight is legendary worldwide, a cultural priority on thinness is spreading—even as obesity rates around the globe skyrocket:

- In traditional Fijian culture, the body ideal for females is, to put it delicately, robust. When a woman started to lose weight in Fiji, this was cause for concern and a sign of probable illness. Then, the island finally got satellite TV feeds that exposed Fijians for the first time to vintage American TV shows, such as *Melrose Place* and *Beverly Hills 90210,* that feature casts of skinny stars. Now the tables have turned, as teenage girls in Fiji exhibit eating disorders. A study found that teens who watched TV three or more nights per week were 50 percent more likely to feel too fat than were other girls. Participants cited actresses such as Heather Locklear as inspiration to change their bodies.[168] As in Fiji, Egyptians traditionally preferred somewhat plumper women—and the belly dancing tradition encouraged this. Now, though, weight-loss diets are fashionable.

- Japan requires companies and local governments to measure the waistlines of citizens between the ages of 40 and 74 as part of their annual checkups. Persons who exceed government limits—33.5 inches for men and 35.4 inches for women—are provided with medical education. Eventually, the government plans to impose financial penalties on organizations that fail to meet weight targets.[169]

The Tangled Web

At least 400 Web sites attract young people with "ana" and "mia," nicknames for anorexia and bulimia. These "communities" offer tips on crash dieting, bingeing, vomiting, and hiding weight loss from concerned parents. *Group dieting* is a growing problem as consumers patronize blog rings devoted to excessive weight loss—especially when they challenge female college students to lose as much weight as possible before events such as spring break. In one typical post, a woman confessed to eating ". . . one cracker, one strawberry and a little bit of soup" in a 24-hour period, whereas another recounted a lunch of a slice of mango and a stick of gum. These sites, often adorned with photos of ultrathin celebrities and slogans such as "Diet Coke Is Life," appeal to followers of an underground movement called *pro-ana* (pro-anorexia) who sometimes identify themselves in public when they wear red bracelets. As one blog proclaims, "Welcome to the Pro-Ana Webring! Our Mission: To assist all who walk Ana's Path in connecting with like-minded individuals who also Live with AN, EDNOS-restrictive subtype, and/or are practitioners of Volitional Anorexia."[167]

College student Galia Slayen created a "life-size" Barbie (39" bust, 18" waist and 33" hips) for an eating disorders awareness event at her college. When she was interviewed on NBC's Today Show about the impact the doll had on her as she was growing up, she commented, "I'm not blaming Barbie [for her own eating disorder]. . . . "I'm blond and blue-eyed and I figured that was what I was supposed to look like. She was my idol. It impacted the way I looked at myself."

Source: Courtesy of Galia Slayen.

● Jump over to Europe, where the diet brand Slim-Fast tackled a common stereotype: British women are the plump ones on the beaches of Europe. The United Kingdom has the highest obesity rate in Europe; nearly one in five of all 15-year-olds are overweight. The company ran ads that rally British women to lose weight or lose face to their sexier Continental counterparts in France, Spain, and Sweden. In one Slim-Fast ad, a French model says, "I love British women. They make me look great." In another spot, a shapely Spanish woman scolds, "Face it, British women, it's not last year's bikini getting smaller."[170]

Cosmetic Surgery

Consumers increasingly choose to have cosmetic surgery to change a poor body image or simply to enhance appearance.[171] In Venezuela, billboards advertise bank loans to obtain breast augmentations; a political candidate even tried to finance his campaign by raffling off a breast lift.[172] As the middle class booms in China, cosmetic surgery is now the fourth most popular way to spend discretionary income—only houses, cars, and travel rank higher. The most popular surgeries make eyes appear larger by adding a crease in the eyelid to form what doctors call a double eyelid. The second most popular operation raises the bridge of the nose to make it more prominent (the opposite of the typical nose job in the West). Young people often request these procedures as a high school graduation present to enhance their prospects in the competitive job market.[173]

According to the American Academy of Cosmetic Surgery, doctors in the United States perform nearly 860,000 cosmetic-surgery procedures each year—and men make up more than 150,000 of the patients. As cosmetic surgery becomes increasingly acceptable (even expected in some circles), consumers and the medical profession expand the scope of body parts they want to alter. Perhaps spurred by fashions such as low-rise jeans and spandex workout gear that call attention to the derrière, for example, buttock augmentation surgery is gaining in popularity. The operation typically costs about $20,000, so clearly it's not intended for the bottom of the market.[174]

The craze for "modifications" even extends to younger consumers who (one would think) don't need it—at least not yet. The American Society of Plastic Surgeons reports that doctors give about 12,000 Botox injections to U.S. teens aged 13 to 19 annually. Although there are some sound medical reasons for this, such as abnormal twitching of the eyelid or involuntary contractions of neck muscles, apparently most young patients elect to have the treatment to address perceived imperfections such as a too-gummy smile and a too-square jaw. Some teenagers mistakenly think that Botox can prevent wrinkles.[175]

Body Image Distortions

In less than two months, four young Brazilian women died in widely publicized cases of anorexia, which sparked an international debate about body image and eating disorders. The first to die was a 21-year-old model who stood 5'8" but who weighed slightly more than 80 pounds when she collapsed at a fashion shoot in Japan. In Spain, the government imposed a controversial ban on extremely thin models as measured by their **body mass index (BMI)** (a formula that takes into account both height and weight). It requires a BMI greater than 17.4 for female models younger than 18 years old, or 18.5 for models older than 18 years old. For a 5-foot, 9-inch model older than 18, that translates to a weight requirement of 126 pounds. Unilever, in turn, banned the use of so-called "size 0" models in its ads for products ranging from Lux shower gel and Sunsilk shampoo to Slim-Fast diet drinks.[176]

Some people exaggerate the connection between self-esteem and appearance to such an extent that they sacrifice their health to attain what they consider to be a desirable body image. Women in particular tend to pick up messages from the media that the quality of their bodies reflects their self-worth, so it is not surprising that most (though certainly not all) major distortions of body image occur among females.

Researchers link a distorted body image to eating disorders, which are particularly prevalent among young women. People with *anorexia* perceive themselves as too fat, and they virtually starve themselves in the quest for thinness. This condition often results in *bulimia,* which involves two stages. First, binge eating occurs (usually in private), in which a person may consume more than 5,000 calories at one time. The binge is followed by induced vomiting, abuse of laxatives, fasting, or overly strenuous exercise—a "purging" process that reasserts the woman's sense of control.

Most eating disorders occur among white, upper-middle-class teens and college-age women. Victims often have brothers or fathers who are hypercritical of their weight; these disorders are also associated with a history of sexual abuse.[177] In addition, one's peers can encourage binge eating; groups such as athletic teams, cheerleading squads, and sororities may reinforce this practice. In one study of a college sorority, members' popularity within the group increased the more they binged.[178]

OBJECTIVE 6

Every culture dictates certain types of body decoration or mutilation.

Body Decoration and Mutilation

People in every culture adorn or alter their bodies in some way. Decorating the self serves a number of purposes:[179]

- **To separate group members from nonmembers**—The Chinook, Native Americans of North America, pressed the head of a newborn between two boards for a year, which permanently altered its shape. In our society, teens go out of their way to adopt distinctive hair and clothing styles that will separate them from adults.
- **To place the individual in the social organization**—Many cultures engage in puberty rites during which a boy symbolically becomes a man. Some young men in part of Ghana paint their bodies with white stripes to resemble skeletons to symbolize the death of their child status. In Western cultures, this rite may involve some form of mild self-mutilation or engaging in dangerous activities.
- **To place the person in a gender category**—The Tchikrin, Native Americans of South America, insert a string of beads in a boy's lip to enlarge it. Western women wear lipstick to enhance femininity. At the turn of the 20th century, small lips were fashionable because they represented women's submissive role at that time.[180] Today, big, red lips are provocative and indicate an aggressive sexuality.
- **To enhance sex-role identification**—We can compare the modern use of high heels, which podiatrists agree are a prime cause of knee and hip problems, backaches, and fatigue, with the traditional Asian practice of foot binding to enhance femininity. As one doctor observed, "When [women] get home, they can't get their high-heeled shoes off fast enough. But every doctor in the world could yell from now until Doomsday, and women would still wear them."[181]
- **To indicate desired social conduct**—The Suya of South America wear ear ornaments to emphasize the importance placed on listening and obedience in their culture. In Western society, some gay men may wear an earring in the left or right ear to signal what role (submissive or dominant) they prefer in a relationship.
- **To indicate high status or rank**—The Hidates, Native Americans of North America, wear feather ornaments that indicate how many people they have killed. In our society, some people wear glasses with clear lenses, even though they do not have eye problems, to enhance their perceived status.
- **To provide a sense of security**—Consumers often wear lucky charms, amulets, and rabbits' feet to protect them from the "evil eye." Some modern women wear a "mugger whistle" around their necks for a similar reason.

Tattoos

Tattoos—both temporary and permanent—today are a popular form of body adornment.[182] Mattel Inc. even released Totally Stylin' Tattoos Barbie, which comes with tiny tattoos her young owners can put on her body. The doll also comes with wash-off tats kids can use to ink themselves.[183]

Although consumers young and old (okay, mostly young) sport body art to make statements about the self, these skin designs actually serve some of the same functions that other kinds of body painting do in primitive cultures. Tattoos (from the Tahitian *ta-tu*) have deep roots in folk art. Until recently, the images were crude and were primarily death symbols (e.g., a skull), animals (especially panthers, eagles, and snakes), pinup women, or military designs. More current influences include science fiction themes, Japanese symbolism, and tribal designs.

Historically, people associated tattoos with social outcasts. For example, authorities in sixth-century Japan tattooed the faces and arms of criminals to identify them, and these markings served the same purpose in 19th-century prisons and 20th-century concentration camps. Marginal groups, such as bikers or Japanese *yakuza* (gang members), often use these emblems to express group identity and solidarity.

Today, a tattoo is a fairly risk-free way to express an adventurous side of the self. A Harris Poll reported that one-third of Americans aged 25 to 29 and one-fourth of those

An interesting tattoo in an Australian liquor ad.
Source: Advertising Agency: JayGrey.
Photographer: Sean Izzard.

between 30 and 39 have tattoos. Consistent with our previous discussion, when we compare respondents who sport a tattoo to those who don't, the latter are more likely to think that people who have one are deviant and rebellious. In contrast, one-third of those who do have a tattoo say it makes them feel sexier.[184]

As more people jump on the tattoo bandwagon (the FDA estimates that 17 million Americans have gotten inked), it's inevitable that some of them will regret this decision later (perhaps when they wake up in the morning?). Tattoo removal centers with names such as Dr. Tattoff, Tat2BeGone, and Tattoo MD meet the need to deal with so-called "tattoo regret." One industry member estimates that as many as 100,000 Americans undergo tattoo removal each year. Unfortunately—at least for now—it's a lot more complicated to remove a tattoo than to put one on you. A design that cost several hundred dollars could require several thousand dollars and many laser sessions to remove. A special laser device shatters tattoo pigment into particles that the body's lymphatic system clears. Full removal takes an average of eight treatments, spaced at least a month apart, using different lasers for different colored inks.[185] The moral: Before you get a significant other's name etched onto your body, be pretty sure you plan to stay together.

Body Piercing

Like tattoos, body piercing evolved from a practice associated with fringe groups to a popular fashion statement. Historians credit the initial impetus for the mainstreaming of what had been an underground West Coast fad to Aerosmith's 1993 video for the song "Cryin'," in which Alicia Silverstone gets both a navel ring and a tattoo.[186] Piercings can range from a hoop protruding from a navel to scalp implants, where metal posts are inserted in the skull (do not try this at home!). Publications such as *Piercing Fans International Quarterly* see their circulations soar, and Web sites attract numerous followers.

MyMarketingLab

Go to **mymktlab.com** to complete the problems marked with this icon ⭐.

CHAPTER SUMMARY

Now that you have finished reading this chapter, you should understand why:

1. The self-concept strongly influences consumer behavior.

Consumers' self-concepts are reflections of their attitudes toward themselves. Whether these attitudes are positive or negative, they will help to guide many purchase decisions; we can use products to bolster self-esteem or to "reward" the self.

2. Products often define a person's self-concept.

We choose many products because we think that they are similar to our personalities. The symbolic interactionist perspective of the self implies that each of us actually has many selves, and we require a different set of products as props to play each role. We view many things other than the body as part of who we are. People use valued objects, cars, homes, and even attachments to sports teams or national monuments to define the self, when they incorporate these into the extended self.

3. A consumer's personality influences the way he responds to marketing stimuli, but efforts to use this information in marketing contexts meet with mixed results.

The concept of *personality* refers to a person's unique psychological makeup and how it consistently influences the way a person responds to her environment. Marketing strategies based on personality differences have met with mixed success, partly because of the way researchers have measured and applied these differences in *personality traits* to consumption contexts. Some analysts try to understand underlying differences in small samples of consumers by employing techniques based on Freudian psychology and variations of this perspective, whereas others have tried to assess these dimensions more objectively in large samples using sophisticated, quantitative techniques

4. Brands have personalities.

A brand personality is the set of traits people attribute to a product as if it were a person. Consumers assign personality qualities to all sorts of inanimate products: Like our relationships with other people, these designations can change over time; therefore, marketers need to be vigilant about maintaining the brand personality they want consumers to perceive. Forging a desirable brand personality often is key to building brand loyalty.

5. The way we think about our bodies (and the way our culture tells us we should think) is a key component of self-esteem.

A person's conception of his or her body also provides feedback to self-image. A culture communicates specific ideals of beauty, and consumers go to great lengths to attain these. Many consumer activities involve manipulating the body, whether through dieting, cosmetic surgery, piercing, or tattooing. Sometimes these activities are carried to an extreme, as people try too hard to live up to cultural ideals. One common manifestation is eating disorders, diseases in which women in particular become obsessed with thinness.

6. Every culture dictates certain types of body decoration or mutilation.

Body decoration or mutilation may serve such functions as separating group members from nonmembers, marking the individual's status or rank within a social organization or within a gender category (e.g., homosexual), or even providing a sense of security or good luck.

KEY TERMS

actual self, 273
animism, 297
anthropomorphism, 296
archetypes, 286
avatars, 279
badges, 277
Big Five personality dimensions, 292
body image, 301
body mass index (BMI), 311
brand personality, 295
computer-mediated environments (CMEs), 279
digital identity management, 279
digital self, 279
Doppelgänger brand image, 297

ego, 282
extended self, 276
fantasy, 274
fattism, 309
geospatial platforms, 277
id, 282
ideal of beauty, 301
ideal self, 273
identity marketing, 298
impression management, 273
lifestream, 279
looking-glass self, 286
motivational research, 283
Myers-Briggs Type Indicator, 292
personality, 280

personality traits, 286
pleasure principle, 282
reality principle, 282
self-concept, 272
self-esteem, 272
self-image congruence models, 297
sexting, 282
social comparison, 273
social footprint, 279
superego, 282
symbolic interactionism, 275
symbolic self-completion theory, 299
torn self, 275
virtual identities, 279

REVIEW

7-1 What is the Big Five?

7-2 In Lifestyle Dimensions, some 13 different personality traits have been identified. List these traits, and give an example of each of them. Identify five that apply to you.

⭐ **7-3** How might the "digital self" differ from a consumer's self-concept in the real world, and why is this difference potentially important to marketers?

⭐ **7-4** Have ideals of beauty in the United States changed during the past 50 years? If so, how? What is fattism?

7-5 How are subjective views of body image exploited by marketers?

CONSUMER BEHAVIOR CHALLENGE

■ DISCUSS

7-6 To what extent do your purchasing habits reflect your own personality?

7-7 According to the Web site Voucher Codes, "pester power" costs U.K. parents U.S. $750 per year.[187] The children were clearly influenced by advertising, and parents often used diversionary tactics to put them off the scent. One parent in 10, according to the study, gave in and made the purchase whether the child needed the item or not. What is pester power, and is it a problem in your country?

7-8 In 2012, a survey carried out by *Glamour Magazine* asked 1,000 women about their attitude toward airbrushed advertisements. Retouching photographs has reached massive levels as technology makes it easier to manipulate images. Younger women seem to be happier with the approach than older ones. Commercial retouching of photographs yielded a pro response rate of 43 percent if the photograph was in a magazine and just 39 percent if it appeared in an advertisement. What is your take on the technique?

■ APPLY

7-9 Construct a "consumption biography" of a friend or family member. Make a list of or photograph his or her favorite possessions, and see if you or others can describe this person's personality just from the information provided by this catalog.

7-10 Interview victims of burglaries, or people who have lost personal property in floods, hurricanes, or other natural disasters. How do they go about reconstructing their possessions, and what effect did the loss appear to have on them? Similarly, poll your class: If their house or apartment was on fire and they could only take one possession with them as they evacuate, what would it be?

7-11 Some people sacrifice their health to attain what they consider to be a desirable body image. Is this a problem in your country?

Case Study

IS BEAUTY MORE THAN SKIN DEEP?

They are thin, possess flawless skin, and have beautiful hair. They are the models and celebrities we see in television, print, and billboard ads that tout the latest shampoos, anti-aging creams, and skin cleansers. The message is clear. Buy our product and you too can look like this.

Beginning in 2004, Dove, a division of Unilever, started to send out a radically different message when the brand launched its "Campaign for Real Beauty." The first step in Dove's campaign, a tactic to support its skin-firming cream, introduced the nation to billboards that showed unretouched photographs of "normal" women of various sizes in just their underwear.

Dove sent the message that women do not need to conform to the standards of beauty the fashion industry determines. Every woman, regardless of her age or body size, is beautiful. The campaign continued to build strongly over the next couple of years, and gained more steam with the viral release of the video "Evolution." The ad featured an average-looking woman who enters a film studio. The video then speeds through a series of hair, makeup, and shocking computer-enhancement techniques. In 60 seconds she emerges as a gorgeous model on a billboard. Immediately after the final shot of the billboard, the video blacks out to the statement, "No wonder our perception of beauty is distorted." This viral video was followed with "Onslaught," an equally powerful ad, which shows the intensity of personal care, diet, and exercise advertising as viewed through the eyes of a young girl. The ad ends with another powerful message, "Talk to your daughter before the beauty industry does." The latest ad in the campaign, "Dove Real Beauty Sketches," shows us how critical some women can be in evaluating and describing their looks. It was inspired by research conducted by Dove that found only 4 percent of women around the world consider themselves beautiful.

An important part of the Campaign for Real Beauty is the Dove Self-Esteem Fund. With young girls reporting alarmingly low levels of self-worth, this arm of the campaign works to provide confidence-building tools and workshops for young girls. Dove partners with the Girl Scouts, the Boys and Girls Clubs of America, and girls.inc to educate girls on the importance of self-esteem.

Dove reaped a lot of public relations benefits from the campaign, but it is not without its critics. Some charge that Unilever, which owns Dove, is as guilty as the rest of the industry in promoting false ideals of beauty. Ads for the company's Axe brand often are cited as flagrant examples of messages that objectify women. In addition, the anti-aging and firming creams Unilever sells thrive on women's insecurities about their looks. If she is supposed to be satisfied with her natural beauty, then why does a woman need these products? In addition, there was controversy concerning the airbrush techniques Dove used to photograph these "normal" women. An article in the *New Yorker* cited a prominent photo editor who claimed that he had done a large amount of retouching and mentioned what a challenge it was to make the women look attractive. Unilever's response was that it did not digitally alter the photos but retouched them only to correct color and remove dust. Still, this was a damaging accusation against Dove and its ad agency Ogilvy & Mather, especially since the "Evolution" campaign criticizes retouching tricks.

Finally, there is the question of whether such an emotionally charged campaign actually boosts sales. It certainly helps to break through the clutter and bring recognition to the brand, but does it resonate with the consumer over the long term? Apparently yes; Dove reported a doubling of its sales in the first 5 years after the campaign launched. Will this unconventional beauty theme continue to strike a chord—while it sells beauty products at the same time?

DISCUSSION QUESTIONS

CS 7-1 Dove's campaign assumes that advertising has the power to determine what we find attractive or unattractive. Do you agree?

CS 7-2 Some people argue that fashion products are "aspirational"; they encourage consumers to think about what they could be rather than what they are. Do women really want to see "average" models in advertising? Why or why not?

Sources: www.dove.us, accessed July 23, 2013; Neol Bussey, "Dove Abandons Its Soapbox to Focus on the Soap," *Campaign* (August 28, 2008); Molly Prior, "Reality Check: Would You Buy Beauty Products from These Women?" *WWD* (April 20, 2007); Jack Neff, "Retouching Ruckus Leaves Dove Flailing," *Advertising Age* (May 12, 2008).

MyMarketingLab

Go to **mymktlab.com** for the following Assisted-graded writing questions:

7-12 What does "the looking-glass self" mean? How do feelings about the self influence the specific brand people buy?

7-13 How do Eastern and Western cultures differ in terms of how people think about the self?

7-14 **Mymktlab Only**—comprehensive writing assignment for this chapter.

NOTES

1. http://wiki.answers.com/Q/Who_has_the_most_Twitter_followers, accessed May 28, 2011.

2. Harry C. Triandis, "The Self and Social Behavior in Differing Cultural Contexts," *Psychological Review* 96, no. 3 (1989): 506–20; H. Markus and S. Kitayama, "Culture and the Self: Implications for Cognition, Emotion, and Motivation," *Psychological Review* 98 (1991): 224–53.

3. Markus and Kitayama, "Culture and the Self."

4. Nancy Wong and Aaron Ahuvia, "A Cross-Cultural Approach to Materialism and the Self," in Dominique Bouchet, ed., *Cultural Dimensions of International Marketing* (Denmark: Odense University, 1995): 68–89.

5. Lisa M. Keefe, "You're So Vain," *Marketing News* (February 28, 2000): 8.

6. Morris Rosenberg, *Conceiving the Self* (New York: Basic Books, 1979); M. Joseph Sirgy, "Self-Concept in Consumer Behavior: A Critical Review," *Journal of Consumer Research* 9 (December 1982): 287–300; www.mediapost.com, accessed February 15, 2007; Roy F. Baumeister, Dianne M. Tice, and Debra G. Hutton, "Self-Presentational Motivations and Personality Differences in Self-Esteem," *Journal of Personality* 57 (September 1989): 547–75; Ronald J. Faber, "Are Self-Esteem Appeals Appealing?" in Leonard N. Reid, ed., *Proceedings of the 1992 Conference of the American Academy of Advertising* (1992): 230–35.

7. John Tierney, "Why You Won't Be the Person You Expect to Be?" *New York Times* (January 3, 2013), http://www.nytimes.com/2013/01/04/science/study-in-science-shows-end-of-history-illusion.html?_r=0, accessed January 23, 2013.

8. Emily Yoffe, "You Are What You Buy," *Newsweek* (June 4, 1990): 59.

9. Derek D. Rucker, David Dubois, and Adam D. Galinsky, "Generous Paupers and Stingy Princes: Power Drives Consumer Spending on Self Versus Others," *Journal of Consumer Research* 37, no. 6 (April 2011): 1015–29.

10. Christine Bittar, "Alberto-Culver Ties Hair Relaxer to Self-Esteem," www.mediapost.com, accessed February 15, 2007; www.texturesoftener.com, accessed May 29, 2009.

11. Michael Hafner, "How Dissimilar Others May Still Resemble the Self: Assimilation and Contrast After Social Comparison," *Journal of Consumer Psychology* 14, nos. 1 & 2 (2004): 187–96.

12. Marsha L. Richins, "Social Comparison and the Idealized Images of Advertising," *Journal of Consumer Research* 18 (June 1991): 71–83; Mary C. Martin and Patricia F. Kennedy, "Advertising and Social Comparison: Consequences for Female Preadolescents and Adolescents," *Psychology & Marketing* 10 (November–December 1993): 513–30; cf. also Claudia Townsend and Sanjay Sood, "Self-Affirmation Through the Choice of Highly Aesthetic Products," *Journal of Consumer Research* Vol. 39, No. 2 (August 2012): pp. 415–28.

13. Philip N. Myers, Jr., and Frank A. Biocca, "The Elastic Body Image: The Effect of Television Advertising and Programming on Body Image Distortions in Young Women," *Journal of Communication* 42 (Summer 1992): 108–33.

14. Charles S. Gulas and Kim McKeage, "Extending Social Comparison: An Examination of the Unintended Consequences of Idealized Advertising Imagery," *Journal of Advertising* 29 (Summer 2000): 17–28.

15. Brent McFerran, Darren W. Dahl, Gavan J. Fitzsimons, and Andrea C. Morales, "Might an Overweight Waitress Make You Eat More? How the Body Type of Others Is Sufficient to Alter Our Food Consumption," *Journal of Consumer Psychology* 20, no. 2 (2010): 146–51; cf. also Michael Häfner and Debra Trampe, "When Thinking Is Beneficial and When It Is Not: The Effects of Thin and Round Advertising Models," *Journal of Consumer Psychology* 19, no. 4 (2009): 619–28; Brent McFerran, Darren W. Dahl, Gavan J. Fitzsimons, and Andrea C. Morales "I'll Have What She's Having: Effects of Social Influence and Body Type on the Food Choices of Others," *Journal of Consumer Research* 36, no. 6 (April 2010): 173–80.

16. For the seminal treatment of this process, cf. Erving Goffman, *The Presentation of Self in Everyday Life* (New York: Doubleday, 1959).

17. Quoted in Michael Slackman, "Fashion and Faith Meet, on Foreheads of the Pious," *New York Times* (December 18, 2007), www.nytimes.com, accessed December 18, 2007.

18. http://www.cloudgirlfriend.com/, accessed March 4, 2013; Quoted in Alexia Tsotsis, "Cloud Girlfriend Launches as a Dating Site, NOT a Virtual Girlfriend Service," *Tech Crunch* (April 26, 2011), http://techcrunch.com/2011/04/26/cloud-girlfriend-launches-as-a-dating-site-not-a-virtual-girlfriend-service/, accessed May 28, 2011.

19. Harrison G. Gough, Mario Fioravanti, and Renato Lazzari, "Some Implications of Self Versus Ideal-Self Congruence on the Revised Adjective Check List," *Journal of Personality & Social Psychology* 44, no. 6 (1983): 1214–20.

20. Steven Jay Lynn and Judith W. Rhue, "Daydream Believers," *Psychology Today* (September 1985): 14.

21. www.taaz.com, accessed May 29, 2009; www.dailymakeover.com, accessed May 29, 2009.

22. Erving Goffman, *The Presentation of Self in Everyday Life* (Garden City, NY: Doubleday, 1959); Michael R. Solomon, "The Role of Products as Social Stimuli: A Symbolic Interactionism Perspective," *Journal of Consumer Research* 10 (December 1983): 319–29.

23. A. Reed, "Activating the Self-Importance of Consumer Selves: Exploring Identity Salience Effects on Judgments," *Journal of Consumer Research* 31, no. 2 (2004): 286–95.

24. Aliakbar Jafari and Christina Goulding, "'We Are Not Terrorists!' UK-Based Iranians, Consumption Practices and the 'Torn Self,'" *Consumption Markets & Culture* 11 (June 2008): 73–91.

25. Quoted in Fred Meier, "Girls Named Zoe Lose Suit Against Renault for Naming Electric Car Zoe," *DriveOn* (November 10, 2010), http://content.usatoday.com/communities/driveon/post/2010/11/girls-lose-renault-zoe-electric-car-lawsuit-over-name/1, accessed April 10, 2011.

26. George H. Mead, *Mind, Self and Society* (Chicago: University of Chicago Press, 1934).

27. Debra A. Laverie, Robert E. Kleine, and Susan Schultz Kleine, "Reexamination and Extension of Kleine, Kleine, and Kernan's Social Identity Model of Mundane Consumption: The Mediating Role of the Appraisal Process," *Journal of Consumer Research* 28 (March 2002): 659–69.

28. Natasha Singer, "If the Mirror Could Talk (It Can)," *New York Times* (March 18, 2007), www.nytimes.com, accessed March 18, 2007.

29. Charles H. Cooley, *Human Nature and the Social Order* (New York: Scribner's, 1902).

30. J. G. Hull and A. S. Levy, "The Organizational Functions of the Self: An Alternative to the Duval and Wicklund Model of Self-Awareness," *Journal of Personality & Social Psychology* 37 (1979): 756–68; Jay G. Hull, Ronald R. Van Treuren, Susan J. Ashford, Pamela Propsom, and Bruce W. Andrus, "Self-Consciousness and the Processing of Self-Relevant Information," *Journal of Personality & Social Psychology* 54, no. 3 (1988): 452–65.

31. Arnold W. Buss, *Self-Consciousness and Social Anxiety* (San Francisco: Freeman, 1980); Lynn Carol Miller and Cathryn Leigh Cox, "Public Self-Consciousness and Makeup Use," *Personality & Social Psychology Bulletin* 8, no. 4 (1982): 748–51; Michael R. Solomon and John Schopler, "Self-Consciousness and Clothing," *Personality & Social Psychology Bulletin* 8, no. 3 (1982): 508–14.

32. Loraine Lau-Gesk and Aimee Drolet, "The Publicly Self-Conscious Consumer: Prepare to Be Embarrassed," *Journal of Consumer Psychology* 18 (April 2008): 127–36.

33. Morris B. Holbrook, Michael R. Solomon, and Stephen Bell, "A Re-Examination of Self-Monitoring and Judgments of Furniture Designs," *Home Economics Research Journal* 19 (September 1990): 6–16; Mark Snyder, "Self-Monitoring Processes," in Leonard Berkowitz, ed., *Advances in Experimental Social Psychology* (New York: Academic Press, 1979): 85–128.

34. Mark Snyder and Steve Gangestad, "On the Nature of Self-Monitoring: Matters of Assessment, Matters of Validity," *Journal of Personality & Social Psychology* 51 (1986): 125–39; Timothy R. Graeff, "Image Congruence Effects on Product Evaluations: The Role of Self-Monitoring and Public/Private Consumption," *Psychology & Marketing* 13 (August 1996): 481–99; Richard G. Netemeyer, Scot Burton, and Donald R. Lichtenstein, "Trait Aspects of Vanity: Measurement and Relevance to Consumer Behavior," *Journal of Consumer Research* 21 (March 1995): 612–26.

35. Ernest Beaglehole, *Property: A Study in Social Psychology* (New York: Macmillan, 1932).

36. https://foursquare.com/user/2509238/badges/foursquare, accessed May 28, 2011; Rob Walker, "Lifelong Earning," *New York Times* (June 11, 2010), http://www.nytimes.com/2010/06/13/magazine/13fob--consumed-t.html?emc=eta1, accessed April 10, 2011.

37. Scott Smith, Dan Fisher, and S. Jason Cole, "The Lived Meanings of Fanaticism: Understanding the Complex Role of Labels and Categories in Defining the Self in Consumer Culture," *Consumption, Markets & Culture* 10 (June 2007): 77–94.

38. Russell W. Belk, "Shoes and Self," *Advances in Consumer Research* (2003): 27–33.

39. Park Ji Kyung and Deborah Roedder John, "Got to Get You into My Life: Do Brand Personalities Rub Off on Consumers?" *Journal of Consumer Research* 37, no. 4 (2010): 655–69.

40. Russell W. Belk, "Possessions and the Extended Self," *Journal of Consumer Research* 15 (September 1988): 139–68.

41. "Virtual Reality Avatars Created," *The Drum* (February 17, 2011), http://www.thedrum.co.uk/news/2011/02/17/18810-virtual-reality-avatars-created/, accessed April 10, 2011.

42. Erving Goffman, *The Presentation of Self in Everyday Life*, (New York: Anchor, 1959); Barry R. Schlenker and Beth A. Pontari, "The Strategic Control of Information: Impression Management and Self-Presentation in Daily Life," in Abraham Tesser, Richard B. Felson, and Jerry Suls, eds., *Psychological Perspectives on Self and Identity* (Washington, DC, American Psychological Association, (2000): 199–232.

43. Michael R. Solomon, "Digital Identity Management: Old Wine in New Bottles?" *Critical Studies in Fashion and Beauty* 1, no. 2 (December 2010): 173–80.

44. Neal Stephenson, *Snow Crash* (New York: Bantam Books, 1992).

45. Katie Kindelan, "Clothing Giant H&M Defends 'Perfect' Virtual Models," ABC News Blogs (December 6, 2011), http://gma.yahoo.com/blogs/abc-blogs/clothing-giant-h-m-defends-perfect-virtual-models-173726573.html, accessed January 11, 2013.

46. "Virtual World Web Reaches 50,000 Virtual Worlds," *San Francisco Chronicle* (March 31, 2011), http://www.sfgate.com/cgi-bin/article.cgi?f=/g/a/2011/03/31/prweb8256005.DTL, accessed May 28, 2011.

47. Natalie Wood and Michael R. Solomon, eds., *Virtual Social Identity* (Newport Beach, CA: Sage, 2010); Peter Svensson, "Study: Virtual Men Are Standoffish Too," *MyFox 21* (February 2007), http://matei.org/ithink/2007/02/22/study-virtual-men-are-standoffish-too-yahoo-news/, accessed February 22, 2007.

48. Liz Neporent, "Getting Naked in the Virtual World—More Women Than Men Show Flesh," *New York Times* (December 26, 2012), http://abcnews.go.com/blogs/health/2012/12/26/getting-naked-in-the-virtual-world-more-women-than-men-show-flesh-2/, accessed January 11, 2013.

49. This section is adapted from Jagdish N. Sheth and Michael R. Solomon, "Extending the Extended Self in a Digital World," *Journal of Marketing Theory and Practice* (2014, in press).

50. Diane Dannenfeldt, "How Prescription Alerts Work," *How Stuff Works*, http://computer.howstuffworks.com/e-mail-messaging/prescription-alerts1.htm, accessed May 28, 2012.

51. Changing Places, MIT Media Lab, http://www.media.mit.edu/research/groups/changing-places, accessed May 28, 2012; "Clever Toilet Checks on Your Health," *CNN Tech* (June 28, 2005), http://articles.cnn.com/2005-06-28/tech/spark.toilet_1_toilet-toto-bathroom?_s=PM:TECH, accessed May 31, 2012.

52. http://itunes.apple.com/us/app/weight-watchers-mobile/id331308914?mt=8, accessed May 28, 2012.

53. Eli Pariser, *The Filter Bubble: What the Internet Is Hiding from You* (New York: The Penguin Press, 2011).

54. Viet Le, "'Haul Videos': The Ultimate in Materialistic PG Porn?" *All Tech Considered*, http://www.npr.org/blogs/alltechconsidered/2010/02/haul_videosthe_ultimate_pg_gir2.html, accessed May 28, 2012.

55. Stephanie Rosenbloom, "Log On, Coordinate, Pose," *New York Times* (February 29, 2012), http://www.nytimes.com/2012/03/01/fashion/virtual-closet-web-sites-like-pinterest-and-stylitics-revise-online-fashion-shopping.html?_r=2&scp=1&sq=log%20on,%20coordinate&st=cse, accessed May 31, 2012.

56. "Haptic Glove," Cornell University, https://courses.cit.cornell.edu/ee476/FinalProjects/s2008/crs54_tz36/crs54_tz36/twocolumn.html, accessed May 31, 2012.

57. Christina Passariello, "Electronic Mirrors Sell Lipstick and a Makeover," *Wall Street Journal* (August 27, 2010), http://professional.wsj.com/article/SB10001424052748703700904575391213196820750.html?mg=reno64-wsj, accessed May 31, 2012.

58. "Pharmacogenetic Testing," Genelex, http://www.healthanddna.com/healthcare-professional/pharmacogenetics.html, accessed May 31, 2012; Stephanie Baum, "DNA Sequencing Platform Could Help Physicians Target Drugs for Each Patient," *MedCity News* (March 20, 2012), http://medcitynews.com/2012/03/dna-sequencing-platform-could-help-physicians-target-drugs-for-each-patient/, accessed May 31, 2012.

59. "Toyota Window to the World—Multimedia System," YouTube (July 4, 2011), http://www.youtube.com/watch?v=dl9eqdZpvJU, accessed May 31, 2012.

60. Robert Stratton, "Interactive LED Art Wall," YouTube (August 24, 2011), http://www.youtube.com/watch?v=33acbSk-mI0, accessed May 31, 2012.

61. Molly Edmonds, "How Smart Homes Work," *HowStuffWorks*, http://home.howstuffworks.com/smart-home.htm, accessed June 1, 2012.

62. See J. Aronoff and J. P. Wilson, *Personality in the Social Process* (Hillsdale, NJ: Erlbaum, 1985); Walter Mischel, *Personality and Assessment* (New York: Wiley, 1968).

63. http://www.reputation.com/, accessed May 29, 2011.

64. Sean D. Hamill, "Students Sue Prosecutor in Cellphone Photos Case," *New York Times* (March 25, 2009), www.nytimes.com/2009/03/26/us/26sext.html, accessed March 26, 2009.

65. Robert R McCraie and Paul T. Costa, "The Stability of Personality: Observations and Evaluations," *Current Directions in Psychological Science* (1994): 173–175.

66. Ernest Dichter, *A Strategy of Desire* (Garden City, NY: Doubleday, 1960); Ernest Dichter, *The Handbook of Consumer Motivations* (New York: McGraw-Hill, 1964); Jeffrey J. Durgee, "Interpreting Dichter's Interpretations: An Analysis of Consumption Symbolism," in *The Handbook of Consumer Motivations* (unpublished manuscript, Rensselaer Polytechnic Institute, Troy, New York, 1989); Pierre Martineau, *Motivation in Advertising* (New York: McGraw-Hill, 1957).

67. Vance Packard, *The Hidden Persuaders* (New York: D. McKay, 1957).

68. Harold Kassarjian, "Personality and Consumer Behavior: A Review," *Journal of Marketing Research* 8 (November 1971): 409–18.

69. Karen Horney, *Neurosis and Human Growth* (New York: Norton, 1950).

70. Joel B. Cohen, "An Interpersonal Orientation to the Study of Consumer Behavior," *Journal of Marketing Research* 6 (August 1967): 270–78; Pradeep K. Tyagi, "Validation of the CAD Instrument: A Replication," in Richard P. Bagozzi and Alice M. Tybout, eds., *Advances in Consumer Research* 10 (Ann Arbor, MI: Association for Consumer Research, 1983): 112–14.

71. For a comprehensive review of classic perspectives on personality theory, see Calvin S. Hall and Gardner Lindzey, *Theories of Personality*, 2nd ed. (New York: Wiley, 1970).

72. See Carl G. Jung, "The Archetypes and the Collective Unconscious," in H. Read, M. Fordham, and G. Adler, eds., *Collected Works*, vol. 9, part 1 (Princeton, NJ: Princeton University Press, 1959).

73. This material was contributed by Rebecca H. Holman, senior vice president and director, Consumer Knowledge Structures, The Knowledge Group, Young & Rubicam Brands, July 2005.

74. Margaret Mark and Carol S. Pearson, *The Hero and the Outlaw: Building Extraordinary Brands Through the Power of Archetypes* (New York: McGraw-Hill, 2001). This section borrows from a discussion in Michael R. Solomon, Rebekah Russell-Bennett, and Josephine Previte, *Consumer Behaviour: Buying, Having, Being*, 3rd ed. (Frenchs Forest, NSW: Pearson Australia, 2012).

75. E. B. Boyd, "How a Personality Test Designed to Pick Astronauts Is Taking the Pain out of Customer Support," *Fast Company* (December 1, 2010), http://www.fastcompany.com/1706766/how-a-system-designed-to-weed-out-nasa-astronauts-is-taking-the-pain-out-of-customer-support-call?partner=homepage_newsletter, accessed April 13, 2011.

76. For an application of trait theory, cf. Adam Duhachek and Dawn Iacobucci, "Consumer Personality and Coping: Testing Rival Theories of Process," *Journal of Consumer Psychology* 15, no. 1 (2005): 52–63.

77. S. Christian Wheeler, Richard E. Petty, and George Y. Bizer, "Self-Schema Matching and Attitude Change: Situational and Dispositional Determinants of Message Elaboration," *Journal of Consumer Research* 31 (March, 2005): 787–97.

78. John L. Lastovicka, Lance A. Bettencourt, Renee Shaw Hughner, and Ronald J. Kuntze, "Lifestyle of the Tight and Frugal: Theory and Measurement," *Journal of Consumer Research* 26 (June 1999): 85–98; The Hartman Group, "The Continuing Economic Maelstrom & the US Consumer: Implications for CPG, Restaurant and Retail January 2009," http://www.hartman-group.com/publications/white-papers/the-continuing-economic-maelstrom-the-us-consumer, accessed September 3, 2011; Joseph Lazzaro, "US Savings Rate Soars to 14-Year High," *Daily Finance* (June 1, 2009), www.dailyfinance.com/2009/06/01/us-savings-rate-soars-to-14-year-high, accessed June 1, 2009; Andrea K. Walker, "Economy Breeds a Frugal Consumer," *Baltimore Sun* (April 20, 2009), www.baltimoresun.com/business/bal-te.bz.shoppinghabits19apr20,0,1577826.story, accessed June 1, 2009.

79. Adapted from information presented in Beth Snyder Bulik, "You Are What You Watch: Market Data Suggest Research Links Personality Traits to Consumers' Viewing Habits, Helps Marketers Match Brands with Audiences," *Advertising Age* (November 1, 2010), http://adage.com/article/news/research-links-personality-traits-tv-viewing-habits/146779/, accessed April 13, 2011.

80. Adapted from https://www.cpp.com/products/mbti/index.aspx, accessed March 6, 2013.

81. Stephanie Buck, "What Type of Social Media Personality Are You?" Mashable.com (August 13, 2012), http://mashable.com/2012/08/13/what-type-of-social-media-personality-are-you-infographic/?utm_medium=email&utm_source=newsletter, accessed March 6, 2013.

82. Jacob Jacoby, "Personality and Consumer Behavior: How Not to Find Relationships," in *Purdue Papers in Consumer Psychology*, no. 102 (Lafayette, IN: Purdue University, 1969); Harold H. Kassarjian and Mary Jane Sheffet, "Personality and Consumer Behavior: An Update," in Harold H. Kassarjian and Thomas S. Robertson, eds., *Perspectives in Consumer Behavior*, 4th ed. (Glenview, IL: Scott Foresman, 1991): 291–353; John Lastovicka and Erich Joachimsthaler, "Improving the Detection of Personality

Behavior Relationships in Consumer Research," *Journal of Consumer Research* 14 (March 1988): 583–87. For an approach that ties the notion of personality more directly to marketing issues, see Jennifer L. Aaker, "Dimensions of Brand Personality," *Journal of Marketing Research* 34 (August 1997): 347–57.

83. See Girish N. Punj and David W. Stewart, "An Interaction Framework of Consumer Decision-Making," *Journal of Consumer Research* 10 (September 1983): 181–96.

84. J. F. Allsopp, "The Distribution of On-Licence Beer and Cider Consumption and Its Personality Determinants Among Young Men," *European Journal of Marketing* 20, no. 3 (1986): 44–62; Gordon R. Foxall and Ronald E. Goldsmith, "Personality and Consumer Research: Another Look," *Journal of the Market Research Society* 30, no. 2 (April 1988): 111–25; J. Z. Sojka and J. L. Giese, "Using Individual Differences to Detect Consumer Shopping Behavior," *International Review of Retail, Distribution and Consumer Research* 13, no. 4 (2003): 337–53; P. Albanese, "Personality and Consumer Behaviour: An Operational Approach," *European Journal of Marketing* 27, no. 8 (1993): 28–37; M. B. Holbrook and T. J. Olney, "Romanticism and Wanderlust: An Effect of Personality on Consumer Preferences," *Psychology and Marketing* 12, no. 3 (1995): 207–22; H. Baumgartner, "Towards a personology of the consumer," *Journal of Consumer Research* 29 (September 2002): 286–92.

85. J. C. Mowen and B. Carlson, "Exploring the Antecedents and Consumer Behavior Consequences of the Trait of Superstition," *Psychology and Marketing* 20, no. 12 (2003): 1045–65; M. Cleveland, M. Kalamas, and M. Laroche, "Shades of Green, Linking Environmental Locus of Control and Pro-environmental Behaviors," *Journal of Consumer Marketing* 22, no. 4/5 (2005): 198–212; J. C. Mowen, *The 3M Model of Motivation and Personality: Theory and Empirical Applications to Consumer Behavior* (Massachusetts: Kluwer Academic Publishers, 2000); M. B. Holbrook and T. J. Olney, "Romanticism and Wanderlust: An Effect of Personality on Consumer Preferences," *Psychology and Marketing* 12, no. 3 (1995): 207–22; S. I. Rick, C. E. Cryder, and G. Loewenstein, "Tightwads and Spendthrifts," *Journal of Consumer Research* 34 (April 2008): 767–81; J. K. Sojka and J. L. Giese, "The Influence of Personality Traits on the Processing of Visual and Verbal Information," *Marketing Letters* 12, no. 1 (2001): 91–106; R. A. Clark and R. E. Goldsmith, "Market Mavens: Psychological Influences," *Psychology and Marketing* 22 (April 2005): 289–312; U. R. Orth, "Consumer Personality and Other Factors in Situational Brand Choice Variation," *Journal of Brand Management* 13, no. 2 (2005): 115–33; M. Marquis and P. Filiatrault, "Understanding Complaining Responses Through Consumers' Self-Consciousness Disposition," *Psychology and Marketing* 19, no. 3 (2002): 267–91; T. A. Mooradian and J. M. Olver, "'I Can't Get No Satisfaction': The Impact of Personality and Emotion on Postpurchase Processes," *Psychology and Marketing* 14, no. 4 (1997): 379–92.

86. Quoted in Stuart O'Brien, "iPad Owners Are 'Self-Centered Workaholics,'" *Mobile Entertainment (*July 30, 2010), http://www.mobile-ent.biz/news/read/ipad-owners-are-self-centered-workaholics, accessed April 13, 2011.

87. Thomas Hine, "Why We Buy: The Silent Persuasion of Boxes, Bottles, Cans, and Tubes," *Worth* (May 1995): 78–83.

88. Jennifer Aaker, Kathleen D. Vohs, and Cassie Mogilner, "Nonprofits Are Seen as Warm and For-Profits as Competent: Firm Stereotypes Matter," *Journal of Consumer Research* 37, no. 2 (August 2010): 224–37.

89. Bradley Johnson, "They All Have Half-Baked Ideas," *Advertising Age* (May 12, 1997): 8.

90. Michael Hiestand, "ESPN Drops Ad Campaign That Was to Portray College Stereotypes," *USA Today* (November 14, 2008), www.usatoday.com/money/advertising/2008-11-13-espn-ad-campaign-killed_N.html, accessed November 14, 2008.

91. Rebecca Piirto Heath, "The Frontiers of Psychographics," *American Demographics* (July 1996): 38–43.

92. Quoted in Erin White, "Volvo Sheds Safe Image for New, Dangerous Ads," *Wall Street Journal* (June 14, 2002), www.wsj.com, accessed June 14, 2002; Viknesh Vijayenthiran, "Volvo's Upmarket Plans Hindered by Brand Image, Poor CO_2 Emissions," *Motor Authority* (November 24, 2008), www.motorauthority.com/volvo-continuing-with-plans-to-move-upmarket.html, accessed June 1, 2009.

93. Shirley Brady, "Volvo's Naughty S60 Experiment," *BrandChannel* (July 28, 2010), http://www.brandchannel.com/home/post/2010/07/28/Volvo-Naughty-S60-Experiment.aspx, accessed April 13, 2011.

94. Yongjun Sung and Spencer F. Tinkham, "Brand Personality Structures in the United States and Korea: Common and Culture-Specific Factors," *Journal of Consumer Psychology* 15, no. 4 (2005): 334–50; Beverly T. Venable, Gregory M. Rose, Victoria D. Bush, and Faye W. Gilbert, "The Role of Brand Personality in Charitable Giving: An Assessment and Validation," *Journal of the Academy of Marketing Science* 33 (July 2005): 295–312.

95. Quoted in Stuart Elliott, "A 1950s Brand Mascot Fights 21st-Century Indigestion," *New York Times* (March 5, 2008), www.nytimes.com, accessed March 5, 2008.

96. Craig J. Thompson, Aric Rindfleisch, and Zeynep Arsel, "Emotional Branding and the Strategic Value of the Doppelganger Brand Image," *Journal of Marketing* 70, no. 1 (2006): 50.

97. Jennifer L. Aaker, "Dimensions of Brand Personality," *Journal of Marketing Research* 34 (August 1997): 347–57.

98. Tim Triplett, "Brand Personality Must Be Managed or It Will Assume a Life of Its Own," *Marketing News* (May 9, 1994): 9.

99. Seth Stevenson, "How to Beat Nike," *New York Times* (January 5, 2003), www.nytimes.com, accessed January 5, 2003.

100. Susan Fournier, "Consumers and Their Brands: Developing Relationship Theory in Consumer Research," *Journal of Consumer Research* 24, no. 4 (March 1998): 343–73.

101. Jennifer L. Aaker, "The Malleable Self: The Role of Self-Expression in Persuasion," *Journal of Marketing Research* 36 (February 1999): 45–57; Sak Onkvisit and John Shaw, "Self-Concept and Image Congruence: Some Research and Managerial Implications," *Journal of Consumer Marketing* 4 (Winter 1987): 13–24. For a related treatment of congruence between advertising appeals and self-concept, see George M. Zinkhan and Jae W. Hong, "Self-Concept and Advertising Effectiveness: A Conceptual Model of Congruency, Conspicuousness, and Response Mode," in Rebecca H. Holman and Michael R. Solomon, eds., *Advances in Consumer Research* 18 (Provo, UT: Association for Consumer Research, 1991): 348–54.

102. C. B. Claiborne and M. Joseph Sirgy, "Self-Image Congruence as a Model of Consumer Attitude Formation and Behavior: A Conceptual Review and Guide for Further Research," paper presented at the Academy of Marketing Science Conference, New Orleans, 1990.

103. Susan Fournier and Julie L. Yao, "Reviving Brand Loyalty: A Reconceptualization within the Framework of Consumer-Brand Relationships," *International Journal of Research in Marketing* 14, no. 5 (December 1997): 451–72; Caryl E. Rusbult, "A Longitudinal Test of the Investment Model: The Development (and Deterioration) of Satisfaction and Commitment in Heterosexual Involvements," *Journal of Personality & Social Psychology* 45, no. 1 (1983): 101–17.

104. Allison R. Johnson, Maggie Matear, and Matthew Thomson, "A Coal in the Heart: Self-Relevance as a Post-Exit Predictor of Consumer Anti-Brand Actions," *Journal of Consumer Research* 38, no. 1 (June 2011): 108–25.

105. A. L. E. Birdwell, "A Study of Influence of Image Congruence on Consumer Choice," *Journal of Business* 41 (January 1964): 76–88; Edward L. Grubb and Gregg Hupp, "Perception of Self, Generalized Stereotypes, and Brand Selection," *Journal of Marketing Research* 5 (February 1986): 58–63.

106. Benedict Carey, "With That Saucy Swagger, She Must Drive a Porsche," *New York Times* (June 13, 2006), www.nytimes.com, accessed June 13, 2006.

107. Ira J. Dolich, "Congruence Relationship Between Self-Image and Product Brands," *Journal of Marketing Research* 6 (February 1969): 80–84; Danny N. Bellenger, Earle Steinberg, and Wilbur W. Stanton, "The Congruence of Store Image and Self Image as It Relates to Store Loyalty," *Journal of Retailing* 52, no. 1 (1976): 17–32; Ronald J. Dornoff and Ronald L. Tatham, "Congruence Between Personal Image and Store Image," *Journal of the Market Research Society* 14, no. 1 (1972): 45–52.

108. Naresh K. Malhotra, "A Scale to Measure Self-Concepts, Person Concepts, and Product Concepts," *Journal of Marketing Research* 18 (November 1981): 456–64.

109. Jack L. Nasar, "Symbolic Meanings of House Styles," *Environment & Behavior* 21 (May 1989): 235–57; E. K. Sadalla, B. Verschure, and J. Burroughs, "Identity Symbolism in Housing," *Environment & Behavior* 19 (1987): 579–87.

110. Solomon, "The Role of Products as Social Stimuli"; Robert E. Kleine III, Susan Schultz-Kleine, and Jerome B. Kernan, "Mundane Consumption and the Self: A Social-Identity Perspective," *Journal of Consumer Psychology* 2, no. 3 (1993): 209–35; Newell D. Wright, C. B. Claiborne, and M. Joseph Sirgy, "The Effects of Product Symbolism on Consumer Self-Concept," in John F. Sherry Jr. and Brian Sternthal, eds., *Advances in Consumer Research* 19 (Provo, UT: Association for Consumer Research, 1992): 311–18; Susan Fournier, "A Person-Based Relationship Framework for Strategic Brand Management" (doctoral dissertation, University of Florida, 1994).

111. www.airnewzealand.com/aboutus/mediacentre/cranial-billboards-campaign.htm, accessed March 5, 2013.

112. A. Dwayne Ball and Lori H. Tasaki, "The Role and Measurement of Attachment in Consumer Behavior," *Journal of Consumer Psychology* 1, no. 2 (1992): 155–72.

113. William B. Hansen and Irwin Altman, "Decorating Personal Places: A Descriptive Analysis," *Environment & Behavior* 8 (December 1976): 491–504.

114. Lan Nguyen Chaplin and Deborah Roedder John, "The Development of Self-Brand Connections in Children and Adolescents," *Journal of Consumer Research* 32 (June 2005): 119–29.

115. R. A. Wicklund and P. M. Gollwitzer, *Symbolic Self-Completion* (Hillsdale, NJ: Erlbaum, 1982).

116. Jack L. Nasar, "Symbolic Meanings of House Styles," *Environment & Behavior* 21 (May 1989): 235–57; E. K. Sadalla, B. Verschure, and J. Burroughs, "Identity Symbolism in Housing," *Environment & Behavior* 19 (1987): 579–87.

117. Paul Glader, "Avid Boarders Bypass Branded Gear," *Wall Street Journal* (July 27, 2007): B1.

118. Erving Goffman, *Asylums* (New York: Doubleday, 1961).

119. Floyd Rudmin, "Property Crime Victimization Impact on Self, on Attachment, and on Territorial Dominance," *CPA Highlights, Victims of Crime Supplement* 9, no. 2 (1987): 4–7.

120. Barbara B. Brown, "House and Block as Territory," paper presented at the Conference of the Association for Consumer Research, San Francisco, 1982.

121. Shay Sayre and David Horne, "I Shop, Therefore I Am: The Role of Possessions for Self-Definition," in Shay Sayre and David Horne, eds., *Earth, Wind, and Fire and Water: Perspectives on Natural Disaster* (Pasadena, CA: Open Door Publishers, 1996): 353–70; cf. also Jill G. Klein and Laura Huang, "After All Is Lost: Meeting the Material Needs of Adolescent Disaster Survivors," *Journal of Public Policy & Marketing* 26, no. 1 (Spring 2007): 1–12.

122. Lisa E. Bolton, Joel B. Cohen, and Paul N. Bloom (2006), "Does Marketing Products as Remedies Create 'Get Out of Jail Free Cards'?" *Journal of Consumer Research* 33 (June): 71–81.

123. Amit Bhattacharjee, Lisa E. Bolton, and Americus Reed, II, "License to Lapse: The Effects of Weight Management Product Marketing on a Healthy Lifestyle," working paper, *Wharton*, 2009.

124. Lisa E. Bolton, Americus Reed II, Kevin Volpp, and Katrina Armstrong, "How Does Drug and Supplement Marketing Affect a Healthy Lifestyle?" *Journal of Consumer Research* 34, no. 5 (2008): 713–26.

125. Sheila Shayon, "Levi's for Women: Shape, Not Size, Matters," *BrandChannel* (September 17, 2010), http://www.brandchannel.com/home/post/2010/09/17/Levis-Women-Curve-ID-Digital.aspx, accessed April 10, 2011; http://us.levi.com/shop/index.jsp?categoryId=3146849&AB=CMS_Home_CurveID_081010, accessed May 28, 2011.

126. http://www.spanx.com/category/index.jsp?categoryId=2992553&clickid=topnav_shapers_txt, accessed May 28, 2011.

127. Samantha Murphy, "No, You're Not Fat—Facebook Just Makes You Think You Are," Mashable (March 30, 2012), http://mashable.com/2012/03/30/facebook-makes-you-feel-fat/?WT.mc_id=en_social-media&utm_campaign=Social%2BMedia&utm_medium=email&utm_source=newsletter, accessed January 11, 2013.

128. Nina Mandell, "Padded Swimsuits for All? Abercrombie and Fitch Marketing Padded Tops to Young Girls," *New York Daily News* (March 27, 2011), http://www.nydailynews.com/lifestyle/fashion/2011/03/27/2011-03-27_padded_swimsuits_for_all_abercrombie_and_fitch_marketing_padded_tops_to_young_gi.html, accessed April 10, 2011.

129. Daniel S. Hamermesh, "Ugly? You May Have a Case," *New York Times Magazine* (August 27, 2011), http://www.nytimes.com/2011/08/28/opinion/sunday/ugly-you-may-have-a-case.html?ref=opinion, accessed January 11, 2013.

130. Sharon Jayson, "Study: Beautiful People Cash in on Their Looks," *USA Today* (March 31, 2011), http://usatoday30.usatoday.com/money/perfi/basics/2011-03-30-beauty30_ST_N.htm, accessed January 11, 2013.

131. "Saving Face," *The Economist* (July 10, 2004): 55.

132. Emily Flynn, "Beauty: Babes Spot Babes," *Newsweek* (September 20, 2004): 10.

133. For some results that provide exceptions to this overall phenomenon, cf. Elizabeth Cashdan, "Waist-to-Hip Ratio Across Cultures: Trade-Offs Between Androgen- and Estrogen-Dependent Traits," *Current Anthropology* 49, no. 6 (2008): 1099–1107.

134. Abigail W. Leonard, "How Women Pick Mates vs. Flings," *LiveScience* (January 2, 2007), www.livescience.com/health/070102_facial_features.html, accessed January 3, 2007.

135. Corky Siemaszko, "Depends on the Day: Women's Sex Drive a Very Cyclical Thing," *New York Daily News* (June 24, 1999): 3.

136. http://science.netscape.com/story/2006/10/10/fertile-women-dress-to-impress, accessed February 1, 2007; Kristina M. Durante, Vladas Griskevicius, Sarah E. Hill, Carin Perilloux, and Norman P. Li, "Ovulation, Female Competition, and Product Choice: Hormonal Influences on Consumer Behavior," *Journal of Consumer Research* 37 (April 2011): 921–34.

137. Amanda B. Bower, "Highly Attractive Models in Advertising and the Women Who Loathe Them: The Implications of Negative Affect for Spokesperson Effectiveness," *Journal of Advertising* 30 (Fall 2001): 51–63.

138. Basil G. Englis, Michael R. Solomon, and Richard D. Ashmore, "Beauty Before the Eyes of Beholders: The Cultural Encoding of Beauty Types in Magazine Advertising and Music Television," *Journal of Advertising* 23 (June 1994): 49–64; Michael R. Solomon, Richard Ashmore, and Laura Longo, "The Beauty Match-Up Hypothesis: Congruence Between Types of Beauty and Product Images in Advertising," *Journal of Advertising* 21 (December 1992): 23–34.

139. Thomas Fuller, "A Vision of Pale Beauty Carries Risks for Asia's Women," *International Herald Tribune Online* (May 14, 2006), accessed May 16, 2006.

140. Seth Mydans, "Oh Blue-Eyed Thais, Flaunt Your Western Genes!" *New York Times* (August 29, 2002), www.nytimes.com, accessed August 29, 2002.

141. Fuller, "A Vision of Pale Beauty Carries Risks for Asia's Women."

142. Norimitsu Onishi, "Globalization of Beauty Makes Slimness Trendy," *New York Times* (October 3, 2002), www.nytimes.com, accessed October 3, 2002.

143. Ellen Knickermeyer, "Full-Figured Females Favored," *Opelika-Auburn News* (August 7, 2001).

144. Amy Chozick, "The 'Love Bra' Catches Fire," *Wall Street Journal* (May 7, 2007): A1.

145. Austin Considine, "A Little Imperfection for That Smile?" *New York Times* (October 21, 2011), http://www.nytimes.com/2011/10/23/fashion/in-japan-a-trend-to-make-straight-teeth-crooked-noticed.html, accessed December 2, 2013.

146. Lois W. Banner, *American Beauty* (Chicago: University of Chicago Press, 1980); for a philosophical perspective, see Barry Vacker and Wayne R. Key, "Beauty and the Beholder: The Pursuit of Beauty Through Commodities," *Psychology & Marketing* 10 (November–December 1993): 471–94.

147. Mark J. Miller, "Macy's Introduces Marilyn Monroe Collection to a Racier Generation," *Brandchannel* (March 6, 2013), http://www.brandchannel.com/home/post/2013/03/06/Macys-Marilyn-Monroe-030613.aspx, accessed March 7, 2013.

148. Elaine L. Pedersen and Nancy L. Markee, "Fashion Dolls: Communicators of Ideals of Beauty and Fashion," paper presented at the International Conference on Marketing Meaning, Indianapolis, IN, 1989; Dalma Heyn, "Body Hate," *Ms.* (August 1989): 34; Mary C. Martin and James W. Gentry, "Assessing the Internalization of Physical Attractiveness Norms," *Proceedings of the American Marketing Association Summer Educators' Conference* (Summer 1994): 59–65.

149. Lisa Bannon, "Barbie Is Getting Body Work, and Mattel Says She'll Be 'Rad,'" *Wall Street Journal Interactive Edition* (November 17, 1997).

150. Lisa Bannon, "Will New Clothes, Bellybutton Create 'Turn Around' Barbie," *Wall Street Journal Interactive Edition* (February 17, 2000).

151. "Report Delivers Skinny on Miss America," *Montgomery Advertiser* (March 22, 2000): 5A.

152. "Study: Playboy Models Losing Hourglass Figures," CNN.com (December 20, 2002), www.CNN.com.

153. Anthony H. Ahrensa, Sarah F. Etua, James J. Graya, James E. Mosimanna, Mia Foley Sypecka, and Claire V. Wisemanb, "Cultural Representations of Thinness in Women, Redux: *Playboy* Magazine's Depiction of Beauty from 1979 to 1999," *Body Image* (September 2006): 229–35.

154. Quoted in Will Lassek, Steve Gaulin, and Hara Estroff Marano, "Eternal Curves," *Psychology Today* (July 03, 2012), http://www.psychologytoday.com/articles/201206/eternal-curves, accessed January 11, 2013.

155. Quoted in Lauren Indvik, Mashable (July 3, 2012), http://mashable.com/2012/07/03/seventeen-real-girls-petition/?utm_source=feedburner&utm_medium=email&utm_campaign=Feed%3A+Mashable+%28Mashable%29, accessed January 11, 2013.

156. Erin White, "Dove 'Firms' with Zaftig Models: Unilever Brand Launches European Ads Employing Non-Supermodel Bodies," *Wall Street Journal* (April 21, 2004): B3.

157. Quoted in Sarah Nassauer, "Project Plus-Size Retailers Put New Focus On Getting the Fit Right; An Hourglass Shape, High Waists Are Key," *Wall Street Journal* (September 1, 2011), http://professional.wsj.com/article/SB10001424053111904332804576540650673343320.html?mg=reno-wsj, accessed January 11, 2013; Stephanie Clifford, "Plus-Size Revelation: Bigger Women Have Cash, Too," *New York Times* (June 18, 2010), http://www.nytimes.com/2010/06/19/business/19plus.html?emc=eta1, accessed April 10, 2011.

158. Geoffrey A. Fowler, "Unilever Gives 'Ugly Betty' a Product-Plug Makeover in China," *Wall Street Journal* (December 29, 2008), www.wsj.com, accessed December 29, 2008.

159. Stephanie Clifford, "High Fashion, No Airbrushing," *New York Times* (October 19, 2012), http://www.nytimes.com/2012/10/20/business/rent-the-runway-uses-real-women-to-market-high-fashion.html?ref=todayspaper&_r=0, accessed January 11, 2013.

160. Jill Neimark, "The Beefcaking of America," *Psychology Today* (November–December 1994): 32.

161. Richard H. Kolbe and Paul J. Albanese, "Man to Man: A Content Analysis of Sole-Male Images in Male-Audience Magazines," *Journal of Advertising* 25 (Winter 1996): 1–20.

162. Douglas Quenqua, "Muscular Body Image Lures Boys into Gym, and Obsession," *New York Times* (November 19, 2012), http://www.nytimes.com/2012/11/19/health/teenage-boys-worried-about-body-image-take-risks.html?hp, accessed January 11, 2013.

163. Nina Lentini, "Levi's Launches 'Ultimate Lift' for Female Derriere," *Marketing Daily* (November 17, 2008), www.mediapost.com/Publications/?Fa=Articles.Showarticle&Art_Aid=94943, accessed November 23, 2008; Miho Inada, "Is a Girdle Just for Men a Stretch? Japanese Company Calls Product 'Exercise Wear,' Says It Tones Muscles," *Wall Street Journal* (December 28, 2007): B3.

164. Jack Loechner, "Appearance and Weight Trumps Disease in Women's Concerns," Center for Media Research (May 26, 2008), http://blogs.mediapost.com/Research_Brief/?P=1714, accessed May 26, 2008.

165. David Goetzl, "Teen Girls Pan Ad Images of Women," *Advertising Age* (September 13, 1999): 32; Carey Goldberg, "Citing Intolerance, Obese People Take Steps to Press Cause," *New York Times* (November 5, 2000), http://www.nytimes.com/2000/11/05/us/fat-people-say-an-intolerant-world-condemns-them-on-first-sight.html, accessed September 1, 2011.

166. Shirley S. Wang, "Diet Pepsi's 'Skinny Can' Campaign Riles Eating Disorders Group," *Wall Street Journal* (February 15, 2011), http://blogs.WallStreetJournal.com/health/2011/02/15/diet-pepsis-skinny-can-campaign-riles-eating-disorders-group/, accessed April 10, 2011.

167. http://www.myproana.com, accessed July 29, 2013; Quoted in http://hub.webring.org/hub/proana, accessed May 29, 2011; Doreen Carvajal, "French Bill Takes Chic Out of Being Too Thin," *New York Times* (April 16, 2008), www.newyorktimes.com, accessed April 16, 2008; Alex Williams, "Before Spring Break, the Anorexic Challenge," *New York Times* (April 2, 2006), www.newyorktimes.com, accessed April 2, 2006.

168. "Fat-Phobia in the Fijis: TV-Thin Is In," *Newsweek* (May 31, 1999): 70.

169. Norimitsu Onishi, "Japan, Seeking Trim Waists, Measures Millions," *New York Times* (June 13, 2008), www.nytimes.com, accessed June 13, 2008.

170. Erin White and Deborah Ball, "Slim-Fast Pounds Home Tough Talk Ads Aimed at U.K. Women," *Wall Street Journal* (May 28, 2004): B3.

171. John W. Schouten, "Selves in Transition: Symbolic Consumption in Personal Rites of Passage and Identity Reconstruction," *Journal of Consumer Research* 17 (March 1991): 412–25; Janet Whitman, "Extreme Makeovers Blur Line Between Medicine and Cosmetics," *Wall Street Journal* (January 7, 2004), www.wsj.com, accessed January 7, 2004.

172. Simon Romero, "Chávez Tries to Rally Venezuela against a New Enemy: Breast Lifts," *New York Times* (March 14, 2011), http://www.nytimes.com/2011/03/15/world/americas/15venezuela.html?scp=1&sq=breast&st=cse, accessed April 10, 2011.

173. Sharon Lafranierek, "For Many Chinese, New Wealth and a Fresh Face," *New York Times* (April 23, 2011), http://www.nytimes.com/2011/04/24/world/asia/24beijing.html?_r=1&ref=todayspaper, accessed April 29, 2011.

174. Natasha Singer, "How to Stuff a Wild Bikini Bottom," *New York Times* (March 2, 2006), www.nytimes.com, accessed March 2, 2006.

175. Catherine Saint Louis, "This Teenage Girl Uses Botox. No, She's Not Alone," *New York Times* (August 11, 2010), http://www.nytimes.com/2010/08/12/fashion/12SKIN.html?_r=1&scp=2&sq=botox&st=cse, accessed April 10, 2011.

176. Caroline Muspratt, "Unilever Bans 'Size Zero' Models in Ads," *London Telegraph* (May 9, 2007), www.telegraph.co.uk, accessed May 9, 2007; Larry Rohter, "Burst of High-Profile Anorexia Deaths Unsettles Brazil," *New York Times* (December 30, 2006), www.nytimes.com, accessed December 30, 2006; Eric Wilson, "Doctors Fault Designers' Stance Over Thin Models," *New York Times* (January 9, 2007), www.nytimes.com, accessed January 9, 2007.

177. Jane E. Brody, "Personal Health," *New York Times* (February 22, 1990): B9.

178. Christian S. Crandall, "Social Contagion of Binge Eating," *Journal of Personality & Social Psychology* 55 (1988): 588–98.

179. Ruth P. Rubinstein, "Color, Circumcision, Tattoos, and Scars," in Michael R. Solomon, ed., *The Psychology of Fashion* (Lexington, MA: Lexington Books, 1985): 243–54; Peter H. Bloch and Marsha L. Richins, "You Look 'Mahvelous': The Pursuit of Beauty and Marketing Concept," *Psychology & Marketing* 9 (January 1992): 3–16.

180. Sondra Farganis, "Lip Service: The Evolution of Pouting, Pursing, and Painting Lips Red," *Health* (November 1988): 48–51.

181. Michelle Hancock, "High Heels: The Agony and the Ecstacy," *The Telegraph* (April 1, 1986), http://news.google.com/newspapers?nid=2209&dat=19860401&id=xp4rAAAAIBAJ&sjid=NfwFAAAAIBAJ&pg=6255,163038, accessed September 19, 2013.

182. Dannie Kjeldgaard and Anders Bengtsson, "Consuming the Fashion Tattoo," in Geeta Menon and Akshay R. Rao, eds., *Advances in Consumer Research* 32 (Duluth, MN: Association for Consumer Research, 2005): 172–77.

183. Tiffany Hsu and Don Lee, "At 50 Years Old, Barbie Gets Tattoos—And a Megastore in China," *Los Angeles Times* (March 6, 2009), http://articles.latimes.com/2009/mar/06/business/fi-tattoobarbie6, accessed March 6, 2009.

184. "Three in Ten Americans with a Tattoo Say Having One Makes Them Feel Sexier," Harris (February 12, 2008), www.harrisinteractive.com/harris_poll/index.asp?PID=868, accessed May 29, 2009.

185. Natasha Singer, "Erasing Tattoos, Out of Regret or for a New Canvas," *New York Times* (June 17, 2007), www.nytimes.com, accessed June 17, 2007.

186. www.pathfinder.com:80/altculture/aentries/p/piercing.html, accessed August 22, 1997.

187. "'Pester power' costs parents £460 a year," *The Telegraph U.K.* (October 17, 2013), http://www.telegraph.co.uk/finance/personalfinance/10385226/Pester-power-costs-parents-460-a-year.html, accessed on December 17, 2013.

Chapter 8 • Attitudes and Persuasion

Chapter Objectives

When you finish reading this chapter you will understand why:

1. It is important for consumer researchers to understand the nature and power of attitudes.

2. Attitudes are more complex than they first appear.

3. We form attitudes in several ways.

4. A need to maintain consistency among all of our attitudinal components often motivates us to alter one or more of them.

5. Attitude models identify specific components and combine them to predict a consumer's overall attitude toward a product or brand.

6. The communications model identifies several important components for marketers when they try to change consumers' attitudes toward products and services.

7. The consumer who processes a message is not the passive receiver of information marketers once believed him or her to be.

8. Several factors influence the effectiveness of a message source.

9. The way a marketer structures his or her message determines how persuasive it will be.

10. Audience characteristics help to determine whether the nature of the source or the message itself will be relatively more effective.

MyMarketingLab™
⭐ Improve Your Grade!
Over 10 million students improved their results using the Pearson MyLabs.
Visit **mymktlab.com** for simulations, tutorials, and end-of-chapter problems.

S aundra is hanging out at the mall, idly texting some friends about some stuff she saw in a few stores. When she checks her Facebook page, she sees several of them are chatting about their college application plans. She groans to herself; it's starting already! She's just starting her senior year of high school, and already everybody's thinking about what happens next year. Saundra realizes it's time to bite the bullet and really start to look into this—her Mom will certainly be happy. But it's all so confusing. She's been getting bombarded with enticing ads and brochures from so many different schools. They're hard to escape—some arrive by snail mail and others keep hitting her with emails and texts. A few have invited her to take virtual campus tours on their Web sites, and one even wants her to enter a virtual world version of the campus as an avatar to walk around and "talk" to current students. It's amazing to see how different their pitches are, too. Sure, some universities tout their academic excellence, but others play up their international programs, job placement programs, and even amenities (rock climbing walls!). Of course, she's familiar with some of the schools that are starting to court her, and she already has a pretty good idea in her mind of what they're about. But others feel like a blank slate; so far at least, she has absolutely no idea about what it would be like to be a student at these schools. As Saundra starts to post some Facebook queries about where people are looking, she realizes it's going to be an intense year.

OBJECTIVE 1

It is important for consumer researchers to understand the nature and power of attitudes.

The Power of Attitudes

People use the term *attitude* in many contexts. A friend might ask you, "What is your attitude toward abortion?" A parent might scold, "Young man, I don't like your attitude." Some bars even euphemistically refer to happy hour as "an attitude adjustment period." For our purposes, though, an **attitude** is a lasting, general evaluation of people (including oneself), objects, advertisements, or issues.[1] We call anything toward which one has an attitude an **attitude object (A_o)**. As Saundra will learn during her college search process, we assimilate information from a variety of sources and often put a lot of effort into forming an attitude toward many things, including a complex attitude object like a university.

An attitude is lasting because it tends to endure over time. It is general because it applies to more than a momentary event, such as hearing a loud noise, though you might, over time, develop a negative attitude toward all loud noises. Consumers have attitudes toward a wide range of attitude objects, from very product-specific behaviors (e.g., you use Crest toothpaste rather than Colgate) to more general, consumption-related behaviors (e.g., how often you should brush your teeth). Attitudes help to determine whom you choose to date, what music you listen to, whether you will recycle aluminum cans, or whether you choose to become a consumer researcher for a living. In this chapter we'll consider the contents of an attitude, how we form attitudes, and how we measure them. We will also review some of the surprisingly complex relationships between attitudes and behavior and then take a closer look at how marketers can change these attitudes.

Psychologist Daniel Katz developed the **functional theory of attitudes** to explain how attitudes facilitate social behavior.[2] According to this pragmatic approach, attitudes exist *because* they serve some function for the person. Consumers who expect that they will need to deal with similar situations at a future time will be more likely to start to form an attitude in anticipation.[3] Two people can each have an attitude toward some object for very different reasons. As a result, it's helpful for a marketer to know *why* an attitude is held before she tries to change it. These are different attitude functions:

- **Utilitarian function**—The **utilitarian function** relates to the basic principles of reward and punishment we learned about in Chapter 6. We develop some attitudes toward products simply because they provide pleasure or pain. If a person likes the taste of a cheeseburger, that person will develop a positive attitude toward cheeseburgers. Ads that stress straightforward product benefits (e.g., you should drink Diet Coke "just for the taste of it") appeal to the utilitarian function.
- **Value-expressive function**—Attitudes that perform a **value-expressive function** relate to the consumer's central values (Chapter 3) or self-concept (Chapter 7). A person forms a product attitude in this case because of what the product says about him as a person. Value-expressive attitudes also are highly relevant to the psychographic analyses we discussed in Chapter 7, which consider how consumers cultivate a cluster of activities, interests, and opinions to express a particular social identity.
- **Ego-defensive function**—Attitudes we form to protect ourselves either from external threats or internal feelings perform an **ego-defensive function**. An early marketing study showed that housewives resisted the use of instant coffee because it threatened their conception of themselves as capable homemakers (this doesn't seem to be a very big issue for most anymore!).[4] Products that promise to help a man project a "macho" image (e.g., Marlboro cigarettes) appeal to his insecurities about his masculinity. Another example is deodorant ads that stress the dire, embarrassing consequences when you're caught with underarm odor in public.
- **Knowledge function**—We form some attitudes because we need order, structure, or meaning. A **knowledge function** applies when a person is in an ambiguous situation ("it's OK to wear casual pants to work, but only on Friday") or she confronts a new product (e.g., "Bayer wants you to know about pain relievers").

OBJECTIVE 2

Attitudes are more complex than they first appear.

The ABC Model of Attitudes

When Subaru of America began work on a new marketing strategy, the automaker discovered that even though most auto buyers had heard of the brand, very few had strong emotional connections to it. However, current Subaru owners expressed strong passion and even love for the brand. To ramp up this emotional connection for nonowners as well, the new campaign targets people who are in three different stages of buying a car—what Subaru calls the *heart*, the *head*, and the *wallet*. The *heart* stage focuses on the love owners show for their cars; commercials share personal stories of their attachment. The *head* stage ads, in contrast, present the rational side of specific models as they emphasize how the cars benefit their owners in terms of reliability, economy, and so on. Then, the *wallet* ads deal with the financial details of actually buying a Subaru; these include special offers from local dealers.[5]

Like the Subaru campaign, an attitude has three components: affect, behavior, and cognition. **Affect** describes how a consumer *feels* about an attitude object. **Behavior** refers to his intentions to *take action* about it (but, as we will discuss at a later point, an intention does not always result in an actual behavior). **Cognition** is what he *believes* to be true about the attitude object. You can remember these three components of an attitude as the **ABC model of attitudes**. If these concepts sound familiar, kudos for staying awake: They relate to the three types of decision-making we discussed back in Chapter 2.

The ABC model emphasizes the interrelationships among knowing, feeling, and doing. We can't determine consumers' attitudes toward a product if we just identify their cognitions (beliefs) about it. For example, a researcher may find that shoppers "know" a particular camcorder has a power zoom lens, auto focus, and a flying erase head, but simply knowing this doesn't indicate whether they feel these attributes are good, bad, or irrelevant, or whether they would actually buy the camcorder.

Hierarchies of Effects

Which comes first: knowing, feeling, or doing? It turns out that each element may lead things off, depending on the situation. Attitude researchers developed the concept of a **hierarchy of effects** to explain the relative impact of the three components. Each hierarchy specifies that a fixed sequence of steps occur en route to an attitude. Again, these sequences correspond to the models of decision-making we've already reviewed in Chapter 2. Figure 8.1 summarizes these three different hierarchies.

The Standard Learning Hierarchy

Think → Feel → Do: The **standard learning hierarchy** assumes that a person approaches a product decision as a problem-solving process. We referred to this in Chapter 2 as cognitive decision-making. First, she forms beliefs about a product as she accumulates knowledge (*beliefs*) regarding relevant attributes. Next, she evaluates these beliefs and forms a feeling about the product (*affect*).[6] Then she engages in a relevant behavior, such as when she buys a product that offers the attributes she feels good about. This hierarchy assumes that a consumer is highly involved when she makes a purchase decision.[7] She's motivated to seek out a lot of information, carefully weigh alternatives, and come to a thoughtful decision.

The Low-Involvement Hierarchy

Do → Feel → Think: The **low-involvement hierarchy of effects** assumes that the consumer initially doesn't have a strong preference for one brand over another; instead, she acts on the basis of limited knowledge and forms an evaluation only *after* she has bought the product.[8] The attitude is likely to come about through behavioral learning, as good or bad experiences reinforce her initial choice. So, this sequence corresponds to the model of habitual decision-making from Chapter 2.

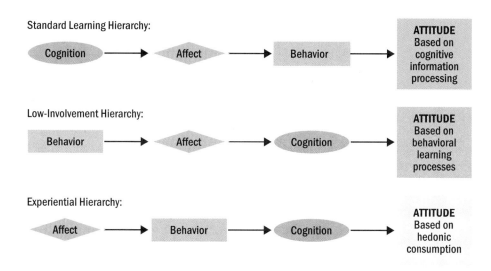

Standard Learning Hierarchy:

Cognition → Affect → Behavior → **ATTITUDE** Based on cognitive information processing

Low-Involvement Hierarchy:

Behavior → Affect → Cognition → **ATTITUDE** Based on behavioral learning processes

Experiential Hierarchy:

Affect → Behavior → Cognition → **ATTITUDE** Based on hedonic consumption

Figure 8.1 HIERARCHIES OF EFFECTS

This ad for New York's famous Smith & Wollensky restaurant emphasizes that marketers and others associated with a product or service are often more involved with it than are their customers.
Source: Courtesy of Smith & Wollensky Steak House.

The possibility that consumers simply don't care enough about many decisions to carefully assemble a set of product beliefs and then evaluate them is important. This implies that all of our well-intentioned efforts to influence beliefs and carefully communicate information about product attributes may fall on deaf ears. Consumers aren't necessarily going to pay attention anyway; they are more likely to respond to simple stimulus–response connections when they make purchase decisions. For example, a consumer who chooses among paper towels might remember that "Bounty is the quicker picker-upper" rather than systematically comparing all the brands on the shelf. Get a life!

The notion of consumers' low involvement is a bitter pill for some marketers to swallow. Who wants to admit that what they market is not very important to the people who buy it? A brand manager for, say, a brand of bubble gum or cat food may find it hard to believe that consumers don't put that much thought into purchasing her product, because she herself spends many of her waking (and perhaps sleeping) hours thinking about it.

For marketers, the ironic silver lining to this low-involvement cloud is that under these conditions, consumers are not motivated to process a lot of complex, brand-related information. Instead, they will be swayed by principles of behavioral learning, such as the simple responses that conditioned brand names or point-of-purchase displays elicit (as we discussed in Chapter 6).

The Experiential Hierarchy

Feel →Do→Think: According to the **experiential hierarchy of effects**, we act on the basis of our emotional reactions. The experiential perspective highlights the idea that intangible product attributes, such as package design, advertising, brand names, and the nature of the setting in which the experience occurs, can help shape our attitudes toward a brand. We may base these reactions on hedonic motivations, such as whether using the product is exciting (like the Nintendo Wii). This sequence corresponds to the process of affective decision-making we covered in Chapter 2.

Even the emotions the communicator expresses have an impact. A smile is infectious; in a process we term *emotional contagion*, messages that happy people deliver enhance our attitude toward the product.[9] Numerous studies demonstrate that the mood a person is in when she sees or hears a marketing message influences how she will process the ad, the likelihood that she will remember the information she sees, and how she will feel about the advertised item and related products in the future.[10]

OBJECTIVE 3
We form attitudes in several ways.

How Do We Form Attitudes?

We all have lots of attitudes, and we don't usually question how we got them. Certainly, you're not born with the heartfelt conviction that, say, Pepsi is better than Coke, or that emo music liberates the soul. From where do these attitudes come?

We form an attitude in several different ways, depending on the particular hierarchy of effects that operates. As we saw in Chapter 6, we simply may form an attitude toward a brand due to classical conditioning: A marketer repeatedly pairs an attitude object such as the Pepsi name with a catchy jingle ("You're in the Pepsi Generation"). Or we can form an attitude due to instrumental conditioning: The marketer reinforces us when we consume the attitude object (e.g., you take a swig of Pepsi and it quenches your thirst). Finally, this learning can result from a very complex cognitive process. For example, a teenager may model the behavior of friends and media endorsers, such as Beyoncé, who drink Pepsi because they believe that this will allow them to fit in with the desirable lifestyle that Pepsi commercials portray.

All Attitudes Are Not Created Equal

It's important to distinguish among types of attitudes, because not all form in the same way.[11] One consumer may be highly brand-loyal; she has an enduring, deeply held positive attitude toward an attitude object, and it would be difficult to weaken this involvement. However, another woman may be a more fickle consumer: She may have a mildly positive attitude toward a product but be quite willing to abandon it when something better comes along. In this section, we'll consider the differences between strongly and weakly held attitudes and briefly review some of the major theoretical perspectives researchers use to explain how attitudes form and relate to our other attitudes.

Consumers vary in their *commitment* to an attitude; the degree of commitment relates to their level of involvement with the attitude object (see Chapter 2).[12] Let's look at three (increasing) levels of commitment:

1 **Compliance**—At the lowest level of involvement, **compliance**, we form an attitude because it helps us to gain rewards or avoid punishment. This attitude is very superficial; it is likely to change when others no longer monitor our behavior or when another option becomes available. You may drink Pepsi because the cafeteria sells it, and it is too much trouble to go elsewhere for a Coca-Cola.

2 **Identification**—**Identification** occurs when we form an attitude to conform to another person's or group's expectations. Advertising that depicts the dire social consequences when we choose some products over others relies on the tendency of consumers to imitate the behavior of desirable models (more on this in Chapter 9).

3 **Internalization**—At a high level of involvement we call **internalization**, deep-seated attitudes become part of our value system. These attitudes are very difficult to change because they are so important to us. The infamous Coke debacle of the 1980s (still a standard in marketing textbooks today) illustrates what can happen when a marketer messes with strongly held attitudes. In this case, Coca-Cola decided to

change its flavor formula to meet the needs of younger consumers who often preferred a sweeter taste (more characteristic of Pepsi). The company conducted rigorous blind *taste tests* that showed people who didn't know what brands they were drinking preferred the flavor of the new formula. Much to its surprise, when New Coke hit the shelves, the company faced a consumer revolt as die-hard Coke fans protested. This allegiance to Coke was obviously more than a minor taste preference for these people; the brand was intertwined with their social identities and took on intense patriotic and nostalgic properties.

OBJECTIVE 4

A need to maintain consistency among all of our attitudinal components often motivates us to alter one or more of them.

The Consistency Principle

Have you ever heard someone say, "Pepsi is my favorite soft drink. It tastes terrible," or "I love my boyfriend. He's the biggest idiot I've ever met"? Probably not (at least until the couple gets married!), because these beliefs or evaluations don't go together. According to the **principle of cognitive consistency**, we value harmony among our thoughts, feelings, and behaviors, and a need to maintain uniformity among these elements motivates us. This desire means that, if necessary, we change our thoughts, feelings, or behaviors to make them consistent with other experiences. That boyfriend may slip up and act like a noob occasionally, but his girlfriend (eventually) will find a way to forgive him—or dump him. The consistency principle is an important reminder that we don't form our attitudes in a vacuum: A big factor is how well they fit with other, related attitudes we already hold.

The **theory of cognitive dissonance** states that when a person is confronted with inconsistencies among attitudes or behaviors, he will take some action to resolve this "dissonance"; perhaps he will change his attitude or modify his behavior to restore consistency. The theory has important ramifications for consumer behavior. We often confront situations in which there is some conflict between our attitudes toward a product or service and what we actually do or buy.[13]

According to the theory, our motivation to reduce the negative feelings of dissonance makes us find a way for our beliefs and feelings to fit together. The theory focuses on situations in which two cognitive elements clash. A *cognitive element* is something a person believes about himself, a behavior he performs, or an observation about his surroundings. For example, the two cognitive elements "I know smoking cigarettes causes cancer" and "I smoke cigarettes" are *dissonant* with one another. This psychological inconsistency creates a feeling of discomfort that the smoker tries to reduce. The magnitude of dissonance depends on both the importance and number of dissonant elements.[14] In other words, we're more likely to observe dissonance in high-involvement situations where there is more pressure to reduce inconsistencies.

We reduce dissonance when we eliminate, add, or change elements. A person can stop smoking (*eliminating*), or remember Great-Aunt Sophie who smoked until the day she died at age 95 (*adding*). Alternatively, he might question the research that links cancer and smoking (*changing*), perhaps by believing industry-sponsored studies that try to refute this connection.

Dissonance theory can help to explain why evaluations of a product tend to increase *after* we buy the product. The cognitive element, "I made a stupid decision," is dissonant with the element, "I am not a stupid person," so we tend to find even more reasons to like something after it becomes ours. A classic study at a horse race demonstrated this *postpurchase dissonance*. Bettors evaluated their chosen horse more highly and were more confident of its success *after* they placed a bet than before. Because the bettor financially commits to the choice, she reduces dissonance as she increases the attractiveness of the chosen alternative relative to the nonchosen ones.[15] One implication of this phenomenon is that consumers actively seek support for their decisions so they can justify them; therefore, marketers should supply their customers with additional reinforcement after they purchase to bolster these decisions.

Advertisers often need to resort to creative imagery to capture consumers' attention and build awareness for their clients.
Source: Courtesy of Energy BBDO.

Motivational Conflicts

A goal has *valence*, which means that it can be positive or negative. We direct our behavior toward goals we value; we are motivated to *approach* the goal and to seek out products that will help us to reach it. However, as we saw in Chapter 6's discussion of negative reinforcement, sometimes we're also motivated to *avoid* a negative outcome rather than achieve a positive outcome. We structure purchases or consumption activities to reduce the chances that we will experience a nasty result. For example, many consumers work hard to avoid rejection by their peers (a negative goal). They stay away from products that they associate with social disapproval. Products such as deodorants and mouthwash frequently rely on consumers' negative motivation when ads depict the onerous social consequences of underarm odor or bad breath.

Because a purchase decision can involve more than one source of motivation, consumers often find themselves in situations in which different motives, both positive and negative, conflict with one another.[16] Marketers attempt to satisfy consumers' needs when they provide possible solutions to these dilemmas. As Figure 8.2 shows, there are three general types of conflicts we should understand. Let's review each kind.

Figure 8.2 TYPES OF MOTIVATIONAL CONFLICTS

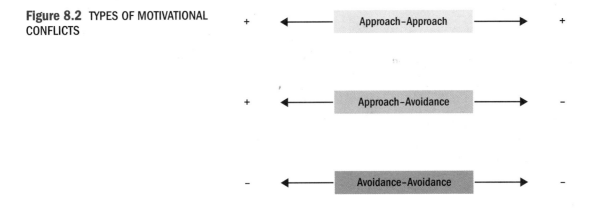

Approach–Approach Conflict

During an **approach–approach conflict**, a person chooses between two desirable alternatives. A student might be torn between going home for the holidays and going on a skiing trip with friends. Or, she might have to choose between two CDs to download (assuming that she's going to pay for one of them!). Because the need to select only one of two goals we want to achieve creates dissonance, we tend to convince ourselves after the fact that the choice we made was the smart one. We may discover additional reasons to support the alternative we did choose or perhaps identify flaws with the option we did not choose (sometimes we call this *rationalization*). A marketer can bundle several benefits together to resolve an approach–approach conflict. For example, Miller Lite's claim that it is "less filling" *and* "tastes great" allows the drinker to "have his beer and drink it too."

Many of the products and services we desire have negative consequences attached to them as well. A person may feel guilty or ostentatious if he or she buys a luxury product like a fur coat or like a glutton if he or she craves a tempting package of Twinkies. An **approach–avoidance conflict** occurs when we desire a goal but wish to avoid it at the same time.

Some solutions to these conflicts include the proliferation of fake furs, which eliminate guilt about harming animals to make a fashion statement, and the success of diet programs like Weight Watchers that promise good food without the calories.[17] Many marketers try to help consumers overcome guilt by convincing them that they deserve these luxuries. As the model for L'Oréal cosmetics exclaims, "Because I'm worth it!"

Sometimes we find ourselves caught "between a rock and a hard place." We may face a choice with two undesirable alternatives: for instance, the option of either spending more money on an old car or buying a new one. Don't you hate when that happens? Marketers frequently address an **avoidance–avoidance conflict** with messages that stress the unforeseen benefits of choosing one option (e.g., when they emphasize special credit plans to ease the pain of car payments).

Self-Perception Theory

Do we always change our attitudes to be in line with our behavior because we're motivated to reduce cognitive dissonance? **Self-perception theory** provides an alternative explanation of dissonance effects.[18] It assumes that we observe our own behavior to determine just what our attitudes are, much as we assume that we know what another person's attitude is when we watch what he does. The theory states that we maintain consistency as we infer that we must have a positive attitude toward an object if we have bought or consumed it (assuming that we freely made this choice). Thus, you might say to yourself, "I guess I must be into Facebook pretty big time. I seem to spend half my life on it."

Self-perception theory helps to explain the effectiveness of a strategy salespeople call the **foot-in-the-door technique**: They know that a consumer is more likely to comply with a big request if he agrees to a smaller one.[19] The name for this technique comes from the old practice of door-to-door selling; salespeople learn to plant their foot in a door so the prospect (they hope) doesn't slam it on them. A good salesperson knows that she is more likely to get an order if she can persuade the customer to open the door and talk. By agreeing to do so, the customer signals that he's willing to listen to the salesperson's pitch. Placing an order is consistent with the self-perception that "I'm the kind of person who is willing to buy something from a salesperson who knocks on my door."[20] Recent research also points to the possibility that when salespeople ask consumers to make a series of choices, these decisions are cognitively demanding and deplete the resources the person has available to monitor his behavior. As a result, the target will opt for easier decisions down the road; in some cases, it may be easier just to comply with the request than to search for reasons why you shouldn't.[21]

Social Judgment Theory

Social judgment theory also assumes that people assimilate new information about attitude objects in light of what they already know or feel.[22] The initial attitude acts as a frame of reference, and we categorize new information in terms of this existing standard. Just as our decision that a box is heavy depends in part on the weight of other boxes we lift, we develop a subjective standard when we judge attitude objects.

One important aspect of the theory is that people differ in terms of the information they will find acceptable or unacceptable. They form **latitudes of acceptance and rejection** around an attitude standard. They will consider and evaluate ideas falling within the latitude favorably, but they are more likely to reject out of hand those that fall outside of this zone. People tend to perceive messages within their latitude of acceptance as more consistent with their position than those messages actually are. We call this exaggeration an *assimilation effect.*

However, we tend to see messages that fall in our latitude of rejection as even more unacceptable than they actually are—this results in an exaggeration we call a *contrast effect.*[23] As a person becomes more involved with an attitude object, her latitude of acceptance gets smaller. In other words, the consumer accepts fewer ideas farther from her own position and she tends to oppose even mildly divergent positions. Discriminating buyers have smaller latitude of acceptance (e.g., "choosy mothers choose Jif peanut butter"). However, relatively uninvolved consumers consider a wider range of alternatives. They are less likely to be brand loyal and are more likely to switch brands.

Balance Theory

Have you ever heard the expression, "Any friend of Joe's is a friend of mine?" How about "My enemy's enemy is my friend?" **Balance theory** considers how a person perceives relations among different attitude objects, and how he alters his attitudes so that these remain consistent (or "balanced").[24] This perspective involves relations (always from the perceiver's subjective point of view) among three elements, so we call the resulting attitude structures *triads.* Each triad contains (1) a person and his perceptions of (2) an attitude object and (3) some other person or object. The theory specifies that we want relations among elements in a triad to be harmonious. If they are unbalanced, this creates tension that we are motivated to reduce by changing our perceptions in order to restore balance.

We link elements together in one of two ways: They can have either a *unit relation,* where we think that a person is somehow connected to an attitude object (something like a belief); or they can have a *sentiment relation,* where a person expresses liking or disliking for an attitude object. You might perceive that a dating couple has a positive sentiment relation. On getting married, they will have a positive unit relation. If they get divorced, they sever the unit relation.

To see how balance theory might work, consider the following scenario:

- Alex would like to date Elliott, who is in her consumer behavior class. In balance theory terms, Alex has a positive sentiment relation with Elliott.
- One day, Elliott shows up in class wearing an earring. Elliott has a positive unit relation with the earring.
- Men who wear earrings are a turnoff to Alex. She has a negative sentiment relation with men's earrings.

According to balance theory, Alex faces an unbalanced triad. As Figure 8.3 shows, she will experience pressure to restore balance by altering some aspect of the triad. How can she do this? She could decide that she does not like Elliott after all. Or her liking for Elliott could prompt her to decide that earrings on men are really pretty cool. She might even try to negate the unit relation between Elliott and the earring by deciding that he must wear it as part of a fraternity initiation (this reduces the free-choice element). Finally, she could choose to "leave the field" by accepting a date with Elliott's roommate Byron who doesn't wear an earring (but who has an awesome tattoo). Note that although the theory does not specify which of these routes Alex will choose, it does predict that she will change one or more of her perceptions to achieve balance. Although this example is an oversimplified representation of most attitude processes, it helps to explain a number of consumer behavior phenomena.

Balance theory reminds us that when we have balanced perceptions, our attitudes also are likely to be stable. However, when we experience inconsistencies, we also are more likely to change our attitudes. Balance theory helps explain why consumers like to be linked to positively valued objects. When you form a unit relation with a popular product (e.g., you wear a popular designer's clothing, drive a hot car, or follow a popular singer), this may improve the chances that other people will include you as a positive sentiment relation in their triads.

This "balancing act" is at the heart of **celebrity endorsements**, in which marketers hope that the star's popularity will transfer to the product or when a nonprofit

Figure 8.3 BALANCE THEORY

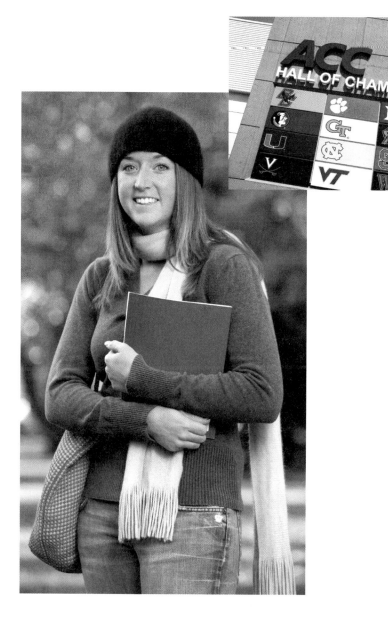

When a school's team wins a game, students (and fans) are more likely to wear merchandise that link them to the institution as they "bask in reflected glory."
Source: © D. Hurst/Alamy;
© Rose-Marie Murray/Alamy.

Marketing Opportunity

Consumers often like to publicize their connections with successful people or organizations (no matter how shaky the connection) to enhance their own standing. Researchers call this tactic **basking in reflected glory**. A series of studies at Arizona State University (ASU) showed how students' desires to identify with a winning image—in this case, ASU's football team—influenced their consumption behaviors. After the team played a game each weekend, observers recorded the incidence of school-related items, such as ASU T-shirts and caps, that students walking around campus wore. The researchers correlated the frequency of these behaviors to the team's performance. If the team won on Saturday, students were more likely to show off their school affiliation (basking in reflected glory) the following Monday than if the team lost. And the bigger the point spread, the more likely they were to observe students who wore clothes with the ASU logo.[25]

At the college level, many schools in addition to ASU reap huge revenues when they license their school's name and logo. Universities with strong athletic programs, such as Michigan, Miami, and Auburn, clean up when they sell millions of dollars worth of merchandise (everything from T-shirts to toilet seats). Yale was a relative latecomer to this game, but the director of licensing explained the decision to profit from the use of the school's name and the likeness of bulldog mascot Handsome Dan: "We recognize that our name means a lot—even to people who didn't go here. Plus, this way we can crack down on the Naked Coed Lacrosse shirts out there with Yale on them."[26]

• • • • • • • • • • • • • • • •

organization recruits a celebrity to discourage harmful behaviors.[27] We will consider this strategy at length later in this chapter. For now, it pays to remember that creating a unit relation between a product and a star can backfire if the public's opinion of the celebrity endorser shifts from positive to negative. For example, Pepsi pulled an ad that featured Madonna after she released a controversial music video involving religion and sex; it also happened when celebrity bad girl Paris Hilton got busted. The strategy can also cause trouble if people question the star–product unit relation: This occurred when the late singer Michael Jackson, who also did promotions for Pepsi, subsequently confessed that he didn't even drink soda.

OBJECTIVE 5
Attitude models identify specific components and combine them to predict a consumer's overall attitude toward a product or brand.

Attitude Models

When market researchers want to assess consumers' attitudes toward beer brands, they might simply go to a bar and ask a bunch of guys, "How do you feel about Budweiser?" However, as we saw earlier, attitudes can be a lot more complex than that. One problem is that many attributes or qualities may link to a product or service; depending on the individual, some of these will be more or less important ("Less filling!" "Tastes great!"). Another problem is that when a person decides to take action toward an attitude object, other factors influence his behavior, such as whether he feels that his family or friends would approve. **Attitude models** specify the different elements that might work together to influence people's evaluations of attitude objects.

Multiattribute Attitude Models

A simple response does not always tell us everything we need to know, either about *why* the consumer feels a certain way toward a product or about what marketers can do to change her attitude. Our beliefs (accurate or not) about a product often are key to how we evaluate it. Warner-Lambert discovered this when it conducted research for its Fresh Burst Listerine mouthwash. A research firm paid families so it could set up cameras in their bathrooms and watch their daily routines (maybe they should have just checked out YouTube). Participants who bought both Fresh Burst and rival Scope said they used mouthwash to make their breath smell good. But Scope users swished around the liquid and then spit it out, whereas Listerine users kept the product in their mouths for a long time (one respondent held the stuff in until he got in the car and finally spit it out in a sewer a block away!). These findings told Listerine that the brand still hadn't shaken its medicine-like image.[28]

Because attitudes are so complex, marketing researchers may use **multiattribute attitude models** to understand them. This type of model assumes that a consumer's attitude toward an attitude object (A_o) depends on the beliefs she has about several of its attributes. When we use a multiattribute model, we assume that we can identify these specific beliefs and combine them to derive a measure of the consumer's overall attitude. We'll describe how these models work with the example of a consumer who evaluates a complex attitude object that should be very familiar to you: a college.

Basic multiattribute models contain three specific elements:[29]

- *Attributes* are characteristics of the A_o. A researcher tries to identify the attributes that most consumers use when they evaluate the A_o. For example, one of a college's attributes is its scholarly reputation.
- *Beliefs* are cognitions about the specific A_o (usually relative to others like it). A belief measure assesses the extent to which the consumer perceives that a brand possesses a particular attribute. For example, a student might believe that the University of North Carolina is strong academically (or maybe this is consistency theory at work, since your humble author got his PhD there!).
- *Importance weights* reflect the relative priority of an attribute to the consumer. Although people might consider an A_o on a number of attributes, some attributes are likely to be more important than others (i.e., consumers will give them greater weight). Furthermore, these weights are likely to differ across consumers. In the case of colleges and universities, for example, one student might stress research opportunities, whereas another might assign greater weight to athletic programs.

The Fishbein Model. The most influential multiattribute model is called the **Fishbein model**, named after its primary developer.[30] The model measures three components of attitude:

- *Salient beliefs* people have about an A_o (i.e., those beliefs about the object a person considers during evaluation).
- *Object-attribute linkages*, or the probability that a particular object has an important attribute.
- *Evaluation* of each of the important attributes.

When we combine these three elements, we compute a consumer's overall attitude toward an object (we'll see later how researchers modify this equation to increase its accuracy). The basic formula is:

$$A_{jk} = \Sigma \beta_{ijk} I_{ik}$$

where

i = attribute
j = brand
k = consumer
I = the importance weight given attribute i by consumer k
β = consumer k's belief regarding the extent to which brand j possesses attribute i
A = a particular consumer's (k's) attitude score for brand j

We obtain the overall attitude score (A) when we multiply a consumer's rating of each attribute for all the brands she considered by the importance rating for that attribute.

To see how this basic multiattribute model works, let's suppose we want to predict which college our friend Saundra from the beginning of the chapter is likely to attend. After months of waiting anxiously, Saundra gets accepted to four schools. Because she must now decide among these, we would first like to know which attributes Saundra will consider when she forms an attitude toward each school. We can then ask Saundra to assign a rating regarding how well each school performs on each attribute and also determine the relative importance of the attributes to her.

By summing scores on each attribute (after we weight each by its relative importance), we compute an overall attitude score for each school. Table 8.1 shows these hypothetical ratings. Based on this analysis, it seems that Saundra has the most favorable attitude toward Smith. She is clearly someone who would like to attend a college for women with a solid academic reputation rather than a school that offers a strong athletic program or a party atmosphere.

Marketing Applications of the Multiattribute Model

Suppose you were the director of marketing for Northland College, another school Saundra considered. How might you use the data from this analysis to improve your image?

TABLE 8.1 The Basic Multiattribute Model: Saundra's College Decision

Attribute (*i*)	Importance (*I*)	Beliefs (*B*) Smith	Princeton	Rutgers	Northland
Academic reputation	6	8	9	6	3
All women	7	9	3	3	3
Cost	4	2	2	6	9
Proximity to home	3	2	2	6	9
Athletics	1	1	2	5	1
Party atmosphere	2	1	3	7	9
Library facilities	5	7	9	7	2
Attitude score		163	142	153	131

Capitalize on Relative Advantage. If prospective students view one brand as superior on a particular attribute, a marketer needs to convince consumers like Saundra that this particular attribute is important. For example, although Saundra rates Northland's social atmosphere highly, she does not believe this attribute is a valued aspect for a college. As Northland's marketing director, you might emphasize the importance of an active social life, varied experiences, or even the development of future business contacts that a student forges when she makes strong college friendships.

Strengthen Perceived Product/Attribute Linkages. A marketer may discover that consumers do not equate his brand with a certain attribute. Advertising campaigns often address this problem when they stress a specific quality to consumers (e.g., "new and improved"). Saundra apparently does not think much of Northland's academic quality, athletic programs, or library facilities. You might develop an informational campaign to improve these perceptions (e.g., "little-known facts about Northland").

Add a New Attribute. Product marketers frequently try to distinguish themselves from their competitors when they add a product feature. Northland College might try to emphasize some unique aspect, such as a hands-on internship program for business majors that takes advantage of ties to the local community.

Influence Competitors' Ratings. Finally, you can decrease your competitors' higher ratings with a *comparative advertising* strategy. In this case, you might publish an ad that lists the tuition rates of a number of area schools with which Northland compares favorably and emphasize the value for the money its students get.

Do Attitudes Predict Behavior?

Consumer researchers have used multiattribute models for many years, but a major problem plagues them: In many cases, a person's attitude doesn't predict her behavior. In a classic demonstration of "do as I say, not as I do," many studies report a very low correlation between a person's reported attitude toward something and her actual behavior toward it. Some researchers are so discouraged that they question whether attitudes are of any use at all when we try to understand behavior.

The Extended Fishbein Model

In response, researchers tinkered with the Fishbein model to improve its predictive ability. They call the newer version the **theory of reasoned action**.[31] This model contains several important additions to the original, and although the model is still not perfect, it does a better job of prediction.[32] Let's look at some of the modifications to this model.

Intentions versus Behavior

Attitudes possess both direction and strength. A person may like or dislike an attitude object with varying degrees of confidence or conviction. It is helpful to distinguish between attitudes we hold firmly and those that are more superficial, especially because a person who holds an attitude with greater conviction is more likely to act on it. One study on environmental issues and marketing activities found, for example, that people who express greater conviction in their feelings regarding environmentally responsible behaviors such as recycling show greater consistency between attitudes and behavioral intentions.[33]

Perhaps most importantly, the theory acknowledges the power of other people to influence what we do. Much as we may hate to admit it, what we think others would *like* us to do may override our own preferences. Thus, **normative influence** can result in a contradiction between what we say we will do and what we actually do when the moment of truth arrives.

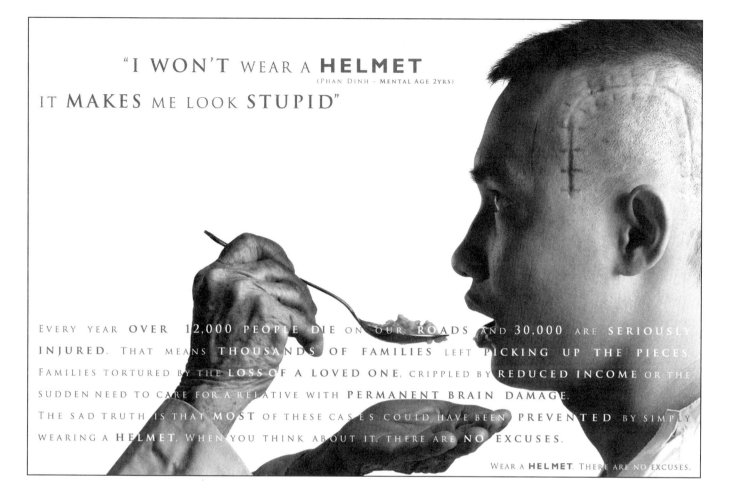

"I WON'T WEAR A **HELMET**
(PHAN DINH - MENTAL AGE 2YRS)
IT **MAKES** ME LOOK **STUPID**"

EVERY YEAR **OVER 12,000 PEOPLE DIE** ON OUR ROADS AND 30,000 ARE **SERIOUSLY INJURED**. THAT MEANS **THOUSANDS OF FAMILIES** LEFT PICKING UP THE PIECES. FAMILIES TORTURED BY THE **LOSS OF A LOVED ONE**, CRIPPLED BY **REDUCED INCOME** OR THE SUDDEN NEED TO CARE FOR A RELATIVE WITH **PERMANENT BRAIN DAMAGE**. THE SAD TRUTH IS THAT **MOST** OF THESE CASES COULD HAVE BEEN **PREVENTED** BY SIMPLY WEARING A **HELMET**. WHEN YOU THINK ABOUT IT, THERE ARE **NO** EXCUSES.

WEAR A **HELMET**. THERE ARE NO EXCUSES.

This Vietnamese ad employs social pressure (the subjective norm) to address people's attitudes toward wearing helmets.
Source: Courtesy of Ogilvy & Mather/Asia Injury Prevention Foundation; Photo by Pro-I Studio.

Let's take a closer look at Saundra's college choice. You can see in Table 8.1 that she was eager to attend a predominantly female school. However, if she felt that this choice would be unpopular (perhaps her friends would think she was too nerdy), she might ignore or downgrade this preference when she made her decision. Researchers added a new element, the **subjective norm (SN)**, to account for the effects of what we believe other people think we should do. They use two factors to measure SN: (1) the intensity of a *normative belief (NB)* that others believe we should take or not take some action and (2) the *motivation to comply (MC)* with that belief (i.e., the degree to which the consumer takes others' anticipated reactions into account when she evaluates a purchase).

The newer model also measures **attitude toward the act of buying (A_{act})**, rather than only the attitude toward the product itself. In other words, it focuses on the perceived consequences of a purchase. Knowing how someone feels about buying or using an object turns out to be more valid than merely knowing the consumer's evaluation of the object itself.[35]

To understand this distinction, consider a marketing researcher who wants to measure college students' attitudes toward safe sex and wearing condoms. Although many college students she interviews would probably report a positive attitude toward condom use, can she conclude from these responses that these respondents will actually buy and use them? She might get more accurate results if she simply asks the same students how likely they are to *buy* condoms. A person might have a positive A_o toward condoms, but A_{act} (attitude toward the act of obtaining the attitude object) might be negative because of the embarrassment or the hassle involved.

Obstacles to Predicting Behavior in the Theory of Reasoned Action

Despite improvements to the Fishbein model, problems arise when researchers misapply it. As our discussion about measuring personality traits in Chapter 7 showed, sometimes researchers use a model in ways it was not intended or where certain assumptions about human behavior may not be warranted.[36] Here are some other obstacles to prediction researchers encounter:

- The model tries to predict actual behavior (e.g., taking a diet pill), not the *outcomes* of behavior that some studies assess (e.g., losing weight).
- Some outcomes are beyond our control, such as when the purchase requires the co-operation of other people. For instance, a woman might *want* to get a mortgage, but this intention will be worthless if she cannot find a banker to give her one.
- The basic assumption that behavior is intentional may be invalid in a variety of cases, including impulsive acts, sudden changes in situation, novelty seeking, or even simple repeat buying. One study found that such unexpected events as having guests, changes in the weather, or reading articles about the healthfulness of certain foods significantly affected actual behaviors.[37]
- Measures of attitude often do not really correspond to the behavior they are supposed to predict, either in terms of the A_o or when the act will occur. One common problem is a difference in the level of abstraction researchers employ. For example, knowing a person's attitude toward sports cars may not predict whether she will purchase a BMW Z3. It is very important to match the level of specificity between the attitude and the behavioral intention.
- A similar problem relates to the *time frame* of the attitude measure. In general, the longer the time between the attitude measurement and the behavior it is supposed to assess, the weaker the relationship will be. For example, predictability improves greatly if we ask a consumer the likelihood that she will buy a house in the next week as opposed to within the next five years.
- We form stronger and more predictive attitudes through direct, personal experience with an A_o than those we form indirectly through advertising.[38] According to the **attitude accessibility perspective**, behavior is a function of the person's immediate perceptions of the A_o, in the context of the situation in which she encounters it. An attitude will guide the evaluation of the object but *only* if a person's memory activates it when she encounters the object. These findings underscore the importance of strategies that induce trials (e.g., by widespread product sampling to encourage the consumer to try the product at home, taste tests in grocery stores, test drives at car dealers, etc.) as well as those that maximize exposure to marketing communications.

In addition, most researchers apply the theory of reasoned action in Western settings. Certain assumptions inherent in the model may not necessarily apply to consumers from other cultures. Several cultural roadblocks diminish the universality of the theory of reasoned action:[39]

- The model predicts the performance of a voluntary act. Across cultures, however, many activities, ranging from taking exams and entering military service to receiving an inoculation or even choosing a marriage partner, are not necessarily voluntary.
- The relative impact of subjective norms may vary across cultures. For example, Asian cultures tend to value conformity and "face saving," so it is possible that subjective norms involving the anticipated reactions of others to the choice will have an even greater impact on behavior for many Asian consumers. Indeed, a study conducted during an election in Singapore successfully predicted how people would vote as it assessed their voting intentions beforehand. These intentions were in turn influenced by such factors as voters' attitudes toward the candidate, attitudes toward the

political party, and subjective norms—which in Singapore includes an emphasis on harmonious and close ties among members of the society.

● The model measures behavioral intentions and thus presupposes that consumers are actively thinking ahead and planning future behaviors. The intention concept assumes that consumers have a linear time sense; they think in terms of past, present, and future. As we'll discuss in Chapter 9, not all cultures subscribe to this perspective on time.

● A consumer who forms an intention implicitly claims that he is in control of his actions. Some cultures (e.g., Muslim peoples) tend to be fatalistic and do not necessarily believe in the concept of free will. Indeed, one study that compared students from the United States, Jordan, and Thailand found evidence for cultural differences in assumptions about fatalism and control over the future.

Trying to Consume

Other theorists propose different perspectives on the attitude–behavior connection. For example, the **multiple pathway anchoring and adjustment (MPAA) model** emphasizes multiple pathways to attitude formation, including outside-in (object-centered) and inside-out (person-centered) pathways.[40]

Another perspective tries to address some of these problems as it focuses instead on consumers' goals and what they believe they have to do to attain them. The **theory of trying** states that we should replace the criterion of behavior in the reasoned action model with *trying* to reach a goal. As Figure 8.4 shows, this perspective recognizes that additional factors might intervene between intent and performance—both personal and environmental barriers might prevent the individual from attaining the goal. For example, a person who intends to lose weight may have to deal with numerous issues: He may not believe he is capable of slimming down, he may have a roommate who loves to cook and who leaves tempting goodies lying around the apartment, his friends may be jealous of his attempts to diet and encourage him to pig out, or he may be genetically predisposed to obesity and cutting down on calories simply will not produce the desired results.[41]

Figure 8.4 THEORY OF TRYING

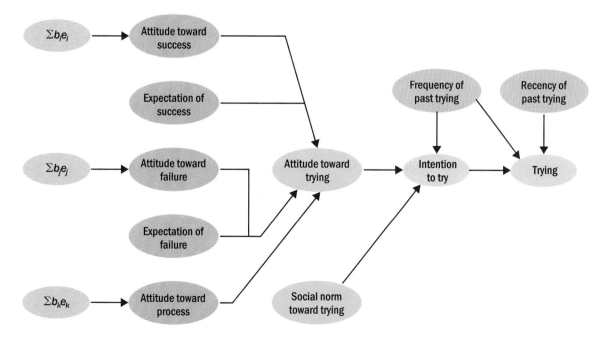

How Do Marketers Change Attitudes?

BUY NOW! Advertisers constantly bombard us with messages imploring us to change our attitudes—and of course buy their products. These persuasion attempts can range from logical arguments to graphic pictures, from peers who try to intimidate us to celebrities who try to charm us. Now we'll review some of the factors that help gauge the effectiveness of marketing communications. Our focus will be on some basic aspects of communication that specifically help to determine how and if consumers will form new attitudes or modify existing ones.

Persuasion involves an active attempt to change attitudes. This is of course Job #1 for many marketing communications. Later we'll learn more about how marketers try to accomplish this, but for now we'll set the stage by listing some basic psychological principles that influence people to change their minds or comply with a request:[42]

- **Reciprocity**—We are more likely to give if first we receive. That's why including money in a mail survey questionnaire (in some cases, as little as a nickel or dime) increases the response rate compared to surveys that come without financial incentives in the envelope.
- **Scarcity**—Like people, items are more attractive when they aren't available. In one study, researchers asked people to rate the quality of chocolate chip cookies. Participants who only got one cookie liked them better than did those who evaluated more of the same kind of cookie. That helps explain why we tend to value "limited-edition" items.
- **Authority**—We believe an authoritative source much more readily than one that is less authoritative. That explains why the American public's opinion on an issue can shift by as much as 2 percent when the *New York Times* (but not the *National Enquirer*) runs an article about it.
- **Consistency**—As we saw earlier in this chapter, people try not to contradict themselves in terms of what they say and do about an issue. In one study, students at an Israeli university who solicited donations to help disabled people doubled the amount they normally collected in a neighborhood if they first asked the residents to sign a petition supporting this cause two weeks before they actually asked for the donations.
- **Liking**—We agree with those we like or admire. A study found that good-looking fund-raisers raised almost twice as much as other volunteers who were not as attractive.
- **Consensus**—We consider what others do before we decide what to do. People are more likely to donate to a charity if they first see a list of the names of their neighbors who have already done so.

Decisions, Decisions: Tactical Communications Options

Suppose Audi wants to create an advertising campaign for a new ragtop it targets to young drivers. As it plans this campaign, the automaker must develop a message that will arouse desire for the car. To craft persuasive messages that might persuade someone to buy this car instead of the many others available, we must answer several questions:

- Who will drive the car in the ad? A NASCAR driver? A career woman? A hip-hop star? The source of a message helps determine whether consumers will accept it.
- How should we construct the message? Should it emphasize the negative consequences of being left out when others drive cool cars and you still tool around in your old clunker? Should it directly compare the car with others already on the market, or maybe present a fantasy in which a tough-minded female executive meets a dashing stranger while she cruises down the highway in her Audi?

- What media should we use? Should the ad run in a magazine? Should we air it on TV? Sell the product door-to-door? Post the material on a Web site or create a Facebook group? Convince bloggers to write about it? Reward shoppers who check in on FourSquare at an Audi dealership? If we do produce a print ad, should we run it in the pages of *Vogue*? *Good Housekeeping*? *Car and Driver*? Sometimes *where* you say something is as important as *what* you say. Ideally, we should match the attributes of the medium with those of what we sell. For example, advertising in magazines with high prestige is more effective when we want to communicate messages about overall product image and quality, whereas specialized expert magazines do a better job when we want to convey factual information.[43]
- What characteristics of the target market might lead its members to accept the ad? If targeted users are frustrated in their daily lives, they might be more receptive to a fantasy appeal. If they're status-oriented, maybe a commercial should show bystanders who swoon with admiration as the car cruises by.

OBJECTIVE 6

The communications model identifies several important components for marketers when they try to change consumers' attitudes toward products and services.

The Elements of Communication

Marketers traditionally rely on the **communications model** shown in Figure 8.5. This model specifies the elements they need to control in order to communicate with their customers. One of these is a *source*, where the communication originates. Another is the *message* itself. There are many ways to say something, and the structure of the message has a significant effect on how we perceive it. We must transmit the message via a *medium*, which could be TV, radio, magazines, billboards, personal contact, or even a matchbook cover. One or more *receivers* interpret the message in light of their own experiences. Finally, the source receives *feedback* so that the marketer can use receivers' reactions to modify aspects of the message as necessary.

An Updated View: Interactive Communications

The traditional communications model is not entirely wrong, but it also doesn't tell the whole story—especially in today's dynamic world of interactivity, where consumers have many more choices available to them and greater control over which messages they *choose* to process.[44]

In fact, the popular strategy we call **permission marketing** acknowledges that a marketer will be much more successful when he communicates with consumers who have already agreed to listen to him; consumers who "opt out" of listening to the message probably weren't good prospects in the first place.[45] In contrast, those who say they want to learn more are likely to be receptive to marketing communications they have chosen

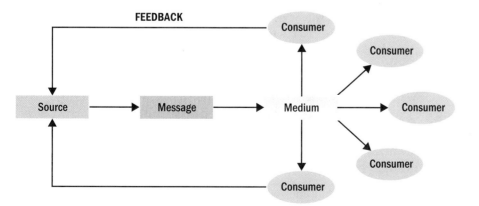

Figure 8.5 THE TRADITIONAL COMMUNICATIONS MODEL

Figure 8.6 AN UPDATED
COMMUNICATIONS MODEL

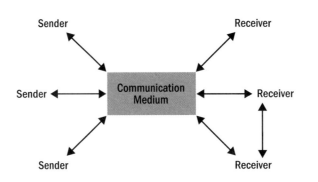

to see or hear. As the permission marketing concept reminds us, we don't have to simply sit there and take it. We have a voice in deciding what messages we choose to see and when—and we exercise that option more and more.

Social scientists developed the traditional model to understand mass communications in which a source transmits information to many receivers at one time—typically via a *broadcast* medium such as television. This perspective essentially views advertising as the process of transferring information to the buyer before a sale. It regards a message as *perishable*—the marketer repeats the same message to a large audience and then the message "vanishes" when a new campaign takes its place. As we'll see, that model doesn't work as well now that we can *narrowcast*, or finely tune our messages to suit very small groups of receivers (sometimes even one person at a time).

OBJECTIVE 7

The consumer who processes a message is not the passive receiver of information marketers once believed him or her to be.

How long has it been since you posted to your Facebook page? Exciting technological and social developments make us rethink the picture of passive consumers as people increasingly play more proactive roles in communications. In other words, we are to a greater extent *partners*—rather than couch potatoes—in the communications process. Our input helps to shape the messages we and others like us receive; furthermore, we may seek out these messages rather than sit home and wait to see them on TV or in the paper. Figure 8.6 illustrates this updated approach to interactive communications.

One of the early instigators of this communications revolution was the humble handheld remote control device. As VCRs (remember them?) began to be commonplace in homes, suddenly consumers had more input into what they wanted to watch—and when. No longer did the TV networks decide when we could watch our favorite shows, and we didn't have to miss the new episode of *Hawaii Five-O* because it was on at the same time as the Bears game.

Since that time, of course, our ability to control our media environment has mushroomed. Just ask some of the millions of us who use digital video recorders (DVRs) such as TiVo to watch TV shows whenever we wish—and who blithely skip over the commercials.[46] Many others have access to video-on-demand or pay-per-view TV. Home-shopping networks encourage us to call in and discuss our passion for cubic zirconium jewelry live on the air. Caller ID devices and answering machines allow us to decide if we will accept a phone call during dinner and to know if a telemarketer lurks on the other end before we pick up the phone. A bit of Web surfing allows us to identify kindred spirits around the globe, to request information about products, and even to provide suggestions to product designers and market researchers.

New Message Formats

An array of new ways to transmit information in both text and picture form offers marketers exciting alternatives to traditional advertising on TV, billboards, magazines, and so on.[47]

M-commerce (mobile commerce), where marketers promote their goods and services via wireless devices, including cell phones, PDAs, and iPods, is red-hot. European and Asian consumers already rely on their cell phones to connect them to the world in ways we are only starting to see in the United States. In Asia, tiny cell phone screens have become electronic wallets that buy Cokes from vending machines and devices that dole out McDonald's coupons on the phone screen. Among the Chinese, cell phones have become such important status symbols that relatives at funeral rites burn paper cell phone effigies so the dead will have their mobiles in the afterlife.

If you're on Facebook, Twitter, or LinkedIn (and the odds are good that you are), you're one of the billions of people to use **social media** applications globally. This label refers to the set of technologies that enable users to create content and share it with thousands or even millions of others. Social media are so widespread that in the United States and other developed countries more people use these platforms than use email—and the time people spend on these networks is growing three times faster than the rate of overall participation online.[48]

Social media platforms include:

- **Blogs**—Users post messages to the Web in diary form. Blogging started as a grassroots movement where individuals shared their thoughts on a range of topics from the mundane to the profound.
- **Video blogging (vlogging)**—You can post video diaries on sites such as YouTube or photos on Flickr.
- **Podcasting**—You can create your own radio show that people can listen to either on their computers or iPods.
- **Virtual worlds**—Immersive-D digital environments (e.g., The Sims).
- **Twitter**—Postings limited to 140 characters. The site continues to grow exponentially as more celebrities tweet to their fans. Teen heartthrob Justin Bieber leads the pack with over 35 million followers, and Lady Gaga and Katy Perry also boast more than 30 million.[49]
- **Widgets**—Small programs that users can download onto their desktops, or embed in their blogs or profile pages, that import some form of live content. For example, a football blogger can place an ESPN.com widget on his blog that displays up-to-the-minute NFL rankings.
- **Transmedia formats**—As new platforms evolve, they mix in intriguing ways because creative marketers harness multiple formats to allow consumers to express themselves and participate in campaigns. These approaches may take the form of **transmedia storytelling**; they typically include communications media that range from Web sites, blogs, and email to recorded phone calls and even graffiti messages scrawled in public spaces. As we saw in Chapter 1, often these take the form of *alternate reality games (ARGs)*, where thousands of people participate in a fictional story or competition to solve a mystery.

OBJECTIVE 8

Several factors influence the effectiveness of a message source.

The Source

Regardless of whether we receive a message by "snail mail" (netheads' slang for the postal service), email, or SMS text, common sense tells us that if different people say or write the very same words, the message can still affect us differently. Researchers have discussed the power of *source effects* for more than 60 years. When we attribute the same message to different sources and measure the degree of attitude change that occurs after listeners hear it, we can isolate which characteristics of a communicator cause attitude change.[52]

Under most conditions, the source of a message can have a big impact on the likelihood that receivers will accept it. Marketers can choose a spokesperson because she is an expert, attractive, famous, or even a "typical" consumer who is both likable and trustworthy. *Credibility* and *attractiveness* are two particularly important source characteristics (i.e., how much we either believe or like the communicator).[53]

Net Profit

The band Nine Inch Nails created a successful ARG campaign to publicize its *Year Zero* album. Players in the game found clues and received phone calls directing them to Web sites revealing images from "the future." The first clue appeared on the back of a shirt promoting Nine Inch Nails' European tour. On the back of the shirt several letters were highlighted that spelled out "I am trying to believe." The words led fans to the Web site iamtryingtobelieve, which describes a drug named "Parepin" that, in the Year Zero story, is being added to the water supply to cloud people's minds.[50] Other clues linked back to the band, such as a USB flash drive left in a bathroom stall at a concert, which in turn led fans to other Web sites that let them download printable stickers, stencils, and posters. Eventually, some players obtained special mobile phones that rang later with instructions to find a bus that took them to—drumroll—a special live performance by the band.[51]

How do marketing specialists decide whether to stress credibility or attractiveness when they select a message source? There should be a match between the needs of the recipient and the potential rewards the source offers. When this match occurs, the recipient is more motivated to process the message. An attractive source, for example, is more effective for receivers who tend to be sensitive about social acceptance and others' opinions, whereas a credible, expert source is more powerful when she speaks to internally oriented people.[54] However, even a credible source's trustworthiness evaporates if she endorses too many products.[55]

The choice may also depend on the type of product. A positive source can reduce risk and increase message acceptance overall, but particular types of sources are more effective to reduce different kinds of risk. Experts excel when we want to change attitudes toward utilitarian products that have high performance risk, such as vacuums, because they are complex and may not work as we expect. Celebrities work better when they focus on products such as jewelry and furniture that have high social risk, where the user is more concerned about the impression others have of him. Finally, "typical" consumers, who are appealing sources because of their similarity to the recipient, tend to be most effective when they provide real-life endorsements for everyday products that are low risk, such as cookies.[56]

Source Credibility

Source credibility refers to a communicator's expertise, objectivity, or trustworthiness. This dimension relates to consumers' beliefs that this person is competent and that she will provide the necessary information we need when we evaluate competing products.

A credible source is particularly persuasive when the consumer has yet to learn much about a product or form an opinion of it.[57] Indeed, a recent study demonstrated that simply letting consumers know a firm is profitable leads them to put more stock in what the company says in its advertising.[58]

Sincerity is particularly important when a company tries to publicize its *corporate social responsibility (CSR)* activities that benefit the community. As we saw in Chapter 4, a company's image can skyrocket when consumers believe it's genuinely doing good things. But this effort can backfire if people question the organization's motivations (e.g., if they think the firm spends more to talk about its good deeds than to actually do them).[59] Not too surprisingly, people who see deceptive advertising experience a feeling of distrust that carries over to other messages from that source and even to other sources, because they are more likely to assume that advertising in general is not very credible—a true case of poisoning the well for other marketers![60]

One widely used technique to generate credibility is to pay an expert or a celebrity to tout a product—but this kind of endorsement doesn't come cheap. However, typically the investment is worth it simply because market analysts use the announcement of an endorsement contract to evaluate a firm's potential profitability, which affects its expected return. On average, then, the impact of endorsements on stock returns appears to be so positive that it offsets the cost of hiring the spokesperson.[61] Indeed, a study on the use of celebrities in marketing reported that ads containing a celebrity endorser produced 9.4 percent higher consumer readership than ads without a celebrity endorser. In its analysis of almost 80,000 print ads, Starch Advertising Research concluded that "in terms of helping with the first task in . . . getting consumers to read your ad, these data show that a celebrity endorsement moves the readership needle."[62]

The drawing power of famous people may even be "wired in": One study found that compared to "ordinary" faces, our brains pay more attention to famous faces and more efficiently process information about these images.[63] Celebrities increase awareness of a firm's advertising and enhance both company image and brand attitudes.[64] A celebrity endorsement strategy can be an effective way to differentiate among similar products. This is especially important when consumers do not perceive many actual differences among competitors, as often occurs when brands are in the mature stage of the product life cycle.

What's more, the early evidence indicates that celebrities exert the same impact on messages we receive from social media platforms. One study found that brand endorsements streamed by celebrities directly to friends and followers on platforms such as Facebook and Twitter are significantly more effective (in fact, greater than 50 percent more) than conventional display ads placed on social media pages. The celebrities in the study included Drew Brees, Snoop Dogg (now Snoop Lion), Matt Hasselbeck, Enrique Iglesias, Khloe Kardashian, Nick Swisher, and Kendra Wilkinson.[65]

Although in general more positive sources tend to increase attitude change, there are exceptions to this rule. Sometimes we can think a source is obnoxious, yet it is still effective. A case in point is the irritating redhead in Wendy's commercials who says "Now That's Better." In some instances the differences in attitude change between positive sources and less positive sources become erased over time. After a while, people appear to "forget" about the negative source and change their attitudes anyway. We call this process the **sleeper effect**.[66]

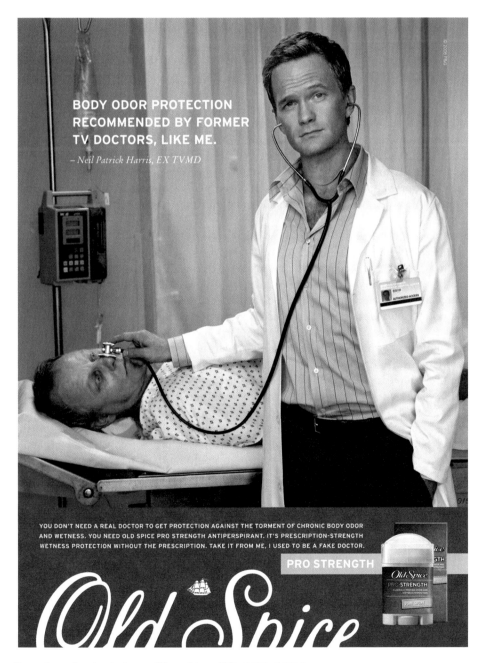

Even actors who play doctors on TV may be credible communicators.

Source: Courtesy of Old Spice/The Procter & Gamble Company.

The Tangled Web

In recent years we've witnessed a new attempt to manipulate attitudes that some call **sock puppeting**. This term describes a company executive or other biased source who poses as someone else as he touts his organization in social media. For example, it came to light that the CEO of Whole Foods had posted derogatory comments about rival Wild Oats without revealing his true identity. More recently, a nonprofit research organization called GiveWell that rates the effectiveness of charities had to discipline two of its founders who pretended to be other people on blogs and then referred people to the group's Web site.[67]

Similar problems may dilute the credibility of Wikipedia, the open-source online encyclopedia that is beloved by many students. Anyone can edit entries, so their reliability is not assured. Although other alert contributors may eventually correct false or self-serving entries, there is still room for organizations to color content in a way that serves their goals. For example, a visitor edited the Wikipedia entry for the SeaWorld theme parks to change all mentions of "orcas" to "killer whales"; he or she also deleted a paragraph that criticized SeaWorld's "lack of respect toward its orcas." It turns out the changes originated at a computer located in Anheuser-Busch—the company that happens to own SeaWorld. An employee of PepsiCo deleted several paragraphs of the Pepsi entry that focused on its detrimental health effects, and a person at Walmart altered an entry about how the retailer pays its employees.

Another form of sock puppeting is so-called *paid influencer programs* that attempt to start online conversations about brands when they encourage bloggers to write about them. These "sponsored conversations" can be effective, but again marketers need to be careful about the potential to distort source recommendations. For example, Kmart awarded a shopping spree to a group of bloggers who agreed to post about their experiences. Panasonic flew bloggers to the Consumer Electronics Show in Las Vegas, where they posted about the show and Panasonic products unveiled there. Mercedes gave a blogger use of an SUV for a week in exchange for posts about it.

This practice got the attention of the U.S. Federal Trade Commission, which recently updated its truth-in-advertising guidelines to require anyone paid in cash or in kind to provide an online endorsement to disclose the financial relationship to the audience. The agency jumped into action in response to the California public relations agency hired by video game developers that had employees pose as consumers and post positive game reviews at the iTunes store.[68]

* * * * * * * * * * * * * * * * *

What Factors Affect Credibility?

A message's credibility increases if receivers think the source's qualifications are relevant to the product he or she endorses. This linkage can overcome other objections people may have to the endorser or the product. Ronald Biggs, whose claim to fame was his role in the Great Train Robbery in the United Kingdom, successfully served as a spokesman in Brazil for a company that makes door locks—a topic about which he is presumably knowledgeable![69]

It's important to note that what is credible to one consumer segment may be a turn-off to another. Indeed, rebellious or even deviant celebrities may be attractive to some simply for that reason. Tommy Hilfiger cultivated a rebellious, street-smart image when he used rapper Snoop Doggy Dogg (who was acquitted of murder charges) to help launch his clothing line and Coolio, a former crack addict and thief, as a runway model.[70] Parents may not be thrilled by these message sources—but isn't that the point? Charlie Sheen, please report to the studio. . . .

A consumer's beliefs about a product's attributes will weaken if he or she perceives that the source is biased.[71] *Knowledge bias* implies that a source's knowledge about a topic is not accurate. *Reporting bias* occurs when a source has the required knowledge but we question his willingness to convey it accurately—as when a racket manufacturer pays a star tennis player to use its products exclusively. The source's credentials might be appropriate, but the fact that consumers see the expert as a "hired gun" compromises believability. The Federal Trade Commission is considering steps to toughen the rules for testimonials by requiring advertisers to produce evidence that the results for a spokesperson are likely to be typical for others. One other possible measure will require celebrities who mention products in TV interviews to disclose any connections they have to the manufacturers of those products. Finally, bloggers who receive free products and recommend them in their blogs will have to document that they got the items at no charge.[72]

Source Attractiveness: "What Is Beautiful Is Good"

A British dairy company enlisted Johnny Rotten, the lead singer of the Sex Pistols, to appear in a commercial (or *advert*, as they say in the United Kingdom) to promote its butter. Sales went up substantially when the punk legend plugged the product (rotten butter?).[73] **Source attractiveness** refers to the social *value* recipients attribute to a communicator. This value relates to the person's physical appearance, personality, social status, or similarity to the receiver (we like to listen to people who are like us).

Some sources like Johnny Rotten appeal to us because they are cool, brainy, or just plain famous. However, many simply are nice to look at. Almost everywhere we turn, beautiful people try to persuade us to buy or do something. As Chapter 7 showed us, our society places a very high premium on physical attractiveness. We assume that good-looking people are smarter, hipper, and happier than the rest of us. This is an example of a *halo effect*, which occurs when we assume that persons who rank high on one dimension excel on others as well. We explain this effect in terms of the consistency principle we discussed earlier in this chapter; we are more comfortable when all of our judgments about a person correspond.

Star Power: Celebrities as Communications Sources

Celebrities hawk everything from grills (George Foreman) to perfumes (J. Lo). As our discussion about the consistency principle illustrates, these messages are more effective when there's a logical connection between the star and the product. When Bob Dylan—who wrote lyrics such as "Advertising signs that con you/Into thinking you're the one/That can do what's never been done/That can win what's never been won . . ." pitches Victoria's Secret lingerie (yes, he really did), marketers may need to reread their consumer behavior textbook.[74] Then again, teen idol Justin Bieber puts his name on almost everything . . . including nail polish![75]

Star power works because celebrities embody *cultural meanings*—they symbolize important categories like status and social class (a "working-class hero," such as Kevin James of *King of Queens*), gender (a "ladies man," such as Brad Pitt), age (the boyish

Marketing Pitfall

Celebrities (and their managers) don't necessarily jump at the chance to endorse just any product. After all, they have a brand image to protect as well. For years one popular strategy has been to film commercials overseas and stipulate that they are not to air at home. The practice is so widespread in Japan that one Web site even coined a term to describe it: *Japander* (a combination of Japanese and pandering)—". . . a western star who uses his or her fame to make large sums of money in a short time by advertising products in Japan that they would probably never use . . . *(see sinecure [sic.], prostitute)* . . . [see text in exhibit at left] to make an ass of oneself in Japanese media." Check out japander.com to see actors such as Arnold Schwarzenegger, George Clooney, and Jennifer Aniston in commercials they'd prefer their American fans didn't see.[77]

Michael J. Fox), and even personality types (the nerdy but earnest Andy Bernard on *The Office*). Ideally, the advertiser decides what meanings the product should convey (that is, how it should position the item in the marketplace) and then chooses a celebrity who embodies a similar meaning. The product's meaning thus moves from the manufacturer to the consumer, using the star as a vehicle.[76]

Nonhuman Endorsers

A celebrity endorsement strategy has its drawbacks. As we previously noted, stars' motives may be suspect if they plug products that don't fit their images or if consumers begin to believe the celebrities never met a product they didn't like (for a fee). They may be involved in a scandal or deviate from a brand's desired image—for example, the Milk Processor Education Program suspended "Got Milk?" ads featuring Mary-Kate and Ashley Olsen after Mary-Kate entered a treatment facility for an undisclosed health issue.

For these reasons, some marketers seek alternative sources, including cartoon characters and mascots. As the marketing director for a company that manufactures costumed characters for sports teams and businesses points out, "You don't have to worry about your mascot checking into rehab."[78] Researchers report that **spokescharacters**, such as the Pillsbury Doughboy, Chester the Cheetah, and the GEICO Gecko, do, in fact, boost viewers' recall of claims that ads make and also yield higher brand attitudes.[79] Some of the most popular spokescharacters in recent years include Old Spice's The Man Your Man Could Smell Like (played by former NFL athlete Isaiah Mustafa), Snoopy (who appears in commercials for MetLife), the talking M&Ms, and Allstate's Mayhem Man.[80]

As we saw in Chapter 7, an *avatar* is one increasingly popular alternative to a flesh-and-blood endorser. *Avatar* is a Hindu term for a deity that appears in superhuman or animal form. In the computing world, it means a character you can move around inside a visual, graphical world. Consumers who inhabit virtual worlds such as *Second Life*, *Habbo Hotel*, and *Entropia Universe* design their avatars to reflect their own unique personalities, desires, and fantasies.

The advantages of using virtual avatars compared to flesh-and-blood models include the ability to change the avatar in real time to suit the needs of the target audience.

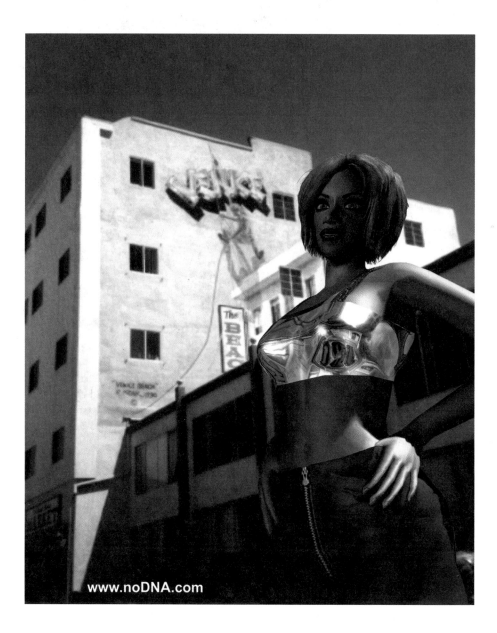

A German firm called NoDNA offers its own stable of cybermodels such as Tyra, who is shown here.
Source: Used with permission of NoDNA c/o Vierte Art.

From an advertising perspective, they are likely to be more cost effective than hiring a real person. From a personal selling and customer service perspective, they handle multiple customers at one time, they are not geographically limited, and they are operational 24/7; therefore, they free up company employees and sales personnel to perform other activities.[81]

OBJECTIVE 9
The way a marketer structures his or her message determines how persuasive it will be.

The Message

A major study of more than 1,000 commercials identified factors that determine whether a commercial message will be persuasive. The single most important feature: Does the communication stress a unique attribute or benefit of the product?[82] Table 8.2 lists some other good and bad elements of commercial messages.

Consumers may find commercials confusing, but what's even worse is when we find them annoying. In a landmark study of irritating advertising, researchers examined more than 500 prime-time network commercials that had registered negative reactions by consumers. The most irritating commercials were for feminine hygiene products, hemorrhoid medication or laxatives, and women's underwear. The researchers identify these as prime offenders:

- The commercial shows a sensitive product (e.g., hemorrhoid medicine) and emphasizes its usage.
- The situation is contrived or overdramatized.
- A person is put down in terms of appearance, knowledge, or sophistication.
- An important relationship, such as a marriage, is threatened.
- There is a graphic demonstration of physical discomfort.
- The commercial created uncomfortable tension because of an argument or an antagonistic character.
- It portrays an unattractive or unsympathetic character.
- It includes a sexually suggestive scene.
- The commercial suffers from poor casting or execution.

TABLE 8.2   Characteristics of Good and Bad Messages

Positive Effects	Negative Effects
Showing convenience of use	Extensive information on components, ingredients, or nutrition
Showing new product or improved features	Outdoor setting (message gets lost)
Casting background (i.e., people are incidental to message)	Large number of on-screen characters
Indirect comparison to other products	Graphic displays
Demonstration of the product in use	
Demonstration of tangible results (e.g., bouncy hair)	
An actor playing the role of an ordinary person	
No principal character (i.e., more time is devoted to the product)	

Source: Adapted from David W. Stewart and David H. Furse, "The Effects of Television Advertising Execution on Recall, Comprehension, and Persuasion," *Psychology & Marketing* 2 (Fall 1985): 135–60. Copyright © 1985 by John Wiley & Sons, Inc. Reprinted by permission.

Characteristics of the message itself help determine its impact on attitudes. These variables include *how* we say the message as well as *what* we say. Depending on the marketer's objectives and the nature of the product, different kinds of messages produce different results. A marketer faces some crucial issues when she creates a message:

- Should she convey the message in words or pictures?
- How often should she repeat the message?
- Should it draw a conclusion, or should this be left up to the listener?
- Should it present both sides of an argument?
- Should it explicitly compare the product to competitors?
- Should it include a blatant sexual appeal?
- Should it arouse negative emotions such as fear?
- How concrete or vivid should the arguments and imagery be?
- Should it be funny?

How Do We Send the Message?

Pictures or Words? The saying "One picture is worth a thousand words" captures the idea that visuals are very effective, especially when the communicator wants to influence receivers' emotional responses. For this reason, advertisers often rely on vivid illustrations or photography.[83]

However, a picture is not always as effective when it communicates factual information. Ads that contain the same information elicit different reactions when the marketer presents them in visual versus verbal form. The verbal version affects ratings on the utilitarian aspects of a product, whereas the visual version affects aesthetic evaluations. Verbal elements are more effective when an accompanying picture reinforces them, especially if they *frame* the illustration (the message in the picture strongly relates to the copy).[84]

Because it requires more effort to process, a verbal message is most appropriate for high-involvement situations, such as print contexts where the reader really pays attention to the advertising. Verbal material decays more rapidly in memory, so these messages require more frequent exposures to obtain the desired effect. Visual images, in contrast, allow the receiver to *chunk* information at the time of encoding (see Chapter 6). Chunking results in a stronger memory trace that aids retrieval over time.[85]

The concrete discussion of a product attribute in ad copy also influences the importance of that attribute, because it draws more attention. For example, in a study where participants read two versions of ad copy for a watch, the version that claimed "According to industry sources, three out of every four watch breakdowns are due to water getting

This British department store ad uses vivid (and perhaps a bit scary?) imagery to communicate.
Source: Courtesy of DDB, London.

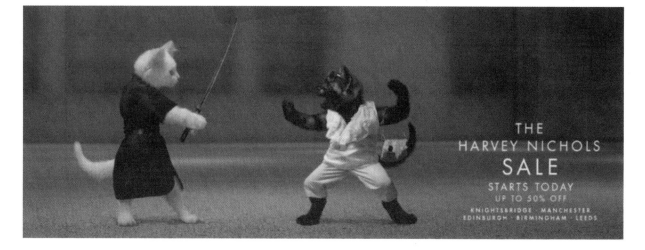

into the case," was more effective than the version that simply said, "According to industry sources, many watch breakdowns are due to water getting into the case."[88]

Repeat the Message? Repetition can be a double-edged sword for marketers. As we noted in Chapter 6, we usually need multiple exposures to a stimulus before learning occurs. Contrary to the saying "familiarity breeds contempt," people tend to like things that are more familiar to them, even if they were not that keen on them initially.[89] Psychologists call this the **mere exposure** phenomenon.

Advertisers find positive effects for repetition even in mature product categories: Repeating product information boosts consumers' awareness of the brand, even though the marketer says nothing new.[90] However, as we saw in Chapter 6, too much repetition creates *habituation*, whereby the consumer no longer pays attention to the stimulus because of fatigue or boredom. Excessive exposure can cause advertising wear-out, which can result in negative reactions to an ad after we see it too much.[91]

The **two-factor theory** explains the fine line between familiarity and boredom; it proposes that two separate psychological processes operate when we repeatedly show an ad to a viewer. The positive side of repetition is that it increases familiarity and thus reduces uncertainty about the product. The negative side is that over time boredom increases with each exposure. At some point the amount of boredom exceeds the amount of uncertainty the message reduces, and this results in wear-out. Figure 8.7 depicts this pattern. Its effect is especially pronounced when each exposure is of a fairly long duration (such as a 30-second commercial).[92]

The two-factor perspective implies that advertisers can overcome this problem if they limit the amount of exposure per repetition (e.g., use 15-second spots instead of longer commercials). They can also maintain familiarity but alleviate boredom if they slightly vary the content of ads over time—although each spot differs, the campaign still revolves around a common theme. Recipients who see varied ads about the product absorb more information about product attributes and experience more positive thoughts about the brand than do those who see the same information repeatedly. This additional information also allows the person to resist attempts to change his or her attitude in the face of a counterattack by a competing brand.[93]

How Do We Structure the Argument?

Many marketing messages are like debates or trials: A source presents an argument and tries to convince the receiver to shift his or her opinion. As you've no doubt guessed, the *way* we present the argument may be as important as *what* we say.

Most messages merely present one or more positive attributes about the product or reasons to buy it. These are *supportive arguments*. An alternative is to use a *two-sided*

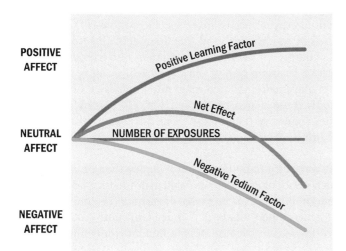

Figure 8.7 TWO-FACTOR THEORY OF MESSAGE REPETITION

message, in which the message presents both positive and negative information. Research indicates that two-sided ads can be quite effective, yet marketers rarely use them.[94]

Why would a marketer want to devote advertising space to publicize a product's negative attributes? Under the right circumstances, **refutational arguments** that first raise a negative issue and then dismiss it can be quite effective. This approach increases source credibility because it reduces *reporting bias*; this means that the receiver assumes the source has carefully considered both sides of the argument. Also, people who are skeptical about the product may be more receptive to a balanced argument instead of a "whitewash."[95] For example, after General Motors declared bankruptcy, an ad declared: "Let's be completely honest: No company wants to go through this."[96] Research evidence indicates that when experts have strong arguments on their side, they are actually more effective if they express some uncertainty rather than stating unequivocally that they are correct.[97]

This doesn't mean the marketer should go overboard and confess to major problems with the product (though hopefully there aren't any major ones to admit to). The typical refutational strategy discusses relatively minor attributes that may present a problem or fall short when the customer compares a product to competitors. Positive, important attributes then refute these drawbacks. For example, Avis got a lot of mileage when it claimed to be only the "No. 2" car rental company, whereas an ad for Volkswagen woefully described one of its cars as a "lemon" because there was a scratch on the glove compartment chrome strip.[98] A two-sided strategy appears to be the most effective when the audience is well educated (and presumably more impressed by a balanced argument).[99] It is also best to use when receivers are not already loyal to the product—"preaching to the choir" about possible drawbacks may raise doubts unnecessarily.

Should the argument draw conclusions, or should the marketer merely present the facts and let the consumer arrive at his own decision? On the one hand, consumers who make their own inferences instead of having ideas spoon-fed to them will form stronger, more accessible attitudes. On the other hand, leaving the conclusion ambiguous increases the chance that the consumer will not form the desired attitude.

The response to this issue depends on the consumer's motivation to process the ad and the complexity of the arguments. If the message is personally relevant, people will pay attention to it and spontaneously form inferences. However, if the arguments are hard to follow or consumers lack the motivation to follow them, it's safer for the ad to draw conclusions.[100]

Should we compare our product to our competitors'? In 1971 the FTC issued guidelines that encouraged advertisers to name competing brands in their ads. The government did this to improve the information available to consumers in ads, and indeed recent evidence indicates that, at least under some conditions, this type of presentation does result in more informed decision-making.[101]

Comparative advertising refers to a message that compares two or more recognizable brands and weighs them in terms of one or more specific attributes.[102] An Arby's campaign to promote its chicken sandwiches used this approach: One commercial, set in a fictitious McDonald's boardroom, featured a young man who tries to convince McDonald's executives to serve a healthier type of chicken as he proclaims, "I propose that McDonald's stops putting phosphates, salt and water into its chicken. Consider replacing your chicken that is only about 70 percent chicken, with 100 percent all-natural chicken." The room erupts in laughter. At the end of the spot, a voice-over chimes in: "Unlike McDonald's, all of Arby's chicken sandwiches are made with 100 percent all-natural chicken. . . ."[103]

This strategy can cut both ways, especially if the sponsor depicts the competition in a nasty or negative way. Although some comparative ads result in desired attitude changes, they may also be lower in believability and stir up *source derogation* (i.e., the consumer may doubt the credibility of a biased presentation).[104] Indeed, in some cultures (such as Asia), comparative advertising is rare because people find such a confrontational approach offensive.

Types of Message Appeals

A persuasive message can tug at the heartstrings or scare you, make you laugh, make you cry, or leave you yearning to learn more. In this section, we'll review the major alternatives available to communicators.

Emotional versus Rational Appeals

Colgate-Palmolive's Total brand was the first toothpaste to claim that it fights gingivitis, a benefit that let Colgate inch ahead of Procter & Gamble's Crest for the first time in decades. Colgate initially made a scientific pitch for its new entry as it emphasized Total's germ-fighting abilities. In newer ads, however, former model Brooke Shields cavorts with two children (not hers) as soft music plays in the background. She states, "Having a healthy smile is important to me. Not just as an actress but as a mom."[105]

So, which is better: to appeal to the head or to the heart? The answer often depends on the nature of the product and the type of relationship consumers have with it. It's hard to gauge the precise effects of rational versus emotional appeals. Although recall of ad content tends to be better for "thinking" ads than for "feeling" ads, conventional measures of advertising effectiveness (e.g., day-after recall) may not be adequate to assess cumulative effects of emotional ads. These open-ended measures assess cognitive responses, and they may penalize feeling ads because the reactions are not as easy to articulate.[106]

Sex Appeals

In a campaign that lit up the Twittersphere, vodka maker Skyy Spirits launched a print and billboard campaign that shows—from the thighs down—a woman in red tights and red heels appearing to have sex with a giant Skyy blue vodka bottle. One critic complained, "This is just ridiculous, it's porn-a-hol. Underage kids will look at this and associate sexual prowess with drinking Skyy."[107]

Echoing the widely held belief that "sex sells," many marketing communications for products from perfumes to autos feature heavy doses of erotic suggestions that range from subtle hints to blatant displays of skin. Of course, the prevalence of sexual appeals varies from country to country. Even American firms run ads elsewhere that would not go over at home. For example, a "cheeky" ad campaign designed to boost the appeal of American-made Lee jeans among Europeans features a series of bare buttocks. The messages are based on the concept that if bottoms could choose jeans, they would opt for Lee: "Bottoms feel better in Lee Jeans."[108]

Perhaps not surprisingly, female nudity in print ads generates negative feelings and tension among female consumers, whereas men's reactions are more positive—although women with more liberal attitudes toward sex are more likely to be receptive.[109] In a case of turnabout being fair play, another study found that males dislike nude males in ads, whereas females responded well to undressed males—but not totally nude ones.[110] Women also respond more positively to sexual themes when they occur in the context of a committed relationship rather than just gratuitous lust.[111]

So, does sex work? Although erotic content does appear to draw attention to an ad, its use may actually be counterproductive. In one survey, an overwhelming 61 percent of the respondents said that sexual imagery in a product's ad makes them *less* likely to buy it.[112] Ironically, a provocative picture can be *too* effective; it can attract so much attention as to hinder processing and recall of the ad's contents. Sexual appeals appear to be ineffective when marketers use them merely as a "trick" to grab attention. They do, however, appear to work when the product is *itself* related to sex (e.g., lingerie or Viagra).[113]

A research firm explored how men and women look at sexually themed ads and what effect, if any, what they choose to look at might have on the ads' effectiveness. One part of the study used special software to follow the visual behavior of respondents as they looked at print ads. The ad sample consisted of two U.S. print ads, one sexual and one nonsexual, from each of five product categories. When the participants looked at a sexual ad, men tended to ignore the text as they focused instead on the woman in it, whereas

This ad from Dubai clearly appeals to the heart.

Source: Courtesy of Y&R Dubai.

STOP USING REGULAR LIGHT BULBS AND WE'LL STOP RUNNING ADS LIKE THIS.

the women participants tended first to explore the ad's text elements. Men said they liked the sexual ads more, they liked the products advertised in them more, and they would be more likely to buy those products. In contrast, women scored the sexual ads lower than the nonsexual ones on all three of those criteria.[114]

Humor Appeals

A TV commercial for Metamucil showed a National Park Service ranger who pours a glass of the laxative down Old Faithful and announces that the product keeps the famous geyser "regular." Yellowstone National Park started getting letters from offended viewers such as this one who wrote, "I suppose that in an era when people sell naming rights to sports arenas . . . that some in the National Park Service would see nothing wrong with selling the image of a National Park ranger for the marketing of a product promoting bowel regularity." Park officials also had their own concerns: They didn't want people to think that the geyser needed "help" or that it's OK to throw things down into it![115]

Does humor work? Overall, humorous advertisements do get attention. One study found that recognition scores for humorous liquor ads were better than average. However, the verdict is mixed as to whether humor affects recall or product attitudes in a significant way.[116] One reason silly ads may shift opinions is that they provide a source of *distraction*. A funny ad inhibits **counterarguing** (in which a consumer thinks of reasons why he doesn't agree with the message); this increases the likelihood of message acceptance because the consumer doesn't come up with arguments against the product.[117]

Fear Appeals

Volkswagen's advertising campaign to promote the safety of its Jetta model really got people's attention. The spots depict graphic car crashes from the perspective of the passengers who chatter away as they drive down the street. Without warning, other vehicles come out of nowhere and brutally smash into their cars. In one spot, viewers see a passenger's head striking an airbag. The spots end with shots of stunned passengers, the damaged Jetta, and the slogan: "Safe happens." The ads look so realistic that consumers called the company to ask if any of the actors were hurt.[119]

Fear appeals emphasize the negative consequences that can occur unless the consumer changes a behavior or an attitude. Fear appeals are fairly common in advertising, although they are more common in social marketing contexts in which organizations encourage people to convert to healthier lifestyles by quitting smoking, using contraception, or relying on a designated driver. Several countries including the United States are looking at tough new guidelines for cigarette advertising and packaging; these include requiring a range of horrific images to appear directly on the cigarette packaging (and in cigarette ads) to show people who have suffered from the ravages of cigarettes.[120]

This tactic may well scare away would-be smokers, but do fear appeals work more generally? Most research on this topic indicates that these negative messages are most effective when the advertiser uses only a moderate threat and when the ad presents a solution to the problem. Otherwise, consumers will tune out the ad because they can do nothing to solve or avoid the threat.[121]

When a weak threat is ineffective, there may be insufficient elaboration of the harmful consequences of the behavior. When a strong threat doesn't work, there may be too much

Marketing Pitfall

A series of funny ads created by a German agency didn't make everyone laugh. Grey Germany did three condom ads for a pharmacy chain. They implied that if more people used condoms the world would have been spared such figures as Mao Tse-Tung, Adolf Hitler, and Osama bin Laden. Each execution depicted a swimming sperm with a likeness of one of the despised characters. Critics complained that the ads were racist, offensive, and inappropriate; the campaign apparently didn't exactly enhance the retailer's image.[118]

A fear appeal from South Africa.
Source: Courtesy of Brandhouse.

elaboration that interferes with the processing of the recommended change in behavior—the receiver is too busy thinking of reasons the message doesn't apply to her to pay attention to the offered solution.[122] A study that manipulated subjects' degree of anxiety about AIDS, for example, found that they evaluated condom ads most positively when the ads used a moderate threat. Copy that promoted use of the condom because "Sex is a risky business" (moderate threat) resulted in more attitude change than either a weaker threat that emphasized the product's sensitivity or a strong threat that discussed the certainty of death from AIDS.[123]

Similarly, scare tactics have not generally been an effective way to convince teenagers to curb their use of alcohol or drugs. Teens simply tune out the message or deny its relevance to them.[124] However, a study of adolescent responses to social versus physical threat appeals in drug prevention messages found that social threat (such as being ostracized by one's peers) is a more effective strategy.[125]

The Message as Art Form: Metaphors Be with You

Just like novelists, poets, and artists, marketers are storytellers. Their communications take the form of stories because they describe intangible product benefits. The storyteller, therefore, must express these in some concrete form so that consumers will get the message.

Advertising creatives rely (consciously or not) on well-known literary devices to communicate these meanings. For example, characters such as Mr. Goodwrench, the Jolly Green Giant, and Charlie the Tuna may personify a product or service. Many ads take the form of an **allegory**; a story about an abstract trait or concept that advertisers tell in the context of a person, animal, vegetable, or object.

A **metaphor** places two dissimilar objects into a close relationship such that "A is B," whereas a **simile** compares two objects, "A is like B." A and B, however dissimilar, share some quality that the metaphor highlights. Metaphors allow the marketer to apply meaningful images to everyday events. In the stock market, "white knights" battle "hostile raiders" with the help of "poison pills"; Tony the Tiger equates cereal with strength and "you're in good hands with Allstate" insurance.[126]

This Chinese detergent ad uses a handcuff metaphor as it urges the viewer, "Free yourself from the burden of handwash."
Source: Courtesy of Saatchi & Saatchi.

为你解开手洗束缚

Resonance is another type of literary device advertisers frequently use. It is a form of presentation that combines a play on words with a relevant picture. Whereas metaphor substitutes one meaning for another by connecting two things that are in some way similar, resonance employs an element that has a double meaning—such as a *pun,* in which two words sound similar but have different meanings. For example, an ad for a diet strawberry shortcake dessert might bear the copy "berried treasure" so that the brand conveys qualities we associate with buried treasure such as valuable and hidden. An ad for ASICS athletic shoes proclaimed, "We believe women should be running the country" as it depicted a woman jogging, while a Bounce fabric softener ad asked "Is there something creeping up behind you?" as it showed a woman's dress bunched up on her back due to static. Because the text departs from expectations, it creates a state of tension or uncertainty on the part of the viewer until he figures out the wordplay. Once the consumer "gets it," he may prefer the ad to a more straightforward message.[127]

Just as a novelist or artist can tell a story in words or pictures, we can choose several ways to address our consumer audiences. Advertisers structure commercials like other art forms; as we've seen, they borrow conventions from literature and art to communicate.[128] One important distinction is between a *drama* and a *lecture.*[129] A lecture is like a speech: The source speaks directly to the audience to inform them about a product or to persuade them to buy it. Because a lecture clearly implies an attempt at persuasion, the audience will regard it as such. Assuming it motivates listeners, they weigh the merits of the message along with the source's credibility. Cognitive responses occur (e.g., "How

CB AS I SEE IT
Professor Edward McQuarrie, *Santa Clara University*

Early in my career, I became fascinated by *wordplay* in magazine advertisements. Puns, rhymes, and much more complex figures of speech abound in advertising headlines. In fact, virtually any figure of speech catalogued by the ancient Greeks can be found in the headlines of American advertisements today. But why is that? After all, advertisers are under a lot of pressure. They have to spend tons of money in the often forlorn hope of getting a consumer to spend a second or two glancing at an ad. Why mess around with complicated wordplay and risk confusing or alienating consumers?

The answer, my colleague Professor David Mick and I discovered, goes to the heart of what makes mass-media advertising a distinctive kind of human communication.[130] The thing to remember is that no one has to look at a magazine ad, or spend much time on it. It's the exact opposite of being in school, where you have to pay attention—or flunk. And that's why advertisers put puns, rhymes, and every other rhetorical device in ad headlines: Such wordplay functions as a lure and a snare for attention. It's fun to get the joke. Result: Consumers linger a second longer, and absorb at least one point from the ad, even if they never read the rest. And a small jot of pleasure gets associated with the brand.

Traditional consumer research is tied to an experimental paradigm in which the subjects are forced to read the whole ad; within that paradigm, there is no way to discover the importance of rhetorical figures. A related problem that I believe continues to handicap consumer research is an excessive focus on persuasion by

means of words. Open a contemporary magazine and look at the full-page color ads: How many words do you see? Not very many anymore. What you will see is carefully crafted photographic imagery, heavily altered by computer graphics software. In fact you will see visual puns, and visual metaphors—figures of speech in pictorial form. My colleague Professor Barbara Phillips and I have shown why it might be smart for advertisers to make their pitch in pictures rather than words; briefly, the very ambiguity of pictorial persuasion makes it more effective, because the reader has to generate more inferences to comprehend the ad.[131]

What I like about being a consumer researcher is that I get to study reality. Every ad represents an attempt by someone working very hard, under the gun to keep his or her job, to get an invisible mass of consumers to spend a second or two more with his or her creation. In my view, it's the study of these real efforts at persuasion that hold the most promise for advancing scientific understanding.

much did Coke pay him to say that?"). Consumers accept the appeal if it overcomes objections and is consistent with their beliefs.

OBJECTIVE 10

Audience characteristics help to determine whether the nature of the source or the message itself will be relatively more effective.

The Source versus the Message: Do We Sell the Steak or the Sizzle?

We've discussed two major components of the communications model: the source and the message. At the end of the day, which component persuades consumers to change their attitudes? Should we worry more about *what* we say or *how* we say it and *who* says it?

Surprise! The answer is it depends. As we saw in Chapter 2, a consumer's level of involvement determines which cognitive processes will activate when she receives a message. This in turn influences which aspects of a communication she processes. Like a traveler who comes to a fork in the road, she chooses one path or the other. The direction she takes determines which aspects of the marketing communication will work and which will fall on deaf ears.

The **elaboration likelihood model (ELM)** assumes that, under conditions of high involvement, we take the *central route* to persuasion. Under conditions of low involvement, we take a *peripheral route* instead. Figure 8.8 diagrams this model.[132]

The Central Route to Persuasion

According to the ELM, when we find the information in a persuasive message relevant or interesting, we pay careful attention to it. In this event, we focus on the arguments the marketer presents and generate *cognitive responses* to this content. An expectant mother who hears a radio message that warns about drinking while pregnant might say to herself, "She's right. I really should stop drinking alcohol now that I'm pregnant." Or she might offer counterarguments, such as, "That's a bunch of baloney. My mother had a cocktail every night when she was pregnant with me, and I turned out fine." If a person generates counterarguments in response to a message, it's less likely that she will yield to the message, whereas if she generates further supporting arguments, it's more likely she'll comply.[133]

The central route to persuasion involves the standard hierarchy of effects we discussed earlier in this chapter. Recall this assumes that we carefully form and evaluate beliefs; the strong attitudes that result in turn guide our behavior. The implication is that message factors, such as the quality of arguments an ad presents, will determine attitude

Figure 8.8 THE ELABORATION LIKELIHOOD MODEL (ELM) OF PERSUASION

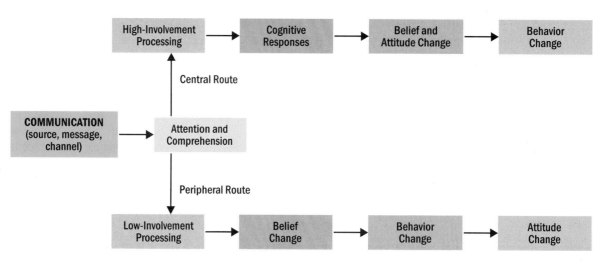

change. Prior knowledge about a topic results in more thoughts about the message and also increases the number of counterarguments.[134]

The Peripheral Route to Persuasion

In contrast, we take the peripheral route when we're not really motivated to think about the marketer's arguments. Instead, we're likely to use other cues to decide how to react to the message. These cues include the product's package, the attractiveness of the source, or the context in which the message appears. We call sources of information extraneous to the actual message *peripheral cues* because they surround the actual message.

The peripheral route to persuasion highlights the **paradox of low involvement**: When we *don't* care as much about a product, the way it's presented (e.g., who endorses it or the visuals that go with it) increases in importance. The implication here is that we may buy low-involvement products chiefly because the marketer designs a "sexy" package, chooses a popular spokesperson, or creates a stimulating shopping environment. In other words, especially when a consumer engages in emotional or behavioral decision-making, these environmental cues become more important than when he or she performs cognitive decision-making; as a result, he or she looks more carefully at the product's performance or other objective attributes.

To recap, the basic idea of the ELM is that highly involved consumers look for the "steak" (e.g., strong, rational arguments). Those who are less involved go for the "sizzle" (e.g., the colors and images in packaging or famous people's endorsements). It is important to remember, however, that the *same* communications variable can be both a central and a peripheral cue, depending on its relation to the attitude object. The physical attractiveness of a model might serve as a peripheral cue in a car commercial, but her beauty might be a central cue for a product such as shampoo where a major product benefit is to enhance attractiveness.[135]

MyMarketingLab

Go to **mymktlab.com** to complete the problems marked with this icon ⭐.

CHAPTER SUMMARY

Now that you have finished reading this chapter, you should understand why:

1. **It is important for consumer researchers to understand the nature and power of attitudes.**

   An *attitude* is a predisposition to evaluate an object or product positively or negatively. We form attitudes toward products and services, and these attitudes often determine whether we will purchase or not.

2. **Attitudes are more complex than they first appear.**

   Three components make up an attitude: beliefs, affect, and behavioral intentions.

3. **We form attitudes in several ways.**

   Attitude researchers traditionally assumed that we learn attitudes in a fixed sequence: First we form beliefs (*cognitions*) about an attitude object, then we evaluate that object (*affect*), and then we take some action (*behavior*). Depending on the consumer's level of involvement and the circumstances, though, his attitudes can result from other hierarchies of effects as well. A key to attitude formation is the function the attitude holds for the consumer (e.g., is it utilitarian or ego defensive?).

4. **A need to maintain consistency among all of our attitudinal components often motivates us to alter one or more of them.**

   One organizing principle of attitude formation is the importance of consistency among attitudinal components— that is, we alter some parts of an attitude to be in line with others. Such theoretical approaches to attitudes as cognitive dissonance theory, self-perception theory, and balance theory stress the vital role of our need for consistency.

5. **Attitude models identify specific components and combine them to predict a consumer's overall attitude toward a product or brand.**

   Multiattribute attitude models underscore the complexity of attitudes: They specify that we identify and combine a set of beliefs and evaluations to predict an overall attitude. Researchers integrate factors such as subjective norms and the specificity of attitude scales into attitude measures to improve predictability.

6. **The communications model identifies several important components for marketers when they try to change consumers' attitudes toward products and services.**

   Persuasion refers to an attempt to change consumers' attitudes. The communications model specifies the elements marketers need to transmit meaning. These include a source, a message, a medium, a receiver, and feedback.

7. **The consumer who processes a message is not the passive receiver of information marketers once believed him or her to be.**

   The traditional view of communications regards the perceiver as a passive element in the process. New developments in interactive communications highlight the need to consider the active roles a consumer plays when he or she obtains product information and builds a relationship with a company. Advocates of permission marketing argue that it's more effective to send messages to consumers who have already indicated an interest in learning about a product than trying to hit people "cold" with these solicitations.

8. **Several factors influence the effectiveness of a message source.**

   Two important characteristics that determine the effectiveness of a source are its attractiveness and credibility. Although celebrities often serve this purpose, their credibility is not always as strong as marketers hope. Marketing messages that consumers perceive as buzz (those that are authentic and consumer generated) tend to be more effective than those they categorize as hype (those that are inauthentic, biased, and company generated).

9. **The way a marketer structures his or her message determines how persuasive it will be.**

   Some elements of a message that help to determine its effectiveness include the following: conveyance of the message in words or pictures; employment of an emotional or a rational appeal; frequency of repetition; conclusion drawing; presentation of both sides of the argument; and inclusion of fear, humor, or sexual references. Advertising messages often incorporate elements from art or literature, such as dramas, lectures, metaphors, allegories, and resonance.

10. **Audience characteristics help to determine whether the nature of the source or the message itself will be relatively more effective.**

    The relative influence of the source versus the message depends on the receiver's level of involvement with the communication. The elaboration likelihood model (ELM) specifies that source effects are more likely to sway a less-involved consumer, whereas a more-involved consumer will be more likely to attend to and process components of the actual message.

KEY TERMS

ABC model of attitudes, 325
affect, 324
allegory, 356
approach–approach conflict, 330
approach–avoidance conflict, 330
attitude, 323
attitude accessibility perspective, 338
attitude models, 334
attitude object (A_o), 323
attitude toward the act of buying (A_{act}), 337
avoidance–avoidance conflict, 330
balance theory, 331
basking in reflected glory, 333
behavior, 324
blogs, 343

celebrity endorsements, 322
cognition, 324
communications model, 341
comparative advertising, 352
compliance, 327
counterarguing, 355
ego-defensive function, 324
elaboration likelihood model (ELM), 358
experiential hierarchy of effects, 326
fear appeals, 355
Fishbein model, 334
foot-in-the-door technique, 331
functional theory of attitudes, 324
hierarchy of effects, 325
identification, 327
internalization, 327

knowledge function, 324
latitudes of acceptance and rejection, 331
low-involvement hierarchy of effects, 325
M-commerce, 343
mere exposure, 351
metaphor, 356
multiattribute attitude models, 334
multiple pathway anchoring and adjustment (MPAA) model, 339
normative influence, 336
paradox of low involvement, 359
permission marketing, 341
persuasion, 340
principle of cognitive consistency, 328

refutational arguments, 352
resonance, 357
self-perception theory, 330
simile, 356
sleeper effect, 345
social judgment theory, 331
social media, 343

sock puppeting, 345
source attractiveness, 346
source credibility, 344
spokescharacters, 348
standard learning hierarchy, 325
subjective norm (SN), 337
theory of cognitive dissonance, 328

theory of reasoned action, 336
theory of trying, 339
transmedia storytelling, 343
two-factor theory, 351
utilitarian function, 324
value-expressive function, 324

REVIEW

8-1 How can an attitude play an ego-defensive function?

8-2 Describe the ABC model of attitudes.

8-3 List the three hierarchies of attitudes, and describe the major differences among them.

8-4 How do levels of commitment to an attitude influence the likelihood that it will become part of the way we think about a product in the long term?

8-5 We sometimes enhance our attitude toward a product after we buy it. How does the theory of cognitive dissonance explain this change?

8-6 What is the foot-in-the-door technique? How does self-perception theory relate to this effect?

8-7 What are latitudes of acceptance and rejection? How does a consumer's level of involvement with a product affect his latitude of acceptance?

8-8 According to balance theory, how can we tell if a triad is balanced or unbalanced? How can consumers restore balance to an unbalanced triad?

8-9 Describe a multiattribute attitude model and list its key components.

8-10 "Do as I say, not as I do." How does this statement relate to attitude models?

8-11 What is a subjective norm, and how does it influence our attitudes?

8-12 What are three obstacles to predicting behavior even if we know a person's attitudes?

8-13 Describe the theory of reasoned action. Why might it not be equally valuable when we apply it to non-Western cultures?

8-14 List three psychological principles related to persuasion.

8-15 Describe the elements of the traditional communications model, and tell how the updated model differs.

8-16 What are blogs and how can marketers use them?

8-17 What is source credibility, and what are two factors that influence our decision as to whether a source is credible?

8-18 What is the difference between buzz and hype? How does this difference relate to the *corporate paradox*?

8-19 What is a halo effect, and why does it happen?

8-20 What is an avatar, and why might an advertiser choose to use one instead of hiring a celebrity endorser?

8-21 When should a marketer present a message visually versus verbally?

8-22 How does the two-factor theory explain the effects of message repetition on attitude change?

8-23 When is it best to present a two-sided message versus a one-sided message?

8-24 Do humorous ads work? If so, under what conditions?

8-25 Should marketers ever try to arouse fear in order to persuade consumers?

8-26 Why do marketers use metaphors to craft persuasive messages? Give two examples of this technique.

8-27 What is the difference between a lecture and a drama?

CONSUMER BEHAVIOR CHALLENGE

■ DISCUSS

8-28 Contrast the hierarchies of effects the chapter outlines. How should marketers take these different situations into account when they choose their marketing mix?

8-29 Corporate sponsorship of universities in the U.S. and the U.K. is commonplace; the sponsored universities have attracted millions of dollars. Chinese universities are following suit. However, this process was strongly criticized following the sponsorship of a building at Tsinghua University in 2011. The No. 4 Teaching Building was adorned with big gold letters proclaiming it to be the Jeanswest Building. Within days of the sign going up it was defaced with spray paint. Students at the university believed the institution had "sold out" and that it was a laughingstock across China. The sign was eventually taken down. The university was trying to raise U.S. $114 million in sponsorship and had offered the naming rights for 14 of its buildings. Has

Tsinghua University crossed the line and brought the institution into disrepute?

8-30 Across the globe there is a growing demand for free mobile phone content, mainly in the form of apps. In turn, this is having a marked influence on mobile advertising. In order to fund the free content, the developers are incorporating advertising.[136] The biggest increase in mobile advertising is taking place in the Asia Pacific region. According to the analyst firm Gartner, the region is the largest market for mobile advertising. Gartner predicts that mobile advertising will grow at a rate of 400 percent until 2016. At that point, the market will be worth an estimated U.S. $24.5 billion. How do you think the marketplace will react to this new advertising medium as it becomes more common?

8-31 Against the backdrop of Chinese consumers' fear of buying contaminated food, a new industry emerged in 2013. Online suppliers promised products directly from the farm. This followed a food scare surrounding contaminated rice and cooking oil. Two of the new businesses, COFO Ltd. and Shunfeng Express, are aiming to capture a market share of the 1.3 billion Chinese consumers in a position to pay for the premium and guaranteed range of organic products. Online sales of fresh produce reached U.S. $6.5 billion in 2013, which represented a growth in excess of 400 percent. Is it ethical to base a business model on fear?

8-32 The Coca-Cola Company pulled a U.K. Internet promotion campaign after parents accused it of targeting children by using references to a notorious pornographic movie. As part of its efforts to reach young social media users for its Dr. Pepper brand, the company took over consenting users' Facebook status boxes. Then, the company would post mildly embarrassing questions such as "Lost my special blankie. How will I go sleepies?" and "What's wrong with peeing in the shower?" But, when a parent discovered that her 14-year-old daughter's profile had been updated with a message that directly referred to a hardcore porn film, the plan backfired and Coke had to pull the promotion.[137] What does it take to get the attention of jaded young people, who get exposed to all kinds of messages in cyberspace? What guidelines (if any) should marketers follow when they try to talk to young people on social media platforms?

8-33 What do you understand by *sock puppeting*, and is it ethical?

8-34 Should corporations use their activities in the field of CSR as marketing tools? Is the point of CSR to be a better corporate neighbor rather than a tool to market products and services?

⭐ 8-35 Discuss some conditions that would cause you to advise a marketer to use a comparative advertising strategy.

8-36 In 2013, Real Madrid's Cristiano Ronaldo signed a multi-million dollar five-year deal to become the official nutrition sponsor of Herbalife. He joined Lionel Messi, who signed a similar agreement in 2010. Should sports icons endorse specific products at the expense of other offerings?

8-37 Fear appeals emphasize the negative consequences that can occur unless the consumer changes a behavior or an attitude. Find some examples of fear appeals in your country.

8-38 Many, many companies rely on celebrity endorsers as communications sources to persuade. Especially when they target younger people, these spokespeople often are "cool" musicians, athletes, or movie stars. In your opinion, who would be the most effective celebrity endorser today, and why? Who would be the least effective? Why?

8-39 Swiss Legend, a watch brand, gets famous people to wear its colorful timepieces. One way it does this is to give away its products at awards shows. Publicists call this common practice "gifting the talent": Companies provide stars with "goody bags" full of complimentary products.[138] What do you think about the practice of "gifting the talent" to accumulate endorsements? Is this a sound strategy? Is it ethical for celebrities to accept these gifts?

■ APPLY

8-40 Think of a behavior someone does that is inconsistent with his or her attitudes (e.g., attitudes toward cholesterol, drug use, or even buying things to make him or her stand out or attain status). Ask the person to elaborate on why he or she does the behavior, and try to identify the way the person resolves dissonant elements.

8-41 Devise an attitude survey for a set of competing automobiles. Identify areas of competitive advantage or disadvantage for each model you include.

8-42 Construct a multiattribute model for a set of local restaurants. Based on your findings, suggest how restaurant managers could improve their establishment's image via the strategies described in this chapter.

8-43 Locate foreign ads at sites like japander.com in which celebrities endorse products that they don't pitch on their home turf. Ask friends or classmates to rate the attractiveness of each celebrity, then show them these ads and ask them to rate the celebrities again. Does the star's "brand image" change after it's paired with cheesy ads? Based on these results, what advice would you give to a manager who has to choose among endorsement offers for a famous client?

8-44 Why would a marketer consider saying negative things about her product? When is this strategy feasible? Can you find examples of it?

8-45 Collect ads that rely on sex appeal to sell products. How often do they communicate benefits of the actual product?

8-46 Observe the process of counterargumentation by asking a friend to talk out loud while he watches a commercial. Ask him to respond to each point in the ad or to write down reactions to the claims the message makes. How much skepticism regarding the claims can you detect?

8-47 Make a log of all the commercials a network television channel shows during a 2-hour period. Assign each to a product category and decide whether each is a drama or an argument. Describe the types of messages the ads use (e.g., two-sided arguments), and keep track

of the types of spokespeople who appear (e.g., TV actors, famous people, animated characters). What can you conclude about the dominant forms of persuasive tactics that marketers currently employ?

8-48 Collect examples of ads that rely on the use of metaphors or resonance. Do you feel these ads are effective? If you were marketing the products, would you feel more comfortable with ads that use a more straightforward, "hard-sell" approach? Why or why not?

8-49 The elaboration likelihood model (ELM) assumes that, under conditions of high involvement, we take the central route to persuasion. What does this mean, and how does it work?

8-50 According to this chapter, "Just like novelists, poets, and artists, marketers are storytellers." To what extent can this be taken seriously? There is certainly a case for it when you consider the fact that communications can often take the form of stories, as they need to illustrate an intangible aspect of product or service. The story is a concrete form of getting the message across. Do you agree?

Case Study

SHAMPOO BUYING: A "BAD HAIR" DAY?

When was the last time you purchased shampoo or other hair care products? How long did it take you to choose? How did you decide?

The hair care aisle of a typical drugstore has over 200 choices for shampoo. The packages promote a myriad of benefits including repair, protection, hydration, control, and nourishment. How does a consumer make the match between his or her needs and the brand benefits? It's not easy to choose, and therefore not a surprise that many of us spend about 20 minutes in this aisle when we select a shampoo brand.

The confusion builds when you consider that it is not just shampoo that we buy. There are gels, mousses, hairsprays, shine enhancers, and conditioners. A recent Mintel survey shows that three-quarters of consumers use conditioner in addition to shampoo, and these numbers are even higher for women.

Advertising agencies work hard to help people make sense of all the options. Hair care product advertising relies heavily on television and print advertising. Sometimes we also see outdoor advertising, most commonly in the form of billboards. Many ad campaigns rely on celebrity endorsers including Kate Winslet and Zooey Deschanel.

And it's not only women in the United States who scratch their heads over these choices. To the women of

Singapore and the Philippines, the choice of hair conditioner poses the same challenges. To connect with women in these countries, Unilever tried a nontraditional campaign to show the benefit of Cream Silk Hair Fall Defense, a conditioner brand the company sells in those countries. Cream Silk's core benefit is the "strength" it gives hair. With the help of advertising agency JWT, Unilever was able to break through the advertising clutter and deliver its message in an entirely new format.

JWT began by contacting Paul Goh, the leading violin bowmaker in Singapore. For this promotion, Mr. Goh was asked to switch out the horsehair violin bows he traditionally used and exchange them with human hair on four of his violin bows. This hair had been washed and conditioned with Cream Silk. To demonstrate the strength of the hair, a string quartet used the bows as it played during a 4-hour concert in a busy shopping mall in Manila. Good news for Unilever: The entire concert concluded without even one broken hair on the violin bows! You can view the video yourself on YouTube; just search "The Human Hair Quartet." The viral video has excellent production quality and includes the advertising message:

"When it comes to showing strong hair, all commercials show it the same way. So we changed the game, by turning the demonstration of STRONG HAIR, into a live performance. . . ."

According to the advertising agency JWT, "The event struck the right chord with Cream Silk's target market. The crowd swelled to 600 at its height, more than 450 Cream Silk samples were given away and the vast majority of consumers we surveyed walked away with a positive perception of the brand." What do you think? If you were looking for stronger hair, would this advertising convince you? How is this approach superior or inferior to others that conditioner brands typically use?

DISCUSSION QUESTIONS

CS 8-1 Describe Cream Silk's promotion within the context of the multiattribute model.

CS 8-2 Will the people who left with the positive attitude purchase the product? What other factors might influence their behavior in addition to this promotion?

Sources: "Shampoo, Conditioners and Styling Products—US—April 2013," Mintel Oxygen, accessed August 4, 2013; "Jwt and Unilever Demonstrate the Power of Cream Silk with First Ever Human Hair Quartet," J. Walter Thompson, http://www.jwt.com/en/news/singapore/singapore/jwtandunileverdemonstratethepowerofcreamsilkwithfirsteverhumanhairquartet/, accessed August 5, 2013.

MyMarketingLab

Go to **mymktlab.com** for the following Assisted-graded writing questions:

8-51 Describe the elaboration likelihood model, and summarize how it relates to the relative importance of *what* is said versus *how* it's said.

8-52 A government agency wants to encourage people who have been drinking to use designated drivers. What advice could you give the organization about constructing persuasive communications? Discuss some factors that might be important, including the structure of the communications, where they should appear, and who should deliver them. Should it use fear appeals? If so, how?

8-53 Mymktlab Only—comprehensive writing assignment for this chapter.

NOTES

1. Robert A. Baron and Donn Byrne, *Social Psychology: Understanding Human Interaction*, 5th ed. (Boston: Allyn & Bacon, 1987).
2. Daniel Katz, "The Functional Approach to the Study of Attitudes," *Public Opinion Quarterly* 24 (Summer 1960): 163–204, Richard J. Lutz, "Changing Brand Attitudes Through Modification of Cognitive Structure," *Journal of Consumer Research* 1 (March 1975): 49–59.
3. Russell H. Fazio, T. N. Lenn, and E. A. Effrein, "Spontaneous Attitude Formation," *Social Cognition* 2 (1984): 214–34.
4. Sharon Shavitt, "The Role of Attitude Objects in Attitude Functions," *Journal of Experimental Social Psychology* 26 (1990): 124–48; see also J. S. Johar and M. Joseph Sirgy, "Value Expressive Versus Utilitarian Advertising Appeals: When and Why to Use Which Appeal," *Journal of Advertising* 20 (September 1991): 23–34.
5. Aaron Baar, "New Subaru Campaign Takes Aim with Cupid's Arrow," *Marketing Daily* (April 28, 2008), http://publications.mediapost.com/Index .Cfm?Fuseaction=Articles.San&S=81435&Nid=420. . ., accessed April 28, 2008.
6. Michael Ray, "Marketing Communications and the Hierarchy-of-Effects," in P. Clarke, ed., *New Models for Mass Communications* (Beverly Hills, CA: Sage, 1973), 147–76.
7. Herbert Krugman, "The Impact of Television Advertising: Learning Without Involvement," *Public Opinion Quarterly* 29 (Fall 1965): 349–56; Robert Lavidge and Gary Steiner, "A Model for Predictive Measurements of Advertising Effectiveness," *Journal of Marketing* 25 (October 1961): 59–62.
8. Stephanie Thompson, "Bad Breakup? There, There, B&J Know Just How You Feel," *Advertising Age* (January 24, 2005): 8.
9. For some recent studies, see Andrew B. Aylesworth and Scott B. MacKenzie, "Context Is Key: The Effect of Program-Induced Mood on Thoughts About the Ad," *Journal of Advertising* 27 (Summer 1998): 17; Angela Y. Lee and Brian Sternthal, "The Effects of Positive Mood on Memory," *Journal of Consumer Research* 26 (September 1999): 115–28; Michael J. Barone, Paul W. Miniard, and Jean B. Romeo, "The Influence of Positive Mood on Brand Extension Evaluations," *Journal of Consumer Research* 26 (March 2000): 386–401. For a study that compared the effectiveness of emotional appeals across cultures, see Jennifer L. Aaker and Patti Williams, "Empathy Versus Pride: The Influence of Emotional Appeals Across Cultures," *Journal of Consumer Research* 25 (December 1998): 241–61. For research that relates mood (depression) to acceptance of health-related messages, see Punam Anand Keller, Isaac M. Lipkus, and Barbara K. Rimer, "Depressive Realism and Health Risk Accuracy: The Negative Consequences of Positive Mood," *Journal of Consumer Research* 29 (June 2002): 57–69.
10. Punam Anand, Morris B. Holbrook, and Debra Stephens, "The Formation of Affective Judgments: The Cognitive–Affective Model Versus the Independence Hypothesis," *Journal of Consumer Research* 15 (December 1988): 386–91; Richard S. Lazarus, "Thoughts on the Relations Between Emotion and Cognition," *American Psychologist* 37, no. 9 (1982): 1019–24; Robert B. Zajonc, "Feeling and Thinking: Preferences Need No Inferences," *American Psychologist* 35, no. 2 (1980): 151–75.
11. See Sharon E. Beatty and Lynn R. Kahle, "Alternative Hierarchies of the Attitude-Behavior Relationship: The Impact of Brand Commitment and Habit," *Journal of the Academy of Marketing Science* 16 (Summer 1988): 1–10.
12. J. R. Priester, D. Nayakankuppan, M. A. Fleming, and J. Godek, "The A(2) SC(2) Model: The Influence of Attitudes and Attitude Strength on Consideration Set Choice," *Journal of Consumer Research* 30, no. 4 (2004): 574–87.

13. Chester A. Insko and John Schopler, *Experimental Social Psychology* (New York: Academic Press, 1972).

14. Ibid.

15. Robert E. Knox and James A. Inkster, "Postdecision Dissonance at Post Time," *Journal of Personality & Social Psychology* 8, no. 4 (1968): 319–23.

16. Thomas Kramer and Song-Oh Yoon, "Approach-Avoidance Motivation and the Use of Affect as Information," *Journal of Consumer Psychology* 17, no. 2 (2007): 128–38.

17. www.weightwatchers.com/index.aspx, accessed June 30, 2009.

18. Daryl J. Bem, "Self-Perception Theory," in Leonard Berkowitz, ed., *Advances in Experimental Social Psychology* (New York: Academic Press, 1972): 1–62; cf. more recently Keisha M. Cutright, Eugenia C. Wu, Jillian C. Banfield, Aaron C. Kay, and Gavan J. Fitzsimons, "When Your World Must Be Defended: Choosing Products to Justify the System," *Journal of Consumer Research* 38, no. 1 (June 2011): 62–77.

19. Jonathan L. Freedman and Scott C. Fraser, "Compliance Without Pressure: The Foot-in-the-Door Technique," *Journal of Personality & Social Psychology* 4 (August 1966): 195–202. For further consideration of possible explanations for this effect, see William DeJong, "An Examination of Self-Perception Mediation of the Foot-in-the-Door Effect," *Journal of Personality & Social Psychology* 37 (December 1979): 221–31; Alice M. Tybout, Brian Sternthal, and Bobby J. Calder, "Information Availability as a Determinant of Multiple-Request Effectiveness," *Journal of Marketing Research* 20 (August 1988): 280–90.

20. David H. Furse, David W. Stewart, and David L. Rados, "Effects of Foot-in-the-Door, Cash Incentives and Follow-ups on Survey Response," *Journal of Marketing Research* 18 (November 1981): 473–78; Carol A. Scott, "The Effects of Trial and Incentives on Repeat Purchase Behavior," *Journal of Marketing Research* 13 (August 1976): 263–69.

21. Bob Fennis, Loes Janssen, and Kathleen D. Vohs, "Acts of Benevolence: A Limited-Resource Account of Compliance with Charitable Requests," *Journal of Consumer Research* (2009): 906–25.

22. See Joan Meyers-Levy and Brian Sternthal, "A Two-Factor Explanation of Assimilation and Contrast Effects," *Journal of Marketing Research* 30 (August 1993): 359–68.

23. Mark B. Traylor, "Product Involvement and Brand Commitment," *Journal of Advertising Research* (December 1981): 51–56.

24. Fritz Heider, *The Psychology of Interpersonal Relations* (New York: Wiley, 1958).

25. Robert B. Cialdini, Richard J. Borden, Avril Thorne, Marcus Randall Walker, Steven Freeman, and Lloyd Reynolds Sloan, "Basking in Reflected Glory: Three (Football) Field Studies," *Journal of Personality & Social Psychology* 34: 366–75.

26. Quoted in Jon Weinbach, "Ad Score! Major League Soccer Teams Will Sell Ad Space on Players' Jerseys," *Wall Street Journal* (September 28, 2006): B1.

27. Debra Z. Basil and Paul M. Herr, "Attitudinal Balance and Cause-Related Marketing: An Empirical Application of Balance Theory," *Journal of Consumer Psychology* 16, no. 4 (2006): 391–403.

28. Leslie Kaufman, "Enough Talk," *Newsweek* (August 18, 1997): 48–49.

29. Allan Wicker, "Attitudes Versus Actions: The Relationship of Verbal and Overt Behavioral Responses to Attitude Objects," *Journal of Social Issues* 25 (Autumn 1969): 65.

30. M. Fishbein, "An Investigation of the Relationships Between Beliefs About an Object and the Attitude Toward that Object," *Human Relations* 16 (1983): 233–40.

31. Icek Ajzen and Martin Fishbein, "Attitude–Behavior Relations: A Theoretical Analysis and Review of Empirical Research," *Psychological Bulletin* 84 (September 1977): 888–918.

32. Morris B. Holbrook and William J. Havlena, "Assessing the Real-to-Artificial Generalizability of Multi-Attribute Attitude Models in Tests of New Product Designs," *Journal of Marketing Research* 25 (February 1988): 25–35; Terence A. Shimp and Alican Kavas, "The Theory of Reasoned Action Applied to Coupon Usage," *Journal of Consumer Research* 11 (December 1984): 795–809.

33. R. P. Abelson, "Conviction," *American Psychologist* 43 (1988): 267–75; R. E. Petty and J. A. Krosnick, *Attitude Strength: Antecedents and Consequences* (Mahwah, NJ: Erlbaum, 1995); Ida E. Berger and Linda F. Alwitt, "Attitude Conviction: A Self-Reflective Measure of Attitude Strength," *Journal of Social Behavior & Personality* 11, no. 3 (1996): 557–72.

34. Noah J. Goldstein, Robert B. Cialdini, and Vladas Griskevicius, "A Room with a Viewpoint: Using Social Norms to Motivate Environmental Conservation in Hotels," *Journal of Consumer Research* 35 (October 2008): 472–82.

35. Blair H. Sheppard, Jon Hartwick, and Paul R. Warshaw, "The Theory of Reasoned Action: A Meta-Analysis of Past Research with Recommendations for Modifications and Future Research," *Journal of Consumer Research* 15 (December 1988): 325–43.

36. Joseph A. Cote, James McCullough, and Michael Reilly, "Effects of Unexpected Situations on Behavior–Intention Differences: A Garbology Analysis," *Journal of Consumer Research* 12 (September 1985): 188–94.

37. Robert E. Smith and William R. Swinyard, "Attitude–Behavior Consistency: The Impact of Product Trial Versus Advertising," *Journal of Marketing Research* 20 (August 1983): 257–67.

38. For a recent similar application, cf. N. T. Tavassoli and G. J. Fitzsimons, "Spoken and Typed Expressions of Repeated Attitudes: Matching Response Modes Leads to Attitude Retrieval Versus Construction," *Journal of Consumer Research* 33, no. 2 (2006): 179–87.

39. Kulwant Singh, Siew Meng Leong, Chin Tiong Tan, and Kwei Cheong Wong, "A Theory of Reasoned Action Perspective of Voting Behavior: Model and Empirical Test," *Psychology & Marketing* 12, no. 1 (January 1995): 37–51; Joseph A. Cote and Patriya S. Tansuhaj, "Culture Bound Assumptions in Behavior Intention Models," in Thom Srull, ed., *Advances in Consumer Research* 16 (Provo, UT: Association for Consumer Research, 1989): 105–9.

40. Joel B. Cohen and Americus Reed, "A Multiple Pathway Anchoring and Adjustment (MPAA) Model of Attitude Generation and Recruitment," *Journal of Consumer Research* 33 (June 2006): 1–15.

41. Richard P. Bagozzi and Paul R. Warshaw, "Trying to Consume," *Journal of Consumer Research* 17 (September 1990): 127–40.

42. Robert B. Cialdini and Kelton V. L. Rhoads, "Human Behavior and the Marketplace," *Marketing Research* (Fall 2001): 13.

43. Gert Assmus, "An Empirical Investigation into the Perception of Vehicle Source Effects," *Journal of Advertising* 7 (Winter 1978): 4–10. For a more thorough discussion of the pros and cons of different media, see Stephen Baker, *Systematic Approach to Advertising Creativity* (New York: McGraw-Hill, 1979).

44. Alladi Venkatesh, Ruby Roy Dholakia, and Nikhilesh Dholakia, "New Visions of Information Technology and Postmodernism: Implications for Advertising and Marketing Communications," in Walter Brenner and Lutz Kolbe, eds., *The Information Superhighway and Private Households: Case Studies of Business Impacts* (Heidelberg: Physica-Verlag, 1996): 319–37; Donna L. Hoffman and Thomas P. Novak, "Marketing in Hypermedia Computer-Mediated Environments: Conceptual Foundations," *Journal of Marketing* 60, no. 3 (July 1996): 50–68. For an early theoretical discussion of interactivity in communications paradigms, see R. Aubrey Fisher, *Perspectives on Human Communication* (New York: Macmillan, 1978).

45. Seth Godin, *Permission Marketing: Turning Strangers into Friends, and Friends into Customers* (New York: Simon & Schuster, 1999).

46. Brad Stone, "The War for Your TV," *Newsweek* (July 29, 2002): 46–47.

47. Geoffrey A. Fowler, "Asia's Mobile Ads," *Wall Street Journal* (April 25, 2005), www.wsj.com, accessed April 25, 2005; Brooks Barnes, "Coming to Your Cell: Paris Hilton," *Wall Street Journal* (March 17, 2005), www.wsj.com, accessed March 17, 2005; Alice Z. Cuneo, "Marketers Dial in to Messaging," *Advertising Age* (November 1, 2004): 18; Stephen Baker and Heather Green, "Blogs Will Change Your Business," *BusinessWeek* (May 2, 2005): 56.

48. "Social Nets and Blogs More Popular than E-Mail," March 17, 2009, www.emarketer.com, accessed March 17, 2009.

49. http://twittercounter.com/pages/100, accessed March 7, 2013.

50. http://www.iamtryingtobelieve.com/, accessed May 30, 2011.

51. Jon Zahlaway, "Nine Inch Nails' *Year Zero* Plot Hits the Web," *SoundSpike*, February 22, 2007, http://www.livedaily.com/news/11570.html?t=102, accessed May 30, 2011.

52. Carl I. Hovland and W. Weiss, "The Influence of Source Credibility on Communication Effectiveness," *Public Opinion Quarterly* 15 (1952): 635–50; for a recent treatment, cf. Yong-Soon Kang and Paul M. Herr, "Beauty and the Beholder: Toward an Integrative Model of Communication Source Effects," *Journal of Consumer Research* 33 (June 2006): 123–30.

53. Herbert Kelman, "Processes of Opinion Change," *Public Opinion Quarterly* 25 (Spring 1961): 57–78; Susan M. Petroshius and Kenneth E. Crocker, "An Empirical Analysis of Spokesperson Characteristics on Advertisement and Product Evaluations," *Journal of the Academy of Marketing Science* 17 (Summer 1989): 217–26.

54. Kenneth G. DeBono and Richard J. Harnish, "Source Expertise, Source Attractiveness, and the Processing of Persuasive Information: A Functional Approach," *Journal of Personality & Social Psychology* 55, no. 4 (1988): 541–46.

55. Joseph R. Priester and Richard E. Petty, "The Influence of Spokesperson Trustworthiness on Message Elaboration, Attitude Strength, and Advertising Effectiveness," *Journal of Consumer Psychology* 13, no. 4 (2003): 408–21.

56. Hershey H. Friedman and Linda Friedman, "Endorser Effectiveness by Product Type," *Journal of Advertising Research* 19, no. 5 (1979): 63–71. For a study that looked at nontarget market effects—the effects of advertising

intended for other market segments—see Jennifer L. Aaker, Anne M. Brumbaugh, and Sonya A. Grier, "Non-Target Markets and Viewer Distinctiveness: The Impact of Target Marketing on Advertising Attitudes," *Journal of Consumer Psychology* 9, no. 3 (2000): 127–40.

57. S. Ratneshwar and Shelly Chaiken, "Comprehension's Role in Persuasion: The Case of Its Moderating Effect on the Persuasive Impact of Source Cues," *Journal of Consumer Research* 18 (June 1991): 52–62.

58. Steven S. Posavac, Michal Herzenstein, Frank R. Kardes, and Suresh Sundaram, "Profits and Halos: The Role of Firm Profitability Information in Consumer Inference," *Journal of Consumer Psychology* 20, no. 3 (2010): 327–37.

59. Yeosun Yoon, Zeynep Gurhan-Canli, and Norbert Schwarz, "The Effect of Corporate Social Responsibility (CSR) Activities on Companies with Bad Reputations," *Journal of Consumer Psychology* 16, no. 4 (2006): 377–90.

60. Peter R. Darke and Robin J. B. Ritchie, "The Defensive Consumer: Advertising Deception, Defensive Processing, and Distrust," *Journal of Marketing Research* 44 (February 2007): 114–27.

61. Jagdish Agrawal and Wagner A. Kamakura, "The Economic Worth of Celebrity Endorsers: An Event Study Analysis," *Journal of Marketing* 59 (July 1995): 56–62.

62. "Report: Charlie Sheen May Not Shine, But Stars Are Aligned as Print Ad Activists," NYSportsJournalism.com (February 25, 2011), http://nysportsjournalism.squarespace.com/study-stars-shine-in-print-ads/?SSScrollPosition=0&VK=94964620, accessed April 30, 2011.

63. Heather Buttle, Jane E. Raymond, and Shai Danziger, "Do Famous Faces Capture Attention?," paper presented at Association for Consumer Research Conference, Columbus, OH (October 1999).

64. Michael A. Kamins, "Celebrity and Noncelebrity Advertising in a Two-Sided Context," *Journal of Advertising Research* 29 (June–July 1989): 34; Joseph M. Kamen, A. C. Azhari, and J. R. Kragh, "What a Spokesman Does for a Sponsor," *Journal of Advertising Research* 15, no. 2 (1975): 17–24; Lynn Langmeyer and Mary Walker, "A First Step to Identify the Meaning in Celebrity Endorsers," in Rebecca H. Holman and Michael R. Solomon, eds., *Advances in Consumer Research* 18 (Provo, UT: Association for Consumer Research, 1991): 364–71.

65. Joe Mandese, "Tweet This: Social Endorsements Beat Social Media Ad Buys," *Online Media Daily* (March 10, 2011), http://www.mediapost.com/publications/?fa=Articles.showArticle&art_aid=146459&nid=124651, accessed April 30, 2011.

66. Anthony R. Pratkanis, Anthony G. Greenwald, Michael R. Leippe, and Michael H. Baumgardner, "In Search of Reliable Persuasion Effects: III. The Sleeper Effect Is Dead, Long Live the Sleeper Effect," *Journal of Personality & Social Psychology* 54 (1988): 203–18.

67. Stephanie Strom, "Nonprofit Punishes a 2nd Founder for Ruse," *New York Times*, January 15, 2008, www.nytimes.com/2008/01/15/us/15givewell.html?ex=1201064400&en=97effb249, accessed January 15, 2008; Ross D. Petty and J. Craig Andrews, "Covert Marketing Unmasked: A Legal and Regulatory Guide for Practices That Mask Marketing Messages," *Journal of Public Policy & Marketing* (Spring 2008): 7–18; James B. Stewart, "Whole Foods CEO Threatens Merger, Fuels Arbitrage," *Smart Money* (July 18, 2007), www.smartmoney.com/investing/stocks/whole-foods-ceo-threatens-merger-fuels-arbitrage-21550/?hpadref=1, accessed June 4, 2009; Brian Morrissey, "'Influencer Programs' Likely to Spread," *Adweek* (March 2, 2009), http://www.adweek.com/news/advertising-branding/influencer-programs-likely-spread-98542, accessed March 2, 2009; Katie Hafner, "Seeing Corporate Fingerprints in Wikipedia Edits," *New York Times* (August 19, 2007), www.nytimes.com/2007/08/19/technology/19wikipedia.html?_r=1&oref=slogin, accessed August 19, 2007; Brian Bergstein, "New Tool Mines: Wikipedia Trustworthiness Software Analyzes Reputations of the Contributors Responsible for Entries," *MSNBC* (September 5, 2007), www.msnbc.msn.com/id/20604175, accessed September 5, 2007; http://wikiscanner.virgil.gr, accessed June 4, 2009.

68. Ameet Sachdev, "FTC Cracks Down on Fake Online Endorsements: Agency Attempts to Punish Fake Reviews, Force Disclosure," *Chicago Tribune* (October 11, 2010), http://articles.chicagotribune.com/2010-10-11/business/ct-biz-1011-web-reviews--20101011_1_ftc-cracks-endorsements-mary-engle, accessed April 15, 2011.

69. "Robber Makes It Biggs in Ad," *Advertising Age* (May 29, 1989): 26.

70. Robert LaFranco, "MTV Conquers Madison Avenue," *Forbes* (June 3, 1996): 138.

71. Alice H. Eagly, Andy Wood, and Shelly Chaiken, "Causal Inferences About Communicators and Their Effect in Opinion Change," *Journal of Personality & Social Psychology* 36, no. 4 (1978): 424–35.

72. Ira Teinowitz, "'Results May Vary' Won't Be Enough Under New FTC Rules, Proposed Changes Could Put Squeeze on Ads for Diet Plans and Fitness Equipment," *Advertising Age* (March 12, 2009), www.adage.com, accessed March 12, 2009.

73. Patrick Loughran, "Sex Pistol Sends Dairy Crest Butter Sales Soaring," *Times of London* (February 3, 2009), www.timesonline.co.uk, accessed February 4, 2009.

74. Brian Steinberg, "Bob Dylan Gets Tangled Up in Pink: Victoria's Secret Campaign Drafts Counterculture Hero; Just Like the Rolling Stones," *Wall Street Journal* (April 2, 2004): B3.

75. Robert Klara, "Brands by Bieber," Brandweek (January 1, 2011), http://www.adweek.com/news/advertising-branding/brands-bieber-126241, accessed February 23, 2011.

76. Grant McCracken, "Who Is the Celebrity Endorser? Cultural Foundations of the Endorsement Process," *Journal of Consumer Research* 16, no. 3 (December 1989): 310–21.

77. Quoted in www.japander.com, accessed March 7, 2013.

78. Nat Ives, "Marketers Run to Pull the Plug When Celebrity Endorsers Say the Darnedest Things," *New York Times* (July 16, 2004), www.nytimes.com, accessed July 16, 2004.

79. Judith A. Garretson and Scot Burton, "The Role of Spokescharacters as Advertisement and Package Cues in Integrated Marketing Communications," *Journal of Marketing* 69 (October, 2005): 118–32.

80. Jeff Bercovici, "America's Most Loved Spokescharacters," *Forbes* (March 14, 2011), http://www.forbes.com/2011/03/11/old-spice-snoopy-m-and-m-most-loved-spokescharacters.html, accessed April 30, 2011.

81. Natalie T. Wood and Michael R. Solomon, eds., *Virtual Social Identity* (Newport, CA: Sage, 2010).

82. Kathy Crosett, "Consumers Confused by TV Commercials," *Adology* (October 4, 2010), http://www.marketingforecast.com/archives/7538, accessed May 30, 2011; David W. Stewart and David H. Furse, "The Effects of Television Advertising Execution on Recall, Comprehension, and Persuasion," *Psychology & Marketing* 2 (Fall 1985): 135–60.

83. R. C. Grass and W. H. Wallace, "Advertising Communication: Print vs. TV," *Journal of Advertising Research* 14 (1974): 19–23.

84. Elizabeth C. Hirschman and Michael R. Solomon, "Utilitarian, Aesthetic, and Familiarity Responses to Verbal Versus Visual Advertisements," in Thomas C. Kinnear, ed., *Advances in Consumer Research* 11 (Provo, UT: Association for Consumer Research, 1984): 426–31.

85. Terry L. Childers and Michael J. Houston, "Conditions for a Picture-Superiority Effect on Consumer Memory," *Journal of Consumer Research* 11 (September 1984): 643–54.

86. John R. Rossiter and Larry Percy, "Attitude Change Through Visual Imagery in Advertising," *Journal of Advertising Research* 9, no. 2 (1980): 10–16.

87. Spencer E. Ante, "Billboards Join Wired Age," *Wall Street Journal* (February 4, 2011), http://professional.wsj.com/article/SB10001424052748703652104576122091475061666.html?mg=reno-wsj, accessed April 15, 2011.

88. Scott B. MacKenzie, "The Role of Attention in Mediating the Effect of Advertising on Attribute Importance," *Journal of Consumer Research* 13 (September 1986): 174–95.

89. Robert B. Zajonc, "Attitudinal Effects of Mere Exposure," *Journal of Personality & Social Psychology* 8 (1968): 1–29.

90. Giles D'Souza and Ram C. Rao, "Can Repeating an Advertisement More Frequently Than the Competition Affect Brand Preference in a Mature Market?" *Journal of Marketing* 59 (April 1995): 32–42.

91. George E. Belch, "The Effects of Television Commercial Repetition on Cognitive Response and Message Acceptance," *Journal of Consumer Research* 9 (June 1982): 56–65; Marian Burke and Julie Edell, "Ad Reactions Over Time: Capturing Changes in the Real World," *Journal of Consumer Research* 13 (June 1986): 114–18; Herbert Krugman, "Why Three Exposures May Be Enough," *Journal of Advertising Research* 12 (December 1972): 11–14.

92. Robert F. Bornstein, "Exposure and Affect: Overview and Meta-Analysis of Research, 1968–1987," *Psychological Bulletin* 106, no. 2 (1989): 265–89; Arno Rethans, John Swasy, and Lawrence Marks, "Effects of Television Commercial Repetition, Receiver Knowledge, and Commercial Length: A Test of the Two-Factor Model," *Journal of Marketing Research* 23 (February 1986): 50–61.

93. Curtis P. Haugtvedt, David W. Schumann, Wendy L. Schneier, and Wendy L. Warren, "Advertising Repetition and Variation Strategies: Implications for Understanding Attitude Strength," *Journal of Consumer Research* 21 (June 1994): 176–89.

94. Linda L. Golden and Mark I. Alpert, "Comparative Analysis of the Relative Effectiveness of One- and Two-Sided Communication for Contrasting Products," *Journal of Advertising* 16 (1987): 18–25; Michael A. Kamins, "Celebrity and Noncelebrity Advertising in a Two-Sided Context," *Journal of Advertising Research* 29 (June–July 1989): 34; Robert B. Settle and Linda L.

Golden, "Attribution Theory and Advertiser Credibility," *Journal of Marketing Research* 11 (May 1974): 181–85.

95. Cf. Alan G. Sawyer, "The Effects of Repetition of Refutational and Supportive Advertising Appeals," *Journal of Marketing Research* 10 (February 1973): 23–33; George J. Szybillo and Richard Heslin, "Resistance to Persuasion: Inoculation Theory in a Marketing Context," *Journal of Marketing Research* 10 (November 1973): 396–403.

96. Rupal Parekh and Jean Halliday, "New Ad Introduces Consumers to 'New GM,'" *Advertising Age* (June 1, 2009), http://adage.com/article?article_id=137010, accessed June 6, 2009.

97. Uma R. Karmarkar and Zakary L. Tormala, "Believe Me, I Have No Idea What I'm Talking About: The Effects of Source Certainty on Consumer Involvement and Persuasion," *Journal of Consumer Research* 36 (April 2009): 1033–49.

98. Golden and Alpert, "Comparative Analysis of the Relative Effectiveness of One- and Two-Sided Communication for Contrasting Products"; Gita Venkataramani Johar and Anne L. Roggeveen, "Changing False Beliefs from Repeated Advertising: The Role of Claim-Refutation Alignment," *Journal of Consumer Psychology* 17, no. 2 (2007): 118–27.

99. George E. Belch, Michael A. Belch, and Angelina Villareal, "Effects of Advertising Communications: Review of Research," in *Research in Marketing* 9 (Greenwich, CT: JAI Press, 1987): 59–117.

100. Frank R. Kardes, "Spontaneous Inference Processes in Advertising: The Effects of Conclusion Omission and Involvement on Persuasion," *Journal of Consumer Research* 15 (September 1988): 225–33.

101. Belch, Belch, and Villareal, "Effects of Advertising Communications: Review of Research"; Cornelia Pechmann and Gabriel Esteban, "Persuasion Processes Associated with Direct Comparative and Noncomparative Advertising and Implications for Advertising Effectiveness," *Journal of Consumer Psychology* 2, no. 4 (1994): 403–32.

102. Cornelia Dröge and Rene Y. Darmon, "Associative Positioning Strategies Through Comparative Advertising: Attribute vs. Overall Similarity Approaches," *Journal of Marketing Research* 24 (1987): 377–89; D. Muehling and N. Kangun, "The Multidimensionality of Comparative Advertising: Implications for the FTC," *Journal of Public Policy & Marketing* (1985): 112–28; Beth A. Walker and Helen H. Anderson, "Reconceptualizing Comparative Advertising: A Framework and Theory of Effects," in Rebecca H. Holman and Michael R. Solomon, eds., *Advances in Consumer Research* 18 (Provo, UT: Association for Consumer Research, 1991): 342–47; William L. Wilkie and Paul W. Farris, "Comparison Advertising: Problems and Potential," *Journal of Marketing* 39 (October 1975): 7–15; R. G. Wyckham, "Implied Superiority Claims," *Journal of Advertising Research* (February–March 1987): 54–63.

103. Suzanne Vranica, "Arby's TV Spots Play Game of Fast-Food Chicken," *Wall Street Journal* (July 5, 2006): A16.

104. Stephen A. Goodwin and Michael Etgar, "An Experimental Investigation of Comparative Advertising: Impact of Message Appeal, Information Load, and Utility of Product Class," *Journal of Marketing Research* 17 (May 1980): 187–202; Gerald J. Gorn and Charles B. Weinberg, "The Impact of Comparative Advertising on Perception and Attitude: Some Positive Findings," *Journal of Consumer Research* 11 (September 1984): 719–27; Terence A. Shimp and David C. Dyer, "The Effects of Comparative Advertising Mediated by Market Position of Sponsoring Brand," *Journal of Advertising* 3 (Summer 1978): 13–19; R. Dale Wilson, "An Empirical Evaluation of Comparative Advertising Messages: Subjects' Responses to Perceptual Dimensions," in B. B. Anderson, ed., *Advances in Consumer Research* 3 (Ann Arbor, MI: Association for Consumer Research, 1976): 53–57.

105. Louise Kramer, "In a Battle of Toothpastes, It's Information vs. Emotion," *New York Times* (January 17, 2007): C6.

106. H. Zielske, "Does Day-After Recall Penalize 'Feeling' Ads?" *Journal of Advertising Research* 22 (1982): 19–22.

107. Bruce Horovitz, "Skyy Pushes the Envelope with Sexy Ad Campaign," *USA Today* (September 28, 2010), http://www.usatoday.com/money/advertising/2010-09-28-vodka28_ST_N.htm?csp=34money&utm_source=feedburner&utm_medium=feed&utm_campaign=Feed%3A+UsatodaycomMoney-TopStories+%28Money+-+Top+Stories%29, accessed April 15, 2011.

108. Allessandra Galloni, "Lee's Cheeky Ads Are Central to New European Campaign," *Wall Street Journal* (March 15, 2002), www.wsj.com, accessed March 15, 2002.

109. Belch, Belch, and Villareal, "Effects of Advertising Communications: Review of Research"; Courtney and Whipple, *Sex Stereotyping in Advertising*; Michael S. LaTour, "Female Nudity in Print Advertising: An Analysis of Gender Differences in Arousal and Ad Response," *Psychology & Marketing* 7, no. 1 (1990): 65–81; B. G. Yovovich, "Sex in Advertising—The Power and the Perils," *Advertising Age* (May 2, 1983): M4–M5. For an interesting

interpretive analysis, see Richard Elliott and Mark Ritson, "Practicing Existential Consumption: The Lived Meaning of Sexuality in Advertising," in Frank R. Kardes and Mita Sujan, eds., *Advances in Consumer Behavior* 22 (1995): 740–45; Jaideep Sengupta and Darren W. Dahl, "Gender-Related Reactions to Gratuitous Sex Appeals," *Journal of Consumer Psychology* 18 (2008): 62–78.

110. Penny M. Simpson, Steve Horton, and Gene Brown, "Male Nudity in Advertisements: A Modified Replication and Extension of Gender and Product Effects," *Journal of the Academy of Marketing Science* 24, no. 3 (1996): 257–62.

111. Jaideep Sengupta and Darren W. Dahl, "Gender-Related Reactions to Gratuitous Sex Appeals," *Journal of Consumer Psychology* 18 (2008): 62–78; Darren W. Dahl, Jaideep Sengupta, and Kathleen Vohs, "Sex in Advertising: Gender Differences and the Role of Relationship Commitment," *Journal of Consumer Research* 36 (August 2009): 215–231.

112. Mark Dolliver, "Seeing Too Much Sex in Ads, or Too Little?" *Adweek* (December 6, 2010), http://teens.adweek.com/aw/content_display/datacenter/research/e3i5b647315f27310efc8f6df37dcb48e9b, accessed April 15, 2011.

113. Michael S. LaTour and Tony L. Henthorne, "Ethical Judgments of Sexual Appeals in Print Advertising," *Journal of Advertising* 23, no. 3 (September 1994): 81–90.

114. "Does Sex Really Sell?" *Adweek* (October 17, 2005): 17.

115. Katharine Q. Seelye, "Metamucil Ad Featuring Old Faithful Causes a Stir," *New York Times* (January 19, 2003), www.nytimes.com, accessed January 19, 2003.

116. Thomas J. Madden, "Humor in Advertising: An Experimental Analysis," working paper, no. 83-27, University of Massachusetts, 1984; Thomas J. Madden and Marc G. Weinberger, "The Effects of Humor on Attention in Magazine Advertising," *Journal of Advertising* 11, no. 3 (1982): 8–14; Weinberger and Spotts, "Humor in U.S. Versus U.K. TV Commercials" *Journal of Advertising* 18, no. 2 (1989): 39–44; see also Ashesh Mukherjee and Laurette Dubé, "The Use of Humor in Threat-Related Advertising" (unpublished manuscript, McGill University, June 2002).

117. David Gardner, "The Distraction Hypothesis in Marketing," *Journal of Advertising Research* 10 (1970): 25–30.

118. Chris Abraham, "Global Web Means Your 'Fart Jokes' Can Be Heard Out of Context," *Advertising Age* (June 15, 2009), http://adage.com/digitalnext/article?article_id=137273, accessed June 16, 2009.

119. Brian Steinberg, "VW Uses Shock Treatment to Sell Jetta's Safety," *Wall Street Journal* (April 19, 2006): B4.

120. Lindsay Goldwert, "FDA to Require Graphic Images on Cigarette Packages to Deter Smoking," *New York Daily News* (November 10, 2010), http://www.nydailynews.com/lifestyle/health/2010/11/10/2010-11-10_fda_proposes_putting_graphic_images_onto_package_of_cigarettes_to_-deter_smoking.html, accessed April 15, 2011.

121. Michael L. Ray and William L. Wilkie, "Fear: The Potential of an Appeal Neglected by Marketing," *Journal of Marketing* 34, no. 1 (1970): 54–62.

122. Punam Anand Keller and Lauren Goldberg Block, "Increasing the Effectiveness of Fear Appeals: The Effect of Arousal and Elaboration," *Journal of Consumer Research* 22 (March 1996): 448–59.

123. Ronald Paul Hill, "An Exploration of the Relationship Between AIDS-Related Anxiety and the Evaluation of Condom Advertisements," *Journal of Advertising* 17, no. 4 (1988): 35–42.

124. Randall Rothenberg, "Talking Too Tough on Life's Risks?" *New York Times* (February 16, 1990): D1.

125. Denise D. Schoenbachler and Tommy E. Whittler, "Adolescent Processing of Social and Physical Threat Communications," *Journal of Advertising* 25, no. 4 (Winter 1996): 37–54.

126. Barbara B. Stern, "Medieval Allegory: Roots of Advertising Strategy for the Mass Market," *Journal of Marketing* 52 (July 1988): 84–94.

127. Edward F. McQuarrie and David Glen Mick, "On Resonance: A Critical Pluralistic Inquiry into Advertising Rhetoric," *Journal of Consumer Research* 19 (September 1992): 180–97.

128. Cf. Linda M. Scott, "The Troupe: Celebrities as Dramatis Personae in Advertisements," in Rebecca H. Holman and Michael R. Solomon, eds., *Advances in Consumer Research* 18 (Provo, UT: Association for Consumer Research, 1991): 355–63; Barbara Stern, "Literary Criticism and Consumer Research: Overview and Illustrative Analysis," *Journal of Consumer Research* 16 (1989): 322–34; Judith Williamson, *Decoding Advertisements* (Boston: Marion Boyars, 1978).

129. John Deighton, Daniel Romer, and Josh McQueen, "Using Drama to Persuade," *Journal of Consumer Research* 16 (December 1989): 335–43.

130. Edward F. McQuarrie and David Glen Mick, "On Resonance: A Critical Pluralistic Inquiry into Advertising Rhetoric," *Journal of Consumer Research* 19 (September 1992): 180–97.

131. Barbara J. Phillips and Edward F. McQuarrie, "Beyond Visual Metaphor: A New Typology of Visual Rhetoric in Advertising," *Marketing Theory* 4 (March/June 2004): 113–36.

132. Richard E. Petty, John T. Cacioppo, and David Schumann, "Central and Peripheral Routes to Advertising Effectiveness: The Moderating Role of Involvement," *Journal of Consumer Research* 10, no. 2 (1983): 135–46.

133. Jerry C. Olson, Daniel R. Toy, and Philip A. Dover, "Do Cognitive Responses Mediate the Effects of Advertising Content on Cognitive Structure?" *Journal of Consumer Research* 9, no. 3 (1982): 245–62.

134. Julie A. Edell and Andrew A. Mitchell, "An Information Processing Approach to Cognitive Responses," in S. C. Jain, ed., *Research Frontiers in Marketing: Dialogues and Directions* (Chicago, IL: American Marketing Association, 1978).

135. Richard E. Petty, John T. Cacioppo, Constantine Sedikides, and Alan J. Strathman, "Affect and Persuasion: A Contemporary Perspective," *American Behavioral Scientist* 31, no. 3 (1988): 355–71.

136. Ingrid Lunden, "Mobile Ad Revenues Will Top $11.4 Billion In 2013, Up 19% On 2012. India, China And Display Fuelling The Boost," *Tech Crunch* (January 17, 2013), http://techcrunch.com/2013/01/17/mobile-ad-revenues-will-top-11-4-billion-in-2013-up-19-on-2012-india-china-fuelling-boost-search-ads-diminishing-in-use/, accessed December 18, 2103.

137. Vikram Dodd, "Coca-Cola Forced to Pull Facebook Promotion After Porn References," *Guardian.co.uk* (July 18, 2010), http://www.guardian.co.uk/business/2010/jul/18/coca-cola-facebook-promotion-porn, accessed April 15, 2011.

138. Rob Walker, "The Gifted Ones," *New York Times Magazine* (November 14, 2004), www.nytimes.com, accessed September 29, 2007.

SECTION 2 NIELSEN NUGGET

Scenario: Xtr Clean Inc. is a large global producer of home cleaning products. With the economy struggling, both manufacturers and retailers are resorting to new and creative promotions, discounts, and price wars in the battle to win consumers. Xtr Clean is interested in strengthening its position through a better understanding of point-of-sale (POS) trade promotion efforts and their effectiveness in catching consumers' attention in the store aisle.

Challenge: To determine strategies to increase promotional effectiveness of POS efforts for home cleaning products. The company believes that a better understanding of the relative effectiveness of in-store promotions will be of key importance in developing effective strategies. Xtr Clean is also interested in understanding why consumers choose *not* to buy home cleaning products.

After reviewing the data provided:

1 Develop recommendations for reducing the number of nonbuyers of home cleaning products.
2 Develop recommendations concerning which in-store promotions should be emphasized.
3 Describe the purchase situation involvement level likely in this case. How could it be affecting consumer choices?

POS Promotions Stimulating Purchases	Effectiveness Rate
Two or more identical products with discount	46%
Two or more different products with discount	31%
One identical additional product free	5%
Cash discount over the total purchase	5%
Second product at half price	5%
Credit card discount	3%
Didn't know/answer	5%

Reasons for Not Buying	Rate (Multiple choices allowed)
Product out of stock at time of purchase	34%
Remembered already having one at home	23%
Just comparing prices and variants	13%
Was not exactly what wanted	4%
Was not sure what product was needed	3%
Product consumed at a very rapid rate	1%
High price	33%
Other	3%

"MY MOM HASN'T ACCEPTED MY FRIEND REQUEST YET. WHAT COULD SHE POSSIBLY BE DOING?"

AVAILABLE WITH ALL-WHEEL DRIVE.
VENZA. *KEEP ON ROLLING.*

Section 3 • External Influences on Consumer Behavior

This third and final section focuses on the external factors that influence our identities as consumers and the decisions we make. Chapter 9 provides an overview of group processes, and it also considers how the particular situation in which we find ourselves affects the choices we make. Chapter 10 discusses the impact of social identity—how we define ourselves within a larger society—and the subcultures and lifestyles that help to determine how we buy and consume. In Chapter 11 we focus on the ways our social status relative to others helps to define who we are, and also how our deep-seated values guide consumer behavior. Finally, in Chapter 12, we dive into the ways we discuss how we connect with others both physically and digitally and focus on the reasons why social media is transforming our lives as consumers.

CHAPTERS AHEAD

Chapter 9 • **Group and Situational Effects on Consumer Behavior**

Chapter 10 • **Consumer Identity I: Sex Roles and Subcultures**

Chapter 11 • **Consumer Identity II: Social Class and Lifestyles**

Chapter 12 • **Networked Consumer Behavior: Word-of-Mouth, Social Media, and Fashion**

Chapter 9 • Group and Situational Effects on Consumer Behavior

Chapter Objectives

When you finish reading this chapter you will understand why:

1. Many factors at the time of purchase dramatically influence the consumer's decision-making process.

2. The information a store's layout, Web site, or salespeople provides strongly influences a purchase decision.

3. Other people and groups, especially those that possess social power, influence our decisions.

4. We seek out others who share our interests in products or services.

5. Our desire to be consistent with other people motivates us to mimic what they buy and use.

6. Marketers often need to understand consumers' behavior rather than a consumer's behavior.

7. The decision-making process differs when people choose what to buy on behalf of an organization rather than for personal use.

8. Our traditional notions about families are outdated.

9. Members of a family unit play different roles and have different amounts of influence when the family makes purchase decisions.

Zach leads a secret life. During the week, he is a straitlaced stock analyst for a major investment firm. He spends a big chunk of the week worrying about whether he'll have a job, so work is pretty stressful these days. However, his day job only pays the bills to finance his real passion: cruising on his Harley-Davidson road glide custom. His Facebook posts are filled with lunchtime laments about how much he'd rather be out on the road (hopefully his boss won't try to friend him). Actually, Zach feels it's worth the risk: He's participating in Harley's free country social media promotion that encourages riders to post their stories ("freedom statements") on Facebook and Twitter to see if they'll include one of his posts on a Harley banner ad.[1] His girlfriend worries a bit about his getting totaled in an accident, but Zach knows if he stays alert the only way that will probably happen is if he can't kick his habit of texting her while he's driving the bike.

Come Friday evening, it's off with the Brooks Brothers suit and on with the black leather, as he trades in his Lexus for his treasured Harley. A dedicated member of HOG (Harley Owners Group), Zach belongs to the "RUBs" (rich urban bikers) faction of Harley riders. Everyone in his group wears expensive leather vests with Harley insignias and owns customized "low riders." Just this week, Zach finally got his new Harley perforated black leather jacket at the company's Motorclothes Merchandise web page.[2] As one of the Harley web pages observed, "It's one thing to have people buy your products. It's another thing to have them tattoo your name on their bodies." Zach had to restrain himself from buying more Harley stuff; there were vests, eyewear, belts, buckles, scarves, watches, jewelry, even housewares ("home is the road") for sale. He settled for a set of Harley salt-and-pepper shakers that would be perfect for his buddy Dan's new crib.

Zach's experiences on social media platforms make him realize the lengths to which some of his fellow enthusiasts go to make sure others know they are hog riders. Two of his riding buddies are in a lively competition to be "mayor" of the local Harley dealership on Foursquare, while many others tweet to inform people about a group ride that will occur later in the day—kind of a flash mob on wheels.

Zach spends a lot of money to outfit himself to be like the rest of the group, but it's worth it. He feels a real sense of brotherhood with his fellow RUBs. The group rides together in two-column formation to bike rallies that sometimes attract up to 300,000 cycle enthusiasts. What a sense of power he feels when they all cruise together—it's them against the world!

Of course, an added benefit is the business networking he's accomplished during his jaunts with his fellow professionals who also wait for the weekend to "ride on the wild side—these days it would be professional suicide to let your contacts get cold, and you can't just count on LinkedIn to stay in the loop."[3]

Situational Effects on Consumer Behavior

Making a purchase is often not a simple, routine matter where you just pop into a store and make a quick choice. As Figure 9.1 illustrates, many contextual factors affect our choice, such as our mood, whether we feel time pressure to make the purchase, and the particular reason we need the product. In some situations, such as when we buy a car or a home, the salesperson or realtor plays a pivotal role in our final selection. Also, people today often use the Web to arm themselves with product and price information before they even enter a dealership or a store; this puts more pressure on retailers to deliver the value their customers expect.

A **consumption situation** includes a buyer, a seller, and a product or service—but also many other factors, such as the reason we want to make a purchase and how the physical environment makes us feel.[4] Common sense tells us that we tailor our purchases to specific occasions and that the way we feel at a specific point in time affects what we want to do—or buy. Smart marketers understand these patterns and plan their efforts to coincide with situations in which we are most prone to purchase. For example, book clubs invest heavily in promotional campaigns in June because many people want to stock up on "beach books" to read during the summer; for the same reason, we get tons of featured fun fiction books for our Kindles and Nooks in April and May. Our moods even change radically during the day, so at different times we might be more or less interested in what a marketer offers. Social media platforms also are looking at ways to adapt quickly to situational changes. Facebook is testing ads targeted in real time based on users' status updates ("What's on your mind?") and wall posts. Theoretically, a user who posts near the end of his workday that "It's Miller time" could immediately be served a promotion from MillerCoors or another beer company.[5]

A study used a technique called the *day reconstruction method* to track these changes. More than 900 working women kept diaries of everything they did during the day, from reading the paper in the morning to falling asleep in front of the TV at night. The next day they relived each diary entry and rated how they felt at the time (annoyed, happy, etc.). Overall, researchers found that the study participants woke up a little grumpy but soon entered a state of mild pleasure. This mood increased by degrees through the day, though it was punctuated by occasional bouts of anxiety, frustration, and anger. Not surprisingly, the subjects were least happy when they engaged in mundane activities like commuting to work and doing housework, whereas they rated sex, socializing with friends, and relaxing as most enjoyable. Contrary to prior findings, however, the women were happier when they watched television than when they shopped or talked on the phone. They ranked taking care of children low, below cooking and not far above housework. The good news: Overall, people seem to be pretty happy, and these ratings aren't influenced very much by factors such as household income or job security. By far, the two factors that most upset daily moods were a poor night's sleep and tight work deadlines.[6]

Figure 9.1 ISSUES RELATED TO PURCHASE AND POSTPURCHASE ACTIVITIES

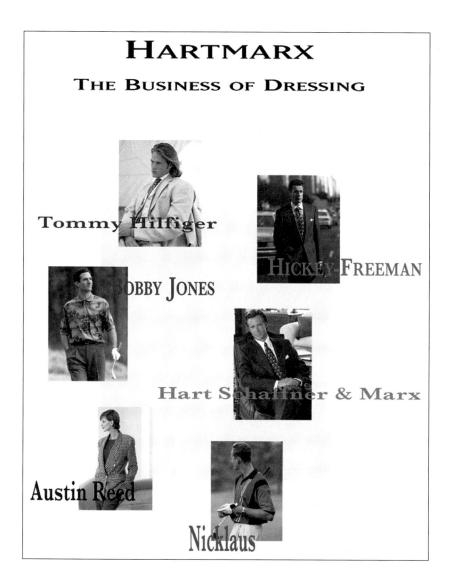

In addition to the functional relationships between products and usage situation, another reason to take environmental circumstances seriously is that a person's *situational self-image*—the role she plays at any one time—helps to determine what she wants to buy or consume.[7] A guy who tries to impress his date as he plays the role of "man-about-town" may spend more lavishly, order champagne instead of beer, and buy flowers—purchases he would never consider when he hangs out with his friends, slurps brew, and plays the role of "one of the boys." Let's see how these dynamics affect the way people think about what they buy.

If we systematically identify important usage situations, we can tailor market segmentation strategies to ensure that our offerings meet the specific needs these situations create. For example, we often tailor our furniture choices to specific settings. We prefer different styles for a city apartment, a beach house, or an executive suite. Similarly, we distinguish motorcycles in terms of how riders use them, including commuting, riding them as dirt bikes, or on a farm versus highway travel.[8]

Table 9.1 gives one example of how a marketer fine-tunes its segmentation strategy to the usage situation. When we list the major contexts in which people use a product (e.g., snow skiing and sunbathing for a suntan lotion) and the different types of people who use the product, we can construct a matrix that identifies specific product features we should emphasize for each situation. During the summer, a lotion manufacturer might promote the fact that the bottle floats and is hard to lose, but during the winter season it could tout its nonfreezing formula.

TABLE 9.1 A Person-Situation Segmentation Matrix for Suntan Lotion

Situation	Young Children		Teenagers		Adult Women		Adult Men		Benefits/Features
	Fair Skin	Dark Skin	Fair Skin	Dark Skin	Fair Skin	Dark Skin	Fair Skin	Dark Skin	
Beach/boat sunbathing	Combined insect repellent				Summer perfume				a. Product serves as windburn protection b. Formula and container can stand heat c. Container floats and is distinctive (not easily lost)
Home-poolside sunbathing					Combined moisturizer				a. Product has large pump dispenser b. Product won't stain wood, concrete, furnishings
Sunlamp bathing					Combined moisturizer and massage oil				a. Product is designed specifically for type of lamp b. Product has an artificial tanning ingredient
Snow skiing					Winter perfume				a. Product provides special protection from special light rays and weather b. Product has antifreeze formula
Person benefit/features	Special protection a. Protection is critical b. Formula is non-poisonous		Special protection a. Product fits in jean pocket b. Product used by opinion leaders		Special protection Female perfume		Special protection Male perfume		

Source: Adapted from Peter R. Dickson, "Person-Situation: Segmentation's Missing Link," *Journal of Marketing* 46 (Fall 1982): 62. By permission of American Marketing Association.

Our Social and Physical Surroundings

A consumer's physical and social environment affects her motives to use a product, as well as how she will evaluate the item. Important cues include her immediate environment as well as the amount and type of other consumers who are there as well. Dimensions of the physical environment, such as decor, odors, and even temperature, can significantly influence consumption. One study even found that if a Las Vegas casino pumped certain odors into the room, patrons fed more money into the slot machines![9] We'll take a closer look at some of these factors a bit later in this chapter when we consider how important store design is to consumer behavior.

Temporal Factors

Time is one of our most precious resources. We talk about "making time" or "spending time" and we frequently remind others that "time is money." Common sense tells us that we think more about what we want to buy when we have the luxury to take our time. Even a normally meticulous shopper who never buys before she compares prices might sprint through the mall at 9:00 P.M. on Christmas Eve to scoop up anything left on the shelves if she needs a last-minute gift. The same logic applies to online marketing; **open rates** (the percentage of people who open an email message from a marketer) vary throughout the day. The peak time for high open rates: mid-day on weekdays (presumably when all those people at work take a lunch break).[10]

Time is an economic variable; it is a resource that we must divide among our activities.[11] We try to maximize satisfaction when we allocate our time to different tasks. Of course, people's allocation decisions differ; we all know people who seem to play all of the time, and others who are workaholics. An individual's priorities determine his **time-style**.[12] People in different countries also "spend" this resource at different rates. A social scientist compared the pace of life in 31 cities around the world as part of a study on timestyles.[13] He and his assistants timed how long it takes pedestrians to walk 60 feet and the time postal clerks take to sell a stamp. Based on these responses, he claims that the fastest and slowest countries are:

Fastest countries—(1) Switzerland, (2) Ireland, (3) Germany, (4) Japan, (5) Italy

Slowest countries—(31) Mexico, (30) Indonesia, (29) Brazil, (28) El Salvador, (27) Syria

Many consumers believe they are more pressed for time than ever before; marketers label this feeling **time poverty**. The problem appears to be more perception than fact. The reality is that we simply have more options for spending our time, so we feel pressured by the weight of all of these choices. The average working day at the turn of the 19th century was 10 hours (6 days per week), and women did 27 hours of housework per week, compared to less than 5 hours weekly now. Of course, there are plenty of husbands who share these burdens more, and in some families it's not as important as it used to be to maintain an absolutely spotless home as our values change. Still, about a third of Americans report always feeling rushed, up from 25 percent of the population in 1964.[14]

"Time flies when you're having fun," but other situations (like some classes—but certainly not Consumer Behavior) seem to last forever. Our experience of time is very subjective; our immediate priorities and needs determine how quickly time flies. It's important for marketers to understand **psychological time** because we're more likely to be in a consuming mood at certain times than we are at others.

A study examined how the timestyles of a group of American women influenced their consumption choices.[15] The researchers identified four dimensions of time: (1) the *social dimension* refers to individuals' categorization of time as either "time for me" or "time with/for others"; (2) the *temporal orientation dimension* depicts the relative significance individuals attach to past, present, or future; (3) the *planning orientation dimension* alludes to different time management styles varying on a continuum from analytic to spontaneous; and (4) the *polychronic orientation dimension* distinguishes between people who prefer to do one thing at a time from those who have multitasking timestyles. After they interviewed and observed these women, the researchers identified a set of five metaphors that they say capture the participants' perspectives on time:

- **Time is a pressure cooker**—These women are usually analytical in their planning, other-oriented, and monochronic in their timestyles. They treat shopping in a methodical manner and they often feel under pressure and in conflict.
- **Time is a map**—These women are usually analytical planners; they exhibit a future temporal orientation and a polychronic timestyle. They often engage in extensive-information search and comparison-shop.
- **Time is a mirror**—Women in this group are also analytical planners and have a polychronic orientation. However, they have a past temporal orientation. Because of their risk averseness in time use, these women are usually loyal to products and services they know and trust. They prefer convenience-oriented products.
- **Time is a river**—These women are usually spontaneous in their planning orientation and have a present focus. They go on unplanned, short, and frequent shopping trips.

Marketing Opportunity

In addition to physical cues, other people who are in the situation affect purchase decisions. In some cases, the sheer presence or absence of **co-consumers**, the other patrons in a setting, actually is a product attribute; think about an exclusive resort or boutique that promises to provide privacy to privileged customers. At other times, the presence of others can have positive value. A sparsely attended ball game or an empty bar can be a depressing sight. The *type* of consumers who patronize a store or service or who use a product affects our evaluations. We often infer something about a store when we examine its customers. For this reason, some restaurants require men to wear jackets for dinner (and supply rather tacky ones if they don't), and bouncers at some "hot" nightspots handpick people who wait in line based on whether they have the right "look" for the club. To paraphrase the comedian Groucho Marx, "I would never join a club that would have me as a member!"

Time poverty is creating opportunities for many new products (like portable soups) that let people multitask.
Source: Courtesy of Campbell Soup Company.

- **Time is a feast**—These women are analytical planners with a present temporal orientation. They view time as something they consume to pursue sensory pleasure and gratification, and for this reason they value hedonic consumption and variety-seeking.

Waiting Time

The psychological dimension of time—how we actually experience it—is an important factor in **queuing theory**, the mathematical study of waiting lines. As we all know, our experience when we wait has a big effect on our evaluations of what we get at the end of the wait. Although we assume that something must be pretty good if we have to wait for it, the negative feelings that long waits arouse can quickly turn people off.[16] In a survey, NCR Corp. found that standing around the local Department or Division of Motor Vehicles is the most dreaded wait of all. Waiting in line at retail outlets came in a close second, followed by registering at clinics or hospitals, checking in at airports, and ordering at fast-food restaurants or deli counters. On average, consumers estimate that they spend more than 2 days per year waiting in line for service, and half believe they waste between 30 minutes and 2 hours each week on lines.[17]

OBJECTIVE 2

The information a store's layout, Web site, or salespeople provides strongly influences a purchase decision.

The Shopping Experience

Our mood at the time of purchase can really affect what we feel like buying.[18] Recall that in Chapter 2 we talked about how we direct our behavior to satisfy certain goal states. If you don't believe it, try grocery shopping on an empty stomach! Or make a decision when you're stressed, and you'll understand how a physiological state impairs information-processing and problem-solving abilities.[19]

Two basic dimensions, *pleasure* and *arousal*, determine whether we will react positively or negatively to a consumption environment.[20] What it boils down to is that you can either enjoy or not enjoy a situation, and you can feel stimulated or not. As Figure 9.2 indicates, different combinations of pleasure and arousal levels result in a variety of emotional states. An arousing situation can be either distressing or exciting, depending on whether the context is positive or negative (e.g., a street riot versus a street festival). So, a specific mood is some combination of pleasure and arousal. The state of happiness is high in pleasantness and moderate in arousal, whereas elation is high on both dimensions.[21] A mood state (either positive or negative) biases our judgments of products and services in that direction.[22] Put simply, we give more positive evaluations when we're in a good mood (this explains the popularity of the business lunch!).

Many factors, including store design, the weather, and whether you just had a fight with your significant other, affect your mood. Music and television programming do as well.[23] When we hear happy music or watch happy programs, we experience more positive reactions to commercials and products.[24] And when we're in a good mood, we process ads with less elaboration. We pay less attention to the specifics of the message and we rely more on heuristics (see Chapter 2).[25]

When the Going Gets Tough, the Tough Go Shopping

We all know some people who shop simply for the sport of it, and others whom we have to drag to a mall. Shopping is how we acquire needed products and services, but social

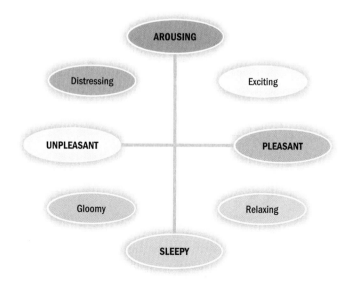

Figure 9.2 DIMENSIONS OF EMOTIONAL STATES

motives for shopping also are important. Thus, shopping is an activity that we can perform for either utilitarian (functional or tangible) or hedonic (pleasurable or intangible) reasons.[26]

So, do people hate to shop or love it? We segment consumers in terms of their **shopping orientation**, or general attitudes about shopping. These orientations vary depending on the particular product categories and store types we consider. One consumer might hate to shop for a car, but love to browse in music stores. A shopper's motivation influences the type of shopping environment that will be attractive or annoying; for example, a person who wants to locate and buy something quickly may find loud music, bright colors, or complex layouts distracting, whereas someone who is there to browse may enjoy the sensory stimulation.[27]

Some scale items that researchers use to assess our shopping motivations illustrate the diverse reasons we may shop. One item that measures hedonic value is "During the trip, I felt the excitement of the hunt." When we compare that type of sentiment to a functional statement, "I accomplished just what I wanted to on this shopping trip," there's a clear contrast between these two dimensions.[28] Hedonic shopping motives include the following:[29]

- **Social experiences**—The shopping center or department store replaces the traditional town square or county fair as a community gathering place. Many people (especially in suburban or rural areas) have almost no other places to spend their leisure time. That probably explains the popularity of late-night games college students in some rural areas play at their local Walmart. In addition to sports such as scavenger hunts, aisle football, and a relay race limbo under the shopping-cart stand, "10 in 10" is a big attraction. To play this game, students form into teams; each team has 10 minutes to put 10 items from anywhere in the store in a shopping cart. Then they turn their cart over to the opposing team, which has to figure out where the items came from and return them to the shelves where they belong (not so easy in a store stocked with more than 100,000 different items). The first team back to the checkout counters with an empty cart wins.[30] Note: If you get busted for playing this game, you did NOT learn about it here.
- **Sharing of common interests**—Stores frequently offer specialized goods that allow people with shared interests to communicate.
- **Interpersonal attraction**—Shopping centers are a natural place to congregate. The shopping mall is a favorite "hangout" for teenagers. It also represents a controlled, secure environment for the elderly, and many malls now feature "mall walkers' clubs" for early morning workouts.
- **Instant status**—As every salesperson knows, some people savor the experience of being waited on, even though they may not necessarily buy anything. One men's clothing salesman offered this advice: "Remember their size, remember what you sold them last time. Make them feel important! If you can make people feel important, they are going to come back. Everybody likes to feel important!"[31] When a team of researchers conducted in-depth interviews with women to understand what makes shopping a pleasurable experience, they found one motivation was role-playing. For example, one respondent dressed up for shopping excursions to upscale boutiques because she liked to pretend she was wealthy and have salespeople fall all over her.[32]
- **The thrill of the hunt**—Some people pride themselves on their knowledge of the marketplace. They may love to haggle and bargain, and even view this process as a sport.

E-Commerce: Clicks Versus Bricks

As more and more Web sites pop up to sell everything from refrigerator magnets to Mack trucks, marketers continue to debate how the online world affects their business.[33] In particular, many lose sleep as they wonder whether e-commerce will replace traditional retailing, work in concert with it, or perhaps even fade away to become another fad your

The experience of acquiring a product or service may be quite different offline versus online. This aspect of the transaction provides value over and above what you actually buy. We clearly see this difference between the two worlds when we compare how people gamble in casinos versus online. When researchers interviewed 30 gamblers to explore these experiences, they found sharp contrasts. Those who enjoy casino gambling have a strong sense of connection to fellow gamblers, so it's very much a social experience. Online gamblers enjoy the anonymity of the Internet. Casino gamblers get turned on by the sensual experiences and excitement of the casino, whereas online gamblers gravitate more to the feeling of safety and control they get because they stay at home. Casino gamblers talked about the friendly atmosphere, while those who stayed online reported behaviors that a real casino wouldn't tolerate, such as taunts and bullying.[34] Although both groups aim to have fun and hope to make money, it's a safe bet that their experiences are quite different.

Source: Shots Studio/Shutterstock.

kids will laugh about someday (OK, that's not real likely). Still, the rising availability of comparison shopping phone apps does threaten the existence of many retailers as consumers engage in what they call **showrooming**. This means that a shopper visits a store like Best Buy to explore options for big-ticket items like TVs or appliances and then he or she finds a cheaper price for the specific model online.

For marketers, the growth of online commerce is a sword that cuts both ways. On the one hand, they reach customers around the world even if they're physically located 100 miles from nowhere. On the other hand, they now compete not only with the store across the street but also with thousands of Web sites that span the globe. Also, when consumers obtain products directly from the manufacturer or wholesaler, this eliminates the intermediary—the loyal, store-based retailers that carry the firm's products and sell them at a marked-up price.[35]

So what makes e-commerce sites successful? Some e-tailers take advantage of technology to provide extra value to their customers that their land-locked rivals can't. eBay offers a feature within its Fashion app called "See It On" that allows the user to virtually

E-commerce sites like Bluefly give shoppers the option of shopping without leaving home.
Source: Courtesy of Bluefly.com.

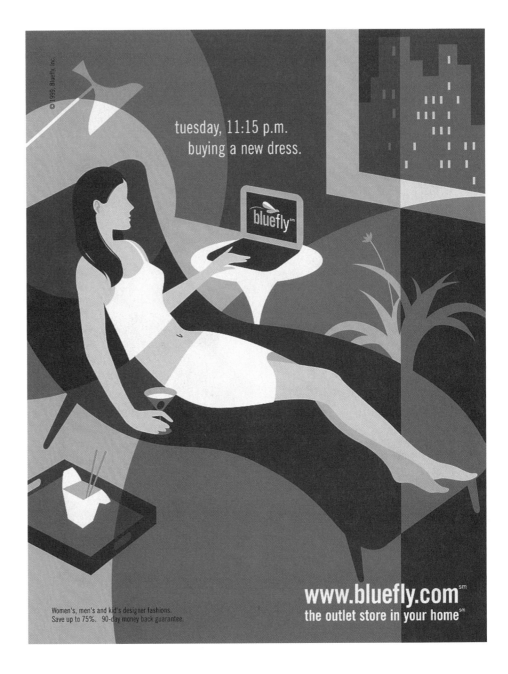

try on sunglasses in real time using an iPhone 4 or iPod Touch. He or she can adjust the fit; choose different styles, frames, lenses, and colors to find the perfect look; and then browse through eBay to find the perfect price.[36] Other new fashion sites, such as Net-a-Porter and Gilt Groupe, directly connect buyers and sellers so that designers can be more nimble and react quickly to changing consumer tastes. Others like Threadless, Mod-Cloth, and Fabricly go a step further: They crowdsource fashion to determine what styles they will actually produce based on what customers tell them they will buy. Indeed, the high-fashion site ModaOperandi bills itself as a **pretailer**; it provides exclusive styles by prodding manufacturers to produce runway pieces they wouldn't otherwise make because store buyers weren't sure anyone would pay the money for them.[37]

More generally, online shoppers value these aspects of a Web site:

- The ability to click on an item to create a pop-up window with more details about the product, including price, size, colors, and inventory availability.
- The ability to click on an item and add it to your cart without leaving the page you're on.

TABLE 9.2	Pros and Cons of E-Commerce

Benefits of E-Commerce	Limitations of E-Commerce
For the Consumer	**For the Consumer**
Shop 24 hours a day	Lack of security
Less traveling	Fraud
Can receive relevant information in seconds from any location	Can't touch items
More choices of products	Exact colors may not reproduce on computer monitors
More products available to less-developed countries	Expensive to order and then return
Greater price information	Potential breakdown of human relationships
Lower prices so that less affluent can purchase	
Participate in virtual auctions	
Fast delivery	
Electronic communities	
For the Marketer	**For the Marketer**
The world is the marketplace	Lack of security
Decreases costs of doing business	Must maintain site to reap benefits
Very specialized business can be successful	Fierce price competition
Real-time pricing	Conflicts with conventional retailers
	Legal issues not resolved

Source: Adapted from Michael R. Solomon and Elnora W. Stuart, *Welcome to Marketing.com: The Brave New World of E-Commerce* (Upper Saddle River, NJ: Prentice Hall, 2001).

- The ability to "feel" merchandise through better imagery, more product descriptions, and details.
- The ability to enter all data related to your purchase on one page, rather than going through several checkout pages.
- The ability to mix and match product images on one page to determine whether they look good together.[38]

Table 9.2 summarizes some of the pros and cons of e-commerce. It's clear that traditional shopping isn't quite dead yet, but brick-and-mortar retailers do need to work harder to give shoppers something they can't get (yet anyway) in the virtual world: a stimulating or pleasant environment. Now let's check out how they're doing that.

Retailing as Theater

At several U.S. malls, shoppers show up in shorts and flip-flops. They're turning out to ride a Flowrider, a huge wave-making machine.[39] Shopping center developers turn to attractions like this to lure reluctant customers back to malls. The competition for customers becomes even more intense as nonstore alternatives, from Web sites and print catalogs to TV shopping networks and home shopping parties, continue to multiply.

With all of these shopping alternatives available, how can a traditional store compete? Many malls are giant entertainment centers, almost to the point that their traditional retail occupants seem like an afterthought. Today, it's commonplace to find carousels, miniature golf, skating rinks, or batting cages in a suburban mall. Hershey opened a make-believe factory smack in the middle of Times Square. It features four steam machines and 380 feet of neon lighting, plus a moving message board that lets visiting chocoloholics program messages to surprise their loved ones.[40]

The quest to entertain means that many stores go all out to create imaginative environments that transport shoppers to fantasy worlds or provide other kinds of stimulation.

Marketing Opportunity

One popular theming strategy is to convert a store into a **being space**. This kind of environment resembles a sort of commercial living room, where we can go to relax, be entertained, hang out with friends, escape the everyday, or even learn. When you think of *being spaces*, Starbucks probably comes to mind. The coffee chain's stated goal is to become our "third place" where we spend the bulk of our time, in addition to home and work. Starbucks led the way when it outfitted its stores with comfy chairs and Wi-Fi. But there are many other marketers who meet our needs for exciting commercial spaces—no matter what those needs are. In Asia, venues such as Manboo and Fujiyama Land provide havens where gamers can do their thing 24/7—and even take a shower on-site during a break. Other spaces cater to the needs of **minipreneurs** (one-person businesses) as they offer work-centered being spaces. At New York's Paragraph, writers who need a quiet place to ruminate can hang out in a loft that's divided into a writing room and a lounge area. TwoRooms ("You Work, They Play") provides office space and child care for home-based workers.[42]

Reflecting the ever-quickening pace of our culture, many of these *being spaces* come and go very rapidly—on purpose. **Pop-up stores** appear in many forms around the world. Typically, these are temporary installations that do business only for a few days or weeks and then disappear before they get old. For example, the Swatch Instant Store sells limited-edition watches in a major city until the masses discover it; then it closes and moves on to another "cool" locale. The Dutch beer brand Dommelsch organized pop-up concerts: Fans entered barcodes they found on cans, beer bottles, and coasters on the brewer's Web site to discover dates and locations. You may even run into a pop-up store on your campus; several brands, including the Brazilian flip-flop maker Havaianas, Victoria's Secret's Pink, and sustainable-clothing brand RVL7, run pop-up projects around the United States.[43]

• • • • • • • • • • • • • • • • •

Source: © Kumar Sriskandan/Alamy.

We call this strategy **retail theming**. Innovative merchants today use four basic kinds of theming techniques:

1 *Landscape themes* rely on associations with images of nature, Earth, animals, and the physical body. Bass Pro Shops, for example, creates a simulated outdoor environment, including pools stocked with fish.
2 *Marketscape themes* build on associations with man-made places. An example is The Venetian hotel in Las Vegas, which lavishly recreates parts of the real Italian city.
3 *Cyberspace themes* build on images of information and communications technology. eBay's retail interface instills a sense of community among its vendors and traders.
4 *Mindscape themes* draw on abstract ideas and concepts, introspection and fantasy, and often possess spiritual overtones. The Kiva day spa in downtown Chicago offers health treatments based on a theme of Native American healing ceremonies and religious practices.[41]

Store Image

As so many stores compete for customers, how do we ever pick one over others? Just like products (see Chapter 7), stores have "personalities." Some shops have very clearly defined images (either good or bad). Others tend to blend into the crowd. What factors shape this personality, or **store image**? Some of the important dimensions of a store's image are location, merchandise suitability, and the knowledge and congeniality of the sales staff.[44]

These design features typically work together to create an overall impression. When we think about stores, we don't usually say, "Well, that place is fairly good in terms of convenience, the salespeople are acceptable, and services are good." We're more likely to proclaim, "That place gives me the creeps," or "It's so much fun to shop there." We quickly get an overall impression of a store, and the feeling we get may have more to do with intangibles, such as interior design and the types of people we find in the aisles, than with the store's return policies or credit availability. As a result, some stores routinely pop up in our consideration sets (see Chapter 2), whereas we never consider others ("Only geeks shop there!").[45]

Atmospherics

Retailers want you to come in—and stay. Careful store design increases the amount of space the shopper covers, and stimulating displays keep them in the aisles longer. This "curb appeal" translates directly to the bottom line: Researchers tracked grocery shopper's movements by plotting the position of their cell phones as they moved about a store. They found that when people lingered just 1 percent longer, sales rose by 1.3 percent.

Of course, grocers know a lot of tricks after years of observing shoppers. For example, they call the area just inside a supermarket's entrance the "decompression zone": People tend to slow down and take stock of their surroundings when they enter the store, so store designers use this space to promote bargains rather than to sell. Similarly, Walmart's "greeters" help customers to settle in to their shopping experience. Once they get a serious start, the first thing shoppers encounter is the produce section. Fruits and vegetables can easily be damaged, so it would be more logical to buy these items at the end of a shopping trip. But fresh, wholesome food makes people feel good (and righteous) so they're less guilty when they throw the chips and cookies in the cart later.[46]

Because marketers recognize that a store's image is a very important part of the retailing mix, store designers pay a lot of attention to **atmospherics**, the "conscious designing of space and its various dimensions to evoke certain effects in buyers."[47] These dimensions include colors, scents, and sounds. For example, stores with red interiors tend to make people tense, whereas a blue decor imparts a calmer feeling.[48]

A store's atmosphere in turn affects what we buy. In one study, researchers asked shoppers how much pleasure they felt 5 minutes after they entered a store. Those who enjoyed their experience spent more time and money.[49] To boost the entertainment value of shopping (and to lure online shoppers back to brick-and-mortar stores), some retailers create **activity stores** that let consumers participate in the production of the products or services they buy there. One familiar example is the Build-A-Bear Workshop chain, where customers dress bear bodies in costumes.[50]

In-Store Decision-Making

Despite all their efforts to "pre-sell" consumers through advertising, marketers increasingly recognize that the store environment exerts a strong influence on many purchases.

Marketing Opportunity

In addition to visual stimuli, all sorts of sensory cues influence us in retail settings.[51] For example, patrons of country-and-western bars drink more when the jukebox music is slower. According to a researcher, "Hard drinkers prefer listening to slower-paced, wailing, lonesome, self-pitying music."[52] Music also can affect eating habits. Another study found that diners who listened to loud, fast music ate more food. In contrast, those who listened to Mozart or Brahms ate less and more slowly. The researchers concluded that diners who choose soothing music at mealtimes can increase weight loss by at least 5 pounds a month![53]

Patrons tend to drink more when they listen to country-and-western music than to other types.
Source: © Radharc Images/Alamy.

Women tell researchers, for example, that store displays are one of the major information sources they use to decide what clothing to buy.[54]

This influence is even stronger when we shop for food: Analysts estimate that shoppers decide on about two out of every three supermarket purchases while they walk through the aisles.[55] Research evidence indicates that consumers use **mental budgets** for grocery trips that are typically composed of both an itemized portion and *in-store slack*. This means they typically decide beforehand on an amount they plan to spend, but then they have an additional amount in mind (slack) they are willing to spend on unplanned purchases—if they come across any they really want to have. Thus, stores should encourage consumers to spend all of their mental budgets by offering samples or posting reminder placards as they approach the checkout lines to remind them of things they may have forgotten.[56]

Mobile shopping apps on smartphones provide imaginative new ways for retailers to guide shoppers through the experience, as they do everything for you: locate merchandise, identify the nearest restroom in a mall, or scout out sales. Some help you remember where you parked your car; others actually provide reward points when you visit certain stores. The apps also promise to provide a solution to the major hassles that drive consumers away from brick-and-mortar stores, especially long checkout times and incompetent sales associates. One survey reported that nearly 3 in 10 store visits ended with an average of $132 unspent because shoppers gave up in frustration and abandoned their carts. The study also found that more than 40 percent of shoppers who received guidance from a retail associate armed with a handheld mobile computer reported an improved shopping experience. To rub salt into the wound, more than half of store employees agreed that because use of online shopping tools is escalating, their customers were more knowledgeable about their products than the salespeople are![57]

The growing practice of mobile couponing encourages in-store decision-making.

Source: Courtesy of Hardees.

Spontaneous Shopping

When a shopper suddenly decides to buy something in the store, one of two different processes explains why:

1. She engages in **unplanned buying** when she's unfamiliar with a store's layout or perhaps she's under some time pressure. Or, if she sees an item on a store shelf, this might remind her she needs it. About one-third of all unplanned buying occurs because a shopper recognizes a new need while she's in the store.[60]
2. She engages in **impulse buying** when she experiences a sudden urge she simply can't resist, like the sketch of a "typical" impulse purchaser an actual consumer drew in Figure 9.3.[61]

Retailers typically place so-called *impulse items*, such as candy and gum, near the checkout to cater to these urges. Similarly, many supermarkets install wider aisles to encourage browsing, and the widest tend to feature products with the highest profit margins. They stack low markup items that shoppers purchase regularly in narrower aisles to allow shopping carts to speed through. Starbucks encourages impulse purchasing when it charges customers who want to download songs they hear over the store's speakers directly onto their iPhones.[62]

Point-of-Purchase Stimuli

A well-designed in-store display boosts impulse purchases by as much as 10 percent. That explains why U.S. companies spend about $19 billion each year on **point-of-purchase (POP) stimuli**.[63] A POP can be an elaborate product display or demonstration, a coupon-dispensing machine, or an employee who gives out free samples of a new cookie in the grocery aisle.

DRAW-A-PICTURE

1. Think about your image of what kind of person an impulse buyer is. In the space provided below, draw a picture of your image of a typical impulse buyer who is about to make an impulse purchase. Be creative and don't worry about your artistic skills! If you feel that some features of your drawing are unclear, don't hesitate to identify them with a written label.

2. After you have completed your drawing, imagine what is going through your character's mind as he or she is about to make his or her impulse purchase. Then write down your shopper's thoughts in a speech balloon (like you might see in a cartoon strip) that connects to your character's head.

Figure 9.3 ONE CONSUMER'S IMAGE OF AN IMPULSE BUYER

Source: Dennis Rock, "Is Impulse Buying (Yet) a Useful Marketing Concept?" (unpublished manuscript, University of Southern California, Los Angeles, 1990): Fig. 7-A.

NXT body wash/moisturizer cans light up on the store shelf.

Source: Courtesy of NXT/Clio Designs Incorporated.

The Salesperson: A Lead Role in the Play

The salesperson is one of the most important players in the retailing drama.[65] As we saw way back in Chapter 1, exchange theory stresses that every interaction involves a trade of value. Each participant gives something to the other and hopes to receive something in return.[66] A (competent) salesperson offers a lot of value because his or her expert advice makes the shopper's choice easier.

A buyer–seller situation is like many other *dyadic encounters* (two-person groups); it's a relationship in which both parties must reach some agreement about the roles of each participant during a process of *identity negotiation*.[67] Some of the factors that help to define a salesperson's role (and effectiveness) are her age, appearance, educational level, and motivation to sell.[68]

In addition, more effective salespersons usually know their customers' traits and preferences better than do ineffective salespersons, and they adapt their approach to meet the needs of each specific customer.[70] The ability to be adaptable is especially vital when customers and salespeople have different *interaction styles*.[71] We each vary in the degree of assertiveness we bring to interactions. At one extreme, *nonassertive* people believe it's not socially acceptable to complain, and sales situations may intimidate them. *Assertive* people are more likely to stand up for themselves in a firm but nonthreatening way. *Aggressives* may resort to rudeness and threats if they don't get their way (we've all run into these folks).[72]

The Tangled Web

At the customerssuck .com Web site, restaurant and store workers who have to grin and bear it all day go to vent. Once off the clock, they share their frustrations about the idiocy, slovenliness, and insensitivity of their customers. Some contributors to the Web site share stupid questions their customers ask, such as "How much is a 99-cent cheeseburger?" whereas others complain about working conditions and having to be nice to not-so-nice people. The slogan of the site is "the customer is never right."[69]

• • • • • • • • • • • • • • • •

Source: www.CustomersSuck.com, Art by Jennie Breeden www.TheDevilsPanties.com.

CB AS I SEE IT

Professor Cele Otnes, *University of Illinois at Urbana-Champaign*

How can retailers make consumers' in-store experiences more meaningful in order to positively influence key attitudinal and behavioral measures, such as brand loyalty and likelihood of repeat purchasing? One research topic that relates to this question is how retailers use in-store rituals to shape consumers' experiences. *Rituals* are expressive, dramatic events we repeat over time (for more on rituals, see Chapter 3).

Our research explores whether and how these types of rituals actually affect customers' experience with a brand. We have interviewed more than 20 retailers and service providers who identify themselves as using rituals designed for their employees or customers in order to enhance their relationships with these stakeholders, to improve efficiency, and to differentiate themselves from their competitors. We're exploring such issues as how consumers resist rituals, how consumers help co-create rituals with other shoppers and with retailers (as is the case at Build-A-Bear, when consumers engage in grooming rituals with the toys they've just created), and whether and how these rituals actually enhance consumers' retail experiences. From a strategic perspective, we will also explore whether ritualizing the shopping experience allows retailers to charge premium prices, to be forgiven more easily if they make mistakes with consumers, and to allocate less of their money to marketing communications. So next time you stand in line at Marble Slab Creamery or wear a "birthday sombrero" on your head at your favorite Mexican restaurant, remember—you've been ritualized!

OBJECTIVE 3

Other people and groups, especially those that possess social power, influence our decisions.

The Social Power of Groups

Humans are social animals. We belong to groups, try to please others, and look to others' behavior for clues about what we should do in public settings. In fact, our desire to "fit in" or to identify with desirable individuals or groups is the primary motivation for many of our consumption behaviors. We may go to great lengths to please the members of a group whose acceptance we covet.[73]

Let's revisit Zach's situation from the beginning of the chapter. His biker group is an important part of his identity, and this membership influences many of his buying decisions. He has spent many thousands of dollars on parts and accessories since he became a RUB. His fellow riders bond via their consumption choices, so total strangers feel an immediate connection with one another when they meet. The publisher of *American Iron*, an industry magazine, observed, "You don't buy a Harley because it's a superior bike, you buy a Harley to be a part of a family."[74]

Zach doesn't model himself after just *any* biker—only the people with whom he really identifies can exert that kind of influence on him. For example, Zach's group doesn't have much to do with outlaw clubs whose blue-collar riders sport big Harley tattoos. The members of his group also have only polite contact with "Ma and Pa" bikers, whose rides are the epitome of comfort and feature such niceties as radios, heated handgrips, and floorboards. Essentially, only the RUBs comprise Zach's *reference group*.

Why are groups so persuasive? The answer lies in the potential power they wield over us. **Social power** describes "the capacity to alter the actions of others."[76] To the degree to which you are able to make someone else do something, regardless of whether that person does it willingly, you have power over that person. The following classification of power bases helps us to distinguish among the reasons a person exerts power over another, the degree to which the influence is voluntary,

Marketing Opportunity

Brands recognize the need to be on social media yet fail to harness group power into convertibles sales. They still judge the group power of social networks which is difficult to put into perspective. A study recognizes that blogs come in third position where 31 percent of consumers say they have influenced their decisions. The firsts—retail and brand Web sites—are still the most influential. However, it is important to note that online group power which was virtually non-existent 10 years ago is now competing with institutional businesses to influence shoppers. Brands have understood the power blogs represent but they are not sure yet how to cultivate this relationship. On average, advertising spending of brands for blogs is 6 percent of their digital budget breakdown, which is insignificant compared to 41 percent on display ads. Facebook, Twitter, Pinterest or Instagram are also deemed influential, but not as much as blogs when considering the group power in social media. Interestingly, enough consumers find that the larger the community, the less power influencers have over consumers' decisions. Online shoppers prefer much smaller networks where trust can be nurtured between members.[75]

and whether this influence will continue to have an effect even when the source of the power isn't around.[77]

- **Referent power**—If a person admires the qualities of a person or a group, he tries to copy the referent's behaviors (e.g., choice of clothing, cars, leisure activities). Prominent people in all walks of life affect our consumption behaviors by virtue of product endorsements (e.g., Lady Gaga for Polaroid), distinctive fashion statements (e.g., Kim Kardashian's displays of high-end designer clothing), or championing causes (e.g., Brad Pitt for UNICEF). **Referent power** is important to many marketing strategies because consumers voluntarily modify what they do and buy in order to identify with a referent.

- **Information power**—A person possesses **information power** simply because she knows something others would like to know. Editors of trade publications such as *Women's Wear Daily* often possess tremendous power because of their ability to compile and disseminate information that can make or break individual designers or companies. People with information power are able to influence consumer opinion by virtue of their (assumed) access to the knowledge that provides some kind of competitive advantage.

- **Legitimate power**—Sometimes we grant power by virtue of social agreements, such as the authority we give to police officers, soldiers, and yes, even professors. The **legitimate power** a uniform confers wields authority in consumer contexts, including teaching hospitals where medical students don white coats to enhance their standing with patients.[78] Marketers "borrow" this form of power to influence consumers. For example, an ad that shows a model who wears a white doctor's coat adds an aura of legitimacy or authority to the presentation of the product ("I'm not a doctor, but I play one on TV").

- **Expert power**—To attract the casual Internet user, U.S. Robotics signed up British physicist Stephen Hawking to endorse its modems. A company executive commented, "We wanted to generate trust. So we found visionaries who use U.S. Robotics technology, and we let them tell the consumer how it makes their lives more productive." Hawking, who has Lou Gehrig's disease and speaks via a synthesizer, said in one TV spot, "My body may be stuck in this chair, but with the Internet my mind can go to the end of the universe."[79] Hawking's **expert power** derives from the knowledge he possesses about a content area. This helps to explain the weight many of us assign to professional critics' reviews of restaurants, books, movies, and cars—even though, with the advent of blogs and open source references such as Wikipedia, it's getting a lot harder to tell just who is really an expert![80]

- **Reward power**—A person or group with the means to provide positive reinforcement (see Chapter 6) has **reward power**. The reward may be the tangible kind, such as the contestants on *Survivor* experience when their comrades vote them off the island. Or it can be more intangible, such as the approval the judges on *American Idol* deliver to contestants.

- **Coercive power**—We exert **coercive power** when we influence someone because of social or physical intimidation. A threat is often effective in the short term, but it doesn't tend to stick because we revert to our original behavior as soon as the bully leaves the scene. Fortunately, marketers rarely try to use this type of power (unless you count those annoying calls from telemarketers!). However, we can see elements of this power base in the fear appeals we talked about in Chapter 8, as well as in intimidating salespeople who try to succeed with a "hard sell."

OBJECTIVE 4
We seek out others who share our interests in products or services.

Reference Groups Aren't Just Any Groups

Just because we find ourselves in the company of others doesn't necessarily mean they influence what we say or do. A **reference group** is an actual or imaginary individual or group that significantly influences an individual's evaluations, aspirations, or

Source: Courtesy of Rock 'n' Roll Fantasy Camp.

Marketing Opportunity

Most consumers only admire their aspirational reference groups from afar; however, more and more of them are now shelling out big bucks to get up close and personal with their heroes. *Fantasy camps* today are a $1 billion industry as people pay for the chance to hang out—and play with—their idols. Baseball camps that mix retired players with fans have been around for many years, but now other types let people mingle with their favorite hockey players, poker players, even members of the U.S. women's national soccer team. At one camp, 80 people each paid about $8,000 to jam with rock stars including Nils Lofgren, Dickey Betts, and Roger Daltrey. One enthusiastic novice gushed afterward, "We all grow up with heroes and never get to share a moment with them. But I got to live out my fantasy."[81]

behavior.[82] Reference groups influence us in three ways: *informational, utilitarian,* and *value-expressive.* Table 9.3 describes these influences.

Recent research on smoking cessation programs powerfully illustrates the impact of reference groups. The study found that smokers tend to quit in groups: When one person quits, this creates a ripple effect that motivates others in his social network to give up the death sticks also. The researchers followed thousands of smokers and nonsmokers for more than 30 years, and they also tracked their networks of relatives, coworkers, and friends. They discovered that over the years, the smokers tended to cluster together (on average in groups of three). As the overall U.S. smoking rate declined dramatically

TABLE 9.3	Three Forms of Reference Group Influence
Informational Influence	• The individual seeks information about various brands from an association of professionals or independent group of experts. • The individual seeks information from those who work with the product as a profession. • The individual seeks brand-related knowledge and experience (such as how Brand A's performance compares to Brand B's) from those friends, neighbors, relatives, or work associates who have reliable information about the brands. • The brand the individual selects is influenced by observing a seal of approval of an independent testing agency (such as Good Housekeeping). • The individual's observation of what experts do (such as observing the type of car that police drive or the brand of television that repairmen buy) influences his or her choice of a brand.
Utilitarian Influencey	• So that he or she satisfies the expectations of fellow work associates, the individual's decision to purchase a particular brand is influenced by their preferences. • The individual's decision to purchase a particular brand is influenced by the preferences of people with whom he or she has social interaction. • The individual's decision to purchase a particular brand is influenced by the preferences of family members. • The desire to satisfy the expectations that others have of him or her has an impact on the individual's brand choice.
Value-Expressive Influence	• The individual feels that the purchase or use of a particular brand will enhance the image others have of him or her. • The individual feels that those who purchase or use a particular brand possess the characteristics that he or she would like to have. • The individual sometimes feels that it would be nice to be like the type of person that advertisements show using a particular brand. • The individual feels that the people who purchase a particular brand are admired or respected by others. • The individual feels that the purchase of a particular brand would help show others what he or she is or would like to be (such as an athlete, successful business person, good parent, etc.).

Source: Adapted from C. Whan Park and V. Parker Lessig, "Students and Housewives: Differences in Susceptibility to Reference Group Influence," *Journal of Consumer Research* 4 (September 1977): 102. Copyright © 1977 JCR, Inc. Reprinted with permission of The University of Chicago Press.

Marketing Pitfall

One criticism of focus groups that provide feedback from consumers is that participants who listen to what others say in the group may change their opinions based on this temporary group influence. Some recent experiments underscore how powerful this effect can be. These studies replicated the live feedback graphs that networks sometimes use to report audience responses during political debates; marketing research firms also use this dial-testing format when they ask focus groups to evaluate TV shows and commercials. In one study that mimicked *American Idol*, several hundred college students watched performances as fake audience feedback appeared on the screen. When the feedback was negative, their evaluations of the contestants dipped also. In a similar study, participants watched an excerpt of a 1984 debate between presidential candidates Ronald Reagan and Walter Mondale (presumably these subjects were just a glimmer in their fathers' eyes when this election happened). Respondents who saw screen feedback that favored Reagan were 2.8 times more likely to say they would have voted for him, whereas those who saw similar feedback in favor of Mondale were 1.8 times more likely to say they would have voted for the Democratic candidate.[88]

during this period, the number of clusters in the sample decreased, but the remaining clusters stayed the same size; this indicated that people quit in groups rather than as individuals. Not surprisingly, some social connections were more powerful than others. A spouse who quit had a bigger impact than did a friend, whereas friends had more influence than siblings. Coworkers had an influence only in small firms where everyone knew one another.[83]

Reference group influences don't work the same way for all types of products and consumption activities. For example, we're not as likely to take others' preferences into account when we choose products that are not very complex, that are low in perceived risk, or that we can try before we buy.[84] In addition, knowing what others prefer may influence us at a general level (e.g., owning or not owning a computer, eating junk food versus health food), whereas at other times this knowledge guides the specific brands we desire within a product category (e.g., if we wear Levi's jeans versus Diesel jeans, or smoke Marlboro cigarettes rather than Virginia Slims).

Although two or more people normally form a group, we often use the term *reference group* a bit more loosely to describe *any* external influence that provides social cues.[85] The referent may be a cultural figure that has an impact on many people (e.g., Michelle Obama) or a person or group whose influence operates only in the consumer's immediate environment (e.g., the "popular" kids in high school). Reference groups that affect consumption can include parents, fellow motorcycle enthusiasts, the Tea Party, or even the Chicago Bears, the Dave Matthews Band, or Spike Lee.

Some people influence us simply because we feel similar to them. Have you ever experienced a warm feeling when you pull up at a light next to someone who drives the exact car as yours? One reason that we feel a bond with fellow brand users may be that many of us are a bit narcissistic (not you, of course); we feel an attraction to people and products that remind us of ourselves.

The need to connect with similar others may explain why we even relate to strangers who happen to share our name. Research on the **name letter effect** finds that, all things equal, we like others who share our names or even initials better than those who don't. When researchers look at large databases like Internet phone directories or Social Security records, they find that Johnsons are more likely to wed Johnsons, women named Virginia are more likely to live in (and move to) Virginia, and people whose surname is Lane tend to have addresses that include the word *lane*, not *street*. During the 2000 presidential campaign, people whose surnames began with B were more likely to contribute to candidate George Bush, whereas those whose surnames began with G were more likely to contribute to candidate Al Gore.[86]

Obviously, some groups and individuals are more powerful than others and affect a broader range of our consumption decisions. For example, our parents may play a pivotal role as we form our values on many important issues, such as attitudes about marriage or where to go to college. This reflects **normative influence**—that is, the reference group helps to set and enforce fundamental standards of conduct. In contrast, a Harley-Davidson club exerts **comparative influence** because it affects members' decisions about specific motorcycle purchases.[87]

Brand Communities and Consumer Tribes

Before it released the popular Xbox game *Halo 2*, Bungie Studios put up a Web site to explain the story line. However, there was a catch: The story was written from the point of view of the Covenant (the aliens who are preparing to attack Earth in the game)—and in *their* language. Within 48 hours, avid gamers around the world shared information in gaming chat rooms to crack the code and translate the text. More than 1.5 million people preordered the game before its release.[89] This cooperative effort illustrates a major trend in consumer behavior.

A **brand community** is a group of consumers who share a set of social relationships based on usage of or interest in a product. Unlike other kinds of communities, these members typically don't live near each other—except when they may meet for brief periods at organized events or **brandfests** that community oriented companies such as Jeep or Harley Davidson sponsor. These events help owners to "bond" with fellow enthusiasts and strengthen their identification with the product as well as with others they meet who share their passion.

Researchers find that people who participate in these events feel more positive about the products as a result, and this enhances brand loyalty. They tend to forgive product failures or lapses in service quality, and they're less likely to switch brands even if they learn that competing products are as good or better. Furthermore, these community members become emotionally involved in the company's welfare, and they often serve as brand missionaries as they carry its marketing message to others.[90] Researchers find that brand community members do more than help the product build buzz; their inputs actually create added value for themselves and other members as they develop better ways to use and customize products. It's common for experienced users to coach "newbies" in ways to maximize their enjoyment of the product so that more and more people benefit from a network of satisfied participants. In other cases, members benefit because their communities empower them to learn; for example, a study that looked at people who suffered from thyroid problems and who indicated they were uninformed and ill prepared to make decisions about their treatment later exhibited more active involvement and informed decision-making after they participated in an online community with others who shared their health issues.[91] Figure 9.4 demonstrates this process of **collective value creation**.[92]

A **consumer tribe** is similar to a brand community; it is a group of people who share a lifestyle and can identify with each other because of a shared allegiance to an activity or a product. Although these tribes are often unstable and short lived, at least for a time members identify with others through shared emotions, moral beliefs, styles of life, and of course the products they jointly consume as part of their tribal affiliation.

Some companies, especially those that are more youth oriented, use a **tribal marketing strategy** that links their product to, say, a group of shredders. However, there also are plenty of tribes with older members, such as car enthusiasts who gather to celebrate such cult products (see Chapter 2) as the Citroën in Europe and the Ford Mustang in the United States, or "foodies" who share their passion for cooking with other Wolfgang Puck wannabes around the world.[93]

Membership versus Aspirational Reference Groups

A **membership reference group** consists of people we actually know; although we don't know those in an **aspirational reference group**, we admire them anyway. These

---

Marketing Opportunity

In virtually any category, you'll find passionate brand communities (in some cases devoted to brands that don't even exist anymore); examples include the 3Com Ergo Audrey (discontinued Internet appliance), Apple Newton (discontinued personal digital assistant), BMW MINI (car), Garmin (GPS device), Jones Soda (carbonated beverage), Lomo and Holga (cameras), Tom Petty and the Heartbreakers (musical group), StriVectin (cosmeceutical), and *Xena: Warrior Princess* (TV program).

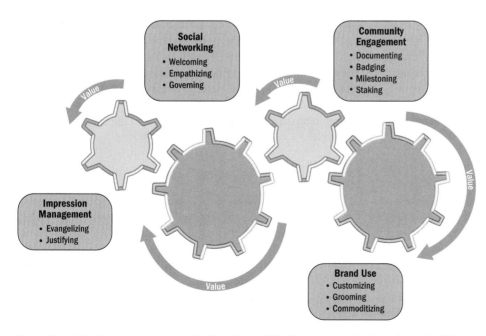

Figure 9.4 THE PROCESS OF COLLECTIVE VALUE CREATION IN BRAND COMMUNITIES

Source: Reprinted with permission from *Journal of Marketing,* published by the American Marketing Association, Schau, Hope Jensen, Albert M. Muniz, and Eric J. Arnould, September 2009, 73, 30–51.

The Web encourages the rise of a new kind of avoidance group: **antibrand communities.** These groups also coalesce around a celebrity, store, or brand—but in this case they're united by their disdain for it. The Rachael Ray Sucks Community on the blogging and social-networking site *LiveJournal* claims more than 1,000 members who don't hesitate to post their latest thoughts about the various shortcomings, flaws, and disagreeable traits of the (otherwise popular) television food personality. They criticize Ray's overuse of chicken stock, her kitchen hygiene, her smile (posters like to compare it to The Joker's of Batman fame), her penchant for saying "Yum-o!" and so on. The community has a basic rule for membership: "You must be anti-Rachael!"[102]

One team of researchers that studies these communities observes that they tend to attract social idealists who advocate non-materialistic lifestyles. After they interviewed members of online communities who oppose Walmart, Starbucks, and McDonald's, they concluded that these antibrand communities provide a meeting place for those who share a moral stance; a support network to achieve common goals; a way to cope with workplace frustrations (many members actually work for the companies they bash!); and a hub for information, activities, and related resources.[103] Another study chronicles the level of opposition the Hummer inspires. For example, whereas brand enthusiasts celebrate the Hummer's road safety because of its size and weight, antibranders who drive smaller cars slam the vehicle's bulk. One driver posted this message: "The H2 is a death machine. You'd better hope that you don't collide with an H2 in your economy car. You can kiss your ass goodbye thanks to the H2's massive weight and raised bumpers. Too bad you couldn't afford an urban assault vehicle of your own."[104]

people are likely to be successful businesspeople, athletes, performers, or anyone else who rocks our world. Not surprisingly, many marketing efforts that specifically adopt a reference group appeal concentrate on highly visible, widely admired figures (such as well-known athletes or performers); they link these people to brands so that the products they use or endorse also take on this aspirational quality. For example, an amateur basketball player who idolizes Miami Heat star Dwyane Wade might drool over a pair of Air Jordan 12 Dwayne Wade PE shoes.[94] One study of business students who aspired to the "executive" role found a strong relationship between products they associated with their *ideal selves* (see Chapter 7) and those they assumed that real executives own.[95]

Of course, as social media usage increases, the line between those we "know" and those we "friend" gets blurrier. Still, whether offline or online, we tend to seek out others who are similar. Indeed, one study even found that people on Twitter tend to follow others who share their mood: People who are happy tend to retweet or reply to others who are happy, while those who are sad or lonely tend to do the same with others who also post negative sentiments.[96]

Because we tend to compare ourselves to similar others, many promotional strategies include "ordinary" people whose consumption activities provide informational social influence. How can we predict which people you know will be part of your membership reference group? Several factors make it more likely:

- **Propinquity**—As physical distance between people decreases and opportunities for interaction increase, they are more likely to form relationships. We call this physical nearness **propinquity**. An early study on friendship patterns in a housing complex showed the strong effects of this factor: All things equal, residents were much more likely to be friends with the people next door than with those who lived only two doors away. Furthermore, people who lived next to a staircase had more friends than those at the ends of a hall (presumably, they were more likely to "bump into" people as they used the stairs).[97]

- **Mere exposure**—We come to like persons or things if we see them more often. We described this *mere exposure phenomenon* in Chapter 8.[98] Greater frequency of contact, even if unintentional, may help to determine one's set of local referents. The same effect holds when we evaluate works of art or even political candidates.[99] One study predicted 83 percent of the winners of political primaries solely by the amount of media exposure each candidate received.[100]

- **Group cohesiveness**—**Cohesiveness** refers to the degree to which members of a group are attracted to each other and how much each values his or her membership in this group. As the value of the group to the individual increases, so too does the likelihood that the group will influence that individual's consumption decisions. Smaller groups tend to be more cohesive, because in larger groups the contributions of each member are usually less important or noticeable. By the same token, groups often try to restrict membership to a select few, which increases the value of membership to those who do get in.

Positive Versus Negative Reference Groups

Reference groups impact our buying decisions both positively and negatively. In most cases, we model our behavior to be in line with what we think the group expects us to do. Sometimes, however, we also deliberately do the *opposite* if we want to distance ourselves from **avoidance groups**. You may carefully study the dress or mannerisms of a group you dislike (e.g., "nerds," "druggies," or "preppies") and scrupulously avoid buying anything that might identify you with that group. Rebellious adolescents do the opposite of what their parents desire to make a statement about their independence. In one study, college freshmen reported consuming less alcohol when they associated it with their avoidance groups.[101]

Marketing Pitfall

Social loafing happens when we don't devote as much time and effort to a task as we could because our contribution is part of a larger group effort.[107] You may have experienced this if you've worked on a group project for a class! Waitpersons are painfully aware of social loafing: People who eat in groups tend to tip less per person than when they eat alone.[108] For this reason, many restaurants automatically tack on a fixed gratuity for groups of six or more.

· · · · · · · · · · · · · · ·

Source: Corepics VOF/Shutterstock.

Your motivation to distance yourself from a negative reference group can be as powerful or more powerful than your desire to please a positive group.[105] That's why advertisements occasionally show an undesirable person who uses a competitor's product. This kind of execution subtly makes the point that you can avoid winding up like *that* kind of person if you just stay away from the products he buys. As a once-popular book reminded us, "Real men *don't* eat quiche!"[106]

Group Shopping

We get away with more when we do it in a group. One simple reason: The more people who are together, the less likely it is that any one member gets singled out for attention. That helps to explain why people in larger groups have fewer restraints on their behavior. For example, we sometimes behave more wildly at costume parties or on Halloween than we do when others can easily identify us. This is the phenomenon of **deindividuation**, a process whereby individual identities become submerged within a group.

Even shopping behavior changes when we do it in groups. For example, people who shop with at least one other person tend to make more unplanned purchases, buy more, and cover more areas of a store than do those who browse solo.[109] Both normative and informational social influence explain this. A group member may buy something to gain the approval of the others, or the group may simply expose her to more products and stores. Either way, retailers are well advised to encourage group-shopping activities.

The famous Tupperware party is a successful example of a **home shopping party** that capitalizes on group pressures to boost sales.[110] In this format that occurs often in **direct selling** companies like Mary Kay, Avon, and Amway, a company representative makes a sales presentation to a group of people who gather at the home of a friend or acquaintance. The shopping party works due to informational social influence: Participants model the behavior of others who provide them with information about how to use certain products, especially because a relatively homogeneous group (e.g., neighborhood homemakers) attends the party. Normative social influence also operates because others can easily observe our actions. Pressures to conform may be particularly intense and may escalate as more and more group members "cave in" (we call this process the *bandwagon effect*).

OBJECTIVE 5

Our desire to be consistent with other people motivates us to mimic what they buy and use.

Conformity

The early Bohemians who lived in Paris around 1830 made a point of behaving, well, differently from others. One flamboyant figure of the time earned notoriety because he walked a lobster on a leash through the gardens of the Royal Palace. His friends drank wine from human skulls, cut their beards in strange shapes, and slept in tents on the floors of their garrets.[111] Sounds a bit like some frats we've visited.

Although in every age there certainly are those who "march to their own drummers," most people tend to follow society's expectations regarding how they should act and look (with a little improvisation here and there, of course). **Conformity** is a change in beliefs or actions as a reaction to real or imagined group pressure. In order for a society to function, its members develop **norms**, or informal rules that govern behavior. Without these rules, we would have chaos. Imagine the confusion if a simple norm such as "always stop for a red traffic light" did not exist.

We conform in many small ways every day, even though we don't always realize it. Unspoken rules govern many aspects of consumption. In addition to norms regarding appropriate use of clothing and other personal items, we conform to rules that include gift-giving (we expect birthday presents from loved ones and get upset if they don't materialize), sex roles (men often pick up the check on a first date), and personal hygiene (our friends expect us to shower regularly). We also observe conformity in the online world; research supports the idea that consumers are more likely to show interest in a product if they see that it is already very popular.

One study analyzed how millions of Facebook users adopted apps to personalize their pages. Researchers tracked, on an hourly basis, the rate at which 50 million Facebook users installed 2,700 apps. They discovered that once an app had reached a rate of about 55 installations a day, its popularity started to soar. Facebook friends were notified when one of their online buddies adopted a new app, and they could also see a list of the most popular ones. Apparently this popularity feedback was the key driver that determined whether still more users would download the software.[112]

Still, we don't mimic others' behaviors all the time, so what makes it more likely that we'll conform? These are some common culprits:[113]

- **Cultural pressures**—Different cultures encourage conformity to a greater or lesser degree. The American slogan "Do your own thing" in the 1960s reflected a movement away from conformity and toward individualism. In contrast, Japanese society emphasizes collective well-being and group loyalty over individuals' needs.
- **Fear of deviance**—The individual may have reason to believe that the group will apply *sanctions* to punish nonconforming behaviors. It's not unusual to observe adolescents who shun a peer who is "different" or a corporation or university that passes over a person for promotion because he or she is not a "team player."
- **Commitment**—The more people are dedicated to a group and value their membership in it, the greater their motivation to conform to the group's wishes. Rock groupies and followers of TV evangelists may do anything their idols ask of them, and terrorists become martyrs for their cause. According to the **principle of least interest**, the person who is *least* committed to staying in a relationship has the most power because that party doesn't care as much if the other person rejects him.[114] Remember that on your next date.
- **Group unanimity, size, and expertise**—As groups gain in power, compliance increases. It is often harder to resist the demands of a large number of people than only a few, especially when a "mob mentality" rules.
- **Susceptibility to interpersonal influence**—This trait refers to an individual's need to have others think highly of him or her. Consumers who don't possess this trait are *role-relaxed*; they tend to be older, affluent, and have high self-confidence. Subaru created a communications strategy to reach role-relaxed consumers. In one of its commercials, a man proclaims, "I want a car. . . . Don't tell me about wood paneling, about winning the respect of my neighbors. They're my neighbors. They're not my heroes."[115]

Collective Decision-Making

OBJECTIVE 6
Marketers often need to understand consumers' behavior rather than a consumer's behavior.

In reality, the individual decision-making process that we described in detail in Chapter 2 often is overly simplistic. That's because in many situations, more than one person participates in the problem-solving sequence—from initial problem recognition and information search to evaluation of alternatives and product choice. To further muddy the waters, these decisions often include two or more people who may not have the same level of investment in the outcome, the same tastes and preferences, or the same consumption priorities. If you've ever debated where to go out to eat with your friends, or perhaps bickered about whose turn it is to do the dishes, you get the picture. You can read 50 restaurant reviews on Yelp!, and still it's like pulling teeth to reach a consensus.

In this section we examine *collective decision-making;* situations where more than one person chooses the products or services that multiple consumers use. In the first part we look at organizational decision-making, in which multiple employees select goods or services on behalf of a larger group. We then focus more specifically on one of the most important organizations to which we belong: the family unit. We'll consider how members of a family negotiate among themselves and how important changes in modern family structure affect this process.

Why do we lump together big corporations and small families? One important similarity is that in both cases individuals or groups play a number of specific roles when they choose products or services for their organizational unit.[116] Depending on the decision, the choice may include some or all of the group members, and different group members play important roles in what can be a complicated process. These roles include the following:

- **Initiator**—The person who brings up the idea or identifies a need.
- **Gatekeeper**—The person who conducts the information search and controls the flow of information available to the group. In organizational contexts, the gatekeeper identifies possible vendors and products for the rest of the group to consider.
- **Influencer**—The person who tries to sway the outcome of the decision. Some people may be more motivated than others to get involved, and participants also possess different amounts of power to get their point across.
- **Buyer**—The person who actually makes the purchase. The buyer may or may not actually use the product.
- **User**—The person who actually consumes the product or service.

B2B Decision-Making

OBJECTIVE 7
The decision-making process differs when people choose what to buy on behalf of an organization rather than for personal use.

Many employees of corporations or other organizations make purchase decisions on a daily basis. **Organizational buyers** are people who purchase goods and services on behalf of companies for the companies' use in manufacturing, distribution, or resale. These individuals buy from **business-to-business (B2B) marketers** who must satisfy the needs of organizations such as corporations, government agencies, hospitals, and retailers. In terms of sheer volume, B2B is where the action is: Roughly $2 trillion worth of products and services change hands among organizations, which is actually *more* than end consumers purchase.

Organizational buyers have a lot of responsibility. They decide on the vendors with whom they want to do business and what specific items they require from these suppliers. The items they consider range in price and significance from paper clips (by the case, not the box) to multimillion-dollar computer systems. Obviously, there are a lot of good reasons for marketers to understand how these organizational consumers make these important decisions—about 2 trillion, which is the amount U.S. companies spend per year to buy what they need to operate!

A number of factors influence the organizational buyer's perception of the purchase situation. These include his or her *expectations* of the supplier (e.g., product quality, the competence and behavior of the firm's employees, and prior experiences in dealing with that supplier), the *organizational climate* of the company (i.e., how it rewards performance and what it values), and the buyer's *assessment* of his or her own performance (e.g., whether he or she believes in taking risks).[117]

Like other consumers, organizational buyers engage in a learning process in which employees share information with one another and develop an "organizational memory" that consists of shared beliefs and assumptions about the best choices to make.[118] Just as our "market beliefs" influence him or her while shopping with the family on the weekend (see Chapter 2), the same thing happens at the office. He or she (perhaps with fellow employees) solves problems as they search for information, evaluate alternatives, and decide.[119] There are, of course, some important differences between the two situations.

How Does B2B Decision-Making Compare to Consumer Decision-Making?

Let's summarize the major differences between organizational and industrial purchase decisions versus individual consumer decisions:[120]

- The purchase decisions that companies make frequently involve many people, including those who do the actual buying, those who directly or indirectly influence this decision, and the employees who will actually use the product or service.
- Organizations and companies often use precise technical specifications that require a lot of knowledge about the product category.
- Impulse buying is rare (industrial buyers do not suddenly get an "urge to splurge" on lead pipe or silicon chips). Because buyers are professionals, they base their decisions on past experience and they carefully weigh alternatives.
- Decisions often are risky, especially in the sense that a buyer's career may ride on his judgment.
- The dollar volume of purchases is often substantial—it dwarfs most individual consumers' grocery bills or mortgage payments. One hundred to two hundred fifty organizational customers typically account for more than half of a supplier's sales volume, which gives the buyers a lot of influence over the supplier.
- Business-to-business marketing often emphasizes personal selling more than advertising or other forms of promotion. Dealing with organizational buyers typically requires more face-to-face contact than when marketers sell to end consumers.

We must consider these important features when we try to understand the purchasing decisions organizations make. Having said that, however, there are actually more similarities between organizational buyers and ordinary consumers than many people realize. True, organizational purchase decisions do tend to have a higher economic or functional component compared to individual consumer choices, but emotional aspects do play a role. Organizational buyers may appear to the outsider to be models of rationality, but at times they base their decisions on brand loyalty, on long-term relationships with particular suppliers or salespeople, or even on aesthetic preferences. Even investors, who are supposed to make cold, calculated judgments about the worth of companies based on financial indicators, sometimes are influenced instead by other concerns; for instance, they may be biased toward companies that provide better working conditions for employees or that are unusual in some other way.[121]

Like end consumers, both internal and external stimuli influence organizational buyers. Internal stimuli include the buyer's unique psychological characteristics, such as his or her willingness to make risky decisions, job experience, and training. External stimuli include the nature of the organization for which the person works as well as the overall economic and technological environment in which the industry operates.

As you'd expect, the organizational decision-making process depends on the purchase. As when individuals choose, the more complex, novel, or risky the decision, the more effort the group devotes to information search and to evaluating alternatives.

However, if these buyers rely upon a fixed set of suppliers for routine purchases, this greatly reduces their information search and effort.[122] Typically, a group of people (members of a **buying center**) plays different roles in more complex organizational decisions. As we will see later on, this joint involvement is somewhat similar to family decision-making, where family members are likely to participate in more important purchases. Note: Unlike a shopping center, a buying center does not refer to a physical place, but rather the group of people who make the decision.

The classic **buyclass theory of purchasing** divides organizational buying decisions into three types that range from the least to the most complex. Three decision-making dimensions describe the purchasing strategies of an organizational buyer:[123]

1 The level of information he or she must gather prior to the decision.
2 The seriousness with which he or she must consider all possible alternatives.
3 The degree to which he or she is familiar with the purchase.

Organizations often assemble teams to make purchasing decisions.
Source: Courtesy: Capstone Turbine Corporation.

TABLE 9.4	Types of Organizational Buying Decisions		
Buying Situation	**Extent of Effort**	**Risk**	**Buyer's Involvement**
Straight rebuy	Habitual decision-making	Low	Automatic reorder
Modified rebuy	Limited problem solving	Low to moderate	One or a few
New task	Extensive problem solving	High	Many

Source: Adapted from Patrick J. Robinson, Charles W. Faris, and Yoram Wind, *Industrial Buying and Creative Marketing* (Boston: Allyn & Bacon, 1967).

In practice, these three dimensions relate to how much cognitive effort the buyer expends when he decides. Three types of "buyclasses," or strategies determined by these dimensions, encompass most organizational decision situations.[124] Table 9.4 summarizes these strategies.

● A **straight rebuy** is an habitual decision. It's an automatic choice, as when an inventory level reaches a preestablished reorder point. Most organizations maintain an approved vendor list, and as long as experience with a supplier is satisfactory, there is little or no ongoing information search or evaluation.

Industrial marketers can be creative when they want to be, as this European ad for a heavy equipment manufacturer demonstrates.
Source: Used courtesy of Komatsu Europe.

Call the experts© for more power at high reach.

Reach further with Komatsu's telescopic handlers. With lifting heights from 9 to over 16 metres and lifting capacities from 3500 to 4500 kg, the range includes machines to suit every application. The state-of-the-art hydraulic system and single PPC joystick let you get the most from the huge power available and deliver precise control of the working equipment even during simultaneous operations. To complete the package, each of these highly versatile machines offers exceptional stability, high travel speed, superb manoeuvrability and best-in-class all-round visibility. Not bad for a telescopic.

KOMATSU

Komatsu Europe International nv - Mechelsesteenweg 586 - B-1800 Vilvoorde - Belgium

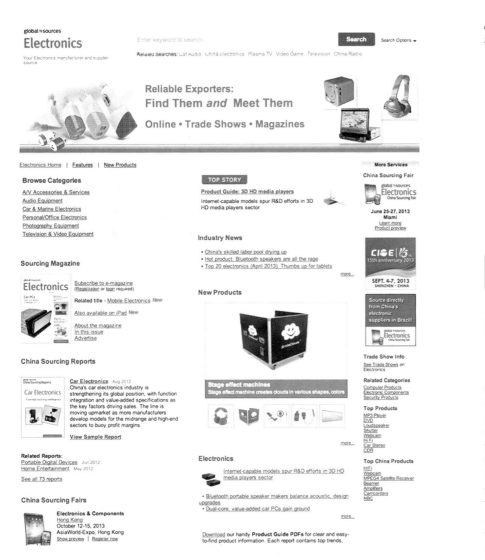

- A **modified rebuy** situation involves limited decision-making. It occurs when an organization wants to repurchase a product or service but also wants to make some minor modifications. This decision might involve a limited search for information among a few vendors. One or a few people will probably make the final decision.
- A **new task** involves extensive problem-solving. Because the company hasn't made a similar decision already, there is often a serious risk that the product won't perform as it should or that it will be too costly. This is when the organization designates a buying center with assorted specialists to evaluate the purchase, and they typically gather a lot of information before they come to a decision.

Prediction Markets

Are all of us smarter than each of us? A **prediction market** is one of the hottest trends in organizational decision-making techniques. This approach asserts that groups of people with knowledge about an industry are, collectively, better predictors of the future than are any of them as individuals.

In a prediction market framework, companies from Microsoft to Eli Lilly and Hewlett-Packard empower their employees as "traders." Like a stock market, traders place bets on what they think will happen regarding future sales, the success of new products, or how other firms in a distribution channel will behave—and they often receive a cash reward if their "stock picks" pan out. For example, the pharmaceutical giant Eli Lilly routinely places multimillion-dollar bets on drug candidates that face overwhelming odds of failure. The

Net Profit

Business-to-business (B2B) e-commerce refers to Internet interactions between two or more businesses or organizations. This includes exchanges of information, products, services, or payments. The Web revolutionized the way companies communicate with other firms and even the way they share information with their own people. More than 50 major corporations that belong to the Worldwide Retail Exchange (WWRE), such as CVS Corporation, Best Buy, Target, Tesco, JC Penney, and The Gap, participate in an online exchange community to complete their commercial transactions. This collaboration allows the members to work together on product development, production planning, and inventory replenishment.[125]

In the simplest form of B2B e-commerce, the Internet provides an online catalog of products and services businesses need. Companies like Dell Computer use their Internet site to deliver online technical support, product information, order status information, and customer service to corporate customers. Early on, Dell discovered that it could serve the needs of its customers more effectively if it tailored its Internet presence to different customer segments. Today Dell's Internet site allows shoppers to get recommendations based on their customer segment (home, home office, government, small business, and education). The company saves millions of dollars a year as it replaces hard-copy manuals with electronic downloads. For its larger customers, Dell provides customer-specific, password-protected pages that allow business customers to obtain technical support or to place an order.[126]

relatively few new compounds that do succeed have to make enough money to cover the losses the others incur. Obviously, the company will benefit if it can separate the winners from the losers earlier in the process. Lilly ran an experiment in which about 50 of its employees involved in drug development, including chemists, biologists, and project managers, traded six mock drug candidates through an internal market. The group correctly predicted the three most successful drugs.[127] At the publicly accessible prediction market Intrade (intrade.com) participants bet on the outcomes of political races, financial activities, or even the market value of rare wines and artwork. Or, surf over to the Hollywood Stock Exchange (hsx.com) to check out which celebrities and new movie releases traders think will succeed or bomb; you can bet Hollywood executives do![128]

Family Decision-Making

OBJECTIVE 8
Our traditional notions about families are outdated.

In 2010, our culture marked a milestone: For the first time married couples made up less than one-half of American households. Back in 1950, fully 78 percent of adults who lived together were married. New Census data also revealed that just a fifth of households were composed of traditional families—married couples with children—compared to 43 percent in 1950.[129] Does this mean that families are obsolete?

Hardly. The reality is that many other *types* of families continue to grow rapidly. Indeed, some experts argue that as traditional family living arrangements wane, we place even greater emphasis on siblings, close friends, and other relatives who provide companionship and social support.[130] Some people join *intentional families,* groups of unrelated people who meet regularly for meals and who spend holidays together.[131] Indeed, for some the act of meeting together to consume homemade food plays a central role in defining family: It is a symbolic way to separate a family unit from other social groups by allowing the cook(s) to personalize the meal and express affection via the effort that went into preparing the feast.[132]

The Modern Family Unit

The **extended family** used to be the most common family unit. It consists of three generations who live together, and it often includes grandparents, aunts, uncles, and cousins. Like the Cleavers of *Leave It to Beaver* and other TV families of the 1950s, the **nuclear family**—a mother, a father, and one or more children (perhaps with a sheepdog thrown in for good measure)—largely replaced the extended family, at least in American society. However, we've witnessed many changes since the days of Beaver Cleaver. Although many people continue to base their image of the typical family on old TV shows, demographic data tell us that this "ideal" image of the family is no longer realistic. The U.S. Census Bureau regards any occupied housing unit as a **household**, regardless of the relationships among the people who live there. Thus, one person living alone, three roommates, or two lovers (whether straight or gay) constitute a household.

Furthermore, as we've already seen, marriage as an institution is evolving. A report released by the U.S. Census Bureau said that nearly half of all women between the ages of 25 and 29 have never been married, up from about a quarter of that age group in 1986. In 1950, the median age of first marriages was 23 for men and 20 for women. In 2009, it was age 28 for men and 26 for women.[133] The recession is also taking its toll on families: The Census Bureau reports a sharp rise in the number of children living with their grandparents as mothers increasingly take jobs outside the home. Overall, 6.5 percent of children in the United States live with their grandparents, which is double the rate from 1970.[134]

The ways people get into (and out of) relationships also continues to evolve, as people increasingly rely on dating sites and social networks to find mates. A survey by the dating site Match.com reported that one in six couples married in the last year met online.[135] Another study by the dating Web site OK Cupid, however, found that the romantic relationships of active Twitter users don't last as long as those of the rest of the population.[136]

Also, due in part to harsh economic conditions, children are more likely to live at home after graduating from college rather than taking their own places. Demographers call these returnees **boomerang kids** (you throw them out . . . they keep coming back). In today's shrinking job market, many young people are forced to redefine the assumption that college graduation automatically means living on their own. Even before the recession we saw this trend quickening. As of 2007, 55 percent of men and 48 percent of women ages 18 to 24 lived with their parents.[137] In addition, many adults care for their own parents as well as for their children. In fact, Americans on average spend 17 years caring for children, but 18 years assisting aged parents.[138] Some label middle-aged people the **Sandwich Generation**, because they must support both the generation above them and the one below them.

Young adults who do leave the nest to live by themselves are relatively unlikely to return, whereas those who move in with roommates are more likely to come back. Young people who move in with a romantic partner are more likely than average to end up back home if the relationship fails![139] If the dismal economic environment continues, it will affect a variety of markets, as boomerang kids spend less on housing and staples and more on discretionary purchases such as entertainment.

CB AS I SEE IT

Professor Alladi Venkatesh, *University of California, Irvine*

As new technologies diffuse into the home, new terminology has begun to emerge as, for example, *smart homes, home automation, digital home, digital living, networked home, home of the future, smart appliances*, and so on. To further complicate the technological scene, we are witnessing enormous growth of social media (Facebook, MySpace, YouTube, etc.). We will use the term *smart home technologies* to describe these and other similar technologies. Although smart home technologies have developed in different directions because of the types of industry players involved, some common themes underlie these developments. For example, family shopping behavior— from online product information search to payments, vacation planning, and communication—are some of the many activities that families undertake using these new technologies. They all seem to point to a great sense of anticipation that home life as we have understood it in the past 50 or 60 years will undergo

some fundamental changes. It is claimed that some of these changes may be the result of advances at the technological frontier.

Embedded in the concept of the smart home are smart appliances, multimedia systems, energy devices, sensors, lighting systems, sensors and control systems, and home robots that manifest basic qualities of programmable machine intelligence. However, their implementation has not been very successful and has been a little slow. Recent developments, however, seem to suggest that smart home concepts are closer to reality and must be taken seriously.

To put these developments in a historical perspective, one can trace all such advances to the early 1980s when the PC was introduced into the home. This was also the period when various electronic gadgets entered the domestic space: VCRs, microwave ovens, answering machines, and cable TV, to name an important few. A lot has happened since then. In the 1990s, the technological scene changed dramatically with the arrival of the Internet, connecting the household to the external environment in some fundamental views. In the beginning of the 21st century, the introduction of mobile phones and wireless technologies has further expanded the technological boundaries. The possibilities seem endless. In this

ever-increasing technological frenzy, some caution must be exercised as new technologies knock on the door to gain acceptance by families. Our previous studies show that families are reluctant to "overtechnologize" their homes, but at the same time are quite open to technologies that fit with their current patterns of behaviors and possibly add value to the family life. It is this balance between too much and too little technology that one must seek.

Given the developments described previously, technology diffusion into the home remains an unexplored area in the field of consumer research. For consumer researchers, the challenging questions are:

- How are smart home technologies diffusing into the home?
- How is the family changing as a result of new technologies coming into the home?
- Who are the innovators? And what are the characteristics of their products and services?
- What are the models of technology and appropriate adoption and use?
- How are the family roles transformed in light of these new changes?
- What are the implications for product advertising in light of social media?

American Girl produces historical-period characters complete with books, dolls, and accessories, as well as modern-period dolls. The company also operates The American Girl Place, where young girls who own the dolls drag their parents and grandparents to attractions including dioramas and a doll hair salon. Consumer researchers who studied the American Girl phenomenon concluded that part of the brand's huge popularity is due to its multigenerational appeal. After they interviewed numerous girls, mothers, and grandmothers, they found that consumers of all ages valued the opportunities for family connection and also learning about their heritage and those of other cultures.[140]

Source: Reprinted with permission of American Girl Inc.

Family Size

Family size depends on such factors as educational level, the availability of birth control, and religion. Demographers define the **fertility rate** as the number of births per year per 1,000 women of childbearing age. Marketers keep a close eye on the population's birth rate to gauge how the pattern of births will affect demand for products in the future. The U.S. fertility rate increased dramatically in the late 1950s and early 1960s, when the parents of *baby boomers* began to reach childbearing age. It declined in the 1970s and began to climb again in the 1980s as baby boomers began to have their own children in a new "baby boomlet" (more on these groups in Chapter 10).

Worldwide, surveys show that many women want smaller families today. This trend is a problem for European countries whose fertility rates have plummeted during past decades, and Japan faces a severe shortage of young people to support older generations. Ironically, while populations boom in many underdeveloped parts of the world, industrialized countries face future crises because there will be relatively fewer young people to support their elders. For population levels to remain constant, the fertility rate has to be 2.0 so that the two children can replace their parents. That's not happening in places such as Spain, Sweden, Germany, and Greece, where the fertility rate is 1.4 or lower. As a benchmark, the U.S. rate is 2.1. More babies were born in the United States in 2007 than in any other year in American history—but this figure mostly reflects a greater number of women of childbearing age.[141]

Some countries are weighing measures to encourage people to have more children. For example, Spain is looking at cheaper utility bills for large families, assisting young couples who are trying to buy homes, and creating hundreds of thousands of new preschools and nursery schools. The Italian government provides mothers with nearly full salary compensation for about half a year of maternity leave, but many women still refuse to have more kids. There are many reasons for this shift from past eras when heavily Catholic countries tended to have large families: Contraception and abortion are more readily available, divorce is more common, and older people who used to look after grandchildren now pursue other activities such as travel. Some experts also cite the fact that many Italian men live with their mothers into their 30s, so when they do get married they're not prepared to help out at home. One analyst commented, "Even the most open-minded guy—if you scratch with the nail a little bit, there's the mother who did everything for him."[142]

In the United States, the National Center of Health Statistics confirms that the percentage of women of childbearing age who define themselves as **voluntarily childless** is on the rise. Twenty percent of women ages 40 to 44 have no children, double the level of 30 years ago. Women with advanced degrees are more likely to be childless, the study found. Of women who gave birth in 2006, 36 percent were separated, widowed, divorced, or never married.[143]

Marketing Opportunity

Childless couples are an attractive market segment for some companies (but obviously not for others, such as Gerber Baby Food). So-called **DINKS** (double income, no kids) couples are better educated on average than are two-income couples with children. According to the U.S. Census Bureau, 30 percent of childless couples consist of two college graduates, compared with 17 percent of those with kids. The childless are more likely to have professional or managerial occupations (24 percent versus 16 percent of dual-employed couples with children). Dave and Buster's, a Dallas-based restaurant chain, caters to this group as it enforces strict policies to deter families with small children. However, many childless couples feel snubbed by a child-oriented society. In recent years they formed networking organizations such as Childfree by Choice to support this lifestyle decision.[144]

Escape to Mum and Dad's £9.50

Escape from Mum and Dad's £9.50

Edinburgh from £9.50 one way.

national express

Many boomerang kids today return home to live with their parents–voluntarily or not.

Source: Copyright Cdp-Travissully Ltd.

Animals Are People Too! Nonhuman Family Members

Almost one-third of all U.S. households have at least one pet, and 92 percent of pet owners consider their furry friends members of the family—83 percent call themselves "Mommy" or "Daddy" when they talk to their pets.[145] Many of us assume that pets share our emotions; perhaps that helps to explain why more than three-quarters of domestic cats and dogs receive presents on holidays and birthdays.[146] We've doubled our spending on our pets in the past decade, and today the pet industry pulls in more revenue (almost $40 billion annually) than either the toy or candy industries. Even in the recession, consumers don't make their pets pay the price, although we pay more for pet food, supplies, and services than ever. Here are a few examples of pet-smart marketing:[147]

- Kennels look a lot more like spas for the furry. At some of them, dogs can hike, swim, listen to music, watch TV, and even get a pedicure—complete with nail polish. Heated tile floors and high-tech ventilation systems are common. When a dog stays in the "ambassador suite" at Club Bow-Wow, a staff member sleeps overnight in the room. PetSmart, the largest U.S. pet-store chain, opened a chain of PetsHotels, where furry guests lounge on hypoallergenic lambskin blankets and snack on lactose-free, fat-free ice cream. The suites feature raised dog beds and a television that plays videos, such as *Lady and the Tramp* and *101 Dalmatians*.
- Companies that make human products, such as Gucci, Juicy Couture, Harley-Davidson, IKEA, Lands' End, Paul Mitchell, and Ralph Lauren, also sell products for pets, ranging from shampoos to nail polish to gold-plated bowls. Harley-Davidson started its pet collection after it noticed that customers at rallies and other events bring along their dogs; some ride shotgun in the motorcycles' saddle bags or side cars. Customers can buy denim and leather jackets for their pets, as well as riding goggles, bandanas, spiked leather collars, and even squeaky toys shaped like oil cans.
- Designer water for dogs? A California company started things off when it introduced a vitamin-enriched water product for dogs. A Florida company sells "DogWater" in containers that double as throwing toys. Then there's K9 Water Inc., a company whose catalog lists products such as "Gutter Water" and chicken-flavored "Toilet Water." Make that a double.

Pets are as important to people in South Africa as they are here.
Source: Courtesy of Euro RSCG South Africa.

The author's pug, Kelbie Rae.
Source: Photo courtesy of Michael Solomon.

● What happens when our four-legged companion goes to the great kennel in the sky? One trend is to freeze-dry the departed pet rather than bury it or cremate it. The bereaved say that turning furry friends into perma-pets helps them deal with loss and maintains a connection to their former companions. Once dried, the animal's body doesn't decay, so it can continue to occupy that special place on the couch.

The Family Life Cycle

Many factors affect what a family spends, including the number of people (children and adults) in the family, their ages, and whether one, two, or more adults work outside of the home. Two especially important factors that determine how a couple spends time and money are (1) whether they have children and (2) whether the woman works.

Because they recognize that family needs and expenditures change over time, marketers apply the **family life cycle (FLC)** concept to segment households. The FLC combines trends in income and family composition with the changes these demands place on this income. As we age, our preferences and needs for products and activities tend to change. Twenty-somethings spend less than average on most products and services because their households are small and their incomes are low (especially today!). Income levels tend to rise (at least until retirement), so that people can afford more over time. Older consumers spend more per capita on luxury items such as gourmet foods and upscale home furnishings.[148] In addition, we don't need to repeat many purchases we make when we start out. For example, we tend to accumulate durable goods such as large appliances and replace them only as necessary.

A life-cycle approach to the study of the family assumes that pivotal events alter role relationships and trigger new stages of life that alter our priorities. In addition to the birth of a first child, other pivotal events include the departure of the last child from the house, the death of a spouse, retirement of the principal wage earner, and divorce. At Web sites like The Bump, women find tools such as an Ovulation Calculator and lists of baby names; The Knot offers a range of wedding-related services when those babies grow up and get hitched. As people move through these life stages, we observe significant changes in expenditures in leisure, food, durables, and services, even after we adjust the figures to reflect changes in income.[149] We simply attribute some of these changes to variations in functional needs, whereas others reflect deeper motivations as we transition from one role to another. For example, researchers find that new mothers undergo profound changes in self-concept during pregnancy and after delivery; these changes influence the types of products they consume to reflect their new identities.[150]

It's particularly useful to get a handle on longitudinal changes in priorities when we want to predict demand for specific product categories over time. For example, the money a couple with no children spends on dinners out and vacations will go to quite different purchases after the birth of a child, when a night on the town becomes a distant memory. Ironically, although the entertainment industry focuses on winning the hearts and wallets of young consumers, it's the senior citizens who have become America's true party animals. The average household headed by a 65- to 74-year-old spends more on entertainment than does the average household in which the primary wage earner is under age 25.[151]

Over the years, researchers have proposed several models to describe family life-cycle stages, but with limited effect because most failed to take into account such important social trends as the changing role of women, the acceleration of alternative lifestyles, childless and delayed-child marriages, and single-parent households. We need to focus on four variables to adequately describe these changes:

1 Age
2 Marital status
3 The presence or absence of children in the home, and
4 The ages of children, if present.

In addition, we have to relax our definition of marital status to include *any* couple living together in a long-term relationship. Thus, although we might not consider roommates "married," for marketing purposes a man and woman who have established a household would be, as would two homosexual men or lesbian women who have a similar understanding. When we update our outlook, we identify a set of categories that includes many more types of family situations.[152] Consumers we classify into these categories show marked differences in consumption patterns:

- Young bachelors and newlyweds are the most likely to exercise; to go out to bars, concerts, movies, and restaurants; and to drink alcohol. Although people in their twenties account for less than 4 percent of all household spending in the United States, their expenditures are well above average in such categories as apparel, electronics, and gasoline.[153]
- Families with young children are more likely to consume health foods such as fruit, juice, and yogurt; those made up of single parents and older children buy more junk foods. The dollar value of homes, cars, and other durables is lowest for bachelors and single parents but increases as people go through the full-nest and childless-couple stages.
- Partly because they score wedding gifts, newlyweds are the most likely to own appliances such as toaster ovens and electric coffee grinders. Babysitter and day-care usage is, of course, highest among single-parent and full-nest households, whereas older couples and bachelors are most likely to employ home maintenance services (e.g., lawn mowing).

OBJECTIVE 9

Members of a family unit play different roles and have different amounts of influence when the family makes purchase decisions.

The Intimate Corporation: Family Decision-Making

The decision process within a household unit resembles a business conference. Certain matters go on the table for discussion, different members advocate different actions based on their differing priorities and agendas, and there may be power struggles to rival any tale of corporate intrigue. In just about every living situation, whether it's a conventional family or students who share a sorority house or apartment, group members assume different roles just as purchasing agents, engineers, account executives, and others do within a company.

When Chevrolet wanted to win drivers over to its Venture minivan, the company sent teams of anthropologists out to observe families in their natural habitats. Conventional wisdom says that minivan buyers are practical; they care about affordability, lots of features, and plenty of room. But these researchers discovered a different story: People see the vehicles as part of the family. When they asked consumers to identify the best metaphor for a minivan, many picked a photo of a hang glider because it represents freedom and families on the go. The advertising slogan for the Venture became, "Let's go."[154]

Families make two basic types of decisions:[155]

1   In a **consensual purchase decision**, members agree on the desired purchase; they disagree only in terms of how they will make it happen. In these circumstances, the family will most likely engage in problem-solving and consider alternatives until they find a way to satisfy everyone in the group. For example, in a family that decides to get a dog, some of the members (you can guess who) voice concerns about who will take care of it. The solution is to draw up a chart that assigns family members to specific duties.

2   In an **accommodative purchase decision**, however, group members have different preferences or priorities and can't agree on a purchase that satisfies everyone's needs. It is here that they use bargaining, coercion, and compromise to achieve agreement on what to buy or who gets to use it. Conflict occurs when there is incomplete correspondence in family members' needs and preferences. Although household spending and budgeting is the most common source of conflict in these disputes, TV viewing choices come in a close second![156]

Decisions create conflict among family members to the extent that the issue is somehow important or novel; conflict also occurs if individuals have strong opinions about good and bad alternatives. The degree to which these factors generate conflict determines the type of decision the family will make.[157] Some specific factors that determine how much family decision conflict there will be include:[158]

● **Interpersonal need**—(a person's level of investment in the group): A teenager may care more about what her family buys for the house than will a college student who lives in a dorm.

● **Product involvement and utility**—(the degree to which a person will use the product to satisfy a need): A mother who is an avid coffee drinker will obviously be more interested in the purchase of a new coffeemaker than will her teenage son who swigs Coke by the gallon.

● **Responsibility**—(for procurement, maintenance, payment, and so on): People are more likely to have disagreements about a decision if it entails long-term consequences and commitments. For example, a family decision about getting a dog may involve conflict over who will be responsible for walking and feeding it.

● **Power**—(or the degree to which one family member exerts influence over the others): In traditional families, the husband tends to have more power than the wife, who in turn has more than the oldest child, and so on. Conflict can arise when one person continually uses the power he has within the group to satisfy his own priorities. For example, if a child believed that his life would end if he did not receive a Kinect for his birthday, he might be more willing to "cash in some chips" and throw a tantrum.

One analysis of family decision-making took a closer look at the idea that family members mutually construct a **family identity** that defines the household both to members and to insiders.[159] According to this perspective (which is similar to the role theory approach to consumer behavior we discussed in Chapter 1), family rituals, narratives (stories the members tell about the family), and everyday interactions help families

The Tangled Web

As avatars socialize in virtual worlds like Kaneva and *Second Life* (SL), it's inevitable that some will pair up. Linden Lab, the creator of SL, reports that more than 35,000 of its residents enter formal partnerships with other residents (a partnership is like a virtual marriage and players include this information on their avatar user profiles). Avatars can have sex with one another in SL, but we won't go there. Suffice it to say that this is a fairly common activity and that there have even been reports of rape. Sometimes these partnerships lead to real-world contact—and as in RL, these relationships can turn bad. It's not unheard of for an SL resident to leave his or her RL partner for an avatar partner. As more people enter virtual worlds, family decision-making research may have to include our virtual partners (and children?) as well.

Even Facebook has an impact on relationships, perhaps because the platform makes it easier for people to rekindle old romances. In a recent survey of attorneys, two-thirds of divorce lawyers identified Facebook as the primary source of evidence in divorce cases. The large majority reports that evidence for infidelity also turns up on online photo albums, profile pages, and Tweets.[160] As one attorney noted, the ". . . huge popularity as well as the lure of sites like Second Life, Illicit Encounters and Friends Reunited are tempting couples to cheat on each other." Apparently many divorces occur when partners find "flirty messages" on their spouse's Facebook wall. She also offered some timely advice to people in the middle of a divorce proceeding: "Avoid posting photos of your new lover until it's all over."[161]

On a more positive note, online video calling services like Skype and iChat may transform family relationships, particularly when they allow family members who live far apart to regularly speak to and see one another onscreen (for free). Many grandparents who previously didn't know an HTML from a VoIP enthusiastically embrace technology when it means they can virtually visit far-away grandchildren up close and personal on a regular basis. The American Association of Retired Persons (AARP) reports that nearly half of American grandparents live more than 200 miles from at least one of their grandchildren. What's more, two-thirds of grandchildren see one or both sets of grandparents at most a few times a year.[162] Digital platforms create a lot of opportunities for family members to connect—and for savvy marketers to connect to them.

maintain their structure, maintain their family character (day-to-day characteristics of family life), and clarify members' relationships to one another. The value of this approach to marketers is that it reminds us of how often products and services help to define the family identity. For example, a father might take his young children out for ice cream every Saturday afternoon, so this becomes a predictable ceremony that defines their relationship. Or, a mom might seek the comfort of her iPod to shield her from the noise when her kids play after school, while a TiVo "saves marriages" because it allows family members to compromise when they decide who gets access to the TV.

Earlier we noted that companies are a lot like families (though some are more dysfunctional than others!). One perspective comes at this idea from the other direction, as it compares families to companies. The researchers looked at the family unit as a set of **customer networks**; in the commercial space, these are structures that invest in products and services to help the family reach collective identity goals, recognizing that these pursuits may compete with rather than complement individual interests. They applied this concept to the context of family vacations to understand how marketers can succeed by reconciling the goals of different family members (especially when some of these are individual goals and others involve cooperation with other members).

Sex Roles and Family Decision-Making Responsibilities

When the Indian composer A. R. Rahman accepted two Oscars for his work on the hit movie *Slumdog Millionaire*, he thanked his mother . . . as an afterthought he also remembered to thank his wife. India's culture strongly encourages a doting relationship between mothers and sons. It's common for many successful men to consult their mothers for advice daily, and some tycoons put their mothers on their boards of directors. Hinduism stresses powerful female gods, and many citizens refer to the country as Mother India. Clearly, older decision-makers in the family unit carry a lot of weight, both in the house and out: Young people often take their parents to their first job interview.[163] Americans may not lag far behind if the number of **helicopter moms** continues to swell: These are overprotective mothers who "hover" around their kids and insert themselves into virtually all aspects of their lives—including, in some cases, job interviews![164]

So, who "wears the pants" in the family? Sometimes it's not obvious which spouse makes the decisions. Indeed, although many men literally wear the pants, it's women who buy them. Haggar's research showed that nearly half of married women bought pants for their husbands without the husbands being present, so the firm started to advertise its menswear products in women's magazines. When one family member chooses a product, this is an **autonomic decision**. In traditional households, for example, men often have sole responsibility to select a car, whereas decorating choices fall to women. **Syncretic decisions**, such as a vacation destination, involve both partners. These choices are common for vacations, homes, appliances, furniture, home electronics, and long-distance phone services. As the couple's educational level increases, they are more likely to make decisions together.[165] A study conducted by the Roper research company reported signs of a shift in marital decision-making toward more compromise and turn-taking. For example, the survey finds that wives tend to win out in arguments about how the house is kept, whereas husbands get control of the remote.[166]

The proportion of autonomic decisions steadily tips more toward women. It's not news to claim that women hold the purse strings in many families. However, this dominance is accelerating because, in a departure from the past, many women are not just the spenders, they are also the earners. Today, the U.S. workforce is almost 50 percent female, and women hold a majority of high-paying management and professional jobs. For every two males who graduate from college or get a higher degree, three women do. Although overall women still earn less than men, about a third of them earn more than their husbands. This shift goes on around the world; some analysts argue that we are entering a **sheconomy** where women will dominate emerging markets.

Here in the United States, a study of 30- to 44-year-olds showed that when a husband is the primary or sole breadwinner, household spending decisions divide roughly

Mothers take on many responsibilities as they care for the family unit.
Source: Courtesy KidCare TV.

equally. He makes about a third of them, she makes a third, and they make a third jointly. But, in the 22 percent of households in which the wife earned more, the wife makes more than twice as many decisions as her husband about where the money goes. The more money women earn, the exponentially more money they manage. These shifts even occur in areas where men traditionally dominate. Women make up almost half of the $200 billion consumer-electronics business, and $105 billion of the $256 billion home-improvement market. In fact, 44 percent of NFL fans are women![167] In contrast, single men remain a powerful and often ignored force in the marketplace. Right now, 3 out of 10 men are single, and more than 80 percent of them make the sole or key big-ticket decisions in their households—at least for now.[168]

Comments from married women who participated in focus groups conducted by *Redbook* magazine illustrate some of the dynamics of autonomic versus syncretic decision-making:

- "We just got our steps done and that was a big project. The contractor would talk (to my husband) and not talk to me. And I said, 'Excuse me, I'm here, too.'"
- "We are looking for a house now, and we're making decisions on which side of town we want it on, what size house do we want, and it's a together decision. That's never how my mother did it."
- "My husband did not want a van, because we have just one child, but I said, 'I want a van. And it's not because everyone else has a van. I want comfort.' He wanted a convertible. And we got a van."[169]

Marketers need to figure out who makes the buying decisions in a family because this information tells them who to target and whether they need to reach both spouses to influence a choice. For example, marketing research in the 1950s indicated that women

The Tangled Web

Johnson & Johnson encountered a firestorm of protest from irate mothers (not a smart group to mess with) after the company ran an online advertisement for its over-the-counter pain pill Motrin. The spot intended to target mothers who get back pain when they carry their babies in slings, but many women felt the ad was an insensitive portrayal of women's pain as well as of their preferred method of carrying their babies. Within days after the launch, calls for a boycott began to gather on blogs, YouTube, and Twitter. J&J quickly pulled the ad—but it learned the hard way how mothers tune into social media today.[170]

were beginning to play a larger role in household purchasing decisions. In response, lawn mower manufacturers emphasized the rotary mower over other power mowers to downplay women's fears of injury. Rotary models, which conceal the cutting blades and engine, began to pop up in ads that depicted young women and smiling grandmothers as they cut the grass.[171]

Researchers pay special attention to which spouse plays the role of the **family financial officer (FFO)**—the individual who keeps track of the family's bills and decides how to spend any surplus funds. Newlyweds tend to share this role, and then over time one spouse or the other takes over these responsibilities.[172] In traditional families (and especially those with low educational levels), women are primarily responsible for family financial management: The man makes it and the woman spends it. Each spouse "specializes" in certain activities.[173]

The pattern is different among families where more modern sex-role norms operate. These couples believe that both people should participate in family maintenance activities. In these cases, husbands assume more responsibility for laundering, housecleaning, grocery shopping, and so on, in addition to such traditionally "male" tasks as home maintenance and garbage removal.[174] Shared decision-making is the norm for most American couples today: A Roper poll reported that 94 percent of partnered women say they make the decision or share equally in home furnishing selections (not a huge surprise), but in addition, 81 percent said the same for financial savings/investments, and 74 percent participate when the couple decides what car to buy.[175]

Working mothers often struggle with what one researcher calls the **juggling lifestyle**: a frenzied, guilt-ridden compromise between conflicting cultural ideals of motherhood and professionalism.[176] This frantic way of life isn't surprising in light of a survey by the U.S. Department of Labor showing that the average working woman spends about twice as much time as the average working man on household chores and the care of children. She also gets about an hour less sleep each night than the average stay-at-home mom.[177]

In general, four factors determine the degree to which one or the other spouse or both jointly will decide what to buy:[178]

1 **Sex-role stereotypes**—Couples who believe in traditional sex-role stereotypes tend to make individual decisions for sex-typed products.
2 **Spousal resources**—The spouse who contributes more resources to the family has the greater influence.
3 **Experience**—Couples who have experience as a decision-making unit make individual decisions more frequently.
4 **Socioeconomic status**—Middle-class families make more joint decisions than do either higher- or lower-class families.

Despite recent changes in decision-making responsibilities, women are still primarily responsible for the continuation of the family's **kin-network system**: They maintain ties among family members, both immediate and extended. Women are more likely to coordinate visits among relatives, stay in touch with family members, send greeting cards, and arrange social engagements.[179] This organizing role means that women often make important decisions about the family's leisure activities, and they are more likely to decide with whom the family will socialize.

The **synoptic ideal** calls for the husband and wife to take a common view and to act as joint decision-makers. According to this view, they would very thoughtfully weigh alternatives, assign one another well-defined roles, and calmly make mutually beneficial consumer decisions. The couple would act rationally and analytically, and use as much information as possible to maximize joint utility. Do you know anyone who does that? In reality, spousal decision-making may be more about choosing whatever option will result in less conflict. A couple "reaches" rather than "makes" a decision. Researchers simply describe this process as "muddling through."[180]

One common technique to simplify the decision-making process uses *heuristics* (see Chapter 2). The following decision-making patterns, which realtors frequently observe when a couple decides on a new house, illustrate how couples use heuristics.

- The couple defines their areas of common preference on obvious, objective dimensions rather than subtler, hard-to-define cues. For example, they may easily agree on the number of bedrooms they need in the new home, but they have a harder time when they need to agree on how the home should look.
- The couple negotiates a system of *task specialization* in which each is responsible for certain duties or decision areas and does not intrude on the other's "turf." For many couples, sex roles often dictate just what these territories are. For example, the wife may do advance scouting for houses that meet their requirements, and the husband determines whether the couple can obtain a mortgage.
- The likelihood of one partner conceding to the wishes of the other depends on how passionately each person desires a specific outcome. One spouse yields to the influence of the other in many cases simply because his or her preference for a certain attribute is not particularly intense. In other situations, he is more willing to fight for what he wants (in other words, "choose your battles").[181] In cases where intense preferences for different attributes exist, rather than attempting to influence each other, spouses will "trade off" a less-intense preference for a more strongly felt desire. For example, a husband who is somewhat indifferent about kitchen design may give in to his wife in exchange for permission to design his own garage workshop.

To what degree are these gender-based decision roles changing? Recent evidence says quite a bit; men and women increasingly express similar attitudes about how they prefer to balance home life and work. Some experts argue that the gender revolution is developing into **gender convergence**. A comprehensive view of current research reported more similarities than differences between American men and women. Most people recognize that mothers work more and do less housework, and that men work less and do more housework and childcare than their fathers, although they still shoulder significantly less of the burden than do women.[182]

MyMarketingLab

Go to **mymktlab.com** to complete the problems marked with this icon ⭐.

CHAPTER SUMMARY

1. Many factors at the time of purchase dramatically influence the consumer's decision-making process.

Many factors affect a purchase. These include the consumer's antecedent state (e.g., his or her mood, time pressure, or disposition toward shopping). Time is an important resource that often determines how much effort and search will go into a decision. Our moods are influenced by the degree of pleasure and arousal a store environment creates.

The usage context of a product is a segmentation variable; consumers look for different product attributes depending on the use to which they intend to put their purchase. The presence or absence of other people (co-consumers)—and the types of people they are—can also affect a consumer's decisions. The shopping experience also is a pivotal part of the purchase decision. In many cases, retailing is like theater: The consumer's evaluation of stores and products may depend on the type of "performance" he witnesses. The actors (e.g., salespeople), the setting (the store environment), and the props (e.g., store displays) influence this evaluation. Like a brand personality, a number of factors, such as perceived convenience, sophistication, and expertise of salespeople, determine store image. With increasing competition from nonstore alternatives, creating a positive shopping experience has never been more important. Online shopping is growing in importance, and this new way to acquire products has both good (e.g., convenience) and bad (e.g., security) aspects.

2. The information a store's layout, Web site, or salespeople provides strongly influences a purchase decision.

Because we don't make many purchase decisions until we're actually in the store, point-of-purchase (POP) stimuli are very important sales tools. These include product samples, elaborate package displays, place-based media, and in-store promotional materials such as "shelf talkers." POP stimuli are particularly useful in promoting impulse buying, which happens when a consumer yields to a sudden urge for a product. Increasingly, mobile shopping apps are also playing a key role. The consumer's encounter with a salesperson is a complex and important process. The outcome can be affected by such factors as the salesperson's similarity to the customer and his or her perceived credibility.

3. Other people and groups, especially those that possess social power, influence our decisions.

We belong to or admire many different groups, and a desire for them to accept us often drives our purchase decisions. Individuals or groups whose opinions or behavior are particularly important to consumers are reference groups. Both formal and informal groups influence the individual's purchase decisions, although such factors as the conspicuousness of the product and the relevance of the reference group for a particular purchase determine how influential the reference group is.

Individuals have influence in a group to the extent that they possess social power. Types of social power include information power, referent power, legitimate power, expert power, reward power, and coercive power.

4. We seek out others who share our interests in products or services.

Brand communities unite consumers who share a common passion for a product. Brandfests, which companies organize to encourage this kind of community, can build brand loyalty and reinforce group membership.

5. Our desire to be consistent with other people motivates us to mimic what they buy and use.

We conform to the desires of others for two basic reasons: (1) People who model their behavior after others because they take others' behavior as evidence of the correct way to act are conforming because of informational social influence; and (2) those who conform to satisfy the expectations of others or to be accepted by the group are affected by normative social influence. Group members often do things they would not do as individuals because their

identities become merged with the group; they become deindividuated.

6. Marketers often need to understand consumers' behavior rather than a consumer's behavior.

More than one person actually makes many purchasing decisions. Collective decision-making occurs whenever two or more people evaluate, select, or use a product or service. In organizations and in families, members play several different roles during the decision-making process. These roles include gatekeeper, influencer, buyer, and user.

7. The decision-making process differs when people choose what to buy on behalf of an organization rather than for personal use.

Organizational buyers are people who make purchasing decisions on behalf of a company or other group. Although many of the same factors that affect how they make decisions in their personal lives influence these buyers, their organizational choices tend to be more rational. Their decisions are also likely to involve more financial risk, and as the choices become more complex, it is probable that a greater number of people will be involved in making the decision. The amount of cognitive effort that goes into organizational decisions relates to internal factors, such as the individuals' psychological characteristics, and external factors, such as the company's willingness to tolerate risk. One of the most important determinants is the type of purchase the company wants to make: The extent of problem-solving required depends on whether the product or service it procures is simply a reorder (a straight rebuy), a reorder with minor modifications (modified rebuy), or something it has never bought before or something complex and risky (new task). Online purchasing sites revolutionize the way organizational decision-makers collect and evaluate product information in business-to-business (B2B) e-commerce.

8. Our traditional notions about families are outdated.

The number and type of U.S. households is changing in many ways, including delays in getting married and having children, and in the composition of family households, which are increasingly headed by a single parent. New perspectives on the family life cycle, which focuses on how people's needs change as they move through different stages in their lives, are forcing marketers to more seriously consider consumer segments such as gays and lesbians, divorced persons, and childless couples when they develop targeting strategies. Many important demographic dimensions of a population relate to family and household structure. *Demographics* are statistics that measure a population's characteristics. Some of the most important of these relate to family structure (e.g., the birth rate, the marriage rate, and the divorce rate). A *household* is an occupied housing unit.

9. **Members of a family unit play different roles and have different amounts of influence when the family makes purchase decisions.**

Marketers have to understand how families make decisions. Spouses in particular have different priorities and exert varying amounts of influence in terms of effort and power. Children are also increasingly influential in everyday purchase decisions.

KEY TERMS

accommodative purchase decision, 409
activity stores, 385
antibrand communities, 394
aspirational reference group, 393
atmospherics, 385
autonomic decision, 410
avoidance groups, 394
being space, 384
boomerang kids, 402
brand community, 392
brandfests, 392
business-to-business (B2B) e-commerce, 401
business-to-business (B2B) marketers, 397
buyclass theory of purchasing, 399
buyer, 397
buying center, 399
co-consumers, 377
coercive power, 390
cohesiveness, 394
collective value creation, 393
comparative influence, 392
conformity, 396
consensual purchase decision, 409
consumer tribe, 393
consumption situation, 374
customer networks, 410
deindividuation, 395
DINKS, 405

direct selling, 395
expert power, 390
extended family, 402
family financial officer (FFO), 412
family identity, 409
family life cycle (FLC), 407
fertility rate, 404
gatekeeper, 397
gender convergence, 413
helicopter moms, 410
home shopping party, 395
household, 402
impulse buying, 387
influencer, 397
information power, 390
initiator, 397
juggling lifestyle, 412
kin-network system, 412
legitimate power, 390
membership reference group, 393
mental budgets, 386
minipreneurs, 384
mobile shopping apps, 386
modified rebuy, 401
name letter effect, 392
new task, 401
normative influence, 392
norms, 396
nuclear family, 402
open rates, 376

organizational buyers, 397
point-of-purchase (POP) stimuli, 387
pop-up stores, 386
prediction market, 401
pretailer, 382
principle of least interest, 396
propinquity, 394
psychological time, 377
queuing theory, 378
reference group, 390
referent power, 390
retail theming, 384
reward power, 390
Sandwich Generation, 403
sheconomy, 410
shopping orientation, 370
showrooming, 381
social loafing, 395
social power, 389
store image, 384
straight rebuy, 400
syncretic decisions, 410
synoptic ideal, 422
time poverty, 377
timestyle, 377
tribal marketing strategy, 393
unplanned buying, 387
user, 397
voluntarily childless, 405

REVIEW

9-1 What is time poverty, and how can it influence our purchase decisions?

9-2 What are the two dimensions that determine whether we will react positively or negatively to a purchase environment?

9-3 List three separate motivations for shopping, and give an example of each.

9-4 What are some important pros and cons of e-commerce?

9-5 List three factors that help to determine store image.

9-6 What is the difference between unplanned buying and impulse buying?

9-7 Name two dimensions that influence whether reference groups affect an individual's purchase decisions.

9-8 List three types of social power, and give an example of each.

9-9 Which tend to influence our behavior more: large formal groups or small informal groups? Why?

9-10 What is a brand community, and why is it of interest to marketers?

9-11 Describe the difference between a membership and an aspirational reference group and give an example of each kind.

9-12 Name one factor that makes it more likely a person will become part of a consumer's membership reference group.

9-13 Define *deindividuation* and give an example of this effect.

9-14 What is the difference between normative and informational social influence?

9-15 Define *conformity* and give an example of it. Name three reasons why people conform.

9-16 How does the principle of least interest relate to your success in a romantic relationship?

9-17 What is *social comparison*? To what type of person do we usually choose to compare ourselves?

9-18 What are some factors that influence how an organizational buyer evaluates a purchase decision?

9-19 What is a prediction market?

9-20 Distinguish between straight rebuy and modified rebuy.

9-21 How can a marketer manipulate the social and physical surroundings in a retail store to influence purchasing decisions? How does it work?

9-22 In terms of temporal factors, what does slow or fast mean?

9-23 Is there such as a thing as the "modern family unit"? Is this too broad a description?

9-24 Non-human family members are pets and other animals that share the household with their owners. How can marketers target these non-humans?

9-25 In many developed countries there is an increasing trend toward the voluntarily childless couple. Why might this be a trend, and what does it mean for marketers?

9-26 Is there such as thing as a typical family life cycle?

9-27 "Helicopter moms" may be an American phenomenon, but is it a feature in your own country?

9-28 Describe the role of "family financial officer." How does this role change over time?

9-29 What is meant by the concept of the synoptic ideal? It is relevant in most cases?

9-30 What is gender convergence, and do you think it is a global trend?

CONSUMER BEHAVIOR CHALLENGE

■ DISCUSS

9-31 Is the customer always right? Why or why not?

9-32 Are pop-up stores simply a fad, or a retailing concept that's here to stay?

9-33 What are some positive and negative aspects of a policy that requires employees who interact with customers to wear a uniform?

9-34 Think about exceptionally good and bad salespeople you have encountered as a shopper. What qualities seem to differentiate them from others?

9-35 Discuss the concept of *timestyle*. Based on your own experiences, how might we segment consumers in terms of their timestyles?

9-36 Several men's clothing retailers nationwide now provide free booze to their male clientele to encourage them to hang out in their stores.[183] Is it ethical to encourage customers to get wasted before they shop?

9-37 Some retailers work hard to cultivate a certain look or image, and they may even choose employees who fit this look. Abercrombie & Fitch, for example, seems to link itself to a clean-cut, all-American image. At one point a lawsuit claimed that Abercrombie & Fitch systematically "refuses to hire qualified minority applicants as brand representatives to work on the sales floor and discourages applications from minority applicants" (Abercrombie replied that it has "zero tolerance for discrimination").[184] We know that the Hooters restaurant chain is notorious for its attractive female waitresses. Should a retailer have the right to recruit employees who are consistent with its image even if this means excluding certain types of people (e.g., non-Caucasians, men) from the sales floor?

★ 9-38 The store environment is heating up as more and more companies put their promotional dollars into point-of-purchase efforts. Some stores confront shoppers with videos at the checkout counter, computer monitors attached to their shopping carts, and ads stenciled on the floors. We're also increasingly exposed to ads in nonshopping environments. For example, a health club in New York was forced to remove TV monitors that showed advertising on the Health Club Media Networks after exercisers claimed that the programming interfered with their workouts. Do you feel that these innovations are overly intrusive? At what point might shoppers rebel and demand some peace and quiet when they shop? Do you see any market potential in the future for stores that "countermarket" by promising a "hands-off" shopping environment?

9-39 Courts often prohibit special-interest groups from distributing literature in shopping malls. Mall managements claim that these centers are private property. However, these groups argue that the mall is the modern-day version of the town square and as such is a public forum. Find some recent court cases involving this free-speech issue, and examine the arguments pro and con. What is the current status of the mall as a public forum? Do you agree with this concept?

9-40 Our emotional reactions to marketing cues are so powerful that some high-tech companies study mood in very small doses (in 1/30 of a second increments) as they analyze people's facial reactions when they see ads or new products. They measure happiness as they look for differences between, for example, a *true smile* (which includes a relaxation of the upper eyelid) and a *social smile* (which occurs only around the mouth). Whirlpool used this technique to test consumers' emotional reactions to a yet-to-be-launched generation of its Duet washers and dryers. The company's goal: To design an appliance that will actually make people happy. Researchers discovered that even though test subjects said they weren't thrilled with some out-of-the-box design options, such as unusual color combinations, their facial expressions said otherwise.[185] Does the ability to study our emotional reactions at such a specific level give marketers an unfair advantage?

9-41 As more people enter virtual worlds, family decision-making research may have to include our virtual partners (and children?) as well.[186] Do you agree? How do you think consumer researchers could use a virtual world to help them understand decision-making in RL?

9-42 Marketers use "tricks" to minimize psychological waiting time. These techniques range from altering customers' perceptions of a line's length to providing distractions that divert attention from waiting:[187]

- One hotel chain received excessive complaints about the wait for elevators, so it installed mirrors near the elevator banks. People's natural tendency to check their appearance reduced complaints, even though the actual waiting time was unchanged.

- Airline passengers often complain about the wait to claim their baggage. In one airport, they would walk 1 minute from the plane to the baggage carousel and then wait 7 minutes for their luggage. When the airport changed the layout so that the walk to the carousel took 6 minutes and bags arrived 2 minutes after that, complaints disappeared.[188]

- Restaurant chains are scrambling to put the "fast" back into fast food, especially for drive-through lanes, which now account for 65 percent of revenues. In a study that ranked the speed of 25 fast-food chains, cars spent an average of 203.6 seconds from the menu board to departure. Wendy's was clocked the fastest at 150.3 seconds. To speed things up and eliminate spills, McDonald's created a salad that comes in a container to fit into car cup holders. Arby's is working on a "high viscosity" version of its special sauce that's less likely to spill. Burger King is testing see-through bags so customers can quickly check their orders before speeding off.[189]

- What are your waiting line "pain points?" How can companies change their processes to make these situations easier or more enjoyable for you?

9-43 Is the family unit dead?

9-44 Discuss the pros and cons of the voluntarily childless movement.

9-45 For each of the following five product categories—groceries, automobiles, vacations, furniture, and appliances—describe the ways in which you believe having children or not affects a married couple's choices.

9-46 When they identify and target newly divorced couples, do you think marketers exploit these couples' situations? Are there instances in which you think marketers may actually be helpful to them? Support your answers with examples.

9-47 Industrial purchase decisions are totally rational. Aesthetic or subjective factors don't—and shouldn't—play a role in this process. Do you agree?

9-48 We can think of college students who live away from home as having a substitute "family." Whether you live with your parents, with a spouse, or with other students, how are decisions made in your college residence "family"? Do some people take on the role of mother, father, or child? Give a specific example of a decision that had to be made and the roles members played.

9-49 The promotional products industry thrives on corporate clients that order $19 billion per year of T-shirts, mugs, pens, and other branded items that are intended to keep their organizations at the forefront of their customers' minds. This has caused a lot of backlash, especially in the medical/pharmaceutical industry where critics worry about the undue influence of these advertising messages. Stanford University Medical Center prohibits its physicians from accepting even small gifts, such as pens and mugs, from pharmaceutical sales representatives under a new policy that it hopes will limit industry influence on patient care and doctor education. The new policy is part of a small but growing movement among medical centers (Yale and the University of Pennsylvania have similar policies). The policy also prohibits doctors from accepting free drug samples and from publishing articles ghostwritten by industry contractors in medical journals (a fairly common practice). These changes come at a time when many of us are concerned about the safety and rising cost of drugs and medical devices. About 90 percent of the pharmaceutical industry's $21 billion marketing budget targets physicians. Some studies have shown that even small gifts create a sense of obligation; one critical study charged that free drug samples are "a powerful inducement for physicians and patients to rely on medications that are expensive but not more effective." Indeed, some industry documents from a civil lawsuit show that big pharmaceutical companies sometimes calculate to the penny the profits that doctors could make from their drugs. Sales representatives shared those profit estimates with doctors and their staffs, the documents show.[190] In response to pressure in the market, the pharmaceutical industry is largely banning the use of promotional products. One result is that the businesses that supply these premiums will lose around $1 billion per year in sales. What do you think about this initiative? Is it fair to deprive an industry of its livelihood in this way? Why or why not? Where is the line between legitimate promotion of one's

products and unethical practice? Should professionals engage in organizational decision-making that has such far-reaching medical and financial ramifications? Is this philosophy selfish?

■ APPLY

9-50 Conduct naturalistic observation at a local mall. Sit in a central location and observe the activities of mall employees and patrons. Keep a log of the nonretailing activity you observe (e.g., special performances, exhibits, socializing, etc.). Does this activity enhance or detract from business the mall conducts? As malls become more like high-tech game rooms, how valid is the criticism that shopping areas only encourage more loitering by teenage boys, who don't spend a lot in stores and simply scare away other customers?

9-51 Select three competing clothing stores in your area and conduct a store image study for them. Ask a group of consumers to rate each store on a set of attributes and plot these ratings on the same graph. Based on your findings, are there any areas of competitive advantage or disadvantage you could bring to the attention of store management?

9-52 Using Table 9.1 as a model, construct a person–situation segmentation matrix for a brand of perfume.

9-53 Many retailers believe that when they pile a lot of stuff around their store, this cluttered look encourages shoppers to hunt for items and eventually buy more. Dollar General recently raised the height of its shelves to more than 6 feet; JC Penney transformed empty walls into jewelry and accessory displays; Old Navy added lanes lined with items like water bottles, candy, and lunchboxes. Best Buy is even testing the impact of filling aisles with bulky items like Segways and bicycles to compensate for the smaller space that thin TVs and smaller speakers take up. Notably, Walmart recently did an abrupt about-face: The company only recently remodeled its stores by eliminating the pallets of items it used to stack in the centers of aisles, and it reduced overall inventory by about 9 percent. Customers loved the leaner, cleaner look. Only one problem: They bought less stuff. As a senior Walmart executive commented, "They loved the experience. They just bought less. And that generally is not a good long-term strategy." Now, Walmart is adding inventory back in and is once again piling stacks of merchandise in aisles.[191] What's your take on these store-stocking strategies? Visit several "big-box" stores in your area, such as Walmart, Target, Best Buy, Costco, and so on. If possible, interview shoppers about their experiences. Do they have trouble navigating around the store? Do they enjoy the clutter? Does it feel like a "treasure hunt" when they have to pick their way around piles

and pallets? If you were designing a store, how would you craft a stocking strategy that would make it easy to shop there?

9-54 Identify three people who own electric coffeemakers. Then, "go to the gemba" by observing them as they actually prepare coffee in the appliance at home. Based on these experiences, what recommendations might you make to the designer of a new coffeemaker model that would improve customers' experiences with the product?

⭐ 9-55 Do you agree that deindividuation encourages binge drinking on campus? What can or should a college do to discourage this behavior?

9-56 The strategy of viral marketing gets customers to sell a product to other customers on behalf of the company. That often means convincing your friends to climb on the bandwagon, and sometimes you get a cut if they buy something.[192] Some might argue that that means you're selling out your friends (or at least selling to your friends) in exchange for a piece of the action. Others might say you're simply sharing the wealth with your buddies. Have you ever passed along names of your friends or sent them to a Web site such as hotmail.com? If so, what happened? How do you feel about this practice?

9-57 Are home shopping parties that put pressure on friends and neighbors to buy merchandise ethical?

9-58 The power of unspoken social norms often becomes obvious only when we violate them. To witness this result firsthand, try one of the following: Stand facing the back wall in an elevator, serve dessert before the main course, offer to pay cash for dinner at a friend's home, wear pajamas to class, or tell someone *not* to have a nice day.

9-59 Identify a set of avoidance groups for your peers. Can you identify any consumption decisions that you and your friends make with these groups in mind?

9-60 Arrange to interview two married couples, one younger and one older. Prepare a response form that lists five product categories—groceries, furniture, appliances, vacations, and automobiles—and ask each spouse to indicate, without consulting the other, whether purchases in each category are made by joint or unilateral decisions, and to indicate whether the unilateral decisions are made by the husband or the wife. Compare each couple's responses for agreement between husbands and wives relative to who makes the decisions, and compare both couples' overall responses for differences relative to the number of joint versus unilateral decisions. Report your findings and conclusions.

9-61 Collect ads for three different product categories that target families. Find another set of ads for different brands of the same items that don't feature families. Prepare a report comparing the probable effectiveness of the two approaches. Which specific categories would most likely benefit from a family emphasis?

9-62 Pick three married couples and ask each husband and wife to list the names of all cousins, second cousins, and so on for both sides of the family. Based on the results, what can you conclude about the relative role of men and women in maintaining the kin-network system?

9-63 Observe the interactions between parents and children in the cereal section of a local grocery store (remember to take earplugs with you). Prepare a report on the number of children who expressed preferences, how they expressed their preferences, and how parents responded, including the number who purchased the child's choice.

9-64 Select a product category and, using the life-cycle stages this chapter describes, list the variables likely to affect a purchase decision for the product by consumers in each stage of the cycle.

9-65 Consider three important changes in the modern family structure. For each, find an example of a marketer who seems to be conscious of this change in its product communications, retailing innovations, or other aspects of the marketing mix. If possible, also try to find examples of marketers who have failed to keep up with these developments.

Case Study

FURNISHING AN EXPERIENCE

Walk into a Jordan's Furniture store on a Saturday afternoon. If you have the time, you can watch the latest 3-D IMAX movie before you pick out your new sofa. This might sound like a crazy in-store activity for a furniture store, but events like this are what drive sales at Jordan's Furniture stores in the Boston area. The company's slogan, "*not just a store . . . an experience*," keeps customers coming every day.

Jordan's calls their store strategy "shopper-tainment." Every location offers food, music, shows, and plenty of surprises. The store in Natick, Massachusetts, provides a marketscape theme by recreating New Orleans Bourbon Street, complete with live Jazz.

Jordan's has been successful with their strategy. When the company was purchased by Berkshire Hathaway in 1999, the *New York Times* reported that Jordan's sold more furniture per square foot than any company in the United States. Their annual revenue was reported as $250 million.

The furniture market is substantial with approximately $60 billion in annual sales. Furniture stores, including Jordan's, still account for most furniture sales, but mass merchandisers (e.g., Target and Walmart), home improvement stores (e.g., Home Depot and Lowes), and warehouse clubs (e.g., Costco and BJ's) are becoming an increasing threat. In a survey by Mintel, 38 percent of those surveyed had purchased furniture at a mass merchandiser and 28 percent had purchased furniture at a home improvement store. If furniture retailers want to stay competitive, they will need to work hard on drawing people into their stores.

What else do customers want? According to Mintel, they want to buy their furniture on sale. Jordan's runs sales regularly and is also known for some unusual promotions. In a recent television ad, Jordan's Furniture president and CEO Eliot Tatelman appeared with former Red Sox pitcher Pedro Martinez and announced the following promotion:

"Buy anything . . . ANYTHING . . . at Jordan's Furniture starting today and it could all be FREE if the Red Sox pitch a perfect game between July 19, 2013 and September 29, 2013."

As Jordan's continues to be innovative in their store atmosphere and promotions, other furniture retailers are also creating innovative products and shopping experiences. IKEA, a major furniture retailer, offers a shopping experience that is fun and engaging. Crate and Barrel has just launched a 3-D room design tool in their stores. With this tool, customers can upload a photo of a room to their 3-D screen and try on different Crate and Barrel merchandise.

If you find yourself in the Boston area in the near future, consider visiting the Avon location of Jordan's Furniture. That location's Motion Odyssey Movie Ride (MOM) will bring you the 4-D thrills of a major theme park ride. After the ride, you just might want to pick up a new desk for your room.

DISCUSSION QUESTIONS

CS 9-1 Evaluate the shopping experience at Jordan's. Why is it so successful?

CS 9-2 If Jordan's were building a new location near colleges, what might they include in their stores to draw young customers?

CS 9-3 How has Jordan's used the brand community around the Boston Red Sox to its' advantage? What other communities could it use?

Sources: "Furniture Retailing—US—August 2012," Mintel Oxygen, accessed July 31, 2013; www.jordans.com, accessed July 31, 2013; "Berkshire Hathaway Buys Furniture Seller," http://www.nytimes.com/1999/10/12/business/berkshire-hathaway-buys-furniture-seller.html, accessed July 31, 2013; "Pedro Martinez Pitches Perfect Game Promotion for Jordan's Furniture," http://www.boston.com/businessupdates/2013/04/03/pedro-martinez-pitches-perfect-game-promotion-for-jordan-furniture/iBw7rZIfRWMSPGRM6eCpWM/story.html, accessed July 31, 2013.

MyMarketingLab

Go to **mymktlab.com** for the following Assisted-graded writing questions:

9-66 What is the difference between a consensual and an accommodative purchase decision? What are some factors that help to determine how much conflict the family will experience when it makes a decision?

9-67 The mall of the future will most likely be less about purchasing products than about exploring them in a physical setting. This means that retail environments will have to become places to build brand images, rather than simply places to sell products. What are some strategies stores can use to enhance the emotional/sensory experiences they give to shoppers?

9-68 **Mymktlab Only**—comprehensive writing assignment for this chapter.

NOTES

1. http://freecountry.harley-davidson.com/landing.php, accessed June 15, 2011.

2. http://www.harley-davidson.com/browse/browse_categories.jsp?WebLogicSession=N3ErFgFyvT2Aiw6MWlyasMkqOsqqZrbOvNQIoR4HpGugrh1zxE0o!-36114594!hiwpbmsp04.ihd.hd!7005!8005&FOLDER%3C%3Efolder_id=1408474395439177&locale=en_US&bmUID=1308066867683&bmLocale=en_US, accessed June 15, 2011.

3. Details adapted from John W. Schouten and James H. McAlexander, "Market Impact of a Consumption Subculture: The Harley-Davidson Mystique," in Fred van Raaij and Gary Bamossy, eds., *Proceedings of the 1992 European Conference of the Association for Consumer Research* (Amsterdam, 1992); John W. Schouten and James H. McAlexander, "Subcultures of Consumption: An Ethnography of the New Bikers," *Journal of Consumer Research* 22 (June 1995): 43-61. See also Kelly Barron, "Hog Wild," *Forbes* (May 15, 2000), http://www.forbes.com/forbes/2000/0515/6511068a.html, accessed September 20, 2013.

4. Pradeep Kakkar and Richard J. Lutz, "Situational Influence on Consumer Behavior: A Review," in Harold H. Kassarjian and Thomas S. Robertson, eds., *Perspectives in Consumer Behavior*, 3rd ed. (Glenview, IL: Scott, Foresman, 1981): 204-14.

5. Christopher Heine, "Will Facebook Ads Soon Reflect 'What's On Your Mind?,'" *ClickZ* (March 23, 2011), http://www.clickz.com/clickz/news/2036901/facebook-ads-soon-reflect-whats-mind, accessed April 17, 2011.

6. Benedict Carey, "TV Time, Unlike Child Care, Ranks High in Mood Study," *New York Times* (December 3, 2004), www.nytimes.com, accessed December 3, 2004.

7. Carolyn Turner Schenk and Rebecca H. Holman, "A Sociological Approach to Brand Choice: The Concept of Situational Self-Image," in Jerry C. Olson, ed., *Advances in Consumer Research 7* (Ann Arbor, MI: Association for Consumer Research, 1980): 610-14.

8. Peter R. Dickson, "Person–Situation: Segmentation's Missing Link," *Journal of Marketing* 46 (Fall 1982): 56-64.

9. Alan R. Hirsch, "Effects of Ambient Odors on Slot-Machine Usage in a Las Vegas Casino," *Psychology & Marketing* 12 (October 1995): 585-94.

10. Tanya Irwin, "ReachMail: Email Marketers Should Focus on Mid-Day," *Marketing Daily* (March 17, 2011), http://www.mediapost.com/publications/?fa5Articles.showArticle&art_aid5146883&nid5124807, accessed April 18, 2011.

11. Carol Felker Kaufman, Paul M. Lane, and Jay D. Lindquist, "Exploring More Than 24 Hours a Day: A Preliminary Investigation of Polychronic Time Use," *Journal of Consumer Research* 18 (December 1991): 392-401.

12. Laurence P. Feldman and Jacob Hornik, "The Use of Time: An Integrated Conceptual Model," *Journal of Consumer Research 7* (March 1981): 407-19; see also Michelle M. Bergadaa, "The Role of Time in the Action of the Consumer," *Journal of Consumer Research* 17 (December 1990): 289-302.

13. Alan Zarembo, "What If There Weren't Any Clocks to Watch?" *Newsweek* (June 30, 1997): 14; based on research reported in Robert Levine, *A Geography of Time: The Temporal Misadventures of a Social Psychologist, or How Every Culture Keeps Time Just a Little Bit Differently* (New York: Basic Books, 1997).

14. Deborah Kotz, "Wives Do More Housework, Study Shows," *U.S. News & World Report* (April 7, 2008), http://health.usnews.com/blogs/on-women/2008/04/07/wives-do-more-housework-study-shows.html, accessed June 8, 2009; John P. Robinson, "Time Squeeze," *Advertising Age* (February 1990): 30-33.

15. June S. Cotte, S. Ratneshwar, and David Glen Mick, "The Times of Their Lives: Phenomenological and Metaphorical Characteristics of Consumer Timestyles," *Journal of Consumer Research* 31 (September 2004): 333-45.

16. Dhruv Grewal, Julie Baker, Michael Levy, and Glenn B. Voss, "The Effects of Wait Expectations and Store Atmosphere Evaluations on Patronage Intentions in Service-Intensive Retail Store," *Journal of Retailing* 79 (2003): 259-68; cf. also Shirley Taylor, "Waiting for Service: The Relationship Between Delays and Evaluations of Service," *Journal of Marketing* 58 (April 1994): 56-69.

17. "We're Hating the Waiting; 43% Prefer Self-Service," *Marketing Daily* (January 23, 2007), www.mediapost.com, accessed January 23, 2007.

18. Laurette Dube and Bernd H. Schmitt, "The Processing of Emotional and Cognitive Aspects of Product Usage in Satisfaction Judgments," in Rebecca H. Holman and Michael R. Solomon, eds., *Advances in Consumer Research* 18 (Provo, UT: Association for Consumer Research, 1991): 52-56; Lalita A. Manrai and Meryl P. Gardner, "The Influence of Affect on Attributions for Product Failure," in Rebecca H. Holman and Michael R. Solomon, eds., *Advances in Consumer Research* 18 (Provo, UT: Association for Consumer Research, 1991): 249-54.

19. Kevin G. Celuch and Linda S. Showers, "It's Time to Stress Stress: The Stress–Purchase/Consumption Relationship," in Rebecca H. Holman and Michael R. Solomon, eds., *Advances in Consumer Research* 18 (Provo, UT: Association for Consumer Research, 1991): 284-89; Lawrence R. Lepisto, J. Kathleen Stuenkel, and Linda K. Anglin, "Stress: An Ignored Situational Influence," in Rebecca H. Holman and Michael R. Solomon, eds., *Advances in Consumer Research* 18 (Provo, UT: Association for Consumer Research, 1991): 296-302.

20. Velitchka D. Kaltcheva and Barton A. Weitz, "When Should a Retailer Create an Exciting Store Environment?" *Journal of Marketing* 70 (January 2006): 107-18.

21. John D. Mayer and Yvonne N. Gaschke, "The Experience and Meta-Experience of Mood," *Journal of Personality & Social Psychology* 55 (July 1988): 102-11.

22. Meryl Paula Gardner, "Mood States and Consumer Behavior: A Critical Review," *Journal of Consumer Research* 12 (December 1985): 281-300; Scott Dawson, Peter H. Bloch, and Nancy M. Ridgway, "Shopping Motives, Emotional States, and Retail Outcomes," *Journal of Retailing* 66 (Winter 1990): 408-27; Patricia A. Knowles, Stephen J. Grove, and W. Jeffrey Burroughs, "An Experimental Examination of Mood States on Retrieval and Evaluation of Advertisement and Brand Information," *Journal of the Academy of Marketing Science* 21 (April 1993): 135-43; Paul W. Miniard, Sunil Bhatla, and Deepak Sirdeskmuhk, "Mood as a Determinant of Postconsumption Product Evaluations: Mood Effects and Their Dependency on the Affective Intensity of the Consumption Experience," *Journal of Consumer Psychology* 1, no. 2 (1992): 173-95; Mary T. Curren

and Katrin R. Harich, "Consumers' Mood States: The Mitigating Influence of Personal Relevance on Product Evaluations," *Psychology & Marketing* 11 (March–April 1994): 91–107; Gerald J. Gorn, Marvin E. Goldberg, and Kunal Basu, "Mood, Awareness, and Product Evaluation," *Journal of Consumer Psychology* 2, no. 3 (1993): 237–56.

23. Gordon C. Bruner, "Music, Mood, and Marketing," *Journal of Marketing* 54 (October 1990): 94–104; Basil G. Englis, "Music Television and Its Influences on Consumers, Consumer Culture, and the Transmission of Consumption Messages," in Rebecca H. Holman and Michael R. Solomon, eds., *Advances in Consumer Research* 18 (Provo, UT: Association for Consumer Research, 1991): 111–14.

24. Marvin E. Goldberg and Gerald J. Gorn, "Happy and Sad TV Programs: How They Affect Reactions to Commercials," *Journal of Consumer Research* 14 (December 1987): 387–403; Gorn, Goldberg, and Basu, "Mood, Awareness, and Product Evaluation"; Curren and Harich, "Consumers' Mood States."

25. Rajeev Batra and Douglas M. Stayman, "The Role of Mood in Advertising Effectiveness," *Journal of Consumer Research* 17 (September 1990): 203; John P. Murry, Jr., and Peter A. Dacin, "Cognitive Moderators of Negative-Emotion Effects: Implications for Understanding Media Context," *Journal of Consumer Research* 22 (March 1996): 439–47; see also Curren and Harich, "Consumers' Mood States"; Gorn, Goldberg, and Basu, "Mood, Awareness, and Product Evaluation."

26. For a scale to assess these dimensions of the shopping experience, see Barry J. Babin, William R. Darden, and Mitch Griffin, "Work and/or Fun: Measuring Hedonic and Utilitarian Shopping Value," *Journal of Consumer Research* 20 (March 1994): 644–56.

27. Kaltcheva and Weitz, "When Should a Retailer Create an Exciting Store Environment?"

28. Babin, Darden, and Griffin, "Work and/or Fun."

29. Edward M. Tauber, "Why Do People Shop?" *Journal of Marketing* 36 (October 1972): 47–48.

30. Ann Zimmerman and Laura Stevens, "Attention, Shoppers: Bored College Kids Competing in Aisle 6," *Wall Street Journal* (February 23, 2005), http://professional.wsj.com/article/SB110911598024661430-H9jfYNklaF4oJ2sZ3IaqiAm5.html?mg5reno-wsj, accessed September 11, 2011.

31. Robert C. Prus, *Making Sales: Influence as Interpersonal Accomplishment* (Newbury Park, CA: Sage Publications, 1989): 225.

32. Michael-Lee Johnstone and Denise M. Conroy, "Dressing for the Thrill: An Exploration of Why Women Dress Up to Go Shopping," *Journal of Consumer Behaviour* 4, no. 4 (2005): 234.

33. Some material in this section was adapted from Michael R. Solomon and Elnora W. Stuart, *Welcome to* Marketing.com: *The Brave New World of E-Commerce* (Upper Saddle River, NJ: Prentice Hall, 2001).

34. June Cotte and Kathryn A. Latour, "Blackjack in the Kitchen: Understanding Online Versus Casino Gambling," *Journal of Consumer Research* 35 (February 2009): 742–58.

35. Rebecca K. Ratner, Barbara E. Kahn, and Daniel Kahneman, "Choosing Less-Preferred Experiences for the Sake of Variety," *Journal of Consumer Research* 26 (June 1999): 1–15.

36. http://www.youtube.com/watch?v=FmYZ1YImWIw&lr=1, accessed March 12, 2013; "Total Immersion and eBay Bring Virtual 'See It On' Feature to eBay's Fashion App," *Business Wire* (February 1, 2011), http://www.businesswire.com/news/home/20110201006053/en/Total-Immersion-eBay-Bring-Virtual-%E2%80%98See-On%E2%80%99, accessed June 3, 2011.

37. http://modaoperandi.com/, accessed March 12, 2013; http://www.net-a-porter.com/, accessed March 12, 2013; http://www.threadless.com/, accessed March 12, 2013; www.modcloth.com, accessed March 12, 2013; www.fabricly.com, accessed March 12, 2013; Alisa Gould-Simon, "How Fashion Retailers Are Redefining E-Commerce with Social Media," Mashable.com (March 7, 2011), http://mashable.com/2011/03/07/fashion-retailers-social-e-commerce/, accessed April 17, 2011.

38. www.allurent.com/newsDetail.php?newsid520, accessed January 29, 2007.

39. http://www.waveloch.com/attraction/flowrider-double, accessed March 12, 2013; Stephanie Rosenbloom, "Malls Test Experimental Waters to Fill Vacancies," *New York Times* (April 4, 2009), www.nytimes.com/2009/04/05/business/05mall.html?_r51, accessed April 4, 2009.

40. Vanessa O'Connell, "Fictional Hershey Factory Will Send Kisses to Broadway," *Wall Street Journal* (August 5, 2002), www.wsj.com, accessed August 5, 2002.

41. Millie Creighton, "The Seed of Creative Lifestyle Shopping: Wrapping Consumerism in Japanese Store Layouts," in John F. Sherry Jr., ed., *Servicescapes: The Concept of Place in Contemporary Markets* (Lincolnwood, IL: NTC Business Books, 1998): 199–228; also cf. Robert V. Kozinets, John F. Sherry, Diana Storm, Adam Duhachek, Krittinee Nuttavuthisit, and Benet

DeBerry-Spence, "Ludic Agency and Retail Spectacle," *Journal of Consumer Research* 31 (December 2004): 658–72.

42. http://www.paragraphny.com/, accessed March 12, 2013.

43. Jennifer Saranow, "Retailers Give It the Old College Try," *Wall Street Journal* (August 28, 2008): B8; *March 2007 Trend Briefing*, www.trendwatching.com/briefing, accessed March 30, 2007.

44. Most measures of store image are quite similar to other attitude measures discussed in Chapter 7. For an excellent bibliography of store image studies, see Mary R. Zimmer and Linda L. Golden, "Impressions of Retail Stores: A Content Analysis of Consumer Images," *Journal of Retailing* 64 (Fall 1988): 265–93.

45. Spiggle and Sewall, "A Choice Sets Model of Retail Selection."

46. "The Science of Shopping: The Way the Brain Buys," *The Economist* (December 18, 2008), www.economist.com, accessed February 2, 2009.

47. Philip Kotler, "Atmospherics as a Marketing Tool," *Journal of Retailing* (Winter 1973–74): 10; Anna Mattila and Jochen Wirtz, "Congruency of Scent and Music as a Driver of In-Store Evaluations and Behavior," *Journal of Retailing* 77, no. 2 (2001): 273–89; J. Duncan Herrington, "An Integrative Path Model of the Effects of Retail Environments on Shopper Behavior," in Robert L. King, ed., *Marketing: Toward the Twenty-First Century* (Richmond, VA: Southern Marketing Association, 1991): 58–62; see also Ann E. Schlosser, "Applying the Functional Theory of Attitudes to Understanding the Influence of Store Atmosphere on Store Inferences," *Journal of Consumer Psychology* 7, no. 4 (1998): 345–69.

48. Joseph A. Bellizzi and Robert E. Hite, "Environmental Color, Consumer Feelings, and Purchase Likelihood," *Psychology & Marketing* 9 (September–October 1992): 347–63.

49. Robert J. Donovan, John R. Rossiter, Gilian Marcoolyn, and Andrew Nesdale, "Store Atmosphere and Purchasing Behavior," *Journal of Retailing* 70, no. 3 (1994): 283–94; cf. also L. W. Turley and Jean-Charles Chebat, "Linking Retail Strategy, Atmospheric Design and Shopping Behaviour," *Journal of Marketing Management* 18, no. 1–2 (2002): 125–44.

50. http://www.buildabear.com/shopping/, accessed March 12, 2013.

51. Charles S. Areni and David Kim, "The Influence of In-Store Lighting on Consumers' Examination of Merchandise in a Wine Store," *International Journal of Research in Marketing* 11, no. 2 (March 1994): 117–25.

52. "Slow Music Makes Fast Drinkers," *Psychology Today* (March 1989): 18.

53. Brad Edmondson, "Pass the Meat Loaf," *American Demographics* (January 1989): 19.

54. "Through the Looking Glass," *Lifestyle Monitor* 16 (Fall–Winter 2002).

55. Jennifer Lach, "Meet You in Aisle Three," *American Demographics* (April 1999): 41.

56. Karen M. Stilley, J. Jeffrey Inman, and Kirk L. Wakefield, "Planning to Make Unplanned Purchases? The Role of In-Store Slack in Budget Deviation," *Journal of Consumer Research* 37, no. 2 (2010): 264–78.

57. "Motorola Survey: Shoppers Better Connected to Information than Store Associates," *Chain Store Age* (January 17, 2011), http://www.chainstoreage.com/article/motorola-survey-shoppers-better-connected-information-store-associates, accessed April 30, 2011; Kris Hudson, "Malls Test Apps to Aid Shoppers," *Wall Street Journal* (April 26, 2011), http://online.wsj.com/article/SB10001424052748704336504576258740640080926.html?mod5dist_smartbrief, accessed April 29, 2011.

58. Manoj Thomas, Kalpesh Kaushik Desai, and Satheeshkumar Seenivasan, "How Credit Card Payments Increase Unhealthy Food Purchases: Visceral Regulation of Vices," *Journal of Consumer Research* 38, no. 1 (June 2011): 126–39.

59. Mukhopadhyay Anirban and Gita Venkataramani Johar, "Indulgence as Self-Reward for Prior Shopping Restraint: A Justification-Based Mechanism," *Journal of Consumer Psychology* 19, no. 3 (2009): 334–45.

60. Easwar S. Iyer, "Unplanned Purchasing: Knowledge of Shopping Environment and Time Pressure," *Journal of Retailing* 65 (Spring 1989): 40–57; C. Whan Park, Easwar S. Iyer, and Daniel C. Smith, "The Effects of Situational Factors on In-Store Grocery Shopping," *Journal of Consumer Research* 15 (March 1989): 422–33.

61. Iyer, "Unplanned Purchasing"; Park, Iyer, and Smith, "The Effects of Situational Factors on In-Store Grocery Shopping."

62. Matt Richtel, "At Starbucks, Songs of Instant Gratification," *New York Times* (October 1, 2007), www.nytimes.com, accessed October 1, 2007.

63. Emily Steel, "Luring Shoppers to Stores," *Wall Street Journal* (August 26, 2010), http://online.wsj.com/article/SB10001424052748704540904575451841980063132.html, accessed April 18, 2011.

64. Quoted in Louise Story, "Product Packages Now Shout to Get Your Attention," *New York Times* (August 10, 2007), www.nytimes.com, accessed August 10, 2007.

65. Cf. Robert B. Cialdini, *Influence: Science and Practice*, 2nd ed. (Glenview, IL: Scott, Foresman, 1988).

66. Richard P. Bagozzi, "Marketing as Exchange," *Journal of Marketing* 39 (October 1975): 32–39; Peter M. Blau, *Exchange and Power in Social Life* (New York: Wiley, 1964); Marjorie Caballero and Alan J. Resnik, "The Attraction

Paradigm in Dyadic Exchange," *Psychology & Marketing* 3, no. 1 (1986): 17–34; George C. Homans, "Social Behavior as Exchange," *American Journal of Sociology* 63 (1958): 597–606; Paul H. Schurr and Julie L. Ozanne, "Influences on Exchange Processes: Buyers' Preconceptions of a Seller's Trustworthiness and Bargaining Toughness," *Journal of Consumer Research* 11 (March 1985): 939–53; Arch G. Woodside and J. W. Davenport, "The Effect of Salesman Similarity and Expertise on Consumer Purchasing Behavior," *Journal of Marketing Research* 8 (1974): 433–36.

67. Mary Jo Bitner, Bernard H. Booms, and Mary Stansfield Tetreault, "The Service Encounter: Diagnosing Favorable and Unfavorable Incidents," *Journal of Marketing* 54 (January 1990): 7–84; Robert C. Prus, *Making Sales* (Newbury Park, CA: Sage Publications, 1989); Arch G. Woodside and James L. Taylor, "Identity Negotiations in Buyer–Seller Interactions," in Elizabeth C. Hirschman and Morris B. Holbrook, eds., *Advances in Consumer Research* 12 (Provo, UT: Association for Consumer Research, 1985): 443–49.

68. Barry J. Babin, James S. Boles, and William R. Darden, "Salesperson Stereotypes, Consumer Emotions, and Their Impact on Information Processing," *Journal of the Academy of Marketing Science* 23, no. 2 (1995): 94–105; Gilbert A. Churchill, Jr., Neil M. Ford, Steven W. Hartley, and Orville C. Walker, Jr., "The Determinants of Salesperson Performance: A Meta-Analysis," *Journal of Marketing Research* 22 (May 1985): 103–18.

69. www.customerssuck.com, accessed June 4, 2011; Keith Naughton, "Tired of Smile-Free Service," *Newsweek* (March 6, 2000): 44–45; www.protest.net, accessed June 4, 2011.

70. Siew Meng Leong, Paul S. Busch, and Deborah Roedder John, "Knowledge Bases and Salesperson Effectiveness: A Script-Theoretic Analysis," *Journal of Marketing Research* 26 (May 1989): 164; Harish Sujan, Mita Sujan, and James R. Bettman, "Knowledge Structure Differences Between More Effective and Less Effective Salespeople," *Journal of Marketing Research* 25 (February 1988): 81–86; Robert Saxe and Barton Weitz, "The SOCCO Scale: A Measure of the Customer Orientation of Salespeople," *Journal of Marketing Research* 19 (August 1982): 343–51; David M. Szymanski, "Determinants of Selling Effectiveness: The Importance of Declarative Knowledge to the Personal Selling Concept," *Journal of Marketing* 52 (January 1988): 64–77; Barton A. Weitz, "Effectiveness in Sales Interactions: A Contingency Framework," *Journal of Marketing* 45 (Winter 1981): 85–103.

71. Jagdish N. Sheth, "Buyer-Seller Interaction: A Conceptual Framework," in *Advances in Consumer Research* 3 (Cincinnati, OH: Association for Consumer Research, 1976): 382–86; Kaylene C. Williams and Rosann L. Spiro, "Communication Style in the Salesperson-Customer Dyad," *Journal of Marketing Research* 22 (November 1985): 434–42.

72. Marsha L. Richins, "An Analysis of Consumer Interaction Styles in the Marketplace," *Journal of Consumer Research* 10 (June 1983): 73–82.

73. Joel B. Cohen and Ellen Golden, "Informational Social Influence and Product Evaluation," *Journal of Applied Psychology* 56 (February 1972): 54–59; Robert E. Burnkrant and Alain Cousineau, "Informational and Normative Social Influence in Buyer Behavior," *Journal of Consumer Research* 2 (December 1975): 206–15; Peter H. Reingen, "Test of a List Procedure for Inducing Compliance with a Request to Donate Money," *Journal of Applied Psychology* 67 (1982): 110–18.

74. Dyan Machan, "Is the Hog Going Soft?," *Forbes* (March 10, 1997): 114–19.

75. Jennine Jacob, "Actually, Bloggers DO Influence People to Buy," *Independent Fashion Bloggers*, http://heartifb.com/2013/03/25/actually-bloggers-do-influence-people-to-buy/, accessed November 5, 2013; "How Twitter, Facebook and Blogs Influence Fashion Shoppers," *NetBase* (July 25, 2013), Gretchen Hoffman, http://www.netbase.com/all-posts/how-twitter-facebook-and-blogs-influence-fashion-shoppers/, accessed November 5, 2013.

76. Kenneth J. Gergen and Mary Gergen, *Social Psychology* (New York: Harcourt Brace Jovanovich, 1981): 312.

77. J. R. P. French, Jr., and B. Raven, "The Bases of Social Power," in D. Cartwright, ed., *Studies in Social Power* (Ann Arbor, MI: Institute for Social Research, 1959): 150–67.

78. Michael R. Solomon, "Packaging the Service Provider," *The Service Industries Journal* 5 (March 1985): 64–72.

79. Tamar Charry, "Unconventional Spokesmen Talk Up U.S. Robotics' Fast Modems in a New TV Campaign," *New York Times* (February 6, 1997), http://www.nytimes.com/1997/02/06/business/unconventional-spokesmen-talk-up-us-robotics-fast-modems-in-a-new-tv-campaign.html?scp=44&sq=Tamar+Charry&st=nyt, accessed September 13, 2011.

80. Patricia M. West and Susan M. Broniarczyk, "Integrating Multiple Opinions: The Role of Aspiration Level on Consumer Response to Critic Consensus," *Journal of Consumer Research* 25 (June 1998): 38–51.

81. Barry Rehfeld, "At These Camps, Everybody Is a Star (If Only for a Day)," *New York Times* (June 12, 2005), http://www.nytimes.com/2005/06/12/business/yourmoney/12fantasy.html?scp=1&sq=Barry%20Rehfeld,%20%E2%80%9CAt%20These%20Camps,%20Everybody%20Is%20a%20Star%20(If%20Only%20for%20a%20Day)&st=cse, accessed June 12, 2005.

82. C. Whan Park and V. Parker Lessig, "Students and Housewives: Differences in Susceptibility to Reference Group Influence," *Journal of Consumer Research* 4 (September 1977): 102–10.

83. Gina Kolata, "Study Finds Big Social Factor in Quitting Smoking," *New York Times* (May 22, 2008), www.nytimes.com/2008/05/22/science/22smoke.html?ex=1369195200&en=0a10910fcde1a1ac&ei=5124&partner=permalink&exprod=permalink, accessed May 22, 2008.

84. Jeffrey D. Ford and Elwood A. Ellis, "A Re-examination of Group Influence on Member Brand Preference," *Journal of Marketing Research* 17 (February 1980): 125–32; Thomas S. Robertson, *Innovative Behavior and Communication* (New York: Holt, Rinehart & Winston, 1980), Ch. 8.

85. Gergen and Gergen, *Social Psychology.*

86. Stephanie Rosenbloom, "Names That Match Forge a Bond on the Internet," *New York Times* (April 10, 2008), www.nytimes.com/2008/04/10/us/10names.html?ref=us, accessed April 10, 2008.

87. Harold H. Kelley, "Two Functions of Reference Groups," in Harold Proshansky and Bernard Siedenberg, eds., *Basic Studies in Social Psychology* (New York: Holt, Rinehart & Winston, 1965): 210–14.

88. Sam Schechner, "When Your Political Opinion Isn't Yours Alone: Broadcasts of Political Debates That Include Live Audience Feedback Can Influence What You're Thinking—Hecklers Can, Too," *Wall Street Journal* (October 10, 2008), http://online.wsj.com/article/SB122359949981721549.html, accessed October 11, 2008.

89. http://halo.xbox.com/en-us/intel/titles/halo2, accessed June 15, 2011; Kris Oser, "Microsoft's Halo 2 Soars on Viral Push," *Advertising Age* (October 25, 2004): 46.

90. Hope Jensen Schau, Albert M. Muñiz, Jr., and Eric J. Arnould, "How Brand Community Practices Create Value," *Journal of Marketing* 73 (September 2009), 30–51; John W. Schouten, James H. McAlexander, and Harold F. Koenig, "Transcendent Customer Experience and Brand Community," *Journal of the Academy of Marketing Science* 35 (2007): 357–68; James H. McAlexander, John W. Schouten, and Harold F. Koenig, "Building Brand Community," *Journal of Marketing* 66 (January 2002): 38–54; Albert Muñiz and Thomas O'Guinn, "Brand Community," *Journal of Consumer Research* (March 2001): 412–32; Scott A. Thompson and Rajiv K. Sinha, "Brand Communities and New Product Adoption: The Influence and Limits of Oppositional Loyalty," *Journal of Marketing* 72 (November 2008): 65–80.

91. Rama K. Jayanti and Jagdip Singh, "Framework for Distributed Consumer Learning in Online Communities," *Journal of Consumer Research* 36, no. 6 (2010): 1058–81.

92. Schau, Muñiz, and Arnould, "How Brand Community Practices Create Value."

93. Veronique Cova and Bernard Cova, "Tribal Aspects of Postmodern Consumption Research: The Case of French In-Line Roller Skaters," *Journal of Consumer Behavior* 1 (June 2001): 67–76.

94. http://www.sneakerfiles.com/2011/06/15/air-jordan-xii-12-dwyane-wade-player-exclusive/, accessed June 15, 2011; Jennifer Edson Escalas and James R. Bettman, "You Are What You Eat: The Influence of Reference Groups on Consumers' Connections to Brands," *Journal of Consumer Psychology* 13, no. 3 (2003): 339–48.

95. A. Benton Cocanougher and Grady D. Bruce, "Socially Distant Reference Groups and Consumer Aspirations," *Journal of Marketing Research* 8 (August 1971): 79–81.

96. Nick Bilton, "Twitter Users Congregate Based on Mood, Study Says," *New York Times* (March 16, 2011), http://bits.blogs.nytimes.com/2011/03/16/twitter-users-congregate-based-on-mood-study-says/, accessed April 29, 2011.

97. A. Benton Cocanougher and Grady D. Bruce, "Socially Distant Reference Groups and Consumer Aspirations."

98. R. B. Zajonc, H. M. Markus, and W. Wilson, "Exposure Effects and Associative Learning," *Journal of Experimental Social Psychology* 10 (1974): 248–63.

99. D. J. Stang, "Methodological Factors in Mere Exposure Research," *Psychological Bulletin* 81 (1974): 1014–25; R. B. Zajonc, P. Shaver, C. Tavris, and D. Van Kreveid, "Exposure, Satiation and Stimulus Discriminability," *Journal of Personality & Social Psychology* 21 (1972): 270–80.

100. J. E. Grush, K. L. McKeogh, and R. F. Ahlering, "Extrapolating Laboratory Exposure Research to Actual Political Elections," *Journal of Personality & Social Psychology* 36 (1978): 257–70.

101. Jonah Berger and Lindsay Rand, "Shifting Signals to Help Health: Using Identity Signaling to Reduce Risky Health Behaviors," *Journal of Consumer Research* 35, no. 3 (2008): 509–18.

102. http://boardoutmind.livejournal.com/, accessed June 15, 2011; Rob Walker, "Anti-Fan Club," *New York Times* (November 26, 2006), www.nytimes.com, accessed November 26, 2006.

103. Candice R. Hollenbeck and George M. Zinkhan, "Consumer Activism on the Internet: The Role of Anti-Brand Communities," *Advances in Consumer Research* 33, no. 1 (2006): 479–85.

104. Marius K. Luedicke, "Brand Community Under Fire: The Role of Social Environments for the Hummer Brand Community," *Advances in Consumer Research* 33, no. 1 (2006): 486–93.

105. Basil G. Englis and Michael R. Solomon, "To Be and Not to Be: Reference Group Stereotyping and the Clustering of America," *Journal of Advertising* 24 (Spring 1995): 13–28; Michael R. Solomon and Basil G. Englis, "I Am Not, Therefore I Am: The Role of Anti-Consumption in the Process of Self-Definition" (special session at the Association for Consumer Research meetings, October 1996, Tucson, Arizona); cf. also Brendan Richardson and Darach Turley, "Support Your Local Team: Resistance, Subculture and the Desire for Distinction," *Advances in Consumer Research* 33, no. 1 (2006): 175–80.

106. Bruce Feirstein, *Real Men Don't Eat Quiche* (New York: Pocket Books, 1982); www.auntiefashions.com, accessed December 31, 2002; Katherine White and Darren W. Dahl, "Are All Out-Groups Created Equal? Consumer Identity and Dissociative Influence," *Journal of Consumer Research* 34 (December 2007): 525–36.

107. B. Latane, K. Williams, and S. Harkins, "Many Hands Make Light the Work: The Causes and Consequences of Social Loafing," *Journal of Personality & Social Psychology* 37 (1979): 822–32.

108. S. Freeman, M. Walker, R. Borden, and B. Latane, "Diffusion of Responsibility and Restaurant Tipping: Cheaper by the Bunch," *Personality & Social Psychology Bulletin* 1 (1978): 584–87.

109. Donald H. Granbois, "Improving the Study of Customer In-Store Behavior," *Journal of Marketing* 32 (October 1968): 28–32; Tamara F. Mangleburg, Patricia M. Doney, and Terry Bristol, "Shopping with Friends and Teens' Susceptibility to Peer Influence," *Journal of Retailing* 80 (2004): 101–16.

110. Len Strazewski, "Tupperware Locks in New Strategy," *Advertising Age* (February 8, 1988): 30.

111. Luc Sante, "Be Different! (Like Everyone Else!)," *New York Times Magazine* (October 17, 1999), www.nytimes.com, accessed October 3, 2007.

112. Tanya Irwin, "Study: Facebook Users Show 'Herding Instinct,'" *Marketing Daily* (October 12, 2010), http://www.mediapost.com/publications/?fa=Articles.showArticle&art_aid=137340&nid=119587, accessed April 29, 2011.

113. For a study that attempted to measure individual differences in proclivity to conformity, see William O. Bearden, Richard G. Netemeyer, and Jesse E. Teel, "Measurement of Consumer Susceptibility to Interpersonal Influence," *Journal of Consumer Research* 15 (March 1989): 473–81.

114. John W. Thibaut and Harold H. Kelley, *The Social Psychology of Groups* (New York: Wiley, 1959); W. W. Waller and R. Hill, *The Family, a Dynamic Interpretation* (New York: Dryden, 1951).

115. Bearden, Netemeyer, and Teel, "Measurement of Consumer Susceptibility to Interpersonal Influence"; Lynn R. Kahle, "Observations: Role-Relaxed Consumers: A Trend of the Nineties," *Journal of Advertising Research* (March–April 1995): 66–71; Lynn R. Kahle and Aviv Shoham, "Observations: Role-Relaxed Consumers: Empirical Evidence," *Journal of Advertising Research* (May–June 1995): 59–62.

116. Fred E. Webster and Yoram Wind, *Organizational Buying Behavior* (Upper Saddle River, NJ: Prentice Hall, 1972).

117. See J. Joseph Cronin, Jr., and Michael H. Morris, "Satisfying Customer Expectations: The Effect on Conflict and Repurchase Intentions in Industrial Marketing Channels," *Journal of the Academy of Marketing Science* 17 (Winter 1989): 41–49; Thomas W. Leigh and Patrick F. McGraw, "Mapping the Procedural Knowledge of Industrial Sales Personnel: A Script-Theoretic Investigation," *Journal of Marketing* 53 (January 1989): 16–34; William J. Qualls and Christopher P. Puto, "Organizational Climate and Decision Framing: An Integrated Approach to Analyzing Industrial Buying," *Journal of Marketing Research* 26 (May 1989): 179–92.

118. James M. Sinkula, "Market Information Processing and Organizational Learning," *Journal of Marketing* 58 (January 1994): 35–45.

119. Allen M. Weiss and Jan B. Heide, "The Nature of Organizational Search in High Technology Markets," *Journal of Marketing Research* 30 (May 1993): 220–33; Jennifer K. Glazing and Paul N. Bloom, "Buying Group Information Source Reliance," *Proceedings of the American Marketing Association Educators' Conference* (Summer 1994): 454.

120. B. Charles Ames and James D. Hlaracek, *Managerial Marketing for Industrial Firms* (New York: Random House Business Division, 1984); Edward F. Fern and James R. Brown, "The Industrial/Consumer Marketing Dichotomy: A Case of Insufficient Justification," *Journal of Marketing* 48 (Spring 1984): 68–77.

121. Jaakko Aspara, "Aesthetics of Stock Investments," *Consumption Markets & Culture* 12 (June 2009): 99–131.

122. Daniel H. McQuiston, "Novelty, Complexity, and Importance as Causal Determinants of Industrial Buyer Behavior," *Journal of Marketing* 53 (April 1989): 66–79.

123. Patrick J. Robinson, Charles W. Faris, and Yoram Wind, *Industrial Buying and Creative Marketing* (Boston: Allyn & Bacon, 1967).

124. Erin Anderson, Wujin Chu, and Barton Weitz, "Industrial Purchasing: An Empirical Examination of the Buyclass Framework," *Journal of Marketing* 51 (July 1987): 71–86.

125. http://wwre.globalsources.com/, accessed June 14, 2011; http://company.monster.com/wre, accessed June 16, 2009.

126. http://www.dell.com/us/business/p/, accessed June 14, 2011.

127. Barbara Kiviat, "The End of Management," *Time Inside Business* (July 12, 2004), www.time.com/time/magazine/article/0,9171,994658,00.html, accessed October 5, 2007.

128. www.intrade.com, accessed June 4, 2011; www.hsx.com, accessed June 4, 2011.

129. Sabrina Tavernise, "Married Couples Are No Longer a Majority, Census Finds," *New York Times* (May 26, 2011), http://www.nytimes.com/2011/05/26/us/26marry.html?_r=2&scp=1&sq=marriage%20rate&st=cse, accessed June 4, 2011.

130. Robert Boutilier, "Targeting Families: Marketing to and Through the New Family," in *American Demographics Marketing Tools* (Ithaca, NY: American Demographics Books, 1993): 4–6; W. Bradford Fay, "Families in the 1990s: Universal Values, Uncommon Experiences," *Marketing Research: A Magazine of Management & Applications* 5 (Winter 1993): 47.

131. Ellen Graham, "Craving Closer Ties, Strangers Come Together as Family," *Wall Street Journal* (March 4, 1996): B1.

132. Risto Moisio, Eric J. Arnould, and Linda L. Price, "Between Mothers and Markets: Constructing Family Identity Through Homemade Food," *Journal of Consumer Culture* 4, no. 3 (2004): 361–84.

133. Sabrina Tavernise, "Study Finds Women Slower to Wed, and Divorce Easing," *New York Times* (May 18, 2011), http://www.nytimes.com/2011/05/19/us/19marriage.html?_r=1&scp=1&sq=age%20of%20marriage&st=cse, accessed June 4, 2011.

134. Sabrina Tavernise, "Grandparents' Role Grows as the Economy Struggles," *New York Times* (November 10, 2010), http://www.nytimes.com/2010/11/11/us/11marriage.html?_r=1&scp=2&sq=grandparent&st=cse, accessed April 19, 2011.

135. "Match.com Releases Study on Trends in Online Dating," *Dating Site Reviews* (April 30, 2010), http://www.datingsitesreviews.com/article.php?story=Match-Releases-Study-Trends-Online-Datin, accessed June 14, 2011.

136. Ben Parr, "Twitter Users Have Shorter Relationships," *Mashable* (April 20, 2011), http://mashable.com/2011/04/19/active-twitter-users-have-shorter-relationships-stats/?utm_source=feedburner&utm_medium=email&utm_campaign=Feed%3A+Mashable+%28Mashable%29, accessed April 30, 2011.

137. Bella English, "The Boomerang Kids," *Boston Globe* (January 13, 2009), www.boston.com/lifestyle/family/articles/2009/01/13/the_boomerang_kids/?page=2, accessed June 16, 2009.

138. "Mothers Bearing a Second Burden," *New York Times* (May 14, 1989): 26.

139. Marcia Mogelonsky, "The Rocky Road to Adulthood," *American Demographics* (May 1996): 26.

140. Nina Diamond, John F. Sherry, Jr., Albert M. Muniz, Jr., Mary Ann McGrath, Robert V. Kozinets, and Stefania Borghini, "American Girl and the Brand Gestalt: Closing the Loop on Sociocultural Branding Research," *Journal of Marketing* 73 (May 2009): 118–34.

141. Erik Eckholm, "'07 U.S. Births Break Baby Boom Record," *New York Times* (March 18, 2009), www.nytimes.com/2009/03/19/health/19birth.html?_r=1, accessed March 18, 2009.

142. Frank Bruni, "Persistent Drop in Fertility Reshapes Europe's Future," *New York Times* (December 26, 2002), www.nytimes.com, accessed December 26, 2002.

143. Katie Zezima, "More Women Than Ever Are Childless, Census Finds," *New York Times* (August 18, 2008), www.nytimes.com, accessed August 19, 2008.

144. P. Paul, "Childless by Choice," *American Demographics* (November 2001): 45–48, 50; www.childfreebychoice.com, accessed June 16, 2009.

145. Rebecca Gardyn, "Animal Magnetism," *American Demographics* (May 2002): 31–37.

146. For a review, cf. Russell W. Belk, "Metaphoric Relationships with Pets," *Society & Animals* 4, no. 2 (1996): 121–46.

147. "Pets Win Prizes as Recession Bites," *Virgin Money* (April 23, 2009), http://uk.virginmoney.com/virgin/news-centre/press-releases/2009/Pets_win_prizes_as_recession_bites.jsp, accessed June 16, 2009; Carla Baranauckas, "A Dog's Life, Upgraded," *New York Times* (September 24, 2006), www.nytimes.com, accessed September 24, 2006; Thom Forbes, "PetSmart's Hotels Offer Doggies the Lap of Luxury," *Marketing Daily* (December 28, 2006), http://www.mediapost.com/publications/?fa=Articles.printFriendly&art_aid$$$=53099, accessed December 28, 2006; Stephanie Thompson, "What's Next, Pup

Tents in Bryant Park?" *Advertising Age* (January 29, 2007): 4; Maryann Mott, "Catering to the Consumers with Animal Appetites," *New York Times on the Web* (November 14, 2004), http://www.nytimes.com/2004/11/14/business/yourmoney/14pet.html, accessed September 9, 2011; http://www.k9waterco.com/, accessed June 14, 2011; Jim Carlton, "For Finicky Drinkers, Water from the Tap Isn't Tasty Enough," *Wall Street Journal* (March 11, 2005), www.wsj.com, accessed March 11, 2005.

148. Brad Edmondson, "Do the Math," *American Demographics* (October 1999): 50–56.

149. www.thebump.com, accessed June 4, 2011; www.theknot.com, accessed June 4, 2011; Edmondson, "Do the Math."

150. The VOICE Group, "Buying into Motherhood? Problematic Consumption and Ambivalence in Transitional Phases," *Consumption Markets & Culture* 13, no. 4 (2010): 373–97.

151. Cheryl Russell, "The New Consumer Paradigm," *American Demographics* (April 1999): 50.

152. These categories are an adapted version of an FLC model proposed by Gilly and Enis (1982). Based on a recent empirical comparison of several competing models, Schaninger and Danko found that this framework outperformed others, especially in terms of its treatment of nonconventional households, though they recommend several improvements to this model as well. See Mary C. Gilly and Ben M. Enis, "Recycling the Family Life Cycle: A Proposal For Redefinition," in Andrew Mitchell, ed., *Advances in Consumer Research* 9 (Ann Arbor: Association for Consumer Research, 1982): 271–76; Schaninger and Danko, "A Conceptual and Empirical Comparison of Alternate Household Life Cycle Models," *Journal of Consumer Research* 19, no. 4 (March 1993): 580–94; Scott D. Roberts, Patricia K. Voli, and Kerenami Johnson, "Beyond the Family Life Cycle: An Inventory of Variables for Defining the Family as a Consumption Unit," in Victoria L. Crittenden, ed., *Developments in Marketing Science* 15 (Coral Gables, FL: Academy of Marketing Science, 1992): 71–75; George P. Moschis, "Life Course Perspectives on Consumer Behaviour," *Journal of the Academy of Marketing Science* 35 (2007): 295–307.

153. Edmondson, "Do the Math."

154. Jennifer Lach, "Intelligence Agents," *American Demographics* (March 1999): 52–60; for a detailed ethnographic study of how households assimilate products, cf. Jennifer Chang Coupland, "Invisible Brands: An Ethnography of Households and the Brands in Their Kitchen Pantries," *Journal of Consumer Research* 33, no. 2 (2005): 106.

155. Harry L. Davis, "Decision-Making Within the Household," *Journal of Consumer Research* 2 (March 1972): 241–60; Michael B. Menasco and David J. Curry, "Utility and Choice: An Empirical Study of Wife/Husband Decision-Making," *Journal of Consumer Research* 16 (June 1989): 87–97; Conway Lackman and John M. Lanasa, "Family Decision-Making Theory: An Overview and Assessment," *Psychology & Marketing* 10 (March–April 1993): 81–94.

156. Shannon Dortch, "Money and Marital Discord," *American Demographics* (October 1994): 11.

157. For research on factors affecting how much influence adolescents exert in family decision-making, see Ellen Foxman, Patriya Tansuhaj, and Karin M. Ekstrom, "Family Members' Perceptions of Adolescents' Influence in Family Decision-Making," *Journal of Consumer Research* 15 (March 1989): 482–91; Sharon E. Beatty and Salil Talpade, "Adolescent Influence in Family Decision-Making: A Replication with Extension," *Journal of Consumer Research* 21 (September 1994): 332–41; for a recent study that compared the influence of parents versus siblings, cf. June Cotte and S. L. Wood, "Families and Innovative Consumer Behavior: A Triadic Analysis of Sibling and Parental Influence," *Journal of Consumer Research* 31, no. 1 (2004): 78–86.

158. Daniel Seymour and Greg Lessne, "Spousal Conflict Arousal: Scale Development," *Journal of Consumer Research* 11 (December 1984): 810–21.

159. Amber M. Epp and Linda L. Price, "Family Identity: A Framework of Identity Interplay in Consumption Practices," *Journal of Consumer Research* 35 (June 2008): 50–70; Robert Lohrer, "Haggar Targets Women with $8M Media Campaign," *Daily News Record* (January 8, 1997): 1.

160. Erik Sass, "Facebook Is Now Leading Source of Evidence in Divorce Cases," *Social Media & Marketing Daily* (March 10, 2011), http://www.mediapost.com/publications/?fa=Articles.showArticle&art_aid=146421&nid=124595, accessed April 19, 2011.

161. Richard Alleyne, "Facebook Increasingly Implicated in Divorce," The Telegraph (UK) (January 21, 2011), http://www.telegraph.co.uk/technology/facebook/8274601/Facebook-increasingly-implicated-in-divorce.html, accessed January 2, 2013.

162. Amy Harmon, "Grandma's on the Computer Screen," *New York Times* (November 26, 2008), www.nytimes.com/2008/11/27/us/27minicam.html?emc=eta1, accessed November 27, 2008.

163. Heather Timmons, "The Hand That Rocks the Cradle Can Call the Shots," *New York Times* (April 3, 2009), http://www.nytimes.com/2009/04/04/business/global/04indiamom.html?scp=113&sq=&st=nyt, accessed April 3, 2009.

164. www.urbanbaby.com/talk/posts/51108366, accessed June 16, 2009; "Helicopter Moms vs. Free-Range Kids," Newsweek.com (April 21, 2008), www.newsweek.com/id/133103, accessed June 16, 2009.

165. Diane Crispell, "Dual-Earner Diversity," *American Demographics* (July 1995): 32–37.

166. "Marriage: The Art of Compromise," *American Demographics* (February 1998): 41.

167. Belinda Luscombe, "Woman Power: The Rise of the Sheconomy," *Time Magazine* (November 22, 2010), http://www.time.com/time/magazine/article/0,9171,2030913-3,00.html, accessed April 19, 2011; Sarah Mahoney, "New Rules of Mama Marketing: Older, Greener," *Marketing Daily* (July 12, 2010), http://www.mediapost.com/publications/?fa=Articles.showArticle&art_aid=131754, accessed April 19, 2011.

168. Tanya Irwin, "Study: Men Defy Marketing Stereotypes," *Marketing Daily* (April 25, 2011), http://www.mediapost.com/publications/?fa=Articles.showArticle&art_aid$$$=149272&nid$$$=126106, accessed April 30, 2011.

169. "Wives and Money," *American Demographics* (December 1997): 34; for a more recent study of decision-making among lesbian couples, cf. Robert Wilkes and Debra A. Laverie, "Purchasing Decisions in Non-Traditional Households: The Case of Lesbian Couples," *Journal of Consumer Behaviour* 6, no. 1 (2007): 60–73.

170. Shirley S. Wang, "J&J Pulls Online Motrin Ad After Social-Media Backlash," *Wall Street Journal* (November 18, 2008): B4.

171. Thomas Hine, *Populuxe* (New York: Knopf, 1986).

172. Boutilier, "Targeting Families: Marketing to and Through the New Family."

173. Karlene Lukovitz, "Women in Wealthy Homes Make 2 of 3 Buying Decisions," *Marketing Daily* (May 15, 2008), www.mediapost.com, accessed May 15, 2008; Dennis L. Rosen and Donald H. Granbois, "Determinants of Role Structure in Family Financial Management," *Journal of Consumer Research* 10 (September 1983): 253–58; Robert F. Bales, *Interaction Process Analysis: A Method for the Study of Small Groups* (Reading, MA: Addison-Wesley, 1950). For a cross-gender comparison of food shopping strategies, see Rosemary Polegato and Judith L. Zaichkowsky, "Family Food Shopping: Strategies Used by Husbands and Wives," *Journal of Consumer Affairs* 28, no. 2 (1994): 278–99.

174. Alma S. Baron, "Working Parents: Shifting Traditional Roles," *Business* 37 (January–March 1987): 36; William J. Qualls, "Household Decision Behavior: The Impact of Husbands' and Wives' Sex Role Orientation," *Journal of Consumer Research* 14 (September 1987): 264–79; Charles M. Schaninger and W. Christian Buss, "The Relationship of Sex-Role Norms to Household Task Allocation," *Psychology & Marketing* 2 (Summer 1985): 93–104.

175. Jennifer Steinhauer, "Mars and Venus: Who Is 'the Decider'?" *New York Times* (April 26, 2006), www.nytimes.com, accessed April 26, 2006; "Tailor-Made," *Advertising Age* (September 23, 2002): 14.

176. Craig J. Thompson, "Caring Consumers: Gendered Consumption Meanings and the Juggling Lifestyle," *Journal of Consumer Research* 22 (March 1996): 388–407.

177. Edmund L. Andrews, "Survey Confirms It: Women Outjuggle Men," *New York Times* (September 15, 2004), www.nytimes.com, accessed September 15, 2004.

178. Gary L. Sullivan and P. J. O'Connor, "The Family Purchase Decision Process: A Cross-Cultural Review and Framework for Research," *Southwest Journal of Business & Economics* (Fall 1988): 43; Marilyn Lavin, "Husband-Dominant, Wife-Dominant, Joint," *Journal of Consumer Marketing* 10, no. 3 (1993): 33–42.

179. Micaela DiLeonardo, "The Female World of Cards and Holidays: Women, Families, and the Work of Kinship," *Signs* 12 (Spring 1942): 440–53.

180. C. Whan Park, "Joint Decisions in Home Purchasing: A Muddling-Through Process," *Journal of Consumer Research* 9 (September 1982): 151–62; see also William J. Qualls and Francoise Jaffe, "Measuring Conflict in Household Decision Behavior: Read My Lips and Read My Mind," in John F. Sherry Jr. and Brian Sternthal, eds., *Advances in Consumer Research* 19 (Provo, UT: Association for Consumer Research, 1992): 522–31.

181. Kim P. Corfman and Donald R. Lehmann, "Models of Cooperative Group Decision-Making and Relative Influence: An Experimental Investigation of Family Purchase Decisions," *Journal of Consumer Research* 14 (June 1987): 1–13.

182. Patricia Cohen, "Signs of Détente in the Battle Between Venus and Mars," *New York Times* (May 31, 2007), www.nytimes.com, accessed May 31, 2007; for a detailed look at couples' goal-setting with regard to artificial reproductive technologies, cf. Eileen Fisher, Cele C. Otnes, and Linda Tuncay, "Pursuing Parenthood: Integrating Cultural and Cognitive Perspectives on Persistent Goal Striving," *Journal of Consumer Research* 34, no. 4 (2007): 425–40.

183. Ray A. Smith, "Belly Up to the Bar and Buy Some Jeans," *Wall Street Journal* (April 2, 2009), http://online.wsj.com/article/SB123862311574879951.html, accessed April 2, 2009.

184. Shelly Branch, "Maybe Sex Doesn't Sell, A&F Is Discovering," *Wall Street Journal* (December 12, 2003), www.wsj.com, accessed December 12, 2003.

185. Jeffrey Zaslow, "Happiness Inc.," *Wall Street Journal* (March 18, 2006): P1.

186. Emily Friedman, "Does Virtual Cheating Still Count?," *ABC News* (August 13, 2007), http://abcnews.go.com/Technology/story?id=3473291&page=1, accessed August 13, 2007; Regina Lynn, "Virtual Rape Is Traumatic, but Is It a Crime?," *Wired* (May 4, 2007); www.wired.com/culture/lifestyle/commentary/sexdrive/2007/05/sexdrive_0504, accessed June 16, 2009; "Representative Kirk Wants to Ban Second Life's 'Rape Rooms' from Schools," *Virtual Worlds News* (May 7, 2008), www.virtualworldsnews.com/2008/05/representative.html?cid=113790134, accessed June 16, 2009.

187. David H. Maister, "The Psychology of Waiting Lines," in John A. Czepiel, Michael R. Solomon, and Carol F. Surprenant, eds., *The Service Encounter: Managing Employee/Customer Interaction in Service Businesses* (Lexington, MA: Lexington Books, 1985): 113–24.

188. David Leonhardt, "Airlines Using Technology in a Push for Shorter Lines," *New York Times* (May 8, 2000), www.nytimes.com, accessed May 8, 2000.

189. Jennifer Ordonez, "An Efficiency Drive: Fast-Food Lanes, Equipped with Timers, Get Even Faster," *Wall Street Journal* (May 18, 2000), www.wsj.com, accessed May 18, 2000.

190. Natasha Singer, "No Mug? Drug Makers Cut Out Goodies for Doctors," *New York Times* (December 30, 2008), www.nytimes.com, accessed December 30, 2008; Alex Berenson, "Cancer Drug Representatives Spelled Out the Way to Profit," *New York Times* (June 12, 2007), www.nytimes.com, accessed June 12, 2007; Andrew Pollack, "Stanford to Ban Drug Makers' Gifts to Doctors, Even Pens," *New York Times* (September 12, 2006), www.nytimes.com, accessed September 12, 2006.

191. Quoted in Stephanie Clifford, "Stuff Piled in the Aisle? It's There to Get You to Spend More," *New York Times* (April 7, 2011), http://www.nytimes.com/2011/04/08/business/08clutter.html?_r=1&hp=&adxnnl=1&adxnnlx=1302264052-gF+9E6s92AG9nsm5jbyIpg, accessed April 18, 2011.

192. Thomas E. Weber, "Viral Marketing: Web's Newest Ploy May Make You an Unpopular Friend," *Wall Street Journal* (September 13, 1999), www.wsj.com, accessed September 13, 1999.

Chapter 10 • Consumer Identity I: Sex Roles and Subcultures

Chapter Objectives

When you have finished reading this chapter you will understand why:

1. Consumer identity derives from "we" as well as "I."

2. Gender identity is a very important component of a consumer's self-concept.

3. Our memberships in ethnic, racial, and religious subcultures often guide our consumption choices.

4. Marketers increasingly use religious and spiritual themes to talk to consumers.

5. We have many things in common with others because they are about the same age.

6. Teens are an important age segment for marketers.

7. Baby Boomers are the most economically powerful age segment.

8. Seniors are a more important market segment than many marketers realize.

9. "Birds of a feather flock together."

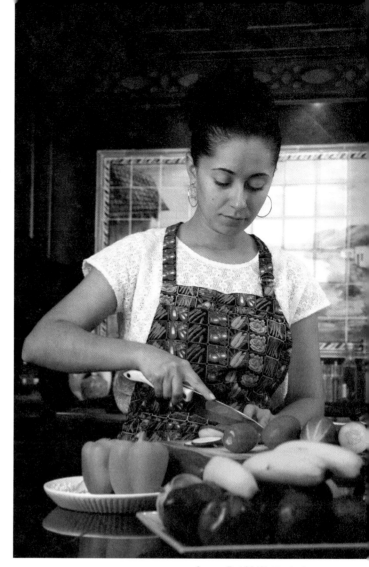

Source: Evok20/Shutterstock.

Maria wakes up early on Saturday morning and braces herself for a long day of errands and chores. As usual, her mother is at work and expects Maria to do the shopping and help prepare dinner for the big family gathering tonight. Of course, her older brother José would never be asked to do the grocery shopping or help out in the kitchen—these are women's jobs.

Family gatherings make a lot of work. Maria wishes that her mother would use prepared foods once in a while, especially on a Saturday when Maria has an errand or two of her own to do. But no, her mother insists on preparing most of her food from scratch. She rarely uses any convenience products, to ensure that the meals she serves are of the highest quality.

Resigned, Maria watches a *telenovela* (soap opera) on Univision while she dresses, and then she heads down to the *carnicería* (small grocery store) to buy a newspaper—almost 40 different Spanish newspapers are published in her area, and she likes to pick up new ones occasionally. Then Maria buys the grocery items her mother wants. The list is full of well-known brand names that she gets all the time, such as Casera and Goya, so she's able to finish quickly. With any luck, she'll have a few minutes to go to the *mercado* (shopping center) to pick up that new Reggaeton CD by Daddy Yankee. She'll listen to it in the kitchen while she chops, peels, and stirs.

Maria smiles to herself: Los Angeles is a great place to live, and what could be better than spending a lively, fun evening with *la familia*?

OBJECTIVE 1
Consumer identity derives from "we" as well as "I."

Consumer Identity

Si, Maria lives in Los Angeles, not Mexico City. More than one in four Californians are Hispanic, and overall the state has more nonwhite than white residents. In fact, more people watch Spanish-language Univision in Los Angeles than any other network.[1]

Maria and other Hispanic Americans have much in common with members of other racial and ethnic groups who live in the United States. They observe the same national holidays, the country's economic health affects what they spend, and they may root for Team USA in the Olympics. Nonetheless, although American citizenship provides the raw material for some consumption decisions, enormous variations in the social fabric of the country profoundly affect many others. The United States truly is a "melting pot" of hundreds of diverse groups, from Italian and Irish Americans to Mormons and Seventh-Day Adventists.

A person's **social identity** is that part of the self that our group memberships define. As we saw in the last chapter, groups exert a lot of influence on our individual consumer decisions. Still, some of our affiliations are more central to our essence than are others.[2] In this chapter we'll look at some of the external linkages that play a very big role in defining who we are and what we value: gender, race/ethnicity, religion, age, and where we live.

Social identity theory argues that each of us has several "selves" that relate to groups. These linkages are so important that we think of ourselves not just as "I," but also as "we." In addition, we favor others that we feel share the same identity—even if that identity is superficial and virtually meaningless. In numerous experiments that employ the **minimal group paradigm** researchers show that even when they arbitrarily assign subjects to one group or another, people favor those who wind up in the same group.[3]

If people distinguish between group members and others based on such a flimsy distinction, imagine the impact our "important" group memberships exert on our feelings, beliefs, and behaviors! For most of us, the groups that "matter" include our gender, age, ethnicity, and other basic characteristics we "inherited" from our parents. In addition, however, important life choices also shape a person's identity, such as identification with a musical genre ("punk," "alternative," etc.), interest in *haute couture* fashion, a belief in the principles of veganism, or passion for a favorite sports team. We'll focus on those choices in the next chapter.

Because our society is so consumption-driven, many of the ways we express our social identities relate to products and services; therefore, we can think of having a **consumer identity** that is a big component of our overall social identity. If to some extent it's true that (as we discussed in Chapter 7) we are what we eat, wear, drive, and so on, then it's fair to say that our consumption choices play a major role in fundamentally defining who we are and who else we want to hang out with. Each of those categories that "matter" is a **subculture**; a group whose members share significant beliefs and common experiences that set them apart from others.

OBJECTIVE 2

Gender identity is a very important component of a consumer's self-concept.

Gender Identity

The Indian government banned a TV spot for Axe men's deodorant: The spot shows a man who turns into a walking chocolate figurine after he sprays himself with the brand's Dark Temptation deodorant. As he walks through the city, women throw themselves at him as they lick him and bite off various parts of his body. Although the same ad played in Argentina and Europe without any problem, traditional Indian culture doesn't approve of such blatant imagery. The government yanked another ad for Amul Macho underwear, in which a young woman comes to a river to do her husband's laundry, pulls out a pair of boxer shorts, and begins to wash them by hand as she gives sultry looks to the camera and throws her head back in a suggestive manner, as a voiceover says, "Amul Macho. Crafted for fantasies." Members of a Hindu organization called The Army of Ram (a Hindu god) attacked a group of female college students in a bar because they were drinking and dancing with men.[4] Clearly, expectations for the appropriate behavior of men and women are not set in stone around the world.

Gender identity is a very important component of a consumer's self-concept. People often conform to their culture's expectations about how those of their gender should act, dress, or speak; we refer to these sets of expectations as **sex roles**. Of course, these guidelines change over time, and they differ radically across societies. In India and elsewhere, for example, a society communicates its assumptions about the proper roles of men and women as it defines ideal behaviors for each gender.

It's not clear to what extent gender differences are innate rather than culturally shaped, but they're certainly evident in many consumption situations. Consider the gender differences market researchers observe when they compare the food preferences of men to those of women. Women eat more fruit; men are more likely to eat meat. As one food writer put it, "Boy food doesn't grow. It is hunted or killed."[5] The sexes also differ sharply in the quantities of food they eat: When researchers at Hershey discovered that women eat smaller amounts of candy, they created a white chocolate confection called Hugs, one of the most successful food introductions of all time. In contrast, a man in a Burger King Whopper ad ditches his date at a fancy restaurant, complaining that he is "too hungry to settle for chick food." Pumped up on Whoppers, a swelling mob of men shake their fists, punch one another, toss a van off a bridge, and sing, "I will eat this meat until my innie turns into an outie," and "I am hungry. I am incorrigible. I am man."[6]

Sex Role Socialization

Children pick up on the concept of gender identity at an earlier age than researchers previously believed—by as young as age 1 in some cases. By the age of 3, most U.S. children categorize driving a truck as masculine and cooking and cleaning as feminine.[7] Even characters that cartoons portray as helpless are more likely to wear frilly or ruffled dresses.[8]

Many commercial sources, in addition to parents and friends, provide lessons in **gender socialization** for both girls and boys. An advertisement for Sony's Bravia televisions is typical: The spot shows a man and a woman gazing through a storefront window at a Bravia LCD. Unaware of each other, the two simultaneously whisper: "Nice picture." Suddenly, two buttons appear on the screen that read: "Ending for Men" and "Ending for Women." The male ending is either a funny clip from a sports show or a cartoon spoof of a martial-arts movie. Women see either a 1950s-era musical centered on shoes or a tearjerker about a female doctor who saves the life of an orphan.[9]

One function of child's play is to rehearse for adulthood. Children act out different roles they might assume later in life and learn about the expectations others have of them. The toy industry provides the props that children use to perform these roles.[10] Depending on which side of the debate you're on, these toys either reflect or teach children about what society expects of males and females. Preschool boys and girls do not exhibit many differences in toy preferences, but after the age of 5 they part company: Girls tend to stick with dolls, whereas boys gravitate toward "action figures" and high-tech diversions.

At Barbie.com, a girl can customize her avatar and her room.[12] Barbie's rebirth as a career woman illustrates how a firm takes concerns about socialization to heart. Although Mattel introduced a Barbie doll astronaut in 1964 and an airline pilot in 1999, it never provided much detail about the careers themselves. Today girls can choose to play

At Barbie.com, a girl can customize her avatar and her room.[11]

Source: Courtesy of Mattel.

with Working Woman Barbie. She comes with a miniature computer and cell phone as well as a CD-ROM about understanding finances. She dresses in a gray suit, but the skirt reverses to a red dress for her to wear with red platform shoes when she goes on after-work adventures with Ken.[13]

Marketers tend to reinforce cultural expectations regarding the "correct" way for boys and girls, men and women, to look and act. Many societies expect males to pursue **agentic goals**, which stress self-assertion and mastery. However, they teach females to value **communal goals**, such as affiliation and building harmonious relations.[14]

One study even found that people perceived a male voice emanating from a computer to be more accurate and authoritative than a female voice that read the very same words. Participants also valued computer-generated words of praise to a greater extent when the voice was male![15] Similarly, an analysis of TV commercials aimed at children in the United States and Australia found that they depict boys as more knowledgeable, active, aggressive, and instrumental.[16] Research indicates that our brains are "wired" to react differently to males and females—and it may help to explain why men tend to objectify women. A study that used brain-scanning technology showed photos of women wearing bikinis to a group of heterosexual male college students and tracked which areas of their brains lit up. The activated areas were the same as those that get aroused when males handle tools. In a follow-up study, men tended to associate bikini-clad women with first-person action verbs such as I "push," "handle," and "grab" instead of the third-person forms such as she "pushes," "handles," and "grabs." In contrast, when they saw photos of fully clothed women, they reverted to the third-person forms, which implied

This Israeli poster that appeared in men's restrooms illustrates cultural assumptions about sex role differences.
Source: Courtesy of Goldstar.

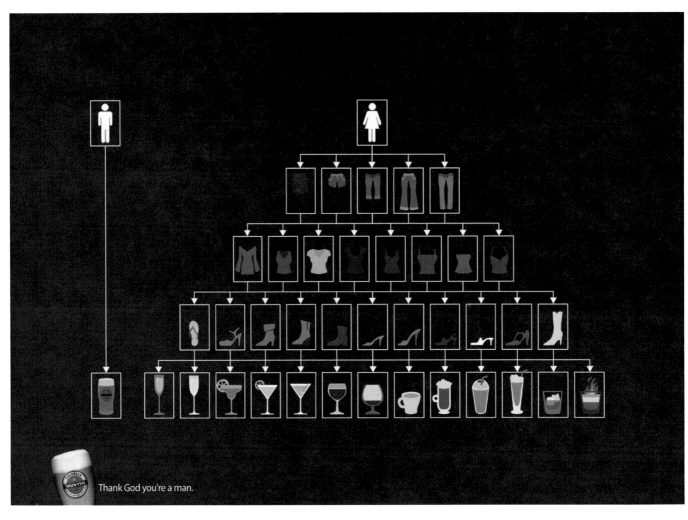

that they perceived these women as being in control of their own actions. Female subjects who responded to both sets of pictures did not display this difference.

These differences in orientation show up early in our development. When Mattel decided to develop Ello, a building toy for girls, its designers carefully observed the play patterns of 5- to 10-year-olds. The toy features interconnecting plastic squares, balls, triangles, squiggles, flowers, and sticks, in pastel colors and with rounded corners, that let users snap pieces together to create houses, people, jewelry, and picture frames. As one of the developers observed, "Boys enjoy stacking blocks and working towards a goal, such as finishing a building. Their play is more physically active, and they like to create conflict between characters. Girls don't like repetitive stacking. They prefer to create relationships between characters, building communities and decorative spaces."[17]

We find the same gender differences in social media: Women are more enthusiastic about connecting with others. Although there are more men online on the global Internet, women spend about 8 percent more time online, averaging 25 hours per month on the Web. Women spend 20 percent more time on retail sites overall than men. In a typical month, about 76 percent of all women globally interact with a social networking site, as compared to only 70 percent of men. Also, women spend significantly more time on social networking sites than men; they average 5.5 hours per month compared to 4 hours for men.[18]

Gender Identity Versus Sexual Identity

Gender-role identity is a state of mind as well as body. A person's biological gender (i.e., male or female) does not totally determine whether he or she will exhibit **sex-typed traits**—characteristics we stereotypically associate with one gender or the other. A consumer's subjective feelings about his or her sexuality are crucial as well.[19]

A male sex-typed product.
Source: IWC Schaffhausen.

Don't fly too high!

Pilot's Watch Double Chronograph. Ref. 3778: A watch? Or a machine? A 46-mm stainless-steel case, mechanical double chronograph movement with a split-seconds hand for intermediate time and a soft-iron inner case to protect the movement against magnetic fields make this timepiece an indestructible, and at the same time high-precision masterpiece from the Schaffhausen-based watch manufacturers. All it needs to make it fly is a pilot. **IWC. Engineered for men.**

Mechanical chronograph movement | Self-winding | 44-hour power reserve when fully wound | Date and day display | Small hacking seconds | Stopwatch function with hours, minutes and seconds | Split-seconds hand for intermediate timing (figure) | Soft-iron inner case for protection against magnetic fields | Screw-in crown | Sapphire glass, convex, antireflective coating on both sides | Water-resistant 6 bar | Stainless steel

Unlike maleness and femaleness, masculinity and femininity are *not* biological characteristics. A behavior that one culture considers to be masculine might get a different response in another. For example, the norm in the United States is that male friends avoid touching each other (except in "safe" situations such as on the football field). In some Latin and European cultures, however, it is common for men to hug and kiss one another as a form of greeting. Note that even this norm continues to evolve, as American teenagers of both sexes adopt the new fad of hugging as a standard form of greeting (sometimes accompanied by the high-five or the fist-bump) and male friends (encouraged by the MTV show of the same name) feel free to talk about having a **bromance** (affection between straight male friends).[20]

Clearly, the "normality" of sex-typed behaviors varies across cultures. For example, although acceptance of homosexuality varies in Asian cultures, it doesn't occur to most Asians to assume that a man with some feminine qualities is gay. A recent survey of Korean consumers found that more than 66 percent of men and 57 percent of women younger than age 40 were living self-described "androgynous" lifestyles—with men having more traditionally female traits and women having more traditionally male ones than they might have years ago. But the respondents didn't link that with sexual orientation. Although Koreans nickname males with feminine interests "flower men," they don't consider this to be a derogatory term.[21] In Japan, men that people call *gyaru-o* ("male gals") are common on city streets. Tanned and meticulously dressed (and usually heterosexual), these fops cruise Tokyo's stylish boutiques.[22]

Sex-Typed Products

A popular book once proclaimed, *Real Men Don't Eat Quiche*. In addition to quiche, marketers promote many **sex-typed products**. They reflect stereotypical masculine

Women consume many products intended to alter their appearance to be in line with cultural expectations.
Source: Agency: Downtown Partners Chicago. Writer: Sean Austin. Art Directors: Joe Stuart and Tom Kim.

Love isn't blind. If it were, there would be no such thing as makeup and pushup bras.

or feminine attributes, and consumers associate them with one gender or another.[23] A vodka brand called Thor's Hammer illustrates this stereotyping. The booze comes in a short, squat bottle, and the company's vice president of marketing describes it as "bold and broad and solid. This is a man's kind of vodka . . . it's not your frosted . . . girly-man vodka." Thor was the Norse god of thunder, and the company claims the name has no connection to the slang phrase "getting hammered," which can happen if you drink too much of the stuff.[24] In contrast, ePad Femme is the ". . . world's first tablet made exclusively for women." It comes preloaded with a pink background and a number of apps related to yoga, grocery shopping, weight loss, and cooking.[25]

Female Sex Roles

In the 1949 movie *Adam's Rib,* Katherine Hepburn played a stylish and competent lawyer. This film was one of the first to show that a woman can have a successful career and still be happily married. Today, the evolution of a new managerial class of women has forced marketers to change their traditional assumptions about women as they target this growing market. For example, Suzuki appeals to the growing number of women in India who achieve financial independence and buy their own cars. Its Zen Estilo (*estilo* means "style" in Spanish) model comes in eight colors, including "purple fusion," "virgin blue," and "sparkling olive."[26]

Still, it's premature to proclaim the death of traditional sex-role stereotypes. This is certainly true in Islamic countries that require women to be completely covered in public and that prohibit them from working as salespeople in stores open to the public (even if the store sells female intimate apparel).[27]

To further complicate matters, sex roles constantly evolve. In a complex society like ours, we often encounter contradictory messages about "appropriate" behavior, and we

This ad for Bijan illustrates how sex role identities are culturally bound by contrasting the expectations of how women should appear in two different countries.

Source: Courtesy of Bijan Fragrances c/o Fashion World.

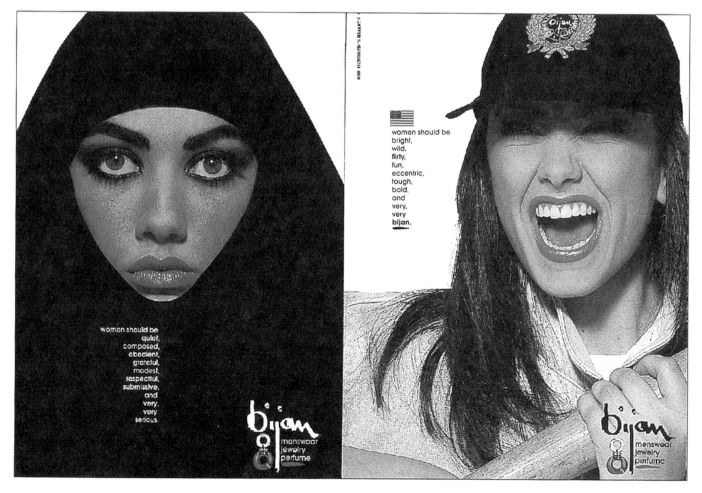

As anyone who understands the logic of market segmentation can explain (see Chapter 1), it's often not realistic to paint a huge group of consumers with the same brush; we often need to subdivide them into segments that share important characteristics. This logic certainly applies to women, and smart marketers know they can't assume that all female consumers have been socialized the same way. For example, a research company called Cohorts identifies nine segments of single women alone. Cohorts describes the three most promising segments:[29]

1. **Megan**—A stylish, tech-savvy student with a median income of $16,000. She reads *Self*, *Rolling Stone*, *InStyle*, and *US Weekly*. She is likely to channel-surf when ads come on TV, and she wouldn't watch TV at all without cable. Her favorite channels are Oxygen, Nickelodeon (Nick at Nite), Disney Channel, MTV, VH1, E!, and TBS. She's turned on by what's cool or the latest thing; she's liberal, seizes opportunities, and spends on a whim.

2. **Allison**—An educated working woman with a median income of $52,000. She reads *Elle*, *Shape*, *Cosmopolitan*, and *Entertainment Weekly*. Her favorite channels are Lifetime, Bravo, Cartoon Network, E!, FX, TBS, and TLC. She's into travel and her career, and she prides herself on her sophisticated tastes.

3. **Elizabeth**—An affluent career woman with a median income of $174,000. She reads *Vogue*, *Harper's Bazaar*, *People*, and *Martha Stewart Living*. When she takes time to watch TV, she tunes in to networks such as Lifetime, WE, Comedy Central, MTV, CNBC, E!, HBO, A&E, Bravo, and AMC. She values foreign travel, fitness, and her career, and she's savvy and spontaneous.

The Axe line of male personal care products puts a twist on an old stereotype by depicting men as sex objects.

Source: Courtesy of Bartle Bogle Hegarty New York aka BBH.

may find ourselves putting on a very different face as we jump from situation to situation. A recent exploration of what the authors labeled **contemporary young mainstream female achievers (CYMFA)** identified different roles these women play in different contexts. For example, as a mother or partner they enact a highly feminine role; as a tough, pitiless businessperson, they play a masculine role; and with a friend they might evoke both roles at once.[28]

Male Sex Roles

A European ad for designer Dolce & Gabbana depicts a group of sweaty men in tight jeans who surround a woman wearing spike heels who is pinned to the ground. Other ads featuring long-time household products spokescharacter Mr. Clean claim that only a strong man is powerful enough to tackle dirt.[30] To promote the new Dr. Pepper Ten drink, the company is sending a mobile "Man Cave" to U.S. cities. The trailer will park in "testosterone zones" such as ball fields or car shows, and gives men a place to watch TV and play video games. The accompanying advertising campaign features a muscled commando type who totes a space-age weapon. "Hey ladies, enjoying the film?" he asks. "'Course not. Because this is our movie, and Dr. Pepper Ten is our soda."[31]

Our culture's stereotype of the ideal male is a tough, aggressive, muscular man who enjoys "manly" sports. When global entrepreneur and CEO of Virgin Airlines Richard

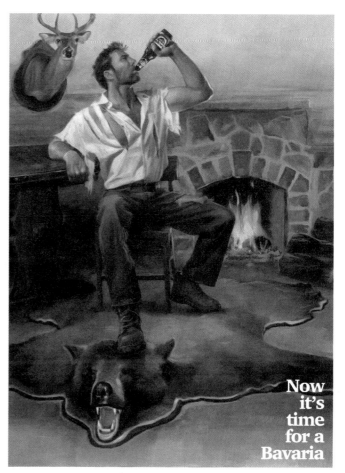

This Dutch beer ad communicates expectations about the male sex role.
Source: KesselsKramer, Amsterdam. KesselsKramer, Sabine Gilhuijs, Lauriergracht 39, 1016 RG Amsterdam. The Netherlands.

Branson lost a racing bet to the owner of Air Asia, his "sentence" was to dress as a female flight attendant for the winner's airline. The winner gloated, "I'm looking forward to him sucking up to me as a stewardess!"[32]

Just as for women, however, the true story is more complicated than being "a man's man." Indeed, scholars of **masculinism** study the male image and the complex cultural meanings of masculinity.[33] Like women, men receive mixed messages about how they are supposed to behave and feel. Chevrolet's "Guy's Night Out" commercial depicts a new dad's night out with friends where they wind up watching his toddler's sing-a-long CD. In another example, Sprint aired a commercial about a boy who is dumped by his girlfriend via text message.[34]

One study examined how American men pursue masculine identities through their everyday consumption. The researchers suggest that men try to make sense out of three different models of masculinity that they call *breadwinner, rebel,* and *man-of-action hero.* On the one hand, the breadwinner model draws from the American myth of success and celebrates respectability, civic virtues, pursuit of material success, and organized achievement. The rebel model, on the other hand, emphasizes rebellion, independence, adventure, and potency. The man-of-action hero is a synthesis that draws from the best of the other two models.[35]

Gay, Lesbian, Bisexual, and Transgender (GLBT) Consumers

The proportion of the population that is gay or lesbian is difficult to determine, and efforts to measure this group have been controversial.[36] Estimates among academics and marketing experts range widely from about 4 percent to 8 percent of the total U.S. population, or between 11 million and 23 million people. The 2000 Census reported 1.2 million same-sex "unmarried" partners in the United States, and this number excludes single

Marketing Opportunity

Smart marketers try to think about new markets for their products. Some companies that sell exclusively to one gender may therefore decide to test the waters with the other sex when they promote **gender-bending products**; traditionally sex-typed items adapted to the opposite gender, such as the recent profusion of merchants that sell pink guns for women. Here are some other gender benders:[37]

Taking a page from a classic *Seinfeld* TV episode, Japanese lingerie retailer Wish Room discovered that some men secretly would like to wear a bra. It sold hundreds of "mansierres."

Rubbermaid introduced a line of grooming tools specifically for men, including tweezers and clippers. As a manager explained, "Most men don't want to go to what we call the 'pink aisle' of the store to get tweezers and clippers that are made for women. They want products that look masculine and are made for their specific grooming needs."

Frito-Lay's salty snacks traditionally appeal to men, but the company is working hard to change that with baked versions of chips and 100-calorie packages of snacks. After conducting extensive research (including asking several hundred women to keep detailed journals of their daily activities), the company's marketers concluded that the typical woman looks for a reminder that she's eating something healthy. As one result of this work, the bag for Baked Lay's will change from shiny yellow to a matte beige that displays pictures of ingredients like spices or ranch dressing.

• • • • • • • • • • • • • • • •

Androgyny describes people who possess both masculine and feminine traits.[38] Researchers make a distinction between sex-typed people, who are stereotypically masculine or feminine, and androgynous people, whose orientation isn't as clearly defined. The **Goth subculture**, inspired by vampire myths and gothic traditions, illustrates an androgynous approach to gender identity. Participants express different forms of sexuality regardless of their biological membership; they use costumes to express hypermasculinity, hyperfemininity, or androgyny (such as skeletons). The vampire narrative also is androgynous, as both males and females can dominate or search for beauty.[39]

Source: Kati Neudert/Shutterstock.

gays and lesbians (the 2010 Census specifically counted same-sex married couples).[40] The respected research company Yankelovich Partners Inc., which has tracked consumer values and attitudes since 1971 in its annual *Monitor*™ survey, now includes a question about sexual identity in its instrument and reports that about 6 percent of respondents identify themselves as gay/homosexual/lesbian. This study was virtually the first to use a sample that reflects the population as a whole instead of polling only smaller or biased groups (such as readers of gay publications) whose responses may not be as representative of all consumers.

To put things in perspective, the GLBT market is at least as large, if not larger, than the Asian American population (currently at about 12 million people). These consumers spend in the range of $250 billion to $350 billion a year. A Simmons study of readers of gay publications found that these readers are almost 12 times more likely to hold professional jobs, twice as likely to own a vacation home, and eight times more likely to own a notebook computer compared to heterosexuals.[41]

Gun Goddess sells feminine accessories to women who own or use firearms.
Source: GunGoddess.com.

Marketing Opportunity

As the movement grows to legalize same-sex marriage, businesses are searching for ways to meet the needs of this new, potentially very lucrative market. Already the online magazine *EquallyWed* offers tips on wedding planning and OutVite.com sells "custom printed gay and lesbian stationery." After it received pressure from gay rights groups, the *Today* show on NBC invited same-sex couples to compete in its annual wedding contest. *Brides'* magazine ran its first feature about a wedding between one of the magazine's photo editors and her longtime girlfriend. A year earlier, *Martha Stewart Weddings* published a pictorial of two gay grooms stomping on a glass and sharing a kiss.[42]

Axe's Anarchy brand is a gender-bender.
Source: Courtesy of Unilever.

CB AS I SEE IT

Professor Susan Dobscha, *Bentley University*

Imagine the excitement a young couple feels when they find out they are pregnant with their first child. They may learn this from a doctor's visit or from a pregnancy test they purchased at the drugstore. Once the pregnancy is confirmed and friends and relatives receive the good news, the couple must now begin the extensive planning process that gets them ready for the new addition to their family. Not surprisingly, a large portion of this process requires the planning and purchasing of goods and services. There are thousands of books on how to be a new parent, most of them geared toward the mother. Although there are several books that give advice on how to be a new father, the book market reflects the still widely accepted cultural norms that mothers are the primary caretakers of children, while fathers largely play a secondary role. A recent study found that although both new mothers and new fathers believed that responsibilities of parenting should be shared equally, the majority of those same

mothers and fathers did not feel that responsibility was equally shared in their household. Sex roles remain fairly stable over time, even if expectations about them change dramatically.

The VOICE Group, an international research team currently undertaking a global study of motherhood, asked new mothers about their husbands' role in the planning process as a run up to the new baby arriving. Despite the fact that most of our participants claimed that their husbands were "excited" and "involved," the reality for most women was that their partner's level of involvement was lower than their own. Our study focused on mothers' perceptions of fathers' attitudes toward consumption decisions related to the introduction of the first child in the family. The data revealed that men, according to their wives' perceptions, used consumption as a virtual umbilical cord, although levels of consumption involvement varied from co-involvement for most purchases, to limited involvement, and/or involvement for big-ticket items, particularly travel systems and technical products. This research also revealed that men partook in highly masculinized forms of "nesting," and in general shunned pregnancy book reading, though some did engage in "research" activities such as searching the Internet for product safety information. We concluded from this study that the transition into parenthood can be

difficult for men due to their lack of a physical connection to the pregnancy, a perception that the baby industry is not designed for them, the continuance of male stereotypes in the media, and also the time available to men to become involved in consumption activities immediately prior to a baby's birth.

An interesting question for consumer researchers is: How do sex roles change over time, and to what extent does the marketplace reflect or in some cases hinder that change? In this study, we found that the books geared toward new dads typically displayed a tongue-in-cheek tone; they implied that new dads are incapable of taking a serious look at their new role as caretaker of a young child. The baby stores are also somewhat intimidating to men (although the women felt just as intimidated by the large box baby stores) because of men's general lack of experience with caring for infants and lack of information on or awareness of what that infant's needs would be once he or she arrived.

If men have an expectation about themselves that they will be coparents, equally responsible in the caretaking of their child, does the lack of marketplace offerings directed at new dads hinder those dads from enacting those new roles? Are there opportunities here for enterprising marketers who can develop products to better meet these needs?

OBJECTIVE 3
Our memberships in ethnic, racial, and religious subcultures often guide our consumption choices.

Ethnic and Racial Subcultures

McDonald's U.S. chief marketing officer (CMO) observes, "The ethnic consumer tends to set trends. So they help set the tone for how we enter the marketplace." He notes that feedback from minority consumers shape McDonald's menu and ad choices, which it then markets to all of its customers. In fact, the chain's American strategy is called "Leading with Ethnic Insights." The company includes a disproportionate number of blacks, Hispanics, and Asians in focus groups. It asks its marketers to imagine how they would sell a product if the U.S. population were *only* African American, Hispanic, or Asian. For example, the fruit combinations in McDonald's latest smoothies reflect taste preferences in minority communities. And when the company started heavily advertising coffee drinks last year, the ads emphasized the indulgent aspects of sweeter drinks like mochas, a message that resonated with African Americans. Ethnic practices also get picked up in mainstream advertising: In one commercial called "Big Day," a young boy at a wedding looks bored while watching the bride and groom kiss and jump over a broom—an African American wedding tradition. His eyes light up when he gets to his seat and finds a Happy Meal.[43]

An **ethnic subculture** is a self-perpetuating group of consumers who share common cultural or genetic ties, where both its members and others recognize it as a distinct category.[44] In some countries like Japan, ethnicity is virtually synonymous with the dominant culture, because most citizens claim the same cultural ties (although even Japan has sizable minority populations, most notably people of Korean ancestry). In a heterogeneous society such as the United States, which incorporates many different cultures, consumers expend great effort to keep their subcultural identification from being submerged into the mainstream of the dominant society.

Marketers like McDonald's cannot ignore the stunning diversity of cultures that reshape mainstream society. Ethnic minorities spend more than $600 billion a year on products and services, so firms must tailor products and communications strategies to their unique needs. This vast market continues to grow: Immigrants now make up 10 percent of the U.S. population and will account for 13 percent by 2050.[45]

The U.S. Census calculates that by 2042, Americans who identify themselves as Hispanic, Black, Asian, American Indian, Native Hawaiian, and Pacific Islander will together outnumber non-Hispanic whites. Furthermore, the Census Bureau predicts that by 2050, people who identify themselves as multiracial will make up almost 4 percent of the U.S. population.[46] Among American children, the multiracial population has increased almost 50 percent, to 4.2 million, since 2000, making it the fastest growing youth group in the country. The number of people of all ages who identified themselves as both white and black soared by 134 percent since 2000 to 1.8 million people.[47]

This important change encourages advertisers to rethink their old strategies, which assumed that virtually all of their customers were Caucasians who hailed from Western Europe. For example, as part of Crest toothpaste's 50th-anniversary celebration, Procter & Gamble revived its "Crest Kid," who first appeared as an apple-cheeked urchin whom Norman Rockwell illustrated in 1956. Now, a Cuban-born girl plays the character. An independent panel chose her because of her sparkling smile, but it's significant that this mainstream American figure now is Hispanic.[48]

It makes good business sense to cater to these segments by (literally) speaking their language when promoting products and services: Surveys repeatedly show that members of ethnic groups get much of their product information from specialized ethnic media; one found that 63 percent of ethnic Californians watch native-language TV daily, and a third of them also read an ethnic newspaper at least once a week.[49] The advertisements that people who view these media see ideally should match up with the way they communicate in daily life.

One important subcultural difference is how abstract or literal the group is. Sociologists make a basic distinction: In a **high-context culture**, group members tend to be tightly knit, and they infer meanings that go beyond the spoken word. Symbols and gestures, rather than words, carry much of the weight of the message. In contrast, people in a **low-context culture** are more literal. Compared to Anglos (who tend to be low-context), many minority cultures are high-context and have strong oral traditions, so consumers are more sensitive to nuances in advertisements that go beyond the message copy.[50]

Ethnic and Racial Stereotypes

A controversial television commercial for Salesgenie.com that ran during a recent Super Bowl illustrates how marketers (intentionally or not) use ethnic and racial stereotypes to

In the past, marketers used ethnic symbolism as shorthand to convey certain product attributes. However, they often employed crude and unflattering images when they depicted African Americans as subservient or Mexicans as bandits.[52] Aunt Jemima sold pancake mix and Rastus was a grinning black chef who pitched Cream of Wheat hot cereal. The Gold Dust Twins were black urchins who peddled a soap powder for Lever Brothers, and Pillsbury hawked powdered drink mixes via characters such as Injun Orange and Chinese Cherry—who had buck teeth.[53] As the civil rights movement gave more power to minority groups and their rising economic status began to command marketers' respect, these negative stereotypes began to disappear. Frito-Lay responded to protests by the Hispanic community and stopped using the Frito Bandito character in 1971, and Quaker Foods gave Aunt Jemima a makeover in 1989.

Even today, unfortunately, miscommunications occur. A recent flap about a Cadbury candy advertising campaign that ran in the UK illustrates these sensitivities. A print and billboard ad for Cadbury's Bliss line of Dairy Milk chocolate ran with the tagline, "Move over Naomi, there's a new diva in town." Many people, including supermodel Naomi Campbell, objected to the racist undertone of the ad; she claimed it "was in poor taste on a number of levels, not least in the way they likened me to their chocolate bar." Cadbury defended the ad, arguing that it intended to poke fun at her reputation as a diva and that no link to her skin color was intended. Although the industry organization that polices England's advertising determined that the message was not racist, the company responded to threats of a global boycott by withdrawing the ad and apologizing to Campbell.[54]

craft promotional communications. The spot featured two animated pandas that spoke in heavy Chinese accents. After complaints from viewers, the company withdrew the commercial.[51]

Many subcultures have powerful stereotypes the general public associates with them. In these cases, outsiders assume that group members possess certain traits. Unfortunately, a communicator can cast the same trait as either positive or negative, depending on his or her biases or intentions. For example, the Scottish stereotype in the United States is largely positive, so we tend to look favorably on their (supposed) frugality. The 3M company uses Scottish imagery to denote value (e.g., Scotch tape), as does Scotch Inns, a motel chain that offers inexpensive lodging. However, the Scottish "personality" might carry quite different connotations to the British or Irish. One person's "thrifty" is another's "stingy."

Ethnicity and Acculturation

Although some people feel uncomfortable with the notion that marketers should explicitly take into account people's racial and ethnic differences when they formulate their strategies, the reality is that these subcultural memberships do shape many needs and wants. Research indicates, for example, that members of minority groups find an advertising spokesperson from their own group more trustworthy, and this enhanced credibility in turn translates into more positive brand attitudes.[55] However, marketers need to avoid the temptation to paint all members of an ethnic or racial group with the same brush; not only are these generalizations inaccurate, but they also are likely to turn off the very people a company wants to reach.[56]

Acculturation is the process of movement and adaptation to one country's cultural environment by a person from another country.[57] This is a very important issue for marketers because of our increasingly global society. As people move from place to place, they may quickly assimilate to their new homes, or they may resist this blending process and choose to insulate themselves from the mainstream culture. It's typical for a new arrival in the United States, for example, to feel ambivalence or conflict about relinquishing old ways (and consumer behaviors) for new ones. Home Depot segments its campaigns when the retailer speaks to the Hispanic market; it creates different ads for "acculturated Hispanics" (second- or third-generation Americans) than it shows to consumers who almost always speak Spanish.[58]

A study of Mexican immigrants that used the research technique of *ethnography* probed their acculturation as they adapted to life in the United States.[59] Indeed, after the researchers interviewed these people in their natural settings, they reported a lot of ambivalence. On the one hand, they are happy about the improvements in the quality of their lives because of greater job availability and educational opportunities for their children. On the other hand, they report bittersweet feelings about leaving Mexico. They miss their friends, their holidays, their food, and the comfort that comes from living in familiar surroundings. Another study looked at how Hispanic children responded to a campaign to promote oral hygiene cosponsored by the Boys and Girls Club of America and the American Dental Association. It reported that immigrants who are relatively less acculturated are more motivated to modify their behaviors in line with the campaign's suggestions because they view these changes as important tools for social acceptance.[60]

Many factors affect the nature of the transition process. Individual differences, such as whether the person speaks English, influence how rocky the adjustment will be. The person's contact with **acculturation agents**—people and institutions that teach the ways of a culture—are also crucial. Some of these agents come from the *culture of origin* (in this case, Mexico), including family, friends, the church, local businesses, and Spanish-language media that keep the consumer in touch with his or her country of origin. Other agents come from the *culture of immigration* (in this case, the United States) and help the consumer to learn how to navigate in the new environment. These include public schools, English-language media, and government agencies.

Several processes come into play as immigrants adapt to their new surroundings. *Movement* refers to the factors that motivate people to physically uproot themselves from one location and go to another. In this case, people leave Mexico because of the scarcity of jobs and the desire to provide a good education for their children. On arrival, immigrants encounter a need for *translation*. This means they try to master a set of rules for operating in the new environment, whether it's learning how to decipher a different currency or figuring out the social meanings of unfamiliar clothing styles. This cultural learning leads to a process of *adaptation*, by which people form new consumption patterns. For example, some of the Mexican women in the study started to wear shorts and pants once they settled in the United States, although people in Mexico frown on this practice.

During the acculturation process, many immigrants undergo *assimilation*, where they adopt products, habits, and values they identify with the mainstream culture. At the same time, there is an attempt at *maintenance* of practices they associate with the culture of origin. Immigrants stay in touch with people in their country and, like Maria, many continue to eat Hispanic foods and read Spanish-language newspapers. Their continued identification with Mexican culture may cause *resistance*, as they resent the pressure to submerge their Mexican identities and take on new roles. Finally, immigrants (voluntarily or not) tend to exhibit *segregation*; they are likely to live and shop in places physically separated from mainstream Anglo consumers. These processes illustrate that ethnicity is a fluid concept and that members of a subculture constantly recreate its boundaries.

The **progressive learning model** helps us to understand the acculturation process. This perspective assumes that people gradually learn a new culture as they increasingly come in contact with it. Thus, we expect that when people acculturate, they will mix the practices of their original culture with those of their new or **host culture**.[62] Research that examines such factors as shopping orientation, the importance people place on various product attributes, media preference, and brand loyalty generally supports this pattern.[63] When researchers take into account the intensity of ethnic identification, they find that consumers who retain a strong ethnic identification differ from their more assimilated counterparts in these ways:[64]

- They have a more negative attitude toward business in general (probably caused by frustration due to relatively low income levels).
- They access more media that's in their native language.
- They are more brand loyal.
- They are more likely to prefer brands with prestige labels.
- They are more likely to buy brands that specifically advertise to their ethnic group.

The acculturation process occurs even when we relocate from one place to another within the same country. If you have ever moved (and it's likely you have), you no doubt remember how difficult it was to give up old habits and friends and adapt to what people in your new location do.

A study of Turkish people who moved from the countryside to an urban environment illustrates how people cope with change and unfamiliar circumstances. The authors describe a process of **warming**, which they describe as transforming objects and places into those that feel cozy, hospitable, and authentic. The study's informants described what happened as they tried to turn a cold and unfamiliar house into a home that is *güzel* ("beautiful and good," "modern and warm"). In this context, that means they integrated symbols of their former village life into their new homes: They blanketed them with the embroidered, crocheted, and lace textiles that people traditionally make by hand for brides' dowries in the villages. The researchers reported that migrants' homes contained far more of these pieces than they would have in their village homes because they used them to adorn their new modern appliances. The dowry textiles symbolize traditional norms and social networks of friends and family in the villages, so they link the "cold" modern objects with the owner's past. Thus, the unfamiliar becomes familiar.[65]

Of course, it's not unusual for consumers who don't belong to a subculture to use products they associate with that group. **Deethnicization** occurs when a product we link to a specific ethnic group detaches itself from its roots and appeals to other groups as well. Think about the popularity of bagels, a staple of Jewish cuisine that's mass-marketed today. Recent variations include jalapeño bagels, blueberry bagels, and even a

Marketing Pitfall

The mass merchandising of ethnic products is a growing practice. Native American Aztec designs appear on sweaters, gym shoes come in *kente* cloth from an African tribe, and greeting cards bear likenesses of Native American sand paintings. However, some worry about the borrowing—and in some cases, misinterpretation—of distinctive symbolism. Consider, for example, the storm of protest from the international Islamic community over a dress in a House of Chanel fashion show. Supermodel Claudia Schiffer wore a strapless evening gown (with a price tag of almost $23,000) that Karl Lagerfeld designed. The dress included Arabic letters that the designer believed spelled out a love poem. Instead, the message was a verse from the Koran, the Muslim holy book. To add insult to injury, the word *God* happened to appear over the model's right breast. Both the designer and the model received death threats, and the controversy subsided only after the company burned the dress. More recently, Nike caught flak from activists when it introduced an athletic shoe specially designed for Native Americans. Along with its trademark swoosh, the Nike Air Native N7 features feathers and arrowheads. One young Spokane/ Coeur d'Alene Indian commented, "The day it was announced, I thought: 'Are they going to have dream catchers on them? Are they going to be beaded? Will they have native bumper stickers on them that say, "Custer had it coming"?'"[61]

The Tangled Web

The release of several popular video games underscores the concern of some critics who argue that these games play on racial stereotypes, including images of African American youths who commit violent street crimes:

- *Grand Theft Auto—San Andreas* is set in a city that resembles gang-ridden stretches of Los Angeles of the 1990s. It features a digital cast of African American and Hispanic men, some of whom wear braided hair and scarves over their faces and aim Uzis from low-riding cars.
- *Def Jam Fight for NY* features hip-hop-style characters (one with the voice of the rapper Snoop Dogg) who slap, kick, and pummel one another in locations such as the 125th Street train station in Harlem.
- *25 to Life* is an "urban action game" that includes a hip-hop soundtrack. It lets gamers play the role of police officers or criminals, and includes lots of images of young gun-toting African American gangsters.
- *Notorious—Die to Drive* features "gangsta-style car combat" with players who compete to "rule the streets of four West Coast neighborhoods." The game's Web site proclaims, "High-priced honeys, the finest bling, and millionaire cribs are just some of the rewards for the notorious few who can survive this most dangerous game. Once you go Notorious, there's no going back."[77]

green bagel for St. Patrick's Day.[66] Bagels now account for 3 to 6 percent of all American breakfasts, and bagel franchisers such as Bruegger's Corporation and the Einstein/Noah Bagel Corporation operate hundreds of stores in cities that had never heard of a bagel just a few years ago.[67]

The dominant American culture historically exerted pressure on immigrants to divest themselves of their origins and integrate with mainstream society. As President Theodore Roosevelt put it in the early part of the 20th century, "We welcome the German or the Irishman who becomes an American. We have no use for the German or the Irishman who remains such."[68]

Indeed, there is a tendency for ethnic groups with a relatively longer history in the United States to view themselves as more mainstream as they relax their identification with their country of origin. When the U.S. Census asked respondents to write up to two ancestries that defined their background, the results showed a clear decline in the number of people who identified themselves as of Irish, German, or other European origin. Compared to other subcultures, more people from these countries simply choose to call themselves "American."[69]

The "Big Three" American Ethnic Subcultures

African Americans, Hispanic Americans, and Asian Americans account for much of America's current growth. The Hispanic population is now the largest ethnic subculture.[70] Asian Americans, though much smaller in absolute numbers, are the fastest-growing racial group.[71]

African Americans

African Americans make up more than 13 percent of the U.S. population.[72] As we saw in the case of McDonald's, many marketers recognize the huge impact of this racial subculture and work hard to identify products and services that will appeal to these consumers. Procter & Gamble launched a "My Black Is Beautiful" program for African American women after the company's research showed that these women think mainstream media does not represent them very well; three-quarters of the women the company surveyed said programs and ads portray them more negatively than other racial groups and that they worry about the negative impact these messages will have on teens.[73]

Sometimes these differences are subtle but still important. When Coffee-Mate discovered that African Americans tend to drink their coffee with sugar and cream much more than do Caucasians, the company mounted a promotional blitz in the African American media and in return benefited from double-digit increases in sales volume and market share for this segment.[74] Volvo North America created its first advertising campaign to target African Americans after research showed that car crashes are the leading cause of death among African American children, who are half as likely to use seat belts as other children.[75]

Research by Unilever illustrates how the body image dynamics we discussed in Chapter 7 vary across subcultures; the personal care products company found that skin takes on a deeper meaning for African Americans. In a poll it ran in *Essence* magazine, the company asked more than 1,400 African American women aged 18 to 64 to describe their skin, and the most common response was "beautiful" (59 percent). Another 30 percent described their skin as "strong." The survey also found that African American women rank skin as "most important to them" (49 percent); more so than their hair, figure, makeup, and clothes. About one-third say their skin is a source of their heritage, one-fourth say it's a source of pride, and "almost half of African American women say their skin tells a story of who they are and identifies them." This deep attachment is clear in posted comments such as "My skin is my life's historian," and "My skin represents the blending of my parents, an outward expression of their love."[76]

CB AS I SEE IT

Professor Sonya Grier, *American University*

What are the social implications when marketers focus their efforts on specific consumer groups in our increasingly multicultural societies? Target marketing is at the heart of an effective marketing strategy, and it's driven by the recognition that a "one size fits all" approach to marketing no longer works among diverse, sophisticated consumers. Targeted strategies may attempt to affect commercial behavior (e.g., "buy this product") or social behavior (e.g., "increase fruit and vegetable consumption to reduce weight gain") or some combination of the two (e.g., "buy this product and 10 percent of profits go to charity"). Increased competitiveness, product proliferation, and changing economic conditions make it more challenging for marketers to reach those who are potential consumers of their products and services.

Moreover, the emphasis of social marketing as an agent of behavior change has increased the use of target marketing as a tool to address the growing array of social challenges among specific consumer groups. My research investigates the "how" and "to what effect" of target marketing strategies directed at consumers defined by race and ethnicity, especially African Americans. I study diverse domains (e.g., obesity, ethnic product crossover, cancer prevention,

and service discrimination) to converge on an understanding of the influence of targeted marketing, both positive and negative, on society.

My initial work in this area asked, "How do consumers respond to targeted advertisements when they are (or are *not*) a member of the targeted group?" Research showed that people used different psychological processes to interpret a racially targeted advertisement, and had different attitudes toward those ads, depending on their own race, the social status of their racial group, and their familiarity with other racial groups.[78] These findings led me to consider how target marketing, with its emphasis on providing different prices, promotions, and access to different consumer segments, might create different marketing environments among targeted consumers and serve as a countervailing force for the socially beneficial behavior changes intended by social marketing efforts.

Currently I am exploring how target marketing may contribute to, as well as help resolve, health disparities between members of ethnic minority and majority groups, with a focus on obesity. The prevalence of obesity in African American and Hispanic children and adults tends to be substantially higher than in white Americans. We know that this disparity is not due solely to differences in income or education, although those factors do play a role. Social marketing programs aimed at obesity prevention often promote the increased intake of healthy foods and decreased intake of less healthy foods. What, then, is the role of target marketing of these less healthy foods in the effectiveness of such strategies (i.e., does it "prevent prevention?"). In a systematic review of the marketing

environment of African Americans, a colleague and I found that targeted food marketing strategies, in the aggregate, may challenge the ability of African American consumers to eat healthfully.[79] Marketers' promotional strategies directed toward African Americans emphasize the awareness of low-cost, low-nutrition food products such as candy, soda, and snacks and are less likely to contain health-oriented messages. We also found that distribution and pricing strategies may constrain the ability of African American consumers to purchase healthy food. It is certainly a challenge for any consumer to eat healthfully when their choices are constrained.

My ongoing research further examines how targeted marketing may be used to encourage more health-oriented behaviors at a community level. Such strategies will entail not only changing individual dietary habits, but also supporting communities when they advocate for increased health-supporting targeted marketing. I am also exploring interactive targeting efforts. As technological advances change the process of targeted marketing, it is important to understand whether consumers' response facilitates or hinders important health behaviors. I believe that through understanding unintended consequences of target marketing, especially aggregate effects among particular target segments, targeted marketing can be a beneficial strategy for commercial and social marketers alike, and can help address important social challenges. I hope my research contributes to this understanding and to the design of more socially responsible marketing practices, effective social marketing efforts, and conscious, equitable marketplaces worldwide.

Marketing Pitfall

Many initial efforts to market to Hispanic Americans were, to say the least, counterproductive. Companies bumbled in their efforts to translate advertising adequately or to compose copy that captured the nuances advertisers intended. These mistakes do not occur so much anymore because marketers are more sophisticated when they talk to this segment and they tend to involve Hispanics in advertising production to ensure that they get it right. These translation mishaps slipped through before Anglos got their acts together:[80]

- The Perdue slogan, "It takes a tough man to make a tender chicken," translated as "It takes a sexually excited man to make a chick affectionate."
- Budweiser was the "queen of beers."
- Braniff (now defunct) promoted the comfortable leather seats on its airplanes with the headline, *Sentado en cuero*, which translates as "Sit naked."
- Coors beer's slogan to "get loose with Coors" appeared in Spanish as "get the runs with Coors."

Hispanic Americans

The umbrella term **Hispanic** describes people of many different backgrounds. Nearly 60 percent of Hispanic Americans are of Mexican descent. The next largest group, Puerto Ricans, make up just fewer than 10 percent of Hispanics. Other groups the Census includes in this category are Central Americans, Dominicans, South Americans, and Cubans.

The Hispanic subculture is a sleeping giant that many U.S. marketers ignored until recently. The growth and increasing affluence of this group now makes it impossible to overlook, and today major corporations avidly court Hispanic consumers. No surprise: The 2010 Census reported a record 50 million Hispanics, or one in every six U.S. residents; this was a 42 percent increase from the 2000 Census. Hispanics are now the nation's second-largest consumer market after white non-Hispanics. Ironically, this segment also resembles our idealized concept of 1950s America. They are young (their median age is about where the whole nation was in 1955) and they more often live in large, traditional, married-with-children families where grandparents log a lot of time. They're

Hispanic consumers are rapidly entering the mainstream market.

Source: Courtesy of *Latina Magazine*.

increasingly moving to the suburbs, they tend to be community-oriented, and they have high aspirations for their children.

More than one in three Hispanics in the United States are under 18 years old. This means they will acculturate much faster than their parents did. Already, almost half report that they are at ease when they speak English. They also are geographically concentrated, which makes it easier for marketers to reach them. About half of Hispanic consumers live in California and Texas. The other six states having more than 1 million Hispanics are Florida, New York, Illinois, Arizona, New Jersey, and Colorado.[81]

Here are some notable current marketing efforts to reach this important ethnic subculture:

- Walmart opened its first Hispanic-focused supermarkets, Supermercado de Walmart, in Phoenix and Houston.[83]
- AT&T launched a Spanish advertising campaign featuring Grammy Award-winning singer Natalia Jimenez.[84]
- L'Oréal USA partnered with the Telemundo Communications Group to sponsor Club de Noveleras, the first official club for fans of the Telemundo broadcast network's mainstay programming of *telenovelas*—the popular serialized dramas that run in weeks-long blocks in prime time.[85]
- Wendy's International, Inc., rolled out a new series of television and radio commercials themed "Sabor de Verdad," roughly translating to "Real Taste." The campaign positions Wendy's as the solution for Hispanic consumers looking to satisfy their "-antojos," or taste cravings, with quality food at affordable prices.[86]

Asian Americans

Asian Americans have surpassed Hispanics as the fastest-growing racial group in the nation and have become the largest group of new immigrants to the United States. This subculture's buying power is projected to reach $700 billion in the coming years.[87]

Asians not only make up the fastest-growing population group, they also are the most affluent, best educated, and most likely to hold technology jobs of any ethnic subculture. Indeed, Asian Americans are much more likely than average Americans to buy high-tech gadgets. They are almost three times as likely to own a digital camcorder and twice as likely to have an MP3 player.[88] About 32 percent of Asian households have incomes of more than $50,000, compared to 29 percent across the entire U.S. population. Estimates put this segment's buying power at $253 billion annually. That explains why the brokerage firm Charles Schwab now employs more than 300 people who speak Chinese, Korean, and Vietnamese at its call centers.[89]

The problems American marketers encountered when they first tried to reach the Hispanic market popped up again when they began to target Asian Americans:[90]

- The Coca-Cola slogan "Coke Adds Life" translated as "Coke brings your ancestors back from the dead" in Japanese.
- Kentucky Fried Chicken described its chicken as "finger-lickin' good" to the Chinese, who don't think it's polite to lick your fingers.
- A footwear ad depicted Japanese women performing foot binding, which only the Chinese did.

Despite its potential, the Asian American subculture can be hard to reach, because it's composed of numerous culturally diverse subgroups that use different languages and dialects.[91] The term *Asian* refers to 20 ethnic groups, with Chinese being the largest and Filipino and Japanese second and third, respectively. Filipinos are the only Asians who speak English predominantly among themselves; like Hispanics, most Asians prefer media in their own languages. The languages Asian Americans speak most frequently are Mandarin Chinese, Korean, Japanese, and Vietnamese.

Not only are Asian consumers the most frequent shoppers of all racial and ethnic groups, but also they are the most brand-conscious. Almost half (43 percent) say they

Marketing Opportunity

Hispanic Americans spend triple the amount of time browsing online that non-Hispanics do, and nearly twice as much time (on average 5 hours per week) on social networks. One factor that accounts for this difference is the relative youth of this segment; Hispanics ages 13 to 34 use social networking sites about three times more than do those over the age of 35. About 30 million Hispanics—or 60 percent of the U.S. Hispanic population—are online. A study from comScore, commissioned by Terra (a Spanish-language media network), suggests that Hispanics are more active online and more receptive to new technology than non-Hispanics. The research also says the Internet is the main media source of information for Hispanics in terms of services and products. The survey of several thousand respondents reported that 37 percent of Hispanics versus 30 percent of non-Hispanics said they would respond to online pitches, and 35 percent of Hispanics versus 27 percent of non-Hispanics said they are more open to advertising on sites where they read or contribute user-generated comments. Thirty-six percent of Hispanics, compared to 24 percent of non-Hispanics, said that Internet advertising has motivated them to visit a retail establishment; 35 percent of Hispanics versus 25 percent of non-Hispanics are likely to attend movies based on their online campaigns. Sixty percent of Hispanics polled, versus 42 percent of non-Hispanics, said they like things like iPad demonstrations, virtual shoppers, mobile coupons, and live streaming. The study also noted that Hispanics are more receptive to updates for offline activities via mobile text alerts, Twitter feeds, and Facebook. They are also more likely to visit a brand's fan page and to follow Twitter updates from artists.[82]

always look for a brand name when they shop. Yet, interestingly, they are also the least brand loyal. Fully a quarter of Asians say they change brands often, compared with 22 percent of Hispanics, 20 percent of African Americans, and 17 percent of whites. Asian consumers are also the most concerned about keeping up appearances. More than a quarter (26 percent) say they buy what they think their neighbors will approve of, compared with 12 percent each of Hispanics and African Americans and only 10 percent of whites. As one Asian American advertising executive noted, "Prosperous Asians tend to be very status-conscious and will spend their money on premium brands, such as BMW and Mercedes-Benz, and the best French cognac and Scotch whiskey."[92]

OBJECTIVE 4

Marketers increasingly use religious and spiritual themes to talk to consumers.

Religious Subcultures

In recent years we've seen an explosion of religion and spirituality in popular culture, including the box office success of Mel Gibson's movie *The Passion of the Christ*, the book *The Da Vinci Code,* and even the Broadway hit *The Book of Mormon*.[93] Mainstream marketers that used to avoid religion like the plague (pardon the pun) now actively court church members.

You don't have to be active in an organized religion to "worship" products. A study of a brand community centered on the Apple Newton illustrates how religious themes spill over into everyday consumption, particularly in the case of "cult products." Apple abandoned the Newton PDA years ago, but many avid users still keep the faith. The researchers examined postings in chat rooms devoted to the product. They found that many of the messages have supernatural, religious, and magical themes, including the miraculous performance and survival of the brand, as well as the return of the brand creator. The most common postings concerned instances in which dead Newton batteries magically come back to life. Here is an excerpt from one story, posted on a listserv under the heading "Another Battery Miracle":

> The battery that came with the 2100 that I just received seemed dead. . . . I figured that the battery was fried and I have nothing to lose. While "charging," I unplugged the adapter until the indicator said it was running on batteries again, and then plugged it back in until it said "charging" . . . after a few times, the battery charge indicator started moving from the left to right and was full within 10 minutes! . . . I've been using the Newt for about 4 hours straight without any problems. Strange. It looks like there has been yet another Newton battery miracle! Keep the faith.[94]

In addition to organized religion, numerous other types of groups serve similar functions for consumers—and indeed, they may be loosely based on religious principles (like the highly successful 12-step program that guides Alcoholics Anonymous and other addiction support groups). Weight Watchers, the world's largest support group for weight loss, similarly follows a **spiritual-therapeutic model** even though it is a profitable business.[95]

In fact, one study found that for some people, a brand logo serves the same function that a religious symbol like a crucifix or a Star of David does for others. For people who aren't deeply religious, visible markers of commercial brands are a form of self-expression and a token of self-worth, just like symbolic expressions of one's faith. In a field study, the researchers analyzed several geographic areas in terms of the number of Apple stores per million people, and the number of brand stores such as Macy's and Gap, and they developed a comparison statistic they called the "brand-discount store ratio." They then compared these rough measures of brand reliance against the number of congregations per thousand and self-reported attendance in church or synagogue, controlling for income, education, and urbanization differences. In every region, they found a negative relationship between brand reliance and religiosity; that is, areas with a lot of branding activity also tended to have lower participation in organized religion.

The team then conducted a series of laboratory experiments to determine if brands might somehow substitute for these religious experiences, using the kind of primes we discussed in Chapter 2 where people are first prompted to think about a topic before they engage in an activity. In one study, a group of college students was primed by being asked to write a short essay on "what your religion means to you personally," while a control group wrote about how they spend their days. Each group was then sent on an imaginary shopping trip in which they chose between products shown two at a time, national brand versus store brand. Some of the products were forms of self-expression, such as sunglasses, watches, and socks. Other products were functional items like bread, batteries, and ibuprofen. The group that had been primed to think about religion was less likely to choose branded products for the purpose of self-expression. Another online study found similar results when participants who were high on self-reported measures of religiosity were compared to those who scored low.[96]

Organized Religion and Consumption

Marketers have not studied organized religion extensively, possibly because many view it as a taboo subject.[97] As one research director noted, "Religion, along with sex and politics, is one of the three taboo topics that we're never supposed to talk about."[98]

Religious sensibilities vary around the world, and big trouble can result if marketers violate taboo subjects in other cultures. Here are some examples:[99]

- Winning entries in the Doritos/Pepsi MAX "Crash the Super Bowl" challenge get broadcast as ads during the Super Bowl. One entry in the 2011 contest caused a lot of controversy: "Feed the Flock" showed a "pastor" succeeding in bringing in new church parishioners by serving Doritos and Pepsi MAX from the altar—a scenario that some Catholics interpreted as mocking the religion's sacrament of Holy Eucharist (formerly Holy Communion). A petition appeal went out to Catholic organizations urging PepsiCo not to approve the entry, which was described as a "horrific blasphemy." The entry wasn't chosen as a finalist and PepsiCo removed it from the gallery of thousands of entries that were posted on the contest's Web site. However, the creators of the video posted it on YouTube, where it generated well over 100,000 views.
- A Lipton ad won the prestigious Gold Lion award in Cannes, but the company had to decline the honor in the face of objections. The ad mocked the Catholic Church as it showed a man standing in the communion line with a bowl of onion dip in his hand.
- In Salt Lake City, a proposed billboard for Polygamy Porter beer aroused the ire of Mormons worldwide. The billboard company under contract with the brewery refused to erect the ad. The board, which was going to show a picture of a scantily clad man, cherubs, and a six-pack of spouses, advises drinkers to "take some home for the wives."
- An ad for Levi's jeans produced in London shows a young man who buys condoms from a pharmacist and then hides them in the small side pocket of his jeans. When he goes to pick up his date, he discovers that her father is the same pharmacist. The commercial was a hit in the United Kingdom, but people in strongly Catholic Italy and Spain didn't appreciate it at all.
- The French car manufacturer Renault withdrew an ad in a Danish campaign in response to protests from the local Catholic community. It depicted a dialogue during confession between a Catholic priest and a repenting man. The man atones for his sins as he prays *Ave Marias* until he confesses to having scratched the paint of the priest's new Renault—then the priest shouts "heathen" and orders the man to pay a substantial penalty to the church.

Born-Again Consumers

Mainstream churches are marketing themselves aggressively these days. In the United States, there are approximately 400 **megachurches**; each serves 2,000 or more congregants per week (some actually attract more than 20,000 to Sunday services!) and boast a

Marketing Opportunity

Despite the occasional blunder, it's clear that religious dietary or dress requirements do create demand for certain products. For example, less than a third of the 6 million consumers who buy the 86,000 kosher products now on the market are Jewish. Seventh-Day Adventists and Muslims have very similar dietary requirements, and other people simply believe that kosher food is of higher quality. Indeed only 15 percent of people who buy kosher do it for religious reasons. That's why some of the nation's largest manufacturers, like Pepperidge Farm, offer a wide range of kosher options.[100]

Not of This World specializes in Christian-themed apparel and accessories.
Source: Courtesy of NOTW.

Marketing Opportunity

Christian bookstores bring in revenues of well over $2 billion per year, and the proliferation of Born Agains (especially younger evangelicals) propels religiously oriented products into more mainstream stores as vendors update their messages for a younger generation (one T-shirt for sale shows a hand with a nail through it along with the caption, "Body Piercing Saved My Life"). C28, a chain of California stores, takes its name from the Bible verse Colossians 2:8, "See to it that no one takes you captive through hollow and deceptive philosophy, which depends on human tradition and the basic principles of this world rather than on Christ." C28 has its own house brand, Not of This World, that features modern designs coupled with biblical verses. The owner claims that hundreds of people have converted to born-again Christianity in his stores: "Our mission is to share the grace, the truth and the love of Jesus. And what better place to do it than a mall?"[105]

combined annual income of $1.85 billion.[101] As a church marketing consultant observes, "Baby boomers think of churches like they think of supermarkets. They want options, choices, and convenience. Imagine if Safeway was open only one hour a week, had only one product, and didn't explain it in English."[102] Clearly, religion is big business.

In the United States, we trace most religious marketing activity to "born-again" Christians, who follow literal interpretations of the Bible and acknowledge being born again through belief in Jesus. Theirs is among the fastest-growing religious affiliations in the United States. One research company reported that about 72 million of the 235 million Christians in the United States say they are born again.[103]

The strength of the evangelical movement has caught the attention of many marketers who want to reach these consumers; marketers involved in faith-based marketing strategies include Pfizer, Merck, Tyson, Smucker's, several major automakers, and even the Curves fitness chain. Suzuki sponsored the Christian rock band Kutless on its national tour to promote its motorcycle and SUV lines.[104]

Islamic Marketing

Muslims will be more than one-quarter of the Earth's population by 2030, and during that same time period analysts expect the number of U.S. Muslims to more than double. If immigration patterns and Muslims' comparatively higher birth rates continue, experts predict that their numbers in the United States will climb from 2.6 million people to 6.2 million. In several European countries, it's predicted that Muslim populations will exceed 10 percent of the country's total population.[106] That's a consumer market to take seriously.

Nike committed a legendary error when it released a pair of athletic shoes in 1996 with a logo on the sole that some Muslims believed resembled the Arabic lettering for Allah. Muslims consider the feet unclean, and the company had to recall 800,000 pairs of the shoes globally. Today, some companies listen more closely to the needs of this religious subculture. For example, a Malaysian commercial for Sunsilk's Lively Clean

& Fresh shampoo depicts a young, smiling woman—but there is not a strand of hair in sight. Her head is completely covered by a *tudung*, the head scarf worn by many Muslim women in that country. Sunsilk's pitch is that it helps remove excess oil from the scalp and hair, a common problem among wearers of *tudungs*.

Mindful of the success of kosher certification, some Muslims recognize that **halal** foods (permissible under the laws of Islam) also may appeal to mainstream consumers. The Islamic Food and Nutrition Council of America certifies halal products with a "crescent M," much like the circled "O" of the Orthodox Union, the largest kosher certifier. Both kosher and halal followers forbid pork, and both require similar rituals for butchering meat. Religious Jews don't mix milk and meat, nor do they eat shellfish, whereas religious Muslims don't drink alcohol. Neither group eats birds of prey or blood.[107]

Halal as a descriptor is being used for more and more commodities, services, and activities, including milk, water, nonprescription medicine, holidays, washing powder, tissues, cosmetics, Web sites, and music. Many major companies are taking steps to reassure consumers that all of their products—not just food—are *halal* by having them officially certified.

- Colgate-Palmolive claims to be the first international company to have obtained *halal* certification in Malaysia for toothpaste and mouthwash products. Some mouthwashes may contain alcohol, which would be forbidden under *halal* guidelines. Colgate's products now bear the *halal* logo, which also is featured in the company's television commercials.
- Nokia introduced a phone for the Middle East and North Africa markets that came loaded with an Islamic Organizer including alarms for the five daily prayers, two Islamic e-books, and an e-card application that lets people send SMS greeting cards for Ramadan.
- Ogilvy & Mather established a new arm, Ogilvy Noor (Noor means "light" in Arabic), which the ad agency describes as "the world's first bespoke Islamic branding practice." Ogilvy also introduced the Noor index, which rates the appeal of brands to Muslim consumers. The index was formulated on the basis of how consumers ranked more than 30 well-known brands for compliance with *Shariah*, or Islamic law. Lipton tea, owned by Unilever, topped the list, followed by Nestlé. Ogilvy's research shows that young Muslim consumers are different from their Western counterparts; they believe that by staying true to the core values of their religion, they are more likely to achieve success in the modern world.[108]

Age Subcultures

OBJECTIVE 5
We have many things in common with others because they are about the same age.

The era in which you grow up bonds you with the millions of others who come of age during the same time period. Obviously, your needs and preferences change as you grow older—often in concert with others of your own age (even though some of us don't really believe we'll ever get older). For this reason, our age is a big part of our identity. All things equal, we are more likely to have things in common with others of our own age than with those younger or older. These similarities can create opportunities for marketers (just ask any social media executive) or they can raise red flags: younger consumers, for example, don't drink nearly as much coffee on a daily basis as do older people.[109]

An **age cohort** consists of people of similar ages who have similar experiences. They share many common memories about cultural icons (e.g., John Wayne versus Brad Pitt), important historical events (e.g., the Great Depression versus the Great Recession), and so on. Although there is no universally accepted way to sort people into age cohorts, each of us seems to have a pretty good idea what we mean when we refer to "my generation." Marketers often target products and services to a specific age cohort; our possessions help us identify with others of a certain age and express the priorities and needs we encounter at each life stage.[110]

Marketing Pitfall

Toys are fun to play with, but often a hidden agenda is that they're also socialization agents that teach kids about life. Sometimes, perhaps, they can be a bit *too* realistic. Some critics objected to a new doll called Baby Alive Learns to Potty. She comes with a pink plastic toilet. When a child presses the doll's bracelet, she chirps, "Sniff sniff. I made a stinky!" The doll also comes with "green beans" and "bananas" that the child feeds to the doll—then they come out the other end. Put Baby Alive on her toilet and a magnet triggers a change in the bowl: The "water" is replaced with "potty waste," which the child can flush (with appropriate sound effects). Critics charge that some things are better left to the land of make-believe. Indeed, most child psychologists agree that the best toys encourage children to use their imaginations.[118]

Although there is general consensus when analysts describe age cohorts, the labels and cutoff dates they use to put consumers into generational categories are subjective. One rough approximation looks like this:[111]

- **The Interbellum Generation**—People born at the beginning of the 20th century.
- **The Silent Generation**—People born between the two World Wars.
- **The War Baby Generation**—People born during World War II.
- **The Baby Boom Generation**—People born between 1946 and 1964.
- **Generation X**—People born between 1965 and 1985.
- **Generation Y**—People born between 1986 and 2002.
- **Generation Z**—People born 2003 and later.

The same offering probably won't appeal to people of different ages, nor will the language and images marketers use to reach them. In some cases, companies develop separate campaigns for age cohorts. For example, Norelco found that younger men are far less likely to use electric shavers than are its core customer base of older men. The firm launched a two-pronged effort, on the one hand, to convince younger men to switch from wet shaving to electric, and, on the other hand, to maintain loyalty among its older following. Ads for Norelco's Speedrazor, aimed at males 18 to 35 years old, ran on late-night TV and in *GQ* and *Details*. Messages about the company's triple-head razors, geared to men older than 35, ran instead in publications that attract older readers, such as *Time* and *Newsweek*.

Children as Decision-Makers: Consumers-in-Training

It's no secret that people spend a lot on their kids (just ask any grandparent). The massive market for items from diapers to Disney World excursions certainly gets the attention of many companies. In fact, Disney even works hard to reach parents and *really* young kids—that is, so young they're not yet born. Disney estimates the North American baby market, including staples like formula, to be worth $36.3 billion annually. A representative of the Disney Baby program that operates in 580 maternity hospitals in the United States visits a new mother and offers a free Disney Cuddly Bodysuit, a variation of the classic Onesie. The rep provides bedside demonstrations and asks mothers to sign up for email alerts from DisneyBaby.com. As one company executive observes, "To get that mom thinking about her family's first park experience before her baby is even born is a home run."[112]

Anyone who has had the "delightful" experience of grocery shopping with children in tow knows that kids often have a say (sometimes a loud, whiny one) in what their parents buy. Children make up three distinct markets:[113]

1 **Primary market**—Kids spend a lot on their own wants and needs, which include toys, apparel, movies, and games. When marketers at M&Ms candy figured out who actually buys a lot of their products, they redesigned vending machines with coin slots lower to the ground to accommodate shorter people, and sales rose dramatically.[114]

2 **Influence market**—**Parental yielding** occurs when a parental decision-maker "surrenders" to a child's request.[115] Yielding drives many product selections because about 90 percent of these requests are for a specific brand. Researchers estimate that children directly influence about $453 billion worth of family purchases in a year. They report that on average children weigh in with a purchase request every 2 minutes when they shop with parents.[116] In recognition of this influence, Mrs. Butterworth's Syrup created a $6 million campaign to target kids directly with humorous ads that show the lengths to which adults will go to get the syrup bottle to talk to them. An executive who worked on the campaign explained, "We needed to create the *nag factor* [where kids demand that their parents buy the product]."[117]

3 **Future market**—Kids have a way of growing up to be adults, so savvy marketers try to lock in brand loyalty at an early age. As they struggle to convince us to buy new cars, carmakers also take time out to woo some people who are still too young to drive. Many advertise in child-oriented areas such as gyms that cater to kids, social networking sites that young people visit frequently, and the Saturday morning

cartoons. In Whyville.net, a virtual world where nearly 2 million children aged 8 to 15 hang out, kids can buy virtual Scion xBs if they have enough "clams" (Whyville's monetary unit). If not, they can meet with Eric, a virtual Toyota Financial Services advisor, to finance an xB replica they can use to tool around while in-world. Small wonder: A study Nickelodeon conducted reported that almost two-thirds of parents now say their children "actively participate" in car-buying decisions.[119]

OBJECTIVE 6

Teens are an important age segment for marketers.

The Youth Market

In 1956, the label *teenage* entered the general American vocabulary when Frankie Lymon and the Teenagers became the first pop group to identify themselves with this new subculture. Believe it or not, the concept of a teenager is a fairly new idea. Throughout most of history a person simply made the transition from child to adult, and many cultures marked this abrupt change in status with some sort of ritual or ceremony, as we discussed in Chapter 3.

Marketing Pitfall

Do marketers try to turn girls into women before they should? Adult products and practices increasingly trickle down to the younger set. Analysts estimate that girls 11 to 14 see about 500 advertisements a day. We read about elementary school students who spend the afternoon at the beauty salon and even 5-year-olds who have spa days and pedicure parties. In 2005, the NPD group reported that the average age at which women began to use beauty products was 17. By 2009, that average had dropped to 13. Another study by Experian found that 43 percent of 6- to 9-year-olds use lipstick or lip gloss, and 38 percent use hairstyling products. In addition to adult shows like *Extreme Makeover*, youngsters learn about makeup from the girls of *Toddlers & Tiaras* and *Little Miss Perfect*.[120]

Now, even feminine hygiene products target young girls. A Kotex Web site designed for mothers asks, "Some girls get their period as young as 8. Have you had the talk?" The company designed a pad specifically for 8- to 12-year-olds that is shorter and narrower than other Kotex pads; it's sold in glittery boxes decorated with hearts, stars, and swirls (which are also printed on the pads themselves). Kotex reports research showing that one out of three girls has no idea what is happening when her first period arrives, while four out of five mothers feel ill-prepared to educate their daughters about menstruation.[121]

Figure 10.1 THE U.S. TEEN POPULATION

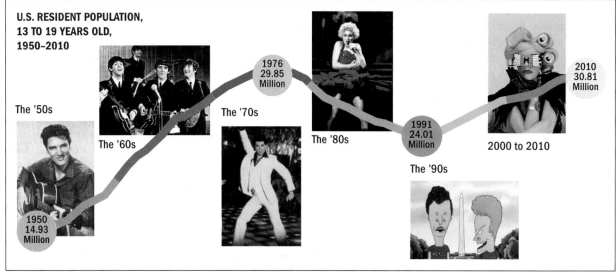

The magazine *Seventeen* was first published in 1944; its founders realized that modern young women didn't want to be little clones of Mom. Following World War II, the teenage conflict between rebellion and conformity began to unfold as teen culture pitted Elvis Presley, with his slicked hair and suggestive pelvis swivels, against the wholesome Pat Boone, with his white bucks and whiter teeth (see Figure 10.1). Today, this rebellion continues to play out as pubescent consumers forsake their Barbies for the likes of Paris Hilton, Lindsay Lohan (when they're not in jail or rehab), Justin Bieber, or the teen heart-throb *du jour*.[122]

The global youth market is massive. It represents about $100 billion in spending power! Much of this money goes toward "feel-good" products: cosmetics, posters, and fast food—with the occasional nose ring thrown in. Because teens are interested in so many different products and have the resources to obtain them, many marketers avidly court them.

As anyone who has been there knows, puberty and adolescence are both the best of times and the worst of times. Many exciting changes happen as we leave the role of child and prepare to assume the role of adult. These transitions create a lot of uncertainty about the self, and the need to belong and to find one's unique identity as a person becomes

Redken, a hairstyling products brand that is owned by L'Oréal and sold only in salons created Busy Scissors, a hairstyling and simulation game for the Nintendo Wii and DS that targets girls ages 8 to 16. Busy Scissors is a role-playing game that allows players to pretend they own a Hollywood salon and cater to what Redken calls "a glamorous and eccentric clientele." Players earn points for giving customers a good hair day (with a choice of 25 styles), by executing proper techniques for cutting, coloring and even shampooing.

Source: Courtesy of Busy Bizzy, LLC.

pressing. At this age, our choices of activities, friends, and clothes are crucial. Teens constantly search for cues for the "right" way to look and behave from their peers and from advertising. Advertising to teens is typically action-oriented and depicts a group of "in" teens who use the product.

Consumers in this age subculture have a number of needs (including some that conflict with one another) such as experimentation, belonging, independence, responsibility, and approval from others. Product usage is a significant medium that lets them satisfy these needs. For example, many kids view smoking cigarettes as a status activity because of the numerous movies they've seen that glorify this practice. In one study, ninth graders watched original movie footage with either smoking scenes or control footage with the smoking edited out. Sure enough, when the young viewers saw the actors smoking, this enhanced their perceptions of smokers' social stature and increased their own intent to smoke. (The good news: When kids see an antismoking advertisement before the film, these effects cancel out.)[123]

Teenagers in every culture grapple with fundamental developmental issues when they transition from childhood to adult. Throughout history young people have coped with insecurity, parental authority, and peer pressure (although each generation has trouble believing it's not the first!). According to Teenage Research Unlimited, the five most important social issues for teens are AIDS, race relations, child abuse, abortion, and the environment. Today's teens often have to cope with additional family responsibilities as well, especially if they live in nontraditional families where they have significant responsibility for shopping, cooking, and housework. It's hard work being a teen in the modern world. The Saatchi & Saatchi advertising agency identified four basic conflicts common to all teens:

- **Autonomy versus belonging**—Teens need to acquire independence, so they try to break away from their families. However, they need to attach themselves to a support structure, such as peers, to avoid being alone.
- **Rebellion versus conformity**—Teens need to rebel against social standards of appearance and behavior, yet they still need to fit in and be accepted by others. They prize "in-your-face" products that cultivate a rebellious image, such as those the retail chain Hot Topic sells, for this reason.
- **Idealism versus pragmatism**—Teens tend to view adults as hypocrites, whereas they see themselves as being sincere. They have to struggle to reconcile their view of how the world should be with the realities they perceive around them.
- **Narcissism versus intimacy**—Teens tend to obsess about their appearance and needs. However, they also feel the desire to connect with others on a meaningful level.[124]

These needs often collide, sometimes in unpleasant ways (there's nothing more venomous than a teenager who's having a bad hair day!). One researcher explored the role of *ridicule* as a mechanism through which adolescents exchange information about consumption norms and values. He found that—often beginning in middle school—adolescents use ridicule to ostracize, haze, or admonish peers who violate consumption norms. One result of this painful process is that kids internalize their peers' stereotypes about aspirational and avoidance groups (remember Chapter 9) and often significantly alter their consumption patterns to try to align themselves with the former and distance themselves from the latter. For example, one of the kids in the study quickly exchanged a pair of white sneakers for more stylish black ones after his peers ridiculed him.[125]

Gen Y

A brand overhaul by Pepsi that included its new smiley-face logo had the so-called **Gen Y** age segment squarely in its sights. Young people have always been Pepsi's lifeblood, starting with its tagline "You're in the Pepsi Generation" that over time evolved into "Generation Next" and "The Choice of a New Generation." But that blood has drained or thinned a bit over the past few years, as young people gravitate toward energy drinks and fortified waters. The company's research showed that this age group—which also goes by the labels **Millennials** and **Echo Boomers**—are hopeful about the future; almost all of them agree that it's important to maintain a positive outlook on life. Pepsi also found that 95 percent of Millennials have positive associations with the word *change* and that they link the word to others like *new, progress, hope*, and *excitement*.[126]

Gen Yers were born between 1984 and 2002. They already make up nearly one-third of the U.S. population, and they spend $170 billion a year of their own and their parents' money. They love brands like Sony, Patagonia, Gap, Aveda, and Apple. Echo Boomers are a reflection of the sweeping changes in American life during the past 20 years. They are also the most diverse generation ever: Thirty-five percent are nonwhite, and, as we saw in Chapter 9, they often grow up in nontraditional families: Today, one in four 21-year-olds was raised by a single parent, and three out of four have a working mother.

Members of Gen Y are "jugglers" who value being both footloose and connected to their "peeps" 24/7. The advertising agency Saatchi & Saatchi labels this new kind of lifestyle **connexity**. To help Millennials feel connected with one another, companies

Couples want their nuptials to reflect their particular story, and brands are adapting marketing campaigns to account for a new set of tastes and needs. Instead of traditional must-haves like engraved invitations or sit-down dinners, the Millennials—people generally in their 20s—seek touches that showcase their interests and personal style.

Source: Gottlieb & Sons.

Every Romance Has A Story. Wear Yours.

I was in London for business and he made plans to meet me in Paris. We'd been dating four years, but we'd never taken a real vacation together. The first three days were perfect. Then I sprained my ankle. Two bottles of red at dinner didn't mix. I had no idea he was planning to pop the question. He was so nervous and I was...well, extremely relaxed. He had to ask me again the next morning! We'll always have Paris. We're going back for our three-year anniversary this fall.

GOTTLIEB & SONS
ESTABLISHED 1949

Designed by Gottlieb & Sons, available at:

Jason Michael JEWELRY

including Apple and Philips developed miniature devices such as the iPod and MP3 key ring that store music and images for kids on the run—and they plug directly into a USB port for up- and downloading. When Toyota developed its youth-oriented Scion model, researchers learned that Echo Boomers practically live in their cars; for example, one-quarter of Gen Yers keep a full change of clothes in their vehicles. So Toyota's designers made the Scion resemble a home on wheels, with fully reclining front seats so drivers can nap between classes and a 15-volt outlet so they can plug in their computers.[127]

Unlike their parents or older siblings, Gen Yers tend to hold relatively traditional values and they prefer to fit in rather than rebel. Their acculturation agents (like those we discussed earlier in this chapter) stress teamwork—team teaching, team grading, collaborative sports, community service, service learning, and student juries. Violent crime among teenagers is down 60 to 70 percent. The use of tobacco and alcohol is at an all-time low, as is teen pregnancy. Five out of ten Echo Boomers say they trust the government, and virtually all of them trust Mom and Dad.[128]

We've already discussed the overwhelming importance of the online world in the lives of consumers, especially young ones. Millennials are the first generation to grow up with computers at home, in a 500-channel TV universe. They are *multitaskers* who easily engage their cell phones, music downloads, and IMs at the same time. They are totally at home in a *thumb culture* that communicates online and by cell phone (more likely via text and IM than by voice).

One pair of researchers took an in-depth look at how 13- and 14-year-olds integrate the computer into their lives, and how they use it to express their *cyberidentities.* These tweens have limited mobility in RL (too young to drive), so they use the computer to transport themselves to other places and modes of being. The researchers explored the metaphors these kids use when they think about their computers. For some, the PC is a "fraternity house" where they can socialize; it also can be a "carnival" where they play games and an "external brain" that helps with homework.[129]

Because modern teens were raised on TV and tend to be more "savvy" than older generations, marketers must tread lightly when they talk to this group. If the message is going to work, they have to see it as authentic and not condescending. As one researcher observed, "They have a B.S. alarm that goes off quick and fast. . . . They walk in and usually make up their minds very quickly about whether it's phat or not phat, and whether they want it or don't want it. They know a lot of advertising is based on lies and hype."[130]

So what are the rules of engagement for young consumers?[131]

- **Rule 1: Don't talk down**—Younger consumers want to draw their own conclusions about products. In the words of one teen: "I don't like it when someone tells me what to do. Those drugs and sex commercials preach. What do they know? Also, I don't like it when they show a big party and say come on and fit in with this product. That's not how it works."
- **Rule 2: Don't try to be what you're not. Stay true to your brand image**—Kids value straight talk. Firms that back up what they say impress them. Procter & Gamble appealed to this value with a money-back guarantee on its Old Spice High Endurance deodorant with an invitation to phone 1-800-PROVEIT.
- **Rule 3: Entertain them. Make it interactive and keep the sell short**—Gen Yers like to find brands in unexpected places. The prospect of catching appealing ads is part of the reason they're watching that TV show in the first place. If they want to learn more, they'll check out your Web site.
- **Rule 4: Show that you know what they're going through, but keep it light**—A commercial for Hershey's Ice Breakers mints subtly points out its benefit when it highlights the stress a guy feels as he psyches himself up to approach a strange girl at a club. "I'm wearing my lucky boxers," he reassures himself. "Don't trip. Don't drool. Relax. How's my breath?"
- **Rule 5: Show that you're authentic and that you give back**—Millennials are inspired by organizations that link to a compelling cause or mission. It's important for them to trust the company. "Deeds work, empty promises don't": In one survey, only 2 percent said celebrity endorsements or pleas motivated them to donate to a cause.[132]

Tweens

The most popular TV network for young adolescents is The Disney Channel, which offers shows like *Phineas* and *Ferb* that these kids love.[133] Disney understands the buying power of **tweens**, the 27 million children aged 8 to 14 who spend $14 billion a year on clothes, CDs, movies, and other "feel-good" products. Tweens are "between" childhood and adolescence, and they exhibit characteristics of both age groups. As one tween commented, "When we're alone we get weird and crazy and still act like kids. But in public we act cool, like teenagers."[134]

A marketing campaign by Victoria's Secret illustrates the fine line marketers must walk when they deal with consumers who are not children but not yet adults, or even full-fledged teens. When the retail chain developed Pink, a lingerie line for younger girls, it wanted to avoid the heat that Abercrombie & Fitch attracted when it sold child-size thong underwear. The company recruited about two dozen (female) students at colleges such as Ohio State, UCLA, and Penn State as brand ambassadors. These older girls became role models for the tween set. Members of Team Pink hand out free gift flyers, give away tickets to special screenings of popular TV shows, and orchestrate stunts such as hiding a thousand pink stuffed animals around campus. "All they are really asking me to do is support another cause," one ambassador explained to her school newspaper, "and the cause happens to be underwear instead of the homeless, child poverty or hunger."[135] Wow.

Big (Wo)Man on Campus

Advertisers spend approximately $100 million a year on campuses to woo college students, and with good reason: Overall, students spend more than $11 billion a year on snacks and beverages, $4 billion on personal care products, and $3 billion on CDs and tapes. Seventy percent of them own a laptop. Many students have plenty of extra cash and free time (not you, of course . . .): On an average day the average student spends 1.7 hours in class and another 1.6 hours studying. This "average" student (or are all students above average?) has about $287 to spend on discretionary items per month. As one marketing executive observed, "This is the time of life where they're willing to try new products. . . . This is the time to get them in your franchise." The college market is also attractive to many companies because these novice consumers are away from home for the first time, so they have yet to form unshakeable brand loyalty in some product categories such as cleaning supplies (bummer!).[136]

Some marketers attend "Trend School" to get up to speed on the best ways to talk to young people.

Source: The Intelligence Group.

ABOUT   PRIVATE TREND SCHOOLS

A DAY OF DISCOVERY

TREND SCHOOL IS IMMERSIVE, INTIMATE, AND INTERACTIVE...AND IT WILL TRANSFORM YOU.

Thousands of executives have gained the awareness and vision necessary to connect with young consumers by attending Trend School. Part grad class, part mini-conference, part networking event, Trend School takes you beyond what's happening with young consumers by delving into why they do what they do. Comprehensive Cassandra Report presentations. Pervasive macro trends. Amazing guest speakers. Product samples. Taste tests. Tech demos. Ideation exercises. Cool music. Hot videos. Gen Y consumer panels. It's all there, in one intense day.

Nevertheless, college students pose a special challenge for marketers because they are hard to reach via conventional media such as newspapers. Of course, online advertising is very effective: Ninety-nine percent of college students go online at least a few times per week, and 90 percent do so daily. Web sites such as mtvU.com and collegehumor .com blossom because they reach students where they live and play.[137] To acknowledge the power of this market, Nielsen Media Research now includes college students who live away from home in its television ratings. Nielsen reports that students watch an average of 24.3 hours of television a week.[138]

Gen X

The **Gen X** age subculture consists of 46 million Americans. This group got the label following publication of the best-selling novel *Generation X: Tales for an Accelerated Culture* by Douglas Coupland. Some called them "slackers" or "baby busters" because of their supposed alienation and laziness, and these stereotypes live on in movies such as *Clueless* and in music groups such as Marilyn Manson.[140]

Advertisers fell all over themselves to create messages that would not turn off the worldly Generation X cohort. Many of them referenced old TV shows such as *Gilligan's Island* or showed commercials that featured disheveled actors in turned-around baseball caps who tried their best to appear blasé. This approach actually turned off a lot of Busters, because it implied that they had nothing else to do but sit around and watch old television reruns. Subaru sponsored one of the first commercials of this genre. It showed a sloppily dressed young man who described the Impreza model as "like punk rock" as he denounced the competition as "boring and corporate." The commercial did not play well with its intended audience, and Subaru eventually switched advertising agencies.

Today, Gen Xers have grown up, and in fact members of this generation are responsible for many culture-changing products and companies such as Google, YouTube, and Amazon. A recent book that laments the bad rap Gen X has gotten sums it up: *X Saves the World: How Generation X Got the Shaft But Can Still Keep Everything from Sucking.*[141]

The Mature Market

Restylane is the top-selling dermal injection to reduce the appearance of wrinkles. The company decided to pitch it directly to consumers for the first time, so in keeping with new media trends it launched a multipronged campaign that recognizes the technical prowess of many middle-aged people. A conventional TV spot features before-and-after results along with women who talk about how frequently men check them out after the treatment. But a second component is a video skit on YouTube that supposedly takes place during a woman's 50th birthday party. While her son works on a video birthday card, Mom gets caught smooching with a younger man on a couch. Viewers don't know the skit is an ad until the last 15 seconds. A third prong is a contest to name the "Hottest Mom in America": Contestants submit videos to a Web site and the winner gets cash, free treatments for a year, and an interview with a modeling agency.[142] Today's Mom isn't exactly June Cleaver. Let's take a closer look at the changing face of mature consumers—some of them aren't as mature as they used to be.

OBJECTIVE 7

Baby Boomers are the most economically powerful age segment.

Baby Boomers

The **Baby Boomer** age subculture consists of people whose parents established families following the end of World War II and during the 1950s when the peacetime economy was strong and stable. As a general rule, when people feel confident about how things are going in the world, they are more

Marketing Opportunity

Research firms that specialize in the youth market have to be innovative because many Millennials don't respond well to traditional survey techniques. Pizza Hut invites teens into its boardroom to eat lunch with company executives and share their opinions about the perfect pie. Some research companies give teens video cameras and ask them to record a "typical" day at school—along with play-by-play commentary to help interpret what's going on. Other marketers pay $2,500 a head to spend a day at Trend School, a monthly one-day forum in New York and Los Angeles. The "students" hang out with über-cool kids to learn about the latest tech, music, and fashion trends.[139]

This 1962 Pepsi ad highlights the emphasis on youth power that began to shape our culture as Baby Boomers came of age in the 1960s.

Source: Courtesy of PepsiCo.

now it's Pepsi–for those who think young

Thinking young is a wholesome attitude, an enthusiastic outlook. It means getting the most out of life, and everyone can join in. This is the life for Pepsi –light, bracing, clean-tasting Pepsi. Think young. Say "Pepsi, please!"

ENJOY THE STEVE ALLEN SHOW PRESENTED BY PEPSI WEEKLY ON ABC-TV

likely to decide to have children, so this was a "boom" time for delivery rooms. As teenagers in the 1960s and 1970s, the "Woodstock generation" created a revolution in style, politics, and consumer attitudes. As they aged, they fueled cultural events as diverse as the Free Speech movement and hippies in the 1960s to Reaganomics and yuppies in the 1980s. Now that they are older, they continue to influence popular culture.

As the Restylane campaign demonstrates, this generation is much more active and physically fit than its predecessors; Baby Boomers are 6 percent more likely than the national average to engage in some kind of sports activity.[143] In addition. Baby Boomers are now in their peak earning years. As one commercial for VH1, the music video network that caters to those who are a bit too old for MTV, pointed out, "The generation that dropped acid to escape reality . . . is the generation that drops antacid to cope with it."

Consumers aged 35 to 44 spend the most on housing, cars, and entertainment. Baby Boomers are busy "feathering their nests": They account for roughly 40 percent of all the money consumers spend on household furnishings and equipment. In addition, consumers aged 45 to 54 spend the most of any age category on food (30 percent above average), apparel (38 percent above average), and retirement programs (57 percent above average).[144] A study found that the majority of Boomers want to be "surprised and delighted" by brands. Offerings that especially appeal to them include Swiffer for the home; Keurig for the palate; Amy's Kitchen for organic foods, Dove, and Trader Joe's.[145]

To appreciate the impact middle-aged consumers have and will have on our economy, consider this: At current spending levels, a 1 percent increase in the population

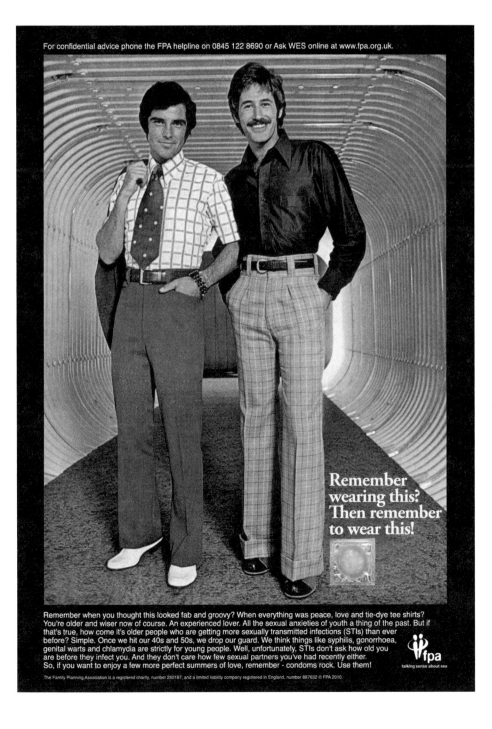

This British AIDS awareness message targets men over the age of 50.
Source: FPA.

of householders aged 35 to 54 results in an additional $8.9 billion in consumer spending. Ironically, however, most marketers neglect this incredibly important group: For example, although Boomers spend 38.5 percent of CPG (consumer packaged goods) dollars, Nielsen estimates that only 5 percent of advertising dollars are currently targeted toward adults 35 to 64 years old. Nielsen's research says that Boomers dominate 1,023 out of 1,083 CPG categories, and watch 9.34 hours of video per day—more than any other segment. They also constitute a third of all TV viewers, online users, social media users, and Twitter users, and are significantly more likely to have broadband Internet. As a Nielsen executive observed, "Marketers have this tendency to think the Baby Boom—getting closer to retirement—will just be calm and peaceful as they move ahead, and that's not true. Everything we see with our behavioral data says these people are going to be active consumers for much longer. They are going to be in better health, and despite the ugliness around the retirement stuff now, they are still going to be more affluent. They are going to be an important segment for a long time."[146]

| OBJECTIVE 8 | **The Senior Market** |

OBJECTIVE 8
Seniors are a more important market segment than many marketers realize.

The Senior Market

The old woman sits alone in her dark apartment while the television blares out a soap opera. Once every couple of days, her arthritic hands slowly and painfully open her triple-locked door as she ventures out to the corner store to buy essentials such as tea, milk, and cereal—of course she always picks the least expensive items. Most of the time she sits in her rocking chair and thinks sadly about her dead husband and the good times they used to have together.

Is this the image you have of a typical elderly consumer? Until recently, many marketers did. They neglected the elderly in their feverish pursuit of the youth market. But as our population ages and we live longer and healthier lives, the game is rapidly changing. A lot of businesses are updating their old stereotype of the poor recluse. The newer, more accurate image is of an active person who is interested in what life has to offer, who is an enthusiastic consumer with the means and willingness to buy many goods and services, and who maintains strong loyalty to favorite brands over the years. And this market grows even as we speak: An American turns 50 every 7 seconds.[147]

Think about this: The United Nations says that people older than 60 are the fastest-growing age group on Earth. There are 700 million of them now, and there will be 2 billion by midcentury. In the United States, by 2030, 20 percent of the population will be over the age of 65.[148] By 2100, there will be 5 million of us who are at least 100 years old.[149]

Few of us may be around then, but we can already see the effects of the **senior market** today. Older adults control more than 50 percent of discretionary income, and worldwide consumers over the age of 50 spend nearly $400 billion a year.[150] The mature market is the second-fastest-growing market segment in the United States, lagging only behind Boomers. We're living longer and healthier because of more wholesome lifestyles (at least some of us), improved medical diagnoses and treatment, and changing cultural expectations about appropriate behaviors for the elderly.

Larger numbers of older people lead more active, multidimensional lives than we assume. Nearly 60 percent engage in volunteer activities, one in four seniors aged 65 to 72 still works, and more than 14 million provide care for their grandchildren.[151] It is also crucial to remember that income alone does not express seniors' spending power. Older consumers are finished with many of the financial obligations that siphon off the income of younger consumers. Eighty percent of consumers older than age 65 own their own homes. In addition, child-rearing costs are over.

Dove soap challenges Western society's "young is beautiful" stereotype.

Source: Courtesy of Unilver.

☐ wrinkled?
☐ wonderful?

Will society ever accept
old can be beautiful?

As the popular bumper sticker proudly proclaims, "We're Spending Our Children's Inheritance!"

Given the economic clout of senior consumers, it's often surprising how many marketers ignore them in favor of younger buyers—even though seniors are among the most brand loyal of any group. Older consumers repurchase a brand more frequently, consider fewer brands and dealers, and choose long-established brands more often.[152] Still, most contemporary advertising campaigns don't recognize these buyers. Even though people over the age of 50 account for half of all the discretionary spending in the United States, watch more television, go to more movies, and buy more CDs than do the young, Americans over age 50 are the focus of less than 10 percent of the advertising![153]

Some of the important areas that stand to benefit from the surging gray market include exercise facilities, cruises and tourism, cosmetic surgery and skin treatments, and "how-to" books and university courses that offer enhanced learning opportunities. In many product categories, seniors spend their money at an even greater rate than other age groups: Householders aged 55 to 64 spend 15 percent more than average per capita. They shell out 56 percent more than the average consumer on women's

Echoing the saying, "You're only as old as you feel," this ad reminds us that a person's perceived age often does not correspond to his or her chronological age.

Source: Courtesy of Atena US Healthcare.

A ROCKING CHAIR IS A PIECE OF FURNITURE.
NOT A STATE OF MIND.

We know people whose lust for life has not and will not diminish because it's the morning after their 65th birthday. They're too busy putting the finishing touches on a book of poems. Tutoring underprivileged kids with their math. Learning the tango. Or taking acting classes. It's an outlook that works rather well with ours. Whether it's annuities, 401(k)s, IRAs, mutual funds or life insurance for your family, we've packaged a unique set of tools to help you realize your life's next great exploit. Which comes naturally when retirement isn't viewed as merely an end. But rather the way you've been living all along: passionately. For a free brochure, call 1-800-AETNA-60 or visit us at http://www.aetna.com.

Build for Retirement. Manage for Life.

Aetna
Retirement Services.

Marketing Opportunity

Research confirms the popular wisdom that age is more a state of mind than of body. A person's mental outlook and activity level have a lot more to do with longevity and quality of life than does *chronological age*, the actual number of years the person has actually been alive. That's why **perceived age**, or how old a person *feels*, is a better yardstick to use. Researchers measure perceived age on several dimensions, including "feel-age" (i.e., how old a person feels) and "look-age" (i.e., how old a person looks).[157] The older consumers get, the younger they feel relative to their actual age.

A recent study investigated what the authors call **consumer identity renaissance**; this refers to the redefinition process people undergo when they retire. The research identified two different types of identity renaissance: revived (revitalization of previous identities) or emergent (pursuit of entirely new life projects). Even though many retirees cope with losses (of professional identity, spouses, and so on), many of them focus on moving forward. They engage in a host of strategies to do this, including affiliation, where they reconnect with family members and friends (in many cases online), and *self-expression*. This latter strategy may involve revisiting an activity they never had time to adequately pursue when they were younger, learning new skills, or perhaps moving into an urban area to reengage with cultural activities.[158]

clothing, and as new grandparents they actually spring for more toys and playground equipment than people aged 25 to 44.[154] In fact, the average grandparent spends an average of about $500 per year on gifts for grandchildren—have you called yours today?[155]

Researchers point to a set of key values relevant to mature consumers. For marketing strategies to succeed, they should link to one or more of these factors:[156]

- **Autonomy**—Mature consumers want to lead active lives and be self-sufficient. The advertising strategy used for Depends, the undergarments for incontinent people made by Kimberly-Clark, centers on senior celebrities such as actress June Allyson, who plays golf and goes to parties without worrying about her condition.
- **Connectedness**—Mature consumers value the bonds they have with friends and family. Quaker Oats successfully tapped into this value with its ads that feature actor Wilford Brimley, who dispenses grandfatherly advice to the younger generation about eating right.

CB AS I SEE IT

Professor George Moschis, *Georgia State University*

Consumer behavior researchers typically study individuals at a given point in time or stage in life in isolation from events and circumstances they experience or anticipate at various stages in life. While researchers have recognized the importance of prior life experiences in shaping patterns of consumer behavior during later stages in life, they have had inadequate tools to investigate consumer behavior issues over the course of life. Consumer research over the life course has been predominantly cross-sectional; it focuses on the consumer behavior of different age groups, and is confined to describing the observed differences that exist across age categories of individuals. For the most part it does not address how and why changes in consumer behavior occur over the life span.

In recent decades, however, an increasing number of researchers in various disciplines have adopted the life course paradigm to study behavior. This perspective views behavior at any stage in life or given point in time as the product of one's actions or responses to earlier life conditions and the way the individual has adapted to social and environmental circumstances. The life course model suggests that changing life conditions in the form of life-event experiences create physical, social, and emotional demands and circumstances to which one must adapt. Development and change in patterns of thought and action may be viewed as an outcome of one's adaptation to various demands and circumstances, with adaptation entailing the change mechanisms or processes of socialization, stress and coping responses, and development/ growth or decline.

The life course approach can help researchers understand how experiences at earlier stages in life, including consumer choices, affect current patterns of consumer behavior. We can study consumer behaviors in relation to earlier life stages within historical and cultural contexts and examine the processes that link time and context to change. Specifically, this approach can be used to study issues related to stability, development, and changes in consumer behaviors in later life by considering their timing, duration, sequence, historical contexts, and conditions under which consumers develop or change their consumption patterns. Marketers must appeal to consumers at a given stage in life differently because their needs differ due to life events and circumstances they have experienced. Previous life experiences, such as becoming a widow or a retiree, affect people's mindsets, consumption needs, and the way they respond to various types of marketing offerings.

● **Altruism**—Mature consumers want to give something back to the world. Thrifty Car Rental found in a survey that more than 40 percent of older consumers would select a rental car company if it sponsors a program that gives van discounts to senior citizens' centers. Based on this research, the company launched its highly successful program, "Give a Friend a Lift."

OBJECTIVE 9

"Birds of a feather flock together."

Place-Based Subcultures

Geodemography refers to analytical techniques that combine data on consumer expenditures and other socioeconomic factors with geographic information about the areas in which people live, in order to identify consumers who share common consumption patterns. Researchers base this approach on the common assumption that "birds of a feather flock together"—people who have similar needs and tastes also tend to live near one another, so it should be possible to locate "pockets" of like-minded people whom marketers can reach more economically by direct mail and other methods. For example, a marketer who wants to reach white, single consumers who are college educated and tend to be fiscally conservative may find that it is more efficient to mail catalogs to zip codes 20770 (Greenbelt, MD) and 90277 (Redondo Beach, CA) than to adjoining areas in either Maryland or California, where there are fewer consumers who exhibit these characteristics.

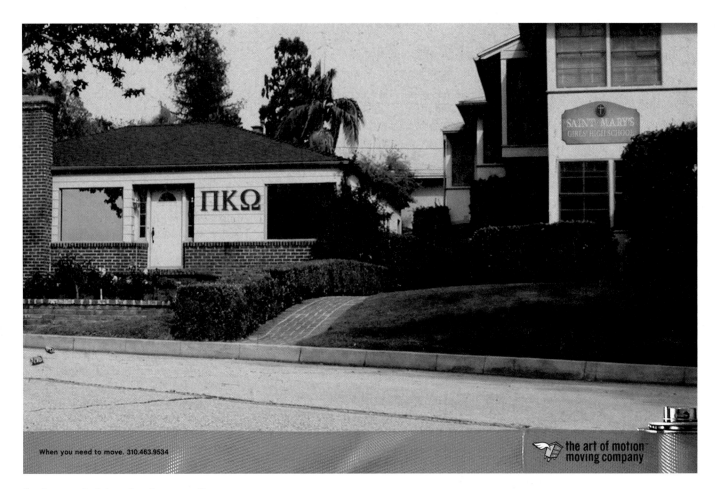

When you need to move. 310.463.9534

the art of motion™
moving company

Geodemography is based on the assumption that "birds of a feather flock together." A frat house next to an all-girls' school means one of them needs to relocate, according to the moving company that created this ad.
Source: Courtesy of 86 The Onion Ad Agency.

One popular clustering technique is Nielsen's **PRIZM** system. This system classifies every U.S. Zip Code into 1 of 66 categories, ranging from the most affluent "Blue-Blood Estates" to the least well-off "Public Assistance."[159] It terms a resident of southern California "Money & Brains" if she lives in Encino (Zip Code 91316), whereas someone living in Sherman Oaks (Zip Code 91423) is a "Young Influential."[160]

Residents of different clusters display marked differences in their consumption of products, from annuities to Ziploc bags. The system also ranks these groupings by income, home value, and occupation (i.e., a rough index of social class) on a ZQ (Zip Quality) scale. Table 10.1 provides an idea of how dramatically different the consumption patterns of two clusters can be. It compares consumption data for "Movers and Shakers," the third-highest-ranking cluster, with "Bedrock America," the third-lowest. You can check out your own Zip Code at MyBestSegments.com.[161]

Although consumers in two very different clusters may purchase a product at an equivalent rate, these similarities end when we take their other purchases into account. These differences highlight the importance of going beyond simple product-category purchase data and demographics to really understand a market (remember the earlier discussion of product complementarity). For example, people in "Urban Gold Coast," "Money & Brains," and "Blue-Blood Estates" communities buy a lot of high-quality binoculars, but so do those in the "Grain Belt," "New Homesteaders," and "Agri-Business" clusters. The difference is that the former groups use the binoculars to watch birds and other wildlife, whereas the latter use them to help line up the animals in their gun sights. Furthermore, whereas the bird watchers do a lot of foreign travel, listen to classical music, and host cocktail parties, the bird hunters travel by bus, like country music, and belong to veterans' clubs.

TABLE 10.1	SA Comparison of Two Very Different PRIZM Clusters

Furs & Station Wagons (ZQ3)		Tobacco Roads (ZQ38)	
New money, parents in 40s and 50s		Racially mixed farm towns in the South	
Newly built subdivisions with tennis courts, swimming pools, gardens		Small downtowns with thrift shops, diners, and laundromats; shanty-type homes without indoor plumbing	
Sample neighborhoods:		Sample neighborhoods:	
Plano, TX (75075)		Belzoni, MI (39038)	
Dunwoody, GA (30338)		Warrenton, NC (27589)	
Needham, MA (02192)		Gates, VA (27937)	
High Usage	**Low Usage**	**High Usage**	**Low Usage**
Country clubs	Motorcycles	Travel by bus	Knitting
Wine by the case	Laxatives	Asthma relief remedies	Live theater
Lawn furniture	Nonfilter cigarettes	Malt liquors	Smoke detectors
Gourmet magazine	Chewing tobacco	*Grit* magazine	*Ms.* magazine
BMW 5 Series	*Hunting* magazine	Pregnancy tests	Ferraris
Rye bread	Chevrolet Chevettes	Pontiac Bonnevilles	Whole-wheat bread
Natural cold cereal	Canned stews	Shortening	Mexican foods

Note: Usage rates as indexed to average consumption across all 40 clusters.
Source: "A Comparison of Two Prizm Clusters" from *The Clustering of America* by Michael J. Weiss. Copyright © 1988 by Michael J. Weiss. Reprinted by permission of the Sagalyn Literacy Agency.

MyMarketingLab

Go to **mymktlab.com** to complete the problems marked with this icon ⭐.

CHAPTER SUMMARY

Now that you have finished reading this chapter, you should understand why:

1. Consumer identity derives from "we" as well as "I."

Consumers identify with many groups that share common characteristics and identities, but some of these affiliations are more central to how we define ourselves. Subcultures are large groups that exist within a society, and membership in them often gives marketers a valuable clue about individuals' consumption decisions. Important sources of consumer identity include gender, race/ethnicity, religion, age, and place of residence.

2. Gender identity is a very important component of a consumer's self-concept.

Sex roles, or a society's conceptions about masculinity and femininity, exert a powerful influence on our expectations about the brands we should consume. Advertising plays an important role because it portrays idealized expectations about gender identity.

3. Our memberships in ethnic, racial, and religious subcultures often guide our consumption choices.

A person's ethnic origins, racial identity, and religious background often are major components of his or her identity. African Americans, Hispanic Americans, and Asian Americans are the three most important ethnic/racial subcultures in the United States. Key issues to reach members of racial/ethnic subcultures are consumers' degree of acculturation into mainstream American society and the recognition of important cultural differences among subgroups (e.g., Puerto Ricans, Cubans, and Mexicans).

4. **Marketers increasingly use religious and spiritual themes to talk to consumers.**

The quest for spirituality influences demand in product categories including books, music, and cinema. Although the impact of religious identification on consumer behavior is not clear, some differences among religious subcultures do emerge. Marketers need to consider the sensibilities of believers carefully when they use religious symbolism to appeal to members of different denominations.

5. **We have many things in common with others because they are about the same age.**

Consumers who grew up at the same time share many cultural memories because they belong to a common age cohort, so they respond well to marketers' nostalgia appeals that remind them of these experiences.

6. **Teens are an important age segment for marketers.**

Teenagers are in the middle of a transition from childhood to adulthood, and their self-concepts tend to be unstable. They are receptive to products that help them to be accepted and enable them to assert their independence. Because many teens earn money but have few financial obligations, they are a particularly important segment for many nonessential or expressive products, ranging from chewing gum to clothing fashions and music. Because of changes in family structure, many teens also are taking more responsibility for their families' day-to-day shopping. College students are an important but hard-to-reach market. In many cases, they live alone for the first time, so they make important decisions about setting up a household. Tweens are kids aged 8 to 14; they are influential purchasers of clothing, CDs, and other "feel-good" products. Many young people belong to youth tribes that influence their lifestyles and product preferences.

7. **Baby Boomers are the most economically powerful age segment.**

Baby Boomers are the most powerful age segment because of their size and economic clout. Boomers continue to affect demands for housing, child care, automobiles, clothing, and many other products.

8. **Seniors are a more important market segment than many marketers realize.**

As the population ages, the needs of older consumers will become increasingly important. Many marketers ignore seniors because of the stereotype that they are too inactive and spend too little. This stereotype is no longer accurate. Many older adults are healthy, vigorous, and interested in new products and experiences—and they have the income to purchase them. Marketing appeals to this age subculture should focus on consumers' perceived ages, which tend to be more youthful than their chronological ages. Marketers also should emphasize concrete benefits of products because this group tends to be skeptical of vague, image-related promotions

9. **"Birds of a feather flock together."**

Geodemography refers to analytical techniques that combine data on consumer expenditures and other socioeconomic factors with geographic information about the areas in which people live, in order to identify consumers who share common consumption patterns. Researchers base this approach on the common assumption that "birds of a feather flock together." Marketers can increase the efficiency of their messages when they focus on the similarities among consumers who choose to live in the same place.

KEY TERMS

acculturation, 440
acculturation agents, 440
age cohort, 449
agentic goals, 430
androgyny, 436
Baby Boomer, 457
bromance, 432
communal goals, 430
connexity, 454
consumer identity, 428

consumer identity renaissance, 462
contemporary young mainstream
    female achievers (CYMFA), 434
deethnicization, 441
Echo Boomers, 454
ethnic subculture, 439
Gen X, 457
Gen Y, 453
gender identity, 428
gender socialization, 429

gender-bending products, 436
geodemography, 463
Goth subculture, 436
halal, 449
high-context culture, 439
Hispanic, 444
host culture, 441
low-context culture, 439
masculinism, 435
megachurches, 447

Millennials, 454

minimal group paradigm, 428

parental yielding, 450

perceived age, 462

PRIZM, 464

progressive learning model, 441

senior market, 460

sex roles, 428

sex-typed products, 432

sex-typed traits, 431

social identity, 427

social identity theory, 428

spiritual-therapeutic model, 446

subculture, 428

tweens, 456

warming, 441

REVIEW

10-1 What is meant by the term "social identity theory"?

10-2 One important subcultural difference is how abstract or literal the group is. What are the distinctions?

10-3 How do marketers market products and services to ethnic subcultures?

10-4 What is deethnicization? Give an example.

10-5 Why are Hispanic American consumers attractive to marketers?

✪ **10-6** What is acculturation? How does it differ from enculturation?

10-7 Who are acculturation agents? Give two examples.

✪ **10-8** Describe the processes involved when a person assimilates into a new host culture.

10-9 Why might a marketer be interested in the second largest ethnic group in a market? Is this group difficult for marketers to reach?

10-10 Identify five brands that are in huge demand and dominate the market. Why is this the case?

10-11 Is it true that religious, cultural, or traditional events impact consumption?

10-12 Can children be considered "consumers-in-waiting"?

10-13 What is parental yielding?

10-14 How important is the global youth market? Suggest products and services they would want to use.

10-15 What are the rules of engagement for young consumers?

10-16 How important is the senior market?

10-17 What is geodemography? Is it straightforward to apply it to any market or country?

CONSUMER BEHAVIOR CHALLENGE

▪ DISCUSS

10-18 One consequence of the continual evolution of sex roles is that men are concerned as never before with their appearance. Men spend $7.7 billion on grooming products globally each year. A wave of male cleansers, moisturizers, sunscreens, depilatories, and body sprays washes up on U.S. shores, largely from European marketers. L'Oréal Paris reports that men's skincare products are now its fastest-growing sector. In Europe, 24 percent of men younger than age 30 use skincare products—and 80 percent of young Korean men do. Mintel reports big growth, especially in products with antiaging and exfoliating ingredients. Even some cosmetics products, like foundation and eyeliner, are catching on in some segments, though men aren't comfortable owning up to using them. In fact, a British makeup product looks like a ballpoint pen so men can apply it secretly at the office.[162] Over the past decade, the media paid a lot of attention to so-called "metrosexuals": straight males who are very interested in fashion, home design, gourmet cooking and personal care products. How widespread is this phenomenon? Do you see men in your age group focusing on these interests? Should marketers change how they think of male sex roles today?

✪ **10-19** Some activists object to Axe's male-focused marketing because they claim it demeans women. In contrast, Dove's "Natural Beauty" campaign gets kudos because it promotes more realistic expectations for girls. Guess what? The same company—Unilever—owns both Axe and Dove. Is it hypocritical for a big company to sponsor positive messages about women in one of its divisions while it sends a different message in another?

10-20 Kurt, the gay character on the hit show *Glee* (played by actor Chris Colfer), has helped to publicize the issues that GLBT consumers face, and gay characters now star in hit shows like *Modern Family*. President Obama uploaded a video on YouTube to let GLBT teens know that "there are people out there who love you and care about you just the way you are."[163] Now the movement toward legalizing gay marriage is going mainstream. What are the marketing implications of the growing acceptance of GLBT consumers by "everyday" consumers?

10-21 Geodemographic techniques assume that people who live in the same neighborhood have other things in common as well. Why do they make this assumption, and how accurate is it?

10-22 Some industry experts feel that it's acceptable to appropriate symbols from another culture even if the buyer does not know their original meaning. They argue that even in the host society there is often disagreement about these meanings. What do you think?

10-23 The prominence of African American characters in video games that contain violent story lines is all the more striking because of the narrow range of video games in which African Americans have been present over the years. One study found that of 1,500 video game characters surveyed, 288 were African American males, and 83 percent of those were athletes.[164] Do you think this is a problem, and if so how would you address it?

10-24 Should members of a religious group adapt marketing techniques that manufacturers customarily use to increase market share for their secular products? Why or why not?

10-25 Several years ago R.J. Reynolds announced plans to test market a menthol cigarette called Uptown specifically to African American consumers. According to the company, about 70 percent of African American smokers prefer menthol, more than twice the average rate. After market research showed that blacks tend to open cigarette packs from the bottom, the company decided to pack Uptowns with the filters facing down. Reynolds cancelled its plans after private health groups and government officials protested. Does a company have the right to exploit a subculture's special characteristics, especially to increase sales of a harmful product such as cigarettes? What about the argument that virtually every business that follows the marketing concept designs a product to meet the needs and tastes of a preselected segment?

10-26 RushmoreDrive.com was touted as the first black search engine, but it shut down only a year after its launch. The idea of a site that would look specifically for black-oriented content and data had been the subject of debate in the blogosphere. Some critics felt the site was racist and separatist, but an African American marketing executive commented, "An African-American search engine not only helps other African Americans find Black-owned business Web sites, but it can also aid corporations looking for minority companies to hire." Should companies develop techniques to allow distinct subcultures to access different parts of the Web?[165]

10-27 Describe the progressive learning model and discuss why this perspective is important when we market to subcultures.

10-28 Born-again Christian groups have been instrumental in organizing boycotts of products advertised on shows they find objectionable, especially those that they feel undermine family values. Church leaders can encourage consumption but, more importantly, they can also *discourage* it—sometimes with powerful effects. The Disney Corporation discovered how effective these movements can be when the Southern Baptist Convention voted to persuade all its members to boycott Disney's operations.[166] The church instituted its anti-Mickey rebellion to protest the "Gay Days" at the theme parks, and advocated a view that Disney had a radical homosexual agenda that it promoted through its broadcasts. Soon other organizations joined the cause, including the American Family Association, the General Council of the Assemblies of God, the Congregational Holiness Church, the Catholic League for Religious and Civil Rights, and the Free Will Baptists. The fallout from the boycott was significant; Disney was forced to lay off 4,000 employees.[167] Do religious groups have a right or a responsibility to dictate what advertising a network should carry?

10-29 Religious symbolism appears in advertising, even though some people object to this practice. For example, a French Volkswagen ad for the relaunch of the Golf showed a modern version of *The Last Supper* with the tagline, "Let us rejoice, my friends, for a new Golf has been born."[168] A group of clergy in France sued the company and the ad was removed from 10,000 billboards. One of the bishops involved in the suit said, "Advertising experts have told us that ads aim for the sacred in order to shock, because using sex does not work anymore." Do you agree? Should religion be used to market products? Do you find this strategy effective or offensive? When and where is this appropriate, if at all?

10-30 The chapter describes efforts by some mainstream marketers to appeal to Muslim consumers by making *halal* products. Given the political attitudes some Americans hold regarding Muslims, is this a dangerous strategy or a courageous one? What are the potential pitfalls of this approach, and how would you handle it?

10-31 This chapter describes members of Gen Y as much more traditional and team oriented than their older brothers and sisters. Do you agree?

10-32 Many parents worry about the time their kids spend online, but this activity may actually be good for them. A study by the MacArthur Foundation claims that surfers gain valuable skills to prepare them for the future. One of the authors observes, "It may look as though kids are wasting a lot of time hanging out with new media, whether it's on MySpace or sending instant messages. But their participation is giving them the technological skills and literacy they need to succeed in the contemporary world. They're learning how to get along with others, how to manage a public identity, how to create a home page." The study also finds that concerns about online predators are over-blown; most kids socialize with friends they know from other situations like school or camp.[169] What's your take on this? Are concerns about excessive Web surfing unjustified?

10-33 What are some of the positives and negatives of target-ing college students? Identify some specific marketing strategies you feel have either been successful or un-successful. What characteristics distinguish the suc-cesses from the failures?

10-34 Is it practical to assume that people age 55 and older constitute one large consumer market? How can mar-keters segment this age subculture? What are some important variables to keep in mind when we tailor marketing messages to this age group?

10-35 Some critics charge that kids' games perpetuate sex-role stereotypes, but toy company executives counter that they simply respond to kids' natural pref-erences.[170] Indeed, after two decades of trying to avoid boy-versus-girl stereotypes, many companies seem to have decided that differences are inevitable. Toys "R" Us unveiled a new store design after it interviewed 10,000 kids; the chain now has separate sections it calls Girls' World and Boys' World. According to the president of Fox Family Channels, "Boys and girls are different, and it's great to celebrate what's special about each." Boys tend to be more interested in battle and competition; girls are more interested in creativ-ity and relationships. This is what experts refer to as "male and female play patterns."[171] Which argument do you support?

10-36 The mainstream media have sent a clear message for the last several years: It's cool to be slutty. Role models like Paris Hilton, Lindsay Lohan, Britney Spears, and even Bratz dolls convey standards about how far pre-teens and teens should go when they broadcast their sexuality. Now, as these messages seem to go over the top (at least in the eyes of some concerned parents), we start to see early signs of a backlash, as some ad-vocate a return to styles that leave almost everything to the imagination. At the *PureFashion* Web site, girls get style tips recommending skirts and dresses that fall no more than four fingers above the knee and no tank tops without a sweater or jacket over them; the *Mod-estApparel* site proclaims, "because a modest woman is a beautiful woman."[172] Is our culture moving from a celebration of "girls gone wild" to "girls gone mild?"

■ APPLY

10-37 Watch a set of ads on TV that feature men and women. Try to imagine the characters with reversed roles (i.e., the male roles played by women and vice versa). Can you see any differences in assumptions about sex-typed behavior?

10-38 Locate current examples of marketing stimuli that de-pend on an ethnic or religious stereotype to communi-cate a message. How effective are these appeals?

10-39 To understand the power of ethnic stereotypes, con-duct your own poll. For a set of ethnic groups, ask people to anonymously provide attributes (including personality traits and products) most likely to charac-terize each group, using the technique of free associa-tion where they simply say what comes to mind when you mention each group. How much agreement do you obtain across respondents? To what extent do the char-acteristics derive from or reflect negative stereotypes? Compare the associations for an ethnic group between actual members of that group and nonmembers.

10-40 One study asked young people in the United States and the Netherlands to write essays about what is "cool" and "uncool" and to create visual collages that represent what it means to be cool.[173] The researchers found that cool has multiple meanings to kids in these two cul-tures. Some of the common dimensions include hav-ing charisma, being in control, and being a bit aloof. Many of the respondents also agreed that being cool is a moving target: The harder you try to be cool, the more uncool you are! Here are some of their actual responses:

- "Cool means being relaxed, to nonchalantly be the boss of every situation, and to radiate that" (Dutch female)
- "Cool is the perception from others that you've got 'something' which is macho, trendy, hip, etc." (Dutch male)
- "Cool has something standoffish, and at the same time, attractive" (Dutch male)
- "Being different, but not too different. Doing your own thing, and standing out, without looking des-perate while you're doing it" (American male)
- "When you are sitting on a terrace in summer, you see those machos walk by, you know, with their mo-bile [phones] and their sunglasses. I always think, 'Oh please, come back to earth!' These guys only want to impress. That is just so uncool" (Dutch female)
- "When a person thinks he is cool, he is absolutely uncool" (Dutch female)
- "To be cool we have to make sure we measure up to it. We have to create an identity for ourselves that mirrors what we see in magazines, on TV, and with what we hear on our stereos" (American male)

Replicate this study in your area. Recruit a group of teenagers to construct individual collages that repre-sent what they feel is "cool." Analyze their choices—what patterns do you see?

10-41 Locate one or more consumers (perhaps family members) who have emigrated from another country. Interview them about how they adapted to their host culture. In particular, what changes did they make in their consumption practices over time?

10-42 Find good and bad examples of advertising that targets older consumers. To what degree does advertising stereotype the elderly? What elements of ads or other promotions appear to determine their effectiveness in reaching and persuading this group?

10-43 Interview some retired people. How are they reconstructing their identities? What opportunities do their desires present for marketers?

Case Study

RIDING THE PLUS-SIZE WAVE

For years, Hollywood and the advertising media perpetuated a stereotypical image of women. As a result, many consumers have the unrealistic expectation that many women are (or should be) poreless, hipless, silken-haired, high-cheekboned, size 0, 20-year-old goddesses. But is this beauty myth finally changing? Companies like Ascena Retail Group, parent to plus-size retailer Lane Bryant, are doing their darnedest to see that it does.

Lane Bryant was founded in 1900 in New York as the first women's apparel retailer devoted exclusively to plus-sizes. In 2012 they were acquired by Ascena Retail Group, who believes that Lane Bryant's iconic brand and market leadership will contribute to Ascena's strategic plan for ongoing growth and profitability.

The future looks bright. The apparel industry defines plus-size as 14 and up—today that includes 62 percent of American women. According to one industry executive, "People are more accepting of their bodies today, and I think there has been a positive influence with role models. Years ago, manufacturers were only interested in making low-end plus-size merchandise because they thought customers were always in transition. Now no longer."

Lane Bryant is fighting this tide. With a new flagship store in New York City, the company sends the message that it's not only OK to be a plus-size, but that women in this category can be as stylish as anyone. Lane Bryant focuses on en vogue styles previously available only to more modestly sized shoppers. Their strategy also includes marketing the Cacique brand of plus-size lingerie, which is known for its appealing fit and fashion styling.

Lane Bryant's sales hit $1 billion in 2012; other retailers are noticing this market and beginning to make a move. One of these companies, online retailer ModCloth, reports that their plus-size customers tend to spend 25 percent more per order and they buy 17 percent more items per order than non plus-size customers.

Plus-size bloggers are grabbing the attention of other retailers who are also increasing their stakes in the game.

H&M, Gap/Old Navy, Target, Lands' End, Saks Fifth Avenue, and Macy's are among national retailers offering or expanding their assortments of plus apparel sizes and increasing promotional efforts for this category. In fact, H&M gained media attention recently by casting a size 12 model for a swimwear photo without labeling the photo with the term *plus-size*. With these industry changes, who knows what images of women the media of the future will celebrate?

DISCUSSION QUESTIONS

CS 10-1 Explain the success that Lane Bryant is currently experiencing in relation to self-concept, self-esteem, and self-consciousness. How can the plus-size industry leverage what we know about consumer behavior to address self-esteem issues?

CS 10-2 Discuss the real-world changes that appear to be occurring with respect to media images of women. What are the reasons for this?

CS 10-3 How do you reconcile the greater degree of acceptance of plus-size women with the parallel emphasis our society continues to place on thinness (as evidenced by the billions we spend on diet products, exercise, and so on)? Given the health problems associated with obesity (heart disease, diabetes, etc.) should the industry continue to encourage this acceptance?

Sources: Tamara Abraham, "The Huge Potential of Plus-Size Clothes: How Fashion Brands Are Waking Up to the Spending Power of Larger Women," http://www.dailymail.co.uk/femai/article-2341742/, accessed July 26, 2013; Ascena Retail Group, 2012 Annual Report, July 28, 2012, p. 2. From http://www.ascenaretai.com/investors.jsp; accessed July 28, 2013; www.spoke.com, accessed May 23, 2009; "Plus Size Teens and Women—US—November 2008," Mintel Oxygen, accessed May 23, 2009; Leigh Gragan, "Looking Good: Plus-Size Styles Are All About the Fashion," *McClatchy Tribune Business News* (March 26, 2008); Keiko Morris, "Finding Both Fashion and Fit: Plus-Size Retailing Is Becoming Hot as Demand Grows for Trendy Clothing in Size 14 and Up," *Knight Ridder Tribune Business News* (May 28, 2007): 1.

MyMarketingLab

Go to **mymktlab.com** for the following Assisted-graded writing questions:

10-44 What are some possible marketing opportunities available at reunions? What effects might attending such events have on consumers' self-esteem, body image, and so on?

10-45 What advice would you give to a marketer who wants to appeal to Gen Y? What are major do's and don'ts? Can you provide some examples of specific marketing attempts that work or don't work?

10-46 **Mymktlab Only**—comprehensive writing assignment for this chapter.

NOTES

1. Jaime Mejia and Gabriel Sama, "Media Players Say 'Si' to Latino Magazines," *Wall Street Journal* (May 15, 2002), www.wsj.com, accessed May 15, 2002.
2. Kay Deaux, "Social Identity," http://www.utexas.edu/courses/stross/ant393b_files/ARTICLES/identity.pdf, accessed March 13, 2013.
3. Henri Tajfel and John C. Turner, "The Social Identity Theory of Intergroup Behaviour," in S. Worchel and W. G. Austin (Eds.), *Psychology of Intergroup Relations* (Chicago, IL: Nelson-Hall, 1986): 7–24.
4. Somini Sengupta, "Attack on Women at an Indian Bar Intensifies a Clash of Cultures," *New York Times* (February 8, 2009), www.nytimes.com, accessed February 8, 2009; Niraj Sheth and Tariq Engineer, "As the Selling Gets Hot, India Tries to Keep Cool, New-Age Dilemma: Too Sexy? Just Fun? The Chocolate Man," *Wall Street Journal* (September 9, 2008), www.wsj.com, accessed September 9, 2008.
5. Diane Goldner, "What Men and Women Really Want . . . to Eat," *New York Times* (March 2, 1994): C1(2).
6. Nina M. Lentini, "McDonald's Tests 'Angus Third Pounder' in California," *Marketing Daily* (March 27, 2007), www.mediapost.com, accessed March 27, 2007.
7. Glenn Collins, "New Studies on 'Girl Toys' and 'Boy Toys,'" *New York Times* (February 13, 1984): D1.
8. Susan B. Kaiser, "Clothing and the Social Organization of Gender Perception: A Developmental Approach," *Clothing & Textiles Research Journal* 7 (Winter 1989): 46–56.
9. Suzanne Vranica, "Sony Tries to Lure DVR Ad-Skippers," *Wall Street Journal* (September 20, 2006): A20.
10. Lori Schwartz and William Markham, "Sex Stereotyping in Children's Toy Advertisements," *Sex Roles* 12 (January 1985): 157–70.
11. http://www.barbie.com/activities/friends/, accessed June 14, 2011.
12. http://www.barbie.com/activities/friends/, accessed March 16, 2013.
13. www.amazon.com/Mattel-Working-Woman-Barbie-Doll/dp/B001871UEO, accessed June 16, 2009; Constance L. Hayes, "A Role Model's Clothes: Barbie Goes Professional," *New York Times* (April 1, 2000), www.nytimes.com, accessed April 1, 2000.
14. Joan Meyers-Levy, "The Influence of Sex Roles on Judgment," *Journal of Consumer Research* 14 (March 1988): 522–30.
15. Anne Eisenberg, "Mars and Venus, on the Net: Gender Stereotypes Prevail," *New York Times* (October 12, 2000), www.nytimes.com, accessed October 12, 2000.
16. Beverly A. Browne, "Gender Stereotypes in Advertising on Children's Television in the 1990s: A Cross-National Analysis," *Journal of Advertising* 27 (Spring 1998): 83–97.
17. Lisa Bannon, "Mattel Sees Untapped Market for Blocks: Little Girls," *Wall Street Journal* (June 6, 2002): B1.
18. Gavin O'Malley, "Study: Men Are from Hulu, Women Are from Facebook," *Online Media Daily* (July 28, 2010), http://www.mediapost.com/publications/?fa=Articles.showArticle&art_aid=132841&nid=117095, accessed April 10, 2011.
19. Eileen Fischer and Stephen J. Arnold, "Sex, Gender Identity, Gender Role Attitudes, and Consumer Behavior," *Psychology & Marketing* 11 (March–April 1994): 163–82.
20. Sarah Kershaw, "For Teenagers, Hello Means 'How About a Hug?'" *New York Times* (May 27, 2009), www.nytimes.com, accessed May 28, 2009.
21. Geoffrey A. Fowler, "Asia's Lipstick Lads," *Wall Street Journal* (May 27, 2005), www.wsj.com, accessed May 27, 2005.
22. Matt Alt and Hiroko Yoda, "Big Primpin' in Tokyo," *Wired* (May 2007): 46.
23. Clifford Nass, Youngme Moon, and Nancy Green, "Are Machines Gender Neutral? Gender-Stereotypic Responses to Computers with Voices," *Journal of Applied Social Psychology* 27, no. 10 (1997): 864–76; Kathleen Debevec and Easwar Iyer, "Sex Roles and Consumer Perceptions of Promotions, Products, and Self: What Do We Know and Where Should We Be Headed," in Richard J. Lutz, ed., *Advances in Consumer Research* 13 (Provo, UT: Association for Consumer Research, 1986): 210–14; Joseph A. Bellizzi and Laura Milner, "Gender Positioning of a Traditionally Male-Dominant Product," *Journal of Advertising Research* (June–July 1991): 72–79.
24. Hillary Chura, "Barton's New High-End Vodka Exudes a 'Macho Personality,'" *Advertising Age* (May 1, 2000): 8; www.thorshammervodka.com, accessed May 29, 2009.
25. Michelle Jaworski, "The 'First Tablet for Women' Is as Awful as It Sounds," *The Daily Dot* (March 13, 2013), http://www.dailydot.com/society/epad-femme-tablet-for-women/, accessed March 15, 2013.
26. Eric Bellman, "Suzuki's Stylish Compacts Captivate India's Women," *Wall Street Journal* (May 11, 2007): B1.
27. Craig S. Smith, "Underneath, Saudi Women Keep Their Secrets," *New York Times* (December 3, 2002), www.nytimes.com, accessed December 3, 2002.
28. Marylouise Caldwell, Ingeborg Astrid Kelppe, and Paul Henry, "Prosuming Multiple Gender Role Identities: A Multi-Country Written and Audio-Visual Exploration of Contemporary Young Mainstream Female Achievers," *Consumption, Markets & Culture* 10 (June 2007): 95–115.
29. Adapted from http://www.ixicorp.com/PDFs/2010-Cohorts-Brief-Descriptions.pdf, accessed March 15, 2013.
30. Doreen Carvajal, "Europe Takes Aim at Sexual Stereotyping in Ads," *New York Times* (September 9, 2008), www.nytimes.com/2008/09/10/Business/Media/10adco.Html?_R=1&Ei=5070&Emc=Et . . ., accessed September 10, 2008.
31. Quoted in Natalie Zmuda, "Can Dr Pepper's Mid-Cal Soda Score a 10 with Men?," *Advertising Age* (February 21, 2011), http://adage.com/article/news/dr-pepper-10-avoid-marketing-missteps-pepsi-coke/148983/, accessed April 10, 2011.
32. Quoted in Barry Silverstein, "Ever the Publicity Hound, Branson Readies to Be an Airline Hostess," *BrandChannel* (November 18, 2010), http://www.brandchannel.com/home/post/2010/11/18/Richard-Branson-Loses-Bet.aspx, accessed April 10, 2011.
33. Barbara B. Stern, "Masculinism(s) and the Male Image: What Does It Mean to Be a Man?," in Tom Reichert and Jacqueline Lambiase, eds., *Sex in Advertising: Multi-Disciplinary Perspectives on the Erotic Appeal* (Mahwah, NJ: Erlbaum, 2003): 215–28.
34. "NBCU Brand Index: Women Love Gender Bender Ads," *Media Daily News* (February 28, 2011), http://www.mediapost.com/publications/?fa=Articles.showArticle&art_aid=145748, accessed April 10, 2011.
35. Douglas B. Holt and Craig J. Thompson, "Man-of-Action Heroes: The Pursuit of Heroic Masculinity in Everyday Consumption," *Journal of Consumer Research* 31 (September): 425–40.

36. Projections of the incidence of homosexuality in the general population often are influenced by assumptions of the researchers, as well as the methodology they employ (e.g., self-report, behavioral measures, fantasy measures). For a discussion of these factors, see Edward O. Laumann, John H. Gagnon, Robert T. Michael, and Stuart Michaels, *The Social Organization of Homosexuality* (Chicago: University of Chicago Press, 1994).

37. Rupal Parekh, "Gender-Bending Brands an Easy Way to Increase Product Reach," *Advertising Age* (March 2, 2009), www.adage.com, accessed March 2, 2009; Sarah Mahoney, "Best Buy Opens Store Designed for Women," *Marketing Daily* (October 6, 2008), www.mediapost.com, accessed October 6, 2008; Kevin Helliker, "The Solution to Hunting's Woes? Setting Sights on Women," *Wall Street Journal* (October 1, 2008), http://online.wsj.com/Article/Sb122281550760292225.Html?Mod=Dist_Smartbrief, accessed October 2, 2008; Stephanie Clifford, "Frito-Lay Tries to Enter the Minds (and Lunch Bags) of Women," *New York Times* (February 24, 2009), www.nytimes.com, accessed February 24, 2009; Karl Greenberg, "Harley Says Guys Ride Back Seat in May," *Marketing Daily* (February 3, 2009), www.mediapost.com, accessed February 3, 2009.

38. Sandra L. Bem, "The Measurement of Psychological Androgyny," *Journal of Consulting & Clinical Psychology* 42 (1974): 155–62; Deborah E. S. Frable, "Sex Typing and Gender Ideology: Two Facets of the Individual's Gender Psychology That Go Together," *Journal of Personality & Social Psychology* 56, no. 1 (1989): 95–108.

39. Christina Goulding and Michael Saren, "Performing Identity: An Analysis of Gender Expressions at the Whitby Goth Festival," *Consumption, Markets & Culture* 12 (March 2009): 27–46; Ayalla Ruvio and Russell Belk, "Conflicting Selves and the Role of Possessions: Exploring Transgenders' Self-Identity Conflict," in eds. Ayalla A. Ruvio and Russell W. Belk, *The Routledge Companion to Identity and Consumption*, Routledge, London (2013): 141–148.

40. Lisa Leff, "2010 Census Will Count Same-Sex Couples in Reversal of Bush Policy," June 19, 2009, *Huffington Post*, http://www.huffingtonpost.com/2009/06/20/210-census-will-count-sam_n_218489.html, accessed May 28, 2011; Lee Condon, "By the Numbers (Census 2000)," *The Advocate: The National Gay & Lesbian Newsmagazine* (September 25, 2001): 37.

41. For a recent academic study of this subculture, cf. Steven M. Kates, "The Dynamics of Brand Legitimacy: An Interpretive Study in the Gay Men's Community," *Journal of Consumer Research* 31 (September 2004): 455–64.

42. Kevin Sack, "When the Bride Takes a Bride, Businesses Respond," *New York Times* (July 15, 2010), http://www.nytimes.com/2010/07/16/us/16marriage.html?emc=eta1,accessed April 10, 2011; http://equallywed.com/, accessed May 28, 2011; http://www.outvite.com/?Cobrand=OutVite&Site=OutVite&vk=1777211146, accessed May 28, 2011.

43. Burt Helm, "Ethnic Marketing: McDonald's Is Lovin' It," *Bloomberg Businessweek* (July 8, 2010), http://www.businessweek.com/magazine/content/10_29/b4187022876832.htm, accessed April 24, 2011.

44. See Frederik Barth, *Ethnic Groups and Boundaries: The Social Organization of Culture Difference* (London: Allen & Unwin, 1969); Janeen A. Costa and Gary J. Bamossy, "Perspectives on Ethnicity, Nationalism, and Cultural Identity," in J. A. Costa and G. J. Bamossy, eds., *Marketing in a Multicultural World: Ethnicity, Nationalism, and Cultural Identity* (Thousand Oaks, CA: Sage, 1995): 3–26; Michel Laroche, Annamma Joy, Michael Hui, and Chankon Kim, "An Examination of Ethnicity Measures: Convergent Validity and Cross-Cultural Equivalence," in Rebecca H. Holman and Michael R. Solomon, eds., *Advances in Consumer Research* 18 (Provo, Utah: Association for Consumer Research, 1991): 150–57; Melanie Wallendorf and Michael Reilly, "Ethnic Migration, Assimilation, and Consumption," *Journal of Consumer Research* 10 (December 1983): 292–302; Milton J. Yinger, "Ethnicity," *Annual Review of Sociology* 11 (1985): 151–80.

45. D'Vera Cohn, "2100 Census Forecast: Minorities Expected to Account for 60% of U.S. Population," *Washington Post* (January 13, 2000): A5.

46. Sam Roberts, "In a Generation, Minorities May Be the U.S. Majority," *New York Times* (August 13, 2008), http://www.nytimes.com/2008/08/14/washington/14census.html?scp=1&sq=In%20a%20Generation,%20Minorities%20May%20Be%20the%20U.S.%20Majority&st=cse&gwh=F531FD97BA1C0FB38BB78D5D88A0AD16, accessed August 14, 2008.

47. Susan Saulny, "Census Data Presents Rise in Multiracial Population of Youths," *New York Times* (March 24, 2011), http://www.nytimes.com/2011/03/25/us/25race.html?_r=2&ref=census, accessed April 24, 2011.

48. Brian Sternberg, "P&G Brushes up Iconic Image of 'Crest Kid' in New Campaign," *Wall Street Journal* (March 29, 2005), www.wsj.com, accessed March 29, 2005.

49. Pui-Wing Tam, "The Growth in Ethnic Media Usage Poses Important Business Decisions," *Wall Street Journal* (April 23, 2002), www.wsj.com, accessed April 23, 2002.

50. Steve Rabin, "How to Sell Across Cultures," *American Demographics* (March 1994): 56–57.

51. Stuart Elliott, "An Ad with Talking Pandas, Maybe, but Not with Chinese Accents," *New York Times* (February 6, 2008), http://www.nytimes.com/2008/02/06/business/media/06adco.html?scp=1&sq=An%20Ad%20with%20Talking%20Pandas,%20Maybe,%20but%20Not%20with%20Chinese%20Accents&st=cse&gwh=6B8FCB2D9ADF9E79D7859A84689E4F68, accessed February 6, 2008.

52. Marty Westerman, "Death of the Frito Bandito," *American Demographics* (March 1989): 28.

53. Stuart Elliott, "Uncle Ben, Board Chairman," *New York Times* (March 30, 2007), www.nytimes.com, accessed March 30, 2007.

54. Adam Sherwin, "ASA Says Cadbury Was Not Racist When It Compared Campbell to Chocolate Bar," *The Independent* (June 21, 2011), http://www.independent.co.uk/news/media/advertising/asa-says-cadbury-was-not-racist-when-it-compared-campbell-to-chocolate-bar-2300278.html, accessed June 22, 2011.

55. Rohit Deshpandé and Douglas M. Stayman, "A Tale of Two Cities: Distinctiveness Theory and Advertising Effectiveness," *Journal of Marketing Research* 31 (February 1994): 57–64.

56. Warren Brown, "The Potholes of Multicultural Marketing," *Washington Post* (June 10, 2007): G2.

57. See Lisa Peñaloza, "*Atravesando Fronteras*/Border Crossings: A Critical Ethnographic Exploration of the Consumer Acculturation of Mexican Immigrants," *Journal of Consumer Research* 21 (June 1994): 32–54; Lisa Peñaloza and Mary C. Gilly, "Marketer Acculturation: The Changer and the Changed," *Journal of Marketing* 63 (July 1999): 84–104; Carol Kaufman-Scarborough, "Eat Bitter Food and Give Birth to a Girl; Eat Sweet Things and Give Birth to a Cavalryman: Multicultural Health Care Issues for Consumer Behavior," *Advances in Consumer Research* 32, no.1 (2005): 226–69; Søren Askegaard, Eric J. Arnould, and Dannie Kjeldgaard, "Postassimilationist Ethnic Consumer Research: Qualifications and Extensions," *Journal of Consumer Research* 32, no. 1 (2005): 160.

58. Stuart Elliott, "1,200 Marketers Can't Be Wrong: The Future Is in Consumer Behavior," *New York Times* (October 15, 2007), www.nytimes.com, accessed October 15, 2007.

59. Peñaloza, "*Atravesando Fronteras*/Border Crossings."

60. Shuili Du, Sankar Sen, and C. B. Bhattacharya, "Exploring the Social and Business Returns of a Corporate Oral Health Initiative Aimed at Disadvantaged Hispanic Families," *Journal of Consumer Research* 35 (October 2008): 483–94.

61. Andrew Adam Newman, "Nike Adds Indian Artifacts to Its Swoosh," *New York Times* (October 3, 2007), www.nytimes.com, accessed October 3, 2007.

62. Wallendorf and Reilly, "Ethnic Migration, Assimilation, and Consumption."

63. Ronald J. Faber, Thomas C. O'Guinn, and John A. McCarty, "Ethnicity, Acculturation and the Importance of Product Attributes," *Psychology & Marketing* 4 (Summer 1987): 121–34; Humberto Valencia, "Developing an Index to Measure Hispanicness," in Elizabeth C. Hirschman and Morris B. Holbrook, eds., *Advances in Consumer Research* 12 (Provo, Utah: Association for Consumer Research, 1985): 118–21.

64. Rohit Deshpandé, Wayne D. Hoyer, and Naveen Donthu, "The Intensity of Ethnic Affiliation: A Study of the Sociology of Hispanic Consumption," *Journal of Consumer Research* 13 (September 1986): 214–20.

65. Güliz Ger, "Warming: Making the New Familiar and Moral," *Journal of European Ethnology* (special issue of the journal *Ethnologia Europea*), Richard Wilk and Orvar Lofgren, eds. (forthcoming) 35, no. 1–2: 19–21.

66. Eils Lotozo, "The Jalapeño Bagel and Other Artifacts," *New York Times* (June 26, 1990): C1.

67. Dana Canedy, "The Shmeering of America," *New York Times* (December 26, 1996): D1.

68. Peter Schrag, *The Decline of the WASP* (New York: Simon & Schuster, 1971): 20.

69. "Nation's European Identity Falls by the Wayside," *Montgomery Advertiser* (June 8, 2002): A5.

70. U.S. Census Bureau, *Census 2000 Brief: Overview of Race and Hispanic Origin* (U.S. Department of Commerce, Economics and Statistics Administration, March 2001).

71. Padmananda Rama, "U.S. Census Show Asians Are Fastest Growing Racial Group," NPR (March 23, 2012), http://www.npr.org/blogs/thetwo-way/2012/03/23/149244806/u-s-census-show-asians-are-fastest-growing-racial-group, accessed March 16, 2013.

72. U.S. Census Bureau, http://quickfacts.census.gov/qfd/states/00000.html, accessed March 16, 2013.

73. www.myblackisbeautiful.com, accessed June 18, 2009; Karl Greenberg, "P&G Borrows 'Black Power' Phrase for Campaign," *Marketing Daily*, (August 10, 2007), www.mediapost.com, accessed August 10, 2007.

74. Bob Jones, "Black Gold," *Entrepreneur* (July 1994): 62–65.

75. Jean Halliday, "Volvo to Buckle Up African-Americans," *Advertising Age* (February 14, 2000): 28.

76. www.skinvoice.com, accessed June 18, 2009; Sarah Mahoney, "Unilever Finds Skin Takes on Deep Meaning Among Black Women," *Marketing Daily* (May 23, 2007), www.mediapost.com, accessed May 23, 2007.

77. Michel Marriott, "The Color of Mayhem, in a Wave of 'Urban' Games," *New York Times* (August 12, 2004), www.nytimes.com, accessed August 12, 2004.

78. Sonya A. Grier and Anne Brumbaugh, "Compared to Whom? The Impact of Status on Third Person Effects in Advertising Persuasion in a South African Context," *Journal of Consumer Behavior* 6, no. 1 (February 2007): 5-18; Sonya A. Grier, Anne Brumbaugh, and C. Thornton, "Crossover Dreams: Consumer Responses to Ethnic-Oriented Products," *Journal of Marketing* 70, no. 2 (April 2006): 35-51; Sonya A. Grier and Rohit Deshpandé, "Social Dimensions of Consumer Distinctiveness: The Influence of Social Status on Group Identity and Advertising Persuasion," *Journal of Marketing Research* 38 (May 2001): 216-24; Jennifer A. Aaker, Anne Brumbaugh, and Sonya A. Grier, "Non-Target Market Effects and Viewer Distinctiveness: The Impact of Target Marketing on Attitudes," *Journal of Consumer Psychology* 9, no. 3 (2000): 127-40; Sonya A. Grier and Anne Brumbaugh, "Noticing Cultural Differences: Advertising Meanings Created by the Target and Non-Target Markets," *Journal of Advertising* 28, no. 1 (Spring 1999): 79-93.

79. Sonya A. Grier and S. K. Kumanyika, "The Context for Choice: Health Implications of Targeted Food and Beverage Marketing to African Americans," *American Journal of Public Health* 98, no. 9 (September 2008): 1616-29.

80. Schwartz, "Hispanic Opportunities," *Joe Schwartz American Demographics* (May 1987): 56-59.

81. Peter Francese, "Hispanic Market Hits Tipping Point," *Advertising Age* (July 26, 2010), http://adage.com/article/hispanic-marketing/hispanic-market-hits-tipping-point/145095/, accessed April 24, 2011.

82. Karl Greenberg, "Study: Hispanics Are Ideal Online Consumers," *Marketing Daily* (January 3, 2011), http://www.mediapost.com/publications/?fa=Articles.showArticle&art_aid=142204&nid=122251, accessed April 24, 2011; Karl Greenberg, "Hispanics' Web Savvy Surpassing Others," *Marketing Daily* (March 25, 2009), www.mediapost.com, accessed March 25, 2009.

83. Jonathan Birchall, "Wal-Mart looks to Hispanic Market," *Financial Times* (March 12, 2009), www.ft.com/cms/s/0/bd371350-0f2c-11de-ba10-0000779fd2ac,dwp_uuid=02e16f4a-46f9-11da-b8e5-00000e2511c8.html?nclick_check=1, accessed March 12, 2009.

84. Aaron Baar, "AT&T Enlists Jimenez in Hispanic Campaign," *Marketing Daily* (April 5, 2011), http://www.mediapost.com/publications/?fa=Articles.showArticle&art_aid=148053&nid=125449, accessed April 24, 2011.

85. Stuart Elliot, "Pretty as a (Census) Picture," *New York Times* (March 28, 2011), http://www.nytimes.com/2011/03/29/business/media/28adnewsletter1.html?nl=business&adxnnl=1&emc=ata1&ref=advertisingemail&adxnnlx=1303681253-toqoRVw+PthkndBiYU0ctQ#, accessed April 24, 2011.

86. Karlene Lukovitz, "Wendy's Launches Hispanic Campaign," *Marketing Daily* (November 1, 2010), http://www.mediapost.com/publications/?fa=Articles.showArticle&art_aid=138648, accessed April 24, 2011.

87. "Pew Social & Demographic Trends. The Rise of Asian Americans Overview," Pew Research Center (June 19, 2012), http://www.pewsocialtrends.org/2012/06/19/the-rise-of-asian-americans/; Bruce Britt, "Marketing to Asian Americans," *Deliver Magazine* (August 23, 2012), https://delivermagazine.com/2012/08/marketing-to-asian-americans/.

88. "Made in Japan," *American Demographics* (November 2002): 48.

89. Hassan Fattah, "Asia Rising," *American Demographics* (July–August 2002), http://findarticles.com/p/articles/mi_m4021/is_2002_July_1/ai_89374125/?tag=content;col1, accessed October 6, 2007.

90. Marty Westerman, "Fare East: Targeting the Asian-American Market," *Prepared Foods* (January 1989): 48-51; Eleanor Yu, "Asian-American Market Often Misunderstood," *Marketing News* (December 4, 1989): 11.

91. For a recent discussion of Asian identity, cf. Julien Cayla and Giana M. Eckhardt, "Asian Brands and the Shaping of a Transnational Imagined Community," *Journal of Consumer Research* 35 (August 2008): 216-30.

92. Donald Dougherty, "The Orient Express," *The Marketer* (July/August 1990): 14.

93. Dan Brown, *The Da Vinci Code* (New York: Doubleday, 2003).

94. Albert M. Muñiz, Jr., and Hope Jensen Schau, "Religiosity in the Abandoned Apple Newton Brand Community," *Journal of Consumer Research* 31 (March 2005): 737-47.

95. Risto Moisio and Mariam Beruchashvili, "Questing for Well-Being at Weight Watchers: The Role of the Spiritual-Therapeutic Model in a Support Group," *Journal of Consumer Research* 36, no. 5 (2010): 857-75.

96. Ron Shachar, Tülin Erdem, Keisha M. Cutright, and Gavan J. Fitzsimons, "Brands: The Opiate of the Non-Religious Masses?" *Marketing Science* 30, no. 1 (January–February 2011): 92-111.

97. For a couple of exceptions, see Michael J. Dotson and Eva M. Hyatt, "Religious Symbols as Peripheral Cues in Advertising: A Replication of the Elaboration Likelihood Model," *Journal of Business Research* 48 (2000): 63-68; Elizabeth C. Hirschman, "Religious Affiliation and Consumption Processes: An Initial Paradigm," *Research in Marketing* (Greenwich, CT: JAI Press, 1983): 131-70.

98. Quoted in Joe Mandese, "MindShare Turns SoulShare, Puts Faith in Evangelicals," *Media Daily News* (May 15, 2008), http://www.mediapost.com/publications/index.cfm?fa=Articles.showArticle&art_aid=82586&passFuseAction=PublicationsSearch.showSearchReslts&art_searched=&page_number=0, accessed May 15, 2008.

99. Karlene Lukovitz, "PepsiCo Pulls Controversial Video Entry from Site," *Marketing Daily* (January 5, 2011), http://www.mediapost.com/publications/?fa=Articles.showArticle&art_aid=142406&nid=122346, accessed April 25, 2011; Jack Neff, "Dip Ad Stirs Church Ire," *Advertising Age* (July 2, 2001): 8; G. Burton, "Oh, My Heck! Beer Billboard Gets the Boot," *Salt Lake Tribune* (November 6, 2001); "Religion Reshapes Realities for U.S. Restaurants in Middle East," *Nation's Restaurant News* 32 (February 16, 1998); Sarah Ellison, "Sexy-Ad Reel Shows What Tickles in Tokyo Can Fade Fast in France," *Wall Street Journal* (March 31, 2000), www.wsj.com, accessed March 31, 2000; Claudia Penteado, "Brazilian Ad Irks Church," *Advertising Age* (March 23, 2000): 11; "Burger King Will Alter Ad That Has Offended Muslims," *Wall Street Journal* (March 15, 2000), www.wsj.com, accessed March 15, 2000.

100. Kim Severson, "For Some, 'Kosher' Equals Pure," *New York Times* (January 12, 2010), http://www.nytimes.com/2010/01/13/dining/13kosh.html?pagewanted=all&_r=0, accessed March 15, 2013.

101. Patricia Leigh Brown, "Megachurches as Minitowns: Full-Service Havens from Family Stress Compete with Communities," *New York Times* (May 9, 2002): D1; Edward Gilbreath, "The New Capital of Evangelicalism: Move Over, Wheaton and Colorado Springs—Dallas, Texas, Has More Megachurches, Megaseminaries, and Mega-Christian Activity Than Any Other American City," *Christianity Today* (May 21, 2002): 38; Tim W. Ferguson, "Spiritual Reality: Mainstream Media Are Awakening to the Avid and Expanding Interest in Religion in the U.S.," *Forbes* (January 27, 1997): 70.

102. Richard Cimino and Don Lattin, *Shopping for Faith: American Religion in the New Millennium* (New York: Jossey-Bass, 2002).

103. Michael Fielding, "The Halo," *Marketing News* (February 1, 2005): 18-20.

104. Mandese, "MindShare Turns SoulShare, Puts Faith in Evangelicals"; Karlene Lukovitz, "Evangelicals More Diverse Than Might Be Assumed," *Marketing Daily* (November 7, 2007), http://www.mediapost.com/publications/?fa=Articles.showArticle&art_aid=70553, accessed November 7, 2007.

105. Rob Walker, "Cross Selling," *New York Times Magazine* (March 6, 2005), www.nytimes.com, accessed March 6, 2005; John Leland, "At Festivals, Faith, Rock and T-Shirts Take Center Stage," *New York Times* (July 5, 2004), www.nytimes.com, accessed July 5, 2004.

106. Cathy Lynn Grossman, "Number of U.S. Muslims to Double," *USA Today* (January 27, 2011), http://www.usatoday.com/news/religion/2011-01-27-1Amuslim27_ST_N.htm, accessed June 22, 2011.

107. Barry Newman, "Halal Meets Kosher in Health-Food Aisle," *Wall Street Journal* (May 5, 2006): B1; Louise Story, "Rewriting the Ad for Muslim-Americans," *New York Times Online* (April 28, 2007), www.nytimes.com, accessed April 28, 2007.

108. Liz Gooch, "Advertisers Seek to Speak to Muslim Consumers," *New York Times* (August 11, 2010), http://www.nytimes.com/2010/08/12/business/media/12branding.html?pagewanted=1&_r=1&ref=media, accessed April 25, 2011.

109. Karlene Lukovitz, "Coffee Marketers Need to Woo Young Adults," *Marketing Daily* (October 8, 2010), http://www.mediapost.com/publications/?fa=Articles.showArticle&art_aid=137318, accessed April 29, 2011.

110. Anil Mathur, George P. Moschis, and Euehun Lee, "Life Events and Brand Preference Changes," *Journal of Consumer Behavior* 3, no. 2 (December 2003): 129-41; James W. Gentry, Stacey Menzel Baker, and Frederic B. Kraft, "The Role of Possessions in Creating, Maintaining, and Preserving Identity: Variations Over the Life Course," in Frank Kardes and Mita Sujan, eds., *Advances in Consumer Research* 22 (Provo, Utah: Association for Consumer Research, 1995): 413-18.

111. Cf. Neil Howe and William Strauss, *Generations: The History of America's Future, 1584 to 2069* (New York: Harper Perennial, 1992). The yearly ranges in this list are the author's synthesis of a variety of generational schemes and as such are approximations.

112. www.disneybaby.com, accessed March 16, 2013; Quoted in Brooks Barnes, "Disney Looking into Cradle for Customers," *New York Times* (February 6, 2011), http://www.nytimes.com/2011/02/07/business/media/07disney.html?_r=1&ref=business#, accessed April 19, 2011.

113. James U. McNeal, "Tapping the Three Kids' Markets," *American Demographics* (April 1998): 3, 737-41.

114. Harris Curtis, "Making Kids Street Smart," *Newsweek* (September 16, 2002): 10.

115. Kay L. Palan and Robert E. Wilkes, "Adolescent-Parent Interaction in Family Decision-Making," *Journal of Consumer Research* 24 (September 1997): 159–69; cf. also Tiffany Meyers, "Kids Gaining Voice in How Home Looks," *Advertising Age* (March 29, 2004): S4.

116. Russell N. Laczniak and Kay M. Palan, "Under the Influence," *Marketing Research* (Spring 2004): 34–39.

117. Stephanie Thompson, "Mrs. Butterworth's Changes Her Target," *Advertising Age* (December 20, 1999): 44.

118. Brigid Schulte, "Baby Dolls Raise a Stink in More Ways than One," *Washington Post* (December 21, 2008): A1.

119. http://whyville.net/smmk/nice, accessed March 16, 2013; Jennifer Saranow, "'This Is the Car We Want, Mommy'—Car Makers Direct More Ads at Kids (And Their Parents)," *Wall Street Journal* (November 9, 2006): D1.

120. Jessica Bennett, "Generation Diva: How Our Obsession with Beauty Is Changing Our Kids," *Newsweek* (March 30, 2009), www.newsweek.com/id/191247, accessed April 8, 2009.

121. Andrew Adam Newman, "A Younger Group for Feminine Products," *New York Times* (April 14, 2011), http://www.nytimes.com/2011/04/15/business/media/15adco.html?_r=1, accessed April 19, 2011.

122. Stephen Holden, "After the War the Time of the Teen-Ager," *New York Times* (May 7, 1995): E4.

123. Cornelia Pechmann and Chuan-Fong Shih, "Smoking Scenes in Movies and Antismoking Advertisements Before Movies: Effects on Youth," *Journal of Marketing* 63 (July 1999): 1–13.

124. Junu Bryan Kim, "For Savvy Teens: Real Life, Real Solutions," *New York Times* (August 23, 1993): S1.

125. Excerpted from David B. Wooten, "From Labeling Possessions to Possessing Labels: Ridicule and Socialization Among Adolescents," *Journal of Consumer Research* 33 (September 2006): 188–98.

126. Natalie Zmuda, "Pepsi Embraces 'Optimistic' Millennials in New TBWA Work," *Advertising Age* (December 11, 2008), http://adage.com/article/news/pepsi-embraces-optimistic-millennials-tbwa-work/133211/, accessed January 12, 2008; James Ledbetter, "Obama, the Pepsi Candidate," *Slate* (August 21, 2008), www.slate.com/id/2198198, accessed June 19, 2009.

127. Michael J. Weiss, "To Be About to Be," *American Demographics* (September 2003): 29–48.

128. Steve Kroft, "The Echo Boomers," *CBS News* (October 3, 2004), www.cbsnews.com, accessed October 3, 2004.

129. Laurel Anderson and Julie L. Ozanne, "The Cyborg Teen: Identity Play and Deception on the Internet," in Connie Pechmann and Linda Price, eds., *Advances in Consumer Research* 33, no. 1 (2006): 12–14.

130. Cyndee Miller, "Phat Is Where It's at for Today's Teen Market," *Marketing News* (August 15, 1994): 6; see also Tamara F. Mangleburg and Terry Bristol, "Socialization and Adolescents' Skepticism Toward Advertising," *Journal of Advertising* 27 (Fall 1998): 11; see also Gil McWilliam and John Deighton, "Alloy.com: Marketing to Generation Y," *Journal of Interactive Marketing* 14 (Spring 2000): 74–83.

131. Adapted from Gerry Khermouch, "Didja C That Kewl Ad?," *BusinessWeek* (August 26, 2002): 158–60.

132. Aaron Baar, "Gen Y Donors Rely on Trust, Not Celebrity," *Marketing Daily* (April 7, 2011), http://www.mediapost.com/publications/?fa=Articles.showArticle&art_aid=148198&nid=125532, accessed April 24, 2011.

133. Shannan Younger, "Disney Channel Rules Tween Screens," *Tween Us* (August 29, 2012), http://www.chicagonow.com/tween-us/2012/08/disney-channel-rules-the-tween-airwaves/, accessed September 25, 2013.

134. Karen Springen, Ana Figueroa, and Nicole Joseph-Goteiner, "The Truth About Tweens," *Newsweek* (October 18, 1999): 62–72.

135. Rob Walker, "Training Brand," *New York Times Magazine* (February 27, 2005), www.nytimes.com, accessed February 27, 2005.

136. Center for Media Research, "Students Rule," www.mediapost.com, accessed August 12, 2008; Rebecca Gardyn, "Educated Consumers," *Demographics* (November 2002): 18; Tibbett L. Speer, "College Come-Ons," *American Demographics* (March 1998): 40–46; Fannie Weinstein, "Time to Get Them in Your Franchise," *Advertising Age* (February 1, 1988): S6.

137. www.mtvU.com, accessed June 21, 2011; www.collegehumor.com, accessed June 21, 2011.

138. Maria Aspan, "Nielsen Will Start to Measure TV Habits of College Students," *New York Times* (February 20, 2006), www.nytimes.com, accessed February 20, 2006.

139. http://www.cassandra.co/live/trendschool/, accessed March 16, 2013; Beth Snyder Bulik, "Want to Build a Hipper Brand? Take a Trip to Trend School: Intelligence Group Endeavor Gives Marketers a Crash Course in Cool," *Advertising Age* (February 19, 2007), www.adage.com, accessed February 19, 2007.

140. Laura Zinn, "Move Over, Boomers," *BusinessWeek* (December 14, 1992): 7.

141. Jeff Gordinier, *X Saves the World: How Generation X Got the Shaft But Can Still Keep Everything from Sucking* (New York: Viking Adult, 2008); M. J. Stephey, "Gen-X: The Ignored Generation?" *Time* (April 16, 2008), www.time.com/time/arts/article/0,8599,1731528,00.html, accessed June 19, 2009.

142. http://www.restylaneusa.com/, accessed March 16, 2013; Angel Jennings, "Contests, YouTube and Commercials Converge for Skin Product," *New York Times Online* (July 26, 2007), http://www.nytimes.com/2007/07/26/business/media/26adco.html?_r=0, accessed September 25, 2013; cf. also Isabelle Szmigin and Marylyn Carrigan, "Consumption and Community: Choices for Women Over Forty," *Journal of Consumer Behaviour* 5, no. 4 (2006): 292.

143. Jennings, "Contests, YouTube and Commercials Converge for Skin Product"; cf. also Szmigin and Carrigan, "Consumption and Community: Choices for Women Over Forty."

144. Amy Merrick, "Gap Plans Five Forth & Towne Stores for Fall," *Wall Street Journal* (April 22, 2005): B1.

145. Gavin O'Malley, "Boomers Value Brands That Champion 'Youthful' Style," *Marketing Daily* (April 13, 2011), http://www.mediapost.com/publications/?fa=Articles.showArticle&art_aid=148507&nid=125673, accessed April 24, 2011.

146. Quoted in Sarah Mahoney, "Nielsen: Time to Recommit to Boomers," *Marketing Daily* (July 21, 2010), http://www.mediapost.com/publications/?fa=Articles.showArticle&art_aid=132364&nid=116838, accessed April 24, 2011.

147. Elkin Tobi, "Sony Ad Campaign Targets Boomers-Turned-Zoomers," *Advertising Age* (October 21, 2002): 6; cf. also Raphaelle Lambert-Pandraud and Gilles Laurent, "Why Do Older Consumers Buy Older Brands? The Role of Attachment and Declining Innovativeness," *Journal of Marketing* 74 (July 2010): 104–21.

148. Hiawatha Bray, "At MIT's AgeLab Growing Old Is the New Frontier," *Boston Globe* (March 23, 2009), www.boston.com/business/technology/articles/2009/03/23/at_mits_agelab_growing_old_is_the_new_frontier/?s_campaign=8315, accessed March 23, 2009.

149. D'Vera Cohn, "2100 Census Forecast: Minorities Expected to Account for 60% of U.S. Population," *Washington Post* (January 13, 2000): A5.

150. Catherine A. Cole and Nadine N. Castellano, "Consumer Behavior," in James E. Binnen, ed., *Encyclopedia of Gerontology*, vol. 1 (San Diego, CA: Academic Press, 1996), 329–39.

151. Rick Adler, "Stereotypes Won't Work with Seniors Anymore," *Advertising Age* (November 11, 1996): 32.

152. Raphaël Lambert-Pandraud, Gilles Laurent, and Eric Lapersonne, "Repeat Purchasing of New Automobiles by Older Consumers: Empirical Evidence and Interpretations," *Journal of Marketing* 69 (April 2005): 97–113.

153. Jonathan Dee, "The Myth of '18 to 34,'" *New York Times Magazine* (October 13, 2002), www.nytimes.com, accessed October 11, 2007; Hillary Chura, "Ripe Old Age," *Advertising Age* (May 13, 2002): 16.

154. Cheryl Russell, "The Ungraying of America," *American Demographics* (July 1997): 12.

155. Jeff Brazil, "You Talkin' to Me?," *American Demographics* (December 1998): 55–59.

156. David B. Wolfe, "Targeting the Mature Mind," *American Demographics* (March 1994): 32–36.

157. Benny Barak and Leon G. Schiffman, "Cognitive Age: A Nonchronological Age Variable," in Kent B. Monroe, ed., *Advances in Consumer Research* 8 (Provo, UT: Association for Consumer Research, 1981): 602–6.

158. Hope Jensen Schau, Mary C. Gilly, and Mary Wolfinbarger, "Consumer Identity Renaissance: The Resurgence of Identity-Inspired Consumption in Retirement," *Journal of Consumer Research* 36 (August 2009): 255–76.

159. http://www.claritas.com/MyBestSegments/Default.jsp?ID=70&&pageName=Nielsen%20PRIZM&menuOption=learnmore, accessed March 16, 2013; Michael J. Weiss, *The Clustering of America* (New York: Harper & Row, 1988).

160. Bob Minzesheimer, "You Are What You Zip," *Los Angeles Times* (November 1984): 175.

161. www.MyBestSegments.com, accessed March 16, 2013.

162. Vivian Manning-Schaffel, "Metrosexuals: A Well-Groomed Market?" *Brand Channel* (May 22, 2006), www.brandchannel.com, accessed May 22, 2006; Jack Neff, "A Lipstick Index for Men? Philips' Norelco Posits That Guys Are Growing Beards to Protest Recession," *Advertising Age* (April 2, 2009), www.adage.com, accessed April 2, 2009; Aaron Baar, "Move Over, Ladies; Men Are Walking Down Beauty Aisles," *Marketing Daily* (December 22, 2008), www.mediapost.com, accessed December 22, 2008.

163. Ben Parr, "Google Chrome Commercial Lets Gay Teens Know 'It Gets Better,'" Mashable.com, http://mashable.com/2011/05/04/google-chrome-it-gets-better/, accessed May 28, 2011.

164. Marriott, "The Color of Mayhem, in a Wave of 'Urban' Games."

165. Quoted in Pepper Miller and John Parikhal, "Do African-Americans Need a Separate Search Engine?," *Advertising Age* (June 25, 2009), www.adage.com, accessed June 26, 2009.

166. www.religioustolerance.org/new1_966.htm, accessed October 6, 2007; www.erlc.com/WhoSBC/Resolutions/1997/97Disney.htm, accessed October 6, 2007.

167. Alex Johnson, "Southern Baptists End 8-Year Disney Boycott," *MSNBC* (June 22, 2005), www.msnbc.com, accessed October 6, 2007.

168. Penteado, "Brazilian Ad Irks Church."

169. Quoted in Tamar Lewin, "Teenagers' Internet Socializing Not a Bad Thing," *New York Times* (November 19, 2008), www.nytimes.com/2008/11/20/us/20internet.html?ex=1384923600&en=c3467e945b431625&ei=5124, accessed November 24, 2008.

170. Joseph Pereira, "Oh Boy! In Toyland, You Get More If You're Male," *Wall Street Journal* (September 23, 1994): B1; Joseph Pereira, "Girls' Favorite Playthings: Dolls, Dolls, and Dolls," *Wall Street Journal* (September 23, 1994): B1.

171. Lisa Bannon, "More Kids' Marketers Pitch Number of Single-Sex Products," *Wall Street Journal* (February 14, 2000), www.wsj.com, accessed February 14, 2000.

172. See D. Bruce Carter and Gary D. Levy, "Cognitive Aspects of Early Sex-Role Development: The Influence of Gender Schemas on Preschoolers' Memories and Preferences for Sex-Typed Toys and Activities," *Child Development* 59 (1988): 782–92; Bernd H. Schmitt, France Le Clerc, and Laurette Dube-Rioux, "Sex Typing and Consumer Behavior: A Test of Gender Schema Theory," *Journal of Consumer Research* 15 (June 1988): 122–27.

173. Gary J. Bamossy, Michael R. Solomon, Basil G. Englis, and Trinske Antonidies, "You're Not Cool If You Have to Ask: Gender in the Social Construction of Coolness," paper presented at the Association for Consumer Research Gender Conference, Chicago, June 2000; see also Clive Nancarrow, Pamela Nancarrow, and Julie Page, "An Analysis of the Concept of Cool and Its Marketing Implications," *Journal of Consumer Behavior* 1 (June 2002): 311–22.

Chapter 11 • Consumer Identity II: Social Class and Lifestyles

Chapter Objectives

When you finish reading this chapter you will understand why:

1. Our confidence in our future, as well as in the overall economy, determines how freely we spend and the types of products we buy.

2. We group consumers into social classes that say a lot about where they stand in society.

3. Individuals' desires to make a statement about their social class, or the class to which they hope to belong, influence the products they like and dislike.

4. A lifestyle defines a pattern of consumption that reflects a person's choices of how to spend his or her time and money, and these choices are essential to define consumer identity.

5. Identifying patterns of consumption can be more useful than knowing about individual purchases when organizations craft a lifestyle marketing strategy.

6. Psychographics go beyond simple demographics to help marketers understand and reach different consumer segments.

Source: Sakala/Shutterstock.

Finally, the big day has come! Phil is going home with Marilyn to meet her parents. He was doing some contracting work at the securities firm where Marilyn works, and it was love at first sight. Even though Phil attended the "School of Hard Knocks" on the streets of Brooklyn and Marilyn was fresh out of Princeton, somehow they knew they could work things out despite their vastly different backgrounds. Marilyn hinted that her family has money, but Phil doesn't feel intimidated. After all, he knows plenty of guys from his old neighborhood who wheeled-and-dealed their way into six figures. He certainly can handle one more big shot in a silk suit who flashes a roll of bills and shows off his expensive modern furniture with mirrors and gadgets everywhere you look.

When they arrive at the family estate in Connecticut, Phil looks for a blinged-out Escalade parked in the circular driveway, but he only sees a beat-up Jeep Cherokee, which must belong to one of the servants. Once inside, Phil is surprised by how simply the house is decorated and by how shabby everything seems. A faded Oriental rug covers the hall entryway and all of the furniture looks really old.

Phil is even more surprised when he meets Marilyn's father. He had half expected Mr. Caldwell to be wearing a tuxedo and holding a large brandy snifter like the rich people he's seen in the movies. In fact, Phil has put on his best shiny Italian suit in anticipation, and he wore his large cubic zirconium pinky ring so this guy would know that he has some money, too. When Marilyn's father emerges from his study wearing an old rumpled cardigan sweater and tennis sneakers, Phil realizes he's definitely not one of those guys from the old neighborhood.

Income and Consumer Identity

OBJECTIVE 1
Our confidence in our future, as well as in the overall economy, determines how freely we spend and the types of products we buy.

As Phil's eye-opening experience at the Caldwells' house suggests, there are many ways to spend money, and there's also a wide gulf between those who have it and those who don't. Perhaps an equally wide gap exists between those who have had it for a long time and those who "made it the hard way—by earning it!" As this chapter begins, we briefly consider how general economic conditions affect the way we allocate our money. Then, to reflect the adage that says, "The rich are different," we'll explore how people who occupy different positions in society consume in very different ways. These consumption differences in turn help to create a unique *lifestyle*, which refers to the broad pattern of how we choose to allocate our time and money. That's a hugely important concept for marketers to understand, so we'll explore some dynamics of lifestyle marketing to close out the chapter.

Income Patterns

A popular saying goes, "You can never be too thin or too rich." As we recover from the Great Recession, the average American's standard of living continues to improve—though many consumers still don't get a full ticket to the American Dream. Two factors

Marketing Opportunity

It's naïve to think that everyone reacts the same way to an economic downturn. The U.K.-based firm M&C Saatchi conducted research to identify eight specific consumer segments that each display different attitudes and behaviors regarding spending and saving money:[6]

1. *Crash Dieters* (26 percent): Try to cut out all nonessential spending until things improve.
2. *Scrimpers* (13 percent): Want to maintain their lifestyle and are reluctant to make sacrifices, so they will trade down to less expensive brands but not stop buying what they like.
3. *Abstainers* (15 percent): Postpone big purchases but look to buy things on credit and pay later.
4. *Balancers* (9 percent): Sacrifice purchases in some categories in order to buy things in other categories.
5. *Treaters* (12 percent): They know they have to cut back, but they have trouble budgeting; therefore, they reward themselves with small treats when they do economize.
6. *Justifiers* (12 percent): They are willing to spend, but they need a good reason to buy something, such as a new model or a really good deal.
7. *Ostriches* (9 percent): They are in denial; they're mostly younger consumers who continue to buy as long as their credit cards hold out.
8. *Vultures* (4 percent): Circle the market, looking to snap up bargains as businesses offer bargain-basement prices.

contribute to an (overall) upward trajectory: a shift in women's roles and increases in educational attainment.[1]

- Mothers with preschool children are the fastest-growing segment of working people. Furthermore, many of them work in high-paying occupations, such as medicine and architecture, which men used to dominate. Although women are still a minority in most professional occupations, their ranks continue to swell. The steady increase in the numbers of working women is a primary cause of the rapid growth of middle- and upper-income families.
- Education also determines who gets a bigger piece of the economic pie. Although picking up the tab for college often entails great sacrifice, it still pays off in the long run. During the course of their lives, college graduates earn about 50 percent more than those who have only gone through high school. Women without high school diplomas earn only 40 percent as much as women who have a college degree.[2] So, hang in there!

To Spend or Not to Spend, That Is the Question

Consumer demand for goods and services depends on both our ability and our willingness to buy. As we've seen over the past few years, although demand for necessities tends to be stable over time, we postpone or eliminate other expenditures if we don't feel that now is a good time to spend money.[3] For example, you may decide to "make do" with your current clunker for another year rather than buy a new car right away. Even businesses like warehouse clubs that sell staples by the case feel the pain when shoppers postpone their purchases; stores such as Costco and Sam's Club post big losses when people no longer buy their discounted jewelry and clothing, even though sales of paper towels and pickles hold steady.[4]

Discretionary income is the money available to a household over and above what it requires to have a comfortable standard of living. Economists estimate that American consumers wield about $400 billion a year in discretionary spending power. People aged 35 to 55, whose incomes are at a peak, account for about half of this amount. As the population ages and income levels rise, the way a typical U.S. household spends its money changes. The most noticeable shift is to allocate a much larger share of a budget to shelter and transportation, and less to food and apparel. (Note: This doesn't mean that higher-income households buy less food and clothing; it's just that the *proportion* of dollars going to these categories decreases.)

Especially in the wake of the Great Recession of 2009, many consumers experience doubts about their individual and collective futures, and they are anxious to hold on to what they have. Of course, not everyone has the same attitudes about money and its importance. We all know **tightwads** who hate to part with even a penny (and who actually experience emotional pain when they hand over their cash), and **spendthrifts** who enjoy nothing more than buying everything in sight. Research on this issue finds that (stereotypes aside) American tightwads outnumber spendthrifts. Men are more likely than women to be tightwads, as are older people and those with more education. How do we tell a tightwad from someone who's just being frugal? One of the researchers puts it this way: "The evidence suggests that frugality is driven by a pleasure of saving, as compared with tightwaddism, which is driven by a pain of paying."[5]

Money has many complex psychological meanings; we equate it with success or failure, social acceptability, security, love, freedom, and yes, even sex appeal.[7] There are therapists who specialize in treating money-related disorders, and they report that some people even feel guilty about their success and deliberately make bad investments to reduce this feeling! Some other clinical conditions include *atephobia* (fear of being ruined), *harpaxophobia* (fear of becoming a victim of robbers), *peniaphobia* (fear of poverty), and *aurophobia* (fear of gold).[8]

A study that approached money as a *social resource* explored some interesting links between our need for acceptance and feelings about cash. In one case participants were either led to believe that a group had rejected them or that it had accepted them. They then completed a number of measures that reflected their desire for money. Those whom the group rejected expressed a greater desire for money. At another stage, subjects counted either real money or pieces of paper and then experienced physical pain. Those who counted money reported they felt less pain than did those who just counted paper![9]

Consumer Confidence

Our expectations about the future affect our current spending, and these individual decisions add up to affect a society's economic well-being.[10] Consumers' beliefs about what the future holds are an indicator of **consumer confidence**. This measure reflects how optimistic or pessimistic people are about the future health of the economy and how they predict they'll fare down the road. These beliefs are important because they influence how much money people pump into the economy when they make discretionary purchases.

Many businesses take forecasts about anticipated spending very seriously, and periodic surveys "take the pulse" of the American consumer. The Conference Board conducts a survey of consumer confidence, as does the Survey Research Center at the University of Michigan. The following are the types of questions they pose to consumers:[11]

- Would you say that you and your family are better off or worse off financially than a year ago?
- Will you be better off or worse off a year from now?
- Is now a good time or a bad time for people to buy major household items, such as furniture or a refrigerator?
- Do you plan to buy a car in the next year?

When people are somewhat pessimistic about their prospects and about the state of the economy, as they are now, they tend to cut back on what they spend and take on less debt. When consumers feel optimistic about the future, they reduce the amount they save, they take on more debt, and they splurge on discretionary items. A range of factors influence the overall savings rate, including individual consumers' pessimism or optimism about their personal circumstances, such as a sudden increase in personal wealth as the result of an inheritance and global events such as the Great Recession. In addition, we see cultural differences in attitudes toward saving (e.g., the Japanese have a much higher savings rate than do Americans, though the latter have definitely been saving more of their incomes in recent years).[12]

The Great Recession and Its Aftermath

In the current economic climate, we have to acknowledge that recent changes in consumer spending—prompted by numerous factors, including frozen credit markets and massive layoffs—almost overnight altered the landscape of consumer behavior. The "go-go" years seem like a distant memory as many people suddenly put the brakes on their BUY NOW mentality. In 2011, median household income was 8.1 percent lower than in 2007, the year before the recession hit the U.S. hard.[13]

Since the 1980s (when we last experienced economic turbulence), Americans' savings rate dropped steadily; it dipped to less than 1 percent in late 2008. In a few short months this rate rocketed to 5 percent, as people cut back wherever they could. The new mantra: Make do with what you have. Save. Question every expense: Do you really need that Starbucks latte, that $80 haircut, that fashion magazine? Thriftiness is in, eye-popping bling is out. Even many *fashionistas* turned into *frugalistas*—they refuse to sacrifice style, but they achieve it on a budget. Now it's cool to visit Web sites and blogs that celebrate frugality, such as Dollar Stretcher (stretcher.com), All Things Frugal (allthingsfrugal.com), and Frugal Mom (frugalmom.net).[14]

Of course, it remains to be seen whether this new frugality will persist when the economy improves (and it will). Young consumers who have grown up with images of

The woman in this Danish ad is fed up with bad financial news. Whether we like it or not, the global recession has affected all of us. Marketers are scrambling to adjust their strategies to this glum economic environment.

Source: Courtesy of Bianco Footwear & Co.

(if not actual) affluence and in-your-face bling may not be prepared to pull such an abrupt about-face. In one survey, 91 percent of young adults say they have financial goals, but only 53 percent stick to a monthly budget, and 42 percent give themselves a grade of D or F to describe how well they save.[15]

Contrary to popular wisdom, not everyone suffers in a recession—and consumers don't uniformly cut back on their spending. Many of them just reallocate their priorities (and perhaps buy less on credit). For now, which companies will feel the pain and which will actually gain? Citigroup strategists coined the term **plutonomy** to describe an economy that's driven by a fairly small number of rich people. Taking a cue from the Standard & Poor's 500-stock index, they created a "basket" of luxury stocks like Bulgari, Porsche, and Sotheby's. Unfortunately, many of those rich people are a lot less rich today, and luxury brands are hurting. Even so, we're starting to see resurgence in expensive categories as sales begin to climb back to higher levels (in some cases, this is largely due to demand in booming economies like China).[16]

In contrast, another team of analysts created their own *Poor Getting Poorer Index.* This basket includes 22 stocks that include retailers, generic brands, repossession agencies, dollar stores, and pawnshops that prosper when others do worse. In a period when the S&P declined by 40 percent, this index actually generated a positive return of about 9 percent. As consumers downscale their eating habits, for example, fast-food chains like McDonald's pick up the surplus. People may not buy as many expensive concert tickets, but they still treat themselves to a movie; box office receipts are holding up well.

Finally, although people are a lot more conscious of price, it's not clear that they've forsaken what was—before the recession hit—a growing emphasis on corporate social responsibility. In one global survey, about seven in ten consumers said that despite the recession, they have given just as much (or more) time and money to causes they deem worthy, and more than half still are prepared to pay more for a brand that supports a good cause. Nearly eight in ten U.S. consumers, although very anxious regarding their personal finances, said they would switch to a brand that supports good causes. As an aside, marketers have their work cut out for them if they want to earn brand loyalty and do good at the same time: Only one-third of the respondents worldwide said they were aware of *any* brand that supports a good cause![17]

Materialism and Economic Conditions

As a by-product of the Great Recession, many consumers have been forced to reconsider the value of their possessions. As one woman observed, "The idea that you need to go bigger to be happy is false. I really believe that the acquisition of material goods doesn't bring about happiness." This doesn't necessarily mean that people will stop buying— but perhaps, at least for a while, they will do so more carefully. In the words of one industry analyst, "We're moving from a conspicuous consumption—which is 'buy without regard'—to a calculated consumption." In 2010, American consumers on average saved more than 6 percent of their incomes—before the Recession the rate was 1 to 2 percent.

Ironically, bad economic conditions may make at least some people happier. Research on the relationship between consumption and happiness tends to show that people are happier when they spend money on experiences instead of material objects, when they relish what they plan to buy long before they buy it, and when they stop trying to outdo their neighbors. One study reported that the only consumption category that was positively related to happiness involved leisure: vacations, entertainment, sports, and equipment like golf clubs and fishing poles. This finding is consistent with changes in buying patterns, which show that consumers have tended to choose experiences over objects during the last couple of years. For example, they may choose to entertain themselves at home rather than going out, or even to forgo a trip to Disney World for a "staycation" in the backyard.

Another factor is just how much of a "buzz" we get from the stuff we buy. The research evidence points to the idea that consumers get more "bang for their buck" when they buy a bunch of smaller things over time, rather than blowing it all on one big purchase. This is due to what psychologists call **hedonic adaptation**; it basically means that to maintain a fairly stable level of happiness, we tend to become used to changes, big or small, wonderful or terrible. That means that over time the rush from a major purchase will dissipate and we're back to where we started (emotionally speaking). So, the next time you get a bonus or find an envelope stuffed with cash on the street, take a series of long weekends instead of splurging on that three-week trip to Maui.[18]

OBJECTIVE 2
We group consumers into social classes that say a lot about where they stand in society.

Social Class and Consumer Identity

Members of every society divide into the "haves" and the "have-nots" (though the amount people "have" is relative). The United States is a place where "all men are created equal," but even so some people seem to be more equal than others. A complex set of variables, including income, family background, and occupation, determines one's standing in society. The place you occupy in the social structure helps to determine not only how much money you spend but also *how* you spend it.

Pick a Pecking Order

In many animal species, a social organization develops whereby the most assertive or aggressive animals exert control over the others and have the first pick of food, living space, and even mating partners. Chickens, for example, exhibit a clearly defined **dominance–submission hierarchy**. Within this hierarchy, each hen has a position in which she is submissive to all the hens above her and she dominates all the ones below her (hence the origin of the term *pecking order*).[19]

People are not much different. We also develop a pecking order that ranks us in terms of our relative standing in society. This rank determines our access to such resources as education, housing, and consumer goods. People try to move up in the social order to improve their ranking. This desire to improve one's lot in life, and often to let others know that one has done so, is at the core of many marketing strategies.

Just as marketers carve society into groups for segmentation purposes, sociologists describe divisions of society in terms of people's relative social and economic resources. Some of these divisions involve political power, whereas others revolve around purely economic distinctions. Karl Marx, the 19th-century economic theorist, argued that a person's relationship to the *means of production* determined his position in a society. The "haves" control resources, and they use the labor of others to preserve their privileged positions. The "have-nots" depend on their own labor for survival, so these people have the most to gain if they change the system. The German sociologist Max Weber showed that the rankings people develop are not one-dimensional. Some involve prestige or "social honor" (he called these *status groups*), some rankings focus on power (or *party*), and some revolve around wealth and property (*class*).[20]

We use the term **social class** more generally to describe the overall rank of people in a society. People who belong to the same social class have approximately equal social standing in the community. They work in roughly similar occupations, and they tend to have similar lifestyles by virtue of their income levels and common tastes. These people tend to socialize with one another and share many ideas and values regarding the way life should be lived.[21]

Indeed, "birds of a feather do flock together." We tend to marry people in a social class similar to our own, a tendency sociologists call **homogamy**, or *assortative mating*. Well over 90 percent of married high school dropouts marry someone who also dropped out or who has only a high school diploma. On the other side of the spectrum, less than 1 percent of the most highly educated Americans have a spouse who did not complete high school.[22]

Social class is as much a state of being as it is of having: It's also a matter of what you do with your money and how you define your role in society. Although we may not like the idea that some members of society are better off or "different" from others, most consumers do acknowledge the existence of different classes and the effect of class membership on consumption. As one wealthy woman observed when researchers asked her to define social class:

> I would suppose social class means where you went to school and how far. Your intelligence. Where you live . . . [w]here you send your children to school. The hobbies you have. Skiing, for example, is higher than the snowmobile. . . . It can't be [just] money, because nobody ever knows that about you for sure.[23]

In school, some kids seem to get all the breaks. They have access to many resources, such as special privileges, fancy cars, large allowances, or dates with other popular classmates. At work, some coworkers get promoted to high-prestige jobs with higher salaries and perks such as a parking space, a large office, or the keys to the executive washroom.

Indeed, in virtually every context some people rank higher than others—even if they just have a larger number of Twitter followers. Patterns of social arrangements evolve whereby some members get more resources than others by virtue of their relative standing, power, or control in the group.[24] The process of **social stratification** refers to this creation of artificial divisions, "those processes in a social system by which scarce and valuable resources are distributed unequally to status positions that become more or less permanently ranked in terms of the share of valuable resources each receives."[25]

Whatever your customers love to do for fun, Libbey refreshes them along the way. Libbey offers glasses to fit any lifestyle and specific taste.☐ You

can satisfy your customers' preferences and reflect your store's distinctiveness, too.☐ Contact your Libbey representative today for a personal viewing. We will come out to see you with so many choices, we know it will be very refreshing indeed.   Libbey

"Peach cooler, please."

"Gimme a brew."

This ad implies that there are social class differences in leisure activities and preferred beverages.
Source: Courtesy of Libbey Glass Co.

Achieved Versus Ascribed Status

You probably agree that in many instances group members seem to get more than their fair share of bennies, whereas other individuals aren't so lucky. Some of these resources probably went to people who earned them through hard work or diligent study (i.e., **achieved status**). But someone may have gotten the goodies because she was lucky enough to be born with "a silver spoon in her mouth." Such good fortune reflects **ascribed status**.

Whether rewards go to the "best and the brightest" or to someone who happens to be related to the boss, allocations are rarely equal within a social group. Most groups exhibit a structure, or **status hierarchy**, in which some members are better off than others. They may have more authority or power, or other members simply like or respect them.

Social Mobility

We've seen that, worldwide, there's an upward drift in terms of access to consumer goods. But to what degree do people actually move from one social class to another? In some societies, such as India, it's difficult to change one's social class; in America, however, we like to say, "anyone can grow up to be president" (though being related to a former president doesn't hurt your chances). **Social mobility** refers to the "passage of individuals from one social class to another."[28]

Horizontal mobility occurs when a person moves from one position to another that's roughly equivalent in social status; for instance, a nurse becomes an elementary school teacher. *Downward mobility* is, of course, movement none of us wants, but unfortunately we observe this pattern fairly often, as farmers and other displaced workers go on welfare

In our society, wealth is more likely to be earned than inherited.

Source: Courtesy of The Phoenix Companies, Inc.

rolls or join the ranks of the homeless. By one estimate, between 2.3 million and 3.5 million Americans experience homelessness in a year's time.[29]

Despite that discouraging trend, demographics decree that overall there must be *upward mobility* in our society. The middle and upper classes reproduce less (i.e., have fewer children per family) than the lower classes (an effect demographers call *differential fertility*), and they tend to restrict family size to below replacement level (i.e., they often have only one child). Therefore, so the reasoning goes, over time those of lower status must fill positions of higher status.[30]

Still, despite America's well-deserved reputation as the "land of opportunity" in reality social mobility is a harder climb in the United States than in many other developed economies such as Canada, Denmark, Australia, Norway, Finland, Sweden, Germany, and Spain, in terms of how freely citizens move up or down the social ladder. One widely cited report, for example, found that the economic advantage of having an affluent father is much more likely to influence the fortune of his son in the United States than in most other Western countries.[31]

Overall, the offspring of blue-collar consumers are blue-collar, and the offspring of white-collar consumers are white-collar.[32] People do improve their positions over time, but these increases are not usually dramatic enough to catapult them from one social class to another. The exception is when a person marries someone considerably richer. This "Cinderella fantasy" is a popular theme in our society; we see it in movies (*Pretty Woman* or *Maid in Manhattan*) and popular TV shows such as *The Bachelor*.

Components of Social Class

When we think about a person's social class, we consider several pieces of information. Two major ones are occupation and income. Let's take a quick look at each.

Occupational Prestige

In a system in which (like it or not) we define people to a great extent by what they do for a living, *occupational prestige* is one way we evaluate their "worth." Hierarchies of occupational prestige tend to be quite stable over time and across cultures. Researchers find similarities in occupational prestige in countries as diverse as Brazil, Ghana, Guam, Japan, and Turkey.[33]

A typical ranking includes a variety of professional and business occupations at the top (e.g., CEO of a large corporation, physician, and college professor); whereas jobs that hover near the bottom include shoe shiner, ditch digger, and garbage collector. Because a person's occupation links strongly to his or her use of leisure time, allocation of family resources, aesthetic preferences, and political orientation, many social scientists consider it the single best indicator of social class.

Income

The distribution of wealth is of great interest to social scientists and to marketers because it determines which groups have the greatest buying power and market potential. Wealth is by no means distributed evenly across the classes. Income *per se* is not often a very good indicator of social class because the *way* in which we spend our money is more telling than *how much* we spend—that's the all-important lifestyle component we'll talk about later in the chapter. Still, people need money to obtain goods and services to express their tastes, so obviously income remains very important.

Although we equate money with social class, the precise relationship between the two concepts is unclear, and social scientists debate it.[34] They are by no means synonymous, which is why many people with a lot of money try to buy their way into a higher social class. One problem is that even if a family adds one or more wage earners and increases its household income, each additional job is likely to be lower in status than the primary wage earner's job. In addition, these members don't necessarily pool their earnings toward the common good of the family.[35]

So, is social class or income a better predictor of consumer behavior? The answer partly depends on the type of product we sell: Do people buy it largely for its functional value (what it does), or for its symbolic value (the impression it conveys to others)?

- Social class is a better predictor of purchases that have symbolic aspects but low to moderate prices (e.g., cosmetics, liquor).
- Income is a better predictor of major expenditures that do not have status or symbolic aspects (e.g., major appliances).
- We need both social class and income data to predict purchases of expensive, symbolic products (e.g., cars, homes).

Targeting the Top of the Pyramid: High-Income Consumers

Many marketers try to target affluent, upscale markets. This often makes sense because these consumers obviously have the resources to spend on costly products that command higher profit margins. However, it is a mistake to assume that we should place everyone with a high income into the same market segment. As we noted earlier, social class involves more than absolute income. It is also a way of life, and several factors—including where they got their money, how they got it, and how long they have had it—significantly affect wealthy people's interests and spending priorities.[36]

Despite our stereotype of rich people who just party all day long, one study found that the typical millionaire is a 57-year-old man who is self-employed, earns a median household income of $131,000, has been married to the same wife for most of his adult life, has children, has never spent more than $399 on a suit or more than $140 for a pair of shoes, and drives a Ford Explorer (the humble billionaire investor Warren Buffett comes to mind). Interestingly, many affluent people don't consider themselves to be rich. One tendency researchers notice is that these people indulge in luxury goods while they

CB AS I SEE IT

Professor George Loewenstein, *Carnegie Mellon University*

The average American spends more on lottery tickets than on reading materials or movies. In 2003, total spending on lotteries was almost $45 billion, or $155 for every man, woman, and child in the United States. Moreover, people at low income levels play the lottery disproportionately; one study found that those with incomes under $10,000 spent almost three times as much on lottery tickets as those with incomes over $50,000.

Why is playing the lottery so attractive, and why is it especially attractive to low-income individuals? My colleagues Emily Haisley and Romel Mostafa and I explored these questions. We hypothesized that one of the attractions of the lottery is that the typical lottery ticket only costs a dollar—peanuts in the budget of even those with low incomes. We went to the Greyhound bus station in Pittsburgh and asked bus travelers if they would complete a survey about their attitudes toward Pittsburgh in

exchange for $5. We then gave them the opportunity to purchase up to five lottery tickets. For some subjects, we handed them the $5 and had them make a single choice of how many tickets to buy (from zero to five). For other subjects, we handed them $1 at a time, five times in a row, and each time asked if they wanted to use the dollar to buy a lottery ticket. Subjects in the latter condition purchased about twice as many lottery tickets. Of course, $1 isn't much, but as the statistics document, many people are forking out the money day after day.

This helps to explain the appeal of the lottery, which is the single most popular form of gambling in the United States despite having the lowest payout rate. Nevertheless, this finding does not explain why low-income individuals are so attracted to playing the lottery. In two follow-up studies we attempted to find out. We reasoned that poor people play the lottery disproportionately because, in contrast to more affluent people, it is their only opportunity, however small, for a dramatic improvement in their economic situation. In the first study we made some Greyhound riders feel rich by asking them in the survey to report their income on a scale that went up in $10,000 increments, peaking at $50,000 or more. We made others feel poor by asking about income with a scale that went up

in $50,000 increments, peaking at $1,000,000 or more. Those made to feel poor bought, on average, about twice as many tickets. In the second study we reasoned that lottery tickets might be attractive to people with low incomes because they have the same opportunity to win as people with higher incomes (in contrast to other areas of life where rich people have advantages). We reminded them of this fact by asking them to report whether poor people, rich people, or neither had an advantage in different areas of life, with one of the areas being "gambling." Those respondents who received this subtle reminder that lotteries give everyone similar odds of winning once again bought more.

The sad fact is that lotteries return only fifty cents on the dollar, making them one of the worst possible investments, and far less lucrative than playing the stock market—even in a bad year. Yet 21 percent of Americans— and 38 percent of those with incomes less than $25,000— report that the lottery is the only way they would be able to accumulate several thousand dollars for retirement. Along with payday loans, rent-to-own establishments, pawn shops, and instant rebate tax services, lotteries are one of the many ways that commercial and state enterprises may be detrimental to the financial well-being of the poor.

---

pinch pennies on everyday items—they buy shoes at Neiman Marcus and deodorant at Walmart, for example.[37]

SRI Consulting Business Intelligence divides consumers into three groups based on their attitudes toward luxury:

1 **Luxury is functional**—These consumers use their money to buy things that will last and have enduring value. They conduct extensive prepurchase research and make logical decisions rather than emotional or impulsive choices.
2 **Luxury is a reward**—These consumers tend to be younger than the first group but older than the third group. They use luxury goods to say, "I've made it." The desire to be successful and to demonstrate their success to others motivates these consumers to purchase conspicuous luxury items, such as high-end automobiles and homes in exclusive communities.

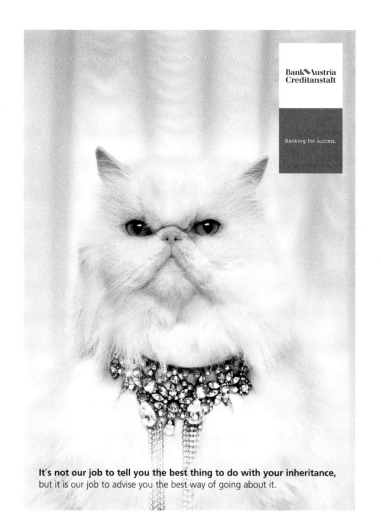

Many companies, like this Austrian bank, aggressively pursue the upper class consumer.
Source: Courtesy of Bank Austria Creditanstalt AG. Photo by Gunter Parth.

3 **Luxury is indulgence**—This group is the smallest of the three and tends to include younger consumers and slightly more males than the other two groups. To these consumers, the purpose of owning luxury is to be extremely lavish and self-indulgent. This group is willing to pay a premium for goods that express their individuality and make others take notice. They have a more emotional approach to luxury spending and are more likely than the other two groups to make impulse purchases.[38]

People who have had money for a long time tend to use their fortunes a lot differently. *Old money* families (e.g., the Rockefellers, DuPonts, Fords, etc.) live primarily on inherited funds. One commentator called this group "the class in hiding."[39] Following the Great Depression of the 1930s, moneyed families became more discreet about exhibiting their wealth. Many fled from mansions such as those we still find in Manhattan (the renovated Vanderbilt mansion now is Ralph Lauren's flagship store) to hideaways in Virginia, Connecticut, and New Jersey.

Mere wealth is not sufficient to achieve social prominence in these circles. You also need to demonstrate a family history of public service and philanthropy, and tangible markers of these contributions often enable donors to achieve a kind of immortality (e.g., Rockefeller University, Carnegie Hall, or the Whitney Museum).[40] "Old money" consumers distinguish among themselves in terms of ancestry and lineage rather than wealth.[41] Furthermore, they're secure in their status. In a sense, they have trained their whole lives to be rich.

In contrast to people with old money, today there are many people—including high-profile billionaires such as Bill Gates, Mark Zuckerberg, and Richard Branson—who

Many consumers still covet luxury products— whether they can afford them or not.
Source: Courtesy of Harry Winston Jewelers.

HARRY WINSTON

NEW YORK BEVERLY HILLS LAS VEGAS BAL HARBOUR HONOLULU DALLAS PARIS GENEVA LONDON TOKYO OSAKA TAIPEI BEIJING HONG KONG

are "the working wealthy."[42] The Horatio Alger myth, where a person goes from "rags to riches" through hard work and a bit of luck, is still a powerful force in our society. That's why a commercial that showed the actual garage where the two cofounders of Hewlett-Packard first worked struck a chord in so many.

Although many people do in fact become "self-made millionaires," they often encounter a problem (although not the worst problem one could think of!) after they have become wealthy and change their social status. The label *nouveau riche* describes consumers who recently achieved their wealth and who don't have the benefit of years of training to learn how to spend it.

Pity the poor **nouveau riches**; many suffer from *status anxiety*. They monitor the cultural environment to ensure that they do the "right" thing, wear the "right" clothes, get seen at the "right" places, use the "right" caterer, and so on.[43] Their flamboyant consumption is an example of *symbolic self-completion* because they try to display symbols they believe have "class" to make up for an internal lack of assurance about the "correct" way to behave.[44] In major Chinese cities such as Shanghai, some people wear pajamas in public as a way to flaunt their newfound wealth. As one consumer explained, "Only people in cities can afford clothes like this. In farming villages, they still have to wear old work clothes to bed."[45]

Targeting the Bottom of the Pyramid: Low-Income Consumers

About 14 percent of Americans live below the poverty line, and most marketers largely ignore this segment. Still, although poor people obviously have less to spend than do

The Tangled Web

Because so much of what happens in the world today happens online, people who don't have access to the Internet can be at a real disadvantage. The so-called **Digital Divide** between the rich and the poor is still a reality. According to a study by the Pew Research Center, 87 percent of U.S. households making more than $75,000 have broadband access at home. In contrast, only 40 percent of U.S. households making less than $30,000 have access. Whereas 95 percent of high-income households use the Internet at home in some fashion, just 57 percent of the poorest do. Not surprisingly, affluent people are also much more likely to own cell phones, computers, e-readers, and other entertainment devices.[48]

rich ones, they have the same basic needs as everyone else. Low-income families purchase staples, such as milk, orange juice, and tea, at the same rates as average-income families. Minimum wage–level households spend more than average on out-of-pocket health-care costs, rent, and the food they eat at home.[46] And, of course, the market size is huge: Although there are 6.6 billion consumers in the world, only 1.5 billion of them possess purchasing power greater than $10,000 to make personal expenditures. The other 5.1 billion people—78 percent of the global population—are low-income consumers.[47] Some analysts refer to this vast number of consumers as the **bottom of the pyramid**.

A lot of companies are taking a second look at marketing to the poor because of their large numbers.[49] Some find innovative ways to tap these vast markets as they revamp their distribution systems or make their products simpler and less expensive. When Nestlé Brazil shrank the package size of its Bono cookies (no relation to the U2 singer) from 200 grams to 140 grams and dropped the price, sales jumped 40 percent. Unilever called a new soap brand Ala so that illiterate people in Latin America could easily recognize it. In Mexico, the cement company CEMEX improved housing in poor areas after it introduced a pay-as-you-go system to buy building supplies.[50] Figure 11.1 provides one framework to help marketers make needed changes to provide for the needs of low-income consumers around the world.

Worldview

A **worldview** is one way to differentiate among social classes. To generalize, the world of the working class (i.e., the lower-middle class) is more intimate and constricted. For example, working-class men are likely to name local sports figures as heroes and are less likely to take long vacation trips to out-of-the-way places.[51] Immediate needs, such as a new refrigerator or TV, tend to dictate buying behavior, whereas the higher classes focus on more long-term goals, such as saving for college tuition or retirement.[52] Working-class consumers depend heavily on relatives for emotional support and tend to orient themselves in terms of the local community rather than the world at large. They are more likely to be conservative and family oriented. Maintaining the appearance of one's home and property is a priority, regardless of the size of the house.

One study that looked at social class and how it relates to consumers' feelings of *empowerment* reported that lower-class men aren't as likely to feel they have the power

Figure 11.1 THE 4 A'S

Source: Anderson and Niels Billou, "Serving the World's Poor: Innovation at the Base of the Economic Pyramid," *Journal of Business Strategy,* 28, 2: 14–21, reprinted in A. T. Kearney, *Serving the Low-Income Consumer: How to Tackle This Mostly Ignored Market,* 2011, http://www.atkearney.com/index.php/Publications/serving-the-low-income-consumer.html.

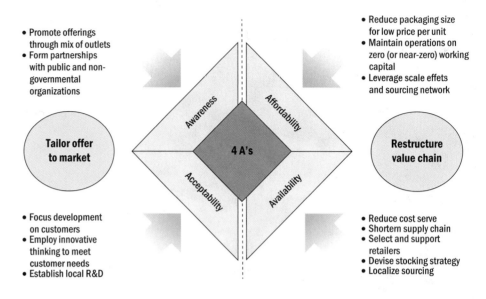

The 4 A's of addressing low-income consumers

- Promote offerings through mix of outlets
- Form partnerships with public and non-governmental organizations

- Reduce packaging size for low price per unit
- Maintain operations on zero (or near-zero) working capital
- Leverage scale effects and sourcing network

Tailor offer to market

Restructure value chain

Awareness   Affordability

4 A's

Acceptability   Availability

- Focus development on customers
- Employ innovative thinking to meet customer needs
- Establish local R&D

- Reduce cost serve
- Shorten supply chain
- Select and support retailers
- Devise stocking strategy
- Localize sourcing

to affect their outcomes. Respondents varied from those who were what the researcher calls *potent actors* (those who believe they have the ability to take actions that affect their world) to *impotent reactors* (those who feel they are at the mercy of their economic situations). This orientation influenced consumption behaviors; for example, the professionals in the study who were likely to be potent actors set themselves up for financial opportunity and growth. They took very broad perspectives on investing and planned their budgets strategically.[53]

Although they would like to have more in the way of material goods, working-class people do not necessarily envy those who rank above them in social standing.[54] They may not view the maintenance of a high-status lifestyle as worth the effort. As one blue-collar consumer commented, "Life is very hectic for those people. There are more breakdowns and alcoholism. It must be very hard to sustain the status, the clothes, and the parties that are expected. I don't think I'd want to take their place."[55]

This person may be right. Although good things appear to go hand-in-hand with higher status and wealth, the picture is not that clear. The social scientist Émile Durkheim observed that suicide rates are much higher among the wealthy; he wrote in 1897, "The possessors of most comfort suffer most."[56] Durkheim's wisdom may still be accurate today. Many well-off consumers seem to be stressed or unhappy despite or even because of their wealth, a condition some call **affluenza**.[57]

Cosmopolitanism is an aspect of worldview that is starting to receive more attention by consumer behavior researchers, who define a cosmopolitan as someone who tries to be open to the world and who strives for diverse experiences (not to be confused with the popular cocktail). This is a quality that used to be linked to the wealthy, but now—with improved access to media and of course the Internet—it's no longer necessary to be rich to express an interest in a range of culturally diverse products. Cosmopolitans respond well to brands that have a "worldly" (i.e., international or global) image. They think it's important to own consumer electronics products and are more likely to engage in electronic media activities such as email, Web surfing, and buying DVDs.[58] A scale to identify these consumers includes statements like these:

- I enjoy exchanging ideas with people from other cultures or countries.
- I am interested in learning more about people who live in other countries.
- I find people from other cultures stimulating.

Social Class in the United States

The United States *in theory* does not have a rigid, objectively defined class system. Nevertheless, Americans tend to maintain a stable class structure in terms of income distribution. Unlike some other countries, however, what *does* change are the groups (ethnic, racial, and religious) that occupy different positions within this structure at different times.[59] The sociologist W. Lloyd Warner proposed the most influential classification of American class structure in 1941. Warner identified six social classes:[60]

1 Upper Upper
2 Lower Upper
3 Upper Middle
4 Lower Middle
5 Upper Lower
6 Lower Lower

These classifications imply that access to resources, such as money, education, and luxury goods, increases as you move up the ladder from Lower Lower to Upper Upper. For example, the richest 20 percent of U.S. households earn roughly half of all the income. In contrast, the poorest 20 percent receive just over 3 percent. However, these figures don't tell the whole story: Some poorer families have access to nontaxable income, or members may be between jobs so their low income is temporary. When you adjust income for other factors and look at the data on a per-person basis (while on average 3.1 people live in a household in the top category, only 1.7 live in one in the bottom category), the richest people actually consume four times more than the poorest.[61]

Other social scientists have proposed variations on this system over the years, but these six levels summarize fairly well the way we still think about class, even though the proportion of consumers who fall into each category fluctuates over time. Figure 11.2 provides one view of the American status structure.

Social Class Around the World

Every society has some type of hierarchical class structure that determines people's access to products and services. Let's take a quick look at a few important ones.

Marketing Pitfall

In the last few years the label **One Percenter** entered our nation's vocabulary. Beginning with the Occupy Wall Street movement where we saw protestors camping out in cities across the United States, the spotlight has been on the people who earn the top 1 perecnt of income in our country. The 2012 presidential campaign focused on disparities in income as some people voiced resentment about the growing income gap between the haves and the have-nots. As of 2010, on average the top 1 percent of taxpayers earned $1.12 million.[62]

Source: Kevork Djansezian/Getty Images.

Figure 11.2 A CLASSIC VIEW OF THE AMERICAN CLASS STRUCTURE

INCOME

UPPER CLASS AMERICANS
Upper-Upper (0.3%): The "capital S society" world of inherited wealth
Lower-Upper (1.2%): The newer social elite, drawn from current professionals
Upper-Middle (12.5%): The rest of college graduate managers and professionals; lifestyle centers on private clubs, causes, and the arts

MIDDLE CLASS AMERICANS
Middle Class (32%): Average pay white-collar workers and their blue-collar friends; live on "the better side of town," try to "do the proper things"
Working Class (38%): Average pay blue-collar workers; lead "working class lifestyle" whatever the income, school, background, and job

LOWER CLASS AMERICANS
"A lower group of people, but not the lowest" (9%): Working, not on welfare; living standard is just above poverty; behavior judged "crude," "trashy"
"Real Lower-Lower" (7%): On welfare, visibly poverty-stricken, usually out of work (or have "the dirtiest jobs"); "bums," "common criminals"

China

An economic boom is rapidly creating a middle class of more than 130 million people that analysts project will grow to more than 400 million in 10 years. During the Cultural Revolution, Mao's Red Guards seized on even the smallest possessions—a pocket watch or silk scarf—as evidence of "bourgeois consciousness." Change came rapidly in the early 1990s, after Mao's successor Deng Xiaoping uttered the phrase that quickly became the credo of the new China: "To get rich is glorious."

Because costs in China are low, a family with an annual income below the U.S. poverty threshold of about $14,000 can enjoy middle-class comforts, including stylish clothes, Chinese-made color televisions, DVD players, and cell phones. Wealthier Chinese entrepreneurs indulge in Cuban Cohiba cigars that sell for $25 each, a quarter of the average Chinese laborer's monthly wage. In bustling Shanghai, newly minted "yuppies" drop their kids off for golf lessons; visit Maserati and Ferrari showrooms; buy some luxury items from Louis Vuitton, Hugo Boss, or Prada; then pick up some Häagen-Dazs ice cream before they head to an Evian spa to unwind.

Nike, which consumers in a survey named China's coolest brand, profits mightily from the rise of the Chinese middle class. Nike shoes are a symbol of success, and the company opens an average of 1.5 new stores a day there. The company worked for a long time to attain this status, starting when it outfitted top Chinese athletes and sponsored all the teams in China's pro basketball league. Still, becoming a fashion icon (and persuading consumers to spend twice the average monthly salary for a pair of shoes) is no mean feat in a country that's not exactly sports crazy. So Nike affiliated with the NBA (which began to televise games in China) and brought over players such as Michael Jordan for visits. Slowly but surely, in-the-know Chinese came to call sneakers "Nai-ke."[63]

Japan

Japan is a highly brand-conscious society where upscale, designer labels are incredibly popular. Although the devastation from the 2011 tsunami reduced demand for luxury goods among many Japanese, their love affair with top brands started in the 1970s when the local economy was booming and many Japanese could buy Western luxury accessories for the first time. Some analysts say Japan's long slump since that time may have fostered a psychological need to splurge on small luxuries to give people the illusion of wealth and to forget their anxieties about the future. Single, working women are largely responsible for fueling Japan's luxury-goods spending; about three-quarters of Japanese women aged 25 to 29 work outside the home. These "office ladies" typically save money

Middle-class Chinese women prize a pale complexion in part because it implies a life free of outdoor manual labor. A popular folk saying goes, "Fair skin conceals a thousand flaws." As consumers have more leisure time and spend more time at the beach, women have to work harder to protect their pallid appearance. Some wear elaborate face masks or "sun protection gloves."[64]
Source: Sim Chi Yin/VII Mentor.

because they live with their parents, so this leaves them with cash on hand to spend on clothes, accessories, and vacations.[65]

The Middle East

In contrast to the Japanese, few Arab women work. This makes a search for the latest in Western luxury brands a major leisure activity for those with money. Dressing rooms are large, with antechambers to accommodate the friends and family members who often come along on shopping sprees. A major expansion of Western luxury brands is under way across the Middle East, home to some of the fashion industry's best customers. High-end retailers such as Saks Fifth Avenue and Giorgio Armani operate opulent stores that cater to this growing market. However, fashion retailers must take cultural and religious considerations into account. Missoni makes sure that collections include longer pants and skirts, and evening gowns with light shawls to cover heads or bare shoulders. Advertising and display options are also more limited: Erotic images don't work. In the strict religious culture of Saudi Arabia, mannequins can't reveal a gender or human shape. At Saks' Riyadh store, models are headless and don't have fingers. Half of the two-level store is off limits to men.[66]

The United Kingdom

England is an extremely class-conscious country, and at least until recently inherited position and family background largely predetermined consumption patterns. Traditionally people defined three classes: upper, middle, and working. Members of the upper class were educated at schools such as Eton and Oxford, and they spoke like Henry Higgins in *My Fair Lady*. We can still find remnants of this rigid class structure. "Hooray Henrys" (wealthy young men) play polo at Windsor and hereditary peers still dominate the House of Lords.

However, the dominance of inherited wealth appears to have faded in Britain's traditionally aristocratic society, as British entrepreneurs like Richard Branson (of the Virgin empire) redefine the economy. The United Kingdom was particularly hard hit by the Great Recession, as was the United States, and a new emphasis on frugality altered people's priorities. In addition, populist outrage grew after it came to light that legislators had billed the government for excessive expenses—among other abuses, British taxpayers footed a £2,000 bill for one M.P. to clean the moat surrounding his castle.[67]

The U.K. came to a virtual standstill during the royal wedding between Prince William and Catherine Middleton in 2011.

Source: waynehowes/Shutterstock.

The Great British Class Survey, a recent survey conducted by the BBC, asked more than 161,000 people for their input about social class. The study concluded the number of distinct classes in the U.K. today has grown from three to seven. These range from the "elite" at the top who possess money, social connections, and upper-crust cultural preferences, to the *precariat* (precarious proletariat) at the bottom who live from day-to-day with severely constrained resources. The new middle categories include the "technical middle class," a group that has a lot of money but few social connections or cultural activity, and "emergent service workers," a young, urban group that has little money but a lot of social connections and cultural interests. Not all Britons agreed with the new classifications. As one wrote to a newspaper, "There are only two classes: those with tattoos, and those without."[68]

India

India's economy is booming despite the global recession, and affluent consumers prize higher-end global brands—even though nearly half of India's population lives on less than $1.25 a day. Brands like Gucci, Jimmy Choo, and Hermès scramble to open stores in high-end hotels or new superluxury malls, where the management often stations guards at the doors to keep the destitute outside.[69]

A recent flap illustrates the rapid changes in Indian society. *Vogue India* ran a 16-page spread of poor people surrounded by luxury goods: a toothless old woman holds a child who wears a Fendi bib, a woman and two other people ride on a motorbike as she sports a Hermès bag that sells for more than $10,000, a street beggar grips a Burberry umbrella. A columnist denounced the spread as "not just tacky but downright distasteful." The magazine's editor commented that the shoot's message is simply that "fashion is no longer a rich man's privilege. Anyone can carry it off and make it look beautiful."[70]

One of Bollywood's biggest stars, Shahrukh Khan, is "brand ambassador" for Tag Heuer watches, which cost thousands of dollars. He gives them away on the Indian version of *Who Wants to Be a Millionaire?*, the show that also formed the basis for the hit movie *Slumdog Millionaire*. India's ascendancy is fairly recent; for decades after the country became independent from Britain, its economy was socialistic and traditional with a very rigid class hierarchy—Dalits, formerly known as the Untouchables, are at the bottom and forced into menial jobs while Brahmins historically occupied the highest rung of the social ladder.[71]

Analysts project that by 2015 there will be about 267 million middle class Indian consumers, a growth of about 67 percent over just a 5-year period. Although the middle class currently represents less than 15 percent of India's population, it still accounts for about one-half of the cars, computers, and air conditioners in the country.[73] Today, young Indian consumers watch MTV and read international fashion magazines. They exert a strong influence on the country's rapid growth, especially since India's population is relatively young—54 percent of the people are under 25 years of age.[74]

How Do We Measure Social Class?

Because social class is a complex concept that depends on a number of factors, it is not surprising that social scientists disagree on the best way to measure it. Early measures included the Index of Status Characteristics from the 1940s and the Index of Social Position from the 1950s.[75] These indices combined individual characteristics (e.g., income, type of housing) to arrive at a label of class standing. The accuracy of these composites is still a subject of debate among researchers; a study claimed that for segmentation purposes, raw education and income measures work as well as composite status measures.[76] Figure 11.3 shows one commonly used measurement instrument.

American consumers generally have little difficulty placing themselves in either the working class (lower-middle class) or middle class.[77] The proportion of consumers who identify themselves as working class tended to rise until about 1960, but it has declined since then. Blue-collar workers with relatively high-prestige jobs still tend to view themselves as working class, even though their income levels are equivalent to those of many white-collar workers.[78] This fact reinforces the idea that the labels of "working class" or "middle class" are very subjective. Their meanings say at least as much about self-identity as they do about economic well-being.

Market researchers were among the first to propose that we can distinguish people from different social classes from one another. Some of these class distinctions still exist,

Figure 11.3 EXAMPLE OF A COMPUTERIZED STATUS INDEX

Interviewer circles code numbers (for the computer) that in his/her judgment best fit the respondent and family. Interviewer asks for detail on occupation, then makes rating. Interviewer often asks the respondent to describe neighborhood in own words. Interviewer asks respondent to specify income—a card is presented to the respondent showing the eight brackets—and records R's response. If interviewer feels this is overstatement or understatement, a "better judgment" estimate should be given, along with an explanation.

EDUCATION:	Respondent	Respondent's Spouse
Grammar school (8 yrs or less)	−1	−1
Some high school (9 to 11 yrs)	−2	−2
Graduated high school (12 yrs)	−3	−3
Some post high school (business, nursing, technical, 1 yr college)	−4	−4
Two, three years of college—possibly Associate of Arts degree	−5	−5
Graduated four-year college (B.A./B.S.)	−7	−7
Master's or five-year professional degree	−8	−8
Ph.D. or six/seven-year professional degree	−9	−9

(Respondent box: R's Age ____ ; Spouse box: Spouse's Age ____)

OCCUPATION PRESTIGE LEVEL OF HOUSEHOLD HEAD: Interviewer's judgment of how head of household rates in occupational status.

(Respondent's description—asks for previous occupation if retired, or if R. is widow, asks husband's: _____)

Chronically unemployed—"day" laborers, unskilled; on welfare	−0
Steadily employed but in marginal semiskilled jobs; custodians, minimum pay factory help, service workers (gas attendants, etc.)	−1
Average-skill assembly-line workers, bus and truck drivers, police and firefighters, route deliverymen, carpenters, brickmasons	−2
Skilled craftsmen (electricians), small contractors, factory foremen, low-pay salesclerks, office workers, postal employees	−3
Owners of very small firms (2–4 employees), technicians, salespeople, office workers, civil servants with average-level salaries	−4
Middle management, teachers, social workers, lesser professionals	−5
Lesser corporate officials, owners of middle-sized businesses (10–20 employees), moderate-success professionals (dentists, engineers, etc.)	−7
Top corporate executives, "big successes" in the professional world (leading doctors and lawyers), "rich" business owners	−9

AREA OF RESIDENCE: Interviewer's impressions of the immediate neighborhood in terms of its reputation in the eyes of the community.

Slum area: people on relief, common laborers	−1
Strictly working class: not slummy but some very poor housing	−2
Predominantly blue-collar with some office workers	−3
Predominantly white-collar with some well-paid blue-collar	−4
Better white-collar area: not many executives, but hardly any blue-collar either	−5
Excellent area: professionals and well-paid managers	−7
"Wealthy" or "society"-type neighborhood	−9

TOTAL SCORE _____

TOTAL FAMILY INCOME PER YEAR:

Under $5,000	−1	$20,000 to $24,999	−5
$5,000 to $9,999	−2	$25,000 to $34,999	−6
$10,000 to $14,999	−3	$35,000 to $49,999	−7
$15,000 to $19,999	−4	$50,000 and over	−8

Estimated Status _____

(Interviewer's estimate: _____ and explanation _____)

R's MARITAL STATUS: Married ____ Divorced/Separated ____ Widowed ____ Single ____ (CODE: ____)

but—as we saw earlier—others (including brand preferences) have changed. Unfortunately, many of these measures are badly dated and have little validity today.[79]

One reason for this is that social scientists designed most measures of social class with the traditional nuclear family in mind; this unit included a male wage earner in the middle of his career and a female full-time homemaker. These measures have trouble accounting for two-income families, young singles living alone, or households headed by women, which are so prevalent today.

Another problem with measuring social class is the increasing anonymity of our society. Earlier studies relied on the *reputational method*, where researchers conducted extensive interviews within an area to determine the reputations and backgrounds of individuals. When they used information and also traced people's interaction patterns, they could generate a very comprehensive view of social standing within a community. However, this approach is virtually impossible to implement in most communities today. One compromise is to interview individuals to obtain demographic data and to combine these data with the interviewer's subjective impressions of each person's possessions and standard of living.

As an example, refer to the items in Figure 11.3. Note that the accuracy of this questionnaire relies largely on the interviewer's judgment, especially regarding the quality of the respondent's neighborhood. The interviewer's own circumstances can bias these impressions because they can affect her standard of comparison. Furthermore, the instrument uses highly subjective terms: *slummy* and *excellent* are not objective measures. These potential problems highlight the need to adequately train interviewers, as well as for some attempt to cross-validate such data, possibly by employing multiple judges to rate the same area.

One problem when we assign any group of people to a social class is that they may not exhibit equal standing on all of the relevant dimensions. A person might come from a low-status ethnic group but have a high-status job, whereas another who did not finish high school may live in a fancy part of town. Social scientists use the concept of **status crystallization** to assess the impact of social class inconsistency.[80] The logic is that when these indicators are not consistent, stress occurs, because the rewards from each part of such an "unbalanced" person's life are variable and unpredictable. People who exhibit such inconsistencies tend to be more receptive to social change than are those whose identities are more firmly rooted.

A related problem occurs when a person's social-class standing creates expectations that he or she can't meet. Some people find themselves in the not-unhappy position of making more money than we expect of those in their social class. This means they are *overprivileged,* a condition we define as an income that is at least 25 to 30 percent greater than the median for one's class.[81] In contrast, *underprivileged* consumers, who earn at least 15 percent less than the median, must often allocate a big chunk of their income to maintaining the impression that they occupy a certain status. For example, some people talk about being "house-poor"; they pay so much for a lavish home that they can't afford to furnish it. Today, many homeowners unfortunately find themselves in this position. In 2012, U.S. banks foreclosed on about 700,000 homes (which at least was less than the 800,000 foreclosures the year before).[82]

We traditionally assume that husbands define a family's social class, whereas wives must live it. Women achieve their social status through their husbands.[83] Indeed, the evidence indicates that physically attractive women do tend to "marry up" (**hierogamy**) in social class to a greater extent than attractive men do. Women trade the resource of sexual appeal, which historically has been one of the few assets they were allowed to possess, for the economic resources of men.[84]

We must strongly question the accuracy of this assumption in today's world. Many women now contribute equally to the family's well-being, and they work in positions of comparable or even greater status than their spouses. Employed women tend to average both their own and their husband's positions when they estimate their own subjective status.[85] Nevertheless, a prospective spouse's social class is often an important "product attribute" when someone in the "marriage market" evaluates his or her options.

Status Symbols and Social Capital

OBJECTIVE 3

Individuals' desires to make a statement about their social class, or the class to which they hope to belong, influence the products they like and dislike.

It's getting more difficult to clearly link certain brands or stores with a specific class. Marketplace changes make it tougher for the casual observer to accurately place a consumer in a certain class by looking at the products he buys. That's because a lot of "affordable luxuries" now are within reach of many consumers who could not have acquired them in the past. Think of college women you may know who buy pricey bags from Louis

Luxury items like diamond engagement rings are valued as status symbols the world over, as this Brazilian ad for a jeweler reminds us. *Source:* Courtesy of Saatchi & Saatchi/Brazil.

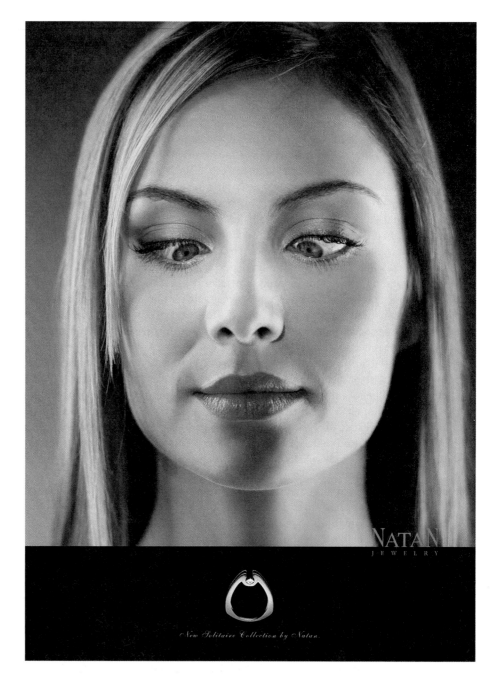

Vuitton or Coach, and then eat ramen noodles for dinner. To make matters even more confusing, a wealthy family may well buy its wine at Costco and its bath towels at Target—and, especially in today's economy, proudly gloat about the steals they got.[86] Luxury brands slash prices to attract more customers, while mass-market brands move upscale. Disney's Couture line sells cashmere sweaters "inspired by Tinker Bell," pricey chandeliers patterned after the Art Deco décor in Mr. Disney's former office, and a $1,400 sequined Mickey Mouse T-shirt from Dolce & Gabbana.[87]

Profound changes in global income distribution drive this shift. Traditionally, it was common to find a huge gulf between the rich and the poor: You were either one or the other. Today, rising incomes in many economically developing countries, such as South Korea and China, coupled with decreasing prices for quality consumer goods and services, level the playing field. The current recession aside, more and more consumers around the globe participate in the global economy. The biggest emerging markets go by the acronym **BRIC nations**: Brazil, Russia, India, and China. These four countries today account for 15 percent of the $60 trillion global economy, but analysts project they will overtake the European and American economies within 20 years.[88]

This change fuels demand for mass-consumed products that still offer some degree of panache. Companies such as H&M, Zara, EasyJet, and L'Oréal provide creature comforts to a consumer segment that analysts label **mass class**. This refers to the hundreds of millions of global consumers who now enjoy a level of purchasing power that's sufficient to let them afford high-quality products—except for big-ticket items such as college educations, housing, or luxury cars. The mass-class market, for example, spawned several versions of affordable cars: Latin Americans have their Volkswagen Beetle (they affectionately call it *el huevito*, "the little egg"); Indian consumers have their Maruti 800 (it sells for as little as US $4,860); and the Fiat Palio, the company's "world car," targets people in emerging countries such as Brazil, Argentina, India, China, and Turkey.[89]

"What Do You Use That Fork For?" Taste Cultures, Codes, and Cultural Capital

A **taste culture** describes consumers in terms of their aesthetic and intellectual preferences. This concept helps to illuminate the important, yet sometimes subtle, distinctions in consumption choices among the social classes.[90] For example, a comprehensive analysis of social class differences using data from 675,000 households supports the mass-class phenomenon we discussed earlier: Differences in consumption patterns between the upper and upper-middle classes and between the middle and working classes are disappearing. However, strong differences still emerge in terms of how consumers spend their discretionary income and leisure time. Upper- and upper-middle-class people are more likely to visit museums and attend live theater, and middle-class consumers are more likely to camp and fish. The upper classes are more likely to listen to all-news programs, whereas the middle classes are more likely to tune in to country music.[91]

In one of the classic studies of social differences in taste, researchers cataloged homeowners' possessions as they sat in their living rooms and asked them about their income and occupation. As Figure 11.4 shows, they identified clusters of furnishings and decorative items that seemed to appear together with some regularity, and they found different clusters depending on the consumer's social status. For example, they tended to find a cluster that consisted of religious objects, artificial flowers, and still-life portraits in relatively lower-status living rooms, whereas they were likely to catalog a cluster of abstract paintings, sculptures, and modern furniture in a higher-status home.[92]

Another approach to social class focuses on the **codes** (the ways consumers express and interpret meanings) people within different social strata use. It's valuable for marketers to map these codes, because they can use concepts and terms that target customers will relate to. Marketing appeals we construct with class differences in mind result in quite different messages. For example, a life insurance ad that a company targets to a lower-class person might depict, in simple, straightforward terms, a hard-working family man who feels good immediately after he buys a policy. A more upscale appeal might depict a more affluent older couple surrounded by photos of their children and grandchildren. It might include extensive copy that plugs the satisfaction of planning for the future.

These two ways to communicate product benefits incorporate different types of codes. **Restricted codes** focus on the content of objects, not on relationships among objects. **Elaborated codes**, in contrast, are more complex and depend on a more sophisticated worldview. These code differences extend to the way consumers approach basic concepts such as time, social relationships, and objects. Table 11.1 summarizes some differences between these two code types.

Clearly, not all taste cultures are created equal. The upper classes have access to resources that enable them to perpetuate their privileged position in society. Pierre

Figure 11.4 LIVING ROOM CLUSTERS AND SOCIAL CLASS

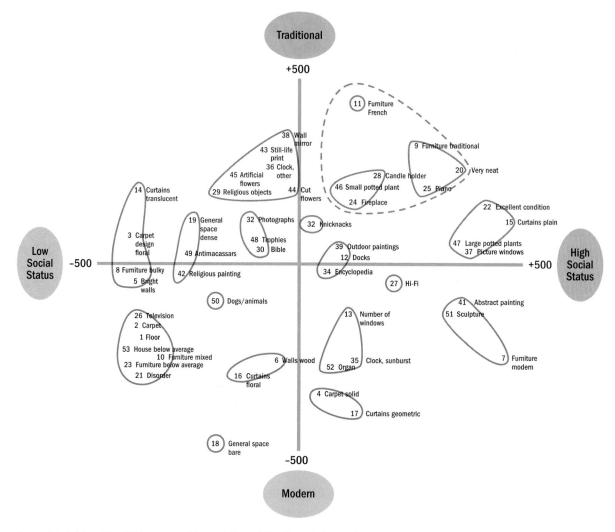

Bourdieu was a French theorist who wrote at length about how people compete for resources, or *capital*. Bourdieu did large-scale surveys to track people's wealth, and he related this "economic capital" to patterns of taste in entertainment and the arts. He concluded that "taste" is a status-marking force, or **habitus**, that causes consumption preferences to cluster together. Later analyses of American consumers largely confirm these relationships; for example, higher-income people are more likely than the average consumer to attend the theater, whereas lower-income people are more likely to attend a wrestling match.[93]

Social Capital

In addition to economic capital (financial resources), Bourdieu pointed to the significance of **social capital** (organizational affiliations and networks). The legions of aspiring professionals who take up golf because they conduct so much business on the greens demonstrate how social capital operates. Although many people genuinely love to hit that ball around, the reality is that a lot of business gets transacted on the course and executives profit from their membership in this community (some business schools even offer academic courses on "golf etiquette"!). Social capital tends to

TABLE 11.1	Effects of Restricted Versus Elaborated Codes	
	Restricted Codes	**Elaborated Codes**
General characteristics	Emphasize description and contents of objects	Emphasize analysis and interrelationship between objects; i.e., hierarchical organization and instrumental connections
	Have implicit meanings (context dependent)	Have explicit meanings
Language	Use few qualifiers, i.e., few adjectives or adverbs	Have language rich in personal, individual qualifiers
	Use concrete, descriptive, tangible symbolism	Use large vocabulary, complex conceptual hierarchy
Social relationships	Stress attributes of individuals over formal roles	Stress formal role structure, instrumental relationships
Time	Focus on present; have only general notion of future	Focus an instrumental relationship between present activities and future rewards
Physical space	Locate rooms, spaces in context of other rooms and places: e.g., "front room," "corner store"	Identify rooms, spaces in terms of usage; formal ordering of spaces; e.g., "dining room," "financial district"
Implications for marketers	Stress inherent product quality, contents (or trustworthiness, goodness of "real-type"), spokesperson	Stress differences, advantages vis-à-vis other products in terms of some autonomous evaluation criteria
	Stress implicit of fit of product with total lifestyle	Stress product's instrumental ties to distant benefits
	Use simple adjectives, descriptions	Use complex adjectives, descriptors

Source: Adapted from Jeffrey F. Durgee, "How Consumer Sub-Cultures Code Reality: A Look at Some Code Types," in Richard J. Lutz, ed., *Advances in Consumer Research* 13 (Provo, UT: Association of Consumer Research, 1986): 332.

be a limited and protected resource. At many country clubs it's not enough just to be rolling in money: You also need to be recommended by current members, so that the organization controls (fairly or not) just who gets to hobnob on the links and in the locker room.

Bourdieu also reminds us of the consequences of **cultural capital**. This refers to a set of distinctive and socially rare tastes and practices—knowledge of "refined" behavior that admits a person into the realm of the upper class.[94] The elites in a society collect a set of skills that enable them to hold positions of power and authority, and they pass these on to their children (think etiquette lessons and debutante balls). These resources gain in value because class members restrict access to them. That's part of the reason why people compete so fiercely for admission to elite colleges. Much as we hate to admit it, the rich *are* different.

Online Social Capital

Typically, a community is healthier and more desirable when it is able to offer a lot of social capital as an inducement for people to join. This is true in the online world as well. You can think of this like a big, beefy nightclub bouncer who decides who he will admit past the velvet rope. In the online world, bloggers acquire social capital when a lot of other people start to rate their posts highly and perhaps re-tweet them.[95] And, like exclusive country clubs, **online gated communities** that selectively allow access to some people may offer a high degree of social capital to the lucky few who pass the test.

Consider, for example, "exclusive" dating sites like hotenough.org that (at least allegedly) weed out unattractive people. The site's home page claims, "Through our screening process, we have filtered the masses leaving only your area's most attractive, fit, trendy singles and have now included an exclusive section for our 40+ singles, the 'BABY BOOMER SECTION.' Hot Enough offers three tiers of hotties, so if you're fit and trendy, then rest assured there is a place for you."[96]

Net Profit

Let's use Foursquare as an example to understand how online social capital works. People visit Foursquare because they can check in at locations and announce their arrivals to their community of friends. Some check-ins can earn badges and coupons from participating retailers. The more people who become involved, the more valuable the community, and involvement grows based on activities that participants value. For instance, people who are into Foursquare crave the status of being designated as "mayor" of a location like their local Starbucks. As long as people value this title, the Foursquare community will attract enthusiastic participants. If and when people move on to something else, the social capital that flows from being a "mayor" will slow to a trickle. At that point, we're on to the next hot site. As it declines, the community experiences a big dropoff in participation, adherence to norms, perceived reputation, and trust among members.[97] Think MySpace or Friendster to understand how platforms can lose their cool almost overnight.

This ad from New Zealand pokes fun at the tendency of some consumers to show off their cultural capital excessively.
Source: DB Breweries.

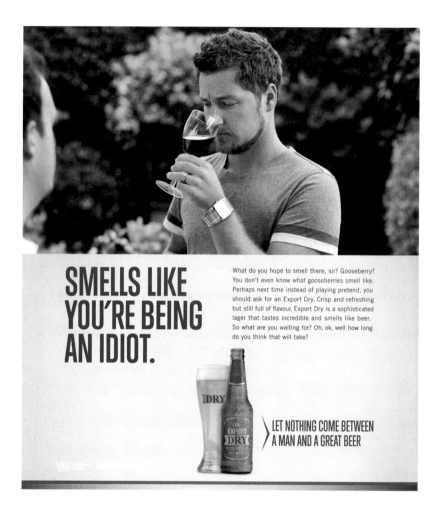

Status Symbols

We tend to evaluate ourselves, our professional accomplishments, our appearance, and our material well-being relative to others. The popular phrase "keeping up with the Joneses" (in Japan, it's "keeping up with the Satos") refers to a desire to compare your standard of living with your neighbors'—and exceed it if you can.

Often it's not enough just to have wealth or fame; what matters is that you have more of it than others. One study demonstrated that we assign value to *loyalty programs* (e.g., when airlines award you special status based on the number of miles you fly) at least in part based on our level in the hierarchy relative to other members. Subjects were assigned to "gold status" in a program where they were in the only tier, or a program where there was also a silver tier. Although both groups were "gold," those in the program that also offered a lower level felt better about it.[98]

A major motivation to buy is not to enjoy these items but rather to let others know that we can afford them. These products are **status symbols**. The popular bumper-sticker slogan, "He who dies with the most toys, wins," summarizes the desire to accumulate these badges of achievement. Status-seeking is a significant source of motivation to procure appropriate products and services that we hope will let others know we've "made it." A study demonstrated how people turn to status symbols to prop up their self-concepts, especially when they feel badly or uncertain about other aspects of their lives. When subjects in auctions were made to feel that they had little power, they spent more to purchase items to compensate for this deficit.[99]

As we discussed earlier in the chapter, the rise of a *mass class* market means that many luxury products have gone down-market. Does this mean that Americans no

Source: © Neil Setchfield/Alamy.

Marketing Pitfall

Luxury goods often serve as status symbols, but the proliferation of inexpensive counterfeit products threatens to diminish their value ("Hey buddy, wanna buy a 'genuine' Rolex for $20?"). Fakes are a major headache for many manufacturers, especially in Asia: Officials in China estimate that 15 to 20 percent of the products made there are counterfeit.[100]

How do people who bought the real thing react when they see imitations of their prized handbags or watches parading by them on the street? Researchers who interviewed consumers who purchased luxury fashion brands in India and Thailand identified three coping strategies:

1. **Flight**—They stop using the brand because they don't want to be mislabeled as a lesser-status person who buys fake brands.
2. **Reclamation**—They go out of their way to emphasize their long relationship with the brand, but express concern that its image will be tarnished.
3. **Abranding**—They disguise their luxury items in the belief that truly high-status people do not need to display expensive logos, whereas those who do betray lower status.[101]

longer yearn for status symbols? Hardly. The market continues to roll out ever-pricier goods and services, from $12,000 mother–baby diamond tennis bracelet sets to $600 jeans, $800 haircuts, and $400 bottles of wine. Although it seems that almost everyone can flaunt a designer handbag (or at least a counterfeit version with a convincing logo), our country's wealthiest consumers employ 9,000 personal chefs, visit plastic surgeons, and send their children to $400-an-hour math tutors. A sociologist explained, "Whether or not someone has a flat-screen TV is going to tell you less than if you look at the services they use, where they live and the control they have over other people's labor, those who are serving them."[102]

Of course, the particular products that count as status symbols vary across cultures and locales:

- Although to most Americans the now-defunct Hummer vehicle is a symbol of excess, Iraqis still regard the huge gas-guzzlers as an alluring symbol of power. An Iraqi Hummer dealer observed, "In Iraq, people judge you by your car, and you're not a man without one." People there use an Arabic phrase to explain the need to have the biggest car: *hasad thukuri,* which roughly translates as "penis envy."[103]
- In China, children are status symbols (partly because the government strongly discourages couples from having more than one baby). Parents want to show off their pampered child and are eager to surround their "little emperors" with luxury goods. Chinese families spend one-third to one-half of their disposable income on their children.[104]
- Largely because of an oil boom, there are at least 25 billionaires and 88,000 millionaires in Russia (though the recession has taken a big bite out of the Russian economy also). Muscovites crave luxury goods to show off their newfound wealth. Some buy the GoldVish cell phone that glitters with 120 carats of diamonds encrusting a case of white gold. The desire to spend as much as possible on indulgences fuels a popular

joke in Moscow: A wealthy businessman tells a friend he bought a tie for $100. The friend responds, "You fool! You can get the same tie for $200 just across the street."[105]

● In Indonesia, as in many countries, a cell phone is a status symbol—but instead of a sleek iPhone, a decade-old Nokia model users call "the Brick" is the one to have. This "smart phone" never took off in the West; its bulky design makes it look dated. But in Jakarta, its heft is what people like about it. At a whopping half-pound, it doesn't fit into a pocket, so it's very visible when models, politicians, and other celebrities cart it around with them. Nokia even sells a gold-plated version for $2,500. In the world of status symbols, anything goes as long as others don't have it.[106]

The social analyst Thorstein Veblen first discussed the motivation to consume for the sake of consuming at the turn of the 20th century. For Veblen, we buy things to create **invidious distinction**; this means that we use them to inspire envy in others through our display of wealth or power. Veblen coined the term **conspicuous consumption** to refer to people's desires to provide prominent visible evidence of their ability to afford luxury goods. The material excesses of his time motivated Veblen's outlook. Veblen wrote in the era of the "Robber Barons," where the likes of J. P. Morgan, Henry Clay Frick, and William Vanderbilt built massive financial empires and flaunted their wealth as they competed to throw the most lavish party. Some of these events were legendary, as this account describes:

> There were tales, repeated in the newspapers, of dinners on horseback; of banquets for pet dogs; of hundred-dollar bills folded into guests' dinner napkins; of a hostess who attracted attention by seating a chimpanzee at her table; of centerpieces in which lightly clad living maidens swam in glass tanks, or emerged from huge pies; of parties at which cigars were ceremoniously lighted with flaming banknotes of large denominations.[107]

Sounds like they really lived it up back in the old days, right? Well, maybe the more things change, the more they stay the same: The recent wave of corporate scandals involving companies such as AIG, Enron, WorldCom, and Tyco infuriated many consumers when they discovered that some top executives lived it up even as other employees were laid off. One account of a $1 million birthday party the chief executive of Tyco threw for his wife is eerily similar to a Robber Baron shindig: The party reportedly had a gladiator theme and featured an ice sculpture of Michelangelo's *David* with vodka streaming from his penis into crystal glasses. The company also furnished the executive's New York apartment with such "essentials" as a $6,000 shower curtain, a $2,200 gilt wastebasket, and a $17,100 "traveling toilette box."[108]

This phenomenon of conspicuous consumption was, for Veblen, most evident among what he termed the **leisure class**; people for whom productive work is taboo. In Marxist terms, such an attitude reflects a desire to link oneself to ownership or control of the means of production, rather than to the production itself. Those who control these resources, therefore, avoid any evidence that they actually have to work for a living, as the term the *idle rich* suggests.

To Veblen, wives are an economic resource. He criticized the "decorative" role of women, as rich men showered them with expensive clothes, pretentious homes, and a life of leisure as a way to advertise their own wealth (note that today he might have argued the same for a smaller number of husbands). Fashions such as high-heeled shoes, tight corsets, billowing trains on dresses, and elaborate hairstyles all conspired to ensure that wealthy women could barely move without assistance, much less perform manual labor. Similarly, the Chinese practice of foot-binding prevented female members of the aristocracy from walking; servants carried them from place to place. In recent years the tables have turned as older women—who increasingly boast the same incomes and social capital as their male peers—seek out younger men as arm candy. These so-called **cougars** (a term popularized by the TV show *Cougar Town*) are everywhere; surveys estimate that about one-third of women over age 40 date younger men.[109]

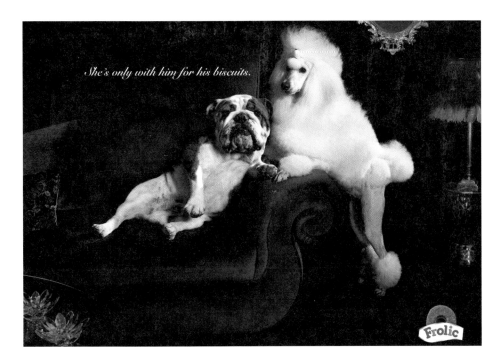

This French ad suggests that even dogs marry "trophy wives."
Source: Courtesy of Mars Petfood.

Consumers engage in conspicuous consumption as a way to display status markers, yet the prominence of these markers varies from products with large recognizable emblems to those with no logo at all. Those "in the know" often can recognize a subtle status marker when another member of their elite group displays it, such as the distinctive design of a bag or watch—these are "quiet signals." In contrast, some people may feel the need to almost hit others over the head with their bling; they use "loud signals."

One set of researchers labels these differences **brand prominence**. They assign consumers to one of four consumption groups (patricians, parvenus, poseurs, and proletarians) based on their wealth and need for status. When they looked at data on luxury goods, the authors found different classes gravitated toward different types of brand prominence. Brands like Louis Vuitton, Gucci, and Mercedes vary in terms of how blatant their status appeals (e.g., prominent logos) are in advertisements and on the products themselves—or in other words, in the type of **status signaling** they employ.

Thinking back to our discussion about "old money" versus "new money" earlier in the chapter, for example, it's not surprising that those who are wealthier and don't have a high need for status (patricians) rely on "quiet signals" and likely will be put off by excessive displays. Marketers for status brands need to understand these distinctions, because their customers may or may not value products with explicit logos and other highly visible cues that signal conspicuous consumption.[110] Figure 11.5 summarizes these four types and provides one set of contrasting products the researchers used in their study: quiet versus loud Gucci sunglasses.

Veblen's inspiration came from anthropological studies of the Kwakiutl Indians, who lived in the Pacific Northwest. At a *potlatch* ceremony, the host showed off his wealth and gave extravagant presents to the guests. The more he gave away, the greater his status. Sometimes, the host employed an even more radical strategy to flaunt his wealth. He would publicly *destroy* some of his property just to demonstrate how much he had.

And the plot thickens: Because guests had to reciprocate by giving a gift of equal value, the host could humiliate a poorer rival with an invitation to a lavish *potlatch*. The hapless guest would eventually be forced into bankruptcy because he needed to give away as much as the host, even though he could not afford to do so. If this practice sounds "primitive," think for a moment about many modern weddings. Parents commonly invest huge sums of money to throw a lavish party and compete with others for the distinction

Figure 11.5 A TYPOLOGY OF STATUS SIGNALING

Note: "Quiet" sunglasses (L) do not include a prominent designer logo, while "Loud" (R) sunglasses do.
Source: Young Jee Han, Joseph C. Nunes, and Xavier Dreza (2010), "Signaling Status with Luxury Goods: The Role of Brand Prominence," *Journal of Marketing* 74 (July), 15–30, from Figures 2 and 3.

of giving their daughter the "best" or most extravagant wedding, even if they have to dip into their retirement savings to do it.

Like the *potlatch* ritual, in modern times our desire to convince others we have a surplus of resources creates the need for us to exhibit the evidence that we do. Accordingly, we may prioritize consumption activities that use up as many resources as possible in nonconstructive pursuits. This *conspicuous waste*, in turn, shows others that we have assets to spare. Veblen wrote, "We are told of certain Polynesian chiefs, who, under the stress of good form, preferred to starve rather than carry their food to their mouths with their own hands."[111]

As the competition to accumulate status symbols escalates, sometimes the best tactic is to switch gears and go in reverse. One way to do this is to deliberately *avoid* status symbols—that is, to seek status by mocking it. Social scientists call this sophisticated form of conspicuous consumption **parody display**.[112] Hence, the popularity of old, ripped blue jeans (or more likely, the ones companies stonewash and treat so that they *look* old and ripped), "utility" vehicles such as Jeeps among the upper classes (like the Caldwells), and brands with a strong blue-collar heritage like Von Dutch truckers' hats and Red Wing boots.

OBJECTIVE 4

A lifestyle defines a pattern of consumption that reflects a person's choices of how to spend his or her time and money, and these choices are essential to define consumer identity.

Lifestyles and Consumer Identity

So far in this chapter we've talked about social class influences on consumer behavior. Still, you can easily find two people who are very similar on most or all social class indicators, yet who make totally different consumption choices. We often see this strong variation among students at the same university, even though many of them come from similar backgrounds. For example, some of the undergraduates at an institution may fall into one of these categories:[113]

● **Metro:** You just can't walk past a Banana Republic store without making a purchase. You own 20 pairs of shoes, half a dozen pairs of sunglasses, just as many watches, and you carry a man-purse. You see a stylist instead of a barber, because barbers don't do highlights. You can make her lamb shanks and risotto for dinner and Eggs Benedict for breakfast . . . all from scratch. You shave more than just your face. You also exfoliate and moisturize.

- **Hesher:** A Reebok-wearing, mulleted person in acid-washed jeans and a Judas Priest T-shirt who still lives in his/her parents' basement, swears that he/she can really rock out on his/her Ibanez Stratocaster copy guitar, and probably owns a Nova that hasn't run in 5 years.
- **Emo:** Someone into softcore punk music that integrates high-pitched, overwrought lyrics and inaudible guitar riffs. He/she wears tight wool sweaters, tighter jeans, itchy scarves (even in the summer), ripped chucks with favorite band's signature, black square-rimmed glasses, and ebony greasy unwashed hair that is required to cover at least three-fifths of the face at an angle.

In traditional societies, class, caste, village, or family largely dictate a person's consumption options. In a modern consumer society, however, each of us is free (at least within our budgets) to select the set of products, services, and activities that define our self and, in turn, create a social identity we communicate to others. **Lifestyle** defines a pattern of consumption that reflects a person's choices of how to spend his or her time and money. These choices play a key role in defining consumer identity.[114]

Whether Tuners, Dead Heads, or skinheads, each lifestyle subculture exhibits its own unique set of norms, vocabulary, and product insignias. At the online Redneck Bank ("where bankin's funner"), you can take care of your "personal bankin' bidness" and earn Redneck Rewards.[116] A study of contemporary "mountain men" in the western United States illustrates the binding influence of a microculture on its members. Researchers found that group members shared a strong sense of identity they expressed in weekend retreats, where they reinforced these ties with authentic items as they used *tipis,* buffalo robes, buckskin leggings, and beaded moccasins to create a sense of community among fellow mountain men.[117]

The "Tuner" subculture consists of single men in their late teens and early twenties, usually in Latino or Asian communities, who share a passion for fast cars, high-tech auto upgrades, and specialized car parts. This consumer identity started with late-night meets among illegal street racers in New York and Los Angeles. Now, Tuners are more mainstream: Magazines like *Import Tuner* and major companies such as Pioneer eagerly court these high-tech hot-rodders. A Honda Civic commercial targeted to Hispanic American consumers showed a fleet of cars in different colors with customized features such as chrome rims and tinted windows.[115]

Source: © Blue Jean Images/Alamy.

These subcultures often form around fictional characters and events, and they help to define the extended self (see Chapter 7). Numerous lifestyles thrive on their collective worship of mythical and not-so-mythical worlds and characters that range from the music group Phish to Hello Kitty.

Marketers also think about lifestyle in terms of how much time we have available to do what we'd like and what we choose to do with that leisure time. In general, consumers work harder than ever, partly to compensate for their economic problems. People aged 32 to 43 work the longest, averaging 55 hours per week. The Harris Poll has tracked American's leisure time since 1973. When the Poll started, the median number of hours people devoted to leisure was 26. By 2008, this number had shrunk to 16 hours per week! It's also interesting to look at how we use the fewer hours we have: Thirty percent of Americans say their favorite activity is reading, 24 percent say it is watching TV, and 17 percent say it is spending time with family and kids. Although we spend a lot of time on computer-related activities, the survey finds that people spend even more time "just checking in" to work via computer or phone, but they don't count this as work time.[119]

A **lifestyle marketing perspective** recognizes that people sort themselves into groups on the basis of the things they like to do, how they like to spend their leisure time, and how they choose to spend their disposable income.[120] The growing number of

Our food preferences say a lot about our lifestyles and values.

Source: Courtesy of Saskatoon Restaurant, Greenville, SC.

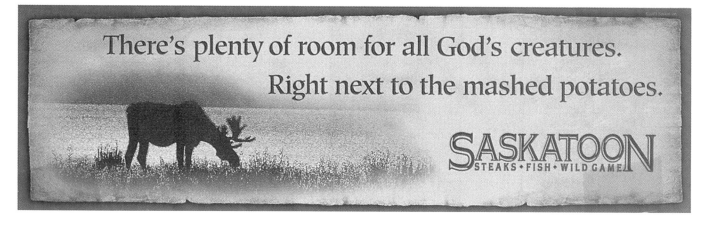

niche magazines and Web sites that cater to specialized interests reflects the spectrum of choices available to us in today's society. The downside of this is obvious to the newspaper industry; several major papers have already had to shut down their print editions because people consume most of their information online.

A lifestyle is much more than how we allocate our discretionary income. It is a statement about who one is in society and who one is not. Group identities, whether of hobbyists, athletes, or drug users, gel around distinctive consumption choices. Social scientists use a number of terms to describe such self-definitions in addition to lifestyle, including *taste public, consumer group, symbolic community,* and *status culture.*[121]

Many people in similar social and economic circumstances may follow the same general consumption pattern. Still, each person also gives a unique "twist" to the pattern that allows him to inject some individuality into a lifestyle. For example, a "typical" college student (if there is such a thing) may dress much like his friends, hang out in the same places, and like the same foods, yet still indulge a passion for marathon running, stamp collecting, or acid jazz. These interests often link a person to others who share it (both offline and online), and the groups that form around these choices also become subcultures.

A goal of lifestyle marketing is to allow consumers to pursue their chosen ways to enjoy their lives and express their social identities. For this reason, a key aspect of this strategy is to focus on people who use products in desirable social settings. The desire to associate a product with a social situation is a long-standing one for advertisers, whether they include the product in a round of golf, a family barbecue, or a night at a glamorous club surrounded by the hip-hop elite.[124] Thus, people, products, and settings combine to express a *consumption style,* as Figure 11.6 diagrams.

OBJECTIVE 5

Identifying patterns of consumption can be more useful than knowing about individual purchases when organizations craft a lifestyle marketing strategy.

Product Complementarity and Co-Branding Strategies

We get a clearer picture of how people use products to define lifestyles when we see how they make choices in a variety of product categories. A lifestyle marketing perspective implies that we must look at *patterns of behavior* to understand consumers. As one study noted, "All goods carry meaning, but none by itself. . . . The meaning is in the relations between all the goods, just as music is in the relations marked out by the sounds and not in any one note."[125]

Indeed, many products and services do seem to "go together," usually because the same types of people tend to select them. In many cases, products do not seem to "make sense" if companion products don't accompany them (e.g., fast food and paper plates, or a suit and tie) or are incongruous in the presence of other products that have a very different personality (e.g., a Chippendale chair in a high-tech office or Lucky Strike cigarettes with a solid gold lighter).

Marketing Opportunity

Our musical choices say a lot about our lifestyles, and today some forward-looking brands that have nothing to do with making music are jumping into the music business to strengthen the connections between musical expressions and brand loyalty. Nike commissioned original workout music for its "Nike + Original Run" series, which you can buy at Apple's iTunes Music Store. It teamed up with Apple to offer the Nike + shoes that feature a built-in pocket under the insole for the Nike + iPod sensor that lets you track your run and set goals while listening to your favorite tunes. It's releasing other CDs featuring music and voice-over coaching in activities such as yoga, dance, and weight training.[122] Rival Converse built a recording studio so that new bands can record their work free to leverage the associations between its shoes and music artists (the brand has been worn by generations of bands, from the Ramones to the Strokes). Levi Strauss, Dr. Martens, Scion, and Bacardi have all sponsored music by under-the-radar artists. Mountain Dew's Green Label Sound label releases free MP3s by blogger favorites like Neon Indian and Chromeo. Starbucks started its own label after its success with albums like Ray Charles's *Genius Loves Company.* The Motel 6 chain even sponsors a Rock Yourself to Sleep program that gives free rooms to touring groups.[123]

• • • • • • • • • • • • • • •

Figure 11.6 CONSUMPTION STYLE

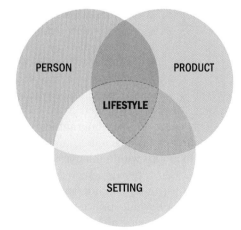

Therefore, an important part of lifestyle marketing is to identify the set of products and services that consumers associate with a specific lifestyle. In fact, research evidence suggests that even a relatively unattractive product becomes more appealing when consumers link it with other products that they do like.[126] The meshing of objects from many different categories to express a single lifestyle idea is at the heart of many consumption decisions, including coordinating an outfit for a big date (shoes, garments, fragrance, etc.), decorating a room (tables, carpet, wallpaper, etc.), and designing a restaurant (menu, ambiance, waitperson uniforms, etc.). Many people today evaluate products not just in terms of function, but also in terms of how well their design coordinates with other objects and furnishings.

Marketers who understand these cross-category relationships may pursue **co-branding strategies** where they team up with other companies to promote two or more items. Some marketers even match up their spokescharacters in ads; the Pillsbury Doughboy appeared in a commercial with the Sprint Guy to pitch cell phones, the lonely Maytag repairman was in an ad for the Chevrolet Impala, and the Taco Bell Chihuahua (now retired) showed up in a commercial for GEICO insurance.[127]

Product complementarity occurs when the symbolic meanings of different products relate to one another.[128] Consumers use these sets of products we call a **consumption constellation** to define, communicate, and perform social roles.[129] For example, we identified the American "yuppie" of the 1980s by such products as a Rolex watch, a BMW automobile, a Gucci briefcase, a squash racket, fresh pesto, white wine, and brie cheese. Researchers find that even children are adept at creating consumption constellations, and as they get older they tend to include more brands in these cognitive structures.[130] Figure 11.7 shows a pair of lifestyle trends.

OBJECTIVE 6

Psychographics go beyond simple demographics to help marketers understand and reach different consumer segments.

Psychographics

When Cadillac introduced its Escalade sport utility vehicle, critics scoffed at the bizarre pairing of this old-line luxury brand with a truck. However, consumers quickly associated the vehicle with the hip-hop lifestyle. Artists such as Jennifer Lopez, Outkast, and Jay-Z referred to it in songs, and Jermaine Dupri proclaimed, "Gotta have me an Escalade." Three years later, Cadillac rolled out its 18-foot Escalade EXT pickup with a sticker price of $50,000.

The Escalade brand manager describes the target customer for luxury pickups as a slightly earthier version of the SUV buyer. She says that although the two drivers may own $2 million homes next door to each other, the typical luxury SUV driver is about 50, has an MBA from Harvard, belongs to a golf club, maintains connections with his college friends, and works hard at keeping up with the Joneses. In contrast, the luxury pickup driver is roughly 5 years younger. He might have inherited his father's construction business, and he's been working since he was 18 years old. He may or may not have attended college, and unlike the SUV driver, he is absolutely still connected to his high school friends.[131]

As this example shows, marketers often find it useful to develop products that appeal to different lifestyle subcultures. When marketers combine personality variables with knowledge of lifestyle preferences, they have a powerful lens they can focus on consumer segments. Adidas, for example, describes different types of shoe buyers in terms of lifestyles so that it can address the needs of segments such as *Gearheads* (hard-core, older runners who want high-performance shoes), *Popgirls* (teeny-boppers who hang out at the mall and wear Skechers), and *Fastidious Eclectus* (bohemian, cutting-edge types who want hip, distinctive products).[132]

This approach, **psychographics**, involves the "use of psychological, sociological, and anthropological factors . . . to determine how the market is segmented by the propensity of groups within the market—and their reasons—to make a particular decision about a product, person, ideology, or otherwise hold an attitude or use a medium."[133] Marketers use many psychographic variables to segment consumers, but all of these dimensions go beyond surface characteristics to investigate consumers' motivations for purchasing and using products. Demographics allows us to describe *who* buys, but psychographics tells us *why* they do. A classic example involves a very popular Canadian

Figure 11.7 LIFESTYLE TRENDS. Many marketers around the globe closely monitor emerging trends, both offline and online, as they try to identify the influences that will shape consumer behavior in the near future as well as in the long term. Canvas 8 is a U.K.-Based *brand consultancy* that issues a periodic report on new lifestyle developments

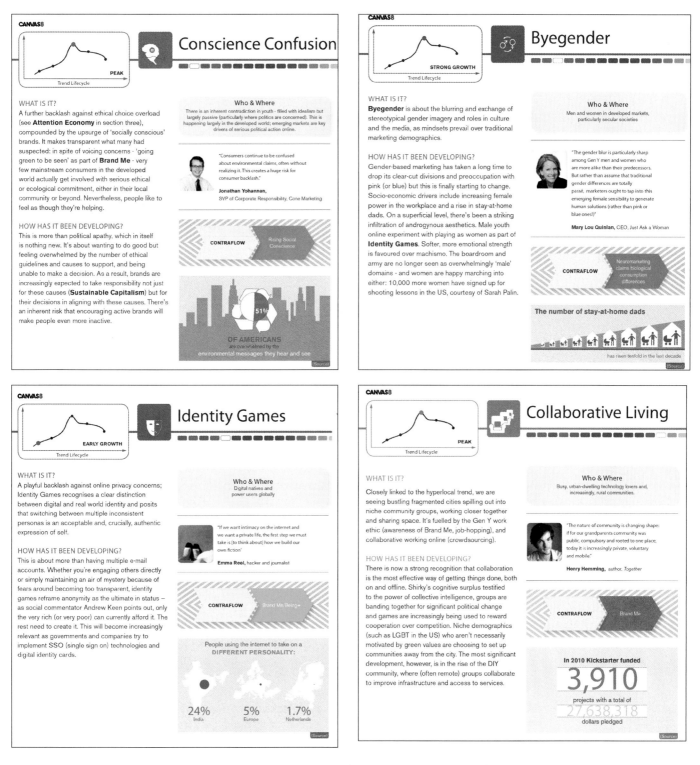

advertising campaign for Molson Export beer that included insights from psychographic findings. The company's research showed that Molson's target customers tend to be like boys who never grew up, who were uncertain about the future, and who were intimidated by women's newfound freedoms. Accordingly, the ads featured a group of men, "Fred and the boys," whose get-togethers emphasized male companionship, protection against change, and the reassuring message that the beer "keeps on tasting great."[134]

The makers of the popular Sigg water bottle, which is available in many different designs, actually choose from about 3,000 different concepts each year with specific customers in mind. These include the *Whole Foods Woman,* who lives in a city, practices yoga, and buys organic produce; and the *Geek Chic Guy,* who listens to Radiohead and wears vintage Converse sneakers.[135]

Source: © Winston Wong/Alamy.

How Do We Perform a Psychographic Analysis?

Psychographic studies take several different forms:

- **A lifestyle profile** looks for items that differentiate between users and nonusers of a product.
- **A product-specific profile** identifies a target group and then profiles these consumers on product-relevant dimensions.
- **A general lifestyle segmentation** places a large sample of respondents into homogenous groups based on similarities of their overall preferences.
- **A product-specific segmentation study** tailors questions to a product category. For example, if a researcher wants to conduct research for a stomach medicine, she might rephrase the item, "I worry too much" as, "I get stomach problems if I worry too much." This allows her to more finely discriminate among users of competing brands.[136]

AIOs

Most contemporary psychographic research attempts to group consumers according to some combination of three categories of variables: activities, interests, and opinions, which we call **AIOs**. Using data from large samples, marketers create profiles of customers who resemble each other in terms of their activities and patterns of product usage.[137] Table 11.2 lists commonly used AIO dimensions.

To group consumers into AIO categories, researchers give respondents a long list of statements and ask them to indicate how much they agree with each one. Thus, we can "boil down" a person's lifestyle by discovering how he spends his time, what he finds interesting and important, and how he views himself and the world around him.

Typically, the first step in conducting a psychographic analysis is to determine which lifestyle segments yield the bulk of customers for a particular product. This strategy reflects *The 80/20 rule* we first discussed in Chapter 1. This rule reminds us that, in many cases, only one or a few lifestyle segments account for the majority of sales.[138]

Psychographic techniques help marketers to identify their heavy users. Then they can better understand how they relate to the brand and the benefits they derive from it.

TABLE 11.2	Lifestyle Dimensions		
Activities	**Interests**	**Opinions**	**Demographics**
Work	Family	Themselves	Age
Hobbies	Home	Social issues	Education
Social events	Job	Politics	Income
Vacation	Community	Business	Occupation
Entertainment	Recreation	Economics	Family size
Club membership	Fashion	Education	Dwelling
Community	Food	Products	Geography
Shopping	Media	Future	City size
Sports	Achievements	Culture	Stage in life cycle

Source: William D. Wells and Douglas J. Tigert, "Activities, Interests, and Opinions," *Journal of Advertising Research* 11 (August 1971): 27–35. © 1971 by The Advertising Research Foundation. Used with permission.

For instance, marketers at the beginning of the walking-shoe craze assumed that all purchasers were basically burned-out joggers. Subsequent psychographic research showed that there were actually several different groups of "walkers," ranging from those who walk to get to work to those who walk for fun. This realization resulted in shoes that manufacturers aimed at different segments, from Footjoy Joy-Walkers to Nike Healthwalkers.

Marketers use the results of these studies to:

- **Define the target market**—This information allows the marketer to go beyond simple demographic or product usage descriptions (e.g., middle-aged men or frequent users).
- **Create a new view of the market**—Sometimes marketers create their strategies with a "typical" customer in mind. This stereotype may not be correct, because the actual customer may not match these assumptions. For example, marketers of a face cream for women were surprised to find that older, widowed women were their heavy users rather than the younger, sociable women to whom they were pitching their appeals.
- **Position the product**—Psychographic information can allow the marketer to emphasize features of the product that fit in with a person's lifestyle.
- **Better communicate product attributes**—The artist or copywriter obtains a much richer mental image of the target consumer than she can simply by looking at dry statistics. For example, research that the Schlitz beer company conducted found that heavy beer drinkers tended to feel that life's pleasures were few and far between. In response, the brewer developed commercials with the tagline, "You only go around once, so reach for all the gusto you can."[139]
- **Develop product strategy**—Understanding how a product fits, or does not fit, into consumers' lifestyles allows the marketer to identify new product opportunities, chart media strategies, and create environments most consistent and harmonious with these consumption patterns.
- **Market social and political issues**—A psychographic study of men aged 18 to 24 who drink and drive highlights the potential for this perspective to help in the eradication of harmful behaviors. Researchers divided this segment into four groups: "good timers," "well adjusted," "nerds," and "problem kids." They found that one group in particular—"good timers"—was more likely to believe that it is fun to be drunk, that the chances of having an accident while driving drunk are low, and that drinking increases one's appeal to the opposite sex. Because the study showed that this group is also the most likely to drink at rock concerts and parties, is most likely to watch MTV, and tends to listen to album-oriented rock radio stations, reaching "good timers" with a prevention campaign became easier.[140]

Marketers constantly search for new insights so they can identify and reach groups of consumers united by common lifestyles. To meet this need, many research companies and advertising agencies develop their own **lifestyle segmentation typologies**. Respondents answer a battery of questions that allow the researchers to cluster them into a set of distinct lifestyle groups. The questions usually include a mixture of AIOs plus other items relating to feelings about specific brands, favorite celebrities, and media preferences. Companies that want to learn more about their customers and potential customers then buy one or more of these systems for their own use.

The best-known lifestyle segmentation system is **The Values and Lifestyles System (VALS2™)** that SRI International developed. The current VALS2™ system uses a battery of 39 items (35 psychological and 4 demographic) to divide U.S. adults into groups, each with distinctive characteristics. As Figure 11.8 shows, the typology arranges groups vertically by their resources (including such factors as income, education, energy levels, and eagerness to buy) and horizontally by self-orientation.

Three self-orientations constitute the horizontal dimension. Consumers with an *Ideals* orientation rely on a belief system to make purchase decisions, and they are not concerned with the views of others. People with an *Achievement* orientation are more competitive; they take into account what their peers will think about their decisions and how these choices will reflect on them. Finally, those with a *Self-Expression* orientation are more concerned with the emotional aspects of purchases and the satisfaction they will personally receive from products and services.

● **Innovators**—The top VALS2™ group, they are successful consumers with many resources. This group is concerned with social issues and is open to change.

Figure 11.8 VALS2™

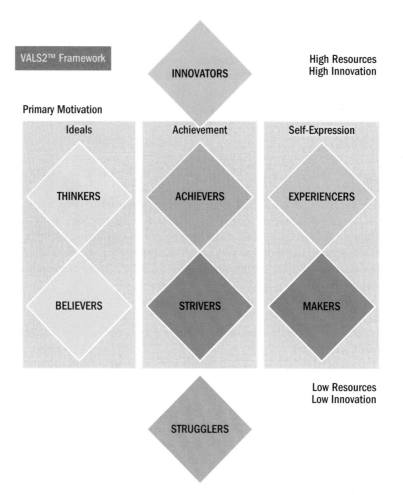

The next three groups also have sufficient resources, but differ in their outlooks on life:[141]

- **Thinkers**—They are satisfied, reflective, and comfortable.
- **Achievers**—They are career oriented and prefer predictability to risk or self-discovery.
- **Experiencers**—They are impulsive, young, and enjoy offbeat or risky experiences.

The next four groups have fewer resources:

- **Believers**—They have strong principles and favor proven brands.
- **Strivers**—They are similar to Achievers but have fewer resources. They are very concerned about the approval of others.
- **Makers**—They are action oriented and tend to focus their energies on self-sufficiency. They will often be found working on their cars, canning their own vegetables, or building their own houses.
- **Strugglers**—They are at the bottom of the economic ladder. They are most concerned with meeting the needs of the moment and have limited ability to acquire anything beyond the basic goods they need for survival.

If you want to see what VALS2™ type you are, go to www.strategicbusinessinsights .com/vals/presurvey.shtml.

MyMarketing Lab

Go to **mymktlab.com** to complete the problems marked with this icon ⭐.

CHAPTER SUMMARY

Now that you have finished reading this chapter, you should understand why:

1. **Our confidence in our future, as well as in the overall economy, determines how freely we spend and the types of products we buy.**

   The field of behavioral economics studies how consumers decide what to do with their money. Consumer confidence—the state of mind consumers have about their own personal situation, as well as their feelings about their overall economic prospects—helps to determine whether they will purchase goods and services, take on debt, or save their money.

2. **We group consumers into social classes that say a lot about where they stand in society.**

   A consumer's *social class* refers to his or her standing in society. Factors including education, occupation, and income determine the class to which we belong. Virtually all groups make distinctions among members in terms of relative superiority, power, and access to valued resources. This social stratification creates a status hierarchy in which consumers prefer some goods to others.

   Although income is an important indicator of social class, the relationship is far from perfect. Factors such as place of residence, cultural interests, and worldview also determine social class. As income distributions change around the world, it is getting more difficult to distinguish among members of social classes; many products succeed because they appeal to a newly emerging group that marketers call the *mass class* (people with incomes high enough to purchase luxury items, at least on a small scale).

3. **Individuals' desires to make a statement about their social class, or the class to which they hope to belong, influence the products they like and dislike.**

   Conspicuous consumption, when a person flaunts his status by deliberately using up valuable resources, is one way to "buy up" to a higher social class. *Nouveau riches,* whose relatively recent acquisition of income rather than ancestry or breeding accounts for their enhanced social mobility, are the most likely to do this. We use status symbols (usually scarce goods or services) to communicate our standing to others. Parody display occurs when we seek status by deliberately avoiding fashionable products.

4. A lifestyle defines a pattern of consumption that reflects a person's choices of how to spend his or her time and money, and these choices are essential to define consumer identity.

A consumer's *lifestyle* refers to the ways she chooses to spend time and money and how her consumption choices reflect these values and tastes. Lifestyle research is useful for tracking societal consumption preferences and also for positioning specific products and services to different segments. Marketers segment based on lifestyle differences; they often group consumers in terms of their AIOs (activities, interests, and opinions).

5. Identifying patterns of consumption can be more useful than knowing about individual purchases when organizations craft a lifestyle marketing strategy.

We associate interrelated sets of products and activities with social roles to form *consumption constellations*.

People often purchase a product or service because they associate it with a constellation that, in turn, they link to a lifestyle they find desirable. *Geodemography* involves a set of techniques that use geographical and demographic data to identify clusters of consumers with similar psychographic characteristics.

6. Psychographics go beyond simple demographics to help marketers understand and reach different consumer segments.

Psychographic techniques classify consumers in terms of psychological, subjective variables in addition to observable characteristics (demographics). Marketers have developed systems to identify consumer "types" and to differentiate them in terms of their brand or product preferences, media usage, leisure time activities, and attitudes toward broad issues such as politics and religion.

KEY TERMS

achieved status, 483
affluenza, 490
AIOs, 512
ascribed status, 483
bottom of the pyramid, 489
brand prominence, 505
BRIC nations, 498
chavs, 495
co-branding strategies, 510
codes, 499
conspicuous consumption, 504
consumer confidence, 479
consumption constellation, 510
cosmopolitanism, 490
cosplay, 508
cougars, 504
cultural capital, 501
Digital Divide, 489
discretionary income, 478

dominance–submission hierarchy, 482
elaborated codes, 499
frugalistas, 479
habitus, 500
hedonic adaptation, 481
hierogamy, 497
homogamy, 482
invidious distinction, 504
leisure class, 504
lifestyle, 507
lifestyle marketing perspective, 508
lifestyle segmentation typologies, 514
mass class, 499
nouveau riches, 488
One Percenter, 491
online gated communities, 501
parody display, 506
plutonomy, 480
product complementarity, 510

psychographics, 510
reputation economy, 482
restricted codes, 499
social capital, 500
social class, 482
social mobility, 483
social stratification, 482
spendthrifts, 478
status crystallization, 497
status hierarchy, 483
status signaling, 505
status symbols, 502
taste culture, 499
The Values and Lifestyles System (VALS2™), 514
tightwads, 478
worldview, 489

REVIEW

⭐ **11-1** How have women contributed to the overall rise in income in our society?

11-2 Define discretionary income.

11-3 How does consumer confidence influence consumer behavior?

11-4 What is a pecking order?

11-5 Explain what is meant by achieved versus ascribed status.

11-6 What is the significance of lower fertility rates in higher- and middle-class families?

11-7 Is income alone a good determinant of social class?

11-8 How are attitudes toward luxury categorized according to SRI Consulting Business Intelligence?

11-9 In some countries it is difficult to measure and quantify social class. Why might this be the case?

11-10 What are the main motivators in purchasing a status symbol?

11-11 What is the term used to describe an individual's aesthetic and intellectual preferences?

11-12 Describe the difference between a restricted and an elaborated code. Give an example of each.

11-13 How do the elites restrict access to their group?

11-14 What are the three identified strategies used by consumers if counterfeiting is common in their preferred brands?

11-15 What is meant by the term "calculated consumption"?

11-16 What is a current example of parody display?

11-17 How do people, products, and setting combine to create a consumption style?

11-18 How is psychographic analysis carried out?

CONSUMER BEHAVIOR CHALLENGE

■ DISCUSS

11-19 Sears, JC Penney, and Walmart tried hard in recent years to upgrade their images and appeal to higher-class consumers. In fact, JC Penney even hired the head of Apple's stores as its new CEO. How successful have these efforts been? Do you believe this strategy is wise?

11-20 What are some of the obstacles to measuring social class in today's society? Discuss some ways to get around these obstacles.

11-21 What consumption differences might you expect to observe between a family we characterize as underprivileged and one whose income is average for its social class?

⭐ **11-22** How do you assign people to social classes, or do you at all? What consumption cues do you use (e.g., clothing, speech, cars, etc.) to determine social standing?

11-23 In today's economy, it's become somewhat vulgar to flaunt your money—if you have any left. Do you think this means that status symbols like luxury products are passé? Why or why not?

11-24 Thorstein Veblen argued that men used women as "trophy wives" to display their wealth. Is this argument still valid today?

11-25 Status symbols are products, such as Rolex watches or expensive sports cars, that we value because they show others how much money or prestige we have. Do you believe that your peer group values status symbols? Why or why not? If yes, what are the products that you think are status symbols for consumers your age? Do you agree with the assertion in this chapter that a cell phone is a status symbol for many young people?

11-26 Wireless devices have quickly become an indispensable part of many consumers' lifestyles. How do you view this rapid development of a situation in which many of us are lost without our "CrackBerrys" or iPhones? What impact on other lifestyle activities do you predict as a result?

⭐ **11-27** As we continue to emerge from a recession, many people live frugally; they cut back on visits to restaurants, buy fewer high-end clothes and other luxury goods, and hold onto their cars much longer. Are we witnessing a long-term shift in consumer behavior, or do you believe this is just a temporary situation?

■ APPLY

11-28 Use the status index in Figure 11.3 to compute a social-class score for people you know, including their parents, if possible. Ask several friends (preferably from different places) to compile similar information for people they know. How closely do your answers compare? If you find differences, how can you explain them?

11-29 Compile a list of occupations and ask a sample of students in a variety of majors (both business and nonbusiness) to rank the prestige of these jobs. Can you detect any differences in these rankings as a function of students' majors?

11-30 Compile a collection of ads that depict consumers of different social classes. What generalizations can you make about the reality of these ads and about the media in which they appear?

11-31 New "types" (or, more often, updated versions of old types) emerge from popular culture on a regular basis, whether they are shredders, tuners, or geeks. In recent years, for example, some analysts have identified the resurrection of the *hipster*. One source describes a person who follows this lifestyle as someone with a "complicated" hairstyle (dyed black or white-blonde) who reads *Nylon* magazine; listens to indie rock; majored in art or writing; drinks Pabst Blue Ribbon beer; wears tight black pants, scarves, and ironic T-shirts; and is addicted to coffee and cigarettes—and denies being a hipster![142] How valid is this lifestyle type in your area? Can you identify people who belong to it, or to a similar group?

11-32 Using media that target college students, construct a consumption constellation for this social role. What set of products, activities, and interests tend to appear in advertisements depicting "typical" college students? How realistic is this constellation?

11-33 Extreme sports. YouTube. Pinterest. Veganism. Can you predict what will be "hot" in the near future? Identify a lifestyle trend that is just surfacing in your universe. Describe this trend in detail, and justify your prediction. What specific styles or products relate to this trend?

Case Study

PARROT HEADS UNITE!

Are you a Parrot Head? If you don't know what that is, then you definitely are not. Jimmy Buffett fans all over the world proudly refer to themselves by this name. In many respects, they represent one of the most dedicated fan bases anywhere. Why the name Parrot Head? In a 1985 concert, a member of the Eagles looked at the audience members with their bright Hawaiian shirts. He announced that they "looked like Deadheads in tropical suits. They're like Parrot Heads."

Some critics think Jimmy Buffett's career peaked in the late 1970s, though between 1978 and 2006 he released eight gold, six platinum, and three multiplatinum records. During this period he gained a reputation for his concerts, wrote five best sellers, and became one of the world's wealthiest musicians through his Margaritaville brand, a multibillion dollar business that includes restaurants and casinos.

Buffett fans gather by the thousands at concerts. A Buffett concert is like a beach party, with fans decked out in Hawaiian shirts and parrot hats. But the concert itself is only part of the event. Fans get to know each other year after year at tailgate parties. So many people party before Buffett concerts, in fact, that many venues charge admission now just to get into the tailgating area.

How die-hard are Buffett fans? Consider that many plan regular vacations around a Buffett concert (some have racked up dozens) or special trips to visit Buffett-themed restaurants in Caribbean destinations. Houses, boats, and RVs decked out in tropical Buffet décor are not uncommon, and there have been a good number of Parrot Head-themed weddings.

Buffett fans come from all walks of life, age groups, and occupations; they typically cite "escapism" as a reason for their devotion. But Parrot Heads do much more than just "wasting away again in Margaritaville." Many spend their free time as volunteers at blood drives, raise thousands of dollars to grant the wishes of sick kids, or build houses for the needy. Parrot Heads in Paradise, a group of fans with more than 220 chapters, has donated more than $29 million to charity.

Buffett's management recognizes the charitable efforts of the Buffett community. Parrot Head clubs get a certain number of tickets allocated to them. Members still have to pay for them, but they get first dibs on the best seats depending on how many Parrot Points (doled out to members when they participate in charitable or volunteer efforts) they earn. As tickets have become harder and harder to obtain, this is indeed a welcome bonus.

DISCUSSION QUESTIONS

CS 11-1 How can we consider Jimmy Buffett fans as members of a reference group? A brand community?

CS 11-2 What kind of opportunities does the existence of the Buffett community present to marketers? Develop a list of specific marketing and promotional tactics.

Sources: Chris Willman, "For Christmas Birthday Boy Jimmy Buffett, Who Needs Record Sales to Be Worth $400 Million?" http://music.yahoo.com/blogs/stop-the-presses, accessed July 25, 2013; www.phip.com, accessed July 25, 2013; Douglas Hanks, "Jimmy Buffett Represents Florida Culture, Lifestyle," *McClatchy Tribune Business News* (May 17, 2009); Alexis Garrobo, "Tropical Tuesday Brings Out the Parrot Heads," *McClatchy Tribune Business News* (July 16, 2008); Geoff Gehman, "A Buffet of Buffett: Tropical Troubadour Sets Sail to Philly," *McClatchy Tribune Business News* (June 5, 2008).

MyMarketingLab

Go to **mymktlab.com** for the following Assisted-graded writing questions:

11-34 What is the difference between achieved and ascribed status? Describe what we mean by the term *mass class* and summarize what causes this phenomenon.

11-35 This chapter observes that some marketers find "greener pastures" when they target low-income people. How ethical is it to single out consumers who cannot afford to waste their precious resources on discretionary items? Under what circumstances should we encourage or discourage this segmentation strategy?

11-36 **Mymktlab Only**—comprehensive writing assignment for this chapter.

NOTES

1. Data in this section adapted from Fabian Linden, *Consumer Affluence: The Next Wave* (New York: The Conference Board, 1994). For additional information about U.S. income statistics, access Occupational Employment and Wage Estimates at www.bls.gov/oes/oes_data.htm.
2. Mary Bowler, "Women's Earnings: An Overview," *Monthly Labor Review* 122 (December 1999): 13–22.
3. Christopher D. Carroll, "How Does Future Income Affect Current Consumption?" *Quarterly Journal of Economics* 109 (February 1994): 111–47.
4. "Costco Net Falls on Weak Discretionary Spending," *Reuters* (May 28, 2009), www.reuters.com/article/newsOne/idUSTRE54R1GJ20090528, accessed June 17, 2009.
5. Quoted in Philip Jackman, "What Makes a Tightwad? Study Finds That People Who Are Stingy Report Feeling Emotional Pain When Spending Money," *Toronto Globe & Mail* (March 19, 2008), www.theglobeandmail.com, accessed March 22, 2008; http://webuser.bus.umich.edu/srick/Globe%20and%20Mail%203-19-08.pdf, accessed September 24, 2011.
6. Center for Media Research, "Coping with Recession" (June 3, 2009), www.mediapost.com, accessed June 3, 2009.
7. José F. Medina, Joel Saegert, and Alicia Gresham, "Comparison of Mexican-American and Anglo-American Attitudes Toward Money," *Journal of Consumer Affairs* 30, no. 1 (1996): 124–45.
8. Kirk Johnson, "Sit Down. Breathe Deeply. This Is Really Scary Stuff," *New York Times* (April 16, 1995): F5; cf. also Matthew J. Bernthal, David Crockett, and Randall L. Rose, "Credit Cards as Lifestyle Facilitators," *Journal of Consumer Research* 32 (June 2005): 130–45.
9. Xinyue Zhou, Kathleen D. Vohs, and Roy F. Baumeister, "The Symbolic Power of Money: Reminders of Money Alter Social Distress and Physical Pain," *Psychological Science* 20, no. 6 (2009): 700–6.
10. Fred van Raaij, "Economic Psychology," *Journal of Economic Psychology* 1 (1981): 1–24.
11. Richard T. Curtin, "Indicators of Consumer Behavior: The University of Michigan Surveys of Consumers," *Public Opinion Quarterly* (1982): 340–52.
12. George Katona, "Consumer Saving Patterns," *Journal of Consumer Research* 1 (June 1974): 1–12.
13. "Income, Poverty, and Health Insurance Coverage in the United States: 2011," U.S. Census Bureau (September 2012), http://www.census.gov/prod/2012pubs/p60-243.pdf, accessed March 17, 2013.
14. Matt Richtel, "Austere Times? Perfect," *New York Times* (April 10, 2009), www.nytimes.com/2009/04/11/business/economy/11cheap.html?_r=1, accessed April 10, 2009; www.stretcher.com, accessed March 16, 2013; www.allthingsfrugal.com, accessed March 16, 2013; www.frugalmom.net, accessed March 16, 2013.
15. Center for Media Research, "Financial Security an Elusive Concept," *Mediapost* (November 20, 2008), www.mediapost.com, accessed November 20, 2008.
16. Elizabeth Holmes, "Luxury Goods Sparkle," *Wall Street Journal* (May 4, 2011), http://professional.wsj.com/article/SB10001424052748703834804576300941315031916.html?mg=reno-secaucus-wsj, accessed June 16, 2011.
17. Michael Bush, "Consumers Continue to Stand by Their Causes During Downturn, Survey Says People Will Still Pay More if They Support Brand's Beliefs," *Advertising Age* (November 17, 2008), http://adage.com/article/news/consumers-continue-stand-downturn/132587/, accessed November 17, 2008; Rob Cox and Aliza Rosenbaum, "The Beneficiaries of the Downturn," *New York Times* (December 28, 2008), www.nytimes.com, accessed December 28, 2008.
18. Stephanie Rosenbloom, "But Will It Make You Happy?," *New York Times* (August 7, 2010), http://www.nytimes.com/2010/08/08/business/08consume.html?pagewanted=1&_r=2&ref=business, accessed April 10, 2011.
19. Floyd L. Ruch and Philip G. Zimbardo, *Psychology and Life*, 8th ed. (Glenview, IL: Scott Foresman, 1971).
20. Jonathan H. Turner, *Sociology: Studying the Human System*, 2nd ed. (Santa Monica, CA: Goodyear, 1981).
21. Richard P. Coleman, "The Continuing Significance of Social Class to Marketing," *Journal of Consumer Research* 10 (December 1983): 265–80; Turner, *Sociology: Studying the Human System*.
22. Rebecca Gardyn, "The Mating Game," *American Demographics* (July-August 2002): 33–34.
23. Richard P. Coleman and Lee Rainwater, *Standing in America: New Dimensions of Class* (New York: Basic Books, 1978): 89.
24. Coleman and Rainwater, *Standing in America: New Dimensions of Class*.
25. Turner, *Sociology: Studying the Human System*.
26. Anya Kamenetz, "The Perils and Promise of the Reputation Economy," *Fast Company* (November 25, 2008), www.fastcompany.com/magazine/131/on-the-internet-everyone-knows-youre-a-dog.html, accessed June 17, 2009.
27. Ruth LaFerla, "A Facebook for the Few," *New York Times* (September 6, 2007), www.nytimes.com, accessed September 6, 2007; www.asmallworld.net, accessed June 16, 2011.
28. Turner, *Sociology: Studying the Human System*, 260.
29. See Ronald Paul Hill and Mark Stamey, "The Homeless in America: An Examination of Possessions and Consumption Behaviors," *Journal of Consumer Research* 17 (December 1990): 303–21; "The Homeless Facts and Figures," NOW (May 2, 2007), www.ask.com/bar?q=What+Percentage+of+Americans+Are+Homeless&page=1&qsrc=6&ab=0&u=http://www.pbs.org/now/shows/305/homeless-facts.html, accessed June 17, 2009.
30. Joseph Kahl, *The American Class Structure* (New York: Holt, Rinehart & Winston, 1961).
31. "A Family Affair: Intergenerational Social Mobility Across OECD Countries," Organization for Economic Co-Operation and Development (2010), http://www.oecd.org/tax/public-finance/chapter%205%20gfg%202010.pdf, accessed March 17, 2013; Dan Froomkin, "Social Immobility: Climbing the Economic Ladder Is Harder in the U.S. Than in Most European Countries," *The Huffington Post* (September 21, 2010), http://www.huffingtonpost.com/2010/03/17/social-immobility-climbin_n_501788.html, accessed September 25, 2013.
32. Leonard Beeghley, *Social Stratification in America: A Critical Analysis of Theory and Research* (Santa Monica, CA: Goodyear, 1978).
33. Coleman and Rainwater, *Standing in America: New Dimensions of Class*.
34. See Coleman, "The Continuing Significance of Social Class to Marketing"; Charles M. Schaninger, "Social Class Versus Income Revisited: An Empirical Investigation," *Journal of Marketing Research* 18 (May 1981): 192–208.
35. Coleman, "The Continuing Significance of Social Class to Marketing."
36. "Reading the Buyer's Mind," *U.S. News & World Report* (March 16, 1987): 59.
37. Shelly Reese, "The Many Faces of Affluence," *Marketing Tools* (November-December 1997): 44–48.
38. Rebecca Gardyn, "Oh, the Good Life," *American Demographics* (November 2002): 34.
39. Paul Fussell, *Class: A Guide Through the American Status System* (New York: Summit Books, 1983): 29.
40. Elizabeth C. Hirschman, "Secular Immortality and the American Ideology of Affluence," *Journal of Consumer Research* 17 (June 1990): 31–42.
41. Coleman and Rainwater, *Standing in America: New Dimensions of Class*, 150.
42. Kerry A. Dolan, "The World's Working Rich," *Forbes* (July 3, 2000): 162.
43. Jason DeParle, "Spy Anxiety: The Smart Magazine That Makes Smart People Nervous About Their Standing," *Washingtonian Monthly* (February 1989): 10.
44. For an examination of retailing issues related to the need for status, cf. Jacqueline Kilsheimer Eastman, Leisa Reinecke Flynn, and Ronald E. Goldsmith, "Shopping for Status: The Retail Managerial Implications," *Association of Marketing Theory & Practice* (Spring 1994): 125–30; also cf. Wilfred Amaldoss and Sanjay Jain, "Pricing of Conspicuous Goods: A Competitive Analysis of Social Effects," *Journal of Marketing Research* 42 (February 2005): 30–42.
45. Martin Fackler, "Pajamas: Not Just for Sleep Anymore," *Opelika-Auburn News* (September 13, 2002): 7A.
46. Paula Mergenhagen, "What Can Minimum Wage Buy?," *American Demographics* (January 1996): 32–36.
47. A. T. Kearney, *Serving the Low-Income Consumer: How to Tackle This Mostly Ignored Market*, 2011, http://www.atkearney.com/index.php/Publications/serving-the-low-income-consumer.html, accessed March 17, 2013.
48. Teddy Wayne, "Digital Divide Is a Matter of Income," *New York Times* (December 12, 2010), http://www.nytimes.com/2010/12/13/business/media/13drill.html?adxnnl=1&src=busln&adxnnlx=1304179556-CFuBrgamrMhyRJjRfjj9Zg, accessed April 30, 2011.
49. C. K. Prahalad, *The Fortune at the Bottom of the Pyramid: Eradicating Poverty Through Profits* (Philadelphia, PA: Wharton School Publishing, 2004).
50. Antonio Regalado, "Marketers Pursue the Shallow-Pocketed," *Wall Street Journal* (January 26, 2007): B3.
51. Ibid.

52. Jeffrey F. Durgee, "How Consumer Sub-Cultures Code Reality: A Look at Some Code Types," in Richard J. Lutz, ed., *Advances in Consumer Research* 13 (Provo, UT: Association for Consumer Research, 1986): 332–37.

53. Paul C. Henry, "Social Class, Market Situation, and Consumers' Metaphors of (Dis)Empowerment," *Journal of Consumer Research* 31 (March 2005): 766–78.

54. David Halle, *America's Working Man: Work, Home, and Politics Among Blue-Collar Owners* (Chicago: University of Chicago Press, 1984); David Montgomery, "America's Working Man," *Monthly Review* (1985): 1.

55. Coleman and Rainwater, *Standing in America: New Dimensions of Class*, 139.

56. Roger Brown, *Social Psychology* (New York: Free Press, 1965).

57. Kit R. Roane, "Affluenza Strikes Kids," *U.S. News & World Report* (March 20, 2000): 55.

58. Mark Cleveland, Michel Laroche, and Nicolas Papadopoulos, "Cosmopolitanism, Consumer Ethnocentrism, and Materialism: An Eight-Country Study of Antecedents and Outcomes," *Journal of International Marketing* 17, no. 1 (2009): 116–46; cf. also Dana Alden, James Kelley, Petra Reifler, Julie Lee, and Geoff Soutar, "The Negative Impact of Global Companies: A Three Country Study on Global Company Animosity," *Journal of International Marketing*, in press, June 2013.

59. James Fallows, "A Talent for Disorder (Class Structure)," *U.S. News & World Report* (February 1, 1988): 83.

60. Coleman, "The Continuing Significance of Social Class to Marketing"; W. Lloyd Warner and Paul S. Lunt, eds., *The Social Life of a Modern Community* (New Haven, CT: Yale University Press, 1941).

61. W. Michael Cox and Richard Alm, "You Are What You Spend," *New York Times* (February 10, 2008), www.nytimes.com/2008/02/10/opinion/10cox.html?scp=1&sq=you+are+what+you+, accessed February 10, 2008.

62. Tami Luhby, "What It Takes to Be a One Percenter," CNNMoney (November 20, 2012), http://money.cnn.com/2012/11/20/news/economy/top-1-percent/index.html, accessed April 11, 2013.

63. Howard W. French, "Chinese Children Learn Class, Minus the Struggle," *New York Times* (September 22, 2006), www.nytimes.com, accessed September 22, 2006; Bay Fang, "The Shanghai High Life," *U.S. News & World Report* (June 20, 2005), www.usnews.com/usnews/biztech/articles/050620/20china.b2.htm, accessed June 20, 2005; Janine Gibson, "Den of Equity," *The Guardian* (May 12, 2001), http://travel.guardian.co.uk/cities/story/0,7450,489488,00.html, accessed June 20, 2005; Russell Flannery, "Long Live the $25 Cigar," *Forbes* (December 27, 2004): 51; Clay Chandler, "China Deluxe," *Fortune* (July 26, 2004): 149–56; Matthew Forney, "How Nike Figured Out China," *Time* (November 2004): A10–A14; J. David Lynch, "Emerging Middle Class Reshaping China," *USA Today* (November 12, 2002): 13A.

64. Dan Levin, "Beach Essentials in China: Flip-Flops, a Towel and a Ski Mask," *New York Times* (August 3, 2012), http://www.nytimes.com/2012/08/04/world/asia/in-china-sun-protection-can-include-a-mask.html?_r=1&ref=todayspaper, accessed January 11, 2013.

65. Sebastian Moffett, "The Japanese Paradox: Pinched by Economic Slump, Women Buy More Handbags from Vuitton, Prada, Hermes," *Wall Street Journal* (September 23, 2003), www.wsj.com, accessed September 23, 2003.

66. Cecilie Rohwedder, "Design Houses Build Stores, Pamper Demanding Shoppers in Fashion-Industry Hot Spot," *Wall Street Journal* (January 23, 2004), www.wsj.com, accessed January 23, 2004.

67. Frank Skinner, "Take Not the Moat Out of the Tory's Eye," *Times of London* (May 15, 2009), www.timesonline.co.uk/tol/comment/columnists/frank_skinner/article6289313.ece, accessed June 17, 2009.

68. Quoted in Sarah Lyall, "Multiplying the Old Divisions of Class in Britain," *New York Times* (April 3, 2013), http://www.nytimes.com/2013/04/04/world/europe/multiplying-the-old-divisions-of-class-in-britain.html?_r=0, accessed April 11, 2013; "Huge Survey Reveals Seven Social Classes in UK," *BBC News UK* (April 3, 2013), http://www.bbc.co.uk/news/uk-22007058, accessed April 11, 2013;

69. Heather Timmons, "Vogue's Fashion Photos Spark Debate in India," *New York Times* (August 31, 2008), www.nytimes.com/2008/09/01/business/worldbusiness/01vogue.html?_r=1&ref=busi; accessed September 1, 2008.

70. Quoted in Timmons, "Vogue's Fashion Photos Spark Debate in India."

71. Sara C. Nelson, "Vagina 'Brightener': Indian Feminine Hygiene Product Promises to Make Genitals 'Many Shades Fairer," *Huffington Post UK* |, http://www.huffingtonpost.co.uk/2012/04/12/vagina-brightener-indian-feminine-hygiene-product-promises-to-make-genitals-many-shades-fairer_n_1420052.html?just_reloaded=1, accessed January 11, 2013.

72. Robert Guy Matthews, "Bawdy British Ads Target Hot Youth," *Wall Street Journal* (April 20, 2005): B9.

73. "India's Middle Class Population to Touch 267 Million in 5 Yrs," *Hindustan Times*, http://www.hindustantimes.com/India-news/NewDelhi/India-s-middle-class-population-to-touch-267-million-in-5-yrs/Article1-659159.aspx, accessed March 17, 2013.

74. "Indian Consumer Market: A Change from Pyramid to Sparkling Diamond," KS Oils, http://www.ksoils.com/whitepapers/KS_WHITEPAPER_INDIAN_CONSUMER_MARKET.pdf, accessed March 17, 2013.

75. August B. Hollingshead and Fredrick C. Redlich, *Social Class and Mental Illness: A Community Study* (New York: Wiley, 1958).

76. John Mager and Lynn R. Kahle, "Is the Whole More Than the Sum of the Parts? Re-evaluating Social Status in Marketing," *Journal of Business Psychology* 10 (Fall 1995): 3–18.

77. Beeghley, *Social Stratification in America: A Critical Analysis of Theory and Research*.

78. R. Vanneman and F. C. Pampel, "The American Perception of Class and Status," *American Sociological Review* 42 (June 1977): 422–37.

79. Coleman, "The Continuing Significance of Social Class to Marketing"; Donald W. Hendon, Emelda L. Williams, and Douglas E. Huffman, "Social Class System Revisited," *Journal of Business Research* 17 (November 1988): 259.

80. Gerhard E. Lenski, "Status Crystallization: A Non-Vertical Dimension of Social Status," *American Sociological Review* 19 (August 1954): 405–12.

81. Richard P. Coleman, "The Significance of Social Stratification in Selling," in Martin L. Bell, ed., *Marketing: A Maturing Discipline: Proceedings of the American Marketing Association 43rd National Conference* (Chicago: American Marketing Association, 1960): 171–84.

82. Alex Veiga, "Number of Homes Facing Foreclosure Rose in July," Yahoo! Finance (August 9, 2012), http://finance.yahoo.com/news/number-homes-facing-foreclosure-rose-040831645.html, accessed March 17, 2013.

83. E. Barth and W. Watson, "Questionable Assumptions in the Theory of Social Stratification," *Pacific Sociological Review* 7 (Spring 1964): 10–16.

84. Zick Rubin, "Do American Women Marry Up?" *American Sociological Review* 33 (1968): 750–60.

85. K. U. Ritter and L. L. Hargens, "Occupational Positions and Class Identifications of Married Working Women: A Test of the Asymmetry Hypothesis," *American Journal of Sociology* 80 (January 1975): 934–48.

86. Jennifer Steinhauer, "When the Joneses Wear Jeans," *New York Times* (May 29, 2005), www.nytimes.com, accessed May 29, 2005.

87. http://www.disneystore.com/adults/disney-couture/mn/1000777+1000808/, accessed March 17, 2013; Brooks Barnes, "Disney, By Design," *New York Times* (November 5, 2008), http://www.nytimes.com/2008/11/06/style/06iht-06disney.17579292.html?scp=1&sq=Disney%20by%20design%20brooks%20barnes&st=cse, accessed November 6, 2008.

88. Gleb Bryanski and Guy Faulconbridge, "BRIC Demands More Clout, Steers Clear of Dollar Talk," *Reuters* (June 16, 2009), www.reuters.com/article/ousiv/idUSTRE55F47D20090616, accessed June 17, 2009; Guy Faulconbridge, "BRIC Seeks Global Voice at First Summit," *Reuters* (June 14, 2009), http://www.reuters.com/article/2009/06/14/us-russia-bric-idUSLE11928120090614, accessed June 17, 2009.

89. Paul F. Nunes, Brian A. Johnson, and R. Timothy S. Breene, "Moneyed Masses," *Harvard Business Review* (July–August 2004): 94–104; *Trend Update: Massclusivity*, report from Reinier Evers and Trendwatching.com, Zyman Institute of Brand Science, Emory University, www.zibs.com, accessed February 25, 2005.

90. Herbert J. Gans, "Popular Culture in America: Social Problem in a Mass Society or Social Asset in a Pluralist Society?" in Howard S. Becker, ed., *Social Problems: A Modern Approach* (New York: Wiley, 1966).

91. Eugene Sivadas, George Mathew, and David J. Curry, "A Preliminary Examination of the Continuing Significance of Social Class to Marketing: A Geodemographic Replication," *Journal of Consumer Marketing* 41, no. 6 (1997): 463–79.

92. Edward O. Laumann and James S. House, "Living Room Styles and Social Attributes: The Patterning of Material Artifacts in a Modern Urban Community," *Sociology & Social Research* 54 (April 1970): 321–42; see also Stephen S. Bell, Morris B. Holbrook, and Michael R. Solomon, "Combining Esthetic and Social Value to Explain Preferences for Product Styles with the Incorporation of Personality and Ensemble Effects," *Journal of Social Behavior & Personality* 6 (1991): 243–74.

93. Morris B. Holbrook, Michael J. Weiss, and John Habich, "Class-Related Distinctions in American Cultural Tastes," *Empirical Studies of the Arts* 22, no. 1 (2004): 91–115.

94. Pierre Bourdieu, *Distinction: A Social Critique of the Judgment of Taste* (Cambridge, UK: Cambridge University Press, 1984); cf. also Douglas B. Holt, "Does Cultural Capital Structure American Consumption?," *Journal of Consumer Research* 1 (June 1998): 1–25; Tuba Ustuner and Douglas B. Holt, "Toward a Theory of Status Consumption in Less Industrialized Countries," *Journal of Consumer Research* 37, no. 1 (2010): 37–56; James S.

Coleman, "Social Capital in the Creation of Human Capital," *American Journal of Sociology* 94 (1988): 95–120.

95. Charla Mathwick, Caroline Wiertz, and Ko de Ruyter, "Social Capital Production in a Virtual P3 Community," *Journal of Consumer Research* 34 (April 2008): 832–49; cf. also Jonah Berger and Morgan Ward, "Subtle Signals of Inconspicuous Consumption," *Journal of Consumer Research* 37, no. 4 (2010): 555–69.

96. Quoted from www.hotenough.org, accessed June 16, 2011.

97. Nicole Ellison, Charles Steinfield, and Cliff Lampe, "The Benefits of Facebook 'Friends': Social Capital and College Students' Use of Online Social Network Sites," *Journal of Computer-Mediated Communication* 12 (2007): 1143–68.

98. Xavier Dréze and Joseph C. Nunes, "Feeling Superior: The Impact of Loyalty Program Structure on Consumers' Perceptions of Status," *Journal of Consumer Research* (April 2009): 890–905.

99. Derek Rucker and Adam D. Galinsky, "Desire to Acquire: Powerlessness and Compensatory Consumption," *Journal of Consumer Research* 35 (August 2008): 257–67.

100. "China: The Land Where Fake Brands Reign Supreme," *WeirdAsia News* (October 22, 2010), http://www.weirdasianews.com/2010/10/22/chinathe-land-fake-brands-reign-supreme/, accessed June 16, 2011.

101. Suraj Commuri, "The Impact of Counterfeiting on Genuine-Item Consumers' Brand Relationships," *Journal of Marketing* 73 (May 2009): 86–98.

102. Quoted in Steinhauer, "When the Joneses Wear Jeans."

103. Rod Nordland, "Iraqis Snap Up Hummers as Icons of Power," *New York Times* (March 29, 2009), http://www.nytimes.com/2009/03/30/world/middleeast/30hummer.html?scp=1&sq=Iraqis%20Snap%20Up%20Hummers%20as%20Icons%20of%20Power&st=cse, accessed March 29, 2009.

104. "Western Companies Compete to Win Business of Chinese Babies," *Wall Street Journal Interactive Edition* (May 15, 1998).

105. Andrew E. Kramer, "New Czars of Conspicuous Consumption," *New York Times* (November 1, 2006), www.nytimes.com, accessed November 1, 2006.

106. Tom Wright, "Ringing Up Sales in Indonesia: Nokia's Bulky Smart Phones Find Niche Following There as Business Status Symbol," *Wall Street Journal* (May 22, 2007): B1.

107. John Brooks, *Showing Off in America* (Boston, MA: Little, Brown, 1981), 13.

108. Naughton Keith, "The Perk Wars," *Newsweek* (September 30, 2002): 42–46.

109. http://www.wikihow.com/Know-if-a-Woman-is-a-Cougar, accessed July 29, 2013; Alexia Elejalde-Ruiz, "Age Gap: She's Old Enough to Be his . . . Wife," *Chicago Tribune* (September 19, 2012), http://articles.chicagotribune.com/2012-09-19/features/sc-fam-0918-age-gap-romance-20120919_1_age-gap-age-difference-age-matters, accessed March 17, 2013; Jessica Leshnoff, "Cougars and Their Cubs," *AARP* (February 2008), www.aarp.org/family/love/articles/cougars_and_their.html, accessed June 17, 2009; Robert Campbell, "For the Mature Woman Who Has Everything: A Boy Toy," Reuters (January 30, 2008), http://www.reuters.com/article/2008/01/30/us-speeddating-odd-idUSN3061371020080130, accessed July 29, 2013.

110. Young Jee Han, Joseph C. Nunes, and Xavier Dreza, "Signaling Status with Luxury Goods: The Role of Brand Prominence," *Journal of Marketing* 74 (July 2010): 15–30.

111. Thorstein Veblen, *The Theory of the Leisure Class* (1899; reprint, New York: New American Library, 1953): 45.

112. Brooks, *Showing Off in America*.

113. These definitions are adapted from entries in *The Urban Dictionary*, www.urbandictionary.com, accessed March 16, 2013.

114. Benjamin D. Zablocki and Rosabeth Moss Kanter, "The Differentiation of Life-Styles," *Annual Review of Sociology* (1976): 269–97; Mary Twe Douglas and Baron C. Isherwood, *The World of Goods* (New York: Basic Books, 1979).

115. www.bullz-eye.com/cars/tuner_cars.htm, accessed June 18, 2009; Brian Steinberg, "Pioneer's Hot-Rod Ads Too Cool for Mainstream," *Wall Street Journal* (March 14, 2003), www.wsj.com, accessed March 14, 2003; Mireya Navarro, "Advertisers Carve out a New Segment," *New York Times* (May 22, 2003), www.nytimes.com, accessed May 22, 2003.

116. www.redneckbank.com, accessed June 20, 2011.

117. Russell W. Belk and Janeen Arnold Costa, "The Mountain Man Myth: A Contemporary Consuming Fantasy," *Journal of Consumer Research* 25 (1998): 218–40.

118. "Cosplay," www.cosplay.com, accessed June 20, 2011; www.acparadise.com, accessed June 20, 2011; Lisa Katayama, "Anatomy of a Nerd; Japanese Schoolgirl Watch," *Wired* (March 2006), www.wired.com/wired/archive/14.03/play.html?pg=3, accessed October 6, 2007.

119. Center for Media Research, "Precious Little Time," www.mediapost.com, accessed December 24, 2008.

120. Zablocki and Kanter, "The Differentiation of Life-Styles."

121. Richard A. Peterson, "Revitalizing the Culture Concept," *Annual Review of Sociology* 5 (1979): 137–66.

122. Stephanie Kang and Ethan Smith, "Music for Runners, Volume 2: Nike Releases Second Recording," *Wall Street Journal* (October 23, 2006): B6; http://nikeplus.nike.com/nikeplus/#tutorials, accessed July 6, 2007.

123. Ben Sisario, "Looking to a Sneaker for a Band's Big Break," *New York Times* (October 6, 2010), http://www.nytimes.com/2010/10/10/arts/music/10brand.html?_r=1&emc=eta1, accessed April 30, 2011.

124. William Leiss, Stephen Kline, and Sut Jhally, *Social Communication in Advertising* (Toronto: Methuen, 1986).

125. Douglas and Isherwood, *The World of Goods*, quoted on pp. 72–73.

126. Christopher K. Hsee and France Leclerc, "Will Products Look More Attractive When Presented Separately or Together?" *Journal of Consumer Research* 25 (September 1998): 175–86.

127. Brian Steinberg, "Whose Ad Is This Anyway? Agencies Use Brand Icons to Promote Other Products; Cheaper Than Zeta-Jones," *Wall Street Journal* (December 4, 2003), www.wsj.com, accessed December 4, 2003.

128. Michael R. Solomon, "The Role of Products as Social Stimuli: A Symbolic Interactionism Perspective," *Journal of Consumer Research* 10 (December 1983): 319–29.

129. Michael R. Solomon and Henry Assael, "The Forest or the Trees? A *Gestalt* Approach to Symbolic Consumption," in Jean Umiker-Sebeok, ed., *Marketing and Semiotics: New Directions in the Study of Signs for Sale* (Berlin: Mouton de Gruyter, 1988), 189–218; Michael R. Solomon, "Mapping Product Constellations: A Social Categorization Approach to Symbolic Consumption," *Psychology & Marketing* 5, no. 3 (1988): 233–58; see also Stephen C. Cosmas, "Life Styles and Consumption Patterns," *Journal of Consumer Research* 8, no. 4 (March 1982): 453–55; Russell W. Belk, "Yuppies as Arbiters of the Emerging Consumption Style," in Richard J. Lutz, ed., *Advances in Consumer Research* 13 (Provo, UT: Association for Consumer Research, 1986): 514–19.

130. Lan Nguyen Chaplin and Tina M. Lowrey, "The Development of Consumer-Based Consumption Constellations in Children," *Journal of Consumer Research*, 36, no. 5 (2010): 757–77.

131. Danny Hakim, "Cadillac, Too, Shifting Focus to Trucks," *New York Times* (December 21, 2001), http://www.nytimes.com/2001/12/21/business/cadillac-too-shifting-focus-to-trucks.html, accessed September 3, 2011.

132. Stevenson, "How to Beat Nike."

133. See Lewis Alpert and Ronald Gatty, "Product Positioning by Behavioral Life Styles," *Journal of Marketing* 33 (April 1969): 65–69; Emanuel H. Demby, "Psychographics Revisited: The Birth of a Technique," *Marketing News* (January 2, 1989): 21; William D. Wells, "Backward Segmentation," in Johan Arndt, ed., *Insights into Consumer Behavior* (Boston: Allyn & Bacon, 1968): 85–100.

134. Ian Pearson, "Social Studies: Psychographics in Advertising," *Canadian Business* (December 1985): 67.

135. Helen Coster, "The $25 Water Bottle," *Forbes* (March 19, 2009), www.forbes.com, accessed March 19, 2009; www.mysigg.com, accessed June 3, 2009.

136. Rebecca Piirto Heath, "Psychographics: Qu'est-Ce Que C'est?," *Marketing Tools* (November–December 1995).

137. Alfred S. Boote, "Psychographics: Mind Over Matter," *American Demographics* (April 1980): 26–29; William D. Wells, "Psychographics: A Critical Review," *Journal of Marketing Research* 12 (May 1975): 196–213.

138. Joseph T. Plummer, "The Concept and Application of Life Style Segmentation," *Journal of Marketing* 38 (January 1974): 33–37.

139. Berkeley Rice, "The Selling of Lifestyles," *Psychology Today* (March 1988): 46.

140. John L. Lastovicka, John P. Murry, Erich A. Joachimsthaler, Gurav Bhalla, and Jim Scheurich, "A Lifestyle Typology to Model Young Male Drinking and Driving," *Journal of Consumer Research* 14 (September 1987): 257–63.

141. www.strategicbusinessinsights.com/vals/presurvey.shtml, accessed March 16, 2013; Martha Farnsworth Riche, "VALS 2," *American Demographics* (July 1989): 25. Additional information provided by William D. Guns, Director, Business Intelligence Center, SBI Consulting, Inc., personal communication, May 1997.

142. Robert Lanham, *The Hipster Handbook* (New York: Anchor, 2003); www.urbandictionary.com/define.php?term=hipster, accessed July 5, 2007.

Chapter 12 • Networked Consumer Behavior: Word-of-Mouth, Social Media, and Fashion

Chapter Objectives

When you finish reading this chapter you will understand why:

1. What other consumers tell us about products (good and bad) is more influential than formal advertising.

2. "Opinion leaders" are particularly likely to influence others' product choices.

3. Social media changes the way companies and consumers interact.

4. Online social networking magnifies the impact of word-of-mouth communication.

5. New products, services, and ideas spread through a population over time. Different types of people are more or less likely to adopt them during this diffusion process.

6. Many people and organizations play a role in the fashion system that creates and communicates symbolic meanings to consumers.

7. Fashions follow cycles and reflect cultural dynamics.

MyMarketingLab™
⭐ Improve Your Grade!
Over 10 million students improved their results using the Pearson MyLabs.
Visit **mymktlab.com** for simulations, tutorials, and end-of-chapter problems.

Source: Lucky Business/Shutterstock.

Natalie quickly sorts through today's mail: bill, ad, bill, fund-raising letter from political candidate, an offer for another credit card. Aha! Here it is—the envelope she's been waiting for: an invitation to a posh cocktail party at her friend Jackie's ad agency. This will be her chance to see and be seen, to mingle, network, and maybe even land a job offer. But, what to wear? Somehow her industrial grunge clothes don't seem appropriate for the new life she imagines as an account executive. Natalie needs help, so she does what comes naturally. First, she tweets her friends to let them know about the event; then she fires up her computer to check out what the *fashionistas* who roam the blogosphere recommend this season. She browses *Polyvore* to see what looks celebrities are posting, and she's immediately grabbed by actress Cate Blanchett's rose pink gown with floral appliqués by Balenciaga. There's also a funkier look that a "regular" person with the screen name *buttonbaby* posted she could grab for 1/10 the price.[1] Natalie quickly copies some snapshots from the site and posts them on her Facebook page to get some quick reactions from her network. It helps a lot to get honest feedback from her "peeps" in addition to advice from fashion industry insiders. As Natalie waits a few minutes for the votes to filter in, she imagines the great *haul video* she's going to post on YouTube when she brings home her outfit.[2] Even if she doesn't land any interviews at the party, no big deal. Just making that little clip of herself recounting her shopping trip for the camera as she triumphantly pulls the clothes and accessories out of her bag will be worth the effort.

OBJECTIVE 1
What other consumers tell us about products (good and bad) is more influential than formal advertising.

Word-of-Mouth Communication

Altoids breath mints have been around for 200 years, but the brand caught fire in the market only near the end of the 20th century. How did this happen? The revival began when the mint attracted a devoted following among smokers and coffee drinkers who hung out in the blossoming Seattle club scene during the 1980s. Until 1993, when Kraft bought manufacturer Callard & Bowser, only those "in the know" sucked the mints. The brand's marketing manager persuaded Kraft to hire advertising agency Leo Burnett to develop a modest promotional campaign. The agency decided to publicize the candy with subway posters sporting retro imagery and other "low tech" media to avoid making the product seem mainstream— that would turn off the original audience.[3] As young people started to tune into this "retro" treat, its popularity skyrocketed.

As the Altoids success story illustrates, today "buzz" makes a hit product. **Word-of-mouth (WOM)** is product information that individuals transmit to other individuals. Because we get the word from people we know, WOM tends to be more reliable and trustworthy than messages from more formal marketing channels. And, unlike advertising, WOM often comes with social pressure to conform to these recommendations.[4]

Net Profit

Varsity Brands is a leading supplier to cheerleaders. The company sponsored a big survey of teenage girls to learn how they decide what to buy. No surprises here: Half of the respondents spend an hour or more each day texting, and another third spend an hour socializing online. In contrast, 44 percent spend less than 15 minutes actually talking on the phone (who uses the phone to talk anymore?). When these girls discover a brand they like, three-quarters say they are likely to recommend it to a friend. About half become online fans of the brand, and 55 percent agree that "[i]f I see a favorable post online about an item, it will likely influence me to buy it." A Varsity marketing executive commented, "When it comes to spreading ideas via social media, teen girls lead the pack. They are more likely to use online time for connecting, self-expression, and relationship building. They are more likely to have used e-mail and are almost twice as likely as boys to have shared photos through a website, posted a comment on a blog or community, blogged themselves or kept an online journal."[5]

· · · · · · · · · · · · · · · · · ·

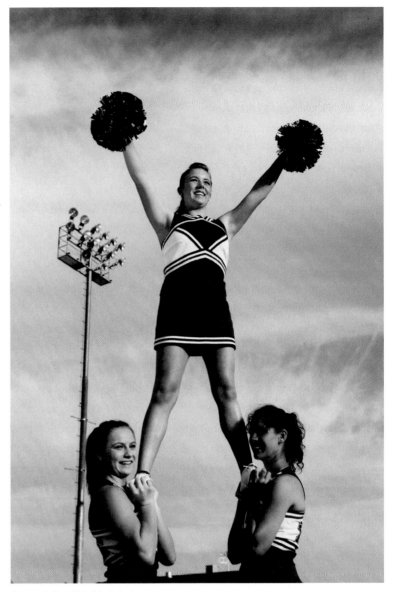

Source: Andrew Rich/istockphoto.com.

Ironically, despite all the money marketers pump into lavish ads, WOM is far more powerful: It influences two-thirds of all consumer goods sales.[6] In one survey, 69 percent of interviewees said they relied on a personal referral at least once over the course of a year to help them choose a restaurant, 36 percent reported that they used referrals to decide on computer hardware and software, and 22 percent got help from friends and associates to decide where to travel.[7]

If you think carefully about the content of your own conversations in the course of a normal day, you will probably agree that much of what you discuss with friends, family members, or coworkers is product related: When you compliment someone on her dress and ask her where she bought it, recommend a new restaurant to a friend, or complain to your neighbor about the shoddy treatment you got at the bank, you engage in WOM.

As far back as the Stone Age (well, the 1950s, anyway), communications theorists challenged the assumption that advertising primarily determines what we buy. As a rule, *advertising is more effective to reinforce our existing product preferences than to create new ones.*[8] Studies in both industrial and consumer purchase settings underscore the idea that although information from impersonal sources is important to create brand awareness, consumers rely on WOM in the later stages of evaluation and adoption.[9] Quite

Source: BzzAgent, Inc.

Net Profit

Marketers have been aware of the power of WOM for many years, but recently they've been more aggressive about trying to promote and control it instead of sitting back and hoping people will like their products enough to talk them up. Companies like BzzAgent enlist thousands of "agents" who try new products and spread the word about those they like.[10] Many sophisticated marketers today also precisely track WOM. For example, the ongoing TalkTrack study reports which brands consumers mention the most in different categories. Based on online surveys of 14,000 women, it reports that middle aged (baby boomer) women talk about Kraft more than any other packaged goods food brand, and they discuss Olay the most among beauty products.[11]

simply, the more positive information consumers get about a product from peers, the more likely they will be to adopt the product.[12]

The influence of others' opinions is at times even more powerful than our own perceptions. In one study of furniture choices, consumers' estimates of how much their friends would like the furniture was a better predictor of purchase than what they thought of it.[13] In addition, consumers may find their own reasons to push a brand that take the manufacturer by surprise. That's what happened with Mountain Dew: Its popularity among younger consumers is due to the "buzz" about the soda's high caffeine content. As an advertising executive explained, "The caffeine thing was not in any of Mountain Dew's television ads. This drink is hot by word of mouth."[14]

WOM is especially powerful when the consumer is relatively unfamiliar with the product category. We would expect such a situation in the case of new products (e.g., medications to prevent hair loss) or those that are technologically complex (e.g., smartphones). One way to reduce uncertainty about the wisdom of a purchase is to talk about it. Talking gives the consumer an opportunity to generate supporting arguments for the purchase and to garner support for this decision from others. For example,

Marketing Opportunity

To boost their brand awareness, Subaru Singapore has been organizing "The MediaCorp Subaru Challenge" in association with Singapore MediaCorp since 2002.[17] This annual contest, held in an open space in front of a shopping mall, requires each contestant to keep the palm of his or her hand on a Subaru vehicle; the specific position on the vehicle is pre-selected by a lucky draw. Many view this as an "endurance contest" because contestants must remain standing, come rain or shine, and are only given a five-minute break every six hours to eat, drink, or relieve themselves. During the competition, they are eliminated if they lift their hands from the vehicle or relieve themselves in their clothes. The last person standing wins the Subaru vehicle. The current record stands at 81 hours 32 minutes. This event was so successful that it went regional in 2008, attracting contestants from surrounding countries such as Hong Kong and Vietnam. The event, currently in its 12th year, has helped Subaru achieve greater brand awareness in Asia.[18]

• • • • • • • • • • • • • • • •

Hoaxkill.com is a Web site dedicated to tracking hoaxes and debunking product rumors.

Source: Courtesy of Joroen Siking Hoaxkill.com.

the strongest predictor of a person's intention to buy a residential solar water heating system is the number of solar heat users the person knows.[15]

Buzz Building

In the "old days," here's how a toy company would launch a new product: Unveil a hot holiday toy during a spring trade fair, run a November–December saturation television ad campaign during cartoon prime time to sell the toy to kids, sit back and watch as desperate parents scrambled through the aisles at Toys "R" Us, and then wait for the resulting media coverage to drive still more sales.

Fast forward to a more recent toy story: A Hong Kong company called Silverlit Toys makes the $30 Picoo Z helicopter. At one point a Google search for the term *Picoo* produced more than 109,000 URLs, with many of those links pointed to major online global gift retailers like Hammacher Schlemmer and Toys "R" Us. Do you think this huge exposure was the result of a meticulously planned promotional strategy? Think again. By most accounts, a 28-year-old tech worker in Chicago started the Picoo Z buzz; he bought his helicopter after he read about it on a hobbyist message board. A few months later, he uploaded his homemade video of the toy on YouTube. Within 2 weeks, 15 of his friends had also bought the toy, and they in turn posted their own videos and pointed viewers to the original video. Internet retailers who troll online conversations for fresh and exciting buzz identified the toy and started to add their own links to the clips. Within a few short months, there were hundreds of Picoo Z videos and more than a million people viewed them.[16]

The grassroots efforts we often witness today epitomize **guerrilla marketing**: promotional strategies that use unconventional means and venues to encourage WOM about products. This has nothing to do with monkey business; the term implies that the marketer "ambushes" the unsuspecting recipient because the message pops up in a place where he or she wasn't expecting to see an advertisement. These campaigns often recruit legions of real consumers who agree to engage in some kind of street theater or other activity to convince others to use the product or service.

Negative WOM: The Power of Rumors

WOM is a two-edged sword that cuts both ways for marketers. Informal discussions among consumers can make or break a product or store. Furthermore, consumers weigh **negative word-of-mouth** more heavily than they do positive comments. According to a study by the White House Office of Consumer Affairs, 90 percent of unhappy customers will not do business with a company again. Each of these people is likely to share his or her grievance with at least nine other people, and 13 percent of these disgruntled customers tell more than 30 people about their negative experience.[19] Before you know it, it's easy to have a real problem on your hands.

Especially when we consider a new product or service, we're likely to pay more attention to negative information than to positive information and to tell others about our nasty experience.[20] Research shows that negative WOM reduces the credibility of a firm's advertising and influences consumers' attitudes toward a product as well as their intention to buy it.[21] Dell found this out the hard way when bloggers denounced the computer maker's quality and service levels; then the popular media picked up this discontent and magnified it.[22]

As Dell discovered, it's incredibly easy to spread negative WOM online. Many dissatisfied customers and disgruntled former employees create Web sites simply to share their tales of woe with others. For example, a Web site for people to complain about the

This Israeli ad illustrates how "facts" often mutate when people repeat them.
Source: Gitam BBDO, Tel Aviv; Karmel Abuzlaf, Guy Bar, Shani Gershi; Eitan Cohen; Arnon Rotem; Miriam Moshinksy.

Marketing Pitfall

In the 1930s, some companies hired "professional rumormongers" to organize word-of-mouth campaigns that pushed their clients' products and criticized competitors'.[25] More recently, Bio Business International, a small Canadian company that markets 100 percent cotton nonchlorine bleached tampons under the name Terra Femme, encouraged women to spread a message that the tampons its American competitors make contain dioxin. There is very little evidence to support the claim that these products are dangerous, but as a result of this rumor, Procter & Gamble received thousands of complaints about its feminine hygiene products.[26]

Dunkin' Donuts chain got to be so popular that the company bought it in order to control the bad press it got. A man created the site because he couldn't get skim milk for his coffee.[23] An in-depth study of 40 complaint Web sites such as walmartsucks.com identified three basic themes:[24]

1 **Injustice**—Consumer protestors frequently talk about their fruitless attempts to contact the company.
2 **Identity**—Posters characterize the violator (often top management) as evil, rather than simply incompetent.
3 **Agency**—Individual Web site creators try to create a collective identity for those who share their anger with a company. They evoke themes of crusade and heroism to rally others to believe that they have the power to change a status quo in which companies can wrong consumers without retribution.

As we transmit information to one another, it tends to change. The resulting message usually does not resemble the original at all. The British psychologist Frederic Bartlett used the method of *serial reproduction* to examine how content mutates. Like the game of "Telephone" many of us played as kids, he asked a subject to reproduce a stimulus, such as a drawing or a story. He then gave another subject this reproduction and asked him to copy it, and repeated this process several times. Figure 12.1 illustrates how a message changes as people reproduce it. Bartlett found that distortions almost inevitably follow a pattern: They tend to change from ambiguous forms to more conventional ones as subjects try to make them consistent with their preexisting schemas (see Chapter 2). He called this process *assimilation* and he noted that it often occurs as people engage in *leveling,* when they omit details to simplify the structure; or *sharpening,* when they exaggerate prominent details.

Figure 12.1 THE TRANSMISSION OF MISINFORMATION

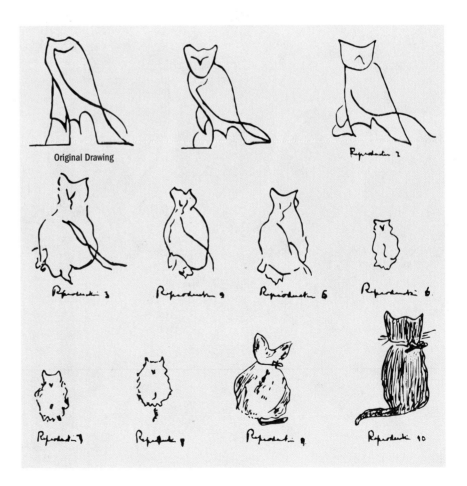

CB AS I SEE IT

Prof. Praveen Aggarwal, *University of Minnesota Duluth*

Though most of us would like to believe that we act independently while making our purchase decisions, the fact of the matter remains that our decisions are heavily influenced by others. The traditional literature on interpersonal influences examines the role of word of mouth (WOM) in decision making. We routinely turn to our friends and family members for advice and information. Many of us even serve as opinion leaders who help others with their decision making. In the context of WOM communications, does it matter if the message being exchanged has specific details or is of a generic nature? For instance, if someone wanted to communicate to you that a particular cell phone's battery was better than average, would it make a difference if they gave a generic advice that "the

cell phone's battery lasts longer than average" rather than giving you more specific information such as "the cell phone's battery lasts an additional five hours per charge"? Our research indicates that WOM communications are more effective if they contain more specific information. Interestingly, this advantage disappears when the sender of the message is seen as an expert or has strong social ties with the receiver.

In a related area of research on interpersonal influences, my colleagues and I examine situations in which people knowingly delegate the task of decision making to someone else. This is different from seeking others' opinions, in the sense that they decide not to decide and instead let someone else make their decisions for them. The individuals to whom the decision-making task is delegated are called *surrogate buyers*. Wardrobe consultants, interior decorators, stock brokers, and wine stewards are some common examples where the end user delegates the choice decision to someone else. What kinds of conditions promote decision delegation? Our research indicates higher levels of delegation when

the differential between the user's and surrogate's expertise is high, and when the surrogate is seen as trustworthy and accountable. It also helps if the surrogate customizes recommendations to the individual's needs and wants.

How can companies find out what kinds of things are being said about their products by their buyers and end users? Although it was difficult to gauge the general sentiment of people's opinions in the pre-Internet era, the vast repository of opinions, reviews, and recommendations available online provides a tantalizing opportunity for managers to gain a summary assessment of the WOM shaping up around their brands. The problem, however, is that the volume of information available is so vast that it is extremely difficult to sift through it and draw summary conclusions. Our research addresses this vexing problem. Drawing on research in lexical text analysis and computational linguistics, we were able to develop a simple mechanism to take massive amounts of information and convert them into simple indices that managers can use to track how the WOM around their brands is evolving![27]

OBJECTIVE 2

"Opinion leaders" are particularly likely to influence others' product choices.

Opinion Leadership

As Cold Stone Creamery expands to Japan, the ice cream store projects a somewhat different image than it has in the United States. The chain wants to be ultracool as it generates a buzz among fashion-conscious "office ladies"—as the Japanese call young, single, female professionals. These women are very influential in Japan; their reactions to a new product can make or break it. To woo this group, Cold Stone sponsored a fashion show for young women (assuming the models can fit into the dresses after sampling a few of the chain's caloric creations), and fashion magazines staged photo shoots at the stores.[28]

Although consumers get information from personal sources, they do not usually ask just *anyone* for advice about purchases. If you decide to buy a new stereo, you will most likely seek advice from a friend who knows a lot about sound systems. This friend may own a sophisticated system, or she may subscribe to specialized magazines such as *Stereo Review* and spend her free time browsing through electronics stores. However, you may have another friend who has a reputation for being stylish and who spends his free time reading *Gentleman's Quarterly* and shopping at trendy boutiques. You might not bring up your stereo problem with him, but you may take him with you to shop for a new fall wardrobe.

Everyone knows people who are knowledgeable about products and whose advice others take seriously. These individuals, called **opinion leaders**, are frequently able to influence others' attitudes or behaviors.[29] Clearly, some people's recommendations carry more weight than others. Opinion leaders are extremely valuable information sources because they possess the social power we discussed earlier in the chapter:

- They are technically competent, so they possess expert power.[30]
- They prescreen, evaluate, and synthesize product information in an unbiased way, so they possess knowledge power.[31]
- They are socially active and highly interconnected in their communities.[32]
- They are likely to hold offices in community groups and clubs and to be active outside of the home. As a result, opinion leaders often wield legitimate power by virtue of their social standing.
- They tend to be similar to the consumer in terms of their values and beliefs, so they possess referent power. Note that although opinion leaders are set apart by their interest or expertise in a product category, they are more convincing to the extent that they are *homophilous* rather than *heterophilous*. **Homophily** refers to the degree to which a pair of individuals is similar in terms of education, social status, and beliefs.[33] Effective opinion leaders tend to be slightly higher in terms of status and educational attainment than those they influence, but not so high as to be in a different social class.
- Opinion leaders are often among the first to buy new products, so they absorb much of the risk. This experience reduces uncertainty for the rest of us who are not as courageous. Furthermore, whereas company-sponsored communications tend to focus exclusively on the positive aspects of a product, the hands-on experience of opinion leaders makes them more likely to impart *both* positive and negative information about product performance. Thus, they are more credible because they have no "axe to grind."

How Influential Is an Opinion Leader?

Ford's prelaunch campaign for its crossover SUV Flex model aimed to get buzz going as it gave opinion leaders an exclusive look at the new car. In five cities, the company invited radio deejays, musicians, and other creative people to take a tour of the Flex. These influentials went on an urban odyssey as fleets of the vehicles took them to art galleries, nightclubs, and other hot spots. In a separate campaign to plug its Fiesta model, the carmaker selected 100 young people who got free use of a car for 6 months in return for blogging about it.[34]

When social scientists initially developed the concept of the opinion leader, they assumed that certain influential people in a community would exert an overall impact on group members' attitudes. Later work, however, questioned the assumption that there is such a thing as a *generalized opinion leader* whose recommendations we seek for all types of purchases. Very few people are capable of being expert in a number of fields (even though they believe otherwise). Sociologists distinguish between those who are *monomorphic*, or expert in a limited field, and those who are *polymorphic*, or expert in several fields.[35] Even opinion leaders who are polymorphic, however, tend to concentrate on one broad domain, such as electronics or fashion. For example, Mediamark Research & Intelligence estimates that 10.5 percent of the U.S. adult population, whom it labels "Big Circle Influentials," are the key influencers for personal finance decisions.[36]

Research on opinion leadership generally indicates that although opinion leaders do exist for multiple product categories, expertise tends to overlap across similar categories. It is rare to find a generalized opinion leader. An opinion leader for home appliances is likely to serve a similar function for home cleaners but not for cosmetics. In contrast, we may consult a fashion opinion leader whose primary influence is on clothing choices for recommendations on cosmetics purchases but not necessarily for her opinions on microwave ovens.[37]

A reexamination of the traditional perspective on opinion leadership reveals that the process isn't as clear-cut as some researchers thought.[38] The original framework is called the **two step flow model of influence**. It proposes that a small group of *influencers* disseminate information because they can modify the opinions of a large number of other people. When the authors ran extensive computer simulations of this process, they found that the influence is driven less by influentials and more by the interaction among those who are easily influenced; they communicate the information vigorously to one another and they also participate in a two-way dialogue with the opinion leader as part of an **influence network**. These conversations create **information cascades** that occur when a piece of information triggers a sequence of interactions (much like an avalanche).

Types of Opinion Leaders

We've seen that early conceptions of the opinion leader role assumed a static, one-way process: The opinion leader absorbs information from the mass media and in turn transmits data to opinion receivers. This view also confuses the functions of several different types of consumers.

Opinion leaders may or may not be purchasers of the products they recommend. Early purchasers also tend to be *innovators*; they like to take risks and try new things. Researchers call opinion leaders who also are early purchasers *innovative communicators*. One study identified characteristics of college men who were innovative communicators for fashion products. These men were among the first to buy new fashions, and other students were likely to follow their lead when they made their own purchases. Other characteristics of the men included the following:[39]

● They were socially active.
● They were appearance conscious and narcissistic (i.e., they were quite fond of themselves and self-centered).

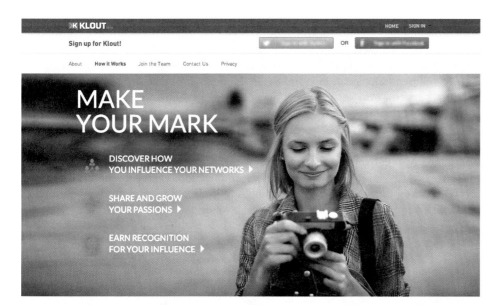

WHAT IS INFLUENCE?

Net Profit

Klout claims to precisely measure just how influential each of us is. It awards pop sensation Justin Bieber, with his 6.4 million Twitter followers, a perfect score of 100; go there and see how influential you are.[40] Although many marketers today focus on identifying key influencers and motivating them to spread the word about a brand, another camp believes that it's more productive simply to get your message out to as many people as possible. They argue that it's very difficult to predict what will trigger a cascade, so it's better to hedge your bets by simply getting the word out as widely as possible.[41] Stay tuned, as the science of understanding online influence races to keep up with the mushrooming usage of these new platforms.

Source: Courtesy of Klout, Inc.

- They were involved in rock culture.
- They were heavy readers of magazines like *Playboy* and *Sports Illustrated*.
- They were likely to own more clothing, and a broader range of styles, than other students.

Opinion leaders also are likely to be *opinion seekers*. They are generally more involved in a product category and so they actively search for information. As a result, they are more likely to talk about products with others and to solicit others' opinions as well.[42] Contrary to the older, static view of opinion leadership, most product-related conversation does not take place in a "lecture" format where one person does all the talking. A lot of product-related conversation occurs in the context of a casual interaction rather than as formal instruction.[43] One study, which found that opinion seeking is especially high for food products, revealed that two-thirds of opinion seekers also view themselves as opinion leaders.[44]

The Market Maven

To publicize Clinical Therapy, a new lotion brand from Vaseline, the company's advertising campaign mapped the social network of a small town in Alaska. In Kodiak, reps took over a storefront and gave away free bottles. In return, the recipients had to identify the person in town who recommended the product to them. Through this process they found a woman whom many of the townspeople named as their source.[45]

The Alaskan woman Vaseline found (no, she isn't Sarah Palin) is a **market maven**—she is a person who likes to transmit marketplace information of all types. These shopaholics are not necessarily interested in certain products and they may not necessarily be early purchasers; they're simply into staying on top of what's happening in the marketplace. They come closer to the function of a generalized opinion leader because they tend to have a solid overall knowledge of how and where to procure products. They're also more confident in their own ability to make smart purchase decisions.

The Surrogate Consumer

In addition to everyday consumers who influence others' purchase decisions, a class of marketing intermediary we call the **surrogate consumer** often guides what we buy. This term refers to a third party we retain to provide input into our purchase decisions. Unlike the opinion leader or market maven, we usually compensate the surrogate for his or her advice. Interior decorators, stockbrokers, professional shoppers, and college consultants are surrogate consumers.

Regardless of whether they actually make the purchase on behalf of the consumer, their recommendations can be enormously influential. The consumer, in essence, relinquishes control over several or all decision-making functions, such as information search, the evaluation of alternatives, or the actual purchase. For example, a client may commission an interior decorator to redo her house, and we may entrust a broker to make crucial buy/sell decisions on our behalf. Marketers tend to overlook surrogates when they try to convince consumers to buy their goods or services. This can be a big mistake, because they may mistarget their communications to end consumers when they should focus on the surrogates who actually sift through product information and recommend a purchase to their clients.[46]

How Do We Find Opinion Leaders?

Companies that want to connect with teens are turning up on the cheerleading circuit. They recognize that cheerleaders often are among the most popular kids in high school, and they're able to influence their classmates' opinions about which products are the coolest. That's why makeup artists who work for P&G's Cover Girl line of cosmetics show up at cheerleading clinics to offer makeup tips to some of the 350,000 people per year who attend these training sessions. Samsung promotes its

Galaxy lineup via the Mobilers program, where active Samsung mobile ambassadors share their own experiences with their respective audiences on social media.[47]

Unfortunately, because most opinion leaders are everyday consumers rather than celebrities, they are harder to find. A celebrity or an influential industry executive is by definition easy to locate. That person has national or at least regional visibility or has a listing in published directories. In contrast, opinion leaders tend to operate at the local level and they may influence only a small group of consumers rather than an entire market segment.

Because it's difficult to identify specific opinion leaders in a large market, most attempts to do so focus instead on *exploratory studies*. In these efforts, researchers identify the profile of a representative opinion leader and then generalize these insights to a larger market. For example, one company that sought out financial opinion leaders found that these consumers were more likely to manage their own finances and tended to use a computer to do so. They also were more likely to follow their investments on a daily basis and to read books and watch television shows devoted to financial issues.[49]

Self-Designation

The most commonly used technique to identify opinion leaders is simply to ask individual consumers whether they consider themselves to *be* opinion leaders. Although respondents who report a greater degree of interest in a product category are more likely to be opinion leaders, we must view the results of surveys that discover self-designated opinion leaders with some skepticism. Some people have a tendency to inflate their own importance and influence, whereas others who really are influential might not admit to this quality or be conscious of it if they are.[50]

Here's the problem: The fact that we transmit advice about products does not mean other people *take* that advice. For someone to be considered a legit opinion leader, opinion seekers must actually heed his or her advice. An alternative is to select certain group members (*key informants*) whom we ask to identify opinion leaders. The success of this approach hinges on locating those who have accurate knowledge of the group.

The self-designating method is not as reliable as a more systematic analysis (where we can verify an individual's self-designation by asking others if they agree), but the advantage is that we can easily apply it to a large group of potential opinion leaders. Figure 12.2 shows one of the measurement scales researchers use for this kind of self-designation.

Figure 12.2 OPINION LEADER SCALE

Please rate yourself on the following scales relating to your interactions with friends and neighbors regarding _____.

1. In general, do you talk to your friends and neighbors about _____:

very often				never
5	4	3	2	1

2. When you talk to your friends and neighbors about _____ do you:

give a great deal of information				give very little information
5	4	3	2	1

3. During the past six months, how many people have you told about a new _____?

told a number of people				told no one
5	4	3	2	1

4. Compared with your circle of friends, how likely are you to be asked about new _____?

very likely to be asked				not at all likely to be asked
5	4	3	2	1

5. In discussion of new _____, which of the following happens most?

you tell your friends about _____				your friends tell you about _____
5	4	3	2	1

6. Overall in all of your discussions with friends and neighbors are you:

often used as a source of advice				not used as a source of advice
5	4	3	2	1

Sociometry: The Kevin Bacon Phenomenon

The play *Six Degrees of Separation* is based on the premise that everyone on the planet indirectly knows everyone else—or at least knows people who in turn know them. Indeed, social scientists estimate that the average person has 1,500 acquaintances and that five to six intermediaries could connect any two people in the United States.[51] A popular game challenges players to link the actor Kevin Bacon with other actors in much the same way.

Sociometric methods trace communication patterns among members of a group. These techniques allow researchers to systematically map out the interactions among group members. Like the Vaseline campaign in Alaska we described earlier, this means we interview consumers and find out who they ask for product information. In many cases, one or a few people emerge as the "nodes" in a map—and *voilá*, we've found our opinion leaders. This method is the most precise, but it is very difficult and expensive to implement because it involves very close study of interaction patterns in small groups. For this reason, it's best to apply a sociometric technique in a closed, self-contained social setting, such as in hospitals, in prisons, and on army bases, where members are largely isolated from other social networks.

A recent sociometric study on obesity (similar to the one we read about earlier regarding clusters of smokers) provides a striking example of how our social networks influence what we do. The researchers analyzed a sample of more than 12,000 people who participated in the Framingham Heart Study, which closely documented their health from 1971 to 2003. They discovered that obesity can spread from person to person, much like a virus. The investigators knew who was friends with whom, as well as who was a spouse or sibling or neighbor, and they knew how much each person weighed at various times over three decades so they could reconstruct what happened over the years if study participants became obese. Guess what? When one person gains weight, close friends tend to gain weight, too: A person's chances of becoming obese if a close friend put on the pounds increased by 57 percent! The friend's influence remained even if he lived hundreds of miles away. The researchers speculated that the reason for this *social contagion* effect is that when our best buds get fat, this alters our perception of normal body weight so we aren't as concerned when we put on a few pounds as well. The moral of the story: Hang out with thin people![52]

Many professionals, such as doctors, accountants, and lawyers, as well as services marketers like lawn-care companies and cleaning services, depend primarily on word-of-mouth to generate business. In many cases, consumers recommend a service provider to a friend or coworker, and in other cases businesspeople make recommendations to their customers. For example, only 0.2 percent of respondents in one study reported that they choose a physician based on advertising. Instead, they rely primarily on advice from family and friends.[53]

We use sociometric analyses to better understand *referral behavior* and to locate strengths and weaknesses in terms of how one's reputation flows through a community.[54] *Network analysis* focuses on communication in social systems, considers the relations among people in a *referral network*, and measures the *tie strength* among them. To understand how a network guides what we buy, consider a study researchers conducted among women who lived together in a sorority house. They found evidence that subgroups, or *cliques*, within the sorority were likely to share preferences for various products. In some cases, the sisters even shared their choices of "private" (i.e., socially inconspicuous) products (probably because of shared bathrooms in the sorority house).[55]

Tie strength refers to the nature of the bond between people. It can range from *strong primary* (e.g., one's spouse) to *weak secondary* (e.g., an acquaintance whom one rarely sees). Although strong ties are important, weak ties are too because they perform a *bridging function*. This type of connection allows a consumer access between subgroups. For example, you might have a regular group of friends that is a primary reference group (strong ties). If you have an interest in tennis, one of these friends might introduce you to a group of people in her dorm who play on the tennis team. As a result, you gain access to their valuable expertise through this bridging function. This referral process demonstrates the *strength of weak ties*.

The Social Media Revolution

OBJECTIVE 3
Social media changes the way companies and consumers interact.

The odds are good that you've already interacted with social media today. If you checked into your Facebook page (of course not during class!), fired off a tweet, read a restaurant review on Yelp, or maybe even killed off some nasty orcs on *World of Warcraft*, you're part of the social media revolution that is changing how consumers interact with the marketplace and with one another. Many of us love to share details about our lives that our parents probably would never discuss in public. Somehow events don't seem "official" until we post them: A change in relationship status on Facebook, a photo of a luscious restaurant appetizer on Instagram, a funky necklace pinned onto Pinterest. We want others in our networks to know what we know; and research indicates we're more likely to share good news than bad. We're also most likely to talk about ourselves; one study reported that 80 percent of tweets focused on the author.[56]

Sometimes people define social media in terms of hardware (like Android smartphones) or software (like Wikipedia), but really it's first and foremost about *community*: the collective participation of members who together build and maintain a site.[57] Indeed, many of us become so enmeshed in our social networks that we feel the need to check them constantly to be sure we stay on top of what our (online) friends are up to 24/7 (oops, better stop reading and scan your Facebook, Twitter, or Foursquare postings!). Some refer to this compulsion as **FOMO** (Fear of Missing Out). Certainly there are advantages to always feeling connected, but perhaps the downside is a vague feeling of regret or inadequacy that lurks in the background in

As people spend more and more time interacting with social media, some critics fret that we're sacrificing the benefits of face-to-face interactions. What do you think (or poll your Facebook friends for a response!).

Source: Chinet® Brand Ad, The Bunlin Group.

case we chose not to be somewhere—or even worse, that we weren't invited in the first place![58]

Our zeal to share and to collect feedback from others before we purchase underscores the key role social media plays in fueling the basic word-of-mouth process. We call the people who supply these reviews **brand advocates**. Yahoo! estimates that 40 percent of people who spend time online are advocates and that they influence purchases two to one over nonadvocates. Marketers who adjust their strategies to acknowledge this impact find it's worth their while. For example, PETCO saw a 500 percent increase in its click-through rate when it included consumers' reviews in its online ads.[59]

Social Media and Community

The Skittles candy brand changed its Web site into a social media hub and in the process significantly boosted consumers' awareness of the product. Instead of seeing corporate-produced content, a visitor to the site finds links to Twitter to read tweets about Skittles (good and bad). Another link guides her to Skittles videos and photos on YouTube and Flickr, and if she clicks "Friends," she'll go directly to the brand's Facebook area.[60]

Marketers like Skittles stumble over one another to adapt their strategies to a Web 2.0 environment. These new communications platforms can be as varied as a social networking site like Facebook, a social shopping site like Groupon, or a virtual world like Twinity. Nonetheless, they share some basic characteristics:

- They improve as the number of users increase. For example, Amazon's ability to recommend books to you based on what other people with similar interests buy gets better as it tracks more and more people who enter search queries.
- Their currency is eyeballs. Google makes money as it charges advertisers according to the number of people who see their ads after they type in a search term.
- They are free and in perpetual beta. Wikipedia, the online encyclopedia, gets updated constantly by volunteer editors who "correct" others' errors.
- They categorize entries according to a **folksonomy** rather than a *taxonomy* (a preestablished labeling hierarchy). Instead, sites rely on users to sort contents. Listeners at Pandora.com create their own "radio stations" that play songs by artists they choose, as well as other similar artists.[61] People who upload their photos to Flickr tag them with the labels *they* think best describe the pictures.

In some ways, online communities are not much different from those we find in our physical environment. The *Merriam-Webster Dictionary* (online version, of course) defines **community** as "a unified body of individuals, unified by interests, location, occupation, common history, or political and economic concerns." In fact, one social scientist refers to an online community as a **cyberplace** where "people connect online with kindred spirits, engage in supportive and sociable relationships with them, and imbue their activity online with meaning, belonging, and identity."[62]

Marketing Opportunity

Viral marketing refers to the strategy where an organization motivates visitors to a Web site to forward information on the site to their friends in order to make still more consumers aware of it. It usually takes off when the online content is entertaining or just plain weird. This approach stirred up a huge amount of interest in lap giraffes, for example. Thousands of people started to look for these novel pets after an online message circulated about them and Sokoblovsky Farms, the place that breeds these petite versions of the gentle creatures we see in zoos. One hitch: There is no such thing as a lap giraffe. The scam was part of a marketing campaign for DirecTV, America's biggest satellite cable TV provider. It started with a TV commercial that starred a rich Russian who "also likes saving zee money." At the end of the spot, he gives a little kiss to a giraffe that's the size of a small lap dog. The company followed up with a fake Web site that included photos of the pets and even a "live camera feed" from the farm, which shows a tiny giraffe grazing. More than half a million people put their names on a waiting list to receive one of the tiny animals. It's not clear if they're still waiting for their pets to arrive, but DirecTV certainly hooked a lot of exposures.[63]

Source: Courtesy of DIRECTV.

Today, it seems that "everyone" is on Facebook—including parents.
Source: Toyota Motor Sales U.S.A., Inc.

When consumers are truly involved with a product, an ad, or a Web site, they enter a **flow state**. This experience is the Holy Grail of Web designers, who want to create sites that are so entrancing the surfer loses all track of time as he becomes engrossed in the site's contents (and hopefully buys stuff in the process!). Flow is an optimal experience with these qualities:

- A sense of playfulness
- A feeling of being in control
- Concentration and highly focused attention
- Mental enjoyment of the activity for its own sake
- A distorted sense of time
- A match between the challenge at hand and one's skills[64]

The Structure of Social Networks

Let's take a closer look at the underlying fabric of social media. Each platform consists of a **social network**, a set of socially relevant nodes connected by one or more relations.[65] **Nodes** are members of the network (e.g., the 900-million-plus Facebook users). Members (or **network units**) are connected by their **ties** (relationships) with one another. Ties stem from affiliations, such as kinship, friendship and affective bonds, shared experiences, and common hobbies and interests. When we think of community, we tend to think of people, but in principle members of a network can be organizations, articles, countries, departments, or any other definable unit. A good example is your university alumni association. The association is a community of networked individuals and organizations. Social networks are sometimes called **social graphs**, though this term may also refer to a diagram of the interconnections of units in a network.

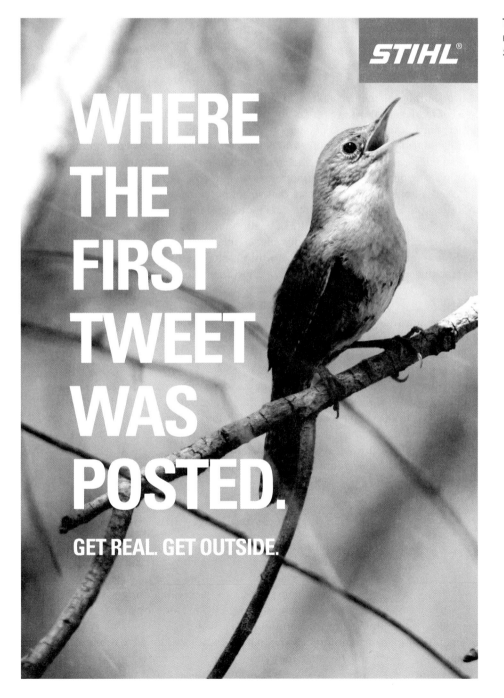

Twitter has emerged as a powerful social network, as this Australian ad reminds us.
Source: STIHL Pty Ltd.

Nodes in a network experience **interactions**; these are behavior-based ties such as talking with each other, attending an event together, or working together. If you chat online with a prospective dating partner on Match.com, you are a node engaging in an interaction with another node (hopefully a node, but not a nerd . . .). And, if that actually works out and you participate in an online forum that shares experiences about wedding photographers in your area, you engage in interactions with other nodes who are also getting married. Interactions are participative in nature; they are shared activities among members in the network.

Flows occur between nodes. Flows are exchanges of resources, information, or influence among members of the network. On Facebook you share news, updates about your life, opinions on your favorite books and movies, photos, videos, and notes. As you share content, you create flows from among those in your network. In social media, these flows of communication go in many directions at any point in time and often on multiple platforms—a condition we term **media multiplexity**. Flows are not simply two way or three way; they may go through an entire community, a list or group within a network, or several individuals independently. Flows of communication also occur outside the community platform. Whereas the online community may exist entirely within a Web space, the flows of communication may extend to other domains as well, like emails, text messages, virtual worlds, and even face-to-face **meetups**, where members of an online network arrange to meet in a physical location.

For marketers, flows are especially important because they are the actionable components of any social network system in terms of the sharing of information, delivery of promotional materials, and sources of social influence. The extent of this social influence (where one person's attitudes or behavior change as a result of others' attempts) varies depending upon the power or attractiveness of other nodes.

Social object theory suggests that social networks will be more powerful communities if there is a way to activate relationships among people and objects. In this perspective, an *object* is something of common interest and its primary function is to mediate the interactions between people. All relationships have social objects embedded in the relationship. In the online world, a site like Facebook provides venues for several object formats to ensure that relationships can thrive within the site's framework. One factor that drives Facebook's stunning success is that it offers so many objects for users to share; these include events, family and friends, quizzes, and so on. Other social networking sites (SNSs) provide a more specialized or focused set of objects. For example, consider how each of these SNSs incorporates objects as part of its mission.

- On Flickr, users participate because they want to share photos. These images are the objects that give meaning to the platform and motivate people to visit.
- Video is the social object around which YouTube centers.
- On the Diigo social bookmarking site, the objects are URLs.
- On Foursquare, the objects are physical locations.
- On Dogster, the objects are our canine companions.

OBJECTIVE 4
Online social networking magnifies the impact of word-of-mouth communication.

The Power of Online Communities

All communities, whether they are online or in the physical world, share important characteristics: Participants experience a feeling of membership, a sense of proximity to one another (even though in online groups other members' physical selves may be thousands of miles away), and in most cases some interest in the community's activities. Members may identify with one another due to a common mission (e.g., a Twitter campaign to donate money for oil spill relief) or simply because they come from the same neighborhood or belong to the same sorority (e.g., Classmates.com connects people who attended the same high school).

Communities help members meet their needs for affiliation, resource acquisition, entertainment, and information. Above all else, communities are social! Whether online or offline, they thrive when the members participate, discuss, share, and interact with others as well as recruit new members to the community. Members do vary in their degree of participation, but the more active the membership, the healthier the community.

Social media provide the fuel that fans the fires of online communities. In the Web 1.0 era, people visited a lot of Web sites to get content that interested them. But these really weren't communities, because the flow of information was all one way. In today's Web 2.0 environment, all that has changed as interactive platforms enable online communities to exhibit the following basic characteristics:[66]

- **Conversations**—Communities thrive on communication among members. These conversations are not based on talking or writing but on a hybrid of the two. If you communicate with a friend via SMS or Facebook chat, you may feel that you actually "talked" to her.
- **Presence**—Though online communities exist virtually rather than at a physical location, the better ones supply tangible characteristics that create the sensation of actually being in a place. This is particularly true for virtual world communities that include three-dimensional depictions of physical spaces, but it also applies to visually simplistic online communities like message board groups. **Presence** describes the effect that people experience when they interact with a computer-mediated or computer-generated environment.[67] Social media sites enhance a sense of presence when they enable interactions among visitors and make the environment look and feel real.[68]
- **Collective interest**—Just as your offline communities are based on family, religious beliefs, social activities, hobbies, goals, place of residence, and so on, your online communities also need commonalities to create bonds among the members. These groups come together to allow people to share their passions, whether these are for indie bands, white wines, or open source apps.
- **Democracy**—The political model of most online communities is democratic (that's with a small d, not the Democratic Party); leaders emerge due to the reputation they earn among the general membership. In this context, **democracy** is a descriptive term that refers to rule by the people. The leaders are appointed or elected by the community based on their demonstrated ability to add value to the group. The huge growth in demand for user reviews in turn fuels new opinion-based sites, such as Yelp for local businesses, TripAdvisor for travel, and Urbanspoon for restaurants. Yelp, for example, offers more than 4 million reviews of everything from corner cafés to dog groomers. People who take the time to post to these sites don't do it for money, but they do generate an income in the form of props for good recommendations. Many thousands of consumers devote significant time to edit Wikipedia entries, serving as brand advocates, or uploading clips to YouTube simply because they enjoy the process and want to boost their reputation as knowledgeable advisors.[70]

Because of the horizontal structure of social media, we typically find that control over what appears on the platform shifts from a small elite to the larger mass. **Media democratization** means that the members of social communities, not traditional media publishers like magazines or newspaper companies, control the creation, delivery, and popularity of content.

- **Standards of behavior**—Virtual communities need rules that govern behavior in order to operate. Some of these rules are spelled out explicitly (e.g., if you buy an item on eBay, you agree that you have entered into a legal contract to pay for it), but many of them are unspoken. A simple example is discouragement of the practice of **flaming**, when a POST CONTAINS ALL CAPITAL LETTERS TO EXPRESS ANGER.
- **Level of participation**—For an online community to thrive, a significant proportion of its members must participate. Otherwise, the site will fail to offer fresh material and ultimately traffic will slow. Participation can be a challenge, though. Most users

Net Profit

The open-source revolution is part of a seismic shift in the way some cutting-edge companies think about their business model. One label for this new approach is **freemium**—you distribute a free version of your product that's supported by a paid premium version. The idea is to encourage the maximum number of people to use your product and eventually convert a small fraction of them to paying customers. In the process, you accumulate a sizable customer base that has value to advertisers (Exhibit A: Google). This also creates a **network effect**, whereby each person who uses the product or service benefits as more people participate. For example, if you check out restaurant reviews on Zagat, you'd rather know what 1,000 diners thought of a place than to settle for feedback from just 10 cranky people.

The freemium model pops up in all sorts of places: People play free online games, they listen to free music on Pandora (legally), they trash their cable service and watch free TV shows and movies on Hulu, and they cancel their landlines in favor of free international calls on Skype. The new and booming market for iPhone apps follows the freemium principle also when you download a program like *Tap Tap Revenge* (like the popular game *Guitar Hero*, you have to hit notes that stream down your screen). Millions of people downloaded the app, and then some of them forked over cash when the creator offered paid versions built around real bands like Weezer and Nine Inch Nails.[69] In the wacky world of Web 2.0, you give something away to make money. Go figure.

Net Profit

ASOS is the largest **pure play retailer** in the U.K. This means it sells online only rather than operating physical stores. The company's Fashion Finder platform is a popular way for shoppers to share ideas with one another and thus create a community around a passion for fashion.

are **lurkers**: That's kind of a creepy term, but it just means they absorb content that others post rather than contributing their own. Researchers estimate that only 1 percent of a typical community's users regularly participate, and another 9 percent do so only intermittently. The remaining 90 percent just observe what's on the site, so they don't add a lot of value—other than adding to the number of "eyeballs" the site can claim when it tries to convince advertisers to buy space.

How can a site convert lurkers into active users? The easier it is to participate, the more likely it is that the community can generate activity among a larger proportion of visitors. In part, this means ensuring that there are several ways to participate that vary in ease of use. Facebook is an example of an online community that has figured out how to offer several forms of participation. Members can post status updates (very easy), make comments, upload pictures, share notes and links, play social games, answer quizzes, decorate their profiles, upload videos, and create events (a bit harder), among other forms of participation.

● **Crowd power**—Social media change the fundamental relationship between marketers and consumers: Companies no longer market to customers, they market *with* them.[71] Although many organizations resist this change, others build new business models on the **wisdom of crowds** perspective (from a book by that name). This model argues that, under the right circumstances, groups are smarter than the smartest people in them. If this is true, it implies that large numbers of consumers can predict successful products.[72] Companies as diverse as Budweiser (which crowdsourced its new Black Crown beer) to handbag designer Alexander Wang today offer products that originated from ideas submitted by employees or customers.[73] ModCloth, an online retailer of affordable women's clothing and accessories, launched an entire private label collection made up mostly of designs submitted and voted upon by its Facebook community. At Kickstarter.com, a crowdsourced funding site, participants have pledged over $320 million to fund over 18,000 projects that range from movies to a bluetooth-enabled watch.[74]

There's no 'u' in Threadless, but there should be. You pick the great ideas, you pick what we sell, you pick the next big thingy!

Net Profit

At Threadless, customers rank T-shirt designs ahead of time, and the company prints the winning ideas. Every week, contestants upload T-shirt designs to the site, where about 700 compete to be among the six that are printed during that time. Threadless visitors score designs on a scale of 0 to 5, and the staff members select winners from the most popular entrants. *Threadless sells out of every shirt it offers.*[75]

Source: Courtesy of Threadless.

Online Opinion Leaders

The Internet makes opinion leaders even more powerful—it's like giving a baseball player steroids (only legal). Instead of reaching only those within earshot, now an influential person can sway the opinions of thousands or even millions of people around the world. In online groups, opinion leaders sometimes are called **power users**. They have a strong communication network that gives them the ability to affect purchase decisions for a number of other consumers, directly and indirectly.[76]

Much like their offline counterparts, power users are active participants at work and in their communities. Their social networks are large and well developed. Others trust them and find them to be credible sources of information about one or more specific topics. They tend to have a natural sense of intellectual curiosity, which may lead them to new sources of information. And they post an awful lot of brand-related content: Forrester Research has dubbed these brand-specific mentions **influence impressions**. In advertising lingo, an *impression* refers to a view or an exposure to an advertising message. Forrester estimates that, each year, American consumers generate 256 billion influence impressions as people talk about their lives with each other, telling stories and experiences that invariably include brands.[77] These influence impressions are primarily delivered by—you guessed it—power users: Only 6.2 percent of social media users are responsible for about 80 percent of these brand mentions. Forrester calls these influencers **Mass Connectors**.

As Mass Connectors spread influence impressions, the impact of the message grows due to the **momentum effect**.[78] Influencers publish the message on blogs, share widgets, place a brand logo on their Facebook pages, and so on. Friends share with friends who share with friends. If a brand is well-liked, relevant, and buzz-worthy, the media value originating from nonpaid, word-of-mouth referrals for the brand can be enormous.

Social Shopping

Social shopping is an emerging form of e-commerce that allows an online shopper to simulate the experience of shopping in a brick-and-mortar store. New technologies allow

The Tangled Web

The Whopper Sacrifice was an advertising campaign Burger King launched to promote its new Angry Whopper sandwich. You could earn a free burger, but to get it you had to sacrifice 10 of your Facebook friends. After you delete these names, you get a coupon in the mail. Your ex-friends get a note informing them that they were dumped for a freebie sandwich. The burger costs $3.69, so when you do the math, each former friend is worth about 37 cents. Although it sounds cruel to give up a friend for this amount, many Facebookers jumped at the chance to purge their friend lists. As one student with several hundred friends commented, "It's a good excuse to get rid of old girlfriends and their families on my account and get a Whopper out of it."[79]

Travelocity enlisted its Roaming Gnome to boost online consumer engagement and trigger a momentum effect. The spokescharacter was (supposedly) outraged that the Aflac Duck had more friends on Facebook, and so Travelocity created International Gnome Day. On his page, the gnome implored fans to share his plea with their friends in the hopes that he could achieve his goal by the big day.
Source: ©2011 Travelocity.com LP.

TABLE 12.1	Social Shopping Applications

Social Shopping Web Site Categories						
Virtual Wish Lists/ Scrapbooking	Try It On Sites and Apps	Pre-purchase Feedback	Competitions	Social Shopping Advocacy	Group Purchasing Sites	Linking and Networking 'Sign On'
Svpply	Gotryiton	ASOS	ASOS	Klout	Living Social	Facebook Connect
Polyvore	Fashionism	Facebook		The Fancy	Groupon	Modcloth
Pinterest	Justboughtit	Twitter		Sneakpeeq	BuyWithMe	Wanelo
vi.sualize.us		Motilo		Fab		
Mydeco		Daily Grommet				

Source: Adapted from Rachel Ashman and Michael R. Solomon, "Bowling Alone" No Longer: Social Shopping in the Digital Age," *Academy of Marketing Science*, 2013.

a consumer to "try on" a garment via an avatar, and also perhaps to access feedback from others in his or her social network either prior to or after deciding on a purchase. As such, social shopping is a hybrid of social networking and online retailing. As the technology continues to mature, social shopping may offer an even more compelling purchase experience than the in-store interactions it replaces. The social shopping mechanisms now being introduced at a rapid rate take the form of product ratings, reviews, product montages, design competitions, style advice, live outfit reviews, visual scrapbooking, and crowdsourced advice. Table 12.1 summarizes some of the current approaches to social shopping.

Social Games and Gamification

A **social game** is a multiplayer, competitive, goal-oriented activity with defined rules of engagement and online connectivity among a community of players. Successful mobile games like *FarmVille* and *Angry Birds* boast millions of avid followers. Brands can utilize social games for marketing in several ways—and they should! When the Microsoft search engine Bing ran an ad that offered players the chance to earn *FarmVille* cash for becoming a fan of Bing on Facebook, the brand won 425,000 new fans in the first day.[80] As we saw in Chapter 6, *gamification* strategies turn routine behaviors into engaging experiences when marketers add gaming elements to the environments where consumers shop or work.

One specific tactic we will see more of in the booming world of social games is **transactional advertising**, which rewards players if they respond to a request as they play a social game.[81] The offers can be for *virtual goods* (which players can use in the game or offer as gifts to friends), *currency* (used to advance in the game), or *codes* (used to unlock prizes and limited-access player experiences). Players are rewarded with the virtual goods, currencies, or codes if they make a purchase, "friend" the brand, watch a commercial, or perhaps answer a survey. ProFlowers used transactional advertising as part of a Valentine's Day promotion in Playfish's *Pet Society* game. Players who sent real flowers from within the game were rewarded with Playfish Cash.[82] The hugely popular *FarmVille* social game teamed with the also hugely popular Lady Gaga to launch a special version of the game called *GagaVille*, which included an entire area inside the game with Gaga-themed items like unicorns. Fans who bought a $25 game card from Best Buy also received her *Born This Way* album as a free download.[83]

Most social games include a few key elements:

- **Leaderboards**—a listing of the leaders in the game competition.
- **Achievement badges**—symbols awarded to show game levels achieved, shared with the community.

● **Friend (buddy) lists** with chat—a list of contacts with whom one plays and the ability to communicate within the game.

Social games are built upon several layers, including platform, mode, milieu, and genre.[84] Let's briefly review the basic dimensions of social games:

● A **game platform** refers to the hardware systems on which the game is played. Platforms include *game consoles* (consoles are interactive, electronic devices used to display video games, such as Sony's PlayStation3, Microsoft's Xbox 360, and Nintendo's Wii), computers (including both online games and those that require software installation on the player's computer hard drive), and portable devices that may include smartphones or devices specifically for game play such as the Sony PSP or Nintendo DS.[85]

● **Mode** refers to the way players experience the game world. It includes aspects such as whether a player's activities are highly structured, whether the game is single-player or multiplayer, whether the game is played in close physical proximity to other players (or by virtual proximity), and whether the game is real-time or turn-based.

● **Milieu** describes the visual nature of the game, such as science fiction, fantasy, horror, and retro.

● The **genre** of a game refers to the method of play. Popular genres include simulation, action, and role-playing. *Simulation games* attempt to depict real-world situations as accurately as possible. There are several subgenres, including racing simulators, flight simulators, and "Sim" games that enable players to simulate the development of an environment. Among social games, simulations include the highly popular *FarmVille*, *Pet Resort*, and *FishVille*. *Action games* consist of two major subgenres: *first-person shooters (FPS)*, where you "see" the game as your avatar sees it, and third-person games. Examples of social action games are *Epic Goal*, a live-action soccer game; *Paradise Paintball*, a first-person shooter social game; and *Texas Hold 'Em*, a social gambling game. In *role-playing games* (RPGs), the players play a character role with the goal of completing some mission. Perhaps the best-known RPG started its life as a tabletop game: *Dungeons and Dragons*. Players adopt the identity of a character in the game story and go about completing tasks and collecting points and items as they strive to accomplish the intended goal.

Net Profit

MMORPGs—*massive multiplayer online role-playing games*—are a type of RPG that truly encompass the social aspects of gaming. *World of Warcraft* is one of the largest MMORPGs with millions of players from around the world. Social RPGs on Facebook include *Haven*, *Mafia Wars*, *Battle Stations*, and *Tennis Mania*.[86] The money people spend in virtual worlds like these grows rapidly. Indeed, **digital virtual consumption (DVC)** may well be the next frontier of marketing. Today in the United States alone, consumers spend well over $2 billion per year (yes, billion) to buy **virtual goods** for the characters they play in online games.[87] Thousands of in-world residents design, create, and purchase clothing, furniture, houses, vehicles, and other products their avatars need—and many do it in style as they acquire the kind of "bling" they can only dream about in real life. Some forward-thinking marketers understand that these platforms are the next stage they can use to introduce their products into people's lives, whether real or virtual. Today, for example, people who play *The Sims* can import actual pieces of furniture from IKEA into their virtual homes; the use of this sort of platform to accelerate purchases for real homes is unplowed ground. With hundreds of these immersive 3-D environments now live or in development, we may well see other social networks like Facebook migrate to these platforms in the near future.

● ● ● ● ● ● ● ● ● ● ● ● ● ● ● ●

Source: Fabrice Dimier/Bloomberg via Getty Images.

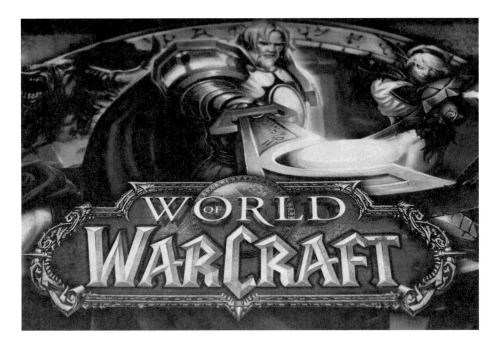

CB AS I SEE IT

Professor Donna L. Hoffman, *The George Washington University*

How and why do consumers use social media? As social media applications continue to proliferate and the dynamics of online social interaction continue to evolve, consumer behavior researchers are calling for a deeper understanding of consumers' use of social media so that theoretically consistent models linking consumer motivations, social media goals, and perceptions of well-being can be constructed. The need for such models is increasingly acute as consumer participation in new forms of social media increases and marketers seek to incorporate into their content applications those social components that best satisfy consumers' basic needs and lead to the most positive outcomes.

My colleague Professor Tom Novak and I have proposed that the fundamental interactivity of social media allows for four higher-order goals: connect, create, consume, and control. These "4Cs" capabilities of social media undoubtedly explain in part why so many people spend so much of their time using social media and why social media are so popular. Although there has been a surge of research lately examining social media usage, few studies are based or focused on a conceptual framework that can help explain what drives use

and how usage goals relate subjective well-being.

To address this gap, we designed two large-scale studies to evaluate how consumer motivations may differentially drive social media goal pursuit and investigate how those goals and subjective well-being are associated. Individuals for whom social media satisfies needs should experience a positive impact on well-being. This line of reasoning is closely related to the idea of optimal online experience we pursued in our previous research, where we found that individuals who experience flow during their online navigational experiences are more likely to achieve positive outcomes compared to individuals who cannot attain these compelling online experiences. For both studies, we used our 4Cs of connecting, creating, consuming, and controlling social media experiences to organize consumers' social media goals.

In the first study, we examined social media goal pursuit in the context of the core social motive of the need to relate, the additional fundamental needs for autonomy and competence, individuals' orientation toward intrinsic and external locus of causality, and two aspects of self-esteem in the context of social identity. Results suggested that connect goals ("social" goals) are associated with relatedness needs, an external locus of control, intrinsic motivation to connect with others, and positive evaluations of the social media groups to which consumers belong (private collective self-esteem). Consumers' pursuit to create goals is associated with autonomy, competence, and relatedness needs; an external locus of control;

higher social media involvement; and contribution to sense of self (identity self-esteem). Consume goals ("nonsocial" goals) appear to be intrinsically motivated and negatively associated with autonomy and competence. Control goals satisfy autonomy and competence needs, and are associated with an external locus of causality and social media knowledge.

In the second study, we evaluated whether individuals with different primary 4Cs social media goals differed in terms of their perceptions of wellbeing. We found a clear link between differential social media goal pursuit and subjective well-being (connectors and creators are happiest), with clear differences in terms of the higher-order focus of the online interaction (connectors are happiest pursuing personinteraction while creators are happiest pursuing content-interaction).

Our findings that different social media goals are supported by different needs and motivations and do not relate equally to perceptions of well-being have important implications for research and marketing practice. The results may help researchers understand whether and how increased participation in social media will enhance well-being. Marketing managers believe that social media offer the potential for the "killer app," and one recurring question is how marketers can develop applications that are more "social." Marketers can use the results to help focus strategic efforts as they examine the relationship between social media goals and consumer response to marketing efforts in interactive media environments.

The Diffusion of Innovations

The originators of skateboarding in 1970s southern California (who were portrayed in the popular documentary *Dogtown and Z-Boys*) wouldn't recognize the sport today. At that time, boarders were outlaws; as one of the main characters in the film says, "We get the beat-down from all over. Everywhere we go, man, people hate us."

Now skateboarding is about as countercultural as *The Simpsons*. More kids ride skateboards than play basketball, and many of them snap up pricey T-shirts, skate shoes, helmets, and other accessories. In fact, boarders spend almost six times as much on "soft goods," such as T-shirts, shorts, and sunglasses (about $4.4 billion in a year), than on hard-core equipment, including the boards themselves.[88]

The progression of skateboarding from a cult-like activity with rebellious undertones to a mainstream hobby mirrors the journey many products and services take through popular culture. **Diffusion of innovations** refers to the process whereby a new product, service, or idea spreads through a population. An **innovation** is any product or service that consumers perceive to be new. It may take the form of an activity (skateboarding), a clothing style (Ed Hardy T-shirts), a new manufacturing technique (the ability to design your own running shoe at nike.com), a new variation on an existing product (Parkay Fun Squeeze Colored Margarine in electric blue and shocking pink), a new way to deliver a product (ordering groceries online and having Peapod deliver them to your home), or a new way to package a current product (Campbell's Soup at Hand Microwaveable Soup that comes in a travel mug).[89]

The social media explosion takes the diffusion process to a whole different level. As we've seen, the media democratization we witness today means that there are fundamental disruptions in the way consumers become aware of new products and the rate at which these innovations reach their markets. In this final section, we'll step back and examine the basic process of diffusion.

If an innovation is successful (most are not!), it spreads through the population. First only a trickle of people decides to try it. Then, more and more consumers decide to adopt it, until sometimes it seems that almost everyone is buying it—if it's a "hit." The rate at which a product diffuses varies. For example, within 10 years after introduction, 40 percent of U.S. households watched cable TV, 35 percent listened to compact discs, 25 percent used answering machines, and 20 percent bought color TVs. It took radio 30 years to reach 60 million users and TV 15 years to reach this number. In contrast, within 3 years 90 million of us surfed the Web.[90]

How Do We Decide to Adopt an Innovation?

Our adoption of an innovation resembles the decision-making sequence we discussed way back in Chapter 2. We move through the stages of awareness, information search, evaluation, trial, and adoption. The relative importance of each stage differs, however, depending on how much we already know about an innovation as well as on cultural factors that affect our willingness to try new things.[91]

A study of 11 European countries found that consumers in individualistic cultures are more innovative than consumers in collective cultures (see Chapter 3).[92] However, even within the same culture, not all people adopt an innovation at the same rate. Some do so quite rapidly, and others never do at all. We place consumers into approximate categories based on the likelihood that they will adopt something new.

As Figure 12.3 shows, roughly one-sixth of the population (innovators and early adopters) are very quick to adopt new products, and one-sixth (**laggards**) are very slow. The other two-thirds, so-called **late adopters**, are somewhere in the middle. These

Figure 12.3 TYPES OF ADOPTERS

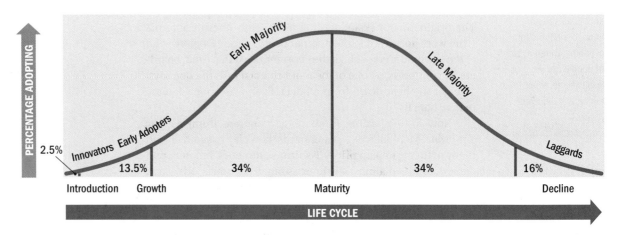

PERCENTAGE ADOPTING — 2.5% Innovators, 13.5% Early Adopters, 34% Early Majority, 34% Late Majority, 16% Laggards. Life cycle: Introduction, Growth, Maturity, Decline. LIFE CYCLE

Marketing Opportunity

How do we locate innovators? Ad agencies and market research companies are always on the prowl for people who stay on top of developing trends. One ad agency surveys taxi drivers about what they see on the streets every day. Others get more sophisticated and use the Internet and their global networks to monitor what "people in the know" do. The agency DDB runs a service it calls SignBank, which collects thousands of snippets of information from its 13,000 employees around the world about cultural change in order to advise its clients on what it all means for them. For example, sign spotters in several markets noticed that dinner-party guests tended to bring their hosts flowers instead of chocolate because of concerns about health and obesity—that's valuable information for a client that makes chocolates.[94]

consumers are the mainstream public. They are interested in new things, but they do not want them to be *too* new. In some cases, people deliberately wait to adopt an innovation because they assume that the company will improve its technology or that its price will fall after it has been on the market awhile (have you been holding off on that iPhone purchase to see what Apple will come up with next?).[93] Keep in mind that the proportion of consumers who fall into each category is an estimate; the actual size of each depends on such factors as the complexity of the product, its cost, and how much risk people associate with it.

Even though **innovators** represent only about 2.5 percent of the population, marketers are eager to identify them. These are the brave souls who are always on the lookout for novel products or services and who are first to try something new. An innovator tends to be a risk-taker. He or she also is likely to have a relatively high educational and income level and to be socially active.

Early adopters share many of the same characteristics as innovators. An important difference is their high degree of concern for social acceptance, especially with regard to expressive products such as clothing and cosmetics. Generally speaking, an early adopter is receptive to new styles because she is involved in the product category and she values being in fashion.

What appears on the surface to be a fairly high-risk adoption (e.g., wearing a skirt three inches above the knee when most people wear them below the knee) is actually not *that* risky. Innovators who truly took the fashion risk have already "field-tested" the style change. We're likely to find early adopters in "fashion-forward" stores that feature the latest "hot" designer brands. In contrast, we're more likely to find true innovators in small boutiques that carry merchandise from as-yet-unknown designers.

Behavioral Demands of Innovations

We categorize innovations by the degree to which they demand adopters to change their behavior. Researchers identify three major types of innovations, though these three categories are not absolutes. They refer, in a relative sense, to the amount of disruption or change they bring to people's lives.

A **continuous innovation** is a modification of an existing product, such as when General Mills introduces a Honey Nut version of Cheerios or Levi's promotes shrink-to-fit jeans. The company makes small changes to position the product, add line extensions, or merely alleviate consumer boredom. Most product innovations are of this type; they are *evolutionary* rather than *revolutionary*.

When a consumer adopts this kind of new product, she only has to make minor changes in her habits. A typewriter company, for example, many years ago modified its product to make it more "user friendly" to secretaries. Its engineers made the tops of the keys concave because women told them it was hard to type with long fingernails on a flat surface. This change endures today on our computer keyboards.

Some innovations present us with a new way to use an existing product. This may be more effective, but we still have to alter our habits to use it. A Japanese clothing company introduced a line of Shower Clean business suits that allow traveling executives to bypass the dry cleaner; they wash their suits in a warm shower and need not press or iron them.[95] A **dynamically continuous innovation** is a significant change to an existing product. When IBM introduced its Selectric typewriter that used a typing ball rather than individual keys, the new design permitted secretaries to instantly change the typeface of manuscripts as they replaced one Selectric ball with another.

In contrast, a **discontinuous innovation** creates really *big* changes in the way we live. Major inventions, such as the airplane, the car, the computer, and the television, radically changed modern lifestyles. The personal computer replaced the typewriter; it also allows some of us to "telecommute" from our homes. Of course, the cycle continues, as new continuous innovations (e.g., new versions of software) constantly update our computers.

What Determines If an Innovation Will Diffuse?

Regardless of how much we have to change what we do, a successful innovation should possess these attributes:[96]

- **Compatibility**—The innovation should be compatible with consumers' lifestyles. A manufacturer of personal care products tried unsuccessfully several years ago to introduce a cream hair remover for men as a substitute for razors and shaving cream. This formulation was similar to what many women use to remove hair from their legs. Although the product was simple and convenient to use, it failed because men were not interested in a product they perceived to be too feminine and thus a threat to their masculine self-concepts.
- **Trialability**—Because we think an unknown product is risky, we're more likely to adopt an innovation if we can experiment with it prior to making a commitment. To reduce this risk, companies may spend a lot of money to distribute free "trial-size" samples of new products.
- **Complexity**—The product should be low in complexity. All things being equal, we will choose a product that's easier to understand and use rather than a more complex one. This strategy requires less effort from us and it also lowers our perceived risk. Manufacturers of DVD recorders, for example, put a lot of effort into simplifying usage (e.g., on-screen programming) to encourage nontechies to adopt them.
- **Observability**—Innovations that are readily apparent are more likely to spread because we can learn about them more easily. The rapid proliferation of fanny packs (pouches people wear around the waist in lieu of wallets or purses) was a result of their high visibility. It was easy for others to see the convenience this alternative offered (even if they were a bit nerdy).
- **Relative advantage**—Most importantly, the product should offer relative advantage over other alternatives. The consumer must believe that it will provide a benefit other products cannot offer. For example, the Bugchaser is a wristband that contains insect repellent. Mothers with young children like it because it's nontoxic and nonstaining—these are clear advantages over alternatives. In contrast, the Crazy Blue Air Freshener, which emits a fragrance when you turn on your car wipers, fizzled: People didn't see the need for the product and felt there were simpler ways to freshen their cars.

Net Profit

M-PESA (M for mobile, pesa is Swahili for money) is a mobile-phone-based money transfer service that is very popular in parts of Africa, where most consumers do not have access to bank branches. As many other people around the world start to transact more of their banking business online, M-PESA provides valuable lessons on how to design an app that transforms how we relate our financial institutions. This service is an example of **reverse innovation** (or trickle-up innovation). This term refers to the process whereby a product is initially to meet the needs of developing nations and then is adapted elsewhere. Battery-operated medical instruments first designed for use in countries with limited infrastructure are another example.

CB AS I SEE IT

Professor Gordon Bruner, *Southern Illinois University*

Several years ago, Professor Kumar (University of South Florida) and I were working with Sprint to develop a way for the company to measure a person's technological innovativeness such that it could be easily implemented in the surveys the company routinely conducted. Sprint's primary interest was in *innovators*—the small group of consumers who have a tendency to be among the first to adopt high-tech goods and services. At the same time, Dr. Kumar and I wanted to learn more about a similar group of adopters we called *gadget lovers*. The term *gad-*

get lover has been tossed around in our country for many decades but no scientific study of them had occurred. We wondered if they were pretty much the same people as tech innovators or if they were different.

After we conducted several studies, the results were rather clear: Although there is overlap between the two groups of consumers, there are also key differences. As a group, innovators adopt a little more quickly than gadget lovers. While gadget lovers tend to adopt much more rapidly than the average consumer, they don't all qualify as innovators. On the other hand, more gadget lovers than innovators qualify as *opinion leaders*. The reasons for this are not perfectly clear, but it seems that gadget lovers, as the name implies, genuinely enjoy playing with technology. That experience and expertise are visible to other consumers who then feel comfortable seeking the gadget lovers' advice. In contrast, innovators seem

to be more interested in the status that comes from being first to adopt. Although they like hightech toys, they don't appear to be as expert at using them as are gadget lovers, nor do they tend to exhibit the infectious enthusiasm that gadget lovers do.

When the gadget lover scale was administered to a large, nationally representative sample of U.S. consumers, the results indicated that males scored much higher than females, younger adults scored slightly higher than older adults, those with greater education scored higher than those with less education, and the major ethnic groups scored higher than white/non-Hispanics.

The bottom line is that even though gadget lovers are similar to innovators in several ways, we believe they are distinct enough to deserve as much or more attention from marketers of hightech innovations, particularly because of the group's seemingly greater influence on what others do.[97]

OBJECTIVE 6

Many people and organizations play a role in the fashion system that creates and communicates symbolic meanings to consumers.

The Fashion System

The **fashion system** includes all the people and organizations that create symbolic meanings and transfer those meanings to cultural goods. Although we often equate fashion with clothing, it's important to keep in mind that fashion processes affect *all* types of cultural phenomena, including music, art, architecture, and even science (i.e., certain research topics and individual scientists are "hot" at any point in time). Even business practices are subject to the fashion process; they evolve and change depending on which management techniques are in vogue, such as TQM (total quality management), JIT (just-in-time inventory control), or MBWO (managing by walking around). All of these domains are affected by the "movement of meaning" in a culture that we discussed in Chapter 3.

At the outset, let's distinguish among some confusing terms. **Fashion** is the process of social diffusion by which some group(s) of consumers adopts a new style. In contrast, *a fashion* (or style) is a particular combination of attributes (say, stovepipe jeans that women wear with a tunic top). To be *in fashion* means that some reference group positively evaluates this combination (i.e., *Vogue* endorses this look as "in" for this season). Thus, the term *Danish Modern* refers to particular characteristics of furniture design (i.e., a fashion in interior design); it does not necessarily imply that Danish Modern is a fashion that consumers currently desire.[98]

Behavioral Science Perspectives on Fashion

Fashion is a very complex process that operates on many levels. At one extreme, it's a societal phenomenon that affects many of us simultaneously. At the other, it exerts a very personal effect on individual behavior. Many of us desire to be in fashion, and this motivates us as to what we buy. Fashion products also are aesthetic objects that reflect a culture's artistic traditions and history. For this reason, there are many perspectives on the origin and diffusion of fashion. Let's summarize some major approaches.[99]

Psychological Models of Fashion.   Many psychological factors help explain what motivates us to be fashionable. These include conformity, desires for variety seeking, the need to express personal creativity, and sexual attraction. For example, many consumers seem to have a "need for uniqueness": They want to be different (though not necessarily *too* different!).[100] As a result, people may conform to the basic outlines of a fashion, but still improvise to make a personal statement within these general guidelines.

One of the earliest theories of fashion argued that "shifting *erogenous zones*" (sexually arousing areas of the body) accounted for fashion changes and that different zones become the object of interest because they reflect societal trends. J. C. Flugel, a disciple of Freud, proposed in the 1920s that sexually charged areas wax and wane as we grow bored with them; clothing styles change to highlight or hide the parts that currently are the focus of attention. For example, it was common for Renaissance-era women to drape their abdomens in fabrics in order to give a swollen appearance; successful childbearing was a priority in the disease-ridden 14th and 15th centuries. Now, some suggest that the current prevalence of the exposed midriff in women's fashion reflects the premium our society places on fitness.[101]

Economic Models of Fashion.   Economists approach fashion in terms of the model of supply and demand. Items in limited supply have high value, whereas our desire decreases for readily available products. Rare items command respect and prestige. As we discussed in Chapter 11, the writer Thorstein Veblen argued that the wealthy practice *conspicuous consumption* to display their prosperity. As we also noted, this approach is somewhat outdated; upscale consumers today engage in *parody display* where they deliberately buy inexpensive products (especially during a recession). Other factors also influence the demand curve for fashion-related products. These include a *prestige–exclusivity effect*, where high prices still create high demand, and a *snob effect*, whereby lower prices actually reduce demand ("If it's that cheap, it can't be any good").[102]

Sociological Models of Fashion.   This perspective focuses on a subculture's adoption of a fashion (idea, style, etc.) and its subsequent diffusion into society as a whole. To understand this process, think about the integration of Goth culture into the mainstream. This fashion started as an expression of rebellion by young outcasts who admired 19th-century romantics and who defied conventional styles with their black clothing (often including over-the-top fashion statements such as Count Dracula capes, fishnet stockings, studded collars, and black lipstick) and punk music from bands such as Siouxsie & the Banshees and Bauhaus. Today, music stores sell vampire-girl lunchboxes, and mall outlets sell tons of clunky cross jewelry and black lace. You can find a T-shirt that looks like a corset at Kmart. At the Hot Topic Web site, teen surfers can buy a "multi-ring choker." Hard-core Goths are not amused, but hey, that's fashion for you.[103]

Trickle-down theory, which the sociologist Georg Simmel first proposed in 1904, is one of the most influential sociological perspectives on fashion. It states that two conflicting forces drive fashion change. First, subordinate groups adopt the status symbols of the groups above them as they attempt to climb up the ladder of social mobility. Dominant styles thus originate with the upper classes and *trickle down* to those below.

Now the second force kicks in: Those people in the superordinate groups keep a wary eye on the ladder below them to be sure followers don't imitate them. When lower-class consumers mimic their actions, they adopt new fashions to distance themselves

This ad for Maidenform illustrates that fashions have accentuated different parts of the female anatomy throughout history.

Source: Courtesy of Maidenform Inc.

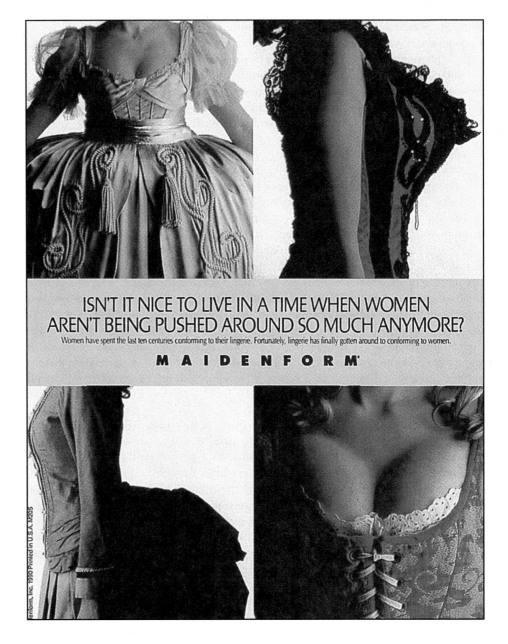

ISN'T IT NICE TO LIVE IN A TIME WHEN WOMEN AREN'T BEING PUSHED AROUND SO MUCH ANYMORE?

Women have spent the last ten centuries conforming to their lingerie. Fortunately, lingerie has finally gotten around to conforming to women.

M A I D E N F O R M

from the mainstream. These two processes create a self-perpetuating cycle of change—the machine that drives fashion.[104]

The integration of hip-hop phrases into our vocabulary illustrates how people who set fashions resist mainstream adoption by the broader society. The street elite shunned some slang terms, such as *bad, fresh,* and *jiggy,* once they became too mainstream. The rap community even held a funeral (with a eulogy by Reverend Al Sharpton) for the word *def* once the *Oxford English Dictionary* included it in its new edition.[105]

Trickle-down theory applies to a society with a stable class structure that allows us to easily identify lower- versus upper-class consumers. This task is no longer so easy. In contemporary Western society, we have to modify this theory to account for new developments in mass culture:[106]

● A perspective we base on class structure can't account for the wide range of styles now available. We have many more choices today because of technological advances that let manufacturers drastically speed up production times and real-time media that keep us informed of style changes in minutes. Stores such as Zara and H&M can replenish their inventories in weeks rather than months. Suburban tweens watch MTV, chat on Facebook, or browse the virtual world Stardoll.com to stay on top of the latest trends; *mass fashion* thus replaces elite fashion because our media allow many market segments to learn about a style simultaneously.

- Consumers today are more influenced by opinion leaders who are similar to them, even if these innovators don't live in the same town or even country. As a result, each social group has its own fashion innovators who determine fashion trends. It's more accurate to speak of a *trickle-across effect*, where fashions diffuse horizontally among members of the same social group.[107]

- Finally, current fashions often originate with the lower classes and *trickle up*. Grassroots innovators typically are people who lack prestige in the dominant culture (e.g., urban youth). Because they are less concerned with maintaining the status quo, they are free to innovate and take risks.[108]

Medical Model of Fashion. For many years, the lowly Hush Puppy was a shoe for nerds. Suddenly—almost overnight—the shoe became a chic fashion statement even though its manufacturer did nothing to promote this image. Why did this style diffuse through the population so quickly? **Meme theory** explains this process with a medical metaphor. A *meme* is an idea or product that enters the consciousness of people over time—examples include tunes, catch-phrases ("You're fired!"), or styles such as the Hush Puppy.

In this view, memes spread among consumers in a geometric progression just as a virus starts off small and steadily infects increasing numbers of people until it becomes an epidemic. Memes "leap" from brain to brain via a process of imitation. The memes that survive tend to be distinctive and memorable, and the hardiest ones often combine aspects of prior memes. For example, the *Star Wars* movies evoke prior memes that relate to the legend of King Arthur, religion, heroic youth, and 1930s adventure serials. Indeed, George Lucas studied comparative religion and mythology as he prepared his first draft of the *Star Wars* saga, *The Story of Mace Windu*.[110]

The diffusion of many products in addition to Hush Puppies seems to follow the same basic path. A few people initially use the product, but change happens in a hurry when the process reaches the moment of critical mass—what one author calls the **tipping point**.[111] For example, Sharp introduced the first low-priced fax machine in 1984 and sold about 80,000 in that year. There was a slow climb in the number of users for the next 3 years. Then, suddenly, in 1987 enough people had fax machines that it made sense for everyone to have one, and Sharp sold a million units. Cell phones followed a similar trajectory. Do you remember when you first heard about Instagram?

OBJECTIVE 7
Fashions follow cycles and reflect cultural dynamics.

Cycles of Fashion Adoption

In the early 1980s, Cabbage Patch dolls were all the rage among American children. Faced with a limited supply of the product, some retailers reported near-riots among adults as they tried desperately to buy the dolls for their children. A Milwaukee dee-jay jokingly announced that people should bring catcher's mitts to a local stadium because an airplane was going to fly overhead and drop 2,000 dolls. He told his listeners to hold up their American Express cards so their numbers could be photographed from the plane. More than two dozen anxious parents apparently didn't get the joke: They showed up in subzero weather, mitts in hand.[112]

The Cabbage Patch craze lasted for a couple of seasons before it eventually died out, and consumers moved on to other things, such as Teenage Mutant Ninja Turtles, which grossed more than $600 million in 1989. The Mighty Morphin Power Rangers eventually replaced the Turtles, and Beanie Babies and Giga Pets in turn deposed them before the invasion of Pokémon, followed by Yu-Gi-Oh! cards, Webkinz, Transformers, Squinkies and Zoobles, Furbys and on and on.[113]

Music, furniture, and other cultural products undergo cycles of fashion adoption.
Source: Creative Director: João Santos,
Art Director: Mariana Moreira,
Copy: Daniel Pereira.

Figure 12.4 illustrates that fashions begin slowly, but if they "make it," they diffuse rapidly through a market, peak, and then retreat into obscurity. We identify different classes of fashion when we look at the relative length of their **acceptance cycles**. Many fashions have a moderate cycle, taking several months or even years to work their way through the stages of acceptance and decline; others are extremely long lived or short-lived.

A **classic** is a fashion with an extremely long acceptance cycle. It is in a sense "anti-fashion" because it guarantees stability and low risk to the purchaser for a long period of time. Keds sneakers, introduced in 1917, appeal to those who are turned off by the high-fashion, trendy appeal of Nike or Reebok. When researchers asked consumers in focus groups to imagine what kind of building Keds would be, a common response was a country house with a white picket fence. In other words, consumers see the shoes as a stable,

Figure 12.4 COMPARISON OF THE ACCEPTANCE CYCLES OF FADS, FASHIONS, AND CLASSICS

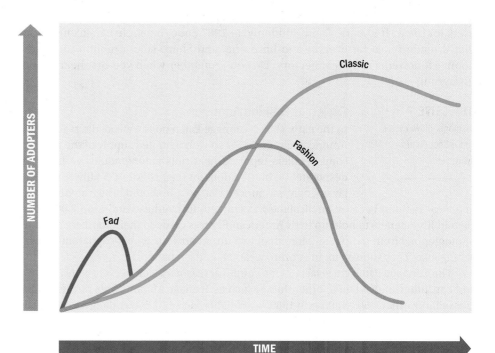

classic product. In contrast, participants described Nikes as steel-and-glass skyscrapers to reflect that brand's more modern image.[114]

A theme park in Japan offers "amusement baths" to visitors, including a wine bath, a green-tea bath, a coffee bath, a sake bath, and even a ramen-noodle bath. When they don their bathing suits and jump into the ramen bath (which looks like a soup bowl), they frolic in pepper-flavored water that contains collagen and garlic extracts the Japanese believe will improve the skin. A man dressed as a chef dispenses noodle-shaped bath additives and soy sauce to everyone in the tub.[115] A **fad** is a very short-lived fashion. Relatively few people adopt a fad product, but it can spread very quickly. Adopters may all belong to a common subculture, and the fad "trickles across" members but rarely breaks out of that specific group.

The *streaking* fad hit college campuses in the mid-1970s as it was briefly popular for students to run nude through classrooms, cafeterias, dorms, and sports venues.

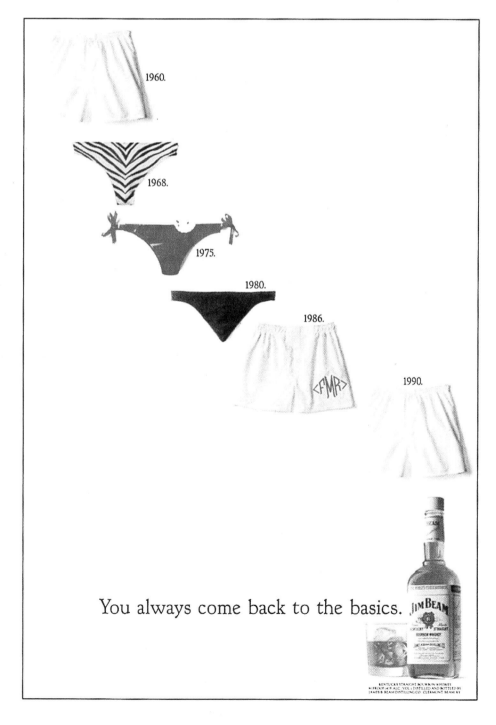

This Jim Beam ad illustrates the cyclical nature of fashion.
Source: Courtesy of Jim Beam Brands.

Marketing Pitfall

Fads often involve frivolous or "weird" behavior, and many consumers may not conform (see Chapter 9) as they refuse to participate (this may make the fad even *more* appealing to devotees). A pair of researchers studied adults who resist the Harry Potter craze. They find some of these consumers avoid the Hogwarts world because they pride themselves on "not being taken in." These adults react negatively to the "evangelical" enthusiasts who try to convert them to fandom. They recount the resentment of one newlywed on her honeymoon (as her new husband related in an essay): "My new page turning obsession did not go down too well with my new life partner. When on our first night in the Maldives and expecting some form of conjugal rites [she found] herself in second place to a fictional 11-year-old trainee wizard and something called the Sorting Hat."[116]

Although the practice quickly spread across many campuses, it was primarily restricted to college settings. Streaking highlights several of a fad's "naked truths:"[117]

- The fad is nonutilitarian—it does not perform any meaningful function.
- The fad often spreads impulsively—people do not undergo stages of rational decision-making before they join in.
- The fad diffuses rapidly, gains quick acceptance, and dies just as quickly.

MyMarketingLab

Go to **mymktlab.com** to complete the problems marked with this icon ⭐.

CHAPTER SUMMARY

Now that you have finished reading this chapter, you should understand why:

1. What other consumers tell us about products (good and bad) is more influential than formal advertising.

Much of what we know about products we learn through word-of-mouth (WOM) communication rather than formal advertising. We tend to exchange product-related information in casual conversations. Guerrilla marketing strategies try to accelerate the WOM process when they enlist consumers to help spread the word. Although WOM often is helpful to make consumers aware of products, it can also hurt companies when damaging product rumors or negative WOM occur.

2. "Opinion leaders" are particularly likely to influence others' product choices.

Opinion leaders who are knowledgeable about a product and whose opinions are highly regarded tend to influence others' choices. Specific opinion leaders are somewhat hard to identify, but marketers who know their general characteristics can try to target them in their media and promotional strategies. Other influencers include market mavens, who have a general interest in marketplace activities; and surrogate consumers, who are compensated for their advice about purchases.

3. Social media changes the way companies and consumers interact.

As Web 2.0 continues to develop, companies and consumers increasingly interact directly. The wisdom-of-crowds perspective argues that under the right circumstances, groups are smarter than the smartest people in them. If this is true, it implies that large numbers of consumers can predict successful products.[118] In a sense, a lot of social networking sites let their members dictate purchase decisions.

4. Online social networking magnifies the impact of word-of-mouth communication.

Social networking platforms significantly increase our access to others' opinions about products and services. Virtual consumption communities unite those who share a common bond—usually enthusiasm about or knowledge of a specific product or service. Emerging marketing strategies try to leverage the potential of the Web to spread information from consumer to consumer extremely quickly. Viral marketing techniques enlist individuals to tout products, services, Web sites, and so on, to others on behalf of companies. Blogging allows consumers to easily post their thoughts about products for others to see.

5. New products, services, and ideas spread through a population over time. Different types of people are more or less likely to adopt them during this diffusion process.

Diffusion of innovation refers to the process whereby a new product, service, or idea spreads through a population. Innovators and early adopters are quick to adopt new products, and laggards are very slow. A consumer's decision to adopt a new product depends on his or her personal characteristics as well as on characteristics of the innovation itself. We are more likely to adopt a new product if it demands relatively little behavioral change, is easy to understand, and provides a relative advantage compared to existing products.

6. Many people and organizations play a role in the fashion system that creates and communicates symbolic meanings to consumers.

The fashion system includes everyone involved in creating and transferring symbolic meanings. Many different products express common cultural categories (e.g., gender distinctions). Many people tend to adopt a new style simultaneously in a process of collective selection. According to meme theory, ideas spread through a population in a geometric progression much as a virus infects many people until it reaches epidemic proportions. Other perspectives on motivations for adopting new styles include psychological, economic, and sociological models of fashion.

7. Fashions follow cycles and reflect cultural dynamics.

The styles prevalent in a culture at any point in time reflect underlying political and social conditions. We term the set of agents responsible for creating stylistic alternatives a culture production system. Factors such as the types of people involved in this system and the amount of competition by alternative product forms influence the choices that eventually make their way to the marketplace for consideration by end consumers.

Fashions follow cycles that resemble the product life cycle. We distinguish between two extremes of fashion adoption, classics and fads, in terms of the length of this cycle.

KEY TERMS

acceptance cycles, 554
brand advocates, 536
classic, 554
community, 537
compatibility, 549
complexity, 549
continuous innovation, 548
cyberplace, 537
democracy, 541
diffusion of innovations, 547
digital virtual consumption (DVC), 545
discontinuous innovation, 549
dynamically continuous innovation, 549
early adopters, 548
fad, 555
fashion, 550
fashion system, 550
flaming, 541
flow state, 538
flows, 540
folksonomy, 537
FOMO, 535
freemium, 541
game platform, 545
genre, 545
guerrilla marketing, 526

homophily, 530
influence impressions, 543
influence network, 531
information cascades, 531
innovation, 547
innovators, 548
interactions, 540
laggards, 547
late adopters, 547
lurkers, 542
market maven, 532
Mass Connectors, 543
media democratization, 541
media multiplexity, 540
meetups, 540
meme theory, 553
milieu, 545
MMORPGs, 545
mode, 545
momentum effect, 543
M-PESA, 549
negative word-of-mouth, 527
network effect, 541
network units, 539
nodes, 539
observability, 549

opinion leader, 530
power users, 543
presence, 541
pure play retailer, 541
relative advantage, 549
reverse innovation, 549
social game, 544
social graphs, 539
social network, 539
social object theory, 540
social shopping, 543
sociometric methods, 534
surrogate consumer, 532
tie strength, 535
ties, 539
tipping point, 553
transactional advertising, 544
trialability, 549
trickle-down theory, 551
two step flow model of influence, 531
viral marketing, 537
virtual goods, 545
wisdom of crowds, 542
word-of-mouth (WOM), 523

REVIEW

12-1 What is buzz building, and how does it work?

12-2 What is meant by *homophily*?

⭐ **12-3** Describe some ways in which marketers use the Internet to encourage positive WOM.

12-4 Could a marketer create a generalized opinion leader?

⭐ **12-5** What is an opinion leader? Give three reasons why they are powerful influences on consumers' opinions. What are some characteristics of opinion leaders?

⭐ **12-6** Is there such a thing as a generalized opinion leader? Why or why not?

12-7 What is Klout, and how is it measured?

12-8 How do you find a suitable opinion leader?

12-9 What is FOMO, and why might it be important?

CONSUMER BEHAVIOR CHALLENGE

■ DISCUSS

12-10 Boots with 6-inch heels were a fashion rage among young Japanese women a few years ago. Several teens died after they tripped over their shoes and fractured their skulls. However, followers of the style claimed they were willing to risk twisted ankles, broken bones, bruised faces, and other dangers the platform shoes caused. One teenager said, "I've fallen and twisted my ankle many times, but they are so cute that I won't give them up until they go out of fashion."[119] Many consumers around the world seem willing to suffer for the sake of fashion. Others argue that we are merely pawns in the hands of designers, who conspire to force unwieldy fashions down our throats. What do you think? What is and what should be the role of fashion in our society? How important is it for people to be in style? What are the pros and cons of keeping up with the latest fashions? Do you believe that we are at the mercy of designers?

12-11 Although social networking is red-hot, could its days be numbered? Many people have concerns about privacy issues. Others feel that platforms like Facebook are too overwhelming. As one media executive comments, "Nobody has 5,000 real friends. At the end of the day it just becomes one big cauldron of noise." What's your stand on this: Can we have too much of a good thing? Will people start to tune out all of these networks?[120]

12-12 The average American teenager spends well over 8 hours a day in front of a screen, whether smartphone, PC, TV, or tablet. One study reported increasing physical isolation among Internet users; it created a controversy and drew angry complaints from some users who insisted that time they spent online did not detract from their social relationships. However, the researchers said they had now gathered further evidence showing that Internet use has lowered the amount of time people spend socializing with friends and even sleeping. According to the study, an hour of time spent using the Internet reduces face-to-face contact with friends, coworkers, and family by 23.5 minutes; lowers the amount of time spent watching television by 10 minutes; and reduces sleep time by 8.5 minutes.[121] What's your perspective on this issue? Does increasing use of the Internet have positive or negative implications for interpersonal relationships in our society?

12-13 SureBzz claims it is the first and leading word-of-mouth marketing service in India. The business works by creating a community of "SureBzzers." This community is then used to spread the word about a brand, product, or service to other consumers. SureBzz uses demographic and behavioral data points to help identify the right kind of person to spread the "buzz" about the brand. Each SureBzzer has the opportunity to experience the product or service firsthand; this is in order to ensure that the "buzz" is genuine. Typically, they are given samples, trials, and coupons. SureBzzers are encouraged to share their opinions on Facebook, Twitter, blogs, and other social media. The SureBzzers submit reports to the company that are then checked.[122] How is the data used from this point?

12-14 Ooredoo is a leading international communications company operating in the Middle East and North Africa. In September 2013 it announced a major sponsorship agreement with four of Tunisia's top football teams – Club Sportif Sfaxien (CSS), Club Africain (CA), Etoile Sportive du Sahel (ESS), and Esperance Sportive de Tunis (EST). What advantages does Ooredoo get from this relationship?

12-15 Riddled with malware and advertisements, and lacking in trust—that's how some people view peer-to-peer sharing. These issues have been around for years, ever since it became possible for computer users to share files. Anything in a digital format is fair game for the sharers. Huge networks have been set up (and shut down) with massive communities of members who are happy to install software and take the associated risks. Are corporations right in trying to end this aspect of the Internet?

■ APPLY

12-16 Who are the fashion opinion leaders in your country? How do they match up with the desired profile for such leaders?

12-17 Choose 10 people and ask them about their latest major purchase of a product or service. How did they decide that they needed that product or service? What made them choose the brand? Were they influenced by the views of an opinion leader in their decision-making process?

12-18 List at least 10 of your friends. They can be close friends or acquaintances. Try to rank them in terms of their influence on your purchasing behavior. To what extent are you more likely to trust and follow the opinions of your closer friends compared to your acquaintances? What types of product and service purchases have they influenced?

Case Study

NEVER STAY HERE! THE POWER OF NEGATIVE ONLINE REVIEWS

If you book a hotel for your next vacation, you will likely view ratings from TripAdvisor. As the world's largest travel site, TripAdvisor has integrated their review system with over 500 major travel partners including online booking site Kayak and leading hotel chains Wyndham, Best Western, and Four Seasons.

TripAdvisor is an online opinion leader whose influence comes from a community of travelers. How important are online reviews? Boston-based Cone Communications research revealed that 89 percent of consumers say they find online channels to be trustworthy sources for product and service reviews. In addition, Cone's research showed that four-out-of-five consumers have changed their minds about a recommended purchase based solely on negative information they found online.

Since online reviews are important, the challenge to marketers is how to manage the reviews, especially the dreaded negative reviews. Everyone knows all reviews cannot be positive, but there are ones that strike a chord of fear for hospitality companies: bed bugs, dirty sheets, discourteous front desk staff . . . the list goes on. The question for every hotel: how do we respond to negative reviews?

There are several options for handling negative reviews. Obviously, the first option is to do nothing at all, and many hotels go this route. The small hotel owner is incredibly busy, so following and responding to online reviews may fall low on his or her list of daily priorities. Perhaps these owners are not social media savvy or they are unaware of social media monitoring tools that will make tracking and responding to comments easier. Some of the more sophisticated monitoring tools are expensive, beginning at $800 a month; that might be beyond the marketing budget for a small business.

Still, most marketers agree that listening and responding to negative reviews is the best strategy. Several hotel chains, including Red Roof Inns, require managers of individual properties to respond to every negative online review. The responses themselves can be tricky; what do you say? It's clear that the overall goal of the response is to satisfy the reviewer and to change the public perception of your property. If the reviewer appears incorrect, how can the hotel politely attempt to correct the information without insulting the reviewer or creating an online argument?

If a reviewer has a truly bad experience, many hotels consider the guest deserving of a discount or a free night at the hotel. But hotels must be careful not to publicly promote this reward or less ethical reviewers might intentionally write bad reviews in the hopes of getting free nights at the hotel.

TripAdvisor has features to help hotels with some of these obstacles. The hotel can send a private message via the TripAdvisor message system offering a coupon to the customer. If the hotel feels a review is incorrect, there is an opportunity to report the review as inappropriate to TripAdvisor in the hopes of removal or correction.

Some businesses have gone more extreme in their reactions to negative reviews. There are a few reports of hotels fining their customers as much as $500 for a bad review. The customer is warned in the fine print of the contract and hotels are deducting the fee from the credit card used at check-in. There are also several cases of small businesses suing customers for defamation in their online reviews.

Online reviews are important for business survival and revenue growth. One study revealed that a one-star increase in a Yelp rating (Yelp is a leading online review site) can lead to as much as a 9 percent increase in revenue. In the competitive world of hotel marketing, social media marketing and visitor review sites will continue to gain influence on travelers' choices.

DISCUSSION QUESTIONS

CS 12-1 What steps do you recommend a hotel take when dealing with a negative online review?

CS 12-2 Do you use online reviews when choosing a hotel or restaurant? How much do these comments influence your choices?

Sources: "Game Changer: Cone Survey Finds 4-out-of-5 Consumers Reverse Purchase Decisions Based on Negative Online Reviews," http://www.conecomm.com/stuff/contentmgr/files/0/286c351989671ae74994fec139863bb2/files/2011_cone_online_influence_trend_tracker_release_and_fact_sheet.pdf, accessed August 9, 2013; "HBS Study Finds Positive Yelp Reviews Boost Business," *Harvard Magazine* (October 5, 2011), http://harvardmagazine.com/2011/10/hbs-study-finds-positive-yelp-reviews-lead-to-increased-business, accessed August 9, 2013; Steve Chenevey, "Hotel Owners Fining Customers for Bad Reviews," (May 29, 2012), http://www.wjla.com/articles/2012/05/hotel-owners-fining-customers-for-bad-reviews-76443.html, accessed August 9, 2013; "Hotel Websites Embrace TripAdvisor, Bad Reviews and All," *USA Today* (December 20, 2012), http://www.usatoday.com/story/hotelcheckin/2012/12/20/tripadvisor-red-roof-latest-hotel-chain-wyndham-best-western/1782313/, accessed August 9, 2013.

MyMarketingLab

Go to **mymktlab.com** for the following Assisted-graded writing questions:

12-19 How can marketers use opinion leaders to help them promote their products or services?

12-20 The chapter mentions the Hush Puppy shoe fad. Clearly, it's a matter of time before consumers tire of these shoes and move on. What can the company do to prolong the life of this brand?

12-21 Mymktlab Only—comprehensive writing assignment for this chapter.

NOTES

1. www.polyvore.com, accessed July 29, 2013.
2. http://www.youtube.com/channel/HCzDHQjv_snsA, accessed July 29, 2013.
3. Pat Wechsler, "A Curiously Strong Campaign," *BusinessWeek* (April 21, 1997): 134.
4. Johan Arndt, "Role of Product-Related Conversations in the Diffusion of a New Product," *Journal of Marketing Research* 4 (August 1967): 291–95.
5. Quoted in Sheila Shayon, "Teen Girls: Shopping and Texting, Texting and Shopping," *BrandChannel* (November 26, 2010), http://www.brandchannel.com/home/post/2010/11/26/Teen-Girls-Snapshot-Shopping-and-Social-Media.aspx, accessed February 23, 2011.
6. John Gaffney, "The Cool Kids Are Doing It. Should You?" *Asiaweek* (November 23, 2001): 1.
7. Douglas R. Pruden and Terry G. Vavra, "Controlling the Grapevine," *MM* (July–August 2004): 23–30.
8. Elihu Katz and Paul F. Lazarsfeld, *Personal Influence* (Glencoe, IL: Free Press, 1955).
9. John A. Martilla, "Word-of-Mouth Communication in the Industrial Adoption Process," *Journal of Marketing Research* 8 (March 1971): 173–78; see also Marsha L. Richins, "Negative Word-of-Mouth by Dissatisfied Consumers: A Pilot Study," *Journal of Marketing* 47 (Winter 1983): 68–78.
10. www.bzzagent.com, accessed March 18, 2013.
11. Les Luchter, "Kraft, Folgers, Olay Top Baby Boomer Gals' WOM," *Marketing Daily* (November 18, 2008), www.mediapost.com/publications/?fa=Articles.showArticle&art_aid=95000, accessed November 18, 2008.
12. Arndt, "Role of Product-Related Conversations in the Diffusion of a New Product."
13. James H. Myers and Thomas S. Robertson, "Dimensions of Opinion Leadership," *Journal of Marketing Research* 9 (February 1972): 41–46.
14. Ellen Neuborne, "Generation Y," *BusinessWeek* (February 15, 1999): 86.
15. Leonard-Barton, "Experts as Negative Opinion Leaders in the Diffusion of a Technological Innovation."
16. youtube.com/watch?v=y6t1R3yB-cs, accessed June 15, 2011.
17. http://www.mediacorpradio.sg/archive098.htm.
18. Tiffany Yap, "MediaCorp Subaru Challenge 2013 kicks off," *Today Online* (October 26, 2013), http://www.todayonline.com/lifestyle/cars/mediacorp-subaru-challenge-2013-kicks.
19. Chip Walker, "Word-of-Mouth," *American Demographics* (July 1995): 38–44; Albert M. Muñiz, Jr., Thomas O'Guinn, and Gary Alan Fine, "Rumor in Brand Community," in Donald A. Hantula, ed., *Advances in Theory and Methodology in Social and Organizational Psychology: A Tribute to Ralph Rosnow* (Mahwah, NJ: Erlbaum, 2005); cf. also Gaby A. C. Schellekens, Peeter W. J. Verlegh, and Ale Smidts, "Language Abstraction in Word of Mouth," *Journal of Consumer Research* 37, no. 2 (2010): 207–23.
20. Richard J. Lutz, "Changing Brand Attitudes Through Modification of Cognitive Structure," *Journal of Consumer Research* 1 (March 1975): 49–59. For some suggested remedies to bad publicity, see Mitch Griffin, Barry J. Babin, and Jill S. Attaway, "An Empirical Investigation of the Impact of Negative Public Publicity on Consumer Attitudes and Intentions," in Rebecca H. Holman and Michael R. Solomon, eds., *Advances in Consumer Research* 18 (Provo, UT: Association for Consumer Research, 1991): 334–41; Alice M. Tybout, Bobby J. Calder, and Brian Sternthal, "Using Information Processing Theory to Design Marketing Strategies," *Journal of Marketing Research* 18 (1981): 73–79; see also Russell N. Laczniak,

Thomas E. DeCarlo, and Sridhar N. Ramaswami, "Consumers' Responses to Negative Word-of-Mouth Communication: An Attribution Theory Perspective," *Journal of Consumer Psychology* 11, no. 1 (2001): 57–73.
21. Robert E. Smith and Christine A. Vogt, "The Effects of Integrating Advertising and Negative Word-of-Mouth Communications on Message Processing and Response," *Journal of Consumer Psychology* 4, no. 2 (1995): 133–51; Paula Fitzgerald Bone, "Word-of-Mouth Effects on Short-Term and Long-Term Product Judgments," *Journal of Business Research* 32 (1995): 213–23.
22. Keith Schneider, "Brands for the Chattering Masses," *New York Times* (December 17, 2006), www.nytimes.com, accessed October 3, 2007.
23. "Dunkin' Donuts Buys Out Critical Web Site," *New York Times* (August 27, 1999), www.nytimes.com, accessed August 27, 1999. For a discussion of ways to assess negative WOM online, cf. David M. Boush and Lynn R. Kahle, "Evaluating Negative Information in Online Consumer Discussions: From Qualitative Analysis to Signal Detection," *Journal of EuroMarketing* 11, no. 2 (2001): 89–105.
24. James C. Ward and Amy L. Ostrom, "Complaining to the Masses: The Role of Protest Framing in Customer-Created Complaint Web Sites," *Journal of Consumer Research* 33, no. 2 (2006): 220.
25. King and Summers, "Overlap of Opinion Leadership Across Consumer Product Categories."
26. Michael Fumento, "Tampon Terrorism," *Forbes* (May 17, 1999): 170.
27. Sung-Youl Jun, Taihoon Cha, and Praveen Aggarwal, "How Much Better? The Effect of Tensile Information on Word-of-Mouth Effectiveness," *Journal of Marketing Theory & Practice* 19, no. 3 (2011): 263–77; Praveen Aggarwal, Rajiv Vaidyanathan, and Alladi Venkatesh, "Using Lexical-Semantic Analysis to Derive Online Brand Perceptions: An Application to Retail Marketing Research," *Journal of Retailing* 85, no. 2 (2009): 145–58; Praveen Aggarwal and Tridib Mazumdar, "Delegation of Purchase Tasks: An Empirical Investigation," *Psychology & Marketing* 25, no. 1 (2008): 73–95.
28. Amy Chozick, "Cold Stone Aims to Be Hip in Japan Ice-Cream Chain, Uses Word-of-Mouth as Part of Bid for an Urban Image," *Wall Street Journal* (December 14, 2006): B10.
29. Everett M. Rogers, *Diffusion of Innovations*, 3rd ed. (New York: Free Press, 1983); cf. also Duncan J. Watts and Peter Sheridan Dodds, "Influentials, Networks, and Public Opinion Formation," *Journal of Consumer Research* 34 (December 2007): 441–58; Morris B. Holbrook and Michela Addis, "Taste Versus the Market: An Extension of Research on the Consumption of Popular Culture," *Journal of Consumer Research* 34 (October 2007): 415–24.
30. Dorothy Leonard-Barton, "Experts as Negative Opinion Leaders in the Diffusion of a Technological Innovation," *Journal of Consumer Research* 11 (March 1985): 914–26; Rogers, *Diffusion of Innovations*; cf. also Jan Kratzer and Christopher Lettl, "Distinctive Roles of Lead Users and Opinion Leaders in the Social Networks of Schoolchildren," *Journal of Consumer Research* (2009): 646–59. Dec 2009, Volume: 36 Issue 4.
31. Herbert Menzel, "Interpersonal and Unplanned Communications: Indispensable or Obsolete?," in Edward B. Roberts, ed., *Biomedical Innovation* (Cambridge, MA: MIT Press, 1981), 155–63.
32. Meera P. Venkatraman, "Opinion Leaders, Adopters, and Communicative Adopters: A Role Analysis," *Psychology & Marketing* 6 (Spring 1989): 51–68.
33. Rogers, *Diffusion of Innovations*.

34. Karl Greenberg, "Ford Puts Trendsetters Behind Wheel in VIP Events," *Marketing Daily* (November 11, 2008), www.mediapost.com/publications/?fa=Articles.san&s=94582&Nid=49281&p=407, accessed November 11, 2008.

35. Robert Merton, *Social Theory and Social Structure* (Glencoe, IL: Free Press, 1957).

36. Center for Media Research, "Inconspicuous, But Influential" (December 26, 2008), www.mediapost.com, accessed December 26, 2008.

37. Charles W. King and John O. Summers, "Overlap of Opinion Leadership Across Consumer Product Categories," *Journal of Marketing Research* 7 (February 1970): 43–50.; see also Ronald E. Goldsmith, Jeanne R. Heitmeyer, and Jon B. Freiden, "Social Values and Fashion Leadership," *Clothing & Textiles Research Journal* 10 (Fall 1991): 37–45; J. O. Summers, "Identity of Women's Clothing Fashion Opinion Leaders," *Journal of Marketing Research* 7 (1970): 178–85.

38. Duncan J. Watts and Peter Sheridan Dodds, "Influentials, Networks, and Public Opinion Formation," *Journal of Consumer Research* 34 (December 2007): 441–58.

39. Steven A. Baumgarten, "The Innovative Communicator in the Diffusion Process," *Journal of Marketing Research* 12 (February 1975): 12–18.

40. http://klout.com/home, accessed June 15, 2011.

41. Matthew Creamer, "Your Followers Are No Measure of Your Influence," *Advertising Age* (January 3, 2011), http://adage.com/article/special-report-influencers-2010/facebook-followers-measure-influence/147957/, accessed April 30, 2011.

42. Laura J. Yale and Mary C. Gilly, "Dyadic Perceptions in Personal Source Information Search," *Journal of Business Research* 32 (1995): 225–37.

43. Russell W. Belk, "Occurrence of Word-of-Mouth Buyer Behavior as a Function of Situation and Advertising Stimuli," in Fred C. Allvine, ed., *Combined Proceedings of the American Marketing Association*, series no. 33 (Chicago: American Marketing Association, 1971): 419–22.

44. Lawrence F. Feick, Linda L. Price, and Robin A. Higie, "People Who Use People: The Other Side of Opinion Leadership," in Richard J. Lutz, ed., *Advances in Consumer Research* 13 (Provo, UT: Association for Consumer Research, 1986): 301–5.

45. Stephanie Clifford, "Spreading the Word (and the Lotion) in Small-Town Alaska," *New York Times* (October 8, 2008), www.nytimes.com/2008/10/09/business/media/09adco.html, accessed October 9, 2008.

46. Michael R. Solomon, "The Missing Link: Surrogate Consumers in the Marketing Chain," *Journal of Marketing* 50 (October 1986): 208–18.

47. http://samsunggeeks.com/samsung-mobilers/#.UvHV9hCSwgv, accessed November 10, 2013.

48. https://www.facebook.com/Samsungninja, accessed November 10, 2013.

49. Barbara Stern and Stephen J. Gould, "The Consumer as Financial Opinion Leader," *Journal of Retail Banking* 10 (1988): 47–49.

50. William R. Darden and Fred D. Reynolds, "Predicting Opinion Leadership for Men's Apparel Fashions," *Journal of Marketing Research* 1 (August 1972): 324–28. A modified version of the opinion leadership scale with improved reliability and validity appears in Terry L. Childers, "Assessment of the Psychometric Properties of an Opinion Leadership Scale," *Journal of Marketing Research* 23 (May 1986): 184–88.

51. Dan Seligman, "Me and Monica," *Forbes* (March 23, 1998): 76.

52. Gina Kolata, "Find Yourself Packing It On? Blame Friends," *New York Times* (July 26, 2007), www.nytimes.com, accessed July 26, 2007.

53. "Referrals Top Ads as Influence on Patients' Doctor Selections," *Marketing News* (January 30, 1987): 22.

54. Peter H. Reingen and Jerome B. Kernan, "Analysis of Referral Networks in Marketing: Methods and Illustration," *Journal of Marketing Research* 23 (November 1986): 370–78.

55. Peter H. Reingen, Brian L. Foster, Jacqueline Johnson Brown, and Stephen B. Seidman, "Brand Congruence in Interpersonal Relations: A Social Network Analysis," *Journal of Consumer Research* 11 (December 1984): 771–83; see also James C. Ward and Peter H. Reingen, "Sociocognitive Analysis of Group Decision-Making Among Consumers," *Journal of Consumer Research* 17 (December 1990): 245–62.

56. John Tierney, "Good News Beats Bad on Social Networks," *New York Times* (March 18, 2013), http://www.nytimes.com/2013/03/19/science/good-news-spreads-faster-on-twitter-and-facebook.html, accessed March 19, 2013.

57. The material in this section is adapted from Tracy Tuten and Michael R. Solomon, *Social Media Marketing* (Englewood Cliffs, NJ: Pearson, 2012).

58. Jenna Wortham, "Feel Like a Wallflower? Maybe It's Your Facebook Wall," *New York Times* (April 9, 2011), http://www.nytimes.com/2011/04/10/business/10ping.html?_r=0, accessed March 19, 2013; Lizzie Crocker, "Are Twentysomethings Too Afraid of Missing Out?" *The Daily Beast* (November 9, 2012), http://www.thedailybeast.com/articles/2012/11/09/are-twentysomethings-too-afraid-of-missing-out.html, accessed March 19, 2013.

59. Emily Burg, "Leverage User-Generated Content to Boost Brands," *Marketing Daily* (March 13, 2007), www.mediapost.com, accessed March 13, 2007.

60. Karlene Lukovitz, "Marketers Praise Skittles' Gutsy Site Move," *Marketing Daily* (March 3, 2009), www.mediapost.com, accessed March 3, 2009.

61. www.pandora.com, accessed June 15, 2011.

62. Barry Wellman, "Physical Place and Cyberplace: The Rise of Personalized Networking," *International Journal of Urban & Regional Research* 24, no. 2 (2001): 227–52.

63. Michael Waltzer, "Petite Lap Giraffe: A Tiny Viral Marketing Success," *Brandchannel* (April 5, 2011), http://www.brandchannel.com/home/post/2011/04/05/Petite-Lap-Giraffe.aspx, accessed June 15, 2011.

64. Mihaly Csikszentmihalyi, *Flow: The Psychology of Optimal Experience* (New York: HarperCollins, 1991); Donna L. Hoffman and Thomas P. Novak, "Marketing in Hypermedia Computer-Mediated Environments: Conceptual Foundations," *Journal of Marketing* (July 1996): 50–68.

65. Alexandra Marin and Barry Wellman, "Social Network Analysis: An Introduction," in *Handbook of Social Network Analysis* (London: Sage, 2010).

66. John Coate, "Cyberspace Innkeeping: Building Online Community" (1998), http://www.cervisa.com/innkeeping, accessed December 31, 2010.

67. T. B. Sheridan, "Further Musings on the Psychophysics of Presence," *Presence: Teleoperators and Virtual Environments* 5 (1994): 241–46.

68. Matthew Lombard and Theresa Ditton, "At the Heart of It All: The Concept of Presence," *Journal of Computer Mediated Communication* 3, no. 2 (1973), http://jcmc.indiana.edu/vol3/issue2/lombard.html, accessed December 31, 2010.

69. Chris Anderson, "The Economics of Giving It Away," *Wall Street Journal* (January 31, 2009), http://online.wsj.com/article/SB123333567842023500.html, accessed January 31, 2009.

70. Sangkil Moon, Paul K. Bergey, and Dawn Iacobucci, "Dynamic Effects Among Movie Ratings, Movie Revenues, and Viewer Satisfaction," *Journal of Marketing* 74 (January 2010): 108–21; http://www.yelp.com/search?find_desc=restaurants&find_loc=Philadelphia%2C+PA&action_search=Search, accessed May 31, 2011; Anya Kamenetz, "The Perils and Promise of the Reputation Economy," *Fast Company* (December 3, 2008), www.fastcompany.com/magazine/131/on-the-internet-everyone-knows-youre-a-dog.html, accessed December 3, 2008.

71. Cf. C. Page Moreau and Kelly B. Herd, "To Each His Own? How Comparisons with Others Influence Consumers' Evaluations of Their Self-Designed Products," *Journal of Consumer Research* 36, no. 5 (February 2010): 806–819; Wendy Liu and David Gal, "Bringing Us Together or Driving Us Apart: The Effect of Soliciting Consumer Input on Consumers' Propensity to Transact with an Organization," *Journal of Consumer Research* 38, no. 2 (August 2011): 242–259.

72. James Surowiecki, *The Wisdom of Crowds* (New York: Anchor, 2005); Jeff Howe, "The Rise of Crowdsourcing," *Wired* (June 2006), www.wired.com/wired/archive/14.06/crowds.html, accessed October 3, 2007.

73. Emma Hutchings, "Budweiser Will Crowdsource Its Next Beer," *Mashable* (November 7, 2012), http://mashable.com/2012/11/07/budweiser-crowdsourced-beer/, accessed March 19, 2013; Stephanie Buck, "Alexander Wang Teams Up with Samsung for Crowdsourced Handbag," *Mashable* (February 11, 2013), http://mashable.com/2013/02/11/alexander-wang-samsung/, accessed March 19, 2013.

74. Lauren Indvik, "ModCloth Launches Clothing Collection of User-Generated Designs," *Mashable* (May 23, 2012), http://mashable.com/2012/05/23/modcloth-user-generated-fashion-label/?WT.mc_id=en_business&utm_campaign=Business&utm_medium=email&utm_source=newsletter, accessed January 10, 2013; kickstarter.com, accessed March 19, 2013.

75. www.threadless.com, accessed March 19, 2013; Mark Weingarten, "Designed to Grow," *Business 2.0* (June 2007): 35–37. For a contrarian view, cf. Joseph P. Simmons, Leif D. Nelson, Jeff Galak, and Shane Frederick, "Intuitive Biases in Choice Versus Estimation: Implications for the Wisdom of Crowds," *Journal of Consumer Research* 38, no. 1 (June 2011): 1–15.

76. Ed Keller and Jon Berry. *The Influentials* (New York: Simon & Schuster, 2003).

77. "Introducing Peer Influence Analysis: 500 Billion Peer Impressions Each Year," *Empowered*, (April 20, 2010), http://forrester.typepad.com/groundswell/2010/04/introducing-peer-influence-analysis.html, accessed December 31, 2010.

78. "MySpace, Isobar & Carat, Never Ending Friending: A Journey into Social Networking," http://creative.myspace.com/groups/_ms/nef/images/40161_nef_onlinebook.pdf, accessed December 31, 2010; cf. also Malcolm Gladwell, *The Tipping Point* (New York: Little, Brown, 2000).

79. Jenna Wortham, "What's the Value of a Facebook Friend? About 37 Cents," *New York Times* (January 9, 2009), www.nytimes.com, accessed January 9, 2009.

80. Drew Elliott, "Opportunities for Brands in Social Games," *Ogilvy PR Blog* (May 2010), http://blog.ogilvypr.com/2010/05/opportunities-for-brands-in-social-games/, accessed July 12, 2010.

81. Andiara Petterle, "Reaching Latinos Through Virtual Goods," *Media Post* (June 10, 2010), http://www.mediapost.com/publications/?fa=Articles.showArticle&art_aid=129857, accessed July 13, 2010.

82. Adapted from Tracy Tuten and Michael R. Solomon, *Social Media Marketing* (Upper Saddle River, NJ: Pearson Education, 2012).

83. "Gagaville," http://gagaville.org/, accessed May 12, 2011.

84. Thomas Apperley, "Genre and Game Studies: Toward a Critical Approach to Video Game Genres," *Simulation & Gaming* 37, no. 1 (2006): 6–23.

85. Interactive Advertising Bureau, *IAB Game Advertising Platform Status Report*, http://www.iab.net/media/file/games-reportv4.pdf, accessed May 31, 2011.

86. Apperley, "Genre and Game Studies: Toward a Critical Approach to Video Game Genres."

87. Mike Snider, "Virtual Goods Spending Topped $2 Billion in U.S. in 2011," *Game Hunters* (February 29, 2012), http://content.usatoday.com/communities/gamehunters/post/2012/02/virtual-goods-spending-topped-2-billion-in-us-in-2011/1, accessed March 19, 2013; Janice Denegri-Knot and Mike Molesworth, "Concepts and Practices of Digital Virtual Consumption," *Consumption Markets & Culture* 13, no. 2 (2010): 109–32; Natalie T. Wood and Michael R. Solomon, "Adonis or Atrocious: Spokesavatars and Source Effects in Immersive Digital Environments," in Matthew S. Eastin, Terry Daugherty, and Neal M. Burns, eds., *Handbook of Research on Digital Media and Advertising: User Generated Content Consumption* (Hershey, PA IGI Global, 2011): 521–34.

88. Damien Cave, "Dogtown, U.S.A.," *New York Times* (June 12, 2005), www.nytimes.com, accessed June 12, 2005.

89. Emily Nelson, "Moistened Toilet Paper Wipes Out After Launch for Kimberly-Clark," *Wall Street Journal* (April 15, 2002), www.wsj.com, accessed April 15, 2002.

90. Robert Hof, "The Click Here Economy," *BusinessWeek* (June 22, 1998): 122–28.

91. Eric J. Arnould, "Toward a Broadened Theory of Preference Formation and the Diffusion of Innovations: Cases from Zinder Province, Niger Republic," *Journal of Consumer Research* 16 (September 1989): 239–67; Susan B. Kaiser, *The Social Psychology of Clothing* (New York: Macmillan, 1985); Thomas S. Robertson, *Innovative Behavior and Communication* (New York: Holt, Rinehart & Winston, 1971).

92. Jan-Benedict E. M. Steenkamp, Frenkel ter Hofstede, and Michel Wedel, "A Cross-National Investigation into the Individual and National Cultural Antecedents of Consumer Innovativeness," *Journal of Marketing* 63, no. 7 (1999): 55–69.

93. Susan L. Holak, Donald R. Lehmann, and Fareena Sultan, "The Role of Expectations in the Adoption of Innovative Consumer Durables: Some Preliminary Evidence," *Journal of Retailing* 63 (Fall 1987): 243–59.

94. DDB Signbank (April 25, 2012), http://issuu.com/jannekedekker/docs/trendreport, accessed March 19, 2013; Eric Pfanner, "Agencies Look Beyond Focus Groups to Spot Trends," *New York Times* (January 2, 2006), www.nytimes.com, accessed January 2, 2006.

95. "Trends in Japan," http://web-japan.org/trends/08_lifestyle/lif080707.html, accessed March 19, 2013.

96. Everett M. Rogers, *Diffusion of Innovations*, 3rd ed. (New York: Free Press, 1983).

97. For more details, see Gordon C. Bruner II and Anand Kumar, "Gadget Lovers," *Journal of the Academy of Marketing Science* 35, no. 3 (2007): 329–39.

98. Melanie Wallendorf, "The Formation of Aesthetic Criteria Through Social Structures and Social Institutions," in Jerry C. Olson, ed., *Advances in Consumer Research 7* (Ann Arbor, MI: Association for Consumer Research, 1980): 3–6.

99. For more details, see Kaiser, *The Social Psychology of Clothing*; George B. Sproles, "Behavioral Science Theories of Fashion," in Michael R. Solomon, ed., *The Psychology of Fashion* (Lexington, MA: Lexington Books, 1985): 55–70.

100. C. R. Snyder and Howard L. Fromkin, *Uniqueness: The Human Pursuit of Difference* (New York: Plenum Press, 1980).

101. Linda Dyett, "Desperately Seeking Skin," *Psychology Today* (May–June 1996): 14; Alison Lurie, *The Language of Clothes* (New York: Random House, 1981). Note: Until very recently, the study of fashion focused almost exclusively on women. Some researchers today also probe the meanings of the fashion system for men, but not nearly to the same extent. Cf., for example, Susan Kaiser, Michael Solomon, Janet Hethorn, Basil Englis, Van Dyk Lewis, and Wi-Suk Kwon, "Menswear, Fashion, and Subjectivity," paper presented in Special Session: Susan Kaiser, Michael Solomon, Janet Hethorn, and Basil Englis (Chairs), "What Do Men Want? Media Representations, Subjectivity, and Consumption," at the ACR Gender Conference, Edinburgh, Scotland, June 2006.

102. Harvey Leibenstein, *Beyond Economic Man: A New Foundation for Microeconomics* (Cambridge, MA: Harvard University Press, 1976).

103. Nara Schoenberg, "Goth Culture Moves into Mainstream," *Montgomery Advertiser* (January 19, 2003): 1G.

104. Georg Simmel, "Fashion," *International Quarterly* 10 (1904): 130–55.

105. Maureen Tkacik, "'Z' Zips into the Zeitgeist, Subbing for 'S' in Hot Slang," *Wall Street Journal* (January 4, 2003), www.wsj.com, accessed January 4, 2003; Tkacik, "Slang from the 'Hood Now Sells Toyz in Target," *Wall Street Journal* (December 30, 2002), http://www.ytlcommunity.com/commnews/shownews.asp?newsid=5112, accessed September 13, 2011.

106. Grant D. McCracken, "The Trickle-Down Theory Rehabilitated," in Michael R. Solomon, ed., *The Psychology of Fashion* (Lexington, MA: Lexington Books, 1985): 39–54.

107. Charles W. King, "Fashion Adoption: A Rebuttal to the 'Trickle-Down' Theory," in Stephen A. Greyser, ed., *Toward Scientific Marketing* (Chicago: American Marketing Association, 1963): 108–25.

108. Alf H. Walle, "Grassroots Innovation," *Marketing Insights* (Summer 1990): 44–51.

109. Adapted from Tracy Tuten and Michael R. Solomon, *Social Media Marketing* (Upper Saddle River, NJ: Pearson, 2012); Jenna Wortham, "Once Just a Site with Funny Cat Pictures, and Now a Web Empire" (June 13, 2010), *New York Times*, http://www.nytimes.com/2010/06/14/technology/internet/14burger.html?emc=eta1, accessed June 23, 2011.

110. Robert V. Kozinets, "Fandoms' Menace/Pop Flows: Exploring the Metaphor of Entertainment as Recombinant/Memetic Engineering," *Association for Consumer Research* (October 1999). The new science of memetics, which tries to explain how beliefs gain acceptance and predict their progress, was spurred by Richard Dawkins who in the 1970s proposed culture as a Darwinian struggle among "memes" or mind viruses. See Geoffrey Cowley, "Viruses of the Mind: How Odd Ideas Survive," *Newsweek* (April 14, 1997): 14.

111. Malcolm Gladwell, *The Tipping Point* (New York: Little, Brown, 2000).

112. "Cabbage-Hatched Plot Sucks in 24 Doll Fans," *New York Daily News* (December 1, 1983).

113. www.Zoobles.com, accessed June 23, 2011; Ann Zimmerman, "How Toy Crazes Are Born: Collectibles Are Designed to Be Cute, Numerous, Affordable and Just Rare Enough," *Wall Street Journal* (December 16, 2010), http://online.wsj.com/article/SB100014240527487048281045760214304349838792.html, accessed April 28, 2011; John Lippman, "Creating the Craze for Pokémon: Licensing Agent Bet on U.S. Kids," *Wall Street Journal* (August 16, 1999), www.wsj.com, accessed August 16, 1999; "Turtlemania," *The Economist* (April 21, 1990): 32.

114. Anthony Ramirez, "The Pedestrian Sneaker Makes a Comeback," *New York Times* (October 14, 1990): F17.

115. Madden, "Japan's Latest Fads—Marketable in U.S.?"

116. Quoted in Stephen Brown and Anthony Patterson, "You're a Wizard, Harry!" Consumer Responses to the Harry Potter Phenomenon," *Advances in Consumer Research* 33, no. 1 (2006): 155–160.

117. B. E. Aguirre, E. L. Quarantelli, and Jorge L. Mendoza, "The Collective Behavior of Fads: The Characteristics, Effects, and Career of Streaking," *American Sociological Review* (August 1989): 569.

118. Surowiecki, *The Wisdom of Crowds*; Howe, "The Rise of Crowdsourcing."

119. Calvin Sims, "For Chic's Sake, Japanese Women Parade to the Orthopedist," *New York Times* (November 26, 1999), www.nytimes.com, accessed November 26, 1999.

120. Quoted in Suzanne Vranica, "Ad Houses Will Need to Be More Nimble, Clients Are Demanding More and Better Use of Consumer Data, Web," *Wall Street Journal* (January 2, 2008): B3.

121. John Markoff, "Internet Use Said to Cut into TV Viewing and Socializing," *New York Times on the Web* (December 30, 2004), http://www.nytimes.com/2004/12/30/technology/30internet.html?_r=1&scp=1&sq=John%20Markoff,%20%E2%80%9CInternet%20Use%20Said%20to%20Cut%20into%20TV%20Viewing%20and%20Socializing&st=cseM, accessed September 13, 2011.

122. http://www.surebzz.com, accessed December 18, 2013.

SECTION 3 NIELSEN NUGGET

Scenario: Healthy Clean, Inc., has a strong presence in surface disinfection under the "Germ Destructor" brand. It is important for the company to enter the hand-hygiene segment, in order to be able to provide a complete range of germ-kill solutions and to maintain the perception of category leadership. Healthy Clean company wants to investigate entering the hand-wash market with the launch of a no-touch dispensing system.

Challenge: Healthy Clean seeks to better understand consumer perceptions as they relate to various product attributes and the general acceptance of the product concept. Among other research objectives, Healthy Clean hopes to determine where it may be able to achieve competitive performance advantages. The company also seeks to identify those product attributes that may have to be adjusted or those consumer perceptions it may seek to influence.

After reviewing the data provided:

1 Identify specific attributes that Healthy Clean should emphasize in promotions if it proceeds with the new product launch.

2 Identify specific attributes, if any, that should be considered for reengineering.

3 Which of the marketing applications of the multiattribute model discussed in this chapter could be suggested by the data?

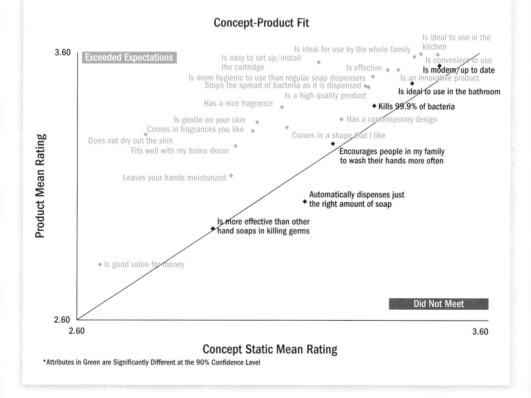

Concept-Product Fit

ABC model of attitudes a multidimensional perspective stating that attitudes are jointly defined by affect, behavior, and cognition

Abandoned products grocery items that shoppers buy but never use

Absolute threshold the minimum amount of stimulation that can be detected on a given sensory channel

Acceptance cycles a way to differentiate among fashions in terms of their longevity

Accommodative purchase decision the process of using bargaining, coercion, compromise, and the wielding of power to achieve agreement among group members who have different preferences or priorities

Acculturation the process of learning the beliefs and behaviors endorsed by another culture

Acculturation agents friends, family, local businesses, and other reference groups that facilitate the learning of cultural norms

Achieved status a relative position in an organization or culture awarded on the basis of accomplishment or mastery of some task

Activation models of memory approaches to memory stressing different levels of processing that occur and activate some aspects of memory rather than others, depending on the nature of the processing task

Activity stores a retailing concept that lets consumers participate in the production of the products or services being sold in the store

Actual self a person's realistic appraisal of his or her qualities

Adaptation the process that occurs when a sensation becomes so familiar that it no longer commands attention

Advergaming online games merged with interactive advertisements that let companies target specific types of consumers

Advertising wear-out the condition that occurs when consumers become so used to hearing or seeing a marketing stimulus that they no longer pay attention to it

Affect the way a consumer feels about an attitude object

Affluenza well-off consumers who are stressed or unhappy despite of, or even because of, their wealth

Age cohort a group of consumers of approximately the same age who have undergone similar experiences

Agentic goals an emphasis on self-assertion and mastery, often associated with traditional male gender roles

AIOs (activities, interests, and opinions) the psychographic variables researchers use to group consumers

Allegory a story told about an abstract trait or concept that has been personified as a person, animal, or vegetable

Alternate-reality game (ARG) an application that blends online and offline clues and encourages players to collaborate to solve a puzzle

Androgyny the possession of both masculine and feminine traits

Animism cultural practices whereby inanimate objects are given qualities that make them somehow alive

Anthropomorphism the tendency to attribute human characteristics to objects or animals

Antibrand communities groups of consumers who share a common disdain for a celebrity, store, or brand

Anticonsumption the actions taken by consumers involving the deliberate defacement or mutilation of products

Antifestival an event that distorts the symbols associated with other holidays

Approach–approach conflict a person must choose between two desirable alternatives

Approach–avoidance conflict a person desires a goal but wishes to avoid it at the same time

Archetypes a universally shared idea or behavior pattern, central to Carl Jung's conception of personality; archetypes involve themes—such as birth, death, or the devil—that appear frequently in myths, stories, and dreams

Art product a creation viewed primarily as an object of aesthetic contemplation without any functional value

Ascribed status relative position in an organization or culture awarded on the basis of family connections or other factors external to the individual

Aspirational reference group high-profile athletes and celebrities used in marketing efforts to promote a product

Associative network a memory system that organizes individual units of information according to some set of relationships; may include such concepts as brands, manufacturers, and stores

Asynchronous interactions message posts that don't require all participants to respond immediately

Atmospherics the use of space and physical features in store design to evoke certain effects in buyers

Attention the assignment of processing activity to selected stimuli

Attitude a lasting, general evaluation of people (including oneself), objects, or issues

Attitude accessibility perspective an attitude will guide the evaluation of the object but *only* if a person's memory activates it when she encounters the object

Attitude models frameworks that identify specific components and combine them to predict a consumer's overall attitude toward a product or brand

Attitude object (A_o) anything toward which one has an attitude

Attitude toward the act of buying (A_{act}) the perceived consequences of a purchase

Audio watermarking a technique where composers and producers weave a distinctive sound/motif into a piece of music that sticks in people's minds over time

Augmented reality technology applications that layer digital information over a physical space to add additional information for users

Autonomic decision when one family member chooses a product for the whole family

Avatar manifestation of a Hindu deity in superhuman or animal form; in the computing world, it has come to mean a cyberspace presence represented by a character that you can move around inside a visual, graphical world

Avoidance-avoidance conflict a choice situation where both alternatives are undesirable

Avoidance groups reference groups that exert a negative influence on individuals because they are motivated to distance themselves from group members

B2C e-commerce businesses selling to consumers through electronic marketing

Baby Boomer a large cohort of people born between the years of 1946 and 1964 who are the source of many important cultural and economic changes

Badges evidence of some achievement consumers display either in the physical world or on social platforms

Balance theory a theory that considers relations among elements a person might perceive as belonging together, and people's tendency to change relations among elements in order to make them consistent or "balanced"

Basking in reflected glory the practice of publicizing connections with successful people or organizations to enhance one's own standing

Behavior a consumer's actions with regard to an attitude object

Behavioral economics the study of the behavioral determinants of economic decisions

Behavioral learning theories the perspectives on learning that assume that learning takes place as the result of responses to external events

Being space a retail environment that resembles a residential living room where customers are encouraged to congregate

Big Data the collection and analysis of extremely large datasets to identify patterns of behavior in a group of consumers

Big Five a set of five dimensions that form the basis of personality: openness to experience, conscientiousness, extroversion, agreeableness, and neuroticism

Binary opposition a defining structural characteristic of many myths in which two opposing ends of some dimension are represented (e.g., good versus evil, nature versus technology)

Bioterrorism a strategy to disrupt the nation's food supply with the aim of creating economic havoc

Blogs messages posted online in diary form

Body image a consumer's subjective evaluation of his or her physical self

Body mass index (BMI) a formula to calculate obesity that takes into account both height and weight

Boomerang kids grown children who return to their parents' home to live

Botnets a set of computers that are penetrated by malicious software known as *malware* that allows an external agent to control their actions

Bounded rationality a concept in behavioral economics that states since we rarely have the resources (especially the time) to weigh every possible factor into a decision, we settle for a solution that is just good enough

Bottom of the pyramid the huge number of consumers around the world who have very low incomes

Brand advocates consumers who supply product reviews online

Brand community a set of consumers who share a set of social relationships based on usage or interest in a product

Brand equity a brand that has strong positive associations in a consumer's memory and commands a lot of loyalty as a result

Brand loyalty repeat purchasing behavior that reflects a conscious decision to continue buying the same brand

Brand personality a set of traits people attribute to a product as if it were a person

Brand prominence the display of blatant status symbols to ensure that others recognize one's luxury brands

Brandfests a corporate-sponsored event intended to promote strong brand loyalty among customers

BRIC nation the bloc of nations with very rapid economic development: Brazil, Russia, India, and China

Bromance a relationship characterized by strong affection between two straight males

Business ethics rules of conduct that guide actions in the marketplace

Business-to-business (B2B) e-commerce Internet interactions between two or more businesses or organizations

Business-to-business (B2B) marketers specialists in meeting the needs of organizations such as corporations, government agencies, hospitals, and retailers

Buyclass theory of purchasing a framework that characterizes organizational buying decisions in terms of how much cognitive effort is involved in making a decision

Buyer the person who actually makes the purchase

Buying center the part of an organization charged with making purchasing decisions

C2C e-commerce consumer-to-consumer activity through the Internet

Category exemplars brands that are particularly relevant examples of a broader classification

Cause marketing a strategy that aligns a company or brand with a cause to generate business and societal benefits

Celebrity endorsements a communications tactic whereby an organization retains a well-known person to tout a product or cause on its behalf

Chavs British term that refers to young, lower-class men and women who mix flashy brands and accessories from big names such as Burberry with track suits

Chunking a process in which information is stored by combining small pieces of information into larger ones

Classic a fashion with an extremely long acceptance cycle

Classical conditioning the learning that occurs when a stimulus eliciting a response is paired with another stimulus that initially does not elicit a response on its own but will cause a similar response over time because of its association with the first stimulus

Closure principle the *Gestalt* principle that describes a person's tendency to supply missing information in order to perceive a holistic image

Co-branding strategies linking products together to create a more desirable connotation in consumer minds

Co-consumers other patrons in a consumer setting

Codes the ways members of a shared culture express and interpret meanings

Coercive power influence over another person due to social or physical intimidation cohesiveness

Cognition the beliefs a consumer has about an attitude object

Cognitive learning theory approaches that stress the importance of internal mental processes; this perspective views people as problem-solvers who actively use information from the world around them to master their environment

Cohesiveness the degree to which members of a group are attracted to each other and how much each values their membership in this group

Collecting the systematic acquisition of a particular object or set of objects

Collective value creation the process whereby brand community members work together to develop better ways to use and customize products

Communal goals an emphasis on affiliation and the fostering of harmonious relations, often associated with traditional female gender roles

Communications model a framework specifying that a number of elements are necessary for communication to be achieved, including a source, message, medium, receivers, and feedback

Community in a digital context, a group of people who engage in supportive and sociable relationships with others who share one or more common interests

Comparative advertising a strategy in which a message compares two or more specifically named or recognizably presented brands and makes a comparison of them in terms of one or more specific attributes

Comparative influence the process whereby a reference group influences decisions about specific brands or activities

Compatibility in the context of diffusion of innovations, the extent to which a new product fits with a consumer's preexisting lifestyle

Compensatory decision rules a set of rules that allows information about attributes of competing products to be averaged in some way; poor standing on one attribute can potentially be offset by good standing on another

Complexity in the context of diffusion of innovation, the extent to which a new product is difficult to use or to integrate into a person's daily life

Compliance belief that we form an attitude because it helps us to gain rewards or avoid punishment

Compulsive consumption the process of repetitive, often excessive, shopping used to relieve tension, anxiety, depression, or boredom

Computer-mediated environment (CME) immersive virtual worlds

Conditioned response (CR) a response to a conditioned stimulus caused by the learning of an association between a conditioned stimulus (CS) and an unconditioned stimulus (UCS)

Conditioned stimulus (CS) a stimulus that produces a learned reaction through association over time

Conformity a change in beliefs or actions as a reaction to real or imagined group pressure

Connexity a lifestyle term coined by the advertising agency Saatchi & Saatchi to describe young consumers who place high value on being both footloose and connected

Conscientious consumerism a new value that combines a focus on personal health with a concern for global health

Consensual purchase decision a decision in which the group agrees on the desired purchase and differs only in terms of how it will be achieved

Consideration set the products a consumer actually deliberates about choosing

Conspicuous consumption the purchase and prominent display of luxury goods to provide evidence of a consumer's ability to afford them

Constructive processing a thought process in which a person evaluates the effort he or she will need to make a particular choice, and then tailors the amount of cognitive "effort" expended to make this decision

Consumed consumers those people who are used or exploited, whether willingly or not, for commercial gain in the marketplace

Consumer a person who identifies a need or desire, makes a purchase, and/or disposes of the product

Consumer addiction a physiological and/or psychological dependency on products or services

Consumer behavior the processes involved when individuals or groups select, purchase, use, or dispose of products, services, ideas, or experiences to satisfy needs and desires

Consumer confidence the extent to which people are optimistic or pessimistic about the future health of the economy

Consumer confusion in legal contexts, the likelihood that one company's logo, product design, or package is so similar to another that the typical shopper would mistake one for the other

Consumer identity the ways we express our social identities that relate to our consumption of products and services

Consumer identity renaissance the redefinition process people undergo when they retire

Consumer satisfaction/dissatisfaction (CS/D) the overall attitude a person has about a product after it has been purchased

Consumer socialization the process by which people acquire skills that enable them to function in the marketplace

Consumerspace marketing environment where customers act as partners with companies to decide what the marketplace will offer

Consumer style a pattern of behaviors, attitudes, and opinions that influences all of a person's consumption activities—including attitudes toward advertising, preferred channels of information and purchase, brand loyalty, and price consciousness

Consumer tribe group of people who share a lifestyle and who can identify with each other because of a shared allegiance to an activity or a product

Consumption communities Web groups where members share views and product recommendations online

Consumption constellation a set of products and activities used by consumers to define, communicate, and perform social roles

Consumption situation includes a buyer, a seller, and a product or service—but also many other factors, such as the reason we want to make a purchase and how the physical environment makes us feel

Contamination when a place or object takes on sacred qualities because of its association with another sacred person or event

Contemporary Young Mainstream Female Achievers (CYMFA) modern women who assume multiple roles

Context effects subtle cues in the environment that influence a person's decisions

Continuous innovation a modification of an existing product

Contrast stimuli that differ from others around them

Conventions norms that regulate how we conduct our everyday lives

Cooptation a cultural process by which the original meanings of a product or other symbol associated with a subculture are modified by members of mainstream culture

Core values common general values held by a culture

Corporate social responsibility (CSR) processes that encourage the organization to make a positive impact on the various stakeholders in its community including consumers, employees, and the environment

Corrective advertising messages an organization releases (voluntarily or not) that inform consumers of previous messages that were inaccurate or misleading

Cosmopolitanism a cultural value that emphasizes being open to the world and striving for diverse experiences

Cosplay a form of performance art in which participants wear elaborate costumes that represent a virtual world avatar or other fictional character

Cougars older women who date younger men

Counteractive construal exaggerating the negative aspects of behaviors that will impede the attainment of a goal as a strategy to avoid them and reach the goal

Counterarguing the tendency for consumers to think of reasons why they should not believe a message

Counterfeiting companies or individuals sell fake versions of real products

Country of origin original country from which a product is produced; it can be an important piece of information in the decision-making process

Covariation assumed associations among events that may or may not actually influence one another

Craft product a creation valued because of the beauty with which it performs some function; this type of product tends to follow a formula that permits rapid production, and it is easier to understand than an art product

Creolization foreign influences are absorbed and integrated with local meanings

Crescive norms unspoken rules that govern social behavior

Cult products items that command fierce consumer loyalty and devotion

Cultural capital a set of distinctive and socially rare tastes and practices that admits a person into the realm of the upper class

Cultural formula a sequence of media events in which certain roles and props tend to occur consistently

Cultural gatekeepers individuals who are responsible for determining the types of messages and symbolism to which members of mass culture are exposed

Cultural selection the process by which some alternatives are selected over others by cultural gatekeepers

Culture the values, ethics, rituals, traditions, material objects, and services produced or valued by the members of a society

Culture jamming strategies that attempt to disrupt or satirize messages from corporations

Culture of participation the driving philosophy behind social media that includes a belief in democracy; the ability to freely interact with other people, companies, and organizations; open access to venues that allow users to share content from simple comments to reviews, ratings, photos, stories, and more; and the power to build on the content of others from your own unique point of view

Culture production system (CPS) the set of individuals and organizations responsible for creating and marketing a cultural product

Curation a source such as a store or a celebrity selects a set of products to simply shoppers' decisions

Custom a norm that controls basic behaviors, such as division of labor in a household

Customer networks groups in companies and families that customer networks invest in products and services to help them reach collective identity goals

Cyberbullying when one or more people post malicious comments online about someone else in a coordinated effort to harass him or her

Cybermediary intermediary that helps to filter and organize online market information so that consumers can identify and evaluate alternatives more efficiently

Cyberplace an online social community

Cyberterrorism deliberate disruption of digital networks to accomplish political, social or financial objectives

Database marketing tracking consumers' buying habits very closely, and then crafting products and messages tailored precisely to people's wants and needs based on this information

Decay structural changes in the brain produced by learning decrease over time

Deethnicization process whereby a product formerly associated with a specific ethnic group is detached from its roots and marketed to other subcultures

Default bias a tendency in decision making that makes it more likely for people to comply with a requirement than to make the effort not to comply

Deindividuation the process whereby individual identities get submerged within a group, reducing inhibitions against socially inappropriate behavior

Democracy in a social media context, a term that refers to rule by the people; community leaders are appointed or elected based on their demonstrated ability to add value to the group

Demographics the observable measurements of a population's characteristics, such as birthrate, age distribution, and income

Desacralization the process that occurs when a sacred item or symbol is removed from its special place, or is duplicated in mass quantities, and becomes profane as a result

Determinant attributes the attributes actually used to differentiate among choices

Differential threshold the ability of a sensory system to detect changes or differences among stimuli

Diffusion of innovations the process whereby a new product, service, or idea spreads through a population

Digital Divide the gulf between wealthy and poor people in terms of online access

Digital identity management the process of manipulating online information to create or maintain an extended self in social networks

Digital native young people who have grown up with computers and mobile technology; multitaskers with cell phones, music downloads, and instant messaging on the Internet; people who are comfortable communicating online and by text and IM rather than by voice

Digital self elements of self-expression that relate to a person's online identity

Digital virtual consumption (DVC) purchases of virtual goods for use in online games and social communities

DINKS acronym for Double Income, No Kids; a consumer segment with a lot of disposable income

Direct selling a multilevel marketing structure that sells a consumer product or service, person-to-person, away from a fixed retail location, marketed through independent sales representatives who are sometimes also referred to as consultants or distributors

Discontinuous innovation a new product or service that radically changes the way we live

Discretionary income the money available to a household over and above that required for necessities

Dominance-submission hierarchy a "pecking order" within a culture that dictates which members are relatively higher in status than other members

Doppelgänger brand image a parody of a brand posted on a Web site that looks like the original but is in fact a critique of it

Drive the desire to satisfy a biological need in order to reduce physiological arousal

Drive theory concept that focuses on biological needs that produce unpleasant states of arousal

Dynamically continuous innovation a significant change to an existing product

Early adopters people who are receptive to new products and adopt them relatively soon, though they are motivated more by social acceptance and being in style than by the desire to try risky new things

Echo Boomers people born between 1986–2002, also known as Gen Y and Millennials

Ecology the way members of a culture adapt to their physical habitat

Economics of information perspective in which advertising is an important source of consumer information emphasizing the economic cost of the time spent searching for products

Ego the system that mediates between the id and the superego

Ego-defensive function attitudes we form to protect ourselves either from external threats or internal feelings

80/20 rule a rule-of-thumb in volume segmentation, which says that about 20 percent of consumers in a product category (the heavy users) account for about 80 percent of sales

Elaborated codes the ways of expressing and interpreting meanings that are more complex and depend on a more sophisticated worldview, which tend to be used by the middle and upper classes

Elaboration likelihood model (ELM) the approach that one of two routes to persuasion (central versus peripheral) will be followed, depending on the personal relevance of a message; the route taken determines the relative importance of the message contents versus other characteristics, such as source attractiveness

Elaborative rehearsal a cognitive process that allows information to move from short-term memory into long-term memory by thinking about the meaning of a stimulus and relating it to other information already in memory

Embeds tiny figures inserted into magazine advertising by using high-speed photography or airbrushing; these hidden figures, usually of a sexual nature, supposedly exert strong but unconscious influences on innocent readers

Emic perspective an approach to studying for (or marketing to) cultures that stresses the unique aspects of each culture

Emotional oracle effect a finding reported by researchers that people who trust their feelings are able to predict future events better than those who do not

Encoding the process in which information from short-term memory enters into long-term memory in a recognizable form

Enculturation the process of learning the beliefs and behaviors endorsed by one's own culture

Episodic memories memories that relate to personally relevant events; this tends to increase a person's motivation to retain these memories

Ethnic subculture a self-perpetuating group of consumers held together by common cultural ties

Ethnocentrism the belief in the superiority of one's own country's practices and products

Etic perspective an approach to studying (or marketing to) cultures that stresses commonalities across cultures

Evaluative criteria the dimensions used by consumers to compare competing product alternatives

Evoked set those products already in memory plus those prominent in the retail environment that are actively considered during a consumer's choice process

Exchange a transaction in which two or more organizations or people give and receive something of value

Expectancy disconfirmation model states that we form beliefs about product performance based on prior experience with the product and/or communications about the product that imply a certain level of quality: (1) if something performs the way we thought it would, we may not think much about it; (2) if it fails to live up to expectations, this may create negative feelings; (3) if performance exceeds our initial expectations, we are satisfied

Expectancy theory the perspective that behavior is largely "pulled" by expectations of achieving desirable outcomes, or positive incentives, rather than "pushed" from within

Experiential hierarchy of effects an attitude is initially formed on the basis of a raw emotional reaction

Expert power influence over others due to specialized knowledge about a subject

Exposure an initial stage of perception during which some sensations come within range of consumers' sensory receptors

Extended family traditional family structure in which several generations live together

Extended self the external objects we consider a part of our self-identity

Extinction the process whereby a learned connection between a stimulus and response is eroded so that the response is no longer reinforced

Eyeball economy the argument that in today's media environment marketers compete for consumers' attention rather than their money

Fad a very short-lived fashion

Family branding an application of stimulus generalization when a product capitalizes on the reputation of its manufacturer's name

Family financial officer (FFO) the individual in the family who is in charge of making financial decisions

Family identity the definition of a household by family members that it presents to members and to those outside the family unit

Family life cycle (FLC) a classification scheme that segments consumers in terms of changes in income and family composition and the changes in demands placed on this income

Fantasy a self-induced shift in consciousness, often focusing on some unattainable or improbable goal; sometimes fantasy is a way of compensating for a lack of external stimulation or for dissatisfaction with the actual self

Fashion the process of social diffusion by which a new style is adopted by some group(s) of consumers

Fashion system those people and organizations involved in creating symbolic meanings and transferring these meanings to cultural goods

Fattism a preference for thin people and/or discrimination against overweight people

Fear appeals an attempt to change attitudes or behavior through the use of threats or by highlighting negative consequences of noncompliance with the request

Feature creep the tendency of manufacturers to add layers of complexity to products that make them harder to understand and use

Fertility rate a rate determined by the number of births per year per 1,000 women of childbearing age

Figure-ground principle the *Gestalt* principle whereby one part of a stimulus configuration dominates a situation whereas other aspects recede into the background

Fishbein model a widely-used perspective that measures several attributes to determine a person's overall attitude

Fixed-interval reinforcement after a specified time period has passed, the first response an organism makes elicits a reward

Fixed-ratio reinforcement reinforcement occurs only after a fixed number of responses

Flaming a violation of digital etiquette when a post is written in all capital letters

Flow exchanges of resources, information, or influence among members of an online social network

Flow state situation in which consumers are truly involved with a product, an ad, or a Web site

Focus groups small set of consumers tries out a new product while being observed by company personnel

Folksonomy an online posting system where users categorize entries themselves rather than relying upon a preestablished set of labels

FOMO "Fear of Missing Out"—a popular explanation for the addictive nature of social networks

Food desert a geographic area where residents are unable to obtain adequate food and other products to maintain a healthy existence

Foot-in-the-door technique approach based on the observation that a consumer is more likely to comply with a request if he or she has first agreed to comply with a smaller request

Fortress brands brands that consumers closely link to rituals; this makes it unlikely they will be replaced

Framing a concept in behavioral economics that the way a problem is posed to consumers (especially in terms of gains or losses) influences the decision they make

Freemium a free version of a product that's supported by a paid premium version; the idea is to encourage the maximum number of people to use the product and eventually convert a small fraction of them to paying customers

Frequency marketing a marketing technique that reinforces regular purchasers by giving them prizes with values that increase along with the amount purchased

Frugalistas fashion-conscious consumers who pride themselves on achieving style on a limited budget

Functional theory of attitudes states that attitudes exist *because* they serve some function for the person; consumers who expect that they will need to deal with similar situations at a future time will be more likely to start to form an attitude in anticipation

Functionally illiterate a person whose reading skills are not adequate to carry out everyday tasks

Game platform an online interface that allows users to engage in games and other social activities with members of a community

Gamification the process of injecting gaming elements into tasks that might otherwise be boring or routine

Gatekeeper the person who conducts the information search and controls the flow of information available to the group

Gemba Japanese term for the one true source of information

Gen X people born between 1965–1985

Gen Y people born between 1986–2002; also known as Echo Boomers and Millennials

Gender-bending product a traditionally sex-typed item adapted to the opposite gender

Gender convergence blurring of sex roles in modern society; men and women increasingly express similar attitudes about balancing home life and work

Gender identity the elements of self-concept that reflect sex roles

Gender socialization elements of culture, including advertising, that provide guidelines regarding "appropriate" sex role behavior for members

Genre in the context of social gaming, the method of play such as simulation, action, and role-playing

Geodemography techniques that combine consumer demographic information with geographic consumption patterns to permit precise targeting of consumers with specific characteristics

Geospatial platforms online applications that use smartphones to identify consumers' physical locations

Gestalt meaning derived from the totality of a set of stimuli, rather than from any individual stimulus

Gift-giving ritual the events involved in the selection, presentation, acceptance, and interpretation of a gift

Global consumer culture a culture in which people around the world are united through their common devotion to brand name consumer goods, movie stars, celebrities, and leisure activities

Globalized consumption ethic the global sharing of a material lifestyle including the valuing of well-known multinational brands that symbolize prosperity

Goal a consumer's desired end state

Golden triangle the portion of a Web site that a person's eyes naturally gravitate to first, which makes it more likely that search results located in that area will be seen

Goth subculture a lifestyle group inspired by vampire myths that illustrates an androgynous approach to gender identity

Green marketing a marketing strategy involving an emphasis on protecting the natural environment

Greenwashing inflated claims about a product's environmental benefits

Gripe sites Web sites that consumers create to share frustrations about bad experiences with companies

Grooming rituals sequences of behaviors that aid in the transition from the private self to the public self or back again

Guerrilla marketing promotional strategies that use unconventional locations and intensive word-of-mouth campaigns

Habitual decision-making choices made with little or no conscious effort

Habitus ways in which we classify experiences as a result of our socialization processes

Halal food and other products whose usage is permissible according to the laws of Islam

Halo effect a phenomenon that occurs when people react to other, similar stimuli in much the same way they respond to the original stimulus

Haptic touch-related sensations

Heavy users a name companies use to identify their customers who consume their products in large volumes

Hedonic adaptation belief that in order to maintain a fairly stable level of happiness we tend to become used to positive and negative events in our lives

Hedonic consumption the multisensory, fantasy, and emotional aspects of consumers' interactions with products

Helicopter moms overprotective mothers who "hover" around their kids and insert themselves into virtually all aspects of their lives

Heuristics the mental rules of thumb that lead to a speedy decision

Hierarchy of effects a fixed sequence of steps that occurs during attitude formation; this sequence varies depending on such factors as the consumer's level of involvement with the attitude object

Hierarchy of Needs (Maslow's) a framework that specifies different levels of motives that depends upon the consumer's personal situation

High-context culture group members tend to be close-knit and are likely to infer meanings that go beyond the spoken word

Highlighting effect the order in which consumers learn about brands determines the strength of association between these brands and their attributes

Hispanic people whose geographic and/or cultural origins are in Latin American countries

Hoarding unsystematic acquisition of objects (in contrast to collecting)

Hofstede Dimensions of National Culture a measurement system that scores a country in terms of its standing on six dimensions so that users can compare and contrast values

Home shopping party a selling format where a company representative makes a sales presentation to a group of people who gather at the home of a friend or acquaintance

Homogamy the tendency for individuals to marry others similar to themselves

Homophily the degree to which a pair of individuals is similar in terms of education, social status, and beliefs

Horizontal revolution a fundamental change in how consumers communicate via social media, whereby information doesn't just flow from big companies and governments; information flows *across* people as well

Host culture a new culture to which a person must acculturate

Household according to the U.S. Census Bureau, an occupied housing unit

Hybrid ad a marketing communication that explicitly references the context (e.g., TV show) in which it appears

Hyperreality the becoming real of what is initially simulation or "hype"

Icon a sign that resembles the product in some way

Id the Freudian system oriented toward immediate gratification

Ideal of beauty a model, or exemplar, of appearance valued by a culture

Ideal self a person's conception of how he or she would like to be

Identification the process of forming an attitude to conform to another person's or group's expectations

Identity marketing a practice whereby consumers are paid to alter some aspects of their selves to advertise for a branded product

Identity theft the unauthorized use of personal information

Ideology the mental characteristics of a people and the way they relate to their environment and social groups

Impression management our efforts to "manage" what others think of us by strategically choosing clothing and other cues that will put us in a good light

Impulse buying a process that occurs when the consumer experiences a sudden urge to purchase an item that he or she cannot resist

Incidental learning unintentional acquisition of knowledge

Index a sign that is connected to a product because they share some property

Inertia the process whereby purchase decisions are made out of habit because the consumer lacks the motivation to consider alternatives

Influence impressions brand-specific mentions on social media posts

Influence network a two-way dialogue between participants in a social network and opinion leaders

Influencer the person who tries to sway the outcome of the decision

Information cascades an online communication process where one piece of information triggers a sequence of interactions

Information power influence over others due to the possession of inside knowledge

Information processing perspective According to this view, people calmly and carefully integrate as much information as possible with what they already know about a product, painstakingly weigh the pluses and minuses of each alternative, and arrive at a satisfactory decision

Information search the process by which the consumer surveys his or her environment for appropriate data to make a reasonable decision

Initiator the person who brings up the idea or identifies a need

Innovation a product or style that is perceived as new by consumers

Innovators people who are always on the lookout for novel developments and will be the first to try a new offering

Instrumental conditioning also known as operant conditioning, occurs as the individual learns to perform behaviors that produce positive outcomes and avoid those that yield negative outcomes

Instrumental values goals endorsed because they are needed to achieve desired end states or terminal values

Intelligent agents software programs that learn from past user behavior in order to recommend new purchases

Interactions in a social media context, behavior-based ties between participants such as talking with each other, attending an event together, or working together

Interference one way that forgetting occurs; as additional information is learned, it displaces the earlier information

Internalization deep-seated attitudes become part of our value system

Interpretant the meaning derived from a sign or symbol

Interpretation the process whereby meanings are assigned to stimuli

Interpretivism as opposed to the dominant positivist perspective on consumer behavior, instead stresses the importance of symbolic, subjective experience and the idea that meaning is in the mind of the person rather than existing "out there" in the objective world

Invidious distinction the use of status symbols to inspire envy in others through display of wealth or power

Involvement the motivation to process product-related information

J.N.D. (just noticeable difference) the minimum difference between two stimuli that can be detected by a perceiver

Juggling lifestyle working mothers' attempts to compromise between conflicting cultural ideals of motherhood and professionalism

Kansei engineering a Japanese philosophy that translates customers' feelings into design elements

Kin-network system the rituals intended to maintain ties among family members, both immediate and extended

Knowledge function the process of forming an attitude to provide order, structure, or meaning

Knowledge structure organized system of concepts relating to brands, stores, and other concepts

Laddering a technique for uncovering consumers' associations between specific attributes and general values

Laggards consumers who are exceptionally slow to adopt innovations

Late adopters the majority of consumers who are moderately receptive to adopting innovations

Lateral cycling a process in which already-purchased objects are sold to others or exchanged for other items

Latitudes of acceptance and rejection in the social judgment theory of attitudes, the notion that people differ in terms of the information they will find acceptable or unacceptable; they form latitudes of acceptance and rejection around an attitude standard—ideas that fall within a latitude will be favorably received, but those falling outside of this zone will not

Learning a relatively permanent change in a behavior caused by experience

Legitimate power influence over others due to a position conferred by a society or organization

Leisure class wealthy people for whom work is a taboo

Licensing popular marketing strategy that pays for the right to link a product or service to the name of a well-known brand or designer

Lifestream the ongoing record of a person's digital life across online platforms

Lifestyle a pattern of consumption that reflects a person's choices of how to spend his or her time and money

Lifestyle marketing perspective strategy based on the recognition that people sort themselves into groups on the basis of the things they like to do, how they like to spend their leisure time, and how they choose to spend their disposable income

Lifestyle segmentation typologies Research projects that cluster a large group of consumers into a set of distinct lifestyle groups

List of Values (LOV) scale identifies consumer segments based on the values members endorse and relates each value to differences in consumption behaviors

Locational privacy the extent to which a person's activities and movements in the physical world are tracked by his or her devices such as smartphones

LOHAS an acronym for "lifestyles of health and sustainability"; a consumer segment that worries about the environment, wants products to be produced in a sustainable way, and spends money to advance what they see as their personal development and potential

Long tail states that we no longer need to rely solely on big hits (such as blockbuster movies or best-selling books) to find profits; instead, companies can also make money if they sell small amounts of items that only a few people want—if they sell enough different items

Long-term memory (LTM) the system that allows us to retain information for a long period of time

Looking-glass self the process of imagining the reaction of others toward oneself

Lovemark a passionate commitment to a brand

Low-context culture in contrast to high-context cultures that have strong oral traditions and that are more sensitive to nuance, low-context cultures are more literal

Low-involvement hierarchy of effects the process of attitude formation for products or services that carry little risk or self-identity

Lurkers passive members of an online community who do not contribute to interactions

M-commerce the practice of promoting and selling goods and services via wireless devices including cell phones, PDAs, and iPods

Market access the extent to which a consumer has the ability to find and purchase goods and services

Market maven a person who often serves as a source of information about marketplace activities

Market segmentation strategies targeting a brand only to specific groups of consumers who share well-defined and relevant characteristics

Masculinism study devoted to the male image and the cultural meanings of masculinity

Mass class a term analysts use to describe the millions of global consumers who now enjoy a level of purchasing power that's sufficient to let them afford many high-quality products

Mass Connectors highly influential members of social media networks

Mass customization the personalization of products and services for individual customers at a mass-production price

Materialism the importance consumers attach to worldly possessions

Maximizing solution the extensive cognitive decision strategies we use when we want to identify the best possible choice

Means-end chain model assumes that people link very specific product attributes (indirectly) to terminal values such as freedom or safety

Media democratization in a social media context, members of social communities, rather than traditional media publishers like magazines or newspaper companies, control the creation, delivery, and popularity of content

Media literacy a consumer's ability to access, analyze, evaluate, and communicate information

Media multiplexity in a social media context, when flows of communication go in many directions at any point in time and often on multiple platforms

Meetups occasion when members of an online network arrange to meet in a physical location

Megachurches very large churches that serve between 2,000 and 20,000 congregants

Megacity a metropolitan area with a total population of more than 10 million people

Membership reference group ordinary people whose consumption activities provide informational social influence

Meme theory a perspective that uses a medical metaphor to explain how an idea or product enters the consciousness of people over time, much like a virus

Memory a process of acquiring information and storing it over time so that it will be available when needed

Mental accounting principle that states that decisions are influenced by the way a problem is posed

Mental budgets consumers' preset expectations of how much they intend to spend on a shopping trip

Mere exposure phenomenon the tendency to like persons or things if we see them more often

Message involvement properties of the medium and message content that influence a person's degree of engagement with the message

Metaphor the use of an explicit comparison ("A" is "B") between a product and some other person, place, or thing

Milieu in the context of social gaming, the visual nature of the game such as science fiction, fantasy, horror, and retro

Millennials people born between 1986–2002; also known as Echo Boomers and Gen Y

Minimal group paradigm the common finding that even when people are arbitrarily assigned to a group they tend to favor those who are placed in the same group

Minipreneurs one-person businesses

Mixed emotions affect with positive and negative components

MMORPGs (massive multiplayer online role-playing games) online role-playing games that typically involve thousands of players

Mobile shopping apps smartphone applications that retailers provide to guide shoppers in stores and malls

Mode in the context of social gaming, the way players experience the game world

Modeling imitating the behavior of others

Modified rebuy in the context of the buyclass framework, a task that requires a modest amount of information search and evaluation, often focused on identifying the appropriate vendor

Momentum effect an accelerating diffusion of a message in social media due to the contributions of influential members

More a custom with a strong moral overtone

Motivation an internal state that activates goal-oriented behavior

Motivational research a qualitative research approach, based on psychoanalytic (Freudian) interpretations, with a heavy emphasis on unconscious motives for consumption

Multiattribute attitude models those models that assume a consumer's attitude (evaluation) of an attitude object depends on the beliefs he or she has about several or many attributes of the object;

the use of a multiattribute model implies that an attitude toward a product or brand can be predicted by identifying these specific beliefs and combining them to derive a measure of the consumer's overall attitude

Multiple-intelligence theory a perspective that argues for other types of intelligence, such as athletic prowess or musical ability, beyond the traditional math and verbal skills psychologists use to measure IQ

Multiple pathway anchoring and adjustment (MPAA) model a model that emphasizes multiple pathways to attitude formation

Multitasking processing information from more than one medium at a time

Myers-Briggs Type Indicator a widely-used personality test based upon the work of Carl Jung

Myth a story containing symbolic elements that expresses the shared emotions and ideals of a culture

Name-letter effect all things equal, we like others who share our names or even initials better than those who don't

Narrative product information in the form of a story

Narrative transportation the result of a highly involving message where people become immersed in the storyline

Natural user interface a philosophy of computer design that incorporates habitual human movements

Need a basic biological motive

Negative reinforcement the process whereby the environment weakens responses to stimuli so that inappropriate behavior is avoided

Negative word-of-mouth consumers passing on negative experiences relating to products or services to other potential customers to influence others' choices

Network effect each person who uses a product or service benefits as more people participate

Network units members of a social network

Neuromarketing a new technique that uses a brain scanning device called functional magnetic resonance imaging (fMRI) that tracks blood flow as people perform mental tasks; scientists know that specific regions of the brain light up in these scans to show increased blood flow when a person recognizes a face, hears a song, makes a decision, senses deception, and so on; therefore, they are now trying to harness this technology to measure consumers' reactions to movie trailers, choices about

automobiles, the appeal of a pretty face, and loyalty to specific brands

New task in the context of the buyclass framework, a task that requires a great degree of effort and information search

Nodes members of a social network connected to others via one or more shared relationships

Noncompensatory decision rules decision shortcuts a consumer makes when a product with a low standing on one attribute cannot make up for this position by being better on another attribute

Normative influence the process in which a reference group helps to set and enforce fundamental standards of conduct

Norms the informal rules that govern what is right or wrong

Nostalgia a bittersweet emotion; the past is viewed with sadness and longing; many "classic" products appeal to consumers' memories of their younger days

Nouveau riches affluent consumers whose relatively recent acquisition of income rather than ancestry or breeding accounts for their enhanced social mobility

Nuclear family a contemporary living arrangement composed of a married couple and their children

Nudge a subtle change in a person's environment that results in a change in behavior

Object in semiotic terms, the product that is the focus of a message

Objectification when we attribute sacred qualities to mundane items

Observability in the context of diffusion of innovations, the extent to which a new product is something that is easy for consumers to see in use in order to motivate others to try it

Observational learning the process in which people learn by watching the actions of others and noting the reinforcements they receive for their behaviors

One Percenter a label applied by the Occupy Wall Street Movement to people who earn the top 1 percent of income

Online gated communities digital social networks that selectively allow access to people who possess criteria such as wealth or physical attractiveness

Open rates the percentage of people who open an email message from a marketer

Opinion leader person who is knowledgeable about products and who frequently is able to influence others' attitudes or behaviors with regard to a product category

Organizational buyers people who purchase goods and services on behalf of companies for use in the process of manufacturing, distribution, or resale

Paradigm a widely accepted view or model of phenomena being studied; the perspective that regards people as rational information processors is currently the dominant paradigm, although this approach is now being challenged by a new wave of research that emphasizes the frequently subjective nature of consumer decision-making

Paradox of low involvement when we *don't* care as much about a product, the way it's presented (e.g., who endorses it or the visuals that go with it) increases in importance

Parental yielding the process that occurs when a parental decision-maker is influenced by a child's product request

Parody display deliberately avoiding status symbols; to seek status by mocking it

Pastiche mixture of images

Perceived age how old a person feels as compared to his or her true chronological age

Perceived risk belief that a product has potentially negative consequences

Perception the process by which stimuli are selected, organized, and interpreted

Perceptual defense the tendency for consumers to avoid processing stimuli that are threatening to them

Perceptual selection process by which people attend to only a small portion of the stimuli to which they are exposed

Perceptual vigilance the tendency for consumers to be more aware of stimuli that relate to their current needs

Permission marketing popular strategy based on the idea that a marketer will be much more successful in persuading consumers who have agreed to let them try

Personality a person's unique psychological makeup, which consistently influences the way the person responds to his or her environment

Personality traits identifiable characteristics that define a person

Persuasion an active attempt to change attitudes

Phantom Vibration Syndrome the tendency to habitually reach for your cell phone because you feel it vibrating, even if it is off or you are not even wearing it at the time

Phishing Internet scams where people receive fraudulent emails that ask them to supply account information

Pleasure principle the belief that behavior is guided by the desire to maximize pleasure and avoid pain

Plinking™ act of embedding a product or service link in a video

Plutonomy an economy that a small number of rich people control

Point-of-purchase (POP) stimuli the promotional materials that are deployed in stores or other outlets to influence consumers' decisions at the time products are purchased

Popular culture the music, movies, sports, books, celebrities, and other forms of entertainment consumed by the mass market

Pop-up stores temporary locations that allow a company to test new brands without a huge financial commitment

Positioning strategy an organization's use of elements in the marketing mix to influence the consumer's interpretation of a product's meaning vis-à-vis competitors

Positive reinforcement the process whereby rewards provided by the environment strengthen responses to stimuli and appropriate behavior is learned

Positivism a research perspective that relies on principles of the "scientific method" and assumes that a single reality exists; events in the world can be objectively measured; and the causes of behavior can be identified, manipulated, and predicted

Postpurchase evaluation the final stage of consumer decision-making when we experience the product or service we selected

Power users opinion leaders in online networks

Prediction market an approach based on the idea that groups of people with knowledge about an industry are jointly better predictors of the future than are any individuals

Presence the effect that people experience when they interact with a computer-mediated environment

Pretailer an e-commerce site that provides exclusive styles by prodding manufacturers to produce runway pieces they wouldn't otherwise make to sell in stores

Priming properties of a stimulus that evoke a schema that leads us to compare the stimulus to other similar ones we encountered in the past

Principle of cognitive consistency the belief that consumers value harmony among their thoughts, feelings, and behaviors and that they are motivated to maintain uniformity among these elements

Principle of least interest the person who is least committed to staying in a relationship has the most power

Principle of similarity the *Gestalt* principle that describes how consumers tend to

group objects that share similar physical characteristics

PRIZM (Potential Rating Index by Zip Market) clustering technique that classifies every zip code in the United States into one of 66 categories, ranging from the most affluent "Blue-Blood Estates" to the least well off "Public Assistance," developed by Claritas, Inc.

Problem recognition the process that occurs whenever the consumer sees a significant difference between his or her current state of affairs and some desired or ideal state; this recognition initiates the decision-making process

Product complementarity the view that products in different functional categories have symbolic meanings that are related to one another

Product disposal choices people make regarding how to get rid of items once they no longer are of value to them

Product involvement a consumer's level of interest in a particular item

Product line extension related products to an established brand

Product placement the process of obtaining exposure for a product by arranging for it to be inserted into a movie, television show, or some other medium

Productivity orientation a continual striving to use time constructively

Profane consumption the process of consuming objects and events that are ordinary or of the everyday world

Progressive learning model the perspective that people gradually learn a new culture as they increasingly come in contact with it; consumers assimilate into a new culture, mixing practices from their old and new environments to create a hybrid culture

Propinquity as physical distance between people decreases and opportunities for interaction increase, they are more likely to form relationships

Prospect theory a descriptive model of how people make choices

Provenance the origin of a product and a preference for "authentic" items

Psychographics the use of psychological, sociological, and anthropological factors to construct market segments

Psychological time a person's subjective evaluation of the passage of time, which may not correspond very closely to the actual time elapsed

Psychophysics the science that focuses on how the physical environment is integrated into the consumer's subjective experience

Punishment the learning that occurs when a response is followed by unpleasant events

Purchase momentum initial impulses to buy in order to satisfy our needs increase the likelihood that we will buy even more

Pure play retailer a merchant that conducts transactions only online and does not maintain a physical store

Queuing theory the mathematical study of waiting lines

Reality engineering the process whereby elements of popular culture are appropriated by marketers and become integrated into marketing strategies

Reality principle principle that the ego seeks ways that will be acceptable to society to gratify the id

Real-time bidding an electronic trading system that sells ad space on the Web pages people click on at the very moment they visit them

Recall the process of retrieving information from memory; in advertising research, the extent to which consumers can remember a marketing message without being exposed to it during the study

Reciprocity norm a culturally learned obligation to return the gesture of a gift with one of equal value

Recognition in advertising research, the extent to which consumers say they are familiar with an ad the researcher shows them

Recommerce the practice of trading or reselling used possessions in the underground economy rather than purchasing new items from retailers

Red market the global market for body parts

Reference group an actual or imaginary individual or group that has a significant effect on an individual's evaluations, aspirations, or behavior

Referent power influence over others because they are motivated to imitate or affiliate with a person or group

Refutational arguments calling attention to a product's negative attributes as a persuasive strategy where a negative issue is raised and then dismissed; this approach can increase source credibility

Relationship marketing the strategic perspective that stresses the long-term, human side of buyer–seller interactions

Relative advantage in the context of diffusion of innovations, the extent to which a new product or service is an improvement over alternatives that are already available in the market

Repetition multiple exposures to a stimulus

Reputation economy a reward system based on recognition of one's expertise by others who read online product reviews

Resonance a literary device, frequently used in advertising, that uses a play on words (a double meaning) to communicate a product benefit

Response bias a form of contamination in survey research in which some factor, such as the desire to make a good impression on the experimenter, leads respondents to modify their true answers

Restricted codes the ways of expressing and interpreting meanings that focus on the content of objects, which tend to be used by the working class

Retail theming strategy where stores create imaginative environments that transport shoppers to fantasy worlds or provide other kinds of stimulation

Retrieval the process whereby desired information is recovered from long-term memory

Retro brand an updated version of a brand from a prior historical period

Reverse innovation the process whereby a product is created initially to meet the needs of developing nations and then is adapted elsewhere

Reward power a person or group with the means to provide positive reinforcement

Rich media elements of an online ad that employ movement to gain attention

Rites of passage sacred times marked by a change in social status

Ritual a set of multiple, symbolic behaviors that occur in a fixed sequence and that tend to be repeated periodically

Ritual artifacts items (consumer goods) used in the performance of rituals

Role theory the perspective that much of consumer behavior resembles actions in a play

Sacralization a process that occurs when ordinary objects, events, or people take on sacred meaning to a culture or to specific groups within a culture

Sacred consumption the process of consuming objects and events that are set apart from normal life and treated with some degree of respect or awe

Salience the prominence of a brand in memory

Sandwich Generation a description of middle-aged people who must care for both children and parents simultaneously

Satisficing solution a decision strategy that aims to yield an adequate solution (rather than the best solution) in order

to reduce the costs of the decision-making process

Schema an organized collection of beliefs and feelings represented in a cognitive category

Script a learned schema containing a sequence of events an individual expects to occur

Self-concept the beliefs a person holds about his or her own attributes and how he or she evaluates these qualities

Self-esteem the positivity of a person's self-concept

Self-image congruence models research that suggests we choose products when their attributes match some aspect of the self

Self-perception theory an alternative (to cognitive dissonance) explanation of dissonance effects; it assumes that people use observations of their own behavior to infer their attitudes toward some object

Self-regulation a person's deliberate efforts to change or maintain his actions over time

Semiotics a field of study that examines the correspondence between signs and symbols and the meaning or meanings they convey

Senior market consumers over the age of 50 who control a large amount of discretionary income

Sensation the immediate response of sensory receptors (eyes, ears, nose, mouth, fingers) to such basic stimuli as light, color, sound, odors, and textures

Sensory marketing marketing strategies that focus on the impact of sensations on our product experiences

Sensory memory the temporary storage of information received from the senses

Sensory overload a condition where consumers are exposed to far more information than they can process

Sensory signature a distinctive sound or aroma that an organization links to its brand identity

Sensory threshold the point at which a stimulus is strong enough to make a conscious impact on a person's awareness

Sentiment analysis a process (sometimes also called *opinion mining*) that scours the social media universe to collect and analyze the words people use when they describe a specific product or company

Serial wardrobers shoppers who buy an outfit, wear it once, and return it

Sex roles a culture's expectations about how members of the male or female gender should act, dress, or speak

Sexting the growing trend of young people posting sexually suggestive photos of themselves online

Sex-typed products products that reflect stereotypical masculine or feminine attributes

Sex-typed traits characteristics that are stereotypically associated with one gender or the other

Shaping the learning of a desired behavior over time by rewarding intermediate actions until the final result is obtained

Sharing sites e-commerce sites that allow users to share, exchange, and rent goods in a local setting

Sheconomy developing countries where analysts predict women will be a dominant force in the local economy

Shopping orientation a consumer's general attitudes and motivations regarding the act of shopping

Short-term memory (STM) the mental system that allows us to retain information for a short period of time

Showrooming the process lamented by traditional retailers whereby consumers shop their stores to obtain product information and then purchase the chosen product online at a lower price

Shrinkage the loss of money or inventory from shoplifting and/or employee theft

Sign the sensory imagery that represents the intended meanings of the object

Simile comparing two objects that share a similar property

Situational involvement the extent to which a shopper is engaged with a store, Web site, or a location where people consume a product or service

Sleeper effect the process whereby differences in attitude change between positive and negative sources seem to diminish over time

Social capital organizational affiliations and experiences that provide access to desirable social networks

Social class the overall rank of people in a society; people who are grouped within the same social class are approximately equal in terms of their income, occupations, and lifestyles

Social comparison the basic human tendency to compare ourselves to others

Social footprint the record a consumer leaves after he or she occupies a specific digital space such as Facebook

Social game a multi-player, competitive, goal-oriented activity with defined rules of engagement and online connectivity among a community of players

Social graphs social networks; relationships among members of online communities

Social identity the part of the self that our group memberships define

Social identity theory a perspective that argues each of us has several "selves" that relate to groups. These linkages are so important that we think of ourselves not just as "I," but also as "we"

Social judgment theory the perspective that people assimilate new information about attitude objects in light of what they already know or feel; the initial attitude acts as a frame of reference, and new information is categorized in terms of this standard

Social loafing the tendency for people not to devote as much to a task when their contribution is part of a larger group effort

Social marketing the promotion of causes and ideas (social products), such as energy conservation, charities, and population control

Social media the set of technologies that enable users to create content and share it with a large number of others

Social media addiction dependency on interaction with social networking platforms to the extent that signs of withdrawal appear if the person is unable to connect

Social mobility the movement of individuals from one social class to another

Social network a group of people who connect with one another online due to some shared interest or affiliation

Social object theory proposes that social networks will be more powerful communities if there is a way to activate relationships among people and objects within them

Social power the capacity of one person to alter the actions or outcome of another

Social shopping an emerging form of e-commerce that allows an online shopper to simulate the experience of shopping in a brick-and-mortar store

Social stratification the process in a social system by which scarce and valuable resources are distributed unequally to status positions that become more or less permanently ranked in terms of the share of valuable resources each receives

Social structure the way members of a culture maintain an orderly social life

Sociometric methods the techniques for measuring group dynamics that involve tracing communication patterns in and among groups

Sock puppeting a company executive or other biased source poses as someone else to tout his organization in social media

Sound symbolism the process by which the way a word sounds influences our assumptions about what it describes and attributes such as size

Source attractiveness the dimensions of a communicator that increase his or her persuasiveness; these include expertise and attractiveness

Source credibility a communication source's perceived expertise, objectivity, or trustworthiness

Spacing effect the tendency to recall printed material to a greater extent when the advertiser repeats the target item periodically rather than presenting it over and over at the same time

Spectacles a marketing message that takes the form of a public performance

Spendthrifts consumers who derive pleasure from large-scale purchasing

Spiritual-therapeutic model organizations that encourage behavioral changes such as weight loss that are loosely based on religious principles

Spokescharacters the use of animated characters or fictional mascots as product representatives

Spontaneous recovery ability of a stimulus to evoke a weakened response even years after the person initially perceived it

Spreading activation meanings in memory are activated indirectly; as a node is activated, other nodes linked to it are also activated so that meanings spread across the network

Stage of cognitive development the ability to comprehend concepts of increasing complexity as a person matures

Standard learning hierarchy the traditional process of attitude formation that starts with the formation of beliefs about an attitude object

State-dependent retrieval people are better able to access information if their internal state is the same at the time of recall as when they learned the information

Status crystallization the extent to which different indicators of a person's status (income, ethnicity, occupation) are consistent with one another

Status hierarchy a ranking of social desirability in terms of consumers' access to resources such as money, education, and luxury goods

Status signaling the extent to which a brand employs prominent signs of status such as a well-known logo on merchandise

Status symbols products whose primary function is to communicate one's social standing to others

Stimulus discrimination the process that occurs when behaviors caused by two stimuli are different, as when consumers learn to differentiate a brand from its competitors

Stimulus generalization the process that happens when the behavior caused by a reaction to one stimulus occurs in the presence of other, similar stimuli

Storage the process that occurs when knowledge in long-term memory is integrated with what is already in memory and "warehoused" until needed

Store image a store's "personality," composed of such attributes as location, merchandise suitability, and the knowledge and congeniality of the sales staff

Straight rebuy in the context of the buyclass framework, the type of buying decision that is virtually automatic and requires little deliberation

Subculture a group whose members share beliefs and common experiences that set them apart from other members of a culture

Subjective norm (SN) an additional component to the multiattribute attitude model that accounts for the effects of what we believe other people think we should do

Subliminal perception the processing of stimuli presented below the level of the consumer's awareness

Superego the system that internalizes society's rules and that works to prevent the id from seeking selfish gratification

Surrogate consumer a professional who is retained to evaluate and/or make purchases on behalf of a consumer

Sustainability An emphasis on creating and maintaining the conditions under which humans and nature can exist in productive harmony, that permit fulfilling the social, economic and other requirements of present and future generations

Symbol a sign that is related to a product through either conventional or agreed-on associations

Symbolic interactionism a sociological approach stressing that relationships with other people play a large part in forming the self; people live in a symbolic environment, and the meaning attached to any situation or object is determined by a person's interpretation of these symbols

Symbolic self-completion theory the perspective that people who have an incomplete self-definition in some context will compensate by acquiring symbols associated with a desired social identity

Synchronous interactions a conversation that requires participants to respond in real-time

Syncretic decision purchase decision that is made jointly by both spouses

Synoptic ideal a model of spousal decision-making in which the husband and wife take a common view and act as joint decision-makers, assigning each other well-defined roles and making mutually beneficial decisions to maximize the couple's joint utility

Taste culture a group of consumers who share aesthetic and intellectual preferences

Terminal values end states desired by members of a culture

Theory of cognitive dissonance theory based on the premise that a state of tension is created when beliefs or behaviors conflict with one another; people are motivated to reduce this inconsistency (or dissonance) and thus eliminate unpleasant tension

Theory of reasoned action an updated version of the Fishbein multiattribute attitude theory that considers factors such as social pressure and A_{act} (the attitude toward the act of buying a product), rather than simply attitudes toward the product itself

Theory of trying states that the criterion of behavior in the reasoned action model of attitude measurement should be replaced with *trying* to reach a goal

Tie strength the nature and potency of the bond between members of a social network

Ties connections between members of a social network

Tightwads consumers who experience emotional pain when they make purchases

Time poverty a feeling of having less time available than is required to meet the demands of everyday living

Timestyle an individual's priorities regarding how he or she spends time as influenced by personal and cultural factors

Tipping point moment of critical mass

Torn self a condition where immigrants struggle to reconcile their native identities with their new cultures

Total quality management (TQM) management and engineering procedures aimed at reducing errors and increasing quality; based on Japanese practices

Trade dress color combinations that become strongly associated with a corporation

Transactional advertising an advertising message in a social game that transactional advertising rewards players if they respond to a request

Transformative Consumer Research (TCR) promotes research projects that include the goal of helping people or bringing about social change

Transitional economies a country that is adapting from a controlled, centralized economy to a free-market system

Transmedia storytelling the use of a mix of social media platforms to create a plot that involves consumers who try to solve puzzles or mysteries in the narrative

Trialability in the context of diffusion of innovations, the extent to which a new product or service can be sampled prior to adoption

Tribal marketing strategy linking a product's identity to an activity-based "tribe" such as basketball players

Trickle-down theory the perspective that fashions spread as the result of status symbols associated with the upper classes "trickling down" to other social classes as these consumers try to emulate those with greater status

Triple bottom-line orientation business strategies that strive to maximize financial, social, and environmental return

Tweens a marketing term used to describe children aged 8 to 14

Two-factor theory the perspective that two separate psychological processes are operating when a person is repeatedly exposed to an ad: repetition increases familiarity and thus reduces uncertainty about the product, but over time boredom increases with each exposure, and at some point the amount of boredom incurred begins to exceed the amount of uncertainty reduced, resulting in wear-out

Two-step flow model of influence proposes that a small group of *influencers* disseminate information since they can modify the opinions of a large number of other people

Unconditioned stimulus (UCS) a stimulus that is naturally capable of causing a response

Underground economy secondary markets (such as flea markets) where transactions are not officially recorded

Unipolar emotions emotional reactions that are either wholly positive or wholly negative

Unplanned buying when a shopper buys merchandise she did not intend to purchase, often because she recognizes a new need while in the store

User the person who actually consumes a product or service

User-generated content consumers voice their opinions about products, brands, and companies on blogs, podcasts, and social networking sites such as Facebook and Twitter, and film their own commercials that they post on sites such as YouTube

Utilitarian function states that we develop some attitudes toward products simply because they provide pleasure or pain

Value a belief that some condition is preferable to its opposite

Value-expressive function states each individual develops attitudes toward products because of what they say about him or her as a person

Value system a culture's ranking of the relative importance of values

Values and Lifestyles System (VALS2™) a psychographic segmentation system

Variable-interval reinforcement the time that must pass before an organism's response is reinforced varies based on some average

Variable-ratio reinforcement method in which you get reinforced after a certain number of responses, but you don't know how many responses are required

Variety seeking the desire to choose new alternatives over more familiar ones

Viral marketing the strategy of getting customers to sell a product on behalf of the company that creates it

Virtual goods digital items that people buy and sell online

Virtual identity the appearance and personality a person takes on as an avatar in a computer-mediated environment like Second Life

Virtual worlds immersive 3-D virtual environments such as Second Life

Voluntarily childless women of childbearing age who consciously decide not to have children

Von Restorff effect techniques like distinctive packaging that increase the novelty of a stimulus and also improve recall

Want the particular form of consumption chosen to satisfy a need

Warming process of transforming new objects and places into those that feel cozy, hospitable, and authentic

Web 2.0 the current version of the Internet as a social, interactive medium from its original roots as a form of one-way transmission from producers to consumers

Weber's Law the principle that the stronger the initial stimulus, the greater its change must be for it to be noticed

Wisdom of crowds a perspective that argues that, under the right circumstances, groups are smarter than the smartest people in them; implies that large numbers of consumers can predict successful products

Word-of-mouth (WOM) product information transmitted by individual consumers on an informal basis

Word–phrase dictionary in sentiment analysis, a library that codes data so that the program can scan the text to identify whether the words in the dictionary appear

Worldview a perspective on social norms and behaviors that tends to differ among social classes

Page numbers with "*n*" refer to endnotes,
Page numbers followed by "*f*" indicate figure
Page numbers followed by "*t*" indicate table

Name

Aaker, David A., 97n80
Aaker, Jennifer, 57n24, 98n107, 146n20, 254, 268n112, 319n88, 319n97, 319n101, 364n9, 479n78
Abelson, R. P., 365n33
Abraham, Chris, 367n118
Abraham, Tamara, 470
Achenreiner, Gwen Bachmann, 267n60
Adamy, Janet, 188n41
Adaval, Rashmi, 148n71, 267n75
Addis, Michela, 560n29
Adele, 29
Adkins, Natalie Ross, 189n67, 189n68
Adler, G., 318n72
Adler, Keith, 226n35
Adler, Rick, 474n151
Aerosmith, 314
Aggarwal, Pankaj, 227n74
Aggarwal, Praveen, 529, 560n27
Agrawal, Jagdish, 366n61
Aguirre, B. E., 562n117
Ahlering, R. F., 422n100
Aholt, Andreas, 97n58
Ahrensa, Anthony H., 320n153
Ahuvia, Aaron, 317n4
Aikman, Tony, 132
Ajzen, Icek, 365n31
Aksoy, Lerzan, 188n34
Alabaster, Jay, 146n11
Alba, Joseph W., 96n16, 97n62, 266n26, 267n69, 268n101, 268n106, 268n109
Albanes, P., 319n84
Albanese, Paul J., 321n161
Al-Breene, Bob, 190n102
Alden, Dana L., 149n106, 520n58
Alger, Horatio, 488
Allen, Chris T., 265n11, 266n38
Allen, MIchael W., 226n46
Allen, Woody, 51
Alleyne, Richard, 424n161
Allsopp, J. F., 319n84
Allvine, Fred C., 561n41
Allyson, June, 462
Alm, Richard, 520n61
Alpert, Frank, 98n99, 226n21
Alpert, Lewis, 521n133
Alpert, Mark I., 366n94, 367n98
Alsop, Ronald, 97n72
Alstead, Christian, 284*t*, 287*f*
Alt, Matt, 471n22
Altman, Irwin, 319n113
Altman, Josh, 115
Alwitt, Linda F., 365n33
Amaldoss, Wilfred, 519n44
Amatriain, Xavier, 95
Ames, B. Charles, 423n120
Amis, John, 150n176
Amjad, Steven, 189n84
Anand, Punam, 149n113, 364n10

Anderson, B. B., 367n104
Anderson, Chris, 97n54, 561n69
Anderson, Erin, 423n124
Anderson, Helen H., 367n102
Anderson, Laurel, 147n42, 474n129
Anderson, Paul, 147n25
Anderson, Ronald D., 190n126
Andreasen, Alan R., 188n32, 188n48
Andrews, Edmund L., 424n177
Andrews, J. Craig, 366n67
Andrus, Bruce W., 317n30
Andruss, Paula Lyon, 267n61
Anirban, Mukhopadhyay, 421n59
Aniston, Jennifer, 347
Ante, Spencer E., 190n113, 366n87
Antonidies, Trinske, 475n173
Apperley, Thomas, 562n84, 562n86
Appleton-Knapp, S. L., 268n93
Aradhna, Krishna, 226n25
Areni, Charles S., 421n51
Ariely, Dan, 95n38, 98n93
Armstrong, Gary, 267n62
Armstrong, Katrina, 320n124
Arndorfer, James B., 266n19
Arndt, Johan, 521n134, 560n4, 560n12
Arnold, Stephen J., 471n19
Arnould, Eric J., 57n51, 149n107, 150n160, 188n12, 422n90, 423n132, 472n57, 562n91
Aronoff, J., 318n62
Arora, Neeraj, 96n18
Arsel, Zeynep, 319n96
Ashford, Susan J., 317n30
Ashman, Rachel, 544*t*
Ashmore, Richard D., 320n138
Aspan, Maria, 474n138
Aspara, Jaakko, 423n121
Assael, Henry, 521n129
Assmus, Gert, 365n43
Atalay, A. Selin, 227n58
Atkinson, Claire, 148n64
Atkinson, R. C., 267n68
Attaway, Jill S., 560n20
Aylesworth, Andrew B., 226n52, 364n9
Azhari, A. C., 366n64

Baar, Aaron, 267n90, 364n5, 473n84, 474n132, 474n162
Babin, Barry J., 421n26, 422n68, 560n20
Bacon, Kevin, 534
Baertlein, Lisa, 190n133
Bagozzi, Richard P., 148n95, 189n88, 269n132, 318n70, 365n41, 421n66
Bahn, Kenneth D., 267n56
Bahr, Howard M., 149n111
Bailay, Rasul, 150n157
Bakalar, Nicholas, 227n70
Baker, Julie, 420n16
Baker, Stacy Menzel, 188n14, 268n124, 473n110
Baker, Stephen, 365n43, 365n47
Baker, William E., 232
Bales, Robert F., 424n173
Ball, A. Dwayne, 319n112
Ball, Deborah, 146n15, 148n87, 321n170

Ball, Jeffrey, 187n5
Bamossy, Gary, 147n26, 226n20, 420n3, 472n44, 475n173
Bandura, Albert, 266n41
Banfield, Jillian C., 365n18
Banner, Lois W., 320n146
Bannon, Lisa, 320n150, 471n17, 475n171
Barak, Benny, 474n157
Baranauckas, Carla, 423n147
Barbaro, Michael, 266n27
Barbosa, David, 57n40
Barboza, David, 150n168
Bardzell, Jeffrey, 148n69
Bardzell, Shaowen, 148n69
Bargh, J. A., 98n88
Barnes, Brooks, 147n48, 150n168, 365n47, 473n112, 520n87
Baron, Alma S., 424n174
Baron, Robert A., 98n98, 265n2, 364n1
Barone, Michael J., 364n9
Barron, Kelly, 420n3
Barrow, Karen, 189n63
Barth, E., 520n83
Barth, Frederik, 472n44
Barthel, Diane, 149n97
Bartlett, Frederic, 528
Barton, Roger, 227n62
Basil, Debra Z., 365n27
Basilico, Justin, 95
Basu, Kunal, 97n62, 421n22, 421n24, 421n25
Batra, Rajeev, 227n61, 421n25
Baum, Stephanie, 318n58
Baumeister, R. F., 267n75
Baumeister, Roy F., 317n6, 519n9
Baumgardner, Michael H., 268n100, 366n66
Baumgarten, Steven A., 561n41
Baumgartner, Hans, 96n34, 319n84
Beaglehole, Ernest, 317n35
Bearak, Barry, 149n116
Bearden, William O., 97n81, 98n94, 423n113, 423n115
Beasley, Deena, 190n112
Beatty, Sharon E., 98n84, 147n24, 364n11, 424n157
Beck, Glenn, 163
Becker, B. W., 147n22
Becker, Howard S., 147n37, 520n90
Beckham, David, 101, 494
Beckham, Victoria, 494
Beeghley, Leonard, 519n32, 520n77
Beethoven, 112
Beirne, Mike, 96n18
Belch, George E., 366n91, 367n99, 367n101, 367n109
Belch, Michael A., 367n99, 367n101, 367n109
Belk, Russell W., 57n28, 57n52, 149n98, 149n101, 149n107, 149n115, 149n122, 149n135, 149n137, 150n145, 150n155, 188n12, 188n22, 188n23, 189n80, 268n121, 268n126, 317n39, 317n40, 423n146, 472n38, 521n117, 521n129, 561n41
Bell, Martin, 520n81
Bell, Stephen, 317n33, 520n92
Bellenger, Danny N., 319n107
Bellizzi, Joseph A., 226n10, 421n48, 471n23
Bellman, Eric, 471n26

Belluck, Pam, 226n14
Bem, Daryl J., 365n18
Bem, Sandra L., 472n37
Bender, Thomas, 226n13
Benet-Martinez, Veronica, 146n20
Bengtsson, Anders, 321n182
Bennett, Jessica, 474n120
Bennett-Russell, Rebekah, 292t, 294t
Bercovici, Jeff, 366n80
Berenson, Alex, 425n190
Bergadaa, Michelle M., 420n12
Berger, Arthur A., 147n43, 227n81
Berger, D. G., 147n35
Berger, Ida E., 365n33
Berger, Jonah, 97n59, 422n101, 521n95
Bergey, Paul K., 561n70
Bergiel, J. Blaise, 266n29
Bergstein, Brian, 366n67
Berkowitz, Leonard, 317n33, 365n18
Bernard, Andy, 347
Berning, Carol K., 189n83
Bernthal, Matthew J., 519n8
Berry, Jon, 561n76
Beruchasvili, Mariam, 473n95
Berzon, Alexandra, 190n113
Best, Arthur, 188n32
Bettelheim, Bruno, 149n108
Bettencourt, Lance A., 318n78
Bettman, James R., 95n1, 96n16, 96n47,
    97n55, 97n76, 190n95, 245n69,
    269n134, 422n70, 422n94
Betts, Dickey, 390
Beverland, Michael, 146n19
Beyoncé, 111, 327
Bhalla, Gurav, 521n140
Bhatla, Sunil, 420n22
Bhattacharjee, Amit, 320n123
Bhattacharya, C. B., 472n60
Bieber, Justin, 308, 343, 531
Biggs, Ronald, 346
Bijmolt, Tammo H. A., 268n95
Bilton, Nick, 189n61, 422n96
bin Laden, Osama, 250
Biocca, Frank A., 317n12
Birdwell, A. L. E., 319n105
Birrell, Susan, 149n131
Birthall, Jonathan, 473n83
Bitner, Mary Jo, 422n67
Bittar, Christine, 317n10
Bizer, George Y., 318n77
Bjork, R. A., 268n93
Blair, Elizabeth M., 147n30
Blair, Margaret Henderson, 268n102
Blakeslee, Sandra, 97n48, 97n58, 99n119
Blanchett, Cate, 523
Blanco, Anthony, 57n10
Blink: The Power of Thinking Without Thinking
    (Gladwell), 81
Bloch, Peter H., 96n15, 96n41, 321n179, 420n22
Block, Lauren G., 130, 267n70, 367n122
Bloom, Paul N., 149n119, 188n47, 320n122,
    423n119
Bogart, Humphrey, 114
Boles, James S., 422n68
Bolton, Lisa E., 300, 320n122, 320n123, 320n124
Bone, Paula Fitzgerald, 226n28, 560n21
Bono, 489
Bonsu, Samuel K., 98n107, 149n115
Booms, Bernard H., 422n67
Boote, Alfred S., 521n137
Borden, R., 423n108
Borden, Richard J., 365n25
Borghini, Stefania, 147n42, 423n140
Bornstein, Robert F., 366n92
Bosmans, Anick, 96n35

Bosworth, Kate, 27
Botticelli, Sandro, 306
Boulding, William, 98n82
Bourdieu, Pierre, 499–500, 520n94
Boush, David M., 560n23
Boutilier, Robert, 423n130, 424n172
Bow, Clara, 305
Bower, Amanda B., 320n137
Bowler, Mary, 519n2
Bowling, Clark, 269n143
Boyd, E. B., 318n75
Bradford, Tonya Williams, 149n106
Bradsher, Keith, 150n167
Brady, Michael K., 188n33
Brady, Shirley, 319n93
Branch, John, 149n125
Branch, Shelly, 425n184
Branson, Richard, 434–435, 487, 493
Brasel, S. Adam, 57n24, 189n84
Braun-LaTour, Kathryn A., 267n73
Bray, Hiawatha, 474n148
Brazil, Jeff, 474n155
Breene, R. Timothy S., 520n89
Brees, Drew, 345
Brenner, L., 266n37
Brenner, Walter, 365n44
Breslau, Karen, 147n40
Brill, Louis M., 225
Brimley, Wilford, 462
Bristol, Terry, 423n109, 474n130
Britt, Bruce, 473n87
Britt, Robert Roy, 189n66
Brody, Jane E., 321n177
Broniarczyk, Susan M., 95n3, 422n80
Brook, Stephen, 56
Brooks, John, 521n107, 521n112
Brosius, Hans-Bernd, 268n118
Brown, Barbar B., 320n120
Brown, Dan, 473n93
Brown, Gene, 367n110
Brown, Jacqueline Johnson, 561n55
Brown, James R., 423n120
Brown, Patricia Leigh, 473n101
Brown, Robbie, 188n36
Brown, Roger, 520n56
Brown, Stephen, 269n141, 562n116
Brown, Warren, 4472n56
Browne, Beverly A., 471n16
Browne, Ray B., 149n114
Brownlie, Douglas, 57n39
Bruce, Grady D., 422n95, 422n97
Brucks, Merrie, 96n16, 267n62
Bruell, Alexandra, 98n106
Brumbaugh, Anne, 473n78
Bruner, Gordon C., 421n23, 550
Bruner, Gordon C., II, 96n40, 562n97
Bruner, J., 267n75
Bruni, Frank, 423n142
Bryant, Adam, 98n103, 226n9
Bryant, Lena, 306
Bryant, Paul "Bear," 112
Brynjolfsson, Erik, 57n20
Bryson, Bill, 150n162
Buck, Stephanie, 318n81, 561n73
Buffett, Jimmy, 518
Buffett, Warren, 485
Bulik, Beth Snyder, 98n94, 267n80, 318n79,
    474n139
Bunn, Austin, 147n50
Burg, Emily, 189n71, 561n59
Burke, Marian, 366n91
Burke, Raymond R., 268n96
Burkitt, Laurie, 265n3
Burks, Arthur W., 227n81
Burnett, Leo, 190n128

Burnkrant, Robert E., 422n73
Burns, Alvin C., 149n120
Burns, Neal M., 265, 562n87
Burris, Joseph, 226n54
Burros, Marian, 266n50
Burroughs, J., 319n109, 320n116
Burroughs, James E., 188n13, 188n15, 188n19
Burroughs, W. Jeffrey, 420n22
Burton, G., 473n99
Burton, Scot, 97n81, 317n34, 366n79
Busch, Paul S., 422n70
Bush, Michael, 519n17
Bush, Ronald F., 97n67, 149n122
Bush, Victoria D., 319n94
Buss, Arnold W., 317n31
Buss, W. Christian, 424n174
Buttle, Heather, 366n63
Byranski, Gleb, 520n88
Byrne, Donn, 364n1
Byron, Ellen, 226n49

Caballero, Marjorie, 421n66
Cacioppo, John T., 368n132, 368n135
Cadei, Emily, 226n12
Caffee, Shannon L., 149n113
Calder, Bobby, 188n47, 365n19, 560n20
Caldwell, Marylouise, 148n90, 471n28
Camargo, Eduardo G., 150n161
Camerer, Colin, 149n106
Campbell, Joseph, 148n77
Campbell, Robert, 521n109
Campomar, Marcos Cortez, 147n25
Canedy, Dana, 472n67
Cantril, Hadley, 227n76
Caplow, Theodore, 149n111
Caravajal, Doreen, 321n167
Carey, Benedict, 227n69, 227n78, 319n106, 420n6
Carlson, B., 319n85
Carlson, Les, 266n49
Carlton, Jim, 424n147
Carney, Scott, 190n117
Carr, Austin, 268n125
Carr, David, 146n7
Carrigan, Marylyn, 474n142
Carroll, Christopher D., 519n2
Carson, Rachel, 163
Carter, D. Bruce, 475n172
Carvajal, Doreen, 471n30
Casey, Marianne, 188n47
Cashdan, Elizabeth, 320n133
Castellano, Nadine N., 474n150
Cave, Damien, 562n88
Cayla, Julien, 473n91
Celsi, Richard, 147n25
Celsi, Richard L., 95n8
Celuch, Kevin G., 420n19
Cerio, Gregory, 150n163
Cha, Taihoon, 560n27
Chadwick, Bruce A., 149n111
Chagall, Marc, 112
Chaiken, Shelly, 366n57, 366n71
Chakravarti, Dipankar, 267n84
Chandler, Clay, 520n63
Chandrashekaran, Murali, 268n91
Chang, Hannah H., 98n111
Chaplin, Charlie, 51
Chaplin, Lan Nguyen, 188n16, 320n114, 521n130
Charles, Ray, 509
Charry, Tamar, 422n79
Chartrand, Tanya, L., 98n88, 98n89
Chatterjee, Subimal, 99n120
Chattopadhyay, Amitava, 97n64, 226n10,
    267n69, 268n101, 268n109
Chebat, Jean-Charles, 421n49
Chenevey, Steve, 559

Chestnut, Robert, 96n19
Chi, Maxwell, 57n55
Childers, T. L., 226n40
Childers, Terry L., 189n58, 190n124, 268n110,
    268n116, 366n85, 561n49
Cho, Angela, 148n71
Chozick, Amy, 320n144, 560n28
Chu, Wujin, 423n124
Chung, Mabel, 267n58
Chura, Hillary, 471n24, 474n153
Churchill, Gilbert A., Jr., 97n82, 269n136,
    422n68
Cialdini, Robert B., 266n37, 365n25, 365n34,
    365n42, 421n65
Cimino, Richard, 473n102
Claiborne, C. B., 319n102, 319n110
Clancy, Kevin J., 96n24
Clark, Gary L., 188n31
Clark, R. A., 319n85
Clark, Terry, 150n168
Clarke, Peter, 149n110, 364n6
Cleveland, Mark, 319n85, 520n58
Clifford, Stephanie, 96n33, 189n75, 226n48,
    320n148, 320n159, 425n190, 472n39,
    561n45
Clinton, William Jefferson, 286
Clooney, George, 347
Close, Angeline, 149n112
Coate, John, 561n66
Cobb, Cathy J., 96n46, 98n84
Cocanougher, A. Benton, 422n95, 422n97
Cohen, Joel B., 97n62, 318n70, 320n122,
    365n40, 422n73
Cohen, Patricia, 424n182
Cohen, William, 96n45
Cohn, D'Vera, 472n45, 474n149
Cole, Catherine A., 190n124, 267n81, 474n150
Cole, S. Jason, 317n37
Coleman, James S., 520–521n94
Coleman, Richard P., 56n9, 519n21, 519n23,
    519n24, 519n33, 519n34, 519n35,
    519n41, 520n55, 520n60, 520n79,
    520n81
Collins, A. M., 267n81
Collins, Glenn, 150n173, 225n4, 471n7
Collins, Janay, 226n35
Commuri, Suraj, 521n101
Compeau, Larry D., 149n114
Condon, Lee, 472n40
Conklin, J. C., 149n118
Conner, P. E., 147n22
Conroy, Denise M., 421n32
Considine, Austin, 320n145
Cooil, Bruce, 188n34
Cook, Daniel, 267n65
Cook, Michael P., 150n179
Cook, William A., 269n137
Cooley, Charles H., 317n29
Coolio, 346
Coon, Gregory S., 149n101
Corfman, Kim P., 424n181
Cornwell, T. B., 267n83
Cornwell, T. Bettina, 147n53
Coskuner-Balli, Gokcen, 147n31
Cosmas, Stephen C., 521n129
Costa, Janeen A., 472n44, 521n117
Costa, Paul T., 57n30, 318n65
Coster, Helen, 521n135
Cote, Joseph A., 365n36, 365n39
Cotte, June, 189n74, 420n15, 421n34, 424n157
Coulter, Keith S., 226n35
Coulter, Robin A., 226n35
Coupland, Jennifer Chang, 424n154
Cousineau, Alain, 422n73
Cova, Bernard, 422n93

Cova, Veronique, 422n93
Covel, Simona, 148n61
Cowley, Geoffrey, 562n110
Cox, Anthony D., 190n126
Cox, Cathryn Leigh, 317n31
Cox, Dena, 190n126
Cox, Rob, 519n17
Cox, W. Michael, 520n61
Craik, Fergus I. M., 267n81
Crandall, Christian S., 321n178
Creamer, Matthew, 561n40
Creighton, Millie, 421n41
Creswell, Julie, 266n27
Crispell, Diane, 424n165
Crittenden, Victoria L., 424
Crocker, Kenneth E., 365n53
Crocker, Lizzie, 561n58
Crockett, David, 519n8
Cronin, J. Joseph, Jr., 423n117
Cronin, Joseph, Jr., 97n80
Crosett, Kathy, 366n82
Crowley, Ayn E., 226n10, 226n24
Cruise, Tom, 212
Cryder, C. E., 319n85
Csikszentmihalyi, Mihaly, 561n64
Cuneo, Alice Z., 365n47
Cunha, Marcus, Jr., 268n107, 268n108
Cunningham, C., 266n30
Curnutte, Mark, 190n125
Curren, Mary T., 420n22
Curry, David J., 424n155, 520n91
Curtin, Richard T., 519n11
Curtis, Harris, 474n114
Cutright, Keisha M., 365n18, 473n96
Czepiel, John A., 267n87, 425n187

Dabholkar, Pratibhar, 189n88
Dacin, Peter A., 421n25
Dahab, Debra J., 189n87
Dahl, Darren W., 96n25, 317n15, 367n109,
    367n111, 423n106
Dalakas, Vassilis, 266n46
Daltrey, Roger, 390
Danko, William D., 56n8, 424n152
Dannenfeldt, Diane, 318n50
Danziger, Shai, 267n88, 366n63
Darden, William R., 421n26, 422n68, 561n49
Darke, Peter R., 226n10, 366n60
Darmody, Aron, 98n107
Darmon, Rene Y., 367n102
Daugherty, Terry, 265, 562n87
Davenport, J. W., 422n66
Davis, Harry L., 424n155
Davis, Teresa, 148n74
Dawkins, Richard, 562n110
Dawson, Scott, 420n22
Day, George S., 188n47
Dean, James, 108
Deberry-Spence, Benet, 421n41
Debevec, Kathleen, 471n23
DeBono, Kenneth G., 365n54
DeCarlo, Thomas E., 560n20
Dee, Jonathan, 474n153
Deighton, John, 367n129, 474n130
DeJong, William, 365n19
DeLorme, Denise E., 148n66
Demby, Emanuel H., 521n133
Denegri-Knot, Janice, 562n87
Deng, Xiaoyan, 227n73
Deng Xiaoping, 492
DeNitto, Emily, 97n74
DeParle, Jason, 519n43
Depp, Johnny, 308
de Ruyter, Ko, 521n95
Desai, Kalpesh Kaushik, 421n58

Deschanel, Zooey, 363
Deshpandé, Rohit, 472n55, 472n64, 473n78
Deturck, Mark A., 269n135
Deutsch, Claudia, 266n19
Deux, Kay, 471n2
Dhar, Ravi, 98n84
Dholakia, Nikhilesh, 57n52, 365n44
Dholakia, Ruby Roy, 365n44
Diamond, Nina, 423n140
Diaz, Ann-Christine, 190n135
Dichter, Ernest, 284, 285, 318n66
Dickson, Peter R., 96n16, 420n8
Diesendruck, Gil, 149n119
Dietvorst, Thomas F., 189n83
Di Justo, Patrick, 190n115, 190n118
DiLeonardo, Micaela, 424n179
Dillinger, John, 108
Di Muro, Fabrizio, 98n107
Ditton, Theresa, 561n68
Dixon, Kenneth M., 57n57
Dobson, Roger, 265n10
Dodd, Vikram, 368n137
Dodds, Peter Sheridan, 560n29, 561n38
Dolan, Kerry A., 519n42
Dolich, Ira J., 319n107
Dolliver, Mark, 189n77, 367n112
Domzal, Teresa J., 150n183, 227n80
Doney, Patricia M., 423n109
Dong, Lily, 150n153
Donovan, Robert J., 421n49
Donthu, Naveen, 266n16, 472n64
Donthu, Yaveroglu, 265n7, 266n16
Dornoff, Ronald J., 267n90, 319n107
Dortch, Shannon, 424n156
Dotson, Michael J., 473n97
Dougherty, Donald, 473n92
Douglas, Mary Twe, 521n114, 521n125
Dover, Philip A., 368n133
Downey, Robert, Jr., 260
Dr. Dre, 108
Drenan, Sarah, 98n100
Dréze, Xavier, 96n18, 267n79, 506f, 521n98,
    521n110
Dröge, Cornelia, 188n29, 367n102
Drolet, Aimee, 98n97, 268n112, 317n32
D'Souza, Giles, 366n90
Du, Shuili, 472n60
Dubachek, Adam, 318n76
Dubé, Laurette, 367n116, 420n18
Dube-Rioux, Laurette, 475n172
Dubner, Stephen G., 98n93
Dubois, David, 317n9
Dugger, Celia W., 146n4
Duhachek, Adam, 421n41
Duncan, Calvin P., 85t, 98n99, 98n104
Duncan, James S., 149n127
Dupri, Jermaine, 510
Durante, Kristina M., 320n136
Durgee, Jeffrey F., 284t, 287f, 318n66, 501t,
    520n52
Durkheim, Émile, 149n30, 490
Dyer, David C., 367n104
Dyett, Linda, 562n101
Dylan, Bob, 346

Eagly, Alice H., 366n71
Eastin, Matthew S., 265, 562n87
Eastman, Jacqueline Kilsheimer, 519n44
Echikson, William, 227n91
Eckardt, Giana M., 473n91
Eckholm, Erik, 423n141
Edell, Julie, 268n106, 268n107, 366n91, 368n134
Edery, David, 227n86
Edmonds, Molly, 318n61
Edmondson, Brad, 421n53, 424n148, 424n153

Effrein, E. A., 364n3
Eggerton, John, 267n66
Eisenberg, Anne, 471n15
Eisenstein, E. M., 266n35
Ekstrom, Karin M., 424n157
Elder, Ryan S., 225n3
Elejalde, Ruiz, Alexia, 521n109
Ellen, Pam Scholder, 226n28
Elliott, Drew, 562n80
Elliott, Richard, 367n109
Elliott, Stuart, 57n18, 97n60, 97n74, 147n54,
   147n55, 227n59, 266n18, 267n64,
   269n139, 319n95, 472n51, 472n52,
   472n58, 473n85
Ellis, Andrew W., 268n108
Ellis, Elwood A., 422n84
Ellison, Nicole, 521n97
Ellison, Sarah, 57n17, 226n37, 473n99
Ello-Martin, Julia A., 227n92
Emme, 306
Engineer, Tariq, 471n4
Engle, Randall W., 265n5, 266n38
Englis, Basil G., 147n30, 147n49, 227n67,
   320n138, 421n23, 422n105, 475n173,
   562n101
English, Bella, 423n137
Enis, Ben M., 424n152
Epp, Amber M., 149n137, 423n159
Erdem, Tülim, 473n96
Ericksen, Mary Kay, 57n32
Ertimur, Burcak, 149n101
Escalas, Jennifer Edson, 190n95, 267n76, 422n94
Esteban, Gabriel, 367n101
Etgar, Michael, 367n104
Etua, Sarah F., 320n153
Evers, Reinier, 520n89

Faber, Ronald J., 190n109, 317n6, 472n63
Fackler, Martin, 190n103, 519n45
Fairs, Charles W., 423n123
Fallows, James, 520n59
Fang, Bay, 520n63
Farganis, Sondra, 321n180
Farnsworth, Clyde H., 150n181
Farrelly, Francis, 146n19
Farris, Paul W., 367n102
Fattah, Hassan, 473n89
Fay, Bradford, 423n130
Fazio, Russell H., 268n111, 364n3
Feick, Lawrence F., 561n44
Feinberg, Richard A., 265n4
Feintuch, Jocelyn, 150n177
Feirstein, Bruce, 423n106
Feldman, Laurence P., 420n12
Felson, Richard B., 318n42
Fennis, Bob, 365n21
Ferguson, M. J., 98n88
Ferguson, Tim W., 473n101
Fern, Edward F., 423n120
Fernandez, Karen V., 148n70
Fielding, Michael, 473n103
Figueroa, Ana, 474n134
Filliatrault, P., 319n85
Fine, Benny, 145
Fine, Gary Alan, 560n19
Fine, Rafi, 145
Finn, Adam, 227n64, 269n133
Fioravanti, Mario, 317n19
Firth, Niall, 147n51
Fischer, Eileen, 471n19
Fishbein, M., 365n30
Fishbein, Martin, 365n31
Fisher, Dan, 317n37

Fisher, Eileen, 424n182
Fisher, R. Aubrey, 365n44
Fiske, Susan T., 267n85
Fitzsimmons, Gavan J., 82, 99n115, 317n15,
   365n18, 365n38, 473n96
Fixx, The, 233
Flannery, Russell, 520n63
Fleming, M. A., 364n12
Florshein, Renee, 267n59
Fluger, J. C., 551
Flynn, Emily, 320n132
Flynn, Laurie J., 98n97
Flynn, Leisa Reinecke, 519n44
Flynn, Leisha R., 95n9
Fodor, Eugene M., 57n34
Folkes, Valerie S., 98n98, 187n2
Foltz, Kim, 147n43, 148n91
Forbes, Thom, 423n147
Ford, Jeffrey D., 422n84
Ford, Neil M., 422n68
Foreman, George, 346
Forney, Matthew, 520n63
Forstenzer, Martin, 147n41
Foster, Brian L., 561n55
Fournier, Susan, 57n24, 57n25, 97n79, 319n100,
   319n103, 319n110
Fowler, Geoffrey A., 150n141, 150n167,
   320n158, 365n47, 471n21
Fox, Michael J., 347
Fox, Susannah, 189n58
Fox, Zoe, 189n60
Foxall, Gordon R., 266n28, 319n84
Foxman, Ellen, 424n157
Frable, Deborah E. S., 472n37
France, Karen Russo, 99n120
Francese, Peter, 473n81
Francis, Connie, 37
Frank, Mark G., 226n15
Fraser, Scott C., 365n19
Frederick, Shane, 561n75
Freedman, Jonathan L., 365n19
Freeman, S., 423n108
Freeman, Steven, 365n25
Freiden, Jon B., 561n37
French, Howard W., 520n63
French, J. R. P., Jr., 422n77
Freud, Sigmund, 282, 284, 285
Frick, Henry Clay, 504
Friedman, Emily, 425n186
Friedman, Hershey H., 365n56
Friedman, Linda, 365n56
Friedman, Monroe, 147n53
Friedmann, Roberto, 227n76
Fromkin, Howard L., 57n35, 562n100
Froomkin, Dan, 519n31
Fuller, Thomas, 148n73, 320n139, 320n141
Fumento, Michael, 560n26
Furse, David H., 96n27, 268n102, 349t, 365n19,
   366n82
Fussell, Paul, 519n39

Gaffney, John, 560n6
Gagnon, John H., 472n36
Gal, David, 561n71
Galak, Jeff, 268n106, 561n75
Galbraith, John Kenneth, 155
Galinsky, Adam D., 317n9, 521n99
Gallagher, Sean, 190n97
Galloni, Allesandra, 367n108
Gangestad, Steve, 317n34
Gans, Herbert J., 147n37, 520n90
Ganziger, S., 267n88
Gardner, David, 98n105, 367n117
Gardner, Meryl Paula, 420n22

Gardyn, Rebecca, 423n144, 474n136, 519n22,
   519n38
Garolera, Jordi, 146n20
Garretson, Judith A., 366n79
Garrett, Dennis E., 188n47
Garrobo, Alexis, 518
Gaschke, Yvonne N., 420n21
Gates, Bill, 487
Gatty, Ronald, 521n133
Gaulin, Steve, 320n154
Gaylord, Becky, 226n47
Geertz, Clifford, 146n2
Gehman, Geoff, 518
Geller, Martinne, 269n139
Gentry, James W., 189n87, 320n149, 473n110
Ger, Güliz, 57n28, 148n92, 149n138, 188n24,
   472n65
Geren, Brenda, 57n54
Gergen, Kenneth J., 422n76, 422n85
Gergen, Mary, 422n76, 422n85
Ghose, Anindya, 96n18
Gibson, Janine, 520n63
Giehal, Gabriel, 267n84
Gielser, Markus, 146n4
Giese, J. K. Sojka, 319n84, 319n85
Giese, J. L., 319n84, 319n85
Giesler, Markus, 147n34, 149n99
Gilbert, Faye W., 319n94
Gilbreath, Edward, 473n101
Gillan, Tamara, 146n18
Gilly, Mary C., 188n29, 424n152, 472n57,
   474n158, 561n41
Gilmore, James H., 96n17
Gilovich, Thomas, 226n15
Girling, Rob, 98n92
Glader, Paul, 320n117
Gladwell, Malcolm, 81, 98n84, 561n78,
   562n111
Glazing, Jennifer K., 423n119
Gobé, Marc, 150n171, 226n18
Godek, J., 364n12
Godfrey, Andrea L., 188n34
Godin, Seth, 365n45
Goetzl, David, 321n165
Goff, Brent G., 190n111
Goffman, Erving, 57n23, 317n17, 317n22,
   318n42, 320n118
Goh, Paul, 363
Goldberg, Marvin E., 85t, 98n99, 148n85,
   149n107, 189n80, 268n126, 421n22,
   421n24, 421n25
Golden, Ellen, 422n73
Golden, Linda L., 366–367n94, 366n94, 367n98,
   421n44
Goldhaber, Gerald M., 269n135
Goldner, Diane, 471n5
Goldsmith, Ronald E., 95n9, 319n84, 319n85,
   519n44, 561n37
Goldstein, Noah J., 365n34
Goldwert, Lindsay, 367n120
Goleman, Daniel, 149n105
Gollwitzer, P. M., 320n115
Gomes, Lee, 150n140, 227n60
Gonzales, Monica, 149n102
Gooch, Liz, 151n190, 473n108
Goodstein, Ronald C., 97n59, 226n52
Goodwin, Stephen A., 367n104
Gordinier, Jeff, 474n141
Gordon, Beverly, 149n136
Gorn, Gerald J., 46n17, 85t, 96n25, 98n99,
   148n85, 189n80, 226n10, 267n59,
   268n126, 367n104, 421n22, 421n24,
   421n25

Gorn, Jerry, 149n107
Goudreau, Jenna, 265n1
Gough, Harrison G., 317n19
Gould, Stephen J., 561n49
Goulding, Christina, 317n23, 472n38
Gould-Simon, Alisa, 147n33
Graeff, Timothy R., 317n34
Gragan, Leigh, 470
Graham, Ellen, 423n131
Granbois, Donald H., 98n83, 423n109, 424n173
Grass, R. C., 366n83
Graves, Michael, 198
Graya, James J., 320n153
Green, Heather, 365n47
Green, Nancy, 471n23
Green, Robert T., 149n106
Greenberg, Karl, 148n88, 148n94, 189n49, 189n52, 266n49, 472n39, 472n73, 473n82, 561n34
Greenfield, Patricia M., 267n58
Greenwald, Anthony G., 268n100, 366n66
Gregan-Paxton, Jennifer, 267n572
Grégoire, Yany, 188n33
Gresham, Alicia, 519n7
Grewal, Dhruv, 188n34, 420n16
Greyser, Stephen A., 188n47, 562nn107
Grier, Sonya A., 266n49, 473n78, 473n79
Griffin, Dale, 268n112
Griffin, Mitch, 421n26, 421n27, 560n20
Griffiths, Rob, 267n71
Griskevicius, Vladas, 320n136, 365n34
Groom, Nicola, 190n112
Grose, Jessica, 149n129
Gross, Barbara L., 147n24
Grossbart, Sanford, 266n49
Grossman, Cathy Lynn, 473n106
Grossman, Randi Priluck, 265n11
Grove, Stephen J., 190n124, 420n22
Grubb, Edward L., 319n105
Grush, J. E., 422n100
Guetta, David, 202
Gulas, Charles S., 317n14
Gumbel, Peter, 150n141
Guns, William D., 521n141
Gupta, Richa, 226n46
Gupta, Shankar, 148n67
Gurhan-Canli, Zeynep, 366n59
Gutman, Evelyn G., 267n87
Gutman, Jonathan, 147n25

Habich, John, 520n93
Hafner, Katie, 366n67
Hafner, Michael, 317n11
Hagerty, James R., 266n21
Hagtvedt, Henrik, 57n29
Haisley, Emily, 486
Hakim, Danny, 187n5, 521n131
Hall, Calvin S., 57n30, 318n71
Hall, Emma, 150n149
Halle, David, 520n54
Halliday, Jean, 96n39, 367n96, 472n75
Halstead, Dianne, 188n29
Hamermesh, Daniel S., 320n130
Hamill, Sean D., 318n64
Han, Sang-Pil, 146n9
Han, Young Jee, 506f, 521n110
Hancock, Michelle, 321n181
Handelman, Jay M., 188n38
Hanks, Douglas, 518
Hanrahan, Dan, 225
Hansen, William B., 319n113
Hantula, Donald A., 560n19
Hargens, L. L., 520n85

Harich, Katrin E., 421n22
Harkins, S., 423n107
Harmon, Amy, 190n116, 424n162
Harnish, Richard J., 365n54
Harris, James Edwin, 189n68
Harris, Marvin, 146n2
Hartley, Steven W., 422n68
Hartshorne, Charles, 227n81
Hartvig-Larsen, Hanne, 284t, 287f
Hartwick, Jon, 365n35
Hasapopoulous, Tedi, 265n8
Hassay, Derek N., 190n108
Hasselbeck, Matt, 345
Hastork, Albert H., 227n76
Haugtvedt, Curtis P., 366n93
Hauser, John R., 95n38, 97n57
Havlena, William J., 269n140, 365n32
Hayes, Constance L., 57n19, 471n13
Heath, Chip, 98n96
Heath, Rebecca Piirto, 319n91, 521n136
Heath, Timothy B., 99n120
Heckler, Susan E., 268n110, 268n116
Heide, Jan B., 423n119
Heider, Fritz, 365n24
Heine, Christopher, 420n5
Heitmeyer, Jeanne R., 561n37
Heller, Steven, 227n82
Helliker, Kevin, 472n39
Helm, Burt, 57n15, 472n43
Henderson, Pamela W., 226n24
Hendon, Donald W., 520n79
Henry, Paul C., 57n38, 148n90, 188n38, 471n28, 520n53
Henry, Walter A., 267n82
Henthorne, Tony L., 367n113
Herd, Kelly B., 561n71
Herr, Paul M., 268n111, 365n27, 365n52
Herrington, J. Duncan, 421n47
Herzenstein, Michael, 366n58
Heslin, Richard, 367n95
Hess, James D., 96n18
Hethorn, Janet, 562n101
Hewer, Paul, 57n39
Heyn, Dalma, 320n149
Hiestand, Michael, 319n90
Higie, Robin A., 561n44
Hill, Julie Skur, 150n178, 150n182
Hill, R., 423n114
Hill, Reuben, 149n111
Hill, Ronald Paul, 367n123, 519n29
Hill, Sarah E., 320n136
Hilton, Paris, 333
Hine, Thomas, 319n87, 424n171
Hirsch, Alan R., 420n9
Hirsch, Paul M., 147n37
Hirschman, Elizabeth C., 97n67, 147n34, 148n81, 149n113, 149n128, 225n5, 268n109, 268n115, 366n84, 422n67, 472n63, 473n97, 519n40
Hite, Robert E., 226n10, 421n48
Hitt, Jack, 226n29
Hjorth-Andersen, C., 98n105
Hlaracek, James D., 423n120
Hoch, Stephen J., 148n92
Hof, Robert, 562n90
Hoffman, Donna L., 365n44, 546, 561n64
Hoffman, Gretchen, 422n75
Hoffman, Jan, 190n106
Hofmann, Deborah, 150n139
Hofstede, Frenkel ter, 562n92
Hofstede, Geert, 150n179
Holak, Susan L., 269n140, 562n93

Holbrook, Morris B., 57n53, 149n113, 225n5, 268n122, 269n142, 317n33, 319n84, 319n85, 364n10, 365n32, 422n67, 472n63, 520n92, 520n93, 560n29
Holden, Stephen, 474n122
Hollenbeck, Candice R., 423n103
Hollingshead, August B., 520n75
Holman, Rebecca H., 97n79, 97n81, 188n29, 188n33, 318n73, 319n101, 366n64, 367n102, 367n128, 420n7, 420n18, 420n19, 421n23, 472n44, 560n20
Holmes, Elizabeth, 519n16
Holmes, Selina J., 268n108
Holson, Laura M., 148n80, 148n94, 150n167
Holt, Douglas, 148n92, 150n183, 151n184, 471n35, 520n94
Homans, George C., 422n66
Homer, Pamela, 147n24
Honea, Heather, 96n25
Hong, Jae W., 319n101
Hong, Jiewen, 226n7
Hood, Jacqueline N., 187n3
Hookway, James, 150n156
Horn, Martin I., 150n177
Horne, David, 320n121
Horney, Karen, 285, 318n69
Hornik, Jacob, 226n38, 420n12
Horovitz, Bruce, 99n115, 189n78, 367n107
Horowitz, David M., 188n33
Horowitz, Rose A., 150n162
Horsley, Kris, 267n58
Horton, Steve, 367n110
Hotz, Robert Lee, 97n48, 97n58
House, James S., 500f, 520n92
Houston, Michael J., 147n21, 188n47, 267n81, 268n116, 366n85
Hovland, Carl I., 365n52
Howard, Lucy, 150n163
Howe, Neil, 473n111
Hoyer, Wayne D., 96n46, 98n84, 98n99, 188n47, 472n64
Hsee, Christopher K., 521n126
Hsu, Michael, 188n34
Hsu, Tiffany, 321n183
Huang, Laura, 320n121
Huang, Peng, 96n44
Huang, Shirley H., 266n49
Huang, Szu-chi, 95n3
Huber, Joel, 96n37, 98n89
Hudson, Kris, 421n57
Hudson, Laurel A., 52t
Huffman, Cynthia, 57n37
Huffman, Douglas E., 520n79
Hughner, Renee Shaw, 318n78
Huh, Ben, 553
Hui, Michael, 472n44
Hull, J. G., 317n30
Humphreys, M. S., 267n83
Hunt, Kevin, 146
Hunt, Shelby, 97n67, 97n81, 149n122
Hupp, Gregg, 319n105
Hutchings, Emma, 561n73
Hutchinson, J. W., 96n16, 97n62, 266n35, 268n105
Hutton, Debra G., 317n6
Hyatt, Eva M., 473n97
Hymowitz, Carol, 150n165

Iacobucci, Dawn, 97n82, 318n76, 561n70
Iglesias, Enrique, 345
Ikeda, Ana Akemi, 147n25
Imus, Don, 163

Inada, Miho, 321n163
Indvik, Lauren, 98n113, 320n155, 561n74
Inkster, James A., 365n15
Inman, J. Jeffrey, 98n95, 421n56
Innis, Daniel E., 97n81
Insko, Chester A., 98n100, 265n11, 365n13
Irons, Jeremy, 138
Irwin, Tanya, 96n12, 98n109, 420n10, 423n112, 424n168
Isherwood, Baron C., 521n114, 521n125
Ives, Nat, 188n45, 366n78
Iwamura, Miki, 149n106
Iyengar, Reghuram, 96n18
Iyer, Easwar, 421n58, 421n61, 471n23

Jackman, Philip, 519n5
Jackson, Anita, 97n79
Jackson, Michael, 116, 333
Jacob, Jennine, 422n75
Jacobson, Robert, 97n80
Jacoby, Jacob, 96n19, 188n47, 189n82, 319n83
Jafari, Aliakbar, 317n23
Jaffe, Francoise, 424n180
Jaffe, Rebecca H., 98n91
Jain, S. C., 368n134
Jain, Sanjay, 519n44
James, Kevin, 346
James, LeBron, 219
Janiszewski, C., 265n6
Janssen, Loes, 365n21
Jargon, Julie, 226n30
Jaworski, Bernard J., 96n27
Jaworski, Michelle, 471n25
Jayanti, Rama, 97n79, 422n91
Jayson, Sharon, 320n130
Jay-Z, 510
Jefferson Airplane, 229
Jennings, Angel, 474n142, 474n143
Jhally, Sut, 187n6, 521n124
Jiang, Lan, 226n6
Jing, Bing, 96n18
Joachimsthaler, Erich, 318n82, 521n140
Johar, Gita Venkataramani, 367n98, 421n59
Johar, J. S., 364n4
John, Deborah Roedder, 188n16, 267n60, 267n86, 317n39, 320n114, 422n70
Johnson, Alex, 475n167
Johnson, Allison R., 319n104
Johnson, Bradley, 319n89
Johnson, Brian A., 520n89
Johnson, Eric J., 95n1, 268n98, 268n104, 268n105
Johnson, Kerenami, 424n152
Johnson, Kirk, 266n20
Johnson, Lauren, 227n89
Johnson, Michael D., 97n68
Johnson Kirk, 519n8
Johnstone, Michael-Lee, 421n32
Jones, Bob, 472n74
Jordan, Michael, 120, 492
Jordan, Miriam, 150n157
Joseph-Goteiner, Nicole, 474n134
Joshi, Yogesh, 96n18
Joy, Annamma, 472n44
Jun, Sung-Youl, 560n27
Jung, Carl, 285–286, 292, 318n72

Kadaba, Lini S., 266n31
Kahl, Joseph, 519n30
Kahle, Lynn R., 147n24, 364n11, 423n115, 520n76, 560n23
Kahn, Barbara E., 96n22, 226n24, 227n73, 421n35

Kahn, Gabriel, 227n82
Kahneman, Daniel, 96n22, 98n98, 99n120, 421n35
Kaiser, Susan B., 471n8, 562n91, 562n99, 562n101
Kakkar, Pradeep, 420n4
Kakutani, Michiko, 147n46
Kalamas, M., 319n85
Kalra, Ajay, 98n82, 226n52
Kaltcheva, Velitchka D., 420n20, 421n27
Kalyanaram, Gurumurthy, 268n91
Kamakura, Wagner A., 147n24, 366n61
Kamen, Joseph M., 366n64
Kamenetz, Anya, 519n26, 561n70
Kamins, Michael A., 187n2, 366n64, 366n94
Kaminski, Peter F., 188n31
Kamvar, Sepandar D., 98n107
Kang, Stephanie, 190n12, 521n122
Kang, Yong-Soon, 365n52
Kangun, N., 367n102
Kanter, Rosabeth Moss, 521n114, 521n120
Kapner, Suzanne, 151n189
Kardashian, Khloe, 345
Kardashian, Kim, 66, 103
Kardes, Frank R., 189n87, 268n91, 366n58, 367n100, 367n109, 473n110
Karmarkar, Uma R., 367n97
Karp, Hannah, 56n6
Karrer, Holli C., 268n124
Kassarjian, Harold H., 266n40, 266n43, 318n68, 318n82, 420n4
Katayama, Lisa, 521n118
Kates, Steven M., 266n43, 472n41
Katona, George, 519n12
Katona, Zsolt, 97n64
Katz, Daniel, 324, 364n2
Katz, Elihu, 560n8
Kaufman, Carol Felker, 420n11
Kaufman, Leslie, 365n28
Kaufman-Scarborough, Carol, 189n58, 472n57
Kavas, Alican, 365n32
Kay, Aaron C., 365n18
Kaye, Leon, 187
Kearney, A. T., 519n47
Keates, Nancy, 148n86
Keats, John, 305
Keefe, Lisa M., 317n5
Keillor, Bruce, 147n53
Keiningham, Timothy L., 188n34
Keith, Naughton, 521n108
Keller, Ed, 561n76
Keller, Kevin Lane, 265n12, 267n84, 268n103, 268n106, 268n107
Keller, Punam Anand, 149n99, 364n9, 367n122
Kelley, Harold H., 422n87, 423n114
Kelley, James, 520n58
Kelly, Gene, 114
Kelman, Herbert, 365n53
Kelppe, Ingeborg Astrid, 471n28
Kennedy, John F., 163
Kennedy, Pagan, 57n22
Kennedy, Patricia, 147n24, 317n12
Kernan, Jerome B., 150n183, 227n80, 319n110, 561n54
Kershaw, Sarah, 471n20
Key, Wayne R., 320n146
Khan, Shahrukh, 494
Khan, Uzma, 98n84
Khermouch, Gerry, 474n131
Kiel, Geoffrey C., 98n84
Kim, Chankon, 472n44
Kim, David, 421n51

Kim, Junu Bryan, 474n124
Kim, Young Chan, 149n101
Kindelan, Katie, 318n45
King, Charles W., 560n25, 561n37, 562n107
King, Robert L., 421n47
Kinkade, Thomas, 112
Kinnear, Thomas C., 188n47, 268n109, 268n117, 366n84
Kinski, Nastassja, 138
Kirmani, Amna, 97n81
Kitayama, S., 317n2, 317n3
Kiviat, Barbara, 423n127
Kjeldgaard, Dannie, 321n182, 472n57
Klara, Robert, 366n75
Klein, Jill G., 149n100, 320n121
Kleine, Robert E., III, 148n85, 317n27, 319n110
Kleine, Susan Schultz, 188n14, 317n27
Kline, Stephen, 187n6, 521n124
K'naan, 202
Knasko, Susan C., 226n24
Knickermeyer, Ellen, 320n143
Knowles, Patricia A., 420n22
Knox, Robert E., 365n15
Koch, Wendy, 189n76
Koenig, Harold F., 422n90
Koh, Yoree, 150n142
Kohák, Erazim, 188n25
Kolata, Gina, 422n83, 561n52
Kolbe, Lutz, 365n44
Kolbe, Richard, 321n161
Kosaka, Hiroshi, 146n3
Kotler, Philip, 188n48, 421n47
Kottak, Conrad Phillip, 148n74, 149n126
Kotz, Deborah, 420n14
Kozinets, Robert V., 188n38, 269n141, 421n41, 423n140, 562n110
Kraft, Frederic B., 473n110
Kragh, J. R., 366n64
Kramer, Andrew E., 521n105
Kramer, Louise, 367n105
Kramer, Thomas, 365n16
Kramer, Tom, 130
Kratzer, Jan, 560n30
Kravets, Olga, 148n74, 149n138
Kreider, Holly, 267n58
Krishna, Aradhna, 201, 225n3, 226n8
Krishnamurthy, Parthasarathy, 95n1
Krober-Riel, Werner, 268n117
Kroft, Steve, 474n128
Kron, Joan, 149n127
Kropp, Fredric, 266n46
Krosnick, J. A., 365n33
Kruez, Roger J., 147n53
Kruger, Justin, 268n106
Krugman, Herbert, 96n23, 266n13, 268n94, 364n7, 366n91
Kuchinskas, Susan, 268n130
Kukar-Kinney, Monika, 190n109
Kumanyika, S. K., 266n49, 473n79
Kumar, Anand, 562n97
Kumar, Vishesh, 96n18
Kuntze, Ronald J., 318n78
Kuse, Allan R., 268n102
Kwon, Wi-Suk, 562n101
Kyung, Park Ji, 317n39

Labroo, Aparna A., 98n90
Lach, Jennifer, 189n85, 421n55, 424n154
Lackman, Conway, 424n155
Laczniak, Gene R., 188n47
Laczniak, Russell N., 474n116, 560n20
Lady Gaga, 28, 117, 271, 343, 544

LaFerla, Ruth, 519n27
Lafferty, Elaine, 150n162
LaFranco, Robert, 366n70
Lafranierek, Sharon, 321n173
Lagerfeld, Karl, 441
Lajos, Joseph, 97n64
Lakshmi-Ratan, Ramnath, 367n57
Lambert-Pandraud, Raphaël, 474n147, 474n152
Lambiase, Jacqueline, 471n33
Lamont, Lawrence R., 146n18
Lampe, Cliff, 521n97
Lanasa, John M., 424n155
Land, Deborah, 267n58
Lane, Paul M., 420n11
Langer, Ellen J., 266n36
Langmeyer, Lynn, 366n64
Lanham, Robert, 521n142
Lapersonne, Eric, 474n152
Lapidus, Richard S., 188n33
Laran, Juliano, 268n107, 268n108
Laroche, Michel, 319n85, 472n44, 520n58
Larsen, V., 227n81
Lassek, Will, 320n154
Lastovicka, John L., 148n70, 188n20, 318n78, 318n82, 521n140
Latane, B., 423n107, 423n108
Latour, Kathryn A., 249, 421n34
LaTour, Michael S., 249, 267n73, 367n109, 367n113
Lattin, Don, 473n102
Lau-Gesk, Loraine, 317n32
Laumann, Edward O., 472n36, 500f, 520n92
Laurent, G., 267n79
Laurent, Gilles, 474n147, 474n152
Laverie, Debra A., 317n27, 424n169
Lavidge, Robert, 364n7
Lavin, Marilyn, 424n178
Layton, Roger A., 98n84
Lazarsfeld, Paul F., 560n8
Lazarus, Richard S., 364n10
Lazer, William, 146n3
Lazzari, Renato, 317n19
Lazzaro, Joseph, 318n78
Le, Viet, 318n54
Learmonth, Michael, 268n129
Leclerc, France, 475n172, 521n126
Ledbetter, James, 474n126
Ledikwe, Jenny H., 227n92
Lee, Angela Y., 364n9
Lee, Don, 321n183
Lee, Euehun, 473n110
Lee, Jaehoon, 188n13
Lee, Julie, 520n58
Lee, Leonard, 98n112
Lee, M. S., 96n46
Leff, Lisa, 472n40
Legoux, Renaud, 188n33
Lehmann, Donald R., 98n84, 424n181, 562n93
Leibenstein, Harvey, 562n102
Leigh, Thomas W., 423n117
Leippe, Michael R., 268n100, 366n66
Leiss, William, 187n6, 187n9, 188n11, 521n124
Leland, John, 473n105
Lenn, T. N., 364n3
Lennon, John, 133
Lenski, Gerhard E., 520n80
Lentini, Nina M., 147n48, 190n130, 321n163, 471n6
Leonard, Abigail W., 320n134
Leonard-Barton, Dorothy, 560n15, 560n30
Leong, Siew Meng, 365n39, 422n70
Leonhardt, David, 96n42, 425n188
Leshnoff, Jessica, 521n109

Lessig, V. Parker, 422n82
Lessne, Greg, 424n158
Lettl, Christopher, 560n30
Lev, Michael, 226n50
Levin, Aron M., 150n179
Levin, Dan, 520n64
Levine, Dan, 190n133
Levin, Irwin P., 150n179
Lévi-Strauss, Claude, 122, 148n78
Levitt, Steven J., 98n93
Levitt, Thomas, 150n166
Levy, A. S., 317n30
Levy, Gary D., 475n172
Levy, Michael, 420n16
Levy, Sidney J., 148n95, 149n105
Lewin, Tamar, 475n169
Lewis, Van Dyk, 562n101
Li, Norman P., 320n136
Lichtenstein, Donald R., 97n81, 317n34
Lieberman, Peter, 98n113
Lin, Carolyn A., 146n13
Linden, Fabian, 519n1
Lindquist, Jay D., 420n11
Lindzey, Gardner, 57n30, 318n71
Lipkus, Isaac M., 364n9
Lippman, John, 562n113
Lipscomb, Thomas, 266n44
Littlefield, Jon, 146n12
Liu, Wendy, 95n5, 97n59, 561n71
Lloyd, B. B., 97n64
Lo, Bryan Ching-Wing, 190n137
Lockhart, Robert S., 267n81
Locklear, Heather, 309
Loechner, Jack, 57n59, 148n67, 321n164
Loewenstein, George, 486
Lofgren, Nils, 390
Loftus, E. F., 249, 267n81
Loftus, Elizabeth, 267n73
Logsdon, Jeanne M., 187n3
Lohrer, Robert, 423n159
Lohse, Gerald L., 227n65
Loken, Barbara, 265n8
Lombard, Matthew, 561n68
Longo, Laura, 320n138
Lopez, Jennifer, 303, 346, 510
Lotozo, Eils, 472n66
Loughran, Patrick, 366n73
Lowenstein, G ., 319n85
Lowrey, Tina, 148n79, 149n100, 149n101, 189n88, 521n130
Lowry, Adam, 198
Lubby, Tami, 520n62
Lucas, George, 553
Luce, Mary Frances, 97n55, 98n97
Luchter, Les, 96n33, 560n11
Luedicke, Marius K., 146n4, 423n104
Lukovitz, Karlene, 151n188, 424n173, 473n86, 473n99, 473n104, 473n109, 561n61
Luna, D., 227n81
Lunden, Ingrid, 368n136
Lunt, Paul S., 520n60
Lurie, Alison, 562n101
Lurie, Nicholas H., 96n18, 96n44, 97n56
Luscombe, Belinda, 424n167
Lutz, Richard J., 146n2, 266n47, 364n2, 420n4, 471n23, 521n129, 560n20, 561n44
Lwin, May O., 226n25
Lyall, Sarah, 95n4, 520n68
Lynch, J. David, 520n63
Lynch, John G., 95n38, 96n35, 268n105, 268n109
Lynes, Russell, 147n37
Lynn, Regina, 425n186

Lynn, Steven Jay, 317n20
Lysonski, Steven, 146n18

MacCannell, Dean, 149n134
MacGregor, James N., 267n78
Machan, Dyan, 422n74
MacInnis, Deborah J., 96n27
MacKenzie, Scott B., 364n9, 366n88
Macklin, M. Carole, 267n55
MacNealy, Mary Sue, 147n53
Madden, Normandy, 150n147
Madden, Thomas J., 265n11, 266n38, 367n116
Madonna, 333
Mager, John, 520n76
Magrath, Allan J., 190n91
Maguire, A. M., 267n83
Mahoney, Sarah, 98n108, 424n167, 472n39, 473n76, 474n146
Maister, David H., 425n187
Malhotra, Naresh K., 319n108
Malkewitz, Keven, 295f
Mandell, Nina, 320n128
Mandese, Joe, 366n65, 473n98, 473n104
Mangalindan, Mylene, 57n21
Mangleburg, Tamara F., 423n109, 474n130
Manilow, Barry, 212
Manning, Kenneth C., 97n59
Manning-Schaffel, Vivian, 474n162
Mao Tse-Tung, 492
Marano, Hara Estroff, 320n14
Marcoolyn, Gillian, 421n49
Marcoux, Jean-Sebastien, 149n98
Mardin, Sandra, 266n32
Marin, Alexandra, 561n65
Mark, Margaret, 318n74
Markee, Nancy L., 320n149
Markham, William, 471n10
Markoff, John, 562n121
Marks, Lawrence, 366n92
Markus, H., 317n2, 317n3
Markus, H. M., 422n98
Marley, Bob, 234
Marley, Cedella, 234
Marley, Rohan, 234
Marmorstein, Howard, 267n69
Marquis, M., 319n85
Marr, Merissa, 148n80, 150n167
Marriott, Michel, 473n77
Martilla, John A., 560n9
Martin, Andrew, 148n68, 189n75, 266n19, 266n52
Martin, Brett A. S., 226n39
Martin, Diane, 178
Martin, Hugo, 268n120
Martin, Ingrid, 188n33
Martin, Mary C., 317n12, 320n149
Martineau, Pierre, 318n66
Marx, Groucho, 377
Marx, Karl, 482
Mascai, Dan, 266n21
Maslow, Abraham, 43, 44, 57n36
Matear, Maggie, 319n104
Mathur, Anil, 473n110
Mathwick, Charla, 521n95
Matthew, George, 520n91
Matthews, Robert Guy, 520n72
Mattila, Anna, 421n47
Mayer, Caroline E., 151n187
Mayer, John D., 420n21
Mazumdar, Tridib, 560n27
Mazur, Glenn H., 188n37, 226n41
Mazzon, Alfonso, 147n24
McAfee, Andrew, 57n20
McAlexander, James H., 420n3, 422n90
McAllister, Leigh, 95n1

McArthur, Leslie Z., 98n91
McCall, George J., 146n14
McCarthy, Michael, 227n67
McCarty, John A., 189n88, 472n63
McCarty, Martin, 150n177
McCracken, Grant, 147n32, 149n128, 366n76, 562n106
McCrae, Robert R., 57n30, 318n65
McCrohan, Kevin, 190n91
McCullough, James, 365n36
McDaniel, Stephen W., 57n30
McFerran, Brent, 96n25, 317n15
McGill, Ann L., 97n82
McGonigal, J., 266n31
McGrath, Mary Ann, 148n93, 149n105, 423n140
McGraw, Patrick F., 423n117
McKeage, Kim, 317n14
McKeogh, K. L., 422n100
McMath, Robert M., 97n63, 97n66, 227n71, 227n77
McMillan, Braeme, 95
McNeal, James U., 57n30, 266n48, 473n113
McQuarrie, Edward F., 95n9, 96n15, 147n21, 268n119, 357, 367n127, 367n130, 368n131
McQueen, Josh, 367n129
McQuiston, Daniel H., 423n122
McWilliam, Gil, 474n130
Mead, George H., 317
Meadows, Susanah, 148n74
Meamber, Laurie, 87
Medina, José F., 519n7
Meier, Barry, 148n68, 188n36
Meier, Fred, 317n25
Mejia, Jaime, 471n1
Mellers, Barbara, 98n107
Menasco, Michael B., 424n155
Mendoza, Jorge L., 562n117
Menon, Geeta, 226n35, 321n182
Mensinger, Janell, 266n49
Menzel, Herbert, 560n31
Mergenhagen, Paula, 519n46
Merrick, Amy, 474n144
Meton, Robert, 561n35
Meyers, Robert J., 148n92
Meyers-Levy, Joan, 97n71, 268n99, 364n22, 471n14
Michael, Robert T., 472n36
Michaels, Stuart, 472n36
Michelangelo, 135
Mick, David Glen, 57n37, 97n79, 227n79, 227n81, 268n119, 284t, 287f, 357, 367n127, 367n130, 420n15
Middleton, Catherine, 494f
Midgley, David F., 96n20
Miku, Hatsune, 116f
Milberg, Sandra, 97n59
Miller, Annetta, 147n43
Miller, Claire Cain, 226n43, 226n44
Miller, Cyndee, 96n21, 97n61, 474n130
Miller, George A., 267n77
Miller, Lynn Carol, 317n31
Miller, Mark J., 147n56, 266n23, 320n157
Miller, Pepper, 475n165
Milner, Laura, 471n23
Mindlin, Alex, 98n84, 268n113
Miniard, Paul W., 364n9, 420n22
Minzesheimer, Bob, 474n160
Miró, Joan, 112
Mischel, Walter, 318n62
Misra, Shekhar, 147n24
Mitchell, Andrew, 95n7, 368n134

Mitchell, Deborah, J., 226n24
Mitra, Sabyasachi, 96n44
Mizrahi, Isaac, 198
Moffett, Sebastian, 520n65
Mogelonsky, Marcia, 423n139
Mogilner, Cassie, 98n107, 319n88
Mohr, Betty, 190n98
Moisio, Risto, 423n132, 473n95
Molesworth, Mike, 562n87
Monga, Ashwani, 98n94
Monnier, Arnaud, 226n46
Monroe, Kent B., 97n81, 98n105, 190n109, 474n157
Monroe, Marilyn, 305, 306
Montgomery, David, 520n54
Moon, Mariella, 189n57
Moon, Sangkil, 561n70
Moon, Youngme, 471n23
Mooradian, T. A., 319n85
Moore, Clement Clarke, 128
Moore, Elizabeth S., 266n47
Moore, William L., 98n84
Moorman, Christine, 96n27
Morales, Andrea C., 99n115, 317n15
Moran, S., 267n88
Moreau, C. Page, 561n71
Morgan, J. P., 504
Morrell, Roger W., 267n89
Morrin, Maureen, 226n8, 226n25
Morris, Keiko, 470
Morris, Michael M., 423n117
Morrissey, Brian, 366n67
Morwitz, Vicki G., 267n70
Moschis, George P., 190n126, 266n45, 424, 473n110
Mosimanna, James E., 320n153
Moss, Kate, 303, 306
Mostafa, Romel, 486
Mott, Maryann, 424n147
Mowen, John C., 96n36, 319n85
Muehling, D., 367n102
Mukherjee, Ashesh, 367n116
Muller, Joann, 56n3
Muñiz, Albert M., Jr., 422n90, 423n140, 473n94, 560n19
Muñoz, Liz, 307
Munson, J. Michael, 147n21
Murata, Shoji, 146n3
Murphy, David, 150n154
Murphy, Patrick E., 188n47
Murphy, Samantha, 320n127
Murray, Henry, 42
Murray, Jeff B., 188n48
Murray, Kyle B., 98n107
Murry, John P., 521n140
Murry, John P., Jr., 421n25
Muspratt, Caroline, 321n176
Mustafa, Isiah, 348
Mydans, Seth, 320n140
Myers, James H., 560n13
Myers, Philip N., Jr., 317n12
Myers-Levy, Joan, 226n6

Nader, Ralph, 163
Nakashima, Ryan, 146n11
Nancarrow, Clive, 475n173
Nancarrow, Pamela, 475n173
Nasar, Jack L., 319n109, 320n116
Nass, Clifford, 471n23
Nassauer, Sarah, 320n148
Natarajan, Anand, 266n19
Natarajan, Rajan, 190n111
Naughton, Keith, 422n69
Navarro, Mireya, 521n115

Nayakankuppan, D., 364n12
Neff, Jack, 56n4, 56n7, 57n50, 151n187, 188n40, 189n72, 316, 473n99, 474n162
Neil, Dan, 266n14
Neimark, Jill, 320n160
Nelson, Emily, 562n89
Nelson, Leif D., 561n75
Nelson, Sara C., 520n71
Neporent, Liz, 318n48
Nesdale, Andrew, 421n49
Neslin, Scott, 96n18
Netemeyer, Richard G., 96n35, 317n34, 423n113, 423n115
Neuborne, Ellen, 560n14
Neuhaus, Carolin, 97n58, 226n13
Newbery, Charles, 150n159
Newman, Andrew Adam, 98n110, 148n96, 472n61, 474n121
Newman, Barry, 473n107
Newman, Bruce J., 147n24
Newman, George E., 149n119
Newman, Kara, 226n33
Newman, L. S., 267n75
Newton, Sir Isaac, 198
Nicholson, Carolyn, 149n114
Nicosia, Franco M., 97n79
Nielsen, Jesper H., 98n90
Nine Inch Nails, 343, 541
Noel, H., 265n6, 268n93
Nordland, Rod, 521n103
Novak, Thomas P., 365n44, 561n64
Nucifora, Alf, 149n103
Nudd, Timm, 146
Nunberg, Geoff, 57n20
Nunes, Joseph C., 506f, 521n98, 521n110
Nunes, Paul F., 520n89
Nusbaum, Kenneth E., 190n96
Nuttavuthisit, Krittinee, 421n41

Oakes, William F., 265n11
Obama, Barack, 35
O'Brien, Jeffrey M., 97n50
O'Brien, Stuart, 319n86
O'Cass, Aron, 149n110
O'Connell, Vanessa, 421n40
O'Connor, P. J., 424n178
O'Donnell, Rosie, 212, 306
O'Donohoe, Stephanie, 149n115
O'Dwyer, Gerald, 150n141
O'Grady, Leonardo, 88
O'Guinn, Thomas, 190n109, 422n90, 472n63, 560n19
Okrant, Robyn, 133
Oldham, Todd, 198
Olin, Dirk, 226n19
Oliver, Suzanne, 227n63
Olney, T. J., 319n84, 319n85
Olofsson, Anna, 147n30
Olsen, Ashley, 347
Olsen, Mary-Kate, 347
Olshavsky, Richard W., 98n83
Olson, Jerry, 147n25
Olson, Jerry C., 95n8, 368n133, 420n7, 562n98
Olver, J. M., 319n85
O'Malley, Gavin, 471n18, 474n145
O'Neill, Molly, 148n72
Onians, Charles, 150n143
Onishi, Norimitsu, 189n86, 320n142, 321n169
Onkvisit, Sak, 319n101
Orden, Erica, 148n57
Ordonez, Jennifer, 57n13, 425n189

Orth, Ulrich R., 295*f*
Orwall, Bruce, 150n167
Oser, Kris, 422n89
Oster, Shai, 150n148
Ostrom, Amy L., 560n24
O'Sullivan,Terry, 266n43
Otnes, Cele C., 148n79, 148n93, 149n101, 424n182
Ozanne, Julie L., 52*t*, 146n12, 164, 188n46, 188n48, 189n67, 189n68, 422n66, 474n129

Pace, Tyler, 148n69
Packard, Vance, 155, 187n7, 318n67
Page, Julie, 475n173
Painter, James, 227n72
Palan, Kay L., 474n115
Palan, Kay M., 474n116
Palin, Sarah, 532
Paltrow, Gwyneth, 303
Pampel, F. C., 520n79
Pantoja, Maurice, 267n58
Papadopoulos, Nicolas, 520n58
Papasolomou-Doukakis, Joanna, 57n52
Parekh, Rupal, 367n96, 472n39
Parikhal, John, 475n165
Pariser, Eli, 318n53
Park, C. Whan, 96n16, 96n47, 97n75, 421n59, 421n60, 422n82, 424n180
Park, Denise C., 267n89
Parmar, Arundhati, 146n16
Parmentier, Marie-Agnes, 98n107
Parr, Ben, 423n136, 475n163
Parry, Wane, 147n52
Passariello, Christina, 318n57
Passy, Charles, 148n86
Patel, Kunur, 268n131
Patrick, Vanessa M., 57n29
Patterson, Anthony, 562n116
Paul, P., 423n144
Paul, Pamela, 226n16
Pavlov, Ivan, 230
Pavone, Michael, 158*t*, 188n27
Payne, John W., 95n1, 96n37, 97n55
Pearson, Carol S., 318n74
Pearson, Ian, 521n134
Pechmann, Cornelia, 367n101, 474n123
Peck, J., 226n40
Peck, Joann, 226n36
Pedersen, Elaine L., 320n149
Peirce, Charles Sanders, 219, 227n81
Peñaloza, Lisa, 147n34, 472n57, 472n59
Pennington, Bill, 151n187
Penteado, Claudia, 473n99, 475n168
Peracchio, L. A., 227n81
Percy, Larry, 366n86
Pereira, Joseph, 475n170
Perilloux, Carin, 320n136
Perkins, Natalie, 56n5
Perry, Katy, 111, 343
Peters, Jeremy W., 96n10
Peterson, Richard A., 147n34, 147n35, 521n121
Petronzio, Matt, 190n107
Petroshius, Susan M., 365n53
Petterle, Andiara, 562n81
Petty, Richard E., 318n77, 365n33, 365n55, 368n132, 368n135
Petty, Ross D., 366n67
Pfanner, Eric, 96n33, 562n94
Pham, Michel Tuan, 98n111, 98n112
Phillips, Barbara J., 95n9, 357, 368n131
Phillips, Lynn, 188n47
Phillips, Melodie R., 149n120

Piaget, Jean, 245, 267n56
Picasso, Pablo, 112, 114
Pickrell, Jacqueline, 267n73
Pieters, Rik G. M., 96n34, 227n61, 268n95
Pimentel, Robert W., 96n11
Pimentel, Ronald W., 149n132
Pine, Joseph B., II, 96n17
Pitt, Brad, 303, 346
Pizarro, David, 98n113
Plambeck, Joseph, 148n58
Plummer, Joseph T., 521n138
Pohlmann, Mali, 149n99
Polegato, Rosemary, 424n173
Pollack, Andrew, 425n190
Pollard, Chris, 190n104
Pollay, Richard W., 85*t*, 98n99, 106*t*, 148n85, 149n107, 189n80, 268n126
Pomazal, Richard J., 96n40
Pontari, Beth A., 318n42
Poon, Leonard W., 267n89
Porter, Eduardo, 148n84
Porter, Michael, 97n49
Posavac, Steven S., 366n58
Postaer, Steffan, 98n110
Postrel, Virginia, 148n89, 226n11
Poulos, Basil, 147n24
Powell, Martha C., 268n111
Poyner, Cait, 97n59
Prada, Paulo, 150n167
Prahalad, C. K., 519n49
Prasad, V. Kanti, 267n59
Pratkanis, Anthony R., 366n66
Pratt, Gerry, 149n127
Prensky, Marc, 57n44
Presley, Elvis, 116, 131
Previte, Josephine, 98n107, 290*t*, 292*t*, 294*t*, 318n74
Price, Linda L., 149n137, 423n132, 423n159, 561n44
Priester, Joseph R., 364n12, 365n55
Princess Diana, 133, 303
Princess Grace, 303
Prince William, 494*f*
Prior, Molly, 316
Prochansky, Harold, 422n87
Proctor, Stella, 57n52
Proctor, Tony, 57n52
Prokopec, Sonja, 95n1
Propson, Pamela, 317n30
Proust, Marcel, 258
Pruden, Douglas R., 560n7
Prus, Robert C., 421n31, 422n67
Punj, Girish N., 96n44, 319n83
Puto, Christopher P., 423n117
Putsis, William P., Jr., 97n77

Qualls, William J., 423n117, 424n174, 424n180
Quarantelli, E. L., 562n117
Queen Latifah, 306
Quelch, John A., 151n184
Quenqua, Douglas, 321n162
Quester, Pascale, 146n19

Raasch, Chuck, 189n50
Rabin, Steve, 472n50
Rados, David L., 365n19
Rafaely, V., 267n88
Rai, Saritha, 150n141
Rainwater, Lee, 519n23, 519n24, 519n33, 519n41, 520n55
Ramaswami, Sridhar N., 560n20
Ramirez, Anthony, 227n75, 562n114
Rampell, Catherine, 226n48

Rand, Lindsay, 422n101
Ransdell, Eric, 148n76
Rao, Akshay R., 97n81, 321n182
Rao, Ram C., 366n90
Rashid, Karim, 198
Ratchford, Brian T., 96n46, 98n84
Ratner, Rebecca K., 96n22, 421n35
Ratneshwar, S., 57n37, 366n57, 420n15
Raven, B., 422n77
Ray, Michael L., 364n6, 367n121
Raymond, Jane E., 366n63
Raymore, Leslie, 146n18
Read, H., 318n72
Read, L., 266n31
Redden, Joseph P., 268n106
Redlich, Fredrick C., 520n75
Reece, Bonnie, 267n63
Reed, Americus, II, 300, 317n23, 320n123, 320n124, 365n40
Reese, Shelly, 519n37
Reeves, B., 266n31
Regalado, Antonio, 519n50
Rehfeld, Barry, 422n81
Reichert, Tom, 471n33
Reid, Leonard N., 148n66, 317n6
Reidenbach, Eric, 188n47
Reifler, Petra, 520n58
Reilly, Michael, 365n36, 472n44, 472n62
Reimann, Martin, 97n58, 226n13
Reingen, Peter H., 146n6, 422n73, 561n54, 561n55
Remembrance of Things Past (Proust), 258
Rescorla, R. A., 265n5
Resnik, Alan J., 421n66
Rethans, Arno, 366n92
Reynolds, Fred D., 561n49
Reynolds, Helen, 190n114
Reynolds, Kristy E., 96n11, 149n132
Reynolds, Thomas J., 147n25
Rhoads, Kelton V. L., 365n42
Rhue, Judith W., 317n20
Rial, Nerea, 57n58
Rice, Berkeley, 521n139
Rich, Motoko, 57n16, 148n65
Richardson, Brendan, 423n105
Riche, Martha Farnsworth, 521n141
Richins, Marsha L., 96n15, 188n17, 188n21, 317n12, 321n179, 422n72, 560n9
Richtel, Matt, 227n56, 421n62, 519n14
Rick, S. I., 319n85
Ridgway, Nancy, 96n41, 190n109, 420n22
Riding, Alan, 150n150
Rihanna, 59, 108
Rimer, Barbara K., 364n9
Rindfleisch, Aric, 188n13, 188n15, 188n19, 319n96
Rink, David R., 188n31
Ritchie, Robin J., 366n60
Ritson, Mark, 367n109
Ritter, K. U., 520n85
Rivkin, Steve, 150n174
Roane, Kit R., 520n57
Roberts, Sam, 472n46
Roberts, Scott D., 424n152
Robertson, Kim, 267n72
Robertson, Thomas S., 266n40, 318n82, 420n4, 422n84, 560n13, 562n91
Robin, Donald P., 188n47
Robinson, Patricia, 266n43
Robinson, Patrick J., 423n123
Rockwell, Norman, 439
Rodgers, Ellison, 190n111
Roedder, Deborah L., 367n57

Rogers, Everett M., 560n29, 560n30, 560n33, 562n96
Roggeveen, Anne L., 367n98
Rohter, Larry, 321n176
Rohwedder, Cecilie, 150n170, 520n66
Rokeach, Milton, 106, 146n8, 147n21
Romeo, Jean B., 364n9
Romer, Daniel, 367n129
Romero, Simon, 321n172
Ronis, David L., 268n100
Rook, Dennis W., 148n85, 148n95, 149n99
Rosa, José Antonio, 189n68
Rosch, Eleanor, 97n64, 97n70
Rose, Gregory M., 266n46, 319n94
Rose, Randall L., 519n8
Rosen, Dennis L., 226n53, 424n173
Rosen, Meg, 226n21
Rosenbaum, Aliza, 519n17
Rosenberg, Morris, 317n6
Rosenbloom, Stephanie, 318n55, 421n39, 422n86, 519n18
Rosenthal, Elisabeth, 150n151
Ross, Ivan, 265n8
Rossellini, Isabella, 138
Rossiter, John R., 366n86, 421n49
Rothenberg, Randall, 367n124
Rothschild, Michael, 95n1, 188n47
Rotten, Johnny, 346
Rottenstreich, Y., 266n37
Rubin, Zick, 520n84
Rubinstein, Ruth P., 321n179
Ruch, Floyd L., 519n19
Rucker, Derek D., 317n9, 521n99
Rudmin, Floyd, 320n119
Rusbult, Caryl E., 319n103
Russell, Cheryl, 424n151, 474n154
Russell, Cristel Antonia, 148n66
Russell, Lillian, 305
Russell-Bennett, Rebekah, 98n107, 290t, 318n74
Russo, J. Edward, 258n105, 268n98, 268n104
Ruth, Julie A., 149n101
Ruvio, Ayalia, 472n38
Ryan, Eric, 198

Saatcioglu, Bige, 188n46
Sabar, Ariel, 188n28
Sachdev, Ameet, 366n68
Sack, Kevin, 472n42
Sadalla, E. K., 319n109, 320n116
Saegert, Joel, 226n53, 519n7
Saint Louis, Catherine, 321n175
Sajeesh, S., 96n18
Sama, Gabriel, 471n1
Samor, Geraldo, 150n170
Sanchanta, Mariko, 150n142
Sandicki, Ozlem, 149n101
Sanger, David E., 189n81
Sante, Luc, 423n111
Santora, Marc, 147n52
Saranow, Jennifer, 421n43, 474n119
Saren, Michael, 472n38
Sass, Erik, 190n101, 266n53, 268n96, 424n160
Satel, Sally L., 266n38
Sauer, Abe, 150n164
Saulny, Susan, 472n47
Savary, Miklos, 97n64
Sawyer, A. G., 265n6
Sawyer, Alan G., 367n95
Saxe, Robert, 422n70
Sayre, Shay, 320n121
Schachar, Ron, 473n96
Schachter, Stanley, 57n33

Schaninger, Charles M., 56n8, 424n152, 424n174
Schau, Hope Jensen, 422n90, 473n94, 474n158
Schechner, Sam, 422n88
Schellekens, Gaby A. C., 560n19
Schenk, Carolyn Turner, 420n7
Scheurich, Jim, 521n140
Schibrowsky, John A., 188n33
Schiffer, Claudia, 441
Schiffman, Leon G., 474n157
Schindler, Robert M., 268n122, 269n142
Schlenker, Barry R., 318n42
Schlosser, Ann E., 268n119, 421n47
Schmitt, Bernd H., 420n18, 475n172
Schneider, Keith, 57n45, 560n22
Schneier, Wendy L., 366n93
Schoenbachler, Denise D., 367n125
Schoenberg, Nara, 562n103
Schopler, John, 317n31
Schouten, John W., 178, 321n171, 420n3, 422n90
Schrag, Peter, 472n67
Schulte, Brigid, 474n118
Schultz, E. J., 99n116
Schultz, Myrna, 226n35
Schultz-Kleine, Susan, 319n110
Schumann, David, 366n93, 368n132
Schurr, Paul H., 422n66
Schutz, Howard, 188n47
Schwartz, Ariel, 99n118
Schwartz, Joe, 473n80
Schwartz, Lori, 471n10
Schwarz, Norbert, 366n59
Schwarzenegger, Arnold, 347
Sciolino, Elaine, 96n28
Scott, Carol A., 365n19
Scott, Jerome E., 146n18
Scott, Linda M., 367n128
Sedikides, Constantine, 368n135
Seelye, Katharine Q., 367n113
Seenivasan, Satheeshkumar, 421n58
Seidenberg, Bernard, 422n87
Seiders, Kathleen, 188n34
Seidman, Stephen B., 561n55
Sela, Aner, 97n59
Seligman, Dan, 561n51
Sen, Sankar, 472n60
Sengupta, Jaideep, 367n109, 367n111
Sengupta, Somini, 471n4
Sennott, Sarah, 148n67
Serchuk, David, 96n31
Settle, Robert B., 366n94
Severson, Kim, 188n36, 473n100
Sex Pistols, 346
Seymour, Daniel, 424n158
Shakur, Tupac, 116
Shaninger, Charles M., 519n34
Sharma, Subhash, 98n102
Sharpton, Al, 552
Shaver, P., 422n99
Shavitt, Sharon, 146n9, 364n4
Shaw, John, 319n101
Shayon, Sheila, 189n51, 226n34, 320n125, 560n5
Sheen, Charlie, 346
Sheffet, Mary Jane, 318n82
Sheluga, David A., 188n47
Sheppard, Blair H., 365n35
Sheridan, T. B., 561n67
Sherrell, Daniel L., 96n41, 149n120
Sherry, John F., Jr., 98n82, 146n2, 147n42, 149n98, 149n104, 149n105, 150n161, 189n90, 190n92, 269n141, 319n110, 421n41, 423n140, 424n180
Sherwin, Adam, 472n54

Sheth, Jagdish N., 147n24, 147n34, 280t, 318n49, 422n71
Sheth, Niraj, 471n4
Shields, Brooke, 353
Shiffrin, I. M., 267n68
Shih, Chuan-Fong, 474n123
Shimp, Terence A., 97n81, 98n102, 265n5, 265n8, 266n38, 266n40, 365n32, 367n104
Shirouzu, Norihiko, 150n172
Shiv, Baba, 98n89
Shoham, Aviv, 423n115
Showers, Linda S., 420n19
Shrum, L. J., 188n13
Shu, Suzanne B., 226n36
Shurm, L. J., 189n88
Siemaszko, Corky, 320n135
Silent Spring (Carson), 163
Silk, Alvin J., 268n132
Silk, Michael L., 150n176
Silverstein, Barry, 471n32
Silverstone, Alicia, 314
Simeon, Roblyn, 56
Simmel, Georg, 551, 562n104
Simmons, J. L., 146n14
Simmons, Joseph P., 561n75
Simonson, Itamar, 96n37, 98n97
Simpson, Penny M., 367n110
Simpson, Richard Neil, 265n9, 266n25
Sims, Calvin, 562n119
Sinclair, Upton, 161
Singer, Natasha, 97n58, 188n39, 189n53, 267n67, 317n28, 321n174, 321n185, 425n190
Singh, Jagdip, 188n29, 422n91
Singh, Kulwant, 365n39
Singh, Surendra N., 226n53, 269n136
Sinha, Rajiv K., 422n90
Sinkula, James M., 423n118
Sinn, Francisca, 97n59
Sirdeskmuhk, Deepak, 420n22
Sirgy, M. Joseph, 57n32, 317n6, 319n102, 319n110, 364n4
Sirianni, Nancy J., 188n20
Sirsi, Ajay K., 146n6
Sisario, Ben, 147n36, 521n123
Sivadas, Eugene, 520n91
Skinner, B. F., 235
Skinner, Frank, 520n67
Slackman, Michael, 317n17
Slayten, Galia, 310f
Sleeth-Keppler, David, 97n59
Sloan, Lloyd Reynolds, 365n25
Slutsky, Irina, 57n43
Smidts, Ale, 560n19
Smith, Craig S., 471n27
Smith, Daniel C., 421n60, 421n61
Smith, Darlene Brannigan, 188n47
Smith, Ethan, 521n122
Smith, James D., 190n91
Smith, Kel, 189n59
Smith, Lois J., 267n59
Smith, Malcolm C., 190n108
Smith, Ray A., 425n183
Smith, Robert E., 97n78, 365n37, 560n21
Smith, Ruth Ann, 149n123
Smith, Scott M., 98n84, 317n37
Smith, Terry, 57n34
Snider, Mike, 562n87
Snipes, Wesley, 303
Snow Crash (Stephenson), 279
Snoop Doggy Dogg, 345, 346
Snyder, C. R., 57n35, 562n100
Snyder, Mark, 317n33, 317n34
Sokolowsky, Jennifer, 148n59
Soll, Jack, 98n96

Solomon, Michael R., 56n2, 57n11, 57n32, 57n48, 97n52, 97n65, 97n67, 97n79, 97n81, 98n91, 98n100, 98n107, 99n117, 147n26, 147n30, 147n34, 147n37, 147n49, 147n53, 149n113, 149n127, 187n4, 188n29, 188n33, 189n59, 190n96, 226n20, 227n67, 227n90, 265, 267n87, 268n109, 268n115, 280t, 290t, 292t, 294t, 317n31, 317n33, 318n43, 318n47, 318n49, 318n51, 318n74, 319n101, 319n110, 320n138, 321n179, 366n64, 366n81, 366n84, 367n102, 367n128, 420n18, 420n19, 421n23, 421n33, 422n78, 422n105, 425n187, 472n44, 475n173, 520n92, 521n129, 544t, 560n20, 561n46, 561n57, 562n82, 562n87, 562n99, 562n101, 562n106, 562n109
Sood, S., 266n37
Sood, Sanjay, 317n12
Sørenson, Elin Brandi, 147n25
Soster, Robin L., 98n94
Soutar, Geoff, 520n58
Spangenberg, Eric R., 226n24
Spangler, Steve, 57n45
Speer, Tibbett L., 188n33
Spence, J. T., 267n67
Spence, K. W., 267n67
Spiegler, Marc, 147n29
Spiller, Stephen A., 96n35
Spiro, Rosann L., 422n71
Spodek, Joshua, 225
Springen, Karen, 474n134
Sproles, George B., 562n99
Sprott, David E., 97n59
Srinivasan, Narasimhan, 97n77, 98n84
Srull, Thomas K., 268n96, 268n105, 268n109
Staelin, Richard, 96n44, 98n82
Stamey, Mark, 519n29
Stang, D. J., 422n99
Stanton, Wilbur W., 319n107
Stanwick, Peter A., 227n93
Stanwick, Sarah D., 227n93
Starck, Philippe, 198
Stayman, Douglas M., 421n25, 472n55
Steel, Emily, 96n34, 188n30, 421n63
Steenkamp, Jan-Benedict E. M., 562n92
Stein, Mark A., 149n133
Steinberg, Brian, 148n63, 227n57, 266n15, 366n74, 367n119, 521n115, 521n127, 561n47
Steinberg, Earle, 319n107
Steiner, Gary, 364n7
Steinfield, Charles, 521n97
Steinhauer, Jennifer, 424n175, 520n86, 521n102
Stephen, Andrew T., 98n112
Stephens, Debra, 364n10
Stephenson, Neal, 279, 318n44
Stephey, M. J., 474n141
Sterling, Greg, 97n51
Stern, Barbara, 367n126, 367n128, 471n33, 561n49
Stern, Linda, 227n68
Sternberg, Brian, 472n48
Sternthal, Brian, 98n82, 319n110, 364n9, 364n22, 365n19, 424n180, 560n20
Stettler, Nicolas, 266n49
Stevens, Laura, 421n30
Stevenson, Seth, 51n100
Stewart, David W., 96n27, 268n102, 319n83, 349t, 365n19, 366n82
Stewart, James B., 366n67
Stigler, George, 95n38, 188n10
Stilley, Karen M., 421n56
Stone, Brad, 365n46

Stone, Simon, 190n134
Storm, Diana, 421n41
Story, Louise, 96n28, 148n67, 421n64, 473n107
Strathman, Alan J., 368n135
Stratton, Robert, 318n60
Strauss, William, 473n111
Strazewski, Len, 423n110
Strebel, Judi, 98n107
Strom, Stephanie, 366n67
Strutton, David, 190n124
Stuart, Elnora W., 56n2, 97n52, 227n90, 265n5, 266n38, 421n33
Stuenkel, J. Kathleen, 266n49
Su, Meng, 96n18
Su, Wanru, 189n87
Sujan, Harish, 422n70
Sujan, Mita, 97n69, 97n76, 189n87, 367n109, 422n70, 473n110
Sukhdial, Ajay, 147n24
Sullivan, Gary L., 424n178
Sullivan, Harry Stack, 285
Suls, Jerry, 318n42
Sultan, Fareena, 562n93
Summers, John O., 560n25, 561n37
Sun, Yacheng, 226n7
Sundaram, Suresh, 366n58
Sung, Yongjun, 319n94
Sunstein, Cass R., 98n92
Suprenant, Carol F., 425n187
Surowiecki, James, 561n72, 562n118
Surprenant, Carol F., 97n82, 267n87
Svensson, Peter, 318n47
Swan, John E., 97n82
Swasy, John, 366n92
Swift, Taylor, 111
Swinyard, William R., 365n37
Swisher, Nick, 345
Syam, Niladri, 96n18
Sypecka, Mia Foley, 320n153, 320n154
Szenasy, Mary Kate, 150n177
Szmigin, Isabelle, 474n142
Szybillo, George J., 367n95
Szymanski, David M., 422n70

Tagliabue, John, 226n45
Tahrai, Elie, 306
Tajfel, Henri, 471n3
Talpade, Salil, 424n157
Tam, Pui-Wing, 472n49
Tan, Chin Tiong, 365n39
Tanaka, Hiroshi, 149n106
Tanner, Robin J., 98n89
Tansuhaj, Patriya S., 365n39, 424n157
Tasaki, Lori H., 319n112
Tatham, Ronald L., 319n107
Tauber, Edward M., 421n29
Tavassoli, N. T., 365n38
Tavernise, Sabrina, 423n129, 423n133, 423n134
Tavris, C., 422n99
Taybout, Alice M., 148n95
Taylor, Curtis L., 190n110
Taylor, Earl L., 151n184
Taylor, James L., 422n67
Taylor, Shelley E., 267n85
Taylor, Shirley, 420n16
Taylor, Steven A., 97n80
Teel, Jesse E., 423n113, 423n115
Teheschi, Bob, 227n88
Teichert, Thorsten, 97n58
Teinowitz, Ira, 366n72
Tellegen, C. L., 267n83
Terhune, Chad, 57n45
Teriz, Ana, 226n23
Tesser, Abraham, 318n42

Tetreault, Mary A. Stansfield, 148n85, 422n67
Thaler, Richard, 96n43, 98n92
Theus, Kathryn T., 226n53
Thibaut, John W., 423n114
Thomas, Jacquelyn, 96n18
Thomas, Manoj, 421n58
Thomas, Paulette, 226n16
Thompson, Adam, 150n148
Thompson, Clive, 97n48, 97n58
Thompson, Craig J., 57n51, 146n4, 147n23, 147n31, 319n96, 424n176, 471n35
Thompson, J. Walter, 364
Thompson, Scott A., 422n90
Thompson, Stephanie, 364n8, 423n147, 474n117
Thomson, Matthew, 319n104
Thorne, Avril, 365n25
Thornton, C., 473n78
Tian Kelly, 150n153
Tice, Dianne M., 317n6
Tierney, John, 317n7, 561n56
Tigert, Douglas J., 513t
Till, Brian D., 265n11
Timmons, Heather, 424n163, 520n69, 520n70
Tinkham, Spencer F., 319n94
Tkacik, Maureen, 562n105
Toberston, Thomas S., 266n43
Tobi, Elkin, 474n147
Toluca, D., 96n46
Tormala, Zakary L., 367n97
Townsend, Claudia, 95n5, 317n12
Toy, Daniel R., 368n133
Trappey, Randolph J., III, 190n111
Trawick, I. Frederick, 97n82
Traylor, Mark B., 365n23
Triandis, Harry C., 317n2
Triplett, Tim, 319n98
Tripp, Thomas M., 188n33
Troester, Maura, 147n23
Trosclair, Christine, 266n29
Trout, Jack, 97n73
Trudel, Remi, 189n74
Tse, David K., 97n79, 97n82
Tsotsis, Alexia, 268n123, 317n18
Tulving, Endel, 267n74
Tuncay, Linda, 424n182
Turley, Darach, 149n115, 423n105
Turley, I. W., 421n49
Turner, John C., 471n3
Turner, Jonathan H., 519n20, 519n25
Tuten, Tracy, 57n11, 57n48, 99n117, 561n57, 562n82, 562n109
Tversky, Amos, 98n98, 99n120
Twiggy, 303
Tyagi, Pradeep K., 318n70
Tybout, Alice M., 97n71, 318n70, 365n19, 560n20
Tyrrell, William Blake, 148n82

Umiker-Sebeok, Jean, 521n129
Underwood, Anne, 149n121
Unnava, H. Rao, 97n81
Unsafe at Any Speed (Nader), 163
Urban, Glenn L., 95n38
Urbany, Joel E., 96n16
U.S. Census Bureau, 472n72
Ustuner, Tuba, 148n92, 520n94
Utter, Lydia, 95

Vacker, Barry, 320n146
Valencia, Humberto, 472n63
Valenzuela, Ana, 98n107
Vanden Bergh, Bruce G., 226n35
Vanderbilt, William, 504
Van Gennep, Arnold, 149n113

Van Grove, Jennifer, 99n117
Vanhuele, M., 267n79
van Ittersum, Koert, 227n72
Van Kreveid, D., 422n99
Vanneman, R., 520n79
van Raaij, Fred, 420n3, 519n10
Van Treuren, Ronald R., 317n30
Vavra, Terry G., 560n7
Veblen, Thorstein, 504, 505, 521n111, 551
Veeck, Ann, 268n124
Veiga, Alex, 520n82
Veludo-de-Oliveira, Tania Modesto, 147n25
Venable, Beverly T., 319n94
Venkatesh, Alladi, 57n52, 365n44
Venkatraman, Meera P., 560n32
Verlegh, Peeter W. J., 560n19
Verschure, B., 319n109, 320n116
Vijayenthiran, Viknesh, 319n92
Villareal, Angelina, 367n99, 367n101, 367n109
Vinciguerra, Thomas, 57n26
Vinson, Donald E., 146n18
Vipat, Padma, 268n92
Visconti, Luca M., 147n42
Viswanathan, Madhubalan, 189n68
Vitell, Scott J., 190n124
Vizedom, Maika B., 149n113
Vogel, Nadine, 189n59
Vogt, Christine A., 560n21
Vohs, Kathleen D., 319n09, 365n21, 367n111, 519n9
Voigt, Daniel Q., 149n131
Voli, Patricia K., 424n152
Volpp, Kevin, 320n124
Voorhees, Clay M., 188n33
Voss, Glenn B., 188n34, 420n16
Vranica, Suzanne, 57n45, 57n49, 147n48, 266n34, 268n114, 367n103, 471n9, 562n120

Wade, Dwayne, 120
Wade, Nicholas, 226n32
Wakefield, Kirk L., 421n56
Walker, Beth A., 147n25, 367n102
Walker, Bob, 368n138, 423n102
Walker, Chip, 560n19
Walker, M., 423n108
Walker, Marcus Randall, 365n25
Walker, Mary, 366n64
Walker, Orville C., Jr., 422n68
Walker, Rob, 189n82, 227n86, 227n87, 473n105, 474n135
Walker, W. W., 423n114
Wallace, W. H., 366n83
Walle, Alf H., 562n108
Wallendorf, Melanie, 147n25, 149n98, 149n107, 188n12, 472n44, 472n62, 562n98
Waltzer, Michael, 561n60
Wang, Alexander, 542
Wang, Shirley S., 321n166, 424n170
Wansink, Brian, 189n84, 227n72
Ward, James C., 146n6, 265n8, 560n24, 561n55
Ward, Morgan, 521n95
Ward, Scott, 266n43
Warhol, Andy, 271
Warlop, Luk, 266n26
Warner, Fara, 148n60
Warner, W. Lloyd, 491, 520n60
Warren, Wendy L., 366n93
Warshaw, Paul R., 365n35, 365n41
Wartzman, Rick, 150n158
Watanabe, Chisake, 146n10
Waters, Audrey, 265
Watson, John, 146n18

Watson, W., 520n83
Watts, Duncan J., 560n29, 561n38
Waxman, Sharon, 227n55
Wayne, Teddy, 519n48
Weber, Bernd, 97n58, 226n13
Weber, Ernst, 207
Weber, Max, 482
Weber, Thomas E., 425n190
Webster, Fred E., 423n116
Wechsler, Pat, 560n3
Wedel, Michel, 227n61, 562n92
Weeks, C. S., 267n83
Weezer, 541
Weinbach, Jon, 365n26
Weinberg, Bruce D., 95n38
Weinberg, Charles B., 367n104
Weinberger, Marc G., 367n116
Weingarten, Mark, 561n76
Weinstein, Fannie, 474n136
Weiss, Allen M., 423n119
Weiss, Michael J., 474n127, 474n159, 520n93
Weiss, Paul, 227n81
Weiss, W., 365n52
Weitz, Barton A., 420n20, 422n70, 423n124
Wellman, Barry, 561n63, 561n65
Wells, William D., 189n48, 513t, 521n133, 521n137
Wernerfelt, Birger, 97n57
West, Kanye, 112
West, Patricia M., 422n80
Westerman, Marty, 472n52, 473n90
Whalen, Bernie, 148n83
Wheeler, S. Christian, 97n59, 318n77
Whitaker, Walter W., III, 149n114
White, Erin, 226n37, 319n92, 320n156, 321n170
White, Joseph B., 226n42
White, Katherine, 423n106
Whitman, Janet, 321n171
Whitney, John C., Jr., 267n86
Whittler, Tommy E., 367n125
Wickens, T. D., 268n93
Wicker, Allan, 365n29
Wicklund, R. A., 320n115
Wiertz, Caroline, 521n95
Wilk, Richard R., 150n160
Wilkes, Robert E., 424n169, 474n115
Wilkie, Maxine, 226n31
Wilkie, William L., 95n7, 96n16, 266n47, 367n102, 367n121
Wilkinson, Kendra, 345
Will.I.Am, 202
Williams, Alex, 321n167
Williams, Emelda L., 520n79
Williams, Kaylene C., 422n71, 423n107
Williams, Margaret, 149n111
Williams, Patti, 364n9
Williams, Raymond, 187n8
Williamson, Judith, 367n128
Willman, Chris, 518
Wilson, Eric, 321n176
Wilson, J. P., 318n62
Wilson, R. Dale, 367n104
Wilson, W., 422n98
Wilton, Peter C., 97n79, 97n82
Wind, Yoram, 423n116, 423n123
Winfrey, Oprah, 133, 306
Wingfield, Nick, 148n69, 266n33
Winski, Joseph M., 150n178, 150n182
Winslet, Kate, 363
Wirtz, Jochen, 421n47
Wiseman, Claire V., 320n153
Witkin, Georgia, 190n111
Wolfe, David B., 474n156

Wolfinbarger, Mary, 474n158
Wong, Kwei Cheong, 365n39
Wong, Nancy, 317n4
Wood, Andy, 366n71
Wood, Natalie T., 189n59, 265, 318n47, 366n81, 562n87
Wood, S. L., 424n157
Wood, Stacy, 97n59
Woodside, Arch G., 190n111, 422n66, 422n67
Woodward, Kenneth I., 149n109
Wooten, Adam, 150n175
Wooten, David B., 474n125
Worth, Robert F., 146n5
Wortham, Jenna, 190n94, 561n58, 561n79, 562n109
Wright, James C., 190n96
Wright, Newell D., 319n110
Wright, Peter, 97n81
Wright, Richard L., 268n108
Wright, Tom, 521n106
Wu, Eugenia C., 99n115, 365n18
Wyckham, R. G., 367n102
Wyer, Robert S., Jr., 267n75

Yale, Laura J., 561n41
Yao, Julie L., 319n103
Yap, Kim-Len, 190n137
Yap, Tiffany, 560n18
Yardley, Jim, 146n17
Yi, Tracey, 226n10
Yinger, Milton J., 472n44
Yoffe, Emily, 317n8
Yogovich, B. G., 367n109
Yoka, Hiroko, 471n22
Yoon, Song-Oh, 365n16
Yoon, Yeosun, 366n59
York, Emily Bryson, 226n27, 266n51
Yorkston, Eric, 226n35
Younger, Shannan, 474n133
Yu, Eleanor, 473n90
Yunis, Muhammad, 164
Yut, Emily, 267n58
Yuwei, Jiang, 148n71

Zablocki, Benjamin D., 521n114, 521n120
Zahlaway, Jon, 365n51
Zaichkowsky, Judith, 95n6, 96n14, 226n13, 265n9, 266n25, 268n92, 424n173
Zajonc, R. B., 422n98
Zajonc, Robert B., 364n10, 366n89
Zammit, Alessandra, 96n35
Zarembo, Alan, 420n13
Zaslow, Jeffrey, 425n185
Zax, David, 189n62
Zeithaml, Valerie, 98n82
Zezima, Kate, 423n143
Zhang, Ying, 95n3
Zhang, Z. John, 96n18
Zhou, Xinyue, 519n9
Zhu, Rui (Juliet), 226n6
Zichermann, G., 266n30
Zielske, H., 367n106
Zifliog'lu, Verichan, 146n7
Zimbardo, Philip G., 519n19
Zimmer, Mary R., 227n76, 421n44
Zimmerman, Ann, 150n170, 421n30, 562n113
Zinkhan, George M., 149n112, 267n73, 319n101, 423n103
Zinn, Laura, 474n140
Zmuda, Natalie, 227n84, 471n31, 474n126
Zuckerberg, Mark, 487
Zuckert, Tim, 148n67

Company/Brand Name

ABC, 47, 94, 115, 118, 208
Abercrombie & Fitch, 301, 456
Ace Ventura, 508
Activision, 119
Adam's Rib, 433
Adbusters, 162, 163*f*
Adidas, 63, 233, 297
Advantage Marketing and Advertising, 355
A&E, 434
Affliction, 108
Aherk!, 238, 239*f*
AIG, 160, 163, 504
Air Asia, 435
Air Jordans, 29
Air Nikes, 120
Alberto-Culver, 272
Alien, 219
Alka-Seltzer, 296
All in the Family, 132
All Things Frugal, 479
Alpha M.O.S., 204
Altoids, 523
Amazon.com, 73, 95, 170, 173, 246, 457, 537
AMC, 434
American Academy of Cosmetic Surgery, 311
American Airlines, 164
American Anthropological Association, 49
American Association for Public Opinion
        Research, 49
American Association of Advertising Agencies, 156*f*
American Association of Family
        and Consumer Sciences, 49
American Association of People with
        Disabilities (AAPD), 164
American Association of Retired Persons
        (AARP), 410
American Dental Association, 440
American Economic Association, 49
American Express, 178, 197, 224, 235, 553
American Heart Association, 247
American Idol, 65, 86, 118, 390
American Iron, 389
American Marketing Association, 49
American Red Cross, 86
American Society of Plastic Surgeons, 311
American Sociological Association, 49
American Statistical Association, 49
America's Army, 118
America's Next Top Model, 118
Amul Macho, 428
Amway, 395
Amy's Kitchen, 459
Android phones, 60, 220, 294, 535
Angry Birds, 108, 544
Apple, 62, 81, 82, 87, 88, 167, 177–178, 197, 198,
        203, 291, 294, 393, 446, 454, 455, 509
Apprentice, The, 118
Aqua Teen Hunger Force, 179
Arab Dairy Company, 355
Arby, 352
Are You Smarter Than a Fifth Grader?, 253
Arizona State University (ASU), 333
Armani, 42
Arm & Hammer, 77
Arthur Andersen, 163
Ascena Retail Group, 470
Asda grocery chain, 203
ASICS, 357
ASmallWorld.net, 482
ASOS, 541

Association for Consumer Research, 48, 49
Aston Martin, 482
AT&T, 296, **4**45
Audi, 30, 291, 340, 341
Aunt Jemima, 440
Austin Reed, 375*f*
Australian Postal Service, 217*f*
Automobile Magazine, 39*f*
Avatar, 279
Avatar Reality, 281*f*
Aveda, 454
Avis, 123, 352
Avon, 165, 395
Axe, 67, 118, 201, 251, 252, 387, 428, 434*f*, 437*f*

Baby Alive, 450
Bacardi, 509
Bachelor, The, 484
Backer Spielvogel Bates, 107
Bad Girls Club, 27
Bag Borrow or Steal, 117
Balenciaga, 523
Banana Republic, 506
Barbie Dolls, 28, 46, 115, 306, 310*f*, 312, 429–430, 429*f*
Barcalounger, 229
Barnes & Noble, 73
Barney & Friends, 246
Bass Export, 65
Bass Pro Shops, 384
Battle Stations, 545
Bavaria, 435*f*
Bayer, 162, 296, 324
BBDO Worldwide, 125
Beacon South Africa, 66
Beanie Babies, 553
Bear Stearns, 160, 163
Ben & Jerry's, 108
Berkshire Hathaway, 419
Bertie Bott's Every Flavor Beans, 219
Best Buy, 118, 167, 229, 381, 401, 544
Best Western, 559
Beverly Hills 90210, 309
Bianco Footwear, 480*f*
Big Bang Theory, 59, 118
Biggest Loser, The, 118
Bijan, 433*f*
Billboard 200, 116
Bing, 73, 544
Bio Business International, 528
Bizrate.com, 59, 73
BJ's, 419
Blackberry, 180
Black & Decker, 213
Black Eyed Peas, 196
Blackspot sneakers, 163*f*
Blade Runner, 219
Blair Witch Project, The, 115
Bluefly.com, 382*f*
Blue's Clues, 246
BMW, 30, 292, 393, 446, 510
Bobby Jones, 375*f*
Body Shop, 307*f*
Book of Mormon, The, 446
Born This Way, 544
Boston Consulting Group, 84
Boston Red Sox, 62
Botox, 311
Bounce, 357
Bounty, 222
Boxtops for Education, 165
Boys and Girls Clubs of America, 316, 440
Boy Scouts, 277
BP, 163
Brain Box, 253

Braniff, 140, 444
Bravia, 429
Bravo, 115, 434
Brides, 437
Bristol-Myers Squibb, 205
Brooks Brothers, 373
Bruegger's Corporation, 442
Bubba Co., 32
Bubba Gump Shrimp Company, 219
Budweiser, 219, 333, 444, 542
Buffalo Bills, 124
Bulgari, 480
Bump, The, 406
Bungie Studios, 392
Burberry, 494
Burger King, 118, 200, 247, 428, 543
Busy Scissors, 452*f*
BzzAgent, 525, 525*f*

Cabbage Patch, 553
Cachet, 43
Cadbury, 440
Cadillac, 224, 510
Callard & Bowser, 523
Calvin Klein, 224
Calvin Klein Eternity, 251
Campbell Soup, 84, 165, 200, 234, 247, 378*f*, 547
Canon, 90
Canvas 8, 511*f*
Cap'n Crunch, 229
Capstone Turbine Corporation, 399*f*
Captain CupCake, 229
Car and Driver, 61, 341
Cartoon Network, 224, 434
Castello Bianco, 200
CBS, 47, 74, 94, 118
CEMEX, 489
Chanel, 251
Chapstick, 179, 181
Charles Schwab, 445
Charlie the Tuna, 296, 356
Charmin, 66, 68*f*, 162
Cheerios, 145, 548
Cheetos, 139
Cheezburger Network, 553
Chevrolet, 260, 409, 435, 510
Chicago Bears, 118
Chick-Fil-A, 62
Children by Choice, 405
Children's Food and Beverage Initiative, 247
China Telecom, 220
Chinet, 536*f*
Chio, 117*f*
Chivas Regal, 137
Chromeo, 509
Chrysler, 204, 291
Church & Dwight, 77, 208
Citigroup, 480
Citroën, 393
Classmates.com, 540
Clearasil, 273
Club Med, 134
Clueless, 457
CNBC, 434
Coach, 498
Coachella music festival, 116
Coca-Cola, 74, 88, 88*f*, 117, 118, 124, 136, 137,
        138, 141, 155, 159, 198, 202, 202*f*, 224,
        229, 233, 247, 327, 328, 343, 445
Coffee-Mate, 248, 442
Cohorts, 434
Cold Stone Creamery, 304, 529
Colgate, 323, 353
Colgate-Palmolive Co., 449

Colgate-Palmolive's Total brand, 353
Collegehumor.com, 457
Comedy Central, 434
ConAgra, 108
Conair Pro Style 1600, 72
Cone Communications, 559
Consumer Product Safety Commission
    (CPSC), 162*t*
Converse, 509
Coors, 387, 444
Cornell Dairy Ice Cream, 234
CosmoGirl.com, 282
Cosmopolitan, 103, 271, 434
Cosmopolitan Turkey, 103
Costco, 112, 419, 478, 498
Cougar Town, 504
Council of Better Business Bureaus, 162, 247
Coyote Girls, 131
Coyote Ugly, 131
Crate and Barrel, 419
Crazy Blue Air Freshener, 549
Crest, 31, 323, 353, 439
C28, 448
Curves, 448
CVS Corporation, 401
Cyburbia Productions, 87
CyWorld, 279

DaimlerChrysler, 74
Dallas, 157
Dallas Cowboys, 132
Dancing with the Stars, 291
Dannon, 247
Danone, 494
Dating 4 Disabled, 168
Dave and Buster's, 405
David's Bridal, 126
Da Vinci Code, The, 446
Dawn, 165
DDB World Communications Group, 107, 548
Def Jam Fight for NY, 442
Dell Computer, 64, 401, 527
Denny's, 201
Denver Broncos, 124
Department of Agriculture, 161, 169
Depends, 462
Details, 450
Dexter, 220
Diageo, 124
Diesel Jeans, 41, 392
Diet Coke, 47, 324
DiGiorno Pizza, 291
Dilbert, 198
Dippin' Dots, 201
DirecTV, 537
Dirty Dancing, 136
Discovery Channel, 224, 256
Disney, 74, 87, 229, 498
DisneyBaby.com, 450
Disney Channel, 434, 456
Disneyland, 133, 254
Disneyland Paris, 138
Disney World, 122, 123, 133, 138, 257, 450, 481
dogdoo.com, 183
Dogtown, 547
DogWater, 406
Dolce & Gabbana, 434, 498
Dollar Stretcher, 479
Domino, 84
Dommelsch, 384
Doonesbury, 124
Dora the Explorer, 246
Doritos, 229, 447

Dove, 306–307, 316, 459, 461*f*
Doyle Dane Bernbach (DDB), 51
Dr. Martens, 509
Dr. Pepper Ten, 434
Dr. Tattoff, 313
Dreyfus Fund, 219
DriveNow, 30
Dropps, 153
Dunder Mifflin Paper Company, 116
Dungeons and Dragons, 545
Dunkin' Donuts, 68, 528
Duracell, 32, 35*f*

E!, 434
Eagles, 518
Eastman Kodak, 200
EasyJet, 499
eBay, 133, 166, 541
Ecko, 108
Ecos, 153
Ed Hardy, 233, 547
Egg Banking, 66
eharmony.com, 286
80sTees.com, 219
Einstein/Noah Bagel Corporation, 442
Electronic Arts, 118
Eli Lilly, 401, 402
Elizabeth Arden Red Door, 251
Elle, 434
Enron, 163, 504
Entertainment Weekly, 434
Entourage, 118
Entropia Universe, 348
Environmental Protection Agency (EPA), 153,
    161, 162*t*, 170
Enyce, 108
ePad Femme, 433
Epic Goal, 545
Epinions, 90
Equally Wed, 437
ESPN, 296, 343
ESPN.com, 343
Essence magazine, 442
Esso, 284
E.T.: The Extra-Terrestrial, 123
Euro Disney, 136, 139
Evian, 291, 387
ExBoyfriendJewelry.com, 127*f*
Experian, 451
Extreme Makeover, 451
Extreme Makeover: Home Edition, 118, 256
Exxon, 219, 284
EZFace system, 275

Fabricly, 109, 382
Facebook, 27, 46*f*, 47, 48, 67, 69, 73, 81, 89, 165,
    172, 180, 229, 233, 234, 239, 257, 258*f*,
    261*f*, 271, 274, 275, 293, 301, 323, 341,
    343, 345, 373, 374, 389, 396, 403, 410,
    445, 482, 523, 535, 536, 539, 540, 541,
    542, 545
Family Guy, 291
Fantasy Kids Resort, 104
FarmVille, 180, 544, 545
Febreze, 89
Federal Communications Commission
    (FCC), 162*t*
Federal Trade Commission (FTC), 161, 162*t*,
    165, 166, 246, 247, 345, 346, 352
Femme Actuelle, 244
Fendi, 494
Ferrari, 74, 482, 492
Ferrero, 117*f*

Fiat, 499
First Alert, 132*f*
FishVille, 545
Fitocracy, 240
Flickr, 31, 257, 343, 536
Flowrider, 383
Folgers, 200, 201
Food and Drug Administration (FDA), 145, 161,
    162, 162*t*
Food Hotel, 117*f*
Footjoy, 513
Foot Locker, 31
Ford Motor Company, 69, 171*f*, 222,
    291, 530
Ford Mustang, 219, 248, 393
Forever 21, 306
Forrester, 543
Forrest Gump, 219
Fossil, 260*f*
Four Seasons, 559
Foursquare, 45, 341, 373, 501, 535
Fox Broadcasting, 212
Framingham Heart Study, 534
Francesco Biasia Handbags, 278*f*
France Telecom, 350*f*
Frankie Lymon and the Teenagers, 451
French Connection, 215*f*
Friends Reunited, 410
Frito-Lay, 72, 74, 139, 236*f*, 436
Frugal Mom, 479
Fudge Australia, 248*f*
Furbys, 553
FX, 434

Gablinger, 101
GagaVille, 544
Game Show Network, 73
Gap Inc., 32, 67, 114, 136, 176, 234, 401,
    446, 454, 470
Garmin, 393
Garmz, 109*f*
GEICO, 115, 348, 510
General Electric (GE), 234, 254
General Foods, 74, 75
General Mills, 145, 165, 247, 548
General Motors (GM), 87, 162,
    163, 352
Gentleman's Quarterly, 530
Gerber Baby Food, 405
Giga Pets, 553
Gillette, 198
Gilligan's Island, 114, 457
Gilt Groupe, 382
Ginger, 89
Giorgio Armani, 493
Girl Scouts, 165, 316
GiveWell, 345
Glade, 200
Glamour, 271
Glee, 291
GlobalScan, 107
GoldVish, 503
Gone with the Wind, 123
Good Housekeeping, 341
Google, 73, 74, 165, 169, 220, 258, 286, 350*f*,
    457, 526, 537, 541
"Got Milk?" ads, 195, 347
GQ, 157, 450
Grand Theft Auto, 442
Grauman's Chinese Theater, 133
Grease, 136
Green Giant, 218
Grey Advertising, 83*f*, 296

Grey Poupon, 222
Grey's Anatomy, 118, 162
Groupe Danone, 494
Groupon, 537
Gucci, 406, 494, 505, 510
Guess, 183
Guinness, 125, 256
Guitar Hero, 541

Häagen-Dazs, 492
Habbo Hotel, 279, 348
Haggar, 410
Halo 2, 392
Hammacher Schlemmer, 526
Handi-Wrap, 260
Happy Ho Ho, 229
Harley-Davidson, 46, 62, 196, 373, 389, 392, 393, 406
Harper's Bazaar, 434
Harris Poll, 508
Harry Potter, 219, 286, 508, 555
Harry Winston Jewelers, 488*f*
Hart Schaffner & Marx, 375*f*
Harvey Nichols, 350*f*
Haven, 545
Hawaii Five-O, 342
HBO, 94, 118, 434
Heineken, 137, 208
Heinz, 234
Hello Kitty, 508
Henkel, 208
HerCampus, 27
Hermès, 494
Hershey Foods, 247, 428, 455
Hewlett-Packard, 401, 488
Hickey-Freeman, 375*f*
hiphopcapital.com, 108
H&M, 470, 499, 552
Hoaxkill.com, 526*f*
Holga camera, 393
Holiday Inn, 80
Hollywood Stock Exchange, 46, 402
Home Depot, 419, 440
Honda, 507
Honey Maid, 207
Hong Kong Disneyland, 139
Hostess, 229
Host Foods, 160
Hot or Not, 281*f*
Hot Topic, 453, 551
House of Chanel, 441
Hugo Boss, 492
Hulu, 95, 541
Hummer, 87, 394, 503
Hush Puppy, 553
Hydrox, 62

iAds, 259
IBM, 81, 82, 549
iChat, 410
IKEA, 139, 406, 419, 545
Illicit Encounters, 410
Import Tuner, 507
Index of Social Position, 495
Index of Status Characteristics, 495
Infiniti, 282
Instagram, 229, 257, 389, 535
Institute of Management Sciences, 49
InStyle, 434
International Communication Association, 49
Interstate Commerce Commission (ICC), 162*t*
iPad, 168, 198, 294, 445
iparty.com, 78*f*
iPhone, 28, 60, 62, 88, 177, 248, 259, 382, 387, 541

iPod, 259, 309, 343, 382, 410, 455
Islamic Food and Nutrition Council of America, 449
iTunes, 346, 509
iVillage.com, 27, 31
Ivory Soap, 84
IWC, 431*f*
Izod Lacoste, 232
Izze Sparkling Pomegranate, 118

Japander.com, 347*f*
JC Penney, 48, 108, 126, 401
Jell-O, 75, 89
JetBlue Airways, 32
Jewelmint.com, 27
Jif, 331
Jim Beam Brands, 234, 555*f*
Jimmy Choo, 286, 494
Johnson & Johnson, 411
Jollibee Food Corp., 137
Jolly Green Giant, 37, 296, 356
Jones Soda, 62, 393
Jordan's Furniture, 419
Journal of Consumer Research, 49
Juicy Couture, 29, 251, 304, 406

Kamashita, 59
Kaneva, 410
Kayak, 559
KaZaa, 126
Keds, 554
Keebler Elves, 296
Keeping Up With the Kardashians, 157
Kellogg, 140, 165, 203, 247
Kentucky Fried Chicken (KFC), 209, 299*f*, 445
Keurig, 459
Kickstarter.com, 542
Kimberly-Clark, 162, 462
Kindle, 374
King Ding Dong, 229
King of Queens, 346
Kitchen Aid, 297
Klout, 531
Kmart, 345, 551
K9 Water Inc., 406
Knot, The, 73, 406
Kodak, 138
Komatsu Europe, 400*f*
Kontera, 145
Kotex, 451
Kraft, 90, 169, 207, 247, 291, 523, 524
Krispy Kreme, 61, 304
Kutless, 448
Kwik-E-Marts, 115*f*

Lada, 140
Lady and the Tramp, 406
Lamborghini, 482
Lamisil, 89
Lands' End, 406, 470
Lane Bryant, 306, 470
LastExitToNowhere.com, 219, 221*f*
Layar, 220
La-Z-Boy, 112
Leave It to Beaver, 402
Lee Jeans, 353
Lehman Brothers, 160
Leo Burnett, 523
Lever Brothers, 440
Levi Strauss & Company, 41, 64, 136, 222, 234, 301, 308, 392, 447, 509, 548
Lexus, 113, 373
Libbey Glass Co., 483*f*
Life cereal, 255

Lifetime, 434
Like Mike, 120
Linden Lab, 410
LinkedIn, 293, 343, 373
Lipton, 134, 447, 449
Listerine, 232, 334
Little Miss Perfect, 451
Little Red Riding Hood, 120–121, 122*f*
LiveJournal, 394
Lomo Cameras, 393
Lord of the Rings, The, 286
L'Oréal, 63*f*, 222, 304, 330, 445, 452*f*, 499
Lorillard Tobacco, 451*f*
Lost Ring, The, 31
Louis Vuitton, 492, 498, 505
LowerMyBills.com, 212
Lowes, 419
LuckySurf.com, 121*f*
LUSH Cosmetics, 86
Lux soap, 304

Maalox, 215
Macy's, 34, 108, 446, 470
Mad Men, 291
Mafia Wars, 545
Magnum 5 Senses Ice Cream, 201
Maidenform, 552*f*
Maid in Manhattan, 484
Major League Baseball, 133
Mall of America, 45
Manolo Blahnik, 62, 83
Marco Polo Hotel, 49*f*
Marks & Spencer, 72
Marlboro, 162, 219, 220, 233, 324, 392
Mars, 247
Mars Snackfood USA, 64
Martha Stewart, 163
Martha Stewart Living, 434
Martha Stewart Weddings, 437
Maruti 800, 499
Mary Kay, 395
Maserati, 482, 492
Match.com, 47, 286, 540
Matrix, The, 279, 508
Mattel, 115, 306, 312, 429, 431
Maytag, 510
Mazda Miata, 204
McCann-Erickson, 182
McDonald's, 31, 32, 43*f*, 121, 128*f*, 135, 136, 137, 162, 195, 215, 233, 244, 247, 343, 352, 394, 438, 439, 442, 480
MCI, 296
M&C Saatchi, 478
Medal of Honor Warfighter, 118
Mediamark Research & Intelligence, 530
Megaupload, 126
Meister Brau, 260
Melrose Place, 117, 309
Mentos, 47
Mercedes, 345, 505
Mercedes-Benz, 30, 446
Merck, 448
Merriam-Webster Dictionary, 537
Metamucil, 354
Metaverse, 279
Method, 153, 198, 198*f*
MetLife, 348
Michelin Man, 296
Mickey Mouse, 102, 137, 498
Microsoft, 235, 279, 401, 544, 545
Mighty Morphin Power Rangers, 553
Milk Industry Foundation, 195
Miller Brewing, 101
MillerCoors, 374

Miller Lite, 330
Mindset Media, 286
Mini Cooper, 118, 257*f*
Minolta, 64*f*
Mintel, 363, 419
Minute Maid, 224
Miracle Whip, 117
Missoni, 493
MIT, 124, 277
MLE/FOCE (Major League Eating/Federation
    of Competitive Eating), 196
M&Ms, 64, 300, 348, 450
ModaOperandi, 382
ModCloth, 109, 382, 470, 542
Molson, 210*f*, 511
Mo'men, 32
Morpheus, 126
Motel 6, 509
Motion Odyssey Movie Ride (MOM), 419
Motrin, 411
Mountain Dew, 229, 509, 525
M-PESA, 549
Mr. Clean, 234, 434
Mr. Goodwrench, 356
Mr. Peanut, 296
Mrs. Butterworth's Syrup, 450
MTV, 37, 136, 141, 245, 432, 434, 458, 495, 513, 553
MTV Europe, 141
mtvU.com, 457
Museum of Bad Art, 37*f*
MyBestSegments.com, 464
My Fair Lady, 493
MySpace, 403
Mythbusters, 256

Nabisco, 207
Nair, 126
NASA, 167, 286
NASCAR, 119, 153, 340
Natan Jewelry (Brazil), 498*f*
National Advertising Division (NAD), 162
National Basketball Association
    (NBA), 136, 492
National Center of Health Statistics, 405
National Eating Disorders Association, 309
National Enquirer, 340
National Football League (NFL), 59, 124, 198,
    220, 343, 411
National Hockey League (NHL), 198
National Institutes of Health, 244
National Park Service, 354
National Religious Partnership for the
    Environment, 155
Nature's Source, 171
Nautica, 108
NBC, 47, 94
NCR Corp., 378
Need for Speed Underground 2, 118
NeighborGoods.com, 177
Neiman Marcus, 158*f*, 486
Neon Indian, 509
Nestlé, 219, 247, 449
Nestlé Brazil, 489
Net-a-Porter, 382
Netflix, 73, 94–95
New Adventures of Old Christine, The, 118
Newman's Own, 165
Newsweek, 450
New York City Department of Health, 89
New York Health and Racquet Club, 212
New York Times, 167, 340, 419
New York Yankees, 133
Nickelodeon, 245, 434, 451
Nicklaus, 375*f*

Nielsen Company, 94, 119, 191, 244, 256, 457,
    460, 463
Nike, 38, 63, 118, 122, 136, 137, 297, 441, 448,
    492, 509, 513, 554, 555
Nintendo Wii, 327, 452*f*, 545
NoDNA, 348*f*
Nokia, 117, 137, 350*f*, 449, 504
Nooks, 374
Noor Index, 449
Norelco, 450
Northwestern Insurance, 222
Notorious-Die to Drive, 442
NPD Group, 451
NXT, 388*f*
Nytol, 72

Objective Logistics, 240
Obsession perfume, 236
Ocean Spray, 240
Office, The, 116, 219, 292, 347
Ogilvy & Mather, 107, 316, 449
Ogilvy Noor, 449
OKCupid, 47
Olay, 126, 304, 524
Old Navy, 470
Old Spice, 118, 260, 285, 345*f*, 348, 455
Olympics, 105
Omega watches, 304
Omni hotels, 197
101 Dalmatians, 406
One Tree Hill, 118
Opower, 240
Oracle, 220
Orbitz, 118
Oregon Humane Society, 192*f*, 370*f*
Oreos, 41, 195, 196
Organization for Economic Cooperation
    and Development (OECD), 154
O: The Oprah Magazine, 31
OurWeddingDay.com, 126
OutVite.com, 437
Owens-Corning Fiberglass Corporation, 196
Oxford English Dictionary, 552
Oxygen.com, 27
Oxygen network, 434

Panasonic, 140, 345
Pandora, 541
Pandora.com, 537
Pantone, Inc., 200
Paradise Paintball, 545
Paragraph, 384
Parkay, 547
Parkwood Entertainment, 112
Parrot Heads, 518
Passion of Christ, The, 446
Patagonia, 454
Paul Mitchell, 406
PayPal, 27
Peapod, 547
Peeps, 38
Pentel, 137
People, 434
Pepperidge Farm, 123, 447
PepsiCo Inc., 74, 75, 77, 112, 118, 179, 203, 204,
    207, 207*f*, 229, 247, 254, 309, 327, 328,
    333, 345, 387, 447, 453, 458*f*
Perdue Chicken, 444
PETCO, 536
Pet Detective, 508
Pet Resort, 545
PetsHotels, 406
PetSmart, 406
Pet Society, 544

Pew Research Center, 489
Pfanni, 67*f*
Pfizer Inc., 448
PGA European Tour, 31
Philips, 455
Philips Electronics, 80
Phish, 508
Pictionary, 241*f*
Piercing Fans International Quarterly, 314
Pillsbury, 182, 285
Pillsbury Doughboy, 37, 296, 510
Pink Panther, 196
Pinterest, 389, 535
Pioneer, 507
Pizza Queen, 32
Planters Peanuts, 217, 260
Playboy, 306, 532
Playfish, 544
Playtex, 107
Plenty of Fish, 47
Pluto the Circus Dog, 138
Pokémon, 553
Polaroid, 390
Polygamy Porter, 447
Polymer Records, 219
Polyvore, 523
POM Wonderful, 117
Pond's Moisturizer, 303
Pontiac, 297
Pop-Tarts, 33
Porsche, 74, 232, 480
Porter Novelli, 32
Prada, 492
Pretty Woman, 484
Pricegrabber.com, 59, 73
Prilosec OTC, 32
Prime Wave, 59, 77, 79
Princeton University, 125
Pringles, 67, 296
Procter & Gamble (P&G), 31, 32, 67, 104, 105,
    138, 153, 154, 162, 165, 198, 208, 219,
    234, 235*f*, 353, 439, 442, 455, 528, 532
ProFlowers, 544
Prozac, 246
Purex, 329*f*
Pussycat Dolls, 118

Quaker Foods, 440
Quaker Oats, 294, 297, 462
Qualcomm, 246
Quick, 32
Quill.com, 116

Rachel Ray Sucks Community, 394
Ragu, 124
Ralph Lauren, 88, 232, 406, 487
Ramones, 509
Rand Corporation, 178
RateMyProfessors.com, 27, 47
Reader's Digest, 107
Real Gilligan's Island, 114
RED, 165
Redbook, 411
Red Bull, 31
Red Cross, 285
Redken, 452*f*
Redneck Bank, 33*f*
Red Shoes, The, 277
Red Wing, 506
Reebok, 38, 507, 554
Renault, 119*f*, 275, 447
Rent the Runway, 308, 308*f*
Reputation.com, 282
Restylane, 457, 458

Right Guard, 66*f*
RJR Nabisco, 216
Roche, 205
Rock 'n' Roll Fantasy Camp, 391*f*
Rolex, 510
Rolling Stone, 107, 434
Roper Research, 410
Roper Starch Worldwide, 272
Rowenta, 72
Royal Caribbean, 224
Rubbermaid, 436
RVL7, 384

Saatchi & Saatchi, 88, 453, 454
Safeway, 448
Saks Fifth Avenue, 470, 493
Salesgenie.com, 439
Sam's Club, 478
Samsung, 40*f*, 250, 533
Samuel Adams, 219
San Francisco Ballet, 199*f*
Sani-Flush, 248
Sara Lee, 140, 247, 272
SAS, 36*f*
Saskatoon Restaurant, 508*f*
S.C. Johnson, 171
Scent Marketing Institute, 202
Schlitz, 513
Scion, 509
Sears, 157
SeaWorld, 345
Second Life, 48, 279, 348, 410
Securities and Exchange Commission, 161
Seinfeld, 42, 182, 436
Self, 434
Sesame Street, 246
7-Eleven, 120
Seven For All Mankind, 41, 250
Seventeen, 306, 452
Seventh Generation, 153, 170
Sex and the City, 117, 277
Sex Pistols, 200, 346
Shape, 434
ShareSomeSugar, 177
Sharp, 553
Shearson, 260
Sidetrack Technologies, 224
Sigg water bottles, 512*f*
SignBank, 548
Silverlit Toys, 526
Simon Fraser University, 124
Simpsons, The, 219, 547
Sims, The, 264, 343, 545
Sims Online, The, 279
Singapore Airlines, 201
Singapore MediaCorp, 526
Sitepal.com, 265
Six Degrees of Separation, 534
Skittles, 536*f*, 537
Skype, 410, 541
Skyy Spirits, 353
Slim-Fast, 310, 311
Slumdog Millionaire, 410, 494
Smash, 305
Smithsonian Institution, 132
Smith & Wesson, 234
Smith & Wollensky, 326*f*
Smucker's, 448
SnapGoods, 177
Snapple, 139, 297
Snow Crash, 279
Society for Consumer Psychology, 48, 49
Society for Personality and Social Psychology, 49
Sony, 119, 167, 204, 429, 454, 545

sooruz.com, 24*f*, 77*f*
Sotheby's, 480
Spanx, 301
Speaking Roses International, 67
Speedo, 82
Spice Girls, 101
SpongeBob SquarePants, 245
Sports Authority, 183
Sports Illustrated, 532
Sprint, 296, 435, 510, 550
Spyder Eclipse, 222
Squinkies, 553
SRI International, 514
Standard & Poor's, 480
Staples, 116, 183
Starbucks, 45, 63, 101, 133, 201, 219, 234, 292, 384, 384*f*, 394, 509
Starch Advertising Research, 344
Stardoll.com, 553
Starlite Urban Drive-In (London), 136
Star Trek, 123, 131, 132
Star Wars, 508, 553
Stereo Review, 529
Stihl, 539*f*
Story of Mace Windu, The, 553
StriVectin, 393
Strokes, The, 509
Subaru, 45*f*, 324, 396, 457, 526
Submedia, 224, 225
Sudoku, 253
Sultan Ayub, 32
Sun Chips, 236*f*
Sunkist, 76*f*
Sunsilk shampoo, 311, 448, 449
Super Bowl, 37, 112, 125, 134, 439, 447
Survivor, 390
Susan G. Komen for the Cure, 165
Suzuki, 433, 448
Swanson, 72
Swatch, 384
Swatch Instant Store, 384
Swiffer, 104, 105, 459

Taco Bell, 510
Tag Heuer, 494
Taproot India, 218*f*
Tap Tap Revenge, 541
Target, 159, 198, 224, 306, 401, 419, 470, 498
Tat2BeGone, 313
Tattoo MD, 313
Taxi, 214
TBS, 434
Teenage Mutant Ninja Turtles, 553
Teenage Research Unlimited, 453
Teen Mom 2, 245
Telemundo Communications Group, 445
Tennis Mania, 545
Terra, 445
Terra Cycle, 174, 175*f*
Terre Femme, 528
Tesco, 72, 401
Texas A&M, 124
Texas A&M Jerky, 234
Texas Hold 'Em, 545
theknot.com, 126
This Is Spinal Tap, 219
Thor's Hammer, 433
Threadless, 109, 382, 542
3Com, 393
3 Doors Down, 115
3M, 440
Thrifty Car Rental, 463
Tide, 153, 154, 235*f*, 248
Tiffany's, 42

Time, 450
Titleist, 251
TiVo, 342, 410
TLC, 434
Today show, 437
Toddlers & Tiaras, 451
Tommy Hilfiger, 108, 220, 346, 375*f*
Tom Petty and the Heartbreakers, 393
TOMS, 164
ToneCheck, 90
Tony Hawk's Underground 2, 119
Tony the Tiger, 356
Torrid, 307
Toyota, 113, 233, 451, 455, 538*f*
Toys "R" Us, 159, 526
Trader Joe's, 459
Transformers, 553
Travelocity, 543*f*
Trend School, 456*f*, 457
TripAdvisor, 541, 559
Triscuit, 387
Trivial Pursuit, 253
Tron franchise (Disney), 229
True Religion, 41
Trulia, 115
Tupperware, 395
TV Guide, 107
25 to Life, 442
Twinity, 537
Twinkies, 40, 330
Twinkie the Kid, 229
Twitter, 47, 69, 73, 89, 90, 177, 229, 257, 271, 293, 343, 345, 373, 389, 394, 411, 445, 460, 531, 535, 536*f*, 540
TwoRooms, 384
Tyco, 504
Tylenol, 179
Tyson, 448

Ugly Betty, 307
Ugly Wudi, 308
UNICEF, 186–187, 390
Unilever, 104, 172, 208, 303, 306, 307, 316, 363, 442, 449, 494
United Airlines, 283*f*
United Arab Emirates, 41*f*
United Nations, 45
Universal Studios, 196
University of California at Santa Barbara, 125
University of Michigan, 125
University of North Carolina, 334
University of Vermont, 124
Univision, 427
Upscale, 31
Urbanspoon, 541
U.S. Census Bureau, 30, 167, 402, 405, 439, 442
U.S. Department of Labor, 412
U.S. Education Department, 169
U.S. Robotics, 390
US Weekly, 434

VALS2™, 107
Valspar, 86, 87
Varsity Brands, 524
Vaseline, 532, 534
Verizon, 246
Versace, 108
VH1, 434, 458
Viagra, 246, 353
Victoria's Secret, 277, 346, 384, 456
Virgin Airlines, 434
Virgin America, 204
Virginia Slims, 392

Virgin Mobile, 117
Viva La Juicy, 196, 251
Vogue, 157, 341, 434
Vogue India, 494
VOICE Group, 438
Volkswagen, 291, 352, 355
Volkswagen Beetle, 51, 499
Volvo, 296, 442
Von Dutch, 506

Wacoal Corp., 308
Wagyu beef, 234
Walmart, 33, 108, 139, 159, 178, 345, 385, 394, 419, 445, 486
walmartsucks.com, 528
Walt Disney Studios, 138
Warner-Lambert, 334
Water Kingdom, Bombay, 102
WE, 434
Webkinz, 28, 279, 553
Wedding Crashers, 35
Weight Watchers, 330, 446
Wendy's International, Inc., 445
Wesleyan College, 124
Weyland-Yutani Corporation, 219
Where the Boys Are, 37
Whirlpool, 297
White Castello, 200
White House Office of Consumer Affairs, 527
Whole Foods, 154, 158, 158*f*, 159, 345
Who Wants to Be a Millionaire?, 494
Whyville.net, 451
Wikipedia, 47, 169, 345, 390, 535, 537, 541
Willy Wonka, 219
Wish Room, 436
Wizard of Oz, The, 132, 277
Women's Wear Daily, 390
Wonder Bread, 260
Wonka candy, 219
Woodstock, 229
World Bank, 138
WorldCom, 504
World Cup, 135, 202
World of Warcraft, 46, 279, 535
Wrangles, 41
Wrigley, 222
Wyndham, 559

Xena: Warrior Princess, 393
Xerox, 159

Yahoo!, 73, 536
Yale University, 125
Yankelovich, Skelly & White, 107
Yankelovich Partners Inc., 436
Yaz, 162
Yellow Pages, 199
Yellowstone National Park, 354
Yelp, 397, 535, 541, 559
Yoplait, 165
Young & Rubicam, 286
YouTube, 31, 47, 73, 88, 120, 126, 172, 259, 297, 334, 343, 403, 411, 457, 523, 526, 536, 540, 541
Yu-Gi-Oh!, 553

Zagat, 541
Zara, 499, 552
Z-Boys, 547
Zima, 76
Ziploc, 464
Zippo Manufacturing Co., 234
Zoobles, 553
Zumba, 85, 86

Subject Index

Abandoned products, 174
ABC model of attitudes, 324–325
Abranding, 502
Absolute threshold, 206
Abstainers, 478
Acceptance cycles, 554
Accommodative purchase decision, 409
Acculturation, 104, 440
    defined, 440
    ethnicity and, 440–442
Acculturation agents, 440
Accuracy, self-concept and, 272
Achieved status, 483
Achievement badges, 544
Achievement orientation, 514
Achievers, 515
Activation models of memory, 251
Activity stores, 385
Actual self, 273
Actual state, 70
Adaptation, 213, 441
Addictive consumption, 180–181
Advance-fee fraud, 182
Advergaming, 118–119
Advertising
    comparative, 352
    corrective, 162
    importance of, 155–156
    subway, 224–225
    transactional, 544
Advertising wear-out, 233
Aesthetic consumption, 87
Affect, 86, 324, 325
    negative, 88–89
    positive, 88
Affective decision-making, 85–90
Affiliation, need for, 42
Affluenza, 490
African Americans, 439, 442
Age cohort, 449
Age groups, as demographic, 31
Agency, 528
Agentic goals, 430
Age subcultures, 449–462
    Baby Boomers, 457–460
    big (wo)man on campus, 456–457
    children, 450–451
    Generation X, 457
    Generation Y, 453–455
    mature market, 457
    senior market, 460–462
    tweens, 456
    youth market, 451–453
Aggregation stage, 130
Aggressiveness, 285
Aggressive people, 388
AIOs, 512–514
Allegory, 356
Alternate reality games (ARGs), 31, 343
Alternatives, deciding among, 73–79
Altruism, 463
American Indians, 439
Analytical psychology, 285
Analytics, 36*f*
Androgyny, 436
Animals, 406–407, 406*f*, 407*f*
Animism, 297
Anorexia, 309, 311
Anthrax scares of 2001, 179
Anthropomorphization, 216, 296
Antibrand communities, 394

Anticonsumption, 183
Antifestival, 129
Antiglobals, 141
Approach-approach conflict, 330
Approach-avoidance conflict, 330
Archetypes, 286, 288*t*–268*t*
Arousal levels, shopping and, 379
Art product, 112
Ascribed status, 483
Asian Americans, 439, 442, 445–446
Aspirational reference groups, 393–394
Assertive people, 388
Assimilation, 441, 528
Assimilation effect, 331
Associative networks, 251, 252*f*
Assortative mating, 482
Asynchronous interactions, 47
Atephobia, 478
Atmospherics, 385
Attention
    defined, 209
    marketers and, 212
    multitasking and, 211–212
    personal selection factors and, 212–213
    stimulus selection factors and, 213–215
Attitude accessibility perspective, 338
Attitude object (A_o), 323, 331
Attitudes
    ABC model of, 324–325
    balance theory, 331–333
    behavior and, 336
    consistency principle, 328
    defined, 323
    extended Fishbein model, 336–339
    forming, 327–328
    functional theory of, 324
    hierarchies of effects, 325–327
    marketers and, 340
    models of, 333–336
    motivational conflicts, 329–330
    multiattribute attitude models, 334
    multiple pathway anchoring and adjustment model, 339
    power of, 323–324
    self-perception theory, 330–331
    social judgment theory, 331
    toward buying, 337
Attractiveness, 343, 344, 346
Attributes, 222, 334
Auctions, 165–166
Audio watermarking, 202
Augmented reality, 220
Aurophobia, 478
Authoritarian parents, 243
Authority, 340
Automaticity, 255
Autonomic decision, 410
Autonomic responses, 230
Autonomy, 42, 453, 462
Avatars, 264–265, 279, 279*f*, 280, 348, 429
Averaging, 259
Avoidance-avoidance conflict, 330
Avoidance groups, 394

Babies for sale, 182
Baby Boomers, 404, 457–460
Baby Boom Generation, 450
Badges, 277
Bait-and-switch, 154
Balancers, 478
Balance theory, 331–333, 332*f*
Bandwagon effect, 395
Basic level category, 75

Basking in reflected glory, 333
Behavior, 324
    intentions *vs.*, 336–339
    patterns of, 509
Behavioral economics, 81
Behavioral learning theories, 229, 230–232
Being space, 384
Beliefs, 252, 325, 334
Belief systems, 102
Believers, 515
Bias
    interpretational, 217–220
    response, 259
Big Data, 34
Big Five personality dimensions, 292, 292*t*
Binary opposition, 122
Binge eating, 311
Biological needs, 40
Bioterrorism, 178
Birthday gift ritual, 127
Blogs, 343
Blood donors, 181, 182
Bobo doll experiment, 242
Body image
    body decoration and mutilation, 312
    body piercing, 314
    cosmetic surgery, 310–311
    defined, 301
    distortions of, 311–312
    fattism, 308–310
    ideals of beauty, 301–308
    tattoos, 312–313
Body mass index (BMI), 311
Bogus ads, 259
Boomerang kids, 402
Born-again consumers, 447–448
Botnets, 166–167
Bottom of the pyramid, 489
Bounded rationality, 81
Brand advocates, 536
BrandAsset Archetypes model, 287*f*
Brand-building strategies, British popular
        culture, 55–56
Brand communities, 392–393, 393*f*
Brand consultancy, 511*f*
Brandfests, 392–393
Brand images, 38
Brand loyalty, 28, 64, 140, 240
Brand-name imprinting, 232
Brand personality, 293, 294–296, 295*f*
Brand prominence, 505
Brand(s), 28
    pioneering, 253
    socializing with, 296–297
Brand switching, 65
Brazil, 311
Bribery, 154
BRIC nations, 498–499
Broadcast medium, 342
Bromance, 432
Bulimia, 309, 311
Business ethics, consumer rights and, 154
Business-to-business (B2B) e-commerce, 401
Business-to-business (B2B) marketers, 397
Buyclass theory of purchasing, 399
Buyer behavior, 29
Buyer role, 397
Buying center, 399
Buzz building, 526–527

Capital, 500
Category exemplars, 76
Caucasians, 439
Cause marketing, 164–165

Celebrity endorsements, 66, 332, 344–345, 345*f*
Central route, to persuasion, 358, 358*f*
Ceremonies, cultural, 119–120
Chavs, 494
Chief marketing officers (CMOs), 160
Childless couples, 405
Children
    cognitive development, 245–247
    consumer socialization, 243–245
    as decision-makers, 450–451
    sex-role socialization, 429–431
Children's Television Act (1990), 246
China, 230, 301, 307, 310–311, 492
Christmas rituals, 128–129
Chronological age, 462
Chunking, 250, 350
Cinderella fantasy, 484
Classical conditioning, 230, 231
Classic fashion, 554
Cliques, 535
Closure principle, 218
Co-branding strategies, 510
Co-consumers, 377
Codes, 499, 544
Coercive power, 390
Cognition, 324
Cognitive decision-making, 69–80, 70*f*
Cognitive development, 245–247
Cognitive element, 328
Cognitive learning principles, marketing
        applications of, 243
Cognitive learning theory, 229, 240–243
Cognitive matching, 297
Cognitive responses, 358
Cohesiveness, 394
Collaborative filtering technologies, 73
Collecting, 132
Collective decision making, 397
Collective interest, 541
Collective self, 271
Collective unconscious, 286
Collective value creation, 393, 393*f*
Colleges, brand personalities of, 296
College students, 456–457
Color palette, 199
Color(s), 197
    forecasts, 200
    of stimulus, 213
Communal goals, 430
Communication
    elements of, 341
    interactive, 341–342
    new message formats, 342–343
    the source, 343–349
    source *vs.* message, 358–359
    traditional model of, 341*f*
    types of appeals, 353–358
    updated model of, 342*f*
Communications subsystem, 111
Communism, fall of, 157
Community
    online, 540–542
    social media and, 536–538
Comparative advertising, 336, 352
Comparative influence, 392
Compatibility, 549
Competitors
    brand's position and, 222
    identifying, 76
Complexity, 549
Compliance, 285, 327
Compulsive consumption, 181
Compulsive shopping disorder (CSD), 181
Computer-mediated environments (CMEs), 279

Conceptual brand meanings, 245
Conditioned response (CR), 230
Conditioned stimulus (CS), 230, 231
Conditioning
    classical, 230, 231
    instrumental (operant), 230, 235–238
    product associations, 233–234
    repetition, 231–232
    stimulus discrimination, 232–233
    stimulus generalization, 232
Conformity, 396
Conjunctive rule, 79
Connectedness, 462
Connexity, 454
Conscientious consumerism, 170
Consensual purchase decision, 409
Consideration set, 74
Consistency principle, 328
Conspicuous consumption, 504, 505
Conspicuous waste, 506
Constructive processing, 60
Consumed consumers, 181–182
Consumer addiction, 179
Consumer behavior
    consumer terrorism, 178–179
    culture and, 102
    dark side of, 177–183
    data explosion and, 34–35
    defined, 28–29
    digital self and, 280*t*
    illegal acquisition and product use,
        182–183
    interdisciplinary influences on study of,
        48–49, 50*t*, 51
    overview, 27–28
    policy issues relevant to, 165–177
    process of, 29–30
    pyramid of, 50*f*
    situational effects on, 374–375
    values and, 105–107
Consumer confidence, 479
Consumer confusion, 234
Consumer fairy tales, 122
Consumer groups, 509
Consumer identity, 427–428
    income and, 477–481
    lifestyles and, 506–515
    social class and, 481–490
Consumer identity renaissance, 462
Consumer involvement. *See* Involvement
Consumerism, 162–163
Consumer research
    focus of, 52
    perspectives on, 51
    trait theory and, 293–294
Consumer researchers, finding, 48
Consumer rights
    business ethics and, 153–154
    product satisfaction and, 158–160
Consumers
    defined, 29
    global "always on," 23
    high-income, 485–488
    impact on marketing strategy, 30–35
    low-income, 488–489, 490*f*
    manipulation of, 154–157
    marketing's impact on, 35–45
    surrogate, 532
Consumer satisfaction/dissatisfaction (CS/D), 80
Consumer socialization, 243–245
Consumerspace, 155
Consumer style, 140
Consumer terrorism, 178–179
Consumer tribes, 393

Consumer welfare, federal legislation, 161, 161*t*
Consumption
    addictive, 180–181
    aesthetic, 87
    compulsive, 181
    emotions and, 86–87
    happiness and, 481
    motives for, 38–41
    organized religion and, 447
    sacred and profane, 131–135
Consumption communities, 28
Consumption constellation, 510
Consumption microcultures, 106
Consumption process, stages in, 29*f*
Consumption situation, 374
Consumption-specific values, 105
Consumption style, 509, 509*f*
Contagion effect, 535
Contamination, 132, 133
Contemporary young mainstream female
    achievers (CYMFA), 434
Content, self-concept and, 272
Context effects, 196
Continuous innovation, 548
Contrast, 213
Contrast effect, 331
Conventions, 105
Conversations, 541
Cooptation, 108
Core values, 103–105
Corporate social responsibility (CSR), 164, 344
Corrective advertising, 162
Cosmetic surgery, 310–311
Cosmological function, of myths, 122
Cosmopolitanism, 490
Cosplay movement, 508, 508*f*
Cougars, 504
Counteractive construal, 60
Counterarguing, 355
Countercultures, 108
Counterfeiting, 183
Counterfeit products, 502
Couponing, mobile, 386*f*
Covariation, 84
Craft product, 112
Crash dieters, 478
Creative subsystem, 111
Credibility, 343, 344, 346, 527
Creolization, 137–138
Crescive norms, 105
Crime, hot zones, 34
Cross-cultural values
    diffusion of consumer culture and, 135–136
    emerging cultures in transitional
        economy, 141
    global marketing and, 140–141
    localized strategy, 138–139
    overview, 135–136
    relevancy to marketers, 140
    standardized strategy, 138
Crowd power, 542
C2C e-commerce, 46
Cued developmental stage, 245
Cult products, 62
Cultural capital, 501
Cultural Creatives, 173
Cultural formula, 113–114
Cultural gatekeepers, 112
Cultural movement, 108–112
Cultural selection, 110
Cultural values, 105
Culture
    concept of self and, 272
    defining, 101–102

ethics, 154
high and low, 112–113, 439
Maslow's Hierarchy of Needs and, 44
production process, 110*f*
sacred and profane consumption, 131–135
stories and ceremonies, 119–120
subjective norms and, 338–339
systems, 102
values, 102–107
Culture Jammers Manifesto, 163
Culture jamming, 162–163
Culture of immigration, 440
Culture of origin, 440
Culture of participation, 47–48
Culture production system (CPS), 111
Culture shock, 101
Curation, 158
Currency, 544
Customer networks, 410
Customer product reviews, 73
Customs, 105
Cyberbullying, 180
Cyberidentities, 455
Cybermediaries, 73
Cyberplace, 537
Cyberspace, 251
Cyberspace retail themes, 384
Cyberterrorism, 178

Danish Modern, 550
Database marketing, 33
Data privacy, 165–167
Day reconstruction method, 374
Dead Heads, 507
Decay, 255
Decision making
    affective, 85–90
    among alternatives, 73–79
    biases and shortcuts, 81–83
    B2B, 397–402
    children's role in, 450–451
    collective, 397
    family, 402–405, 408–410
    habitual, 80–81
    heuristics and, 413
    information search, 70–73
    in-store, 385–387
    problem recognition, 69–70
    problem solving, 59–61
    product choice and, 79–80
"Declaration of Consumer Rights, The," 141
Decompression zone, 385
Deep processing, 251
Deethnicization, 441
Default bias, 81
Defendance, 42
Deindividuation, 395
Delayed gratification, 41
Democracy, 541
Demographics, 27, 30–31
Depth interviews, 283
Desacralization, 135
Dessert categories, levels of abstraction in, 75*f*
Detachment, 285
Determinant attributes, 77
Differential fertility, 484
Differential threshold, 206
Diffusion of innovations, 547
Digital Divide, 489
Digital homes, 403
Digital identity management, 279
Digital living, 403
Digital Native, 47
Digital self, 279–280, 280*t*

Digital video recorder (DVR), 212, 342
Digital virtual consumption (DVC), 545
DINKS (double income, no kids), 405
Direction, motivation and, 41
Directories, 73
Direct selling, 395
Disabilities, market access and,
    167–168, 168*f*
Discontinuous innovation, 549
Discretionary income, 478
Discrimination, adaptation and, 213
Dissonance theory, 328
Distractions, 355
Dominance-submission hierarchy, 482
Doppelgänger brand image, 297
Downward mobility, 483–484
Drama, lecture *vs.,* 357
Dramaturgical perspective, 275
Drive, 40
Drive theory, 40, 41
Dyadic encounters, 388
Dynamically continuous innovation, 549

Early adopters, 547, 548, 548*f*
Eastern Europe, 157
Eating disorders, 309, 311
Echo Boomers, 454
Ecology, cultural system and, 102
e-commerce, 177, 380–383, 383*t*, 401
Economic exchange, 126
Economics of information, 69
E-consumers, 46
Ego, 282
Ego-defensive function, 324
80/20 Rule, 30, 512
Elaborated codes, 499, 501*t*
Elaboration Likelihood Model (ELM), 358,
    358*f*, 359
Elaborative rehearsal, 250
Electronic marketing, 46
Elimination-by-aspects rule, 79
Embeds, 209
Emic perspective, 139
Emo, 507
Emotional appeals, 353
Emotional contagion, 327
Emotional oracle effect, 86
Emotional states, dimensions of, 379*f*
Emotions
    consumption and, 86–87
    mixed, 254, 256
    social media and, 89–90
    unipolar, 256
Employee performance, 240
Empowerment, 489
Enacted norms, 104
Encoding, memory, 247
Enculturation, 104
Environmental bottom line, 170
Episodic memories, 249
Ethics, 154
Ethnicity
    acculturation and, 440–442
    as demographic, 31–32
Ethnic stereotypes, 439–440
Ethnic subcultures, 427, 438–442
Ethnocentrism, 84
Ethnography, 440
Ethos, 102
Etic perspective, 138
Evaluation, 334
Evaluative criteria, 77–79, 77*f*
Evoked set, 74
Exchange, 29

Exchange theory, 29
Exemplar, 301
Exemplar products, creating, 76
Expectancy disconfirmation model, 80
Expectancy theory, 41
Experiencers, 515
Experiential hierarchy, 325f, 326–327
Expert power, 390
Exploratory studies, 533
Exposure
    adaptation and, 213
    defined, 206
    sensory thresholds, 206
    subliminal perception, 207, 209
Extended family, 402
Extended self, 276–278
External memory, 247
External search, 71, 72
Extinction, 232, 237, 237f
Extroversion, 286, 292
Eyeball economy, 210

Facial Recognition Technology (FRT), 68f
Fads, 555
Fair Trade principles, 171
Familiar brand names, 84
Familiarity, recall and, 255–256
Family
    animals and, 406–407
    children and, 404–405
    as decision makers, 402–405, 408–410
    life cycle, 407–408
    modern, 402–403
    size of, 404–405
Family branding, 234
Family financial officer (FFO), 412
Family identity, 409–410
Family life cycle (FLC), 407–408
Family structure, as demographic, 31
Fan clubs, 73
Fantasy, 274
Fantasy camps, 391, 391f
Fashion
    adoption cycles, 553–556
    behavioral science perspectives on,
      551–553
    defined, 550
    economic models of, 551
    hip-hop, 108
    medical model of, 553
    psychological models of, 551
    sites, 109f
    sociological models of, 551–553
Fashion system, 550–556
Fastidious Eclectus, 510
Fatalism, 339
Fattism, 308–310
Fear appeals, 355–356
Feature creep, 80
Feedback, 341
Female sex roles, 433–434
Femme fatale self, 275
Fertility rate, 404
Figure-ground principle, 219
Fijian culture, 309
Financial bottom line, 169
Fishbein model, 334–335
Fixed-interval reinforcement, 237
Fixed-ratio reinforcement, 238
Flaming, 541
Flashbulb memories, 249
Flavor houses, 204
Flight, 502
Flows, 538, 540

Flow state, 538
Focus groups, 160, 392
Folksonomy, 537
Follower brands, 253
FOMO (Fear of Missing Out), 535
Food desert, 169
Food insecurity, 169
Foot-in-the-door technique, 331
Forgetting, 255
Fortress brands, 125
Forums, 73
Framing, 81–82, 350
Fraud, 182–183
Freemium, 541
Free recall tests, 259
Frequency marketing, 238
Friend (buddy) lists, 545
Frugalistas, 479
Frugality, 286
Functionally illiterate, 169
Functional magnetic resonance imaging
    (fMRI), 74
Functional risk, 65f
Functional theory of attitudes, 324
Funeral ceremonies, 131
Fusiform face area, 74

Gadget lovers, 550
Gambling, 181
    casino vs. online, 381, 381f
Game consoles, 545
Game platform, 545
Gamification, 238, 240
Gatekeeper role, 397
Gatekeepers, cultural, 112
Gay, lesbian, bisexual, and transgender (GLBT)
    consumers, 435–436, 437f
Gearheads, 510
Gemba, 160, 160f
Gender
    as demographic, 31
    sex appeals and, 353–354
    sexual identity vs., 431–432
    socialization and, 104
Gender-bending products, 436
Gender convergence, 413
Gender identity, 428–437
    sex-typed products, 432–433
    sexual identity vs., 431–432
Gender socialization, 429–431
Generalized opinion leader, 530
Generation X, 450, 457
Generation Y, 450, 453–455
Generation Z, 450
Genre, 545
Geodemography, 463
Geography, as demographic, 32
Geospatial platforms, 277
Gestalt psychology, 217
Gestation stage, 127
Gift-giving rituals, 126–128
Global agnostics, 141
Global citizens, 141
Global consumer culture, 135–141
Global dreamers, 141
Global marketing, 140–141
Goals, 40
Golden triangle, 213, 214f
Goth subculture, 436
Grass-roots innovators, 553
Gray market, 460–462
Great Depression, 487
Great Recession, 160, 171, 286, 477, 478, 479–481
Green marketing, 153–154, 170–171, 172f

Greenwashing, 172
Gripe sites, 159
Grooming rituals, 126
Group cohesiveness, 394
Group dieting, 309
Groups, social power of, 389–390
Guerrilla marketing, 186–187, 526

Habitual decision-making, 80–83
Habituation, 351
Habitus, 500
Hacking, 167
Hair donors, 181, 182
Halal, 449
Halloween rituals, 129
Halo effect, 232, 346
Happiness, consumption and, 481
Haptic (touch) sense, 204
Harpaxophobia, 478
Head banging, 125
Health remedies, labeling of, 300
Heavy users, 30
Hedonic adaptation, 481
Hedonic consumption, 196
Hedonic needs, 39, 41, 62
Hedonic shopping motives, 380
Helicopter moms, 410
Hero tale, 134
Hesher, 507
Heuristics, 78f, 84
    in joint decision-making, 413
Hierarchical value maps, 107
Hierarchies of effects, 325–327
Hierarchy of Needs, 43, 44, 44f
Hierogamy, 497
High-context culture, 439
High-income consumers, 485–488
High-involvement medium, 65
Highlighting effect, 255
Hispanic Americans, 442, 444–445, 444f
Hoarding, 132
Hofstede Dimensions of National Culture, 140
Holiday rituals, 128–129
Home automation technologies, 403
Home of the future, 403
Home shopping party, 395
Homogamy, 482
Homophily, 530
Horizontal mobility, 483
Horizontal revolution, 47
Host culture, 441
Hot zones, crime, 34
Households, 402
H-point, 204
Humorous appeals, 354–355
Hurricane Sandy, 32
Hybrid ads, 256
Hyperreality, 220

Icons, 219
Id, 282
Idealism vs. pragmatism, 453
Ideal self, 273, 394
Ideals of beauty
    defined, 301
    male, 308
    over time, 305–306
    realistic, 306–308
    universality of, 301–303
    Western, 303–304
Ideals orientation, 514
Ideal state, 70
Identification, 327
Identity, 528

Identity marketing, 298
Identity negotiation, 388
Identity theft, 166–167
Ideology, cultural system and, 102
Idle rich, 504
Illiteracy, 169
Importance weights, 334
Impotent reactors, 490
Impression management, 273, 274, 279
Impulse buying, 80, 387
Impulse items, 387
Incidental brand exposure, 82
Incidental learning, 229
Income
    consumer identity and, 477–481
    as demographic, 31
    discretionary, 478
    patterns of, 477–478
    social class and, 485
Index, 219
India, social class in, 494–495
Indicator of consumer confidence, 479
Individualism, 140
Indulgence *vs.* restraint, 140
Indulgent parents, 243
Inertia, 62
Influence impressions, 543
Influencer, 29, 397
Informational influence, 391, 391*t*
Information power, 390
Information processing, 206
Information-processing approach, 247
Information-processing perspective, 69
Information search, 70–73
Information seekers, 140
Initiator role, 397
Injustice, 528
Innovations
    adopting, 547–548
    behavioral demands of, 548–549
    continuous, 548
    defined, 547
    diffusion of, 547–549
    discontinuous, 549
    dynamically continuous, 549
    fashion system, 550–556
    overview of, 547
Innovative communicators, 531
Innovators, 514, 531, 547, 548, 548*f*
Innumeracy, 169
In-store slack, 386
Instrumental (operant) conditioning, 230,
    235–238
Instrumental values, 106, 106*t*
Intelligent agents, 73
Intensity
    adaptation and, 213
    self-concept and, 272
Intentional families, 402
Intentions, behavior *vs.*, 336–339
Interactions, 540
Interaction styles, 388
Interbellum Generation, 450
Interdependence, 38
Interference, 255
Internalization, 327–328
Internal memory, 247
Internal search, 71
Internet, 47
Internet addiction, 180
Interpersonal needs, 409
Interpretants, 219
Interpretation
    biases, 217–219

defined, 215
hyperreality, 220
perceptual positioning, 221–222
semiotics, 219–220
stimulus organization, 216–217
Interpretivism, 51, 52*t*
Introversion, 292
Invidious distinction, 504
Involvement
    conceptualizing, 61*f*
    defined, 61
    inertia, 62
    measuring, 62*t*
    message, 65–67
    product, 63–65
    situational, 68
    types of, 63
iPhone, 248
Islamic marketing, 448–449

Japan, 304, 309, 492–493, 508, 529, 555
Japanese gift-giving rituals, 127–128
J.N.D. (just noticeable difference), 206
Juggling Lifestyle, 412
Jungle, The (Sinclair), 161
Justifiers, 478

Ketamine, 179*f*
Key informants, 533
Kin-network system, 412
Kinsei engineering, 204
Knowledge, levels of, 252
Knowledge bias, 346
Knowledge function, 324
Knowledge structures, 74, 251

Laddering, 107
Laggards, 547, 548*f*
Landscape retail themes, 384
Lanham Act, 234
Late adopters, 547
Latent motives, 283
Lateral cycling, 176
Latitudes of acceptance and rejection, 331
Leaderboards, 544
Learning
    behavioral theories, 230–232
    cognitive theory, 240–243
    conscious *vs.* unconscious, 241–242
    defined, 229
    incidental, 229
    instrumental, 235
    observational, 242
Lecture, drama *vs.*, 357
Legitimate power, 390
Leisure class, 504
Leveling, 528
Lexicographic rule, 79
Library, 90
Licensing, 234
Life course paradigm, 463
Lifestream, 279
Lifestyle dimensions, 294*t*, 513*t*
Lifestyle marketing perspective, 508–509
Lifestyle profile, 512
Lifestyles, 477
    brand's position and, 222
    defined, 507
    as demographic, 32
    as group identities, 506–515
    materialists, 157–158
    products as building blocks of, 509–510
Lifestyle segmentation, 512, 514
Lifestyle statement, 28

Limbic system, 201
Liminality stage, 130
Limited developmental stage, 245
List of values (LOV) scale, 107
"Little Man" pattern, 51
Localized strategy, 138–139
Locational privacy, 167
Logos, 234
LOHAS market sectors, 173, 174*t*, 178
Long tail, 73
Long-term memory (LTM), 250
Long-term orientation, 140
Look-alike packaging, 234
Looking-glass self, 276
Loss aversion, 83
Lotteries, 486
Love, 38
Lovemark, 88
Low-context culture, 439
Low-income consumers, 488–489, 490*f*
Low-involvement hierarchy, 325–326, 325*f*
Low-involvement medium, 65, 67*f*
Lurkers, 542
Luxury products, changes in, 157–158

Magnetic resonance imaging (MRI), 74
Makers, 515
Male sex roles, 434–435
Malware, 167
Managerial subsystem, 111
Mark and Pearson brand archetypes, 288–290*t*
Market access, 167–169
    disabilities, 167–168, 168*f*
    food deserts, 169
    literacy, 169
Market beliefs, 85*t*
Marketerspace, 155
Marketing
    database, 33
    electronic, 46
    identity, 298
    impact on consumers, 35–45
    necessity of, 155–156
    relationship, 32
Marketing applications
    of classic conditioning principles, 233–235
    of instrumental conditioning principles,
        238–240
Marketing messages, measuring consumers'
    recall of, 258–259
Marketing strategies
    consumer impact on, 30–35
    ethnicity and, 443, 444–446
Market maven, 532
Market regulation, 160–162, 162*t*
Marketscape themes, 384
Market segmentation strategies, 28
Masculinism, 435
Masculinity, 140
Masking effects, 242
Maslow's Hierarchy of Needs, 43–44
Mass class, 499, 502
Mass Connectors, 543
Mass customization, 64
Mass fashion, 553
Massive multiplayer online games (MMOGs), 46
Materialism, 157–158, 481
Mature market, 457–462
Maximizing solution, 81
MBWO (managing by walking around), 550
M-commerce, 343
Meaning, 252
    of products, 38
    types of, 248–250

Means-end chain model, 107
Means of production, 482
Media democratization, 511
Media literacy, 169
Media multiplexity, 540
Mediating figures, 122
Medium, 341
Meetups, 540
Megachurches, 447–448
Megacity, 45
Membership reference groups, 393–394
Meme theory, 553
Memory
  defined, 247
  episodic, 249
  information encoding and, 247, 248–250
  information storage and, 250–252
  lapses, 259
  long-term, 250
  measuring, 258–259
  nostalgia and, 229, 259–260, 261f
  overview, 247–248
  pictures and, 256–257
  retrieving, purchasing and, 253–254
  sensory, 250
  short-term, 250
  storage, 247
  types of, 247f
Men
  ideals of beauty, 308
  sex appeals and, 353–354
  sex roles, 410–413
Mental accounting, 82
Mental budgets, 60, 386
Mere exposure phenomenon, 351, 394
Message appeals
  emotional vs. rational, 353
  fear, 355–356
  humor, 354–355
  metaphors, 356–358
  sex, 353–354
Message comprehension, 246–247
Message involvement, 65–67
Message(s)
  good and bad, 349t
  new formats, 342–343
  sending, 350–351
  source vs., 341
Metaphors, 356–358
Metaphysical function, of myths, 122
Metro, 506–507
Microcultures, 106, 507–508
Middle East, social class in, 493
Milieu, 545
Milk Processor Education Program, 347
Millennials, 454
Mindlessness, 241
Mindscape retail themes, 384
Minimal group paradigm, 428
Minipreneurs, 384
Minnesota Multiphasic Personality Inventory (MMPI), 282
Misinformation, transmission of, 528, 528f
Mixed emotions, 254, 256
MMOGs (massively multiplayer online games), 545
Mnemonic qualities, 258
Mobile shopping apps, 386
Mode, 545
Modeling, 242
Modernism, 51
Modified rebuy, 401
Momentum effect, 543
Monetary risk, 65f

Monomorphic, 530
Mores, 105
Motivation
  conflicts in, 329–330, 330f
  consumer involvement and, 38–39
  consumer needs classification and, 42–44
  defined, 39
  Maslow's Hierarchy of Needs, 43–44
  needs vs. wants, 41–42
  overview, 39–41
  strength of, 41
Motivational research, 283–285, 284t
Motivation to comply (MC), 337
Mountain men, 507
Movement, 440
  cultural, 108–112
  of meaning, 108f
Multiattribute attitude models, 334–336, 335t
Multiple-intelligence theory, 246
Multiple pathway anchoring and adjustment (MPAA) model, 339
Multiple selves, 274–275
Multiple-store perspective, 250
Multitaskers, 455
Multitasking, 377
  attention and, 210–212
  defined, 211
Music industry, cultural specialists in, 111t
Myers-Briggs Type Indicator, 292
Mystery ads, 256
Myths, 120, 122–124

Nag factor, 450
Name letter effect, 392
Naming consultants, 246
Narcissism vs. intimacy, 453
Narratives, 137, 250
Narrative transportation, 65
Narrowcast, 342
National character, 139
Native Hawaiians, 439
Natural user interface, 204
Need for Touch (NFT) scale, 204
Need for uniqueness, 43
Need recognition, 70
Needs
  for affiliation, 42
  artificial, 155
  biological vs. learned, 40
  classifying, 42–45
  for power, 42
  wants vs., 41–42
Negative affect, 88–89
Negative reference groups, 394–395
Negative reinforcement, 236, 237f
Negative word-of-mouth, 527–528
Neglecting parents, 243
Neo-Freudian theories, 285–286
Neo-Personality Inventory, 292
Nervous systems, 230
Network analysis, 535
Networked homes, 403
Network effect, 541
Network units, 539
Neuromarketing, 74
New task, 401
New Vintage, 115
Nigeria, 304
Nodes, 539
Nonassertive people, 388
Noncompensatory rule, 78
Nonconscious procedural knowledge, 241
Nonhuman endorsers, 347–349
Normative belief (NB), 337

Normative influence, 336, 392
Norms, 104–105, 396
Nostalgia, 229, 229f, 259–260, 261f
Nostalgia Index, 260
Nostalgic attachment, 38
Nouveau riche, 488
Novelty, of stimulus, 213–214
Novice consumers, 72
Nuclear family, 402
Nudge, 81

Obesity, 244, 247, 306, 310, 534
Object-attribute linkages, 334
Objectification, 132
Objects, 219, 277
Observability, 549
Observational learning, 242, 242f
Occasions, brand's position and, 222
Occupational prestige, 485
Occupy Wall Street movement, 491
Odors, 200–202
Old money, 487
Omitting, 259
One Percenter, 491
Ongoing search, 71
Online communities, 537, 540–542
Online gated communities, 501
Online social capital, 501
Open rates, 376
Operant (instrumental) conditioning, 235–238
Opinion leaders/leadership, 529–535
  finding, 532–535
  influence of, 530–531
  online, 543–545
  overview, 529–530
  scale, 534f
  types of, 531–532
Opinion mining, 90
Opinion seekers, 532
Opportunity recognition, 70
Organ donors, 181–182
Organizational climate, 398
Organizational decision making
  B2B e-commerce, 397–398
  family, 402–405
  organizational buyers, 397
  overview, 397
  types of, 400t
Ostriches, 478
Overprivileged consumers, 497
Oxytocin, 177

Pacific Islanders, 439
Package schematics, 216
Pack rats, 174
Paid influencer programs, 345
Paradigm, 51
Paradigm shift, 51
Paradox of low involvement, 359
Parental yielding, 450
Parents, consumer socialization and, 243
Parody display, 506
Parrot Heads, 518
Participatory action research (PAR), 163
Partners, 342
Parvenus, 505, 506f
Pastiche, 51
Patricians, 505, 506f
Patterns of behavior, 509
Peak experiences, 44
Pecking order, 481–482
Peniaphobia, 478
Perceived age, 462
Perceived risk, 63, 65f

Perception
    attention, 210–215
    defined, 196, 206
    exposure, 206–210
    interpretation, 215–222
    overview, 206f
    sensory systems, 198–205
Perceptual defense, 213
Perceptual positioning, 221–222
Perceptual selection, 212
Perceptual vigilance, 212
Peripheral cues, 359
Peripheral route, to persuasion, 358, 358f, 359
Perishable messages, 342
Personal accomplishment, 42
Personality
    Big Five dimensions, 292–293, 292t
    defined, 280
    Freudian theory, 282
    motivational research, 283–285
    neo-Freudian theories, 285–286
    overview, 280–282
    trait theory, 286, 291–292
Personality traits, 286
Personal selection factors, 212–213
Person-segmentation matrix, 376t
Persuasion, 340
Pets, 406–407, 406f, 407f
Phallic symbols, 282
Phantom Limb Syndrome, 181
Phantom Vibration Syndrome, 181
Phishing, 166
Phonemes, 203, 246
Physical environment, 376
Physical risk, 65f
Pictorial cues, verbal cues vs., 256–258
Pictures, 256–257
Piercings, 314
Pioneering brands, 253
Place-based subcultures, 463–464
Planning orientation dimension of time, 377
Play, 42
Pleasure levels, shopping and, 379
Pleasure principle, 282
Plinking, 118
Plus-size consumers, 307, 470
Plutonomy, 480
Podcasting, 343
Point-of-purchase (POP) stimuli, 387
Polychronic orientation dimension of time, 377
Polymorphic, 530
Poor Getting Poorer Index, 480
Popgirls, 510
Popular culture, 37
Pop-up stores, 384
Portals, 73
Poseurs, 505, 506f
Position, of stimulus, 213
Positioning strategy, 75, 221
Positive affect, 88
Positive reference groups, 394
Positive reinforcement, 236, 237, 237f
Positivism, 51, 52t
Positivity, self-concept and, 272
Postmodernism, 51
Post-purchase dissonance, 328
Postpurchase evaluation, 80
Post-traumatic stress disorder (PTSD), 167, 168
Potent actors, 490
Potlatch ceremony, 505
Power
    family decision making and, 409
    need for, 42

Power distance, 140
Power users, 543
Precariat, 494
Prediction markets, 401–402
Preoperational stage of development, 245
Preparing for battle ritual, 125
Prepurchase search, 70
Presence, 541
Presentation stage, 127
Pretailer, 382
Price leadership, brand's position and, 222
Price-quality relationship, 84
Price-sensitive consumers, 140
Priming, 81, 241
Principle of cognitive consistency, 328
Principle of least interest, 396
Principle of similarity, 218, 218f
Private response, to dissatisfaction, 159
PRIZM system, 464, 465t
Proactive interference, 255
Pro-ana movement, 309
Problem recognition, 69–70, 71f
Problem solving, consumers and, 59–61
Process Communication Model, 286
Product categorization, 75–77
Product class, brand's position and, 222
Product complementarity, 510
Product involvement, 63–65, 68f
Productivity orientation, 42
Product labels, 72, 72f
Product line extension, 234
Product placement, 117–118
Products
    categorizing, 74
    disposal of, 173, 175f, 176–177
    involvement and utility, 409
    locating in store, 76–77
    meaning of, 38
    as memory markers, 257–258
    positioning, 75
    repositioning, 296
    types of relationships with, 38
Product satisfaction, consumer rights and, 158–160
Product-specific profile, 512
Product-specific segmentation study, 512
Product-specific values, 105
Profane consumption, 131
Progressive learning model, 441
Proletarians, 505, 506f
Propinquity, 394
Proposition, 252
Prospect theory, 83
Prostitution, 181
Prototypical, 75
Provenance, 158
Psychic economy, 212
Psychogenic needs, 42
Psychographics, 510–515
    addictive consumption, 180–181
    AIOs, 512–514
    compulsive consumption, 181
    consumed consumers, 181–182
    defined, 510
    geodemography, 463
    illegal activities, 182–183
    overview, 510
    segmentation typologies, 514
Psychological function, of myths, 122
Psychological risk, 65f
Psychological time, 377
Psychophysics, 206
Public self-consciousness, 276
Punishment, 236, 237, 237f

Puns, 357
Purchase momentum, 80
Pure play retailer, 541

Quality, brand's position and, 222
Queuing theory, 378

Race, as demographic, 31–32
Racial stereotypes, 439–440
Racial subcultures, 438–442
Ramadan, 135
Rational appeals, 353
Rationalization, 330
Reality engineering, 115–117
Reality principle, 282
Real-time bidding, 165
Rebellion vs. conformity, 453
Recall, 258–259
    familiarity and, 255–256
    salience and, 256
Recall bias, 254
Receivers, 341
Reciprocity, 126, 340
Reciprocity norm, 127
Reclamation, 502
Recognition, 259
Recognition test, 259
Recommerce, 177
Recycling, 175f, 176, 176f
Red market, 181
Reference groups, 389, 390–392
    conformity and, 396
    defined, 390–391
    forms of, 391t
    importance of, 392
    membership vs. aspirational, 393–394
    positive vs. negative, 394–395
Referent power, 390
Referral behavior, 535
Referral network, 535
Reformulation stage, 127
Refutational arguments, 352
Regulatory agencies, 160–162, 162t
Reinforcement, 236–238, 237f
Relationship marketing, 32
Relative advantage, 549
Relevance, adaptation and, 213
Religion, 135
Religious subcultures, 446–449
Repetition, 231–232, 351
    marketing applications of, 233
Reporting bias, 346, 352
Reposition, 296
Reputational method, 497
Reputation economy, 482
Resonance, 357
Response bias, 259
Responsibility, family decision making and, 409
Restricted codes, 499, 501t
Retailing, as theater, 383–384
Retail theming, 384
Retrieval, 247, 253
Retroactive interference, 255
Retro brand, 260, 261f
Reverse innovation, 549
Reverse product placement, 219
Reward power, 390
Rhymes, 357
Rich media, 212
Ridicule, 453
Risk, kinds of, 64, 65f
Risk capital, 64
Rites of passage, 129–131

Ritual artifacts, 126
Rituals, 124–131, 389
    defined, 124
    gift-giving, 126–128
    grooming, 126
    holiday, 128–129
    online, 126
    overview, 124–125
    rites of passage, 129–131
Rokeach Value Survey, 106
Role identities, 275
Role-relaxed consumers, 396
Role theory, 37

Sacralization, 131–133
Sacred consumption, 131, 133–134
Sacred events, 134
Sacred people, 133
Sacred places, 133
Salespersons, 388
Salience, 256
Salient beliefs, 334
Sanctions, 396
Sandwich Generation, 403
Satisficing, 81
Scarcity, 340
Scents, 200–202
Schema, 215, 252
Scrimpers, 478
Script, 252
Secret shoppers, 238
Segmentation typologies, 514
Selective savers, 174
Selective search, 72
Self
    digital, 279–280
    existence of, 271–272
    extended, 276–278
    fantasy, 274
    ideal, 273
    looking-glass, 276
    multiple selves, 274–275
    real, 273
    symbolic interactionism, 275–276
Self-administered conditioning, 239f
Self-concept, 272
Self-concept attachment, 38
Self-consciousness, 276
Self-designation, 533
Self-esteem, 272–273
Self-expression, 462, 514
Self-fulfilling prophecy, 276
Self-image congruence models, 297
Self-monitors, 276
Self-perception theory, 330–331
Self-regulation, 60
Semantic meaning, 249
Semiotics, 219–220, 220f
Senior market, 460–462
Sensation, defined, 196
Sensory inputs, 196
Sensory marketing
    defined, 197, 201
    scents, 200–202
    sound, 202
    taste, 204–205
    touch, 203, 204, 204f
    vision, 197–200
Sensory meaning, 248–249
Sensory memory, 250
Sensory overload, 210
Sensory signature, 201
Sensory systems
    hedonic consumption, 196

    overview, 195–197
    sensory marketing, 197–205
Sensory threshold, 206
Sentiment analysis, 90
Sentiment relation, 331
Separation stage, 129
Serial reproduction, 528
Serial wardrobers, 183
Service scripts, 252
Sex appeals, 353–354
Sex roles, 428
    cultural assumptions about, 430f
    decision-making and, 410–413
    defined, 428
    female, 433–434
    GLBT consumers, 435–436, 437f
    male, 434–435
    socialization and, 429–431
Sexting, 282
Sex-typed products, 432–433, 432f
Sex-typed traits, 431
Sexual dimorphic markers, 306
Sexual identity, gender identity *vs.*, 431–432
Shadows, 286
Shampoo buying, 363–364
Shaping, 235
Sharing sites, 177
Sharpening, 528
Sheconomy, 410
Shoplifting, 182–183
Shopping
    compulsive, 181
    e-commerce, 380–383
    group, 395
    in-store decision making, 385–387
    overview, 379–380
    salesperson and, 388
    spontaneous, 387
    store image, 384–385
    as theater, 383–384
Shopping orientation, 380
Short-term memory (STM), 250
Showrooming, 381
Shrinkage, 182–183
Signs, 219
Silent Generation, 450
Simile, 356
Simulation games, 545
Situational effects, on consumer behavior, 374–375
Situational involvement, 68
Situational self-image, 375
Size, of stimulus, 213
Skateboarding, 547
Skinheads, 507
Sleeper effect, 345
Smart appliances, 403
Smart home technologies, 403
Social attractiveness, 243
Social bottom line, 169
Social capital, 500–501
    cultural, 501
    online, 501
Social class
    achieved *vs.* ascribed status, 483
    around the world, 491–495
    components of, 484–485
    consumer identity and, 481–490
    consumer spending and economic
        behavior, 478–479
    defined, 482
    as demographic, 31, 33f
    income and, 485
    living room clusters and, 500f

    measuring, 495–497
    recession and, 479–481
    status symbols and, 497–499
    structure of, 481–484
    in United States, 491, 492f
    worldview and, 489–490
Social comparison, 273
Social dimension of time, 377
Social environment, 376
Social footprint, 279
Social games, 544
Social graphs, 539
Social identity, 427
Social identity theory, 428
Social isolates, 169
Socialization agents, 104
Social judgment theory, 331
Social loafing, 395
Social marketing, 164, 240
Social media, 45–48, 73, 89–90, 343, 403, 535–542
    addiction to, 180
    community and, 536–538
    emotions and, 89–90
    4Cs of, 546
Social mobility, 483–484
Social networking sites (SNSs), 540
Social networks, structure of, 539–540
Social object theory, 540
Social power, 389–390
Social pressure, 336
Social risk, 65f, 66f
Social shopping, 543–544, 544t
Social stratification, 482
Social structure, cultural system and, 102
Social value, 346
Sociological function, of myths, 122
Sociometric methods, 534–535
Sock puppeting, 345
Sound, 202
Sound symbolism, 203
Source
    attractiveness of, 346
    credibility of, 344–346
    of the message, 341
Source derogation, 352
Source effects, 343
Spacing effect, 253
Spain, 311
Spectacles, 212
Spendthrifts, 478
Spiritual-therapeutic model, 446
Spokescharacters, 37, 348
Spontaneous recovery, 258
Spontaneous shopping, 387
Spreading activation, 251
Spring Break, 37, 38f
Stability, self-concept and, 272
Stage of cognitive development, 245
Standardized strategy, 138
Standard learning hierarchy, 325, 325f
Standard of comparison, 70
State-dependent retrieval, 255
Status anxiety, 488
Status crystallization, 497
Status culture, 509
Status groups, 482
Status hierarchy, 483
Status index, 496f
Status signaling, 505, 506f
Status symbols, 497–499, 502–506
Stereotypes, ethnic and racial, 439–440
Stimulus discrimination, 232–233
Stimulus generalization, 232
    marketing applications of, 234–235

Stimulus organization, 216–217
Stimulus selection factors, 213–215
Storage, memory, 247
Store image, 384
Store loyalty, 240
Stories, cultural, 119–120
Straight rebuy, 400
Strategic developmental stage, 245
Streaking, 555–556
Street art, 112
Strength, of motivation, 41
Strivers, 515
Strugglers, 515
Subcultures, 108, 278
    age, 449–462
    "big three," 420, 444–446
    defined, 428
    ethnic and racial, 438–442
    microcultures, consumer identity and,
        507–508
    place-based, 463–464
    religious, 446–449
Subjective norm (SN), 337, 338
Subliminal perception, 209
Subordinate category, 75
Subway advertising, 224–225
Sunk-cost fallacy, 82
Superego, 282
Superordinate category, 75
Superstitions, 130
Supportive arguments, 351
Surrogate buyers, 529
Surrogate consumers, 532
Surveys, 107
Sustainability, 170
Sustainable business model, 169
Symbol, 219
Symbolic community, 509
Symbolic exchange, 126
Symbolic interactionism, 275–276
Symbolic self-completion, 488
Symbolic self-completion theory, 299
Synchronous interactions, 47
Syncretic decisions, 410
Syndicated surveys, 107
Synoptic ideal, 412

Tactical communications options,
    340–341
Tailgating, 124, 124f
Target marketing, 443
Task specialization, 413
Taste, 204–205
Taste culture, 499–500
Taste public, 509
Taste tests, 328
Tattoos, 312–313, 313f
Taxonomy, 537
Teaser ads, 212
Technology, in homes, 403
Teenagers, 451, 452f
Telescoping, 259
Television, 244–245
Temporal factors, 376–378
Temporal orientation dimension of
    time, 377

Terminal values, 106, 106t
Terrorist attacks of 9/11, 178
Thailand, 304
Theft, 182–183
Theory of cognitive dissonance, 328
Theory of memory reconstruction, 249
Theory of reasoned action, 336, 338
Theory of trying, 339, 339f
Thinkers, 515
Third-party response, to dissatisfaction, 159
Throughput sector, 112
Thumb culture, 455
Ties, 539
Tie strength, 535
Tightwads, 478
Time frame, of attitude measure, 338
Time poverty, 377, 378f
Time-style, 377
Tipping point, 553
Torn self, 275
Total quality management (TQM), 160, 550
Touch, 203, 203f, 204, 204f
Touch-to-speak technology, 168
Tourism, 134
Trade dress, 200
Trait theory, 286, 291–292
Transactional advertising, 544
Transformative consumer research (TCR),
    163, 164
Transitional economies, 157
Translation, 441
Transmedia storytelling, 343
Treaters, 478
Triads, 331, 332
Trialability, 549
Tribal marketing strategy, 393
Trickle-across effect, 553
Trickle-down theory, 551
Trickle up, 553
Trigger feature, 241
Triple bottom-line orientation, 169
Tuners, 507, 507f
TV set, hypothetical alternatives for, 79t
Tweens, 456
Two-factor theory, 351, 351f
Two-sided messages, 351–352
Two step flow model of influence, 531

UHT pasteurized milk, 195
Uncertainty avoidance, 140
Unconditioned stimulus (UCS), 230, 231
Underground economy, 176–177
Underprivileged consumers, 497
Unipolar emotions, 256
United Kingdom, social class in, 493–494
United States, social class in, 491, 492f
Unit relation, 331
Unplanned buying, 387
Upward mobility, 484
User-generated content, 47
User groups, 73
User role, 397
Users, brand position and, 222
Utilitarian function, 324
Utilitarian influence, 391, 391t
Utilitarian needs, 39, 41, 42f, 62

Valence, 329
Valentine's Day rituals, 129
Value-expressive function, 324
Value-expressive influence, 391, 391t
Values
    consumer behavior and, 105–107
    core, 103–105
    cross-cultural, 102–107
    defined, 102
    instrumental, 106, 106t
    materialism and, 157–158
    terminal, 106, 106t
    universal, 154
Values and Lifestyles System (VALS2), 514–515
Value system, 104
Variable-interval reinforcement, 237–238
Variable-ratio reinforcement, 238
Variety seekers, 140
Variety seeking, 65
VCRs, 342
Venezuela, 310
Verbal cues, pictorial cues vs., 256–258
Vicarious learning, 242
Video blogging (vlogging), 343
Viewing context, 256
Viral marketing, 537
Virtual brand communities, 46
Virtual goods, 544, 545
Virtual identities, 279
"Virtual Iraq," 146
Virtual makeovers, 274
Virtual mirror, 275
Virtual worlds, 264, 265, 343
Vision, 197–200
Visual channel, 197
Voice response, to dissatisfaction, 159
Voluntarily childless, 405
Voluntary acts, 338
von Restorff Effect, 256
Vultures, 478

Waist-hip ratios, 303
Waiting time, 378–379
Wants, needs vs., 41–42
War Baby Generation, 450
Warming, 441
Weber's Law, 208, 213
Web 2.0, 47, 541
Widgets, 343
Wikipedia, 47
Wisdom of crowds, 542
Women
    sex appeals and, 353–354
    sex roles and, 410–413
Word-of-mouth (WOM), 523–526, 529, 535
Word-phrase dictionary, 90
Working memory, 250
Working wealthy, 488
Worldview, 102, 489–490
World Wide Web, 244–245, 251

Yankelovich Monitor, 107
Youth market, 451–453

Zebibah, 273
ZIP Quality (ZQ) scale, 464